ECONOMICS FOR BUSINESS

ECONOMICS FOR BUSINESS

Seventh edition

John Sloman

The Economics Network, University of Bristol
Visiting Professor, University of the West of England

Dean Garratt

Nottingham Business School

Jon Guest

Warwick Business School

Elizabeth Jones

University of Warwick

PEARSON

Harlow, England • London • New York • Boston • San Francisco • Toronto • Sydney
Auckland • Singapore • Hong Kong • Tokyo • Seoul • Taipei • New Delhi
Cape Town • São Paulo • Mexico City • Madrid • Amsterdam • Munich • Paris • Milan

Pearson Education Limited
Edinburgh Gate
Harlow CM20 2JE
United Kingdom
Tel: +44 (0)1279 623623
Web: www.pearson.com/uk

———————

First published by Prentice Hall 1998 (print)
Second edition published 2001 (print)
Third edition published 2004 (print)
Fourth edition published 2007 (print)
Fifth edition published 2010 (print)
Sixth edition published 2013 (print and electronic)
Seventh edition published 2016 (print and electronic)

ISBN: 978–1–292–08210–3 (print)
     978–1–292–08211–0 (PDF)
     978–1–292–08217–2 (ePub)

British Library Cataloguing-in-Publication Data
A catalogue record for the print edition is available from the British Library

Library of Congress Cataloguing-in-Publication Data
A catalogue record for the print edition is available from the Library of Congress

10 9 8 7 6 5 4 3 2 1
20 19 18 17 16

Front cover images and all part and chapter images © John Sloman

Print edition typeset in 8/12pt ITC Stone Serif Std by Lumina Datamatics
Print edition printed and bound by L.E.G.O.S.P.A, Italy

NOTE THAT ANY PAGE CROSS REFERENCES REFER TO THE PRINT EDITION

About the authors

John Sloman was Director of the Economics Network (www.economicsnetwork.ac.uk) from 1999 to 2012. The Economics Network is a UK-wide organisation based at the University of Bristol and provides a range of services designed to promote and share good practice in learning and teaching economics. John is now a Visiting Fellow at Bristol and a Senior Associate with the Economics Network.

John is also Visiting Professor at the University of the West of England, Bristol, where, from 1992 to 1999, he was Head of School of Economics. He taught at UWE until 2007. John has taught a range of courses, including economic principles on social science and business studies degrees, development economics, comparative economic systems, intermediate macroeconomics and managerial economics. He has also taught economics on various professional courses.

He is also the co-author with Alison Wride and Dean Garratt of *Economics* (Pearson Education, 9th edition 2015), with Dean Garratt of *Essentials of Economics* (Pearson Education, 7th edition 2016) and with Elizabeth Jones of *Essential Economics for Business* (4th edition 2014). Translations or editions of the various books are available for a number of different countries with the help of co-authors around the world.

John is very interested in promoting new methods of teaching economics, including group exercises, experiments, role playing, computer-aided learning and the use of audience response systems and podcasting in teaching. He has organised and spoken at conferences for both lecturers and students of economics throughout the UK and in many other countries.

As part of his work with the Economics Network he has contributed to its two sites for students and prospective students of economics: Studying Economics (www.studyingeconomics.ac.uk) and Why Study Economics? (www.whystudyeconomics.ac.uk)

From March to June 1997, John was a visiting lecturer at the University of Western Australia. In July and August 2000, he was again a visiting lecturer at the University of Western Australia and also at Murdoch University in Perth.

In 2007, John received a Lifetime Achievement Award as 'outstanding teacher and ambassador of economics' presented jointly by the Higher Education Academy, the Government Economic Service and the Scottish Economic Society.

Dean Garratt is a Principal Lecturer in Economics at Nottingham Business School (NBS), Assistant Head of Economics and the course leader for the School's MSc Economics programme. In 2014/15 Dean worked as a Principal Teaching Fellow in Economics at the University of Warwick having previously been at NBS from 2001, including a period as course leader for the undergraduate economics courses.

Dean teaches economics at a variety of levels to students both on economics courses and non-economics courses. He is passionate about encouraging students to communicate economics more intuitively, to deepen their interest in economics and to apply economics to a range of issues.

Earlier in his career Dean worked as an economic assistant at both HM Treasury and at the Council of Mortgage Lenders. While at these institutions Dean was researching and briefing on a variety of issues relating to the household sector and to the housing and mortgage markets.

Dean is a Senior Fellow of the Higher Education Academy and an Associate of the Economics Network helping to promote high-quality teaching practice. Dean has been involved in several projects promoting a problem-based approach in the teaching of economics.

In 2006 Dean was awarded the Outstanding Teaching Prize by the Economics Network. The award recognises exemplary teaching practice that deepens and inspires interest in economics. In 2013, Dean won the student-nominated Nottingham Business School teacher of the year award.

Dean is an academic assessor for the Government Economic Service (GES). In this role he helps to assess potential recruits to the GES with particular focus on the ability of candidates to articulate their understanding of economics and its applications.

Outside of work, Dean is an avid watcher of most sports. Having been born in Leicester, he is a season ticket holder at both Leicester City Football Club and Leicestershire County Cricket Club.

Jon Guest is a Principal Teaching Fellow in economics at Warwick Business School. He joined the University of Warwick in 2015 having previously spent over 20 years as a Lecturer, Senior Lecturer and Principal Lecturer in the Economics Department at Coventry University.

Jon has taught a range of courses including Principles of Microeconomics, Intermediate Microeconomics, Economics of Human Resource Management and Behavioural Economics. He has also taught economics on various professional courses for the Government Economic Service and HM-Treasury.

His approach towards teaching is one that tries to convey his own enthusiasm for the subject combined with material that presents abstract economics concepts in the context of the everyday life of the student. Questions such as 'Why do I never stick to my revision timetable?' help to create lively discussions and develop students' ability to think like an economist. He has also published chapters in textbooks on the economics of professional team sports and is an editor and regular contributor for the Economic Review.

Jon has worked on developing teaching methods that promote a more active learning environment in the classroom. In particular, he has published journal articles and carried out a number of funded research projects on the impact of games and experiments on student learning. These include an on-line version of the TV show 'Deal No Deal' and games that involve students acting as buyers and sellers in the classroom. He has also recently created a series of short videos and implemented elements of the flipped classroom into his teaching.

Through his work as an Associate of the Economics Network, Jon has run sessions on innovative pedagogic practices at a number of universities and major national events. He is also an academic assessor for the Economic Assessment Centres run by the Government Economic Service. This involves interviewing candidates and evaluating their ability to apply economic reasoning to a range of policy issues.

The quality of his teaching was formally recognised when he became the first Government Economic Service Approved Tutor in 2005 and won the student nominated award from the Economics Network in the same year. In 2011 Jon was awarded a National Teaching Fellowship by the Higher Education Academy.

Outside of work Jon is a keen runner and has completed the London Marathon. He is also a long suffering supporter of Portsmouth Football Club.

Elizabeth Jones is a Principal Teaching Fellow in the Economics Department at the University of Warwick. She joined the University of Warwick in 2012 and was the Deputy Director of Undergraduate Studies for 2 years. Since 2014, she has been the Director of Undergraduate Studies, with overall responsibility for all Undergraduate Degree programmes within the Economics Department. She is also a Fellow for the Warwick International Higher Education Academy and through this, she is involved in developing and sharing best practice in teaching and learning within Higher Education.

She is also the Academic Co-ordinator for the Warwick Economics Summer School and teaches on the Microeconomics and Principles of Economics Courses. She has also been involved in delivering the Warwick Economics Summer School in New Delhi, India, which delivers introductory courses in Economics to 16-18 year olds and has delivered taster events to schools in Asia about studying Economics at University.

Prior to being at Warwick, Elizabeth was a Lecturer at the University of Exeter within the Business School and was in this position for 5 years, following the completion of her MSc in Economics. She also taught A level Economics and Business Studies at Exeter Tutorial College and continues to work as an Examiner in Economics for AQA. She is also a member of the OCR Consultative Forum and has previously been involved in reviewing A level syllabi for the main Examining bodies.

Elizabeth has taught a range of courses including Principles of Economics; Economics for Business; Intermediate Microeconomics; Economics of Social Policy; Economics of Education and Applied Economics. She has won multiple student-nominated awards for teaching at Warwick and Exeter University and loves interacting with students in the classroom. She has a passion for teaching Economics and particularly enjoys teaching Economics to non-economists and spends much of her time at Warwick investing in innovative approaches to teaching and learning. She is also a contributor to the Sloman Economics News Site and uses the blogs within her teaching.

Elizabeth has taught on a number of professional courses, with EML Learning Ltd, where she teaches Economics for Non-economists and Intermediate Microeconomics to the public sector. She has delivered courses across all government Departments, including BIS, Department for Transport, HM-Treasury and the Department for Health. She has also been involved in teaching on the induction programme for new HM-Treasury employees, looking at economics, the role of policy, analysing and using evidence and the implementation of policy.

Outside of work, Elizabeth loves any and all sports. She is an avid fan of Formula 1, tennis and football and provides ongoing support to her father's beloved Kilmarnock FC.

Brief contents

Detailed contents

Custom publishing

Custom publishing allows academics to pick and choose content from one or more textbooks for their course and combine it into a definitive course text.

Here are some common examples of custom solutions which have helped over 1000 courses across Europe:

- different chapters from across our publishing imprints combined into one book;
- lecturer's own material combined together with textbook chapters or published in a separate booklet;
- third-party cases and articles that you are keen for your students to read as part of the course;
- any combination of the above.

The Pearson Education custom text published for your course is professionally produced and bound – just as you would expect from any Pearson Education text. Since many of our titles have online resources accompanying them we can even build a Custom website that matches your course text.

If you are teaching a first year Economics course you may have a large teaching team with different lecturers teaching the micro and macroeconomics sections. Do you find that it can be difficult to agree on one textbook? If you do, you might find combining the macro and micro halves from different Pearson textbooks a useful solution. You may teach a mixed ability class and would like to be able to provide some advanced material from Sloman's larger economics text or perhaps you take more of a business focus where chapters from Sloman's *Economics for Business* might be useful.

Custom publishing has enabled adopters of this text to employ these different solutions.

If, once you have had time to review this title, you feel Custom publishing might benefit you and your course, please do get in contact. However minor, or major the change – we can help you out.

For more details on how to make your chapter selection for your course please go to www.pearsoned.co.uk/sloman and select the custom publishing link.

You can contact us at: **www.pearsoncustom.co.uk** or via your local representative at: **www.pearsoned.co.uk/replocator**.

Preface

If you are studying economics on a business degree or diploma, then this book is written for you. Although we cover all the major principles of economics, the focus throughout is on the world of business. For this reason we also cover several topics that do not appear in traditional economics textbooks.

As well as making considerable use of business examples throughout the text, we have included many case studies (in boxes). These illustrate how economics can be used to understand particular business problems or aspects of the business environment. Many of these case studies cover issues that you are likely to read about in the newspapers. Some cover general business issues; others look at specific companies. Nearly all of them cover topical issues including, the rise of online business, the video gaming market, entrepreneurship, competition and growth strategy, the banking crisis of the late 2000s, the sluggish recovery from recession, quantitative easing, the role of global trade and increased competition from newly industrialised countries.

The style of writing is direct and straightforward, with short paragraphs to aid rapid comprehension. There are also questions interspersed throughout the text in 'Pause for thought' panels. These encourage you to reflect on what you are learning and to see how the various ideas and theories relate to different issues. Definitions of all key terms are given in definition boxes, with defined terms appearing in bold. Also we have highlighted 44 'Key ideas', which are fundamental to 'thinking like an economist'. We refer back to these every time they recur in the book. This helps you to see how the subject ties together, and also helps you to develop a toolkit of concepts that can be used in a host of different contexts.

Summaries are given at the end of each chapter, with points numbered according to the section in which they appeared. These summaries should help you in reviewing the material you have covered and in revising for exams. Each chapter finishes with a series of questions. These can be used to check your understanding of the chapter and help you to see how its material can be applied to various business problems. References to various useful websites are listed at the end of each Part of the book.

The book also has a blog, The Sloman Economics News Site, with several postings each week by the authors. The blog discusses topical issues, links to relevant articles, videos and data and asks questions for you to think about.

In addition to the blog, the book is accompanied by an interactive website, MyEconLab. This is a personalised and innovative online study and testing resource. It also contains an online version of the book, 145 additional case studies, answers to 'Pause for Thought' questions, animations of key models in the book with audio explanations, a set of videoed interviews with businesspeople about decision-making and the relevance of economics to their businesses, hotlinks to 278 websites, plus other materials to improve your understanding of concepts and techniques used in economics.

We hope that, in using this book, you will share some of our fascination for economics. It is a subject that is highly relevant to the world in which we live. And it is a world where many of our needs are served by business – whether as employers or as producers of the goods and services we buy. After graduating, you will probably take up employment in business. A thorough grounding in economic principles should prove invaluable in the business decisions you may well have to make.

The aim of this book is to provide a course in economic principles as they apply to the business environment. It is designed to be used by first-year undergraduates on business studies degrees and diplomas where economics is taught from the business perspective. It is also suitable for students studying economics on postgraduate courses in management, including the MBA, and various professional courses.

Being essentially a book on economics, we cover all the major topics found in standard economics texts – indeed, some of the material in the principles sections is drawn directly from *Economics* (9th edition). But in addition there are several specialist business chapters and sections to build upon and enliven the subject for business studies students. These have been fully updated and revised for this new edition. The following are some examples of these additional topics:

- The business environment
- Business organisations
- Characteristics theory
- Advertising and marketing of products
- Business strategy
- Alternative aims of firms
- Growth strategy
- Strategic alliances and various other forms of co-operation between firms
- The small-firm sector
- Pricing in practice, including topics such as mark-up pricing, an extended analysis of first-, second- and third-degree price discrimination in various contexts, multiple product pricing, transfer pricing and pricing over the product life cycle
- Government and the firm, including policies towards research and development (R&D) and policies towards training
- Government and the market, including environmental policy and transport policy
- Financial markets and the funding of business investment
- The financial well-being of firms, households and governments and its impact on the business environment
- The multinational corporation
- Globalisation and business
- Trading blocs and their development
- Monetary union, the future of the eurozone and implications for business

The text is split into 32 chapters. Each chapter is kept relatively short to enable the material to be covered in a single lecture or class. Each chapter finishes with a summary and review questions, which can be used for seminars or discussion sessions.

The chapters are grouped into 11 Parts:

- Part A Business and economics (Chapters 1–3) establishes the place of business within the economy and the relevance of economics to business decision making.
- Part B Business and markets (Chapters 4 and 5) looks at the operation of markets. It covers supply and demand analysis and examines the importance of the concept of elasticity for business decisions.

- Part C Background to demand (Chapters 6–8) considers the consumer – how consumer behaviour can be predicted and how, via advertising and marketing, consumer demand can be influenced.
- Part D Background to supply (Chapters 9 and 10) focuses on the relationship between the quantity that businesses produce and their costs, revenue and profits.
- Part E Supply: short-run profit maximisation (Chapters 11 and 12) presents the traditional analysis of market structures and the implications that such structures have for business conduct and performance.
- Part F Supply: alternative strategies (Chapters 13–17) starts by looking at business strategy. It then considers various alternative theories of the firm. It also examines how business size can influence business actions, and why pricing strategies differ from one firm to another and how these strategies are influenced by the market conditions in which firms operate.
- Part G The firm in the factor market (Chapters 18 and 19) focuses on the market for labour and the market for capital. It examines what determines the factor proportions that firms use and how factor prices are determined.
- Part H The relationship between government and business (Chapters 20–22) establishes the theoretical rationale behind government intervention in the economy, and then assesses the relationship between the government and the individual firm and the government and the market.
- Part I Business in the international environment (Chapters 23–25) starts by examining the process of globalisation and the growth of the multinational business. It then turns to international trade and the benefits that accrue from it. It also examines the issue of protection and international moves to advance free trade. Finally it examines the expansion of regional trading agreements.
- Part J The macroeconomic environment (Chapters 26–29) considers the macroeconomic framework in which firms operate. We focus on the principal macroeconomic variables, investigate the role of money in the economy, and briefly outline the theoretical models underpinning the relationships between these variables.
- Part K Macroeconomic policy (Chapters 30–32) examines the mechanics of government intervention at a macro level as well as its impact on business and its potential benefits and drawbacks. Demand-side and supply-side policy and economic policy co-ordination between countries are all considered.

SPECIAL FEATURES

The book contains the following special features:

- A direct and straightforward written style, with short paragraphs to aid rapid comprehension. The aim all the time is to provide maximum clarity.

- Attractive full-colour design. The careful and consistent use of colour and shading makes the text more attractive to students and easier to use by giving clear signals as to the book's structure.

- Key ideas highlighted and explained where they first appear. There are 44 of these ideas, which are fundamental to the study of economics. Students can see them recurring throughout the book, and an icon appears in the margin to refer back to the page where the idea first appears. Showing how ideas can be used in a variety of contexts helps students to 'think like an economist' and to relate the different parts of the subject together. All 44 Key ideas are defined in a special section at the end of the book.
- Pause for thought' questions integrated throughout the text. These encourage students to reflect on what they have just read and make the learning process a more active one. Answers to these questions appear in the student section of MyEconLab.
- Double-page opening spreads for each of the 11 Parts of the book. These contain an introduction to the material covered and an article from the *Financial Times* on one of the topics.
- All technical terms are highlighted and clearly defined in definition panels on the page on which they appear. This feature has proved very popular in previous editions and is especially useful for students when revising.
- A comprehensive glossary of all technical terms.
- Additional applied material to that found in the text can be found in the boxes within each chapter. All boxes include questions which relate the material back to the chapter in which the box is located. The extensive use of applied material makes learning much more interesting for students and helps to bring the subject alive. This is particularly important for business students who need to relate economic theory to their other subjects and to the world of business generally. The boxes are current and include discussion of a range of companies and business topics. They are ideal for use as case studies in class. Answers to the questions in boxes can be found in the lecturer past of MyEconLab, which you can make available to students if you choose.
- Additional case studies with questions appearing in MyEconLab are referred to at the end of each Part. Again, they can be used for class, with answers available on the lecturer part of MyEconLab.
- Detailed summaries appear at the end of each chapter with the points numbered by the chapter section in which they are made. These allow students not only to check their comprehension of the chapter's contents, but also to get a clear overview of the material they have been studying.
- Each chapter concludes with a series of review questions to test students' understanding of the chapter's salient points. These questions can be used for seminars or as set work to be completed in the students' own time. Again, answers are available to lecturers on MyEconLab.
- References at the end of each Part to a list of relevant websites, details of which can be found in the Web appendix at the end of the book. You can easily access any of these sites from the book's own website (at www. pearsonblog.campaignserver.co.uk/). When you enter the site, click on 'Hotlinks'. You will find all the sites from the Web appendix listed. Click on the one you want and the 'hotlink' will take you straight to it.
- A comprehensive index, including reference to all defined terms. This enables students to look up a definition as required and to see it used in context.

SUPPLEMENTS

Blog

Visit the book's blog, The *Sloman Economics News Site*, at www.pearsonblog.campaignserver.co.uk/ This refers to topical issues in economics and relates them to particular chapters in the book. There are several postings per week, with each one providing an introduction to the topic, and then links to relevant articles, videos, podcasts, data and official documents, and then questions which students and lecturers will find relevant for homework or class discussion.

MyEconLab for students

MyEconLab provides a comprehensive set of online resources. A student access code card may have been included with this textbook at a reduced cost. If you do not have an access code, you can buy access to MyEconLab and the eText – an online version of the book – at www.myeconlab.com.

Central to MyEconLab is an interactive study plan with questions and answers. You will also find a variety of tools to enable you to assess your own learning. A personalised Study Plan identifies areas to concentrate on to improve grades, and specific tools are provided to enable you to direct your studies in a more efficient way. Other resources include:

- An etext version of the book to enable you to access it via the Internet
- Animations of key models with audio explanations
- 145 case studies with questions for self-study, ordered Part-by-Part and referred to in the text
- Updated list of 278 hot links to sites of use for economics
- Answers to all in-chapter (Pause for Thought) questions
- Videoed interviews with a number of businesspeople, where the discuss business decision-making and the relevance of economic concepts to them
- Glossary flashcards to test and check your knowledge of all technical concepts

MyEconLab for lecturers and tutors

MyEconLab can be set up by you as a complete virtual learning environment for your course or embedded into Blackboard, WebCT or Moodle. You can customise its look and feel and its availability to students. You can use it to provide support to your students in the following ways:

■ My EconLab's gradebook automatically records each student's time spent and performance on the tests and Study Plan. It also generates reports you can use to monitor your students' progress.

■ You can use MyEconLab to build your own test, quizzes and homework assignments from the question base provided to set your own students' assessment.

■ Questions are generated algorithmically so they use different values each time they are used.

■ You can create your own exercises by using the econ exercise builder.

Additional resources for lecturers and tutors

There are many additional resources for lecturers and tutors that can be downloaded from the lecturer site of MyEconLab. These have been thoroughly revised for the seventh edition. These include:

■ PowerPoint® slide shows in full colour for use with a data projector in lectures and classes. These can also be made available to students by loading them on to a local network. There are several types of slideshows:

– *All figures from the book and most of the tables.* Each figure is built up in a logical sequence, thereby allowing tutors to show them in lectures in an animated form.

– *Customisable lecture slideshows.* There is one for each chapter of the book. Each one can be easily edited, with points added, deleted or moved, so as to suit particular lectures. A consistent use of colour is made to show how the points tie together. They come in various versions:

  • Lecture slideshows with integrated diagrams. These include animated diagrams, charts and tables at the appropriate points.
  • Lecture slideshows with integrated diagrams and questions. These are like the above but also include multiple-choice questions, allowing lectures to become more interactive. They can be used with or without an audience response system (ARS). ARS versions are available for InterWrite PRS® and two versions of TurningPoint® and are ready to use with appropriate 'clickers'.
  • Lecture plans without the diagrams. These allow you to construct your own diagrams on the blackboard or whiteboard, or use an OHP or visualiser.

■ Case studies. These, also available in the student part of MyEconLab, can be reproduced and used for classroom exercises or for student assignments. Answers are also provided (not available on the student site).

■ Workshops. There are 24 of these, each one covering one or more chapters. They are in Word® and can be reproduced for use with large groups (up to 200 students) in a lecture theatre or large classroom. Suggestions for use are given in an accompanying file. Answers to all workshops are given in separate Word® files.

■ Teaching/learning case studies. There are 20 of these. They examine various approaches to teaching introductory economics and ways to improve student learning of introductory economics.

■ Answers to all end-of-chapter questions, pause for thought questions, questions in boxes, questions in the case studies in MyEconLab, the 24 workshops.

ACKNOWLEDGEMENTS

As with previous editions, we've had great support from the team at Pearson, including Kate Brewin, Caitlin Lisle, Louise Hammond, Tim Parker, Zoe Smith and Melanie Beard. We'd like to thank all of them for their hard work and encouragement. Thanks too to the many users of the book who have given us feedback. We always value their comments. Please continue to send us your views.

Kevin Hinde and Mark Sutcliffe, co-authors with John on previous editions, have moved on to new ventures. However, many of their wise words and ideas are still embedded in this edition and, for that, we offer a huge thanks.

Our families have also been remarkably tolerant and supportive throughout the writing of this new edition. Thanks especially to Alison, Pat, and Helen, Elizabeth, Douglas and Harriet who seem to have perfected a subtle blend of encouragement, humour, patience and tolerance.

John, Dean, Elizabeth and Jon

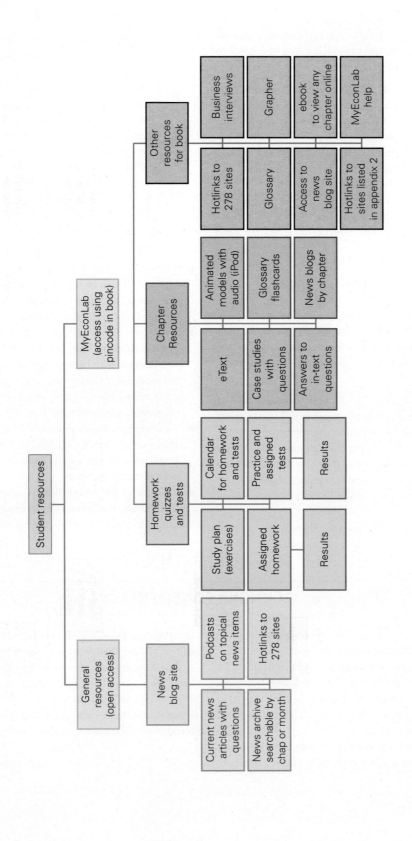

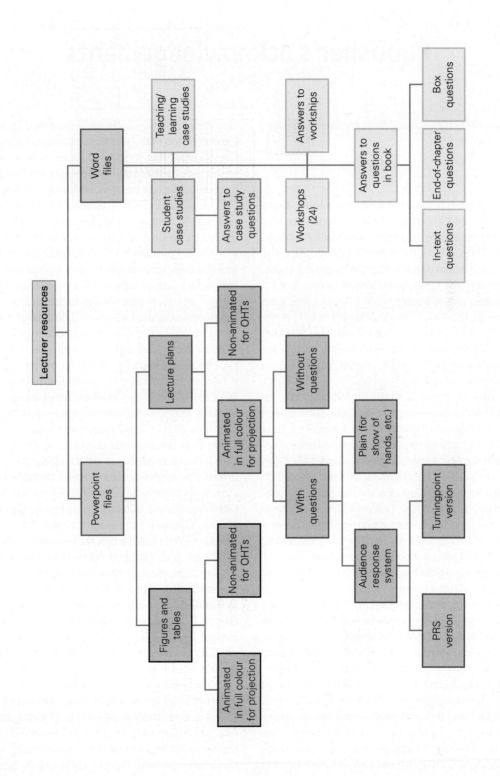

Publisher's acknowledgements

We are grateful to the following for permission to reproduce copyright material:

Figures

Figure 1.1 after data in Time series data, series KKP5, KKD5, KKD9, KKD7 and KKJ7 (ONS, 2015), Office for National Statistics (ONS); Figure 1.2 after Labour Market Statistics data, series DYDC, JWR5, JWR6, JWT8 (ONS, 2015), Office for National Statistics (ONS), Office for National Statistics licensed under the Open Government Licence v.3.0. ; Figure 1.3 after data in Gross Domestic Product time series data, series KL8S, KL8T, KL8V, KL9D, KL9F, KL9R, KL9X, KLA4, KLA6 (ONS, 2015), Office for National Statistics (ONS), Office for National Statistics licensed under the Open Government Licence v.3.0. ; Figure 1.4 after Labour Market Statistics, series JWR5–9, JWS2–9, JWT2–7 (ONS, 2015), Office for National Statistics (ONS), Office for National Statistics licensed under the Open Government Licence v.3.0. ; Figure 2.3 after Statistical Annex of the European Economy, Table 20 (EC, 2015), European Union, Contains public sector information licensed under the Open Government Licence v3.0. © European Union, 1995-2015.; Figure 2.4 after Statistical Annex of the European Economy, Tables 10 and 20 (EC, 2015), European Union, Contains public sector information licensed under the Open Government Licence v3.0. © European Union, 1995-2015.; Figures 2.5 after Mintel Cider UK Report, February 2012, Mintel Group Ltd; Figures 2.6 from Mintel Cider UK Report, February 2012, Mintel Group Ltd; Figure in Box 4.1 after data in Halifax House Price Index (Lloyds Banking Group), Lloyds Banking Group plc; Figure in Box 7.1 after data in Family Food datasets, Table 2.1 (defra), https://www.gov.uk/government/statistical-data-sets/family-food-datasets, Department for Environment, Food & Rural Affairs. UK government., Contains public sector information licensed under the Open Government Licence (OGL) v3.0. http://www.nationalarchives.gov.uk/doc/open-government-licence; Figure 8.2 from H. A. Lipson and J. R. Darling, Introduction to Marketing: an administrative approach (John Wiley & Sons, Inc., 1971). Reproduced with permission of the Estate of Professor Harry Lipson; Figure 8.3 after warc.com © and database right Warc Limited 2015.; Figure 12.2 after Kantar Worldpanel, TNS UK Limited; Figure 13.2 from Michael E. Porter, Competitive Strategy: Techniques for Analyzing Industries and Competitors by. Reprinted with the permission of the Free Press of Simon & Schuster, Inc., Copyright © 1980, 1988 by The Free Press. All Rights Reserved. Free Press of Simon & Schuster, Inc., With the permission of The Free Press, a Division of Simon & Schuster, Inc., from (publication) by (author). Copyright © (date) by (author). All rights reserved.; Figures in Box 14.1 after data in '2014 Year on Year Sales and Market Share Update', VGChartz (9 January 2015), VGChartz Limited; Figures in Box 15.1 from 'Cross Border Mergers & Acquisitions', World Investment Report Annex Tables (UNCTAD, June 2014), Tables 9 and 11, United Nations Conference on Trade and Development Palais des Nations (UNCTAD); Figure in Box 15.3 after Times Online, data available from http://timesonline.hemscott.com/timesonline/timesonline.jsp?page=company-chart&companyId=3497&from=1/1/2007&to=22/2/2008&returnPeriod=2; Figure (a) in Box 16.1 after data in Global Entrepreneurship Monitor 2014, Executive Report (Global Enterprise Research Association, 2015), Global Enterprise Research Association; Figure (b) in Box 16.1 after data in Key Indicators database, Global Entrepreneurship Monitor (GEM), Global Entrepreneurship Research Association; Figure 18.2 after Time series Data, series BBFW (ONS), Office of National Statistics (ONS), Office for National Statistics licensed under the Open Government Licence v.3.0.; Figure 18.10 after data from StatExtracts (OECD), Organisation for Economic Co-Operation and Development (OECD); Figure 18.12 after data in ASHE 1997 to 2014 selected estimates, Tables 2 and 6 (National Statistics, 2014), Office of National Statistics (ONS), Office for National Statistics licensed under the Open Government Licence v.3.0.; Figure 18.13 from the Institute of Manpower Studies, The Flexible Firm (MS, 1984) Reproduced with permission. Emerald Group Publishing; Figure 21.1 after data in Main Science and Technology Indicators (OECD, 2015), Organisation for Economic Co-Operation and Development (OECD); Figures 21.2, 21.3 after data from BIS FE data library: apprenticeships (BIS, 2015), Department for Business, Innovation and Skills, UK government (BIS), GOV.UK, Contains public sector information licensed under the Open Government Licence (OGL) v3.0. http://www.nationalarchives.gov.uk/doc/open-government-licence; Figure 22.1 after data in Environmentally Related Taxes Database (OECD), Organisation for Economic Co-Operation and Development (OECD); Figure 22.2 after data in EU

Transport in Figures (European Commission, 2014), European Union, Contains public sector information licensed under the Open Government Licence v3.0. © European Union, 1995-2015; Figure 22.3 after data from Annex Web Table 9, World Investment Report (UNCTAD), United Nations Conference on Trade and Development; Figure 23.1 adapted from World Investment Report 2014 (UNCTAD), page, xiii Figure 1, United Nations Conference on Trade and Development; Figure (a) in Box 23.1 after data from Annex Web Table 9, World Investment Report (UNCTAD), United Nations Conference on Trade and Development Palais des Nations (UNCTAD); Figure (b) in Box 23.1 after data from Annex Web Table 19, World Investment Report (UNCTAD), United Nations Conference on Trade and Development Palais des Nations (UNCTAD); Figure 23.2 from World Investment Report 2014 (UNCTAD), United Nations Conference on Trade and Development; Figure (a) in Box 23.2 after data from UNCTADstat (UNCTAD), United Nations Conference on Trade and Development; Figure (b) in Box 23.2 after data in Foreign Direct Investment (FDI) Involving UK Companies, 2013 (Directional Principle) (ONS, January 2015), Office for National Statistics (ONS), Office for National Statistics licensed under the Open Government Licence v.3.0.; Figure 24.2 after data in WTO Statistics Database, World Trade Organization (WTO); Figure 24.3 after data in WTO Statistics Database World Trade Organization (WTO); Figure 24.4 from WTO Statistics database (WTO), World Trade Organization (WTO); Figure 24.5 from International Trade Statistics, 2014 (WTO), Table II.2, World Trade Organization (WTO); Figures 24.6, 26.1, 26.4, 26.7, 26.8, 27.1, 29.1 after data in AMECO Database (European Commission, DGECFIN), European Union, Contains public sector information licensed under the Open Government Licence v3.0. © European Union, 1995-2015.; Figure in Box 25.2 from Internal Market scoreboard., http://ec.europa.eu/internal_market/scoreboard/performance_by_governance_tool/transposition/index_en.htm#maincontentSec4. (European Commission), European Union c/o European Commission, Contains public sector information licensed under the Open Government Licence v3.0. © European Union, 1995-2015.; Figure 26.1 after data from AMECO database (European Commission, DGECFIN) European Union, Contains public sector information licensed under the Open Government Licence v3.0. © European Union, 1995-2015.; Figure (a) in Box 26.2 after data from Labour Market Statistics, series YBWF, YBWG and YBWH (National Statistics), Office for National Statistics (ONS), Office for National Statistics licensed under the Open Government Licence v.3.0.; Figure (b) in Box 26.2 after data from Labour Market Statistics (National Statistics), Office for National Statistics (ONS), Office for National Statistics licensed under the Open Government Licence v.3.0.; Figure in Box 26.3 after data from World Bank Commodity Data (Pink Sheet) (World Bank), The World Bank; Figure 26.9 after Time series data, series IHYU, D7G7 and KAC3 (National Statistics), Office for National Statistics (ONS), Office for National Statistics licensed under the Open Government Licence v.3.0. ; Figure 26.14 from Blue Book Tables - Series (ONS, 2014) (http://www.ons.gov.uk/ons/datasets-and-tables/data-selector.html?table-id=2.3&dataset=bb, Office for National Statistics (ONS), Source: Office for National Statistics licensed under the Open Government Licence v.3.0.; Figure 27.2 after data from Balance of Payments quarterly First Release (National Statistics) Office for National Statistics (ONS), Office for National Statistics licensed under the Open Government Licence v.3.0.; Figures 27.3, 27.6 after data in Monthly Review of External Statistics (National Statistics), Office for National Statistics (ONS), Office for National Statistics licensed under the Open Government Licence v.3.0.; Figure in Box 27.4 from Federal Reserve Bank, European Central Bank, Bank of England and Monthly Review of External Trade Statistics (National Statistics), Office for National Statistics (ONS), Source: Office for National Statistics licensed under the Open Government Licence v.3.0.; Figure in Box 28.3 after data from Statistical Interactive Database, Bank of England, series LPQB3XE and LPQB3HK (data published 2/3/15). Bank of England, Contains public sector information licensed under the Open Government Licence v3.0. http://www.nationalarchives.gov.uk/doc/open-government-licence/version/3/; Figure 28.3 after data from Statistical Interactive Database, series IUMAMIH and IUMVNEA (Bank of England) (data published 7/6/15). Bank of England, Contains public sector information licensed under the Open Government Licence v3.0. http://www.nationalarchives.gov.uk/doc/open-government-licence/version/3/; Figure 28.4 after on series LPMBL22 (reserves), LPMAVAB (notes and coin) and LPMAUYN (M4) from Statistical Interactive Database, Bank of England (data published 2 March 2015, seasonally adjusted except for reserves)., Contains public sector information licensed under the Open Government Licence v3.0. http://www.nationalarchives.gov.uk/doc/open-government-licence/version/3/; Figure (a) in Box 28.4 from Statistical Interactive Database (Bank of England), Series LPQVWNL, LPQVWNQ and LPQVWNV (data published 2/6/15, seasonally adjusted)., Contains public sector information licensed under the Open Government Licence v3.0. http://www.nationalarchives.gov.uk/doc/open-government-licence/version/3/; Figure (b) in Box 28.4 from Statistical Interactive Database (Bank of England), Series LPQBC44, LPQBC56 and LPQBC57 (data published 2/6/15, seasonally adjusted). Bank of England, Contains public sector information licensed under the Open Government Licence v3.0. http://www.nationalarchives.gov.uk/doc/open-government-licence/version/3/; Figure 28.5 from M4 growth rate from Statistical Interactive Database Series LPQVQJW (data published 2/6/15, seasonally adjusted), Contains public sector information licensed under the Open Government Licence v3.0. http://www.nationalarchives.gov.uk/doc/open-government-licence/version/3/; Figure in Box 29.2 after data from National Balance Sheet (National Statistics), Office for National Statistics (ONS),

Office for National Statistics licensed under the Open Government Licence v.3.0.; Figure 29.13 after Time Series Data, series MGSX and CZBH (National Statistics), Office for National Statistics (ONS), Office for National Statistics licensed under the Open Government Licence v.3.0.; Figure 29.14 after data in Underemployment and Overemployment in the UK, 2014 (Office for National Statistics, December 2014), Office for National Statistics (ONS), Office for National Statistics licensed under the Open Government Licence v.3.0.; Figure 29.15 from Forecasts for the UK Economy (HM Treasury, various years), UK government, GOV. UK, Source: Contains public sector information licensed under the Open Government Licence v3.0. http://www. nationalarchives.gov.uk/doc/open-government-licence/ version/3/; Figure 29.16 after data in Quarterly National Accounts, series KGZ7, KG7T and IHYR (National Statistics), Office for National Statistics (ONS), Office for National Statistics licensed under the Open Government Licence v.3.0.; Figures 30.1 and Figure (a) from Box 30.2 from Public Finances Databank (Office for Budget Responsibility), Office of Budget Responsibility (OBR), Source: Open Government Licence v3.0 Contains public sector information licensed under the Open Government Licence (OGL). http://www .nationalarchives.gov.uk/doc/open-government-licence; Figure (a) in Box 30.1 from Public Sector Finances Databank (OBR), Office of Budget Responsibility (OBR), Source: Open Government Licence v3.0 Contains public sector information licensed under the Open Government Licence (OGL) http://www.nationalarchives.gov.uk/doc/open-government-licence.; Figure (b) in Box 30.1 after Public Sector Finances Databank (OBR) and Quarterly National Accounts, series YBHA (ONS), Office for National Statistics (ONS), Office for National Statistics licensed under the Open Government Licence v.3.0.; Figure 30.2a after data in Statistical Annex to the European Economy (European Commission), European Union, Contains public sector information licensed under the Open Government Licence v3.0. © European Union, 1995-2015.; Figure in Box 31.1 after data from AMECO database (European Commission), European Union, Contains public sector information licensed under the Open Government Licence v3.0. © European Union, 1995-2015.; Figure 31.1 after data from World Economic Outlook Database (IMF), International Monetary Fund; Figure in Box 31.2 after data in Human Capital Estimates, 2013 (ONS, 2014) Office for National Statistics (ONS), Office for National Statistics licensed under the Open Government Licence v.3.0.; Figure 31.2 after data from OECD.StatExtracts (OECD), Organisation for Economic Co-Operation and Development (OECD); Figures in Box 31.3 after data in International Comparisons of Productivity (National Statistics, 2015), Office for National Statistics (ONS), Office for National Statistics licensed under the Open Government Licence v.3.0.; Figure in Box 32.1 after data in World Economic Outlook, April 2015 (International Monetary Fund), International Monetary Fund; Figure 32.1 after data in UNCTADstat (UNCTAD), United Nations Conference on Trade and Development (UNCTAD)

Tables

Tables 1.1, 1.2 after Standard Industrial Classification 2007, Office for National Statistics (ONS), Office for National Statistics licensed under the Open Government Licence v.3.0. ; Table 2.1 after Statistical Annex of the European Economy (EC, 2015). 2015 and 2016 are forecast. European Union, Contains public sector information licensed under the Open Government Licence v3.0. © European Union, 1995-2015.; Table 2.2 after Statistical Annex of the European Economy (EC, 2015). 2015 and 2016 are forecast, European Union, Contains public sector information licensed under the Open Government Licence v3.0. © European Union, 1995-2015.; Table 2.3 from Mintel Cider UK Report, February 2012, Mintel Group Ltd; Table 2.4 from Time series data, series K22A and L2NC (ONS, 2015), Office for National Statistics (ONS), Source: Office for National Statistics licensed under the Open Government Licence v.3.0. ; Tables in Box 8.1 from Mintel Reports (2014), Mintel Group Ltd; Tables 8.1, 8.2, 8.4 from warc.com © and database right Warc Limited 2015. All warranties and liabilities disclaimed to the fullest extent permitted by law. Used by permission.; Table 8.3 from Nielsen and MPP Consulting. Available from www. rankingthebrands.com, reproduced with permission. SyncForce; Table in Box 9.3 after EU Cluster Observatory, www .clusterobservatory.eu, European Union, Contains public sector information licensed under the Open Government Licence v3.0. © European Union, 1995-2015.; Table (b) in Box 9.4 from The Single Market Review, Subseries V: Impact on Competition and Scale Effects, European Commission. Office for Official Publications of the European Communities 2 rue Mercier, L-2985 Luxembourg ISBN 92-827-8804-0 Catalogue number: C1 -71 -96-004-EN-C, Table 3.3. EOS potential and SM sensitivity of EU manufacturing sectors listed in decending order of EOS potential, page 35., © European Union, 1995-2015; Table in Box 11.1 after data in Table 8.31 of United Kingdom Input–Output Analyses 2006 (National Statistics), Office for National Statistics (ONS), Office for National Statistics licensed under the Open Government Licence v.3.0.; Tables 16.2 and 16.3 from Business Population Estimates for the UK and Regions (BIS, 2014). Department for Business, Innovation and Skills, GOV. UK, Source: Contains public sector information licensed under the Open Government Licence v3.0. http://www .nationalarchives.gov.uk/doc/open-government-licence/ version/3/; Table 16.4 from D. J. Storey, Understanding the Small-Business Sector (Routledge, 1994). Reproduced with permission of Cengage Learning (EMEA) Ltd., ISBN-13: 978-1861523815; Table 18.1 after Annual Survey of Hours and Earnings (Office for National Statistics, 2014), Office of National Statistics (ONS), Office for National Statistics licensed under the Open Government Licence v.3.0.; Table in Box 21.2 after data from 2014 EU Industrial R&D Investment Scorecard (European Commission), European Commission Joint Research Centre, European Union, Contains public sector information licensed under the Open Government Licence v3.0. © European Union, 1995-2015.;

Table 22.2 from Transport Statistics Great Britain 2014 (Department for Transport, National Statistics 2014), Office of National Statistics (ONS), Source: Office for National Statistics licensed under the Open Government Licence v.3.0.; Table 23.1 from George S. Yip Total global strategy managing for worldwide competitive advantage (Business school ed)., Reproduced by permission of Pearson Education, Inc., Upper Saddle River, NJ, US; Table in Box 23.1 after data from World Investment Report, Annex Tables 10 and 18 (UNCTAD, 2015), United Nations Conference on Trade and Development; Table 23.3 adapted from data from UNCTADstat United Nations Conference on Trade and Development; Tables 26.1 from United Kingdom National Accounts (National Statistics), Office for National Statistics (ONS), Source: Office for National Statistics licensed under the Open Government Licence v.3.0.; Tables 26.2 from United Kingdom National Accounts (National Statistics), Office for National Statistics (ONS), Source: Office for National Statistics licensed under the Open Government Licence v.3.0.; Table 27.1 from Balance of Payments, Quarter 4 and Annual 2014 (Office for National Statistics, 2015) Office for National Statistics (ONS), Source: Office for National Statistics licensed under the Open Government Licence v.3.0.; Table 28.1 after data in Bankstats (Monetary and Financial Statistics) (Bank of England), March 2015. Bank of England, Contains public sector information licensed under the Open Government Licence v3.0. http://www.nationalarchives.gov.uk/doc/open-government-licence/version/3/; Table 28.5 from Statistical Interactive Database, 2 March 2015, Contains public sector information licensed under the Open Government Licence v3.0. http://www.nationalarchives.gov.uk/doc/open-government-licence/version/3/; Table in Box 29.2 after data from National Balance Sheet, 2014 Estimates and Quarterly National Accounts (National Statistics), Office for National Statistics (ONS), Office for National Statistics licensed under the Open Government Licence v.3.0.; Table 30.1 after data from AMECO database, Tables 16.3 and 18.1 (European Commission, DG ECFIN), European Union, Contains public sector information licensed under the Open Government Licence v3.0. © European Union, 1995-2015.; Table 31.1 after AMECO database, European Commission, DGECFIN, Tables 3.2 and 6.1. European Union, Contains public sector information licensed under the Open Government Licence v3.0. © European Union, 1995-2015.

Text

Article on page 2 from Tim Bradshaw, The Financial Times, 26 October 2015, Financial Times Limited, © The Financial Times Limited. All Rights Reserved; Quote on page 3 from John Kay, Everyday economics makes for good fun at parties, Financial Times, 2 May 2006, http://www.ft.com/cms/s/1/39850c1a-d938-11da-8b06-0000779e2340.html#axzz3hxi6DvLn., Financial Times Limited, © The Financial Times Limited. All Rights Reserved.; Article on page 48 from Emiko Terazono, The Financial Times, 10 September 2015, Financial Times Limited, © The Financial Times Limited. All Rights Reserved; Box on page 84 from Gavyn Davies, 'Fundamentals and speculation in commodity markets' The Financial Times 16 May 2011. http://blogs.ft.com/gavyndavies/2011/05/16/fundamentals-and-speculation-in-commodity-markets/, Financial Times Limited, © The Financial Times Limited. All Rights Reserved; Article on page 88 from Michael Pooler, The Financial Times, 11 October 2015, Financial Times Limited, © The Financial Times Limited. All Rights Reserved; Quote on page 89 from Philip Collins (2009) Chairman of the Office of Fair Trading, Preserving and Restoring Trust and Confidence in Markets. Keynote address to the British Institute of International and Comparative Law at the Ninth Annual Trans-Atlantic Antitrust Dialogue. April 30th. Available at http://www.oft.gov.uk/shared_oft/speeches/2009/spe0809.pdf, Source: Contains public sector information licensed under the Open Government Licence v3.0. http://www.nationalarchives.gov.uk/doc/open-government-licence/version/3/ ; Article on page 138 from Jamie Smyth, The Financial Times, 20 August 2015, Financial Times Limited, © The Financial Times Limited. All Rights Reserved.; Quote on page 138 from Michael Pooler, 29 September 2015, The Financial Times, © The Financial Times Limited. All Rights Reserved; Quote on page 169 from David Blair, Gerrit Wiesmann and Ausha Sakoui, RWE considers pulling plug on NPower. The Financial Times, 5 July 2011, http://www.ft.com/cms/s/0/e7fe61ec-a737-11e0-b6d4-00144feabdc0.html, The Financial Times Limited, © The Financial Times Limited. All Rights Reserved; Article on page 172 from Murad Ahmed, The Financial Times, 25 October 2015 The Financial Times, © The Financial Times Limited. All Rights Reserved; Quote on page 173 from Andrea Felstead, 25 June 2015, The Financial Times Limited, © The Financial Times Limited. All Rights Reserved; Quote on page 195 from Simon Stenning, strategy director at Allegra Foodservice in Owen McKeon, 'Street Food set to boost UK's eating out sector', http://www.evolvehospitality.co.uk/evolve-hospitality-news-detail/street-food-set-to-boost-uk-s-eating-out-sector/159, Allegra Foodservice (William Reed Business Media Ltd), Used by permission.; Article on page 214 from Chris Bryant, The Financial Times, 2 August 2015, The Financial Times Limited, © The Financial Times Limited. All Rights Reserved; Quote on page 215 from Michael E. Porter, 'The five competitive forces that shape competition', Harvard Business Review, January 2008, p. 93; Quote on pages 216-17 from Mission Statement; 3 interrelated parts, http://www.benjerry.com/values, Source: (c) Ben & Jerry's; Quote on page 270 from Our Unique Cocoa Plantation – The Rabot Estate, St Lucia, September 2012., http://www.hotelchocolat.co.uk; Article on page 296 from Sam Fleming, The Financial Times, 11 October 2015, The Financial Times Limited, © The Financial Times Limited. All Rights Reserved; Quote on page 297 from Zero-hour contracts hold their place in UK labour market, 2 September 2015, The Financial Times,

Business and economics

The FT Reports . . .

The Financial Times, 26 October 2015

FT

Apple investors worry the iPhone is losing its shine

By Tim Bradshaw

When Apple reports its earnings this week, Wall Street wants to know just one thing: will iPhone sales keep growing?

Apple's smartphone has become one of the most profitable products the technology industry has ever produced. In the three months to December last year [2014], so lucrative was the iPhone that Apple reported the most profitable quarter of any US company on record.

But the euphoria of that achievement soon gave way to the daunting challenge of matching or even exceeding such a record profit.

Most analysts predict that iPhone unit growth . . . will slow from about 35 per cent over the past year to the low single-digits for the next few quarters. But given the strength of its performance a year ago, concerns remain that even that may be a stretch.

"Sentiment on Apple is a-changin", wrote analysts at Berenberg in a recent note . . . Tim Cook, Apple's Chief Executive, dismissed questioning by analysts three months ago about the impact of Chinese macroeconomic fluctuations on iPhone demand in its most important growth market.

Nonetheless, even Apple analysts who are normally more bullish have acknowledged the concern that iPhone sales might soon see a year-on-year drop for the first time since its launch.

Gene Munster of Piper Jaffray predicts a 3 per cent rise in iPhone unit sales over the coming year, a sharp slowdown from its growth rate of 25 per cent in the three months to September, which Apple is expected to report this week. . . .

Worries about iPhone growth will put renewed focus on which new products may be able to take up some of the slack.

Mr Cook's comments a week ago that carmakers face "massive change" because of technology trends may bolster confidence among investors that Apple is serious about entering the automotive industry with a vehicle of its own in the coming years.

But in the near term, investor focus will be on Apple's Watch . . . and its TV box and larger iPads . . . Apple has not disclosed sales figures for the Watch but a software update in September has made modest improvements to the user experience, according to a recent study . . . Wristly found that 90 per cent of owners wear the Apple Watch every day, seen as a higher rate than other wearable devices such as fitness trackers, which are often abandoned a few months after purchase.

I dread admitting I am an economist. The cab driver quizzes you on what is going to happen to the economy, the dinner companion turns to talk to the person on the other side and the immigration officer says, with heavy sarcasm, that his country needs people like you.

John Kay, 'Everyday economics makes for good fun at parties', *Financial Times*, 2 May 2006

Businesses play a key role in all our lives. Whatever their size, and whatever the goods or services they provide, they depend on us as consumers to buy their products.

But just as businesses rely on us for their income, many of us also rely on them for our income. The wages we earn depend on our employer's success, and that success in turn depends on us as suppliers of labour.

And it is not just as customers and workers that we are affected by business. The success of business in general affects the health of the whole economy and thus the lives of us all.

The extract from the *Financial Times* takes the case of Apple and the iPhone. To be successful, firms must be capable of responding to changes in the market environment in which they operate. This requires a thorough understanding of economics. Developing a business strategy that simultaneously responds to technological changes, changes in consumer tastes and the activities of rival companies is not an easy task. Fortunately, economics provides frameworks for thinking about these issues, and many more.

In Part A of this text, we consider the relationship between business and economics.

In Chapter 1 we look at the structure of industry and its importance in determining firms' behaviour. We also look at a range of other factors that are likely to affect business decisions and how we can set about analysing the environment in which a firm operates in order to help it devise an appropriate business strategy.

Then, in Chapter 2 we ask what it is that economists do and, in particular, how economists set about analysing the world of business and the things businesses do. In particular, we focus on rational decision making – how to get the best outcome from limited resources.

Finally, in Chapter 3 we look at the different ways in which firms are organised: at their legal structure, at their internal organisation and at their goals.

Key terms

The business environment
PEST and STEEPLE analysis
Production
Firms
Industries
Industrial sectors
Standard Industrial Classification (SIC)
Industrial concentration
Structure–conduct–performance
Scarcity
Factors of production
Macroeconomics
Microeconomics
Opportunity cost
Marginal costs
Marginal benefits
Rational choices
Circular flow of income
Transaction costs
Principal and agent
Business organisation
Price taker
Perfectly competitive market
Price mechanism
Demand
Supply

Chapter 1

The business environment and business economics

What is business economics?

What is the role of *business economics*? What will you study in this text?

The global business environment has been rather uncertain since the start of the financial crisis in 2008/9. Furthermore, the world economy has experienced many changes in recent decades and they have had profound effects on businesses across the world. An economist's approach to the world of business requires that we examine *firms*: the environment in which they operate, the decisions they make, and the effects of these decisions – on themselves, on their customers, on their employees, on their business rivals, on the public at large and on the domestic and international economy.

All firms are different, but they are all essentially concerned with using inputs to make output. Inputs cost money and output earns money. The difference between the revenue earned and the costs incurred constitutes the firm's profit. Firms will normally want to make as much profit as possible, or at the very least avoid a decline in profits. In order to meet these and other objectives, managers will need to make choices: choices of what types of output to produce, how much to produce and at what price; choices of what techniques of production to use, how many workers to employ and of what type, what suppliers to use for raw materials, equipment, etc. In each case, when weighing up alternatives, managers will want to make the best choices. Business economists study these choices. They study economic decision making by firms.

The study of decision making can be broken down into three stages.

The external influences on the firm (the 'business environment'). Here we are referring to the various factors that affect the firm that are largely outside its direct control. Examples are the competition it faces, the prices its suppliers charge for raw materials, the state of the economy (e.g. whether growing or in recession) and the level of interest rates. Businesses need a clear understanding of their environment before they can set about making the right decisions.

Internal decisions of the firm. Given a firm's knowledge of these external factors, how will it then decide on prices, output, inputs, marketing, investment, etc.? Here the business economist can play a major role in helping firms achieve their business objectives.

The external effects of business decision making. When the firm has made its decisions and acted on them, how do the results affect the firm's rivals, its customers and the wider public? In other words, what is the impact of a firm's decision making on people outside the firm? Are firms' actions in the public interest, or is there a case for government intervention?

What do business economists do?

Our study of business will involve three types of activity:

- *Description*. We will describe the objectives of businesses (e.g. making profit or increasing market share), the types of market in which firms operate (e.g. competitive or non-competitive) and the constraints on decision making (e.g. the costs of production, the level of consumer demand and the state of the economy).
- *Analysis* We will analyse how a firm's costs might vary with the amount of output it produces and how its revenues will be affected by a change in consumer demand or a change in the price charged by rivals. We will also analyse the upswings and downswings in the economy: something that will have a crucial bearing on the profitability of many companies.
- *Recommendations*. Given the objectives of a firm, the business economist can help to show how those objectives can best be met. For example, if a firm wants to maximise its profits, the business economist can advise on what prices to charge, how much to invest, how much to advertise, etc. Of course, any such recommendations will only be as good as the data on which they are based. In an uncertain environment, recommendations will necessarily be more tentative.

In this chapter, as an introduction to the subject of business economics, we shall consider the place of the firm within its business environment, and assess how these external influences are likely to shape and determine its actions. In order to discuss the relationship between a business's actions and its environment, we first need to define what the business environment is.

1.1 THE BUSINESS ENVIRONMENT

It is normal to identify four dimensions to the business environment: political, economic, social/cultural and technological.

Political factors. Firms are directly affected by the actions of government and other political events. These might be major events affecting the whole of the business community, such as the collapse of communism, the problems in Syria and Iraq, the troubles between Russia and Ukraine or a change of government. Alternatively, they may be actions affecting just one part of the economy. For example, the ban on smoking in public places affects the tobacco industry; a minimum price on alcohol would affect breweries, pubs, supermarkets, etc.

Economic factors. There are numerous and diverse economic factors that affect businesses and these must be taken into account when businesses devise and act upon their strategy. Economic factors include the rising costs of raw materials; the market entry of a new rival; the latest Budget; changes

in policy abroad; the current availability of investment funds and the economic performance of the domestic and world economy.

It is normal to divide the economic environment in which the firm operates into two levels:

- *The microeconomic environment.* This includes all the economic factors that are *specific* to a particular firm operating in its own particular market. Thus one firm may be operating in a highly competitive market, whereas another may not; one firm may be faced by rapidly changing consumer tastes (e.g. a designer clothing manufacturer), while another may be faced with a virtually constant consumer demand (e.g. a potato merchant); one firm may face rapidly rising costs, whereas another may find that costs are constant or falling.
- *The macroeconomic environment.* This is the *national* and *international* economic situation in which business as a whole operates. Business in general will fare much better when the economy is growing, as opposed to when it is

| BOX 1.1 | A PERFECT PARTNERSHIP |

Making the best of your business environment

John Spedan Lewis created John Lewis in 1864 with the opening of a single shop on Oxford Street, London. In 1937, it bought Waitrose, which at the time had 10 shops. However, prior to this, in 1929, the first Trust Settlement was created making the John Lewis Partnership legal. Since then the Partnership has grown to include 43 John Lewis shops across the UK, 31 department stores, 10 John Lewis At Home, shops at St Pancras International and Heathrow Terminal 2, 33 Waitrose supermarkets, and an online and catalogue business, a production unit and a farm.

The John Lewis Partnership has over 90 000 permanent staff and it is they who own the business. The interests of these employees are the first priority of the John Lewis Partnership and they benefit if the company does well. They share in the profits and their opinions are taken into account in decision making, creating a democratic and transparent business. The Partnership has annual gross sales of over £10 billion and provides a wide range of goods and services. John Lewis itself has over 350 000 lines available in store and more than 280 000 lines available online. In addition, it offers other services, such as credit cards, insurance and broadband, to name a few.

The John Lewis Partnership is a unique one, in particular due to its organisational structure that puts its employees at its heart. Despite this very different focus from most businesses, the Partnership has been a success, expanding its reach over the past century. But how has it continued to be successful? What lessons are there for other businesses? How has its performance been affected by its business environment – by consumer tastes, by the actions of its rivals, by the state of the national and world economies and by government policy?

In particular, how would an economist analyse the Partnership's performance so as to advise it on its best strategy for the future? This is the sort of thing that business economists do and the sort of thing we will be doing throughout this text. We will also look at the impact of the behaviour of businesses on their customers, on employees, on competitors and on society in general. So let's take a closer look at the John Lewis Partnership and relate its business in general to the topics covered in this text.

The market environment

To be successful, it is important for the John Lewis Partnership to get its product right. This means understanding the markets that it operates in and how consumer demand responds to changes in prices and to the other services being offered. For example, in 2008, John Lewis responded to challenging conditions by increasing the number of products available for national delivery, prioritising customer service and introducing free delivery across the UK. Its investment in customer service clearly achieved its goal, helping John Lewis to rank as the best company in the 2009 UK Customer Satisfaction Survey. It has maintained good quality customer service since then and in the 2014 Verdict Customer Satisfaction Awards, it won various awards including Best Overall Retailer. John Lewis also enforced its commitment to being 'Never Knowingly Undersold', which helped the company to maintain its market share. It added lines such as Jigsaw to its fashion ranges to continue to meet customer demand and keep up with the fast-moving women's fashion industry.

The John Lewis Partnership as a whole has clearly had success in meeting the needs of its customers, having performed exceptionally well in the Which? Surveys. John Lewis won Best Retailer in 2014 for the second year in a row and Waitrose took the top spot in the Which? Supermarket survey in 2014 and was awarded the Best Food & Grocery Retailer prize in Verdict's Customer Satisfaction Awards.[1]

We look at how markets work in general in Chapters 4 and 5 and then look specifically at consumer demand and methods of stimulating it in Chapters 6 to 8.

The store 'John Lewis' operates in a highly competitive market, facing competition in its fashion departments from firms such as Debenhams, Selfridges, Next, etc., and in other departments from firms such as Currys and DFS.

The products it sells are crucial for its success, but the prices charged are equally important. Consumers will not be willing to pay any price, especially if they can buy similar products from other stores. Thus when setting prices and designing products, consideration must be given to what rival companies are doing. John Lewis's prices must be competitive to maintain its sales, profitability and its position in the global market. The same applies to Waitrose, as the supermarket industry is highly competitive and with growth in demand for the low-cost retailers, it has been a difficult time for Waitrose and its more high-end competitors, such as Marks & Spencer.

With the emergence of the Internet and online shopping, John Lewis has had to adapt its strategy and consider which markets to target. Back in 2011, John Lewis expanded its online market to continental Europe as part of a £250 million investment programme. Backed up by excellent customer service, online sales have expanded rapidly – for the half year to July 2014 they were up 25 per cent at £552 million.[2] This reflects a changing national and global market environment where consumers are increasingly shopping online.

The John Lewis Partnership has typically been UK based, but Waitrose ventured into the Channel Islands in 2011, following approval by the Jersey Competition Regulatory Authority (JCRA) in August 2010 for it to purchase five Channel Island supermarkets.[3] If the Partnership were to think about expanding further into the global marketplace, such as into the USA and Asia, careful consideration would need to be given to the competitors in these nations and to the tastes of consumers. Tesco, for example, had little success with its foray into the United States. The factors behind this would be something that the Partnership would need to consider before making any significant global move.

Strategic decisions such as growth by expansion in the domestic and global economy are examined in Chapters 13, 16 and 23.

---

[1] www.johnlewispartnership.co.uk/about/john-lewis.html

[2] www.johnlewispartnership.co.uk/media/press/y2014/press-release-11-september-2014-john-lewis-partnership-plc-interim-results-for-the-half-year-ended-26-July-2014.html

[3] John Whiteaker, 'Waitrose invades Channel Islands', *Retail Gazette*, 26 August 2010.

Production and employment

Being a profitable business depends not just on being able to sell a product, but on how efficiently the product can be produced. This means choosing the most appropriate technology and deploying the labour force in the best way. John Lewis and Waitrose, as with other companies, must decide on how many workers to employ, what wage rates to pay and what the conditions of employment should be. We explore production and costs in Chapters 9 and 10 and the employment of labour in Chapter 18.

The John Lewis Partnership has over 90 000 permanent members of staff employed in a variety of areas. However, despite rising sales in difficult trading conditions, in 2013 John Lewis cut over 300 managerial positions, the biggest cut seen since 2009 when hundreds of call-centre workers lost their jobs. Workers typically have involvement in decisions given the nature of the organisational structure, but the enforced job cuts came as a shock, especially given the good Christmas trading when sales were 13 per cent up on the same period in the previous year. However, much of those sales came from its online trading, further suggesting a change in the way we shop and a need for companies to adapt. At the time, this was reinforced by the collapse of companies such as HMV, which was facing increased competition from online companies, such as Amazon. However in 2013, all 90 000 workers received a bonus of 17 per cent of their annual salary and this was backed up by a further 15 per cent bonus in 2014.[4]

On the production side, the Partnership is a vertically integrated company, with a production unit and a farm. John Lewis makes its own-brand textiles in Lancashire and also has a small fabric weaving operation creating thousands of products for its stores every week. Its efficient operations also allow John Lewis to operate a seven-day delivery system on orders of many types of product. However, the growth in this area did require changes, as the Managing Director, Ron Bartram pointed out:

> To support that growth we've had to change the way we work . . . We need to expand our output in every area but our factory is very tight for space . . . We have to be flexible to handle the peaks and troughs of demand, and many Partners have been cross-trained so they can help out in different areas of the factory.[5]

In addition to selling its own-brand items in both John Lewis and Waitrose, numerous other brands are sold and this does create a need for awareness concerning the ethical nature of the business and what is known as 'corporate social responsibility'. We examine these broader social issues in Chapter 20, along with government policies to encourage, persuade or force firms to behave in the public interest.

The Partnership has been active in diversifying its suppliers and creating opportunities for small and medium-sized enterprises (SMEs) to access their supply chain, creating wider social benefits. In addition, Waitrose became the first supermarket to commit to stocking 100 per cent British in its own-label dairy products and, as stated on the website, Waitrose 'looks to buy local with buyers seeking out the finest local and regional products, helping to boost the economy in many rural areas and enabling customers to sample the very best foods made locally'.[6]

The John Lewis Partnership remains a success story of Britain's high streets and it has been hailed by the government as a 'model of responsible capitalism'.

The economy

So do the fortunes of the John Lewis Partnership and other companies depend solely on their policies and those of their competitors? The answer is no. One important element of a company's business environment is largely beyond its control: the state of the national economy and, for internationally trading companies, of the global economy. When the world economy is booming, sales and profits are likely to grow without too much effort by the company. However, when the global economy declines, as we saw in the economic downturn from 2008, trading conditions will become much tougher. In the years after the financial crisis, the global economy remained in a vulnerable position and this led to many companies entering administration, such as Woolworths, Jessops, HMV, Comet, Blockbuster and Peacocks.

In the Annual Report by the John Lewis Partnership from 2009, its Chairman said:

> As the economic downturn gained momentum, the focus of the Partnership has been to achieve the right balance between continuing to meet the needs and expectations of our customers and Partners while making sufficient profit to support our growth plans, by controlling our costs tightly and managing our cash efficiently.[7]

John Lewis experienced a slowdown in its sales of large value purchases in its home market, such as furnishings and electrical appliances, as the financial crisis began to spread. This decline in sales was largely driven by the collapse of the housing market, which remained weak for several years and has only recently begun to recover. Operating profit for the Partnership (excluding property profits) was down 17.7 per cent in April 2009 (compared to the same time the year before) at £316.8 million. For John Lewis itself, gross sales fell by 0.1 per cent and this pushed its operating profit down by £54.6 million from April 2008 to April 2009. Like-for-like sales were also down 3.4 per cent.

Due to the nature of the products being sold, Waitrose was somewhat more insulated against the financial crisis and in the same tax year experienced a 5.2 per cent increase in gross sales; a like-for-like sales growth of 0.4 per cent, but a fall in operating profit (excluding property profits) of 3.4 per cent. However, since then the supermarket industry has become more vulnerable, with low-cost retailers such as Aldi and Lidl posing a very real threat.

As difficult conditions prevailed in the economy, the Partnership turned things around, delivering 'market-beating

---

[4]'John Lewis staff get 15% annual bonus', *BBC News*, 6 March 2014.

[5]Katy Perceval, 'Material world', *JLP e-Zine*, 21 May 2010.

[6]www.johnlewispartnership.co.uk/about/waitrose/products-and-services.html

[7]The John Lewis Partnership Annual Report and Accounts 2009.

▶

sales growth' and healthy profits.[8] Prior to 2009, John Lewis' advertising investment seemed largely ineffective and part of its strategy to boost demand since then has been the use of a new approach to advertising. Its highly emotive TV advertising campaigns stimulated interest in the brand and it led to increased numbers of shoppers visiting its stores and increased sales. According to the Institute of Practitioners in Advertising (IPA), the campaign generated £1074 million of extra sales and £261 million of extra profit in just over two years. In 2012, John Lewis was the Grand Prix winner, receiving the Gold Award in the IPA's Effectiveness Awards.

Gross sales in the 2011 to 2012 fiscal year rose by 9.1 per cent to £8.47 billion and the Group operating profit increased by 15.8 per cent to £409.6 million. This was the second year that both John Lewis and Waitrose saw significant growth in their sales and operating profit, suggesting a reversal of fortunes since the onset of the financial crisis.[9] The positive trend has continued: gross sales for the Partnership were up by 6 per cent in the half year to July 2014, with both Waitrose and John Lewis outperforming the industry. Profit before tax and exceptional items was 12 per cent up on 2013, recorded at £129.8 million. However, John Lewis' figures had to offset those from Waitrose, as the supermarket industry remains vulnerable. Waitrose saw its profits fall by 9.4 per cent in the six months to July 2014, despite its sales rising to £3.15 billion.[10]

We examine the national and international business environment in Chapters 23 to 29. We also examine the impact on business of government policies to affect the economy – policies such as changes in taxation, interest rates, exchange rates and customs duties in Chapters 30 to 32.

 Choose a well-known company that trades globally and do a Web search to find out how well it has performed in recent years and how it has been influenced by various aspects of its business environment.

[8] www.johnlewispartnership.co.uk/content/dam/cws/pdfs/financials/annual%20reports/John _Lewis_plc_annual_report_and_accounts_2009.pdf
[9] The John Lewis Partnership Annual Report and Accounts 2011.
[10] 'John Lewis' 62% profits soar off-sets poor Waitrose first half results', *The Drum*, 11 September 2014.

in recession, as we have seen since the onset of the financial crisis. In examining the macroeconomic environment, we will also be looking at the policies that governments adopt in their attempt to steer the economy, since these policies, by affecting things such as taxation, interest rates and exchange rates, will have a major impact on firms.

Social/cultural factors. This aspect of the business environment concerns social attitudes and values. These include attitudes towards working conditions and the length of the working day, equal opportunities for different groups of people (whether by ethnicity, gender, physical attributes, etc.), the nature and purity of products, the use and abuse of animals, and images portrayed in advertising. The social/cultural environment also includes social trends, such as an increase in the average age of the population, or changes in attitudes towards seeking paid employment while bringing up small children. In recent times, various ethical issues, especially concerning the protection of the environment, have had a big impact on the actions of business and the image that many firms seek to present.

Technological factors. Over the past 30 years there has been significant technological change, which has had a huge impact on how firms produce, advertise and sell their products. The growth in online shopping means that firms can compete in global markets, but it has created problems for high street retailers. It has also changed how business is organised, providing opportunities for smaller online retailers, many of which are yet to be realised. The use of robots and other forms of computer-controlled production has changed the nature of work for many workers. The information-technology revolution has enabled much more rapid communication and has made it possible for firms across the world to work together more effectively. The working environment has become more flexible and efficient, with many workers able to do their job from home, while travelling or from another country.

The division of the factors affecting a firm into political, economic, social and technological is commonly known as a *PEST analysis*. However, we can add a further three factors to create *STEEPLE analysis*. The additional elements are:

Environmental (ecological) factors. This has become an increasingly important issue in politics and business, with many firms aiming to take a greener approach to business. Consumers are more environmentally aware and a green image can be useful in generating finance from investors and government. Business attitudes towards the environment are examined in section 22.1.

Legal factors. Businesses are affected by the legal framework in which they operate. Examples include industrial relations legislation, product safety standards, regulations

Definitions

PEST analysis Where the political, economic, social and technological factors shaping a business environment are assessed by a business so as to devise future business strategy.

STEEPLE analysis In addition to the four categories of factors considered in PEST analysis, STEEPLE analysis takes into account environmental, legal and ethical factors.

BOX 1.2   **THE BIOTECHNOLOGY INDUSTRY**

Its business environment

There are few areas of business that cause such controversy as biotechnology. It has generated new medicines, created pest-resistant crops, developed eco-friendly industrial processes and, through genetic mapping, is providing incalculable advances in gene therapy. These developments, however, have raised profound ethical issues. Many areas of biotechnology are uncontentious, but genetic modification and cloning have met with considerable public hostility, colouring many people's views of biotechnology in general.

Biotechnology refers to the application of knowledge about living organisms and their components to make new products and develop new industrial processes. For many it is seen as the next wave in the development of the knowledge-based economy. The global biotechnology industry was worth some $500 billion in 2015. The growth of the sector has made a significant contribution to job creation over the past 15 years.

The global structure of the industry

In global terms, the USA dominates this sector. According to the Organisation for Economic Co-operation and Development (OECD), out of a worldwide total of nearly 20 000 firms involved in biotechnology, the USA has 6862, of which 2178 are dedicated biotechnology firms, and between 2010 and 2012 these firms accounted for 41 per cent of all patent applications. Spain is the European leader in terms of biotechnology firms, with 3070, followed by France with 1950 firms, although France has more dedicated biotechnology firms than Spain. When compared to Europe as a whole, the US biotechnology sector spends over twice as much on research and development (R&D) – $26 billion – and generates twice as much in revenues. The UK is seventh in the league table with some 614 biotech companies, 66 per cent of which are estimated to engage in R&D.

The industry is dominated by small and medium-sized businesses. Most biotechnology firms (approximately 80% in the UK) have fewer than 50 employees. However, the larger firms dominate the sector in terms of R&D. In the USA and France, the countries with the largest R&D expenditure, some 88 and 84 per cent of this was carried out by firms with over 50 employees. In most countries biotech firms are geographically clustered, forming industry networks around key universities and research institutes. In the UK, such clusters can be found in Cambridge, Oxford and London. The link with universities and research institutes taps into the UK's strong science base.

In addition to such clustering, the biotech industry is well supported by the UK government and charitable organisations such as the Wellcome Trust. Such support helps to fund what is a highly research-intensive sector. The UK government not only provides finance, but also encourages firms to form collaborative agreements, and through such collaboration hopes to encourage better management and use of the results that research generates. It also offers help for biotechnology business start-ups, and guidance on identifying and gaining financial support.

The EU too provides a range of resources to support business within the biotech sector. The EUREKA programme, founded in 1985, attempts to help create pan-EU partnerships. Now consisting of 40 members including the EU itself, it provides support for such collaborative ventures through a series of National Project Co-ordinators who help to secure national or EU funding. Successful projects are awarded the internationally recognised Eureka label.

Such support by governments is seen as a crucial requirement for the creation of a successful biotechnology sector, as product development within the industry can take up to 12 years.

Funding, growth and consolidation in the sector

The majority of funding for the industry comes from 'venture capital' (investment by individuals and firms in new and possibly risky sectors). Even though the UK is Europe's largest venture capital market, such funding is highly volatile. Following significant share price rises in 1999 and 2000, many of the biotech companies listed on the stock market saw their share prices collapse, along with those of various high-tech companies. With a depressed stock market, raising finance became much more difficult.

Then, after growth between 2000 and 2007, there was a collapse in investment in both the EU (−79%) and the US (−62%) biotechnology industry. This had a serious impact on the viability of some businesses in the sector. Some were forced to close and others had to scale back their activities. However, the sector as a whole weathered the downturn relatively well. Investment recovered quickly and by 2011 the amount of capital raised globally by biotechnology firms was higher than that for any year since 2000. Since 2012 biotechnology shares have soared, with many tripling in value in just three years.

Growth in research and development has also recovered and in 2013 industry R&D spending increased by 14 per cent; however, this included a 20 per cent increase in the USA, but a 4 per cent decline in Europe.[11] This is another indication of the impact of the financial crisis and indeed the more constrained finance faced across Europe. With the growth in R&D expenditure, there has been a decline in the industry's net income.

In recent years there has been considerable consolidation in the sector. Mergers and acquisitions (M&As) have increased, involving both public and private biotech companies. The EY Firepower Index, which measures biotech companies' ability to take over or merge with other companies based on the strength of its balance sheet, has suggested that since 2013 there have been more viable competitors for any particular transaction than in previous years.[12] 2014 was a record year for deal making, with worldwide biopharma M&As alone exceeding $200 billion in value. And it was not just consolidation: there was a record number of new biotech companies, with 63 new US companies alone listed on the stock market.

High growth rates in coming years are expected. Forecasts indicate annual growth of the biotechnology sector of 10.8 per cent per year for the 10 years until 2019.[13] Furthermore, Jonathon Porritt, a leading environmentalist in the UK, estimates that the global market for biotechnology could lie somewhere between £150 billion and £360 billion by 2025. The differential between these estimates is substantial, but nevertheless it gives some indication as to the likely trend for this industry and where significant job growth may arise.

 From the brief outline above, identify the political, economic, social and technological dimensions shaping the biotechnology industry's business environment.

[11]'Beyond borders: Biotechnology Industry Report 2014', Ernst & Young, 23 June 2014.

[12]Elton Licking, 'Firepower fireworks drive record M&A in 2014. What's ahead for 2015?', Ernst & Young, 7 January 2015.

[13]Global Technology Market Research Report, IBIS Word, January 2015.

governing pricing in the privatised industries and laws preventing collusion between firms. We examine some of these laws in Chapter 21.

Ethical factors. Firms are increasingly under pressure to adopt a more socially responsible attitude towards business, with concerns over working conditions, product safety and quality and truthful advertising. Business ethics and corporate responsibility are examined in section 20.5.

This framework is widely used by organisations to audit their business environment and to help them establish a strategic approach to their business activities. It is nevertheless important to recognise that there is a great overlap and interaction among these sets of factors. Laws and government policies reflect social attitudes; technological factors determine economic ones, such as costs and productivity; technological progress often reflects the desire of researchers to meet social or environmental needs; and so on.

As well as such interaction, we must also be aware of the fact that the business environment is constantly changing. Some of these changes are gradual, some are revolutionary. To be successful, a business will need to adapt to these changes and, wherever possible, take advantage of them. Ultimately, the better business managers understand the environment in which they operate, the more likely they are to be successful, either in exploiting ever-changing opportunities or in avoiding potential disasters.

> ## Pause for thought
>
> *Under which heading of a PEST or STEEPLE analysis would you locate training and education?*

KEY IDEA 1

The behaviour and performance of firms is affected by the business environment. The business environment includes economic, political/legal, social/cultural and technological factors, as well as environmental, legal and ethical ones.

Although we shall be touching on political, social and technological factors, it is economic factors that will be our main focus of concern when examining the business environment.

1.2 THE STRUCTURE OF INDUSTRY

One of the most important and influential elements of the business environment is the *structure of industry*. How a firm performs depends on the state of its particular industry and the amount of competition it faces. Knowledge of the structure of an industry is therefore crucial if we are to understand business behaviour and its likely outcomes.

In this section we will consider how the production of different types of goods and services is classified and how firms are located in different industrial groups.

Classifying production

When analysing production it is common to distinguish three broad categories:

- ***Primary production.*** This refers to the production and extraction of natural resources such as minerals and sources of energy. It also includes output from agriculture.
- ***Secondary production.*** This refers to the output of the manufacturing and construction sectors of the economy.
- ***Tertiary production.*** This refers to the production of services, and includes a wide range of sectors such as finance, the leisure industry, retailing and transport.

Figures 1.1 and 1.2 show the share of output (or ***gross domestic product (GDP)***) and employment of these three sectors in 1974 and 2015. They illustrate how the tertiary sector has expanded rapidly. In 2015, it contributed some 80.2 per cent to total output and employed 83.1 per cent of all workers. By contrast, the share of output and employment of the secondary sector has declined. In 2015,

it accounted for only 17.9 per cent of output and 15.4 per cent of employment.

This trend is symptomatic of a process known as ***deindustrialisation*** – a decline in the share of manufacturing in GDP. Many commentators argue that this process of deindustrialisation is inevitable and that the existence of a large and growing tertiary sector in the UK economy reflects its maturity.

Furthermore, it is possible to identify part of the tertiary sector as a fourth or 'quarternary' sector. This refers to the knowledge-based part of the economy and includes services such as education, information generation and sharing, research and development, consultation, culture and parts of government. This sector has been growing as a proportion of the tertiary sector.

The classification of production into primary, secondary and tertiary, and even quarternary, allows us to consider

> ## Definitions
>
> **Primary production** The production and extraction of natural resources, plus agriculture.
>
> **Secondary production** The production from manufacturing and construction sectors of the economy.
>
> **Tertiary production** The production from the service sector of the economy.
>
> **Gross domestic product (GDP)** The value of output produced within the country over a 12-month period.
>
> **Deindustrialisation** The decline in the contribution to production of the manufacturing sector of the economy.

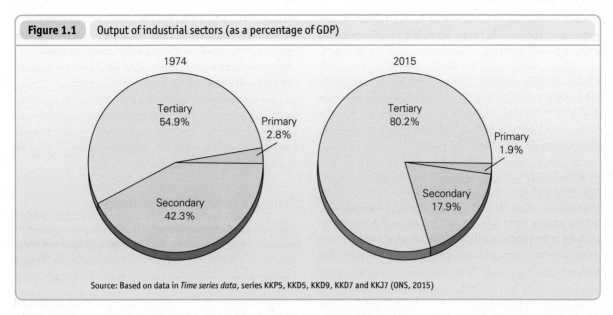

Figure 1.1 Output of industrial sectors (as a percentage of GDP)

Source: Based on data in *Time series data*, series KKP5, KKD5, KKD9, KKD7 and KKJ7 (ONS, 2015)

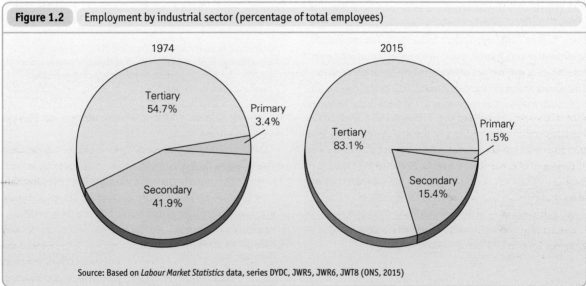

Figure 1.2 Employment by industrial sector (percentage of total employees)

Source: Based on *Labour Market Statistics* data, series DYDC, JWR5, JWR6, JWT8 (ONS, 2015)

broad changes in the economy. However, if we require a more comprehensive analysis of the structure of industry and its changes over time, we need to classify firms into *particular* industries. The following section outlines the classification process used in the UK and the EU.

Classifying firms into industries

An *industry* refers to a group of firms that produce a particular category of product. Thus we could refer to the electrical goods industry, the holiday industry, the aircraft industry or the insurance industry. Industries can then be grouped together into broad *industrial sectors*, such as manufacturing, or mining and quarrying, or construction, or transport.

Classifying firms into industrial groupings and sub-groupings has a number of purposes. It helps us to analyse various trends in the economy and to identify areas of growth and areas of decline. It helps to identify parts of the economy with specific needs, such as training or transport

infrastructure. Perhaps most importantly, it helps economists and businesspeople to understand and predict the behaviour of firms that are in direct competition with each other. In such cases, however, it may be necessary to draw the boundaries of an industry quite narrowly.

To illustrate this, take the case of the vehicle industry. The vehicle industry produces cars, lorries, vans and coaches. The common characteristic of these vehicles is that they are self-propelled road transport vehicles. In other words, we could draw the boundaries of an industry in terms

Definitions

Industry A group of firms producing a particular product or service.

Industrial sector A grouping of industries producing similar products or services

of the broad physical or technical characteristics of the products it produces. The problem with this type of categorisation, however, is that these products may not be substitutes in an *economic* sense. If I am thinking of buying a new vehicle to replace my car, I am hardly likely to consider buying a coach or a lorry! Lorries are not in competition with cars. If we are to group together products which are genuine competitors for each other, we will want to divide industries into more narrow categories, e.g. family cars, sports cars, etc.

On the other hand, if we draw the boundaries of an industry too narrowly, we may end up ignoring the effects of competition from another closely related industry. For example, if we are to understand the pricing strategies of electricity supply companies in the household market, it might be better to focus on the whole domestic fuel industry.

Thus how narrowly or broadly we draw the boundaries of an industry depends on the purposes of our analysis. You should note that the definition of an industry is based on the *supply* characteristics of firms, not on the qualities that consumers might attribute to products. For example, we classify cars into several groups according to size, price, engine capacity, design, model (e.g. luxury, saloon, seven-seater and sports), etc. These are demand-side characteristics of motor cars determined by consumers' tastes. The government, on the other hand, will categorise a company such as Nissan as belonging to the 'motor car' industry

because making cars is its principal activity, and it does this even though Nissan produces a variety of models each with numerous features to suit individual consumer needs.

Both demand- and supply-side measures are equally valid ways of analysing the competitive behaviour of firms, and governments will look at both when there is a particular issue of economic importance, such as a merger between car companies. However, the supply-side measure is more simply calculated and is less susceptible to change, thereby making it preferable for general use.

Standard Industrial Classification

The formal system under which firms are grouped into industries is known as the ***Standard Industrial Classification (SIC)***. It was first introduced in 1948, aiming to provide a uniform and comparable body of data on industry. Revisions to the SIC have been made in order to reflect changes

> **Definition**
>
> **Standard Industrial Classification (SIC)** The name given to the formal classification of firms into industries used by the government in order to collect data on business and industry trends.

Table 1.1 Standard Industrial Classification (2007)

Section	Division (manufacturing)
A Agriculture, forestry and fishing	
B Mining and quarrying	
C Manufacturing ———————————————	10 Manufacture of food products
D Electricity, gas, steam and air conditioning supply	11 Manufacture of beverages
E Water supply, sewerage, waste management and remediation activities	12 Manufacture of tobacco products
	13 Manufacture of textiles
F Construction	14 Manufacture of wearing apparel
G Wholesale and retail trade, repair of motor vehicles and motor cycles	15 Manufacture of leather and related goods
	16 Manufacture of wood and of products of wood and cork, except furniture; manufacture of articles of straw and plaiting materials
H Transport and storage	17 Manufacture of paper and paper products
I Accommodation and food service activities	18 Printing and reproduction of recorded media
J Information and communication	19 Manufacture of coke and refined petroleum products
K Financial and insurance activities	20 Manufacture of chemicals and chemical products
L Real estate activities	21 Manufacture of basic pharmaceutical products and pharmaceutical preparations
M Professional, scientific and technical activities	22 Manufacture of rubber and plastic products
N Administrative and support service activities	23 Manufacture of other non-metallic mineral products
O Public administration and defence; compulsory social security	24 Manufacture of basic metals
P Education	25 Manufacture of fabricated metal products, except machinery and equipment
Q Human health and social work activities	26 Manufacture of computer, electrical and optical equipment
R Arts, entertainment and recreation	27 Manufacture of electrical equipment
S Other service activities	28 Manufacture of equipment not elsewhere specified
T Activities of households as employers; undifferentiated goods and services producing activities of households for own use	29 Manufacture of motor vehicles, trailers and semi-trailers
	30 Manufacture of other transport equipment
	31 Manufacture of furniture
U Extra-territorial organisations and bodies	32 Other manufacturing
	33 Repair and installation of machinery and equipment

Source: Based on *Standard Industrial Classification 2007* (National Statistics)

Table 1.2	The classification of the manufacture of a tufted carpet
Section C	Manufacturing (comprising divisions 10 to 33)
Division 13	Manufacture of textiles
Group 13.9	Manufacture of other textiles
Class 13.93	Manufacture of carpets and rugs
Subclass 13.93/1	Manufacture of woven or tufted carpets and rugs

Source: Based on *Standard Industrial Classification 2007* (National Statistics)

in the UK's industrial structure, such as the emergence of new products and industries. The most recent revision in 2007 brought the UK and EU systems of industry classification further into alignment with each other, helping the process of effectively monitoring business across the EU.

SIC (2007) is divided into 21 sections (A–U), each representing a production classification (see Table 1.1). These sections are then divided into 88 divisions, which are in turn divided into 272 groups. The groups are then divided into 615 classes and finally 191 subclasses. Table 1.2 gives an example of how a manufacturer of a tufted carpet would be classified according to this system.

Changes in the structure of the UK economy

Given such a classification, how has UK industry changed over time? Figures 1.3 and 1.4 show the changes in output and employment of the various sectors identified by the SIC

between 1990 and 2014. Note that output is measured in terms of *real values*: i.e. market values corrected for inflation (see pages 484–5).

The figures reveal that output of the services industries (G–S) grew rapidly throughout the period from 1990 to 2008, but then there was a temporary decline in some sectors following the recession of 2008–10. Construction too (F) grew for most of the period, but again declined in the recession and also in the earlier slowdown of the early 1990s. Since 1990, there has been little long-term growth in agricultural output (A) but the value of output has fluctuated year by year depending on harvests and prices. The value of output of the mining and extraction sector (B) has been quite volatile, reflecting the decline in the coal industry in the mid-1980s, the expansion and then decline of the oil industry and volatile prices of oil and gas; output has tailed away significantly in recent years. Manufacturing (C) experienced modest growth until the late 1990s. Since then it has experienced a slight decline.

In respect to employment, significant variations once again occur between sections and indeed divisions. The financial services sector (K) has seen rapid growth in employment, but there has been a decline in employment in parts of the retail banking sector (fewer counter staff are required in high street banks, given the growth in cash machines, direct debits, debit cards, etc.). Real estate (L) is another sector that has expanded more recently and, as with construction (F), can be very susceptible to the strength of the economy. Manufacturing (C) has seen a general decline in employment since the 1980s, in particular in traditional

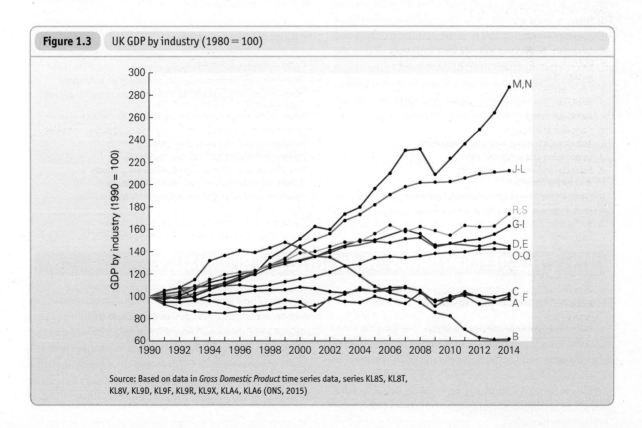

Figure 1.3 UK GDP by industry (1980 = 100)

Source: Based on data in *Gross Domestic Product* time series data, series KL8S, KL8T, KL8V, KL9D, KL9F, KL9R, KL9X, KLA4, KLA6 (ONS, 2015)

Figure 1.4   UK employment by industry (1980 = 100)

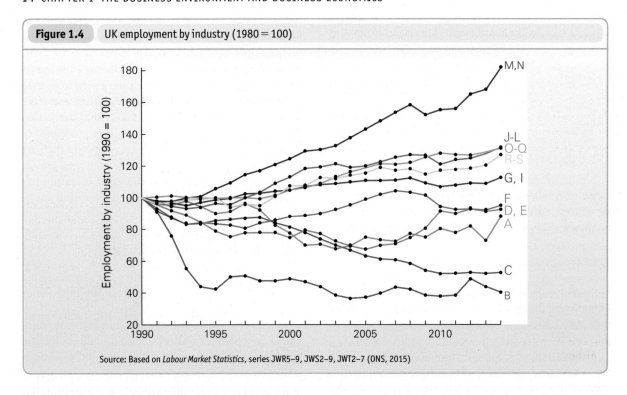

Source: Based on *Labour Market Statistics*, series JWR5–9, JWS2–9, JWT2–7 (ONS, 2015)

areas such as shipbuilding and metal manufacturing. However, there has been a growth in employment in some of the more 'high-tech' industries. Similar falls have occurred in mining, quarrying and extraction (B), electricity, gas and water supply (D and E).

When considering the changes in the structure of UK industry, it is important to examine the subsections and divisions within the SIC. For example, we might look solely at manufacturing and note the decline in output and employment, but taking a closer look will show us that the process of deindustrialisation has not been experienced by all manufacturing industries. Certain divisions, such as instruments and electrical engineering, are in fact among the fastest growing in the whole UK economy.

Analysing industrial concentration

The SIC also enables us to address wider issues such as changes in **industrial concentration**.

When we examine the size structure of UK industry, we find that some sectors are dominated by large business units

(those employing 250 or more people), such as electricity, gas and the mining and quarrying sectors. In contrast, the bulk of output in the service sector, agriculture, forestry and fishing is produced by small or medium-sized enterprises (SMEs). We look at industrial structure in more detail at various points in the text, with a particular focus on the small-firm sector in Chapter 16.

> **Pause for thought**
>
> *Give some examples of things we might learn about the likely behaviour and performance of businesses in an industry by knowing something about the industrial concentration of that industry.*

> **Definition**
>
> **Industrial concentration** The degree to which an industry is dominated by large business enterprises.

1.3   THE DETERMINANTS OF BUSINESS PERFORMANCE

Structure–conduct–performance

KI 1
p 10

It should be apparent from our analysis thus far that business performance is strongly influenced by the market structure within which the firm operates. This is known as the *structure–conduct–performance paradigm*.

The structure of an industry depends on many factors, such as consumer tastes, technology and the availability of

resources. These factors determine the competitiveness of an industry and influence firms' behaviour, as a business operating in a highly competitive market structure will conduct its activities differently from a business in a market with relatively few competitors. For example, the more competitive the market, the more aggressive the business may have to be in order to sell its product and remain competitive.

Such conduct will in turn influence how well businesses perform. Performance can be measured by several different indicators, such as profitability, market share or growth in market share, and changes in share prices, especially relative to those of other firms in the industry, to name some of the most commonly used.

Throughout the text, we will see how market structure affects business conduct, and how business conduct affects business performance. Chapters 11 and 12 are particularly relevant here.

It would be wrong, however, to argue that business performance is totally shaped by external factors such as market structure. In fact, the internal aims and organisation of business may be very influential in determining success.

Internal aims and organisation

Economists have traditionally assumed that businesses aim to maximise their profits. This traditional 'theory of the firm' shows the output that a firm should sell and at what price, if its objective is to make as much profit as possible.

Although this is still the case for many firms, as businesses have grown and become increasingly complex, more specialist managers have been employed to make the day-to-day decisions. This complexity of organisation makes the assumption of profit maximisation too simplistic in many cases.

With complex products and production lines, we have seen the emergence of increasingly distinct groups within firms, including the owners (shareholders) and the managers who are employed for their specialist knowledge. The problem is that the objectives of managers and owners may well differ and are often in conflict.

The owners of a business may want to maximise profits by selling a particular level of output at a certain price. However, the managers may want to maximise sales and reduce prices to achieve this goal. This action may reduce

profits, creating a conflict between objectives. Understanding these possible conflicts is crucial when trying to establish the objectives of a business. Whose objectives are being pursued? We will look at these conflicts and solutions in Chapters 3 and 14.

It is not only the aims of a business that affect its performance. Performance also depends on the following:

- *Internal structure.* The way in which the firm is organised (e.g. into departments or specialised units) will affect its costs, its aggressiveness in the market, its willingness to innovate, etc.
- *Information.* The better informed a business is about its markets, about its costs of production, about alternative techniques and about alternative products it could make, the better will it be able to fulfil its goals.
- *The competence of management.* The performance of a business will depend on the skills, experience, motivation, dedication and sensitivity of its managers.
- *The quality of the workforce.* The more skilled and the better motivated is a company's workforce, the better will be its results.

Systems. The functioning of any organisation will depend on the systems in place: information systems, systems for motivation (rewards, penalties, team spirit, etc.), technical systems (for sequencing production, for quality control, for setting specifications), distributional systems (transport, ordering and supply), financial systems (for accounting and auditing), and so on. We shall be examining many of these features of internal organisation in subsequent chapters.

> **Pause for thought**
>
> KI 7
> p 38
>
> *Other than profit and sales, what other objectives might managers have and how would you expect this to affect the price charged and output sold?*

SUMMARY

1a Business economics is about the study of economic decisions made by business and the influences upon this. It is also concerned with the effects that this decision making has upon other businesses and the performance of the economy in general.

1b The business environment refers to the environment within which business decision making takes place. When analysing a business's environment it has been traditional to divide it into four dimensions: political, economic, social and technological (PEST). It is common practice nowadays, however, to add a further three dimensions: environmental, ethical and legal (STEEPLE).

1c The economic dimension of the business environment is divided into two: the microeconomic environment and the macroeconomic environment. The microenvironment concerns factors specific to a particular firm

in a particular market. The macroenvironment concerns how national and international economic circumstances affect all business, although to different degrees.

2a Production is divided into primary, secondary or tertiary. In most advanced countries the tertiary sector has grown relative to the secondary sector.

2b Firms are classified into industries and industries into sectors. Such classification enables us to chart changes in industrial structure over time and to assess changing patterns of industrial concentration, its causes and effects.

3 The performance of a business is determined by a wide range of both internal and external factors, such as business organisation, the aims of owners and managers, and market structure.

MyEconLab

This book can be supported by MyEconLab, which contains a range of additional resources, including an online homework and tutorial system designed to test and build your understanding.

You need both an access card and a course ID to access MyEconLab:

1. Is your lecturer using MyEconLab? Ask your lecturer for your course ID.

2. Has an access card been included with the book at a reduced cost? Check the inside back cover of the book.

3. If you have a course ID but no access card, go to: http://www.myeconlab.com/ to buy access to this interactive study programme.

REVIEW QUESTIONS

1 Assume you are a Japanese car manufacturer with a plant located in the UK and are seeking to devise a business strategy for the twenty-first century. Conduct a STEEPLE analysis on the UK car industry and evaluate the various strategies that the business might pursue.

2 What is the Standard Industrial Classification (SIC)? In what ways might such a classification system be useful? Can you think of any limitations or problems such a system might have over time?

3 Into which of the three sectors would you put (a) the fertiliser industry; (b) a marketing agency serving the electronics industry?

4 In Chapter 1 we have identified some of the major changes in the UK's industrial structure and concentration in recent times. What were these changes and what might they tell us about changes in the UK economy?

5 Outline the main determinants of business performance. Distinguish whether these are micro- or macroeconomic.

Economics and the world of business

Business issues covered in this chapter

■ How do economists set about analysing business decision making?
■ What are the core economic concepts that are necessary to understand the economic choices that businesses have to make, such as what to produce, what inputs and what technology to use, where to locate their production and how best to compete with other firms?
■ What is meant by 'opportunity cost'? How is it relevant when people make economic choices?
■ What is the difference between microeconomics and macroeconomics?
■ How can you represent simple economic relationships in a graph?
■ What are the relative merits of presenting data in a chart or in a table?
■ What is meant by a functional relationship?

2.1 WHAT DO ECONOMISTS STUDY?

This text aims to give you a better understanding of the economic influences on business in a dynamic world.

Since 2007 we have seen many changes in the global financial system. Many banks and financial institutions failed and there was considerable intervention by governments and central banks across the world to rescue the financial system and restore economic growth.

But intervention could not prevent recession. Businesses of all sizes were adversely affected by difficult lending conditions and falling consumer demand; many still are. It is likely to take many years for some economies to recover to pre-crisis levels. In the UK, GDP remains some 17 per cent lower than if growth had continued on its pre-2008 trajectory.

As we look forward, key economic challenges include making further reforms to the financial system and reducing levels of sovereign debt.

The global economy is changing, perhaps more dramatically than in the recent past, but you will be glad to know that most of the principles of economics do not. This text therefore aims to give you a much better understanding of the economic influences on the world of business in a constantly changing world.

Tackling the problem of scarcity

In the previous chapter we looked at various aspects of the business environment and the influences on firms. We also looked at some of the economic problems that businesses face. But what contribution can economists make to the analysis of these problems and to recommending solutions?

To answer this question we need to go one stage back and ask what it is that economists study in general. What is it that makes a problem an *economic* problem? The answer

KEY IDEA 2

Scarcity is the excess of human wants over what can actually be produced. Because of scarcity, various choices have to be made between alternatives.

is that there is one central problem faced by all individuals, firms, governments and in all societies. This is the problem of *scarcity*.

Of course, we do not all face the problem of scarcity to the same degree. A poor person unable to afford enough to eat or a decent place to live will hardly see it as a 'problem' that a rich person cannot afford a second Ferrari. But economists do not claim that we all face an *equal* problem of scarcity. The point is that people, both rich and poor, want more than they can have and this will cause them to behave in certain ways. Economics studies that behaviour.

Pause for thought

If we would all like more money, why doesn't the government or central bank print a lot more? Could this solve the problem of scarcity 'at a stroke'?

Two of the key elements in satisfying wants are **consumption** and **production**. As far as consumption is concerned, economics studies how much the population spends; what the pattern of consumption is in the economy; and how much people buy of particular items. The business economist, in particular, studies consumer behaviour; how sensitive consumer demand is to changes in prices, advertising, fashion and other factors; and how the firm can seek to persuade the consumer to buy its products.

As far as production is concerned, economics studies how much the economy produces in total; what influences the rate of growth of production; and why the production of some goods increases and the production of others falls. The business economist tends to focus on the role of the firm in this process: what determines the output of individual businesses and the range of products they produce; what techniques firms use and why; and what determines their investment decisions and how many workers they employ.

The production of goods and services involves the use of inputs, or *factors of production* as they are often called. These are of three broad types:

- Human resources: *labour*. The labour force is limited both in number and in skills.
- Natural resources: *land and raw materials*. The world's land area is limited, as are its raw materials.
- Manufactured resources: *capital*. Capital consists of all those inputs that themselves have had to be produced in the first place. The world has a limited stock of capital: a limited supply of factories, machines, transportation and other equipment. The productivity of capital is limited by the state of technology.

We will be studying the use of these resources by firms for the production of goods and services: production to meet consumer demand – production which will thus help to reduce the problem of scarcity.

Demand and supply

We said that economics is concerned with consumption and production. Another way of looking at this is in terms of *demand* and *supply*. In fact, demand and supply and the relationship between them lie at the very centre of economics. But what do we mean by the terms, and what is their relationship with the problem of scarcity?

Demand is related to wants. If goods and services were free, people would simply demand and consume whatever they wanted. Such wants are virtually boundless: perhaps only limited by people's imagination. *Supply*, on the other hand, is limited. The amount that firms can supply depends on the resources and technology available.

Given the problem of scarcity, given that human wants exceed what can actually be produced, *potential* demands will exceed *potential* supplies. Society therefore has to find some way of dealing with this problem. Somehow it has to try to match demand and supply. This applies at the level of the economy overall: *aggregate* demand will need to be balanced against *aggregate* supply. In other words, total spending in the economy must balance total production. It also applies at the level of individual goods and services. The demand and supply of cabbages must balance, as must the demand and supply of TVs, cars, houses and bus journeys.

KI 2
p 18

But if potential demand exceeds potential supply, how are *actual* demand and supply to be made equal? Either demand has to be curtailed or supply has to be increased, or a combination of the two. Economics studies this process. It studies how demand adjusts to available supplies, and how supply adjusts to consumer demands.

The business economist studies the role of firms in this process: how they respond to demand, or, indeed, try

Definitions

Scarcity The excess of human wants over what can actually be produced to fulfil these wants.

Consumption The act of using goods and services to satisfy wants. This will normally involve purchasing the goods and services.

Production The transformation of inputs into outputs by firms in order to earn profit (or meet some other objective).

Factors of production (or resources) The inputs into the production of goods and services: labour, land and raw materials, and capital.

Labour All forms of human input, both physical and mental, into current production.

Land (and raw materials) Inputs into production that are provided by nature: e.g. unimproved land and mineral deposits in the ground.

Capital All inputs into production that have themselves been produced: e.g. factories, machines and tools.

to create demand for their products; how they combine their inputs to achieve output in the most efficient way; how they decide the amount to produce and the price to charge their customers; and how they make their investment decisions. Not only this, the business economist also considers the wider environment in which firms operate and how they are affected by it: the effect of changes in the national and international economic climate, such as upswings and downswings in the economy, and changes in interest rates and exchange rates. In short, the business economist studies supply: how firms' output is affected by a range of influences, and how firms can best meet their objectives.

Dividing up the subject

Economics is traditionally divided into two main branches – *macroeconomics* and *microeconomics*, where 'macro' means big, and 'micro' means small.

- *Macroeconomics* examines the economy as a whole. It is thus concerned with **aggregate demand** and **aggregate supply**. By 'aggregate demand' we mean the total amount of spending in the economy, whether by consumers, by overseas customers for our exports, by the government, or by firms when they buy capital equipment or stock up on raw materials. By 'aggregate supply' we mean the total national output of goods and services.

- *Microeconomics* examines the individual parts of the economy. It is concerned with the factors that determine the demand and supply of particular goods and services and resources: cars, butter, clothes and haircuts; electricians, shop assistants, blast furnaces, computers and oil. It explores issues in competition between firms and the rationale for trade.

Business economics, because it studies firms, is largely concerned with microeconomic issues. Nevertheless, given that businesses are affected by what is going on in the economy as a whole, it is still important for the business economist to study the macroeconomic environment and its effects on individual firms.

Definitions

Macroeconomics The branch of economics that studies economic aggregates (grand totals): e.g. the overall level of prices, output and employment in the economy.

Aggregate demand The total level of spending in the economy.

Aggregate supply The total amount of output in the economy.

Microeconomics The branch of economics that studies individual units: e.g. households, firms and industries. It studies the interrelationships between these units in determining the pattern of production and distribution of goods and services.

2.2 BUSINESS ECONOMICS: THE MACROECONOMIC ENVIRONMENT

Because things are scarce, societies are concerned that their resources are being used as *fully as possible*, and that over time the national output should *grow*. Governments are keen to boast to their electorate how much the economy has grown since they have been in charge!

The achievement of growth and the full use of resources is not easy, however, as demonstrated by the periods of high unemployment and stagnation that have occurred from time to time throughout the world (e.g. in the 1930s, the early 1980s, the early 1990s and the late 2000s). Furthermore, attempts by governments to stimulate growth and employment have often resulted in inflation and a large rise in imports. Even when societies do achieve growth, it can be short lived. Economies typically experience cycles, where periods of growth alternate with periods of stagnation, such periods varying from a few months to a few years.

Macroeconomics, then, studies the determination of national output and its growth over time. It also studies the problems of stagnation, unemployment, inflation, the balance of international payments and cyclical instability, and the policies adopted by governments to deal with these problems.

Macroeconomic problems are closely related to the balance between aggregate demand and aggregate supply.

If aggregate demand is *too high* relative to aggregate supply, inflation and balance of payments deficits are likely to result.

- *Inflation* refers to a general rise in the level of prices throughout the economy. If aggregate demand rises substantially, firms are likely to respond by raising their prices. After all, if demand is high, they can probably still sell as much as before (if not more) even at the higher prices, and thus make more profit. If firms in general put up their prices, inflation results.

- *Balance of trade deficits* are the excess of imports over exports. If aggregate demand rises, part of the extra demand will be spent on imports, such as US tablets, Japanese MP3 players, German cars and Chilean wine. Also if inflation is high, home-produced goods will become uncompetitive with foreign goods. We are likely, therefore, to buy more foreign imports, and people abroad are likely to buy fewer of our exports.

Definitions

Rate of inflation The percentage increase in the level of prices over a 12-month period.

Balance of trade Exports of goods and services minus imports of goods and services. If exports exceed imports, there is a 'balance of trade surplus' (a positive figure). If imports exceed exports, there is a 'balance of trade deficit' (a negative figure).

If aggregate demand is *too low* relative to aggregate supply, unemployment and recession may well result.

- A *recession* is defined as where output in the economy declines for two consecutive quarters or more: in other words, where growth becomes negative over that time. A recession is associated with a low level of consumer spending. If people spend less, shops are likely to find themselves with unsold stocks. As a result they will buy less from the manufacturers, which in turn will cut down on production.
- *Unemployment* is likely to result from cutbacks in production. If firms are producing less, they will need a smaller labour force.

Government macroeconomic *policy*, therefore, tends to focus on the balance of aggregate demand and aggregate supply. It can be *demand-side policy*, which seeks to influence the level of spending in the economy. This in turn will affect the level of production, prices and employment. Or it can be *supply-side policy*. This is designed to influence the level of production directly: for example, by creating more incentives for businesses to innovate.

Macroeconomic policy and its effects on business

KI 1
p 10

Both demand-side and supply-side policy will affect the business environment. Take demand-side policy. If there is a recession, the government might try to boost the level of spending (aggregate demand) by cutting taxes, increasing government spending or reducing interest rates. If consumers respond by purchasing more, then this will clearly have an effect on businesses. But firms will want to be stocked up ready for an upsurge in consumer demand. Therefore, they will want to estimate the effect on their own particular market of a boost to aggregate demand. Studying the macroeconomic environment and the effects of government policy, therefore, is vital for firms when forecasting future demand for their product.

It is the same with supply-side policy. The government may introduce tax incentives for firms to invest, or for people to work harder; it may introduce new training schemes;

it may build new motorways. These policies will affect firms' costs and hence the profitability of production. So, again, firms will want to predict how government policies are likely to affect them, so that they can plan accordingly.

The circular flow of income

One of the most useful diagrams for illustrating the macroeconomic environment and the relationships between producers and consumers is the *circular flow of income* diagram. This is illustrated in Figure 2.1.

The consumers of goods and services are labelled 'households'. Some members of households, of course, are also workers, and in some cases are the owners of other factors of production too, such as land. The producers of goods and services are labelled 'firms'.

Firms and households are in a twin 'demand and supply' relationship.

First, on the right-hand side of the diagram, households demand goods and services, and firms supply goods and services. In the process, exchange takes place. In a money economy (as opposed to a *barter economy*), firms exchange

Definitions

Recession A period where national output falls. The official definition is where real GDP declines for two or more consecutive quarters.

Unemployment The number of people who are actively looking for work but are currently without a job. (Note that there is much debate as to who should officially be counted as unemployed.)

Demand-side policy Government policy designed to alter the level of aggregate demand, and thereby the level of output, employment and prices.

Supply-side policy Government policy that attempts to alter the level of aggregate supply directly.

Barter economy An economy where people exchange goods and services directly with one another without any payment of money. Workers would be paid with bundles of goods.

| **Figure 2.1** | Circular flow of goods and incomes |

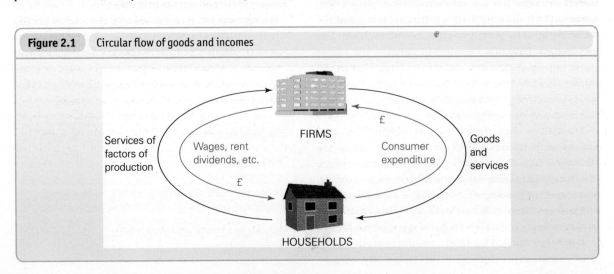

BOX 2.1   **LOOKING AT MACROECONOMIC DATA**

Assessing different countries' macroeconomic performance

	Unemployment (% of workforce)				Inflation (%)				Economic growth (%)				Balance on current account[1] (% of national income)			
	USA	Japan	Germany	UK	USA	Japan	Germany	UK	USA	Japan	Germany	UK	USA	Japan	Germany	UK
1961–70	4.8	1.3	0.6	1.7	2.4	5.6	2.7	4.0	4.2	10.1	4.4	2.8	0.5	0.6	0.9	0.2
1971–80	6.4	1.8	2.2	3.8	7.0	8.8	5.2	13.4	3.2	4.4	2.9	2.0	0.9	0.5	1.1	−0.7
1981–90	7.1	2.5	6.0	9.6	4.5	1.8	2.6	6.2	3.2	4.6	2.3	2.7	−1.7	2.3	2.6	−1.4
1991–2000	5.6	3.3	7.8	7.9	2.2	0.5	1.8	3.2	3.4	1.2	2.1	2.5	−1.6	2.5	−0.7	−1.5
2001–6	5.3	4.8	9.2	5.1	2.7	−0.4	1.6	1.6	2.4	1.4	1.1	2.5	−5.0	3.3	3.3	−2.2
2007–15[2]	7.7	4.1	6.3	7.0	1.5	0.3	1.2	2.3	1.2	0.2	1.2	1.2	−2.3	1.2	6.7	−2.1

Notes: [1] The current account balance is the balance of trade plus other income flows from and to abroad
[2] 2015 figures based on forecasts
Source: Based on *Statistical Annex of the European Economy* (EC, 2015)

Rapid economic growth, low unemployment, low inflation and the avoidance of balance of trade deficits are the major macroeconomic policy objectives of most governments around the world. To help them achieve these objectives they employ economic advisers. But when we look at the performance of various economies, the success of government macroeconomic policies seems decidedly 'mixed'.

The table shows data for the USA, Japan, Germany and the UK from 1961 to 2015.

If the government does not have much success in managing the economy, it could be for the following reasons:

■ Economists have incorrectly analysed the problems and hence have given the wrong advice.

■ Economists disagree and hence have given conflicting advice.
■ Economists have based their advice on inaccurate forecasts.
■ Governments have not heeded the advice of economists.
■ There is little else that governments could have done: the problems were insoluble.

1. *Has the UK generally fared better or worse than the other three countries?*

2. *Was there a common pattern in the macroeconomic performance of each of the four countries over this period of just over 50 years?*

---

goods and services for money. In other words, money flows from households to firms in the form of consumer expenditure, while goods and services flow the other way – from firms to households.

This coming together of buyers and sellers is known as a *market* – whether it be a street market, a shop, an auction, a mail-order system or whatever. Thus we talk about the market for apples, the market for oil, for cars, for houses, for televisions, and so on.

Second, firms and households come together in the market for factors of production. This is illustrated on the left-hand side of the diagram. This time the demand and supply roles are reversed. Firms demand the use of factors of production owned by households – labour, land and capital. Households supply them. Thus the services of labour and other factors flow from households to firms, and in exchange firms pay households money – namely, wages, rent, dividends and interest. Just as we referred to particular goods markets, so we can also refer to particular factor markets – the market for bricklayers, for secretaries, for hairdressers, for land, etc.

There is thus a circular flow of incomes. Households earn incomes from firms and firms earn incomes from households. The money circulates. There is also a circular flow of goods and services, but in the opposite direction. Households supply factor services to firms, which then use them to supply goods and services to households.

Macroeconomics is concerned with the total size of the flow. If consumers choose to spend more, firms will earn more from the increased level of sales. They will probably respond by producing more or raising their prices, or some combination of the two. As a result, they will end up paying more out to workers in the form of wages, and to shareholders in the form of profits. Households will thus have gained additional income. This will then lead to an additional increase in consumer spending, and, therefore, a further boost to production.

Definition

Market The interaction between buyers and sellers.

The effect does not go on indefinitely, however. When households earn additional incomes, not all of it is spent: not all of it recirculates. Some of the additional income will be saved; some will be paid in taxes; and some will be spent on imports (and thus will not stimulate domestic production). The bigger these 'withdrawals', as they are called, the less will production carry on being stimulated.

It is important for firms to estimate the eventual effect of an initial rise in consumer demand (or a rise in government expenditure, for that matter). Will there be a boom in the economy, or will the rise in demand merely fizzle out? A study of macroeconomics helps business people to understand the effects of changes in aggregate demand, and the effects that such changes will have on their own particular business.

We examine the macroeconomic environment and the effects on business of macroeconomic policy in Chapters 26–32.

2.3 BUSINESS ECONOMICS: MICROECONOMIC CHOICES

Microeconomics and choice

 Because resources are scarce, choices have to be made. There are three main categories of choice that must be made in any society:

- *What* goods and services are going to be produced and in what quantities, given that there are not enough resources to produce all the things that people desire? How many cars, how much wheat, how much insurance, how many rock concerts, etc. will be produced?
- *How* are things going to be produced, given that there is normally more than one way of producing things? What resources are going to be used and in what quantities? What techniques of production are going to be adopted? Will cars be produced by robots or by assembly-line workers? Will electricity be produced from coal, oil, gas, nuclear fission, renewable resources or a mixture of these?

- *For whom* are things going to be produced? In other words, how is the nation's income going to be distributed? After all, the higher your income, the more you can consume of the nation's output. What will be the wages of farm workers, printers, cleaners and accountants? How much will pensioners receive? How much profit will owners of private companies receive or will state-owned industries make?

All societies have to make these choices, whether they be made by individuals, by groups or by the government. These choices can be seen as *micro*economic choices, since they are concerned not with the *total* amount of national output, but with the *individual* goods and services that make it up: what they are, how they are made and who gets the incomes to buy them.

BOX 2.2 WHAT, HOW AND FOR WHOM

Who answers these questions?

As we have seen, in microeconomics there are three key questions: what to produce; how to produce; for whom to produce. These questions have to be answered because of the problem of scarcity. However, the scarcity problem does not tell us anything about who answers these questions and how the problems are addressed.

In some economies, it is the government or some central planning authority that answers these questions. This is known as a *planned* or *command economy*. At the other end of the spectrum is a *free-market* or *laissez-faire economy*, where there is no government intervention at all and it is individuals and firms who answer the questions above.

In practice, all economies are *mixed economies*, where decisions are taken by government, individuals and firms. It is the degree of government intervention that distinguishes different economic systems and determines how far towards each end of the spectrum an economy lies.

In countries such as China or Cuba, the government has a large role, whereas in the USA and various other Western economies, the government plays a much smaller role. Furthermore, governments differ in the type of intervention, such as regulation, taxation and public ownership, so any

Definitions

Planned or **command economy** An economy where all economic decisions are taken by the central (or local) authorities.

Free-market or **laissez-faire economy** An economy where all economic decisions are taken by individual households and firms, with no government intervention.

Mixed economy An economy where economic decisions are made partly through the market and partly by the government.

BOX 2.2 | **WHAT, HOW AND FOR WHOM** (*Continued*)

comparisons between countries and the amount of intervention should be made with caution.

Over the past 30 years, there has been a general shift towards the free-market end of the spectrum, as more and more countries have abandoned central planning. So, why are more countries increasingly relying on the free market to answer the questions of what, how and for whom to produce?

The command economy

In a command economy, it is the role of the state to allocate resources. It will decide how much should be invested and in what industries. It may tell each industry and individual firms which goods to produce, how much to produce and how they should be producing: e.g. the technology to use and labour requirements.

The state will also have a role in deciding how output should be distributed between consumers, i.e. the 'for whom' question. Government may distribute goods based on its judgement of its people's needs; it could distribute goods and services directly through rationing or could determine the distribution of income and perhaps prices to influence consumer expenditure.

Although countries have moved towards the free-market end of the spectrum, there are advantages of this type of economic system. Governments can achieve high rates of growth through its allocation of resources to investment and also avoid unemployment by dictating the allocation of labour. Goods and services such as education, policing, national defence would be provided and governments could take account of 'bad' things, such as pollution, which is unlikely to be the case in an economy where there is no government intervention. However, there is likely to be a significant amount of bureaucracy and the administrative costs of a command economy are prohibitive, as modern economies are very complex, meaning that planning would require a huge amount of complex information.

Furthermore, incentives may be very limited. For example, if income is distributed relatively equally between individuals, this could reduce the incentive to work harder or to train. Or if firms are rewarded by meeting targets for output, they may reduce the quality of goods in order to meet the targets.

Consumers and producers may lack individual liberty, being told what to produce and consume and this, in turn, could create shortages and surpluses. Government may dictate what is produced, but what happens if consumers don't want the goods that the government requires firms to produce? A shortage will emerge and, with the state setting prices, the price cannot adjust to eliminate the shortage. Conversely, too much of some goods may be produced, given consumer tastes, and, once again, the price cannot adjust to eliminate the surplus. In both cases, there is an inefficient use and allocation of resources.

Most of these problems were experienced in the former Soviet Union and the other Eastern bloc countries, and were part of the reason for the overthrow of their communist regimes.

The free-market economy

In a free-market economy, it is the firms who decide what to produce and they will respond to consumer tastes. As consumer demand or supply conditions change, prices can adjust. A shortage will push prices up and a surplus will push them down. And so, unlike in a command economy, shortages and surpluses can be eliminated.

This is one of the main advantages of a free-market economy. Resources will be used more efficiently, as firms and consumers have an incentive to act in their own self-interest. And these incentives can help to minimise the economic problem of scarcity. It also has the advantage of allowing individuals to have their liberty and make their own decisions, and because planning is not required, the bureaucracy and administrative costs are low.

Despite the movement towards this type of economic system, it does still have its disadvantages. Without any government, some goods and services may not be produced, such as national defence and street lights. Others may be under- or overproduced, including education and polluting products respectively. Unemployment may be high and society could be very unequal, perhaps through some firms dominating the market and earning substantial profits, and those people with power and influence exploiting those without.

The mixed economy

Given that there are disadvantages to both a free-market and a command economy, it is hardly surprising that all economies are mixed. Some goods/services are left entirely to the free market, where producers respond to signals from consumers when deciding what to produce. Other goods and services have some light-touch intervention, perhaps through regulation of price, quality or information. However, as we saw in the section above, a free-market economy may not produce some goods and services at all and it is in these cases where there may be a much larger role for the government to ensure an efficient allocation of resources. But it is worth bearing in mind that while markets can fail, so can governments. We consider various forms of government intervention in Chapters 20, 21 and 22.

1. *Draw a spectrum of economic systems ranging from command economy to free-market economy. Pick some countries and decide where you think they lie. Think about the role of government in each country and in which areas the government intervenes.*

2. *How would the positioning of countries along the spectrum of economic systems change if you were considering the 1980s?*

Choice and opportunity cost

Choice involves sacrifice. The more food you choose to buy, the less money you will have to spend on other goods. The more food a nation produces, the fewer resources will there be for producing other goods. In other words, the production or consumption of one thing involves the sacrifice of alternatives. This sacrifice of

KEY IDEA 3 The *opportunity cost* of something is what you give up to get it/do it. In other words, it is cost measured in terms of the best alternative forgone.

BOX 2.3   **THE OPPORTUNITY COSTS OF STUDYING ECONOMICS**

What are you sacrificing?

You may not have realised it, but you probably consider opportunity costs many times a day. The reason is that we are constantly making choices: what to buy, what to eat, what to wear, whether to go out, how much to study, and so on. Each time we make a choice to do something, we are in effect reject-ing doing some alternative – after all, we can't do everything. This alternative forgone is the opportunity cost of our action.

Sometimes the opportunity costs of our actions are the direct monetary costs we incur. Sometimes it is more complicated.

Take the opportunity costs of your choices as a student of economics.

Buying a textbook costing £54.99

This does involve a direct money payment. What you have to consider is the alternatives you could have bought with the £54.99. You then have to weigh up the benefit from the best alternative against the benefit of the textbook.

1. *What might prevent you from making the best decision?*

Coming to classes

You may or may not be paying course fees. Even if you are, there is no extra (marginal) monetary cost in coming to classes once the fees have been paid. You will not get a refund by skipping classes!

So are the opportunity costs zero? No: by coming to classes you are not working in the library; you are not having an extra hour in bed; you are not sitting drinking coffee with friends, and so on. If you are making a rational decision to come to classes, then you will consider such possible alternatives.

2. *If there are several other things you could have done, is the opportunity cost the sum of all of them?*

Choosing to study at university or college

What are the opportunity costs of being a student in higher education?

At first it might seem that the costs would include the following:

- Tuition fees.
- Books, stationery, etc.
- Accommodation expenses.
- Transport.
- Food, entertainment and other living expenses.

But adding these up does not give the opportunity cost. The opportunity cost is the sacrifice entailed by going to university or college rather than doing something else. Let us assume that the alternative is to take a job that has been offered. The correct list of opportunity costs of higher educa-tion would include:

- Tuition fees.
- Books, stationery, etc.
- Additional accommodation and transport expenses over what would have been incurred by taking the job.
- Wages that would have been earned in the job less any student grant or loan interest subsidy received.

Note that tuition fees would not be included if they had been paid by someone else: for example, as part of a scholarship or a government grant.

3. *Why is the cost of food not included?*
4. *Make a list of the benefits of higher education.*
5. *Is the opportunity cost to the individual of attending higher education different from the opportunity costs to society as a whole?*

---

alternatives in the production (or consumption) of a good is known as its *opportunity cost*.

If the workers on a farm can produce either 1000 tonnes of wheat or 2000 tonnes of barley, then the opportunity cost of producing 1 tonne of wheat is the 2 tonnes of barley forgone. The opportunity cost of buying a textbook is the new pair of jeans you also wanted that you have had to go without. The opportunity cost of working overtime is the leisure you have sacrificed.

Rational choices

Economists often refer to *rational choices*. This simply means the weighing up of the *costs* and *benefits* of any activ-ity, whether it be firms choosing what and how much to produce, workers choosing whether to take a particular job or to work extra hours, or consumers choosing what to buy.

Imagine you are doing your shopping in a supermar-ket and you want to buy some meat. Do you spend a lot of money and buy best steak, or do you buy cheap mince instead? To make a rational (i.e. sensible) decision, you

Pause for thought

Assume that you are looking for a job and are offered two. One is more pleasant to do, but pays less. How would you make a rational choice between the two jobs?

will need to weigh up the costs and benefits of each alter-native. Best steak may give you a lot of enjoyment, but it has a high opportunity cost: because it is expensive, you will need to sacrifice quite a lot of consumption of other goods if you decide to buy it. If you buy the mince, how-ever, although you will not enjoy it so much, you will

Definitions

Opportunity cost The cost of any activity measured in terms of the best alternative forgone.

Rational choices Choices that involve weighing up the benefit of any activity against its opportunity cost.

have more money left over to buy other things: it has a lower opportunity cost.

Thus rational decision making, as far as consumers are concerned, involves choosing those items that give you the best value for money: i.e. the *greatest benefit relative to cost*.

The same principles apply to firms when deciding what to produce. For example, should a car firm open up another production line? A rational decision will again involve weighing up the benefits and costs. The benefits are the revenues that the firm will earn from selling the extra cars. The costs will include the extra labour costs, raw material costs, costs of component parts, etc. It will be profitable to open up the new production line only if the revenues earned exceed the costs entailed: in other words, if it earns a profit.

 KEY IDEA 4
Rational decision making involves weighing up the marginal benefit and marginal cost of any activity. If the marginal benefit exceeds the marginal cost, it is rational to do the activity (or to do more of it). If the marginal cost exceeds the marginal benefit, it is rational not to do it (or to do less of it).

In the more complex situation of deciding which model of car to produce, or how many of each model, the firm must weigh up the relative benefits and costs of each: i.e. it will want to produce the most profitable product mix.

Marginal costs and benefits

In economics we argue that rational choices involve weighing up **marginal costs** and **marginal benefits**. These are the costs and benefits of doing a little bit more or a little bit less of a specific activity. They can be contrasted with the *total* costs and benefits of the activity.

Take a familiar example. What time will you set the alarm clock to go off tomorrow morning? Let us say that you have to leave home at 8.30. Perhaps you will set the alarm for 7.00. That will give you plenty of time to get up and get ready, but it will mean a relatively short night's sleep. Perhaps then you will decide to set it for 7.30 or even 8.00. That will give you a longer night's sleep, but much more of a rush in the morning to get ready.

So how do you make a rational decision about when the alarm should go off? What you have to do is to weigh up the costs and benefits of *additional* sleep. Each extra minute in bed gives you more sleep (the marginal benefit), but gives you more of a rush when you get up (the marginal cost).

The decision is therefore based on the costs and benefits of *extra* sleep, not on the *total* costs and benefits of a whole night's sleep.

This same principle applies to rational decisions made by consumers, workers and firms. For example, the car firm we were considering just now will weigh up the marginal costs and benefits of producing cars: in other words, it will compare the costs and revenue of producing *additional* cars. If additional cars add more to the firm's revenue than to its costs, it will be profitable to produce them.

Microeconomic choices and the firm

All economic decisions made by firms involve choices. The business economist studies these choices and their results.

We will look at the choices of how much to produce, what price to charge the customer, how many inputs to use, what types of input to use and in what combination. Firms will also need to make choices that have a much longer-term effect, such as whether to expand the scale of its operations, whether to invest in new plants, engage in research and development, whether to merge with or take over another company, diversify into other markets, or increase the amount it exports.

The right choices (in terms of best meeting the firm's objectives) will vary according to the type of market in which the firm operates, its predictions about future demand, its degree of power in the market, the actions and reactions of competitors, the degree and type of government intervention, the current tax regime, the availability of finance, and so on. In short, we will be studying the whole range of economic choices made by firms and in a number of different scenarios.

In all these cases, the owners of firms will want the best possible choices to be made: i.e. those choices that best meet the objectives of the firm. Making the best choices, as we have seen, will involve weighing up the marginal benefits against the marginal opportunity costs of each decision. **KI 4** **p 25**

Definitions

Marginal costs The additional cost of doing a little bit more (or 1 unit more if a unit can be measured) of an activity.

Marginal benefits The additional benefits of doing a little bit more (or 1 unit more if a unit can be measured) of an activity.

SUMMARY

1a The central economic problem is that of scarcity. Given that there is a limited supply of factors of production (labour, land and capital), it is impossible to provide everybody with everything they want. Potential demands exceed potential supplies.

1b The subject of economics is usually divided into two main branches: macroeconomics and microeconomics.

2a Macroeconomics deals with aggregates such as the overall levels of unemployment, output, growth and prices in the economy.

2b The macroeconomic environment will be an important determinant of a business's profitability.

3a Microeconomics deals with the activities of individual units within the economy: firms, industries, consumers, workers, etc. Because resources are scarce, people have to make choices. Society has to choose by some means or other *what* goods and services to produce, *how* to produce them and *for whom* to produce them. Microeconomics studies these choices.

3b Rational choices involve weighing up the marginal benefits of each activity against its marginal opportunity costs. If the marginal benefit exceeds the marginal cost, it is rational to choose to do more of that activity.

3c Businesses are constantly faced with choices: how much to produce, what inputs to use, what price to charge, how much to invest, etc. We will study these choices.

MyEconLab

This book can be supported by MyEconLab, Which contains a range of additional resources, including an online homework and tutorial system designed to test and build your understanding.

You need both an access card and a course ID to access MyEconLab:

1. Is your lecturer using MyEconLab? Ask your lecturer for your course ID.

2. Has an access card been included with the book at a reduced cost? Check the inside back cover of the book.

3. If you have a course ID but no access card, go to: http://www.myeconlab.com/ to buy access to this interactive study program.

REVIEW QUESTIONS

1 Virtually every good is scarce in the sense we have defined it. There are, however, a few exceptions. Under *certain circumstances*, water and air are not scarce. When and where might this be true for (a) water and (b) air? Why is it important to define water and air very carefully before deciding whether they are scarce or abundant? Under circumstances where they are *not* scarce, would it be possible to charge for them?

2 Which of the following are macroeconomic issues, which are microeconomic ones and which could be either depending on the context?

   (a) Inflation.
   (b) Low wages in certain service industries.
   (c) The rate of exchange between the pound and the euro.
   (d) Why the price of cabbages fluctuates more than that of cars.
   (e) The rate of economic growth this year compared with last year.

   (f) The decline of traditional manufacturing industries.

3 Make a list of three things you did yesterday. What was the opportunity cost of each?

4 A washing machine manufacturer is considering whether to produce an extra batch of 1000 washing machines. How would it set about working out the marginal opportunity cost of so doing?

5 How would a firm use the principle of weighing up marginal costs and marginal benefits when deciding whether (a) to take on an additional worker; (b) to offer overtime to existing workers?

6 We identified three categories of withdrawal from the circular flow of income. What were they? There are also three categories of 'injection' of expenditure into the circular flow of income. What do you think they are?

APPENDIX: SOME TECHNIQUES OF ECONOMIC ANALYSIS

When students first come to economics, many are worried about the amount of mathematics they will encounter. Will it all be equations and graphs, and will there be lots of hard calculations to do and difficult theories to grasp?

Economics can involve a lot of mathematics, but it doesn't have to and as you will see if you glance through the pages of this text, there are many diagrams and tables, but only a few equations. The mathematical techniques that you will have to master are relatively limited, but they are ones which we use many times in many different contexts. You will find that, if you are new to the subject, you will very quickly become familiar with these techniques. If you are not new to the subject, perhaps you could reassure your colleagues who are!

Diagrams as pictures

On many occasions, we use diagrams simply to provide a picture of a relationship. Just as a photograph in a newspaper can often provide a much more vivid picture of an event than any description in words, so too a diagram in economics can often picture a relationship with a vividness and clarity that could never be achieved by description alone.

For example, we may observe that as people's incomes rise, they spend a lot more on entertainment and only a little more on food. We can picture this relationship very nicely by the use of a simple graph.

In Figure 2.2, an individual's income is measured along the horizontal axis and the expenditure on food and entertainment is measured up the vertical axis. There are just two lines on this diagram: the one showing how the person's expenditure on entertainment rises as income rises, the other how the expenditure on food rises as income rises.

Now we could use a diagram like this to plot actual data. But we may simply be using it as a sketch – as a picture. In this case we do not necessarily need to put figures on the two axes. We are simply showing the relative *shapes* of the two curves. These shapes tell us that the person's expenditure on entertainment rises more quickly than that on food, and that above a certain level of income the expenditure on entertainment becomes greater than that on food.

If you were to describe in words all the information that this sketch graph depicts, you would need several lines of prose.

Figure 2.1 (the circular flow diagram) was an example of a sketch designed to give a simple, clear picture of a relationship: a picture stripped of all unnecessary detail.

Pause for thought

What else is the diagram telling us?

Representing real-life statistics

In many cases we will want to depict real-world data. We may want to show, for example, how the level of business investment has fluctuated over a given period of time, or we may want to depict the market shares of the different firms within a given industry. In the first case we will need to look at time-series data. In the second we will look at cross-section data.

Time-series data

Table 2.1 shows annual percentage changes in investment in the European Union between 1980 and 2016 (the data

---

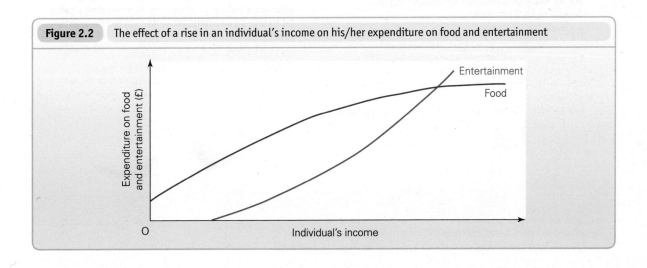

| Figure 2.2 | The effect of a rise in an individual's income on his/her expenditure on food and entertainment |

Table 2.1	Investment in the EU(15): percentage changes from previous year at 2010 market prices

1981	1982	1983	1984	1985	1986	1987	1988	1989	1990	1991	1992	1993	1994	1995	1996	1997	1998
−4.2	−1.0	0.5	2.2	3.2	4.0	5.1	8.9	6.9	3.7	−0.6	−0.3	−5.4	3.1	3.3	2.5	3.5	6.2

1999	2000	2001	2002	2003	2004	2005	2006	2007	2008	2009	2010	2011	2012	2013	2014	2015	2016
5.5	4.6	0.6	−0.8	1.4	2.8	2.4	5.2	4.9	−1.3	−11.6	0.4	1.8	−2.5	−1.6	1.9	2.8	4.5

Source: Based on *Statistical Annex of the European Economy* (EC, 2015). 2015 and 2016 are forecast

refer simply to the 15 countries that were members prior to 2004).

A table like this is a common way of representing *time-series data*. It has the advantage of giving the precise figures, and is thus a useful reference if we want to test any theory and see whether it predicts accurately.

Notice that in this particular table the figures are given annually. Depending on the period of time over which we want to see the movement of a variable, it may be more appropriate to use a different interval of time. For example, if we wanted to see how investment had changed over the past 50 years, we might use intervals of five years or more. If, however, we wanted to see how investment had changed over the course of a year, we would probably use monthly figures.

Time-series data can also be shown graphically. In fact the data from a table can be plotted directly on to a graph. Figure 2.3 plots the data from Table 2.1. Each dot on the graph corresponds to one figure from the table. The dots are then joined up to form a single line.

Thus if you wanted to find the annual percentage change in investment in the EU at any time between 1981 and 2016, you would simply find the appropriate date on the horizontal axis, read vertically upward to the line you have drawn, then read across to find the annual rate of change in investment.

Although a graph like this cannot give you quite such an accurate measurement of each point as a table does, it gives a much more obvious picture of how the figures have moved over time and whether the changes are getting

Definition

Time-series data Information depicting how a variable (e.g. the price of eggs) changes over time.

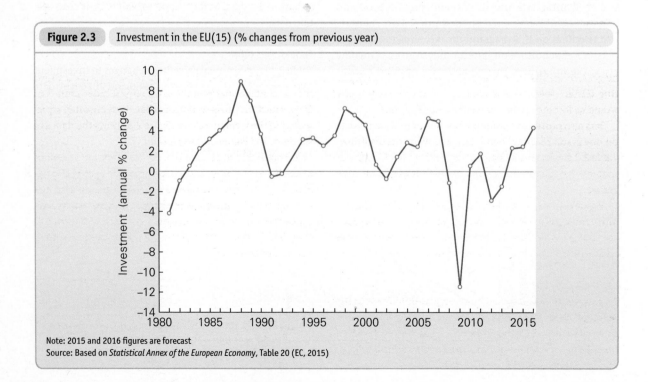

Figure 2.3	Investment in the EU(15) (% changes from previous year)

Note: 2015 and 2016 figures are forecast
Source: Based on *Statistical Annex of the European Economy*, Table 20 (EC, 2015)

Figure 2.4 Economic growth and growth in investment in the EU(15)

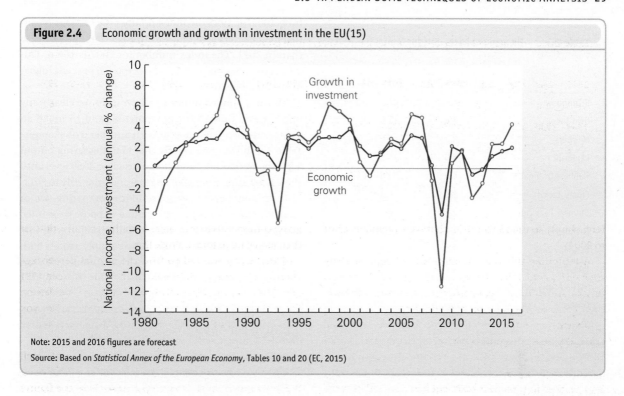

Note: 2015 and 2016 figures are forecast

Source: Based on *Statistical Annex of the European Economy*, Tables 10 and 20 (EC, 2015)

Table 2.2 National income in the EU(15): percentage changes from previous year (economic growth rates) at 2010 market prices

1981	1982	1983	1984	1985	1986	1987	1988	1989	1990	1992	1993	1993	1994	1995	1996	1997	1998
0.2	1.1	1.8	2.5	2.5	2.8	2.8	4.2	3.7	3.0	1.8	1.3	−0.1	2.9	2.6	1.9	2.9	3.0

1999	2000	2001	2002	2003	2004	2005	2006	2007	2008	2009	2010	2011	2012	2013	2014	2015	2016
3.0	3.8	2.1	1.2	1.3	2.3	1.9	3.2	2.9	0.3	−4.5	2.1	1.6	−0.5	−0.1	1.2	1.4	1.9

Source: Based on *Statistical Annex of the European Economy* (EC, 2015). 2015 and 2016 are forecast

bigger (the curve getting steeper) or smaller (the curve getting flatter). We can also read off what the likely figure would be for some point *between* two observations.

It is also possible to combine *two* sets of time-series data on one graph to show their relative movements over time. Table 2.2 shows annual percentage changes in EU national income (i.e. economic growth rates) for the same time period.

Figure 2.4 plots these data along with those from Table 2.1. This enables us to get a clear picture of how annual percentage changes in investment and in national income moved in relation to each other over the period in question.

Cross-section data

Cross-section data show different observations made at the *same point in time*. For example, they could show the quantities of food and clothing purchased at various levels of household income, or the costs to a firm or industry of producing various quantities of a product.

Table 2.3 gives an example of cross-section data. It shows the percentage shares of the UK's largest cider brands in 2009 and 2011. Cross-section data like these are often represented in the form of a chart. Figure 2.5 shows the data as a *bar chart*, and Figure 2.6 as a *pie chart*.

It is possible to represent cross-section data at two or more different points in time, thereby presenting the figures as a time series. In Table 2.3, figures are given for just two years. With a more complete time series we could graph the movement of the market shares of each of the brands over time. In doing this, we create a very complete dataset, known as panel data.

Definition

Cross-section data Information showing how a variable (e.g. the consumption of eggs) differs between different groups or different individuals at a given time.

Table 2.3	UK market shares of cider brands	
	2009 (%)	**2011 (%)**
Strongbow	28.5	27.2
Own-label	8.6	7.9
Magners	8.3	7.5
Lambrini	6.5	4.5
Bulmers Original	4.5	3.8
Frosty Jack's	2.9	4.1
Bulmers Pear cider	2.8	2.6
Jacques Fruits De Bois	2.7	2.2
Scrumpy Jack	2.5	2.4
Kopparberg	1.7	2.2
Stella Artois Cidre	n/a	3.2
Others	31.0	32.4
	100.0	100.0

Source: Mintel Cider UK Report, February 2012

Index numbers

Time-series data are often expressed in terms of *index numbers*. Consider the data in the top row of each part of Table 2.4. It shows index numbers of manufacturing output in the UK from 1985 to 2014.

One year is selected as the *base year*, and this is given the value of 100. In our example this is 2011. The output for other years is then shown by their percentage variation from 100. For 1985 the index number is 83.2. This means that manufacturing output was 16.8 per cent lower in 1985 than in 2011. The index number for 2007 is 106.6. This means that manufacturing output was 6.6 per cent higher in 2007 than in 2011.

The use of index numbers allows us to see clearly any upward and downward movements, and to make an easy comparison of one year with another. For example, Table 2.4 shows quite clearly that manufacturing output fell from 1989 to 1992 and did not reach its 1989 level until 1994. It fell again from 2007 to 2009 and from 2011 to 2013.

Index numbers are very useful for comparing two or more time series of data. For example, suppose we wanted to compare the growth of manufacturing output with that of the service industries. To do this we simply express both sets of figures as index numbers with the same base year. This is again illustrated in Table 2.4.

Pause for thought

Does this mean that the value of manufacturing output in 2007 was 6.6 per cent higher in money terms than in 2011?

Definitions

Index number The value of a variable expressed as 100 plus or minus its percentage deviation from a base year.

Base year (for index numbers) The year whose index number is set at 100.

Figure 2.5	UK market shares of cider brands

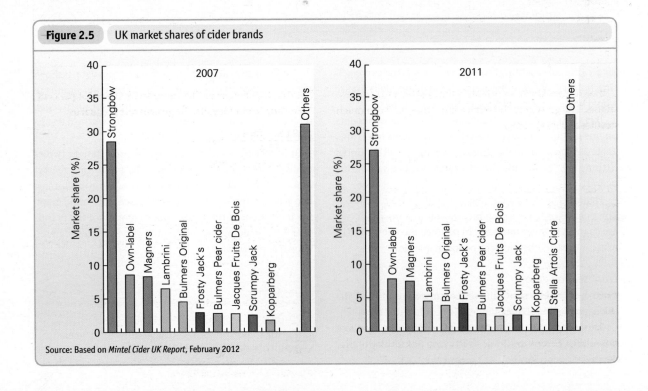

Source: Based on *Mintel Cider UK Report*, February 2012

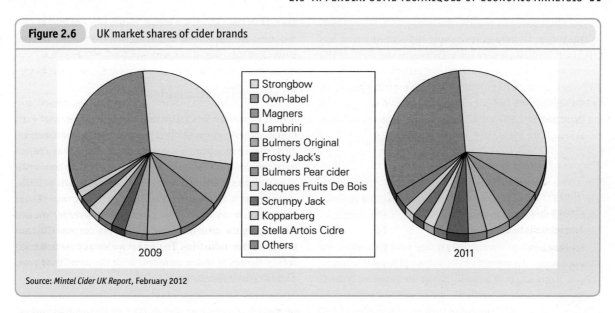

Figure 2.6 UK market shares of cider brands

- Strongbow
- Own-label
- Magners
- Lambrini
- Bulmers Original
- Frosty Jack's
- Bulmers Pear cider
- Jacques Fruits De Bois
- Scrumpy Jack
- Kopparberg
- Stella Artois Cidre
- Others

2009   2011

Source: *Mintel Cider UK Report*, February 2012

Table 2.4 UK manufacturing output at constant 2011 prices: 2011 = 100

1985	1986	1987	1988	1989	1990	1991	1992	1993	1994	1995	1996	1997	1998	1999
Output of manufacturing														
83.2	84.3	88.4	94.8	98.6	98.5	93.5	93.4	94.8	99.3	100.8	101.5	103.3	103.7	104.3
Output of services														
48.3	50.3	52.4	54.8	55.9	56.7	56.9	57.6	59.7	62.0	63.6	65.5	67.3	70.5	73.4

2000	2001	2002	2003	2004	2005	2006	2007	2008	2009	2010	2011	2012	2013	2014
Output of manufacturing														
106.6	105.0	102.3	101.7	103.6	103.5	105.8	106.6	103.5	93.8	98.2	100.0	98.7	98.0	100.5
Output of services														
76.8	79.6	81.9	86.6	88.6	92.4	95.9	98.9	99.4	96.6	98.0	100.0	102.0	104.0	107.1

Source: *Time series data*, series K22A and L2NC (ONS, 2015)

The figures show a quite different pattern for the two sectors. The growth of the service industries has been much steadier and more rapid.

Using index numbers to measure percentage changes

To find the annual percentage growth rate in any one year, we simply look at the percentage change in the index from the previous year. To work this out, we use the following formula:

$$\frac{I_t - I_{t-1}}{I_{t-1}} \times 100$$

where I_t is the index in the year in question and I_{t-1} is the index in the previous year.

Thus, using Table 2.4, to find the growth rate in manufacturing output from, say, 1987 to 1988, we first see how much the index has risen, $I_t - I_{t-1}$. The answer is $94.8 - 88.4 = 6.4$.

But this does *not* mean that the growth rate is 6.4 per cent. According to our formula, the growth rate is equal to:

$$\frac{94.8 - 88.4}{88.4} \times 100$$
$$= 6.4/88.4 \times 100$$
$$= 7.24\%.$$

The price index

Perhaps the best known of all price indices is the ***consumer prices index (CPI)***.[1] It is an index of the prices of goods and

Definition

Consumer prices index (CPI) An index of the prices of goods bought by a typical household.

---

[1] Previously another measure, the *retail price index* (RPI), was the major measure of consumer prices. Although the RPI is still used, it has been largely replaced by the CPI, which is a more sophisticated measure.

services purchased by the average household. Movements in this index, therefore, show how the cost of living has changed. Annual percentage increases in the CPI are the commonest definition of the rate of inflation. Thus if the CPI went up from 100 to 103 over a 12-month period, we would say that the rate of inflation was 3 per cent. If it went up from 150 to 156 over 12 months, the rate of inflation would be $(156 - 150)/150 \times 100 = 4$ per cent.

The use of weighted averages

The CPI is a **weighted average** of the prices of many items. The index of manufacturing output that we looked at above was also a weighted average: an average of the output of many individual products.

To illustrate how a weighted average works, consider the case of a weighted average of the output of just three industries, A, B and C. Let us assume that in the base year (year 1) the output of A was £7 million, of B £2 million and of C £1 million, giving a total output of the three industries of £10 million. We now attach weights to the output of each industry to reflect its proportion of total output. Industry A is given a weight of 0.7 because it produces seven-tenths of total output. Industry B is given a weight of 0.2 and industry C of 0.1. We then simply multiply each industry's index by its weight and add up all these figures to give the overall industry index.

The index for each industry in year 1 (the base year) is 100. This means that the weighted average index is also 100. Table 2.5 shows what happens to output in year 2. Industry A's output falls by 10 per cent, giving it an index of 90 in year 2. Industry B's output rises by 10 per cent and industry C's output rises by 30 per cent, giving indices of 110 and 130, respectively. But as you can see from the table, despite the fact that two of the three industries have had a rise in output, the total industry index has *fallen* from 100 to 98. The reason is that industry A is so much larger than the other two that its decline in output outweighs their increase.

The consumer prices index is a little more complicated. This is because it is calculated in two stages. First, products are grouped into categories such as food, clothing and services. A weighted average index is worked out for each group. Thus the index for food would be the weighted

average of the indices for bread, potatoes, cooking oil, etc. Second, a weight is attached to each of the groups in order to work out an overall index.

Functional relationships

Business economists frequently examine how one economic variable affects another: how the purchases of cars are affected by their price; how consumer expenditure is affected by taxes, or by incomes; how the cost of producing washing machines is affected by the price of steel; how business investment is affected by changes in interest rates. These relationships are called **functional relationships**. We will need to express these relationships in a precise way. This can be done in the form of a table, as a graph or as an equation.

Simple linear functions

These are relationships which, when plotted on a graph, produce a straight line. Let us take an imaginary example of the relationship between total saving in the economy (S) and the level of national income (Y). This functional relationship can be written as:

$$S = f(Y)$$

This is simply shorthand for saying that saving is a function of (i.e. depends on) the level of national income.

If we want to know just *how much* will be saved at any given level of income, we will need to spell out this functional relationship. Let us do this in each of the three ways.

As a table. Table 2.6 gives a selection of values of Y and the corresponding level of S. It is easy to read off from the table

---

Definitions

Weighted average The average of several items where each item is ascribed a weight according to its importance. The weights must add up to 1.

Functional relationships The mathematical relationships showing how one variable is affected by one or more others.

Table 2.5	Constructing a weighted average index				
			Year 1		**Year 2**
Industry	Weight	Index	Index times weight	Index	Index times weight
A	0.7	100	70	90	63
B	0.2	100	20	110	22
C	0.1	100	10	130	13
Total	1.0		100		98

Table 2.6	A saving function
National income (£bn per year)	**Total saving (£bn per year)**
0	0
10	2
20	4
30	6
40	8
50	10

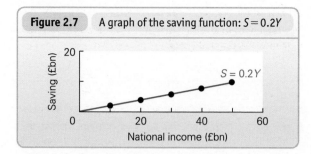

Figure 2.7 A graph of the saving function: $S = 0.2Y$

and thus will draw from their past savings: they will have *negative* saving.

When a graph does not pass through the origin, its equation will have the form:

$$y = a + bx$$

where this time y stands for the dependent variable (not 'income') and x for the independent variable, and a and b will have numbers assigned in an actual equation. For example, the equation might be:

$$y = 4 + 2x$$

This would give Table 2.7 and Figure 2.8.

Notice two things about the relationship between the equation and the graph:

The point where the line crosses the vertical axis (at a value of 4) is given by the constant (a) term. If the a term were negative, the line would cross the vertical axis *below* the horizontal axis.

The slope of the line is given by the b term. The slope is 2/1: for every 1 unit increase in x there is a 2 unit increase in y.

the level of saving at one of the levels of national income listed. It is clearly more difficult to work out the level of saving if national income were £23.4 billion or £47.4 billion.

As a graph. Figure 2.7 plots the data from Table 2.6. Each of the dots corresponds to one of the points in the table. By joining the dots up into a single line we can easily read off the value for saving at some level of income other than those listed in the table. A graph also has the advantage of allowing us to see the relationship at a glance.

It is usual to plot the *independent variable* (i.e. the one that does not depend on the other) on the horizontal or x-axis, and the *dependent variable* on the vertical or y-axis. In our example, saving *depends* on national income. Thus saving is the dependent variable and national income is the independent variable.

As an equation. The data in the table can be expressed in the equation:

$$S = 0.2Y$$

This has the major advantage of being precise. We could work out *exactly* how much would be saved at any given level of national income.

This particular function starts at the origin of the graph (i.e. the bottom left-hand corner). This means that when the value of the independent variable is zero, so too is the value of the dependent variable. Frequently, however, this is not the case in functional relationships. For example, when people have a zero income, they will still have to live,

Non-linear functions

These are functions where the equation involves a squared term (or other power terms). Such functions will give a curved line when plotted on a graph. As an example, consider the following equation:

$$y = 4 + 10x - x^2$$

Table 2.8 and Figure 2.9 are based on it.

As you can see, y rises at a decelerating rate and eventually begins to fall. This is because the negative x^2 term is becoming more and more influential as x rises, and eventually begins to outweigh the $10x$ term.

The actual relationship that exists between two variables will determine the mathematical function that is used (linear or non-linear) and this will then affect the shape of the curve.

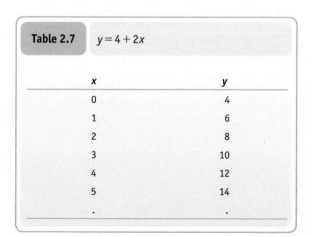

Table 2.7 $y = 4 + 2x$

x	y
0	4
1	6
2	8
3	10
4	12
5	14
.	.

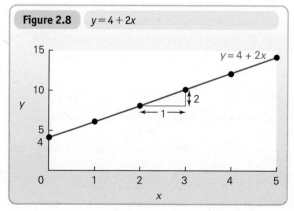

Figure 2.8 $y = 4 + 2x$

Figure 2.9 $y = 4 + 10x - x^2$

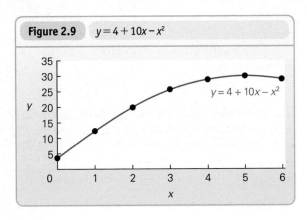

$y = 4 + 10x - x^2$

Table 2.8 $y = 4 + 10x - x^2$

x	y
0	4
1	13
2	20
3	25
4	28
5	29
6	28
.	.

SUMMARY TO APPENDIX

1 Diagrams in economics can be used as pictures, to sketch a relationship so that its essentials can be perceived at a glance.

2 Tables, graphs and charts are also used to portray real-life data. These can be time-series data or cross-section data or both.

3 Presenting time-series data as index numbers gives a clear impression of trends and is a good way of comparing how two or more series (perhaps originally measured in different units) have changed over the same time period. A base year is chosen and the index for that year is set at 100. The percentage change in the value of a variable is given by the percentage change in the index. The formula is:

$$\frac{I_t - I_{t-1}}{I_{t-1}} \times 100$$

4 Several items can be included in one index by using a weighted value for each of the items. The weights must add up to 1 and each weight will reflect the relative importance of that particular item in the index.

5 Functional relationships can be expressed as an equation, a table or a graph. In the linear (straight-line) equation $y = a + bx$, the a term gives the vertical intercept (the point where the graph crosses the vertical axis) and the b term gives the slope. When there is a power term (e.g. $y = a + bx + cx^2$), the graph will be a curve.

REVIEW QUESTIONS TO APPENDIX

1 What are the relative advantages and disadvantages of presenting information in (a) a table; (b) a graph; (c) an equation?

2 If the CPI went up from 125 to 130 over 12 months, what would be the rate of inflation over that period?

3 On a diagram like Figure 2.8, draw the graphs for the following equations.

$$y = -3 = 4x$$
$$y = 15 - 3x$$

4 What shaped graph would you get from the following equations?

$$y = -6 + 3x + 2x^2$$
$$y = 10 - 4x + x^2$$

If you cannot work out the answer, construct a table like Table 2.8 and then plot the figures on a graph.

Business organisations

Business issues covered in this chapter

- How are businesses organised and structured?
- What are the aims of business?
- Will owners, managers and other employees necessarily have the same aims? How can those working in the firm be persuaded to achieve the objectives of their employers?
- What are the various legal categories of business and how do different legal forms suit different types of business?
- How do businesses differ in their internal organisation? What are the relative merits of alternative forms of organisation?

If you decide to grow strawberries in your garden or allotment, or if you decide to put up a set of shelves in your home, then you have made a production decision. Most production decisions, however, are not made by the individuals who will consume the product. Most production decisions are made by firms: whether by small one-person businesses or by giant multinational corporations, such as General Motors or Sony.

In this chapter we are going to investigate the firm: what is its role in the economy; what are the goals of firms; how do firms differ in respect to their legal status; and in what ways are they organised internally?

3.1 THE NATURE OF FIRMS

As firms have grown and become more complex, so the analysis of them has become more sophisticated. They are seen less and less like a 'black box', where inputs are fed in one end, used in the most efficient way and then output emerges from the other end. Instead, the nature and organisation of firms are seen to be key determinants of how they behave and of the role they play in respect to resource allocation and production.

Complex production

Very few goods or services are produced by one person alone. Most products require a complex production process that will involve many individuals. But how are these individuals to be organised in order to produce such goods and services? Two very different ways are:

- within markets via price signals;
- within firms via a hierarchy of managerial authority.

In the first of these two ways, each stage of production would involve establishing a distinct contract with each separate producer. Assume that you wanted to produce a woollen jumper. You would need to enter a series of separate contracts: to have the jumper designed, to buy the wool, to get the wool spun, to get it dyed, to have the jumper knitted. There are many other stages in the production and distribution process that might also be considered. With each contract a price will have to be determined, and that price will reflect current market conditions. In most cases, such a form of economic organisation would prove to be highly inefficient and totally impractical. Consider the number of contracts that might be necessary if you wished to produce a motor car!

With the second way of organising production, a single *firm* (or just a few firms) replaces the market. The co-ordination of the conversion of inputs into output takes place *within* the firm: not through the market mechanism, but by management issuing orders as to what to produce and the manner in which this is to take place. Hence the distinguishing feature of the firm is that the price mechanism plays little role in allocating resources within it.

The benefits of organising production within firms

The function of the firm is to bring together a series of production and distribution operations, doing away with the need for individuals to enter into narrowly specified contracts. If you want a woollen jumper, you go to a woollen jumper retailer.

According to Ronald Coase,[1] the key advantage of organising production and distribution through firms, as opposed to the market, is that it involves lower **transaction costs**. Transaction costs are the costs of making economic arrangements about production, distribution and sales.

> **KEY IDEA 5**
>
> **Transaction costs.** The costs incurred when firms buy inputs or services from other firms as opposed to producing them themselves. They include the costs of searching for the best firm to do business with, the costs of negotiating, drawing up, monitoring and enforcing contracts, and the costs of transporting and handling products between the firms. These costs should be weighed against the benefits of outsourcing through the market.

Definitions

The firm An economic organisation that co-ordinates the process of production and distribution.

Transaction costs Those costs incurred when making economic contracts in the marketplace.

The transaction costs associated with individual contracts made through the market are likely to be substantial for the following reasons:

- The *uncertainty* in framing contracts. It is unlikely that decision makers will have perfect knowledge of the production process. Given, then, that such contracts are established on imperfect information, they are consequently subject to error.
- The *complexity* of contracts. Many products require multiple stages of production. The more complex the product, the greater the number of contracts that would have to be made. The specifications within contracts may also become more complex, requiring high levels of understanding and knowledge of the production process, which raises the possibility of error in writing them. As contracts become more complex they raise a firm's costs of production and make it more difficult to determine the correct price for a transaction.
- *Monitoring* contracts. Entering into a contract with another person may require you to monitor whether the terms of the contract are fulfilled. This may incur a significant time cost for the individual, especially if a large number of contracts require monitoring.
- *Enforcing* contracts. If one party breaks its contract, the legal expense of enforcing the contract or recouping any losses may be significant. Many individuals might find such costs prohibitive, and as a consequence be unable to pursue broken contracts through the legal system.

What is apparent is that, for most goods, the firm represents a superior way to organise production. The actions of management replace the price signals of the market and overcome many of the associated transaction costs.

Goals of the firm

Economists have traditionally assumed that firms will want to maximise profits. The 'traditional theory of the firm', as it is called, shows how much output firms should produce and at what price, in order to make as much profit as possible. But do firms necessarily want to maximise profits?

It is reasonable to assume that the *owners* of firms will want to maximise profits: this much most of the critics of the traditional theory accept. The question is, however, whether it is the owners that make the decisions about how much to produce and at what price.

The divorce of ownership from control

As businesses steadily grew over the nineteenth and twentieth centuries, many owner-managers were forced, however reluctantly, to devolve some responsibility for the running of the business to other individuals. These new managers brought with them technical skills and business expertise, a crucial prerequisite for a modern successful business enterprise.

[1]Ronald H. Coase, 'The Nature of the Firm', *Economica*, Vol. 4, No. 16, Nov. 1937, pp. 386–405.

The managerial revolution that was to follow, in which business owners (shareholders) and managers became distinct groups, called into question what the precise goals of the business enterprise might now be. This debate was to be further fuelled by the growth of the **joint-stock company** (a structure first recognised in England in the sixteenth century) in which the ownership of the enterprise was progressively dispersed over a large number of shareholders. The growth in the joint-stock company was a direct consequence of business owners looking to raise large amounts of investment capital in order to maintain or expand business activity.

This twin process of managerial expansion and widening share ownership led Berle and Means[2] to argue that the *ownership* of stocks and shares in an enterprise no longer meant *control* over its assets. They subsequently drew a distinction between 'nominal ownership', namely getting a return from investing in a business, and 'effective ownership', which is the ability to control and direct the assets of the business. The more dispersed nominal ownership becomes, the less and less likely it is that there will be effective ownership by shareholders. (This issue will be considered in more detail in Chapter 14.)

The modern company is *legally* separate from its owners (as you will discover in section 3.2). Hence the assets are legally owned by the business itself. Consequently, the group *in charge* of the business is that which controls the use of these assets: i.e. the group which determines the business's objectives and implements the necessary procedures to secure them. In most companies this group is the managers.

Berle and Means argued that, as a consequence of this transition from owner to manager control, conflicts are likely to develop between the goals of managers and those of the owners. But what are the objectives of managers? Will they want to maximise profits, or will they have some other aim?

Managers may want to maximise their *own* interests, such as pursuing higher salaries, greater power or prestige, greater sales, better working conditions or greater popularity with their subordinates. Different managers in the same firm may well pursue different aims. But these aims may conflict with profit maximisation.

Managers will still have to ensure that *sufficient* profits are made to keep shareholders happy, but that may be very different from *maximising* profits. Alternative theories of the firm to those of profit maximisation, therefore, tend to assume that large firms are **profit 'satisficers'**. That is, managers strive hard for a minimum target level of profit, but are less interested in profits above this level.

Such theories fall into two categories: first, those theories which assume that firms attempt to maximise some other aim, provided that sufficient profits are achieved; and second, those theories which assume that firms pursue a number of potentially conflicting aims, of which sufficient profit is merely one. (These alternative theories are examined more fully in Chapter 14.)

 The nature of institutions and organisations is likely to influence behaviour. There are various forces influencing people's decisions in complex organisations. Assumptions that an organisation will follow one simple objective (e.g. short-run profit maximisation) are thus too simplistic in many cases.

The principal–agent relationship

Can the owners of a firm ever be sure that their managers will pursue the business strategy most appropriate to achieving the owners' goals (which traditional economic theory tells us is the maximisation of profit)? This is an example of what is known as the **principal–agent problem**.

One of the features of a complex modern economy is that people (principals) have to employ others (agents) to carry out their wishes. If you want to go on holiday, it is easier to go to a travel agent to sort out the arrangements than to do it all yourself. Likewise, if you want to buy a house, it is more convenient to go to an estate agent.

The crucial advantage that agents have over their principals is specialist knowledge and information. This is frequently the basis upon which agents are employed. For example, owners employ managers for their specialist knowledge of a market or their understanding of business

> ## Definitions
>
> **Joint-stock company** A company where ownership is distributed between a large number of shareholders.
>
> **Profit satisficing** Where a firm or manager aims to achieve a target level of profit that is regarded as satisfactory. By not aiming for the maximum profit, this allows managers to pursue other objectives, such as sales maximisation or their own salary or prestige.
>
> **Principal–agent problem** One where people (principals), as a result of lack of knowledge, cannot ensure that their best interests are served by their agents.

---

[2] A. A. Berle and G. C. Means, *The Modern Corporation and Private Property* (Macmillan, 1933).

practice. But this situation of *asymmetric information* – that one party (the agent) knows more than the other (the principal) – means that it will be very difficult for the principal to judge in whose interest the agent is operating. Are managers pursuing their own goals rather than the goals of the owner?

> **KEY IDEA 7**
>
> *The principal–agent problem.* Where people (principals), as a result of a lack of knowledge, cannot ensure that their best interests are served by their agents. Agents may take advantage of this situation to the disadvantage of the principals.

Principals may attempt to reconcile the fact that they have imperfect information, and are thus in an inherently weak position, in the following ways:

- *Monitoring* the performance of the agent. Shareholders could monitor the performance of their senior managers through attending annual general meetings. The managers could be questioned by shareholders and ultimately replaced if their performance is seen as unsatisfactory.

- Establishing a series of *incentives* to ensure that agents act in the principals' best interest. For example, managerial pay could be closely linked to business performance (e.g.

Definition

Asymmetric information A situation in which one party in an economic relationship knows more than another.

BOX 3.1 EXPLOITING ASYMMETRIC INFORMATION

Examples of the principal–agent relationship

The issue of asymmetric information and its implications for the principal–agent relationship is not just a problem within firms. It exists in many walks of life where two parties are involved in some sort of transaction, but where one party has more information than the other and it may be in their interests to use that extra information to gain an advantage.

Housing

When you want to buy or sell a house, you probably lack information about the values of houses and so you will go to an estate agent. However, the reason you go to the estate agent is because they have better information than you – and they know this. The buyer (or seller) is the principal and the estate agent is the agent.

Assume you want to sell a house. It could be in the estate agent's interests to try to convince you that it is necessary to accept a lower price for your house, while the real reason is to save the agent time, effort and expense.

It is a similar story if you want to buy a house. The estate agent may tell you that the heating is excellent and cheap, but it is in their interests to say this and they know much better than you if they are telling the truth! The fact that the estate agent has better information than you (the buyer) means that they can use this information to gain an advantage: a higher price or a quick sale.

Second-hand cars

Assume you want to buy a second-hand car and go to a second-hand car dealer. When looking at a particular car, you might look at the mileage, the upholstery and whether there any scratches on the bodywork or any obvious damage. You'll ask about any problems or reliability issues.

But even if you have expert knowledge about cars, the dealer will have much better information than you as to how good (or bad) it really is. They may 'neglect' to tell you about the rust on the underside of the car, the problems of starting it on a cold morning or its history of unreliability. By omitting certain bad things about the car, they will hope to gain a higher price and thus use the problem of asymmetric information to their advantage.

Elections

Whether it is at school, college, university or even in government, you need votes to win an election. Depending on the context, there will be certain things that are more likely to lead to victory. Perhaps at school, it's campaigning for shorter days or no uniforms. At university, it might be about providing more contact with academic staff and at a general election it might be about redistributing income, protecting education or health care, or investing money in regeneration projects.

But here too there is a problem of asymmetric information. Whatever the campaign promises, the people seeking election (the agents) generally know better than the electorate (the principals) whether or not their manifesto is viable; whether they will stick to their promises or if they are merely promises to gain votes.

Internet dating

The world of online dating has grown significantly over the past few years, with more and more people taking to the web to find their perfect match. But here is another classic example of the problem of asymmetric information. Dating sites (so we're told!) require you to upload a picture and complete some general information about you: your likes, dislikes, height, age, education, salary, occupation, location, etc.

However, when you complete that information, only you know how much of it is completely true. There are inevitably certain characteristics that make people's profiles more attractive – perhaps you exaggerate your height or salary or take a few years off your age. Whatever 'white lies' you tell, you have much better information as to your own profile than those looking at it. Of course, the same applies to you when you accept a date with someone who has seen your profile – they have more information than you as to whether their picture is recent or taken a decade ago!

 Give some other examples of where asymmetric information might cause problems for one party.

profitability). Schemes such as profit sharing encourage managers (agents) to act in the owners' (principals') interests, thereby aligning their objectives. However, this is likely to be more effective with a larger incentive: e.g. the larger the share in company profits, the more inclined managers will be to act in the owners' interests. However, the larger the incentive the more costly it is likely to be to the owners.

Within any firm there will exist a complex chain of principal–agent relationships – between workers and managers, between junior managers and senior managers, between senior managers and directors, and between directors and shareholders. All groups will hold some specialist knowledge which might be used to further their own distinct goals. Predictably, the development of effective monitoring and evaluation programmes and the creation of performance-related pay schemes have been two central themes in the development of business practices in recent years – a sign that the principal is looking to fight back.

Staying in business

Aiming for profits, sales, salaries, power, etc. will be useless if the firm does not survive! Trying to *maximise* any of the various objectives may be risky. For example, if a firm tries to maximise its market share by aggressive advertising or price cutting, it might invoke a strong response from its rivals. The resulting war may drive it out of business. Some of the managers may easily move to other jobs and may actually gain from the experience, but the majority are likely to lose. Concern with survival, therefore, may make firms cautious.

Not all firms, however, make survival the top priority. Some are adventurous and are prepared to take risks. Adventurous firms are most likely to be those dominated by a powerful and ambitious individual – an individual prepared to take gambles.

The more dispersed the decision-making power is in the firm, and the more worried managers are about their own survival, the more cautious are their policies likely to be: preferring 'tried and trusted' methods of production, preferring to stick with products that have proved to be popular, and preferring to expand slowly and steadily.

If a firm is too cautious, however, it may not survive. It may find that it loses market share to more innovative or aggressive competitors. Ultimately, a firm must balance caution against keeping up with competitors, ensuring that the customer is sufficiently satisfied and that costs are kept sufficiently low by efficient management and the introduction of new technology.

The efficient operation of the firm may be strongly influenced by its internal organisational structure. We will consider this in more detail (see section 3.3), but first we must consider how the *legal* structure of the firm might influence its conduct within the marketplace.

3.2 THE FIRM AS A LEGAL ENTITY

 The legal structure of the firm is likely to have a significant impact on its conduct, and subsequent performance, within the marketplace. In the UK, there are several types of firm, each with a distinct legal status.

The sole proprietor

Here, the business is owned by just one person. Usually such businesses are small, with only a few employees. Retailing, construction and farming are typical areas where sole proprietorships are found. Such businesses are easy to set up and may require only a relatively small initial capital investment. They may well flourish if the owner is highly committed to the business, and can respond to changing market conditions. They suffer two main disadvantages, however:

■ *Limited scope for expansion.* Finance is limited to what the owner can raise personally, e.g. through savings or a bank loan. Also there is a limit to the size of an organisation that one person can effectively control.
■ *Unlimited liability.* The owner is personally liable for any losses that the business might make. This could result in the owner's house, car and other assets being seized to pay off any outstanding debts, should the business fail.

The partnership

This is where two or more people own the business. In most partnerships there is a legal limit of 20 partners. Partnerships are common in the same fields as sole proprietorships. They are also common in the professions: solicitors, accountants, surveyors, etc. With more owners, there is more scope for expansion, as extra finance can be raised. Also, as partners can each specialise in one aspect of the business, larger organisations are often more viable. However, taking on partners does mean a loss of control through shared decision making.

Although since 2001 it has been possible to form limited liability partnerships, many partnerships still have unlimited liability. This problem could be very serious. The mistakes of one partner could jeopardise the personal assets of all the other partners.

Where large amounts of capital are required and/ or when the risks of business failure are relatively high, partnerships without limited liability are not an appropriate form of organisation. In such cases it is best to form a company (or 'joint-stock company' to give it its full title).

Companies

A company is legally separate from its owners. This means that it can enter into contracts and own property. Any debts are *its* debts, not the owners'. The owners of the company are the shareholders and the size of each owner's shareholdings will vary, depending on the amount invested. Each shareholder receives his or her share of the company's distributed profit. These payments are called 'dividends'.

The owners have only *limited liability*. This means that, if the company goes bankrupt, the owners will lose the amount of money they have invested in the company, but no more. Their personal assets cannot be seized. This has the advantage of encouraging people to become shareholders, and indeed large companies may have thousands of shareholders – some with very small holdings and others, including institutional shareholders such as pension funds, with very large holdings. Without the protection of limited liability, many of these investors would never put their money into any company that involved even the slightest risk. It also means that companies can raise significant finance, thus creating greater scope for expansion.

Shareholders often take no part in the running of the firm. They may elect a board of directors which decides broad issues of company policy. The board of directors in turn appoints managers who make the day-to-day decisions. There are two types of company: public and private.

Public limited companies. A public limited company is not a nationalised industry: it is still in the private sector. It is 'public' because it can offer new shares publicly: by issuing a prospectus, it can invite the public to subscribe to a new share issue. In addition, many public limited companies are quoted on a stock exchange, where existing shareholders can sell some or all of their shares. The prices of these shares will be determined by demand and supply. A public limited company must hold an annual shareholders' meeting. Examples of well-known UK public limited companies are Marks & Spencer, BP, Barclays, BSkyB and Tesco.

Private limited companies. Private limited companies cannot offer their shares publicly. Shares have to be sold privately. This makes it more difficult for private limited companies to raise finance, and consequently they tend to be smaller than public companies. They are, however, easier to set up than public companies. One of the most famous examples of a private limited company was Manchester United football club (which used to be a public limited company until it was bought out by the Glazer family in 2005). It then became a public limited company again in August 2012 when 10 per cent of the shares were floated on the New York Stock Exchange.

Consortia of firms

It is common, especially in large civil engineering projects that involve very high risks, for many firms to work together as a consortium. The Channel Tunnel and Thames Barrier are products of this form of business organisation. Within the consortium one firm may act as the managing contractor, while the other members may provide specialist services. Alternatively, management may be more equally shared.

Co-operatives

These are of two types.

Consumer co-operatives. These, like the old high street Co-ops, are officially owned by the consumers. Consumers in fact play no part in the running of these co-operatives. They are run by professional managers.

Producer co-operatives. These are firms that are owned by their workers, who share in the firm's profit according to some agreed formula. They are sometimes formed by people in the same trade coming together: for example, producers of handicraft goods. At other times they are formed by workers buying out their factory from the owners; this is most likely if it is due to close, with a resultant loss of jobs. Producer co-operatives, although still relatively few in number, have grown in recent years. One of the most famous is the department store chain, John Lewis, with its supermarket division, Waitrose (see Box 1.1).

Public corporations

These are state-owned enterprises such as the BBC, the Bank of England and nationalised industries.

Public corporations have a legal identity separate from the government. They are run by a board, but the members of the board are appointed by the relevant government minister. The boards have to act within various terms of reference laid down by Act of Parliament. Profits of public corporations that are not reinvested accrue to the Treasury. Since 1980 most public corporations have been 'privatised': that is, they have been sold directly to other firms in the private sector (such as Austin Rover to British Aerospace) or to the general public through a public issue of shares (such as British Gas). However, in response to turmoil in the financial markets, the UK government nationalised two banks in 2008, Northern Rock (see Box 15.3) and Bradford and Bingley. It also partly nationalised two others, the Royal Bank of Scotland and the Lloyds Banking Group (HBOS and Lloyds TSB).

The issue of privatisation is considered in Chapter 22.

MANAGERS AND PERFORMANCE

Are high CEO salaries justified?

In the year to June 2014, according to a report by Incomes Data Services (IDS),[3] chief executives of the top 100 listed UK companies earned an average of £3.34 million, more than 120 times greater than the average UK wage of £27 200. Directors on average earned £2.43 million per year.

The differential between executive pay and that of employees has accelerated significantly over the past 15 years. In the year to June 2014 alone, directors' earnings (pay, bonuses, shares, etc.) rose by 21 per cent, compared with median pay of employees rising by a mere 0.1 per cent. In 2000, chief executives earned on average 'only' 47 times more than the average employee. The IDS report also noted that between 2000 and 2014, 'the median total earnings for FTSE 100 bosses rose by 278 per cent, while the corresponding rise in total earnings for full-time employees was 48 per cent'.[4]

The awards given to executive 'fat cats' have met with considerable protest in recent years. So how can such high pay awards to top executives be justified? The two main arguments put forward to justify such generosity are as follows:

■ 'The best cost money.' Failure to offer high rewards may encourage the top executives within an industry to move elsewhere.
■ 'High rewards motivate.' High rewards are likely to motivate not only top executives, but also those below them. Managers, especially those in the middle of the business hierarchy, will compete for promotion and seek to do well with such high rewards on offer.

However, this view has been challenged, not least by the Business Secretary in the 2010–15 Conservative/Liberal Democrat Coalition government, Vince Cable.

Vince Cable, Britain's outspoken business secretary, is fulminating about 'outrageous' executive pay awards... . 'There's a serious problem, because executive pay has got way out of line with company performance ...'.

Is the link between executive pay and performance as broken as critics say – and if it is, can anything meaningful be done?

The phenomenon has been building for years. FTSE 100 chief executives' pay was 47 times that of average employees in 1998 but had risen to 120 times by 2010... . Bosses' packages have more than doubled in value over that period, while share prices have barely changed. ...

The High Pay Commission says the growth of performance-related pay has itself added to the complexity of remuneration and boosted the amount that can be received. ... Some academics argue that over-powerful executives have been able to extract excessive awards.

Not everyone agrees with the consensus view, however. Thomas Noe, professor of management studies at Oxford's Said Business School, says it is fundamentally incorrect... . In the US, he argues – and probably in the UK, too – most of the increase in executive pay can be accounted for by an increase in company size. ... for a large company, it can make sense to pay a premium for a chief executive who may deliver a slightly better performance than its rivals. 'You are much more willing to pay for tiny differences in performance, because now they are getting multiplied by a much bigger base.' ... 'If shareholders were unhappy', he adds, 'they would vote against company pay policies.'

Robert Talbut, chief investment officer at Royal London Asset Management and a member of the High Pay Commission says: 'Shareholders are engaging but the tools available to them are very limited, because all we do is get an advisory vote once the remuneration committee have decided what they want to do.'

The real problem, he says, is that remuneration committees are showing 'insufficient steel' and not doing the job that shareholders want them to do. 'The whole system gives the impression of having been captured by the insiders.'[5]

1. Explain how excessive executive remuneration might illustrate the principal–agent problem.
2. In the UK, many of the highest-paid executives head former public utilities. Why might the giving of very high rewards to such individuals be a source of public concern?

[3]'Directors' Pay Report 2014/15', *Incomes Data Services* (Thomson Reuters, October 2014).

[4]'Directors "earn 120 times more than average employee"', *BBC News*, 13 October 2014.

[5]Brian Groom, 'Executive pay: The trickle-up effect', *Financial Times*, 27 July 2011. © The Financial Times Limited. All Rights Reserved.

3.3   THE INTERNAL ORGANISATION OF THE FIRM

The internal operating structures of firms are frequently governed by their size. Small firms tend to be centrally managed, with decision making operating through a clear managerial hierarchy. In large firms, however, the organisational structure tends to be more complex, although technological change is forcing many organisations to reassess the most suitable organisational structure for their business.

Pause for thought

Before you read on, consider in what ways technology might influence the organisational structure of a business.

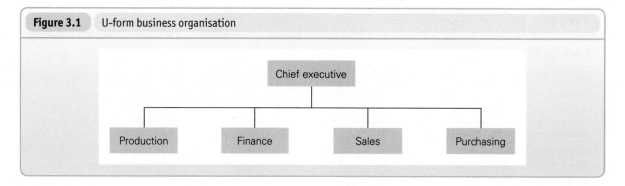

Figure 3.1 U-form business organisation

U-form

In small to medium-sized firms, the managers of the various departments – marketing, finance, production, etc. – are normally directly responsible to a chief executive, whose function is to co-ordinate their activities: relaying the firm's overall strategy to them and being responsible for interdepartmental communication. We call this type of structure *U (unitary) form* (see Figure 3.1).

When firms expand beyond a certain size, however, a U-form structure is likely to become inefficient. This inefficiency arises from difficulties in communication, co-ordination and control. It becomes too difficult to manage the whole organisation from the centre. The problem is that the chief executive suffers from **bounded rationality** – a limit on the rate at which information can be absorbed and processed. When facing complex decisions they typically make satisfactory rather than optimal decisions, relying on rules-of-thumb and tried and tested methods. As the firm grows, more decisions are required. This leads to less time per decision and ultimately poorer decisions. The chief executive effectively loses control of the firm.

 KEY IDEA 8 *Good decision making requires good information.* Where information is poor, or poorly used, decisions and their outcomes may be poor. This may be the result of bounded rationality.

In attempting to regain control, it is likely that a further managerial layer will be inserted. The chain of command thus becomes lengthened as the chief executive must now co-ordinate and communicate via this intermediate managerial level. This leads to the following problems:

- Communication costs increase.
- Messages and decisions may be misinterpreted and distorted.
- The firm experiences a decline in organisational efficiency as various departmental managers, freed from central control, seek to maximise their personal departmental goals.

M-form

To overcome these organisational problems, the firm can adopt an *M (multi-divisional) form* of managerial structure (see Figure 3.2).

This suits medium to large firms. The firm is divided into a number of 'divisions'. Each division could be responsible for a particular product or group of products, or a particular market (e.g. a specific country). The day-to-day running and even certain long-term decisions of each division would be the responsibility of the divisional manager(s). This leads to the following benefits:

- Reduced length of information flows.
- The chief executive being able to concentrate on overall strategic planning.
- An enhanced level of control, with each division being run as a mini 'firm', competing with other divisions for the limited amount of company resources available.

The flat organisation

The shift towards the M-form organisational structure was primarily motivated by a desire to improve the process of decision making within the business. This involved adding layers of management. Recent technological innovations, especially in respect to computer systems such as e-mail and management information systems, have encouraged many organisations to think again about how to establish an efficient and effective organisational structure. The *flat organisation* is one that fully embraces the latest

Definitions

U-form business organisation One in which the central organisation of the firm (the chief executive or a managerial team) is responsible both for the firm's day-to-day administration and for formulating its business strategy.

Bounded rationality Individuals are limited in their ability to absorb and process information. People think in ways conditioned by their experiences (family, education, peer groups, etc.).

M-form business organisation One in which the business is organised into separate departments, such that responsibility for the day-to-day management enterprise is separated from the formulation of the business's strategic plan.

Flat organisation One in which technology enables senior managers to communicate directly with those lower in the organisational structure. Middle managers are bypassed.

Figure 3.2   M-form business organisation

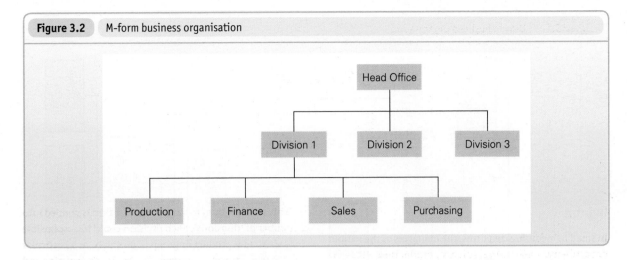

developments in information technology, and by so doing is able to reduce the need for a large group of middle managers. Senior managers, through these new information systems, can communicate easily and directly with those lower in the organisational structure. Middle managers are effectively bypassed.

The speed of information flows reduces the impact of bounded rationality on the decision-making process. Senior managers are able to re-establish and, in certain cases, widen their span of control over the business organisation.

In many respects the flat organisation represents a return to the U-form structure. It is yet to be seen whether we also have a return to the problems associated with this type of organisation.

Multinationals and business organisation

Further types of business organisation which we might identify are closely linked to the expansion and development of the multinational enterprise. Such organisational structures have developed as a response to these businesses attempting to control their business activities on a global scale. Three forms of multinational business organisation are identified below.

H-form. The H-form or *holding company* is in many respects a variation on the M-form structure. A holding company (or parent company) is one which owns a controlling interest in other subsidiary companies. These subsidiaries, in turn, may also have controlling interests in other companies.

H-form organisational structures can be highly complex. While the parent company has ultimate control over its various subsidiaries, it is likely that both tactical and strategic decision making is left to the individual companies within the organisation. Many multinationals are organised along the lines of an international holding company, where overseas subsidiaries pursue their own independent strategy. The Walt Disney Company (Holding Company) represents a good example of an H-form business organisation.

Figure 3.3 shows the firm's organisational structure and the range of assets it owns.

Integrated international enterprise. The **integrated international enterprise** is an organisational structure where a company's international subsidiaries, rather than pursuing independent business strategies, co-ordinate and integrate their activities in pursuit of shared corporate aims and objectives. The co-ordination of such activities can be either at a regional level – for example, within the European market – or on a truly global scale. In such an organisation, the distinction between parent company and subsidiary is of less relevance than the identification of a clear corporate philosophy which dominates business goals and policy.

Transnational association. A further form of multinational business organisation is the **transnational association**. Here the business headquarters holds little equity investment in its subsidiaries. These are largely owned and managed by local people. These subsidiaries receive managerial and technical assistance from the headquarters, in exchange for contractual agreements that output produced by the subsidiary is sold to the headquarters. Such output is most likely to take the form of product components rather than finished products. The headquarters then acts as an assembler, marketer or

Definitions

Holding company A business organisation in which the present company holds interests in a number of other companies or subsidiaries.

Integrated international enterprise One in which an international company pursues a single business strategy. It co-ordinates the business activities of its subsidiaries across different countries.

Transnational association A form of business organisation in which the subsidiaries of a company in different countries are contractually bound to the parent company to provide output to or receive inputs from other subsidiaries.

Figure 3.3 Organisational structure of The Walt Disney Company (Holding Company)

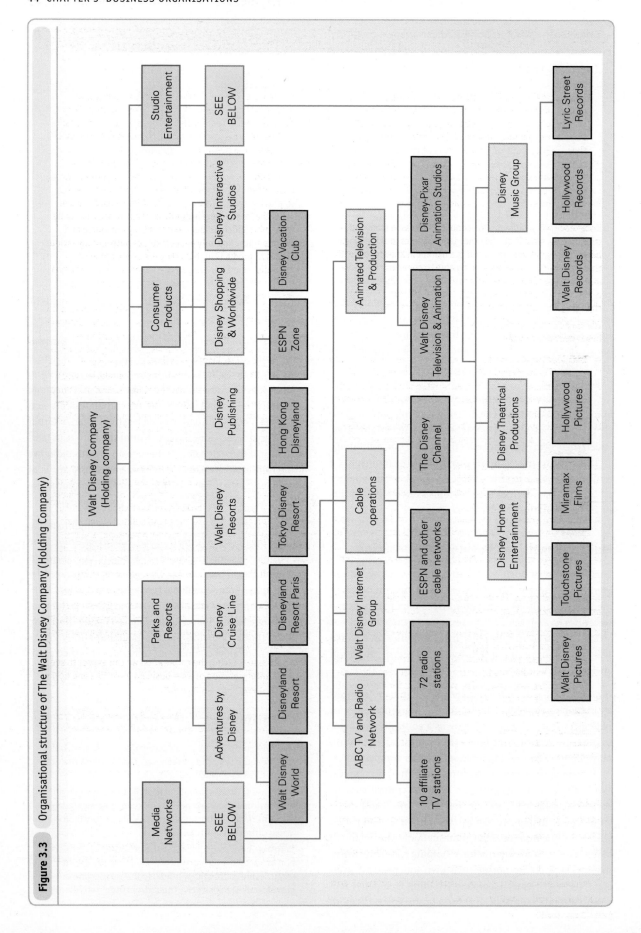

BOX 3.3 THE CHANGING NATURE OF BUSINESS

Knowledge rules

In the knowledge-driven economy, innovation has become central to achievement in the business world. With this growth in importance, organisations large and small have begun to re-evaluate their products, their services, even their corporate culture in the attempt to maintain their competitiveness in the global markets of today. The more forward-thinking companies have recognised that only through such root and branch reform can they hope to survive in the face of increasing competition.[6]

Knowledge is fundamental to economic success in many industries, and for most firms, key knowledge resides in skilled members of the workforce. The result is a market in knowledge, with those having the knowledge being able to command high salaries and often being 'head hunted'. The 'knowledge economy' is affecting people from all walks of life, and fundamentally changing the nature, organisation and practice of business.

The traditional business corporation was based around five fundamental principles:

■ Individual workers needed the business and the income it provided more than the business needed them. After all, employers could always find alternative workers. As such, the corporation was the dominant partner in the employment relationship.
■ Employees who worked for the corporation tended to be full time, and depended upon the work as their sole source of income.
■ The corporation was integrated, with a single management structure overseeing all the various stages of production. This was seen as the most efficient way to organise productive activity.
■ Suppliers, and especially manufacturers, had considerable power over the customer by controlling information about their product or service.
■ Technology relevant to an industry was developed within the industry.

In more recent times, with the advent of the knowledge economy, the principles above have all but been turned on their head.

■ The key factor of production in a knowledge economy is knowledge itself, and the workers that hold such knowledge. Without such workers, the corporation is unlikely to succeed. As such, the balance of power between the business and the worker in today's economy is far more equal.
■ Even though the vast majority of employees still work full time, the diversity in employment contracts, such as

part-time and short-term contracts and consultancy, means that full-time work is not the only option. (We examine this in section 18.7.) The result is an increasing number of workers offering their services to business in non-conventional ways.
■ As the domestic economy increasingly spills into the global economy, the complexity of the marketplace facing business means that few businesses have the expertise to provide an integrated product. With communication costs that are largely insignificant, businesses are likely to be more efficient and flexible if they outsource and de-integrate. Not only are businesses outsourcing various stages of production, but many are also employing specialist companies to provide key areas of management, such as HRM (human resource management): hiring, firing, training, benefits, etc.
■ Whereas in the past businesses controlled information, today access to information via sources such as the Internet means that power is shifting towards the consumer.
■ Today, unlike in previous decades, technological developments are less specific to industries. Knowledge developments diffuse and cut across industry boundaries. What this means for business, in a knowledge-driven economy, is that they must look beyond their own industry if they are to develop and grow. We frequently see partnerships and joint ventures between businesses that cut across industry types and technology.

What is clear from the above is that the dynamics of the knowledge economy require a quite fundamental change in the nature of business. Organisationally it needs to be more flexible, helping it to respond to the ever-changing market conditions it faces. Successful companies draw upon their core competencies to achieve market advantage, and thus ultimately specialise in what they do best. Businesses must learn to work with others, either through outsourcing specialist tasks, or through more formal strategic partnerships.

Within this new business model the key assets are the specialist people in the organisation – its knowledge workers. How will businesses attract, retain and motivate the best? Will financial rewards be sufficient, or will workers seek more from their work and the organisation they work for?

With such issues facing the corporation we can expect to see a radical reinterpretation of what business looks like and how it is practised over the coming years.

 How is the development of the knowledge economy likely to affect the distribution of wage income? Will it become more equal or less equal?

[6]European Commission, Directorate-General for Enterprise, *Innovation Management and the Knowledge-Driven Economy* (ECSC-EC-EAEC Brussels-Luxembourg, 2004).

distributor of such output, or some combination of all three. It retains the decisive role within the international business, but the use of **global sourcing** means that distinct production sites are used to produce large numbers of single components and this helps to reduce costs.

We shall investigate the organisational structures and issues surrounding multinational corporations more fully (see Chapter 23).

Definition

Global sourcing Where a company uses production sites in different parts of the world to provide particular components for a final product.

SUMMARY

1a The firm's role in the economy is to eliminate the need for making individual contracts through the market, and to provide a more efficient way to organise production.

1b Using the market to establish a contract is not costless. Transaction costs will mean that the market is normally less efficient than the firm as an allocator of resources.

1c The divorce of ownership from control implies that the objectives of owners and managers may diverge, and similarly the objectives of one manager from another. Hence the goals of firms may be diverse. What is more, as ownership becomes more dispersed, so the degree of control by owners diminishes yet further.

1d Managers might pursue maximisation goals other than profit, or look to achieve a wide range of targets in which profit acts as a constraint on other business aims.

1e The problem of managers not pursuing the same goals as the owners is an example of the *principal–agent problem*. Agents (in this case the managers) may not always carry out the wishes of their principals (in this case the owners). Because of asymmetric information, managers are able to pursue their own aims, just so long as they produce results that will satisfy the owners. The solution for owners is for there to be better means of monitoring the performance of managers, and incentives for the managers to behave in the owners' interests.

2a The legal status of the firm will influence both its actions and performance within the marketplace.

2b There are several types of legal organisation of firms: the sole proprietorship, the partnership, the private limited company, the public limited company, consortia of firms, co-operatives and public corporations. In the first two cases, the owners have unlimited liability: the owners are personally liable for any losses the business might make. With companies, however, shareholders' liability is limited to the amount they have invested. This reduced risk encourages people to invest in companies.

3a The relative success of a business organisation will be strongly influenced by its organisational structure. As a firm grows, its organisational structure will need to evolve in order to account for the business's growing complexity. This is particularly so if the business looks to expand overseas.

3b As firms grow, so they tend to move from a U-form to an M-form structure. In recent years, however, with the advance of information technology, many firms have adopted a flat organisation – a return to U-form.

3c Multinational companies often adopt relatively complex forms of organisation. These vary from a holding company (H-form) structure, to the integrated international enterprise, to transnational associations.

MyEconLab

This book can be supported by MyEconLab, which contains a range of additional resources, including an online homework and tutorial system designed to test and build your understanding.

You need both an access card and a course ID to access MyEconLab:

1. Is your lecturer using MyEconLab? Ask your lecturer for your course ID.

2. Has an access card been included with the book at a reduced cost? Check the inside back cover of the book.

3. If you have a course ID but no access card, go to: http://www.myeconlab.com/ to buy access to this interactive study programme.

REVIEW QUESTIONS

1 What is meant by the term 'transaction costs'? Explain why the firm represents a more efficient way of organising economic life than relying on individual contracts.

2 Explain why the business objectives of owners and managers are likely to diverge. How might owners attempt to ensure that managers act in their interests and not in the managers' own interests?

3 Compare and contrast the relative strengths and weaknesses of the partnership and the public limited company.

4 Conduct an investigation into a recent large building project, such as the 2012 London Olympics or the Football World Cup in Brazil. Identify what firms were involved and the roles and responsibilities they had. Outline the advantages and disadvantages that such business consortia might have.

5 If a business is thinking of reorganisation, why and in what ways might new technology be an important factor in such considerations?

6 What problems are multinational corporations, as opposed to domestic firms, likely to have in respect to organising their business activity? What alternative organisational models might multinationals adopt? To what extent do they overcome the problems you have identified?

ADDITIONAL PART A CASE STUDIES IN THE *ECONOMICS FOR BUSINESS* MyEconLab (www.pearsoned.co.uk/sloman)

A.1 **The UK defence industry.** A PEST analysis of the changes in the defence industry in recent years.

A.2 **Scarcity and abundance.** If scarcity is the central economic problem, is anything truly abundant?

A.3 **Global economics.** This examines how macroeconomics and microeconomics apply at the global level and identifies some key issues.

A.4 **Buddhist economics.** A different perspective on economic problems and economic activity.

A.5 **Downsizing and business reorganisation.** Many companies in recent years have 'downsized' their operations and focused on their core competencies. This looks particularly at the case of IBM.

A.6 **Positive and normative statements.** A crucial distinction when considering matters of economic policy.

WEBSITES RELEVANT TO PART A

Numbers and sections refer to websites listed in the Web appendix and hotlinked from this text's website at **www.pearsoned.co.uk/sloman**

■ For a tutorial on finding the best economics websites, see site C8 (Internet for Economics).

■ For news articles relevant to Part A, see the Economics News Articles link from the text's website.

■ For general economics news sources, see websites in section A of the Web appendix at the end of the text, and particularly A1–9, 35, 36. See also A38, 39, 42, 43, 44 for links to newspapers worldwide.

■ For business news items, again see websites in section A of the Web appendix at the end of the text, and particularly A1–4, 8, 20–26, 35, 36.

■ For sources of economic and business data, see sites in section B and particularly B1–5, 27–9, 32, 36, 39, 43.

■ For general sites for students of economics for business, see sites in section C and particularly C1–7.

■ For sites giving links to relevant economics and business websites, organised by topic, see sites I4, 7, 8, 11, 12, 17, 18.

■ For details on companies, see site A3.

Business and markets

The FT Reports . . .

The Financial Times, 10 September 2015

FT

Cost of breakfast drops to a five-year low

By Emiko Terazono

At last some good news from the commodities rout – the cost of breakfast is at its lowest in five years.

Prices of breakfast commodities – from wheat to pork to coffee – have fallen this year thanks to benign weather, plentiful supplies and the recent sell-off in raw materials. The rise in the US dollar has also made exports from America uncompetitive, adding to pressure on grain and oil seed prices.

An equal weighted average of six commodities – wheat, milk, coffee, orange juice, sugar and lean hogs – is at levels not seen since 2010.

Although the *Financial Times'* breakfast index is a simple average and only shows a notional value of the morning meal, it does reflect the food deflation that is affecting farmers, as well as consumers, this year.

"The ingredients for breakfast have been falling rapidly," says Abdolreza Abbassian, senior grains economist at the UN Food and Agriculture Organization in Rome.

Cheap breakfast is "in line with the FAO food price index", says Mr Abbassian, pointing to the latest figure in August, which registered the largest monthly fall since December 2008. The index is at its lowest level in six years.

An upward revision in yield forecasts for grains and oilseeds from the US Department of Agriculture, improving weather, as well as worries about the impact of the Chinese market turmoil on the country's consumption, have all contributed to the sharp price declines in the past few weeks, say analysts.

"All in all, that has caused this massive correction in prices," says Daryna Kovalska, analyst at Macquarie.

Although there are concerns about future supplies, the world remains burdened with excess inventories of agricultural crops. According to the latest data from the International Grains Council, global grain inventory is standing at a 29-year high of 447m tonnes.

"We struggle to find any strong bullish indicators for agricultural commodities in the near future," says Ms Kovalska.

The situation is in strong contrast to the first half of 2014, when prices of breakfast commodities soared on adverse weather, hitting raw materials such as coffee and milk. Disease boosted pork prices and Russia's incursion into Crimea pushed wheat prices higher.

There are a handful of agricultural commodities that have remained strong. Breakfast with a cup of tea or cocoa will be more expensive, as tea has jumped 67 per cent this year on supply shortfalls due to a severe drought earlier this year, while cocoa has risen 13 per cent on concerns about the effects of the El Niño weather phenomenon.

> *Uncertainty is also the defining characteristic of business competition today. Competing in volatile markets can feel a lot like entering the ring against George Foreman in his prime – or, even worse, like stumbling into a barroom brawl. The punches come from all directions, include a steady barrage of body blows and periodic haymakers, and are thrown by a rotating cast of characters who swing bottles and bar stools as well as fists.*
>
> Donald Sull, 'How to survive in turbulent markets', *Harvard Business Review*, February 2009, p. 80

Markets dominate economic life, from buying and selling raw materials, to supplying the final product to the customer. It would be difficult to imagine a world without markets. In fact we talk about economies today as 'market economies', with economic decisions made primarily by business, consumers and employees interacting with each other in a market environment.

The determination of a market price is a complex business and often subject to great fluctuation (as the *Financial Times* article illustrates). This is particularly so when you consider commodities, such as coffee, wheat and orange juice, which are highly dependent upon the weather and subject to considerable speculative buying and selling.

In Part B of this text we shall explore how the market system operates. In Chapter 4 we will consider those factors that influence both demand and supply, and how via their interaction we are able to derive a market price. We see how markets transmit information from consumers to producers and from producers to consumers. We see how prices act as an incentive – for example, if consumers want more mobile phones, how this increased demand leads to an increase in their price and hence to an incentive for firms to increase their production.

Changes in price affect the quantity demanded and supplied. But how much? How much will the demand for DVDs go up if the price of DVDs comes down? How much will the supply of new houses go up if the price of houses rises? In Chapter 5 we develop the concept of *elasticity* of demand and supply to examine this responsiveness. We also consider some of the issues the market raises for business, such as the effects on a business's revenue of a change in the price of the product, the impact of time on demand and supply and how businesses deal with the risk and uncertainty markets generate. We also look at speculation – people attempting to gain by anticipating price changes.

Key terms

Price mechanism
Demand and demand curves
Income and substitution effects
Supply and supply curves
Equilibrium price and quantity
Shifts in demand and supply curves
Price elasticity of demand
Income elasticity of demand
Cross-price elasticity of demand
Price elasticity of supply
Speculation
Risk and uncertainty
Spot and futures markets

The working of competitive markets

Business issues covered in this chapter

- How do markets operate?
- How are market prices determined and when are they likely to rise or fall?
- Under what circumstances do firms have to accept a price given by the market rather than being able to set the price themselves?
- What are the influences on consumer demand?
- What factors determine the amount of supply coming on to the market?
- How do markets respond to changes in demand or supply?

4.1 BUSINESS IN A COMPETITIVE MARKET

If a firm wants to increase its profits, should it raise its prices, or should it lower them? Should it increase its output, or should it reduce it? Should it modify its product, or should it keep the product unchanged? The answer to these and many other questions is that it depends on the market in which the firm operates. If the market is buoyant, it may well be a good idea for the firm to increase its output in anticipation of greater sales. It may also be a good idea to raise the price of its product in the belief that consumers will be willing to pay more. If, however, the market is declining, the firm may decide to reduce output, or cut prices, or diversify into an alternative product.

The firm is thus greatly affected by its market environment, an environment that is often outside the firm's control and subject to frequent changes. For many firms, prices are determined not by them, but by the market. Even where they do have some influence over prices, the influence is only slight. They may be able to put prices up a small

amount, but if they raise them too much, they will find that they lose sales to their rivals.

The market dominates a firm's activities. The more competitive the market, the greater this domination becomes. In the extreme case, the firm may have no power at all to change its price: it is what we call a *price taker*. It has to accept the market price as given. If the firm attempts to raise the price above the market price, it will simply be unable to sell its product: it will lose all its sales to its competitors. Take the case of farmers selling wheat. They have to accept the price as dictated by the market. If individually they try to sell above the market price, no one will buy.

Definition

Price taker A person or firm with no power to be able to influence the market price.

In competitive markets, consumers too are price takers. When we go into shops we have no control over prices. We have to accept the price as given. For example, when you get to the supermarket checkout, you cannot start haggling with the checkout operator over the price of a can of beans or a tub of margarine.

So how does a competitive market work? For simplicity we will examine the case of a *perfectly competitive market*. This is where both producers and consumers are too numerous to have any control over prices whatsoever: a situation where everyone is a price taker.

Clearly, in other markets, firms will have some discretion over the prices they charge. For example, a manufacturing company such as Ford will have some discretion over the prices it charges for its Fiestas or Mondeos. In such cases the firm has some 'market power'. (We will examine different degrees of market power in Chapters 11 and 12.)

The price mechanism

In a *free market* individuals are free to make their own economic decisions. Consumers are free to decide what to buy with their incomes: free to make demand decisions. Firms are free to choose what to sell and what production methods to use: free to make supply decisions. The resulting demand and supply decisions of consumers and firms are transmitted to each other through their effect on *prices*: through the *price mechanism*.

The price mechanism works as follows. Prices respond to *shortages* and *surpluses*. Shortages cause prices to rise. Surpluses cause prices to fall.

If consumers decide they want more of a good (or if producers decide to cut back supply), demand will exceed supply. The resulting *shortage* will cause *the price of the good to rise*. This will act as an incentive to producers to supply more, since production will now be more profitable. At the same time, it will discourage consumers from buying so much. *The price will continue rising until the shortage has thereby been eliminated.*

If, on the other hand, consumers decide they want less of a good (or if producers decide to produce more), supply will exceed demand. The resulting *surplus* will cause *the price of the good to fall*. This will act as a disincentive to producers,

who will supply less, since production will now be less profitable. It will encourage consumers to buy more.

The price will continue falling until the surplus has thereby been eliminated.

This price, where demand equals supply, is called the *equilibrium price*. By *equilibrium* we mean a point of balance or a point of rest: in other words, a point towards which there is a tendency to move.

The same analysis can be applied to labour markets (and those for other factors of production), except that here the demand and supply roles are reversed. Firms are the demanders of labour. Households are the suppliers. If there is a surplus of a particular type of labour, the wage rate (i.e. the price of labour) will fall until demand equals supply. Many economies fell into recession in 2008, and in the next few years the demand for goods and services fell, reducing the demand for labour. The surplus of labour (unemployment) that emerged in many labour markets led to a fall in wage rates in these markets.

Likewise, if the demand for a particular type of labour exceeds its supply, the resulting shortage will drive up the wage rate, as employers compete with each other for labour. The higher wages will curb firms' demand for that type of labour and encourage more workers to take up that type of job. As economies have recovered from recession, wages have risen in many labour markets and they should continue to do so until demand equals supply, thus eliminating the shortage in those markets.

As with price, the wage rate where the demand for labour equals the supply is known as the *equilibrium* wage rate.

The response of demand and supply to changes in price illustrates a very important feature of how economies work.

 KEY IDEA 9 *People respond to incentives.* It is important, therefore, that incentives are appropriate and have the desired effect.

The effect of changes in demand and supply

How will the price mechanism respond to changes in consumer demand or producer supply? After all, the pattern of consumer demand changes over time. For example, people may decide they want more downloadable music and

Definitions

Perfectly competitive market (preliminary definition) A market in which all producers and consumers of the product are price takers. There are other features of a perfectly competitive market; these are examined in Chapter 11.

Free market One in which there is an absence of government intervention. Individual producers and consumers are free to make their own economic decisions.

The price mechanism The system in a market economy whereby changes in price in response to changes in demand and supply have the effect of making demand equal to supply.

Equilibrium price The price where the quantity demanded equals the quantity supplied: the price where there is no shortage or surplus.

Equilibrium A position of balance. A position from which there is no inherent tendency to move away.

fewer CDs. The pattern of supply also changes. For example, changes in technology may allow the mass production of microchips at lower cost, while the production of hand-built furniture becomes relatively expensive.

In all cases of changes in demand and supply, the resulting changes in *price* act as both *signals* and *incentives*.

A change in demand

 A rise in demand for a good creates a shortage, which causes a rise in its price. This then acts as an incentive for firms to supply more of it. They will divert resources from goods with lower prices relative to costs (and hence lower profits) to this good, which is now more profitable.

A fall in demand for a good creates a surplus, which causes a fall in its price. This then acts as an incentive for firms to supply less, as these goods are now less profitable to produce.

A change in supply

A rise in supply creates a surplus and causes a fall in price. This then acts as an incentive for consumers to demand more. A fall in supply creates a shortage, causing a rise in price. This then acts as an incentive for consumers to buy less.

> **KEY IDEA 10**
>
> *Changes in demand or supply cause markets to adjust.* Whenever such changes occur, the resulting 'disequilibrium' will bring an automatic change in prices, thereby restoring equilibrium (i.e. a balance of demand and supply).

The interdependence of markets

The interdependence of goods and factor markets

 A rise in demand for a good will raise its price and profitability. Firms will respond by supplying more. But to do this they will require more inputs. Thus the demand for the inputs will rise, which, in turn, will raise the price of the inputs. The suppliers of these inputs will respond to this incentive by supplying more. This can be summarised as follows:

Goods market

- Demand for the good rises.
- This creates a shortage.
- This causes the price of the good to rise.
- This eliminates the shortage by choking off some of the demand and encouraging firms to produce more.

Factor market

- The increased supply of the good causes an increase in the demand for factors of production (i.e. inputs) used in making it.
- This causes a shortage of those inputs.
- This causes their prices to rise.
- This eliminates their shortage by choking off some of the demand and encouraging the suppliers of inputs to supply more.

Goods markets thus affect factor markets. Figure 4.1 summarises this sequence of events. (It is common in economics to summarise an argument like this by using symbols.)

Interdependence exists in the other direction too: factor markets affect goods markets. For example, the discovery of raw materials will lower their price. This will lower the costs of production of firms using these raw materials and increase the supply of the finished goods. The resulting surplus will lower the price of the good, which, in turn, will encourage consumers to buy more.

The interdependence of different goods markets

Many goods markets are also interdependent, such that a rise in the price of one good may encourage consumers to buy alternatives. This will drive up the price of alternatives, which will encourage producers to supply more of the alternatives.

Let us now turn to examine each side of the market – demand and supply – in more detail.

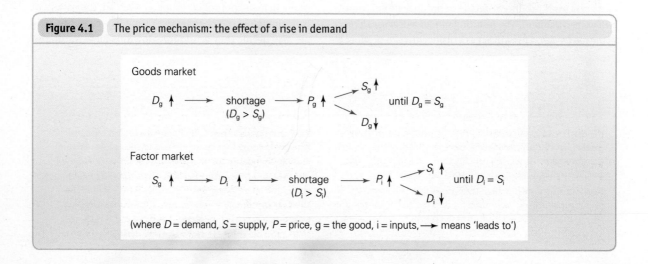

| Figure 4.1 | The price mechanism: the effect of a rise in demand |

Goods market

$$D_g \uparrow \longrightarrow \text{shortage} \longrightarrow P_g \uparrow \begin{array}{c} \nearrow S_g \uparrow \\ \searrow D_g \downarrow \end{array} \text{until } D_g = S_g$$
$$(D_g > S_g)$$

Factor market

$$S_g \uparrow \longrightarrow D_i \uparrow \longrightarrow \text{shortage} \longrightarrow P_i \uparrow \begin{array}{c} \nearrow S_i \uparrow \\ \searrow D_i \downarrow \end{array} \text{until } D_i = S_i$$
$$(D_i > S_i)$$

(where D = demand, S = supply, P = price, g = the good, i = inputs, $\longrightarrow$ means 'leads to')

4.2 DEMAND

The relationship between demand and price

The headlines announce: 'Major crop failures in Brazil and East Africa: coffee prices soar.' Shortly afterwards you find that coffee prices have doubled in the shops. What do you do? Presumably you will cut back on the amount of coffee you drink. Perhaps you will reduce it from, say, six cups per day to two. Perhaps you will give up drinking coffee altogether.

This is simply an illustration of the general relationship between price and consumption: *when the price of a good rises, the quantity demanded will fall*. This relationship is known as the *law of demand*. There are two reasons for this law:

■ People will feel poorer. They will not be able to afford to buy so much of the good with their money. The purchasing power of their income (their *real income*) has fallen. This is called the *income effect* of a price rise.
■ The price has risen *relative to other goods*. People will thus switch to alternative or 'substitute' goods. This is called the *substitution effect* of a price rise.

Similarly, when the price of a good falls, the quantity demanded will rise. People can afford to buy more (the income effect), and they will switch away from consuming alternative goods (the substitution effect).

Therefore, returning to our example of the increase in the price of coffee, we will not be able to afford to buy as much as before, and we will probably drink more tea, cocoa, fruit juices or even water instead.

A word of warning: be careful about the meaning of the words *quantity demanded*. They refer to the amount consumers are willing and able to purchase at a given price over a given time period (for example, a week or a month). They do *not* refer to what people would simply *like* to consume. You might like to own a luxury yacht, but your demand for luxury yachts will almost certainly be zero.

The demand curve

Consider the hypothetical data in Table 4.1. The table shows how many kilos of potatoes per month would be purchased at various prices.

Columns (2) and (3) show the *demand schedules* for two individuals, Tracey and Darren. Column (4), by contrast, shows the total *market demand schedule*. This is the total demand by all consumers. To obtain the market demand schedule for potatoes, we simply add up the quantities demanded at each price by *all* consumers: i.e. Tracey, Darren and everyone else who demands potatoes. Notice that we are talking about demand *over a period of time* (not at a *point* in time). Thus we would talk about daily demand or weekly demand or whatever.

Table 4.1	The demand for potatoes (monthly)			
	Price (pence per kg) (1)	Tracey's demand (kg) (2)	Darren's demand (kg) (3)	Total market demand (tonnes: 000s) (4)
A	20	28	16	700
B	40	15	11	500
C	60	5	9	350
D	80	1	7	200
E	100	0	6	100

Definitions

The law of demand The quantity of a good demanded per period of time will fall as the price rises and rise as the price falls, other things being equal (*ceteris paribus*).

Income effect The effect of a change in price on quantity demanded arising from the consumer becoming better or worse off as a result of the price change.

Substitution effect The effect of a change in price on quantity demanded arising from the consumer switching to or from alternative (substitute) products.

Quantity demanded The amount of a good that a consumer is willing and able to buy at a given price over a given period of time.

Demand schedule for an individual A table showing the different quantities of a good that a person is willing and able to buy at various prices over a given period of time.

Market demand schedule A table showing the different total quantities of a good that consumers are willing and able to buy at various prices over a given period of time.

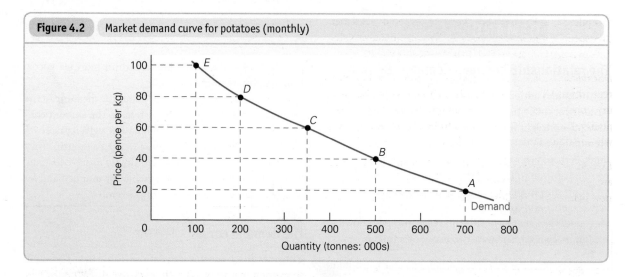

Figure 4.2 Market demand curve for potatoes (monthly)

The demand schedule can be represented graphically as a *demand curve*. Figure 4.2 shows the market demand curve for potatoes corresponding to the schedule in Table 4.1. The price of potatoes is plotted on the vertical axis. The quantity demanded is plotted on the horizontal axis.

Point *E* shows that at a price of 100p per kilo, 100 000 tonnes of potatoes are demanded each month. When the price falls to 80p we move down the curve to point *D*. This shows that the quantity demanded has now risen to 200 000 tonnes per month. Similarly, if the price falls to 60p, we move down the curve again to point *C*: 350 000 tonnes are now demanded. The five points on the graph (*A–E*) correspond to the figures in columns (1) and (4) of Table 4.1. The graph also enables us to read off the likely quantities demanded at prices other than those in the table.

A demand curve could also be drawn for an individual consumer. Like market demand curves, individuals' demand curves generally slope downward from left to right (they have negative slopes): the lower the price of a product, the more a person is likely to buy.

Two points should be noted at this stage:

- In textbooks, demand curves (and other curves too) are only occasionally used to plot specific data. More frequently they are used to illustrate general theoretical arguments. In such cases the axes will simply be price and quantity, with the units unspecified.
- The term 'curve' is used even when the graph is a straight line! In fact, when using demand curves to illustrate arguments we frequently draw them as straight lines – it's easier.

Other determinants of demand

Price is not the only factor that determines how much of a good people will buy. Think about your own consumption of any good – which other factors would cause you to buy more or less of it? Here are just some of the factors that might affect demand:

Tastes. The more desirable people find the good, the more they will demand. Your tastes are probably affected by advertising, fashion, observing what your friends and other consumers buy, considerations of health and your experiences from consuming the good on previous occasions.

The number and price of substitute goods (i.e. competitive goods). The higher the price of *substitute goods*, the higher will be the demand for this good as people switch from the substitutes. For example, the demand for coffee will depend on the price of tea. If tea goes up in price, the demand for coffee will rise.

The number and price of complementary goods. Complementary goods are those that are consumed together: cars and petrol, shoes and polish, bread and butter. The higher the price of complementary goods, the fewer of them will be bought and hence the less the demand for this good. For example, the demand for Xbox games will depend on the price of an XBox. If the price of an XBox goes up, so that fewer are bought, the demand for Xbox games will fall.

Income. As people's incomes rise, their demand for most goods will rise. Such goods are called *normal goods*. There are

---

Definitions

Demand curve A graph showing the relationship between the price of a good and the quantity of the good demanded over a given time period. Price is measured on the vertical axis; quantity demanded is measured on the horizontal axis. A demand curve can be for an individual consumer or a group of consumers, or more usually for the whole market.

Substitute goods A pair of goods which are considered by consumers to be alternatives to each other. As the price of one goes up, the demand for the other rises.

Complementary goods A pair of goods consumed together. As the price of one goes up, the demand for both goods will fall.

Normal goods Goods whose demand rises as people's incomes rise.

exceptions to this general rule, however. As people get richer, they spend less on *inferior goods*, such as supermarkets' value lines or bus travel, and switch to better-quality goods.

Distribution of income. If, for example, national income were redistributed from the poor to the rich, the demand for luxury goods would rise. At the same time, as the poor got poorer, they might have to turn to buying inferior goods, whose demand would thus rise too.

KI 13
p78 *Expectations of future price changes.* If people think that prices are going to rise in the future, they are likely to buy more now before the price does go up, so demand will increase.

> **Pause for thought**
>
> 1. *By referring to each of these six determinants of demand, consider what factors would cause a rise in the demand for butter.*
> 2. *Do all these six determinants of demand affect both an individual's demand and the market demand for a product?*
> 3. *Identify any other factors that would affect (a) your demand for goods and services and (b) the market demand for goods and services.*

Movements along and shifts in the demand curve

A demand curve is constructed on the assumption that 'other things remain equal' (*ceteris paribus*). In other words, it is assumed that none of the determinants of demand, other than price, changes. The effect of a change in price is then simply illustrated by a movement along the demand curve: for example, from point *B* to point *D* in Figure 4.2 when price rises from 40p to 80p per kilo.

What happens, then, when one of these other determinants does change? The answer is that we have to construct a whole new demand curve: the curve shifts. Consider a change in one of the determinants of your demand for books, excluding the price of books: say your income rises. Assuming books are a normal good, this increase in income will cause you to buy more books at any price: the whole curve will shift to the right. This shows that at each price more books will be demanded than before. Thus in Figure 4.3 at a price of *P*, a quantity of Q_0 was originally

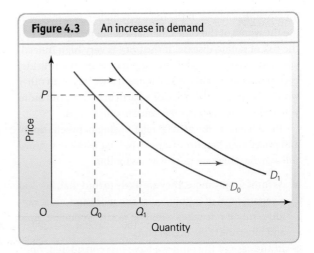

Figure 4.3   An increase in demand

demanded. But now, after the increase in demand, Q_1 is demanded. (Note that D_1 is not necessarily parallel to D_0.)

If a change in a determinant other than price causes demand to fall, the whole curve will shift to the left.

To distinguish between shifts in and movements along demand curves, it is usual to distinguish between a change in *demand* and a change in the *quantity demanded*. A shift in demand is referred to as a ***change in demand***, whereas a movement along the demand curve as a result of a change in price is referred to as a ***change in the quantity demanded***.

> **Pause for thought**
>
> *By referring to the determinants of demand, consider what factors would cause a rightward shift in the demand for family cars.*

> **Definitions**
>
> **Inferior goods** Goods whose demand falls as people's incomes rise.
>
> **Change in demand** The term used for a shift in the demand curve. It occurs when a determinant of demand *other* than price changes.
>
> **Change in the quantity demanded** The term used for a movement along the demand curve to a new point. It occurs when there is a change in price.

4.3   SUPPLY

Supply and price

Imagine you are a farmer deciding what to do with your land. Part of your land is in a fertile valley. Part is on a hillside where the soil is poor. Perhaps, then, you will consider growing vegetables in the valley and keeping sheep on the hillside.

Your decision will depend to a large extent on the price that various vegetables will fetch in the market, and likewise the price you can expect to get from sheep and wool. As far as the valley is concerned, you will plant the vegetables that give the best return. If, for example, the price of potatoes is high, you will probably use a lot of the valley for growing potatoes. If the price gets higher, you may well use the whole of the valley, perhaps being prepared to run the risk of potato disease. If the price is very high indeed, you may even consider growing potatoes on the hillside, even though the yield per acre is much lower there. In other words, the higher the price of a particular crop, the more you are likely to grow in preference to other crops.

This illustrates the general relationship between supply and price: *when the price of a good rises, the quantity supplied will also rise*. There are three reasons for this:

■ As firms supply more, they are likely to find that, beyond a certain level of output, costs rise more and more rapidly. Only if price rises will it be worth producing more and incurring these higher costs.

■ In the case of the farm we have just considered, once potatoes have to be grown on the hillside, the costs of producing them will increase. Also if the land has to be farmed more intensively, say by the use of more and more fertilisers, again the cost of producing extra potatoes is likely to rise quite rapidly. It is the same for manufacturers. Beyond a certain level of output, costs are likely to rise rapidly as workers have to be paid overtime and as machines approach their full capacity. If higher output involves higher costs of production, producers will need to get a higher price if they are to be persuaded to produce extra output. We consider how costs rise with rises in output in more detail in Chapter 9.

■ The higher the price of the good, the more profitable it becomes to produce. Firms will thus be encouraged to produce more of it by switching from producing less profitable goods.

■ Given time, if the price of a good remains high, new producers will be encouraged to set up in production. Total market supply thus rises.

The first two determinants affect supply in the short run. The third affects supply in the long run. (We distinguish between short-run and long-run supply later, in section 5.4.)

The supply curve

The amount that producers would like to supply at various prices can be shown in a *supply schedule*. Table 4.2 shows a monthly supply schedule for potatoes, both for an individual farmer (farmer X) and for all farmers together (the whole market).

The supply schedule can be represented graphically as a *supply curve*. A supply curve may be an individual firm's supply curve or a market supply curve (i.e. that of the whole industry).

Figure 4.4 shows the *market* supply curve of potatoes. As with demand curves, price is plotted on the vertical axis and quantity on the horizontal axis. Each of the points *a–e*

Definitions

Supply schedule A table showing the different quantities of a good that producers are willing and able to supply at various prices over a given time period. A supply schedule can be for an individual producer or group of producers, or for all producers (the market supply schedule).

Supply curve A graph showing the relationship between the price of a good and the quantity of the good supplied over a given period of time.

Table 4.2	The supply of potatoes (monthly)

	Price of potatoes (pence per kg)	Farmer X's supply (tonnes)	Total market supply (tonnes: 000s)
a	20	50	100
b	40	70	200
c	60	100	350
d	80	120	530
e	100	130	700

Figure 4.4 Market supply curve of potatoes (monthly)

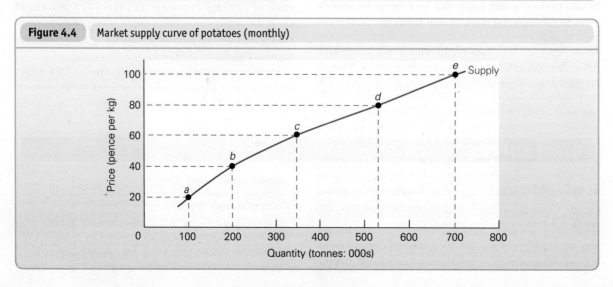

corresponds to a figure in Table 4.2. Thus, for example, a price rise from 60p per kilogram to 80p per kilogram will cause a movement along the supply curve from point *c* to point *d*: total market supply will rise from 350 000 tonnes per month to 530 000 tonnes per month.

Not all supply curves will be upward sloping (positively sloped). Sometimes they will be vertical, or horizontal, or even downward sloping. This will depend largely on the time period over which firms' response to price changes is considered. This question is examined in Chapter 5 (page 76).

Pause for thought

1. *How much would be supplied at a price of 70p per kilo?*
2. *Draw a supply curve for farmer X. Are the axes drawn to the same scale as in Figure 4.4?*

Other determinants of supply

Like demand, supply is not determined simply by price. The other determinants of supply are as follows.

KI 3
p 23
The costs of production. The higher the costs of production, the less profit will be made at any price. As costs rise, firms will cut back on production, probably switching to alternative products whose costs have not risen so much.

The main reasons for a change in costs are as follows:

- Change in input prices: costs of production will rise if wages, raw material prices, rents, interest rates or any other input prices rise.
- Change in technology: technological advances can fundamentally alter the costs of production. Consider, for example, how the microchip revolution has changed production methods and information handling in virtually every industry in the world.
- Organisational changes: various cost savings can be made in many firms by reorganising production.
- Government policy: costs will be lowered by government subsidies and raised by various taxes.

The profitability of alternative products (substitutes in supply). Many firms produce a range of products and will move resources from the production of one good to another as circumstances change. If some alternative product (a *substitute in supply*) becomes more profitable to supply than before, producers are likely to switch from the first good to this alternative; so supply of the first good falls. Other goods are likely to become more profitable if their prices rise or their costs of production fall. For example, if the price of carrots goes up, or the cost of producing carrots comes down, farmers may decide to produce more carrots. The supply of potatoes is therefore likely to fall.

The profitability of goods in joint supply. Sometimes when one good is produced, another good is also produced at the same time. These are said to be *goods in joint supply*. An example is the refining of crude oil to produce petrol. Other grade fuels will be produced as well, such as diesel and paraffin. If more petrol is produced, due to a rise in demand, then the supply of these other fuels will rise too.

Nature, 'random shocks' and other unpredictable events. In this category we would include the weather and diseases affecting farm output, wars affecting the supply of imported raw materials, the breakdown of machinery, industrial disputes, earthquakes, floods and fire, etc.

The aims of producers. A profit-maximising firm will supply a different quantity from a firm that has a different aim, such as maximising sales.

Pause for thought

With reference to each of the above determinants of supply, identify what would cause (a) the supply of potatoes to fall and (b) the supply of leather to rise.

KI 13
p 78
Expectations of future price changes. If price is expected to rise, producers may temporarily reduce the amount they sell. Instead they are likely to build up their stocks and only release them on to the market when the price does rise. At the same time they may plan to produce more, by installing new machines, or taking on more labour, so that they can be ready to supply more when the price has risen.

The number of suppliers. If new firms enter the market, supply is likely to rise.

Movements along and shifts in the supply curve

The principle here is the same as with demand curves. The effect of a change in price is illustrated by a movement along the supply curve: for example, from point *d* to point *e* in Figure 4.4 when price rises from 80p to 100p. Quantity supplied rises from 530 000 to 700 000 tonnes.

If any other determinant of supply changes, the whole supply curve will shift. A rightward shift illustrates an increase in supply. A leftward shift illustrates a decrease in

---

Definitions

Substitutes in supply These are two goods where an increased production of one means diverting resources away from producing the other.

Goods in joint supply These are two goods where the production of more of one leads to the production of more of the other.

supply. Thus in Figure 4.5, if the original curve is S_0, the curve S_1 represents an increase in supply (more is supplied at each price), whereas the curve S_2 represents a decrease in supply (less is supplied at each price).

A movement along a supply curve is often referred to as a *change in the quantity supplied*, whereas a shift in the supply curve is simply referred to as a *change in supply*.

> ### Pause for thought
>
> *By referring to the determinants of supply, consider what factors would cause a rightward shift in the supply of family cars.*

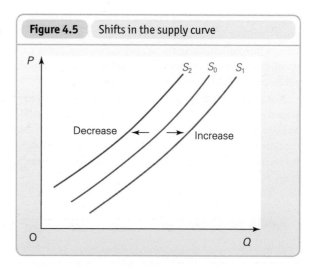

Figure 4.5 Shifts in the supply curve

4.4 PRICE AND OUTPUT DETERMINATION

Equilibrium price and output

We can now combine our analysis of demand and supply. This will show how the actual price of a product and the actual quantity bought and sold are determined in a free and competitive market.

Let us return to the example of the market demand and market supply of potatoes, and use the data from Tables 4.1 and 4.2. These figures are given again in Table 4.3.

What will be the price and output that actually prevail? If the price started at 20p per kilogram, demand would exceed supply by 600 000 tonnes ($A - a$). Consumers would be unable to obtain all they wanted and would thus be willing to pay a higher price. Producers, unable or unwilling to supply enough to meet the demand, will be only too happy to accept a higher price. The effect of the shortage, then, will be to drive up the price. The same would happen at a price of 40p per kilogram. There would still be a shortage; price would still rise. But as the price rises, the quantity demanded falls and the quantity supplied rises. The shortage is progressively eliminated.

What would happen if the price started at a much higher level: say, at 100p per kilogram? In this case supply would exceed demand by 600 000 tonnes ($e - E$). The effect of this surplus would be to drive the price down as farmers competed against each other to sell their excess supplies. The same would happen at a price of 80p per kilogram. There would still be a surplus; the price would still fall.

In fact, only one price is sustainable. This is the price where demand equals supply: namely 60p per kilogram, where both demand and supply are 350 000 tonnes. When supply matches demand the market is said to *clear*. There is no shortage and no surplus.

The price, where demand equals supply, is called the *equilibrium price* (see pages 51–2) or market clearing price. In Table 4.3, if the price starts at any level other than 60p per kilogram, there will be a tendency for it to move towards 60p. The equilibrium price is the only price at which producers' and consumers' wishes are mutually reconciled: where the producers' plans to supply exactly match the consumers' plans to buy.

Table 4.3	The market demand and supply of potatoes (monthly)	
Price of potatoes (pence per kg)	**Total market demand (tonnes: 000s)**	**Total market supply (tonnes: 000s)**
20	700 (A)	100 (a)
40	500 (B)	200 (b)
60	350 (C)	350 (c)
80	200 (D)	530 (d)
100	100 (E)	700 (e)

> ### Definitions
>
> **Change in the quantity supplied** The term used for a movement along the supply curve to a new point. It occurs when there is a change in price.
>
> **Change in supply** The term used for a shift in the supply curve. It occurs when a determinant other than price changes.
>
> **Market clearing** A market clears when supply matches demand, leaving no shortage or surplus. The market is in equilibrium.

Figure 4.6 The determination of market equilibrium (potatoes: monthly)

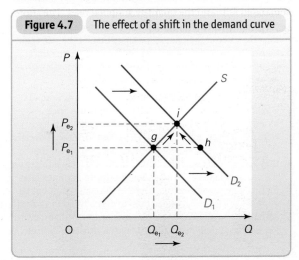

KEY IDEA 11

Equilibrium is the point where conflicting interests are balanced. Only at this point is the amount that demanders are willing to purchase the same as the amount that suppliers are willing to supply. It is a point which will be automatically reached in a free market through the operation of the price mechanism.

Demand and supply curves

The determination of equilibrium price and output can be shown using demand and supply curves. Equilibrium is where the two curves intersect.

Figure 4.6 shows the demand and supply curves of potatoes corresponding to the data in Table 4.3. Equilibrium price is P_e (60p) and equilibrium quantity is Q_e (350 000 tonnes).

At any price above 60p, there would be a surplus. Thus at 80p there is a surplus of 330 000 tonnes ($d - D$). More is supplied than consumers are willing and able to purchase at that price. Thus a price of 80p fails to clear the market. Price will fall to the equilibrium price of 60p. As it does so, there will be a movement along the demand curve from point D to point C, and a movement along the supply curve from point d to point c.

At any price below 60p, there would be a shortage. Thus at 40p there is a shortage of 300 000 tonnes ($B - b$). Price will rise to 60p. This will cause a movement along the supply curve from point b to point c and along the demand curve from point B to point C.

Point Cc is the equilibrium: where demand equals supply.

Movement to a new equilibrium

KI 11 p 59 The equilibrium price will remain unchanged only so long as the demand and supply curves remain unchanged. If either of the curves shifts, a new equilibrium will be formed.

A change in demand

KI 10 p 52

If one of the determinants of demand changes (other than price), the whole demand curve will shift. This will lead to a movement *along* the *supply* curve to the new intersection point.

For example, in Figure 4.7, if a rise in consumer incomes led to the demand curve shifting to D_2, there would be a shortage of $h - g$ at the original price P_{e1}. This would cause price to rise to the new equilibrium P_{e2}. As it did so there would be a movement along the supply curve from point g to point i, and along the new demand curve (D_2) from point h to point i. Equilibrium quantity would rise from Q_{e1} to Q_{e2}.

Pause for thought

What would happen to price and quantity if the demand curve shifted to the left? Draw a diagram to illustrate your answer.

The effect of the shift in demand, therefore, has been a movement *along* the supply curve from the old equilibrium to the new: from point g to point i.

Figure 4.7 The effect of a shift in the demand curve

A change in supply

Likewise, if one of the determinants of supply (other than price) changes, the whole supply curve will shift. This will lead to a movement *along* the *demand* curve to the new intersection point.

For example, in Figure 4.8, if costs of production rose, the supply curve would shift to the left: to S_2. There would be a shortage of $g - j$ at the old price of P_{e1}. Price would rise from P_{e1} to P_{e3}. Quantity would fall from Q_{e1} to Q_{e3}. In other words, there would be a movement along the demand curve from point g to point k, and along the new supply curve (S_2) from point j to point k.

To summarise: a shift in one curve leads to a movement along the other curve to the new intersection point.

Sometimes a number of determinants might change. This may lead to a shift in *both* curves. When this happens, equilibrium simply moves from the point where the old curves intersected to the point where the new ones intersect.

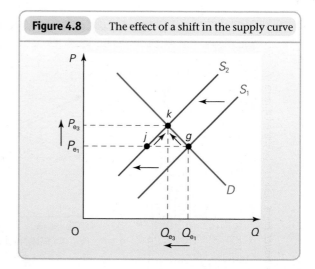

Figure 4.8   The effect of a shift in the supply curve

BOX 4.1   **UK HOUSE PRICES**

The ups and downs of the housing market

If you are thinking of buying a house sometime in the future, then you may well follow the fortunes of the housing market with some trepidation. It is an exceptionally important market to consumers and government, with households spending more on housing as a proportion of their income than on anything else. The housing market is affected by many factors, thus it is hardly surprising that there have been many ups and downs.

In the late 1980s there was a housing price explosion in the UK: between 1984 and 1989 house prices doubled. With people expecting further rises, there was a rush to buy houses and hence borrowing increased significantly. Banks and building societies had plenty of money to lend and many people took out very large mortgages. By the end of 1988 (the peak of boom), house prices were rising at an annual rate of 34 per cent.

However, from 1990 to 1995 house prices fell by 12.2 per cent and this sent many households into *negative equity*. This occurs when the size of a household's mortgage is greater than the value of their house, meaning that if they sold their house, they would still owe money! Many people therefore found themselves in a situation where they were unable to move house.

In the latter part of the 1990s house prices rose by around 5 per cent per annum, but then the rate of house price inflation accelerated and by the end of 2002 house prices were rising by an annual rate of 26 per cent. For home-owners this was good news, but for first-time buyers it meant that they were priced out of the market and hence unable to get on the property ladder. The gross house-price-to-earnings ratio for first-time buyers was just over 2 in the mid-1990s, but by 2007 the price of a house had risen to over 5 times the size of a first-time buyer's earnings. For those on low incomes, owning a home of their own was becoming increasingly difficult.

With the financial crisis of 2007–8 and subsequent recession, house prices started to decline. By early 2009, they were falling at an annual rate of 17.5 per cent. This caused people to postpone buying, once again hoping that prices would continue to fall, but they remained relatively flat for several years (see chart), mirroring the lack of growth in the economy.

First-time buyers now had a greater chance of getting on the property ladder, if they were able to obtain the necessary finance, but many were still reluctant, fearing that prices might continue to decline, seeing a return to the problem of negative equity that occurred in the 1990s.

However, by late 2013, prices were once again rising, especially in the south-east of England and London in particular. In July 2014, the UK's annual house price inflation rate was 11.7 per cent, but this was made up of 19.1 and 12.2 per cent in London and the South East, respectively. Elsewhere in the UK, the average rate was 7.9 per cent. Similar trends continued throughout the rest of 2014 and into 2015, reflecting the relative rates of economic growth in the various regions of the UK.[1]

The determinants of house prices

House prices are determined by demand and supply. If demand rises (i.e. shifts to the right) or if supply falls (i.e. shifts to the left), the equilibrium price of houses will rise. Similarly, if demand falls or supply rises, the equilibrium price will fall.

So why did UK house prices rise so rapidly in the 1980s, the late 1990s through to 2007 and once more from 2013? Why did they also fall in the early 1990s and then fall again from 2008 to 2013? The answer lies primarily in changes in the

---

[1] 'House Price Indices', ONS, October 2014.

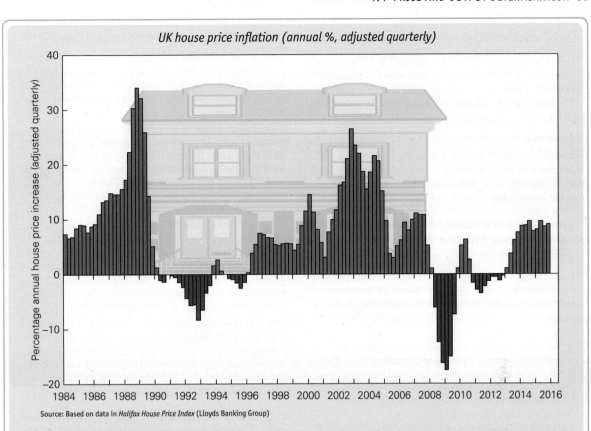

UK house price inflation (annual %, adjusted quarterly)

Source: Based on data in *Halifax House Price Index* (Lloyds Banking Group)

demand for housing. Let us examine the various factors that affected the demand for houses.

Incomes (actual and anticipated)

The second half of the 1980s, 1996 to 2007 and from 2013 were periods of rising incomes or recovery. The economy was experiencing an economic 'boom' or, in the most recent period, a recovery from the financial crisis. Many people wanted to spend their extra incomes on housing: either buying a house for the first time, or moving to a better one. What is more, many people thought that their incomes would continue to grow, and were thus prepared to stretch themselves financially in the short term by buying an expensive house, confident that their mortgage payments would become more and more affordable over time.

The early 1990s and from 2008 to 2012, by contrast, were periods of low or negative growth, with rising unemployment and falling incomes. People had much less confidence about their ability to afford large mortgages.

The desire for home ownership

The desire for home ownership has increased over the years. In recent times this has been fuelled by a host of television programmes focused on buying and selling property. Factors such as increased life expectancy, changing demographics, such as more single-parent families and flows of workers from EU countries, have also caused a significant growth in the desire for home ownership.

The cost of mortgages

During the second half of the 1980s, mortgage interest rates were generally falling. This meant that people could afford larger mortgages, and thus afford to buy more expensive houses. In 1989, however, this trend was reversed. Mortgage interest rates were now rising. Many people found it difficult to maintain existing payments, let alone to take on a larger mortgage. From 1996 to 2003 mortgage rates were generally reduced again, once more fuelling the demand for houses. From 2003 to 2007 interest rates rose again, but this was not enough to deter the demand for housing. From 2008 to 2015 (and perhaps beyond) interest rates remained low. Until 2013, this did not cause an increase in housing demand due to the continued economic uncertainty created by the financial crisis and banks being cautious over their lending. But the recovery in housing demand from around 2013, although driven partly by the recovery of the economy, was helped by continuing low interest rates.

The availability of mortgages

In the late 1980s, mortgages were readily available. Banks and building societies were prepared to accept smaller deposits on houses, and to grant mortgages of 3.5 times a person's annual income, compared with 2.5 times in the early 1980s. In the early 1990s, however, banks and building societies were more cautious about granting mortgages. They were aware that, with falling house prices, rising unemployment and the growing problem of negative equity, there was a growing danger that borrowers would default on payments.

With the recovery of the economy in the mid-1990s, however, and with a growing number of mortgage lenders, mortgages became more readily available and for greater amounts relative to people's income. This pushed up prices. In 2001 the average house price was 3.4 times greater than a person's earnings, but this rose steadily to reach 5.74 times a person's earnings in 2007.

From late 2007 to 2012, however, problems in acquiring loans from the banking sector, falling house prices and rising unemployment all signalled a repeat of the early 1990s.

Many mortgage lenders were asking for deposits of at least 25 per cent – over £40 000 for an average house in the UK. This requirement was relaxed through 2013 and 2014 and government-backed 'Help to Buy' schemes were introduced to help borrowers get a mortgage with a 5 per cent deposit. This was another factor that contributed towards accelerating house prices.

Speculation

A belief that house prices will continue to move in a particular direction can exacerbate house price movements. In other words, speculation tends to increase house price volatility. In the 1980s and from the mid-1990s to 2007, people generally believed that house prices would continue rising. This encouraged people to buy as soon as possible, and to take out the biggest mortgage possible, before prices went up any further. There was also an effect on supply. Those with houses to sell held back until the last possible moment in the hope of getting a higher price. The net effect was for a rightward shift in the demand curve for houses and a leftward shift in the supply curve. The effect of this speculation, therefore, was to help bring about the very effect that people were predicting (see section 5.4).

In the early 1990s, and again from 2008, the opposite occurred. People thinking of buying houses held back, hoping to buy at a lower price. People with houses to sell tried to sell them as quickly as possible before prices fell any further. Again the effect of this speculation was to aggravate the change in prices – this time a fall in prices.

Supply

While speculation about changing house prices is perhaps the biggest determinant of housing supply in the short term, over the long term supply depends on house building. Governments' housing policy is often focused on how to encourage the building industry by providing tax and other incentives and streamlining planning regulations. But house building may bring adverse environmental and social problems and people often oppose new housing developments in their area.

A global dimension to falling house prices

The fall in UK house prices in 2008 had global origins. The dramatic growth in mortgage lending in the UK was also a feature of many other industrialised countries at this time, most notably the USA, where there had been similar dramatic rises in house prices.

Banks and other mortgage lenders bundled up these large mortgage debts into 'financial instruments' and sold them on to other global financial institutions so that they could meet their everyday liquidity requirements of paying bills and meeting customers' demands for cash. This worked well while there was economic prosperity and people could pay their mortgages. However, it became apparent in 2007 that many of the mortgages sold, notably in the USA, were to people who could not meet their repayments.

As the number of mortgage defaults increased, the value of the mortgage-laden financial instruments sold on to other financial institutions fell. As banks found it increasingly difficult to meet their liquidity requirements, they reduced the number of mortgages to potential home owners.

Although housing markets in many countries have recovered as more housing finance has become available and as confidence has returned, the world economy has continued to become more interdependent. This means that the state of the global economy and global finance will increasingly be felt in housing markets around the world.

1. *Draw supply and demand diagrams to illustrate what was happening to house prices (a) in the second half of the 1980s and from the late 1990s to 2007; (b) in the early 1990s and 2008–12; (c) in London and the South East of England in 2014.*

2. *Are there any factors on the supply side that contribute to changes in house prices? If so, what are they?*

3. *Find out what has happened to house prices over the past three years. Attempt an explanation of what has happened.*

BOX 4.2   STOCK MARKET PRICES

Demand and supply in action

Firms that are quoted on the stock market (see page 40 and section 19.5) can raise money by issuing shares. These are sold on the 'primary stock market'. People who own the shares receive a 'dividend' on them, normally paid six-monthly. This varies with the profitability of the company.

People or institutions that buy these shares, however, may not wish to hold on to them for ever. This is where the 'secondary stock market' comes in. It is where existing shares are bought and sold. There are stock markets, primary and secondary, in all the major countries of the world.

There are 2446 companies whose shares are listed on the London Stock Exchange, as of the beginning of 2015 and shares are traded each Monday to Friday (excluding bank holidays). The prices of shares depend on demand and supply. For example, if the demand for Tesco shares at any one time exceeds the supply on offer, the price will rise until demand and supply are equal. Share prices fluctuate

throughout the trading day and sometimes price changes can be substantial.

To give an overall impression of share price movements, stock exchanges publish share price indices. The best known one in the UK is the FTSE 100, which stands for the 'Financial Times Stock Exchange' index of the 100 largest companies' shares. The index represents an average price of these 100 shares. The chart shows movements in the FTSE 100 from 1995 to 2015. The index was first calculated on 3 January 1984 with a base level of 1000 points. It reached a peak of 6930 points on 30 December 1999 and fell to 3287 on 12 March 2003; it then rose again, reaching a high of 6730 on 12 October 2007. In the midst of the financial crisis the index fell to a low of 3781 on 21 November 2008, but by early 2010 it had partially recovered, passing 6000 for a brief period, before levelling out and fluctuating around an average of 5500 to mid-2012, only to rise above 6000 again at the start of 2013. Between

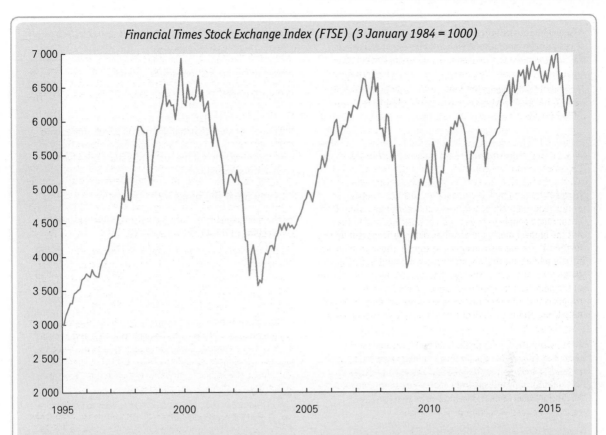

Financial Times Stock Exchange Index (FTSE) (3 January 1984 = 1000)

2013 and the start of 2015 (when writing), it remained above 6500, reaching a high of 6887 by February 2015.

But what causes share prices to change? Why were they so high in 1999, but only just over half that value just three years later, and why has this trend repeated itself in the late 2000s? The answer lies in the determinants of the demand and supply of shares.

Demand

There are five main factors that affect the demand for shares.

The dividend yield

This is the dividend on a share as a percentage of its price. The higher the dividend yields on shares the more attractive they are as a form of saving. One of the main explanations of rising stock market prices from 2003 to 2007 was high profits and resulting high dividends. Similarly, the slowdown in the world economy after 2007 led to falling profits and falling dividends.

The price of and/or return on substitutes

The main substitutes for shares in specific companies are other shares. Thus if, in comparison with other shares, Tesco shares are expected to pay high dividends relative to the share price, people will buy Tesco shares. As far as shares in general are concerned, the main substitutes are other forms of saving. Thus if the interest rate on savings accounts in banks and building societies fell, people with such accounts would be tempted to take their money out and buy shares instead. Another major substitute is property. If house prices rise rapidly, as they did from the late 1990s to 2007, this will reduce the demand for shares as many people switch to buying property in anticipation of even higher prices, as we saw in Box 4.1. If

house prices level off, this makes shares relatively more attractive as an investment and can boost the demand for them.

From late 2007, when house prices and share prices fell dramatically, investors looked towards other, safer, investments such as gold, government debt (Treasury bills and gilts) or even holding cash.

But then with interest rates, including those on savings accounts, being dramatically cut as a result of Bank of England measures to stimulate the economy in 2009, many people saw shares as an attractive alternative to bank and building society accounts. The stock market began rising again.

Incomes

If the economy is growing rapidly and people's incomes are thus rising rapidly, they are likely to buy more shares. Thus in the mid-to-late 1990s, when UK incomes were rising at an average annual rate of over 3 per cent, share prices rose rapidly (see chart). As growth rates fell in the early 2000s, so share prices fell. Similarly, when economic growth improved from 2003 to 2007 share prices increased, but they fell back with the global financial crisis in 2007–8 and the onset of recession and declining real incomes from 2008, only to rise again as the recovery took hold from around 2013.

Wealth

'Wealth' is people's accumulated savings and property. Wealth rose in the 1990s and 2000s, and many people used their increased wealth to buy shares.

Expectations

From 2003 to 2007 people expected share prices to go on rising. They were optimistic about continued growth in the

▶

economy. But as people bought shares, this pushed their prices up even more, thereby fuelling further speculation that they would go on rising and encouraging further share buying.

The global banking crisis in 2007–8 and fears of impending recession started a dramatic fall in share prices in 2008 and, as a result, confidence was shaken. Uncertainty over how and when the global economy would recover caused share prices to be volatile for a few years after the financial crisis, but they began a steady upward trend once the worst of the downturn was over.

Supply

The factors affecting supply in the secondary market are largely the same as those affecting demand, but in the opposite direction.

If the return on alternative forms of saving falls, people with shares are likely to hold on to them, as they represent a better form of saving. The supply of shares to the market will fall. If incomes or wealth rise, people again are likely to want to hold on to their shares.

As far as expectations are concerned, if people believe that share prices will rise, they will hold on to the shares they have. Supply to the market will fall, thereby pushing up prices. If, however, they believe that prices will fall (as they did in 2008), they will sell their shares now before prices do fall. Supply will increase, driving down the price.

Share prices and business

Companies are crucially affected by their share price. If a company's share price falls, this is taken as a sign that 'the

market' is losing confidence in the company, as we saw with Tesco during the latter part of 2014. This will make it more difficult to raise finance, not only by issuing additional shares in the primary market, but also from banks.

It will also make the company more vulnerable to a takeover bid. This is where one company seeks to buy out another by offering to buy all its shares. A takeover will succeed if the owners of more than half of the company's shares vote to accept the offered price. Shareholders are more likely to agree to the takeover if the company's share price has not been performing very well.

Can you buck the market?

Many individuals like to play the market, thinking that they can make easy profits. However, beware! The 'efficient markets hypothesis' predicts that historical share price information, such as that shown in the chart or in the pages of today's financial press, provides no help whatsoever in determining future share prices. Why? Because the current share price already reflects what people anticipate will happen. Future share price movements will occur only as new (unanticipated) information arrives – and it's pure chance; you can't predict the unanticipated! In this purist view, the market for shares is said to be a perfectly efficient market (see section 19.5 for further analysis).

 If the rate of economic growth in the economy is 3 per cent in a particular year, why are share prices likely to rise by more than 3 per cent that year?

BOX 4.3   CONTROLLING PRICES

Efforts to curb binge drinking

Throughout this chapter we have been looking at the way in which the price mechanism works in competitive markets. When a determinant of demand and/or supply changes, the price mechanism eliminates any resulting shortage or surplus: price moves to a new equilibrium level which equates demand and supply.

Over the years there has been a general shift in economies across the world to a more market-based system that allows the price mechanism to work. This means consumers and many producers responding to prices, creating a more efficient market, as we saw in Box 2.2. However, is there an argument against the price mechanism and in favour of government intervention to fix prices? The equilibrium price is not necessarily the 'best' price in a market and we do see governments setting prices either above or below the equilibrium.

When a price is set above the equilibrium, it is known as a *minimum price* (or price floor). Such a price will create a surplus, as the quantity supplied will exceed the quantity demanded, as shown in chart (a). Normally, a surplus would be eliminated by a fall in price but, with a minimum price set above the equilibrium, the surplus persists. One minimum price control that you will be familiar with and may benefit from is the National Minimum Wage, which is covered in more detail in Chapter 18.

When a price is set below the equilibrium, it is known as a *maximum price* (or price ceiling). In this case a shortage emerges, as the quantity demanded will exceed the quantity supplied, as shown in chart (b). Again, the shortage will persist, as the price mechanism no longer adjusts to eliminate it. Governments in some countries have set maximum prices for various basic foodstuffs. The aim is to help the poor. The problem, however, is that it is likely to create shortages of food. The quantity demanded will be higher and the low price is likely discourage farmers from producing so much.

Minimum price for alcohol

Another market where price controls have been extensively discussed is that of alcohol. In early 2010, the UK House of Commons Health Select Committee proposed a minimum price per unit of alcohol in England and Wales (amongst other policies) to combat the growing problem of binge drinking.

It was argued that it would reduce the demand for alcohol by heavy drinkers by raising the price of otherwise cheap drinks, such as those found on offer in supermarkets, and in bars during 'happy hours'.

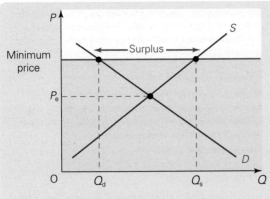

(a) *Minimum Price: Price Floor*

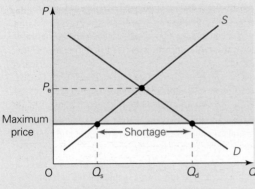

(b) *Maximum Price: Price Ceiling*

The report suggested that a minimum price of alcohol of 50p would save more than 3000 lives per year and would go some way to tackling the costs to the National Health Service of excessive drinking. Estimates by the Royal College of Physicians suggested that the total cost of excessive drinking is £6 billion, £3 billion of which is directly related to higher costs for the NHS.

Few countries have a minimum price for alcohol but Saskatchewan, Canada, is an exception. Evidence from there suggests that a 10 per cent rise in the prices of alcoholic drinks leads to an 8 per cent fall in consumption. While their policy is somewhat different, with the minimum price varying for different drinks, it has furthered the argument in favour of minimum pricing in the UK.[2]

Critics of the minimum price argue that it will be ineffective, because those at whom it is primarily aimed (binge drinkers) will be largely unresponsive to the higher price. Instead it

[2]'The battle over alcohol pricing', BBC News, 30 January 2013.

would be the 'sensible' drinkers who suffer from having to pay a higher price for alcohol. Furthermore, there are concerns that it will adversely affect pubs and small supermarkets. However, an independent MP and member of the Commons Health Select Committee said:

> The evidence we took showed that minimum pricing was the most effective way forward and at the moment you can sometimes buy beer cheaper than water. Our message is that the price would be put up but only by a little for moderate drinkers. Surely that is a sacrifice to pay for the good health of young people.[3]

Legislation for a minimum price of 50p per unit has already been passed in Scotland, though it is being challenged, and calls remain for a minimum price to be imposed in other parts of the UK too. If such a price were imposed above the equilibrium, then a surplus would emerge, as firms would be willing to supply more at the price floor, but consumers would cut back their demand (or at least that's the idea). Further intervention may then be needed to deal with the resulting surpluses that are always associated with minimum prices. There is the danger that the surpluses may be sold illicitly at cut prices.

In the meantime, the UK Coalition government decided in July 2013 not to go ahead with minimum unit pricing. There would instead be a ban on the sale of alcohol below cost price.

1. What methods could be used by the government to deal with:
   a the surpluses from minimum price controls?
   b the shortages that result from maximum price controls?
2. How will the policy of a minimum or maximum price control be affected by a change in the relative steepness of the demand and supply curves? (This concept will be considered in more detail in Chapter 5.)
3. Give some examples of items where the government might choose to set a maximum price. What problems might arise from doing so?

Definitions

Minimum price A price floor set by the government or some other agency. The price is not allowed to fall below this level (although it is allowed to rise above it).

Maximum price A price ceiling set by the government or some other agency. The price is not allowed to rise above this level (although it is allowed to fall below it).

[3]'Alcohol: First Report of Session 2009–10', House of Commons Health Committee, April 2010.

SUMMARY

1a A firm is greatly affected by its market environment. The more competitive the market, the less discretion the firm has in determining its price. In the extreme case of a perfect market, the price is entirely outside the control of firms and consumers. The price is determined by demand and supply in the market, and both sides have to accept this price: they are price takers.

1b In a perfect market, price changes act as the mechanism whereby demand and supply are balanced. If there is a shortage, price will rise until the shortage is eliminated. If there is a surplus, price will fall until that is eliminated.

2a When the price of a good rises, the quantity demanded per period of time will fall. This is known as the 'law of demand'. It applies both to individuals' demand and to the whole market demand.

2b The law of demand is explained by the income and substitution effects of a price change.

2c The relationship between price and quantity demanded per period of time can be shown in a table (or 'schedule') or as a graph. On the graph, price is plotted on the vertical axis and quantity demanded per period of time on the horizontal axis. The resulting demand curve is downward sloping (negatively sloped).

2d Other determinants of demand include tastes, the number and price of substitute goods, the number and price of complementary goods, income, the distribution of income and expectations of future price changes.

2e If price changes, the effect is shown by a movement along the demand curve. We call this effect 'a change in the quantity demanded'.

2f If any other determinant of demand changes, the whole curve will shift. We call this effect 'a change in demand'. A rightward shift represents an increase in demand; a leftward shift represents a decrease in demand.

3a When the price of a good rises, the quantity supplied per period of time will usually also rise. This applies both to individual producers' supply and to the whole market supply.

3b There are two reasons in the short run why a higher price encourages producers to supply more: (a) they are now willing to incur higher costs per unit associated with producing more; (b) they will switch to producing this product and away from now less profitable ones. In the long run there is a third reason: new producers will be attracted into the market.

3c The relationship between price and quantity supplied per period of time can be shown in a table (or schedule) or as a graph. As with a demand curve, price is plotted on the vertical axis and quantity per period of time on the horizontal axis. The resulting supply curve is upward sloping (positively sloped).

3d Other determinants of supply include the costs of production, the profitability of alternative products, the profitability of goods in joint supply, random shocks and expectations of future price changes.

3e If price changes, the effect is shown by a movement along the supply curve. We call this effect 'a change in the quantity supplied'.

3f If any determinant *other* than price changes, the effect is shown by a shift in the whole supply curve. We call this effect 'a change in supply'. A rightward shift represents an increase in supply; a leftward shift represents a decrease in supply.

4a If the demand for a good exceeds the supply, there will be a shortage. This will lead to a rise in the price of the good.

4b If the supply of a good exceeds the demand, there will be a surplus. This will lead to a fall in the price.

4c Price will settle at the equilibrium. The equilibrium price is the one that clears the market, such that demand equals supply. This is shown in a demand and supply diagram by the point where the two curves intersect.

4d If the demand or supply curve shifts, this will lead either to a shortage or to a surplus. Price will therefore either rise or fall until a new equilibrium is reached at the position where the supply and demand curves *now* intersect.

MyEconLab

This book can be supported by MyEconLab, which contains a range of additional resources, including an online homework and tutorial system designed to test and build your understanding.

You need both an access card and a course ID to access MyEconLab:

1. Is your lecturer using MyEconLab? Ask your lecturer for your course ID.

2. Has an access card been included with the book at a reduced cost? Check the inside back cover of the book.

3. If you have a course ID but no access card, go to: http://www.myeconlab.com/ to buy access to this interactive study programme.

REVIEW QUESTIONS

1 Using a diagram like Figure 4.1, summarise the effect of (a) a reduction in the demand for a good; (b) a reduction in the costs of production of a good.

2 Referring to Table 4.1, assume that there are 200 consumers in the market. Of these, 100 have schedules like Tracey's and 100 have schedules like Darren's. What would be the total market demand schedule for potatoes now?

3 Again referring to Table 4.1, draw Tracey's and Darren's demand curves for potatoes on one diagram. (Note that you will use the same vertical scale as in Figure 4.2, but you will need a quite different horizontal scale.) At

what price is their demand the same? What explanations could there be for the quite different shapes of their two demand curves? (This question is explored in Chapter 5.)

4 The price of pork rises and yet it is observed that sales of pork increase. Does this mean that the demand curve for pork is upward sloping? Explain.

5 This question is concerned with the supply of oil for central heating. In each case consider whether there is a movement along the supply curve (and in which direction) or a shift in it (and whether left or right): (a) new oil fields start up in production; (b) the demand for central heating rises; (c) the price of gas falls; (d) oil companies

anticipate an upsurge in the demand for central-heating oil; (e) the demand for petrol rises; (f) new technology decreases the costs of oil refining; (g) all oil products become more expensive.

6   For what reasons might the price of foreign holidays rise? In each case, identify whether these are reasons affecting demand or supply (or both).

7   The price of cod is much higher today than it was 30 years ago. Using demand and supply diagrams, explain why this should be so.

8   The number of owners of compact disc players has grown rapidly and hence the demand for compact discs has also grown rapidly. Yet the price of CDs has fallen. Why? Use a supply and demand diagram to illustrate your answer.

9   What will happen to the equilibrium price and quantity of butter in each of the following cases? You should state whether demand or supply or both have shifted and in which direction: (a) a rise in the price of margarine; (b) a rise in the demand for yoghurt; (c) a rise in the price of bread; (d) a rise in the demand for bread; (e) an expected increase in the price of butter in the near future; (f) a tax on butter production; (g) the invention of a new, but expensive, process of removing all cholesterol from butter, plus the passing of a law which states that butter producers must use this process. In each case, assume *ceteris paribus*.

10 If both demand and supply change, and if we know in which direction they have shifted but not by how much, why is it that we will be able to predict the direction in which *either* price or quantity will change, but not both? (Clue: consider the four possible combinations and sketch them if necessary: *D* left, *S* left; *D* right, *S* right; *D* left, *S* right; *D* right, *S* left.)

Business in a market environment

In Chapter 4 we examined how prices are determined in perfectly competitive markets: by the interaction of market demand and market supply. In such markets, although the *market* demand curve is downward sloping, the demand curve faced by the individual firm will be horizontal. This is illustrated in Figure 5.1.

The market price is P_m. The individual firm can sell as much as it likes at this market price: it is too small to have any influence on the market – it is a price taker. It will not force the price down by producing more because, in terms of the total market, this extra output would be an infinitesimally small amount. If a farmer doubled the output of wheat sent to the market, it would be too small an increase to affect the world price of wheat!

In practice, however, many firms are not price takers; they have some discretion in choosing their price. Such firms will face a downward-sloping demand curve. If they raise their price, they will sell less; if they lower their price, they will sell more. But firms and economists will want to know more than this. They will want to know just *how much* the quantity

KEY IDEA 12

Elasticity. The responsiveness of one variable (e.g. demand) to a change in another (e.g. price). This concept is fundamental to understanding how markets work. The more elastic variables are, the more responsive is the market to changing circumstances.

Figure 5.1 Market demand curve for an individual firm under conditions of perfect competition

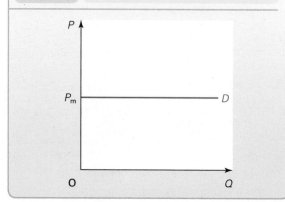

demanded will fall. In other words, they will want to know how *responsive* demand is to a rise in price. This responsiveness is measured using a concept called 'elasticity'.

The responsiveness of quantity demanded to a change in price

The demand for an individual firm

For any firm considering changing its price, it is vital to know the likely effect on the quantity demanded. Take the case of two firms facing very different demand curves. These are shown in Figure 5.2.

Firm A can raise its price quite substantially – from £6 to £10 – and yet its level of sales only falls by a relatively small amount – from 100 units to 90 units. This firm will probably be quite keen to raise its price. After all, it could make significantly more profit on each unit sold (assuming no rise in costs per unit), and yet sell only slightly fewer units.

Firm B, however, will think twice about raising its price. Even a relatively modest increase in price – from £6 to £7 – will lead to a substantial fall in sales from 100 units to 40 units. What is the point of making a bit more profit on those units it manages to sell, if in the process it ends up selling a lot fewer units? In such circumstances the firm may contemplate lowering its price.

The responsiveness of market demand

Economists too will want to know how responsive demand is to a change in price: except in this case it is the responsiveness of *market* demand that is being considered. This information is necessary to enable them to predict the effects of a shift in supply on the market price of a product.

Figure 5.3 shows the effect of a shift in supply with two quite different demand curves (D and D'). Assume that initially the supply curve is S_1, and that it intersects with both demand curves at point a, at a price of P_1 and a quantity of Q_1. Now supply shifts to S_2. What will happen to price and quantity? Economists will want to know! The answer is that it depends on the shape of the demand curve. In the case of demand curve D, there is a relatively large rise in price (to P_2) and a relatively small fall in quantity (to Q_2): equilibrium is at point b. In the case of demand curve D', however, there is only a relatively small rise in price (to P_3), but a relatively large fall in quantity (to Q_3): equilibrium is at point c.

Defining price elasticity of demand

What we will want to compare is the size of the change in quantity demanded of a given product with the size of the

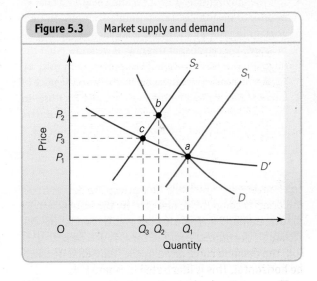

Figure 5.3 Market supply and demand

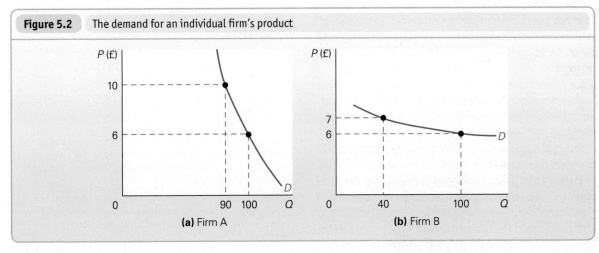

Figure 5.2 The demand for an individual firm's product

(a) Firm A

(b) Firm B

change in price. *Price elasticity of demand* does just this. It is defined as follows:

$$P\varepsilon_{\mathrm{D}} = \frac{\text{Proportionate (or percentage)}}{\text{Proportionate (or percentage) change in price}}$$

If, for example, a 20 per cent rise in the price of a product causes a 10 per cent fall in the quantity demanded, the price elasticity of demand will be:

$-10\%/20\% = -0.5$

Three things should be noted at this stage about the figure that is calculated for elasticity.

The use of proportionate or percentage measures

Elasticity is measured in proportionate or percentage terms for the following reasons:

■ It allows comparison of changes in two qualitatively different things, which are thus measured in two different types of unit: i.e. it allows comparison of quantity changes (quantity demanded) with monetary changes (price).

■ It is the only sensible way of deciding *how big* a change in price or quantity is. Take a simple example. An item goes up in price by £1. Is this a big increase or a small increase? We can answer this only if we know what the original price was. If a can of beans goes up in price by £1, that is a huge price increase. If, however, the price of a house goes up by £1, that is a tiny price increase. In other words, it is the percentage or proportionate increase in price that we look at in deciding how big a price rise it is.

The sign (positive or negative)

If price increases (a positive figure), the quantity demanded will fall (a negative figure). If price falls (a negative figure), the quantity demanded will rise (a positive figure). Thus price elasticity of demand will be negative: a positive figure is being divided by a negative figure (or vice versa).

The value (greater or less than 1)

If we now ignore the sign and just concentrate on the value of the figure, this tells us whether demand is *elastic* or *inelastic*.

Elastic ($\varepsilon > 1$). This is where a change in price causes a proportionately larger change in the quantity demanded. In this case the price elasticity of demand will be greater than 1, since we are dividing a larger figure by a smaller figure.

Inelastic ($\varepsilon < 1$). This is where a change in price causes a proportionately smaller change in the quantity demanded. In this case the price elasticity of demand will be less than 1, since we are dividing a smaller figure by a larger figure.

Unit elastic ($\varepsilon = 1$). *Unit elasticity* is where the quantity demanded changes proportionately the same as price. This will give an elasticity equal to 1, since we are dividing a figure by itself.

The determinants of price elasticity of demand

The price elasticity of demand varies enormously from one product to another. But why do some products have a highly elastic demand, whereas others have a highly *in*elastic demand? What determines price elasticity of demand?

The number and closeness of substitute goods

This is the most important determinant. The more substitutes there are for a good and the closer they are as substitutes, the more people will switch to these alternatives when the price of the good rises, and the greater, therefore, will be the price elasticity of demand.

For example, the price elasticity of demand for a particular brand of a product will probably be fairly high, especially if there are many other, similar brands. If its price goes up, people can simply switch to another brand: there is a large substitution effect. By contrast, the demand for a product in general will normally be pretty inelastic. If the price of food in general goes up, demand for food will fall only slightly. People will buy a little less, since they cannot now afford so much: this is the *income* effect of the price rise. But there is no alternative to food that can satisfy our hunger: there is therefore virtually no *substitution* effect.

The proportion of income spent on the good

The higher the proportion of our income we spend on a good, the more we will be forced to cut consumption when

---

Definitions

Price elasticity of demand A measure of the responsiveness of quantity demanded to a change in price.

Elastic If demand is (price) elastic, then any change in price will cause the quantity demanded to change proportionately more. Ignoring the negative sign, it will have a value greater than 1.

Inelastic If demand is (price) inelastic, then any change will cause the quantity demanded to change by a proportionately smaller amount. Ignoring the negative sign, it will have a value less than 1.

Unit elasticity When the price elasticity of demand is unity, this is where quantity demanded changes by the same proportion as the price. Price elasticity is equal to 1.

its price rises: the bigger will be the income effect and the more elastic will be the demand.

Thus salt has a very low price elasticity of demand. This is because we spend such a tiny fraction of our income on salt that we would find little difficulty in paying a relatively large percentage increase in its price: the income effect of a price rise would be very small. By contrast, there will be a much bigger income effect when a major item of expenditure rises in price. For example, if mortgage interest rates rise (the 'price' of loans for house purchases), people may have to cut down substantially on their demand for housing – being forced to buy somewhere much smaller and cheaper, or to live in rented accommodation.

> ### Pause for thought
>
> *Think of two products and estimate which is likely to have the higher price elasticity of demand. Explain your answer.*

The time period

When price rises, people may take a time to adjust their consumption patterns and find alternatives. The longer the time period after a price change, then, the more elastic is the demand likely to be.

5.2 THE IMPORTANCE OF PRICE ELASTICITY OF DEMAND TO BUSINESS DECISION MAKING

A firm's sales revenue

One of the most important applications of price elasticity of demand concerns its relationship with a firm's sales revenue. The **total sales revenue (TR)** of a firm is simply price multiplied by quantity: $TR = P \times Q$

For example, 3000 units (Q) sold at £2 per unit (P) will earn the firm £6000 (TR).

KI 12
p 68
Let us assume that a firm wants to increase its total revenue. What should it do? Should it raise its price or lower it? The answer depends on the price elasticity of demand.

Elastic demand and sales revenue

As price rises, so quantity demanded falls, and vice versa. When demand is elastic, quantity changes proportionately more than price. Thus the change in quantity has a bigger effect on total revenue than does the change in price. This can be summarised as follows:

P rises; *Q* falls proportionately more; therefore *TR* falls.
P falls; *Q* rises proportionately more; therefore *TR* rises.

In other words, total revenue changes in the same direction as *quantity*.

This is illustrated in Figure 5.4. The areas of the rectangles in the diagram represent total revenue. But why? The area of a rectangle is its height multiplied by its length. In this case, this is price multiplied by quantity purchased, which, as we have seen, gives total revenue.

Demand is elastic between points *a* and *b*. A rise in price from £4 to £5 causes a proportionately larger fall in quantity demanded: from 20 to 10. Total revenue *falls* from £80 (the striped area) to £50 (the shaded area).

When demand is elastic, then, a rise in price will cause a fall in total revenue. If a firm wants to increase its revenue, it should *lower* its price.

> ### Pause for thought
>
> *If a firm faces an elastic demand curve, why will it not necessarily be in the firm's interests to produce more? (Clue: you will need to distinguish between revenue and profit. We will explore this relationship in Chapter 10.)*

| **Figure 5.4** | Elastic demand between two points |

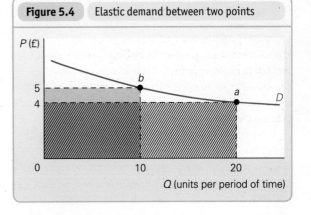

> ### Definition
>
> **Total (sales) revenue (TR)** The amount a firm earns from its sales of a product at a particular price. $TR = P \times Q$. Note that we are referring to *gross* revenue: that is, revenue before the deduction of taxes or any other costs.

Inelastic demand and sales revenue

When demand is inelastic, it is the other way around. Price changes proportionately more than quantity. Thus the change in price has a bigger effect on total revenue than does the change in quantity. To summarise the effects:

P rises; *Q* falls proportionately less; *TR* rises.
P falls; *Q* rises proportionately less; *TR* falls.

In other words, total revenue changes in the same direction as price.

This is illustrated in Figure 5.5. Demand is inelastic between points *a* and *c*. A rise in price from £4 to £8 causes a proportionately smaller fall in quantity demanded: from 20 to 15. Total revenue *rises* from £80 (the striped area) to £120 (the shaded area).

If a firm wants to increase its revenue in this case, therefore, it should *raise* its price.

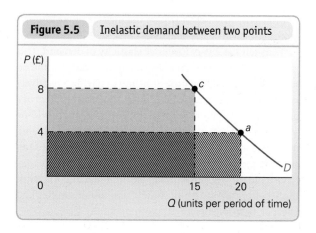

Figure 5.5 Inelastic demand between two points

Special cases

Figure 5.6 shows three special cases: (a) a totally inelastic demand ($P\varepsilon_D = 0$), (b) an infinitely elastic demand ($P\varepsilon_D = 1$) and (c) a unit elastic demand ($P\varepsilon_D = -1$).

BOX 5.1	THE MEASUREMENT OF ELASTICITY

The average or 'mid-point' formula

We have defined price elasticity as the percentage or proportionate change in quantity demanded divided by the percentage or proportionate change in price. But how, in practice, do we measure these changes for a specific demand curve?

A common mistake that students make is to think that you can talk about the elasticity of a whole *curve*. The mistake here is that in most cases the elasticity will vary along the length of the curve.

Take the case of the demand curve illustrated in diagram (a). Between points *a* and *b*, total revenue rises ($P_2Q_2 > P_1Q_1$): demand is thus elastic between these two points. Between points *b* and *c*, however, total revenue falls ($P_3Q_3 < P_2Q_2$). Demand here is inelastic.

Normally, then, we can refer to the elasticity only of a *portion* of the demand curve, not of the *whole* curve.

There is, however, an exception to this rule. This is when the elasticity just so happens to be the same all the way along a curve, as in the three special cases illustrated in Figure 5.6.

Although we cannot normally talk about the elasticity of a whole curve, we can nevertheless talk about the elasticity between any two points on it. Remember the formula we used was:

$$\frac{\%\ or\ Proportionate\ \Delta Q}{\%\ or\ Proportionate\ \Delta P}$$

(where Δ means 'change in').

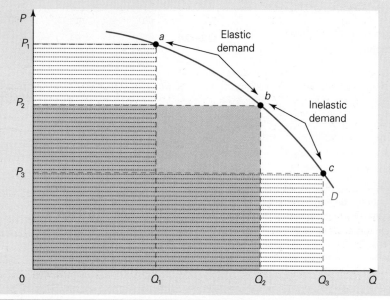

(a) *Different elasticities along different portions of a demand curve*

Figure 5.6 (a) Totally inelastic demand ($P\varepsilon_D = 0$); (b) Infinitely elastic demand ($P\varepsilon_D = \infty$); (c) Unit elastic demand ($P\varepsilon_D = -1$).

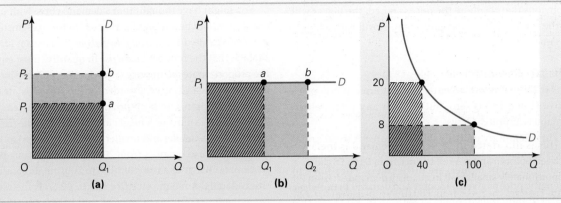

(a)   (b)   (c)

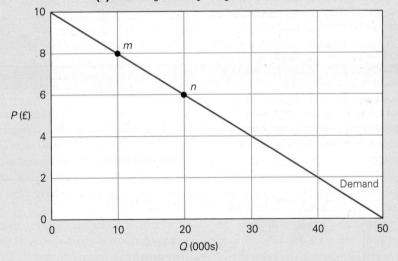

(b) *Measuring elasticity using the arc method*

The way we measure a proportionate change in quantity is to divide that change by the level of Q: i.e. $\Delta Q/Q$. Similarly, we measure a proportionate change in price by dividing that change by the level of P: i.e. $\Delta P/P$. Price elasticity of demand can thus now be rewritten as:

$$\frac{\Delta Q}{Q} \div \frac{\Delta P}{P}$$

But just what value do we give to P and Q? Consider the demand curve in diagram (b). What is the elasticity of demand between points *m* and *n*? Price has fallen by £2 (from £8 to £6), but what is the proportionate change? Is it −2/8 or −2/6? The convention is to express the change as a proportion of the average of the two prices, £8 and £6: in other words to take the mid-point price, £7. Thus the proportionate change is −2/7.

Similarly the proportionate change in quantity between points *m* and *n* is 10/15, since 15 is mid-way between 10 and 20.

Thus using the *average (or 'mid-point') formula*, elasticity between *m* and *n* is given by:

$$\frac{\Delta Q}{\text{average} Q} \div \frac{\Delta P}{\text{average} P} = \frac{10}{10} \div \frac{-2}{7} = -2.33$$

Since 2.33 is greater than 1, demand is elastic between *m* and *n*.

Referring again to diagram (b), what is the price elasticity of demand between a price of (a) £6 and £4; (b) £4 and £2? What do you conclude about the elasticity of a straight-line demand curve as you move down it?

Totally inelastic demand

This is shown by a vertical straight line. No matter what happens to price, quantity demanded remains the same. It is obvious that the more the price is raised, the bigger will be the revenue. Thus in Figure 5.6(a), P_2 will earn a bigger revenue than P_1.

Infinitely elastic demand

This is shown by a horizontal straight line. At any price above P_1 demand is zero. But at P_1 (or any price below) demand is 'infinitely' large.

This seemingly unlikely demand curve is in fact relatively common. Many firms that are very small (like the small-scale grain farmer) are price takers. They have to accept the price as given by supply and demand in the *whole market*. If individual farmers were to try to sell above this price, they would sell nothing at all. At this price, however, they can sell to the market all they produce. (Demand is not *literally* infinite, but as far as the farmer is concerned it is.) In this case, the more the individual farmer produces, the more revenue will be earned. In Figure 5.6(b), more revenue is earned at Q_2 than at Q_1.

Unit elastic demand

This is where price and quantity change in exactly the same proportion. Any rise in price will be exactly offset by a fall in quantity, leaving total revenue unchanged. In Figure 5.6(c), the striped area is exactly equal to the shaded area: in both cases total revenue is £800.

You might have thought that a demand curve with unit elasticity would be a straight line at 45° to the axes. Instead it is a curve called a *rectangular hyperbola*. The reason for its shape is that the proportionate *rise* in quantity must equal the proportionate *fall* in price (and vice versa). As we move down the demand curve, in order for the *proportionate* (or percentage) change in both price and quantity to remain constant, there must be a bigger and bigger *absolute* rise in quantity and a smaller and smaller absolute fall in price. For example, a rise in quantity from 200 to 400 is the same proportionate change as a rise from 100 to 200, but its absolute size is double. A fall in price from £5 to £2.50 is the same percentage as a fall from £10 to £5, but its absolute size is only half.

> **Pause for thought**
>
> *Two customers go to the fish counter at a supermarket to buy some cod. Neither looks at the price. Customer A orders 1 kilo of cod. Customer B orders £3 worth of cod. What is the price elasticity of demand of each of the two customers?*

5.3 OTHER ELASTICITIES

As we know, there are many factors that affect our demand for a product besides price. Firms will thus be interested to know the responsiveness of demand to a change in these other variables, such as consumers' incomes and the prices of goods that are substitute or complementary to theirs. They will want to know the **income elasticity of demand** – the responsiveness of demand to a change in consumers' incomes (Y); and the **cross-price elasticity of demand** – the responsiveness of demand for their good to a change in the price of another (whether a substitute or a complement).

Income elasticity of demand ($Y\varepsilon_D$)

We define the income elasticity of demand for a good as follows:

$$Y\varepsilon_D = \frac{\text{Proportionate (or percentage) change in demand}}{\text{Proportionate (or percentage) change in income}}$$

For example, if a 2 per cent rise in consumer incomes causes an 8 per cent rise in a product's demand, then its income elasticity of demand will be:

$8\%/2\% = 4$

The major determinant of income elasticity of demand is the degree of 'necessity' of the good.

In a developed country, the demand for luxury goods expands rapidly as people's incomes rise, whereas the demand for more basic goods, such as bread, rises only a little. Thus items such as cars and foreign holidays have a high income elasticity of demand, whereas items such as potatoes and bus journeys have a low income elasticity of demand.

As we saw in the last chapter, the demand for inferior goods decreases as income rises. As people earn more, so they switch to better-quality goods. Unlike normal goods, therefore, which have a positive income elasticity of demand, inferior goods have a negative income elasticity of demand (a rise in income leads to a *fall* in demand).

> **Definitions**
>
> **Income elasticity of demand** The responsiveness of demand to a change in consumer incomes: the proportionate change in demand divided by the proportionate change in income.
>
> **Cross-price elasticity of demand** The responsiveness of demand for one good to a change in the price of another: the proportionate change in demand for one good divided by the proportionate change in price of the other.

Income elasticity of demand and the firm

Income elasticity of demand is an important concept to firms considering the future size of the market for their product. If the product has a high income elasticity of demand, sales are likely to expand rapidly as national income rises, but may also fall significantly if the economy moves into recession.

Firms may also find that some parts of their market have a higher income elasticity of demand than others, and may thus choose to target their marketing campaigns on this group. For example, middle-income groups may have a higher income elasticity of demand for certain high-tech products than lower-income groups (which are unlikely to be able to afford such products even if their incomes rise somewhat) or higher-income groups (which can probably afford them anyway, and thus would not buy much more if their incomes rose). For this reason, changes in the distribution of income can be an important factor for firms to consider when making decisions about which products to sell.

The current state of the economy and expectations of how average incomes could change will also be a key factor for firms to consider in helping them decide where to invest resources, based on their predictions about the types of goods that people will demand.

> ### Pause for thought
>
> *Assume that you decide to spend a quarter of your income on clothes. What is (a) your income elasticity of demand; (b) your price elasticity of demand?*

Cross-price elasticity of demand ($C\varepsilon_{Dab}$)

This is often known by its less cumbersome title of 'cross elasticity of demand'. It is a measure of the responsiveness of demand for one product to a change in the price of another (either a substitute or a complement). It enables us to predict how much the demand curve for the first product will shift when the price of the second product changes. For example, knowledge of the cross elasticity of demand for Coca-Cola with respect to the price of Pepsi would allow Coca-Cola to predict the effect on its own sales if the price of Pepsi were to change.

We define cross-price elasticity as follows:

$$C\varepsilon_{Dab} = \frac{\text{Proportionate (or percentage)}}{\text{Proportionate (or percentage) change}}\atop\text{in price of good b}$$

If good b is a *substitute* for good a, a's demand will *rise* as b's price rises. For example, the demand for bicycles will rise as the price of public transport rises. In this case, cross elasticity will be a positive figure. If b is *complementary* to a, however, a's demand will *fall* as b's price rises and thus as the quantity of b demanded falls. For example, the demand for petrol falls as the price of cars rises. In this case, cross elasticity will be a negative figure.

Cross-price elasticity of demand and the firm

The major determinant of cross elasticity of demand is the closeness of the substitute or complement. The closer it is, the bigger will be the effect on the first good of a change in the price of the substitute or complement, and hence the greater will be the cross elasticity – either positive or negative.

Firms will wish to know the cross elasticity of demand for their product when considering the effect on the demand for their product of a change in the price of a rival's product (a substitute). If firm b cuts its price, will this make significant inroads into the sales of firm a? If so, firm a may feel forced to cut its prices too; if not, then firm a may keep its price unchanged. The cross-price elasticities of demand between a firm's product and those of each of its rivals are thus vital pieces of information for a firm when making its production, pricing and marketing plans.

Similarly, a firm will wish to know the cross-price elasticity of demand for its product with any complementary good. Car producers will wish to know the effect of petrol price increases on the sales of their cars.

KI 1 p10
KI 8 p42

Price elasticity of supply ($P\varepsilon_S$)

Just as we can measure the responsiveness of demand to a change in one of the determinants of demand, so too we can measure the responsiveness of supply to a change in one of the determinants of supply. The *price elasticity of supply* refers to the responsiveness of supply to a change in price. We define it as follows:

$$P\varepsilon_S = \frac{\text{Proportionate (or percentage)}}{\text{Proportionate (or percentage) change in price}}\atop{\text{change in quantity supplied}}$$

Thus if a 15 per cent rise in the price of a product causes a 30 per cent rise in the quantity supplied, the price elasticity of supply will be:

30%/15% = 2

In Figure 5.7, curve S_2 is more elastic between any two prices than curve S_1. Thus, when price rises from P_1 to P_2 there is a larger increase in quantity supplied with S_2 (namely, Q_1 to Q_3) than there is with S_1 (namely, Q_1 to Q_2).

Determinants of price elasticity of supply

The amount that costs rise as output rises. The less the additional costs of producing additional output, the more firms will be encouraged to produce for a given price rise: the more elastic will supply be.

> ### Definition
>
> **Price elasticity of supply** The responsiveness of quantity supplied to a change in price: the proportionate change in quantity supplied divided by the proportionate change in price.

BOX 5.2   ELASTICITY AND THE INCIDENCE OF TAX

Who bears the tax?

Taxes on goods are known as 'indirect taxes' because they tax people indirectly through higher prices while it is the shops or other firms that actually pay the taxes. Such taxes include value added tax (VAT) and excise duties on cigarettes, petrol and alcoholic drinks. These taxes can be a fixed amount per unit sold (a 'specific tax') or a percentage of the price (an 'ad valorem tax').

But just how much of the tax will be passed on to the consumer and how much will firms absorb through reduced profit? This 'incidence' of taxation depends on the demand and supply curves for the product being taxed.

A tax represents an increase in a firm's production costs and so the effect will be to shift the firm's supply curve upwards to the left, as discussed in section 4.3 and as shown in diagram (a). The supply curve shifts from S_1 to S_2, where the vertical distance between S_1 and S_2 represents the amount of the tax per unit. This is shown by the arrow.

The price that consumers pay is forced up from P_1 to P_2 and the equilibrium quantity sold falls from Q_1 to Q_2. Notice that the rise in price from P_1 to P_2 is smaller than the total size of the tax. This means that the burden of the tax must be shared between consumers and producers.

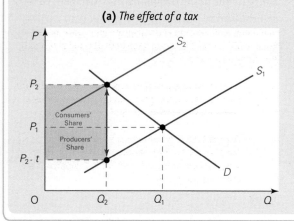

(a) *The effect of a tax*

When a firm's product is taxed, it would probably like to pass the cost increase on to its customers in the form of a higher price, thus protecting its profit margins. However, the law of demand tells us that any increase in price will cut the quantity demanded and this will therefore limit the amount of the tax that a firm can pass on to its customers. The price that the consumer pays with the tax has increased from P_1 to P_2, but the rest of the tax must be paid for by the producer. The producer's share of the tax is the difference between the initial price, P_1, and the price P_{2-tax}. Therefore, consumers pay to the extent that price rises, whereas producers pay to the extent that this rise in price is not sufficient to cover the tax.

The consumers' and producers' shares of the tax are shown by the two shaded areas: namely, the shares of the tax per unit multiplied by the number of units sold (Q_2).

Elasticity and the incidence of taxation

A key question for any firm to answer, when faced with a specific tax being imposed on its good, is just how much of the tax the consumer can pay. The more of the tax that is passed on to the consumer, the bigger will be the potential loss in customers. But if only a small amount is paid by the consumer, the firm will suffer a loss in revenue, as the price it gets to keep will be lower.

The burden faced by each group will depend on the price elasticities of demand and supply.

Take the case of demand. If the demand curve is relatively inelastic, any increase in price will cause a smaller proportionate fall in quantity demanded. As such, the firm will be able to pass a large percentage of the total tax on to its customers in the form of a higher price, knowing that while demand will fall, it will not fall by much. The incidence of taxation falls mainly on the consumer.

Conversely, if the firm's product has relatively elastic demand, any price increase will cause a proportionately larger fall in quantity demanded and so the firm will be reluctant to increase the price to its customers by too much. In this case, the tax burden will fall primarily on the producer.

| Figure 5.7 | Price elasticity of supply |

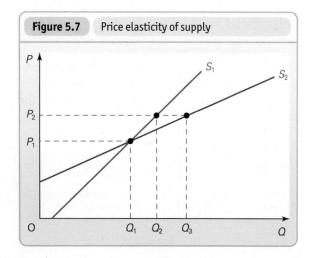

Pause for thought

Return to question 2 in Box 4.3, where we considered the impact of minimum and maximum price controls and how the shape of the demand and supply curves could affect the size of the resulting surplus and shortages. How is the price elasticity of demand and supply relevant in the context of a minimum price on alcohol or any other product?

Supply is thus likely to be elastic if firms have plenty of spare capacity, if they can readily get extra supplies of raw materials, if they can easily switch away from producing alternative products and if they can avoid having to introduce overtime working (at higher rates of pay). If all these conditions hold, costs will be little affected by a rise in out-

(b) *Inelastic demand: the incidence of tax*

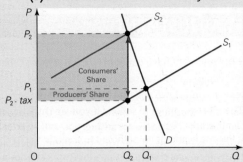

In diagram (b), you can see the impact on the consumer's and producer's share of the tax with a relatively inelastic demand curve. The tax shifts the supply from S_1 to S_2 and consumers now face a significant increase in price from P_1 to P_2. The consumer's share of the tax is therefore the difference in these prices multiplied by the new equilibrium quantity, Q_2 (the red area).

The firm still has to pay some of the tax – the difference between P_1 and P_{2-tax} – but this green area is relatively small. It is therefore in a firm's interest to make its product relatively price inelastic, by advertising its unique qualities and persuading consumers that there are no substitutes, as this will enable the firm to minimise the amount of tax it has to bear.

 1. *Draw a diagram showing an elastic demand curve and explain how this will affect the burden of tax borne by consumers and producers.*

Tax policy

If we combine the red and green areas in diagram (b), we can find the total amount that the firm will pay in tax. This is the same as the amount of revenue earned by the government. So, how can governments use the concept of elasticity to help increase tax revenue? It is easy to see that the less elastic

demand is, the smaller will be the fall in quantity sold following the imposition of a tax. This means that the government is able to receive a given per unit tax on a larger quantity when demand is relatively price inelastic. It therefore has an incentive to impose taxes on products that have a relatively inelastic demand, as a means of generating the highest amount of tax revenue.

This is what we observe in many countries, where products such as cigarettes, petrol and alcohol are the major targets for indirect taxes, as taxes raise a lot of revenue and do not curb demand significantly. Indeed, in the UK, fuel duty (a specific tax) and VAT (an *ad valorem* tax), together account for between 60 and 75 per cent of the cost of petrol, depending on the price of petrol.

The elasticity of supply also has an impact on the burden of tax borne by consumers and producers and crucially on the amount of tax revenue generated. The more elastic supply is, the smaller will be the producer's share of the tax and hence firms have an incentive to make their supply as responsive as possible to a change in price. However, the greatest amount of government revenue will be generated from imposing a tax on a firm that has a relatively inelastic supply curve. Such a tax will cause a relatively small decrease in the quantity sold compared to an elastic supply curve and hence there are many more units to tax.

Combining both demand and supply analysis, government revenue will be at its greatest when both demand and supply are relatively inelastic.

 2. *Using the same approach we did for demand in diagram (b), show how the burden of tax borne by consumers and producers will vary as the elasticity of supply is changed.*

3. *Demand tends to be more elastic in the long run than in the short run. Assume that a tax is imposed on a good that was previously untaxed. How will the incidence of this tax change as time passes?*

put, and supply will be relatively elastic. The less these conditions apply, the less elastic will supply be.

Time period (see Figure 5.8)

- Immediate time period. Firms are unlikely to be able to increase supply by much immediately. Supply is virtually fixed, or can vary only according to available stocks. Hence, supply is highly inelastic. In the diagram SI is drawn with $P\varepsilon_s = 0$. If demand increases to D2, supply will not be able to respond. Price will rise to P2. Quantity will remain at Q1. Equilibrium will move to point *b*.

- Short run. If a slightly longer time period is allowed to elapse, some inputs can be increased (e.g. raw materials), while others will remain fixed (e.g. heavy machinery). Supply can increase somewhat. This is illustrated by S_s. Equilibrium will move to point *c* with price falling again, to P_3, and quantity rising to Q_3.

| **Figure 5.8** | Supply in different time periods |

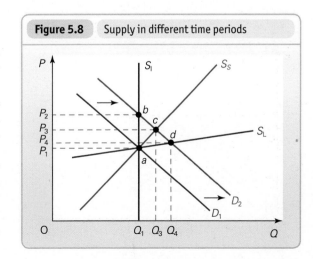

■ Long run. In the long run, there will be sufficient time for all inputs to be increased and for new firms to enter the industry. Supply, therefore, is likely to be highly elastic. This is illustrated by curve S_L. Long-run equilibrium will be at point d with price falling back even further, to P_4, and quantity rising all the way to Q_4. In some circumstances the supply curve may even slope downward. (See the section on economies of scale in Chapter 9, pages 149–51.)

5.4 THE TIME DIMENSION OF MARKET ADJUSTMENT

KI 35
p 354

The full adjustment of price, demand and supply to a situation of disequilibrium will not be instantaneous. It is necessary, therefore, to analyse the time path which supply takes in responding to changes in demand, and which demand takes in responding to changes in supply.

Short-run and long-run adjustment

As we have already seen, elasticity varies with the time period under consideration. The reason is that producers and consumers take time to respond to a change in price. The longer the time period, the bigger the response, and thus the greater the elasticity of supply and demand.

This is illustrated in Figures 5.9 and 5.10. In both cases, as equilibrium moves from points a to b to c, there is a large short-run price change (P_1 to P_2) and a small short-run quantity change (Q_1 to Q_2), but a small long-run price change (P_1 to P_3) and a large long-run quantity change (Q_1 to Q_3).

Price expectations and speculation

In a world of shifting demand and supply curves, prices will constantly be moving up and down. If prices are likely to change in the foreseeable future, this will affect the behaviour of buyers and sellers *now*. If, for example, it is now December and you are thinking of buying a new winter coat, you might decide to wait until the January sales, and in the meantime make do with your old coat. If, on the other hand, when January comes you see a new summer jacket in the sales, you might well buy it now and not wait until the summer, for fear

that the price will have gone up by then. Thus a belief that prices will go up will cause people to buy now; a belief that prices will come down will cause them to wait.

The reverse applies to sellers. If you are thinking of selling your house and prices are falling, you will want to sell it as quickly as possible. If, on the other hand, prices are rising sharply, you will wait as long as possible so as to get the highest price. Thus a belief that prices will come down will cause people to sell now; a belief that prices will go up will cause them to wait.

> **KEY IDEA 13**
>
> ***People's actions are influenced by their expectations.*** People respond not just to what is happening now (such as a change in price), but to what they anticipate will happen in the future.

This behaviour of looking into the future and making buying and selling decisions based on your predictions is called *speculation*. Speculation is often partly based on current trends in price behaviour. If prices are currently rising, people may try to decide whether they are about to peak and go back down again, or whether they are likely to go on rising. Having made their prediction, they will then act on it. This speculation will thus affect demand and supply, which in turn will affect price. Speculation is commonplace in many markets: the stock exchange (see Box 4.2), the foreign exchange market and the housing market (see Box 4.1) are three examples. Large firms often employ specialist buyers who choose the right time to buy inputs, depending on what they anticipate will happen to their price.

Figure 5.9	Response of supply to an increase in demand

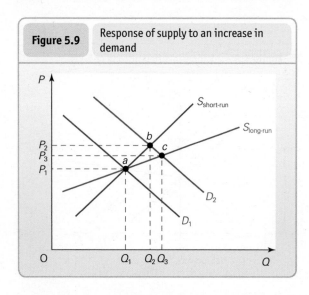

Figure 5.10	Response of demand to an increase in supply

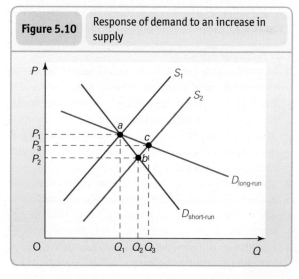

Speculation tends to be *self-fulfilling*. In other words, the actions of speculators tend to bring about the very effect on prices that speculators had anticipated. For example, if speculators believe that the price of BP shares is about to rise, they will buy more BP shares, shifting demand to the right. But by doing this they will ensure that the price *will* rise. The prophecy has become self-fulfilling.

Speculation can either help to reduce price fluctuations or aggravate them: it can be stabilising or destabilising.

Stabilising speculation

Speculation will tend to have a *stabilising* effect on price fluctuations when suppliers and/or demanders believe that a change in price is only *temporary*.

Assume, for example, that there has recently been a rise in price, caused, say, by an increase in demand. In Figure 5.11 (a) demand has shifted from D_1 to D_2. Equilibrium has moved from point *a* to point *b*, and price has risen from P_1 to P_2. How do people react to this rise in price?

Given that they believe this rise in price to be only temporary, suppliers bring their goods to market now, before price falls again. Supply shifts from S_1 to S_2. Demanders, however, hold back until price does fall. Demand shifts from D_2 to D_3. The equilibrium moves to point *c*, with price falling back towards P_1.

A good example of stabilising speculation is that which occurs in agricultural commodity markets. Take the case of wheat. When it is harvested in the autumn there will be a plentiful supply. If all this wheat were to be put on the market, the price would fall to a very low level. Later in the year, when most of the wheat would have been sold, the price would then rise to a very high level. This is all easily predictable.

So what do farmers do? The answer is that they speculate. When the wheat is harvested they know its price will tend to fall, and so instead of bringing it all to market they put a lot of it into store. The more price falls, the more they will put into store *anticipating that the price will later rise*. But this holding back of supplies prevents prices from falling. In other words, it stabilises prices.

Later in the year, when the price begins to rise, they will gradually release grain on to the market from the stores. The more the price rises, the more they will release on to the market *anticipating that the price will fall again by the time of the next harvest*. But this releasing of supplies will again stabilise prices by preventing them rising so much.

Destabilising speculation

Speculation will tend to have a *destabilising* effect on price fluctuations when suppliers and/or buyers believe that a change in price heralds similar changes to come.

Assume again that there has recently been a rise in price, caused by an increase in demand. In Figure 5.11(b), demand has shifted from D_1 to D_2 and price has risen from P_1 to P_2. This time, however, believing that the rise in price heralds further rises to come, suppliers wait until the price rises further. Supply shifts from S_1 to S_2. Demanders buy now before any further rise in price. Demand shifts from D_2 to D_3. As a result the price continues to rise: to P_3.

Box 4.1 examined the housing market. In this market, speculation is frequently destabilising. Assume that people

KI 13
p 78

KI 10
p 52

Definitions

Speculation This is where people make buying or selling decisions based on their anticipations of future prices.

Self-fulfilling speculation The actions of speculators tend to cause the very effect that they had anticipated.

Stabilising speculation This is where the actions of speculators tend to reduce price fluctuations.

Destabilising speculation This is where the actions of speculators tend to make price movements larger.

Figure 5.11 Speculation (initial rise in price)

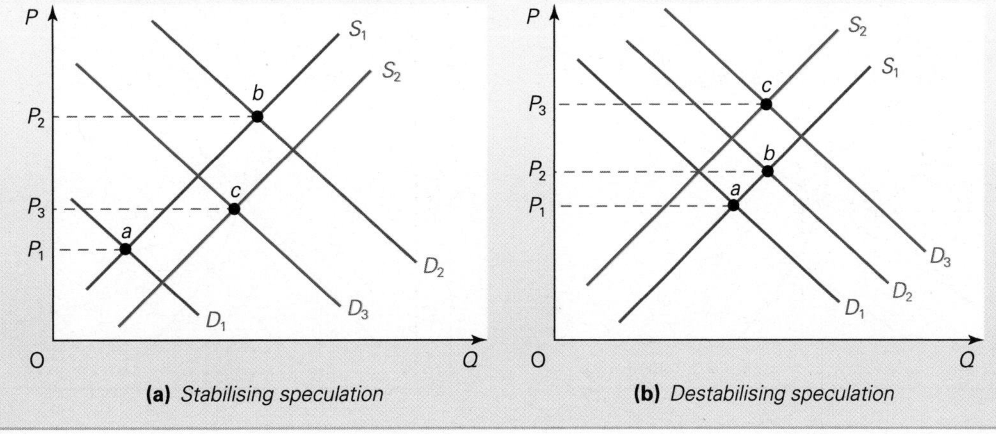

(a) *Stabilising speculation*

(b) *Destabilising speculation*

see house prices beginning to move upward. This might be the result of increased demand brought about by a cut in mortgage interest rates or by growth in the economy. People may well believe that the rise in house prices signals a boom in the housing market: that prices will go on rising. Potential buyers will thus try to buy as soon as possible before prices rise any further. This increased demand (as in Figure 5.11(b)) will thus lead to even bigger price rises. This is precisely what happened in the UK housing market in 1999–2007.

> ### Pause for thought
>
> *Draw two diagrams like Figures 5.11(a) and (b), only this time assume an initial fall in demand and hence price. The first diagram should show the effects of stabilising speculation and the second the effect of destabilising speculation.*

BOX 5.3   ADJUSTING TO OIL PRICE SHOCKS

Short-run and long-run demand and supply responses

Between December 1973 and June 1974, the Organization of Petroleum Exporting Countries (OPEC) put up the price of oil from $3 to $12 per barrel. It was further raised to over $30 in 1979. In the 1980s the price fluctuated, but the trend was downward. Except for a sharp rise at the time of the Gulf War in 1990, the trend continued through most of the 1990s, at times falling as low as $11.

In the early 2000s, oil prices were generally higher, first fluctuating between $19 and $33 per barrel and then, from 2004 to 2006, steadily rising. The price then increased dramatically from January 2007, when it was just over $50 per barrel, to mid-2008 when it reached $147 per barrel. By late 2008 the price had fallen back sharply to under $50 per barrel as fears of a world recession cut the demand for oil.

As the global economy began to recover, the oil price rose steadily, reaching $128 per barrel by early 2011. Prices then stabilised at just above $100 per barrel through to 2013, reaching a peak of $114 in August 2013 before falling back to $100 and then rising again to $112 in June 2014. These figures represented the high points of 2014, as the price of oil then began to plummet, reaching a low of $46.07 in February 2015. The price movements can be explained using simple demand and supply analysis.

The initial rise in price

In the 1970s OPEC raised the price from P_1 to P_2 (see diagram (a)). To prevent surplus at that price, OPEC members restricted their output by agreed amounts. This had the effect of shifting the supply curve to S_2, with Q_2 being produced. This reduction in output needed to be only relatively small because the short-run demand for oil was highly price inelastic: for most uses there are no substitutes in the short run.

Long-run effects on demand

The long-run demand for oil was more elastic (see diagram (b)). With high oil prices persisting, people tried to find ways of cutting back on consumption. People bought smaller cars. They converted to gas or solid-fuel central heating. Firms switched to other fuels. Less use was made of oil-fired power stations for electricity generation. Energy-saving schemes became widespread both in firms and in the home.

This had the effect of shifting the short-run demand curve from D_1 to D_2. Price fell back from P_2 to P_3. This gave a long-run demand curve of D_L: the curve that joins points A and C.

The fall in demand was made bigger by a world recession in the early 1980s.

Long-run effects on supply

With oil production so much more profitable, there was an incentive for non-OPEC oil producers to produce oil. Prospecting went on all over the world and large oil fields were discovered and opened up in the North Sea, Alaska, Mexico, China and elsewhere. In addition, OPEC members were tempted to break their 'quotas' (their allotted output) and sell more oil.

The net effect was an increase in world oil supplies. In terms of the diagrams, the supply curve of oil started to shift to the right from the mid-1980s onwards, causing oil prices to fall through most of the period up to 1998.

Back to square one?

By the late 1990s, with the oil price as low as $10 per barrel, OPEC once more cut back supply. The story had come full circle. This cut-back is once more illustrated in diagram (a).

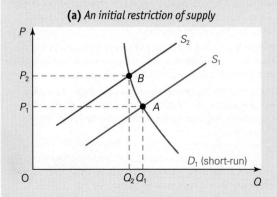

(a) *An initial restriction of supply*

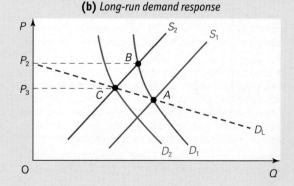

(b) *Long-run demand response*

Conclusion

In some circumstances, then, the action of speculators can help keep price fluctuations to a minimum (stabilising speculation). This is most likely when markets are relatively stable in the first place, with only moderate underlying shifts in demand and supply.

The trouble this time was that worldwide economic growth was picking up. Demand was shifting to the right. The result was a rise in oil prices to around $33, which then fell back again in 2001 as the world slipped into recession and the demand curve shifted to the left.

There were then some very large price increases, first as a result of OPEC in late 2001 attempting once more to restrict supply (a leftward shift in supply), and then, before the Iraq war of 2003, because of worries about possible adverse effects on oil supplies (a rightward shift in demand as countries stocked up on oil). The worries about long-run security of supply continued after the invasion of Iraq and the continuing political uncertainty in the region.

The rises in the price of oil from 2004 through to mid-2008 were fuelled partly by rapidly expanding demand (a rightward shift in short-run demand), especially in countries such as China and India, and by speculation on the future price of oil. On the supply side, producers could not respond rapidly to meet this demand and there was further disruption to supply in some oil-producing countries, including Nigeria and Algeria (a leftward shift in short-run supply). However, the dramatic rise in oil prices fuelled inflation across the world. Consumers and industry faced much higher costs and looked at methods to conserve fuel.

In late 2008, the global financial crisis was followed by recession. The price of oil began to fall back as the demand curve for oil shifted leftwards. It fell from a peak of $147 per barrel in July 2008 to a mere $34 per barrel by the end of the year. But then, as the world economy slowly recovered, and the demand for oil rose, so oil prices rose again. By early 2011, oil was trading at around $128 per barrel.

New sources of supply

The fall in oil prices from the latter part of 2014 might seem somewhat surprising. With continuing conflicts in key oil-producing countries, the normal impact would be a rise in prices, as supply falls. But two things were happening on the supply side.

First, new sources of supply were becoming available, in particular large amounts of shale oil from the USA were coming onto the market. This had a large downward effect on prices. Second, rather than OPEC attempting to push prices up by restricting output, it stated that it would not cut its production, even if the crude oil price were to fall to $30. It hoped, thereby, to make shale oil production unprofitable for many US producers.

These two factors on the supply side, plus continuing weak demand in the eurozone and other parts of the world, pushed

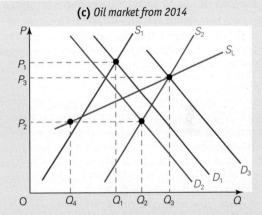

(c) *Oil market from 2014*

oil prices below $50. The demand for oil will inevitably rise at some point, but as long as supply remains high, prices are likely to remain well below the $100 mark.

These effects can be illustrated in diagram (c). The starting point is mid-2014. Global demand and supply are D_1 and S_1; price is above $100 per barrel ($P_1$) and output is Q_1. Demand now shifts to the left (to D_2) as growth in the eurozone and elsewhere falls; and supply shifts to the right (to S_2). Price falls to around $40 per barrel and, given the bigger shift in supply than demand, output rises to Q_2. At a price of P_2, however, output of Q_2 cannot be sustained: investing in new shale oil wells becomes unprofitable. Thus at P_2, long-run supply (shown by S_L) is only Q_4.

But with growth in the global economy in the latter part of the 2010s, demand shifts to the right: say, to D_3. Price rises to P_3 – possibly around $80 per barrel. This gives a short-run output of Q_3, but at that price it is likely that supply will be sustainable in the long run as it makes investment in shale oil sufficiently profitable. Thus curve D_3 intersects with both S_2 and S_L at this price and quantity.

With both demand and supply being price *inelastic* in the short run, large fluctuations in price are only to be expected. And these are amplified by speculation.

The problem is made worse by an income elastic demand for oil. Demand can rise rapidly in times when the global economy is booming, only to fall back substantially in times of recession.

In other circumstances, however, speculation can make price fluctuations much worse. This is most likely in times of uncertainty, when there are significant changes in the determinants of demand and supply. Given this uncertainty, people may see price changes as signifying some trend. They then 'jump on the bandwagon' and do what the rest are doing, further fuelling the rise or fall in price.

5.5   DEALING WITH UNCERTAINTY

Risk and uncertainty

KI 8
p 42

When price changes are likely to occur, buyers and sellers will try to anticipate them. Unfortunately, on many occasions no one can be certain just what these price changes will be. Take the case of stocks and shares. If you anticipate that the price of, say, BP shares is likely to go up substantially in the near future, you may decide to buy some now and then sell them after the price has risen. But you cannot be certain that they will go up in price: they may fall instead. If you buy the shares, therefore, you will be taking a gamble.

Gambles can be of two types. The first is where you know the probability of each possible outcome occurring. Let us take the simplest case of a gamble on the toss of a coin. Heads you win; tails you lose. You know that the probability of winning is precisely 50 per cent. If you bet on the toss of a coin, you are said to be operating under conditions of **risk**. *Risk is when the probability of an outcome is known.* Risk itself is a measure of the *variability* of an outcome. For example, if you bet £1 on the toss of a coin, such that heads you win £1 and tails you lose £1, then the variability is –£1 to +£1.

The second form of gamble is the more usual. This is where the probabilities are not known or are only roughly known. Gambling on the Stock Exchange is like this. You may have a good idea that a share will go up in price, but is it a 90 per cent chance, an 80 per cent chance or what? You are not certain. Gambling under these sorts of conditions is known as operating under **uncertainty**. *This is when the probability of an outcome is not known.*

You may well disapprove of gambling and want to dismiss people who engage in it as foolish or morally wrong. But 'gambling' is not just confined to horses, cards, roulette and the like. Risk and uncertainty pervade the whole of economic life and we are always making decisions, despite not knowing an outcome with any certainty. Even the most morally upright person must decide which career to go into, whether and when to buy a house, or even something as trivial as whether or not to take an umbrella when going out. Each of these decisions and thousands of others are made under conditions of uncertainty (or occasionally risk).

We shall be examining how risk and uncertainty affect economic decisions at several points throughout the text. For example, in the next chapter we will see how it affects people's attitudes and actions as consumers, and how taking out insurance can help to reduce their uncertainty. At this point, however, let us focus on firms' attitudes when supplying goods.

Stock holding as a way of reducing the problem of uncertainty. A simple way that suppliers can reduce risks is by holding stocks. Take the case of the wheat farmers we saw in the previous section. At the time when they are planting the wheat in the spring, they are uncertain as to what the price of wheat will be when they bring it to market. If they keep no stores of wheat, they will just have to accept whatever the market price happens to be at harvest time. If, however, they have storage facilities, they can put the wheat into store if the price is low and then wait until it goes up. Alternatively, if the price of wheat is high at harvest time, they can sell it straight away. In other words, they can wait until the price is right.

> **Pause for thought**
>
> *The demand for pears is more price elastic than the demand for bread and yet the price of pears fluctuates more than that of bread. Why should this be so? If pears could be stored as long and as cheaply as flour, would this affect the relative price fluctuations? If so, how?*

Purchasing information. One way of reducing uncertainty is to buy information. A firm could commission various forms of market research or purchase the information from specialist organisations. It is similar for consumers. You might take advice on shares from a stockbroker, or buy a copy of a consumer magazine, such as *Which?*. The buying and selling

KEY IDEA 14

People's actions are influenced by their attitudes towards risk. Many decisions are taken under conditions of risk or uncertainty. Generally, the lower the probability of (or the more uncertain) the desired outcome of an action, the less likely will people be to undertake the action.

> **Definitions**
>
> **Risk** This is when an outcome may or may not occur, but where its probability of occurring is known.
>
> **Uncertainty** This is when an outcome may or may not occur and where its probability of occurring is not known.

of information in this way helps substantially to reduce uncertainty.

Better information can also, under certain circumstances, help to make any speculation more stabilising. With poor information, people are much more likely to be guided by rumour or fear, which could well make speculation destabilising as people 'jump on the bandwagon'. If people generally are better informed, however, this is likely to make prices go more directly to a long-run stable equilibrium.

Dealing in futures markets

Another way of reducing or even eliminating uncertainty is by dealing in *futures* or *forward markets*. Let us examine the activities first of sellers and then of buyers.

Sellers

Suppose you are a farmer and want to store grain to sell some time in the future, expecting to get a better price then than now. The trouble is that there is a chance that the price will go down. Given this uncertainty, you may be unwilling to take a gamble.

An answer to your problem is provided by the *commodity futures market*. This is a market where prices are agreed between sellers and buyers *today* for delivery at some specified date in the *future*.

For example, if it is 20 October today, you could be quoted a price *today* for delivery in six months' time (i.e. on 20 April). This is known as the six-month *future price*. Assume that the six-month future price for wheat is £60 per tonne. If you agree to this price and make a six-month forward contract, you are agreeing to sell a specified amount of wheat at £60 on 20 April. No matter what happens to the *spot price* (i.e. the current market price) in the meantime, your selling price has been agreed. The spot price could have fallen to £30 (or risen to £100) by April, but your selling price when 20 April arrives is fixed at £60. There is thus *no risk to you whatsoever of the price going down*. You will, of course, lose out if the spot price is *more* than £60 in April.

Buyers

Now suppose that you are a flour miller. In order to plan your expenditures, you would like to know the price you will have to pay for wheat, not just today, but also at various future dates. In other words, if you want to take delivery of wheat at some time in the future, you would like a price quoted *now*. You would like the risks removed of prices going *up*.

Let us assume that today (20 October) you want to *buy* the same amount of wheat on 20 April that a farmer wishes to sell on that same date. If you agree to the £60 future price, a future contract can be made with the farmer. You are then guaranteed that purchase price, no matter what happens to the spot price in the meantime. There is thus *no risk to you whatsoever of the price going up*. You will, of course, lose out if the spot price is *less* than £60 in April.

The determination of the future price

Prices in the futures market are determined in the same way as in other markets: by demand and supply. For example, the six-month wheat price or the three-month coffee price will be that which equates the demand for those futures with the supply. If the five-month sugar price is currently £200 per tonne and people expect by then, because of an anticipated good beet harvest, that the spot price for sugar will be £150 per tonne, there will be few who will want to buy the futures at £200 (and many who will want to sell). This excess of supply of futures over demand will push the price down.

Speculators

Many people operate in the futures market who will never actually handle the commodities themselves. They are neither producers nor users of the commodities. They merely speculate. Such speculators may be individuals, but they are more likely to be financial institutions.

Let us take a simple example. Suppose that the six-month (April) coffee price is £1000 per tonne and that you, as a speculator, believe that the spot price of coffee is likely to rise above that level between now (October) and six months' time. You thus decide to buy 20 tonnes of April coffee futures now.

But you have no intention of taking delivery. After four months, let us say, true to your prediction, the spot price (February) has risen and as a result the April price (and other future prices) have risen too. You thus decide to *sell* 20 tonnes of April (two-month) coffee futures, whose price, let us say, is £1200. You are now 'covered'.

When April comes, what happens? You have agreed to buy 20 tonnes of coffee at £1000 per tonne and to sell 20 tonnes of coffee at £1200 per tonne. All you do is hand the futures contract to buy to the person to whom you agreed to sell. They sort out delivery between them and you make £200 per tonne profit.

If, however, your prediction had been wrong and the price had *fallen*, you would have made a loss. You would have been forced to sell coffee contracts at a lower price than you had bought them for.

Speculators in the futures market thus incur risks, unlike the sellers and buyers of the commodities, for whom the futures market eliminates risk. Financial institutions offering futures contracts will charge for the service: for taking on the risks.

Definitions

Futures or forward market A market in which contracts are made to buy or sell at some future date at a price agreed today.

Future price A price agreed today at which an item (e.g. commodities) will be exchanged at some set date in the future.

Spot price The current market price.

BOX 5.4   DON'T SHOOT THE SPECULATOR

Well not yet, anyway!

In February 2008 the Food and Agricultural Organization of the United Nations stated that the price of cereals had risen 83 per cent over the previous 12 months, with dire consequences for developing nations in particular. In July 2008 the price of oil rose to the unprecedented high of $147 per barrel, with devastating consequences for the millions of users of oil and oil-based products. Between early September and late October 2008 the FTSE 100 fell by 35 per cent, from a high of 5646 to a low of 3665 (see Box 4.3), a fall that had not been seen since October 1987, causing misery to millions of ordinary investors and those with pensions.

Much of the blame for these dramatic changes is placed on speculators who are seen as exacerbating the problem. They are seen as greedy and acting immorally, and affecting the lives of millions of ordinary people through their actions. Thankfully, no one in power has yet adopted Vladimir Lenin's declaration to a meeting at the Petrograd Soviet in 1918: 'Speculators who are caught and fully exposed as such shall be shot ... on the spot.' However, religious leaders, politicians and regulators have been calling for, and getting, stricter controls over their operations.

This commonly held view of the speculator, however, is not held by everyone. Consider the following taken from *The Financial Times* in regard to the rapid rise in commodity prices in early 2011.

> [W]here are commodity prices headed next?
>
> There are many problems in understanding, let alone forecasting, the behaviour of commodity prices. In the long term, which means decades, the real price of commodities is determined by the supply side costs of extraction, ... over shorter term horizons, these factors are incapable of explaining commodity price fluctuations, because they change so slowly. Prices, on the other hand, can change dramatically over short periods. Since demand and supply curves are both very steep (especially for oil), a very small shift in either curve can have very large effects on oil prices, making them very hard to predict.
>
> There are two possible explanations for the surge in commodity prices since last August. The first and 'fundamental' explanation is that the growth in global industrial production has been maintained at levels well above long term trends... .
>
> The second, and 'speculative' explanation is that the Fed's decision to expand liquidity has leaked into all risk assets, including commodities, via financial market demand for these assets... . Paul Krugman and others have argued that the 'speculative' explanation can be eliminated on a priori grounds, because financial operators never take delivery of physical commodities. Ultimately they do not increase the real demand for commodities, and therefore they can have no effect on the price. Financial demand can of course alter the prices for futures and options on commodities, but since the prices of these derivative contracts must eventually home in on the price for the physical, this will eventually be a zero sum game. On this argument, financial speculation is irrelevant.
>
> ... but it seems to me that for short periods ... rising futures prices could lead to the expectation of higher prices for physical commodities, in which case physical players might decide to 'hoard' stocks, and reduce the rate of extraction so that they can benefit from the subsequent rise in prices. By changing inventory levels and extraction rates, this type of real activity could tighten the physical market and, at least for a time, raise prices... .
>
> So which of these explanations best fits the evidence? ... The calculations suggest that while a large part of the rise in oil and other commodity prices may have been caused by fundamentals, nevertheless commodity prices may have overshot their 'equilibrium' levels at times in recent months.[1]

Are speculators largely adjusting their decisions in line with changing circumstances? In other words, are they being efficient? Or are they being inefficient and causing increased price volatility?

 How might it be beneficial for the economy if speculators were less efficient?

[1]Gavyn Davies, 'Fundamentals and speculation in commodity markets', *The Financial Times*, 16 May 2011. © The Financial Times Limited. All Rights Reserved.

SUMMARY

1a Price elasticity of demand measures the responsiveness of demand to a change in price. It is defined as the proportionate (or percentage) change in quantity demanded divided by the proportionate (or percentage) change in price.

1b If quantity demanded changes proportionately more than price, the figure for elasticity will be greater than 1 (ignoring the sign): it is elastic. If the quantity demanded changes proportionately less than price, the figure for elasticity will be less than 1: it is inelastic. If they change by the same proportion, the elasticity has a value of 1: it is unit elastic.

1c Given that demand curves are downward sloping, price elasticity of demand will have a negative value.

1d Demand will be more elastic the greater the number and closeness of substitute goods, the higher the proportion of income spent on the good and the longer the time period that elapses after the change in price.

1e Demand curves normally have different elasticities along their length. We can thus normally refer only to the specific value for elasticity between two points on the curve or at a single point.

2a It is important for firms to know the price elasticity of demand for their product whenever they are considering a price change. The reason is that the effect of the price change on the firm's sales revenue will depend on the product's price elasticity.

2b When the demand for a firm's product is price elastic, a rise in price will lead to a reduction in consumer expenditure on the good and hence to a reduction in the total revenue of the firm.

2c When demand is price inelastic, however, a rise in price will lead to an increase in total revenue for the firm.

3a Income elasticity of demand measures the responsiveness of demand to a change in income. For normal goods it has a positive value. Demand will be more income elastic the more luxurious the good and the less rapidly demand is satisfied as consumption increases.

3b Cross-price elasticity of demand measures the responsiveness of demand for one good to a change in the price of another. For substitute goods the value will be positive; for complements it will be negative. The cross-price elasticity will be greater the closer the two goods are as substitutes or complements.

3c Price elasticity of supply measures the responsiveness of supply to a change in price. It has a positive value. Supply will be more elastic the less costs per unit rise as output rises and the longer the time period.

4a A complete understanding of markets must take into account the time dimension.

4b Given that producers and consumers take a time to respond fully to price changes, we can identify different equilibria after the elapse of different lengths of time. Generally, short-run supply and demand tend to be less price elastic than long-run supply and demand. As a result any shifts in demand or supply curves tend to have a relatively bigger effect on price in the short run and a relatively bigger effect on quantity in the long run.

4c People often anticipate price changes and this will affect the amount they demand or supply. This speculation will tend to stabilise price fluctuations if people believe that the price changes are only temporary. However, speculation will tend to destabilise these fluctuations (i.e. make them more severe) if people believe that prices are likely to continue to move in the same direction as at present (at least for some time).

5a Much economic decision making is made under conditions of risk or uncertainty.

5b Risk is when the probability of an outcome occurring is known. Uncertainty is when the probability is not known.

5c One way of reducing risks is to hold stocks. If the price of a firm's product falls unexpectedly, it can build up stocks rather than releasing its product on to the market. If the price later rises, it can then release stocks on to the market. Similarly with inputs: if their price falls unexpectedly, firms can build up their stocks, only to draw on them later if input prices rise.

5d A way of eliminating risk and uncertainty is to deal in the futures markets. When firms are planning to buy or sell at some point in the future, there is the danger that price could rise or fall unexpectedly in the meantime. By agreeing to buy or sell at some particular point in the future at a price agreed today (a 'future' price), this danger can be eliminated. The bank or other institution offering the price (the 'speculator') is taking on the risk, and will charge for this service.

REVIEW QUESTIONS

1 Why does price elasticity of demand have a negative value, whereas price elasticity of supply has a positive value?

2 Rank the following in ascending order of elasticity: jeans, black Levi jeans, black jeans, black Levi 501 jeans, trousers, outer garments, clothes.

3 Would a firm want demand for its brand to be more or less elastic? How might a firm set about achieving this?

4 Will a general item of expenditure like food or clothing have a price elastic or inelastic demand?

5 Assuming that a firm faces an inelastic demand and wants to increase its total revenue, how much should it raise its price? Is there any limit?

6 Can you think of any examples of goods which have a totally inelastic demand (a) at all prices; (b) over a particular price range?

7 Which of these two pairs are likely to have the highest cross-price elasticity of demand: two brands of coffee, or coffee and tea?

8 Why are both the price elasticity of demand and the price elasticity of supply likely to be greater in the long run?

9 Redraw Figure 5.11, only this time assume that it was an initial shift in supply that caused the price to change in the first place.

10 Give some examples of decisions you have taken recently that were made under conditions of uncertainty. With hindsight, do you think you made the right decisions? Explain.

11 What methods can a firm use to reduce risk and uncertainty?

12 If speculators believed that the price of cocoa in six months was going to be below the six-month future price quoted today, how would they act?

MyEconLab

This book can be supported by MyEconLab, which contains a range of additional resources, including an online homework and tutorial system designed to test and build your understanding.

You need both an access card and a course ID to access MyEconLab:

1. Is your lecturer using MyEconLab? Ask your lecturer for your course ID.

2. Has an access card been included with the book at a reduced cost? Check the inside back cover of the book.

3. If you have a course ID but no access card, go to: http://www.myeconlab.com/ to buy access to this interactive study programme.

ADDITIONAL PART B CASE STUDIES IN THE *ECONOMICS FOR BUSINESS* MyEconLab (www.pearsoned.co.uk/sloman)

B.1 The interdependence of markets. A case study of the operation of markets, examining the effects on a local economy of the discovery of a large shale oil deposit.

B.2 Adam Smith (1723–1790). Smith, the founder of modern economics, argued that markets act like an 'invisible hand' guiding production and consumption.

B.3 Shall we put up our price? Some examples of firms charging high prices in markets where demand is relatively inelastic.

B.4 Any more fares? Pricing on the buses: an illustration of the relationship between price and total revenue.

B.5 Elasticities of demand for various foodstuffs. An examination of the evidence about price and income elasticities of demand for food in the UK.

B.6 Adjusting to oil price shocks. An extended version of Box 5.3 showing how demand and supply analysis can be used to examine the price changes in the oil market since 1973.

B.7 Income elasticity of demand and the balance of payments. This examines how a low income elasticity of demand for the exports of many developing countries can help to explain their chronic balance of payments problems.

B.8 The cobweb. An outline of the theory that explains price fluctuations in terms of time lags in supply.

B.9 The role of the speculator. This assesses whether the activities of speculators are beneficial or harmful to the rest of society.

B.10 Rationing. A case study in the use of rationing as an alternative to the price mechanism. In particular, it looks at the use of rationing in the UK during the Second World War.

B.11 Rent control. This shows how setting (low) maximum rents is likely to lead to a shortage of rented accommodation.

B.12 Agriculture and minimum prices. This shows how setting (high) minimum prices is likely to lead to surpluses.

B.13 The fallacy of composition. An illustration from agricultural markets of the fallacy of composition: 'what applies in one case will not necessarily apply when repeated in all cases'.

B.14 Coffee prices. An examination of the coffee market and the implications of fluctuations in the coffee harvest for growers and coffee drinkers.

B.15 Response to changes in petrol and ethanol prices in Brazil. This case examines how drivers with 'flex-fuel' cars responded to changes in the relative prices of two fuels: petrol and ethanol (made from sugar cane).

WEBSITES RELEVANT TO PART B

Numbers and sections refer to websites listed in the Web appendix and hotlinked from this text's website at
www.pearsoned.co.uk/sloman

- For news articles relevant to Part B, see the Economics News Articles link from the text's website.

- For general news on markets, see websites in section A, and particularly A2, 3, 4, 5, 8, 9, 20–25, 35, 36. See also site A43 for links to economics news articles from newspapers worldwide.

- For links to sites on markets, see the relevant sections of B1, I4, 7, 14, 17.

- For data on the housing market (Box 4.2), see sites B7–11.

- For student resources relevant to Part B, see sites C1–7, 9, 10, 19.

- For sites favouring the free market, see C17 and E34.

Background to demand

The FT Reports . . .

The Financial Times, 11 October 2015

FT

Online Shopping Boom Leads to Record Increase in Vans

By Michael Pooler

The boom in online shopping and revived construction activity has led to record levels of investment in vans and trucks, as British businesses enlarge their fleets.

Finance for commercial vehicles on lease and hire-purchase agreements rose 10 per cent to £6.5bn in the year ending in August, according to the Finance and Leasing Association, a trade body.

The figures point to the broader economic recovery, as well as a shift in how consumers buy – and receive – goods.

Driving the growth was the buoyant retail sector and an increase in people setting up businesses, said BNP Paribas Leasing Solutions, with some of the strongest demand for vans coming from self-employed workers in the building and associated trades.

'It's very easy to get vehicles financed on very competitive rates these days,' said Brian Templar, of logistics consultancy Davies and Robson.

Following a drop in demand for trucks last year due to changes in legislation, registrations have jumped 36 per cent in 2015. The number of vans on the road has continued to rise thanks to online shopping, with 17 per cent more added this year, according to the Society of Motor Manufacturers and Traders.

This reflects how retailers and logistics companies are making fewer large deliveries to stores but more small deliveries to homes. Online sales account for a fifth of all non-food retail sales in Britain.

'Logistics is the next big battleground in ecommerce. [Retailers] have always delivered larger items like furniture but now they will be able to offer it even for smaller items,' said Anita Balchandani, partner at OC&C. The consultancy put the UK ecommerce market size at £42bn last year and forecasts it will rise to £61bn by 2018.

Argos challenged its online and bricks-and-mortar rivals last week as it became the first high-street brand to launch same-day deliveries seven days a week throughout the country. Amazon Prime Now offers shipments within an hour in Coventry and London, and has been introducing a similar service for frozen and chilled foods in parts of the capital.

Meanwhile Ocado, the upmarket online grocer, spent £12.5m on vehicle leases in 2014, against £9m the previous year.

The need for expanded vehicle fleets was underlined on 'Black Friday' in November last year, when a number of companies were caught out by a record-breaking day of online shopping. Delivery delays resulted.

Evidence of the fierce competition in the parcel delivery market was seen when City Link collapsed into administration last Christmas Eve making about 2400 staff redundant and laying off 1000 self-employed drivers. ...

Consumers, that is, the 'demand side', are just as important as the supply side: after all, it is they who ultimately pay for the goods and services provided, while the shape and size of their current and future demand choices is critical to the investment decisions that businesses make.

Philip Collins (2009) Chairman of the Office of Fair Trading, Preserving and Restoring Trust and Confidence in Markets. Keynote address to the British Institute of International and Comparative Law at the Ninth Annual Trans-Atlantic Antitrust Dialogue, 30 April, www.oft.gov.uk/shared_oft/speeches/2009/spe0809.pdf

If a business is to be successful, it must be able to predict the strength of demand for its products and be able to respond to any changes in consumer tastes, particularly when the economic environment is uncertain. It will also want to know how its customers are likely to react to changes in its price or its competitors' prices, or to changes in income. In other words, it will want to know the price, cross-price and income elasticities of demand for its product. The better the firm's knowledge of its market, the better will it be able to plan its output to meet demand, and the more able will it be to choose its optimum price, product design, marketing campaigns, etc.

In Chapter 6 we will go behind the demand curve to gain a better understanding of consumer behaviour. We will consider how economists analyse consumer satisfaction and how it varies with the amount consumed. We will then relate this to the shape of the demand curve.

Then, in Chapter 7, we will investigate how data on consumer behaviour can be collected and the problems that businesses face in analysing such information and using it to forecast changes in demand.

Chapter 8 explores how firms can expand and develop their markets by the use of various types of non-price competition. It looks at ways in which firms can differentiate their products from those of their rivals. The chapter also considers how a business sets about deriving a marketing strategy, and assesses the role and implications of product advertising. However, as the *Financial Times* article shows, if businesses are successful in expanding their markets, they must have the means of supplying them.

Key terms

Marginal utility
Diminishing marginal utility
Consumer surplus
Rational consumer
Asymmetric information
Adverse selection
Moral hazard
Product characteristics
Indifference curves
Efficiency frontier
Market surveys
Market experiments
Demand function
Forecasting
Non-price competition
Product differentiation
Product marketing
Advertising

Demand and the consumer

Business issues covered in this chapter

- What determines the amount of a product that consumers wish to buy at each price? How does consumer satisfaction or 'utility' affect purchasing decisions?
- Why are purchasing decisions sometimes risky for consumers?
- How do attitudes towards risk vary between consumers?
- How can insurance help to reduce or remove the level of risk?
- Why may insurance companies have to beware of high-risk consumers being more likely to take out insurance ('adverse selection') and people behaving less carefully when they have insurance ('moral hazard')?
- How do product characteristics influence consumer choice?
- How will changing a product's characteristics and/or its price influence consumers' choices between products?

Given our limited incomes, we have to make choices about what to buy. You may have to choose between that new economics textbook you feel you ought to buy and going to a rock concert, between a new pair of jeans and a meal out, between saving up for a car and having more money to spend on everyday items, and so on. Business managers are interested in finding out what influences your decisions to consume, and how they might price or package their product to increase their sales.

In this section it is assumed that as consumers we behave 'rationally': that we consider the relative costs and benefits of our purchases in order to gain the maximum satisfaction possible from our limited incomes. Sometimes we may act 'irrationally'. We may purchase goods impetuously with little thought to their price or quality. In general, however, it is a reasonably accurate assumption that people behave rationally.

This does not mean that you get a calculator out every time you go shopping! When you go round the supermarket, you are hardly likely to look at every item on the shelf and weigh up the satisfaction you think you would get from it against the price on the label. Nevertheless, you have probably learned over time the sort of things you like and the prices they cost. You can probably make out a 'rational' shopping list quite quickly.

With major items of expenditure such as a house, a car, a carpet or a foreign holiday, we are likely to take much more care. Take the case of a foreign holiday: you will probably spend quite a long time browsing through brochures comparing the relative merits of various holidays against their relative costs, looking for a holiday that gives good value for money. This is rational behaviour.

6.1 MARGINAL UTILITY THEORY

Total and marginal utility

People buy goods and services because they get satisfaction from them. Economists call this satisfaction 'utility'.

An important distinction must be made between *total utility* and *marginal utility*.

Total utility (*TU*) is the total satisfaction that a person gains from all those units of a commodity consumed within a given time period. Thus if Tracey drank 10 cups of tea a day, her daily total utility from tea would be the satisfaction derived from those 10 cups.

Marginal utility (*MU*) is the additional satisfaction gained from consuming one *extra* unit within a given period of time. Thus we might refer to the marginal utility that Tracey gains from her third cup of tea of the day or her eleventh cup.

Diminishing marginal utility

Up to a point, the more of a commodity you consume, the greater will be your total utility. However, as you become more satisfied, each extra unit you consume will probably give you less additional utility than previous units. In other words, your marginal utility falls as you consume more. This is known as the **principle of diminishing marginal utility**. For example, the second cup of tea in the morning gives you less additional satisfaction than the first cup. The third cup gives less satisfaction still.

>
> **KEY IDEA 15**
>
> *The principle of diminishing marginal utility.* The more of a product a person consumes over a given period of time, the less will be the additional utility gained from one more unit.

Pause for Thought

Are there any goods or services where consumers do not experience diminishing marginal utility?

At some level of consumption, your total utility will be at a maximum. No extra satisfaction can be gained by the consumption of further units within that period of time. Thus marginal utility will be zero. Your desire for tea may be fully satisfied at 12 cups per day. A thirteenth cup will yield no extra utility. It may even give you displeasure (i.e. negative marginal utility).

The optimum level of consumption: The simplest case – one commodity

Just how much of a good should people consume if they are to make the best use of their limited income? To answer this question we must tackle the problem of how to measure utility. The problem is that utility is subjective. There is no way of knowing what another person's experiences are really like. Just how satisfying does Brian find his first cup of tea in the morning? How does his utility compare with Tracey's? We do not have utility meters that can answer these questions!

One solution to the problem is to measure utility with money. In this case, total utility becomes the value that people place on their consumption, and marginal utility becomes the maximum amount of money that a person would be prepared to pay to obtain one more unit: in other words, what that extra unit is worth to that person. If Darren is prepared to pay 70p to obtain an extra packet of crisps, then that packet yields him 70p worth of utility: $MU = 70p$.

So how many packets should he consume if he is to act rationally? To answer this we need to introduce the concept of *consumer surplus*.

Marginal consumer surplus

Marginal consumer surplus (MCS) is the difference between the maximum amount that you are willing to pay for one more unit of a good (i.e. your marginal utility) and what you are actually charged (i.e. the price). If Darren was willing to pay 70p for another packet of crisps which in fact cost him only 55p, he would be getting a marginal consumer surplus of 15p.

$$MCS = MU - P$$

Definitions

Total utility The total satisfaction a consumer gets from the consumption of all the units of a good consumed within a given time period.

Marginal utility The extra satisfaction gained from consuming one extra unit of a good within a given time period. In money terms, it is what you are willing to pay for one more unit of the good.

Principle of diminishing marginal utility As more units of a good are consumed, additional units will provide less additional satisfaction than previous units.

Consumer surplus The difference between the maximum amount a person would have been prepared to pay for a good (i.e. the utility) and what that person actually paid.

Marginal consumer surplus The excess of utility from the consumption of one more unit of a good (*MU*) over the price paid: $MCS = MU - P$.

Total consumer surplus

Total consumer surplus (TCS) is the sum of all the marginal consumer surpluses you have obtained from all the units of a good you have consumed. It is the difference between the total utility from all the units and your expenditure on them. If Darren consumes four packets of crisps, and if he would have been prepared to spend £2.60 on them and only had to spend £2.20, then his total consumer surplus is 40p.

$$TCS = TU - TE$$

where TE is the total expenditure on a good: i.e. $P \times Q$.

(Note that total expenditure (TE) is a similar concept to total revenue (TR). They are both defined as $P \times Q$. But in the case of total expenditure, Q is the quantity *purchased* by the consumer(s) in question, whereas in the case of total revenue, Q is the quantity *sold* by the firm(s) in question.)

Rational consumer behaviour

Let us define **rational consumer behaviour** as the attempt to maximise (total) consumer surplus.

The process of maximising consumer surplus can be shown graphically. Let us take the case of Tina's annual purchases of petrol. Tina has her own car, but as an alternative she can use public transport or walk. To keep the analysis simple, let us assume that Tina's parents bought her the car and pay the licence duty, and that Tina does not have the option of selling the car. She does, however, have to buy the petrol. The current price is 130p per litre. Figure 6.1 shows her consumer surplus.

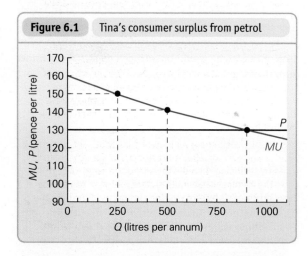

| **Figure 6.1** | Tina's consumer surplus from petrol |

If she were to use just a few litres per year, she would use them for very important journeys for which no convenient alternative exists. For such trips she may be prepared to pay up to 160p per litre. For the first few litres, then, she is getting a marginal utility of around 160p per litre, and hence a marginal consumer surplus of around 30p (i.e. 160p – 130p).

By the time her annual purchase is around 250 litres, she would only be prepared to pay around 150p for additional litres. The additional journeys, although still important, would be less vital. Perhaps these are journeys where she could have taken public transport, albeit at some inconvenience. Her marginal consumer surplus at 250 litres is 20p (i.e. 150p – 130p).

Gradually additional litres give less and less additional utility as fewer and fewer important journeys are undertaken. The 500th litre yields 141p worth of extra utility. Marginal consumer surplus is now 11p (i.e. 141p – 130p).

By the time she gets to the 900th litre, Tina's marginal utility has fallen to 130p. There is no additional consumer surplus to be gained. Her total consumer surplus is at a maximum. She thus buys 900 litres, where $P = MU$.

Her total consumer surplus is the sum of all the marginal consumer surpluses: the sum of all the 900 vertical lines between the price and the MU curve. This is represented by the total *area* between the dashed P line and the MU curve.

This analysis can be expressed in general terms. In Figure 6.2, if the price of a commodity is P_1, the consumer will consume Q_1. The person's total expenditure (TE) is P_1Q_1, shown by area 1. Total utility (TU) is the area under the marginal utility curve: i.e. areas 1 + 2. Total consumer surplus ($TU - TE$) is shown by area 2.

We can now state the general rule for maximising total consumer surplus. If $MU > P$ people should buy more. As they do so, however, MU will fall (diminishing marginal utility). People should stop buying more when MU has fallen to equal P. At that point, total consumer surplus is maximised.

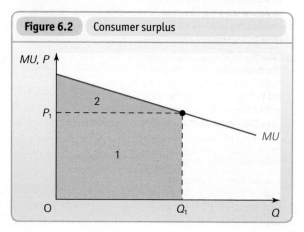

| **Figure 6.2** | Consumer surplus |

Definitions

Total consumer surplus The excess of a person's total utility from the consumption of a good (TU) over the amount that person spends on it (TE): $TCS = TU - TE$.

Rational consumer behaviour The attempt to maximise total consumer surplus.

Marginal utility and the demand curve for a good

An individual's demand curve

Individual people's demand curves for any good will be the same as their marginal utility curve for that good, measured in terms of money.

This is demonstrated in Figure 6.3, which shows the marginal utility curve for a particular person and a particular good. If the price of the good were P_1, the person would consume Q_1: where $MU = P_1$. Thus point a would be one point on that person's demand curve. If the price fell to P_2, consumption would rise to Q_2, since this is where $MU = P_2$. Thus point b is a second point on the demand curve. Likewise if price fell to P_3, Q_3 would be consumed. Point c is a third point on the demand curve.

Thus as long as individuals seek to maximise consumer surplus and hence consume where $P = MU$, their demand curve will be along the same line as their marginal utility curve.

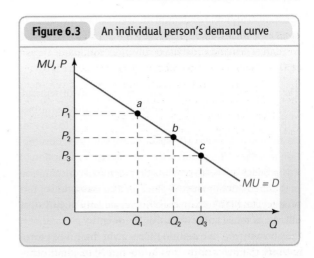

| Figure 6.3 | An individual person's demand curve |

The market demand curve

The market demand curve will simply be the (horizontal) sum of all individuals' demand curves and hence MU curves. Similarly, total consumer surplus is the sum of the

---

What can we learn from eBay?

The idea of a maximum willingness to pay might sound a little strange to most consumers. If you go into a sandwich shop at lunchtime and buy a tuna baguette for £2.50, it is unlikely that you will consider what you might have been willing to pay if the price had been higher. The only thing we can tell from your decision is that the price must be below the maximum amount you are willing to pay. There is some consumer surplus in the transaction but it is difficult to tell how much. We have one piece of information, the price; but we do not have the other information – the amount you were willing to pay – required to make the calculation.

Perhaps one of the only situations where most consumers will be asked about their willingness to pay is when they bid for an item on eBay and are asked for their maximum bid price. This information is not revealed to either the other potential buyers or the seller. Instead, it is used by eBay to make the smallest bid required on behalf of the customer in order for them to become the highest bidder.

Take the following simple example. Robert currently has the highest bid for an item of £10. Unknown to the other buyers and the seller, the maximum amount Robert will bid is £15. If Jon sees the item and places a maximum bid of £12 the price will increase to £12.50. Robert would still have the highest bid as his willingness to pay is greater than Jon's willingness to pay. However, with the bid price increasing, Robert's potential consumer surplus will have fallen from £5 to £2.50.

Assume now that Charlotte sees the item with a current highest bid price of £12.50 and bids with a maximum willingness to pay of £20. The price will now adjust to £15.50 and

Charlotte will be the highest bidder. The software does not make her bid £20. Instead it makes it just high enough to be larger than Robert' maximum willingness to pay of £15. Her consumer surplus if she wins the item at this price would be £4.50.

Unfortunately for economists who want to calculate consumer surplus, eBay does not release data on maximum bid prices. As eBay is a second price auction all that is observable is a price which is just above the maximum willingness to pay of the consumer who just misses out on winning the auction. Even if the data on maximum bid prices were publicly available, they might not fully reflect the maximum amount people were willing to pay.

To try to overcome these problems Bapna et al.[1] set up a website which bid on eBay for customers at the last moment – known as sniping. In order to use the site people had to enter the maximum amount they were willing to pay for the items they were interested in. The authors used the data this software generated on more than 4500 auctions on eBay. They projected that the consumer surplus on eBay auctions was $7 billion in 2003 and $19 billion in 2007.

 What are the differences between eBay and other types of auctions?

Why might some customers not enter their true willingness to pay when placing their maximum bid on eBay?

[1] R. Bapna, P. Goes, A. Gupta and G. Karuga, 'Predicting bidders' willingness to pay in online multi-unit ascending auctions: Analytical and empirical insights', *INFORMS Journal on Computing* 20 (2008), 345–355.

consumer surplus of each individual consumer: i.e. the sum of all individuals' area 2 in Figure 6.2.

Market demand and market consumer surplus are shown in Figure 6.4, where it is assumed that market price is P_m.

The shape of the demand curve. The price elasticity of demand, at any given price, will reflect the rate at which *MU* diminishes. If there are close substitutes for a good, it is likely to have an elastic demand, and its *MU* will diminish slowly as consumption increases. The reason is that increased consumption of this product will be accompanied by *decreased* consumption of the alternative product(s). Since total consumption of this product *plus* the alternatives has increased only slightly (if at all), the marginal utility will fall only slowly.

For example, the demand for a given brand of petrol is likely to have a fairly high price elasticity, since other brands are substitutes. If there is a cut in the price of Texaco petrol (assuming the prices of other brands stay constant), consumption of Texaco will increase a lot. The *MU* of Texaco petrol will fall slowly, since people consume less of other brands. Petrol consumption *in total* may

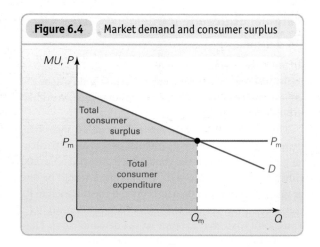

Figure 6.4   Market demand and consumer surplus

be only slightly greater and hence the *MU* of petrol only slightly lower.

Shifts in the demand curve. How do *shifts* in demand relate to marginal utility? For example, how would the marginal

---

BOX 6.2   THE MARGINAL UTILITY REVOLUTION: JEVONS, MENGER, WALRAS

Solving the diamonds–water paradox

What determines the market value of a good? We already know the answer: demand and supply. So if we find out what determines the position of the demand and supply curves, we will at the same time be finding out what determines a good's market value.

This might seem obvious. Yet for years economists puzzled over just what determines a good's value.

Some economists like Karl Marx and David Ricardo concentrated on the supply side. For them, value depended on the amount of resources used in producing a good. This could be further reduced to the amount of *labour* time embodied in the good. Thus, according to the *labour theory of value*, the more labour that was directly involved in producing the good, or indirectly in producing the capital equipment used to make the good, the more valuable would the good be.

Other economists looked at the demand side. But here they came across a paradox. Adam Smith in the 1760s gave the example of water and diamonds. 'How is it', he asked, 'that water which is so essential to human life, and thus has such a high "value-in-use", has such a low market value (or "value-in-exchange")? And how is it that diamonds which are relatively so trivial have such a high market value?' The answer to this paradox had to wait over 100 years until the marginal utility revolution of the 1870s. William Stanley Jevons (1835–82) in England, Carl Menger (1840–1921) in Austria, and Leon Walras (1834–1910) in Switzerland all independently claimed that the source of the market value of a good was its *marginal* utility, not its *total* utility.

This was the solution to the diamonds–water paradox. Water, being so essential, has a high total utility: a high 'value in use'. But for most of us, given that we consume so much already, it has a very low marginal utility. Do you leave the cold tap running when you clean your teeth? If you do, it shows just how trivial water is to you *at the margin*. Diamonds, on the other hand, although they have a much lower total utility, have a

much higher marginal utility. There are so few diamonds in the world, and thus people have so few of them, that they are very valuable at the margin. If, however, a new technique were to be discovered of producing diamonds cheaply from coal, their market value would fall rapidly. As people had more of them, so their marginal utility would rapidly diminish.

Marginal utility still only gives the demand side of the story. The reason why the marginal utility of water is so low is that *supply* is so plentiful. Water is very expensive in Saudi Arabia! In other words, the full explanation of value must take into account both demand *and* supply.

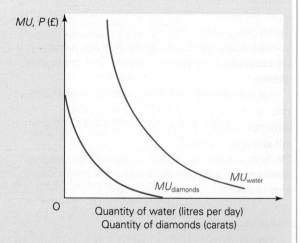

 The diagram illustrates a person's MU curves of water and diamonds. Assume that diamonds are more expensive than water. Show how the MU of diamonds will be greater than the MU of water. Show also how the TU of diamonds will be less than the TU of water. (Remember: TU is the area under the MU curve.)

utility of (and hence demand for) margarine be affected by a rise in the price of butter? The higher price of butter would cause less butter to be consumed. This would increase the marginal utility of margarine, since if people are using less butter, their desire for margarine is higher. The *MU* curve (and hence the demand curve) for margarine thus shifts to the right.

Weaknesses of the one-commodity version of marginal utility theory

A change in the consumption of one good will affect the marginal utility of substitute and complementary goods. It will also affect the amount of income left over to be spent on other goods. Thus a more satisfactory explanation of demand would involve an analysis of choices between goods, rather than looking at one good in isolation. (We examine such choices in section 6.3.)

Nevertheless, the assumptions of diminishing marginal utility and of the consumer making rational choices by considering whether it is 'worth' paying the price being charged are quite realistic assumptions about consumer behaviour. It is important for businesses to realise that the demand for their product tends to reflect consumers' perceptions of the *marginal* utility they expect to gain, rather than the *total* utility.

6.2 DEMAND UNDER CONDITIONS OF RISK AND UNCERTAINTY

The problem of imperfect information

So far we have assumed that when people buy goods and services, they know exactly what price they will pay and how much utility they will gain. In many cases this is a reasonable assumption. When you buy a bar of chocolate, you clearly do know how much you are paying for it and have a very good idea how much you will like it. But what about a mobile phone, or a tablet, or a car, or a washing machine, or any other *consumer durable*? In each of these cases you are buying something that will last you a long time, and the further into the future you look, the less certain you will be of its costs and benefits to you.

Take the case of a washing machine costing you £400. If you pay cash, your immediate outlay involves no uncertainty: it is £400. But washing machines can break down. In two years' time you could find yourself with a repair bill of £100. This cannot be predicted and yet it is a price you will have to pay, just like the original £400. In other words, when you buy the washing machine, you are uncertain as to the full 'price' it will entail over its lifetime.

Not only are the costs of the washing machine uncertain, so too are the benefits. You might have been attracted to buy it in the first place by the manufacturer's glossy brochure, or by the look of it, or by adverts on TV, in magazines, etc. When you have used it for a while, however, you will probably discover things you had not anticipated. The spin dryer does not get your clothes as dry as you had hoped; it is noisy; it leaks; the door sticks; and so on.

Buying consumer durables thus involves uncertainty. So too does the purchase of assets, whether a physical asset such as a house or financial assets such as shares. In the case of assets, the uncertainty is over their future *price*, which you cannot know for certain.

Attitudes towards risk and uncertainty

So how will uncertainty affect people's behaviour? The answer is that it depends on their attitudes towards taking a gamble. To examine these attitudes let us assume that a person does at least know their *chances* when taking a gamble (i.e. the *probabilities involved* in doing so). In other words, the person is operating under conditions of *risk* rather than *uncertainty*. Consider the following example.

Imagine that as a student you only have £105 left out of your student loan to spend. You are thinking of buying an instant lottery ticket/scratch card. The lottery ticket costs £5 and there is a 1 in 4 or 25 per cent chance that it will be a winning ticket. A winning ticket pays a prize of £20. Would you buy the lottery ticket? This will depend on your attitude towards risk.

In order to explain people's attitude towards risk it is important to understand the concept of expected value. The **expected value** of a gamble is the amount the person would earn on average if the gamble were repeated many times. To calculate the expected value of a gamble you simply multiply each possible outcome by the probability that it will occur. These values are then added together. In this example the gamble has only two possible outcomes – you purchase a winning ticket or a losing ticket. There is a

> ### Definitions
>
> **Consumer durable** A consumer good that lasts a period of time, during which the consumer can continue gaining utility from it.
>
> **Expected value** The average value of a variable after many repetitions: in other words, the sum of the value of a variable on each occasion divided by the number of occasions.

25 per cent chance it is a winning ticket, which will give you a total of £120 to spend (£100 left out of your loan plus a £20 prize). There is a 75 per cent chance it is a losing ticket, in which case you will only have £100 left to spend out of your student loan. Therefore the expected value of this gamble is:

$$EV = 0.25(120) + 0.75(100) = 105.$$

Probability it is a winning ticket | Outcome from a winning ticket | Probability it is a losing ticket | Outcome from a losing ticket

If you do not purchase the ticket then you will have £105 to spend for sure.

$$EV = 1(105) = 105$$

There are three possible categories of attitude towards risk.

- *Risk neutral*. If people are risk neutral they will always choose the option with the highest expected value. Therefore a student who is risk neutral would be indifferent between buying or not buying the instant lottery ticket, as each outcome has the same expected value of £105.
- *Risk averse*. If people are risk averse they will never choose a gamble if it has the same expected value as the pay-off from not taking a gamble. Therefore a student who is risk averse would definitely not buy the instant lottery ticket.

  It is too simplistic, however, to say that a risk averse person will never take risks. Such a person may choose a gamble if it has a greater expected value than the pay-off from not taking the gamble. If the probability of purchasing a winning instant lottery ticket in the previous example was 75 per cent instead of 25 per cent, then a risk averse student might nevertheless buy the ticket, as the expected value of the gamble would be greater than the certain pay-off.

  Whether or not risk averse people do take a gamble depends on the *strength* of their aversion to risk, which will vary from one individual to another. The greater people's level of risk aversion, the greater the expected value of a gamble they are willing to give up in order to have a certain pay-off.

- *Risk loving*. If people are risk loving they would always choose a gamble if it had the same expected value as the pay-off from not taking the gamble. Therefore a risk loving student would definitely purchase the instant lottery ticket.

  Once again, it is too simplistic to say that risk loving people will always choose a gamble. They may choose a certain pay-off if it has a higher expected value than the gamble. For example, if the probability of purchasing a winning instant lottery ticket in the previous example were 5 per cent instead of 25 per cent, then even a risk loving student might choose not to buy the ticket. It would depend on the extent to which that person enjoyed taking risks. The more risk loving people are, the greater the return from a certain pay-off they are willing to sacrifice in order to take a gamble.

Pause for thought

1. What is the expected value of the above gamble if the chances of purchasing a winning lottery ticket are 75 per cent? How much of the expected value of the gamble do risk averse people sacrifice if they decide against purchasing a ticket?
2. What is the expected value of the gamble if the chances of purchasing a winning lottery ticket are 5 per cent? How much of a certain pay-off do risk loving people sacrifice if they decide to purchase the lottery ticket?

Diminishing marginal utility of income and attitudes towards risk taking

Avid gamblers may be risk lovers. People who spend hours in the betting shop or at the race track may enjoy the risks, knowing that there is always the chance that they might win. On average, however, such people will lose. After all, the bookmakers have to take their cut and thus the odds are generally unfavourable.

Most people, however, for most of the time are risk averse. We prefer to avoid insecurity. But why? Is there a simple reason for this? Economists use marginal utility analysis to explain why.

They argue that the gain in utility to people from an extra £1000 is less than the loss of utility from forgoing £1000. Imagine your own position. You have probably adjusted your standard of living to your income (or are trying to!). If you unexpectedly gained £1000, that would be very nice: you could buy some new clothes or have a weekend away. But if you lost £1000, it could be very hard indeed. You might have very serious difficulties in making ends meet. Thus if you were offered the gamble of a 50:50 chance of winning or losing £1000, you would probably decline the gamble.

This risk-averse behaviour accords with the principle of *diminishing marginal utility*. Up to now in this chapter we have been focusing on the utility from the consumption of individual goods: Tracey and her cups of tea; Darren and his packets of crisps. In the case of each individual good, the more we consume, the less satisfaction we gain from each additional unit: the marginal utility falls. But the same principle applies if we look at our *total* consumption. The higher our level of total consumption, the less additional satisfaction will be gained from each additional £1 spent.

What we are saying here is that there is a **diminishing marginal utility of income**. The more you earn, the lower

Definition

Diminishing marginal utility of income Where each additional pound earned yields less additional utility than the previous pound.

Figure 6.5 The total utility of income given diminishing marginal utility of income

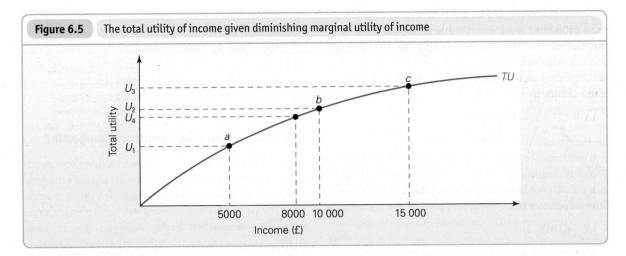

will be the utility from each *extra* £1. If people on low incomes earn an extra £1000, they will feel a lot better off: the marginal utility they will get from that income will be very high. If rich people earn an extra £1000, however, their gain in utility will be less.

Why, then, does a diminishing marginal utility of income make us risk averse? The answer is illustrated in Figure 6.5, which shows the *total* utility you get from your income.

The slope of this curve gives the *marginal* utility of your income. As the curve gets flatter it is illustrating that the marginal utility of income diminishes. A rise in income from £5000 to £10 000 will cause a movement along the curve from point *a* to point *b*. Total utility rises from U_1 to U_2. A similar rise in income from £10 000 to £15 000, however, will lead to a move from point *b* to point *c*, and hence a *smaller* rise in total utility from U_2 to U_3.

Now assume that your income is £10 000 and you are offered a chance of gambling £5000 of it. You are offered a 50:50 chance of gaining an extra £5000 (i.e. doubling it) or losing it. Effectively, then, you have an equal chance of your income rising to £15 000 or falling to £5000. The expected value of the gamble is £10 000, the same as the pay-off from not taking the gamble.

The total utility you obtain from an income of £10 000 is U_2. If the gamble pays off and as a result your income rises to £15 000, your total utility will rise to U_3. If it does not pay off, you will be left with only £5000 and a utility of U_1. Given that you have a 50:50 chance of winning, your *average* or *expected utility* will be midway between U_1 and U_3 i.e. $= \frac{U_1 + U_3}{2} = U_4$. But this is the same utility that would be gained from a certain income of £8000. Given that you would prefer U_2 to U_4 you will choose not to take the gamble. Thus risk aversion is part of rational utility-maximising behaviour.

On most occasions we will not know the probabilities of taking a gamble. In other words, we will be operating under conditions of *uncertainty*. This could make us very cautious indeed. The more pessimistic we are, the more cautious we will be.

Insurance: a way of removing risks

Insurance is the opposite of gambling. It takes the risk away. If, for example, you risk losing your job if you are injured, you can remove the risk of loss of income by taking out an appropriate insurance policy.

Given that many people are risk averse, they may be prepared to pay the premiums even though it will leave them with less than the expected value from taking the gamble. The total premiums paid to insurance companies, and hence the revenue generated, will be *more* than the amount the insurance companies pay out: that is, after all, how the companies make a profit.

But does this mean that the insurance companies are less risk averse than their customers? Why is it that the insurance companies are prepared to shoulder the risks that their customers were not? The answer is that the insurance company is able to *spread its risks*.

The spreading of risks

Take the following simple example. Assume you have £100 000 worth of assets (i.e. savings, car, property, etc.) and there is a 1 in 20 (or 5 per cent) chance that you will be involved in a car accident that results in your car being a write-off. The market value of the car is £20 000. The expected value of taking the gamble and not purchasing any car insurance is $0.95(100\,000) + 0.05(80\,000) = £99\,000$.

Definition

Spreading risks (for an insurance company) The more policies an insurance company issues and the more independent the risks of claims from these policies are, the more predictable will be the number of claims.

If you are risk averse you would be willing to pay more than £1000 to purchase a car insurance policy that covers you for a year. For example, you may be willing to pay £1500 a year for a policy that pays out the full £20 000 if you have the accident. Having paid £1500 out of your total assets of £100 000, you would be left with £98 500 for sure. If you are risk averse this may give you a higher level of utility than not purchasing the insurance and taking the gamble that you do not have the accident.

The insurance company, however, is not just insuring you. It is insuring many others like you at the same time. Assume that it has many customers with exactly the same assets as you and facing the same 5 per cent risk of a car accident. As the number of its customers increases the outcome will become closer to its expected or average value. Therefore the insurance company can predict with increasing confidence that, on average, five out of every 100 customers will have an accident and make a claim of £20 000 while 95 out of every 100 will not have an accident and not make a claim.

This means that the insurance company will pay out £100 000 in claims for every 100 customers: i.e. five will each make a claim of £20 000. This works out at £1000 per customer. If each customer is willing to pay £1500 for the policy, the insurance company will generate more in revenue than it is paying out in claims. Assuming that less than £500 is enough to cover the administrative costs of providing each policy per customer, the insurance company can make a profit.

This is an application of the *law of large numbers*. What is unpredictable for an individual becomes highly predictable in the mass. The more people the insurance company insures, the more predictable the final outcome becomes. In other words, an insurance company will be able to convert your *uncertainty* into their *risk*.

In reality, people taking out insurance will not all have the same level of wealth and the same chances of having an accident. However, using statistical data the insurance company will be able to work out the average chances of an event occurring for people in similar situations. Basing premiums on average chances can, however, create some problems for the insurance supplier, which will be discussed later in the chapter.

The independence of risks. The spreading of risks does not just require that there should be a large number of policies. It also requires that the risks should be **independent**. This means that if one person makes a claim it does not increase the chances of another person making a claim too. If the risks are independent in the previous example, then if one person has a car accident the risk of another person having a car accident remains unchanged at 5 per cent.

Now imagine a different example. If any insurance company insured 1000 houses *all in the same neighbourhood*, and there was a major fire in the area, the claims would be enormous. The risks of fire would *not* be independent, as if one house catches fire it increases the chances of the surrounding houses catching fire. If, however, a company provided fire insurance for houses scattered all over the country, the risks *are* independent.

Another way in which insurance companies can spread their risks is by **diversification**. The more types of insurance a company offers (car, house, life, health, etc.), the greater is likely to be the independence of the risks.

Problems for unwary insurance companies

A major issue for insurance companies is that they operate in a market where there is significant asymmetric information (see page 38). Asymmetric information exists in a market if one party has some information that is relevant to the value of that transaction that the other party does not have. In the insurance market the buyer often has private information about themselves that the insurance company does not have access too.

Asymmetric information is often split into two different types – unobservable characteristics and unobservable actions. Each separate type of asymmetric information generates a different problem. Unobservable characteristics generate the problem of *adverse selection*; unobservable actions generate the problem of *moral hazard*. We consider each in turn.

Potential problems caused by unobservable characteristics – adverse selection

Different potential consumers of insurance will have different characteristics. Take the case of car insurance: some drivers may be very skilful and careful, while others may be less able and enjoy the thrill of speeding. Or take the case of life assurance: some people may lead a very healthy lifestyle by eating a well-balanced diet and exercising regularly. Others may eat large quantities of fast food and do little or no exercise.

In each of these cases the customer is likely to know more about their own characteristics than the insurance company. These characteristics will also influence the cost to the firm of providing insurance. For example, less able drivers are more likely to be involved in an accident and make a claim on their insurance than more able drivers. The problems this might cause can best be explained with a simple numerical example.

In the example of car insurance we considered earlier (page 97), we assumed that all the customers had the same characteristics: i.e. they all had a 5 per cent chance per year of being involved in a car accident, where a car accident

---

Definitions

Law of large numbers The larger the number of events of a particular type, the more predictable will be their average or expected outcome.

Independent risks Where two risky events are unconnected. The occurrence of one will not affect the likelihood of the occurrence of the other.

Diversification Where a firm expands into new types of business.

costs, on average, £20 000. In reality, because of their different characteristics, the chances of having a car accident will vary from one customer to another. To keep the example simple, we will assume that an insurance company has only two types of potential customer. One half of them are very skilful drivers and have a 1 per cent chance per year of being involved in a car accident, while the other half are less able drivers who each have a 9 per cent chance per year of being involved in an accident. The problem for the insurance company is that when a customer purchases the insurance it does not know if they are a skilful or a less able driver.

When faced with this situation the insurance company could set a profit-making risk premium on the assumption that half of its customers will be highly competent drivers, while the other half have relatively poor driving skills. Using the law of large numbers, the firm can predict that 1 in 20 (5 per cent) of its customers will make a claim and so the average pay-out would be £1000 per customer (i.e. £20 000/20). Once again, assuming less than £500 of administrative costs, a premium of greater than £1500 per customer would in theory enable the firm to make a profit.

The problem is that the skilful drivers might find this premium very unattractive. For them the expected value of the gamble (i.e. not taking out the insurance) is 0.99(100 000) + 0.01(80 000) = £99 800. Taking out the insurance would leave them with £98,500 i.e. their initial wealth of £100 000 minus the premium. Unless they were very risk averse, the maximum amount they would be willing to pay is likely to be lower than £1500 (assuming they had a choice).

On the other hand, the less skilful drivers might find the offer from the insurance company very attractive. Their expected value from taking the gamble is 0.91(100 000) + 0.09(80 000) = £98 200. Their maximum willingness to pay is likely to be greater than £1500. In fact, if they were all risk averse they might all purchase the policy if it was £1800.

The insurance company could end up with only the less able drivers purchasing the insurance. If this happens then nine out of every 100 customers would make a claim of 20 000 each. The average pay-out per customer would be £1800. Therefore the firm would be paying out far more in claims than they would be generating from the premiums.

If, however, the insurer *knew* a potential customer was a skilful driver then it could offer the insurance policy at a much lower price: one that the risk averse careful driver would be willing to pay. If all the customers purchasing the policy were skilful drivers then only one in 100 would make a claim for £20 000. The average claim per customer would only be £200. All the skilful and risk averse customers would be willing to pay more than £200 for the insurance policy.

But if the insurance company does not know who is careful and who is not, this asymmetric information will block mutually beneficial sale of insurance from taking place.

This example has illustrated the problem of *adverse selection* in insurance markets. This is where customers with the least desirable characteristics from the sellers' point of view (i.e. those with the greatest chance of making a claim) are more likely to take out the insurance policy at a price based on the average risk of all the potential customers. This can result in the insurance market for low risk individuals collapsing even though mutually beneficial trade would be possible if symmetric information was present.

KEY IDEA 16

Adverse selection. Where information is imperfect, high-risk groups will be attracted to profitable market opportunities, to the disadvantage of the average buyer (or seller). In the context of insurance, it refers to those who are most likely to take out insurance posing the greatest risks to the insurer.

The potential problem of adverse selection is not unique to the insurance market. Unobservable characteristics are present in many other markets and may relate to the buyer, the seller or the product that is being traded. Table 6.1 provides some examples.

Definition

Adverse selection A market process whereby either buyers, sellers or products with certain unobservable characteristics (e.g. high risk or low quality) are more likely to enter the market at the current market price. The process can have a negative impact on economic efficiency and causes some potentially profitable markets to collapse.

Table 6.1   Adverse selection in various markets

Market	Hidden characteristic	Informed party	Uniformed party
The labour market	Innate ability of the worker/preference for working hard	The potential employee: i.e. the seller of labour services	The employer: i.e. the buyer of labour services
The credit market	Ability of people to manage their money effectively	The customer applying for credit	The firm lending the money
A street market with haggling	How much the person is willing to pay	The customer	The seller of the product
The electronic market: e.g. eBay	The quality/condition of the product	The seller of the product	The buyer of the product

More generally, adverse selection is a market process whereby either buyers, sellers or products with certain unobservable characteristics (e.g. high risk or low quality) are more likely to enter the market at its current price. This process can have a negative impact on economic efficiency and causes some potentially profitable markets to collapse.

Tackling the problem of adverse selection. Are there any ways that the potential problems caused by adverse selection can be overcome? One way would be for the person or party who is uninformed about the relevant characteristics of the other parties to ask them for information. For example an insurance company may require people to fill out a questionnaire so that the company can assess their own particular risk and set an appropriate premium. There may need to be legal penalties for people caught lying! This process of the uninformed trying to get the information from the informed is called screening.

An alternative would be for the person or party who is informed about the relevant characteristics to take action to reveal it to the uninformed person or party. This is called *signalling*. For example, a potentially hardworking and intelligent employee could signal this fact to potential employers by obtaining a good grade in an economics degree or to work for a period of time as an unpaid intern.

Pause for thought

What actions can either the buyers or sellers take in each of the examples in Table 6.1 to help overcome some of the potential problems caused by the unobservable characteristics?

Potential problems caused by unobservable actions – moral hazard

Imagine in the previous example if the different characteristics of the drivers were perfectly observable to the insurance company: i.e. the insurance company could identify which drivers were more able or careful and could charge them a lower premium than those who were less able or careful. The company might still face problems caused by *unobservable actions*.

Once drivers have purchased the insurance their driving behaviour may change. All types of driver now have an incentive to take less care when they are driving. If they are now involved in an accident all the costs will be covered by the insurance policy and so the marginal benefit from taking greater care will have fallen. This will result in the chances of a skilful driver having an accident rising above 1 per cent and of the less skilful driver rising above 9 per cent. The problem for the insurer is that these changes in driving behaviour are difficult to observe. The companies may end up in a position where the amount of money claimed by both the skilful and less able drivers increases above the revenue that they are collecting

in premiums based on the risk before the insurance was taken out.

This is called *moral hazard* and can more generally be defined as where the actions/behaviour of one party to a transaction change in a way that reduces the pay-off to the other party. It is caused by a change in incentives once a deal has been reached. It can only exist if there are unobservable actions.

 KEY IDEA 17

Moral hazard. Following a deal, there is an increased likelihood that one party will engage in problematic (immoral and hazardous) behaviour to the detriment of another. In the context of insurance, it refers to people taking more risks when they have insurance than they would have if they did not have insurance.

The problem of moral hazard may occur in many different markets and different situations. For example once a person has a permanent contract of employment they might not work as hard as the employer would have expected. Another good example is that of debt. If someone else is willing to pay your debts (e.g. your parents) it is likely to make you less careful in your spending! If the banks knew that the government would pay off their debts then perhaps they would implement more risky lending strategies. The argument has been used by some rich countries for not cancelling the debts of poor countries. See Box 6.4 for another example.

Are there any ways that the potential problems caused by moral hazard could be overcome? One approach would be for the uninformed party to devote more resources to monitoring the actions and behaviour of the informed party. However, this may be difficult and expensive. An alternative would be to change the terms of the deal so that the party with the unobservable actions has an incentive to behave in ways which are in the interests of the uninformed party.

Pause for thought

How will the following reduce the moral hazard problem?

a. A no-claims bonus in an insurance policy.
b. Having to pay the first so many pounds of any insurance claim.
c. The use of performance-related pay.

Definition

Moral hazard Following a deal, there is an increased likelihood that one party will engage in problematic (immoral and hazardous) behaviour to the detriment of another.

BOX 6.3   ADVERSE SELECTION IN THE INSURANCE MARKET

Can consumer incompetence save the market?

If the buyers in the insurance market have characteristics that are impossible or very costly for the insurance supplier to observe, then the market may suffer from adverse selection. For example, it may be very difficult for an insurance supplier to observe the driving ability of their potential customers. Some will be more able and less likely to have an accident, while others will be less able and more likely to have an accident.

If an insurer cannot tell its customers apart, then it will have to base its premiums on the average ability level of all of its potential customers. However, premiums based on this information tend to be above the maximum amount that the more able drivers are willing to pay and below the maximum amount the less able drivers are willing to pay This results in only the less able drivers purchasing the policy and the insurance company paying out more in claims than the revenue they are generating from the premiums (as we saw on page 99). According to standard economic theory the market suffers from adverse selection.

However, this argument is based on the assumption that people can accurately assess their own driving skills. Do less able drivers realise that they are less able drivers and therefore more likely to have an accident?

A number of psychologists have argued that people often find it very difficult to judge accurately their own ability and competence in a range of activities. In particular, many people tend to be overconfident and think that they are better than average. This is called *illusory superiority*. For example, in a study by McCormick, Walkey and Green,[2] 178 participants were asked to judge their driving skill compared to other people; 80 per cent believed that their driving ability was above that of the average driver.

The Dunning–Kruegar effect

Although there is a large amount of evidence that many people are overconfident in their own ability, studies have also found that the level of this overconfidence varies considerably between individuals.

In a well-known piece of research, the psychologists Dunning and Kruegar carried out a number of experiments to try to identify the factors that influence the extent of this overconfidence. The participants in their study had to complete a number of exercises that were designed to test their skills in a number of different areas. These included logical reasoning, grammar and judging how funny a series of jokes were!

After completing each test, the participants were asked to judge how well they thought they had done. The study found that the least able participants in each skill (i.e. those who achieved the lowest scores on the test) were the most over-confident. The most able (i.e. those who achieved the highest scores on the test) tended to be slightly under-confident but much more accurate. The authors concluded that the skills that make a person good at a particular activity tend to be the same skills that enable them to evaluate if they are good at that same activity. This has become known as the *Dunning-Kruegar effect*.

Similar research has been undertaken to assess how accurately students can judge the quality of their own academic work on the course they are studying. For example, Guest and Riegler [3] examined how precisely undergraduate students of economics could estimate their mark on an assessed essay. When submitting the essay students were asked to complete a form which asked them the following question: 'What do you honestly consider would be a fair and appropriate mark for the essay you have written?' A marks bonus was provided for accurate estimates. The results were very similar to those of Dunning and Kruegar, with the students who achieved the lowest marks being the most overconfident about the quality of the essay they had written.

These research findings have interesting implications for the predictions of standard economic theory when analysing the impact of unobservable characteristics on a market.

1. If the least able drivers overestimate their driving skills, what impact will this have on their willingness to pay for an insurance policy?
2. If the most able drivers underestimate their driving skills, what impact will this have on their willingness to pay for an insurance policy?
3. To what extent could the experience of the driver over time have an impact on either their under- or overconfidence?
4. What implications do your answers to question 1 and 2 have on the likelihood of adverse selection occurring in a market with unobservable characteristics?

[2] I. A. McCormick, F. H. Walkey and D. E. Green, 'Comparative perceptions of driver ability – a confirmation and expansion', *Accident Analysis & Prevention* 18 (3) (1986), pp. 205–8.

[3] J. Guest and R. Riegler, 'An qnalysis of the factors that determine the self-assessment skills of undergraduate economics students', *Economics Department Working paper, Coventry University, No14*.

BOX 6.4	ROGUE TRADERS

Buyer beware!

Markets are usually an efficient way of letting buyers and sellers exchange goods and services. However, this does not stop consumers making complaints about the quality of the goods or services they receive.

It is impossible to get a true measure of customer dissatisfaction because aggrieved consumers do not always complain and data are collected by a number of separate agencies. However, particular sectors seem to be more vulnerable to 'rogue traders' than others.

Ombudsman Services is an organisation that provides independent dispute resolution for the communications, energy, property, copyright licensing and glazing industries. They deal with more than a quarter of a million queries and resolve around 28 000 formal complaints each year.

In 2013/14 Ombudsman Services resolved 28 640 complaints out of 173 664 initial contacts. The table summarises the number of initial contacts, the number of cases resolved and the main types of queries in each of the three sectors.

Complaints resolved by Ombudsman Services in the communications sector 2013/14

Sector	Initial queries	Complaints resolved	Main reasons for complaint (and percentage for that sector)
Communications	80 476	12 909	Customer service (28%), quality of service (24%), contract issues (18%)
Energy	87 542	15 031	Billing (82%), transfer (13%), sales (3%)
Property	5 350	697	Valuations/surveys (41%), residential managing agent (13%), building and condition survey (10%)
Other	296	3	
Total	173 664	28 640	

 Which other sectors would you expect to have a large number of customer complaints? Why?

Consumer complaints are also of concern to cross-border sales as the growth of buying over the Internet has blossomed in recent times. Data gathered by econsumer.gov covering 30 countries show that the largest proportion of complaints relating to e-commerce transactions concern catalogue sales, Internet auction sites, computers (equipment and software), credit cards, phones, Internet access services, banking, healthcare products, jewellery, travel, business opportunities, timeshare, cars and Internet information services. Interestingly, only 767 of the 23 437 complaints were reported by UK consumers, while 1213 complaints were against UK online retailers!

The chart shows the types of consumer complaints about e-commerce. The percentages are based on the 23 608 e-consumer law violations during 2014, not the total number of complaints; one complaint may have multiple law violations.

Adverse selection and moral hazard

But why does a market, which you would think would respond to consumer wishes, give rise to consumer complaints? Why is it that rogue traders can continue in business? The problems arise because of the presence of asymmetric information in the market. Unobservable characteristics can results in the problem of adverse selection while unobservable action can result in the problem of moral hazard. It is an example of the 'principal–agent problem'. The buyer (the 'principal') has poorer information about the product than the agent (the 'seller').

Information asymmetries Complaints by consumers are likely to be few if the product is fairly simple and information about the exchange process is publicly available. For

example, if I buy apples from a market trader but subsequently return them because some are damaged, they are likely to exchange the apples, or offer a full refund, because failure to do so would lead to the trader's sales falling as information gets out that they sell poor-quality fruit. Here information asymmetries are minimal.

However, where the product is more complex, perhaps with consumers making large outlays, and information is more private, the situation can be very different. The greater the information 'gap' between sellers and consumers, the greater the scope for deception and fraud and the more likely are rogue traders to thrive. In these situations the number of consumer complaints increases.

Consider the sale of a conservatory, a large extension to a house usually comprising a number of various building products, including double-glazed windows and doors. A product such as this involves an expensive outlay for consumers, but they may have very limited information about the price of materials and labour, as well as the method of building a conservatory. There is asymmetric information about both the quality of the materials being used and the skills of the people doing the job.

Assume that there is a standard-sized conservatory and that a high-quality seller would be prepared to supply this product at a price of £10 000. Such a price would reflect the quality of their work and would keep them in the business of selling high-quality products. On the other hand, assume that a poor-quality supplier, a 'rogue trader', could provide this conservatory at £5000.

Given information asymmetry, let us assume that consumers are not aware of who is a high-quality or low-quality seller. Assume, however, that they believe that 80 per cent of traders sell the high-quality product and 20 per cent are 'rogue traders'. This means that the 'risk-neutral' consumer will be willing to pay £9000, i.e. (£10 000 × 0.8) + (£5000 × 0.2), for a standard-sized conservatory.

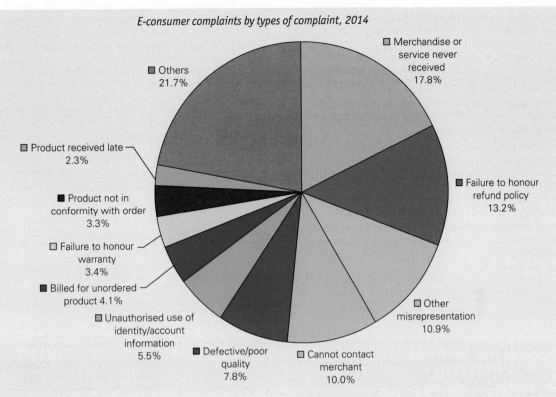

E-consumer complaints by types of complaint, 2014

- Merchandise or service never received 17.8%
- Failure to honour refund policy 13.2%
- Other misrepresentation 10.9%
- Cannot contact merchant 10.0%
- Defective/poor quality 7.8%
- Unauthorised use of identity/account information 5.5%
- Billed for unordered product 4.1%
- Failure to honour warranty 3.4%
- Product not in conformity with order 3.3%
- Product received late 2.3%
- Others 21.7%

Source: www.econsumer.gov

Adverse selection This price of £9000, however, is not enough to cover the costs of high-quality sellers, and so they will not want to offer their services to build high-quality conservatories. On the other hand, 'rogue traders' will find this price very profitable and it will attract a higher than normal number of such sellers into the market. Of course, if consumers know that the only sellers in the market are likely to be 'rogue traders', they will not buy conservatories and the market will collapse.

The problem just described is an example of adverse selection. In this case a group of sellers ('rogue traders') have been attracted to the market by prices considerably greater than their costs even before any transactions have taken place.

Moral hazard Of course, the market in conservatories is thriving. Consumers do try to find out about sellers before they buy and most consumers get a good product. However, 'rogue traders' also make sales.

Once a contract has been signed, the problem of moral hazard may occur. In our example, the rogue trader might initially agree to supply and install the conservatory to meet particular high standards of quality for a particular price. However, unless the buyer has full information about the construction of conservatories or can keep a constant watch over the work, defective materials or poor-quality workmanship may be supplied. But the buyer will not know this until a later date when problems start to appear with the conservatory!

Moral hazard results because the seller has an incentive to behave in ways which are difficult to observe and to the detriment of the buyer. The 'hazard' arises because of asymmetric information: the consumer has poorer information than the supplier. Rogue traders are tempted to supply an inferior product and exert little effort on the job, believing that they can get away with it.

Usually, the process of law would work in favour of the buyer because a contract had been established, but in many cases involving 'rogue traders' the business has been declared bankrupt or the costs to buyers of pursuing a legal case are too great.

Consider the customer complaints in the communications sector (telephones, Internet, etc.) received by Ombudsman Services (see table). Use the concepts of adverse selection and moral hazard to explain why this sector may be predisposed to a high number of complaints.

Solutions

So how can sellers signal to buyers that they offer high-quality products? And how can consumers trust this information? A number of methods exist.

Establishing a reputation A single firm can establish a reputation for selling high-quality goods, usually over a number of years, or perhaps it has created a valued brand name through advertising. Alternatively, firms can offer guarantees and warranties on their products, although a 10-year guarantee on the building work associated with a conservatory is of no use if the firm has gone bankrupt!

Trade associations and other third parties Firms can also band together collectively and establish a trade association. Examples include the Federation of Master Builders and the Association of British Travel Agents (ABTA). Firms that belong to a trade association have benefits that can extend beyond that of acting alone. For example, if one firm provides a poor-quality product, then consumers may get compensation via the association. ABTA, for example, guarantees to make sure customers will complete their holiday, or obtain a refund, if they have purchased it from a member that has gone bankrupt.

Trade associations are a means by which firms can demonstrate that they regulate themselves rather than have governments impose rules on them.

Sometimes third parties can help firms to signal high quality. The online auction site eBay, for example, has provided a feedback system for buyers and sellers so they can register their happiness or otherwise with sales. Likewise, the Competition and Markets Authority (CMA), under the auspices of the Enterprise Act (2002), has created an Approved Codes of Practice scheme whereby trade associations and their members will guarantee that customers will receive high-quality service. Successful associations can display a CMA Approved Codes logo.

Government intervention On the whole, recent UK governments have not liked to intervene in particular industries, preferring a sector to regulate itself. However, in the case of the financial services industry, the government has directly intervened because the impact of the industry on consumers in recent times has been widespread and financially devastating. Following a number of financial scandals, including the mis-selling of pensions and mortgages, the government replaced ineffective self-regulation in 2000 with the Financial Services Authority (FSA), an independent industry regulator with statutory powers, whose board was appointed by and accountable to the Treasury. In this instance the level of product complexity and information asymmetry between buyer and seller was viewed to be too great for the industry to control itself.

However the FSA was widely criticised for failing to do anything about the lending boom which led to the financial crisis in 2007. The FSA was abolished in April 2013 and replaced by the Financial Conduct Authority (FCA), which has greater powers. (See section 21.1 for a more general discussion of competition policy and regulation.)

 What are the disadvantages of trade associations?

6.3 THE CHARACTERISTICS APPROACH TO ANALYSING CONSUMER DEMAND

This section is optional. You may skip straight to the next chapter if you prefer.

To get a better understanding of consumer demand, we need to analyse how consumers choose *between* products (as we concluded in section 6.1). In other words, we must look at products not in isolation, but in relation to other products. Any firm wanting to understand the basis on which consumers demand its products will want to know why they might choose *its* product rather than those of its rivals. A car manufacturer will want to know why consumers might choose one of its models rather than those of its competitors.

 Such choices depend not only on price but also on the characteristics of the products. If you were buying a car, in addition to its price you would consider features such as style, performance, comfort, reliability, durability, fuel economy, safety and various added features (such as air conditioning, stereo system, air bags, electric windows, etc.). Car manufacturers will thus design their cars to make them as attractive as possible to consumers, relative to the cost of manufacture. In fact, most firms will constantly try to find ways of improving their products to make them more appealing to consumers.

What we are saying here is that consumers derive utility from the various characteristics that a product possesses. To understand choices, then, we need to look at the attributes of different products and how these influence consumer choices between them. *Characteristics theory* (sometimes called 'attributes theory') was developed by the economist Kelvin Lancaster[4] in the mid-1960s to analyse such choices and to relate them to the demand for a product.

Characteristics theory is based on four key assumptions:

- All products possess various characteristics.
- Different brands possess them in different proportions.
- The characteristics are measurable: they are 'objective'.
- The characteristics, along with price and consumers' incomes, determine consumer choice.

Identifying and plotting products' characteristics

Let us take a simple case of a product where consumers base their choice between brands on price and just two characteristics. For example, assume that consumers choose between different brands of breakfast cereal on the basis of

> **Definition**
>
> **Characteristics (or attributes) theory** The theory that demonstrates how consumer choice between different varieties of a product depends on the characteristics of these varieties, along with prices of the different varieties, the consumer's budget and the consumer's tastes.

---

[4] K. Lancaster, 'A new approach to consumer theory', *Journal of Political Economy*, 74 (April 1966), pp. 132–57.

taste and health-giving properties. To keep the analysis simple, let us assume that taste is related to the amount of sugar in the cereal and that health-giving properties are related to the amount of fibre.

Plotting the characteristics of different brands

The combinations of these two characteristics, sugar and fibre, can be measured on a diagram. In Figure 6.6, the quantity of sugar is measured on the horizontal axis and the quantity of fibre on the vertical axis. One brand, Healthbran, contains a lot of fibre, but only a little sugar. Another, Tastyflakes, contains a lot of sugar, but only a little fibre.

The ratio of the two attributes, fibre and sugar, in each of the two brands is given by the slope of the two rays out from the origin. Thus by consuming a certain amount of Healthbran, given by point h_1 on the Healthbran ray, the consumer is getting f_1 of fibre and s_1 of sugar. The consumption of more Healthbran is shown by a movement up the ray, say to h_2. At this point the consumer gets f_2 of fibre and s_2 of sugar. Notice that the ratio of fibre to sugar is the same in both cases. The ratio is given by f_1/s_1 ($= f_2/s_2$), which is simply the slope of the Healthbran ray.

The consumer of Tastyflakes can get relatively more sugar, but less fibre. Thus consumption at point t_1 gives s_3 of sugar, but only f_3 of fibre. The ratio of fibre to sugar for Tastyflakes is given by the slope of its ray, which is f_3/s_3.

Any number of rays can be put on the diagram, each one representing a particular brand. In each case, the ratio of fibre to sugar is given by the slope of the ray.

Changes in a product's characteristics. If a firm decides to change the mix of characteristics of a product, the slope of the ray will change. Thus if Healthbran were made sweeter, its ray would become shallower.

The budget constraint

The amount that a consumer buys of a brand will depend in part on the consumer's budget and on the price of the product. Assume that, given the current price of Healthbran, Jane's budget for breakfast cereals allows her to buy at h_1 per month: in other words, the amount of Healthbran that gives f_1 of fibre and s_1 of sugar. (This assumes that she only buys Healthbran and not some other brand too.)

A change in the budget. If she allocates more of her income to buying breakfast cereal, and sticks with Healthbran, she would move up the ray: say, to h_2. In other words, by buying more Healthbran, she would be buying more fibre and more sugar. Similarly, a reduction in expenditure on a product would be represented by a movement down its ray.

A change in price. If a product rises in price and the budget allocated to it remains the same, less will be purchased. There will be a movement down its ray.

The efficiency frontier

In practice, many consumers will buy a mixture of brands. Some days you may prefer one type of breakfast cereal, some days you may prefer another type. People get fed up with consuming too much of one brand or variety: they experience diminishing marginal utility from that particular mix of characteristics. You may allocate a certain amount of money for a summer holiday each year, but you may well want to go to a different place each year, since each place has a different mix of characteristics.

Assume that, given her current budget for breakfast cereals, the prices of Healthbran and Tastyflakes allow Jane to buy at either point a or point b in Figure 6.7. By switching completely from Healthbran to Tastyflakes, her consumption of fibre would go down from f_1 to f_2, and her consumption of sugar would go up from s_1 to s_2. She could, however, spend part of her budget on Healthbran and part on Tastyflakes. In fact, she could consume anywhere along the straight line joining points a and b. This line is known as

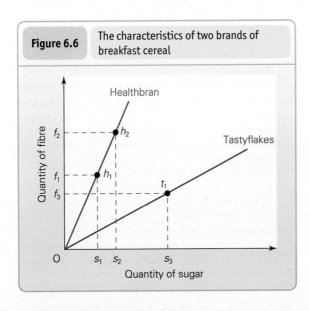

Figure 6.6 The characteristics of two brands of breakfast cereal

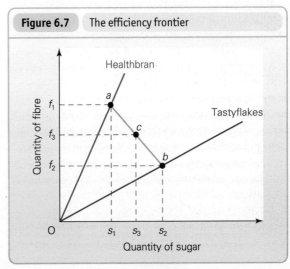

Figure 6.7 The efficiency frontier

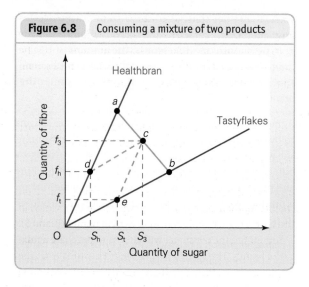

Figure 6.8 Consuming a mixture of two products

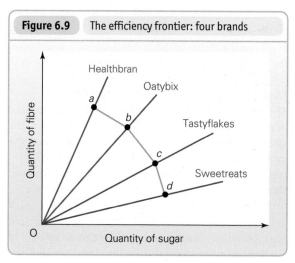

Figure 6.9 The efficiency frontier: four brands

the *efficiency frontier*. For example, by buying some of each brand, she could consume at point c, giving her f_3 of fibre and s_3 of sugar.

If she did consume at point c, how much of the two characteristics would she get from each of the two brands? This is shown in Figure 6.8 by drawing two lines from point c, each one parallel to one of the two rays. Consumption of the two brands takes place at points d and e respectively, giving her f_h units of fibre and s_h units of sugar from Healthbran, and f_t units of fibre and s_t units of sugar from Tastyflakes. The total amount of fibre and sugar from the two brands will be f_3 $(= f_h + f_t)$ and s_3 $(= s_h + s_t)$.[5]

It is easily possible to show an efficiency frontier between several brands, each with their own particular blend of characteristics. This is illustrated in Figure 6.9, which shows the case of four breakfast cereals, each with different combinations of fibre and sugar.

Any of the four points through which the efficiency frontier passes can change if the price of that brand changes. So if Oatybix went up in price, point b would move down the Oatybix ray, thereby altering the shape of the efficiency frontier.

If any of the brands changed their mix of characteristics, then the respective ray would pivot. If the consumer's budget changed, then the whole efficiency frontier would move parallel up or down all the rays.

The optimum level of consumption

Indifference curves

We have seen that by switching between brands, consumers can obtain different mixtures of characteristics. But what, for any given consumer, is the optimum mixture? This can be shown by examining a consumer's preferences, and the way we do this is to construct *indifference curves*.

This is illustrated in Figure 6.10, which shows five indifference curves, labelled I_1 to I_5.

An indifference curve shows all the different combinations of the two characteristics that yield an equal amount of satisfaction or utility. Thus any combination of characteristics along curve I_1 represents the same given level of utility. The consumer is, therefore, 'indifferent' between all points along curve I_1. Although the actual level of utility is not measured in the diagram, the further out the curve, the higher the level of utility. Thus all points on curve I_5 are preferred to all points along curve I_4, and all points along curve I_4 are preferred to all points along curve I_3, and so on. In fact, indifference curves are rather like contours on a map. Each contour represents all points on the ground that are a particular height above sea level. You can have as many contours as you like on the map, depending at what interval you draw them: 100 metres, 25 metres, 10 metres, or whatever. Similarly you could have as many indifference curves as you like on an *indifference map*. In Figure 6.10, we have drawn just five such curves, as that is all that is necessary to illustrate consumer choice, in this example.

---

[5] This follows because of the shape of the parallelogram Odce. Being a parallelogram makes the distance f_3–f_h equal to f_t–O. Thus adding f_h and f_t gives f_3, which must correspond to point c. Similarly the distance s_3–s_t must equal s_h–O. Thus adding sh and s_t gives s_3, which also must correspond to point c.

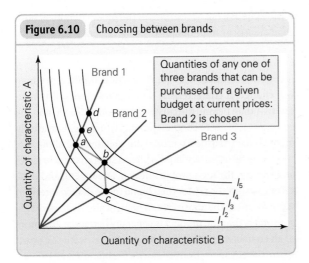

Figure 6.10 Choosing between brands

Quantity of characteristic A

Brand 1

d
e
a
b

Brand 2

Brand 3

I_5
I_4
I_3
I_2
I_1

c

Quantities of any one of three brands that can be purchased for a given budget at current prices: Brand 2 is chosen

Quantity of characteristic B

The shape of indifference curves. Indifference curves are drawn as downward sloping. The reason is that if consumers get less of one characteristic, they would need more of the other to compensate, if their total level of utility was to stay the same. Take the case of washing powder. For any given expenditure, you would only be prepared to give up a certain amount of one characteristic, say whiteness, if you got more of another characteristic, such as softness.

Notice that the indifference curves are not drawn as straight lines. They are bowed in towards the origin. The reason is that people generally are willing to give up less and less of one characteristic for each additional unit of another. For example, if you were buying a new PC, you might be prepared to give up some RAM to get extra hard disk space, but for each extra GB of disk space you would probably be prepared to give up less and less RAM. We call

KI 15
p91

this a ***diminishing marginal rate of substitution*** between the two characteristics. The reason is that you get diminishing marginal utility from any characteristic the more of it you consume, and are thus prepared to give up less and less of another characteristic (whose marginal utility rises as you have less of it).

Indifference curves for different consumers. Different consumers will have different indifference maps. The indifference map in Figure 6.10 is drawn for a particular consumer, say

James. If another consumer, Henry, gets relatively more satisfaction from characteristic B than does James, Henry's indifference curves would be steeper. In other words, he would be prepared to give up more units of A to get a certain amount of B than would James.

The optimum combination of characteristics

We are now in a position to see how a 'rational' consumer would choose between brands. Figure 6.10 shows the rays for three brands of a product, with, at given prices, the efficiency frontier passing through points *a*, *b* and *c*. The consumer would choose to consume Brand 2, since point *b* is on a higher indifference curve than point *a* (Brand 1), which in turn is on a higher indifference curve than point *c* (Brand 3).

Sometimes the consumer will choose to purchase a mixture of brands. This is shown in Figure 6.11, which takes the simple case of just two brands in the market. By consuming at point *a* (i.e. a combination of point *b* on the Brand 1 ray and point *c* on the Brand 2 ray), the consumer is on a higher indifference curve than by consuming only Brand 1 (point *d*) or Brand 2 (point *e*).

Response to changes

We can now show how consumers would respond to changes in price, income, product characteristics and tastes.

Changes in price

Referring back to Figure 6.10, if the price of a brand changes, there is a shift in the efficiency frontier, so that it crosses the ray for that brand at a different point. For example, if the price of Brand 1 fell, there would be a movement of the efficiency frontier up the Brand 1 ray from point *a*. If the price fell far enough that the efficiency frontier now passed through point *d*, the consumer would switch from consuming just Brand 2 to just Brand 1. If the price fell less than this, so that the efficiency frontier passed through point *e*, then the consumer would buy a mixture of both brands. The optimum consumption point would lie on an indifference curve a little above I_4.

KI 15
p91

Pause for thought

Can you think of any instances where the indifference curve will not be bowed in towards the origin?

Definition

Diminishing marginal rate of substitution of characteristics The more a consumer gets of characteristic A and the less of characteristic B, the less and less of B the consumer will be willing to give up to get an extra unit of A.

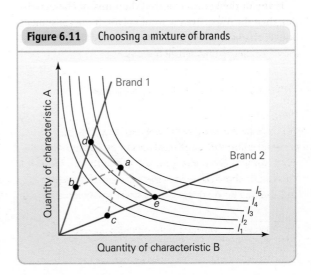

Figure 6.11 Choosing a mixture of brands

Quantity of characteristic A

Brand 1

d
a
b

Brand 2

e
c

I_5
I_4
I_3
I_2
I_1

Quantity of characteristic B

We can relate this analysis to the concept of cross-price elasticity of demand (see page 75). If two products are very close substitutes, they will have a high cross-price elasticity of demand. But what makes them close substitutes? The answer is that they are likely to have similar characteristics; their rays will have a similar slope. Even a slight rise in the price of one of them (i.e. a small movement along its ray) can lead the consumer to switch to the other. This will occur when the rays are close together: when they have a similar slope.

Changes in income

If there is a change in consumer incomes, so that people allocate a bigger budget to the product in question, then there will be a parallel movement outwards of the efficiency frontier. Whether this will involve consumers switching between brands depends on the shape of the indifference map.

Changes in the characteristics of a product (real or perceived)

If consumers believe that a brand now yields relatively more of characteristic B than A, the ray will become less steep. How far out will the efficiency point be on this new ray? This depends on the total perceived amount of the two characteristics that is obtained from the given budget spent on this brand.

To illustrate this, consider Figure 6.12. The firm producing Brand 1 changes its specifications, so that for a given budget a lot more characteristic B can be obtained and a little more characteristic A. The result is that the brand's ray shifts inwards and the efficiency frontier which originally connected points *a* and *b* now connects points *c* and *b*. In this case the consumer represented by the indifference curves shown switches consumption from Brand 2 at point *b* to Brand 1 at point *c*.

If there is a proportionate increase in both characteristics (i.e. the brand has generally improved), the slope of the ray will not change. Instead, there will be a movement of the efficiency frontier outward along the ray. Graphically the effect

is the same as a fall in the price of the product: more of both characteristics can be obtained for a given budget.

Changes in tastes

If consumers' tastes change, their whole indifference map will change. If characteristic B now gives more utility relative to A than before, the curves will become steeper, and the consumer is likely to choose a product which yields relatively more of characteristic B (i.e. one with a relatively shallow ray).

Clearly firms will attempt to predict such changes in tastes and will try, through product design, advertising and marketing, to shift the ray for their brand in the desired direction (downwards in the above case). They will also try to persuade consumers that the product is generally better (i.e. has more of all characteristics) and thereby move outward the point where the efficiency frontier crosses the brand's ray.

Business and the characteristics approach

Characteristics analysis can help us understand the nature of consumer choice. When we go shopping and compare one product with another, it is the differences in the features of the various brands, along with price, that determine which products we end up buying. If firms, therefore, want to compete effectively with their rivals, it is not enough to compete solely in terms of price; it is important to focus on the specifications of their product and how these compare with those of their rivals' products. KI 8 p42

Characteristics analysis can help firms study the implications of changing their product's specifications (and of their rivals changing theirs). It also allows firms to analyse the effects of changes in their price, or their rivals' prices; the effects of changes in the budgets of various types of consumer; the effects of changes in consumer tastes; and the effects of repositioning themselves in the market.

Take the producer of Brand 1 in Figure 6.13. Clearly the firm would like to persuade consumers like the one illus-

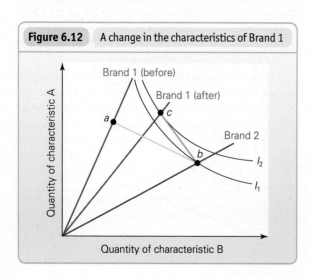

| Figure 6.12 | A change in the characteristics of Brand 1 |

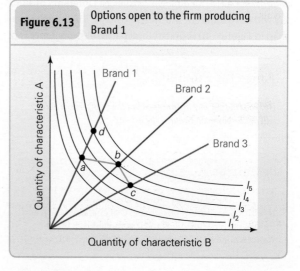

| Figure 6.13 | Options open to the firm producing Brand 1 |

trated to switch away from Brand 2 to Brand 1. It could do this by lowering its price. But a small reduction in price will have no effect on this consumer. Only when the price has fallen far enough for the efficiency frontier to rise nearly to point *d* will the consumer start switching; and only when the price has fallen further still, so that the efficiency frontier passes through a point a little above point *d*, will the consumer switch completely.

An alternative would be for the firm to reposition its product. It could introduce more of characteristic B into its product, thereby swinging the Brand 1 ray clockwise towards the Brand 2 ray. Clearly, it would have to be careful about its price too. The closer its brand became in quality to Brand 2, the more elastic would demand become, since Brand 1 would now be a closer substitute for Brand 2. In the extreme case of its ray becoming the same as that for Brand 2, its price would have to be low enough for the consumer to buy at or above point *b*. Depending on consumer tastes (and hence the shape of the indifference curves), it may choose to reposition its brand between the Brand 2 and Brand 3 rays. Again, a careful mix of product characteristics and price may enable it to capture a larger share of the market.

Another alternative would be for the firm to attempt to influence consumer tastes. In Figure 6.13, if it could persuade consumers to attach more value to characteristic A, the indifference curves would become shallower (i.e. less characteristic A would now be needed to give consumers a given level of utility). If the curves swung downwards enough, point *a* could be now on a higher indifference curve than point *b*. The consumer concerned would switch from Brand 2 to Brand 1. Clearly, the more consumers are influenced in this way, the more sales of Brand 1 will rise.

If a firm is thinking of launching a new product, again it will need to see how the characteristics of its product compare with those of the existing firms in the market. It will need to see where its ray would be compared with those of other firms, and whether the price it is thinking of charging would enable it to take sales away from its rivals.

Pause for thought

Before you read on, what do you think are the limitations of characteristics analysis?

Limitations of characteristics analysis

Characteristics analysis, as we have seen, can help firms to understand their position in the market and the effects of changing their strategy. Nevertheless it cannot provide firms with a complete analysis of demand. There are four key limitations of the approach:

- It is sometimes difficult to identify and measure characteristics in a clear and unambiguous way. Take the look or design of a product, whether it be furniture, clothing, a painting or a car. What makes it visually appealing depends on the personal tastes of the consumer, and such tastes are virtually impossible to quantify.
- Most products have several characteristics. The analysis we have been examining, however, is limited to just two characteristics: one on each axis. By using mathematical analysis it is possible to extend the number of characteristics, but the more characteristics that are included in the analysis, the more complex it becomes.
- Indifference curves, while being a good means of understanding consumer choice in theory, have practical limitations. To draw an indifference map for just one consumer would be very difficult, given that consumers would often find it hard to imagine a series of combinations of characteristics between which they were indifferent. To draw indifference curves for millions of consumers would be virtually impossible. At best, therefore, they can provide a rough guide to consumer choice.
- Consumer tastes change. In what ways consumer tastes will change and how these changes will influence the shape of the indifference curves are very difficult to predict.

Despite these problems, there are many useful insights that firms can gain from the analysis. Firms, through their market research, could gain considerable information about consumer attitudes towards their products' characteristics and thus the general shape, if not precise position, of indifference curves.

What is more, many markets divide into different **market segments** with consumers in each segment having similar tastes (and hence similar sets of indifference curves). For example, different models of car fall into different groups (such as medium-sized saloons, high-performance small cars, people carriers and small 'tall' cars), as do different types of restaurant and different types of holiday. Thus a tour operator will first identify the particular segment of the market it is aiming for (e.g. a young person's package holiday with the characteristics of guaranteed sunshine and plenty of nightlife) and then position itself in that particular market relative to its rival tour operators.

What is clear is that firms need good information about the demand for their products and to develop a careful marketing strategy. In Chapter 7 we look at how firms attempt to get information about demand, and in Chapter 8 we examine how firms set about developing, marketing and advertising their products.

Definition

Market segment A part of a market for a product where the demand is for a particular variety of that product.

SUMMARY

1a Economists call consumer satisfaction 'utility'. Marginal utility diminishes as consumption increases. This means that total utility will rise less and less rapidly as people consume more. At a certain point, total utility will reach a maximum, at which point marginal utility will be zero. Beyond this point, total utility will fall; marginal utility will be negative.

1b Consumers will attempt to maximise their total utility. They will do this by consuming more of a good as long as its marginal utility to them (measured in terms of the price they are prepared to pay for it) exceeds its price. They will stop buying additional amounts once *MU* has fallen to equal the price. At this point, the consumer's surplus will be maximised.

1c An individual's demand curve lies along the same line as the individual's marginal utility curve. The market demand curve is the sum of all individuals' marginal utility curves.

2a When people buy consumer durables they may be uncertain of their benefits and any additional repair and maintenance costs. When they buy financial assets they may be uncertain of what will happen to their price in the future. Buying under these conditions of imperfect knowledge is therefore a form of gambling. When we take such gambles, if we know the probabilities, we are said to be operating under conditions of *risk*. If we do not know the probabilities, we are said to be operating under conditions of *uncertainty*.

2b People can be divided into risk lovers, risk averters and those who are risk neutral. Because of the diminishing marginal utility of income it is rational for people to be risk averters (unless gambling is itself pleasurable).

2c Insurance is a way of eliminating risks for policy-holders. Being risk averters, people are prepared to pay premiums in order to obtain insurance. Insurance companies, on the other hand, are prepared to take on these risks because they can spread them over a large number of policies. According to the law of large numbers, what is unpredictable for a single policy-holder becomes highly predictable for a large number of them provided that their risks are independent of each other.

2d When there is asymmetric information buyers and/or sellers can experience the problems of adverse selection and moral hazard. For example, insurance companies that offer health insurance without taking into account the health of their potential policy-holders will attract those individuals who are most likely to benefit from a health policy, i.e. those prone to illness and injury. This is the problem of adverse selection. Further, once individuals have taken out an insurance policy, they may engage in more risky behaviour. This is the problem of moral hazard.

3a Consumers buy products for their characteristics. Characteristics can be plotted on a diagram and a ray drawn out from the origin for each product. The slope of the ray gives the amount of the characteristic measured on the vertical axis relative to the amount measured on the horizontal axis.

3b The amount purchased will depend on the consumer's budget. An efficiency frontier can be drawn showing the maximum quantity of various alternative brands (or combinations of them) that can be purchased for that budget.

3c An indifference map can be drawn on the same diagram. The map shows a series of indifference curves, each one measuring all the alternative combinations of two characteristics that give the consumer a given level of utility. The consumer is thus indifferent between all combinations along an indifference curve. Indifference curves further out to the right represent higher levels of utility and thus preferred combinations. Indifference curves are bowed in to the origin. This reflects a diminishing marginal rate of substitution between characteristics.

3d The optimum combination of characteristics is where the efficiency frontier is tangential to (i.e. just touches) the highest indifference curve. The 'rational' consumer will thus purchase at this point.

3e A change in a product's price, or a change in the consumer's budget, is represented by a movement along the product's ray. A change in the mix of characteristics of a product is represented by a swing in the ray (i.e. a change in its slope). A change in consumer tastes is represented by a shift in the indifference curves. They will become steeper if tastes shift towards the characteristic measured on the horizontal axis.

3f Although (a) some characteristics are difficult or impossible to measure, (b) only two characteristics can be measured on a simple two-dimensional diagram and (c) the position of indifference curves is difficult to identify in practice, characteristics theory gives useful insights into the process of consumer choice. It can help firms analyse the implications of changing their or their rivals' product specifications, changes in consumer tastes and changes in their or their rivals' prices.

MyEconLab

This book can be supported by MyEconLab, which contains a range of additional resources, including an online homework and tutorial system designed to test and build your understanding.

You need both an access card and a course ID to access MyEconLab:

1. Is your lecturer using MyEconLab? Ask your lecturer for your course ID.

2. Has an access card been included with the book at a reduced cost? Check the inside back cover of the book.

3. If you have a course ID but no access card, go to: http://www.myeconlab.com/ to buy access to this interactive study programme.

REVIEW QUESTIONS

1 Do you ever purchase things irrationally? If so, what are they and why is your behaviour irrational?

2 If you buy something in the shop on the corner when you know that the same item could have been bought more cheaply two miles up the road in the supermarket, is your behaviour irrational? Explain.

3 How would marginal utility and market demand be affected by a rise in the price of a complementary good?

4 Why do we get less consumer surplus from goods where our demand is relatively price elastic?

5 Explain why the price of a good is no reflection of the *total* value that consumers put on it.

6 Give some numerical examples of risk taking where the expected value of the gamble (a) is greater than the pay-off from the certain outcome; (b) equal to the pay-off from the certain outcome; (c) lower than the pay-off from the certain outcome.

7 If people are generally risk averse, why do so many people around the world take part in national lotteries?

8 Why are insurance companies unwilling to provide insurance against losses arising from war or 'civil insurrection'? Name some other events where it would be impossible to obtain insurance.

9 Assume that the insurance company is able to observe whether or not a potential customer is a skilful driver. If drivers do not take out the insurance there is a 1 per cent chance they will be involved in an accident that results in the car being written off. Based on this risk, the insurance company charges a premium of £250 per customer. Assume also that having taken out the insurance drivers take less care when driving. Using a numerical example, explain how this might cause problems for the insurance company.

10 In March 2011 the European Court of Justice banned insurance companies from charging different premiums to men and women solely because of their gender. This change in the law came into effect in December 2012. What impact might this ruling be having on the market for car insurance? What actions might an insurance company or a driver take in response to the change in the law?

11 Euro NCAP carries out crash tests on new cars in order to assess the extent to which they are safer than the minimum required standard. The cars are given a percentage score in four different categories, including adult occupant protection and child occupant protection. An overall safety rating is then awarded. Based on the test results in November 2014, the Volvo V40 hatchback was judged to be the safest car on the market. If you observed that these cars were *more* likely to be involved in traffic accidents, could this be an example of adverse selection or moral hazard? Explain.

12 The UK Government and the Association of British insurers have agreed to the 'Concordat and Moratorium on Genetics and Insurance'. As part of this agreement the providers of income protection insurance and critical illness insurance cannot ask potential customers for the results from predictive genetic tests: i.e. tests that predict the likelihood of you becoming ill at some point in the future as a result of a genetic condition. What impact might this agreement have on the market for these insurance policies?

13 Make a list of characteristics of shoes. Which of these could be easily measured and which are more 'subjective'?

14 If two houses had identical characteristics, except that one was near a noisy airport and the other was in a quiet location, and if the market price of the first house was £300 000 and the second was £400 000, how would that help us to put a value on the characteristic of peace and quiet?

15 Assume that Rachel is attending university and likes to eat a meal at lunchtime. Assume that she has three options of where to eat: the university refectory, a nearby pub or a nearby restaurant. Apart from price, she takes into account the quality of the food and the pleasantness of the surroundings when choosing where to eat.

Sketch her indifference map for the two characteristics: food quality and pleasantness of surroundings. Now, making your own assumptions about which locations provide which characteristics, the prices they charge and Rachel's weekly budget for lunches, sketch the rays for the three locations and draw a weekly efficiency frontier. Mark Rachel's optimum consumption point.

Now illustrate the following (you might need to draw separate diagrams):

a) A rise in the price of meals at the local pub, but no change in the price of meals at the other two locations.

b) A shift in Rachel's tastes in favour of food quality relative to pleasantness of surroundings.

c) The refectory is refurbished and is now a much more attractive place to eat.

16 Why would consumption at a point inside the efficiency frontier not be 'rational'?

WEB APPENDIX IN THE CASE STUDIES SECTION OF MyEconLab

Indifference analysis. This examines the choices consumers make between products and shows how these choices are affected by the prices of the products. It is the traditional analysis on which Characteristics Theory (examined in section 6.3) is based.

Demand and the firm

Business issues covered in this chapter

- ■ How can businesses set about estimating the strength of demand for their products?
- ■ How do businesses set about gathering information on consumer attitudes and behaviour?
- ■ How do businesses calculate the importance of various factors (such as tastes, consumer incomes and rivals' prices) in determining the level of demand?
- ■ What methods can they use to forecast the demand for their products?
- ■ How useful are past trends in predicting future ones?

Given our analysis in Chapter 6, how might a business set about discovering the wants of consumers and hence the intensity of demand? The more effectively a business can identify such wants, the more likely it is to increase its sales and be successful. The clearer idea it can gain of the rate at which the typical consumer's utility will decline as consumption increases, the better estimate it can make of the product's price elasticity.

Also the more accurately it can assess the relative utility to the consumer of its product compared with those of its rivals, the more effectively it will be able to compete by differentiating its product from theirs. In this chapter we shall consider the alternative strategies open to business for collecting data on consumer behaviour, and how it can help business managers to estimate and forecast patterns of demand.

7.1 ESTIMATING DEMAND FUNCTIONS

If a business is to make sound strategic decisions, it must have a good understanding of its market. It must be able to predict things such as the impact of an advertising campaign, or the consequences of changing a brand's price or specifications. It must also be able to predict the likely growth (or decline) in consumer demand, both in the near future and over the longer term.

The problem is that information on consumer behaviour can be costly and time-consuming to acquire, and there is

no guarantee as to its accuracy. As a result, business managers are frequently making strategic decisions with imperfect knowledge, never fully knowing whether the decision they have made is the 'best' one: i.e. the one which yields the most profit or sales, or best meets some other more specific strategic objective (such as driving a competitor from a segment of a market).

But despite the fact that the information which a firm acquires is bound to be imperfect, it is still usually better than relying on hunches or 'instinct'. Once the firm has obtained information on consumer behaviour, there are two main uses to which it can be put:

■ *Estimating demand functions*. Here the information is used to show the relationship between the quantity demanded and the various determinants of demand, such as price, consumers' incomes, advertising, the price of substitute and complementary goods, etc. Once this relationship (known as a *demand function*) has been established, it can be used to predict what would happen to demand if one of its determinants changed.

■ *Forecasting future demand*. Here the information is used to project future sales potential. This can then be used as the basis for output and investment plans.

In this section we concentrate on the first of these two uses. We examine methods for gathering data on consumer behaviour and then see how these data can be used to estimate a demand function. (Forecasting is considered in section 7.2.)

Methods of collecting data on consumer behaviour

There are three general approaches to gathering information about consumers. These are: **observations of market behaviour**, **market surveys** and **market experiments**.

Market observations

The firm can gather data on how demand for its product has changed over time. Virtually all firms will have detailed information of their sales broken down by week, and/or month, and/or year. They will probably also have information on how sales have varied from one part of the market to another.

In addition, the firm will need to obtain data on how the various determinants of demand (such as price, advertising and the price of competitors' products) have themselves changed over time. Firms are likely to have much of this information already: for example, the amount spent on advertising and the prices of competitors' products. Other information might be relatively easy to obtain by paying an agency to do the research.

Having obtained this information, the firm can then use it to estimate how changes in the various determinants have affected demand in the past, and hence what effect they will be likely to have in the future (we examine this estimation process later in this section).

Even the most sophisticated analysis based on market observations, however, will suffer from one major drawback. Relationships that held in the past will not necessarily hold in the future. Consumers are human, and humans change their minds. Their perceptions of products change (something that the advertising industry relies on!) and their tastes change. It is for this reason that many firms turn to market surveys or market experiments to gain more information about the future.

Market surveys

It is not uncommon to be stopped in a city centre, or to have a knock at the door, and be asked whether you would kindly answer the questions of some market researcher. If the research interviewer misses you, then a postal questionnaire may well seek out the same type of information. A vast quantity of information can be collected in this way. It is a relatively quick and cheap method of data collection. Questions concerning all aspects of consumer behaviour might be asked, such as those relating to present and future patterns of expenditure, or how a buyer might respond to changing product specifications or price, both of the firm in question and of its rivals.

A key feature of the market survey is that it can be targeted at distinct consumer groups, thereby reflecting the specific information requirements of a business. For example, businesses selling luxury goods will be interested only in consumers falling within higher income brackets. Other samples might be drawn from a particular age group or gender, or from those with a particular lifestyle, such as eating habits.

The major drawback with this technique concerns the accuracy of the information acquired. Accurate information requires various conditions to be met.

A random sample. If the sample is not randomly selected, it may fail to represent a cross-section of the population being surveyed. As a result, it may be subject to various forms of research bias. For example, the sample might not contain the correct gender and racial balance. The information might then over-emphasise the views of a particular group (e.g. white men).

Clarity of the questions. It is important for the questions to be phrased in an unambiguous way, so as not to mislead the respondent.

Avoidance of leading questions. It is very easy for the respondent to be led into giving the answer the firm wants to hear. For example, when asking whether the person would buy a new product that the firm is thinking of launching, the questionnaire might make the product sound really desirable. The respondents might, as a result, say that they would buy the product, but later, when they see the product in the shops, they might realise that they do not want it.

Definitions

Observations of market behaviour Information gathered about consumers from the day-to-day activities of the business within the market.

Market surveys Information gathered about consumers, usually via a questionnaire, that attempts to enhance the business's understanding of consumer behaviour.

Market experiments Information gathered about consumers under artificial or simulated conditions. A method used widely in assessing the effects of advertising on consumers.

Willingness of respondents. People might refuse to answer particular questions, possibly due to their personal nature. This may then lead to partial or distorted information.

Truthful response. It is very tempting for respondents who are 'keen to please' to give the answer that they think the questioner wants, or for other somewhat reluctant respondents to give 'mischievous' answers. In other words, people may lie!

Stability of demand. By the time the product is launched, or the changes to an existing product are made, time will have elapsed. The information may then be out of date. Consumer demand may have changed, as tastes and fashions have shifted, or as a result of the actions of competitors. The essence of the problem of market surveys is that they ask consumers what they are likely to do. People can and do change their mind.

As well as surveying consumers, businesses might survey other businesses, or panels of experts within a particular market. Both could yield potentially valuable information to the business.

Market experiments

Rather than asking consumers questions and getting them to *imagine* how they *would* behave, the market experiment involves observing consumer *behaviour* under simulated conditions. It can be used to observe consumer reactions to a new product or to changes in an existing product.

A simple experiment might involve consumers being asked to conduct a blind taste test for a new brand of toothpaste. The experimenter will ensure that the same amount of paste is applied to the brush, and that the subjects swill their mouths prior to tasting a further brand. Once the experiment is over, the 'consumers' are quizzed about their perceptions of the product.

More sophisticated experiments could be conducted. For example, a *laboratory shop* might be set up to simulate a real shopping experience. People could be given a certain amount of money to spend in the 'shop' and their reactions to changes in prices, packaging, display, etc. could be monitored.

The major drawback with such 'laboratories' is that consumers might behave differently because they are being observed. For example, they might spend more time comparing prices than they otherwise would, simply because they think that this is what a *good*, rational consumer should do. With real shopping, however, it might simply be habit, or something 'irrational' such as the colour of the packaging, that determines which product they select.

Another type of market experiment involves confining a marketing campaign to a particular town or region. The campaign could involve advertising, or giving out free samples, or discounting the price, or introducing an improved version of the product, but each confined to that particular locality. Sales in that area are then compared with sales in other areas in order to assess the effectiveness of the various campaigns.

> ### Pause for thought
>
> *Before you read on, try to identify some other drawbacks in using market experiments to gather data on consumer behaviour.*

Using the data to estimate demand functions

Once the business has undertaken its market analysis, what will it do with the information? How can it use its new knowledge to aid its decision making?

One way the information might be used is for the business to attempt to estimate the relationship between the quantity demanded and the various factors that influence demand. This would then enable the firm to predict how the demand for the product would be likely to change if one or more of the determinants of demand changed.

We can represent the relationship between the demand for a product and the determinants of demand in the form of an equation. This is called a ***demand function***. It can be expressed in general terms or with specific values attached to the determinants.

General form of a demand function

In its general form the demand function is effectively a list of the various determinants of demand.

$$Q_d = f(P_g; T; P_{s_1}, P_{s_2} \ldots P_{s_n}; P_{c_1}, P_{c_2}; \ldots P_{c_m}; Y; P^e_{g_{t+1}}; U)$$

This is merely saying in symbols that the quantity demanded (Q_d) is a 'function of' (f) – i.e. depends on – the price of the good itself (P_g), tastes (T), the price of a number of substitute goods ($P_{s_1}, P_{s_2} \ldots P_{s_n}$;), the price of a number of complementary goods ($P_{c_1}, P_{c_2}, \ldots P_{c_m}$) total consumer incomes (Y), the expected price of the good (P^e_g) at some future time ($t+1$) and other factors (U) such as the distribution of income, the demographic profile of the population, etc. The equation is thus just a form of shorthand.

Note that this function could be extended by dividing determinants into sub-categories. For example, income could be broken down by household type, age, gender or any other characteristic. Similarly, instead of having one term labelled 'tastes', we could identify various characteristics of the product or its marketing that determine tastes.

In this general form, there are no numerical values attached to each of the determinants. As such, the function has no predictive value for the firm.

> ### Definition
>
> **Demand function** An equation showing the relationship between the demand for a product and its principal determinants.

Estimating demand equations

To make predictions, the firm must use its survey or experimental data to assign *values* to each of the determinants. These values show just how much demand will change if any one of the determinants changes (while the rest are held constant). For example, suppose that an electricity distributor believes that there are three main determinants of demand (Q_d) for the electricity it supplies: its price (P), total consumer incomes (Y) and the price of gas (P_g). It will wish to assign values to the terms a, b, c and d (known as *coefficients*) in the following equation:

$$Q_d = a + bP + cY + dP_g$$

But how are the values of the coefficients to be estimated? This is done using a statistical technique called **regression analysis**. To conduct regression analysis, a number of observations must be used. For example, the electricity company could use its market observations (or the results from various surveys or experiments).

Using simple regression analysis. To show how these observations are used, let us consider the very simplest case: that of the effects of changes in just one determinant – for example, price. In this case the demand equation for the regression analysis would simply be of the form:

$$Q_d = a + bP + \varepsilon$$

where 'a' is a constant which provides an estimate of the quantity demanded if the price is zero; the coefficient 'b' indicates the strength of the impact of a price change and should be negative because of the law of demand; and ε is an error term, which captures the combined impact of *other* factors that influence the demand for electricity but have not been included in the regression.[1]

The observations might be like those illustrated in Figure 7.1. The red points show the amounts of electricity per time period actually consumed at different prices. (Note that the axes are labelled the other way round from the demand curve diagrams in Chapter 4 as it is conventional to put the dependent variable, in this case quantity consumed, on the horizontal axis.)

We could visually try to construct an approximate line of best fit through these points. Alternatively, we could do this much more accurately by using **regression analysis**. The goal is to find the values of a and b in the equation:

$$Q_d = a + bP$$

If we did, then we could use the equation to draw the line of best fit. This is shown as the blue line in Figure 7.1. It illustrates the estimated values of the demand for electricity at each price. For example, at a price of P_1 the estimated

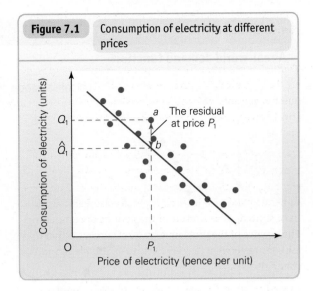

Figure 7.1 Consumption of electricity at different prices

consumption is $\hat{Q}_1$, given on the line of best fit at point b. Actual demand for electricity, however, is Q_1, at point a. The difference between the estimated and the actual value of demand at each price is known as the 'residual', which is also illustrated in Figure 7.1 for P_1.

Simple linear regression analysis produces an equation (i.e. the values of the a and b terms) that minimises the sum of the squares of the residuals. (We do not explain regression analysis in detail in this text, but most business statistics textbooks cover the topic.)

Multiple regression analysis. Of course, in reality, there are many determinants of the demand for electricity. If we can obtain data on these variables it is better to include them in the regression equation, otherwise our model might suffer from a problem called 'omitted variable bias' – this is discussed in more detail in Box 7.1. Omitting variables can cause the estimated coefficients to be unreliable.

Regression analysis can also be used to determine these more complex relationships: to derive the equation that best fits the data on changes in a number of variables. Unlike a curve on a diagram, which simply shows the relationship between two variables, an equation can show the relationship between *several* variables. Multiple regression analysis can be used to find the 'best fit' equation from data on changes in a number of variables.

For example, regression analysis could be applied to data showing the quantity of electricity consumed at various levels of price (P), consumer incomes (Y) and the price of

---

[1] To be precise, the error term only captures the combined impact of other factors if a number of assumptions are met. These can be found in most introductory statistics textbooks.

BOX 7.1	THE DEMAND FOR LAMB

A real-world demand function

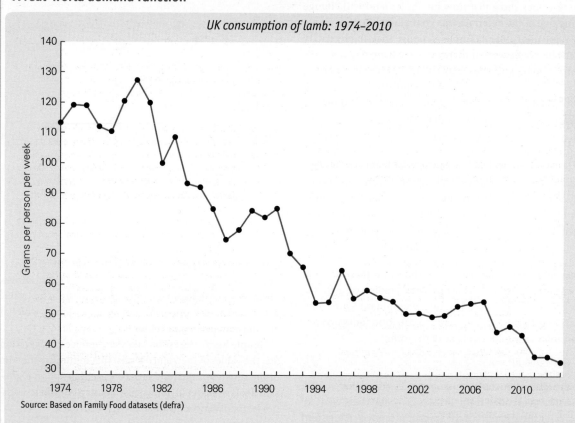

UK consumption of lamb: 1974–2010

Grams per person per week

Source: Based on Family Food datasets (defra)

The diagram shows what happened to the consumption of lamb in the UK over the period 1974–2013. How can we explain this dramatic fall in consumption? One way of exploring this issue is to make use of a regression model, which should help us to see which variables are relevant and how they are likely to affect demand.

The following is an initial model fitted (using Gretl, a free, open source, statistical software package) to annual data for the years 1974–2010.

$$Q_L = 144.0 - 0.137P_L - 0.034P_B + 0.214P_P - 0.00513Y + \varepsilon \quad (1)$$

where:

Q_L is the quantity of lamb sold in grams per person per week;
P_L is the 'real' price of lamb (in pence per kg, 2000 prices);
P_B is the 'real' price of beef (in pence per kg, 2000 prices);
P_P is the 'real' price of pork (in pence per kg, 2000 prices);
Y is households' real disposable income per head (£ per year, 2000 prices);
    is the error term that attempts to capture the impact of any other variables that have an impact on the demand for lamb.

This model makes it possible to predict what would happen to the demand for lamb if any one of the four explanatory variables changed, assuming that the other variables remained constant. We will assume that the estimated coefficients used throughout this box are all statistically significant.

 Using equation (1), calculate what would happen – ceteris paribus – to the demand for lamb if:

a)   the real price of lamb went up by 10p per kg;
b)   the real price of beef went up by 10p per kg;
c)   the real price of pork fell by 10p per kg;
d)   real disposable income per head rose by £100 per annum.
Are the results as you would expect?

There is a serious problem with estimated demand functions like these if there are unobserved factors that change over time and have an impact on the demand for lamb. By omitting explanatory variables, we can say that the model is mis-specified and this introduces a bias into the estimated coeffi-cients. For example the estimated coefficient on Y is negative and quite close to zero. This suggests that household income has little effect on demand. Is this what we would expect? Also the coefficient on P_B is negative which suggests that lamb and beef are complements in consumption. Once again this appears to be a counterintuitive result.

One factor that did change over time was tastes. During the 37-year period covered by the data there was a shift in demand away from lamb and other meats, partly for health reasons, and partly because of an expansion in the availability of and demand for vegetarian and low-meat alternatives. On the assumption that this shift in tastes took place steadily over time, a new demand equation was estimated for the same years:

$$Q_L = 121.4 - 0.151P_L - 0.0213P_B + 0.180P_P$$
$$- 0.000391Y - 1.728TIME \qquad (2)$$

where $TIME = 1$ in 1974, 2 in 1975, 3 in 1976, etc.

1. How does the introduction of the variable TIME affect the relationship between the demand for lamb and (a) its real price; (b) real disposable income per head?
2. Does lamb appear to be a normal good or an inferior good?
3. What does the negative coefficient of P_B indicate?

It can be argued that model (2) is a better model than model (1) because it appears to have a better 'goodness of fit'. This is indicated by something called the 'R-squared' statistic. If $R^2 = 1$ this suggests the model can explain all of the variation in the data on the demand for lamb, whereas if $R^2 = 0$ it indicates that the model cannot explain any of the variation in the data.

In model (2), the adjusted $R^2 = 0.913$[3] compared with 0.908 for model (1). This means that model (2) can explain 91.3 per cent of the variation in the consumption of lamb during the period 1974 to 2010, whereas model (1) can explain 90.8 per cent.

While model (2) appears to be a small improvement on model (1),[4] it still has problems. The estimated coefficient of Y remains negative and is still very close to zero while the coefficient on P_B remains negative. The model might still be mis-specified because of other omitted variables. For example, consumers' purchases of lamb in a given year might be influenced by what they were consuming the previous year. The model also includes the real prices of two substitutes for lamb, but does not include the real prices of any complements.

To take the above points into account, the following third model was estimated, using data for 1975 to 2010.

$$Q_L = -37.520 - 0.128P_L + 0.0757P_B + 0.122P_P + 0.00415Y$$
$$- 1.529TIME + 0.679LQ_L - 0.0519P_C + \varepsilon \qquad (3)$$

where LQ_L is the lagged consumption of lamb (i.e. consumption in the previous year) and P_C is the real price of a complement (potatoes). $R^2 = 0.958$ and the coefficients are all significant.

1. To what extent is model (3) an improvement on model (2)? (Hint: is lamb now a normal or inferior good?)
2. Use the three equations and also the data given in the table below to estimate the demand for lamb in 2000 and 2010. Which model works the best in each case? Why? Explain why the models are all subject to error in their predictions.
3. Use model (3) and the data given in the table to explain why the demand for lamb fell so dramatically between 1980 and 2010.
4. The formula for the elasticity of demand (price elasticity, income elasticity or cross elasticity) can be written as $dQ/dX \div Q/X$, where dQ/dX represents the coefficient for a given variable, X. For example, in equation (3), 0.0757 gives the value of the term dQ_L/dP_B when working out the cross-price elasticity of demand for lamb with respect to changes in the price of beef. Using equation (3) and the table below, work out the following for 2010:
   a) the price elasticity of demand for lamb;
   b) the income elasticity of demand for lamb;
   c) the cross-price elasticity of demand for lamb with respect to (i) beef, (ii) pork, (iii) potatoes.

	Q_L	LQ_L	P_L	P_B	P_P	Y	$TIME$	P_C
1980	128	121	421.7	546.0	414.6	10 498	7	26.7
2000	54	56	467.0	480.5	381.1	17 797	27	44.9
2010	44	46	506.2	470.1	381.1	19 776	37	53.5

Sources: Nominal food prices were calculated by dividing expenditure by consumption. These nominal prices in pence per kg were then adjusted to 'real' prices by dividing by the RPI (retail price index) for total food (2000 = 100) and multiplying by 100. www.defra.gov.uk/statistics/foodfarm/food/familyfood/datasets/ (expenditure and consumption); www.ons.gov.uk/ (income and RPI food)

---

[3] The R^2 must be adjusted for the number of variables because simply adding more variables will always cause the unadjusted R^2 figure to increase.

[4] Care must be taken not to judge a model by simply looking at the R^2 figure. It had been referred to as 'the most over-used and abused of all statistics'.

gas (P_g). An equation similar to the following might be estimated:

$$Q_d = 2000 - 500P + 0.4Y + 200P_g + \varepsilon$$

where Q_d is measured in millions of gigawatts per annum, P in pence per kilowatt hour, Y in £ millions, P_g in pence per kilowatt hour and ε is the error term. Once again an error term must be included because, although data have been included on Y and P_g, there may still be other factors that we are unable to observe or measure that influence the demand for electricity.

The equation shows that if, say, the price of electricity were 5p per kilowatt hour, consumer incomes were £20 billion and the price of gas were 2p per kilowatt hour, then the demand for electricity would be 7900 million gigawatts per annum. This is calculated by substituting these values into the equation as follows:

$$Q_d = 2000 - (500 \times 5) + (0.4 \times 20\,000) + (200 \times 2)$$
$$= 2000 - 2500 + 8000 + 400 = 7900$$

Testing the equation. It is important to test to see if each of the coefficients that have been estimated is significant. This is typically done by completing a 't' test.[2]

What happens if the 't' test indicates that the coefficient is not significant? This means that we cannot be sure that the true value of the coefficient is not in fact zero instead of the value that has been estimated. In other words the variable may have no impact on the demand for electricity.

Interpreting the equation. If the estimated coefficients on each of the variables in the regression equation *are* statistically significant, the equation tells us the impact on the demand for electricity of a marginal or one unit change

---

[2]A 't' statistic is calculated by dividing the estimated coefficient by its standard error. More detail can be found in most business statistics textbooks.

Table 7.1	Effect on the demand for electricity of a 1 unit rise in each determinant	
Determinant	**Change**	**Effect on demand for electricity**
Price of electricity (P)	1p per kilowatt rise	Fall by 500 gigawatts
Consumer incomes (Y)	£1 million rise	Rise by 0.4 gigawatts
Price of gas (P_g)	1p per kilowatt rise	Rise by 200 gigawatts

in each determinant, while holding each of the other determinants constant. In the equation above, this would give the effects on the demand for electricity shown in Table 7.1.

The branch of economics that applies statistical techniques to economic data is known as *econometrics*. The problem with using such techniques, however, is that they cannot produce equations and graphs that allow totally reliable predictions to be made. The data on which the equations are based are often incomplete or unreliable, and the underlying relationships on which they are based (often ones of human behaviour) may well change over time. Therefore these techniques do not provide an exact quantification of the strength of any relationships between variables. They simply provide an estimate. Thus econometrics cannot provide a business manager with 'the answer', but when properly applied it is more reliable than relying on 'hunches' and instinct.

Definition

Econometrics The branch of economics which applies statistical techniques to economic data.

7.2 FORECASTING DEMAND

Demand functions are useful in that they show what will happen to demand *if* one of the determinants changes. But businesses will want to know more than the answer to an 'If . . . then' question. They will want to know what will actually happen to the determinants and, more importantly, what will happen to demand itself as the determinants change. In other words, they will want *forecasts* of future demand. After all, if demand is going to increase, they may well want to invest *now* so that they have the extra capacity to meet the extra demand. But it will be a

costly mistake to invest in extra capacity if demand is not going to increase.

We now, therefore, turn to examine some of the forecasting techniques used by business.

Simple time-series analysis

Simple time-series analysis involves directly projecting from past sales data into the future. Thus if it is observed that sales of a firm's product have been growing steadily by

3 per cent per annum for the past few years, the firm can use this to predict that sales will continue to grow at approximately the same rate in the future. Similarly, if it is observed that there are clear seasonal fluctuations in demand, as in the case of the demand for holidays or ice cream or winter coats, then again it can be assumed that fluctuations of a similar magnitude will continue into the future. In other words, using simple time-series analysis assumes that demand in the future will continue to behave in the same way as in the past.

Using simple time-series analysis in this way can be described as 'black box' forecasting. No *explanation* is offered as to *why* demand is behaving in this way: any underlying model of demand is 'hidden in a black box'. In a highly stable market environment, where the various factors affecting demand change very little or, if they do, change very steadily or regularly, such time-series analysis can supply reasonably accurate forecasts. The problem is that, without closer examination of the market, the firm cannot know whether changes in demand of the same magnitude as in the past will continue into the future. Just because demand has followed a clear pattern in the past, it does not follow that it will continue to exhibit the same pattern in the future. After all, the determinants of demand may well change.

Successful forecasting, therefore, will usually involve a more sophisticated analysis of trends.

The decomposition of time paths

One way in which the analysis of past data can be made more sophisticated is to identify different elements in the time path of sales. Figure 7.2 illustrates one such time path: the (imaginary) sales of woollen jumpers by firm X. It is shown by the continuous red line, labelled 'Actual sales'.

Four different sets of factors normally determine the shape of a time path like this.

Trends. These are increases or decreases in demand over a number of years. In our example, there is a long-term decrease in demand for this firm's woollen jumpers up to year 7 and then a slight recovery in demand thereafter.

Trends may reflect longer-term factors such as changes in population structure, or technological innovation or longer-term changes in fashion. Thus if wool were to become more expensive over time compared with other fibres, or if there were a gradual shift in tastes away from woollen jumpers and towards acrylic or cotton jumpers, or towards sweatshirts, this could explain the long-term decline in demand up to year 7. A gradual shift in tastes back towards natural fibres, and to wool in particular, or a gradual reduction in the price of wool, could then explain the subsequent recovery in demand.

Alternatively, trends may reflect changes over time in the structure of an industry. For example, an industry might become more and more competitive with new firms joining. This would tend to reduce sales for existing firms (unless the market were expanding very rapidly).

Cyclical fluctuations. In practice, the level of actual sales will not follow the trend line precisely. One reason for this is the cyclical upswings and downswings in business activity in the economy as a whole. In some years, incomes are rising rapidly and thus demand is buoyant. In other years, the economy will be in recession, with incomes falling. In these years, demand may well also fall. In our example, in boom years people may spend much more on clothes (including woollen jumpers), whereas in a recession, people may make do with their old clothes. The cyclical variations line thus rises above the trend line in boom years and falls below the trend line during a recession.

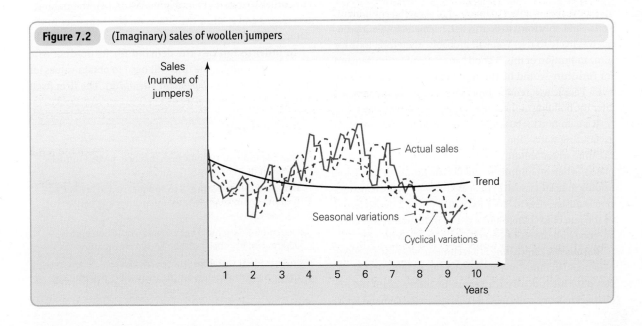

Figure 7.2   (Imaginary) sales of woollen jumpers

Seasonal fluctuations. The demand for many products also depends on the time of year. In the case of woollen jumpers, the peak demand is likely to be as winter approaches or just before Christmas. Thus the seasonal variations line is above the cyclical variations line in winter and below it in summer.

Short-term shifts in demand or supply. Finally, the actual sales line will also reflect various short-term shifts in demand or supply, causing it to diverge from the smooth seasonal variations line.

There are many reasons why the demand curve might shift. A competitor might increase its price, or there may be a sudden change in fashion, caused, say, by a pop group deciding to wear woollen jumpers for their new video: what was once seen as unfashionable by many people now suddenly becomes fashionable! Alternatively, there may be an unusually cold or hot, or wet or dry spell of weather.

Likewise there are various reasons for sudden shifts in supply conditions. For example, there may be a sheep disease which ruins the wool of infected sheep. As a result, the price of wool goes up, and sales of woollen jumpers fall.

These sudden shifts in demand or supply conditions are often referred to as 'random shocks' because they are usually unpredictable and temporarily move sales away from the trend. (Note that *long-term* shifts in demand and supply will be shown by a change in the trend line itself.)

Even with sophisticated time-series analysis, which breaks time paths into their constituent elements, there is still one major weakness: time-series analysis is merely a projection of the *past*. Most businesses will want to anticipate *changes* to sales trends – to forecast any deviations from the current time path. One method for doing this is *barometric forecasting*.

Barometric forecasting

Assume that you are a manager of a furniture business and are wondering whether to invest in new capital equipment. You would only want to do this if the demand for your product was likely to rise. You will probably, therefore, look for some indication of this. A good barometer of future demand for furniture would be the number of new houses being built. People will tend to buy new furniture some months after the building of their new house has commenced.

It is common for businesses to use **leading indicators** such as 'housing starts' (the number of houses built measured at the time when building starts rather than when it is completed) when attempting to predict the future. In fact some leading indicators, such as increased activity in the construction industry, rises in Stock Exchange prices, a depreciation of the rate of exchange and a rise in industrial confidence, are good indicators of a general upturn in the economy.

Barometric forecasting is a technique whereby forecasts of demand in industry A are based on an analysis of time-series data for industry (or sector, or indicator) B, where changes in B normally precede changes in the demand for A.

If B rises by *x* per cent, it can be assumed (other things being equal) that the demand for A will change by *y* per cent.

Barometric forecasting is widely used to predict *cyclical* changes: the effects of the upswings and downswings in the economy. It is thus useful not only for individual firms, but also for governments, which need to plan their policies to counteract the effects of the business cycle: the unemployment associated with recessions, or the inflation associated with booms in the economy.

Barometric forecasting suffers from two major weaknesses. The first is that it only allows forecasting a few months ahead – as far ahead as is the time lag between the change in the leading indicator and the variable being forecast. The second is that it can only give a general indication of changes in demand. It is simply another form of time-series analysis. Just because a relationship existed in the past between a leading indicator and the variable being forecast, it cannot be assumed that exactly the same relationship will exist in the future.

Normally, then, firms use barometric forecasting merely to give them a rough guide as to likely changes in demand for their product: i.e. whether it is likely to expand or contract, and by 'a lot' or by 'a little'. Nevertheless information on leading indicators is readily available in government or trade statistics.

To get a more precise forecast, firms must turn to their demand function, and estimate the effects of predicted changes in the determinants of the demand for their product.

Using demand functions in forecasts

We have seen (section 7.1) how demand functions can be used to show the effects of changes in the determinants of demand. For example, in the following model:

$$Q_d = a + bP + cP_s + dY + eA$$

where the demand for the product (Q_d) is determined by its price (P), the price of a substitute product (P_s), consumer incomes (Y) and advertising (A), the parameters (b, c, d and e) show the effects on Q_d of changes in the determinants.

In order to forecast the demand for its product (the **dependent variable**), the firm will need to obtain values for P, P_s, Y and A (the **independent variables**). The firm itself

---

Definitions

Leading indicators Indicators that help predict future trends in the economy.

Barometric forecasting A technique used to predict future economic trends based upon analysing patterns of time-series data.

Dependent variable That variable whose outcome is determined by other variables within an equation.

Independent variables Those variables that determine the dependent variable, but are themselves determined independently of the equation they are in.

chooses what price to charge and how much to advertise, and thus will decide the values of P and A. Forecasts of consumer incomes are readily available from a number of sources, such as the Bank of England, the Office for Budget Responsibility, HM Treasury and various private forecasting agencies, such as Ernst & Young's ITEM club. As far as P_s is concerned, here the firm will have to make an informed guess. Most firms will have a pretty good idea of the likely policies of their competitors.

Obviously, the accuracy of the forecasts will depend on the accuracy of the model as a description of the past relationship between demand and its determinants. Fortunately, this can be tested using various econometric techniques, and the reliability of the model can be determined. What is more, once the forecast is made, it can be compared with the actual outcome and the new data can be used to refine the model and improve its predictive power for next time.

The major strength of these econometric models is that they attempt to show how the many determinants affect demand. They also allow firms to feed in different assumptions to see how they will affect the outcome. Thus one forecast might be based on the assumption that the major competitor raises its price by x per cent, another that it raises its price by y per cent, and another that it leaves its price unchanged. The firm can then see how sensitive its sales will be to these possible changes. This is called *sensitivity analysis* and its use allows the firm to assess just how critical its assumptions are: would a rise in its rival's price by x per cent rather than y per cent make all the difference between a profit and a loss, or would it make little difference?

Econometric models can be highly complex, involving several equations and many variables. For example, there might be a separate variable for each of the prices and spec-ifications of all the various products in competition with this one.

Problems with econometric forecasting

But despite the apparent sophistication of some of the econometric models used by firms or by forecasting agencies, the forecasts are often wrong.

One reason for this is that the variables specified in the model cannot explain all the variation in the demand for the product. As we explained earlier in the chapter, it is normal to include an *error term* (ε) in order to take some account of these missing independent variables. But this error term will probably cover a number of unspecified determinants which are unlikely to move together over time. It does not therefore represent a stable or predictable 'determinant'. The larger the error term, the less confident we can be about using the equation to predict future demand.

Another reason for the inaccuracy of forecasts is that certain key determinants are difficult, if not impossible, to measure with any accuracy. This is a particular problem with subjective variables like taste and fashion. How can taste be modelled?

Perhaps the biggest weakness of using demand functions for forecasting is that the forecasts are themselves based on forecasts of what will happen to the various determinants. Take the cases of just two determinants: the specifications of competitors' products and consumer tastes. Just what changes will competitors make to their products? Just how will tastes change in the future? Consider the problems a clothing manufacturer might have in forecasting demand for a range of clothing! Income, advertising and the prices of the clothing will all be significant factors determining demand, but so too will be the range offered by other manufacturers and also people's perception of what is and what is not fashionable. But predicting changes in competitors' products and changes in fashion is notoriously difficult.

This is not to say that firms should give up in their attempt to forecast demand. Rather it suggests that they might need to conduct more sophisticated market research, and even then to accept that forecasts can only give an approximate indication of likely changes to demand.

Definition

Sensitivity analysis Assesses how sensitive an outcome is to different variables within an equation.

SUMMARY

1a Businesses seek information on consumer behaviour so as to predict market trends and improve strategic decision making.

1b One source of data is the firm's own information on how its sales have varied in the past with changes in the various determinants of demand, such as consumer incomes and the prices of competitors' products.

1c Another source of data is market surveys. These can generate a large quantity of cheap information. Care should be taken, however, to ensure that the sample of consumers investigated reflects the target consumer group.

1d Market experiments involve investigating consumer behaviour within a controlled environment. This method is particularly useful when considering new products where information is scarce.

1e Armed with data drawn from one or more of these sources, the business manager can attempt to estimate consumer demand using various statistical techniques, such as regression analysis.

1f The estimation of the effects on demand of a change in a particular variable, such as price, depends upon the assumption that all other factors that influence demand remain constant. However, factors that influence the demand for a product are constantly changing, hence there will always be the possibility of error when estimating the impact of change.

▶

2a It is not enough to know what will happen to demand if a determinant changes. Businesses will want to forecast what will actually happen to demand. To do this they can use a variety of methods: time-series analysis, barometric forecasting and econometric modelling.

2b Time-series analysis bases future trends on past events. Time-series data can be decomposed into different elements: trends, seasonal fluctuations, cyclical fluctuations and random shocks.

2c Barometric forecasting involves making predictions based upon changes in key leading indicators.

2d If a firm has estimated its demand function (using econometric techniques), it can then feed into this model forecasts of changes in the various determinants of demand and use the model to predict the effect on demand. The two main problems with this approach are: the reliability of the demand function (although this can be tested using econometric techniques), and the reliability of forecasts of changes in the various determinants of demand.

MyEconLab

This book can be supported by MyEconLab, which contains a range of additional resources, including an online homework and tutorial system designed to test and build your understanding.

You need both an access card and a course ID to access MyEconLab:

1. Is your lecturer using MyEconLab? Ask your lecturer for your course ID.

2. Has an access card been included with the book at a reduced cost? Check the inside back cover of the book.

3. If you have a course ID but no access card, go to: http://www.myeconlab.com/ to buy access to this interactive study programme.

REVIEW QUESTIONS

1 What are the relative strengths and weaknesses of using (a) market observations, (b) market surveys and (c) market experiments as means of gathering evidence on consumer demand?

2 You are working for a record company which is thinking of signing up some new bands. What market observations, market surveys and market experiments could you conduct to help you decide which bands to sign?

3 You are about to launch a new range of cosmetics, but you are still to decide upon the content and structure of your advertising campaign. Consider how market surveys and market experiments might be used to help you assess consumer perceptions of the product. What limitations might each of the research methods have in helping you gather data?

4 The following is an estimate of an historical UK market demand curve for instant coffee. It has been derived (using a computer regression package) from actual data for the years 1973–85.

$$Q_c = 0.042 + 0.068P_c + 0.136P_T + 0.0067Y$$

where:

Q_c is the quantity of instant coffee purchased in ounces per person per week;

P_c and P_T are respectively the 'real' prices of instant coffee and tea, calculated by dividing their market prices in pence per lb by the retail price index for all food (RPI) (1980 = 100);

Y is an index of real personal disposable income (1980 = 100): i.e. household income after tax.

The following table gives the prices of coffee and tea and real disposable income for three years (1973, 1985 and 1990).

Year	Market price of coffee (MP_c) (pence per lb)	RPI of all food (1980 = 100)	Real price of coffee ($P_c = MP_c/RPI \times 100$)	Market price of tea (MP_T) (pence per lb)	Real price of tea ($P_T = MP_T/RPI \times 100$)	Index of real disposable income (Y) (1980 = 100)
1973	111.33	35.20		35.53		89.30
1985	511.65	131.40		184.39		106.10
1990	585.19	165.89		212.77		128.62

a) Fill in the columns for the real price of coffee (P_c) and the real price of tea (P_T).

b) Use the above equation to estimate the demand for instant coffee in 1973.

c) Calculate the percentage growth in the market over the 13-year sample period (1973–85).

d) The equation was used to forecast the demand for instant coffee in 1990. Purchases were estimated at 0.7543 ounces per person per week.

   (i) Verify this from the equation.

   (ii) The actual level of purchases is recorded as 0.48 ounces per week. Suggest reasons why the equation seriously over-estimates the level of demand for 1990.

5 Outline the alternative methods a business might use to forecast demand. How reliable do you think such methods are?

6 Imagine that you are an airline attempting to forecast demand for seats over the next two or three years. What, do you think, could be used as leading indicators?

Products, marketing and advertising

Business issues covered in this chapter

■ In what ways can firms differentiate their products from those of their rivals?
■ What strategies can firms adopt for gaining market share, developing their products and marketing them?
■ What elements are likely to be contained in a marketing strategy?
■ How extensive is advertising in the UK and how does it vary from product to product?
■ What are the effects of advertising and what makes a successful advertising campaign?

For most firms, selling their product is not simply a question of estimating demand and then choosing an appropriate price and level of production. In other words, they do not simply take their market as given. Instead they will seek to *influence* demand. They will do this by developing their product and differentiating it from those of their rivals, and then marketing it by advertising and other forms of product promotion. KI 1 p 10

What firms are engaging in here is *non-price competition*. In such situations the job of the manager can be quite complex. It is likely to involve making a series of strategic decisions, not just concerning price, but also concerning each product's design and quality, its marketing and advertising, and the provision of various forms of after-sales service.

Central to non-price competition is *product differentiation*. Most firms' products differ in various ways from those of their rivals. Take the case of washing machines. Although all washing machines wash clothes, and as such are close substitutes for each other, there are many differences between brands. They differ not only in price, but also in their capacity, their styling, their range of programmes, their economy in the use of electricity, hot water and detergent, their reliability, their noise, their after-sales service, etc. Firms will attempt to design their product so that they can stress its advantages (real or imaginary) over the competitor brands. Just think of the specific features of particular models of car, hi-fi equipment or brands of cosmetic, and then consider the ways in which these features are stressed by advertisements. In fact, think of virtually any advertisement and consider how it stresses the features of that particular brand.

Definitions

Non-price competition Competition in terms of product promotion (advertising, packaging, etc.) or product development.

Product differentiation Where a firm's product is in some way distinct from its rivals' products.

8.1 PRODUCT DIFFERENTIATION

Features of a product

A product has many dimensions, and a strategy to differentiate a product may focus on one or more of these dimensions.

- *Technical standards.* These relate to the product's level of technical sophistication: how advanced it is in relation to the current state of technology. This would be a very important product dimension if, for example, you were purchasing a PC.
- *Quality standards.* These relate to aspects such as the quality of the materials used in the product's construction and the care taken in assembly. These will affect the product's durability and reliability. The purchase of consumer durables, such as televisions, tablets and toys, will be strongly influenced by quality standards.
- *Design characteristics.* These relate to the product's direct appeal to the consumer in terms of appearance or operating features. Examples of design characteristics are colour, style and even packaging. A major reason for the success of Apple's iPhone has been its design and appearance. This is a characteristic its leading rival Samsung has focused on with the launch of the Galaxy 6 Edge. The demand for fashion products such as clothing will also be strongly influenced by design characteristics.
- *Service characteristics.* This aspect is not directly concerned with the product itself, but with the support and back-up given to the customer after the product has been sold. Servicing, product maintenance and guarantees would be included under this heading. When purchasing a new car, the quality of after-sales service might strongly influence the choice you make.

Any given product will possess a 'bundle' of the above attributes. Within any product category, each brand is likely to have a different mix of technical and quality standards and design and service characteristics. Consumers will select the bundle of attributes or characteristics they most prefer (see section 6.3). The fact that these different dimensions exist means that producers can focus the marketing of their product on factors other than price – they can engage in non-price competition.

Vertical and horizontal product differentiation

When firms are seeking to differentiate their product from those of their rivals (product differentiation), one important distinction they must consider is that between *vertical* and *horizontal* differentiation.

Vertical product differentiation. This is where products differ in quality, with some being perceived as superior and others as inferior. In general, the better the quality, the more expensive will the product be. Take the case of a mobile phone handset. The cheaper (inferior) models will just have basic functions. More expensive models will have more and better functions, such as higher screen resolution, cameras with more megapixels, louder speakers, better video quality and faster charging times.

Vertical product differentiation will usually be in terms of the quantity and quality of functions and/or the durability of the product (often a reflection of the quality of the materials used and the care spent in making the product). Thus a garment will normally be regarded as superior if it is better made and uses high-quality cloth. In general, the vertical quality differences between products will tend to reflect differences in production costs.

Horizontal product differentiation. This refers to differences between products that are not generally regarded as superior or inferior, but merely reflections of the different tastes of different consumers. One person may prefer black shoes and another brown. One may prefer milk chocolate, another plain. Within any product range there may be varieties which differ in respect to style, design, flavour, colour, etc. Such attributes are neither better, nor worse, but are simply different.

Horizontal differences within a range do not significantly alter the costs of production, and it is common for the different varieties to have the same price. A pot of red paint is likely to be the same price as a pot of blue (of the same brand). The point is that the products, although horizontally different, are of comparable quality.

> **Pause for thought**
>
> *Identify two other products that are vertically differentiated, two that are horizontally differentiated and two that are both.*

In practice, most product ranges will have a mixture of horizontal and vertical differentiation. For example, some of the differences between different makes and models of motor car will be vertical (e.g. luxury or basic internal fittings, acceleration and fuel consumption); some will be horizontal (e.g. hatchback or saloon, colour and style).

> **Definitions**
>
> **Vertical product differentiation** Where a firm's product differs from its rivals' products with respect to quality.
>
> **Horizontal product differentiation** Where a firm's product differs from its rivals' products, although the products are seen to be of a similar quality.

Market segmentation

Different features of a product will appeal to different consumers. This applies both to vertically differentiated features and to horizontally differentiated ones. Where features are quite distinct, and where particular features or groups of features can be seen to appeal to a particular category of consumers, it might be useful for producers to divide the market into segments. Taking the example of cars again,

the market could be divided into luxury cars, large, medium and small family cars, sports cars, multi-terrain vehicles, six-seater people carriers, etc. Each type of car occupies a distinct market segment, and within each segment the individual models are likely to be both horizontally and vertically differentiated from competitor models.

When consumer tastes change over time, or where existing models do not cater for every taste, a firm may be able to

---

BOX 8.1	THE BATTLE OF THE BRANDS

The rise, fall and rise of own-label brands

From fairly humble beginnings, supermarket own-label brands really took off in the late 1980s and early 1990s. By 1995 they accounted for over half of supermarket sales in the UK.

However, by the mid-2000s own-label brands' share of supermarket sales had fallen to around one-third. They became popular again in the late 2000s and the growth in sales continued into the early years of this decade. UK retail sales of own-label food and non-alcoholic drink were estimated to be £46.8 billion in 2013.[1] This represented a market share of 48 per cent.

The sales of these goods are much higher in some product categories than they are in others. For example, market shares vary from close to 100 per cent for fresh fruit to below 10 per cent for products such as baby food and chocolate.

So, how do own-label brands compete? Why have they been far more successful in some categories than others? Why have their fortunes fluctuated over time?

They don't have significant differences in costs of production . . .

Branded manufacturers were always thought to be able to take advantage of large economies of scale in sourcing and production. However, new technologies and close working relationships between retailers and suppliers have allowed supermarkets to provide own-label products in smaller batches but at lower costs, thus offsetting any advantage that brand manufacturers may have. Technology has also helped to improve the quality of products, making it possible for own-label producers to imitate the ideas of brand manufacturers and engage in their own innovations.

. . . but they do offer different product characteristics

Own-label products are not a homogenous group all with the same characteristics. Instead they can be placed into three broad categories – value/economy, standard and premium.

As the name suggests, the value/economy own-label products are the cheapest. Research by Mintel, illustrated in Table (a), shows that relatively more consumers believe that these products offer value for money and are not overpriced. However, only 8 per cent of people associate them with high quality, whereas for branded goods the figure is 52 per cent. Examples of economy own-label products include Tesco 'Everyday Value', Sainsbury's 'Basics' and Aldi's 'Everyday Essentials'.

The widest variety of own-label products is the standard range. Their prices fall somewhere between those of the premium and economy products. Slightly more consumers perceive them as being of higher quality than the value range, whereas slightly fewer consumers think they are value for money. Standard own-label products usually just display the name of the supermarket such as Tesco or Sainsbury's, although Asda uses the label 'Chosen by you'.

Premium own-label products are positioned in the higher end of the market and are much more associated with quality than the other own-label products. Compared with branded goods, they are still less likely to be associated with high quality and other positive characteristics, such as being trustworthy and authentic. However, they do score better on value for money. Examples of premium own-label products include Sainsbury's 'Taste the Difference', Tesco's 'Finest' and Morrison's 'M Signature'. Interestingly there appears to be very little difference between any of the own-label and branded products on consumer perceptions such as ethically responsible or caring about my health.

The balance between quality and price remains a difficult combination for supermarkets to get right. A low price on its own is not enough as the sales of standard own-label products are still significantly greater than value own-label products.

(a) Perceived characteristics of branded and own-label products, 2013

	Percentage of respondents			
	Branded product	Own-label product		
Characteristic		Value/ econ	Standard	Premium
High quality	52	8	13	36
Trustworthy	42	16	22	20
Overpriced	30	1	2	25
Authentic	29	6	7	10
Worth paying for	25	3	3	15
Ethically responsible	6	4	6	5
Value for money	10	68	63	24
Cares about my health	5	4	6	5

Source: From *Mintel Reports (2014)*, Mintel Group Ltd

---

[1]Mintel, *The private label food consumer*, 2014.

They take advantage of changing economic prosperity

The decline in market share of own-brands from the early 1990s to 2007 was partly due to a period of prolonged economic growth. The rise in disposable income during this period led to increased conspicuous consumption, and many branded goods are associated with affluence and increased quality of lifestyle.

The recessions of the early 1990s and 2008–9, by contrast, saw a growth in the market share of own-label brands as consumers sought to economise. Supermarkets were able to tap into the price sensitivity of consumers with a range of value-for-money own-label products. Research carried out by Mintel found that 27.4 per cent of survey respondents stated that in the 12 months prior to January 2011 they had switched from buying branded to cheaper own-label groceries.

Even with sustained economic growth since the beginning of 2013, the sales of own-label products has continued to grow. With very moderate increases in their real income, consumers have remained very price sensitive.

Nevertheless, customers still value brands. Brand manufacturers rely on consumers developing a loyal attachment to a product over a number of years. This is strengthened by substantial investments in advertising and marketing. Branding is concerned with conveying an image and a style of living, as well as showing the product's function, its convenience and its value. All this takes time to develop, and successful brands, such as Kellogg's and Hovis, have been popular for over 100 years.

Brands dominate many market segments . . .

While the trend in recent times has been for customers to switch back to own-label brands, it is important to recognise that there is still substantial variability in own-label penetration across products. As Table (b) illustrates, in some product segments, the penetration of supermarkets' own-brands is considerable (e.g. fresh fruit and vegetables, ready meals, milk and pasta). In others, however, branded products dominate (e.g. baby food, chocolate and carbonated soft drinks).

Where products are viewed by the customer as fairly homogeneous, or require limited technological input, product differentiation or unique selling points (USP) are difficult for brands to achieve. Fruit, vegetables, milk and pasta are clear examples of this. For example, 4 in 10 consumers believe that own-label dry pasta is tastier than branded varieties whereas only 28 per cent believe that the branded products are tastier. For these types of products supermarket own-labels can compete effectively on price. The example of ready meals is perhaps more interesting as differentiation is more likely. However, when ready meals were first introduced they were predominately own-label products and branded versions may have found it difficult to enter the market because of the limited chilled cabinet space in supermarkets.

For other goods that can be more easily differentiated, consumers may identify the quality of a product with a particular brand. Carbonated soft drinks (CSDs) are a good example, with famous names such as Coca-Cola and Pepsi. When surveyed, two-thirds of consumers agreed that they preferred the taste of a branded CSD to an own-label product. This has made it difficult for own-label products to compete and they have only managed to obtain a market share of 8.4 per cent. Another example of perceived quality differences is in the market for washing-up liquid. The Fairy brand is said to last twice as long as its own-label competitors.

Branded products may also target a particular group (defined by gender, age or socioeconomic status), or reflect a certain style of living (e.g. healthy eating). People are also more likely to choose a branded item when it is being purchased as a treat or a present. In these types of market, brands do not have to compete strictly on price as successful differentiation enables them to charge premium prices. Research by Mintel indicated that 54 per cent of people were willing to pay a higher price for branded chocolate, while 40 per cent were willing to pay a higher price for branded breakfast cereals.

(b) Market penetration of own-label products in selected UK markets, 2014

Market segment	Market share (%)
Fresh fruit and vegetables	95.1
Ready meals	87.2
Milk	66.0
Pasta	62.5
Cakes	48.7
Ice cream	25.6
Breakfast cereals	20.8
Biscuits	18.4
Sugar confectionery	14.4
Carbonated soft drinks	8.4
Chocolate confectionery	4.9
Baby food and drink	0.8

Source: From *Mintel Reports (2014)*, Mintel Group Ltd

One disadvantage for own-label products is that the advertising expenditure by supermarkets is largely concerned with branding the store rather than a particular product. This makes their promotional expenditures rather diluted. Brand manufacturers, on the other hand, are specialists in targeting their advertising and promotional expenditures towards particular markets. They achieve economies from marketing the brand, with the result that their sales per pound of promotional expenditure are higher. Economies of scale in marketing provide a powerful competitive advantage for brand manufacturers.

. . . but brand manufacturers still have to be responsive to competitive pressures from low-cost own-label rivals

The suppliers of branded goods could respond to the increase in competition from own-label products in a number of different ways – innovation intensity, advertising and cutting prices.

Greater product innovation by the suppliers of branded goods might be an effective way of reducing the sales of own-label products. There is evidence that some suppliers have responded in this way. For example, 61 per cent of new product launches in food and non-alcoholic drink from January to September 2014 were by the suppliers of branded products whereas 39 per cent were from own-labels.

An alternative response might be to increase expenditure on advertising in an attempt to differentiate the product further

▶

in the minds of consumers. Interesting recent examples have occurred in the market for food and drink that people buy as treats, such as biscuits, chocolate and CSDs. Rather than focusing on the attributes or functionality of the product, a number of recent advertising campaigns have focused on emotional cues such as how consuming the product makes people feel. For example, McVitie's launched a £12 million media campaign in 2014 that centred on how eating its biscuits would 'sweeten' the day. Cadbury's recent advertising has also stressed the 'Feel the joy' factor of eating its chocolate products.

A final response might be for the supplier of branded products to cut prices. However, this is likely to be only a temporary option, such as a 'special offer'. The impact of sustained price cuts might have a negative impact on the consumers' perception of the brand. It will also reduce profitability if the supplier is unable to reduce its costs sufficiently.

1. *How has the improvement in the quality of own-brands affected the price elasticity of demand for branded products? What implications does this have for the pricing strategy of brand manufacturers?*
2. *Why don't brand manufacturers readily engage in the production of supermarket own-label products?*
3. *How might brand manufacturers respond to the development of a new product line?*

identify a new segment of the market – a **market niche**. Having identified the appropriate market niche for its product, the marketing division within the firm will then set about targeting the relevant consumer group(s) and developing an appropriate strategy for promoting the product. (In the next section we will explore more closely those factors which are likely to influence a business's marketing strategy.)

> **Definition**
>
> **Market niche** A part of a market (or new market) that has not been filled by an existing brand or business.

8.2 MARKETING THE PRODUCT

What is marketing?

There is no single accepted definition of marketing. It is generally agreed, however, that marketing covers the following activities: establishing the strength of consumer demand in existing parts of the market, and potential demand in new niches; developing an attractive and distinct image for the product; informing potential consumers of various features of the product; fostering a desire by consumers for the product; and, in the light of all these, persuading consumers to buy the product.

Clearly, marketing must be seen within the overall goals of the firm. There would be little point in spending vast sums of money in promoting a product if it led to only a modest increase in sales and sales revenue.

Product/market strategy

KI 23
p 197

Once the nature and strength of consumer demand (both current and potential) have been identified, the business will set about meeting and influencing this demand. In most cases it will be hoping to achieve a growth in sales. To do this, one of the first things the firm must decide is its *product/market strategy*. This will involve addressing two major questions:

- Should it focus on promoting its existing product, or should it develop new products?
- Should it focus on gaining a bigger share of its existing market, or should it seek to break into new markets?

In 1957 Igor Ansoff illustrated these choices in what he called a *growth vector matrix*. This is illustrated in Figure 8.1.

> **Definition**
>
> **Growth vector matrix** A means by which a business might assess its product/market strategy.

> **Figure 8.1** Growth vector components 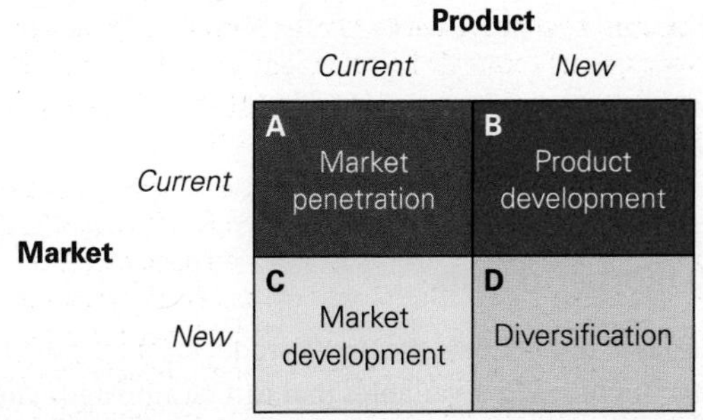
>
> | | | Product | |
> | | | Current | New |
> | **Market** | Current | **A** Market penetration | **B** Product development |
> | | New | **C** Market development | **D** Diversification |
>
> Source: I. Ansoff, *Corporate Strategy* (McGraw-Hill, 1965); 'Strategies for diversification', *Harvard Business Review*, (September–October 1957)

The four boxes show the possible combinations of answers to the above questions: Box A – *market penetration* (current product, current market); Box B – *product development* (new product, current market); Box C – *market development* (current product, new market); Box D – *diversification* (new product, new market).

- *Market penetration.* In the market penetration strategy, the business will seek not only to retain existing customers, but also to expand its customer base with current products in current markets. Of the four strategies, this is generally the least risky: the business will be able to play to its product strengths and draw on its knowledge of the market. The business's marketing strategy will tend to focus upon aggressive product promotion and distribution. Such a strategy, however, is likely to lead to fierce competition from current business rivals, especially if the overall market is not expanding and if the firm can therefore gain an increase in sales only by taking market share from its rivals.
- *Product development.* Product development strategies will involve introducing new models and designs in current markets. This may involve either vertical differentiation (e.g. the introduction of an upgraded model) or horizontal differentiation (e.g. the introduction of a new style).
- *Market development.* With a market development strategy the business will seek increased sales of current products by expanding into new markets. These may be in a different geographical location (e.g. overseas), or new market segments. Alternatively, the strategy may involve finding new uses and applications for the product.
- *Diversification.* A diversification strategy will involve the business expanding into new markets with new products. Of all the strategies, this is the most risky given the unknown factors that the business is likely to face.

Once the product/market strategy has been decided upon, the business will then attempt to devise a suitable *marketing strategy*. This will involve looking at the marketing mix.

> ### Pause for thought
>
> *What unknown factors is the business likely to face following a diversification strategy?*

The marketing mix

In order to differentiate the firm's product from those of its rivals, there are four variables that can be adjusted. These are as follows:

- product;
- price;

- place (distribution);
- promotion.

The particular combination of these variables, known as 'the four Ps', represents the business's **marketing mix**, and it is around a manipulation of them that the business will devise its marketing strategy.

Figure 8.2 illustrates the various considerations that might be taken into account when looking at product, price, place and promotion.

- *Product considerations.* These involve issues such as quality and reliability, as well as branding, packaging and after-sales service.
- *Pricing considerations.* These involve not only the product's basic price in relation to those of competitors' products, but also opportunities for practising price discrimination (the practice of charging different prices in different parts of the market: see Chapter 17), offering discounts to particular customers, and adjusting the terms of payment for the product.
- *Place considerations.* These focus on the product's distribution network, and involve issues such as where the business's retail outlets should be located, what warehouse facilities the business might require, and how the product should be transported to the market.
- *Promotion considerations.* These focus primarily upon the amount and type of advertising the business should use. In addition, promotion issues might also include selling techniques, special offers, trial discounts and various other public relations 'gimmicks'.

Every product is likely to have a distinct marketing *mix* of these four variables. Thus we cannot talk about an ideal value for one (e.g. the best price), without considering the other three. What is more, the most appropriate mix will vary from product to product and from market to market. If you wanted to sell a Rolls-Royce, you would be unlikely to sell any more by offering free promotional gifts or expanding the number of retail outlets. You might sell more Rolls-Royces, however, if you were to improve their specifications or offer more favourable methods of payment.

What the firm must seek to do is to estimate how sensitive demand is to the various aspects of marketing. The greater the sensitivity (elasticity) in each case, the more the firms should focus on that particular aspect. It must be careful, however, that changing one aspect of marketing does not conflict with another. For example, there would be lit-

> ### Definition
>
> **Marketing mix** The mix of product, price, place (distribution) and promotion that will determine a business's marketing strategy.

Figure 8.2   Model of the customer market offering dimensions of the marketing mix

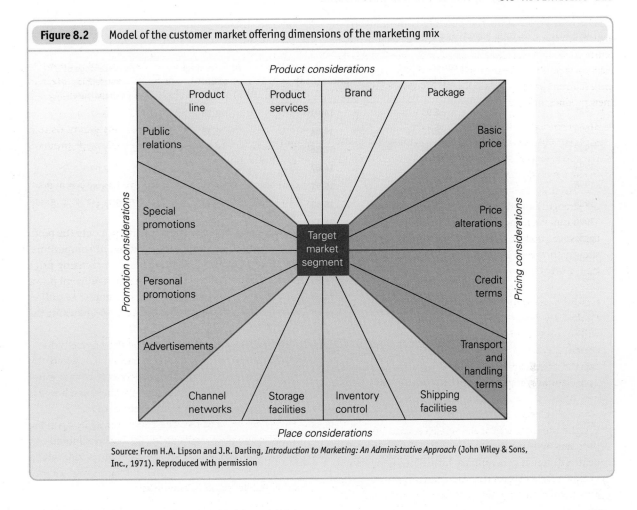

Source: From H.A. Lipson and J.R. Darling, *Introduction to Marketing: An Administrative Approach* (John Wiley & Sons, Inc., 1971). Reproduced with permission

tle point in improving the product's quality if, at the same time, the product was promoted by the use of marketing gimmicks that led consumers to believe they were buying an inferior, 'mass consumption' product.

Another consideration that must be taken into account is the stage in the product's life cycle (see section 17.6). The most appropriate marketing mix for a new and hence unfamiliar product, and one which may be facing little in the way of competition, may well be totally inappropriate for a product that is long established and may be struggling against competitors to maintain its market share.

8.3   ADVERTISING

One of the most important aspects of marketing is advertising. The major aim of advertising is to sell more products, and businesses spend a vast quantity of money on advertising to achieve this goal. By advertising, the business will not only be informing the consumer of the product's existence and availability, but also deliberately attempting to persuade and entice the consumer to purchase the good. In doing so, it will tend to stress the specific and unique qualities of this firm's product over those of its rivals. This will be discussed in more detail below.

Advertising facts and figures

Advertising and the state of the economy

Advertising expenditure, like other business expenditures, is subject to the cyclical movement of the national economy. Indeed, advertising is particularly sensitive to the ups and downs in the economy. In times of rising demand and growing profitability of business, expenditure on advertising tends to rise substantially. Thus between 1984 and 1989, when UK GDP in real terms (i.e. after accounting for

Table 8.1	UK total advertising expenditure			
	At current prices (£bn)	At constant (2014) prices (£bn)	As percentage of GDP*	As percentage of household expenditure
1988	6.95	14.01	1.36	2.37
1990	8.17	14.64	1.33	2.34
1992	8.05	12.86	1.20	2.04
1994	9.21	14.07	1.24	2.09
1996	10.95	15.91	1.31	2.20
1998	13.10	18.41	1.42	2.31
2000	15.37	21.13	1.50	2.41
2002	15.24	20.45	1.36	2.20
2004	16.81	21.96	1.34	2.18
2006	16.33	20.43	1.16	1.92
2007	17.08	20.88	1.15	1.90
2008	16.59	19.57	1.09	1.79
2009	14.50	16.75	0.98	1.60
2010	15.68	17.53	1.01	1.64
2011	16.10	17.23	1.00	1.63
2012	17.17	17.87	1.04	1.68
2013	17.88	18.15	1.04	1.69
2014	18.58	18.58	1.04	1.68

Note: *Based on nominal values

Source: Based on data from Advertising Association/WARC, *Expenditure Report*, AA/WARC UK Expenditure (various years), reproduced with permission

inflation) increased by 22 per cent, advertising expenditure increased by 48 per cent in real terms. Similarly, in the long period of economic growth from 1992 to 2000, advertising expenditure in real terms grew faster, accounting for a higher and higher proportion of household expenditure (see Table 8.1).

Conversely, in times of recession or very low economic growth, advertising budgets tend to be cut. Thus there was a 15 per cent fall in advertising expenditure in real terms between 1989 (the peak of the 1980s boom) and 1991 (a year of recession). During the most recent recession there was a fall in real terms of 6.3 per cent in 2008 and 14.4 per cent in 2009.

With the return to economic growth advertising expenditure has started to increase once again, with a 2.2 per cent increase in real terms in 2014. However, it is still some way below the peak of the mid-2000s.

Advertising media

When considering advertising expenditure by the main categories of media, there has been a long historical trend over which total press advertising (national, local and magazine) has fallen as a proportion of total advertising. It fell from a peak of nearly 90 per cent in 1953 to 18.7 per cent in 2014, although there was some growth in expenditure

on digital adverts, which partly offset the fall in printed adverts.

Advertising on television (which only started in the UK in the mid-1950s with the birth of ITV) now accounts for some 25.4 per cent of total advertising expenditure. The majority of this expenditure (91 per cent) is on sports advertising.

The most dramatic growth in advertising expenditure, however, is on the Internet, which increased from virtually nothing in 1998 to 26.1 per cent in 2012 and 37.2 per cent in 2014.

Figure 8.3 compares the proportions in 2014 with 2005.

Product sectors

The distribution of advertising expenditure by product sectors shows that some 23 per cent of advertising expenditure is for consumables: i.e. food, drink, cosmetics, etc. A further 17 per cent is for consumer durables such as household appliances and equipment, and 11 per cent for retailers, such as supermarkets. Both these sectors tend to be dominated by just a few firms producing each type of product. This type of market is known as an 'oligopoly', which is Greek for 'few sellers'. Oligopolists often compete heavily in terms of product differentiation and advertising. (Oligopoly is examined in Chapter 12.)

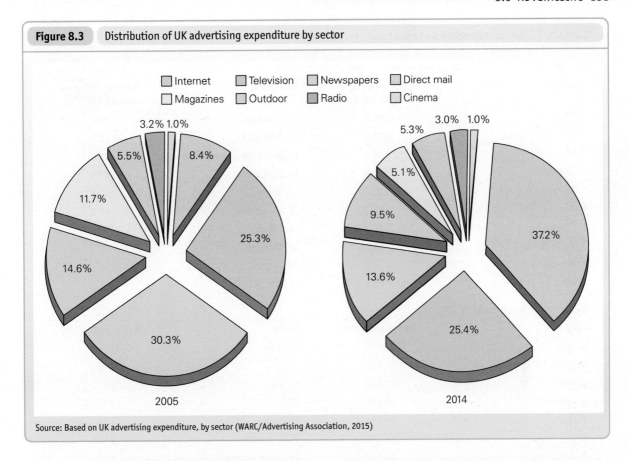

Figure 8.3 Distribution of UK advertising expenditure by sector

Legend: Internet, Television, Newspapers, Direct mail, Magazines, Outdoor, Radio, Cinema

2005: 3.2%, 1.0%, 8.4%, 5.5%, 11.7%, 25.3%, 14.6%, 30.3%

2014: 3.0%, 1.0%, 5.3%, 5.1%, 9.5%, 37.2%, 13.6%, 25.4%

Source: Based on UK advertising expenditure, by sector (WARC/Advertising Association, 2015)

Details of the allocation of advertising expenditure between the different product sectors are given in Table 8.2.

If we take the 20 companies with the highest advertising expenditure, most are within the consumables, consumer durables and retail sectors. The same applies to the 20 most valuable brands (see Table 8.3).

Pause for thought

Try to use the ideas of the growth vector matrix and marketing mix to explain the reasons for the high advertising expenditures of a few of the companies in Table 8.3.

The advertising/sales ratio

If we wished to consider the intensity of advertising within a given product sector, we could construct an ***advertising/sales ratio***. This relates the total expenditure on advertising for a particular product to the total value of product sales. A selection of products and their advertising/sales ratios in the USA can be seen in Table 8.4.

Transportation services have the highest advertising/sales ratio at 26.7 per cent. This tells us that 26.7 per cent of all earnings by firms supplying transportation services (rail, air, taxis, etc.) goes on advertising their product. At the other extreme, companies producing and/or selling computer storage devices spend only 0.3 per cent of their sales revenue on advertising their products.

Table 8.2 UK advertising expenditure by product sector (percentage of total advertising expenditure)

	1986	1990	1995	2000	2005	2008	2014
Retail	14	12	18	14	15	14	11
Industrial	9	7	8	17	13	12	15
Financial	10	11	10	12	14	13	12
Government	3	3	3	2	5	6	5
Services	9	11	11	11	16	17	17
Durables	21	20	20	21	17	17	17
Consumables	35	36	31	24	20	21	23
Total	100	100	100	100	100	100	100

Source: Based on data from Advertising Association/WARC, *Expenditure Report*, AA/WARC UK Expenditure (2014), reproduced with permission

The wide variation in advertising intensity can be put down to two factors: market structure and product characteristics. As mentioned above, oligopolistic markets are

Definition

Advertising/sales ratio A ratio that reflects the intensity of advertising within a market.

Table 8.3	The top advertisers and advertising brands in the UK

(a) The top 20 advertisers by expenditure in the UK (2013)

Advertiser	Total spending on advertising (£m)	Advertiser	Total spending on advertising (£m)
1. BSkyB	264.3	11. Vodafone	74.5
2. Procter & Gamble	117.2	12. McDonald's	72.1
3. BT	149.7	13. Reckitt Benckiser	68.9
4. Unilever UK	119.1	14. L'Oréal Paris	63.5
5. Tesco	116.2	15. Nestlé	63.1
6. Asda	97.0	16. Lloyds Bank	62.2
7. TalkTalk Group	92.5	17. Sainsbury's	60.4
8. Virgin Media	88.3	18. Microsoft	60.2
9. Morrison's	81.5	19. British Gas	60.1
10. DFS	75.6	20. Aldi	56.5

(b) The top 20 brands in the UK (2015)

Brand	Market value ($m)	Brand	Market value ($m)
1. Shell	30 716	11. Tesco	11 052
2. Vodafone	27 287	12. EY	10 994
3. HSBC	27 280	13. Sky	8 699
4. Orange	19 867	14. O$_2$	8 359
5. PwC	17 330	15. Asda	8 031
6. BT	16 175	16. Prudential	7 877
7. BP	14 743	17. Lloyds Banking	6 995
8. Deloitte	14 694	18. Sainsbury's	6 694
9. Barclays	14 179	19. Land Rover	6 521
10. KPMG	12 332	20. Aviva	6 194

Source: Nielsen and Brand Finance. Available from www.rankingthebrands.com, reproduced with permission

Table 8.4	US Advertising/sales ratio: 2014

Product category	Advertising/ sales ratio (%)	Product category	Advertising/ sales ratio (%)
Transportation services	26.7	Paints, varnishes, lacquers	2.3
Perfumes, cosmetics, etc.	21.1	Dairy products	2.1
Soap, detergent, toilet preparations	12.3	Household appliances	1.8
Educational services	11.1	Personal credit institutions	1.7
Motion picture, videotape production	8.7	Hotels and motels	1.3
Household furniture	6.8	Accident and health insurance	1.0
Amusement parks	6.1	Industrial organic chemicals	0.9
Food and kindred products	5.5	Farm machinery and equipment	0.6
Sugar and confectionery products	4.6	Management consulting services	0.6
Department stores	4.4	Computer and office equipment	0.6
Beverages	3.9	Hospital and medical svc plans	0.4
Investment advice	3.1	Computer storage devices	0.3
Motor vehicles and car bodies	2.6		

Source: Based on data from Advertising Association/WARC, *2014 Advertising Ratios and Budgets*, Schonfeld and Associates, Inc. (2015), reproduced with permission

likely to see high advertising outlays. But what types of product will be the most heavily advertised? There are three main categories here.

The first category is goods that represent a large outlay for consumers (e.g. furniture, electrical goods and other consumer durables). Consumers will not want to make a wrong decision: it would be an expensive mistake. They will thus tend to be cautious in their purchasing decision and will be likely to search for information before selecting a particular product. Advertisers will seek to provide information (but, of course, only information relating to their particular product).

The second category is new products which producers are attempting to establish on the market. The third category is goods, such as educational services, which experience constant changes in their customer base.

Products with the lowest advertising/sales ratio will, by contrast, tend to be those goods whose specifications change very little, or where competition is minimal, or where they are selling to just a few large companies that will be familiar with the equipment or other inputs they are buying. This helps to explain why the figure for product categories such as computer storage devices and hospital and medical plans is so low.

The intended effects of advertising

We have argued that the main aim of advertising is to sell more of the product. But when we are told that brand X will make us more beautiful, enrich our lives, wash our clothes whiter, give us get-up-and-go, give us a new taste sensation or make us the envy of our friends, just what are the advertisers up to? Are they merely trying to persuade consumers to buy more?

In fact, there is a bit more to it than this. Advertisers are trying to do two things:

- shift the product's demand curve to the right;
- make it less price elastic.

This is illustrated in Figure 8.4. D_1 shows the original demand curve with price at P_1 and sales at Q_1. D_2 shows the curve after an advertising campaign. The rightward shift allows an increased quantity (Q_2) to be sold at the original price. If, at the same time, the demand is made less elastic, the firm can also raise its price and still experience an increase in sales. Thus in the diagram, price can be raised to P_2 and sales will be Q_3 – still substantially above Q_1. The total gain in revenue is shown by the shaded area.

How can advertising bring about this new demand curve?

Shifting the demand curve to the right. This will occur if the advertising brings the product to more people's attention and if it increases people's desire for the product.

Making the demand curve less elastic. This will occur if the advertising creates greater brand loyalty (i.e. lowering the

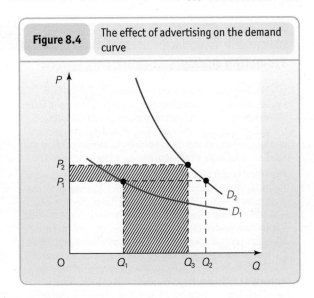

Figure 8.4 The effect of advertising on the demand curve

product's cross-elasticity of demand). People must be led to believe (rightly or wrongly) that competitors' brands are inferior. This will allow the firm to raise its price above that of its rivals with no significant fall in sales. There will be only a small substitution effect of this price rise because consumers have been led to believe that there are no close substitutes.

The more successful an advertising campaign is, the more it will shift the demand curve to the right and the more it will reduce the price elasticity of demand.

Assessing the effects of advertising

The supporters of advertising claim that not only is it an important freedom for firms, but it also provides specific benefits for the consumer. By contrast, critics of advertising suggest that it can impose serious costs on the consumer and on society in general. In this section we will assess the basis of this difference.

> ### Pause for thought
>
> *Before considering the points listed below, see if you can identify the main arguments both for and against the use of advertising.*

The arguments put forward in favour of advertising include the following:

- Advertising provides information to consumers on what products are available.
- Advertising may be necessary in order to introduce new products. Without it, firms would find it difficult to break into markets in which there were established brands. In other words, it is a means of breaking down barriers to the entry of new firms and products.

KI 8
p 42

BOX 8.2 ADVERTISING AND THE LONG RUN

Promoting quality

It is relatively straightforward to measure the short-term impact of an advertising campaign; a simple before and after assessment of sales will normally give a good indication of the advertising's effectiveness. But what about the medium- and longer-term effects of an advertising campaign? How will sales and profits be affected over, say, a five-year period?

The typical impact of advertising on a product's sales is shown in Figure (a). Assume that there is an advertising campaign for the product between time T_1 and T_2. There is a direct effect on sales while the advertising lasts and shortly afterwards. Sales rise from S_1 to S_2. After a while (beyond time T_3), the direct effect of the advertising begins to wear off, and wears off completely by time T_4. This is illustrated by the dashed line. But the higher level of sales declines much more slowly, given that many of the new customers continue to buy the product out of habit. Sales will eventually level off (at point T_5). It is likely, however, that sales will not return to the original level of S_1; there will be some new customers who will stick with the product over the long term. This long-term effect is shown by the increase in sales from S_1 to S_3.

But just what is this long-term effect? One way to explore the impact of advertising over the long run is to evaluate how advertising and profitability in general are linked.

In Figure (b) the argument is made that advertising shapes the key element of profitability, namely relative customer value. Customer value is determined by the product's perceived quality (and hence utility) relative to price. The more that advertising can enhance the perceived quality of a product, the more it will increase the product's profitability.

How this benefits the business over the longer term is best seen through examples.

Examples of successful long-term marketing strategies

Purina Petcare. Purina Petcare is the world's leading pet care company. It produces a range of pet-food brands, including Felix, Winalot, Go Cat, Bonio and Bakers. Bakers is a success story of a long-term advertising campaign that began in 1994,

when the dog-food market was dominated by tinned meat and Bakers was one of a small number of dry dog-food brands. Working with a small advertising agency, Purina developed an advertising campaign around the idea that 'dogs would choose Bakers'. This campaign was awarded a gold medal by the Institute of Practitioners in Advertising, the UK trade body and professional institute, which noted:

> 10 years on, this powerful campaign is still running. Bakers achieved both its short-term objective of becoming the market leader and long-term objective of increasing the size of the market. The length of the campaign is testament to the strong sales response, having so far delivered an estimated £58.3 million for the brand.[2]

PG Tips. Launched in 1930, PG Tips is another brand that continues to be a leader in its respective market. Mintel estimated that it had a market share of 23 per cent of the UK tea market in 2013–14. The 'chimp' adverts, then the Aardman T-Birds and more recently Johnny Vegas and Monkey, have established a clear brand image, enabling PG Tips to hold its ground in a highly competitive market and charge a price premium. (Blind tests have revealed that consumers cannot distinguish between any of the leading tea brands!)

Market analysis shows that PG Tips has a price elasticity of demand of −0.4 compared with its nearest rival, Tetley, which has an elasticity of −1.4. It was estimated that between 1980 and 2000 advertising the PG Tips brand cost £100 million but generated in the region of £2 billion in extra sales.

However, consumer tastes are changing and this may present a real challenge to the brand in the future. The sales of standard black tea have declined, while the market for herbal tea has increased rapidly. Leading rivals Tetley, Typhoo and

---

[2] www.ipaeffectivenessawards.co.uk/pdfs/Embargoed_2005_winners_release.pdf

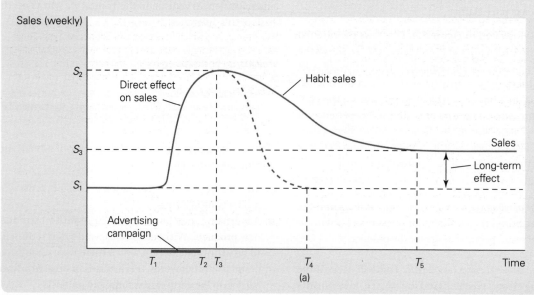

(a)

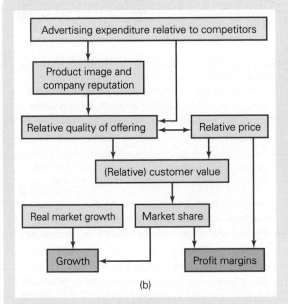

(b)

Twinings have all moved successfully into this segment of the market.

Audi. Another example of a successful long-term campaign is Audi, which was one of the winners of the 2011 Institute of Practitioners in Advertising (IPA) Effectiveness Awards. Praising the advertising campaign's focus on design, performance and innovation, the IPA acknowledged that Audi went from being the understated alternative to Mercedes and BMW, to the fastest growing prestige car brand of the last eight years.

In 1999, against ambitious growth targets, the communications strategy was overhauled to position Audi as the leader in the prestige sector. 'Vorsprung durch Technik' – the relentless desire to challenge and evolve – became the focus of the campaign which generated an incremental 50 000 car sales and payback of £7.50 for every £1 spent.[3]

In 2000, Audi had a 1.5 per cent share of the UK market. By 2010, this had grown to 5.3 per cent.

Marketing and advertising in recessions

An alternative way to illustrate the impact of advertising on longer-term profitability is to assess how companies approach advertising in a recession. What happens when advertising expenditure is cut, and how does profitability return once the recession is over and advertising expenditure once again begins to rise?

Recessions place many firms under significant pressures due to declining consumer demand. A study[4] published in 2011 examined the impact of marketing, in recessionary periods, upon long-term profitability. It reviewed 18 previous academic articles and reports. Firm-wide pressures to cut costs often result in large declines in advertising expenditure. However, the study found that these cutbacks may be short-sighted. The long-term prospects of some firms can be improved during economic downturns. Firms that are able to engage in marketing activities during recessions are asso-

ciated with superior shareholder value, customer loyalty and long-term profitability. Those which rein in expenditures put future profits, and perhaps ultimately their survival, at risk.

Use of social media: a case study

Companies have increasingly made use of social media to support their advertising activity on the television and support long-running campaigns.

One of the clearest examples of this new integrated approach was implemented by the price comparison website *Compare the Market*. In January 2009, the company launched its 'Compare the Meerkat' advert on the television. This centred on a CGI animated Russian Meerkat, Alexandr Orlov, complaining about the confusion between the 'Compare the Meerkat' and the *Compare the Market* websites. The company launched a real 'Compare the Meerkat' website in order to promote its brand further.

The impact of the campaign was immediate. In the week following its first broadcast, the number of Internet searches containing the word 'meerkat' increased by 817 per cent. Within nine weeks the requested number of insurance quotes via the *Compare the Market* website increased by 80 per cent.

The company quickly created a Facebook page for the Alexandr Orlov character, which as of December 2014 had over half a million fans. A Twitter account was also established which by May 2015 had 67 000 followers!

A series of television adverts continues to follow the story of Alexandr and has introduced new characters including friends and family members. The 'Meerkat Movies' promotion has recently been introduced which gives customers two-for-one tickets to cinemas.

The on-line promotion has also continued to expand. Wallpapers, ringtones, text alerts and voicemail messages can be downloaded from the 'Compare the Meerkat' website. There is even an iPhone app that provides 'meerkat' pronunciations of various English phrases.

Conclusions

The message is that advertising should continually seek to promote a product's quality. This is the key to long-term sales and profits.

What is also apparent is that successful brands have advertising campaigns which have been consistent over time. They have also increasingly made use of social media. A brand image of quality is not created overnight, and once it is established, it requires continued investment if it is to endure and yield profits over the longer term.

 1. *How are long-run profits and advertising linked?*
2. *Why does quality 'win out' in the end?*

[3] www.ipaeffectivenessawards.co.uk/IPA-Brand-Films
[4] L. O'Malley, V. Story and V. O'Sullivan, 'Marketing in a recession: retrench or invest', Journal of Strategic Marketing, 19(3) (2011) 285-310.

- It can aid product development by helping the firm emphasise the special features of its product.
- It may encourage price competition, if prices feature significantly in the advertisement.
- By increasing sales, it may allow the firm to gain economies of scale (see section 9.4), which in turn will help to keep prices down.

On the other side, the following arguments are put forward against advertising:

- Advertising is designed to persuade people to buy the product. Consumers do not have perfect information and may thus be misled into purchasing goods whose qualities may be inferior to those goods which are not advertised.
- **KI 2** **p 18** Scarcity is defined as the excess of human wants over the means of fulfilling them. Advertising is used to *create* wants. It could thus be argued to increase scarcity.
- It increases materialism.
- Advertising costs money: it uses resources. These resources could be put to alternative uses in producing more goods.
- If there are no reductions in costs to be gained from producing on a larger scale, the costs of advertising will tend to raise the price paid by the consumer. Even if the firm has potential economies of scale, it may be prevented from expanding its sales by retaliatory advertising from its rivals.
- Advertising can create a barrier to the entry of new firms by promoting brand loyalty to *existing* firms' products. New firms may not be able to afford the large amount of advertising necessary to create a new brand image, whereas existing firms can spread the cost of their advertising over their already large number of sales. In other words, there are economies of scale in advertising which act as a barrier to entry (see page 182–3).

This barrier is strengthened if existing firms sell many brands each (for example, in the washing powder industry many brands are produced by just two firms). This makes it even harder for new firms to introduce a new brand successfully, since the consumer already has so many to choose from.

The fewer the competitors, the less elastic will be the demand for each individual firm, and the higher will be the profit-maximising price (see Chapter 12).

- People are constantly subjected to advertisements, whether on television, in magazines, on bill-boards, etc., and often find them annoying, tasteless or unsightly. Thus advertising imposes costs on society in general. These costs are external to the firm: that is, they do not cost the firm money, and hence are normally ignored by the firm.

The effects of advertising on competition, costs and **KI 1** **p 10** prices are largely an empirical issue (an issue of *fact*), and clearly these effects will differ from one product to another. However, many of the arguments presented here involve judgements as to whether the effects are socially desirable or undesirable. Such judgements involve questions of taste and morality: things that are questions of opinion and cannot be resolved by a simple appeal to the facts.

SUMMARY

1a When firms seek to differentiate their product from those of their competitors, they can adjust one or more of four dimensions of the product: its technical standards, its quality, its design characteristics, and the level of customer service.

1b Products can be vertically and horizontally differentiated from one another. Vertical differentiation is where products are superior or inferior to others. Horizontal differentiation is where products differ, but are of a similar quality.

2a Marketing involves developing a product image and then persuading consumers to purchase it.

2b A business must choose an appropriate product/market strategy. Four such strategies can be identified: market penetration (focusing on current product and market); product development (new product in current market); market development (current product in new markets); diversification (new products in new markets).

2c The marketing strategy of a product involves the manipulation of four key variables: product, price, place and promotion. Every product has a distinct marketing mix. The marketing mix is likely to change over the product's life cycle.

3a Advertising expenditure is cyclical, expanding and contracting with the upswings and downswings of the economy.

3b Most advertising expenditure goes on consumables and durable goods.

3c The advertising intensity within a given product sector can be estimated by considering the advertising/sales ratio. The advertising/sales ratio is likely to be higher the more oligopolistic the market, the more expensive the product, the newer the product, and the more that the customer base for a product is subject to change.

3d The aims of advertising are to increase demand and make the product less price elastic.

3e Supporters of advertising claim that it: provides consumers with information; brings new products to consumers' attention; aids product development; encourages price competition; and generates economies of scale through increasing sales.

3f Critics of advertising claim that it: distorts consumption decisions; creates wants; pushes up prices; creates barriers to entry; and produces unwanted side effects, such as being unsightly.

REVIEW QUESTIONS

1 How might we account for the growth in non-price competition within the modern developed economy?

2 Distinguish between vertical and horizontal product differentiation. Give examples of goods that fall into each category.

3 Consider how the selection of the product/market strategy (market penetration, market development, product development and diversification) will influence the business's marketing mix. Identify which elements in the marketing mix would be most significant in developing a successful marketing strategy.

4 Why might the advertising/sales ratio be a poor guide to the degree of exposure of the consumer to advertisements for a particular category of product?

5 Imagine that 'Sunshine' sunflower margarine, a well-known brand, is advertised with the slogan, 'It helps you live longer' (the implication being that butter and margarines high in saturates shorten your life). What do you think would happen to the demand curve for a supermarket's own brand of sunflower margarine? Consider both the direction of shift and the effect on elasticity. Will the elasticity differ markedly at different prices? How will this affect the pricing policy and sales of the supermarket's own brand? Could the supermarket respond other than by adjusting the price of its margarine?

6 On balance, does advertising benefit (a) the consumer; (b) society in general?

MyEconLab

This book can be supported by MyEconLab, which contains a range of additional resources, including an online homework and tutorial system designed to test and build your understanding.

You need both an access card and a course ID to access MyEconLab:

1. Is your lecturer using MyEconLab? Ask your lecturer for your course ID.

2. Has an access card been included with the book at a reduced cost? Check the inside back cover of the book.

3. If you have a course ID but no access card, go to: http://www.myeconlab.com/ to buy access to this interactive study programme.

ADDITIONAL PART C CASE STUDIES IN THE *ECONOMICS FOR BUSINESS* MyEconLab (www.pearsoned.co.uk/sloman)

C.1 Bentham and the philosophy of utilitarianism. This looks at the historical and philosophical underpinning of the ideas of utility maximisation.

C.2 Choices within the household. Is what is best for the individual best for the family?

C.3 Taking account of time. The importance of the time dimension in consumption decisions.

C.4 The demand for butter. An examination of a real-world demand function.

C.5 What we pay to watch sport. Consideration of the demand function for season tickets to watch spectator sports such as football.

WEBSITES RELEVANT TO PART C

Numbers and sections refer to websites listed in the Web appendix and hotlinked from this book's website at **www.pearsoned .co.uk/sloman**

■ For news articles relevant to Part C, see the *Economics News Articles* link from the book's website.

■ For general news on demand, consumers and marketing, see websites in section A, and particularly A2, 3, 4, 8, 9, 11, 12, 23, 24, 25, 36. See also site A41 for links to economics news articles and to search particular topics (e.g. advertising).

■ For data, information and sites on products and marketing, see sites B1, 3, 14, 27.

■ For student resources relevant to Part C, see sites C1–7, 19.

■ For data on advertising, see site E37.

■ For links to sites on various aspects of advertising and marketing, see section *Industry and Commerce > Consumer Protection > Advertising* in sites I7 and 11.

Background to supply

The Financial Times, 20 August 2015

FT

Qantas turnround gains altitude with swing to profit

By Jamie Smyth

Qantas Airways' recovery gained altitude as the airline soared back into the black and outlined bullish plans to buy new aircraft, return cash to its shareholders and reduce debt.

Buoyed by deep cost-cutting, lower fuel prices and a truce in a bruising capacity war with its domestic rival Virgin Australia, the Australian flag carrier on Thursday posted a A$975m (US$716m) underlying pre-tax profit for the year ended June 2015. This was a marked turnround from a A$646m underlying loss and record A$2.8bn net annual loss a year earlier.

However, the carrier's 2014-15 underlying profit marginally undershot analysts' consensus forecasts of A$982m, and Qantas shares – which have trebled over the past 18 months – closed down 6.1 per cent at A$3.53 on Thursday.

"We are delivering one of the biggest turnrounds in Australia's corporate history," said Alan Joyce, Qantas chief executive. "This is the best first-half [financial] result in four years and the best second-half result in the company's history."

The "Flying Kangaroo" has faced difficulty in recent years due to increasing competition from Virgin Australia at home, tough competition from Middle Eastern and Asian carriers on international routes, high fuel prices and a strong Australian dollar.

It lost its investment-grade credit rating in 2013 and its shares fell to a record low of A$0.96, which prompted rumours the airline would need a government bailout to survive.

Mr Joyce is in the midst of a four-year A$2bn cost-cutting plan that involves axing 5,000 jobs, early retirement of aircraft and wage freezes. The company said it has implemented $1.1bn in cost and revenue benefits so far and expects to realise a further A$450m in benefits during 2015–16.

On Thursday, Qantas said lower fuel costs provided annual cost reduction of A$597m, while the transformation programme provided A$894m in cost benefits. Qantas is proposing to return capital to shareholders equivalent to A$0.23 per share, while also reducing the number of shares on issue. ...

Qantas also said it would exercise options to buy eight Boeing 787-9 Dreamliners for its international fleet. The new aircraft would enable Qantas to operate more efficiently, retiring older aircraft and opening up new routes...

All the airline's divisions were profitable in 2015, with Qantas International and Jetstar, its budget offshoot, returning to an underlying full-year profit. The statutory pre-tax profit of A$789m in the year to end June 2015 compared with a statutory loss of A$3.98bn a year earlier.

[Steelworks across Europe] have been hit by falling prices, weak demand and a flood of cheap imports as the slowdown in China stifles the appetite of the world's biggest steel consumer. These have combined with high operating costs to weigh heavily on their finances, raising questions about the sustainability of the UK's domestic industry. While such factors have squeezed the steelmakers across Europe, their British counterparts say they face additional burdens of higher business rates and energy costs, as well as the impact of a strong pound.

'UK steel hit by perfect storm of falling prices and high costs', *Financial Times,* 29 September 2015

In Part D we turn to supply. In other words, we will focus on the amount that firms produce. In Parts E and F we shall see how the supply decision is affected by the environment in which a firm operates, and in particular by the amount of competition it faces. In this part of the text, however, we take a more general look at supply and its relationship to profit.

Profit is made by firms earning more from the sale of goods than the goods cost to produce. A firm's total profit ($T\Pi$) is thus the difference between its total sales revenue (TR) and its total costs of production (TC):

$$T\Pi = TR - TC$$

(Note that we use the Greek Π (pi) for 'profit'.)

Businesses can increase their profitability either by increasing their revenue (by selling more of their product or adjusting their price) or by reducing their costs of production. As the *Financial Times* article opposite shows, both policies can be vital in helping a struggling company, such as the airline Qantas to return to profit. Sometimes, however, as the quote above illustrates, a combination of falling demand, low prices and rising costs may make losses inevitable.

In order, then, to discover how a firm can maximise its profit, or even get a sufficient level of profit, we must first consider what determines costs and revenue. Chapter 9 examines production, productivity and costs. Chapter 10 considers revenue, and then puts costs and revenue together to examine profit. We will discover the output at which profits are maximised and how much profit is made at that output.

Key terms

Opportunity cost
Explicit and implicit costs
Short and long run
Law of diminishing (marginal) returns
Returns to scale (increasing, constant and decreasing)
Economies of scale (internal)
External economies of scale
Diseconomies of scale
Specialisation and division of labour
Fixed and variable factors
Fixed and variable costs
Total average and marginal costs and revenue
Price takers and price makers/choosers
Profit maximisation
Normal profit
Supernormal profit

Costs of production

Business issues covered in this chapter

- What do profits consist of?
- How are costs of production measured?
- What is the relationship between inputs and outputs in both the short and long run?
- How do costs vary with output in both the short and long run?
- What are meant by 'economies of scale' and what are the reasons for such economies?
- How can a business combine its inputs in the most efficient way?

9.1 THE MEANING OF COSTS

Opportunity cost

When measuring costs, economists always use the concept of *opportunity cost*. Opportunity cost is the cost of any activity measured in terms of the sacrifice made in doing it: in other words, the cost measured in terms of the opportunities forgone (see Chapter 2). If a car manufacturer can produce ten small saloon cars with the same amount of inputs as it takes to produce six large saloon cars, then the opportunity cost of producing one small car is 0.6 of a large car. If a taxi and car hire firm uses its cars as taxis, then the opportunity cost includes not only the cost of employing taxi drivers and buying fuel, but also the sacrifice of rental income from hiring its vehicles out.

Measuring a firm's opportunity costs

To measure a firm's opportunity cost, we must first discover what factors of production it has used. Then we must measure the sacrifice involved in using them. To do this it is necessary to put factors into two categories.

Factors not owned by the firm: explicit costs
The opportunity cost of those factors not already owned by the firm is simply the price that the firm has to pay for them. Thus if the firm uses £100 worth of electricity, the opportunity cost is £100. The firm has sacrificed £100 which could have been spent on something else.

These costs are called *explicit costs* because they involve direct payment of money by firms.

Factors already owned by the firm: implicit costs
When the firm already owns factors (e.g. machinery), it does not as a rule have to pay out money to use them. Their

Definitions

Opportunity cost Cost measured in terms of the next best alternative forgone.

Explicit costs The payments to outside suppliers of inputs.

opportunity costs are thus *implicit costs*. They are equal to what the factors *could* earn for the firm in some alternative use, either within the firm or hired out to some other firm.

Here are some examples of implicit costs:

■ A firm owns some buildings. The opportunity cost of using them is the rent it could have received by letting them out to another firm.

■ A firm draws £100 000 from the bank out of its savings in order to invest in new plant and equipment. The opportunity cost of this investment is not just the £100 000 (an explicit cost), but also the interest it thereby forgoes (an implicit cost).

■ The owner of the firm could have earned £15 000 per annum by working for someone else. This £15 000 is the opportunity cost of the owner's time.

If there is no alternative use for a factor of production, as in the case of a machine designed to produce a specific product, and if it has no scrap value, the opportunity cost of using it is *zero*. In such a case, if the output from the machine is worth more than the cost of all the *other* inputs involved, the firm might as well use the machine rather than let it stand idle.

What the firm paid for the machine – its *historic cost* – is irrelevant. Not using the machine will not bring that money back. It has been spent. These are sometimes referred to as *sunk costs*.

Pause for thought

Assume that a farmer decides to grow wheat on land that could be used for growing barley. Barley sells for £100 per tonne. Wheat sells for £150 per tonne. Seed, fertiliser, labour and other costs of growing crops are £80 per tonne for both wheat and barley. What are the farmer's costs and profit per tonne of growing wheat?

Likewise, the *replacement cost* is irrelevant. That should be taken into account only when the firm is considering replacing the machine.

 The 'bygones' principle states that sunk (fixed) costs should be ignored when deciding whether to produce or sell more or less of a product. Only variable costs should be taken into account.

BOX 9.1 **THE FALLACY OF USING HISTORIC COSTS**

Or there's no point crying over spilt milk

'What's done is done.'

'Write it off to experience.'

'You might as well make the best of a bad job.'

These familiar sayings are all everyday examples of a simple fact of life: once something has happened, you cannot change the past. You have to take things as they are *now*.

If you fall over and break your leg, there is little point in saying: 'If only I hadn't done that I could have gone on that skiing holiday; I could have taken part in that race; I could have done so many other things (sigh).' Wishing things were different won't change history. You have to manage as well as you can *with* your broken leg.

It is the same for a firm. Once it has purchased some inputs, it is no good then wishing it hadn't. It has to accept that it has now got them, and make the best decisions about what to do with them.

Take a simple example. The local convenience store in early December decides to buy 100 Christmas trees for £10 each.

At the time of purchase this represents an opportunity cost of £10 each, since the £10 could have been spent on something else. The shopkeeper estimates that there is enough local demand to sell all 100 trees at £20 each, thereby making a reasonable profit (even after allowing for handling costs).

But the estimate turns out to be wrong. On 23 December there are still 50 trees unsold. What should be done? At this stage the £10 that was paid for the trees is irrelevant. It is a historic cost. It cannot be recouped: the trees cannot be sold back to the wholesaler!

In fact the opportunity cost is now zero. It might even be negative if the shopkeeper has to pay to dispose of any unsold trees. It might, therefore, be worth selling the trees at £10, £5 or even £1. Last thing on Christmas Eve it might even be worth giving away any unsold trees.

 Why is the correct price to charge (for the unsold trees) the one at which the price elasticity of demand equals −1? (Assume no disposal costs.)

KI 3
p 23

9.2 PRODUCTION IN THE SHORT RUN

The cost of producing any level of output will depend on the amount of inputs used and the price that the firm must pay for them. Let us first focus on the quantity of inputs used.

 Output depends on the amount of resources and how they are used. Different amounts and combinations of inputs will lead to different amounts of output. If output is to be produced efficiently, then inputs should be combined in the optimum proportions.

Short-run and long-run changes in production

If a firm wants to increase production, it will take time to acquire a greater quantity of certain inputs. For example, a manufacturer can use more electricity by turning on switches, but it might take a long time to obtain and install more machines, and longer still to build a second or third factory.

If, then, the firm wants to increase output in a hurry, it will only be able to increase the quantity of certain inputs. It can use more raw materials, more fuel, more tools and possibly more labour (by hiring extra workers or offering overtime to its existing workforce). But it will have to make do with its existing buildings and most of its machinery.

The distinction we are making here is between *fixed factors* and *variable factors*. A *fixed* factor is an input that cannot be increased within a given time period (e.g. buildings). A *variable* factor is one that can.

The distinction between fixed and variable factors allows us to distinguish between the *short run* and the *long run*.

The short run is a time period during which at least one factor of production is fixed. This means that in the short run output can be increased only by using more variable factors. For example, if a shipping line wanted to carry more passengers in response to a rise in demand, it could accommodate more passengers on existing sailings if there was space. It could increase the number of sailings with its existing fleet, by hiring more crew and using more fuel. But in the short run it could not buy more ships: there would not be time for them to be built.

The long run is a time period long enough for *all* of a firm's inputs to be varied. Thus in the long run, the shipping company could have a new ship built to cater for the increase in demand.

The actual length of the short run will differ from firm to firm. It is not a fixed period of time. Thus if it takes a farmer a year to obtain new land, buildings and equipment, the short run is any time period up to a year and the long run is any time period longer than a year. But if it takes a shipping company three years to obtain an extra ship, the short run is any period up to three years and the long run is any period longer than three years.

For this and the next section we will concentrate on *short-run* production and costs. We will look at the long run in sections 9.4 and 9.5.

Pause for thought

How will the length of the short run for the shipping company depend on the state of the shipbuilding industry?

Production in the short run: the law of diminishing returns

Production in the short run is subject to *diminishing returns*, which we first alluded to in section 4.3. You may well have heard of 'the law of diminishing returns': it is one of the most famous of all 'laws' of economics. To illustrate how this law underlies short-run production, let us take the simplest possible case where there are just two factors: one fixed and one variable.

Take the case of a farm. Assume the fixed factor is land and the variable factor is labour. Since the land is fixed in supply, output per period of time can be increased only by increasing the number of workers employed. But imagine what would happen as more and more workers crowded on to a fixed area of land. The land cannot go on yielding more and more output indefinitely. After a point the additions to output from each extra worker will begin to diminish.

We can now state the *law of diminishing (marginal) returns*.

 The law of diminishing marginal returns. When increasing amounts of a variable factor are used with a given amount of a fixed factor, there will come a point when each extra unit of the variable factor will produce less additional output than the previous unit.

A good example of the law of diminishing returns is given in Case D.3 in MyEconLab. The case looks at diminishing returns to the application of nitrogen fertiliser on farmland. There is also an article on the Sloman News Site, 'Tackling diminishing returns in food production', which provides another good application of this core concept.

Definitions

Fixed factor An input that cannot be increased in supply within a given time period.

Variable factor An input that *can* be increased in supply within a given time period.

Short run The period of time over which at least one factor is fixed.

Long run The period of time long enough for *all* factors to be varied.

Law of diminishing (marginal) returns When one or more factors are held fixed, there will come a point beyond which the extra output from additional units of the variable factor will diminish.

The short-run production function: total product

Let us now see how the law of diminishing returns affects total output or *total physical product* (*TPP*).

The relationship between inputs and output is shown in a *production function*. In the simple case of the farm with only two factors – namely, a fixed supply of land $\bar{L}n$ and a variable supply of farm workers (*Lb*) – the production function would be:

$$TPP = f(\bar{L}n, Lb)$$

This states that total physical product (i.e. the output of the farm) over a given period of time is a function of (i.e. depends on) the quantity of land and labour employed.

KI 19
p 142

Definitions

Total physical product The total output of a product per period of time that is obtained from a given amount of inputs.

Production function The mathematical relationship between the output of a good and the inputs used to produce it. It shows how output will be affected by changes in the quantity of one or more of the inputs.

Table 9.1	Wheat production per year from a particular farm (tonnes)		
	Number of workers (*Lb*)	*TPP*	*APP* (= *TPP/Lb*)	*MPP* (= $\Delta TPP / \Delta Lb$)
a	0	0	–	
				3
	1	3	3	
				7
	2	10	5	
b				14
	3	24	8	
				12
c	4	36	9	
				4
	5	40	8	
				2
	6	42	7	
d				0
	7	42	6	
				–2
	8	40	5	

The production function can also be expressed in the form of a table or a graph. Table 9.1 and Figure 9.1 show a hypothetical production function for a farm producing wheat. The first two columns of Table 9.1 and the top

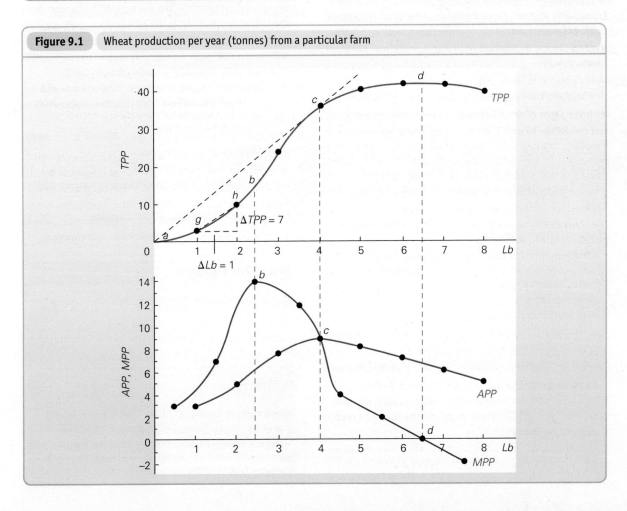

| Figure 9.1 | Wheat production per year (tonnes) from a particular farm |

diagram in Figure 9.1 show how wheat output per year varies as extra workers are employed on a fixed amount of land.

With nobody working on the land, output will be zero (point *a*). As the first farm workers are taken on, wheat output initially rises more and more rapidly. The assumption behind this is that with only one or two workers efficiency is low, since the workers are spread thinly across multiple tasks. With more workers, however, they can work as a team – each, perhaps, doing some specialist job and becoming more productive at it – and thus they can use the land more efficiently. In the top diagram of Figure 9.1, output rises more and more rapidly up to the employment of the second worker.

After point *b*, however, diminishing marginal returns set in: output rises less and less rapidly, and the *TPP* curve correspondingly becomes less steeply sloped.

When point *d* is reached, wheat output is at a maximum: the land is yielding as much as it can. Any more workers employed after that are likely to get in each other's way. Thus beyond point *d*, output is likely to fall again: eight workers produce less than seven workers.

The short-run production function: average and marginal product

In addition to total physical product, two other important concepts are illustrated by a production function: namely, ***average physical product (APP)*** and ***marginal physical product (MPP)***.

Average physical product

This is output (*TPP*) per unit of the variable factor (*Qv*). In the case of the farm, it is the output of wheat per worker.

$$APP = TPP/Qv$$

Thus in Table 9.1 the average physical product of labour when four workers are employed is $36/4 = 9$ tonnes per year.

Marginal physical product

This is the *extra* output (ΔTPP) produced by employing *one more* unit of the variable factor, (where the symbol Δ denotes 'a change in').

Thus in Table 9.1 the marginal physical product of the fourth worker is 12 tonnes. The reason is that, by employing the fourth worker, wheat output has risen from 24 tonnes to 36 tonnes: a rise of 12 tonnes.

In symbols, marginal physical product is given by:

$$MPP = \Delta TPP/\Delta Qv$$

Thus in our example:

$$MPP = 12/1 = 12$$

The reason why we divide the increase in output (ΔTPP) by the increase in the quantity of the variable factor (ΔQv)

is that some variable factors can be increased only in multiple units. For example, if we wanted to know the *MPP* of fertiliser and we found out how much extra wheat was produced by using an extra 20 kg bag, we would have to divide this output by 20 (ΔQv) to find the *MPP* of *one* more kilogram.

Note that in Table 9.1 the figures for *MPP* are entered in the spaces between the other figures. The reason is that *MPP* is the *difference* in output *between* one level of input and another. Thus in the table the differences in output between five and six workers is 2 tonnes.

The figures for *APP* and *MPP* are plotted in the lower diagram of Figure 9.1. We can draw a number of conclusions from these two diagrams.

- The *MPP* between two points is equal to the slope of the *TPP* curve between those two points. For example, when the number of workers increases from 1 to 2 ($\Delta Lb = 1$), *TPP* rises from 3 to 10 tonnes ($\Delta TPP = 7$). *MPP* is thus 7: the slope of the line between points *g* and *h*.
- *MPP* rises at first: the slope of the *TPP* curve gets steeper.
- *MPP* reaches a maximum at point *b*. At that point the slope of the *TPP* curve is at its steepest.
- After point *b*, diminishing returns set in. *MPP* falls. *TPP* becomes less steep.
- *APP* rises at first. It continues rising as long as the addition to output from the last worker (*MPP*) is greater than the average output (*APP*): the *MPP* pulls the *APP* up. This continues beyond point *b*. Even though *MPP* is now falling, the *APP* goes on rising as long as the *MPP* is still above the *APP*. Thus *APP* goes on rising to point *c*.
- Beyond point *c*, *MPP* is below *APP*. New workers add less to output than the average. This pulls the average down: *APP* falls.
- As long as *MPP* is greater than zero, *TPP* will go on rising: new workers add to total output.
- At point *d*, *TPP* is at a maximum (its slope is zero). An additional worker will add nothing to output: *MPP* is zero.
- Beyond point *d*, *TPP* falls. *MPP* is negative.

Pause for thought

What is the significance of the slope of the line ac in the top part of Figure 9.1?

Definitions

Average physical product (*APP*) Total output (*TPP*) per unit of the variable factor (*Qv*) in question: $APP = TPP/Qv$.

Marginal physical product (*MPP*) The extra output gained by the employment of one more unit of the variable factor: $MPP = \Delta TPP/\Delta Qv$.

KI 20
p 142

9.3 COSTS IN THE SHORT RUN

Having looked at the background to costs in the short run, we now turn to examine short-run costs themselves. We will be examining how costs change as a firm changes the amount it produces and hence responds to short-run market conditions. Obviously, if it is to decide how much to produce, it will need to know just what the level of costs will be at each level of output.

Costs and inputs

A firm's costs of production will depend on the factors of production it uses. The more factors it uses, the greater will its costs be. More precisely, this relationship depends on two elements.

The productivity of the factors. The greater their physical productivity, the smaller will be the quantity of them that is needed to produce a given level of output, and hence the lower will be the cost of that output. In other words, there is a direct link between *TPP*, *APP* and *MPP* and the costs of production.

The price of the factors. The higher their price, the higher will be the costs of production. In the short run, some factors are fixed in supply. Therefore, the total costs (*TC*) of these inputs are fixed and thus do not vary with output. Consider a piece of land that a firm rents: the rent it pays will be a **fixed cost**. Whether the firm produces a lot or a little, it will not change.

The cost of variable factors, however, does vary with output. The cost of raw materials is a **variable cost**. The more that is produced, the more raw materials are used and therefore the higher is their total cost.

Total cost

The **total cost (TC)** of production is the sum of the *total variable costs* (*TVC*) and the *total fixed costs* (*TFC*) of production.

$$TC = TVC + TFC$$

Consider Table 9.2 and Figure 9.2. They show the total costs for an imaginary firm for producing different levels of output (*Q*). Let us examine each of the three cost curves in turn.

Table 9.2	Total costs for firm X		
Output (Q)	**TFC (£)**	**TVC (£)**	**TC (£)**
0	12	0	12
1	12	10	22
2	12	16	28
3	12	21	33
4	12	28	40
5	12	40	52
6	12	60	72
7	12	91	103

Definitions

Fixed costs Total costs that do not vary with the amount of output produced.

Variable costs Total costs that do vary with the amount of output produced.

Total cost (*TC*) the sum of total fixed costs (*TFC*) and total variable costs (*TVC*): *TC* = *TFC* + *TVC*.

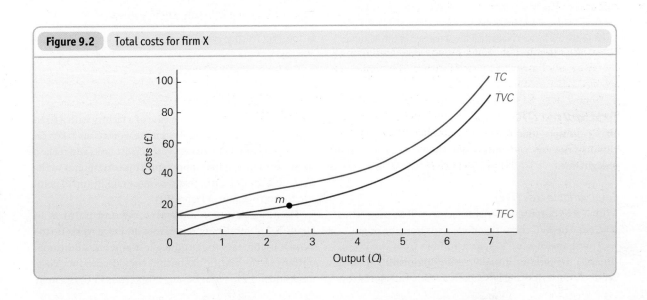

Figure 9.2 Total costs for firm X

BOX 9.2 | HOW VULNERABLE ARE YOU?

The importance of costs

The business environment is uncertain and we see some firms grow and succeed, while others fail. What is it that makes some firms more vulnerable to the economic environment, while other firms are much more insulated? In this box, we look at one aspect of the answer to this question by focusing on the shape of a firm's cost curves and the impact this has on its economic vulnerability.

Type 1 vulnerability

A typical firm will have a U-shaped average cost curve. It falls at first, reflecting rapidly falling average fixed costs, as they are spread over a greater output, plus a more efficient deployment of variable factors of production. Then, as diminishing marginal returns become relatively more important than falling average fixed costs, average costs will rise. The question is how quickly do average costs first fall and then rise as output changes. This is an important determinant of how vulnerable a firm is.

Consider two firms, A and B. Each firm's average cost curve is shown in Figure (a). Assume, for simplicity, that each firm achieves minimum average cost at point x, namely at the same output Q_0 and at the same average cost, AC_0. But now consider what would happen if there was a recession, as we saw across the world following the financial crisis of 2007–8. Assume that both firms experience a fall in demand and, as a result, cut output to Q_1.

With a U-shaped AC curve, both firms see per unit costs begin to rise, but firm A's costs rise significantly faster than firm B's, because firm A has a very steep AC curve. The same fall in quantity pushes firm A's average costs up from AC_0 to AC_1 (point a) but only causes firm B's costs to increase to AC_2 (point b) as firm B's AC curve is very flat – sometimes called flute-shaped.

Returning to point x, now assume that, instead of a recession, there is an expansion in demand. Both firms consequently increase output. Again, firm A's costs rise more rapidly than firm B's.

Therefore, firm A is much more susceptible to any change in demand than firm B. Any small decrease (or increase) in output will have a significant effect on firm A's costs and hence on its profit margin and profits, making it a much more vulnerable firm.

What are the factors that affect the steepness of the AC curve and hence make one firm more vulnerable than another?

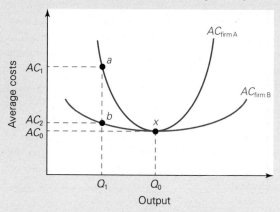

(a) Average cost for firms A and B: change in output

- If a firm has high ratio of fixed factors to variable factors then it is likely to face a steep AC curve. Total fixed costs do not change with output and hence, if output falls, it implies that its high fixed costs are being spread over fewer and fewer units of output and this causes average costs to rise rapidly.
- If a firm is relatively inflexible in its use of inputs, it may find that a cut in production means that efficiency goes down and average cost rises rapidly. Similarly if it wishes to expand output beyond Q_0, it may find it difficult to do so without incurring considerable extra costs, for example by employing expensive agency staff or hiring expensive machinery.

 Conduct some research on a firm of your choice, looking into its data on costs, and decide whether or not you think this firm would suffer from type 1 vulnerability.

Type 2 vulnerability

Most firms purchase inputs to the production process from other companies, but their reliance on other firms and, in some cases on materials where there is a volatile global market, can vary significantly. The second type of economic vulnerability concerns a firm's reliance on external or bought-in factors of production (inputs).

Total fixed cost (TFC)

In our example, total fixed cost is assumed to be £12. Since this does not vary with output, it is shown by a horizontal straight line.

Total variable cost (TVC)

With a zero output, no variable factors will be used. Thus $TVC = 0$. The TVC curve, therefore, starts from the origin.

The shape of the TVC curve follows from the law of diminishing returns. Initially, *before* diminishing returns set in, TVC rises less and less rapidly as more variable factors

KI 20
p 142

are added. For example, in the case of a factory with a fixed supply of machinery, initially as more workers are taken on the workers can do increasingly specialist tasks and make a fuller use of the capital equipment. This corresponds to the portion of the *TPP* curve that rises more rapidly (up to point b in the top diagram of Figure 9.1).

Then, as output is increased beyond point m in Figure 9.2, diminishing returns set in. Extra workers (the extra variable factors) produce less and less additional output, so the additional output they do produce costs more and more in terms of wage costs. Thus TVC rises more

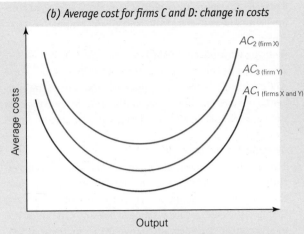

(b) Average cost for firms C and D: change in costs

AC_2 (firm X)

AC_3 (firm Y)

AC_1 (firms X and Y)

Average costs

Output

For example, some firms may be heavily dependent on oil or another raw material and, as such, if the price of oil changes, it can have a very big effect on the firm's costs of production, its profit margins and its profit. During an economic boom or period of high growth, production tends to increase and so demand for oil often rises as well. As the demand for oil increases, its price will rise. A firm that is very dependent on oil to produce will see a significant effect on its costs of production and its *AC* curve will shift vertically upwards, possibly by a considerable extent. However, for a firm that does not use much oil during production, or has alternative inputs, changes in the global price of oil or another input may cause only a very small shift in the *AC* curve.

In Figure (b), both firms X and Y have the same shaped *AC* curve, which we will assume is initially the same (i.e. AC_1). But let us also assume that firm X is very dependent on oil, whereas firm Y is not.

Assume that oil prices now rise. This will lead to a large upward shift in firm X's *AC* curve from AC_1 to AC_2, but a smaller upward shift in firm Y's *AC* curve from AC_1 to AC_3. There is a much larger cost penalty imposed on firm X than on firm Y, due to the reliance on oil as a factor of production.

In 2010, oil prices rose significantly, so firms which were big users of oil, either directly into the production process or for transporting their inputs and produce, saw their costs rise and their profits eroded. However, in late 2014 and early 2015, oil prices fell considerably and so those firms which were heavily dependent on oil saw their AC curves shift downwards significantly, thereby helping to increase their profits. Other firms which were less reliant on oil, however, did not benefit so much from low global prices for oil.

 Now look at some data on a firm of your choice and decide whether or not you think this firm would suffer from type 2 vulnerability. Is it the same firm as you discussed in question 1? If your data suggest the firms would be vulnerable in both ways, what might this mean for the firm?

Nippon Steel & Sumitomo Metal Corporation (NSSMC)

One final thing to consider is a firm that is vulnerable in both ways. That is, a firm that is heavily dependent on external or bought-in costs and at the same time has a high proportion of fixed costs. This might mean that as economies move from economic boom to economic recession, these firms are always vulnerable to changes in costs of production.

A good example is the Japanese steel producer, NSSMC. Its fixed costs as a percentage of internal costs are very high, suggesting a steep *AC* curve and vulnerability to a fall in output. However, this firm's external costs also account for a high percentage of its total costs, suggesting heavy reliance on costs that are beyond its control.

Therefore, during an economic downturn, as we saw in 2009, NSSMC reduced its output to just above 50 per cent of its maximum capacity. This fall in output made the firm very vulnerable to rising short-run average costs. And just the previous year the company had been in trouble again, but this time because costs of production had been rising due to increases in the prices of oil and various raw materials.

These types of vulnerability create uncertainty in the business environment. They can help to explain why some firms are successful and can survive periods of falling output, while others have little chance of survival.

and more rapidly. The *TVC* curve gets steeper. This corresponds to the portion of the *TPP* curve that rises less rapidly (between points *b* and *d* in Figure 9.1).

Total cost (TC)

Since $TC = TVC + TFC$, the *TC* curve is simply the *TVC* curve shifted vertically upwards by £12.

Average and marginal cost

Average cost (AC) is cost per unit of production.

$$AC = TC/Q$$

Thus if it costs a firm £2000 to produce 100 units of a product, the average cost would be £20 for each unit (£2000/100).

Like total cost, average cost can be divided into the two components, fixed and variable. In other words, average

Definition

Average (total) cost (*AC*) Total cost (fixed plus variable) per unit of output: $AC = TC/Q = AFC + AVC$.

cost equals **average fixed cost** (AFC = TFC/Q) plus **average variable cost** (AVC = TVC/Q).

$$AC = AFC + AVC$$

Marginal cost (MC) is the *extra* cost of producing *one more unit*: that is, the rise in total cost per one unit rise in output.

$$MC = \frac{\Delta TC}{\Delta Q}$$

where Δ means 'a change in'.

For example, assume that a firm is currently producing 1 000 000 boxes of matches a month. It now increases output by 1000 boxes (another batch): $\Delta Q = 1000$. As a result its total costs rise by £30: $\Delta TC = £30$. What is the cost of producing *one* more box of matches? It is:

$$MC = \frac{\Delta TC}{\Delta Q} = \frac{\#30}{1000} = 3p$$

(Note that all marginal costs are variable, since, by definition, there can be no extra fixed costs as output rises.)

Given the TFC, TVC and TC for each output, it is possible to derive the AFC, AVC, AC and MC for each output using the above definitions. For example, using the data in Table 9.2, Table 9.3 can be constructed.

What will be the shapes of the MC, AFC, AVC and AC curves? These follow from the nature of the MPP and APP curves (which we looked at in section 9.2).

Marginal cost (MC)

The shape of the MC curve follows directly from the law of diminishing returns. Initially, in Figure 9.3, as more of the variable factor is used, extra units of output cost less than previous units. This means that MC falls. This corresponds to the portion of the TVC curve in Figure 9.2 to the left of point *m*.

Beyond a certain level of output, diminishing returns set in. This is shown as point *x* in Figure 9.3 and corresponds to point *m* in Figure 9.2. Thereafter MC rises. Additional units

of output cost more and more to produce, since they require ever-increasing amounts of the variable factor.

Average fixed cost (AFC)

This falls continuously as output rises, since *total* fixed costs are being spread over a greater and greater output.

Average variable cost (AVC)

The shape of the AVC curve depends on the shape of the APP curve. As the average product of workers rises, the average labour cost per unit of output (the AVC) falls: up to point *y* in Figure 9.3. Thereafter, as APP falls, AVC must rise.

Average (total) cost (AC)

This is simply the vertical sum of the AFC and AVC curves. Note that, as AFC falls, the gap between AVC and AC narrows. Although AVC and MC curves are usually drawn as a U-shape, they are not always shaped like this. Case study D.7 in MyEconLab considers alternative shapes for these curves.

> ### Pause for thought
>
> *Before you read on, can you explain why the marginal cost curve will always cut the average cost curve at its lowest point?*

> ### Definitions
>
> **Average fixed cost (AFC)** Total fixed cost per unit of output: AFC = TFC/Q.
>
> **Average variable cost (AVC)** Total variable cost per unit of output: AVC = TVC/Q.
>
> **Marginal cost (MC)** The cost of producing one more unit of output: MC = ΔTC/ΔQ.

Table 9.3		Costs					
Output (Q) (units)	**TFC** (£)	**AFC (TFC/Q)** (£)	**TVC** (£)	**AVC (TVC/Q)** (£)	**TC (TFC + TVC)** (£)	**AC (TC/Q)** (£)	**MC (ΔTC/ ΔQ)** (£)
0	12	–	0	–	12	–	
							10
1	12	12	10	10	22	22	
							6
2	12	6	16	8	28	14	
							5
3	12	4	21	7	33	11	
							7
4	12	3	28	7	40	10	
							12
5	12	2.4	40	8	52	10.4	
							20
6	12	2	60	10	72	12	
							31
7	12	1.7	91	13	103	14.7	

The relationship between average cost and marginal cost

This is simply another illustration of the relationship that applies between *all* averages and marginals.

As long as the cost of additional units of output is less than the average, their production must pull the average cost down. That is, if *MC* is less than *AC*, *AC* must be falling. Likewise, if additional units cost more than the average, their production must drive the average up. That is, if *MC* is greater than *AC*, *AC* must be rising. Therefore, the *MC* crosses the *AC*, and also the *AVC*, at their minimum points (point *z* and *y* respectively in Figure 9.3).

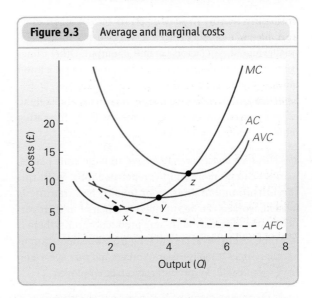

Figure 9.3 Average and marginal costs

9.4 PRODUCTION IN THE LONG RUN

In the long run *all* factors of production are variable. There is time for the firm to build a new factory (maybe in a different part of the country), to install new machines, to use different techniques of production, and in general to combine its inputs in whatever proportion and in whatever quantities it chooses.

Therefore, when planning for the long run a firm will have to make a number of decisions: about the scale of its operations, the location of its operations and the techniques of production it will use. These decisions will affect the firm's costs of production and can be completely irreversible, so it is important to get them right.

The scale of production

If a firm were to double all of its inputs – something it could do only in the long run – would it double its output? Or would output more than double or less than double? We can distinguish three possible situations.

- *Constant returns to scale.* This is where a given percentage increase in inputs will lead to the same percentage increase in output.
- *Increasing returns to scale.* This is where a given percentage increase in inputs will lead to a larger percentage increase in output.
- *Decreasing returns to scale.* This is where a given percentage increase in inputs will lead to a smaller percentage increase in output.

Notice the terminology here. The words 'to scale' mean that *all* inputs increase by the same proportion. Decreasing returns to *scale* are therefore quite different from *diminishing* marginal returns (where only the *variable* factor increases). The differences between marginal returns to a variable factor and returns to scale are illustrated in Table 9.4.

Table 9.4 Short-run and long-run increases in output

| | Short run | | | Long run | |
Input 1	Input 2	Output	Input 1	Input 2	Output
3	1	25	1	1	15
3	2	45	2	2	35
3	3	60	3	3	60
3	4	70	4	4	90
3	5	75	5	5	125

In the short run, input 1 is assumed to be fixed in supply (at 3 units). Output can be increased only by using more of the variable factor (input 2). In the long run, however, both inputs are variable.

In the short-run situation, diminishing returns can be seen from the fact that output increases at a decreasing rate (25 to 45 to 60 to 70 to 75) as input 2 is increased. In the long-run situation, the table illustrates increasing returns to scale. Output increases at an *increasing* rate (15 to 35 to 60 to 90 to 125) as both inputs are increased.

Economies of scale

The concept of increasing returns to scale is closely linked to that of *economies of scale*. A firm experiences economies of scale if costs per unit of output fall as the scale of roduction increases. Clearly, if a firm is getting

Definition

Economies of scale When increasing the scale of production leads to a lower cost per unit of output.

increasing returns to scale from its factors of production, then as it produces more, it will be using smaller and smaller amounts of factors per unit of output. Other things being equal, this means that it will be producing at a lower unit cost.

There are a number of reasons why firms are likely to experience economies of scale. Some are due to increasing returns to scale; some are not.

Specialisation and division of labour. In large-scale plants, workers can do more simple, repetitive jobs. With this **specialisation and division of labour**, less training is needed; workers can become highly efficient in their particular job, especially with long production runs; there is less time lost in workers switching from one operation to another; supervision is easier. Workers and managers who have specific skills in specific areas can be employed.

Indivisibilities. Some inputs are of a minimum size. They are indivisible. The most obvious example is machinery. Take the case of a combine harvester. A small-scale farmer could not make full use of one. They only become economical to use, therefore, on farms above a certain size. The problem of **indivisibilities** is made worse when different machines, each of which is part of the production process, are of a different size. Consider a firm that uses two different machines at different stages of the production process: one produces a maximum of 6 units a day; the other can package a maximum of 4 units a day. Therefore if all machines are to be fully utilised, a minimum of 12 units per day will have to be produced, involving two production machines and three packaging machines.

The 'container principle'. Any capital equipment that contains things (blast furnaces, oil tankers, pipes, vats, etc.) will tend to cost less per unit of output, the larger its size. This is due to the relationship between a container's volume and its surface area. A container's cost will depend largely on the materials used to build it and hence roughly on its *surface area*. Its output will depend largely on its *volume*. Large containers have a bigger volume relative to surface area than do small containers. For example, a container with a bottom, top and four sides, with each side measuring 1 metre, has a volume of 1 cubic metre and a surface area of 6 square metres (6 surfaces of 1 square metre each). If each side were now to be doubled in length to 2 metres, the volume would be 8 cubic metres and the surface area 24 square metres (6 surfaces of 4 square metres each). Therefore a fourfold increase in the container's surface area and thus an approximate fourfold increase in costs has led to an eightfold increase in capacity.

Greater efficiency of large machines. Large machines may be more efficient, in the sense that more output can be gained for a given amount of inputs. For example, whether a machine is large or small, only one worker may be required to operate it. Also, a large machine may make more efficient use of raw materials.

By-products. With production on a large scale, there may be sufficient waste products to enable them to make some by-product. For example, a wood mill may produce sufficient sawdust to make products such as charcoal briquettes or paper.

Multistage production. A large factory may be able to take a product through several stages in its manufacture. This saves time and cost moving the semi-finished product from one firm or factory to another. For example, a large cardboard-manufacturing firm may be able to convert trees or waste paper into cardboard and then into cardboard boxes in a continuous sequence.

All the above are examples of **plant economies of scale**. They are due to an individual factory or workplace or machine being large. There are other economies of scale that are associated with the firm being large – perhaps with many factories.

Organisational. With a large firm, individual plants can specialise in particular functions. There can also be centralised administration of the firms. Often, after a merger between two firms, savings can be made by **rationalising** their activities in this way.

Spreading overheads. Some expenditures are economic only when the *firm* is large, such as research and development: only a large firm can afford to set up a research laboratory. This is another example of indivisibilities, only this time at the level of the firm rather than the plant. The greater the firm's output, the more these **overhead costs** are spread.

Financial economies. Large firms may be able to obtain finance at lower interest rates than small firms, as they are perceived as having lower default risks or have more power to negotiate a better deal. Additionally larger firms may be able to obtain certain inputs more cheaply by purchasing in bulk. This follows from the concept of opportunity cost, as the larger a firm's order, the more likely it is that the supplier will offer a discount, as the opportunity cost of losing the business is getting higher. This helps to reduce the cost per unit.

Definitions

Specialisation and division of labour Where production is broken down into a number of simpler, more specialised tasks, thus allowing workers to acquire a high degree of efficiency.

Indivisibilities The impossibility of dividing a factor of production into smaller units.

Plant economies of scale Economies of scale that arise because of the large size of the factory.

Rationalisation The reorganising of production (often after a merger) so as to cut out waste and duplication and generally to reduce costs.

Overheads Costs arising from the general running of an organisation, and only indirectly related to the level of output.

Economies of scope. Often a firm is large because it produces a range of products. This can result in each individual product being produced more cheaply than if it was produced in a single-product firm. The reason for these *economies of scope* is that various overhead costs and financial and organisational economies can be shared between the products. For example, a firm that produces a whole range of CD players, DVD players and recorders, games consoles, TVs and so on can benefit from shared marketing and distribution costs and the bulk purchase of electronic components.

Many companies will experience a variety of economies of scale and you can find examples in practice from a variety of sources. On the Sloman News Site, you will find blogs that discuss economies of scale, such as those experienced by companies using cloud computing (Operating in a cloud), the possibility of achieving economies of scale through takeovers (Take over?) and whether big supermarkets can use economies of scale to their advantage (Supermarket wars: a pricing race to the bottom). The economies of scale for large cloud providers is also discussed in numerous articles, including an article by Randy Bias[1] and another that considers the case of Microsoft.[2]

Diseconomies of scale

When firms get beyond a certain size, costs per unit of output may start to increase. There are several reasons for such *diseconomies of scale*:

- Management problems of co-ordination may increase as the firm becomes larger and more complex, and as lines of communication get longer. There may be a lack of personal involvement and oversight by management.
- Workers may feel 'alienated' if their jobs are boring and repetitive, and if they feel an insignificant, and undervalued, small part of a large organisation. Poor motivation may lead to shoddy work.
- Industrial relations may deteriorate as a result of these factors and also as a result of the more complex interrelationships between different categories of worker.
- Production-line processes and the complex interdependencies of mass production can lead to great disruption if there are hold-ups in any one part of the firm.

Whether firms experience economies or diseconomies of scale will depend on the conditions applying in each individual firm.

Location

In the long run, a firm can move to a different location. The location will affect the cost of production, since locations differ in terms of the availability and cost of raw materials, suitable land and power supply, the qualifications, skills and experience of the labour force, wage rates, transport and communications networks, the cost of local services, and banking and financial facilities. In short, locations differ in terms of the availability, suitability and cost of the factors of production.

Transport costs will be an important influence on a firm's location. Ideally, a firm will wish to be as near as possible to both its raw materials and the market for its finished product. When market and raw materials are in different locations, the firm will minimise its transport costs by locating somewhere between the two. In general, if the raw materials are more expensive to transport than the finished product, the firm should locate as near as possible to the raw materials. This will normally apply to firms whose raw materials are heavier or more bulky than the finished product. Thus heavy industry, which uses large quantities of coal and various ores, tends to be concentrated near the coal fields or near the ports. If, on the other hand, the finished product is more expensive to transport (e.g. bread or beer), the firm will probably be located as near as possible to its market.

When raw materials or markets are in many different locations, transport costs will be minimised at the 'centre of gravity'. This location will be nearer to those raw materials and markets whose transport costs are greater per mile.

The size of the whole industry

As an *industry* grows in size, this can lead to *external economies of scale* for its member firms. This is where a firm, whatever its own individual size, benefits from the *whole industry* being large. For example, the firm may benefit from having access to specialist raw material or component suppliers, labour with specific skills, firms that specialise in marketing the finished product, and banks and other financial institutions with experience of the industry's requirements. What we are referring to here is the *industry's infrastructure*: the facilities, support services, skills and experience that can be shared by its members. As you will see in Box 9.3, this is one reason why we see industrial clusters emerging.

---

[1]Randy Bias, 'Understanding cloud datacenter economies of scale', cloudscaling, 4 October 2010, www.cloudscaling.com/blog/cloud-computing/understanding-cloud-datacenter-economies-of-scale/
[2]Charles Babcock, 'Microsoft: "incredible economies of scale" await cloud users', *InformationWeek*, 5 November 2011, www.informationweek.com/cloud/software-as-a-service/microsoft-incredible-economies-of-scale-await-cloud-users/d/d-id/1097690?

> ### Definitions
>
> **Economies of scope** When increasing the range of products produced by a firm reduces the cost of producing each one.
>
> **Diseconomies of scale** Where costs per unit of output increase as the scale of production increases.
>
> **External economies of scale** Where a firm's costs per unit of output decrease as the size of the whole *industry* grows.
>
> **Industry's infrastructure** The network of supply agents, communications, skills, training facilities, distribution channels, specialised financial services, etc. that support a particular industry.

The member firms of a particular industry might experience *external diseconomies of scale*. For example, as an industry grows larger, this may create a growing shortage of specific raw materials or skilled labour. This will push up their prices, and hence the firms' costs.

> ### Pause for thought
>
> *Would you expect external economies of scale to be associated with the concentration of an industry in a particular region? Explain.*

The optimum combination of factors

In the long run, all factors can be varied. The firm can thus choose what techniques of production to use: what design of factory to build, what types of machine to buy, how to organise the factory, and whether to use highly automated processes or more labour-intensive techniques. It must be very careful in making these decisions. Once it has built its factory and installed the machinery, these then become fixed factors of production, maybe for many years: the subsequent 'short-run' time period may in practice last a very long time!

For any given scale, how should the firm decide what technique to use? How should it decide the optimum 'mix' of factors of production?

The profit-maximising firm will obviously want to use the least costly combination of factors to produce any given output. It will therefore substitute factors, one for another, if by so doing it can reduce the cost of a given output. What, then, is the optimum combination of factors?

The simple two-factor case
Take first the simplest case where a firm uses just two factors: labour (L) and capital (K). The least-cost combination of the two will be where:

$$\frac{MPP_L}{P_L} = \frac{MPP_K}{P_K}$$

In other words, it is where the extra product (MPP) from the last pound spent on each factor is equal. But why should this be so? The easiest way to answer this is to consider what would happen if they were not equal.

If they were not equal, it would be possible to reduce cost per unit of output, by using a different combination of labour and capital. For example, if:

$$\frac{MPP_L}{P_L} > \frac{MPP_K}{P_K}$$

KI 4
p25
more labour should be used relative to capital, since the firm is getting a greater physical return for its money from extra workers than from extra capital. As more labour is used per unit of capital, however, diminishing returns to labour set
KI 20
p142
in. Thus MPP_L will fall. Likewise, as less capital is used per unit of labour, the MPP_K will rise. This will continue until:

$$\frac{MPP_L}{P_L} = \frac{MPP_K}{P_K}$$

At this point, the firm will stop substituting labour for capital.

Since no further gain can be made by substituting one factor for another, this combination of factors or 'choice of techniques' can be said to be the most efficient. It is the least-cost way of combining factors for any given output. Efficiency in this sense of using the optimum factor proportions is known as *technical or productive efficiency*.

The multifactor case
Where a firm uses many different factors, the least-cost combination of factors will be where:

$$\frac{MPP_a}{P_a} = \frac{MPP_b}{P_b} = \frac{MPP_c}{P_c} = \frac{MPP_n}{P_n}$$

where a ... n are different factors of production.

The reasons are the same as in the two-factor case. If any inequality exists between the MPP/P ratios, a firm will be able to reduce its costs by using more of those factors with a high MPP/P ratio and less of those with a low MPP/P ratio until the ratios all become equal. A major problem for a firm in choosing the least-cost technique is in predicting future factor price changes.

If the price of a factor were to change, the MPP/P ratios would cease to be equal. The firm, to minimise costs, would then like to alter its factor combinations until the MPP/P ratios once more become equal. The trouble is that, once it has committed itself to a particular technique, it may be several years before it can switch to an alternative one. Thus if a firm invests in labour-intensive methods of production and is then faced with an unexpected wage rise, it may regret not having chosen a more capital-intensive technique.

Postscript: decision making in different time periods

We have distinguished between the short run and the long run. Let us introduce two more time periods to complete the picture. The complete list then reads as follows.

Very short run (immediate run). All factors are fixed. Output is fixed. The supply curve is vertical. On a day-to-day basis, a firm may not be able to vary output at all. For example, a flower seller, once the day's flowers have been purchased from the wholesaler, cannot alter the amount of flowers

> ### Definitions
>
> **External diseconomies of scale** Where a firm's costs per unit of output increase as the size of the whole industry increases.
>
> **Technical or productive efficiency** The least-cost combination of factors for a given output.

BOX 9.3   UK COMPETITIVENESS: MOVING TO THE NEXT STAGE

The importance of location

In May 2003 Professor Michael Porter and Christian Ketels of Harvard Business School published a review of the UK's competitiveness on behalf of the UK government. The authors declared that since 1980 the UK had done remarkably well in halting its economic decline on world markets, and had in fact matched and even bettered its main rivals in many industrial sectors. However, they were quick to sound a note of caution.

> The UK currently faces a transition to a new phase of economic development. The old approach to economic development is reaching the limits of its effectiveness, and government, companies, and other institutions need to rethink their policy priorities. This rethinking is not a sign of the past strategy's failure; it is a necessary part of graduating to the new stage.[3]

Porter's view is that economic development is achieved through a series of stages. The factor-driven stage identifies factors of production as the basis of competitive advantage: you have an advantage in those industries where you have a plentiful supply of the relevant factors of production. The investment-driven stage of development focuses upon efficiency and productivity as the key to competitive success. The third stage, into which Porter believes the UK is shifting, is innovation-driven. Here competitive advantage is achieved through the production of innovative products and services.

The importance of industrial clusters

One of the key characteristics of a successful innovation-led development strategy is the existence of industrial clusters.

> Clusters are geographically proximate groups of interconnected companies, suppliers, service providers, and associated institutions in a particular field, linked by commonalties and complementarities.[4]

Porter suggests that clusters are vital for competitiveness in three crucial respects:

- Clusters improve productivity. The close proximity of suppliers and other service providers enhances flexibility.
- Clusters aid innovation. Interaction among businesses within a cluster stimulates new ideas and aids their dissemination.
- Clusters contribute to new business formation. Clusters are self-reinforcing, in so far as specialist factors such as dedicated venture capital, and labour skills, help reduce costs and lower the risks of new business start-up.

Given that national economies tend to specialise in certain industrial clusters, we can identify where clusters occur, and their importance, by considering their share of national output and export earnings. Export earnings in particular are a good indicator of how globally competitive a cluster might be.

The UK's industrial clusters were seen by Porter as being relatively weak, and in fact many traditional clusters, such as steel and car manufacturing, had thinned to the point where they now lacked critical mass and failed to benefit from the clustering effect. The UK had strengths in the areas of services, such as financial services and media, defence, products for personal use, health care and tele-communications.

Porter and Katels concluded that, to improve its competitiveness, the UK must not only support what clusters it has but also 'mount a sustained programme of cluster development to create a more conducive environment for productivity growth and innovation through the collective action of companies and other institutions'.[5]

The UK government responded to this report and currently supports cluster development in a number of ways, including through the creation of Enterprise Zones. These zones aim to create jobs and boost business in 24 areas across England, including the Humber Estuary Renewable Energy Cluster and the Modern Manufacturing and Technology Growth area in Sheffield. Eligible companies within these zones receive benefits such as reductions in business rates and simplified planning regulations. Cluster development has become an integral part of the remit of other policy areas, including science and innovation, export and foreign investment promotion and small and medium-sized enterprise policies.

Recent evidence

The performance of UK clusters has not changed greatly since the earlier report by Porter and Katels, but more information is coming to light. You can access data on a number of countries, including the UK, from the European Cluster Observatory. This is an EU project, which has identified locations where employment is highly concentrated in particular industrial clusters across Europe.[6]

The table shows the UK position. Information from the Observatory also shows that the UK leads the rest of Europe in cluster developments in areas such as Education and Knowledge Creation, Business Services, Finance and Transportation and Logistical Services, with most of these clusters occurring in London and the South East.

---

[3] M.E. Porter and C.H.M. Ketels, 'UK competitiveness: moving to the next stage' (DTI and ESRC, May 2003), p. 5.
[4] Ibid., p. 46.

[5] Ibid., p. 27.
[6] See www.clusterobservatory.eu

The top UK industry clusters ranked by employment, 2011

Region	Cluster category	Employees	Size (%)	Specialisation (quotient)	Focus (%)
Inner London	Financial services	233 734	4.31	3.01	9.82
Inner London	Business services	219 044	3.13	2.19	9.21
Outer London	Business services	122 757	1.76	1.75	7.33
Outer London	Transportation and logistics	100 707	2.10	2.09	6.02
Berks, Bucks and Oxon	Business services	95 295	1.36	2.06	8.66
Inner London	Education and knowledge creation	89 444	3.03	2.12	3.76
Surrey, E and W Sussex	Business services	81 724	1.17	1.71	7.18
Inner London	Media and publishing	76 111	4.08	2.85	3.20
Inner London	Transportation and logistics	69 632	1.45	1.02	2.93
Greater Manchester	Business services	65 071	0.93	1.34	5.61
W Midlands	Business services	64 883	0.93	1.30	5.45
Hants and Isle of Wight	Business services	62 199	0.89	1.78	7.47
Beds and Herts	Business services	60 947	0.87	2.31	8.20
Gloucs, Wilts and N Som	Business services	60 111	0.86	1.36	5.72
E Scotland	Financial services	59 747	1.10	2.03	6.62
Berks, Bucks and Oxon	Education and knowledge creation	58 363	1.97	2.99	5.30
Inner London	Tourism and hospitality	53 701	1.83	1.28	2.26
SW Scotland	Business services	48 878	0.70	1.14	4.78
W Yorks	Financial services	47 764	0.88	1.49	4.85
W Yorks	Business services	46 675	0.67	1.13	4.74
Berks, Bucks and Oxon	IT	30 184	1.96	3.01	2.74
NE Scotland	Oil and gas	11 792	3.98	25.22	4.45

Source: Based on EU Cluster Observatory, www.clusterobservatory.eu

Notes:

The European Cluster Observatory uses three measures to define a cluster, all based on employment. The three measures are size, specialisation and focus. If, for each measure, a location meets a specific criterion it is awarded a star. Only industries that achieved three stars are included in the above table.

The criteria for awarding a star are as follows:

Size: This gives employment in the cluster as a percentage of European employment in that industry. If a cluster is in the top 10 per cent of similar clusters in Europe in terms of employees, it receives a star (Europe is defined as the EU-27, Iceland, Israel, Norway, Switzerland and Turkey).

Specialisation: If a specialisation quotient of 2 or more is achieved, it is awarded a star. The specialisation quotient is given by

$$\frac{\text{UK employment in a region in a cluster category/total UK employment}}{\text{European employment in a cluster category/total European employment}}$$

Focus: This shows the extent to which the regional economy is focused upon the industries comprising the cluster category. This measure shows employment in the cluster as a percentage of total employment in the region. The top 10 per cent of clusters which account for the largest proportion of their region's total employment receive a star.

The UK has been very successful relative to the rest of Europe in developing clusters in the provision of Education and Knowledge Creation, notably in Oxford, Cambridge and East Scotland. Outside of these sectors the UK advantage relative to the rest of Europe is very limited, although there are pockets of success. For example, the UK has achieved some success in IT (around Oxford and the south coast of England), oil and gas (around Aberdeen in Scotland) and the automotive industry (in the West Midlands). These locations have achieved the size, specialisation and focus that have enabled them to develop positive spillovers and linkages which create local prosperity. Much more, though, has to be done.

 What policies or initiatives might a 'programme of cluster development' involve? Distinguish between policies that government and business might initiate.

available for sale on that day. In the very short run, all that may remain for a producer to do is to sell an already-produced good.

Short run. At least one factor is fixed in supply. More can be produced by increasing the quantity of the variable factor, but the firm will come up against the law of diminishing returns as it tries to do so.

Long run. All factors are variable. The firm may experience constant, increasing or decreasing returns to scale. But although all factors can be increased or decreased, they are of a fixed *quality*.

Very long run. All factors are variable, *and* their quality and hence productivity can change. Labour productivity can increase as a result of education, training, experience and social factors. The productivity of capital can increase as a result of new inventions (new discoveries) and innovation (putting inventions into practice).

Improvements in factor quality will increase the output they produce: *TPP*, *APP* and *MPP* will rise. These curves will shift vertically upward.

Just how long the 'very long run' is will vary from firm to firm. It will depend on how long it takes to develop new techniques, new skills or new work practices.

It is important to realise that decisions *for* all four time periods can be made *at* the same time. Firms do not make short-run decisions *in* the short run and long-run decisions *in* the long run. They can make both short-run and long-run decisions today. For example, assume that a firm experiences an increase in consumer demand and anticipates that it will continue into the foreseeable future. It thus wants to increase output. Consequently, it makes the following four decisions *today*:

- *(Very short run)* It accepts that for a few days it will not be able to increase output. It informs its customers that they will have to wait. It may temporarily raise prices to choke off some of the demand.
- *(Short run)* It negotiates with labour to introduce overtime working as soon as possible, to tide it over the next few weeks. It orders extra raw materials from its

suppliers. It launches a recruitment drive for new labour so as to avoid paying overtime longer than is necessary.
- *(Long run)* It starts proceedings to build a new factory. The first step may be to discuss requirements with a firm of consultants.
- *(Very long run)* It institutes a programme of research and development and/or training in an attempt to increase productivity.

> **Pause for thought**
>
> 1. What will the long-run market supply curve for a product look like? How will the shape of the long-run curve depend on returns to scale?
> 2. Why would it be difficult to construct a very long-run supply curve?

Although we distinguish these four time periods, it is the middle two we are primarily concerned with. The reason for this is that there is very little that the firm can do in the very short run. And in the very long run, although the firm will obviously want to increase the productivity of its inputs, it will not be in a position to make precise calculations of how to do it. It will not know precisely what inventions will be made, or just what will be the results of its own research and development.

9.5 COSTS IN THE LONG RUN

When it comes to making long-run production decisions, the firm has much more flexibility. It does not have to operate with plant and equipment of a fixed size. It can expand the whole scale of its operations. All its inputs are variable, and thus the law of diminishing returns does not apply. The firm may experience economies of scale or diseconomies of scale, or its average costs may stay constant as it expands the scale of its operations.

Since there are no fixed factors in the long run, there are no long-run fixed costs. For example, the firm may rent more land in order to expand its operations. Its rent bill therefore goes up as it expands its output. All costs, then, in the long run are variable costs.

Long-run average costs

Although it is possible to draw long-run total, marginal and average cost curves, we will concentrate on *long-run average cost (LRAC) curves*. These curves can take various shapes, but a typical one is shown in Figure 9.4.

It is often assumed that, as a firm expands, it will initially experience economies of scale and thus face a downward-sloping *LRAC* curve. While it is possible for a firm

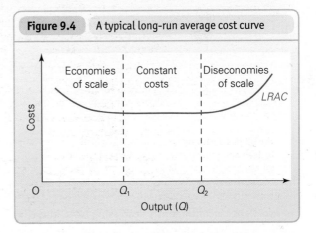

Figure 9.4 A typical long-run average cost curve

> **Definition**
>
> **Long-run average cost (*LRAC*) curve** A curve that shows how average cost varies with output on the assumption that *all* factors are variable. (It is assumed that the least-cost method of production will be chosen for each output.)

BOX 9.4   MINIMUM EFFICIENT SCALE

The extent of economies of scale in practice

Two of the most important studies of economies of scale have been those made by C.F. Pratten[7] in the late 1980s and by a group advising the European Commission[8] in 1997.
Both studies found strong evidence that many firms, especially in manufacturing, experienced substantial economies of scale.

In a few cases long-run average costs fell continuously as output increased. For most firms, however, they fell up to a certain level of output and then remained constant.

The extent of economies of scale can be measured by looking at a firm's *minimum efficient scale* (*MES*). The *MES* is the size beyond which no significant additional economies of scale can be achieved: in other words, the point where the *LRAC* curve flattens off. In Pratten's studies he defined this level as the minimum scale above which any possible doubling in scale would reduce average costs by less than 5 per cent (i.e. virtually the bottom of the *LRAC* curve). In the diagram *MES* is shown at point *a*.

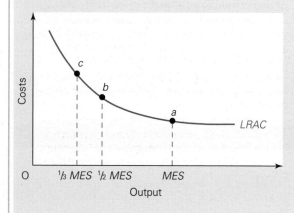

[7] C. F. Pratten, 'A survey of the economies of scale', in *Research on the 'Costs of Non-Europe'*, vol. 2 (Office for Official Publications of the European Communities, 1988).

[8] European Commission/Economists Advisory Group Ltd, 'Economies of scale', *The Single Market Review*, subseries V, vol. 4 (Office for Official Publications of the European Communities, 1997).

Table (a)

Product	MES as % of production		% additional cost at 1/2 MES
	UK	EU	
Individual plants			
Cellulose fibres	125	16	3
Rolled aluminium semi-manufactures	114	15	15
Refrigerators	85	11	4
Steel	72	10	6
Electric motors	60	6	15
TV sets	40	9	9
Cigarettes	24	6	1.4
Ball-bearings	20	2	6
Beer	12	3	7
Nylon	4	1	12
Bricks	1	0.2	25
Tufted carpets	0.3	0.04	10
Shoes	0.3	0.03	1
Firms			
Cars	200	20	9
Lorries	104	21	7.5
Mainframe computers	>100	n.a.	5
Aircraft	100	n.a.	5
Tractors	98	19	6

Sources: Based on C. F. Pratten, and M. Emerson, *The Economics of 1992* (Oxford University Press, 1988, data from tables on pp. 126–40, Section 6.1 'Size phenomena: economies of scale'

The *MES* can be expressed in terms either of an individual factory or of the whole firm. Where it refers to the minimum efficient scale of an individual factory, the *MES* is known as *the minimum efficient plant size* (*MEPS*).

---

to experience a continuously decreasing *LRAC* curve, in most cases, after a certain point (Q_1 in Figure 9.4), all such economies will have been achieved and thus the curve will flatten out.

Then, possibly after a period of constant *LRAC* (between Q_1 and Q_2), the firm will get so large that it will start experiencing diseconomies of scale and thus a rising *LRAC*. At this stage, production and financial economies begin to be offset by the managerial problems of running a giant organisation. Evidence does indeed show diseconomies of scale in many businesses arising from managerial

problems and industrial relations, especially in growing businesses, but there is little evidence to suggest technical diseconomies.

The effect of these factors is to give an L-shaped or saucer-shaped curve.

Assumptions behind the long-run average cost curve

We make three key assumptions when constructing long-run average cost curves.

Table (b)

Plants	MES as % of total EU production
Aerospace	12.19
Tractors and agricultural machinery	6.57
Electric lighting	3.76
Steel tubes	2.42
Shipbuilding	1.63
Rubber	1.06
Radio and TV	0.69
Footwear	0.08
Carpets	0.03

Source: European Commission/Economists Advisory Group Ltd, 'Economies of scale', *The Single Market Review*, subseries V, vol. 4 (Office for Official Publications of the European Communities, 1997)

The *MES* can then be expressed as a percentage of the total size of the market or of total domestic production. Table (a), based on the Pratten study, shows *MES* for plants and firms in various industries. The first column shows *MES* as a percentage of total UK production. The second column shows *MES* as a percentage of total EU production. Table (b), based on the 1997 study, shows *MES* for various plants as a percentage of total EU production.

Expressing *MES* as a percentage of total output gives an indication of how competitive the industry could be. In some industries (such as footwear and carpets), economies of scale were exhausted (i.e. *MES* was reached) with plants or firms that were still small relative to total UK production and even smaller relative to total EU production. In such industries there would be room for many firms and thus scope for considerable competition.

In other industries, however, even if a single plant or firm were large enough to produce the whole output of the industry in the UK, it would still not be large enough to experience the full potential economies of scale: the *MES* is greater than 100 per cent. Examples from Table (a) include factories producing cellulose fibres, and car manufacturers.

In such industries there is no possibility of competition. In fact, as long as the *MES* exceeds 50 per cent there will not be room for more than one firm large enough to gain full economies of scale. In this case the industry is said to be *a natural monopoly*. As we shall see in the next few chapters, when competition is lacking, consumers may suffer by firms charging prices considerably above costs.

A second way of measuring the extent of economies of scale is to see how much costs would increase if production were reduced to a certain fraction of *MES*. The normal fractions used are ½ or ⅓ *MES*. This is illustrated in the diagram. Point *b* corresponds to ½ *MES*; point *c* to ⅓ *MES*. The greater the percentage by which *LRAC* at point *b* or *c* is higher than at point *a*, the greater will be the economies of scale to be gained by producing at *MES* rather than at ½ *MES* or ⅓ *MES*. For example, in the table there are greater economies of scale to be gained from moving from ½ *MES* to *MES* in the production of electric motors than in cigarettes.

The main purpose of the studies was to determine whether the single EU market is big enough to allow both economies of scale and competition. The tables suggest that in all cases, other things being equal, the EU market is large enough for firms to gain the full economies of scale *and* for there to be enough firms for the market to be competitive.

The second study also found that 47 of the 53 manufacturing sectors analysed had scope for further exploitation of economies of scale.

In the 2007–13 Research Framework, the European Commission agreed to fund a number of research projects. These will conduct further investigations of *MES* across different industries and consider the impact of the expansion of the EU.

1. *Why might a firm operating with one plant achieve MEPS and yet not be large enough to achieve MES? (Clue: are all economies of scale achieved at plant level?)*
2. *Why might a firm producing bricks have an MES which is only 0.2 per cent of total EU production and yet face little effective competition from other EU countries?*

Factor prices are given. At each level of output, a firm will be faced with a given set of factor prices. If factor prices *change*, therefore, both short- and long-run cost curves will shift. For example, an increase in wages would shift the curves vertically upwards.

However, factor prices might be different at *different* levels of output. For example, one of the economies of scale that many firms enjoy is the ability to obtain bulk discount on raw materials and other supplies. In such cases the curve does *not* shift. The different factor prices are merely experienced at different points along the curve, and are reflected

in the shape of the curve. Factor prices are still given for any particular level of output.

The state of technology and factor quality are given. These are assumed to change only in the very long run. If a firm gains economies of scale, it is because it is able to exploit existing technologies and make better use of the existing factors of production. As technology improves the curves will shift downwards.

Firms choose the least-cost combination of factors for each output. The assumption here is that firms operate efficiently:

BOX 9.5 | **FASHION CYCLES**

Costs and prices in the clothing industry

For many products, style is a key component of their success. A good example is clothing. If manufacturers can successfully predict or even drive a new fashion, then sales growth can be substantial.

With any new fashion, growth is likely to be slow at first. Then, as the fashion 'catches on' and people want to be seen wearing this fashionable item, sales grow until a peak is eventually reached. In the case of clothing, if it is 'this year's fashion' then the peak will be reached within a couple of months. Then, as the market becomes saturated and people await the next season's fashions, so sales will fall.

This rise and fall is known as the 'fashion cycle' and is illustrated in the following diagram, which shows five stages: introduction of a style; growth in popularity; peak in popularity; decline in popularity; obsolescence.

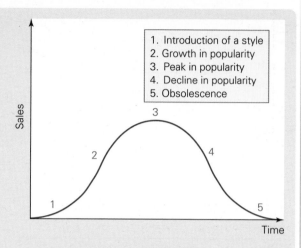

1. Introduction of a style
2. Growth in popularity
3. Peak in popularity
4. Decline in popularity
5. Obsolescence

The variation of costs and prices over the fashion cycle

Costs and prices tend to vary with the stages of the fashion cycle. At the introductory stage of a new fashion item, average costs are likely to be high. Within that stage, the fixed costs of design, setting up production lines, etc. are being spread over a relatively small output; average fixed costs are high. Also, there is a risk to producers that the fashion will not catch on and thus they are likely to factor in this risk when estimating costs. Finally, those consumers who want to be ahead in fashion and wearing the very latest thing will be willing to pay a high price to obtain such items. The result of all these factors is that price is likely to be high in the introductory stage.

Assuming the fashion catches on and more units are produced to cater for this higher demand, average costs will begin to fall. This will allow prices to fall and, as a result, the fashion is likely to be taken up by cheaper High Street chains, further driving demand.

Beyond the peak, costs are unlikely to fall much further, but intense competition between retailers is likely to continue driving prices down. The garments may end up on sales rails. (Note that with fashions that do not catch on, the price may fall rapidly quite early on as producers seek to cut their losses.)

Then, with the new season's fashions, the cycle begins again.

1. If consumers are aware that fashion clothing will fall in price as the season progresses, why do they buy when prices are set high at the start of the season? What does this tell us about the shape of the demand curve for a

given fashion product (a) at the start, and (b) at the end of the season?

The greater the importance of fashion for a particular type of garment, the greater is likely to be the seasonable price variability. The taller the 'bell' in the diagram, i.e. the greater the rise and fall in sales, the greater is likely to be the difference in price between the different stages.

Technology and the fashion cycle

We have seen that costs are an important element in the fashion cycle and in prices and sales through the different phases of the cycle. Fixed costs are highly dependent on technology. Advances in the textile industry have included more easily adaptable machines which are relatively easily programmed and design software which allows designers to change fashion parameters on the screen rather than with physical materials. These advances have meant that the fixed costs of introducing new fashions have come down. With lower fixed costs, average costs will tend to decline less steeply as output rises.

2. How might we account for the changing magnitudes of the fashion price cycles of clothing? What role do fixed costs play in the explanation?

3. Despite new technology in the car industry, changing the design and shape of cars has increased as a share of the total production costs. How is this likely to have affected the fashion cycle in the car industry?

---

that they choose the cheapest possible way of producing any level of output. In other words, at every point along the LRAC curve the firm will adhere to the cost-minimising formula:

$$\frac{MPP_a}{P_a} = \frac{MPP_b}{P_b} = \frac{MPP_c}{P_c} \cdots = \frac{MPP_n}{P_n}$$

where a … n are the various factors that the firm uses.

If the firm did not choose the optimum factor combination, it would be producing at a point above the *LRAC* curve.

Definition

Envelope curve A long-run average cost curve drawn as the tangency points of a series of short-run average cost curves.

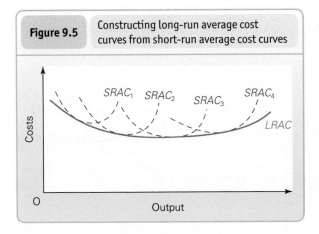

Figure 9.5 Constructing long-run average cost curves from short-run average cost curves

In the long run, it can build more factories or expand its existing facilities. If it thereby experiences economies of scale (due, say, to savings on administration), each successive factory will allow it to produce with a new lower *SRAC* curve. Thus with two factories it will face curve $SRAC_2$; with three factories curve $SRAC_3$, and so on. Each *SRAC* curve corresponds to a particular amount of the factor that is fixed in the short run: in this case, the factory. (There are many more *SRAC* curves that could be drawn between the ones shown, since factories of different sizes could be built or existing ones could be expanded.)

From this succession of short-run average cost curves we can construct a long-run average cost curve. This is shown in Figure 9.5 and is known as the ***envelope curve***, since it envelops the short-run curves.

The relationship between long-run and short-run average cost curves

Take the case of a firm which has just one factory and faces a short-run average cost curve illustrated by $SRAC_1$ in Figure 9.5.

> ### Pause for thought
>
> *Will the envelope curve be tangential to the bottom of each of the short-run average cost curves? Explain why it should or should not be.*

SUMMARY

1a When measuring costs of production, we should be careful to use the concept of opportunity cost.

1b In the case of factors not owned by the firm, the opportunity cost is simply the explicit cost of purchasing or hiring them. It is the price paid for them.

1c In the case of factors already owned by the firm, it is the implicit cost of what the factor could have earned for the firm in its next best alternative use.

2a A production function shows the relationship between the amount of inputs used and the amount of output produced from them (per period of time).

2b In the short run it is assumed that one or more factors (inputs) are fixed in supply. The actual length of the short run will vary from industry to industry.

2c Production in the short run is subject to diminishing returns. As greater quantities of the variable factor(s) are used, so each additional unit of the variable factor will add less to output than previous units: total physical product will rise less and less rapidly.

2d As long as marginal physical product is above average physical product, average physical product will rise. Once *MPP* has fallen below *APP*, however, *APP* will fall.

3a With some factors fixed in supply in the short run, their total costs will be fixed with respect to output. In the case of variable factors, their total cost will increase as more output is produced and hence as more of them are used.

3b Total cost can be divided into total fixed and total variable cost. Total variable cost will tend to increase less rapidly at first as more is produced, but then, when diminishing returns set in, it will increase more and more rapidly.

3c Marginal cost is the cost of producing one more unit of output. It will probably fall at first (corresponding to the part of the *TVC* curve where the slope is getting shallower), but will start to rise as soon as diminishing returns set in.

3d Average cost, like total cost, can be divided into fixed and variable costs. Average fixed cost will decline as more output is produced, as the total fixed cost is spread over a greater and greater number of units of output. Average variable cost will tend to decline at first, but once the marginal cost has risen above it, it must then rise.

4a In the long run, a firm is able to vary the quantity it uses of all factors of production. There are no fixed factors.

4b If a firm increases all factors by the same proportion, it may experience constant, increasing or decreasing returns to scale.

4c Economies of scale occur when costs per unit of output fall as the scale of production increases. This can be due to a number of factors, some of which are directly caused by increasing (physical) returns to scale, such as specialisation and division of labour. Other economies of scale arise from the financial and administrative benefits of large-scale organisations having a range of products (economies of scope).

4d Long-run costs are also influenced by a firm's location. The firm will have to balance the need to be as near as possible both to the supply of its raw materials and to its market. The optimum balance will depend on the relative costs of transporting the inputs and the finished product.

4e To minimise costs per unit of output, a firm should choose that combination of factors which gives an equal marginal product for each factor relative to its price: i.e. $MPP_a/P_a = MPP_b/P_b = MPP_c/P_c$, etc. (where a, b and c are different factors). If the MPP/P ratio for any factor is greater than that for another, more of the first should be used relative to the second.

5a In the long run, all factors are variable. There are thus no long-run fixed costs.

5b When constructing long-run cost curves, it is assumed that factor prices are given, that the state of technology is given and that firms will choose the least-cost combination of factors for each given output.

5c The $LRAC$ curve can be downward sloping, upward sloping or horizontal, depending in turn on whether there

are economies of scale, diseconomies of scale or neither. Typically, $LRAC$ curves are drawn as saucer-shaped or L-shaped. As output expands, initially there are economies of scale. When these are exhausted, the curve will become flat. When the firm becomes very large, it may begin to experience diseconomies of scale. If this happens, the $LRAC$ curve will begin to slope upward again.

5d An envelope curve can be drawn which shows the relationship between short-run and long-run average cost curves. The $LRAC$ curve envelops the short-run AC curves: it is tangential to them.

MyEconLab

This book can be supported by MyEconLab, Which contains a range of additional resources, including an online homework and tutorial system designed to test and build your understanding.

You need both an access card and a course ID to access MyEconLab:

1. Is your lecturer using MyEconLab? Ask your lecturer for your course ID.

2. Has an access card been included with the book at a reduced cost? Check the inside back cover of the book.

3. If you have a course ID but no access card, go to: http://www.myeconlab.com/ to buy access to this interactive study programme.

REVIEW QUESTIONS

1 Are all explicit costs variable costs? Are all variable costs explicit costs?

2 Roughly how long would you expect the short run to be in the following cases?

a) A mobile disco firm.
b) Electricity power generation.
c) A small grocery retailing business.
d) 'Superstore Hypermarkets plc'.

In each case, specify your assumptions.

3 Given that there is a fixed supply of land in the world, what implications can you draw from Figure 9.1 about the effects of an increase in world population for food output per head?

4 The following are some costs incurred by a shoe manufacturer. Decide whether each one is a fixed cost or a variable cost or has some element of both.

a) The cost of leather.
b) The fee paid to an advertising agency.
c) Wear and tear on machinery.
d) Business rates on the factory.
e) Electricity for heating and lighting.
f) Electricity for running the machines.
g) Basic minimum wages agreed with the union.
h) Overtime pay.
i) Depreciation of machines as a result purely of their age (irrespective of their condition).

5 Assume that you are required to draw a TVC curve corresponding to Figure 9.1. What will happen to this TVC curve beyond point d?

6 Why is the minimum point of the AVC curve at a lower level of output than the minimum point of the AC curve?

7 Which economies of scale are due to increasing returns to scale and which are due to other factors?

8 What economies of scale is a large department store likely to experience?

9 Why are many firms likely to experience economies of scale up to a certain size and then diseconomies of scale after some point beyond that?

10 Why are bread and beer more expensive to transport per mile than the raw materials used in their manufacture?

11 Name some industries where external economies of scale are gained. What are the specific external economies in each case?

12 How is the opening up of trade and investment between eastern and western Europe likely to affect the location of industries within Europe that have (a) substantial economies of scale; (b) little or no economies of scale?

13 If factor X costs twice as much as factor Y ($P_x/P_y = 2$), what can be said about the relationship between the $MPPs$ of the two factors if the optimum combination of factors is used?

14 Could the long run and the very long run ever be the same length of time?

15 Examine Figure 9.4. What would (a) the firm's long-run total cost curve and (b) its long-run marginal cost curve look like?

16 Under what circumstances is a firm likely to experience a flat-bottomed $LRAC$ curve?

Revenue and profit

Business issues covered in this chapter

- How does a business's sales revenue vary with output?
- How does the relationship between output and sales revenue depend on the type of market in which a business is operating?
- How do we measure profits?
- At what output will a firm maximise its profits? How much profit will it make at this output?
- At what point should a business call it a day and shut down?

In this chapter we will identify the output and price at which a firm will maximise its profits, and how much profit will be made at that level. Remember that we defined a firm's total profit ($T\Pi$) as its total revenue minus its total costs of production.

$$T\Pi = TR - TC$$

In the previous chapter we looked at costs in some detail. We must now turn to the revenue side of the equation. As with costs, we distinguish between three revenue concepts: total revenue (TR), average revenue (AR) and marginal revenue (MR).

10.1 REVENUE

Total, average and marginal revenue

Total revenue (TR)

Total revenue is the firm's total earnings per period of time from the sale of a particular amount of output (Q).

For example, if a firm sells 1000 units (Q) per month at a price of £5 each (P), then its monthly total revenue will be £5000: in other words, £5 × 1000 ($P \times Q$). Thus:

$$TR = P \times Q$$

Average revenue (AR)

Average revenue is the average amount the firm earns per unit sold. Thus:

$$AR = TR/Q$$

Definition

Total revenue A firm's total earnings from a specified level of sales within a specified period: $TR = P \times Q$.

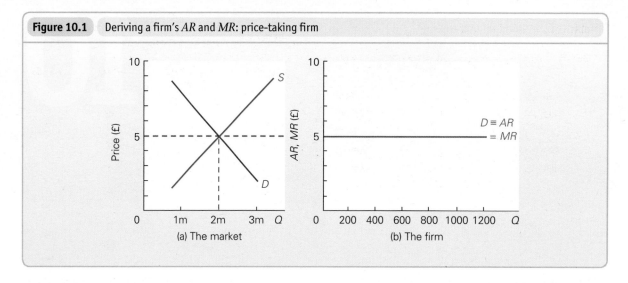

Figure 10.1 Deriving a firm's *AR* and *MR*: price-taking firm

(a) The market

(b) The firm

So if the firm earns £5000 (*TR*) from selling 1000 units (*Q*), it will earn £5 per unit. But this is simply the price! Thus:

$AR = P$

The only exception to this is when the firm is selling its products at different prices to different consumers. In this case *AR* is simply the (weighted) average price.

Marginal revenue (MR)

Marginal revenue is the extra total revenue gained by selling one more unit per time period. So if a firm sells an extra 20 units this month compared with what it expected to sell, and in the process earns an extra £100, then it is getting an extra £5 for each extra unit sold: $MR = £5$. Thus:

$MR = \Delta TR/\Delta Q$

We now need to see how each of these three revenue concepts (*TR*, *AR* and *MR*) varies with output. We can show this relationship graphically in the same way as we did with costs.

The relationship will depend on the market conditions under which a firm operates. A firm which is too small to be able to affect market price will have differently shaped revenue curves from a firm which has some choice in setting its price. Let us examine each of these two situations in turn.

Revenue curves when price is not affected by the firm's output

Average revenue

If a firm is very small relative to the whole market, it is likely to be a **price taker**. That is, it has to accept the price given by the intersection of demand and supply in the whole market. At this price, the firm can sell as much as it is capable of producing, but if it increases the price it would lose all its sales to competitors. Charging a lower price would not be rational

as the firm can sell as much as it is capable of producing at the prevailing price. This is illustrated in Figure 10.1.

Diagram (a) shows market demand and supply. Equilibrium price is £5. Diagram (b) looks at the demand for an individual firm which is tiny relative to the whole market. (Look at the difference in the scale of the horizontal axes in the two diagrams.)

Being so small, any change in the firm's output will be too insignificant to affect the market price. The firm thus faces a horizontal demand 'curve' at this price. It can sell any output up to its maximum capacity, without affecting this £5 price.

Average revenue is thus constant at £5. The firm's average revenue curve must therefore lie along exactly the same line as its demand curve.

Marginal revenue

In the case of a horizontal demand curve, the marginal revenue curve will be the same as the average revenue curve, since selling one more unit at a constant price (*AR*) merely adds that amount to total revenue. If an extra unit is sold at a constant price of £5, an extra £5 is earned.

Total revenue

Table 10.1 shows the effect on total revenue of different levels of sales with a constant price of £5 per unit.

Definitions

Average revenue Total revenue per unit of output. When all output is sold at the same price, average revenue will be the same as price: $AR = TR/Q = P$.

Marginal revenue The extra revenue gained by selling one or more unit per time period: $MR = \Delta TR/\Delta Q$.

Price taker A firm that is too small to be able to influence the market price.

Table 10.1	Deriving total revenue	
Quantity (units)	Price = AR = MR (£)	TR (£)
0	5	0
200	5	1000
400	5	2000
600	5	3000
800	5	4000
1000	5	5000
1200	5	6000
.	.	.

Table 10.2	Revenues for a firm facing a downward-sloping demand curve		
Q (units)	P = AR (£)	TR (£)	MR (£)
1	8	8	
			6
2	7	14	
			4
3	6	18	
			2
4	5	20	
			0
5	4	20	
			−2
6	3	18	
			−4
7	2	14	

Figure 10.2 Total revenue curve for a price-taking firm

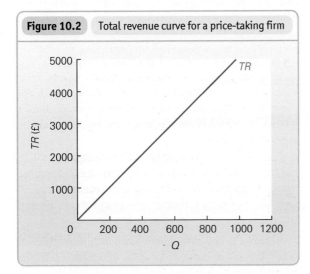

As price is constant, total revenue will rise at a constant rate as more is sold. The *TR* 'curve' will therefore be a straight line through the origin, as in Figure 10.2.

Pause for thought

What would happen to the TR curve if the market price rose to £10? Try drawing it.

Revenue curves when price varies with output

Rather than accepting (or taking) the market price, firms would generally prefer to be a **price maker**. This means that if a firm wants to sell more, it must lower its price. Alternatively, it could raise its price, if it was willing to accept a fall in demand. As such, a firm that is a price maker will face a downward-sloping demand curve. Firms will tend to be benefit from being price makers, as is discussed in an article from Harvard Business School.[1]

The three curves (*TR*, *AR* and *MR*) will look quite different when price does vary with the firm's output.

Average revenue

Remember that average revenue equals price. If, therefore, the price has to be reduced to sell more output, average revenue will fall as output increases.

Table 10.2 gives an example of a firm facing a downward-sloping demand curve. The demand curve (which shows how much is sold at each price) is given by the first two columns.

Note that, as in the case of a price-taking firm, the demand curve and the *AR* curve lie along exactly the same line. The reason for this is simple: $AR = P$, and thus the curve relating price to quantity (the demand curve) must be the same as that relating average revenue to quantity (the *AR* curve).

Pause for thought

Consider the items you have recently purchased. Classify them into products purchased from markets where sellers were price takers and those where the sellers were price makers.

Marginal revenue

When a firm faces a downward-sloping demand curve, marginal revenue will be less than average revenue, and may even be negative. But why?

Definition

Price maker A firm that has the ability to influence the price charged for its good or service.

---

[1]Benson P. Shapiro, 'Commodity busters: be a price maker not a price taker', *Working Knowledge*, Harvard University, 10 February 2003.

If a firm is to sell more per time period, it must lower its price (assuming it does not advertise). This will mean lowering the price not just for the extra units it hopes to sell, but also for those units it would have sold had it not lowered the price.

Thus the marginal revenue is the price at which it sells the last unit, *minus* the loss in revenue it has incurred by reducing the price on those units it could otherwise have sold at the higher price. This can be illustrated with Table 10.2.

Assume that price is currently £7. Two units are thus sold. If the firm wishes to sell an extra unit, it must lower the price, say to £6. It thus gains £6 from the sale of the third unit, but loses £2 by having to reduce the price by £1 on the two units previously sold at £7. Its net gain is therefore £6 − £2 = £4. This is the marginal revenue: it is the extra revenue gained by the firm from selling one more unit. Try using this method to check out the remaining figures for *MR* in Table 10.2. (Note that in the table the figures for *MR* are entered in the spaces between the figures for the other three columns.)

There is a simple relationship between marginal revenue and *price elasticity of demand*. Remember from Chapter 5 (see pages 71–2) that if demand is price elastic, a *decrease* in price will lead to a proportionately larger increase in the quantity demanded and hence an *increase* in revenue. Marginal revenue will thus be positive. If, however, demand is inelastic, a decrease in price will lead to a proportionately smaller increase in sales. In this case the price reduction will more than offset the increase in sales and as a result revenue will fall. Marginal revenue will be negative.

If, then, marginal revenue is a positive figure (i.e. if sales per time period are four units or fewer in Figure 10.3), the demand curve will be elastic at that point, since a rise in quantity sold (as a result of a reduction in price) would lead to a rise in total revenue. If, on the other hand, marginal

revenue is negative (i.e. at a level of sales of five or more units in Figure 10.3), the demand curve will be inelastic at that point, since a rise in quantity sold would lead to a *fall* in total revenue.

Thus, even though we have a straight-line demand (*AR*) curve in Figure 10.3, the price elasticity of demand is not constant along it. The curve is elastic to the left of point *r* and inelastic to the right.

Total revenue

Total revenue equals price times quantity. This is illustrated in Table 10.2. The *TR* column from Table 10.2 is plotted in Figure 10.4.

Unlike in the case of a price-taking firm, the *TR* curve is not a straight line. It is a curve that rises at first and then falls. But why? As long as marginal revenue is positive (and hence demand is price elastic), a rise in output will raise total revenue. However, once marginal revenue becomes negative (and hence demand is inelastic), total revenue will fall. The peak of the *TR* curve will be where *MR* = 0. At this point, the price elasticity of demand will be equal to −1.

Shifts in revenue curves

We saw (Chapter 4) that a change in *price* will cause a movement along a demand curve. It is similar with revenue curves, except that here the causal connection is in the other direction. Here we ask what happens to revenue when there is a change in the firm's *output*. Again the effect is shown by a movement along the curves.

A change in any *other* determinant of demand, such as tastes, income or the price of other goods, will shift the demand curve. By affecting the price at which each level of output can be sold, it will cause a shift in all three revenue curves. An increase in revenue is shown by a vertical shift upwards; a decrease by a shift downwards.

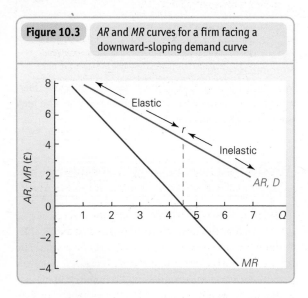

Figure 10.3 *AR* and *MR* curves for a firm facing a downward-sloping demand curve

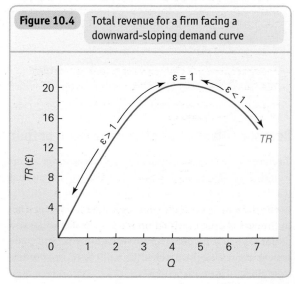

Figure 10.4 Total revenue for a firm facing a downward-sloping demand curve

| BOX 10.1 | COSTS, REVENUE AND PROFITS |

Strategies to increase total revenue

A firm's profit depends on two key factors: costs and revenue. If a firm's costs increase, while its revenue remains constant, then profits will fall. Whereas if a firm can increase its total revenue, without incurring a rise in costs, then profits will rise. If both total revenue and total costs change in the same direction, then we are unable to determine the impact on profits, unless we know the amount by which they each changed. In this box, we consider some strategies to increase revenue, while also considering the potential effect of such strategies on costs and, in turn, profits.

Total revenue is determined by price and quantity, so a change in either factor will affect total revenue. How might a firm go about boosting sales at the current price? Firms may look to find new markets for their products, as we have seen with companies such as Apple, which have expanded into Asian markets.

Another strategy used by firms is product differentiation. This aims to distinguish their product from others and encourage consumers to switch to it. Alternatively, a firm may engage in advertising to try to persuade consumers to buy the product.

With successful implementation of these strategies, at any given price, quantity should now rise and hence so will total revenue. But, does this mean that profits increase?

Advertising, product innovation and market research require time, resources and money and so can be very expensive. While the outcome of such investment might be an increase in total revenue, the means of achieving it will be an increase in total costs. This means that unless we know the relative increase in total revenue and total costs, the impact on profits will be unknown.

Furthermore, the increase in costs will occur as soon as work starts on the process of product differentiation or market research, or at the beginning of an advertising campaign. The increase in revenue may not be felt for some time, as advertising campaigns, entrance into a new market and a differentiated product can take many months before having their anticipated effect. Any firm engaging in such a strategy may therefore experience a time period in which its costs are rising while revenue is remaining fairly constant. In other words, profits decline, until the sales figures respond to the firm's strategy. In 2013, Starbucks implemented a strategy to boost profits, as is discussed in an article by Tucker Dawson.[2]

Pricing, elasticity and profits

Another option for the firm could be to look at its pricing strategy. The Law of Demand tells us that if the price of a good falls, the quantity demanded will rise. The key question is by how much will quantity demanded rise?

When demand is price inelastic, any decrease in price leads to a proportionately smaller increase in demand and so total revenue would fall (as we saw in Chapter 5). But if the firm were to *increase* the price of such a product, total revenue would rise.

 1. *How will total revenue be affected by (a) a price rise and (b) a price fall if the product was relatively elastic?*

Therefore, if a firm knows its product's price elasticity of demand, it can use this to help it increase total revenue.

But what about the impact on profits? Let us consider a product with an *elastic* demand and think about the impact of a price cut on both revenue and costs. The cut in price will boost revenue, as the quantity demanded rises proportionately more than price falls. But with an increased demand, the firm may have to increase production, which means its total variable costs will rise, and possibly its average variable costs too (although average fixed costs will fall). If, however, the firm has sufficient stocks to satisfy the higher demand, then the impact on costs may be less severe. With an elastic demand, the impact on profit depends on whether total revenue increases by more or less than total costs.

But what about the situation where a product has an inelastic demand? This time it is an *increase* in price that will boost total revenue, as the resulting fall in quantity will be proportionately smaller than the rise in price. If production is reduced even by a small amount, it will reduce the firm's demand for raw materials and in doing so cut its total variable costs. In this case, the impact on profit is somewhat more predictable, as total revenue is increasing, while total costs are falling.

There are many factors that can influence profitability and whenever a firm considers a change in strategy, it is important to consider the impact on both costs and revenue and the timing of such changes. This may make the difference between a company's success and failure.

 2. *Consider a firm that introduced a new policy of using only environmentally friendly inputs and locally sourced products in its production process. Analyse the impact of this strategy on the firm's costs and revenue. How do you think profits will be affected?*

[2] Tucker Dawson, 'How Starbucks uses pricing strategy for profit maximization', *Price Intelligently*, 30 June 2013.

| 10.2 | PROFIT MAXIMISATION |

We are now in a position to put costs and revenue together to find the output at which profit is maximised, and also to find out how much that profit will be. At this point, you may find an article by Renee O'Farrell[3] interesting: it considers the advantages and disadvantages of pursuing a strategy of profit maximisation.

There are two ways of determining the level of output at which a firm will maximise profits. The first and simpler method is to use total cost and total revenue curves. The second method is to use marginal and average cost and marginal and average revenue curves. Although this method is a little more complicated, it makes things easier when we come to compare profit maximising under different market conditions (see Chapters 11 and 12).

We will look at each method in turn. In both cases we will concentrate on the short run: namely that period in which one or more factors are fixed in supply. In both cases we take the case of a firm facing a downward-sloping demand curve: i.e. a price maker.

Short-run profit maximisation: using total curves

Table 10.3 shows the total revenue figures from Table 10.2. It also shows figures for total cost. These figures have been chosen so as to produce a *TC* curve of a typical shape.

Total profit (*TΠ*) is found by subtracting *TC* from *TR*. This can be seen in Table 10.3. Where (*TΠ*) is negative, the firm is making a loss. Total profit is maximised at an output of three units: where there is the greatest gap between total revenue and total costs. At this output, total profit is £4 (£18 − £14).

Table 10.3	Total revenue, costs and profit		
Q (units)	**TR (£)**	**TC (£)**	**TΠ (£)**
0	0	6	−6
1	8	10	−2
2	14	12	2
3	18	14	4
4	20	18	2
5	20	25	−5
6	18	36	−18
7	14	56	−42
.	.	.	.

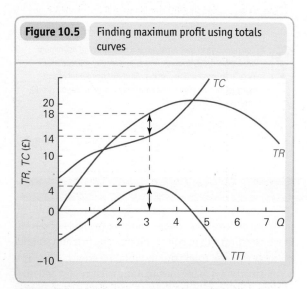

Figure 10.5 Finding maximum profit using totals curves

[3] Renee O'Farrell, 'Advantages and disadvantages of profit maximization', *Small Business*Chron.com, Houston Chronicle*, 24 June 2011.

The *TR*, *TC* and *TΠ* curves are plotted in Figure 10.5. The size of the maximum profit is shown by the arrows.

Short-run profit maximisation: using average and marginal curves

Finding the maximum profit that a firm can make is a two-stage process. The first stage is to find the profit-maximising output. To do this we use the *MC* and *MR* curves. The second stage is to find out just how much profit is at this output. To do this we use the *AR* and *AC* curves.

Stage 1: Using marginal curves to arrive at the profit-maximising output

There is a very simple **profit-maximising rule**: if profits are to be maximised, *MR must equal MC*. From Table 10.4 it can be seen that *MR = MC* at an output of 3 (Table 10.4 is based on the figures in Table 10.3). This is shown as point *e* in Figure 10.6.

> **Pause for thought**
>
> *Why are the figures for MR and MC entered in the spaces between the lines in Table 10.4?*

But why are profits maximised when *MR = MC*? The simplest way of answering this is to see what the position would be if *MR* did not equal *MC*.

Referring to Figure 10.6, at a level of output below 3, *MR* exceeds *MC*. This means that by producing more units there will be a bigger addition to revenue (*MR*) than to cost (*MC*). Total profit will *increase*. *As long as MR exceeds MC, profit can be increased by increasing production*.

At a level of output above 3, *MC* exceeds *MR*. All levels of output above 3 thus add more to cost than to revenue and

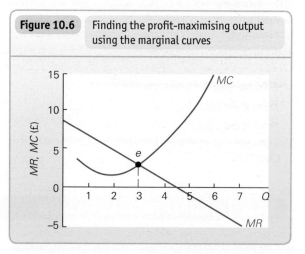

Figure 10.6 Finding the profit-maximising output using the marginal curves

> **Definition**
>
> **Profit-maximising rule** Profit is maximised where marginal revenue equals marginal cost.

Table 10.4	Revenue, costs and profit							
Q(units)	P = AR (£)	TR (£)	MR (£)	TC (£)	AC (£)	MC (£)	TΠ (£)	AΠ (£)
0	9	0		6	–		-6	–
			8			4		
1	8	8		10	10		-2	-2
			6			2		
2	7	14		12	6		2	1
			4			2		
3	6	18		14	4.67		4	-1.33
			2			4		
4	5	20		18	4.5		2	-0.5
			0			7		
5	4	20		25	5		-5	-1
			-2			11		
6	3	18		36	6		-18	-3
			-4			20		
7	2	14		56	8		-42	-6

hence *reduce* profit. *As long as MC exceeds MR, profit can be increased by cutting back on production.*

Profits are thus maximised where $MC = MR$: at an output of 3. This can be confirmed by examining the $T\Pi$ column in Table 10.4.

Students worry sometimes about the argument that profits are maximised when $MR = MC$. Surely, they say, if the last unit is making no profit, how can profit be at a *maximum*? The answer is very simple. If you cannot *add* anything more to a total, the total must be at the maximum. Take the simple analogy of going up a hill. When you cannot go any higher, you must be at the top.

Stage 2: Using average curves to measure the size of the profit

Once the profit-maximising output has been discovered, we now use the average curves to measure the *amount* of profit at the maximum. Both marginal and average curves corresponding to the data in Table 10.4 are plotted in Figure 10.7.

First, average profit ($A\Pi$) is found. This is simply $AR - AC$. At the profit-maximising output of 3, this gives a figure for $A\Pi$ of $£6 - £4^2/_3 = £1^1/_3$. Then total profit is obtained by multiplying average profit by output:

$$T\Pi = A\Pi \times Q$$

This is shown as the shaded area. It equals $£1^1/_3 \times 3 = £4$. This can again be confirmed by reference to the $T\Pi$ column in Table 10.4.

Some qualifications

Long-run profit maximisation

Assuming that the AR and MR curves are the same in the long run as in the short run, long-run profits will be

maximised at the output where MR equals the *long-run MC*. The reasoning is the same as with the short-run case.

The meaning of 'profit'

One element of cost is the opportunity cost to the owners of the firm incurred by being in business. This is the minimum return that the owners must make on their capital in order to prevent them from eventually deciding to close down and perhaps move into some alternative business. It is a *cost* since, just as with wages, rent, etc., it has to be covered if the firm is to continue producing. This opportunity cost to the owners is sometimes known as **normal profit**, and *is included in the cost curves.*

What determines this normal rate of profit? It has two components. First, someone setting up in business invests capital in it. There is thus an opportunity cost of capital. This is the interest that could have been earned by lend-

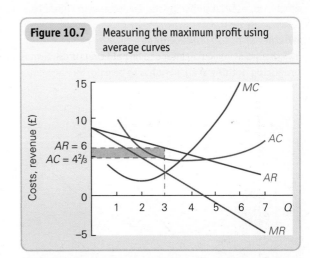

Figure 10.7 Measuring the maximum profit using average curves

Pause for thought

What will be the effect on a firm's profit-maximising output of a rise in fixed costs?

Definition

Normal profit The opportunity cost of being in business. It consists of the interest that could be earned on a riskless asset, plus a return for risk-taking in this particular industry. It is counted as a cost of production.

ing it in some riskless form (e.g. by putting it in a savings account in a bank). Nobody would set up a business unless they expected to earn at least this rate of profit. Running a business is far from riskless, however, and hence a second element is a return to compensate for risk. Thus:

normal profit (%) = rate of interest on a riskless loan + a risk premium

The risk premium varies according to the line of business. In those with fairly predictable patterns, such as food retailing, it is relatively low. Where outcomes are very uncertain, such as mineral exploration or the manufacture of fashion garments, it is relatively high.

Thus if owners of a business earn normal profit, they will (just) be content to remain in that industry. If they earn more than normal profit, they will (obviously) prefer to stay in this business. If they earn less than normal profit, then after a time they will consider leaving and using their capital for some other purpose.

Given that normal profits are included in costs, any profit that is shown diagrammatically (e.g. the shaded area in Figure 10.7) must therefore be over and above normal profit. It is known by several alternative names: **supernormal profit, pure profit, economic profit, abnormal profit** or sometimes simply **profit**. They all mean the same thing: the excess of profit over normal profit, or where *AR* is greater than *AC*. The article 'Milk prices: who gets the cream?', from the Sloman News Site, considers profitability in the milk industry.

Loss minimising

It may be that there is no output at which the firm can make a profit. Such a situation is illustrated in Figure 10.8: the *AC* curve is above the *AR* curve at all levels of output.

In this case, the output where $MR = MC$ will be the loss-minimising output. The amount of loss at the point where $MR = MC$ is shown by the shaded area in Figure 10.8.

Whether or not to produce at all

The short run. Fixed costs have to be paid even if the firm is producing nothing at all. Rent has to be paid, business rates

KI 18
p 141

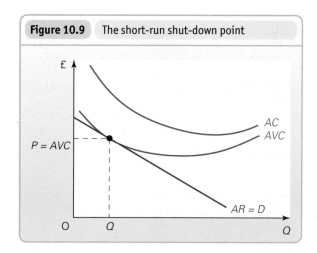

Figure 10.9 The short-run shut-down point

have to be paid, etc. Providing, therefore, that the firm is more than covering its *variable* costs, it can go some way to paying off these fixed costs and therefore will continue to produce.

Therefore, the firm will shut down if the loss it would make from doing so (i.e. the fixed costs that must still be paid) is less than the loss it makes from continuing to produce. That is, a firm will shut down if it cannot cover its variable costs. In Figure 10.9, this will be where the price (*AR*) is below the *AVC* curve: i.e. if it is below the **short-run shut-down point**, where $AR = AVC$.

The long run. All costs are variable in the long run. If, therefore, the firm cannot cover its long-run average costs (which include normal profit), it will close down. The **long-run shut-down point** will be where the *AR* curve is tangential to the *LRAC* curve.

Pause for thought

Why might it make sense for a firm which cannot sell its output at a profit to continue in production for the time being?

Definitions

Supernormal profit (also known as **pure profit, economic profit, abnormal profit** or simply **profit**) The excess of total profit above normal profit.

Short-run shut-down point This is where the AR curve is tangential to the AVC curve. The firm can only just cover its variable costs. Any fall in revenue below this level will cause a profit-maximising firm to shut down immediately.

Long-run shut-down point This is where the AR curve is tangential to the LRAC curve. The firm can just make normal profits. Any fall in revenue below this level will cause a profit-maximising firm to shut down once all costs have become variable.

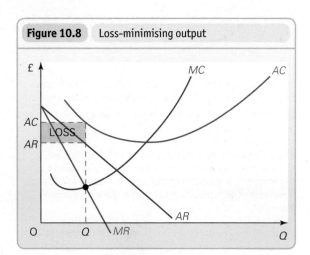

Figure 10.8 Loss-minimising output

BOX 10.2 **OPPORTUNITY COST OF CAPITAL IN PRACTICE**

Opportunity costs of capital and company structures

Opportunity costs of capital play an important role in determining the structure of large corporations. The RWE Group is one of Europe's largest electricity and gas companies. Its core operations are in Germany, the Netherlands and the UK. In the UK it operates through its npower subsidiary, which it purchased in 2002.

Should npower be sold?

By 2011 Jürgen Grossmann, RWE's chief executive, was considering if npower should remain part of the RWE portfolio. According to the *Financial Times*:

> RWE has been reviewing its strategic options, advised by Goldman Sachs, as it grapples with net debt of €27.5bn (£24.7bn).
>
> To reduce this burden, Mr Grossmann has pledged asset disposals of up to €8bn a year between 2011 and 2013. Selling npower, which generates about 9 per cent of the UK's electricity, will go a long way towards hitting this target ....
>
> Analysts point out that npower has significantly underperformed its counterparts in RWE. Last year, npower's return on capital employed was 5.3 per cent, making Britain the worst performing geographical area in the RWE group.
>
> Last year, RWE's annual report showed that npower's return fell below the group's cost of capital of 9 per cent before tax, ... [However] npower remains a cash-generating business, achieving an operating profit of €277m last year.[4]

At the time when Mr Grossmann was making his decision, he was not only looking at past performance, but would also have assessed npower's prospects for the future. On the demand side, there was (and still is) a consumer perception that gas and electricity companies are charging 'unfair' prices. This can make producers reluctant to raise prices, fearing the effects of negative publicity – though we have seen all of the

big six energy suppliers push up prices since then. On the supply side, more powerful emissions regulations were to be introduced from 2013 and this, together with rising distribution costs, would exert additional upward pressure on costs.

Finally, the decision as to whether to sell the company would also have taken into account the prospects for the rest of the RWE Group. Were the prospects of the other constituent parts better or worse than npower's?

The decision and subsequent events

Npower did remain part of RWE and perhaps a key determinant of this outcome was the future prospects of the company and a new Chief Executive Officer for RWE, in the form of Peter Terium, from 1 July 2012.

In November 2012, npower raised its energy prices by 9 per cent and in the same year lost 70 000 customers. Despite this, its profits rose by nearly 25 per cent (£77 million) to £390 million, as its remaining customers increased their energy usage. Its revenues increased to £1.9 billion after the price rise. It also saw an increase in its electricity generation as new power station infrastructure came online.[5]

However, at the start of 2014 its fortunes were reversed, as profits plummeted by 38 per cent – not dissimilar to the 40 per cent decline in operating profits for RWE itself. Various factors contributed to this decline, including warm weather and falling oil prices. Both of these factors are very variable and key drivers of profits and revenues for companies such as npower. As long as they remain uncertain, it is likely that company performance will also remain volatile.

1. *Explain why, even though npower generated €277 million in profit in 2010 and saw profits rise by £77 million in 2012, it still might have made sense for RWE to sell the company.*
2. *Under what circumstances would another company consider buying npower?*

[4]David Blair, Gerrit Wiesmann and Ausha Sakoui, 'RWE considers pulling plug on Npower', *Financial Times*, 5 July 2011. © The Financial Times Limited. All Rights Reserved.

[5]'npower profits soar, despite loss of 70,000 customers', *The Telegraph*, 5 March 2013, www.telegraph.co.uk/finance/personalfinance/household-bills/9911104/npower-profits-soar-despite-loss-of-70000-customers.html

---

BOX 10.3 **SELLING ICE CREAM WHEN I WAS A STUDENT**

John's experience of competition

When I was a student, my parents lived in Exeter in Devon, and at that time the city's bypass became completely jammed on a summer Saturday as holidaymakers made their way to the coast. Traffic queues were several miles long.

For a summer job, I drove a small ice-cream van. Early on, I had the idea of selling ice cream from a tray to the people queuing in their cars. I made more money on a Saturday than the rest of the week put together. I thought I was on to a good thing.

But news of this lucrative market soon spread, and each week new ice-cream sellers appeared – each one reducing my earnings! By the middle of August there were over 30 ice-cream

sellers from five different ice-cream companies. Most tried to get to the beginning of the queue, to get ahead of their rivals.

Imagine the scene. A family driving to the coast rounds a bend and is suddenly met by a traffic jam and several ice-cream sellers all jostling to sell them an ice cream. It was quite surreal. Not surprisingly, many of the potential customers refused to buy, feeling somewhat intimidated by the spectacle. It was not long before most of us realised that it was best to disperse and find a section of the road where there were no other sellers.

▶

But with so many ice-cream sellers, no one made much money. My supernormal earnings had been reduced to a normal level. I made about the same on Saturday selling to people stuck in queues as I would have done if I had driven my van around the streets.

 Imagine that you live in a popular and sunny seaside town and that the local council awarded you the only licence to sell ice cream in the town. Would you be earning normal or supernormal profit? Explain your answer.

SUMMARY

1a Just as we could identify total, average and marginal costs, so too we can identify total, average and marginal revenue.

1b Total revenue (TR) is the total amount a firm earns from its sales in a given time period. It is simply price times quantity: $TR = P \times Q$.

1c Average revenue (AR) is total revenue per unit: $AR = TR/Q$. In other words, $AR = P$.

1d Marginal revenue is the extra revenue earned from the sale of one more unit per time period.

1e The AR curve will be the same as the demand curve for the firm's product. In the case of a price taker, the demand curve and hence the AR curve will be a horizontal straight line and will also be the same as the MR curve. The TR curve is an upward-sloping straight line from the origin.

1f A firm that faces a downward-sloping demand curve must also face the same downward-sloping AR curve. The MR curve will also slope downwards, but will be below the AR curve and steeper than it. The TR curve will be an arch shape starting from the origin.

1g When demand is price elastic, marginal revenue will be positive and the TR curve will be upward sloping. When demand is price inelastic, marginal revenue will be negative and the TR curve will be downward sloping.

1h A change in output is represented by a movement along the revenue curves. A change in any other determinant of revenue will shift the curves up or down.

2a Total profit equals total revenue minus total cost. By definition, then, a firm's profits will be maximised at the point where there is the greatest gap between total revenue and total cost.

2b Another way of finding the maximum-profit point is to find the output where marginal revenue equals marginal cost. Having found this output, the level of maximum profit can be found by finding the average profit ($AR - AC$) and then multiplying it by the level of output.

2c Normal profit is the minimum profit that must be made to persuade a firm to stay in business in the long run. It is counted as part of the firm's cost. Supernormal profit is any profit over and above normal profit.

2d For a firm that cannot make a profit at any level of output, the point where $MR = MC$ represents the loss-minimising output.

2e In the short run, a firm will close down if it cannot cover its variable costs. In the long run, it will close down if it cannot make normal profits.

MyEconLab

This book can be supported by MyEconLab, which contains a range of additional resources, including an online homework and tutorial system designed to test and build your understanding.

You need both an access card and a course ID to access MyEconLab:

1. Is your lecturer using MyEconLab? Ask your lecturer for your course ID.

2. Has an access card been included with the book at a reduced cost? Check the inside back cover of the book.

3. If you have a course ID but no access card, go to: http://www.myeconlab.com/ to buy access to this interactive study programme.

REVIEW QUESTIONS

1 Draw a downward-sloping demand curve. Now put in scales of your own choosing for both axes. Read off various points on the demand curve and use them to construct a table showing price and quantity. Use this table to work out the figures for a marginal revenue column. Now use these figures to draw an MR curve. Explain the position of your MR curve in relation to demand.

2 Copy Figures 10.3 and 10.4 (which are based on Table 10.2). Now assume that incomes have risen and that, as a result, two more units per time period can be sold at each price. Draw a new table and plot the resulting new AR, MR and TR curves on your diagrams. Are the new curves parallel to the old ones? Explain.

3 What can we say about the slope of the TR and TC curves at the maximum-profit point? What does this tell us about marginal revenue and marginal cost?

4 Using the following information, construct a table like Table 10.3.

Q	0	1	2	3	4	5	6	7
P	12	11	10	9	8	7	6	5
TC	2	6	9	12	16	21	28	38

Use your table to draw diagrams like Figures 10.5 and 10.7. Use these two diagrams to show the profit-maximising output and the level of maximum profit. Confirm your findings by reference to the table you have constructed.

5 The following table shows the average cost and average revenue (price) for a firm at each level of output.

a) Construct a table to show *TC*, *MC*, *TR* and *MR* at each level of output (put the figures for *MC* and *MR* midway between the output figures).

b) Using *MC* and *MR* figures, find the profit-maximising output.

c) Using *TC* and *TR* figures, check your answer to (b).

d) Plot the *AC*, *MC*, *AR* and *MR* figures on a graph.

e) Mark the profit-maximising output and the *AR* and *AC* at this output.

f) Shade in an area to represent the level of profits at this output.

Output	1	2	3	4	5	6	7	8	9	10
AC (£)	7.00	5.00	4.00	3.30	3.00	3.10	3.50	4.20	5.00	6.00
AR (£)	10.00	9.50	9.00	8.50	8.00	7.50	7.00	6.50	6.00	5.50

6 Normal profits are regarded as a cost (and are included in the cost curves). Explain why.

7 What determines the size of normal profit? Will it vary with the general state of the economy?

8 A firm will continue producing in the short run even if it is making a loss, providing it can cover its variable costs. Explain why. Just how long will it be willing to continue making such a loss?

9 Would there ever be a point in a firm attempting to continue in production if it could not cover its *long-run* average (total) costs?

10 The price of pocket calculators and digital watches fell significantly in the years after they were first introduced and at the same time demand for them increased substantially. Use cost and revenue diagrams to illustrate these events. Explain the reasoning behind the diagram(s) you have drawn.

11 In February 2000, Unilever, the giant consumer products company, announced that it was to cut 25 000 jobs, close 100 plants and rely more on the Internet to purchase its supplies. It would use part of the money saved to increase promotion of its leading brands, such as Dove skincare products, Lipton tea, Omo detergents and Calvin Klein cosmetics. The hope was to boost sales and increase profits. If it meets these targets, what is likely to have happened to its total costs, total revenue, average costs and average revenue? Give reasons for your answer.

ADDITIONAL PART D CASE STUDIES IN *THE ECONOMICS FOR BUSINESS* MyEconLab (www.pearsoned.co.uk/sloman)

D.1 **Malthus and the dismal science of economics.** A gloomy warning, made over 200 years ago by Robert Malthus, that diminishing returns to labour would lead to famine for much of the world's population.

D.2 **Division of labour in a pin factory.** This is the famous example of division of labour given by Adam Smith in his *Wealth of Nations* (1776).

D.3 **Diminishing returns to nitrogen fertiliser.** This case study provides a good illustration of diminishing returns in practice by showing the effects on grass yields of the application of increasing amounts of nitrogen fertiliser.

D.4 **Diminishing returns in the bread shop.** An illustration of the law of diminishing returns.

D.5 **The relationship between averages and marginals.** An examination of the rules showing how an average curve relates to a marginal curve.

D.6 **Deriving cost curves from total physical product information.** This shows how total, average and marginal costs can be derived from a total product information and the price of inputs.

WEBSITES RELEVANT TO PART D

Numbers and sections refer to websites listed in the Web appendix and hotlinked from this text's website at **www.pearsoned.co.uk/sloman**

■ For news articles relevant to Part D, see the *Economics News Articles* link from the text's website.

■ For student resources relevant to Part D, see sites C1–7, 9, 10, 14, 19, 20.

■ For a case study examining costs, see site D2.

■ For sites that look at companies, their scale of operation and market share, see E4, 10; G7, 8.

■ For links to sites on various aspects of production and costs, see section *Microeconomics > Industrial Organization* in site I 11.

Supply: short-run profit maximisation

The FT Reports . . .

The Financial Times, 25 October 2015   FT

Taxi groups unite to fight Uber with $250m start-up

By Murad Ahmed

An unexpected new combatant is set to join the taxi app wars: a 10-month-old start-up has raised $250m, with plans to raise more than $1bn, in an ambitious attempt to take on Uber.

Karhoo, a little-known group founded by a British entrepreneur and based in New York, said it will launch its taxi comparison app in January next year with the support of several high-profile partnerships and backers.

The service will open in London, New York and Singapore after securing a network of 200,000 cars by striking deals with local taxi and minicab fleet owners.

This includes partnerships with Addison Lee, the UK's largest minicab group Comcab, the London black cab operator; New York private hire firms Carmel and Dial 7; and 10,000 yellow and green cab drivers in the city. Karhoo is working on further deals to expand into more cities in the coming months.

The newcomer is the latest challenger in a fiercely competitive market, with rival taxi app groups also building formidable war chests to fund their expansion plans.

Sources familiar with the matter said Karhoo has raised about $250m so far. The company said it is in talks with "several parties to raise in excess of $300m and we expect this to rise to more than $1bn in around 18 months time"....

Uber's main US competitor, San Francisco-based Lyft, has raised $1bn. Hailo, a UK group that has raised $100m, pulled out of North America last year, saying it could not be profitable due to pricing squeeze created by Uber and Lyft.

In Europe, Israeli group Gett has raised around $220m and has made inroads into key cities including London and Moscow. Earlier this month, Madrid-based Cabify secured $12m in investment from Rakuten, Japan's largest ecommerce company by sales, to fuel a push into Latin America. The dominant Chinese player, Didi Kuaidi, has raised almost $4.5bn, while India's Ola has raised close to $1bn.

But Karhoo's chief executive and founder Daniel Ishag said: "[Uber] can't subsidise prices forever; they have to be profitable, especially if they want to IPO. We can go in and we can level the playing field."

He added that by working with licensed taxi companies, Karhoo will avoid the regulatory troubles that have hampered other groups such as Uber.

"We're able to work in markets where the peer-to-peer networks aren't allowed to work, simply because we empowered the incumbents," he said.

Some analysts believe that more upmarket food and drink retailers – from Waitrose to Majestic Wines – are coming under pressure as Aldi and Lidl push into more upmarket products – from fine wines to pulled pork – and their move into more affluent areas. ...Not only is the vicious supermarket price war hurting the big four supermarkets – Tesco, Asda, J Sainsbury and Wm Morrison – but the collateral damage is spreading upmarket. ..."There is not a retail market that I know of anywhere that is insulated, including the people right at the top," says Richard Hyman, the independent retail analyst. "I have seen shoppers in Harvey Nichols with Lidl bags... People are much more value-conscious right across the piece."

'Supermarket price war moves upmarket' *The Financial Times*, 25 June 2015. © The Financial Times Limited. All Rights Reserved

As we saw in Chapter 10, a firm's profits are maximised where its marginal cost equals its marginal revenue. But we will want to know more than this.

- What determines the *amount* of profit that a firm will make? Will profits be large, or just enough for the firm to survive, or so low that it will be forced out of business?
- Will the firm produce a high level of output or a low level?
- Will it be producing efficiently?
- Will the price charged to the consumer be high or low?
- And, more generally, will the consumer benefit from the decisions that a firm makes?

The answers to all these questions depend on the amount of *competition* that a firm faces. A firm in a highly competitive environment will behave quite differently from a firm facing little or no competition.

In Part E we will look at *different types of market structure*: from highly competitive markets ('perfect competition'), to ones with no competition at all ('monopoly'). We will also look at the intermediate cases of 'imperfect competition': monopolistic competition (where there are quite a lot of firms competing against each other) and oligopoly (where there are just a few).

As the article from the *Financial Times* opposite shows, changes in technology, such as the development of apps, can have a fundamental effect on the nature of competition in an industry (in this case taxis). Also the development of new types of product can even affect firms that, up to now, have had a monopoly of a particular product. However, it is also the case that firms may collude to restrict competition and the development of new technology, as we will see in this Part and Chapter 21. Consumers may then end up with less choice and paying higher prices.

Key terms

Market structures
Perfect competition
Monopoly
Natural monopoly
Competition for corporate control
Barriers to entry
Contestable markets
Sunk costs
Monopolistic competition
Product differentiation
Oligopoly
Interdependence
Collusive and non-collusive oligopoly
Open and tacit collusion
Price leadership
Benchmark pricing
Game theory
Dominant and non-dominant strategy games
Prisoners' dilemma
Nash equilibrium
Credible threat
First-mover advantage
Decision tree
Countervailing power

11 Chapter

Profit maximisation under perfect competition and monopoly

Business issues covered in this chapter

- What determines the degree of market power of a firm?
- Why does operating under conditions of perfect competition make being in business a constant battle for survival?
- How do firms get to become monopolies and remain so?
- At what price and output will a monopolist maximise profits and how much profit will it make?
- How well or badly do monopolies serve the consumer compared with competitive firms?
- Why will the size of entry barriers to an industry (the degree of 'contestability' of a market) affect the amount of profit a monopolist can make?

11.1 ALTERNATIVE MARKET STRUCTURES

In this section, we are beginning to think about firms' behaviour and the factors that determine this. What we are particularly concerned with is the degree of competition that exists within a market and which factors make an industry more or less competitive.

There are various reasons as to why we are interested in analysing the competitiveness of an industry. It can affect the prices charged to consumers and paid to suppliers, how much profit firms make, and the incentives to invest and innovate. In particular, it affects firms' behaviour and sometimes that may be against the public interest. In such cases governments or regulators may wish to intervene.

Factors affecting the degree of competition

So what influences the degree of competition in an industry? There are four key determinants:

- The number of firms.
- The freedom of entry and exit of firms into the industry.
- The nature of the product.
- The shape of the demand curve.

We will consider each factor to determine exactly what impact it has on the degree of competition within a market and then look at how these features vary between different market structures. We should then be able to place different industries into one of four key market structures.

The number of firms. The more firms there are competing against each other, the more competitive any market is likely to be, with each firm trying to steal customers from its rivals. Though there are many ways by which this can be done, one strategy will be to keep prices low. This will generally be in the consumer's interest.

If, however, there are only a few firms in the market, there may be less intense price competition, though, as we shall see, this is not always the case.

The freedom of entry and exit of firms into the industry. A key factor that will affect the number of firms in an industry is how easy it is for a new firm to set up in competition. In some markets, there may be barriers to entry which prevent new firms from entering and this then acts to restrict the number of competing firms in the market. A key question here is, just how great are the barriers to the entry of new firms?

Pause for thought

1. Consider a situation where you have set up a business selling a brand new product, which is not available anywhere else. As the only seller of this product, what could you do in terms of price?
2. Why could the ease with which a firm can leave an industry be a factor that determines the degree of competition within that industry?

The nature of the product. If firms produce an identical product – in other words, if there is no product differentiation within the industry – there is little a firm can do to gain an advantage over its rivals. If, however, firms produce their own particular brand or model or variety, this may enable them to charge a higher price and/or gain a larger market share from their rivals.

The shape of the demand curve. Finally, the degree of competition is affected by the degree of control the firm has over its price. Is the firm a price taker, with no control over price? Or can it choose its price? And if it can, how will changing its price affect its profits? The degree of control is clearly affected by the three factors above, but it has important implications for the shape of the firm's demand curve. How elastic is it? If it puts up its price, will it lose (a) all its sales (a horizontal demand curve), or (b) a large proportion of its sales (a relatively elastic demand curve), or (c) just a small proportion of its sales (a relatively inelastic demand curve)?

 KEY IDEA 21

Market power benefits the powerful at the expense of others. When firms have market power over prices, they can use this to raise prices and profits above the perfectly competitive level. Other things being equal, the firm will gain at the expense of the consumer. Similarly, if consumers or workers have market power, they can use this to their own benefit.

Market structures

Traditionally, we divide industries into categories based on the factors above, which determine the degree of competition that exists between the firms. There are four such categories.

At the most competitive extreme is a market structure referred to as *perfect competition.* This is a situation where there are a large number of firms competing. Each firm is so small relative to the whole industry that it has no power to influence market price. It is a price taker.

At the least competitive extreme is *monopoly*, where there is just one firm in the industry, and hence no competition from *within* the industry, often due to very high barriers to entry.

In the middle there are two forms of imperfect competition. *Monopolistic competition* is the more competitive, which involves quite a lot of firms competing and freedom for new firms to enter the industry. Examples of monopolistic competition can be found by flicking through the *Yellow Pages*! The other type of imperfect competition is *oligopoly,* where there are only a few firms and where the entry of new firms is difficult. Some or all of the existing firms will be dominant – that is, they will tend to have a relatively high market share and can influence prices, advertising, product design, etc.

Table 11.1 shows the differences between the four categories.

Definitions

Perfect competition A market structure in which there are many firms; where there is freedom of entry to the industry; where all firms produce an identical product; and where all firms are price takers.

Monopoly A market structure where there is only one firm in the industry.

Monopolistic competition A market structure where, like perfect competition, there are many firms and freedom of entry into the industry, but where each firm produces a differentiated product and thus has some control over its price.

Oligopoly A market structure where there are few enough firms to enable barriers to be erected against the entry of new firms.

KI 12
p 68

Table 11.1	Features of the four market structures				
Type of market	**Number of firms**	**Freedom of entry**	**Nature of product**	**Examples**	**Implication for demand curve for firm**
Perfect competition	Very many	Unrestricted	Homogeneous (undifferentiated)	Cabbages, foreign exchange (these approximate to perfect competition)	Horizontal. The firm is a price taker
Monopolistic competition	Many/ several	Unrestricted	Differentiated	Builders, restaurants, hairdressers	Downward sloping, but relatively elastic. The firm has some control over price
Oligopoly	Few	Restricted	1. Undifferentiated or 2. Differentiated	1. Cement 2. Cars, electrical appliances, supermarkets	Downward sloping, relatively inelastic but depends on reactions of rivals to a price change
Monopoly	One	Restricted or completely blocked	Unique	Local water company, many prescription drugs	Downward sloping, more inelastic than oligopoly. Firm has considerable control over price

Pause for thought

Based on the characteristics outlined above for each market structure, can you think of a few examples that fit into each of the four market structures?

KI 1
p 10

Structure, conduct and performance

The market structure under which a firm operates will determine its behaviour. Firms under perfect competition behave quite differently from firms that are monopolists, which behave differently again from firms under oligopoly or monopolistic competition.

This behaviour, or 'conduct', will in turn affect the firm's performance: its prices, profits, efficiency, etc. In many cases it will also affect other firms' performance: *their* prices, profits, efficiency, etc. The collective conduct of all the firms in the industry will affect the whole industry's performance.

Some economists thus see a causal chain running from market structure, through conduct, to the performance of that industry.

Structure → Conduct → Performance

This does not mean, however, that all firms operating in a particular market structure will behave in exactly the same way. For example, some firms under oligopoly may be highly competitive, whereas others may collude with each other to keep prices high. This conduct may then, in turn, influence the development of the market structure. For example, the interaction between firms may influence the development of new products or new production methods, and may encourage or discourage the entrance of new firms into the industry.

It is also important to remember that some firms with different divisions and products may operate in more than market structure. As an example, consider the case

of Microsoft. Its Internet Explorer competes with more successful rivals, such as Chrome and Firefox and, as a result, has little market power in the browser market. Its Office products, by contrast, have a much bigger market share and dominate the word processor, presentation and spreadsheet markets.

Also, some firms under oligopoly are highly competitive and may engage in fierce price cutting, while others may collude with their rivals to charge higher prices. It is for this reason that government policy towards firms – known as 'competition policy' – prefers to focus on the *conduct* of individual firms, rather than simply on the market structure within which they operate. Regulators focus on aspects of conduct such as price fixing and other forms of collusion. Indeed, competition policy in most countries accepts that market structures evolve naturally (e.g. because of economies of scale or changing consumer preferences) and do not necessarily give rise to competition problems.

Nevertheless, market structure still influences firms' behaviour and the performance of the industry, even though it does not, in the case of oligopoly and monopoly, rigidly determine it. We look at these influences in this chapter and the next.

First, we look at the two extreme market structures: perfect competition and monopoly (this chapter). Then we turn to look at the two intermediate cases of monopolistic competition and oligopoly (Chapter 12).

As we have seen, these two intermediate cases are sometimes referred to collectively as ***imperfect competition***. The vast majority of firms in the real world operate under imperfect competition. It is still worth studying the two extreme

Definition

Imperfect competition The collective name for monopolistic competition and oligopoly.

cases, however, because they provide a framework within which to understand the real world. They provide important benchmarks for comparison. For example, regulators would find it difficult to identify anti-competitive behaviour if they could not show how outcomes would differ in a more competitive environment.

Some industries tend more to the competitive extreme, and thus their performance corresponds to some extent to perfect competition. Other industries tend more to the other extreme: for example, when there is one dominant firm and a few much smaller firms. In such cases, their performance corresponds more to monopoly.

BOX 11.1 **CONCENTRATION RATIOS**

Measuring the degree of competition

We can get some indication of how competitive a market is by observing the number of firms: the more firms, the more competitive the market would seem to be. However, this does not tell us anything about how *concentrated* the market might be. There may be *many* firms (suggesting a situation of perfect competition or monopolistic competition), but the largest two firms might produce 95 per cent of total output. This would make these two firms more like oligopolists.

Thus even though a large number of producers may make the market *seem* highly competitive, this could be deceiving. Another approach, therefore, to measuring the degree of competition is to focus on the level of concentration of firms.

The simplest measure of industrial concentration involves adding together the market share of the largest so many firms: e.g. the largest three, five or fifteen. This gives the '3-firm', '5-firm' or '15-firm concentration ratios'. The resulting figures can be used to assess whether or not the largest firms in an industry dominate the market. There are different ways of estimating market share: by revenue, by output, by profit, etc.

The table, based on the latest data from the Office for National Statistics, shows the 5-firm concentration ratios of selected industries in the UK by output in 2004. As you can see, there was an enormous variation in the degree of concentration from one industry to another.

One of the main reasons for this is differences in the percentage of total industry output at which economies of scale

are exhausted (see Box 9.4). If this occurs at a low level of output, there will be room for several firms in the industry which are all benefiting from the maximum economies of scale. If it occurs at a much higher level of output, then it may only be possible for a small number of firms to benefit from maximum economies of scale and so these firms will dominate the market.

The degree of concentration will also depend on the barriers to entry of other firms into the industry (see pages 182–4) and on various factors such as transport costs and historical accident. It will also depend on how varied the products are within any one industrial category. For example, in categories as large as furniture and construction there is room for many firms, each producing a specialised range of products.

So is the degree of concentration a good guide to the degree of competitiveness of the industry? The answer is that it is *some* guide, but on its own it can be misleading. In particular, it ignores the degree of competition from abroad, and from other industries within the country.

1. *What are the advantages and disadvantages of using a 5-firm concentration ratio rather than a 10-firm, 3-firm or even a 1-firm ratio?*
2. *Why are some industries like bread baking and brewing relatively concentrated, in that a few firms produce a large proportion of total output (see case studies E.8 and E.9 in MyEconLab), and yet there are also many small producers?*

Concentration ratios for business by industry (2004)

Industry	5-firm ratio	15-firm ratio	Industry	5-firm ratio	15-firm ratio
Sugar	99	99	Alcoholic beverages	50	78
Tobacco products	99	99	Soap and toiletries	40	64
Oils and fats	88	95	Accountancy services	36	47
Confectionary	81	91	Motor vehicles	34	54
Gas distribution	82	87	Glass and glass products	26	49
Soft drinks, mineral water	75	93	Fishing	16	19
Postal/courier services	65	75	Advertising	10	20
Telecommunications	61	75	Wholesale distribution	6	11
Inorganic chemicals	57	80	Furniture	5	13

Source: based on data in Table 8.31 of *United Kingdom Input-Output Analyses* (National Statistics, 2006)

11.2 PERFECT COMPETITION

The theory of perfect competition illustrates an extreme form of capitalism. Firms have no power whatsoever to affect the price of the product. The price they face is that determined by the interaction of demand and supply in the whole *market*.

Assumptions

The model of perfect competition is built on four assumptions:

1. Firms are *price takers*. There are so many firms in the industry that each one produces an insignificantly small proportion of total industry supply, and therefore has *no power whatsoever* to affect the price of the product. Hence it faces a horizontal (perfectly elastic) demand 'curve' at the market price: the price determined by the interaction of demand and supply in the whole market.
2. There is complete *freedom of entry* into the industry for new firms. Existing firms are unable to stop new firms setting up in business. Setting up a business takes time, however. Freedom of entry therefore applies in the long run.
3. All firms produce an *identical product*. The product is 'homogeneous': i.e. all products in the market are identical and are perfect substitutes for each other. There is therefore no branding or advertising.
4. Producers and consumers have *perfect knowledge* of the market. That is, producers are fully aware of prices, costs, technology and market opportunities. Consumers are fully aware of price, quality and availability of the product.

These assumptions are very strict. Few, if any, industries in the real world meet these conditions. Certain agricultural markets perhaps are closest to perfect competition. The market for fresh vegetables is an example.

> ### Pause for thought
>
> 1. *It is sometimes claimed that the market for various stocks and shares is perfectly competitive, or nearly so. Take the case of the market for shares in a large company, such as BP. Go through each of the four assumptions above and see if they apply in this case. (Don't be misled by the first assumption. The 'firm' in this case is not BP itself, but rather the owners of the shares.)*
> 2. *Is the market for gold or silver perfectly competitive?*

The short-run equilibrium of the firm

In the **short run**, we assume that the number of firms in the industry cannot be increased; there is simply no time for new firms to enter the market.

Figure 11.1 shows a short-run equilibrium for both industry and a firm under perfect competition. Both parts of the diagram have the same scale for the vertical axis. The horizontal axes have totally different scales, however. For example, if the horizontal axis for the firm were measured in, say, thousands of units, the horizontal axis for the whole industry might be measured in millions or tens of millions of units, depending on the number of firms in the industry.

Let us examine the determination of price, output and profit in turn.

> ### Definition
>
> **The short run under perfect competition** The period during which there is too little time for new firms to enter the industry.

> **Figure 11.1** Short-run equilibrium of industry and firm under perfect competition

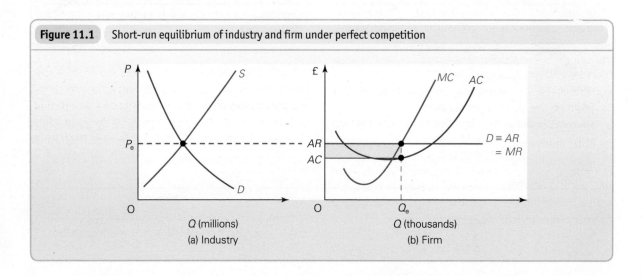

(a) Industry   (b) Firm

Figure 11.2 Loss minimising under perfect competition

Q (millions)

(a)

Q (thousands)

(b)

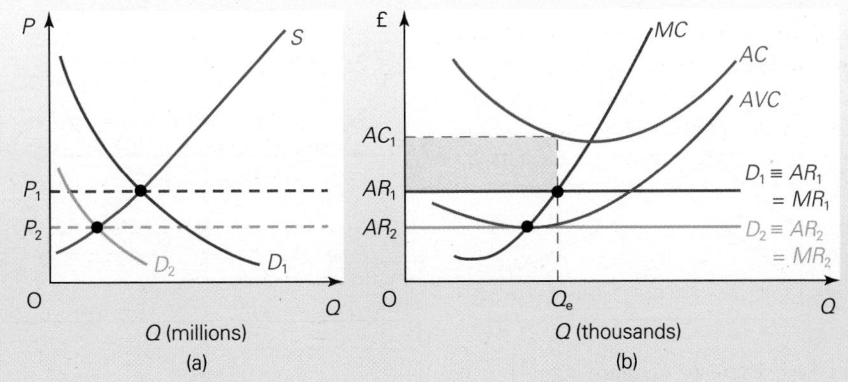

Price

The price is determined in the industry by the intersection of market demand and supply. The firm faces a horizontal demand (or average revenue) 'curve' at this price. It can sell all it can produce at the market price (P_e). It would sell nothing at a price above P_e, however, since competitors would be selling identical products at a lower price.

Pause for thought

If the industry under perfect competition faces a downward-sloping demand curve, why does an individual firm face a horizontal demand curve?

Output

KI 4
p 25
The firm will maximise profit where marginal cost equals marginal revenue ($MR = MC$), at an output of Q_e. Note that, since the price is not affected by the firm's output, marginal revenue will equal price (see pages 161–2 and Figure 10.1). Thus the firm's MR 'curve' and AR 'curve' (= demand 'curve') are the same horizontal straight line.

Profit

If the average cost (AC) curve (which includes normal profit) dips below the average revenue (AR) 'curve', the firm will earn supernormal profit. Supernormal profit per unit at Q_e is the vertical difference between AR and AC at Q_e. Total supernormal profit is the shaded rectangle in Figure 11.1 (i.e. profit per unit times quantity sold).

What happens if the firm cannot make a profit at *any* level of output? This situation would occur if the AC curve were above the AR curve at all points. This is illustrated in Figure 11.2 where the market price is P_1. In this case, the point where $MC = MR$ represents the *loss-minimising* point (where loss is defined as anything less than normal profit). This amount of the loss is represented by the shaded rectangle.

KI 18
p 141
Whether the firm is prepared to continue making a loss in the short run or whether it will close down immediately

depends on whether it can cover its *variable* costs (as we saw in Chapter 10). Provided price is above average variable cost (AVC), the firm will continue producing in the short run: it can pay its variable costs and go some way to paying its fixed costs. It will shut down in the short run only if the market price falls below P_2 in Figure 11.2: i.e. when variable costs of production cannot be covered.

The long-run equilibrium of the firm

In the *long run*, if typical firms are making supernormal profits, new firms will be attracted into the industry. Likewise, if existing firms can make supernormal profits by increasing the scale of their operations, they will do so, since all factors of production are variable in the long run.

The effect of the entry of new firms and/or the expansion of existing firms is to increase industry supply, meaning that at every price level the quantity produced would be higher. This is illustrated in Figure 11.3.

Pause for thought

Before you read on, can you explain why perfect competition and substantial economies of scale are likely to be incompatible?

KI 10
p 52
The industry supply curve shifts to the right. This in turn leads to a fall in price. Supply will go on increasing, and price falling, until firms are making only normal profits. This will be when price has fallen to the point where the demand 'curve' for the firm just touches the bottom

Definition

The long run under perfect competition The period of time which is long enough for new firms to enter the industry.

| **Figure 11.3** | Long-run equilibrium under perfect competition |

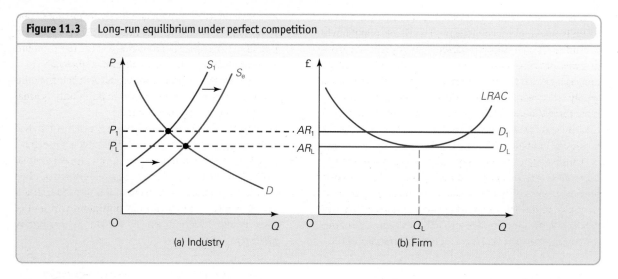

(a) Industry   (b) Firm

| **Figure 11.4** | Long-run equilibrium of the firm under perfect competition |

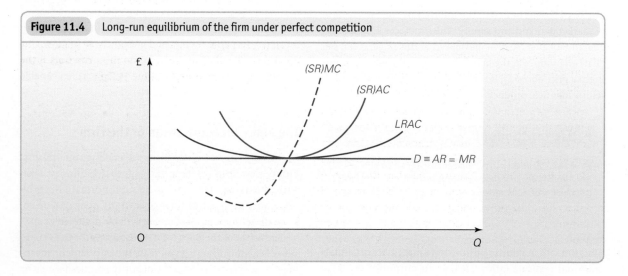

of its long-run average cost curve. Q_L is thus the long-run equilibrium output of the firm, with P_L the long-run equilibrium price.

Since the $LRAC$ curve is tangential to all possible short-run AC curves (see section 9.5), the full long-run equilibrium will be as shown in Figure 11.4 where:

$$LRAC = AC = MC = MR = AR$$

The incompatibility of perfect competition and substantial economies of scale

Why is perfect competition so rare in the real world – if it even exists at all? One important reason for this has to do with economies of scale.

In many industries, firms may have to be quite large if they are to experience the full potential economies of scale. But perfect competition requires there to be *many* firms. Firms must therefore be small under perfect competition: too small in most cases for them to achieve economies of scale.

Once a firm expands sufficiently to achieve economies of scale, it will usually gain market power. It will be able to undercut the prices of smaller firms, which will thus be driven out of business. Perfect competition is destroyed. Perfect competition could only exist in any industry, therefore, if there were no (or virtually no) economies of scale.

Does the firm benefit from operating under perfect competition?

Under perfect competition the firm faces a constant battle for survival. If it becomes less efficient than other firms, it will make less than normal profits and be driven out of business. If it becomes more efficient, it will earn supernormal profits. But these supernormal profits will not last for long. Soon other firms, in order to survive themselves, will be forced to copy the more efficient methods of the new firm. They are able to do this because the perfect knowledge assumption implies that new methods can be copied by all producers.

It is the same with the development of new products. If a firm is able to produce a new product that is popular with consumers, it will be able to gain a temporary advantage over its rivals. But again, any supernormal profits will last only as long as it takes other firms to respond. Soon the increase in supply of the new product will drive the price down and eliminate these supernormal profits. Similarly, the firm must be quick to copy new products developed by its rivals. If it does not, it will soon make a loss and be driven out of the market.

Thus being in perfect competition is a constant battle for survival. Most firms in such a highly competitive environment would love to be able to gain some market power: power to be able to restrict competition and to retain supernormal profits into the long run. We look at the extreme case of market power, where the firm has a monopoly, in section 11.3.

Does the consumer benefit from perfect competition?

Generally it is argued that competition benefits the consumer, and that the more perfect an industry becomes the better it is for consumers. The argument centres around the question of efficiency. There are three elements to the argument.

- Price equals marginal cost. Why is this desirable? To answer this, consider what would happen if they were not equal. If price were greater than marginal cost, this would mean that consumers were putting a higher value (P) on the production of extra units than they cost to produce (MC). Therefore more ought to be produced. If price were less than marginal cost, consumers would be putting a lower value on extra units than they cost to produce. Therefore less ought to be produced. When they

are equal, therefore, production levels are just right. But, as we shall see later, it is only under perfect competition that $MC = P$. This idea of producing just the right amount of the product is referred to as **_allocative efficiency_**.

- The combination of (long-run) production being at minimum average cost and the firm making only normal profit keeps prices at a minimum.
- As we have seen, perfect competition is a case of 'survival of the fittest'. Inefficient firms will be driven out of business, since they will not be able to make even normal profits. This encourages firms to be as efficient as possible and, where possible, to invest in new improved technology. This idea of production at minimum cost and of costs being driven down is known as **_productive efficiency_**.

 KEY IDEA 22 **_Economic efficiency_** is achieved when each good is produced at the minimum cost and where consumers get maximum benefit from their income.

However, perfect competition is not always best for the consumer, any more than it is for the firm. We develop the arguments in the next section and in Chapter 12.

Definitions

Allocative efficiency A situation where the current combination of goods produced and sold gives the maximum satisfaction for each consumer at their current levels of income.

Productive efficiency A situation where firms are producing the maximum output for a given amount of inputs, or producing a given output at the least cost.

11.3 MONOPOLY

What is a monopoly?

This may seem a strange question because the answer seems obvious. A monopoly exists when there is only one firm in the industry.

But whether an industry can be classed as a monopoly is not always clear. It depends on how narrowly the industry is defined. For example, a textile company may have a monopoly on certain types of fabric, but it does not have a monopoly on fabrics in general. The consumer can buy fabrics other than those supplied by the company. A rail company may have a monopoly over rail services between two cities, but it does not have a monopoly over public transport between these two cities. People can travel by coach or air. They could also use private transport. Consider the blog on the Sloman News Site, which asks Is Amazon a monopolist?[1]

To some extent, the boundaries of an industry are arbitrary. What is more important for a firm is the amount of monopoly _power_ it has, and that depends on the closeness of substitutes produced by rival industries. The Post Office, before 2006, had a monopoly over the delivery of letters, but it still faced competition in communications from telephone, faxes and e-mail. Now, with the ending of the monopoly over the delivery of letters, the Post Office criticises the 'unfair' competition it faces from other firms, such as whistl, which delivers mail, packets and parcels, but _only_ in more profitable urban areas. An article from Post and Parcel[2] considers this competition to the Royal Mail.

---

[1]http://pearsonblog.campaignserver.co.uk/?p=14509
[2]http://postandparcel.info/62638/news/companies/royal-mails-challenger-tnt-post-uk-to-rebrand-as-whistl/

BOX 11.2 · E-COMMERCE

A modern form of perfect competition?

The relentless drive towards big business in recent decades has seen many markets become more concentrated and increasingly dominated by large producers. However, forces are at work that are undermining this dominance and bringing more competition to markets. One of these forces is *e-commerce*.

In this case study, we will consider just how far e-commerce is returning 'power to the people'.

Moving markets back towards perfect competition?

Let us reconsider three of the assumptions of perfect competition and the impact of e-commerce on them: a large number of firms; freedom of entry; and perfect knowledge.

A large number of firms. With the global reach of the Internet, the number of firms in any market has increased. Firms must now compete with others across the world, as consumers have access to the global marketplace. They must keep an eye on the prices and products of competitors worldwide and be aware of the continual emergence of new smaller businesses.

Freedom of entry. The Internet has had a key role to play here, reducing the costs of business start-ups. The traditional idea of rented office space, large start-up and fixed costs is no longer the only way to run a business. Small online companies have been created from home, with little more than a computer, and many companies are transferring their purchases to the Internet, finding that prices can be significantly cheaper.

Marketing costs for small Internet-based companies can be relatively low, especially with powerful search engines, and many of these new online companies are more specialist, relying on interest 'outsourcing' (buying parts, equipment and other supplies through the Internet) rather than making everything themselves. They are also more likely to use delivery firms rather than having their own transport fleet.

Not only do all the above factors make markets more price competitive, they also bring other benefits. Costs are driven down, as firms economise on stock holding, rely more on outsourcing and develop more efficient relationships with suppliers. 'Procurement hubs', online exchanges and trading communities are now well established in many industries. All of these factors have made it relatively cheap for new firms to set up and begin trading over the Internet. Many of these firms are involved in 'B2C' (business-to-consumers) e-commerce, where they are selling directly to us as consumers. However, many have begun to sell to other firms, known as 'B2B' (business-to-business).

One particularly interesting example is eBay and the way in which it has caused a blurring between firms and consumers. Setting up a small business from home is now incredibly easy and, via eBay, consumers can become businesses with just one click. With around 130 million active users worldwide and hundreds of thousands of users running a business via eBay in the UK, buying and selling 'junk' has become a viable source of income. Estimates suggest that at any one time, there are over 800 million 'listings' on eBay.

eBay itself is an example of a business that expanded with the growth of the Internet. Founded in 1995, eBay grew rapidly, reaching half a million users and revenues of $4.7 billion in the USA within three years. In 2014, eBay's revenue was $17.9 billion, up from $8.7 billion five years earlier. In more recent years it has experienced some difficulties from increased competition, as there are many other sites offering similar services. However, eBay's global reach and volume of customers, courtesy of the Internet, has enabled rapid growth to continue. Although it is just one company, the fact that it has millions of users, acting as businesses, means that it has provided a highly competitive environment.

The increase in competition from the rise of e-commerce, in whatever form, has led to firms' demand curves becoming more price elastic. This is especially the case for goods which are cheap to transport or for services, such as travel agents, insurance and banking. While some large firms, such as Amazon, do provide competition for the more traditional firms, the greater freedom of entry for new firms that has been created by the Internet is providing an ever-increasing degree of competition, as more and more small businesses are set up every day. This has also created a more innovative environment, where the quality and range of products is also growing daily.

Perfect knowledge. The Internet has also added to consumer knowledge. There are some obvious ways, such as facts, and figures through sites such as Wikipedia, where to eat, what to read, etc. However, it has also improved consumer knowledge through greater transparency. Online shopping agents such as Kelkoo and Google and online comparison sites such as GoCompare and MoneySupermarket can quickly locate a list of alternative suppliers and their prices. There is greater information on product availability, quality and consumer feedback. Virtual shopping malls, full of e-retailers, place the high street retailer under intense competitive pressure.

We have seen evidence of this online competition, with the downfall of some well-known high street retailers, such as HMV, Comet, Peacocks and Borders. Although the weak

Barriers to entry

For a firm to maintain its monopoly position, there must be barriers to the entry of new firms. Barriers also exist under oligopoly, but in the case of monopoly they must be high enough to block the entry of new firms. Barriers can take various forms.

Economies of scale. If the monopolist's average costs go on falling significantly up to the output that satisfies the whole market, the industry may not be able to support more than one producer. This case is known as **natural monopoly**. This is more likely if the market is small. For example, two

Definition

Natural monopoly A situation where long-run average costs would be lower if an industry were under monopoly than if it were shared between two or more competitors.

trading conditions following the economic downturn after 2007 were partly to blame, it has also been the sheer volume of competition these companies face from the Internet. HMV faces steep competition from companies like Amazon, as DVDs, BluRay and CDs can be sold much more cheaply online. LoveFilm and Netflix also provide a new way of watching films.

Google shopping allows consumers to compare prices on larger consumer durables such as fridges, cookers and washing machines, and with the large supermarkets offering such items online and price comparisons being so easy, consumers are finding bargains on the Internet. These competitive pressures from online retailing certainly added to the woes of Comet and other companies.

It is not just the traditional consumer that has benefited from greater knowledge. Many firms are also consumers, purchasing inputs from other firms. It is now commonplace for firms to use the Internet to search for cheaper sources of supply. This is even more relevant now that many firms operate in a worldwide marketplace and can source their supplies from across the globe.

1. *Give three examples of products that are particularly suitable for selling over the Internet and three that are not. Explain your answer.*
2. *Before reading ahead, consider your own shopping and buying habits – how much shopping do you do online? What do you think are the limits to e-commerce? Compare your answers with a friend and try to determine the key factors that explain any differences and what, then, are the limits to e-commerce.*

What are the limits to e-commerce?

In 20 years, will we be doing all our shopping on the Internet? Will the only shopping malls be virtual ones? Although e-commerce is revolutionising some markets, it is unlikely that things will go anything like that far.

The benefits of 'shop shopping' are that you get to see the good, touch it and use it. You can buy the good there and then, and take instant possession of it: you don't have to wait. Although you can order things online and get next day delivery, it's still not quite instant possession. Furthermore, shopping is an enjoyable experience. Many people like wandering round the shops, meeting friends, seeing what takes their fancy, trying on clothes, browsing through DVDs, and so on. 'Retail therapy' for many is a leisure activity. Many consumers are willing to pay a 'premium' for these advantages.

Online shopping is limited by current technology and infrastructure. The quality of Internet access has improved significantly as broadband has become widely available, but online purchases can still be hampered by busy sites or slow connections.

And what if deliveries are late or fail completely? (See Box 6.4.) The busiest time for Internet shopping is in the run-up to Christmas. In 2011 Yodel, the UK's second largest household delivery company (after the Royal Mail), failed to deliver around 15 000 parcels per day as Christmas approached.[1] Similar problems occurred in 2014, when 10 days before Christmas, Yodel announced that it was no longer collecting parcels for delivery due to a backlog (see articles in *The Guardian*[2] and the *Mail Online*[3]). Their delivery infrastructure simply could not cope with the increase in demand from online shopping and, clearly, over three years, it had not found a solution.

Additionally, online shopping requires access to a credit or debit card, which might not be available to everyone, particularly younger consumers and those on low incomes.

Also costs might not always be as low as expected. How efficient is it to have many small deliveries of goods? How significant are the lost cost savings from economies of scale that larger producers or retailers are likely to generate?

Nevertheless, e-commerce has made many markets, both retail and B2B, more competitive. This is especially so for services and for goods whose quality is easy to identify online. Many firms are being forced to face up to having their prices determined by the market.

1. *Why may the Internet work better for replacement buys than for new purchases?*
2. *In 2008 eBay sellers called for a boycott of the site, following changes in the fees being charged and the removal of their ability to leave feedback on buyers. Explain how eBay can both increase competition across the economy and simultaneously acquire very substantial monopoly power.*

[1] 'Surge in online orders hits deliveries', *Financial Times*, 23 December 2011.

[2] 'Yodel warns of parcel backlog as Christmas deliveries face delay', *The Guardian*, 12 December 2014.

[3] Ben Wilkinson, 'Delivery firm Yodel's boss forced into apology after delays mean thousands of customers may not receive parcels in time for Christmas', *Mail Online*, 24 December 2014.

bus companies might find it unprofitable to serve the same routes, each running with perhaps only half-full buses, whereas one company with a monopoly of the routes could make a profit. The blog post Fair Fares?[3] on the Sloman News Site considers the bus industry. Electricity transmission via a national grid is another example of a natural monopoly.

Even if a market could support more than one firm, a new entrant is unlikely to be able to start up on a very large scale. Thus the monopolist which is already experiencing economies of scale can charge a price below the cost of the new entrant and drive it out of business. If, however, the new entrant is a firm already established in another industry, it may be able to survive this competition.

[3]http://pearsonblog.campaignserver.co.uk/?p=2573

Economies of scope. These are the benefits in terms of lower average costs of production, because a firm produces a range of products. For example, a large pharmaceutical company producing a range of drugs and toiletries can use shared research, marketing, storage and transport facilities across its range of products. These lower costs make it difficult for a new single-product entrant to the market, since the large firm will be able to undercut its price and drive it out of the market.

Product differentiation and brand loyalty. If a firm produces a clearly differentiated product, where the consumer associates the product with the brand, it will be very difficult for a new firm to break into that market. Rank Xerox invented, and patented, the plain paper photocopier. After this legal monopoly (see below) ran out, people still associated photocopiers with Rank Xerox. It is still not unusual to hear someone say that they are going to 'Xerox the article' or, for that matter, 'Hoover their carpet'. Other examples of strong brand image include Guinness, Kelloggs Cornflakes, Coca-Cola, Nescafé and Sellotape.

Lower costs for an established firm. An established monopoly is likely to have developed specialised production and marketing skills. It is more likely to be aware of the most efficient production and marketing techniques and the most reliable and/or cheapest suppliers. It is also likely to have access to cheaper finance, as we saw with larger companies in section 3.3 (see page 40). For these reasons it is likely to be operating on a lower average total cost curve. New firms would therefore find it hard to compete on price, given their higher average costs and would be likely to lose any price war.

> ## Pause for thought
>
> *Illustrate the situation described above using AC curves for both a new entrant and an established firm.*

Ownership of, or control over, key inputs or outlets. If a firm governs the supply of vital inputs (say, by owning the sole supplier of some component part), it can deny access to these inputs to potential rivals. On a world scale, the de Beers company has a monopoly in fine diamonds because all diamond producers market their diamonds through de Beers.

Similarly, if a firm controls the outlets through which the product must be sold, it can prevent potential rivals from gaining access to consumers. For example, Wall's (a division of Unilever) used to supply freezers free to shops on the condition that they stocked only Wall's ice cream in them. On the Sloman News Site, two blog posts, Making UK energy supply more productive[4] and The Big Six: for how much longer?[5] show how vertical and horizontal integration act as a barrier to entry in the energy market.

---

[4]http://pearsonblog.campaignserver.co.uk/?p=12358
[5]http://pearsonblog.campaignserver.co.uk/?p=12350

Legal protection. The firm's monopoly position may be protected by patents on essential processes, by copyright, by various forms of licensing (allowing, say, only one firm to operate in a particular area) and by tariffs (i.e. customs duties) and other trade restrictions to keep out foreign competitors. Examples of monopolies, or near monopolies, protected by patents include most new medicines developed by pharmaceutical companies (e.g. anti-AIDS drugs), Microsoft's Windows operating systems and agro-chemical companies, such as Monsanto, with various genetically modified plant varieties and pesticides.

While patents do help monopolists to maintain their market power, they are also essential in encouraging new product innovation, as R&D is very expensive. Patents allow firms that engage in R&D to reap the rewards of that investment.

Mergers and takeovers. The monopolist can put in a takeover bid for any new entrant. The sheer threat of takeovers may discourage new entrants.

Retained profits and aggressive tactics. An established monopolist is likely to have some retained profits behind it. If a new firm enters the market, the established firm could start a price war, mount a massive advertising campaign, offer attractive after-sales service and introduce new brands to compete with the new entrant. Using its retained profits, it can probably sustain losses until the new entrant leaves the market, returning its monopoly status.

Equilibrium price and output

Since there is, by definition, only one firm in the industry, the firm's demand curve is also the industry demand curve.

Compared with other market structures, demand under monopoly will be relatively inelastic at each price. The monopolist can raise its price and consumers have no alternative firm to turn to within the industry. They either pay the higher price, or go without the good altogether. | KI 12 p 68

Unlike the firm under perfect competition, the monopolist is thus a 'price maker'. It can choose what price to charge. Nevertheless, it is still constrained by its demand curve. A rise in price will reduce the quantity demanded.

As with firms in other market structures, a monopolist will maximise profit where $MR = MC$. In Figure 11.5 profit is maximised by producing a quantity of Q_m. The supernormal profit obtained is shown by the shaded area. | KI 4 p 25

These profits will tend to be larger, the less elastic is the demand curve (and hence the steeper is the MR curve), and thus the bigger is the gap between MR and price (AR). The actual elasticity will depend on whether reasonably close substitutes are available in *other* industries.

The demand for a rail service will be much less elastic (and the potential for profit greater) if there is no bus service between the same destinations.

Since there are barriers to the entry of new firms, a monopolist's supernormal profits will not be competed | KI 21 p 175

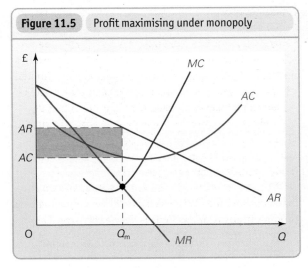

Figure 11.5 Profit maximising under monopoly

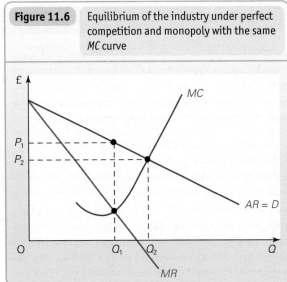

Figure 11.6 Equilibrium of the industry under perfect competition and monopoly with the same *MC* curve

away in the long run. The only difference, therefore, between short-run and long-run equilibrium is that in the long run the firm will produce where *MR = long-run MC*.

Comparing monopoly with perfect competition

Because it faces a different type of market environment, the monopolist will produce a quite different output and at a quite different price from a perfectly competitive industry. Let us compare the two.

The monopolist will produce a lower output at a higher price in the short run. Figure 11.6 compares the profit-maximising position for an industry under monopoly with that under perfect competition. Note that we are comparing the monopoly with the whole *industry* under perfect competition. That way we can assume, for the sake of comparison, that they both face the same demand curve. We also assume for the moment that they both face the same cost curves.

The monopolist will produce Q_1 at a price of P_1. This is where *MC = MR*.

If the same industry were under perfect competition, however, it would produce at Q_2 and P_2 – a higher output and a lower price. But why? The reason for this is that for each of the firms in the industry – and it is at this level that the decisions are made – marginal revenue is the same as price. Remember that the firm under perfect competition faces a perfectly elastic demand (*AR*) curve, which also equals *MR* (see Figure 11.1). Thus producing where *MC = MR* also means producing where *MC = P*. When all firms under perfect competition do this, price and quantity in the industry will be given by P_2 and Q_2 in Figure 11.6.

The monopolist may also produce a lower output at a higher price in the long run. Under perfect competition, freedom of entry

eliminates supernormal profit and forces firms to produce at the bottom of their *LRAC* curve, keeping long-run prices down. A monopolist, however, because of barriers to entry can continue to earn supernormal profits in the long run and is not forced to operate at the bottom of the *AC* curve. Thus, other things being equal, long-run prices will tend to be higher, and hence output lower, under monopoly. (In section 20.2 we examine this in more detail by considering the impact of monopoly on consumer and producer surplus. You might wish to take a preliminary look at pages 343–4 now.)

Pause for thought

If the shares in a monopoly (such as a water company) were very widely distributed among the population, would the shareholders necessarily want the firm to use its monopoly power to make larger profits?

Costs under monopoly. The sheer survival of a firm in the long run under perfect competition requires that it uses the most efficient known technique, and develops new techniques wherever possible. The monopolist, however, sheltered by barriers to entry, can still make large profits even if it is not using the most efficient technique. It has less incentive, therefore, to be efficient.

On the other hand, the monopoly may be able to achieve substantial economies of scale due to larger plant, centralised administration and the avoidance of unnecessary duplication (e.g. a monopoly water company would eliminate the need for several sets of rival water mains under each street). If this results in an *MC* curve substantially below that of the same industry under perfect competition, the monopoly may even produce a *higher* output at a *lower* price.

Another reason why a monopolist may operate with lower costs is that it can use part of its supernormal profits for research and development and investment. It may not

BOX 11.3   WINDOWS CLEANING

Challenging Microsoft's monopoly power

Network effects

Microsoft is a vertically integrated firm (see pages 245–8), with a dominant position in the operating system market (i.e. *Windows*) and in certain application software (*Office* and *Windows Media Player*) markets. It has built this position by creating networks of users. These networks bring both benefits and costs to society.

Network economies arise when consumers of a product benefit from it being used by *other* consumers. In the case of Microsoft's products, firms benefit from lower training costs because individuals who have learnt to use Microsoft products elsewhere can be readily absorbed into the firm. Individuals benefit too because they do not have to learn to use new software when they move to another organisation and the learning costs are fairly low as a new version of the software is introduced.

The negative aspect of developing strong networks is that users can get 'locked in' to using the software and they become reluctant to switch to alternative systems. Protecting the network is vital to Microsoft's competitive edge.

> An operating system attracts software developed around that operating system, thereby discouraging new competition, since any alternative faces not only the challenge of creating a better operating system but competing against a whole array of already existing software applications. . . . These so-called 'network effects' give an incredible anti-competitive edge to companies like Microsoft that control so many different parts of the network.[6]

It is these negative network effects that have led to Microsoft being under seemingly constant investigation by competition authorities for over two decades. By controlling the *Windows* operating software, Microsoft attempted to force its own Internet browser, *Internet Explorer*, on to consumers and computer manufacturers and this led to Microsoft being accused of abusing its market power and seeking to crush its rivals.

Microsoft and the US court findings

Interest in Microsoft's practices began in 1991, with a Federal Trade Commission inquiry into its monopoly abuse of the PC operating system market. However, perhaps the most famous investigation began on 18 May 1998, when the US Justice Department alleged that Microsoft had committed the following anti-competitive actions:

- In May 1995 Microsoft attempted to collude with Netscape Communications to divide the Internet browser market. Netscape Communications refused.
- Microsoft had forced personal computer manufacturers to install Internet Explorer in order to obtain a Windows operating licence.
- Microsoft insisted that PC manufacturers conformed to a Microsoft front screen for Windows. This included specified icons, one of which was Microsoft's Internet Explorer.
- It had set up reciprocal advertising arrangements with America's largest Internet service providers, such as

America Online. Here Microsoft would promote America Online via Windows. In return, America Online would not promote Netscape's browsers.

One solution, posed by Federal Judge Thomas Penfield Jackson in 2000, was that Microsoft be split into two companies to prevent it operating as a monopoly. One would produce and market the *Windows* operating system; the other would produce and market the applications software, such as *Microsoft Office* and the web browser, *Internet Explorer*.

This was overturned on appeal in June 2001 and Microsoft agreed to provide technical information about *Windows* to other companies so that potential rivals could write software that would compete with Microsoft's own software. Also Microsoft would not be allowed to retaliate against computer manufacturers that installed rival products or removed icons for Microsoft applications.

Microsoft and the European Commission findings

It is not only in the US where Microsoft has faced legal action and accusations of abuse of a dominant position. In March 2004 the European Commission fined Microsoft €497 million for an Abuse of a Dominant Position in the operating system market. It found that Microsoft had harmed competition in the media player market by bundling *Windows Media Player* with its operating system.

Further, Microsoft had refused to supply information about its secret software code to suppliers of alternative network software at reasonable rates. Such code was needed to allow non-Windows network software to be interoperable with ('talk' to) Windows network software. Without it, firms that had purchased *Windows Network* servers would be solely tied in to Microsoft server software. This, in turn, would discourage the development of application software products by Microsoft's rivals.

In April 2006, Microsoft launched an appeal against the judgment claiming that the EU's ruling violated international law by forcing the company to share information with rivals. However, the Court of First Instance found in the Commission's favour. Microsoft complied with the first ruling and unbundled *Windows Media Player* from its operating systems, much to the annoyance of computer suppliers who argued that their customers could easily upload alternative media players from the Web.

However, until October 2007 Microsoft continued to charge high royalty rates and fees for interoperability information that would allow competitors to access secret source codes on the *Windows Network System*. As a result, in February 2008 the Commission penalised Microsoft a further €899 million for non-compliance with its 2004 decision and Microsoft became the first company in 50 years of EU competition policy to be fined for non-compliance with a Commission decision (see

Definition

Network economies The benefits to consumers of having a network of other people using the same product or service.

[6] N. Newman, from 'MS Word to MS world: how Microsoft is building a global monopoly' (1997), www.netaction.org/msoft/world

the European Commission Press Release).[7] Microsoft took the Commission to court in an attempt to overturn the fine, losing its case in 2012, though the fine was reduced to €860 million, following a 'miscalculation'.

This was not the end of Microsoft's dealings with the European Commission. In 2009 the Commission announced an investigation into the bundling of *Internet Explorer* with *Windows*. The bundling was thought to be restricting competition in the market for web browsers.[8] Microsoft took the Commission seriously and agreed to remove *Explorer* from the European versions of *Windows 7*. To promote competition it offered users an option of downloading one browser from a list of 12, including Mozilla *Firefox*, Google's *Chrome*, Apple's *Safari* and *Opera*. However, it was found that between May 2011 and July 2012, thousands of customers in Europe did not have this choice available and, as such, the European Commission imposed a €561 million fine on Microsoft (see the European Commission Press Release).[9]

Microsoft has been warned by the Commission about anti-competitive behaviour with its *Windows 8* product and has been told that severe penalties will be imposed if it breaks the 2009 bundling agreement.

Is Microsoft playing a 'game' with the competition authorities – maximising profits by pushing as hard as possible against the legal framework?

Microsoft and the public interest

These lawsuits raise an important issue: is Microsoft acting for or against the public interest?

The classic case against monopoly suppliers is that they charge higher prices and offer lower quantities to consumers than would be the case under perfect competition. In addition, the supernormal profit that monopolies earn may be detrimental to society if it is used to continue to support the monopoly position, say by lobbying or bribing government officials. Further, if no competition prevails then monopoly suppliers may become more inefficient.

However, the competition authorities have never penalised Microsoft simply for possessing monopoly power. It has been fined when it has *abused* its market power. That is, it is not the monopoly market structure that matters per se to competition authorities; rather, it is the behaviour of the firm when it has monopoly power. Through its actions, Microsoft had raised barriers to entry by restricting the opportunities for potential rival firms to offer alternative products to customers. Choice was thereby restricted.

In its defence, Microsoft has argued that it has continually sought to reinvest its profits in new product development and offered a number of innovative solutions over the past 30 years for individuals and businesses alike. (Can you think of all the versions of *Windows* and the 'free updates' there have been?)

Further, in an environment where technology is changing rapidly, Microsoft's control over standards gives the user a measure of stability, knowing that any new products and applications will be compatible with existing ones. In other words, new software can be incorporated into existing systems. In this respect Microsoft can be viewed as operating in society's interest. Microsoft would argue that it has a right to protect its in-house software code from competitors and receive a fair price for it. Indeed, it is a natural response for a firm to protect its intellectual property rights. Failure to do so could lead to the firm's demise.

Challenges to Microsoft monopoly

Microsoft is facing increasing competitive pressure. The recent challenges from competition authorities (referred to above) have opened up the browser market, for example. Microsoft's *Internet Explorer* is no longer the dominant browser; since the mid-2000s its market share has fallen significantly as other browsers have become widely used. In July 2003, it had an 82.7 per cent share of the global browser market; by Quarter 4, 2015, this had fallen to 10.3 per cent for all browsers – third behind Google's *Chrome* (52.8 per cent) and Apple's *Safari* (12.4 per cent) and only just ahead of *Firefox* (9.3 per cent) (although *Firefox's* share had been as high as 32 per cent in 2009).[10]

There is also a growing challenge from new Internet firms, such as Google and Facebook. Both Google and Facebook have created enormous networks of users, who are then targeted with tailored adverts paid for by firms who want to reach these vast audiences.

This is a very different business model from that of Microsoft and, as part of the desire to create large networks of users, free products are being released that will compete with those of Microsoft. For example, Google's *Google Docs* and Apache's *Open Office* compete with Microsoft's *Office*. These are becoming increasingly well known and have growing market shares.

Microsoft's dominance has certainly been tested in many parts of the industry, but its market leading position for its various operating systems is still intact. NetMarketShare and StatCounter put *Window's* market share (all versions) of the desktop and laptop markets at just below 90 per cent, with Apple's operating system making some gains. However, with the rise of tablet computers and smart phones, we are seeing a growing number of competitors, such as Google's Linux opensource operating system, *Android*. With the rise of tablets with detachable keyboards that double as a laptop, this sector is likely to see many changes over the coming years.

You might want to follow subsequent events as the news unfolds (see section A of the Hotlinks section of Sloman Economics News site for links to newspaper sites).

1. *In what respects might Microsoft's behaviour be deemed to have been: (a) against the public interest; (b) in the public interest?*
2. *Being locked in to a product or technology is only a problem if such a product can be clearly shown to be inferior to an alternative. What difficulties might there be in establishing such a case?*

[7] European Commission, 'Antitrust: Commission imposes €899 million penalty on Microsoft for non-compliance with March 2004 Decision', *European Commission Press Release IP/08/318*, 27 February 2008.
[8] See European Commission, 'Antitrust: Commission confirms sending of a Statement of Objections to Microsoft on the tying of Internet Explorer to Windows Reference', *European Commission Press Release MEMO/09/15*, 17 January 2009.
[9] European Commission, 'Commission fines Microsoft for non-compliance with browser choice commitments', *European Commission Press Release IP/13/196*, 6 March 2013.
[10] For figures on browser usage, see http://en.wikipedia.org/wiki/Usage_share_of_web_browsers

have the same *incentive* to become efficient as the perfectly competitive firm which is fighting for survival, but it may have a much greater *ability* to become efficient than a small firm with limited funds.

Although a monopoly faces no competition in the goods market, it may face an alternative form of competition in financial markets. A monopoly, with potentially low costs, which is currently run inefficiently, is likely to be subject to a takeover bid from another company. This **competition for corporate control** may thus force the monopoly to be efficient in order to prevent being taken over.

Innovation and new products. The promise of supernormal profits, protected perhaps by patents, may encourage the development of new (monopoly) industries producing new products. It is this chance of making monopoly profits that encourages many people to take the risk of going into business.

Definitions

Competition for corporate control The competition for the control of companies through takeovers.

11.4 POTENTIAL COMPETITION OR POTENTIAL MONOPOLY? THE THEORY OF CONTESTABLE MARKETS

Potential competition

In recent years, economists have developed the theory of contestable markets. This theory argues that what is crucial in determining price and output is not whether an industry is *actually* a monopoly or competitive, but whether there is the real *threat* of competition.

If a monopoly is protected by high barriers to entry – say that it owns all the raw materials – then it will be able to make supernormal profits with no fear of competition.

If, however, another firm *could* take over from it with little difficulty, it will behave much more like a competitive firm. The threat of competition has a similar effect to actual competition.

As an example, consider a catering company that is given permission by a factory to run its canteen. The catering company has a monopoly over the supply of food to the workers in that factory. However, if it starts charging high prices or providing a poor service, the factory could

---

BOX 11.4 'IT COULD BE YOU'

Bidding for the UK National Lottery

Since its launch in November 1994, the UK National Lottery has struck at the heart of the British psyche because it offers the opportunity to win a fortune and support worthwhile ventures. By the start of 2015, the lottery had created over 3700 millionaires and multi-millionaires, with £53 billion paid out as prizes. However, research by VoucherCodesPro estimated that weekly National Lottery players will lose on average almost £150 over the year. The UK National Lottery also generates an estimated £33 million weekly for 'Good Causes', bringing the total to £33 billion since 1994 and contributed £2.2 billion to the 2012 London Olympic and Paralympic Games.

Around 70 per cent of UK adults play the lottery, spending on average about £3 per week. For the year ending 31 March 2014, for every pound spent on the lottery, approximately 52p was paid in prizes, 26p went to the National Lottery Distribution Fund, which is distributed to arts (20 per cent), sports (20 per cent), health, education, environment and charitable causes (40 per cent) and heritage (20 per cent). A further 12p goes to the government in the form of Lottery Tax, 5p goes to the retailer and 5p goes to Camelot, the operator, and its Canadian parent company, Ontario Teachers' Pension Plan.

Sales of lottery tickets grew dramatically in the early years of operation but waned around the turn of the century. In 2002, a second lottery was launched and this did lead to a recovery in sales and, with the growth of EuroMillions, more people are being encouraged to participate in all lotteries. Sales grew by 12 per cent in the five years to 2012. The 2012/13 financial year

saw the highest annual sales total since 1994, recorded at £6.98 billion, though Camelot said it was boosted by the Olympics.

Sales in the 2013/14 financial year were just behind the previous year at £6.7 billion, making it the second highest annual sales total since 1994. Initially sales were looking weak in the 2013/14 financial year, but they were turned around with a controversial decision to double Loto ticket price to £2 in autumn 2013. This created a £245 million boost to sales, as discussed in a Telegraph article.[11]

The institutional framework

There are a number of institutions involved in providing the lottery. The Department of Culture, Media and Sport oversees the lottery as directed by the National Lottery Act and dictates its strategic direction. It appoints the National Lottery Commission (NLC), which ensures that bids for the lottery licence and the running of the lottery games maximise the returns for 'Good Causes'. There are also a number of distribution bodies that provide lottery funds to thousands of local projects.

The main point of contact for lottery buyers is Camelot, which runs the lotto and scratchcard games via retail outlets, mobile phones, digital television and the Internet.

---

[11] Nathalie Thomas, 'National Lottery sales boosted by £2 ticket price', *The Telegraph*, 20 May 2014.

▶

Camelot won the first, second and third licences for the right to run the UK National Lottery from 1994, 2002 and 2009 respectively. Camelot's extended third-term licence will expire in 2023.

The rationale for a monopoly supplier

Camelot is a monopoly supplier of the UK National Lottery, although it need not be so. The legislation currently allows for two licences, one to operate the infrastructure and another to run the games. It is possible for other companies to run games on the computer network owned by Camelot, much in the same way that Network Rail owns the railway tracks, tunnels, etc. and allows competition between firms on particular routes on the network. Indeed, this option was briefly undertaken by Camelot in 1998, when Vernons Pools sold its 'Easy Play' game using the National Lottery retailer network. Its sales, though, were poor and it was scrapped in May 1999.

However, the government has a strong preference for a single owner of the infrastructure and a single supplier of National Lottery games. The rationale for having a single owner of the infrastructure is fairly standard; this is a natural monopoly and it would be pointless having two lottery computer networks, just as it would be having two separately owned rail lines from Edinburgh to London. With one firm controlling the infrastructure, economies of scale can be reaped.

One of the arguments for having a single supplier of games is known, rather bizarrely, as 'peculiar economies of scale'.[12] This is a situation in which a company that offered a portfolio of innovative lottery games would be more likely to induce additional players to participate in games because they can raise the size of the prize to be won. In other words, good game design can lead to more and bigger jackpots and thus more people buying lottery tickets. This reduces the average costs of supplying tickets and increases the money for 'Good Causes'.

Arguably, more than one firm may be able to supply an innovative portfolio of games if the market is large enough. However, the government is concerned about the risks involved in regulating relationships between network owners and network users (a problem that has occurred in regulating the railways – see Box 22.4). For example, there might be a lengthy legal dispute if a supplier of games is accused of unacceptable performance but it, in turn, accuses the network owner of poor service. This would then have a detrimental effect on the money raised for 'Good Causes'. Thus the government has always preferred a single-firm framework for running the National Lottery.

Bidding for the National Lottery monopoly

Unlike auctions to run national rail franchises or a local bus route, bidding for the lottery does not involve any payment on the part of the successful bidder. The bid is purely a detailed business plan outlining all aspects of running the lottery, but its main emphasis is on providing likely revenue scenarios from games that would maximise money for 'Good Causes' and safeguard players. It was the uncertainty over future revenue flows that led the government in 1994 to require a paper-based bidding scheme for the first lottery licence. This view did not change when subsequent licences came up for renewal.

The NLC is responsible for evaluating the bids and awarding the licence. There were seven bidders for the first licence but for the second licence there were only two tabled 'bids', one from Camelot and other from Sir Richard Branson's The People's Lottery (and initially the NLC rejected both before settling on the incumbent).

For the third licence, the NLC tried to encourage as many bids as possible to come forward. Only one other bidder, Sugal and Dumani UK Ltd, submitted a bid. Camelot won because the NLC believed that, at a similar level of sales, they would be slightly more generous to 'Good Causes' and that 'there was a higher probability that they would achieve higher sales over the length of the licence'.[13]

Clearly, incumbent firms like Camelot have considerable advantages over potential rivals when contracts have to be renewed and thus the number of new bidders is likely to be low. Two problems, in particular, stand out for rivals.

The 'Winner's Curse'

If a potential entrant outbids the incumbent in an auction to run (say) a local bus service, then it could be that winner has paid too much. After all, the incumbent has more knowledge about running the bus service and the likely revenues that may prevail. This situation is known as the 'Winner's Curse' and a similar scenario may occur in respect of the lottery. Potential bidders may be put off bidding because they don't have the same knowledge about the UK lottery market.

Arguably, the lottery market might be considered a mature market and more is now known about lottery sales and the gaming market in general. However, there are strong incentives for risk-averse regulators to continue with accepting bids from incumbent firms because they are known to provide a certain level of sales and service.

The handover problem

If Camelot were to lose the lottery licence, there would be some large risks in transferring to the new bidder. Arguably, Camelot could sell its infrastructure to the new lottery provider, but there is a valuation dilemma. In terms of opportunity cost, Camelot would value the infrastructure at scrap value (if it has no alternative use for it), whereas a winner with no alternative source for such infrastructure would value Camelot's assets at close to their replacement value. This could lead to some difficult negotiations.

Because of this difficulty, the NLC did require bidders for the third lottery licence to provide new infrastructure, but recognised that this would take time to have in place (imagine trying to replace 30 000 retail terminals as well as to make online, television and mobile games work well). Given this difficulty, it is not surprising that there was only one rival bidder to Camelot.

Camelot managed to achieve a first-mover advantage (see page 209) by winning the initial lottery licence in 1994. It is now to continue providing the UK National Lottery until 2023 and so will have been sole monopoly provider for 29 years. Removing Camelot after that date could prove to be difficult.

1. *If Camelot is maximising revenue, what is the price elasticity of demand for lottery tickets?*
2. *To what extent is the National Lottery market a contestable market?*

[12] See, for example, P. Daffern, 'Assessment of the effects of competition on the National Lottery', *Technical Paper No. 6*, Department of Culture, Media and Sport, 2006.

[13] NLC press release, 'Preferred bidder announced for the third National Lottery licence', 7 August 2007.

offer the running of the canteen to an alternative catering company. This threat may force the original catering company to charge 'reasonable' prices and offer a good service.

Perfectly contestable markets

A market is *perfectly contestable* when the costs of entry and exit by potential rivals are zero, and when such entry can be made very rapidly. In such cases, the moment the possibility of earning supernormal profits occurs, new firms will enter, thus driving profits down to a normal level. The sheer threat of this happening, so the theory goes, will ensure that the firm already in the market will (a) keep its prices down, so that it just makes normal profits, and (b) produce as efficiently as possible, taking advantage of any economies of scale and any new technology. If the existing firm did not do this, entry would take place and potential competition would become actual competition.

Contestable markets and natural monopolies

So why in such cases are the markets not *actually* perfectly competitive? Why do they remain monopolies?

The most likely reason has to do with economies of scale and the size of the market. To operate at the minimum efficient scale, the firm may have to be so large relative to the market that there is only room for one such firm in the industry. If a new firm does come into the market, then one firm will not survive the competition. The market is simply not big enough for both of them.

If, however, there are no entry or exit costs, new firms will be perfectly willing to enter even though there is only room for one firm, provided they believe that they are more efficient than the existing firm. The existing firm, knowing this, will be forced to produce as efficiently as possible and with only normal profit.

The importance of costless exit

Setting up in a new business usually involves large expenditures on plant and machinery. Once this money has been spent, it becomes part of the fixed costs. If these fixed costs are no higher than those of the existing firm, then the new firm could win the battle. But, of course, there is always the risk that it might lose.

But does losing the battle really matter? Can the firm not simply move to another market?

It does matter if there are substantial costs of exit. This will be the case if the capital equipment cannot be transferred to other uses. In this case these fixed costs are known as *sunk costs*. The losing firm will exit the industry, but is left with capital equipment that it cannot use and this may deter the firm from entering in the first place. The market is not perfectly contestable, and the established firm can make supernormal profit.

If, however, the capital equipment can be transferred, the exit costs are zero (or at least very low), and new firms will be more willing to risk entering the market. For example, a rival coach company may open up a service on a route previously operated by only one company, and where there is still only room for one operator. If the new firm loses the resulting battle, it can still use the coaches it has purchased. It simply uses them for a different route or sells them for a fair price on the second-hand market. The cost of the coaches is not a sunk cost.

Costless exit, therefore, encourages firms to enter an industry, knowing that, if unsuccessful, they can always transfer their capital elsewhere.

The lower the exit costs, the more contestable the market. This implies that firms already established in other similar markets may provide more effective competition against monopolists, since they can simply transfer capital from one market to another. For example, studies of airlines in the USA show that entry to a particular route may be much easier for an established airline, which can simply transfer planes from one route to another.

Assessment of the theory

Simple monopoly theory merely focuses on the existing structure of the industry and makes no allowance for potential competition. The theory of contestable markets, however, goes much further and examines the *size* of entry barriers and exit costs. The bigger these are, the less contestable the market and therefore the greater the monopoly power of the existing firm. Various attempts have been made to measure monopoly power in this way.

One criticism of the theory, however, is that it does not take sufficient account of the possible reactions of the established firm. Entry and exist may be costless (i.e. a perfectly contestable market), but the established firm may let it be known that any firm that dares to enter will face all-out war, thus deterring new entrants! In the meantime, the established firm may charge high prices and make supernormal profits.

If a monopoly operates in a perfectly contestable market, it might bring the 'best of both worlds' for the consumer. Not only will it be able to achieve low costs through economies of scale, but also the potential competition will keep profits and hence prices down.

KI 18
p 141

> ### Pause for thought
>
> *Think of two examples of highly contestable monopolies (or oligopolies). How well is the consumer's interest served?*

> ### Definitions
>
> **Perfectly contestable market** A market where there is free and costless entry and exit.
>
> **Sunk costs** Costs that cannot be recouped (e.g. by transferring assets to other uses).

SUMMARY

1a There are four alternative market structures under which firms operate. In ascending order of firms' market power, they are: perfect competition, monopolistic competition, oligopoly and monopoly.

1b The market structure under which a firm operates will affect its conduct and its performance.

2a The assumptions of perfect competition are: a very large number of firms, complete freedom of entry, a

▶

homogeneous product and perfect knowledge of the good and its market by both producers and consumers.

2b In the short run of perfect competition, there is not time for new firms to enter the market, and thus supernormal profits can persist. In the long run, however, any supernormal profits will be competed away by the entry of new firms.

2c The short-run equilibrium for the firm under perfect competition will be where the price, as determined by demand and supply in the market, is equal to marginal cost. At this output the firm will be maximising profit.

2d The long-run equilibrium in a perfectly competitive market will be where the market price is just equal to firms' long-run average cost.

2e There are no substantial economies of scale to be gained in a perfectly competitive industry. If there were, the industry would cease to be perfectly competitive as the large, low-cost firms drove the small, high-cost ones out of business.

3a A monopoly is where there is only one firm in an industry. In practice, it is difficult to determine where a monopoly exists because it depends on how narrowly an industry is defined.

3b Barriers to the entry of new firms will normally be necessary to protect a monopoly from competition. Such barriers include economies of scale (making the firm a natural monopoly or at least giving it a cost advantage over new

(small) competitors), control over supplies of inputs or over outlets, patents or copyright, and tactics to eliminate competition (such as takeovers or aggressive advertising).

3c Profits for the monopolist (as for other firms) will be maximised where $MC = MR$.

3d If demand and cost curves are the same in a monopoly and a perfectly competitive industry, the monopoly will produce a lower output and at a higher price than the perfectly competitive industry.

3e On the other hand, any economies of scale will in part be passed on to consumers in lower prices, and the monopolist's high profits may be used for research and development and investment, which in turn may lead to better products at possibly lower prices.

4a Potential competition may be as important as actual competition in determining a firm's price and output strategy.

4b The greater the threat of this competition, the lower are the entry and exit costs to and from the industry. If the entry and exit costs are zero, the market is said to be *perfectly* contestable. Under such circumstances, an existing monopolist will be forced to keep its profits down to the normal level if it is to resist entry of new firms. The lower the exit costs, the lower are the sunk costs of the firm.

4c The theory of contestable markets provides a more realistic analysis of firms' behaviour than theories based simply on the *existing* number of firms in the industry.

MyEconLab

This book can be supported by MyEconLab, which contains a range of additional resources, including an online homework and tutorial system designed to test and build your understanding.

You need both an access card and a course ID to access MyEconLab:

1. Is your lecturer using MyEconLab? Ask your lecturer for your course ID.

2. Has an access card been included with the book at a reduced cost? Check the inside back cover of the book.

3. If you have a course ID but no access card, go to: http://www.myeconlab.com/ to buy access to this interactive study programme.

REVIEW QUESTIONS

1 Why do economists treat normal profit as a cost of production? What determines (a) the level and (b) the rate of normal profit for a particular firm?

2 Why is perfect competition so rare?

3 Why does the market for fresh vegetables approximate to perfect competition, whereas that for frozen or tinned ones does not?

4 Illustrate on a diagram similar to Figure 11.3 what would happen in the long run if price were initially below P_L.

5 We discussed e-commerce in Box 11.2, but are there any other examples of the impact of technological development on the competitiveness of markets or on meeting specific assumptions of perfect competition?

6 As an illustration of the difficulty in identifying monopolies, try to decide which of the following are monopolies: a train-operating company; your local evening newspaper; British Gas; the village post office; the Royal Mail; Interflora; the London Underground; ice creams in the cinema; Guinness; food on trains; TippEx; the board game 'Monopoly'.

7 Try this brain teaser. A monopoly would be expected to face an inelastic demand. After all, there are no direct substitutes. And yet if it produces where $MR = MC$, MR must be positive, demand must therefore be elastic. Therefore the monopolist must face an elastic demand! Can you solve this conundrum?

8 For what reasons would you expect a monopoly to charge (a) a higher price and (b) a lower price than if the industry were operating under perfect competition?

9 'The outcomes of perfect competition are always good, whereas monopolies are always bad.' Discuss this statement.

10 In which of the following industries are exit costs likely to be low: (a) steel production; (b) market gardening; (c) nuclear power generation; (d) specialist financial advisory services; (e) production of fashion dolls; (f) production of a new drug; (g) contract catering; (h) mobile discos; (i) car ferry operators? Are these exit costs dependent on how narrowly the industry is defined?

11 Think of three examples of monopolies (local or national) and consider how contestable their markets are.

Profit maximisation under imperfect competition

Business issues covered in this chapter

■ How will firms behave under monopolistic competition (i.e. where there are many firms competing, but where they produce differentiated products)?
■ Why will firms under monopolistic competition make only normal profits in the long run?
■ How are firms likely to behave when there are just a few of them competing ('oligopolies')?
■ What determines whether oligopolies will engage in all-out competition or instead collude with each other?
■ What strategic 'games' are oligopolists likely to play in their attempt to out-do their rivals?
■ Why might such games lead to an outcome where all the players are worse off than if they had colluded?
■ Does oligopoly serve the consumer's interests?

Very few markets in practice can be classified as perfectly competitive or as a pure monopoly. The vast majority of firms do compete with other firms, often quite aggressively, and yet they are not price takers: they do have some degree of market power. Most markets, therefore, lie between the two extremes of monopoly and perfect competition, in the realm of 'imperfect competition'. There are two types of imperfect competition: namely, monopolistic competition and oligopoly (see section 11.1).

12.1 MONOPOLISTIC COMPETITION

Monopolistic competition is towards the competitive end of the spectrum (as we saw in section 11.1). It can best be understood as a situation where there are a lot of firms competing, but where each firm does nevertheless have some degree of market power (hence the term 'monopolistic' competition): each firm has some discretion as to what price to charge for its products because they are differentiated from those of other firms.

Assumptions of monopolistic competition

■ There is *quite a large number of firms*. As a result, each firm has only a small share of the market and, therefore, its actions are unlikely to affect its rivals to any great extent. This means that when a firm makes its decisions, it will not have to worry about how its rivals will react. It assumes that what its rivals choose to do will not be influenced by what it does.

Figure 12.1 Equilibrium of the firm under monopolistic competition: (a) short run; (b) long run

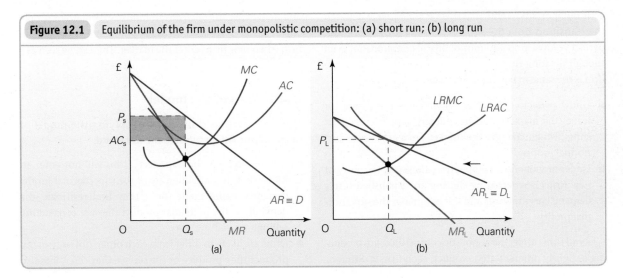

(a)

(b)

This is known as the assumption of *independence*. As we shall see later, this is not the case under oligopoly.

■ There is freedom of entry of new firms into the industry. If any firm wants to set up in business in this market, it is free to do so.

In these two respects, therefore, monopolistic competition is like perfect competition.

■ Unlike perfect competition, however, each firm produces a product or provides a service that is in some way different from its rivals. As a result, it can raise its price without losing all its customers. Thus its demand curve is downward sloping, albeit relatively elastic given the large number of competitors to which customers can turn. This is known as the assumption of *product differentiation*.

Petrol stations, restaurants, hairdressers and builders are all examples of monopolistic competition – as is the case of busking, which is discussed on the Freakonomics blog.[1]

When considering monopolistic competition it is important to take account of the distance consumers are willing to travel to buy a product. In other words, the geographical size of the market matters. For example, McDonald's is a major global and national fast-food restaurant. However, in any one location it experiences intense competition in the 'informal eating-out' market from Indian, Chinese, Italian and other restaurants (see Box 12.1). So in any one local area, there is competition between firms each offering differentiated products.

Definitions

Independence (of firms in a market) When the decisions of one firm in a market will not have any significant effect on the demand curves of its rivals.

Product differentiation When one firm's product is sufficiently different from its rivals', it can raise the price of the product without customers all switching to the rivals' products. This gives a firm a downward-sloping demand curve.

[1]http://freakonomics.com/2012/05/21/the-economics-of-busking/

Equilibrium of the firm

Short run

As with other market structures, profits are maximised at the output where $MC = MR$. The diagram will be the same as for the monopolist, except that the AR and MR curves will be more elastic. This is illustrated in Figure 12.1(a). As with perfect competition, it is possible for the monopolistically competitive firm to make supernormal profit in the short run. This is shown as the shaded area.

Just how much profit the firm will make in the short run depends on the strength of demand: the position and elasticity of the demand curve. The further to the right the demand curve is relative to the average cost curve, and the less elastic the demand curve is, the greater will be the firm's short-run profit. Thus a firm facing little competition and whose product is considerably differentiated from its rivals may be able to earn significant short-run profits.

KI 4
p 25

KI 12
p 68

Pause for thought

Which of these two items is a petrol station more likely to sell at a discount: (a) engine oil; (b) sweets? Why?

Long run

If typical firms are earning supernormal profit, new firms will enter the industry in the long run. As new firms enter, they will take some of the customers away from established firms. The demand for the established firms' products will therefore fall. Their demand (*AR*) curve will shift to the left, and will continue doing so as long as supernormal profits remain and thus new firms continue entering.

Long-run equilibrium will be reached when only normal profits remain: when there is no further incentive for new firms to enter. This is illustrated in Figure 12.1(b). The firm's demand curve settles at D_L, where it is tangential to (i.e. just touches) the firm's $LRAC$ curve. Output will be Q_L: where $AR_L = LRAC$. (At any other output, $LRAC$ is greater than AR and thus less than normal profit would be made.)

KI 10
p 52

KI 11
p 59

It is important to note that there is a difference between the transition from the short run to the long run under perfect competition and monopolistic competition, even though the long-run equilibrium of normal profits for the firm is the same in both market structures.

■ Under perfect competition, when new firms enter (or leave) the market, it is the industry supply curve that shifts, which changes the market price and leaves just normal profits.

■ Under monopolistic competition, however, the entry of new firms is reflected by shifting an established firm's demand curve inwards and this eliminates the supernormal profits.

As all firms under monopolistic competition are producing a slightly differentiated product, each firm is different and hence we cannot create an industry demand or supply curve. Instead, we have to focus on the effect on a given firm when new firms enter the market. This can be seen as a limitation of the model, as we discuss next.

Limitations of the model

There are various problems in applying the model of monopolistic competition to the real world:

■ Information may be imperfect. Firms will not enter an industry if they are unaware of the supernormal profits currently being made, or if they underestimate the demand for the particular product they are considering selling.

■ Firms are likely to differ from each other, not only in the product they produce or the service they offer, but also

---

A monopolistically competitive sector

The 'eating-out' sector (i.e. takeaways, cafés, restaurants and pubs) is a highly competitive market in the UK, with sales, in 2012, of some £77 billion, according to the Office for National Statistics.[2] The sector has grown less strongly in recent years than in the late 1990s and early 2000s. The financial crisis and subsequent recession had an impact on sales in this sector and, according to a PwC discussion document,[3] from 2007 to 2011, the average growth in sales revenue was just 2.1 per cent – not enough to keep up with inflation (which averaged 3.1 per cent over the period). However, according to the Coffer Peach Business Tracker,[4] January 2015 recorded the 22nd consecutive month of positive like-for-like growth in sales based on its sample.

The sector exhibits many of the characteristics of a monopolistically competitive market.

■ *Large number of local buyers*. According to a Mintel survey in 2011, around 94 per cent of UK adults had eaten out within the previous three months; and in 2014, Ernst and Young found that 31 per cent of UK consumers would eat out at least once a week, up from 17 per cent in 2011.[5] According to PwC, there 'has been a structural shift over the last c. 20 years' and 'eating out has become embedded in UK consumer behaviour'.[6]

■ *Large number of firms*. Research from Horizons indicates that there are 23 514 restaurants and 49 953 pubs in the UK.[7] This means that in many areas there are a significant number of competing places to eat and hence consumer choice. In the cases of both restaurants and pubs, there are more independent companies than those belonging to a group – again providing significant choice.

■ *Competitive prices*. Margins are very tight because firms have to price very competitively to catch local custom. Only around 60 per cent of these businesses survive longer than three years.

■ *Differentiated products*. To attract customers, suppliers must each differentiate their product in various ways, such as food type, ambience, comfort, service, quality, advertising and opening hours. Firms have to cater for the dynamic nature of consumer preferences and respond to the behaviour of competitors. They must constantly adapt or go under.

Casual dining

One area that has out-performed traditional restaurants and pubs has been casual dining, which includes street food, coffee shops and fast-food outlets. Worth £4 billion of the total eating-out sector, this area grew by 11.6 per cent in the five years to March 2014.[8] This translates to 47 million more visits to these places in 2014 than in 2009. It has also proved much more resilient to the economic downturn.

The growth has been driven by both demand- and supply-side factors. The report by PwC cited above found that casual dining places provide greater affordability for consumers. This in turn has been driving a change in tastes, with people seeing eating out as a habit and not just a special treat; they would often stop to refuel rather than have a three-course meal. But this means that, while more people are eating out, the average spend on each visit tends to be falling.

Another part of the casual dining sector is the sandwich and lunchtime food outlets. These too have undergone significant growth. As lunch is seen by many as a refuelling exercise rather than a leisure activity, the convenience, fast service and value for money provided by many of these new casual dining places is a key factor behind this sector's growth.

---

[2] *Input-Output Supply and Use Tables*, ONS, 2014.
[3] *UK Casual Dining Market: Discussion Document*, PwC, December 2013.
[4] *Coffer Peach Business Tracker*, CGA Peach, February 2015.
[5] *Restaurant and Casual Dining Insight Report*, Ernst and Young, September 2014.
[6] *UK Casual Dining Market*, PwC
[7] *Insight Report*, Ernst and Young, p. 5.
[8] Ibid., based on data from NPD group.

in their size and in their cost structure. What is more, entry may not be completely unrestricted. For example, two petrol stations could not set up in exactly the same place – on a busy crossroads, say – because of local authority planning controls. Thus although the typical or 'representative' firm may only earn normal profit in the long run, other firms may be able to earn long-run supernormal profit. They may have some cost advantage or produce a product that is impossible to duplicate perfectly.

■ Existing firms may make supernormal profits, but if a new firm entered, this might reduce everyone's profits below the normal level. Thus a new firm will not enter and supernormal profits will persist into the long run. An example would be a small town with two chemist shops. They may both make more than enough profit to persuade them to stay in business. But if a third set up (say midway between the other two), there would not be enough total sales to allow them all to earn even normal profit. This is a problem of indivisibilities. Given the overheads of a chemist shop, it is not possible to set up one small enough to take away just enough customers to leave the other two with normal profits.

■ One of the biggest problems with the simple model outlined above is that it concentrates on price and output decisions. In practice, the profit-maximising firm under monopolistic competition will also need to decide the exact variety of product to produce, and how much to spend on advertising it. This will lead the firm to take part in non-price competition (which we examined in Chapter 8).

Indeed, Mintel found that only 3 per cent of those purchasing weekday lunches found the time to sit down in a restaurant, café or bar. But many customers still place importance on value-added and are willing to pay a premium to have sandwiches made in front of them, perceiving this as providing them with greater choice and a fresher final product.

Chain restaurants

Another factor behind the growth in eating out has been the expansion of many chain restaurants, such as Pizza Express, Nandos, Carluccio's and Wagamama. While they differ from each other, and thus offer consumers greater choice and constant innovation, they offer a common menu *within* each chain and sometimes loyalty programmes for repeat diners. This product differentiation with clear product characteristics is a key characteristic of monopolistically competitive markets, where prices can vary but the market is still highly competitive.

The Internet

As with many other areas, the Internet has had a big influence on the eating-out sector. The use of social media has created a new way for restaurants and casual dining places to advertise. This has meant that sole traders, starting out with a van selling street food, can now compete with the bigger chains. By marketing through social media, they can reach any customer with a smartphone or anyone who accesses sites such as Twitter and Facebook. This has therefore reduced barriers to entry, creating an even more competitive market, with growing consumer choice.

Consumers post reviews of dining experiences or will post a comment about a great meal they just ate. In addition, more and more people take photos of what they eat, posting them online and encouraging others to try out a new place. According to the Ernst and Young report cited above, research published on eMarketer in April 2014 showed that photos of food or meals received the most engagement on Facebook. As the saying goes: 'A picture is worth a thousand words'.

Another development in the take-out industry has been the emergence of companies such as Hungry House. Co-founded in 2003 and launched in 2006, it allows households to enter their postcode online and then search through sometimes hundreds of restaurants and local take-aways to pick out exactly what they want. These orders are then delivered to your door. This is another innovation where an online platform is bringing eating outlets into direct competition with each other and making it easier for consumers to eat out. With different types of food going in and out of fashion, this allows consumers to have access to almost any type of food they could want and perhaps provides some of the smaller companies with another opportunity to break into this highly competitive market.

It seems inevitable that the eating-out sector will continue to grow over the next decade and it will be interesting to see the innovations and trends that occur. Simon Stenning, strategy director at Allegra Foodservice, said:

> The growth will be hard fought for in an increasingly competitive trading environment and gains will be patchy across the market. The onus on operators will remain innovating on product, refining menu price architectures and adding greater value across the consumer experience to build stronger customer loyalty.[9]

1. What are the main barriers to entry in the eating-out sector?
2. What can be said about the price elasticity and cross-price elasticity of demand for meals at pubs/restaurants/hotels/ casual dining places?
3. What are the main reasons for the growth in the popularity of eating out and the switch towards casual dining?

---

[9] Owen McKeon, 'Street Food set to boost UK's eating out sector', *Evolve*, www.evolvehospitality.co.uk/evolve-hospitality-news-detail/street-food-set-to-boost-uk-s-eating-out-sector/159

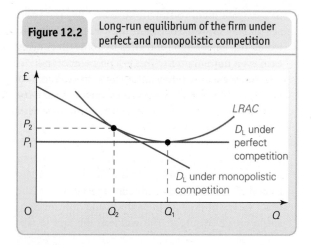

Figure 12.2 Long-run equilibrium of the firm under perfect and monopolistic competition

than optimum output, and thus being forced to charge a price above that which they could charge if they had a bigger turnover.

> ### Pause for thought
>
> *Which would you rather have: five restaurants to choose from, each with very different menus and each having spare tables so that you could always guarantee getting one; or just two restaurants to choose from, charging a bit less but with less choice and making it necessary to book well in advance?*

Comparing monopolistic competition with perfect competition and monopoly

Comparison with perfect competition

It is often argued that monopolistic competition leads to a less efficient allocation of resources than perfect competition.

Figure 12.2 compares the long-run equilibrium positions for two firms. One firm is under perfect competition and thus faces a horizontal demand curve. It will produce an output of Q_1 at a price of P_1. The other is under monopolistic competition and thus faces a downward-sloping demand curve. It will produce the lower output of Q_2 at the higher price of P_2. A crucial assumption here is that a firm would have the *same* long-run average cost (*LRAC*) curve in both cases. Given this assumption, we can make the following two predictions about monopolistic competition:

- Less will be sold and at a higher price.
- Firms will not be producing at the least-cost point.

By producing more, firms would move to a lower point on their *LRAC* curve. Thus firms under monopolistic competition are said to have *excess capacity*. In Figure 12.2 this excess capacity is shown as $Q_1 - Q_2$. In other words, monopolistic competition is typified by quite a large number of firms (e.g. petrol stations), all operating at less

So how does this affect the consumer? Although the firm under monopolistic competition may charge a higher price than under perfect competition, the difference may be very small. Although the firm's demand curve is downward sloping, it is still likely to be highly elastic due to the large number of substitutes. Furthermore, the consumer may benefit from monopolistic competition by having a greater variety of products to choose from. Each firm may satisfy some particular requirement of particular consumers.

Comparison with monopoly

The arguments are very similar here to those when comparing perfect competition and monopoly.

On the one hand, freedom of entry for new firms and hence the lack of long-run supernormal profits under monopolistic competition are likely to help keep prices down for the consumer and encourage cost saving. On the other hand, monopolies are likely to achieve greater economies of scale and have more funds for investment and research and development.

> ### Definition
>
> **Excess capacity (under monopolistic competition)** In the long run, firms under monopolistic competition will produce at an output below that which minimises average cost per unit.

12.2 OLIGOPOLY

Oligopoly occurs when just a few firms between them share a large proportion of the industry. Some of the best-known companies are oligopolists, including Ford, Coca-Cola, BP and Nintendo. On the Sloman News Site, you will find many blogs written about different oligopolies and it is both useful and interesting to compare the outcomes. Some examples of powerful oligopolies include toothbrush manufacturers, supermarkets and energy.

There are, however, significant differences in the structure of industries under oligopoly, and similarly significant differences in the behaviour of firms. The firms may produce a virtually identical product (e.g. metals, chemicals, sugar, petrol). Most oligopolists, however, produce differentiated products (e.g. cars, soap powder, soft drinks, electrical appliances). Much of the competition between such oligopolists is in terms of the marketing of their particular brand. Marketing practices may differ considerably from one industry to another.

The two key features of oligopoly

Despite the differences between oligopolies, there are two crucial features that are common to oligopolies, one of which distinguishes oligopoly from other market structures.

Barriers to entry

Unlike firms under monopolistic competition, there are various barriers to the entry of new firms. These are similar to those under monopoly (see pages 182–4). The size of the barriers, however, will vary from industry to industry. In some cases entry is relatively easy, whereas in others it is virtually impossible, perhaps due to patent protection or prohibitive research and development costs.

Interdependence of the firms

Because there are only a few firms under oligopoly, each firm will take account of the behaviour of the others when making its own decisions. This means that they are mutually dependent: they are ***interdependent***. Each firm is affected by its rivals' actions. If a firm changes the price or specification of its product, for example, or the amount of its advertising, the sales of its rivals will be affected.

The rivals may then respond by changing their price, specification or advertising. No firm can therefore afford to ignore the actions and reactions of other firms in the industry and must always consider its rival's behaviour before making any decisions. It is this feature that differentiates oligopolies from the other market structures. It is illustrated in the blog post Pizza price wars.

> **KEY IDEA 23**
>
> *People often think and behave strategically.* How you think others will respond to your actions is likely to influence your own behaviour. Firms, for example, when considering a price or product change will often take into account the likely reactions of their rivals.

It is impossible, therefore, to predict the effect on a firm's sales of, say, a change in its price without first making some assumption about the reactions of other firms. Different assumptions will yield different predictions. For this reason there is no single, generally accepted theory of oligopoly and no common response to a given market situation in terms of prices, output and profits. Firms may react differently and unpredictably.

Competition and collusion

Oligopolists are pulled in two different directions:

- The interdependence of firms may make them wish to *collude* with each other. If they can club together and act as if they were a monopoly, they could jointly maximise industry profits.
- On the other hand, they will be tempted to *compete* with their rivals to gain a bigger share of industry profits for themselves.

These two policies are incompatible. The more fiercely firms compete to gain a bigger share of industry profits, the smaller these industry profits will become! For example, price competition drives down the average industry price, while competition through advertising raises industry costs. Either way, industry profits fall.

Sometimes firms will collude. Sometimes they will not. The following sections examine first *collusive oligopoly*, where we consider both formal agreements and tacit collusion, and then *non-collusive oligopoly*.

Collusive oligopoly

When firms under oligopoly engage in collusion, they may agree on prices, market share, advertising expenditure, etc. Such collusion reduces the uncertainty they face. It reduces the fear of engaging in competitive price cutting or retaliatory advertising, both of which could reduce total industry profits and probably each individual firm's profit.

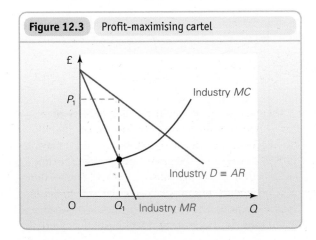

Figure 12.3 Profit-maximising cartel

> ### Definitions
>
> **Interdependence (under oligopoly)** This is one of the two key features of oligopoly. Each firm is affected by its rivals' decisions and its decisions will affect its rivals. Firms recognise this interdependence and take it into account when making decisions.
>
> **Collusive oligopoly** When oligopolists agree, formally or informally, to limit competition between themselves. They may set output quotas, fix prices, limit product promotion or development, or agree not to 'poach' each other's markets.
>
> **Non-collusive oligopoly** When oligopolists have no agreement between themselves – formal, informal or tacit.

Cartels

A formal collusive agreement is called a *cartel*. The cartel will maximise profits by acting like a monopolist, with the members behaving as if they were a single firm. This is illustrated in Figure 12.3.

The total market demand curve is shown with the corresponding market *MR* curve. The cartel's *MC* curve is the *horizontal* sum of the *MC* curves of its members (since we are adding the *output* of each of the cartel members at each level of marginal cost). Profits are maximised at Q_1 where $MC = MR$. The cartel must therefore set a price of P_1 (at which Q_1 will be demanded).

Having agreed on the cartel price, the members may then compete against each other using *non-price competition*, to gain as big a share of resulting sales (Q_1) as they can.

Alternatively, the cartel members may somehow agree to divide the market between them. Each member would be given a *quota*. These quotas could be the same for every firm, or they might be allocated according to the current market share of the firm. Whatever the method of allocation, the sum of all the quotas must add up to Q_1. If the quotas exceeded Q_1, either there would be output unsold if price remained fixed at P_1, or the price would fall to clear the market.

In many countries cartels are illegal, being seen by the government as a means of driving up prices and profits and thereby as being against the public interest. (Government policy towards cartels is examined in Chapter 21.)

The most famous example of a cartel is OPEC, which was set up in 1960 by the five major oil-exporting countries. You may want to investigate the behaviour of OPEC and how it has influenced oil prices. There are numerous blogs on the Sloman News Site that consider this most famous of cartels: see, for example, the blog titled The price of oil in 2015 and beyond. See also Case study E.10 in MyEconLab.

Where open collusion is illegal, firms may simply break the law, or find ways to get round it. Alternatively, firms may stay within the law, but still *tacitly* collude by watching each other's prices and keeping theirs similar. Firms may tacitly 'agree' to avoid price wars or aggressive advertising campaigns.

Tacit collusion

One form of *tacit collusion* is where firms keep to the price that is set by an established leader. The leader may be the largest firm: the firm which dominates the industry. This is known as *dominant firm price leadership*. Alternatively, the price leader may simply be the one that has proved to be the most reliable to follow: the one that is the best barometer of market conditions. This is known as *barometric firm price leadership*. Let us examine each of these two types of price leadership in turn.

Dominant firm price leadership. This is a 'sequential game', where one firm (the leader) moves first and then the followers, having observed the leader's choice of price, move second. We will discuss sequential games in more detail in section 12.3. Here we are interested in determining how

Definitions

Cartel A formal collusive agreement.

Quota (set by a cartel) The output that a given member of a cartel is allowed to produce (production quota) or sell (sales quota).

Tacit collusion When oligopolists follow unwritten 'rules' of collusive behaviour, such as price leadership. They will take care not to engage in price cutting, excessive advertising or other forms of competition.

Dominant firm price leadership When firms (the followers) choose the same price as that set by a dominant firm in the industry (the leader).

Barometric firm price leadership Where the price leader is the one whose prices are believed to reflect market conditions in the most satisfactory way.

Figure 12.4 A price leader aiming to maximise profits for a given market share

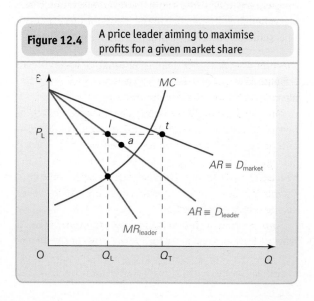

the leader sets the price. This depends on the assumptions it makes about its rivals' reactions to its price changes. If it assumes that rivals will simply follow it by making exactly the same percentage price changes up or down, then a simple model can be constructed. This is illustrated in Figure 12.4. The leader assumes that it will maintain a constant market share (say 50 per cent).

The leader will maximise profits where its marginal revenue is equal to its marginal cost. It knows its current position on its demand curve (say, point a). It then estimates how responsive its demand will be to industry-wide price changes and thus constructs its demand and MR curves on that basis. It then chooses to produce Q_L at a price of P_L: at point l on its demand curve (where $MC = MR$). Other firms then follow that price. Total market demand will be Q_T, with followers supplying that portion of the market not supplied by the leader: namely, $Q_T - Q_L$.

There is one problem with this model. That is the assumption that the followers will want to maintain a constant market share. It is possible that, if the leader raises its price, the followers may want to supply more, given that the new price (= MR for a price-taking follower) may well be above their marginal cost. On the other hand, the followers may decide merely to maintain their market share for fear of invoking retaliation from the leader, in the form of price cuts or an aggressive advertising campaign.

Barometric firm price leadership. A similar exercise can be conducted by a barometric firm. Although the firm is not dominating the industry, its price will be followed by the others. It merely tries to estimate its demand and MR curves – assuming, again, a constant market share – and then produces where $MR = MC$ and sets price accordingly.

In practice, which firm is taken as the barometer may change frequently. Whether we are talking about oil companies, car producers or banks, any firm may take the initiative in raising prices. If the other firms are merely waiting for someone to take the lead – say, because costs have risen – they will all quickly follow suit. For example, if one of the bigger building societies or banks raises its mortgage rates by 1 per cent, this is likely to stimulate the others to follow suit.

Other forms of tacit collusion. An alternative to having an established leader is for there to be an established set of simple 'rules of thumb' that everyone follows.

One such example is *average cost pricing*. Here producers, instead of equating MC and MR, simply add a certain percentage for profit on top of average costs. Thus, if average costs rise by 10 per cent, prices will automatically be raised by 10 per cent. This is a particularly useful rule of thumb in times of inflation, when all firms will be experiencing similar cost increases.

Another rule of thumb is to have certain *price benchmarks*. Thus clothes may sell for £9.99, £24.99 or £39.99 (but not, say, £12.31 or £36.42). If costs rise, then firms simply raise their price to the next benchmark, knowing that other

firms will do the same. (Average cost pricing and other pricing strategies are considered in more detail in Chapter 17.)

Rules of thumb can also be applied to advertising (e.g. you do not criticise other firms' products, only praise your own); or to the design of the product (e.g. lighting manufacturers tacitly agreeing not to bring out an everlasting light bulb).

> ### Pause for thought
>
> *If a firm has a typical-shaped average cost curve and sets prices 10 per cent above average cost, what will its supply curve look like?*

Factors favouring collusion

Collusion between firms, whether formal or tacit, is more likely when firms can clearly identify with each other or some leader and when they trust each other not to break agreements. It will be easier for firms to collude if the following conditions apply:

- There are only very few firms, all well known to each other.
- They are open with each other about costs and production methods.
- They have similar production methods and average costs, and are thus likely to want to change prices at the same time and by the same percentage.
- They produce similar products and can thus more easily reach agreements on price.
- There is a dominant firm.
- There are significant barriers to entry and thus there is little fear of disruption by new firms.
- The market is stable. If industry demand or production costs fluctuate wildly, it will be difficult to make agreements, partly due to difficulties in predicting market conditions and partly because agreements may frequently have to be amended. There is a particular problem in a declining market where firms may be tempted to undercut each other's price in order to maintain their sales.
- There are no government measures to curb collusion.

Non-collusive oligopoly: the breakdown of collusion

In some oligopolies, there may be only a few (if any) factors favouring collusion. In such cases, the likelihood of price competition is greater.

> ### Definitions
>
> **Average cost pricing** Where a firm sets its price by adding a certain percentage for (average) profit on top of average cost.
>
> **Price benchmark** This is a price which is typically used. Firms, when raising prices, will usually raise them from one benchmark to another.

Even if there is collusion, there will always be the temptation for individual oligopolists to 'cheat', by cutting prices or by selling more than their allotted quota. The danger, of course, is that this would invite retaliation from the other members of the cartel, with a resulting price war. Price would then fall and the cartel could well break up in disarray.

When considering whether to break a collusive agreement, even if only a tacit one, a firm will ask: (1) 'How much can we get away with without inviting retaliation?' and (2) 'If a price war does result, will we be the winners? Will we succeed in driving some or all of our rivals out of business and yet survive ourselves, and thereby gain greater market power?'

The position of rival firms, therefore, is rather like that of generals of opposing armies or the players in a game. It is a question of choosing the appropriate *strategy*: the strategy that will best succeed in outwitting your opponents. The strategy that a firm adopts will, of course, be concerned not just with price, but also with advertising and product development.

Non-collusive oligopoly: assumptions about rivals' behaviour

Even though oligopolists might not collude, they will still need to take account of rivals' likely behaviour when deciding their own strategy. Firms will make assumptions about how they believe their rivals will behave and are likely to base these assumptions on past behaviour. There are three well-known models, each based on a different set of assumptions.

Assumption that rivals produce a given quantity: the Cournot model

One assumption is that rivals will produce a particular *quantity*. This is most likely when the market is stable and the rivals have been producing a relatively constant quantity for some time. The task, then, for the individual oligopolist is to decide its own price and quantity given the presumed output of its competitors.

The earliest model based on this assumption was developed by the French economist Augustin Cournot in 1838. The ***Cournot model*** (which is developed in Web Appendix 4.2) takes the simple case of just two firms (a ***duopoly***) producing an identical product: for example, two electricity generating companies supplying the whole country.

This is illustrated in Figure 12.5, which shows the profit-maximising price and output for firm A. The total market demand curve is shown as D_M. Assume that firm A believes that its rival, firm B, will produce Q_{B1} units. Thus firm A perceives its own demand curve (D_{A1}) to be Q_{B1} units less than total market demand. In other words, the horizontal gap between D_M and D_{A1} is Q_{B1} units. Given its perceived demand curve of D_{A1}, its marginal revenue curve will be MR_{A1} and the profit-maximising output will be Q_{A1}, where $MR_{A1} = MC_A$. The profit-maximising price will be P_{A1}.

If firm A believed that firm B would produce *more* than Q_{B1}, its perceived demand and MR curves would be further to the left and the profit-maximising quantity and price would both be lower.

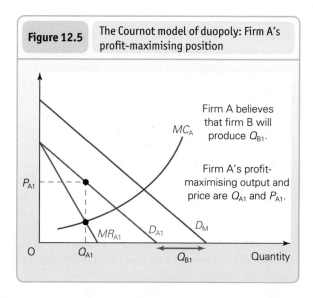

Figure 12.5 The Cournot model of duopoly: Firm A's profit-maximising position

Firm A believes that firm B will produce Q_{B1}.

Firm A's profit-maximising output and price are Q_{A1} and P_{A1}.

At the same time as firm A makes an assumption about firm B's output, firm B will also be making an assumption about how much it thinks firm A will produce. This is therefore a 'simultaneous game', as both firms are making their decisions at the same time, as we will discuss in section 12.3.

Profits in the Cournot model. Industry profits will be *less* than under a monopoly or a cartel. The reason is that price will be lower than the monopoly price. This can be seen from Figure 12.5. If this were a monopoly, then to find the profit-maximising output, we would need to construct an MR curve corresponding to the market demand curve (D_M). This would intersect with the MC curve at a higher output than Q_{A1} and a *higher* price (given by D_M). Nevertheless, profits in the Cournot model will be higher than under perfect competition, since price is still above marginal cost.

Assumption that rivals set a particular price: the Bertrand model

An alternative assumption is that rival firms set a particular price and stick to it. This scenario is more realistic when firms do not want to upset customers by frequent price changes or want to produce catalogues which specify prices. The task, then, for a given oligopolist is to choose its own price and quantity in the light of the prices set by rivals.

The most famous model based on this assumption was developed by another French economist, Joseph Bertrand, in 1883. Bertrand again took the simple case of a duopoly, but its conclusions apply equally to oligopolies with three or more firms.

Definitions

Cournot model A model of duopoly where each firm makes its price and output decisions on the assumption that its rival will produce a particular quantity.

Duopoly An oligopoly where there are just two firms in the market.

Figure 12.6 (a) Kinked demand for a firm under oligopoly; (b) stable price under conditions of a kinked demand curve

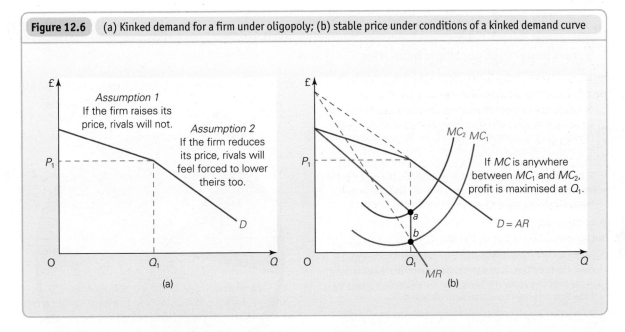

The outcome is one of price cutting until all supernormal profits are competed away. The reason is simple. If firm A assumes that its rival, firm B, will hold price constant, then firm A should undercut this price by a small amount and, as a result, gain a large share of the market. At this point, firm B will be forced to respond by cutting its price. What we end up with is a price war until price is forced down to the level of average cost, with only normal profits remaining.

As with the Cournot model above, this is also a simultaneous move game, except here the variable of interest is price. The supermarket industry is a good example of a market where price wars are a constant feature: see, for example, the blog on the Sloman News Site titled Supermarket price wars and the effect on suppliers.

Nash equilibrium. The equilibrium outcome in either the Cournot or Bertrand models is not in the *joint* interests of the firms. In each case, total profits are less than under a monopoly or cartel. But, in the absence of collusion, the outcome is the result of each firm doing the best it can given its assumptions about what its rivals are doing. The resulting equilibrium is known as a **Nash equilibrium**, after John Nash, a US mathematician (and subject of the film *A Beautiful Mind*) who introduced the concept in 1951. We will return to this concept in section 12.3.

In practice, when competition is intense, as in the Bertrand model, the firms may seek to collude long before profits have been reduced to a normal level. Alternatively, firms may put in a **takeover bid** for their rival(s).

The kinked demand-curve assumption

In 1939 a theory of non-collusive oligopoly was developed simultaneously on both sides of the Atlantic: in the USA by Paul Sweezy and in Britain by R. L. Hall and C. J. Hitch. This **kinked demand theory** has since become perhaps the most famous of all theories of oligopoly. Economists noted that

even when oligopolists did not collude over price, the price charged across the industry often remained relatively stable. The kinked demand curve model was developed to explain this observation and it rests on two asymmetrical assumptions:

- If a firm cuts its price, its rivals will feel forced to follow suit and cut theirs, to prevent losing customers to the first firm.
- If a firm raises its price, its rivals will *not* follow suit since, by keeping their prices the same, they will thereby gain customers from the first firm.

On these assumptions, each oligopolist will face a demand curve that is *kinked* at the current price and output (see Figure 12.6(a)). A rise in price will lead to a large fall in sales as customers switch to the now relatively lower-priced rivals. The firm will thus be reluctant to raise its price. Demand is relatively elastic above the kink. On the other hand, a fall in price will bring only a modest increase in sales, since rivals lower their prices too and therefore customers do not switch. The firm will thus also be reluctant to lower its price. Demand is relatively inelastic below the kink. Thus oligopolists will be reluctant to change prices at all.

Definitions

Nash equilibrium The position resulting from everyone making their optimal decision based on their assumptions about their rivals' decisions.

Takeover bid Where one firm attempts to purchase another by offering to buy the shares of that company from its shareholders.

Kinked demand theory The theory that oligopolists face a demand curve that is kinked at the current price: demand being significantly more elastic above the current price than below. The effect of this is to create a situation of price stability.

BOX 12.2	OLIGOPOLIES: THE GOOD, THE BAD AND THE UGLY

Market power in oligopolistic industries

KI 21
p175

Oligopolies are complex markets and the behaviour of firms within them can be very different. We see some highly competitive oligopolies and others where collusive agreements emerge. One thing they often have in common is being of interest to the relevant country's competition authorities. Many will be under seemingly constant scrutiny or investigation over anti-competitive practices. We examine competition policy in section 21.1. In this box, we consider two classic oligopolies: the supermarket industry and the energy market. You will also find many other examples of oligopolies discussed on the Sloman News Site.

Supermarkets

In the UK supermarket industry, the largest four supermarket chains have a combined market share of over 70 per cent, as shown in the chart. Although this combined share has fallen in the past few years, it still represents market dominance by a few firms – a key characteristic of oligopoly.

Oligopolies are often the subject of inquiries by the Competition authorities, as the market power held by the dominant firms can be abused. In the case of the supermarket industry, it has faced two major inquiries: first in 2000, concerning their relationship with suppliers, and then in May 2006, when they were referred to the Competition Commission (CC) by the Office of Fair Trading (OFT). (The OFT and CC have since been replaced by the Competition and Markets Authority.)

In 2007, the Competition Commission said that it was 'concerned with whether Tesco, or any other supermarket, can get into such a strong position, either nationally or locally, that no other retailer can compete effectively'.[10] The government's Office of Fair Trading had identified four major areas where the supermarkets might gain from the use (or abuse) of market power: (i) barriers to entry to new competitors; (ii) the relationship between the large supermarket chains and their suppliers; (iii) the lack of effective price competition; and (iv) reducing competition in the convenience store sector.

 1. *What do you think are the main barriers to entry in the supermarket industry?*

The Competition authorities have had particular concerns about the big four supermarkets attempting to restrict competition and hence consumer choice at the local and national level. Key barriers to entry, such as buying up tracts of land where rival retailers could set up, or using large economies of scale to make it impossible for new firms to compete on price, have enabled the big supermarkets to maintain market dominance. To this end, the Commission proposed a 'competition test' in planning decisions and action to prevent land agreements, both of which would lessen the market power of supermarkets in local areas.

However, despite the high market share enjoyed by the big four, some price competition does exist and the TV adverts since the recession in 2008 have highlighted this, with each supermarket indicating that they have thousands of baskets of goods cheaper than their rivals! But is there really true price competition?

The supermarket chains have adopted a system of 'shadow pricing', whereby they observe each other's prices and ensure that they remain at similar levels – often similarly high levels rather

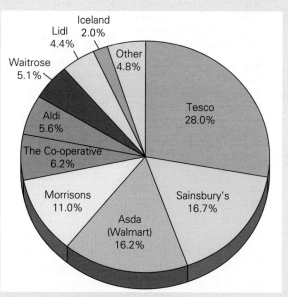

UK supermarket food market share (12 weeks to 6/12/2015)

Source: Based on data from *Kantar Worldpanel*

than similarly low levels! This has limited the extent of true price competition, and the resulting high prices have seen profits grow. Nevertheless, in 2008 the Competition Commission reported that it found little evidence of tacit collusion between the supermarkets.[11]

Furthermore, intense price competition has tended to be only over basic items, such as the own-brand 'value' products. To get to the basic items, you normally have to pass the more luxurious ones, which are much more highly priced and often marketed to make them stand out! Supermarkets rely on shoppers making impulse buys of the more expensive lines, which have much higher profit margins.

However, with the rapid growth of Aldi and Lidl, these discount retailers are placing more and more demands on the big four to bring their prices down or at least identify their target market. With their current structures and costs, Asda, Sainsbury's, Morrisons and Tesco cannot compete with Aldi and Lidl on price and they are not selling the 'up-market' foods of Marks and Spencer and Waitrose. As these retailers have increased their market share, it is the big four who have lost out, despite still retaining a significant advantage.

 2. *Have supermarkets reduced competition in the convenience store sector? In what ways might convenience stores be able to compete with the big supermarkets?*

Although the large supermarkets have huge selling power in the industry, another cause for concern is the *buying power* that they have. Suppliers have complained about the 'heavy-handed tactics' employed by the large supermarkets, which can drive costs down by forcing suppliers to offer discounts. One might suggest that this isn't a bad thing if it means lower prices for the final consumer, but these cost savings do not appear to have been passed on from supplier to shopper. So, while this has enabled the supermarkets to increase their profits, it has had a detrimental effect on suppliers, whose profit margins have been cut to the bone.

The CC also found that this may have had an inhibiting effect on innovation. Accountancy firm Moore Stephens has blamed the supermarket price war for the rise in insolvencies in the food production sector. Duncan Swift from this firm said:

---

[10] Peter Freeman, Chairman of the Competition Commission and Inquiry Chairman, 'Grocery enquiry goes local', *News Release*, Competition Commission, 22 January 2007.

[11] *The Supply of Groceries in the UK Market Investigation*, Competition Commission, 30 April 2008.

The supermarkets are going through the bloodiest price war in nearly two decades and are using food producers as the cannon fodder ... Supermarkets have engaged in questionable buying practices for years, but it's getting worse and clearly wreaking havoc on the UK food production sector.[12]

In order to regulate this relationship, a new Groceries Supply Code of Practice was proposed, to be enforced by an independent ombudsman. Attempts to create a voluntary code of practice failed and so a consultation on the creation of such an ombudsman began in 2010, with Christine Tacon being appointed in 2013.[13]

In this classic oligopoly, we can see interdependence between the firms and the price wars that have emerged. In some cases, this does act in the consumer's interest, but it has repercussions for the suppliers. There are high barriers to entry and this does restrict competition and so we are likely to see continued monitoring of this sector by the Competition Authorities.

 3. *Explain why manufacturers of food products continue to supply supermarkets, despite concerns that they are not always treated fairly.*

Who has the energy to switch?

Another well-known oligopoly is the energy sector, dominated by six big firms (the 'Big Six'), which sell to over 90 per cent of UK households. You can find many articles about the energy sector on the Sloman News Site, considering the barriers to entry; the referral to the CMA and the savings that are possible from switching suppliers.

Barriers to entry

As with most oligopolies, a key problem in the energy sector is the existence of barriers to entry. In this industry, there is both vertical and horizontal integration within firms (see Chapter 15), such that the big six energy suppliers are involved in both generation of power and the local distribution of it (vertical integration) and offer 'dual-fuel' deals, where customers can receive a discount from buying electricity and gas from the same supplier (horizontal integration).

The vertical integration, in particular, has made it difficult for smaller suppliers to enter the market, as they have had to buy wholesale from one of the big six. Thus a key focus of the industry regulator, Ofgem (the Office of Gas and Electricity markets: see section 21.1), has been how to reduce the barriers to entry to make the market more competitive. Through an increased number of suppliers, competition should increase and this should keep prices down, thereby benefiting households.

 4. *Does vertical integration matter if consumers still have a choice of supplier and if generators are still competing with each other?*

In June 2014, following months of political pressure, Ofgem referred the industry to the Competition and Markets Authority (CMA) to see if there was a possible breach of a dominant market position. Ofgem asked the CMA to investigate accusations of profiteering by the big six and discuss mechanisms to reduce structural barriers to entry that undermine competition, including the potential breaking up of these dominant firms. The Chief Executive of Ofgem, Dermot Nolan, said:

A CMA investigation should ensure there are no barriers to stop effective competition bearing down on prices and delivering the benefits of these changes to consumers.[14]

Consumer inertia

As well as the traditional barriers to entry discussed above, new competitors face another obstacle, which also acts to reduce competition between existing firms. In some sense it is a form of brand loyalty, where customers are reluctant to switch to an alternative supplier, making it difficult for new entrants to attract customers.

However, in the case of energy firms, a big criticism levelled at the Big Six was that it was 'impossible' to switch. By 2011, there were more than 300 different tariffs available to domestic consumers and, although choice is often seen as a benefit of competition, there appears to have been too much choice, leading to very confused consumers. This then created inertia, whereby households simply stayed with their existing supplier, even if they were not the cheapest. The suppliers were thus accused of exploiting these 'loyalty' customers. An updated Issues Statement, by the CMA said:

Comparing all available domestic tariffs – including those offered by the independent suppliers – we calculate that, over the period Quarter 1 2012 to Quarter 2 2014, over 95% of the dual fuel customers of the Six Large Energy Firms could have saved by switching tariff and/or supplier and that the average saving available to these customers was between £158 and £234 a year (depending on the supplier).[15]

By making it difficult for customers to switch between tariffs and between companies, competition is limited and this can make it very difficult for new firms to enter the market and gain a sufficient number of customers to make a profitable business.

In 2013, Ofgem introduced a full set of pricing rules in the retail sector. Energy companies had to publish simple 'per-unit' prices, allowing customers to compare tariffs at a glance. The aim of this was to encourage consumers to switch to the cheapest tariff and hence create a more competitive market, where companies are forced to offer the best deals to retain their customers.

Furthermore, from March 2014, the Big Six and the largest independent generators have had to trade fairly with independent suppliers or face penalties. In particular, they have to publish prices up to two years in advance to ensure more effective competition.

In both the wholesale and retail sector, Ofgem, and more recently the Competition and Markets Authority, have taken continuous steps to break down the barriers to entry in the industry in an attempt to make the market genuinely competitive. Critics suggest that the current reforms have still not gone far enough, with the combined market share of the Big Six remaining well above 90 per cent in both sectors.

 5. *The Big Six have been required to open up their finances to greater scrutiny and publish prices up to two years in advance. How will this help to boost competition?*

[12] 'Supermarket price war heaps pressure on food producers as insolvencies jump 28%', *Moore Stevens blog*, 24 November 2014.

[13] 'Christine Tacon named as supermarket ombudsman', *BBC News*, 21 January 2013.

[14] 'Ofgem refers the energy market for a full competition investigation', *Press Release*, Ofgem, 26 June 2014.

[15] *Energy Market Investigation: Updated Issues Statement*, Competition and Markets Authority, 18 February 2015.

This price stability can be shown formally by drawing in the firm's marginal revenue curve, as in Figure 12.6(b).

To see how this is done, imagine dividing the diagram into two parts either side of Q_1. At quantities less than Q_1 (the left-hand part of the diagram), the MR curve will correspond to the shallow part of the AR curve. At quantities greater than Q_1 (the right-hand part), the MR curve will correspond to the steep part of the AR curve. To see how this part of the MR curve is constructed, imagine extending the steep part of the AR curve back to the vertical axis. This and the corresponding MR curve are shown by the dotted lines in Figure 12.6(b).

As you can see, there will be a gap between points a and b. In other words, there is a vertical section of the MR curve between these two points.

Profits are maximised where $MC = MR$. Thus, if the MC curve lies anywhere between MC_1 and MC_2 (i.e. between points a and b), the profit-maximising price and output will be P_1 and Q_1. Thus prices will remain stable *even with a considerable change in costs*.

Oligopoly and the consumer

If oligopolists act collusively and jointly maximise industry profits, they will in effect be acting as a monopoly. In such cases, prices may be very high. This is clearly not in the best interests of consumers.

Furthermore, in two respects, oligopoly may be more disadvantageous than monopoly:

■ Depending on the size of the individual oligopolists, there may be less scope for economies of scale to lower costs and mitigate the effects of market power.
■ Oligopolists are likely to engage in much more extensive advertising than a monopolist. This will raise costs. Consumers could thus end up paying higher prices, though it may lead to product development and better information about the product's characteristics.

These problems will be less severe, however, if oligopolists do not collude, if there is some degree of price competition and if barriers to entry are weak. For example, in the Bertrand model, prices end up being set at the perfectly competitive level.

Moreover, the power of oligopolists in certain markets may to some extent be offset if they sell their product to other powerful firms. Thus oligopolistic producers of baked beans or soap powder sell a large proportion of their output to giant supermarket chains, which can use their market power to keep down the price at which they purchase these products. This phenomenon is known as ***countervailing power***.

In some respects, oligopoly may be more beneficial to the consumer than other market structures:

> ### Pause for thought
>
> *Assume that two brewers announce that they are about to merge. What information would you need to help you decide whether the merger would be in the consumer's interests?*

■ Oligopolists, like monopolists, can use part of their supernormal profit for research and development. Unlike monopolists, however, oligopolists will have a considerable *incentive* to do so. If the product design is improved, this may allow the firm to capture a larger share of the market, and it may be some time before rivals can respond with a similarly improved product. If, in addition, costs are reduced by technological improvement, the resulting higher profits will improve the firm's capacity to withstand a price war.
■ Non-price competition through product differentiation may result in greater choice for the consumer. Take the case of tablets or mobile phones. Non-price competition has led to a huge range of different products of many different specifications, each meeting the specific requirements of different consumers.

It is difficult to draw any general conclusions about the outcomes in this market structure, since oligopolies differ so much in their behaviour and performance. Although an oligopoly is closer to the non-competitive end of the spectrum, it can still be a highly competitive market structure.

Oligopoly and contestable markets

The theory of contestable markets has been applied to oligopoly as well as to monopoly, and similar conclusions are drawn.

The lower the entry and exit costs for new firms, the more difficult it will be for oligopolists to collude and make supernormal profits. If oligopolists do form a cartel (whether legal or illegal), it will be difficult to maintain it if there is a threat of competition from new entrants. What a cartel has to do in such a situation is to erect entry barriers, thereby making the 'contest' more difficult. For example, the cartel could form a common research laboratory, denied to outsiders. It might attempt to control the distribution of the finished product by buying up wholesale or retail outlets. Or it might simply let it be known to potential entrants that they will face all-out price, advertising and product competition from all the members if they should dare to set up in competition.

The industry is thus likely to behave competitively if entry and exit costs are low, with all the benefits and

> ### Definition
>
> **Countervailing power** When the power of a monopolistic/oligopolistic seller is offset by powerful buyers who can prevent the price from being pushed up.

costs to the consumer of such competition – even if the new firms do not actually enter. However, if entry and/or exit costs are high, the degree of competition will simply depend on the relations between existing members of the industry.

12.3 GAME THEORY

The interdependence between oligopolists requires firms to think strategically and *game theory* was developed by economists to examine the best strategy that a firm can adopt, given the assumptions it makes about its rivals' behaviour.

This section will provide some useful insights into firms' behaviour, but it is also worth bearing in mind that game theory can be applied to a huge range of areas. In the BBC News article, 'What exactly is "game theory"?',[16] we can see the application of game theory by Greek Finance Minister Yanis Varoufakis in 2015 in his approach to negotiations over Greek debt.

Single-move games

As we have seen, the firm's choice of strategy under non-collusive oligopoly depends, in part, on how it thinks its rivals will react to its decisions on prices, new products, advertising, etc. The simplest type of 'game' is a single-move or single-period game. This involves just one 'move' by each firm in the game. For example, two or more firms are bidding for a contract which will be awarded to the lowest bidder. When the bids are all made, the contract will be awarded to the lowest bidder; the 'game' is over.

Simple dominant strategy games

Many single-period games have predictable outcomes, no matter what assumptions each firm makes about its rivals' behaviour. Such games are known as ***dominant strategy games***. The simplest case is where there are just two firms with identical costs, products and demand. They are both considering which of two alternative prices to charge. Table 12.1 shows typical profits they could each make.

Let us assume that at present both firms (X and Y) are charging a price of £2 and that they are each making a profit of £10 million, giving a total industry profit of £20 million. This is shown in the top left-hand cell (A).

Now assume they are both (independently) considering reducing their price to £1.80. In making this decision, they will need to take into account what their rival might do, and how this will affect them. Let us consider X's position. In our simple example there are just two things that its rival, firm Y, might do. Either Y could cut its price to £1.80, or it could leave its price at £2. What should X do?

To answer this question we need to take each of firm Y's two possible actions and look at firm X's best response to each. If we assume that firm Y chooses a price of £2, firm X could decide to keep its price at £2 giving it £10m in profit. This is shown by cell A. Alternatively, firm X could cut its price to £1.80 and earn £12m in profit, in cell B. Firm X's best response is therefore to cut price to £1.80, preferring a profit of £12m to one of £10m.

What about if we now assume that firm Y charges £1.80 – how should firm X best respond? If firm X charged £2, we would end up in cell C and firm X would earn only £5m in profit. On the other hand, firm X could also cut its price to £1.80, moving us to cell D and it would earn £8m profit. By comparing these two profit outcomes, we can see that firm X's best response to firm Y lowering its price to £1.80 is to cut its own price to £1.80 as well, preferring a profit of £8m to a profit of £5m.

		Table 12.1	Profits for firms X and Y at different prices

		X's price	
		£2	£1.80
Y's price	£2	**A** £10 m each	**B** £5 m for Y £12 m for X
	£1.80	**C** £12 m for Y £5 m for X	**D** £8 m each

---
[16]Chris Stokel-Walker, 'What exactly is "game theory"?', *BBC News Magazine*, 18 February 2015.

Note that firm Y will argue along similar lines, cutting price to £1.80 as well, no matter what it assumes that firm X will do.

This game is a dominant strategy game, since the firm's best response is always to play the same (dominant) strategy (namely, cutting price to £1.80) irrespective of what it thinks the other firm will do. Both firms do what is best for them, given their assumptions about their rivals' behaviour. The result is that we end up in cell D, with each firm earning a profit of £8 million.

As we saw in the previous section, this equilibrium outcome, when there is no collusion between players, is known as a *Nash equilibrium*. This occurs when all players do what's best for themselves, given the assumptions they make about their rivals' behaviour.

Nash equilibrium. The position resulting from everyone making their optimal decision based on their assumptions about their rivals' decisions. Without collusion, there is no incentive for any firm to move from this position.

However, it is important to note that the profits earned by each firm in the Nash equilibrium (cell D) are lower than they would have been had the firms colluded and charged the higher price (cell A). Each firm would have earned £10 million.

But even with collusion, both firms would be tempted to cheat, or renege, on the agreement and cut prices. This is known as the *prisoners' dilemma* (see Box 12.3). You can watch the scene on YouTube[17] from the film *A Beautiful Mind*, where John Nash begins to formulate the famous 'Nash Equilibrium' concept.

More complex games

More complex 'games' can be devised with more than two firms, many alternative prices, differentiated products and various forms of non-price competition (e.g. advertising). We may also see 'games', where the best response for each firm depends on the assumptions made, meaning there is no dominant strategy. Consider the payoff matrix in Table 12.2.

Definitions

Prisoners' dilemma Where two or more firms (or people), by attempting independently to choose the best strategy, based upon what other(s) are likely to do, end up in a worse position than if they had co-operated from the start.

Tit-for-tat Where a firm will cut prices, or make some other aggressive move, *only* if the rival does so first. If the rival knows this, it will be less likely to make an initial aggressive move.

[17]www.youtube.com/watch?v=2d_dtTZQyUM

Table 12.2	Profits for firms X and Y at different prices

		X's price	
		£25	£19
Y's price	£20	**A** £6m for Y £6m for X	**B** £2m for Y £5m for X
	£15	**C** £4m for Y £3m for X	**D** £4m for Y £4m for X

If firm X assumes that firm Y will charge £20, then firm X will either earn £6m in profit if it charges £25 or £5m in profit if it charges £19. Firm X's best response would be to charge £25 (cell A). However, if it assumes that firm Y will charge £15, then firm X's best response will now be to charge £19, preferring £4m in profit (cell D) to £3m in profit (cell C). We no longer have a dominant strategy. Firm X's best response depends on its assumption about Y's price.

Pause for thought

What is firm Y's best response to each of firm X's possible choices in the game shown in Table 12.2? Does it have a dominant strategy in this game?

In many situations, firms will have a number of different options open to them and a number of possible reactions by rivals. Such games can become highly complex.

The better the firm's information about (a) its rivals' costs and demand, (b) the likely reactions of rivals to its actions and (c) the effects of these reactions on its own profit, the better the firm's 'move in the game' is likely to be. It is similar to a card game: the more you know about your opponents' cards and how your opponents are likely to react to your moves, and the better you can calculate the effects of their moves on you, the better your moves in the game are likely to be.

Multiple-move games

In many situations, firms will *react* to what their rivals do; their rivals, in turn, will react to what they do. In other words, the game moves back and forth from one 'player' to the other like a game of chess or cards. Firms will still have to think strategically (as you do in chess), considering the likely responses of their rivals to their own actions. These multiple-move games are known as *repeated games*.

One of the simplest strategies in a repeated game is *tit-for-tat*. This is where a firm will cut prices, or make some other aggressive move, *only* if the rival does so first. To illustrate this in a multiple-move situation let us look again at the example we considered in Table 12.1, but this time we will extend it beyond one time period.

Assume that firm X is adopting the tit-for-tat strategy. If firm Y cuts its price from £2.00 to £1.80, then firm X will respond in round 2 by also cutting its price. The two firms will end up in cell D – worse off than if neither had cut their price. If, however, firm Y had left its price at £2.00 then firm X would respond by leaving its price unchanged

too. Both firms would remain in cell A with a higher profit than cell D.

As long as firm Y knows that firm X will respond in this way, it has an incentive not to cut its price. Thus it is in X's interests to make sure that Y clearly 'understands' how X will react to any price cut. To do this X can make a threat.

The importance of threats and promises

In many situations, an oligopolist will make a threat or promise that it will act in a certain way. As long as the threat or promise is *credible* (i.e. its competitors believe it), the firm can gain and it will influence its rivals' behaviour.

BOX 12.3   THE PRISONERS' DILEMMA

Game theory is relevant not just to economics. A famous non-economic example is the prisoners' dilemma.

Nigel and Amanda have been arrested for a joint crime of serious fraud. They are both guilty. Each is interviewed separately and given the following alternatives:

- First, if they say nothing, the court has enough evidence to sentence both to a year's imprisonment.
- Second, if either Nigel or Amanda alone confesses, he or she is likely to get only a three-month sentence but the partner could get up to ten years.
- Third, if both confess, they are likely to get three years each.

These outcomes are illustrated in the diagram. What should Nigel and Amanda do?

Let us consider Nigel's dilemma. Should he confess in order to get the short sentence (the maximax strategy)? This is better than the year he would get for not confessing. There is, however, an even better reason for confessing. Suppose Nigel doesn't confess but, unknown to him, Amanda does confess. Then Nigel ends up with the long sentence (cell B). Better than this is to confess and to get no more than three years (cell D). Nigel's best response is always to confess.

Amanda is in the same dilemma and so the result is simple. When both prisoners act in their own self-interest by confessing, they both end up with relatively long prison terms (cell D). Only when they collude will they end up with relatively short ones, the best combined solution (cell A). However, for

each of these prisoners, the more certain they are that their compatriot will maintain their innocence, the greater the incentive for them to confess and reduce their sentence!

Of course the police know this and will do their best to prevent any collusion. They will keep Nigel and Amanda in separate cells and try to persuade each of them that the other is bound to confess.

Thus the choice of strategy depends on:

- Nigel's and Amanda's risk attitudes: i.e. are they 'risk lovers' or 'risk averse'?
- Nigel's and Amanda's estimates of how likely the other is to own up.

1. Why is this a dominant strategy game?

2. How would Nigel's choice of strategy be affected if he had instead been involved in a joint crime with Adam, Ashok, Diana and Rikki, and they had all been caught?

Let us now look at two real-world examples of the prisoners' dilemma.

Standing at concerts

When people go to some public event, such as a concert or a match, they often stand in order to get a better view. But once people start standing, everyone is likely to do so: after all, if they stayed sitting, they would not see at all. In this Nash equilibrium, most people are worse off, since, except for tall people, their view is likely to be worse and they lose the comfort of sitting down.

Too much advertising

Why do firms spend so much on advertising? If they are aggressive, they do so to get ahead of their rivals. If they are cautious, they do so in case their rivals increase their advertising. Although in both cases it may be in the individual firm's best interests to increase advertising, the resulting Nash equilibrium is likely to be one of excessive advertising: the total spent on advertising (by all firms) is not recouped in additional sales.

3. Give one or two other examples (economic or non-economic) of the prisoners' dilemma.

UK supermarket food market share (end March 2015)

		Amanda's alternatives	
		Not confess	Confess
Nigel's alternatives	Not confess	**A** Each gets 1 year	**B** Nigel gets 10 years Amanda gets 3 months
	Confess	**C** Nigel gets 3 months Amanda gets 10 years	**D** Each gets 3 years

Figure 12.7	A decision tree

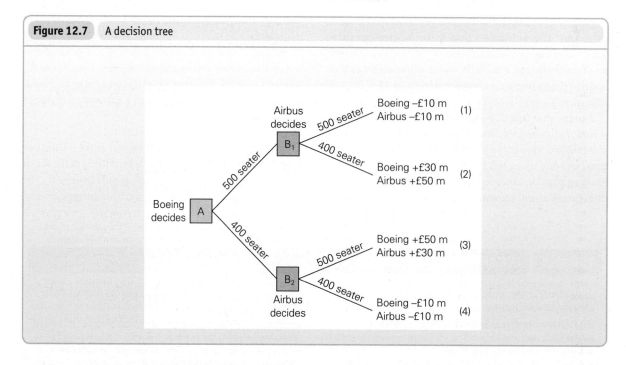

Take the simple situation where a large oil company, such as Esso, states that it will match the price charged by any competitor within a given radius. Assume that competitors believe this 'price promise' but also that Esso will not try to *undercut* their price. In the simple situation where there is only one other filling station in the area, what price should it charge? Clearly it should charge the price which would maximise its profits, assuming that Esso will charge the *same* price. In the absence of other filling stations in the area, this is likely to be a relatively high price.

Now assume that there are several filling stations in the area. What should the company do now? Its best choice is probably to charge the same price as Esso and hope that no other company charges a lower price and forces Esso to cut its price. Assuming that Esso's threat is credible, other companies are likely to reason in a similar way. Prices will therefore be kept high, because of the credible threat made by Esso.

The importance of timing

Most decisions by oligopolists are made by one firm at a time rather than simultaneously by all firms. Sometimes a firm will take the initiative. At other times it will respond

to decisions taken by other firms. Here we are considering a 'sequential game' where the 'order of play' is important.

Take the case of a new generation of large passenger aircraft which can fly further without refuelling. Assume that there is a market for a 500-seater version of this type of aircraft and a 400-seater version, but that the individual markets for each aircraft are not big enough for the two manufacturers, Boeing and Airbus, to share them profitably. Let us also assume that the 400-seater market would give an annual profit of £50 million to a single manufacturer and the 500-seater would give an annual profit of £30 million, but that if both manufacturers produced the same version, they would each make an annual loss of £10 million.

Assume that Boeing announces that it is building the 400-seater plane. What should Airbus do? The choice is illustrated in Figure 12.7. This diagram is called a ***decision tree*** and shows the sequence of events. The small square at the left of the diagram is Boeing's decision point (point A). If it had decided to build the 500-seater plane, we would move up the top branch. Airbus would now have to make a decision (point B_1). If it too built the 500-seater plane, we would move to outcome 1: a loss of £10 million for both manufacturers. Clearly, with Boeing building a 500-seater plane, Airbus would choose the 400-seater plane: we would move to

Definitions

Credible threat (or promise) One that is believable to rivals because it is in the threatener's interests to carry it out.

Decision tree (or game tree) A diagram showing the sequence of possible decisions by competitor firms and the outcome of each combination of decisions.

BOX 12.4 THE HUNGER GAMES

To sleep or not to sleep?

Suzanne Collins published the first book of the trilogy, The Hunger Games in 2008 and since then it has been made into four films (with the final book, *Mockingjay* being split into two parts). *The Hunger Games* is the story of Katniss Everdeen, living in an unknown future time where the country has been divided into Districts, ranging from the wealthy Capitol that rules the other 12 Districts. Each year, one girl and one boy from every District are chosen randomly and they must compete to the death against each other in the Hunger Games, which is set in a dangerous and very public arena. Katniss Everdeen volunteers in place of her younger sister and enters the arena with Peeta, the male 'Tribute' and so the use of strategic thinking and game theory begins.[18]

The Hunger Games lasts until all but one 'Tribute' is left alive (although there is a slight deviation in the 74th Hunger Games). However, survival is not just about avoiding being killed by one of the other 'Tributes' as the Games could last for weeks. Survival is also about having enough sleep to sustain yourself. The problem is, when you are asleep there is the chance of a stealth attack by another competitor, but if you don't sleep, you become more susceptible to any future attack, due to sleep deprivation.

 Try constructing a matrix and determine the Nash equilibrium in this game.

One thing you might have considered in answering the question above is even if you don't sleep and everyone else does, will it necessarily mean that you can find and kill another Tribute? One thing that happens in the Games is that a coalition is formed between a group of Tributes – they agree to work together, but still know that they are competing against each other and hence at some point, each of them would have to try to kill their rivals. They are camping together and so within that group, they know where everyone is.

 Does the Nash equilibrium in the game change if we are now thinking about the decision of one member of the coalition, given the possible responses of the other members of the coalition?

The value that each member places on sleep and getting closer to the finishing line is obviously a key factor in determining how any member should behave. Also, with sleep being a natural response to being tired, there are only so many nights when you can go without sleep and the more nights you do this, the more likely it becomes that you will be susceptible to an attack.

Many stabs in the dark

Looking at the matrix that you have constructed and perhaps making some assumptions about the relative value of sleep versus progress, the likely outcome seems to be 'Don't sleep' for everyone. After all, being sleep deprived is better than being dead. This would suggest that all members of the coalition should avoid sleep, knowing that if they do fall asleep, they are very vulnerable to an attack from another member of the coalition. So, why do the members of the coalition get any sleep?

The Hunger Games goes on for many nights, so it is not just a one-shot game, but a repeated game. Perhaps if the Games had to be over in one night, we would see a clear incentive not to sleep. But, in the Hunger Games, no player knows when their last night will be. The members of the coalition will have to make the sleep decision night after night, knowing that every night they don't sleep they may make progress, but will become more vulnerable to other attacks.

Furthermore, as there are multiple members of the coalition, each member will become less trustworthy if others are killed during the night. So, perhaps the best response in this infinitely repeated game is to co-operate from the start and thus trust everyone within the Coalition – everyone gets some sleep. However, if one night a member is killed, then the next night we would probably see each player once again best responding by remaining awake. Perhaps here would be a typical 'tit-for-tat' strategy, until a winner emerges.

This is just one more example of the application of game theory to areas beyond traditional economics.

 Search for the game show Golden Balls online or go onto YouTube and watch a clip of the very last part of the game '£66,885 Split or Steal?'[19] Try constructing a matrix for this game and working out what the Nash equilibrium is.

---

[18]Samuel Arbesman, 'Probability and game theory in The Hunger Games', *Wired*, 10 April 2012.
[19]www.youtube.com/watch?v=yM38mRHY150

---

outcome 2, with Boeing making a profit of £30 million and Airbus a profit £50 million. Airbus would be very pleased!

KI 24 p 206 Boeing's best strategy at point A, however, would be to build the 400-seater plane. We would then move to Airbus's decision point B_2. In this case, it is in Airbus's interests to build the 500-seater plane. Its profit would be only £30 million (outcome 3), but this is better than a £10 million loss if it too built the 400-seater plane (outcome 4). With Boeing deciding first, the Nash equilibrium will thus be outcome 3.

There is clearly a *first-mover advantage* here. Once Boeing has decided to build the more profitable version of the plane, Airbus is forced to build the less profitable one. Naturally, Airbus would like to build the more profitable one and be the first mover. Which company succeeds in going first depends on how advanced they are in their research and development and in their production capacity.

Definition

First-mover advantage When a firm gains from being the first one to take action.

More complex decision trees. The aircraft example is the simplest version of a decision tree, with just two companies and each one making only one key decision. In many business situations, much more complex trees could be constructed. The 'game' would be more like one of chess, with many moves and several options on each move. If there were more than two companies, the decision tree would be more complex still.

Pause for thought

Give an example of decisions that two firms could make in sequence, each one affecting the other's next decision.

The usefulness of game theory

The advantage of the game-theory approach is that the firm does not need to know which response its rivals will make. It does, however, need to be able to measure the effect of each possible response. This will be virtually impossible to do when there are many firms competing and many differ-ent responses that could be made. The approach is only useful, therefore, in relatively simple cases, and even here the estimates of profit from each outcome may amount to no more than a rough guess.

It is thus difficult for an economist to predict with any accuracy what price, output and level of advertising the firm will choose. This problem is compounded by the difficulty of predicting the type of strategy – safe, high risk, compromise – that the firm will adopt.

In some cases, firms may compete hard for a time (in price or non-price terms) and then realise that maybe no one is winning. Firms may then jointly raise prices and reduce advertising. Later, after a period of tacit collusion, competition may break out again. This may be sparked off by the entry of a new firm, by the development of a new product design, by a change in market demand, or simply by one or more firms no longer being able to resist the temptation to 'cheat'. In short, the behaviour of particular oligopolists may change quite radically over time.

If you are interested in reading more about game theory, then the website 'Game Theory .net' provides some useful resources.

SUMMARY

1a Monopolistic competition occurs where there is free entry to the industry and quite a large number of firms operating independently of each other, but where each firm has some market power as a result of producing differentiated products or services.

1b In the short run, firms can make supernormal profits. In the long run, however, freedom of entry will drive profits down to the normal level. The long-run equilibrium of the firm is where the (downward-sloping) demand curve is tangential to the long-run average cost curve.

1c The long-run equilibrium is one of excess capacity. Given that the demand curve is downward sloping, its tangency point with the *LRAC* curve will not be at the bottom of the *LRAC* curve. Increased production would thus be possible at *lower* average cost.

1d In practice, supernormal profits may persist into the long run: firms have imperfect information; entry may not be completely unrestricted; there may be a problem of indivisibilities; firms may use non-price competition to maintain an advantage over their rivals.

1e Monopolistically competitive firms, because of excess capacity, may have higher costs, and thus higher prices, than perfectly competitive firms, but consumers gain from a greater diversity of products.

1f Monopolistically competitive firms may have less economies of scale than monopolies and conduct less research and development, but the competition may keep prices lower than under monopoly. Whether there will be more or less choice for consumers is debatable.

2a An oligopoly is where there are just a few firms in the industry with barriers to the entry of new firms. Firms recognise their mutual dependence and each firm must consider the reactions of rivals to any changes it makes.

2b Oligopolists may aim to maximise their joint profits. This will tend to make them collude to keep prices high. On the other hand, they will want the biggest share of industry profits for themselves. This will tend to make them compete.

2c They are more likely to collude: if there are few of them; if they are open with each other; if they have similar products and cost structures; if there is a dominant firm; if there are significant entry barriers; if the market is stable; and if there is no government legislation to prevent collusion.

2d A formal collusive agreement is called a 'cartel'. A cartel aims to act as a monopoly. It can set the price and leave the members to compete for market share, or it can assign quotas. There is always a temptation for cartel members to 'cheat' by undercutting the cartel price if they think they can get away with it and not trigger a price war.

2e Tacit collusion can take the form of price leadership. This is where firms follow the price set by either a dominant firm in the industry or one seen as a reliable 'barometer' of market conditions. Alternatively, tacit collusion can simply involve following various rules of thumb such as average cost pricing and benchmark pricing.

2f Even when firms do not collude they will still have to take into account their rivals' behaviour. In the Cournot model, firms assume that their rivals' output is given and then choose the profit-maximising price and output in the light of this assumption. The resulting price and profit are lower than under monopoly, but still higher than under perfect competition. In the Bertrand model, firms assume that their rivals' price is given. This will result in prices being competed down until only normal profits remain.

2g In the kinked-demand curve model, firms are likely to keep their prices stable unless there is a large shift in costs or demand.

2h Non-collusive oligopolists will have to work out a price strategy. This will depend on their attitudes towards risk and on the assumptions they make about the behaviour of their rivals.

2i Whether consumers benefit from oligopoly depends on: the particular oligopoly and how competitive it is; whether there is any countervailing power; whether the firms engage in extensive advertising and of what type; whether product differentiation results in a wide range of choice for the consumer; how much of the profits are ploughed back into research and development; and how contestable the market is. Since these conditions vary substantially from oligopoly to oligopoly, it is impossible to state just how well or how badly oligopoly in general serves the consumer's interest.

3a Game theory is a way of modelling behaviour in strategic situations where the outcome for an individual or firm depends on the choices made by others. Thus game theory examines various strategies that firms can adopt when the outcome of each is not certain.

3b The simplest type of 'game' is a single-move or single-period game. Many single-period games have predictable outcomes, no matter what assumptions each firm makes about its rivals' behaviour. Such games are known as dominant strategy games.

3c Non-collusive oligopolists will have to work out a price strategy. By making the best decisions based on assumptions about their rivals' behaviour we can arrive at a Nash equilibrium. However, a 'Nash' equilibrium may not always be the most efficient strategy for the firms collectively. It is possible that both could do better by co-operating or colluding.

3d In multiple-move games, play is passed from one 'player' to the other sequentially. Firms will respond not only to what firms do, but also to what they say they will do. To this end, a firm's threats or promises must be credible if they are to influence rivals' decisions.

3e A firm may gain a strategic advantage over its rivals by being the first one to take action (e.g. launch a new product). A decision tree can be constructed to show the possible sequence of moves in a multiple-move game.

MyEconLab

This book can be supported by MyEconLab, which contains a range of additional resources, including an online homework and tutorial system designed to test and build your understanding.

You need both an access card and a course ID to access MyEconLab:

1. Is your lecturer using MyEconLab? Ask your lecturer for your course ID.
2. Has an access card been included with the book at a reduced cost? Check the inside back cover of the book.
3. If you have a course ID but no access card, go to: http://www.myeconlab.com/ to buy access to this interactive study programme.

REVIEW QUESTIONS

1 Think of 10 different products or services and estimate roughly how many firms there are in the market. You will need to decide whether 'the market' is a local one, a national one or an international one. In what ways do the firms compete in each of the cases you have identified?

2 Imagine there are two types of potential customer for jam sold by a small food shop. One is the person who has just run out and wants some now. The other is the person who looks in the cupboard, sees that the pot of jam is less than half full and thinks, 'I will soon need some more'. How will the price elasticity of demand differ between these two customers?

3 Why may a food shop charge higher prices than supermarkets for 'essential items' and yet very similar prices for delicatessen items?

4 How will the position and shape of a firm's short-run demand curve depend on the prices that rivals charge?

5 Assuming that a firm under monopolistic competition can make supernormal profits in the short run, will there be any difference in the long-run and short-run elasticity of demand? Explain.

6 Firms under monopolistic competition generally have spare capacity. Does this imply that if, say, half of the petrol stations were closed down, the consumer would benefit? Explain.

7 Is the supermarket sector an oligopoly or monopolistically competitive? Explain.

8 Will competition between oligopolists always reduce total industry profits?

9 In which of the following industries is collusion likely to occur: bricks, beer, margarine, cement, crisps, washing powder, blank audio or video cassettes, carpets?

10 Draw a diagram like Figure 12.4. Illustrate what would happen if there were a rise in market demand.

11 Devise a box diagram like that in Table 12.1, only this time assume that there are three firms, each considering the two strategies of keeping price the same or reducing it by a set amount. Is the game still a 'dominant strategy game'?

12 Having watched the clip from the film *A Beautiful Mind*, can you work out why the situation that Russell Crowe describes as being a 'Nash equilibrium' is actually not a Nash equilibrium? Specifically, in the example used, would all of the males be best responding if they behave as John Nash suggests they should?

13 What are the limitations of game theory in predicting oligopoly behaviour?

14 Which of the following are examples of effective countervailing power?
   a) A power station buying coal from a large local coal mine.
   b) A large factory hiring a photocopier from Rank Xerox.
   c) Marks and Spencer buying clothes from a garment manufacturer.
   d) A small village store (but the only one for miles around) buying food from a wholesaler.

   Is it the size of the purchasing firm that is important in determining its power to keep down the prices charged by its suppliers?

ADDITIONAL PART E CASE STUDIES IN *THE ECONOMICS FOR BUSINESS* MyEconLab (www.pearsoned.co.uk/Sloman)

E.1 **Is perfect best?** An examination of the meaning of the word 'perfect' in perfect competition.

E.2 **B2B electronic marketplaces**. This case study examines the growth of firms trading with each other over the Internet (business to business or 'B2B') and considers the effects on competition.

E.3 **Measuring monopoly power**. An examination of how the degree of monopoly power possessed by a firm can be measured.

E.4 **X-inefficiency**. A type of inefficiency suffered by many large firms, resulting in a wasteful use of resources.

E.5 **Competition in the pipeline**. An examination of attempts to introduce competition into the gas industry in the UK.

E.6 **Airline deregulation in the USA and Europe**. Whether the deregulation of various routes has led to more competition and lower prices.

E.7 **The motor vehicle repair and servicing industry**. A case study of monopolistic competition.

E.8 **Bakeries: oligopoly or monopolistic competition**. A case study on the bread industry, showing that small-scale local bakeries can exist alongside giant national bakeries.

E.9 **Oligopoly in the brewing industry**. A case study showing how the UK brewing industry is becoming more concentrated.

E.10 **OPEC**. A case study examining OPEC's influence over oil prices from the early 1970s to the current day.

E.11 **Cut throat competition**. An examination of the barriers to entry to the UK razor market.

WEBSITES RELEVANT TO PART E

Numbers and sections refer to websites listed in the Web appendix and hotlinked from this text's website at **www.pearsoned .co.uk/sloman**

- For news articles relevant to Part E, see the Economics News Articles link from MyEconLab or the Sloman Economics News site.

- For general news on companies and markets, see websites in section A, and particularly A1, 2, 3, 4, 5, 8, 9, 18, 23, 24, 25, 26, 35, 36. See also A38–44 for links to newspapers worldwide.

- For student resources relevant to Part E, see sites C1–7, 9, 10, 14, 19, 25.

- For models and simulations relevant to Part E, see sites D3, 5, 7, 8, 10, 13, 14, 16–20

- For sites that look at competition and market power, see B2; E4, 10, 20; G7, 8. See also links in B1; I7, 11, 14 and 17.

- For a sites on game theory, see D4; C20; I17 and 4 (in the EconDirectory section).

Supply: alternative strategies

The FT Reports . . .

The Financial Times, 2 August 2015

FT

Industrial giants caught in LED headlights

Philips, Osram and GE face decline of traditional light bulb units as new technology takes off

By Chris Bryant

Lighting is starting to become part of the "internet of things" – where different devices are all connected on telecoms networks – but for incumbent manufacturers this rapid technological shift is causing huge upheaval.

Industrial giants Philips, Siemens and General Electric for decades enjoyed an oligopoly in the hitherto slow-moving lighting market, which James Stettler, an analyst at Barclays, compares with a "licence to print money", partly because people have to regularly replace their bulbs.

Now LEDs are fast displacing traditional light sources such as incandescent, halogen and fluorescent bulbs, catalysed partly by double-digit annual price declines in components.

Government regulations also have supported the growth of LEDs because of their energy efficiency. They produce light using semiconductors — whereas traditional light bulbs rely on filaments — and therefore consume less electricity.

LEDs also last much longer than old-style bulbs and are far more sophisticated. For example, the new 68-storey International Youth Culture Centre in Nanjing, China, has 700,000 LED lights capable of illuminating the building façade in different colours at night.

Frost & Sullivan estimates the global LED lighting market grew 35 per cent to $32.3bn last year, and it is forecast to more than double to $70bn by 2019. LED as a proportion of the total lighting market is set to near 50 per cent by the end of 2015 and reach 84 per cent by 2020.

The incumbents saw the tech revolution coming and are now among the biggest players, but the rapid growth in LEDs has attracted new low-cost competitors, particularly from Asia.

The incumbents are responding to these challenges in different ways, but broadly speaking they are restructuring legacy, high-volume lighting units and regearing their business models towards "smart" and "connected lighting".

"In 10 years there might not be a single light bulb left. If your core competence isn't needed any more, then you need to adapt — the challenge is to move from being a general lighting company to a solution provider," says Ms Nocchi. ...

Although sales of traditional light bulbs are in structural decline, the market remains profitable because there is so little competition. The incumbents therefore talk about a "long" or "golden tail".

"From an investor perspective, this is a cash cow and a solid one, despite the top line decline," says Frans van Houten, Philips chief executive.

The competitive forces reveal the drivers of industry competition. A company strategist who understands that competition extends well beyond existing rivals will detect wider competitive threats and be better equipped to address them. At the same time, thinking comprehensively about an industry's structure can uncover opportunities: differences in customers, suppliers, substitutes, potential entrants, and rivals that can become the basis for distinct strategies yielding superior performance. In a world of more open competition and relentless change, it is more important than ever to think structurally about competition.

Michael E. Porter, 'The five competitive forces that shape competition', *Harvard Business Review*, January 2008, p. 93

Many small companies, especially those facing fierce competition, may be forced to pursue profit as their overriding goal, merely to survive. With large companies, however, where mere survival is not the overriding concern, the pursuit of short-run profit is likely to be only one of many business objectives.

The modern business enterprise is often a complex organisation, with many different departments and divisions. What is more, the ownership and control of the firm are often in totally different hands: i.e. shareholders and managers. With many competing interests there are often several objectives being pursued simultaneously.

In Part F we will consider what these alternative objectives might be and the strategies that businesses might adopt in their pursuit. Having the correct strategy is crucial for business survival. For example, a strategy for lighting manufacturers that worked well for many years may no longer be appropriate as new types of lighting, such as LEDs, replace older types (see the *Financial Times* article on the left).

We start, in Chapter 13, by introducing you to the world of business strategy. We show how crucial the degree of competition is in shaping not only business success but also the strategic approaches open to business.

In Chapter 14 we will outline various alternative theories of the firm – alternative, that is, to the traditional theory of short-run profit maximisation. Then, in Chapter 15, we will focus on one particular strategy: that of growth. Should a firm seek to grow by simply expanding the scale of its operations, or should it merge with other firms or enter into alliances with them? Chapter 16 looks at the small-firm sector, and compares the objectives and behaviour of small firms with those of their bigger rivals.

Finally, in Chapter 17, we will look at alternative pricing strategies and how they vary with market structure and the different aims that firms might pursue.

Key terms

Porter's five forces
Strategic management
Value chain
Core competence
Profit satisficing
Managerial utility
Behavioural theories of the firm
Organisational slack
Internal expansion
External expansion
Transaction costs
Takeover constraint
Horizontal and vertical integration
Vertical restraints
Diversification
Merger
Enterprise
Strategic alliance
Networks
Logistics
SME
Cost-based pricing
Price discrimination
Transfer pricing
Peak-load pricing
Inter-temporal pricing
Product life cycle

An introduction to business strategy

Business issues covered in this chapter

- What are the objectives of strategic management?
- What are the key competitive forces affecting a business?
- What choices of strategy towards competitors are open to a business?
- What internal strategic choices are open to a business and how can it make best use of its core competencies when deciding on its internal organisation?
- How does a business's strategy relate to its vision and mission? What is the role of various stakeholders in shaping strategy?
- Should a business 'go global'?

Ben & Jerry's is founded on and dedicated to a sustainable corporate concept of linked prosperity. Our mission consists of 3 interrelated parts:

Social Mission: To operate the Company in a way that actively recognizes the central role that business plays in society by initiating innovative ways to improve the quality of life locally, nationally and internationally.

Product Mission: To make, distribute and sell the finest quality all natural ice cream and euphoric concoctions with a continued commitment to incorporating wholesome, natural ingredients and promoting business practices that respect the Earth and the Environment.

Economic Mission: To operate the Company on a sustainable financial basis of profitable growth, increasing value for our stakeholders and expanding opportunities for development and career growth for our employees.

Underlying the mission of Ben & Jerry's is the determination to seek new and creative ways of addressing all three parts, while holding a deep respect for individuals inside and outside the company and for the communities of which they are a part.

Source: © Ben & Jerry's Homemade Holdings Inc.

Being a successful business means what? According to its mission statement, for Ben & Jerry's it means producing a high-quality product, returning a profit, presiding over business growth and enhancing shareholder value. The company also claims that a successful business rests upon a 'deep respect for individuals' and that it wants to initiate ways of improving the quality of life. What strategy or strategies will Ben & Jerry's need to adopt in order to achieve these goals?

Ben & Jerry's was formed in 1978 by Ben Cohen and Jerry Greenfield. In 2000, it was taken over by Unilever, the Anglo-Dutch multinational, but it still maintains its identity and its mission. Since its early years as a two-person operation, Ben & Jerry's has expanded to have operations in 26 countries. However, as the mission statement suggests, the founders of Ben & Jerry's were in search of more than profits from their business activities. With a clear philosophy of social responsibility, the business strategy has been one in which the search for profit has been regulated by a wider set of social and environmental goals.

13.1 WHAT IS STRATEGY?

Defining strategy

KI 23
p 197

Business strategy describes the way in which an organisation addresses its fundamental challenges over the medium to long term. Usually, the term 'strategy' is applied to the decision-making processes of the senior management team, but it can be applied at all levels of the organisation.

The term can also be applied to a number of everyday situations. Thus, an individual may have a strategy to keep fit that involves a healthy diet and going to the gym. A student may have a career strategy that involves passing examinations.

Businesses use strategy in an attempt to be more competitive than their rivals. Sometimes these strategies are successful: businesses outperform their competitors. Similarly, individuals' strategy may be successful: people keep their weight under control; students pass exams.

Sometimes, however, strategies fail. Businesses underperform; individuals put on weight; students fail their exams. If this is the case, then a re-evaluation of existing goals and strategies has to take place with new strategies being developed to meet long-term objectives. For a business that has failed to perform, this is an opportunity to regain its competitive position.

Clearly the type of business 'strategy' that is appropriate depends upon the context in which the strategy is being developed. In an attempt to capture the diversity of the term, Henry Mintzberg[1] suggests that we need to look at the 'five Ps' of business strategy. A strategy can be:

- a plan;
- a ploy;
- a pattern of behaviour;
- a position with respect to others;
- a perspective.

A plan. This represents the most common use of the term strategy. It involves, as Mintzberg states, a 'consciously intended course of action to deal with a situation'. Plans most commonly operate over a given period of time, in which the business outlines where it would like to be at a given point in the future. This might be in terms of its market

share or its level of profitability, or some other combination of criteria upon which business progress or success might be evaluated. As such, plans tend to focus on long-term issues facing the business rather than operational details.

A ploy. In contrast to the long-term nature of the plan, strategy as a ploy is generally short term in its application. It often focuses on a specific manoeuvre by business in order to outwit or counteract the behaviour of rivals. Aggressive pricing policy and the use of special offers by supermarkets is a frequently adopted ploy to gain, or more commonly protect, market share. Such a strategy may have limited objectives and be liable to frequent changes.

A pattern of behaviour. Rather than a consciously planned framework of action, business strategy may in fact emerge naturally from a consistent response to events: e.g. introducing a new product variety each year. Such consistent action involves a pattern of behaviour, which takes on a strategic form. Such strategies tend to evolve as circumstances change. There is no clear long-term objective; unlike plan and ploy, here strategy just happens.

A position with respect to others. Here strategy is determined by the position of the business in its market. For example, a firm may attempt to gain or defend market share. Thus a car company such as BMW may set out to defend its position as a manufacturer of high-quality motorcars by focusing on design and performance in its product development and advertising campaigns. Conversely, Aldi and Lidl might focus on defending and developing their claim to have some of the lowest prices in grocery retailing.

A perspective. In this respect strategy is based upon establishing a common way of perceiving the world, primarily within the organisation itself. It may be that this perspective of the world is based on the views of a forceful leader or a strong senior management team, though it can also involve a consensus between stakeholders in the organisation. Businesses with strong ethical and environmental objectives, such as Ben & Jerry's, would see a shared perspective as an important part of their business strategy. Employees are encouraged to take on board the company's philosophy. This, it is hoped, will not only contribute to the business's success through motivation and commitment, but also encourage employees to feel good about what they do.

---

[1] Henry Mintzberg, 'The strategy concept I: five Ps for strategy', *California Management Review*, vol. 30, no. 1, 1987, pp. 11–24.

BOX 13.1　BUSINESS STRATEGY THE SAMSUNG WAY

Staying ahead of the game

Samsung is a major South Korean conglomerate involved in a number of industries, including the machinery and heavy engineering, chemical, financial services and consumer electronic sectors. In its various divisions it has over 489 000 employees globally and is a major international investor and exporter.

This box outlines some of the strategic initiatives that have been taken in recent times by one of its most successful divisions, Samsung Electronics, which has become the world's largest mobile phone producer. The unit sales of its devices overtook those of long time market leader Nokia in the first quarter of 2012.

By 2014, it had a 20.9 per cent share of the global mobile phone market, in contrast to its leading rival Apple, which had 10.2 per cent. It was also the world's biggest producer of LCD TVs in 2014 and the second biggest producer of tablet computers, with global market shares of 21.8 per cent and 14.5 per cent respectively. Samsung Electronics is also one of the world's largest producers of memory semiconductors and employs 280 000 people in more than 80 countries.

The division's success over the past few years is quite an achievement, given the massive financial problems it faced following the Asian financial crisis in the late 1990s. Since that time it has managed not only to shake off its debts and post significant improvements in profits, but also to reposition itself in the upmarket segment of the consumer electronics industry.

The key features of Samsung's strategy

How has Samsung achieved this? What have been the keys to its success?

First, it has a strong management team led by Mr Kwon Oh-Hyun, vice-chairman and CEO of Samsung Electronics. Together they have a clear vision of the future of the sector.

Second, there has been a dramatic streamlining of the business and the decision-making structure following poor financial performance in the mid-1990s and an association with low-end brands in televisions and air-conditioning units. The management team took aggressive measures to improve the division's finances by cutting jobs, closing unprofitable factories, reducing inventory levels and selling corporate assets. They then 'delayered' the company, ensuring that managers had to go through fewer layers of bureaucracy, thereby speeding up the approval of new products, budgets and marketing plans.

Third, Samsung Electronics has been investing heavily in research and development (R&D) to increase its product portfolio and reduce the lead time from product conception to product launch. In 2014 the division invested $13.4 billion in R&D – a 28 per cent increase on the previous year. This made it the second biggest R&D spending company in the world behind Volkswagen. Between 2010 and 2014 it increased its employment of R&D staff by 27 per cent and employed 63 628 people across its 34 R&D units.

It has also engaged in a number of strategic alliances with major players such as Sony, IBM and Hewlett-Packard to share R&D costs.

One way of measuring the output of successful R&D activity is by looking at the number of patents a business has been awarded. In the USA, Samsung was ranked second behind International Business Machines (IBM), having successfully registered 4952 patents in 2014. It has been in second place behind IBM in every year from 2006 to 2013. In the EU Samsung was ranked in first place in 2014 having filed 2541 cases with the European Patent Office.

Samsung has a vision of achieving $400 billion in revenue and becoming one of the world's top five brands by 2020. To achieve this end, Mr Kwon Oh-Hyun and his team recognised that most of its flagship products will be obsolete in 10 years' time. This is why innovation is central to Samsung's 2020 vision. The company intends to build on its existing capabilities in three areas: new technology, innovative products and creative solutions.

Mintzberg notes in his analysis of the term 'strategy' that businesses might adopt any number of approaches to strategic behaviour. Pursuing strategy as a plan, for example, does not preclude using strategy as a ploy or as a position in respect to others. Businesses may interpret strategy in a number of ways simultaneously. What these different understandings of strategy do is to enable us to analyse different aspects of business behaviour and organisation.

Strategic management

For most of the time, most managers have as their primary function the managing of the routine day-to-day activities of the business, such as dealing with personnel issues, checking budgets and looking for ways to enhance efficiency. In other words, they are involved in the detailed operational activities of the business.

Some managers, however, especially those high up in the business organisation, such as the managing director, will be busy in a different way, thinking about big, potentially complex issues, which affect the whole company. For example, they might be analysing the behaviour of competitors, or evaluating the company's share price or considering ways to expand the business. In other words, these managers are involved in the strategic long-term activities of the business.

Both types of management are equally important in the management process, as each contributes in its own way to the business's overall success. However, what is clear is that strategic and operational management are quite distinct managerial functions.

Strategic management comprises three main components.

■ *Strategic analysis* is concerned with examining those factors which underpin an organisation's mission (or purpose) and its long-term vision. These factors are key in determining a business's performance and include internal factors, such as the development of business skills and knowledge,

Fourth, Samsung is concerned about volumes from which it can achieve economies of scale. To this end it invests heavily in modern factories that can cope with large production runs. To help achieve these economies, Samsung also supplies components to its competitors as well as making them for its own product range. For example, it sells flash memory chips for Apple's iPod, Nokia phones and digital cameras. Further, production systems are flexible enough to allow customisation for individual buyers, ensuring that selling prices are above the industry average.

Alongside longer production runs, Samsung is concerned with ensuring that production costs are minimised by making its own business units compete with external rivals. For example, Samsung buys colour filters from Sumitomo Chemical Company of Japan and from its own factories.

Finally, Samsung has been developing its global brand name in consumer electronics and marketing, particularly sports marketing. For example, it sponsored Chelsea football club from 2006 to 2015 and was one of the eleven official partners of the London 2012 Olympics. The company recently announced that it has extended its sponsorship deal with the International Olympics Committee until 2020. It also has a $100 million sponsorship deal in the USA with the National Basketball Association (NBA).

As a result of these changes, Samsung Electronics rose from 42nd in BusinessWeek/Interbrand's list of the top 100 global brands in 2001 to 7th in 2014.

Recent developments

The dramatic growth of Samsung Electronics has been largely achieved since the turn of the twenty-first century. In 2010 the company altered its top management team to include a slightly younger team. It also restructured some of its divisions, producing a better fit with changes in the market and product offerings. This was intended to support Samsung in maintaining its growth into the foreseeable future.

However, Samsung Electronics had a difficult year in 2014. It made an annual net profit of $21.3 billion, which may give the impression that its performance was excellent. This was however a 27 per cent fall on the previous year. It struggled, in particular, in the mobile phone market where sales of its products fell by 21 per cent.

The major reason for this decline was increasing competition from other handset makers. For example, it faced strong competition in the high end premium segment of the market from Apple. Its successful launch of the larger screen iPhone6 and iPhone6 plus in September 2014 removed one of the key competitive advantages that Galaxy phones had over its key rival.

It has also faced more intense competition from producers of lower price Android devices in emerging markets. For example Huawei, Lenovo and Xiami have recently become significant rivals in the Chinese market. Xiami was the leader in the 4th quarter of 2014, with a market share of 13.7 per cent, while both Lenovo and Huawei were ahead of Samsung which was down in 5th place. Although it remained the market leader in India, it also faced increasingly strong competition from local companies such as Micromax, Lava and Karbonn.

In March 2015, Samsung launched the new Galaxy 6 Edge handset. Many of the changes were focused on trying to improve the design and appearance of the phone with a new curved screen, metal frame and glass back. It will be interesting to see if Samsung will remain focused on its battle with Apple in the premium segment of the market or whether it will start to cut prices aggressively in response to its new low-cost rivals.

1. *What dangers do you see with Samsung's recent business strategy?*
2. *Given Mintzberg's five Ps, which would you say fit(s) Samsung's approach to strategy most closely and why?*

and external factors, such as the competitive environment, resource availability and changes in technology.

- *Strategic choice*, by contrast, is primarily concerned with the formulation and evaluation of alternative courses of action that might be adopted in order to achieve the business's strategic objectives. What strategic choices are available? How suitable are such strategies, given their risks and constraints such as time, cost and the business's values?

- *Strategic implementation* is concerned with how strategic choices might be put into effect. In other words, it considers how a strategy might be translated into action. Who is responsible for its implementation? How will it be managed? How is its success or otherwise to be monitored?

In the following sections of this chapter we are going to consider these three dimensions of strategic management and the issues they raise for the conduct of business. Before we

do so, it is worth considering what strategic management means for different business types. How might businesses differ in respect to their analysis, choice and implementation of strategy?

Big business/small business. The strategic requirements of a small local computer assembler and Microsoft are clearly going to be massively different. A small business, operating in a niche market, providing a limited range of products or services, would certainly not require the complex strategic assessment of a large business operating in many markets and providing a whole range of products. Not only would

Definition

Strategic management The management of the strategic long-term activities of the business, which includes strategic analysis, strategic choice and strategic implementation.

the strategy for a small business usually be simpler, it would probably be easier to formulate, given that the managers of small businesses are often the owners and generally the principal creators of the businesses strategy.

Manufacturing business/service provider business. Although in many respects the strategic commitments of both a manufacturer and a service-sector business might be similar, in some crucial respects the focus of strategy will differ. Manufacturers will tend to focus a large part of their strategic effort on product issues (technology, design, inputs, etc.), whereas service providers will tend to focus on strategic issues related to the customer, especially in the area of retailing.

Domestic business/multinational business. The crucial difference in strategic thinking between a domestic business and a multinational business concerns the geographic spread of the multinational corporation. The multinational will need to focus its strategy not only in global terms but possibly also within the context of each international market within which it operates. Depending upon the diversity of these markets, this may require a quite distinct strategic approach

within each. Similarly, a business serving a national market will have more complex strategic issues to consider than one serving a local market.

Private-sector business/public-sector business. Quite clearly the strategic considerations of the National Health Service will in many respects be quite different from, say, Ford, but how different will they be from those of BUPA, the private-sector medical care provider? Increasingly, public-sector organisations, like their private-sector counterparts, are having to adopt a more business-orientated approach to service provision. Stakeholders may be different and profit may not be the principal motivation of business activity, but efficiency, targets and accountability are increasingly becoming public-sector as well as private-sector organisational goals.

For-profit organisations/not-for-profit organisations. Not-for-profit businesses such as charities are essentially based upon a mission underpinned by principles of value. In shaping their strategic goals, such values will be paramount in determining the direction and focus of strategic behaviour.

13.2 STRATEGIC ANALYSIS

In order for an organisation to make strategic decisions, it must first analyse what the organisation is about (its mission) and how it envisages where it wants to be (its vision). In other words, the mission and vision will affect the strategic choices made. Take the case of Ben & Jerry's. Its proclaimed ethical stance limits potential strategic avenues.

Strategic choices also depend on an analysis of (a) the external business environment and (b) the organisation's internal capabilities.

■ How much competition does the firm face and what forms does it take?
■ What other external factors, such as laws and regulations, technological changes and changes in consumer tastes, are likely to affect the firm's decisions?
■ Similarly, what internal factors drive an organisation's performance?

In the case of Ben & Jerry's, the nature of its supply chain is likely to affect not only the quality of the product but also the ability of the company to develop and grow.

Vision and mission

At the beginning of this chapter, we referred to the mission statement of Ben & Jerry's, in which the company clearly expresses a purpose for its business: a purpose that goes far beyond simply making a profit. Such wider social,

environmental and ethical considerations are increasingly shaping business thinking, as expectations regarding corporate responsibility grow.

It is now widely expected that a business must look beyond 'the bottom line' (i.e. profitability) and take account of the interests of a wide group of stakeholders, such as employees, customers, creditors and the local community, and not just the owners of the business. It would be a risky business strategy indeed that pursued profit without taking into account the social, environmental and ethical implications that this might entail (see section 20.5). As such, the formulation of strategy must take into account the purpose of the organisation and the values and objectives that such a purpose involves. Organisational purpose is most often found in a business's mission statement, which is in turn shaped by a number of distinct influences (see Figure 13.1).

Corporate governance. Corporate governance refers to the way in which a business is run and the structure of decision making. It also includes the monitoring and supervision, and in some cases regulation, of executive decisions. The way a business is run depends on the purposes of the business and in *whose interests* it is run.

Stakeholders. Stakeholders differ in power and influence, but ultimately they might all shape the purpose of the organisation in certain respects. Given the wide number of stakeholders, many conflicts of interest can arise.

Figure 13.1 Factors influencing organisational purpose

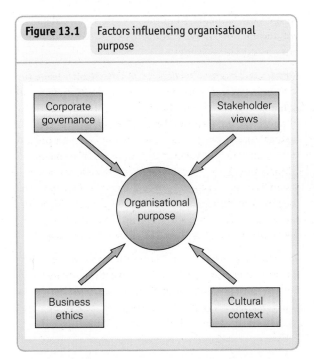

Corporate governance

Stakeholder views

Organisational purpose

Business ethics

Cultural context

Business ethics. A business's ethical position might, as in the case of Ben & Jerry's, be driven by the values of its founders. Alternatively, ethics might be determined and shaped by wider cultural values and standards that determine what is and what is not acceptable behaviour. As previously remarked, business today would find it very difficult to pursue a strategy that failed to exhibit a degree of social responsibility.

High-profile cases can have a significant impact on a firm's reputation and standing in both the business community and society in general. For example, Oxfam produce a 'Behind the Brands Scorecard' which ranks the ten biggest food companies based on seven ethical standards. They call on people to use social media to put pressure on these companies to introduce more ethical policies. Since the campaign started in 2013, Oxfam claims that a number of these businesses have improved their practices.

An example of a company responding to criticism is Apple. It has received damning reports from a number of sources about the working conditions at factories managed by its suppliers. In response to this, it now produces an annual Supplier Responsibility Progress Report. Many firms recognise that ethically sound behaviour is good for business and the bottom line.

Cultural context. How does the cultural context of the organisation influence its objectives? Not only will national culture be significant here, but also the subculture of managers. Wider questions are also raised given the growth in multinational business activity, and the cross-cultural nature of such organisations. Recognising differing cultural contexts

might be crucial in shaping business success within such increasingly global markets.

The business environment

We considered the various dimensions of the business environment and how they shape and influence business activity (Chapter 1). We divided the business environment into four distinct sets of factors: political, economic, social and technological. Such factors comprise what we call a PEST analysis. In this section we will take our analysis of the business environment forward and consider more closely those factors that are likely to influence the competitive advantage of the organisation.

> ### Pause for thought
>
> *Give some examples of cultural differences between countries or regions which might influence business strategy.*

The Five Forces Model of competition

Developed by Professor Michael Porter of Harvard Business School in 1980, the Five Forces Model sets out to identify those factors which are likely to affect an organisation's competitiveness (see Figure 13.2). This then helps a firm choose an appropriate strategy to enhance its competitive opportunities and to protect itself from competitive threats. The five forces that Porter identifies are:

- the bargaining power of suppliers;
- the bargaining power of buyers;
- the threat of potential new entrants;
- the threat of substitutes;
- the extent of competitive rivalry.

The bargaining power of suppliers. Most business organisations depend upon suppliers to some extent, whether to provide raw materials or simply stationery. Indeed, many businesses have extensive supply or 'value chain' networks (as we shall discuss later in this section). Such suppliers can have a significant and powerful effect on a business when:

- there are relatively few suppliers in the market, reducing the ability of the firm to switch from one supply source to another;
- there are no alternatives to the supplies they offer;
- the prices of suppliers form a large part of the firm's total costs;
- a supplier's customers are small and fragmented, and as such have little power over the supplying business.

Car dealers often find that car manufacturers can exert considerable pressure over them in terms of pricing, display and after-sales service.

Figure 13.2	Porter's Five Forces Model

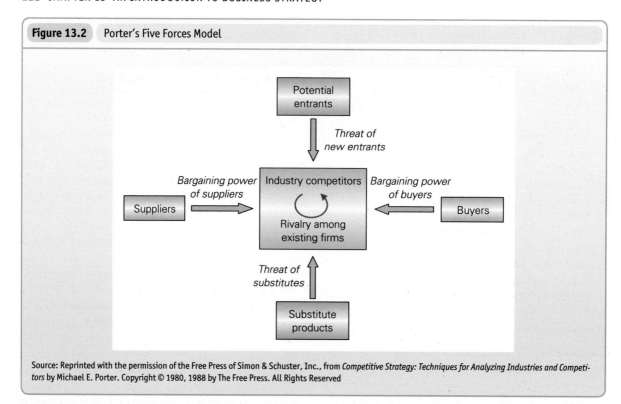

The bargaining power of buyers. The bargaining power of companies that purchase a firm's products will be greater when:

- these purchasing companies are large and there are relatively few of them;
- there are many other firms competing for their custom, and hence a firm that produces an undifferentiated product is likely to be more prone to 'buyer power' than one that produces a unique or differentiated product;
- the costs for the purchasing companies of switching to other suppliers are low;
- purchasing companies are able to backward integrate and effectively displace the supplying firm.

The UK grocery-retailing sector up until recently was dominated by a small number of large supermarket chains such as Tesco, Sainsbury and Asda Wal-Mart. These exert massive levels of buyer power over farmers and food processing companies. Not only do such supermarkets dominate the market, but also they can normally find many alternative supply sources, both domestic and international, at relatively low switching costs. Also, all the supermarkets sell own-brand labels, either produced themselves or through agreement with existing manufacturers, and these are often sold at prices considerably below those of equivalent branded products (see Box 8.1 on page 125).

KI 1
p 10 *The threat of potential new entrants.* The ability of new entrants to enter the marketplace depends largely upon the existence and effectiveness of various barriers to entry.

These barriers to entry were described fully in section 11.3 (pages 182–4), but are listed here as a reminder:

- economies of scale and scope;
- product differentiation;
- capital requirements;
- lower costs of established firm;
- ownership of/control over key factors of production;
- ownership of/control over wholesale or retail outlets;
- legal protection;
- aggressive tactics and retaliation.

Barriers to entry tend to be very industry, product and market specific. Nevertheless, two useful generalisations can be made. First, companies with products that have a strong brand identity will often attempt to use this form of product differentiation to restrict competition; second, manufacturers will tend to rely on economies of scale and low costs as a basis for restricting competitive pressure.

The threat of substitutes. The availability of substitutes can be a major threat to a business and its profitability. Issues that businesses need to consider in relation to the availability of substitute products are:

- the ability of and cost to customers of switching to the substitute;
- the threat of competitors bringing out a more advanced or up-to-date product;
- the impact that substitute products are likely to have on pricing policy.

The makers of games consoles such as Sony, Nintendo and Microsoft have had to face the arrival of substitutes into the market (as discussed in Box 14.1, page 234). People can now play games such as *Minecraft* and *Candy Crush* on their Smartphones and tablets instead of using a PlayStation 4 or Xbox One. The *Steam* download service owned by Valve also means that games such as *Call of Duty* can be downloaded and played on a personal computer as a substitute to using a console.

The relatively good sales of static games consoles in 2014/15 suggest that they have been able to withstand the competition so far, whereas the sale of handheld consoles has fallen considerably. It is highly likely that another new substitute will enter the market. For example, the company Valve is working in partnership with more gaming-focused PC manufacturers to produce custom-built computers which can be plugged into a TV in the same way as a games console. Firms operating in the games console market will need to reconsider their strategies as the market continues to change.

The extent of competitive rivalry. The previous two chapters focused on market structure and were primarily concerned with how businesses respond to differing levels of competition. Clearly the degree of competition a firm faces is a crucial element in shaping its strategic analysis. Competitive rivalry will be enhanced when there is the potential for new firms to enter the market, when there is a real threat from substitute products and when buyers and suppliers have some element of influence over the firm's performance. In addition to this, competitive rivalry is likely to be enhanced in the following circumstances:

- Competitors are of equal size.
- Markets are growing slowly. This makes it difficult to acquire additional sales without taking market share from rivals.
- There are high fixed costs, which require the firm to gain a large market share in order to break even.
- Productive capacity in an industry increases in large increments, often resulting in over-production in the short term. This adds to competitive pressure by putting downward pressure on prices.
- Product differentiation is difficult to achieve; hence product switching by consumers is a real threat.
- There are high exit costs. When a business invests in non-transferable fixed assets, such as highly specialist capital equipment, it may be reluctant to leave a market. It may thus compete fiercely to maintain its market position. On the other hand, as we have seen in the section on contestable markets (page 190), high exit costs may deter firms from entering a market in the first place and thus make the market less contestable.
- There exists the possibility for merger and acquisition. This competition for corporate control may have considerable influence on the firm's strategy.

> ### Pause for thought
>
> *Given that the stronger the competitive forces, the lower the profit potential for firms, describe what five force characteristics an attractive and unattractive industry might have.*

Limitations of the Five Forces Model

One of the great values of the Five Forces Model is that it creates a structured framework for a business to analyse the strategic issues that it faces. However, it does have a number of weaknesses.

First, the Five Forces Model presents a largely static view of the business environment, whereas in reality it is likely to be constantly changing.

Second, the model starts from the premise that the business environment is a competitive threat to the business organisation, which, if the business is to be successful, needs to be manipulated in particular ways. Often, however, success might be achievable not via competition but rather through co-operation and collaboration. For example, a business might set up close links with one of its major buyers; or businesses in an industry might establish links either to build barriers or to share costs via some form of collaborative research and development. In such instances, the business environment of the Five Forces Model might be viewed as a collaborative opportunity rather than a competitive threat. (The section on strategic alliances in Chapter 15 (section 15.6) will offer a fuller evaluation of collaborative business agreements.)

Finally, critics of the model argue that it fails to take sufficient account of the microenvironment of the organisation and its human resources. For example, factors such as country culture and management skills might have a decisive impact on a firm's choice of strategy and its successful implementation.

Value chain analysis and sustainable competitive advantage

As with the Five Forces Model, value chain analysis was developed by Michael Porter, and as such the two concepts are closely related. A *value chain* shows how value is added to a product as it moves through each stage of production: from the raw material stage to its purchase by the final consumer. Value chain analysis is concerned with evaluating how each of the various operations within and around an organisation, such as handling

> ### Definition
>
> **Value chain** The stages or activities that help to create product value.

Figure 13.3 The value chain

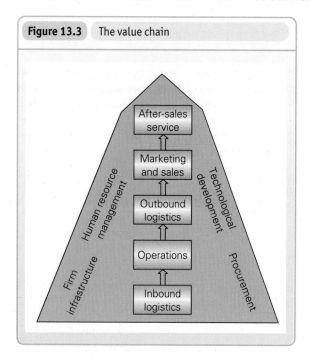

inputs, manufacturing the product and marketing it, contributes to the competitive position of the business. Ultimately it is these value-creating activities which shape a firm's strategic capabilities. A firm's value chain can be split into two separate sets of activities: primary and support (see Figure 13.3).

Primary activities

Primary activities are those directly concerned with the production, distribution and sales of the firm's product. Such primary activities can be grouped into five categories:

- *Inbound* **logistics.** Here we are concerned with the handling of inputs, storage and distribution of such inputs throughout the business.
- *Operations.* These activities involve the conversion of inputs into the final product or service. Operations might include manufacturing, packaging and assembly.
- *Outbound logistics.* These are concerned with transferring the final product to the consumer. Such activities would include warehousing and transport.

KI 19 p 142

Definition

Logistics The process of managing the supply of inputs to a firm and the outputs from a firm to its customers.

- *Marketing and sales.* This section of the value chain is concerned with bringing the product to the consumer's attention and would involve product advertising and promotion.
- *Service.* This can include activities such as installation and repair, as well as customer requirements such as training.

A business might attempt to add value to its activities by improving its performance in one or more of the above categories. For example, it might attempt to lower production costs or be more efficient in outbound logistics.

Support activities

Such primary activities are underpinned by support activities. These are activities that do not add value directly to any particular stage within the value chain. They do, however, provide support to such a chain and ensure that its various stages are undertaken effectively. Support activities include:

- *Procurement.* This involves the acquisition of inputs by the firm.
- *Technological development.* This includes activities within the business that support new product and process developments, such as the use of research departments.
- *Human resource management.* Activities in this category include things such as recruitment, training, and the negotiation and determination of wage rates.
- *Firm infrastructure.* This category includes activities such as financial planning and control systems, quality control and information management.

As well as creating value directly themselves, most firms buy in certain value chain activities, such as employing another firm to do its advertising, or using an external delivery firm to distribute its products. The outsourcing of these activities might prove to be far more beneficial to a business than providing the activities itself. You can employ the best advertisers or the most efficient and reliable distributors.

Thus the value system extends beyond the individual organisation and encompasses the value chains of all those individual businesses that the organisation might deal with. The implication is that the value chain and the value system may be highly complex, and the competitive position of a business may extend well beyond the immediate value chain of the organisation. This will have significant implications for the formulation and choice of business strategy.

Having now discussed the background to strategic analysis, we can shift our focus to consider strategic choice and implementation. What strategies are potentially open to businesses and how do they choose the right ones and set about implementing them?

13.3 STRATEGIC CHOICE

Theories of strategic choice fall into two main categories: market based and resources based.

Market-based theories argue that strategic choices are ultimately determined by the competitive environment that the business faces. As such, understanding this competitive environment and identifying appropriate ways to deal with it will determine whether you are successful or not.

Resource-based theory also looks at the firm's competitive position, but focuses on its internal situation. It considers how strategic decision making is affected by the ownership, control and use of an organisation's resources. It is seen that such resources ultimately deliver profits and it is through a manipulation of such resources that a business can maintain and enhance its competitive position.

Clearly market- and resource-based explanations of strategic choice overlap and interact, and in practice most businesses will attempt to evaluate both their resource base and the threats posed by competitors. However, the two types of explanation do address the issue of strategic choice from quite distinct starting points and this, as we shall see, affects the strategic solutions they offer.

Environment or market-based strategy

As with many other areas in this field, our analysis of market-based theory starts with the observations of Michael Porter. As an extension of his Five Forces Model of competition, Porter argued that there are three fundamental (or 'generic') strategies that a business might adopt:

- cost leadership;
- differentiation;
- focus.

In order to identify which of these was the most appropriate strategy, a business would need to establish two things: (a) the basis of its competitive advantage – whether it lies in lower costs or differentiation; (b) the nature of the target market – is it broad or a distinct market niche?

Cost leadership

As the title implies, a business that is a low-cost leader is able to manufacture and deliver its product more cheaply than its rivals, thereby gaining competitive advantage. The strategic emphasis here is on driving out inefficiency at every stage of the value chain. 'No-frills' budget airlines, such as easyJet and Ryanair, are classic examples of companies that pursue a cost-leadership strategy.

A strategy based upon cost leadership may require a fundamentally different use of resources or organisational structure if the firm is to stay ahead of its rivals. Wal-Mart's hub and spoke distribution system would be an example in point. Here the company distributes its products to shops from regional depots in order to minimise transport costs.

In addition, firms which base their operations on low costs in order to achieve low prices (although that may not necessarily be the aim of low costs) are unlikely to have a high level of brand loyalty. In other words, if customer choice is going to be driven largely by price, demand is likely to be relatively price elastic. Other virtues of the product that might tie in buyers, such as quality or after-sales service, are largely absent from such firms' strategic goals.

Differentiation

A differentiation strategy aims to emphasise and promote the uniqueness of the firm's product. As such, high rather than low prices are often attached to such products. Product characteristics such as quality, design and reliability are the basis of the firm's competitive advantage. Hence a strategy that adds to such differences and creates value for the customer needs to be identified.

Such a strategy might result in higher costs, especially in the short term, as the firm pursues constant product development through innovation, design and research. However, with the ability to charge premium prices, revenues may increase more than costs: in other words, the firm may achieve higher profits. Mobile phone handset producers such as Apple and Samsung provide a good example. Even though they are in fierce competition with each other, both firms focus their strategy on trying to differentiate their products from their rival's. This differentiation is in terms of features and performance, not price. Screen size, camera quality (megapixels), speakers, screen resolution, availability of apps, operating systems, battery life and overall design are all characteristics used in the competitive battle.

Differentiation strategies are not, however, risk free. Pricing differentiated products can be problematic. At what point does the price premium for the product deter potential buyers, such that the differentiated nature of the product is insufficient to outweigh such price considerations? The fact that tastes and fashion change could also have a significant impact upon the sales of a differentiated product.

Laura Ashley clothing was a case in point. In an attempt to differentiate itself from other high street clothing rivals, Laura Ashley promoted a strategy producing rather exclusive good-quality clothing for women, which was very feminine and rooted in a country lifestyle. During the early 1980s Laura Ashley's profits grew as its differentiated product attracted a large following. But the fickle nature of fashion had turned by the early 1990s and Laura Ashley's fashion products were seen as dated and stuffy.

But while its differentiated product and brand image had become somewhat of a liability *in the clothing market*, the company has successfully diversified into the home decorations and furniture market. Here the existing brand image was used to create an affluent customer base.

Focus strategy

Rather than considering a whole market as a potential for sales, a focus strategy involves identifying market niches and designing and promoting products for such niches. Such a strategy may or may not be applicable to other niches. As such, a business might pursue any number of different strategies simultaneously for different market niches. In such cases, a business that does not hold a competitive advantage in a market in general may be able to identify distinct market segments in which it might exploit some advantage it might have over its rivals, whether in terms of costs, or product difference. Ben & Jerry's ice cream would be a case in point. The mass low-cost ice-cream market is served by a number of large multinational food manufacturers and processors, but the existence of niche high-quality ice-cream markets offers opportunities for companies like Ben & Jerry's and Häagen-Dazs. By focusing on such consumers they are able to sell and market their product at premium prices.

Niche markets, however profitable, are by their nature small and as such are limited in their growth potential. Hence firms that focus upon niche market opportunities are likely to have limited growth prospects. There is also the possibility that niches shift or disappear over time. This would require businesses to be flexible in setting out their strategic position.

Sometimes a focus strategy may be combined with a cost-leadership strategy to develop a niche market into a mass market. Amazon.com, the online bookseller, was until relatively recently a business that had a clear cost focus strategy. With low overheads it was able to sell books at knockdown prices to online customers (its niche market segment) and over time, thanks to lower costs, lower prices and the spread of the Internet, this has become a mass market.

Resource-based strategy

Resource-based strategy, as already mentioned, focuses on exploiting a firm's internal organisation and production processes in order to develop its competitive advantage. It is the firm's *distinctiveness* that sets it apart from its competitors. If a business does not have a distinctive feature then it needs to set about creating one.

Core competencies

Core competencies are those skills, knowledge and technologies that underpin the organisation's competitive advantage. These competencies are likely to differ from one business to another, reflecting the uniqueness of each individual organisation, and ultimately determining its potential for success. Given these differences, how does a firm select an appropriate strategy?

When a firm has unique competencies, its strategy should seek to sustain and exploit these, whether in the design of the product or in its methods of production. In many cases, however, firms do not have any competencies that give them a distinctive competitive advantage, even though they may still be profitable. In such instances, strategy often focuses upon either developing such resources or more effectively using the resources the firm already has.

What defines a core competence?

A core competence must satisfy the following four capabilities to serve as a source of competitive advantage for the business. It must be:

- *valuable*: a competence that helps the firm deal with threats or contributes to business opportunities;
- *rare*: a competence or resource that is not possessed by competitors;
- *costly to imitate*: a competence or resource that other firms find difficult to develop and copy;
- *non-substitutable*: a competence or resource for which there is no alternative.

> **Pause for thought**
>
> *Referring back to Box 13.1, what core competencies does Samsung have? Remember, you must justify a core competence in terms of all four listed criteria.*

KEY IDEA 25

Core competencies. The key skills of a business that underpin its competitive advantage. A core competence is valuable, rare, costly to imitate and non-substitutable. Firms will normally gain from exploiting their core competencies.

Clearly then, whether we adopt a market-based view of strategic choice or a resource-based view will have significant implications for how a firm can develop and exploit competitive advantage.

Before we consider issues of how to implement strategy, there is one dimension of the business environment that we need to consider and that is the impact of globalisation on the world economy in general and business activity in particular. Few businesses have been left untouched by the phenomenon. So how has globalisation affected strategic analysis and strategic choice?

> **Definition**
>
> **Core competence** The key skills of a business that underpin its competitive advantage.

| BOX 13.2 | HYBRID STRATEGY |

Are the big four UK supermarkets stuck in the middle?

Michael Porter,[2] in his analysis of alternative business strategies, suggested that it could be disastrous for a business to be 'stuck in the middle', having no clear strategic direction. Attempting both to differentiate its product and to offer lower prices would be a serious strategic error. According to Porter, consumers would be confused, as the business would have no clear market identity to which they could relate. His advice was to pick one strategy and stick with it exclusively.

But is a single generic strategy always the best choice? Is a mixed strategy always inappropriate? Consumers often demand a range of product characteristics that cover not only issues such as quality and reliability, but also price and convenience. As such, businesses are often forced to adopt a strategic position that attempts to capture both difference and low prices simultaneously.

Hybrid theories that focus on a combination of strategies are greatly influenced by the market in which the business is operating. Grocery retailing in the UK offers a clear example of hybrid strategy. The various supermarket chains not only look to differentiate themselves from their rivals in terms of the look and feel of their stores, customer service, and loyalty schemes such as Sainsbury's Nectar card and Tesco's Clubcard, but also compete fiercely over price.

Then there is the range of their products. At the 'bottom' end of the range, with their own-branded 'basic' products, the supermarkets compete primarily in terms of price (e.g. the Tesco 'Value' and Morrisons 'M Savers' ranges). But with more upmarket products, they compete in terms of the variety of lines stocked and their quality (e.g. Asda's 'Extra Special' and Sainsbury's 'Taste the Difference' ranges).

A mixed strategy that appears to work well in a market at one point in time might not be so effective if conditions change. This appears to be the case in the grocery market. The impact of the recession and the continued squeeze on consumer incomes during the economic recovery appears to have made many customers more price sensitive.

One downside with following a hybrid strategy is that it means the business has to offer a large number of different products.

For example, a large Tesco store will typically stock over 40 000 different product lines. This generates relatively high administration costs and hence higher prices. In contrast, companies such as Lidl and Aldi that focus on a strategy of cost leadership stock far fewer product lines – normally around 1600. This generates much lower administration costs and so enables the companies to charge lower prices.

The recent success of the cost leadership strategy of Lidl and Aldi has seen their combined market share increase from 5.2 per cent in 2009 to 9.4 per cent in 2014. The hybrid strategies followed by the 'big four' supermarkets (Tesco, Asda, Morrisons, Sainsbury) that were once so successful have resulted in their combined market share falling from 75.6 per cent in 2009 to 71.6 per cent in 2014. A number of observers have commented that the big four are struggling because they are 'stuck in the middle' between the discounters at the bottom end of the market, and companies like Waitrose and Marks & Spencer in the higher-quality segment of the market.

Another problem for the 'big four' is that an increasing number of people are changing the way they buy their groceries. For a number of years the norm for many customers was to travel to a large out-of-town supermarket and do a weekly shop. Instead many shoppers are now buying online many of the basic goods they consume regularly, using their mobile phones or tablets. They then make more regular visits to local convenience stores to 'top up' on purchases of fresh goods.

In April 2015, Tesco announced a record annual pre-tax loss of £6.4 billion for the year to the end of February. Around £4.7 billion of these losses were caused by a big fall in the property value of its UK stores – a direct consequence of far fewer people shopping at out-of-town supermarkets. Losses were also announced by Sainsbury's and Morrisons.

1. *Choose three supermarket chains and identify the strategy or strategies they adopt. To what extent have they changed over the past few years?*
2. *Do you feel the classification of business strategy options into cost leadership, differentiation and focus is adequate to describe the strategic approaches that businesses might adopt?*

[2] M. E. Porter, *Competitive Advantage: Creating and Sustaining Superior Performance* (Free Press, 1985).

13.4 BUSINESS STRATEGY IN A GLOBAL ECONOMY

In many respects a firm's global strategy is simply an extension of its strategy within its own domestic market. However, opening up to global markets can present many new business opportunities: access to new markets, new customers, new supply sources, new ideas and skills. In addition to such opportunities, the global marketplace can also present competitive threats, as new market entrants from abroad arrive with lower costs, innovative products and marketing, or some other core competency which the domestic firm finds difficult to match. In this section we explore the strategic implications for business in facing up to the global economic system.

Why go global?

The following are reasons why a business may wish to expand beyond its domestic market.

Market size

International markets can potentially offer a business massive new opportunities for growth and expansion. Such markets would be particularly attractive to a business where domestic growth opportunities are limited as a result of either the maturity of the market or shifting consumer taste. Businesses that conduct extensive research and development (R&D) would also be attracted to larger markets as potential returns can be used to offset the firm's R&D investment costs and risk.

Increased profitability

Expanding beyond the domestic economy offers a number of opportunities for increasing profits.

Location economies. The internationalisation of a firm's value chain would enable it to place each value-creating activity in the most appropriate or effective geographic location. So if production costs are lower in one country, it could locate production there. If another country has the specialist skills to offer superior product design and research facilities, then these functions could be located there. Nike, the US training shoe and sportswear manufacturer, undertakes most of its manufacturing at production sites in South East Asia. However, product innovation and research, along with marketing and promotion, are largely undertaken in the USA.

As businesses relocate many dimensions of their value chain, the structure and organisation of the business takes on a web-like appearance, with its various operations being spread throughout the world.

> ### Pause for thought
>
> *Identify some of the potential strengths and weaknesses of businesses having their value chains located in a variety of different countries.*

Scope for significant cost reductions. It is widely observed that over the life cycle of a product a firm's average costs fall. This is partly the result of economies of scale as the firm gets bigger and plants can specialise in particular functions. Clearly, these cost reductions can be greater by expanding globally.

Cost reductions over time are also the result of what is known as 'learning by doing'. This is where skills and productivity improve with experience. Such learning effects apply not only to workers in production, sales, distribution, etc., but also to managers, who learn to develop more efficient forms of organisation. When a firm expands globally, there may be more scope for learning by doing. For example, if a firm employs low-cost labour in developing countries, initially the lower cost per worker will to some extent be offset by lower productivity. As learning by doing takes place, and productivity increases, so initial small cost advantages may become much more substantial.

 Using core competencies. A firm may be able to exploit its core competencies in competing effectively in global markets. The firm might look to expanding first in those countries where it has a clear competitive advantage over already established companies. Wal-Mart's logistic expertise is one example of a business that might exploit such an advantage, in particular overseas markets.

Learning from experience in diverse markets. Successful businesses will learn from their global operations, copying or amending production techniques, organisation, marketing, etc. from one country to another as appropriate. In other words, they can draw lessons from experiences in one country for use in another.

Spreading risk (diversification)

Clearly one of the main reasons a business might have for going global is to spread risk, avoiding being overly reliant on any specific market or geographic region. As such, falling profitability in one region of the global economy might be effectively offset by improved or more favourable economic conditions elsewhere.

Brewery companies have diversified globally in order to reduce their reliance on domestic markets, which in recent years have been growing either very slowly or contracting. For example, SABMiller, the second biggest brewer in the world, posted half yearly profits to 30 September 2014 of $1.97 billion: a 15 per cent rise on a year earlier. This was despite falling sales of lager in Europe and Asia. They were able to do this because of strongly growing sales in both Africa and Latin America.

Keeping up with rivals

Increasingly it seems that the globalisation of business is like a game of competitive leapfrog, with businesses having to look overseas in order to maintain their competitive position in respect to their rivals. A fiercely competitive global environment, in which small cost differences or design improvements can mean the difference between business success and failure, ensures that strategic thinking within a global context is high on the business agenda.

It would seem that at this point we need to raise a few notes of caution regarding the adoption of a global strategy. It is clearly not without its potential pitfalls. Within any global strategy there exists a high degree of both economic and political risk. Investing in developing economies or emerging markets, such as China, is likely to be much riskier than investing in developed market economies. However, it is often within emerging markets that the greatest returns are achieved. It is essentially this trade-off between potential returns and risk that a firm needs to consider in its strategic decisions.

A global business will need a strategy for effectively embracing foreign cultures and traditions into its working practices, and for devising an efficient system for global logistics. Some businesses may be more suited to deal with such global issues than others.

The global strategy trade-off

A firm's drive to reduce costs and enhance profitability by embracing a global strategy is tempered by one critical consideration – the need to meet the demands of customers in foreign markets. To minimise costs, a firm may seek to standardise its product and its operations throughout the world. However, to meet foreign buyers' needs and respond to local market conditions, a firm may be required to differentiate both its product and its operations, such as marketing. In such cases, customisation will *add* to costs and generate a degree of duplication within the business. If a business is required to respond to local market conditions in many different markets, it might be faced with significantly higher costs. But if it fails to take into account the uniqueness of the market in which it wishes to sell, it may lose market share.

The trade-off between cost reduction and local responsiveness can be a key strategic consideration for a firm when

KI 3
p 23

selling or producing overseas. As a general rule we tend to find that cost pressures are greatest in those markets where price is the principal competitive weapon. Where product differentiation is high, and attributes such as quality or some other non-price factor predominates within the competitive process, local responsiveness will tend to shape business thinking. In other words, cost considerations will tend to be secondary.

13.5 STRATEGY: EVALUATION AND IMPLEMENTATION

Evaluation

In deciding what strategy to pursue, global or otherwise, the business will need to evaluate the alternatives open to it. How feasible are they? Are they acceptable strategic goals given the business's mission and vision and other stakeholder demands? How will the strategy contribute to the business's competitive position?

If the choice of strategy is deliberate or prescriptive, i.e. planned in advance, then evaluation tools such as investment appraisal and cost–benefit analysis (CBA) might be used to help identify the best strategy (see section 19.3). Most strategies, however, tend to be emergent: in other words, they evolve over time as conditions change and as the success or otherwise of the firm's decisions becomes apparent. The result is that techniques such as investment appraisal have limited value, given the incomplete information available at the time an appraisal is conducted.

KI 8
p 42

Implementation

When a business considers implementing a strategy this often involves an assessment of three areas:

- resourcing;
- business culture and structure;
- managing change.

Resourcing

All businesses need to evaluate the resource implications of their strategic choices. What resources will be required? Where might such resources be drawn from within the organisation? What new resources will need to be brought into the organisation? From where will the finance for such resources come? Predictably, the more adventurous the strategy, the greater the impact on resources it is likely to have.

Business culture and structure

Similarly, the more radical the strategic shift, the greater the impact this is likely to have on a business's culture and structure. Is the organisation of the business flexible enough to adapt to the new strategic demands placed upon it? This might be particularly relevant if the strategic shift in the business is towards a greater focus on the global marketplace.

Managing change

Managing change can be both difficult and time-consuming. With change often comes uncertainty for employees, especially if the changes are not understood or managers are not trusted. The greater the uncertainty, the more difficult managing change becomes. In addition to barriers to change from employees, there may be organisational barriers. Entrenched power structures and control systems may be quite unsuitable for the new strategy. There may need to be fundamental organisational restructuring before the new strategy can be implemented.

In this chapter we have introduced you to the basic principles underpinning the determination, choice and evaluation of business strategy. This is a massive subject area, and we can only hope to cover a small fraction of the material here. However, from what we have covered you can see how the market environment in which a business operates has a significant impact on its strategic behaviour – and it is such behaviour that ultimately determines its success.

KI 1
p 10

As we have seen, one key factor in determining a business's choice of strategy is its vision and mission – in other words, its aims. In traditional microeconomic theory the firm is assumed to aim for maximum profit. In the next chapter we turn to 'alternative theories of the firm'. These examine the effects of pursuing aims other than simple profit maximisation, especially on prices and output.

SUMMARY

1a Business strategy describes the way in which an organisation addresses its fundamental challenges over the medium to long term.

1b Strategy can be understood in many ways. It can be a plan, a ploy, a pattern of behaviour, a position in respect to others, a perspective, or any combination of them.

▶

1c Strategic management differs from operational management (the day-to-day running of the business) as it focuses on issues which affect the whole business, usually over the long term.

1d Strategic management is composed of three components: strategic analysis (factors affecting business performance), strategic choice (the formulation and evaluation of alternative sources of action) and strategic implementation (how strategic choices are put into effect).

1e Different strategic issues will face different types of business, depending on whether they are large or small, manufacturing or service providers, domestic or multinational, private sector or public sector, and whether they are for-profit or not-for-profit organisations.

2a The Five Forces Model of competition identifies those factors that are most likely to influence the competitive environment of a business. The five forces are: the bargaining power of suppliers, the bargaining power of buyers, the threat of potential new entrants, the threat of substitutes and the extent of competitive rivalry.

2b The weakness of the Five Forces Model is that not only is it a static view of the business environment, but also it does not see the business environment as a collaborative opportunity but merely as a competitive threat. Critics also argue that it underplays the impact of country culture and management skills on strategic choice and implementation.

2c A business value chain shapes its strategic capabilities. The value chain can be split into primary and support activities. Primary activities are those that directly create value, such as operations and marketing and sales. Support activities are those that underpin value creation in other areas, such as procurement and human resource management.

2d A business's vision and mission are shaped by a number of considerations: in whose interest the business is run,

the influence of different stakeholder groups, the prevailing ethical expectations of society or the business owners, and the cultural context of the environment in which the organisation operates.

3a Strategic choices are determined either by the competitive nature of the environment within which the organisation operates, or by the internal resources controlled by the business. Strategic choice often involves a consideration of both internal and external factors.

3b Environment- or market-based strategies are of three types: cost-leadership strategy, where competitiveness is achieved by lower costs; differentiation strategy, where the business promotes the uniqueness of its product; focus strategy, where competitiveness is achieved by identifying market niches and tailoring products for different groups of consumers.

3c The resource-based view of strategy involves identifying core competencies as the key to a business's competitive advantage. A core competence will be valuable, rare, costly to imitate and non-substitutable.

4a A firm might go global in order to increase market size, increase profitability, spread risk and keep up with rivals.

4b When a firm does go global it must weigh up the potential benefits against ensuring it meets the local markets' needs. There is a trade-off between cost reduction and local responsiveness.

5a The impact of a chosen strategy is difficult to evaluate, as the strategy often evolves over time as conditions change.

5b When implementing a strategy, a business must consider the following: the resource implications of the strategic choice, how the strategic choice might fit (or not fit) into existing business culture and structure, and the difficulties in managing the change resulting from the new strategic direction of the business.

MyEconLab

This book can be supported by MyEconLab, which contains a range of additional resources, including an online homework and tutorial system designed to test and build your understanding.

You need both an access card and a course ID to access MyEconLab:

1. Is your lecturer using MyEconLab? Ask your lecturer for your course ID.

2. Has an access card been included with the book at a reduced cost? Check the inside back cover of the book.

3. If you have a course ID but no access card, go to: http://www.myeconlab.com/ to buy access to this interactive study programme.

REVIEW QUESTIONS

1 What do you understand by the term 'business strategy'?

2 Explain why different types of business will see strategic management in different ways. Give examples.

3 Outline the Five Forces Model of competition. Identify both the strengths and weaknesses of analysing industry in this manner.

4 Distinguish between a business's primary and support activities in its value chain. Why might a business be inclined to outsource its support activities? Can you see any weaknesses in doing this?

5 Explain what is meant by a business's vision and mission. What implications might different missions have for its strategic decision making?

6 Distinguish between a market-based and a resource-based view of strategic choice.

7 What do you understand by the term 'core competence' when applied to a business?

8 How might going global affect a business's strategic decision making?

9 'Going global, thinking local.' Explain this phrase, and identify the potential conflicts for a business in behaving in this way.

10 Why is the choice of business strategy and its potential for success difficult to evaluate?

11 When implementing a business strategy, what issues does it raise for a firm?

Chapter 14

Alternative theories of the firm

Business issues covered in this chapter

- Why is it often difficult for a firm to identify its profit-maximising price and output?
- Why may managers pursue goals other than maximising profit?
- What other goals might they pursue?
- What will be the effect of alternative business objectives on price and output?
- Why might businesses have multiple objectives and, if they do, how do they reconcile conflicts between them?

14.1 PROBLEMS WITH TRADITIONAL THEORY

The traditional profit-maximising theories of the firm have been criticised for being unrealistic. The criticisms are mainly of two sorts: (a) that firms wish to maximise profits, but for some reason or other are unable to do so; or (b) that firms have aims other than profit maximisation. Let us examine each in turn.

Difficulties in maximising profit

One criticism of traditional theory sometimes put forward is that firms do not use *MR* and *MC* concepts. This may be true, but firms could still arrive at maximum profit by trial and error adjustments of price, or by finding the output where *TR* and *TC* are furthest apart. Provided they end up maximising profits, they will be equating *MC* and *MR*, even if they do not know it!

In mature industries, where all firms have access to similar technology, an evolutionary process may ensure that the firms which survive are the ones closest to profit maximisation. Firms that are not maximising profits will be forced

out of the market by their more profitable rivals. In this case, traditional models will still be useful in predicting price and output.

Lack of information

The main difficulty in trying to maximise profits is a lack of information.

Firms may well use accountants' cost concepts not based on opportunity cost (see section 9.1). If it is thereby impossible to measure true profit, a firm will not be able to maximise profit except by chance.

More importantly, firms are unlikely to know precisely (or even approximately) their demand curves and hence their *MR* curves. Even though (presumably) they will know how much they are selling at the moment, this only gives them one point on their demand curve and no point at all on their *MR* curve. In order to make even an informed guess about marginal revenue, they must have some idea of how responsive demand will be to a change in price. But how are they to estimate this price elasticity?

KI 8
p 42

Market research may help. But even this is frequently very unreliable.

The biggest problem in estimating the firm's demand curve is in estimating the actions and reactions of *other* firms and their effects. Collusion between oligopolists or price leadership would help, but there will still be a considerable area of uncertainty, especially if the firm faces competition from abroad or from other industries.

Game theory may help a firm decide its price and output strategy: it may choose to pursue a risky strategy of, say, aggressively competing with rivals, but one which potentially might yield high profits if it wins the competitive battle; or it may instead go for the safe strategy of making few if any changes, but getting probably at least reasonable profits. But even this assumes that it knows the consequences for its profits of each of the possible reactions of its rivals. In reality, it will not even have this information to any degree of certainty, because it simply will not be able to predict just how consumers will respond to each of its rivals' alternative reactions.

> ### Pause for thought
>
> *What cost concepts are there other than those based on opportunity cost? Would the use of these concepts be likely to lead to an output greater or less than the profit-maximising one?*

Time period

Finally, there is the problem in deciding the *time period* over which the firm should be seeking to maximise profits. Firms operate in a changing environment. Demand curves shift; supply curves shift. Some of these shifts occur as a result of factors outside the firm's control, such as changes in competitors' prices and products, or changes in technology. Some, however, change as a direct result of a firm's policies, such as an advertising campaign, the development of a new improved product, or the installation of new equipment.

The firm is not, therefore, faced with static cost and revenue curves from which it can read off its profit-maximising price and output. Instead it is faced with a changing (and often highly unpredictable) set of curves. If it chooses a price and an output that maximise profits this year, it may as a result jeopardise profits in the future.

Take a simple example. The firm may be considering whether to invest in new expensive equipment. If it does, its costs will rise in the short run and thus short-run profits will fall. On the other hand, if the quality of the product thereby increases, demand is likely to increase over the longer run. Also variable costs are likely to decrease if the new equipment is more efficient. In other words, long-run profit is likely to increase, but probably by a highly uncertain amount.

Given these extreme problems in deciding profit-maximising price and output, firms may adopt simple rules of thumb for pricing. (These are examined in Chapter 17.)

Alternative aims

An even more fundamental attack on the traditional theory of the firm is that firms do not even *aim* to maximise profits (even if they could).

The traditional theory of the firm assumes that it is the *owners* of the firm that make price and output decisions. It is reasonable to assume that owners *will* want to maximise profits: this much most of the critics of the traditional theory accept. The question is, however, whether the owners do in fact make the decisions.

In public limited companies there is generally a separation of ownership and control (see Chapter 3). The shareholders are the owners and presumably will want the firm to maximise profits so as to increase their dividends and the value of their shares. Shareholders elect directors. Directors in turn employ professional managers, who are often given considerable discretion in making decisions. But what are the objectives of managers? Will *they* want to maximise profits, or will they have some other aim?

Managers may be assumed to want to *maximise their own utility*. This may well involve pursuits that conflict with profit maximisation. They may, for example, pursue higher salaries, greater power or prestige, better working conditions, greater sales, etc. Different managers in the same firm may well pursue different aims.

Managers will still have to ensure that *sufficient* profits are made to keep shareholders happy, but that may be very different from *maximising* profits.

Alternative theories of the firm to those of profit maximisation, therefore, tend to assume that large firms are **profit satisficers**. That is, managers strive hard for a minimum target level of profit, but are less interested in profits above this level.

Such theories fall into two categories: first, those theories that assume that firms attempt to maximise some other aim, provided that sufficient profits are achieved (these are examined in section 14.2); and second, those theories that assume that firms pursue a number of potentially conflicting aims, of which sufficient profit is merely one (these theories are examined in section 14.3).

> ### Definition
>
> **Profit satisficing** Where decision makers in a firm aim for a target level of profit rather than the absolute maximum level.

14.2 ALTERNATIVE MAXIMISING THEORIES

Long-run profit maximisation

The traditional theory of the firm is based on the assumption of *short-run* profit maximisation. Many actions of firms may be seen to conflict with this aim and yet could be consistent with the aim of **long-run profit maximisation**. For example, policies to increase the size of the firm or the firm's share of the market may involve heavy advertising or low prices to the detriment of short-run profits. But if this results in the firm becoming larger, with a larger share of the market, the resulting economic power may enable the firm to make larger profits in the long run.

At first sight, a theory of long-run profit maximisation would seem to be a realistic alternative to the traditional short-run profit-maximisation theory. In practice, however, the theory is not a very useful predictor of firms' behaviour and is very difficult to test.

A claim by managers that they were attempting to maximise long-run profits could be an excuse for virtually any policy. When challenged as to why the firm had, say, undertaken expensive research, or high-cost investment, or engaged in a damaging price war, the managers could reply: 'Ah, yes, but in the long run it will pay off.' This is very difficult to refute (until it is too late!).

Even if long-run profit maximisation *is* the prime aim, the means of achieving it are extremely complex. The firm will need a plan of action for prices, output, investment, etc., stretching from now into the future. But today's prices and marketing decisions affect tomorrow's demand. Therefore, future demand curves cannot be taken as given. Similarly, today's investment decisions will affect tomorrow's costs. Therefore, future cost curves cannot be taken as given. These shifts in demand and cost curves will be very difficult to estimate with any precision. Quite apart from this, the actions of competitors, suppliers, unions and so on are difficult to predict. Thus the picture of firms making precise calculations of long-run profit-maximising prices and outputs is a false one.

It may be useful, however, simply to observe that firms, when making current price, output and investment decisions, try to judge the approximate effect on new entrants, consumer demand, future costs, etc., and try to avoid decisions that would appear to conflict with long-run profits. Often this will simply involve avoiding making decisions (e.g. cutting price) that may stimulate an unfavourable reaction from rivals (e.g. rivals cutting their price).

Managerial utility maximisation

One of the most influential of the alternative theories of the firm, **managerial utility maximisation**, was developed by O. E. Williamson[1] in the 1960s. Williamson argued that, provided satisfactory levels of profit are achieved, managers often have the discretion to choose what policies to pursue. In other words, they are free to pursue their own interests. And what are the managers' interests? To maximise their own utility, argued Williamson.

Williamson identified a number of factors that affect a manager's utility. The four main ones were salary, job security, dominance (including status, power and prestige) and professional excellence.

Of these only salary is *directly* measurable. The rest have to be measured indirectly. One way of doing this is to examine managers' expenditure on various items, and in particular on *staff*, on *perks* (such as a company car and a plush office) and on *discretionary investment*. The greater the level of expenditure by managers on these items, the greater is likely to be their status, power, prestige, professional excellence and job security, and hence utility.

Having identified the factors that influence a manager's utility, Williamson developed several models in which managers seek to maximise their utility. He used these models to predict managerial behaviour under various conditions and argued that they performed better than traditional profit-maximising theory.

One important conclusion was that average costs are likely to be higher when managers have the discretion to pursue their own utility. For example, perks and unnecessarily high staffing levels add to costs. On the other hand, the resulting 'slack' allows managers to rein in these costs in times of low demand (see page 239). This enables them to maintain their profit levels. To support these claims he conducted a number of case studies. These did indeed show that staff and perks were cut during recessions and expanded during booms, and that new managers were frequently able to reduce staff levels without influencing the productivity of firms.

KI 6
p37

Sales revenue maximisation (short run)

Perhaps the most famous of all alternative theories of the firm is that developed by William Baumol in the late 1950s.

Definitions

Long-run profit maximisation An alternative theory which assumes that managers aim to shift cost and revenue curves so as to maximise profits over some longer time period.

Managerial utility maximisation An alternative theory which assumes that managers are motivated by self-interest. They will adopt whatever policies are perceived to maximise their own utility.

---

[1] *The Economics of Discretionary Behaviour* (Prentice Hall, 1964), p. 3.

BOX 14.1 IN SEARCH OF LONG-RUN PROFITS

The video games war

Traditional economic theory argues that firms will seek to maximise their short-run profits, and therefore adopt a range of strategies to achieve this goal. There are, however, plenty of examples from the world of business to suggest that firms often take a longer-term perspective. One example is the long-running video games war between the big three companies in the industry – Sony, Nintendo and Microsoft.

The static games console market

Market share in the static console games market fluctuates between the different models produced by the big three businesses. New console developments, which occur every few years, have a dramatic impact on the shape of the industry. For example, Nintendo was the industry leader with its GameCube until the mid-1990s when Sony launched its PlayStation 1. Sony retained its position as market leader when it released the PlayStation 2 in 2000. This became the most successful static game console of all time and has sold over 155 million units worldwide.

However, Sony faced new competition when Microsoft entered the market for the first time in November 2001 with the Xbox, and became the market leader in 2006 with the introduction of the Xbox360. This seventh generation console was released 12 months ahead of those of its rivals, at a price of £209 for the basic model and £280 for the premium model. Sony suffered technical difficulties with the launch of the PlayStation 3 and failed to deliver it on schedule. It also priced the console significantly above its rival at £425.

Nintendo released the Wii in November 2006 at a price of £179. The company targeted a much wider audience of casual and non-gamers as well as hard-core gamers. Its innovative movement sensor play system helped to catapult it into first place in the market. By 2007 its sales had already surpassed those of the Xbox360 even though it was released a year later. It sold over 22 million units worldwide in both 2008 and 2009 and has sold over 100 million units in total. Although its sales fell very rapidly after 2010 (see chart (a)), research carried out by Mintel in 2014[2] indicates that it is still the most widely owned games console in the UK.

Between 2012 and 2013 the 'big three' released the eighth generation of games consoles onto the market. Nintendo released the WiiU in November 2012. The basic edition of the console was priced at £250 in the UK. Sony released the PlayStation 4 (PS4) in November 2013 for a price of £349 in the UK and $399 in the USA. Microsoft released the Xbox One in the same month for a price of £429 in the UK and $499 in the US.

As illustrated in chart (a), the sales of the WiiU console have proved rather disappointing for Nintendo and the company reported a loss of £57 million for the second quarter of 2014. The company had forecast sales for 2013/14 of 9 million consoles but only sold 2.7 million despite cutting the price by $50.

The PS4 has been much more successful. It has outsold its key rivals by quite some margin. In the financial year 2013/14 Sony sold more games consoles than Nintendo for the first time in eight years. It reported profits of £148 million for the second quarter of 2014.

The sales performance of the Xbox One has been in between its two leading rivals. One initial problem was its price – it was $100 more expensive than the PS4 in the USA and £80 more expensive in the UK. Only three months after its launch, Microsoft reduced the price of the console in the UK to £399.

[2] 'Video games – UK', Mintel, November 2014.

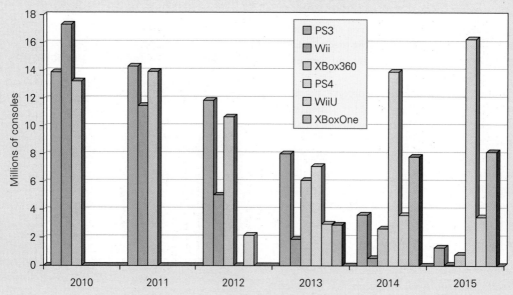

(a) *Global sales of static consoles per year*

Source: Based on data in '2015 Year on Year Sales and Market Share Update', VGChartz, 14 January 2016

It also offered a cheaper version of the product without the Kinect camera for motion tracking. The Xbox One actually outsold the PS4 in November and December 2014 but the PS4 considerably outsold the Xbox One in 2015. As of January 2016, the cumulative sales of the three consoles since they were first launched was as follows – 35.3 million PS4s, 19.2 million Xbox Ones and 12.4 million WiiUs.

The market for mobile gaming hardware

The other strand of the market is the mobile gaming sector, and this segment has seen the most significant changes in the past few years. Traditionally it was dominated by handheld consoles and in particular those produced by Nintendo. The original Gameboy was launched in 1989 and sold nearly 120 million units. Nintendo then introduced the DS in 2004 which became the best-selling handheld console of all time with total sales of over 150 million. The 3DS was released in 2011.

Sony also successfully entered this market in 2004 with its own handheld console, the PlayStation Portable PSP, which was described as the first real competitor to challenge Nintendo's domination. It has sold over 82 million units. Sony launched the PS Vita in 2011.

Unlike in the static games consoles market, Microsoft has never entered the mobile segment of the market. Chart (b) clearly shows how the demand for these handheld consoles has fallen dramatically in the past few years. In 2009 approximately 39.5 million units were sold. This fell to 12.5 million in 2014. The PS Vita has sold fewer units in three years than the PSP did in just its first four months. The major reason for this decline in the sales of handheld consoles is the increased competition in the mobile gaming sector from smartphones and tablets.

Gaming with smartphones and tablets. The launch of the iPhone in 2007, which enabled consumers to play games on the device, changed the mobile gaming market dramatically. Just 100 days after Apple launched its online App Store in late 2008, there had been 200 million downloads. By October 2014 this figure had risen to a staggering 85 billion.

Google Play Store also had 50 billion downloads over the same period. In 2014 the revenue generated from games on smartphones and tablets was $25 billion.[3] It is forecast to exceed the revenue generated from console titles in 2015.

Out of the top ten paid apps that were downloaded onto iPads in the USA in 2014, nine were games. These included *Minecraft*, *Cut the Rope* 2, *Heads Up!* and *Plants vs Zombies*.[4]

The secret of success

The gaming market is a rich source of income and has grown rapidly in recent times. Mintel[5] estimated that the video game market in the UK was worth £2.2 billion in 2014 and projected that it would increase to £5.4 billion in 2019. In its Internet survey in 2014 it found that 21 per cent of the respondents aged 16 and over in the UK classed themselves as regular gamers (play once a week but not every day), 8 per cent classed themselves as hard-core gamers (play every day or most days), 24 per cent classed themselves as casual or social gamers (play every now and then) while 40 per cent classed themselves as non-gamers.

---

[3] 'Quarterly global games market update', *Newzoo*, October 2014.
[4] 'Apple outs most downloaded apps of 2014', gadgets.NDTV.com, 25 December 2014.
[5] 'Video games – UK', Mintel, November 2014.

(b) *Global sales of handheld consoles per year*

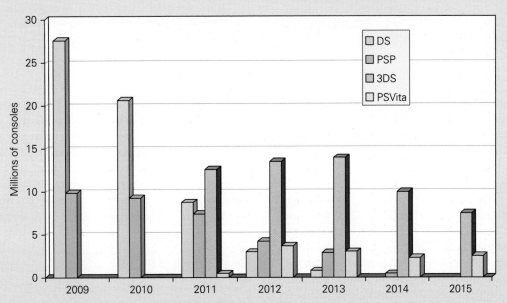

A study by the Internet Advertising Bureau, published in September 2014, reported that seven in ten people in Britain had played a video game in the previous six months. It also found that more people aged 44 and over were playing games than children and teenagers. The research findings also indicated that more females (52 per cent) were playing games than men (48 per cent).

The importance of the games themselves. Static and mobile console sales are only successful if they have games and other features that are attractive to consumers. Therefore the relationship between the companies that produce the games and those that make the consoles is an important one.

The games are actually written and produced by game developers. Writing games is a time-consuming and expensive process. Sometimes games developers receive funding from a games publisher which then releases and markets the games.

Game developers may be employed by an independent company, a games publisher or one of the console producers. For example an independent development company called Infinity Ward created the famous game – *Call of Duty*. It received significant funding from the publisher Activision to help finance the costs of writing the game. The day after *Call of Duty* was released in 2003, Infinity Ward was purchased by Activision and so became a division of this publisher.

Bungie was also an independent company that was developing the game *Halo* in 2000. Before *Halo* was completed and released the company was purchased by Microsoft and so became a division of that console producer. Bungie split from Microsoft and became an independent company again in 2010 and entered into a 10-year deal with Activision. It recently produced the game *Destiny*.

Some games are exclusive to a particular console because the game developers work directly for that company. This was the case with *Halo*, which is available only for the Xbox, *Gran Turismo*, which is available only for the PlayStation and Mario games (*Mario Kart 8*, *Super Mario 3D World*), which are available only for Nintendo consoles.

Games that are released by a games publisher are often available on different consoles and so tend to be the most popular. For example, the three biggest selling games in the UK in 2014 were *FIFA15*, released by EA Sports, *Call of Duty: Advanced Warfare*, released by Activision, and *Grand Theft Auto V*, released by RockStar Games.

Most games are now available to download, and sales through this medium have risen rapidly. Of the £2.45 billion spent on games in 2014, just over £1.5 billion came from digital downloads. This was an increase of 18.8 per cent on the previous year, whereas the sale of physical games fell by 6.6 per cent.

Online gaming. Another important feature of these best-selling static and mobile gaming machines is online gaming capability and global connectivity. Console owners can play a favourite game online against a stranger in another part of the world. Moreover, connection to the Internet has facilitated a move towards the use of consoles as 'digital entertainment centres', in which users can download content, including TV channels, films and music.

All three companies – Nintendo, Sony and Microsoft – know how to be successful in the gaming industry: technological excellence and innovation, appropriate pricing strategies and visionary marketing. With the increased competition from smartphones and iPads some people predicted the end of the console market in 2013.

However, a year after their launch, the combined sales of the PS4 and Xbox One are 60 per cent higher than those of the PS3 and Xbox360 a year after their launch. The release of *Super Smash Bros.* in November 2014 also helped to boost sales of the WiiU.

Perhaps the biggest challenge to the big three static console producers will come from the company Valve, which is working with PC manufacturers to produce custom-built computers which can be plugged into a TV. It already operates the *Steam* download service.

Both Nintendo and Sony have found it more difficult to deal with the increasing competition from smartphones and tablets in the mobile gaming market.

1. *What factors have affected the price elasticity of demand for static and handheld games consoles?*
2. *How does the maximisation of long-run profits conflict with the maximisation of short-run profits?*
3. *What factors might favour collusion in the video games market? What factors might make collusion unlikely?*

This is the theory of **sales revenue maximisation**. Unlike the theories of long-run profit maximisation and managerial utility maximisation, it is easy to identify the price and output that meet this aim – at least in the short run.

So why should managers want to maximise their firm's sales revenue? The answer is that the success of managers, and especially sales managers, may be judged according to the level of the firm's sales. Sales figures are an obvious barometer of the firm's health. Managers' salaries, power and prestige may depend directly on sales revenue. The firm's sales representatives may be paid commission on their sales. Thus sales revenue maximisation may be a more dominant aim in the firm than profit maximisation, particularly if it has a dominant sales department.

Sales revenue will be maximised at the top of the *TR* curve at output Q_1 in Figure 14.1. Profits, by contrast, would be maximised at Q_2. Thus, for given total revenue and total cost curves, sales revenue maximisation will tend to lead to a higher output and a lower price than profit maximisation.

The firm will still have to make sufficient profits, however, to keep the shareholders happy. Thus firms can be seen to be operating with a profit constraint. They are *profit satisficers*.

KI 7
p 38

Definition

Sales revenue maximisation An alternative theory of the firm which assumes that managers aim to maximise the firm's short-run total revenue.

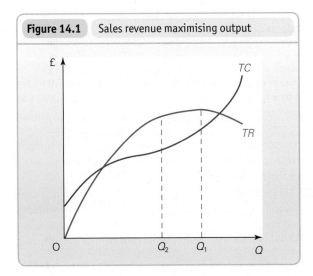

Figure 14.1 Sales revenue maximising output

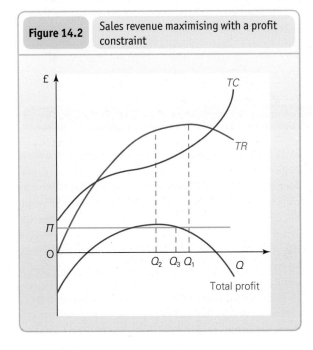

Figure 14.2 Sales revenue maximising with a profit constraint

The effect of this profit constraint is illustrated in Figure 14.2. The diagram shows a total profit curve. (This is found by simply taking the difference between TR and TC at each output.) Assume that the minimum acceptable profit is Π (whatever the output). Any output greater than Q_3 will give a profit less than Π. Thus the sales revenue maximiser who is also a profit satisficer will produce Q_3 not Q_1. Note, however, that this output is still greater than the profit-maximising output Q_2.

If the firm could maximise sales revenue and still make more than the minimum acceptable profit, it would probably spend this surplus profit on advertising to increase revenue further. This would have the effect of shifting the TR curve upward and also the TC curve (since advertising costs money).

Sales revenue maximisation will tend to involve more advertising than profit maximisation. Ideally the profit-maximising firm will advertise up to the point where the marginal revenue of advertising equals the marginal cost of advertising (assuming diminishing returns to advertising). The firm aiming to maximise sales revenue will go beyond this, since further advertising, although costing more than it earns the firm, will still add to total revenue. The firm will continue advertising until surplus profits above the minimum have been used up.

Growth maximisation

Rather than aiming to maximise *short-run* revenue, managers may take a longer-term perspective and aim for **growth maximisation** in the size of the firm. They may gain utility directly from being part of a rapidly growing 'dynamic' organisation; promotion prospects are greater in an expanding organisation, since new posts tend to be created; large firms may pay higher salaries; managers may obtain greater power in a large firm.

Growth is probably best measured in terms of a growth in sales revenue, since sales revenue (or 'turnover') is the simplest way of measuring the size of a business. An alternative would be to measure the capital value of a firm, but this will depend on the ups and downs of the stock market and is thus a rather unreliable method.

If a firm is to maximise growth, it needs to be clear about the time period over which it is setting itself this objective. For example, maximum growth over the next two or three years might be obtained by running factories to absolute maximum capacity, cramming in as many machines and workers as possible, and backing this up with massive advertising campaigns and price cuts. Such policies, however, may not be sustainable in the longer run. The firm may simply not be able to finance them. A longer-term perspective (say, 5–10 years) may therefore require the firm to 'pace' itself, and perhaps to direct resources away from current production and sales into the development of new products that have a potentially high and growing long-term demand.

Equilibrium for a growth-maximising firm

What will a growth-maximising firm's price and output be? Unfortunately, there is no simple formula for predicting this.

In the short run, the firm may choose the profit-maximising price and output – so as to provide the greatest funds for investment. On the other hand, it may be prepared to sacrifice some short-term profits in order to mount an advertising campaign. It all depends on the strategy it considers most suitable to achieve growth.

> **Definition**
>
> **Growth maximisation** An alternative theory which assumes that managers seek to maximise the growth in sales revenue (or the capital value of the firm) over time.

In the long run, prediction is more difficult still. The policies that a firm adopts will depend crucially on the assessments of market opportunities made by managers. But this involves judgement, not fine calculation. Different managers will judge a situation differently.

One prediction can be made though. Growth-maximising firms are likely to diversify into different products, especially as they approach the limits to expansion in existing markets. (Alternative growth strategies are considered in Chapter 15.)

Alternative maximising theories and the consumer

It is difficult to draw firm conclusions about how the behaviour of firms in these alternative maximising theories will affect the consumer's interest.

In the case of sales revenue maximisation, a higher output will be produced than under profit maximisation, but the consumer will not necessarily benefit from lower prices,

since more will be spent on advertising – costs that will be passed on to the consumer.

In the case of growth and long-run profit maximisation, there are many possible policies that a firm could pursue. To the extent that a concern for the long run encourages firms to look to improved products, new products and new techniques, the consumer may benefit from such a concern. To the extent, however, that growth encourages a greater level of industrial concentration through merger, the consumer may lose from the resulting greater level of monopoly power.

As with the traditional theory of the firm, the degree of competition that a firm faces is a crucial factor in determining just how responsive it will be to the wishes of the consumer.

> ### Pause for thought
>
> *How will competition between growth-maximising firms benefit the consumer?*

KI 21
p175

KI 6
p37

14.3 MULTIPLE AIMS

Satisficing and the setting of targets

Firms may have more than one aim. For example, they may try to achieve increased sales revenue *and* increased profit. The problem with this is that, if two aims conflict, it will not be possible to maximise both of them. For example, sales revenue will probably be maximised at a different price and output from that at which profits are maximised. Where firms have two or more aims, a compromise may be for targets to be set for individual aims which are low enough to achieve simultaneously, and yet which are sufficient to satisfy the interested parties. This is known as 'satisficing' (as opposed to maximising) behaviour.

Such target setting is also likely when the maximum value of a particular aim is unknown. If, for example, the maximum achievable profit is unknown, the firm may well set a target for profit which it feels is both satisfactory and achievable.

Behavioural theories of the firm: the setting of targets

A major advance in alternative theories of the firm has been the development of *behavioural theories*.[6] Rather than setting up a model to show how various objectives could in theory be achieved, behavioural theories of the firm are based on observations of how firms *actually* behave.

Large firms are often complex institutions with several departments (sales, production, design, purchasing, personnel, finance, etc.). Each department is likely to have its own specific set of aims and objectives, which may possibly come into conflict with those of other departments. These aims in turn will be constrained by the interests of shareholders, workers, customers and creditors (collectively known as *stakeholders*), who will need to be kept sufficiently happy.

Behavioural theories do not lay down rules of how to *achieve* these aims, but rather examine what these aims are, the motivations underlying them, the conflicts that can arise between aims, and how these conflicts are resolved.

In many firms, targets are set for production, sales, profit, stockholding, etc. If, in practice, target levels are not achieved, a 'search' procedure will be started to find what

> ### Definitions
>
> **Behavioural theories of the firm** Theories that attempt to predict the actions of firms by studying the behaviour of various groups of people within the firm and their interactions under conditions of potentially conflicting interests.
>
> **Stakeholders (in a company)** People who are affected by a company's activities and/or performance (customers, employees, owners, creditors, people living in the neighbourhood, etc.). They may or may not be in a position to take decisions, or influence decision taking, in the firm.

---

[6] See in particular: R. M. Cyert and J. G. March, *A Behavioural Theory of the Firm* (Prentice Hall, 1963).

went wrong and how to rectify it. If the problem cannot be rectified, managers will probably adjust the target downwards. If, on the other hand, targets are easily achieved, managers may adjust them upwards. Thus the targets to which managers aspire depend to a large extent on the success in achieving *previous* targets. Targets are also influenced by expectations of demand and costs, by the achievements of competitors and by expectations of competitors' future behaviour. For example, if it is expected that the economy is likely to move into recession, sales and profit targets may be adjusted downwards.

If targets conflict, the conflict will be settled by a bargaining process between managers. The outcome of the bargaining, however, will depend on the power and ability of the individual managers concerned. Thus a similar set of conflicting targets may be resolved differently in different firms.

Behavioural theories of the firm: organisational slack

Since changing targets often involves search procedures and bargaining processes and is therefore time consuming, and since many managers prefer to avoid conflict, targets tend to be changed fairly infrequently. Business conditions, however, often change rapidly. To avoid the need to change targets, therefore, managers will tend to be fairly conservative in their aspirations. This leads to the phenomenon known as *organisational slack*.

When the firm does better than planned, it will allow slack to develop. This slack can then be taken up if the firm does worse than planned. For example, if the firm produces more than it planned, it will build up stocks of finished goods and draw on them if production subsequently falls. It would not, in the meantime, increase its sales target or reduce its production target. If it did, and production then fell below target, the production department might not be able to supply the sales department with its full requirement.

Thus keeping targets fairly low and allowing slack to develop allows all targets to be met with minimum conflict.

Organisational slack, however, adds to a firm's costs. If firms are operating in a competitive environment, they may be forced to cut slack in order to survive. In the 1970s, many Japanese firms succeeded in cutting slack by using *just-in-time* methods of production. These involve keeping stocks to a minimum and ensuring that inputs are delivered as required. Clearly, this requires that production is tightly controlled and that suppliers are reliable. Many firms today have successfully cut their warehouse costs by using such methods. (These methods are examined in section 18.7.)

Multiple goals: some predictions of behaviour

Conservatism

Some firms may be wary of what they consider to be unnecessary change. In some circumstances it may be optimal for the firm to alter its strategies. However, if the managers suffer from loss aversion, then this can create a bias in favour of the status quo. They may prefer to stick with tried and tested practices even though alternatives would generate a better return. This could apply to pricing policies, marketing techniques, product design and range, internal organisation of the firm, etc.

If a policy is clearly not working managers will probably change it. However, they may be conservative and implement only a cautious change: perhaps imitating successful competitors. A policy may only be judged as not working if profits fall below some reference point. This reference point may be determined by the performance of other similar firms, as discussed in the next section.

This safe, satisficing approach makes predicting a firm's behaviour relatively easy. You simply examine its past behaviour. Making generalisations about all such cautious firms, however, is more difficult. Different firms are likely to have established different rules of behaviour depending on their own particular experiences of their market.

Comparison with other firms

Managers may judge their success by comparing their firm's performance with that of rival firms. For example, growing market share may be seen as a more important indicator of 'success' than simple growth in sales. Similarly, they may compare their profits, their product design, their technology or their industrial relations with those of rivals. To many managers it is *relative* performance that matters, rather than absolute performance.

What predictions can be made if this is how managers behave? The answer is that it depends on the nature of competition in the industry. The more profitable, innovative and efficient are the competitors, the more profitable, innovative and efficient will managers try to make their particular firm.

The further ahead of their rivals firms try to stay, the more likely it is that there will be a 'snowballing' effect: each firm trying to outdo the other.

Pause for thought

Will this type of behaviour tend to lead to profit maximisation?

Definitions

Organisational slack When managers allow spare capacity to exist, thereby enabling them to respond more easily to changed circumstances.

Just-in-time methods Where a firm purchases supplies and produces both components and finished products as they are required. This minimises stockholding and its associated costs.

BOX 14.2 STAKEHOLDER POWER

Who governs the firm?

The concept of the 'stakeholder economy' became fashionable in the late 1990s. Rather than the economy being governed by big business, and rather than businesses being governed in the interests of shareholders (many of whom are big institutions, such as insurance companies and pension funds), the economy should serve the interests of everyone. But what does this mean for the governance of firms?

The stakeholders of a firm include customers, employees (from senior managers to the lowest-paid workers), shareholders, suppliers, lenders and the local and national communities.

The supporters of a stakeholding economy argue that *all* these interest groups ought to have a say in the decisions of the firm. Trade unions or workers' councils ought to be included in decisions affecting the workforce, or indeed all company decisions. They could be represented on decision-making bodies and perhaps have seats on the board of directors. Alternatively, the workforce might be given the power to elect managers.

Banks or other institutions lending to firms ought to be included in investment decisions. In Germany, where banks finance a large proportion of investment, banks are represented on the boards of most large companies.

Local communities ought to have a say in any projects (such as new buildings or the discharge of effluent) that affect the local environment. Customers ought to have more say in the quality of products being produced, for example by being given legal protection against the production of shoddy or unsafe goods. Where interest groups cannot be directly represented in decision making, then companies ought to be regulated by the government in order to protect the interests of the various groups. For example, if farmers and other suppliers to supermarkets are paid very low prices, then the purchasing behaviour of the supermarkets could be regulated by some government agency.

But is this vision of a stakeholder economy likely to become reality? Trends in the international economy suggest that the opposite might be occurring. The growth of multinational corporations, with their ability to move finance and production to wherever it is most profitable, has weakened the power of employees, local interest groups and even national governments.

Employees in one part of the multinational may have little in the way of common interests with employees in another. In fact, they may vie with each other, for example over which plant should be expanded or closed down. What is more, many firms are employing a larger and larger proportion of casual, part-time, temporary or agency workers. With these new 'flexible labour markets' such employees have far less say in the company than permanent members of staff: they are 'outsiders' to decision making within the firm (see section 18.7).

Also, the widespread introduction of share incentive schemes for managers (whereby managers are rewarded with shares) has increasingly made profits their driving goal. Finally, the policies of opening up markets and deregulation, policies that were adopted by many governments round the world up to the mid-1990s, have again weakened the power of many stakeholders.

 Are customers' interests best served by profit-maximising firms, answerable primarily to shareholders, or by firms where various stakeholder groups are represented in decision taking?

Satisficing and the consumer's interest

Firms with multiple goals will be satisficers. The greater the number of goals of the different managers, the greater is the chance of conflict and the more likely it is that organisational slack will develop. Satisficing firms are therefore likely to be less responsive to changes in consumer demand and changes in costs than profit-maximising firms. They may thus be less efficient.

On the other hand, such firms may be less eager to exploit their economic power by charging high prices, or to use aggressive advertising, or to pay low wages.

The extent to which satisficing firms do act in the public interest will, as in the case of other types of firm, depend to a large extent on the amount and type of competition they face, and their attitudes towards this competition. Firms that compare their performance with that of their rivals are more likely to be responsive to consumer wishes than firms that prefer to stick to well-established practices. On the other hand, they may be more concerned to 'manipulate' consumer tastes than the more traditional firm.

SUMMARY

1a There are two major types of criticism of the traditional profit-maximising theory: (a) firms may not have the information to maximise profits; (b) they may not even want to maximise profits.

1b Lack of information on demand and costs and on the actions and reactions of rivals, and a lack of use of opportunity cost concepts, may mean that firms adopt simple 'rules of thumb' for pricing.

1c In large companies there is likely to be a divorce between ownership and control. The shareholders (the owners) may want maximum profits, but it is the managers who make the decisions, and managers are likely to aim to maximise their own utility rather than that of the shareholders. This leads to profit 'satisficing'. This is where managers aim to achieve sufficient profits to keep shareholders happy, but this is a secondary aim to one or more alternative aims.

1d Some alternative theories assume that there is a single alternative aim that firms seek to maximise. Others assume that managers have a series of (possibly conflicting) aims.

2a Rather than seeking to maximise short-run profits, a firm may take a longer-term perspective. It is very difficult, however, to predict the behaviour of a long-run profit-maximising firm, since (a) different managers are likely to make different judgements about how to achieve maximum profits, and (b) demand and cost curves may shift unpredictably both in response to the firm's own policies and as a result of external factors.

2b Managers may seek to maximise their own utility, which, in turn, will depend on factors such as salary, job security, power within the organisation and the achievement of professional excellence. Given, however, that managerial utility depends on a range of variables, it is difficult to use the theory to make general predictions of firms' behaviour.

2c Managers may gain utility from maximising sales revenue. However, they will still have to ensure that a satisfactory level of profit is achieved. The output of a firm which seeks to maximise sales revenue will be higher than that for a profit-maximising firm. Its level of advertising will also tend to be higher. Whether price will be higher or lower depends on the relative effects on demand and the cost of the additional advertising.

2d Many managers aim for maximum growth of their organisation, believing that this will help their salaries, power, prestige, etc.

2e As with long-run profit-maximising theories, it is difficult to predict the price and output strategies of a growth-maximising firm. Much depends on the judgements of particular managers about growth opportunities.

3a In large firms, decisions are taken by, or influenced by, a number of different people, including various managers, shareholders, workers, customers, suppliers and creditors. If these different people have different aims, then a conflict between them is likely to arise. A firm cannot maximise more than one of these conflicting aims. The alternative is to seek to achieve a satisfactory target level of a number of aims.

3b Behavioural theories of the firm examine how managers and other interest groups actually behave, rather than merely identifying various equilibrium positions for output, price, investment, etc.

3c If targets were easily achieved last year, they are likely to be made more ambitious next year. If they were not achieved, a search procedure will be conducted to identify how to rectify the problem. This may mean adjusting targets downwards, in which case there will be some form of bargaining process between managers.

3d Life is made easier for managers if conflict can be avoided. This will be possible if slack is allowed to develop in various parts of the firm. If targets are not being met, the slack can then be taken up without requiring adjustments in other targets.

3e Satisficing firms may be less innovative, less aggressive and less willing to initiate change. If they do change, it is more likely to be in response to changes made by their competitors. Managers may judge their performance by comparing it with that of rivals.

3f Satisficing firms may be less aggressive in exploiting a position of market power. On the other hand, they may suffer from greater inefficiency.

MyEconLab

This book can be supported by MyEconLab, which contains a range of additional resources, including an online homework and tutorial system designed to test and build your understanding.

You need both an access card and a course ID to access MyEconLab:

1. Is your lecturer using MyEconLab? Ask your lecturer for your course ID.
2. Has an access card been included with the book at a reduced cost? Check the inside back cover of the book.
3. If you have a course ID but no access card, go to: http://www.myeconlab.com/ to buy access to this interactive study programme.

REVIEW QUESTIONS

1 In the traditional theory of the firm, decision makers are often assumed to have perfect knowledge and to be able to act, therefore, with complete certainty. It is now widely accepted that in practice firms will be certain about very few things. Of the following: (a) production costs; (b) demand; (c) elasticity; (d) supply; (e) consumer tastes; (f) technology; (g) government policy, which might they be certain of? Which might they be uncertain of?

2 Make a list of six aims that a manager of a high street department store might have. Identify some conflicts that might arise between these aims.

3 When are increased profits in a manager's personal interest?

4 Draw a diagram with *MC* and *MR* curves. Mark the output (a) at which profits are maximised; (b) at which sales revenue is maximised.

5 Since advertising increases a firm's costs, will prices necessarily be lower with sales revenue maximisation than with profit maximisation?

6 We have seen that a firm aiming to maximise sales revenue will tend to produce more than a profit-maximising firm. This conclusion certainly applies under monopoly and oligopoly. Will it also apply under (a) perfect competition and (b) monopolistic competition, where in both cases there is freedom of entry?

7 A frequent complaint of junior and some senior managers is that they are frequently faced with new targets from above, and that this makes their life difficult. If their complaint is true, does this conflict with the hypothesis that managers will try to build in slack?

8 What evidence about firms' behaviour could be used to refute the argument that firms will tend to build in organisational slack and as a result be inherently conservative?

Growth strategy

Whether businesses wish to grow or not, many are forced to. The dynamic competitive process of the market drives producers on to expand in order to remain in the marketplace. If a business fails to grow, this may benefit its more aggressive rivals. They may secure a greater share of the market, leaving the first firm with reduced profits. Thus business growth is often vital if a firm is to survive.

The goal of business growth is closely linked to the key objectives of managers. Managerial status, prestige, promotion and salary might be more directly related to such a goal rather than to that of profit maximisation (as mentioned in Chapter 14). Business growth might also be essential if the business is successfully to manage change and deal with many of the inherent uncertainties of the business environment.

In this chapter we shall consider the various growth strategies open to firms and assess their respective advantages and disadvantages. First, however, we need to look at the relationship between a firm's growth and its profitability, and also at those factors which are likely to constrain the growth of the business.

15.1 GROWTH AND PROFITABILITY

In using traditional theories of the firm, economists often assume that there is a limit to the expansion of the firm: that there is a level of output beyond which profits will start to fall. The justification for this view can be found on both the supply side and the demand side.

On the supply side, it is assumed that if a firm grows beyond a certain size, it will experience rising long-run average costs. In other words, the long-run average cost curve is assumed to be U-shaped, possibly with a horizontal section at the bottom (see pages 155–9). This argument is often based on the assumption that it is *managerial* diseconomies of scale which start driving costs up once a firm has expanded beyond a certain point: there are no more plant economies to be achieved (the firm has passed its **minimum efficient scale (MES)** – see Box 9.4); instead, the firm is faced with a more complex form of organisation, with longer lines of management, more difficult labour relations and a greater possibility of lack of effort going unnoticed.

On the demand side it is assumed that the firm faces a downward-sloping demand curve (and hence marginal revenue curve) for its product. Although this demand curve can be shifted by advertising and other forms of product promotion, finite demand naturally places a constraint on the expansion of the firm.

These two assumptions can be challenged, however. On the supply side, with a multidivisional form of organisation and systems in place for monitoring performance, it is quite possible to avoid diseconomies of scale.

As far as demand is concerned, although the demand (or at least its rate of growth) for any one product may be limited, the firm could diversify into new markets.

It is thus incorrect to say that there is a limit to the size of a business. An individual business may be able to go on expanding its capacity or diversifying its interests indefinitely. There does, however, exist an upper limit on the firm's *rate* of growth – the *speed* at which it can expand its capacity or diversify. The reason behind this constraint is that growth is determined by the profitability of the business. The growth rate/profitability relationship can operate in two ways:

- *Growth depends upon profitability*. The more profitable the firm, the more likely it is to be able to raise finance for investment.
- *Growth affects profitability*. In the short run, growth above a certain rate may reduce profitability. Some of the finance for the investment necessary to achieve growth may have to come from the firm's sales revenue. A firm wishing to expand its operations in an existing market will require greater advertising and marketing; and a firm seeking to diversify may have to spend considerable sums on market research and employing managers with specialist knowledge and skills. In both cases, investment is likely to be needed in new plant and machinery. In other words, the firm may have to sacrifice some of its short-run profits for the long-run gains that greater growth might yield.

But what about long-run profits? Will growth increase or decrease these? The answer depends on the nature of the growth. If growth leads to expansion into new markets in which demand is growing, or to increased market power, or to increased economies of scale, then growth may well increase long-run profits – not only total profits, but the rate of profit on capital, or the ratio of profits to revenue. If, however, growth leads to diseconomies of scale, or to investment in risky projects, then growth may well be at the expense of long-run profitability.

To summarise: greater profitability may lead to higher growth, but higher growth, at least in the short run, may be at the expense of profits.

15.2 CONSTRAINTS ON GROWTH

However much a firm may want to grow, it might simply not be possible. There are several factors that can restrict the ability of a business to expand.

Pause for thought

Before you read on, what constraints on its growth do you feel a business might experience?

Financial conditions. Financial conditions determine the ability of a firm to fund its growth. Growth can be financed in three distinct ways: from internal funds, from borrowing or from the issue of new shares.

The largest source of finance for investment in the UK is **internal funds** (i.e. ploughed-back profit). The principal limitation in achieving growth via this means is that such funds are linked to business profitability, and this in turn is subject to the cyclical nature of economic activity – to the

booms and slumps that the economy experiences. Profitability tends to fall in a recession along with the level of sales. In such times it is often difficult for a firm to afford new investment.

The *borrowing* of finance to fund expansion may be constrained by a wide range of factors, from the availability of finance in the banking sector to the creditworthiness of the business.

Definitions

Minimum efficient scale (MES) The size of the individual factory or of the whole firm, beyond which no significant additional economies of scale can be gained. For an individual factory the MES is known as the *minimum efficient plant size* (MEPS).

Internal funds Funds used for business expansion that come from ploughed-back profit.

The *issuing of new shares* to fund growth depends not only on confidence within the stock market in general, but on the stock market's assessment of the potential performance of the individual firm in particular. It should be noted that finance from this source is not open to all firms. For most small and medium-sized enterprises (i.e. those not listed on the Stock Exchange), raising finance through issuing new shares must be done privately, and normally this source of finance is very limited and hence difficult to access.

(We will examine the financing of investment in more detail in sections 19.4 and 19.5.)

Shareholder confidence. Whichever way growth is financed – internal funds, borrowing or new share issues – the likely outcome in the short run is a reduction in the firm's share dividend. If the firm *retains* too much *profit*, there will be less to pay out in dividends. Similarly, if the firm *borrows* too much, the interest payments that it incurs are likely to make it difficult to maintain the level of dividends to shareholders. Finally, if it attempts to raise capital by a *new issue of shares*, the distributed profits will have to be divided between a larger number of shares.

Whichever way it finances investment, therefore, the more it invests, the more the dividends on shares in the short run will probably fall. Unless shareholders are confident that *long*-run profits and hence dividends will rise again, thus causing the share price to remain high in the long run, they may well sell their shares. This will cause share prices to fall. If they fall too far, the firm runs the risk of being taken over and certain managers risk losing their jobs.

This risk of takeover gives rise to a concept referred to as the **takeover constraint**. The takeover constraint requires that the growth-maximising firm needs to distribute sufficient profits to avoid being taken over. Hence the rate of business growth is influenced not only by market opportunities but also by shareholder demands and expectations and the fear of takeover.

The converse of this situation is also true. If a business fails to grow fast enough, it may be that a potential buyer sees the firm as a valuable acquisition, whose resources might be put to more profitable use over the longer term. Hence businesses must avoid being overcautious and paying high share dividends, but, as a result, failing to invest and failing to exploit their true potential.

The likelihood of takeover depends in large part on the stock market's assessment of the firm's potential: how is the firm's investment strategy perceived to affect its future performance and profitability? The views of the stock market are reflected in the **valuation ratio** of the firm. This is the ratio of the stock market value of the firm's shares (the number of issued shares times the current share price) to the book value of the firm's assets. This is sometimes referred to as the **price to book ratio**. A low ratio means that the real assets of the business are effectively undervalued: that they can be purchased at a low market price. The business is thus likely to be more attractive to potential bidders. Conversely,

firms with a high valuation ratio are seen as overvalued and are unlikely to be the target of takeover bids.

In the long run, a rapidly growing firm may find its profits increasing, especially if it can achieve economies of scale and a bigger share of the market. These profits can then be used to finance further growth. The firm will still not have unlimited finance, however, and therefore will still be faced by the takeover constraint if it attempts to grow too rapidly.

Demand conditions. Our analysis of business growth has shown that finance for growth is largely dependent upon the business's profitability. The more profit it makes, the more it can draw on internal funds; the more likely financial institutions will be to lend; and the more readily will new share issues be purchased by the market. The profitability of a business is in turn dependent upon market demand and demand growth. If the firm is operating in an expanding market, profits are likely to grow and finance will be relatively easy to obtain.

If, on the other hand, the firm's existing market is not expanding, it will find that profits and sales are unlikely to rise unless it diversifies into related or non-related markets. One means of overcoming this demand constraint is to expand overseas, either by attempting to increase export sales or by locating new production facilities in foreign markets.

Managerial conditions. The growth of a firm is usually a planned process, and as such must be managed. But the management team might lack entrepreneurial vision, or various organisational skills.

Equally, as with other resources within the business, the management team might grow, or alternatively its composition might change in order to reflect the new needs of the growing business. However, new managers take time to be incorporated into, and become part of, an effective management team. They must undergo a period of training and become integrated into their new firm and its culture. It takes time to integrate into a team of managers already accustomed to working together. The rate of growth of business is thus constrained by this process of managerial expansion.

In the sections below we will explore the alternative growth strategies open to businesses and the various advantages and limitations that such strategies present.

Definitions

Takeover constraint The effect that the fear of being taken over has on a firm's willingness to undertake projects that reduce distributed profits.

Valuation ratio or price to book ratio The ratio of stock market value to book value. The stock market value is an assessment of the firm's past and anticipated future performance. The book value is a calculation of the current value of the firm's assets.

15.3 ALTERNATIVE GROWTH STRATEGIES

In pursuit of growth, a firm will seek to increase its markets: whether at home or internationally. In either case the firm will need to increase its capacity. This may be achieved by internal or external expansion.

Internal expansion. This is where a business looks to expand its productive capacity by adding to existing plant or by building new plant. There are three main ways of doing this:

- The firm can expand or *differentiate its product* within existing markets, by, for example, updating or restyling its product, or improving its technical characteristics.
- Alternatively, the business might seek to expand via *vertical integration*. This involves the firm expanding within the same product market, but at a different stage of production. For example, a car manufacturer might wish to produce its own components. This is known as 'backward' vertical integration (sometimes called 'upstream' integration). Alternatively, it might decide to distribute and sell its own car models. This is described as 'forward' (or 'downstream') vertical integration.
- As a third option, the business might seek to expand outside of its current product range, and move into new markets. This is known as a process of *diversification*.

External expansion. This is where the firm engages with another in order to expand its activities. It may do this in one of two ways:

- It can join with another firm to form a single legal identity either by merger or by acquisition (takeover).
- Alternatively, it may form a *strategic alliance* with one or more firms. Here firms retain their separate identities.

The term 'strategic alliance' is used to cover a wide range of alternative collaborative arrangements. A strategic alliance might involve a joint venture between one or more firms to complete a particular project or to produce a particular product. It might also involve firms making an informal or a contractual agreement to supply or distribute goods. A key characteristic of a strategic alliance is that the parties involved retain their own legal identity outside of the alliance.

As with internal expansion, external expansion, whether by merger or alliance, can be vertical or horizontal, or involve diversification. In the case of mergers, we use the terms 'horizontal merger', 'vertical merger' and 'conglomerate merger'.

Figure 15.1 outlines the main routes to a firm's growth and the various stages at which it can take place. These will be considered in the following sections.

A further dimension of business growth that we should note at this point is that all of the above-mentioned growth paths can be achieved by the business looking beyond its national markets. In other words, the business might decide to become multinational and invest in expansion overseas. This raises a further set of advantages, issues and problems that a business might face. (These will be discussed in Chapter 23 when we consider multinational business.)

We have already considered business expansion through product differentiation (see Chapter 8). In this chapter, therefore, we will focus on the other possibilities facing the firm: internal expansion via vertical integration or diversification, and external expansion via merger or takeover (whether horizontal, vertical or conglomerate). We will also investigate the increasing tendency for business to enter into strategic alliances with other businesses as an alternative to all of the above.

Definitions

Internal expansion Where a business increases its productive capacity by adding to existing plant or by building new plant.

Product differentiation In the context of growth strategies, this is where a business upgrades existing products or services so as to make them different from those of rival firms.

Vertical integration A business growth strategy that involves expanding within an existing market, but at a different stage of production. Vertical integration can be 'forward', such as moving into distribution or retail, or 'backward', such as expanding into extracting raw materials or producing components.

Diversification A business growth strategy in which a business expands into new markets outside of its current interests.

External expansion Where business growth is achieved by merger, takeover, joint venture or an agreement with one or more other firms.

Strategic alliance Where two firms work together, formally or informally, to achieve a mutually desirable goal.

Figure 15.1 Alternative growth strategy

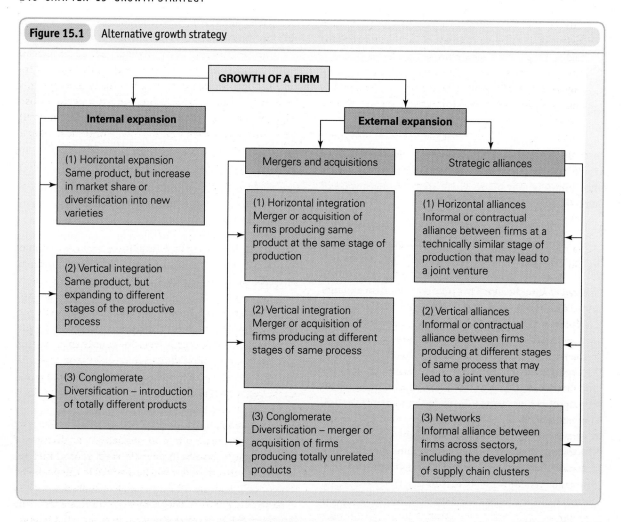

15.4 INTERNAL GROWTH

Firms can extend their product range in a number of ways and for a number of reasons. One method is that of horizontal expansion. This involves the firm producing multiple products within a similar and related activity for which there may be economies of scope (see page 184). Likewise there may be gains for the firm in providing different varieties of the product (as discussed in Chapter 8). Given our extensive discussions on this method of internal growth therefore, we concentrate in the next two sections on vertical integration and conglomerate diversification.

Growth through vertical integration

We can identify a number of specific reasons why a business might wish to expand via vertical integration. (These reasons also apply to external expansion by merger or acquisition.)

Greater efficiency. When vertical integration results in a fall in a business's long-run average costs, it is effectively experiencing various economies of scale. We can identify four categories under which vertical integration might lead to cost savings.

- *Production economies.* These occur when a business, through integration, lowers its costs by performing *complementary* stages of production within a single business unit. The classic example of this is the steel manufacturer combining the furnacing and milling stages of production, saving the costs that would have been required to reheat the iron had such operations been undertaken by independent businesses. Clearly, for most firms, performing more than one stage on a single site is likely to reduce transport costs, as semi-finished products no longer have to be moved from one plant to another.

- *Co-ordination economies.* Such economies arise from the internal structure of the business and its ability to transfer intermediate products between its various divisions. The business is able to avoid purchasing and selling expenses, including those related to the marketing and advertising

KI 22
p 181

of the product(s). If a firm can accurately forecast its intermediate product demand it may be able to reduce costs by holding lower stocks of intermediate products.

- *Managerial economies.* Even though each production stage or division might have its own management or administrative team, economies can be gained from having a single source of supervision.
- *Financial economies.* A vertically integrated business may gain various financial economies. Given the link between vertical integration and business size, such companies may be more able to negotiate favourable deals from key suppliers and secure lower borrowing rates of interest from the financial markets.

(For a more detailed analysis of economies of scale, you should refer back to Chapter 9.)

Reduced uncertainty. A business that is not vertically integrated may find itself subject to various uncertainties in the marketplace. Examples include: uncertainty over future price movements, supply reliability or access to markets.

Backward vertical integration will enable the business to control its supply chain. Without such integration the firm may feel very vulnerable, especially if there are only a few suppliers within the market. In such cases the suppliers would be able to exert considerable control over price. Alternatively, suppliers may be unreliable.

Forward vertical integration creates greater certainty in so far as it gives the business guaranteed access to distribution and retailing on its own terms. As with supply, forward markets might be dominated by large monopsonists (monopoly buyers) which are able not only to dictate price, but also to threaten market foreclosure (being shut out from a market). Forward vertical integration can remove the possibility of such events occurring.

Innovation. Having a more integrated supply chain may lead to more innovation and higher rates of technical change. Enclosing multiple stages of production within the same business should improve communication between component producers and consumers. Dialogue between component designers, manufacturers and users leads to increased possibilities for the development of productivity-improving innovations.

Monopoly power. Forward or backward vertical integration may allow the business to acquire a greater monopoly/monopsony position in the market. Depending upon the type of vertical integration, the business might be able to set prices both for final products and for factor inputs.

Barriers to entry. Vertical integration may give the firm greater power in the market by enabling it to erect entry barriers to potential competitors. For example, a firm that undertakes backward vertical integration and acquires a key input resource can effectively close the market to potential new entrants, either by simply refusing to supply a competitor,

or by charging a very high price for the factor such that new firms face an absolute cost disadvantage.

A further barrier to entry might arise from an increase in the minimum efficient size of the business. As the firm becomes more integrated, it is likely to experience greater economies of scale (i.e. long-run average costs that go on falling below their previous minimum level). New entrants are then forced to come into the market at the level of integration that existing firms are operating under. Failure to do so will mean that new entrants will be operating at an instant cost disadvantage, and hence will be less competitive.

Problems with vertical integration

The major problem with vertical integration as a form of expansion is that the security it gives the business may reduce its ability to respond to changing market demands. A business that integrates, either backward or forward, ties itself to particular supply sources or particular retail outlets. If, by contrast, it were free to choose between suppliers, inputs might be obtained at a lower price than the firm could achieve by supplying itself. Equally, the ability to shift between retail outlets would allow the firm to locate in the best market positions. This may not be possible if it is tied to its own retail network.

As with all business strategy, one course of action may well preclude the pursuit of an alternative. The decision of the business to expand its operations via vertical integration means that resources will be diverted to this goal. The potential advantages from other growth strategies, such as the spreading of risk through diversification, are lost. This is not a problem of vertical integration as such, but it represents the opportunity costs of selecting this strategy to the *exclusion* of others.

Tapered vertical integration

How can a firm gain the benefits of vertical integration but avoid the costs? One alternative means of expansion is *tapered vertical integration*. This is where a business begins producing some of an input itself, while still buying some from another firm (often through subcontracting). This growth strategy is different from a situation where you are relying totally on subcontractors to provide supply (which we will explore in section 15.7). For example, Coca-Cola and Pepsi are large vertically integrated enterprises. They have, as part of their operations, wholly owned bottling subsidiaries. However, in certain markets they subcontract

---

> **Definition**
>
> **Tapered vertical integration** Where a firm is partially integrated with an earlier stage of production: where it produces *some* of an input itself and buys some from another firm.

to independent bottlers both to produce and to market their product.

The advantages of both making and buying an input are:

- The firm, by making an input or providing a service in-house, will have information concerning the costs and profitability of such an operation. Such information helps in the negotiation of contracts with independent producers. In addition, the firm will be able to use the threat of producing more itself to ensure that independent suppliers do not exploit their supply position, which they might be able to do if they held a monopolistic position within the supply chain. The firm is not totally at the mercy of an independent third party over which it has no control.
- The firm does not require the same level of capital outlay that would be required if it were to rely solely on an input or service produced by itself. As such it is able to externalise some of the costs and risks of its business operations.

The major drawback with this growth strategy is that shared production might fail to generate economies of scale, and is hence less efficient than might otherwise be the case. In other words, if Coca-Cola bottled all its own cola, then it might achieve significantly greater economies of scale than by sharing bottling with other firms. None might be large enough to achieve the efficiency gains that a single production site might generate.

Other significant costs with subcontracting are largely borne by the firm doing the subcontracted work, not by the contractor. Many small and medium-sized enterprises (SMEs), which might see doing subcontracted work for a large firm as a means of expanding their business and hence of growing themselves, find that the relationship between them and the large firm is often a highly unequal one. SMEs find that they not only bear some of the large firm's risk, but are also easily expendable. Such vulnerability intensifies, the greater the proportion of the SME's production that is done for a particular customer. When a high level of reliance occurs, the SME finds that its business is, in essence, vertically integrated with its customer, but without the benefits that such a position should confer.

Growth through diversification

Diversification is the process whereby a firm shifts from being a single-product to a multi-product producer. Such products need not cover similar activities. We can in fact identify four directions in which diversification might be undertaken:

- using the existing technological base and market area;
- using the existing technological base and new market area;

- using a new technological base and existing market area;
- using a new technological base and new market area.

Categorising the strategies in this way would suggest that the direction of diversification is largely dependent upon both the nature of technology and the market opportunities open to the firm. But the ability to capitalise on these features depends on the experience, skills and market knowledge of the managers of the business. In general, diversification is likely to occur in areas where the business can use and adapt existing technology and knowledge to its advantage.

A good example of a highly diversified company is Virgin. The brand began as the name of a small record shop in London. It now embraces an airline, trains, banking and finance, gift 'experiences', holidays, hotels, soft drinks, mobile phones, a digital television service, Internet service provision, radio, online books, an online wine store, cosmetics, health clubs, balloon rides and even, with its Virgin Galactic brand, space travel!

Why diversification?

There are three principal factors which might encourage a business to diversify.

- *Stability*. So long as a business produces a single product in a single market, it is vulnerable to changes in that market's conditions. If a farmer produces nothing but potatoes, and the potato harvest fails, the farmer is ruined. If, however, the farmer produces a whole range of vegetable products, or even diversifies into livestock, then he or she is less subject to the forces of nature and the unpredictability of the market. Diversification therefore enables the business to *spread risk*.
- *Maintaining profitability*. Businesses might also be encouraged to diversify if they wish to protect existing profit levels. It may be that the market in which a business is currently located is saturated and that current profitability is perceived to be at a maximum. Alternatively, the business might be in a market where demand is stagnant or declining. In such cases the business is likely to see a greater return on its investment by diversifying into new product ranges located in dynamic expanding markets.
- *Growth*. If the current market is saturated, stagnant or in decline, diversification might be the only avenue open to the business if it wishes to maintain a high growth performance. In other words, it is not only the level of profits that may be limited in the current market, but also the growth of sales.

15.5 EXTERNAL GROWTH THROUGH MERGER

A *merger* is a situation in which, as a result of mutual agreement, two firms decide to bring together their business operations. A merger is distinct from a *takeover* in so far as a takeover involves one firm bidding for another's shares (often against the will of the directors of the target firm). One firm thereby acquires another.

The distinction between merger and takeover is an important one. For example, an important difference is that, in order to acquire a firm, a business will require finance, whereas a merger might simply involve two firms swapping their existing shares for shares in the newly created merged company. A further difference might concern managerial relations between the two businesses. A merger implies that managers, through negotiation, have reached an agreement acceptable to both sides, whereas a takeover involves one group of managers, working in opposition to another group, looking to fend off the aggressor. The acquired firm usually finds its management team dismissed following such action!

In order to avoid confusion at this stage, we will use the term 'merger' to refer to *both* mergers ('mutual agreements') and takeovers ('acquisitions'), although where necessary we will draw a distinction between the two. Before proceeding we need to give some consideration to the types of merger and acquisition. We distinguished three types in Figure 15.1.

- A *horizontal merger* is where two firms at the same stage of production within an industry merge. An example of this is the acquisition of Esporta by Virgin Active in 2011. This expanded the number of fitness centres and racket clubs owned by Virgin Active in the UK from 69 to 124. An example from the technology sector was the acquisition in 2012 of the photo sharing business Instagram by Facebook for £628 million.
- A *vertical merger* is where businesses at different stages of production within the same industry merge. As such we might identify backward and forward vertical mergers for any given firm involved. One example of this is where TomTom, the Dutch producer of portable navigation devices (e.g. satnavs in cars), bought TeleAtlas, the Dutch provider of navigable maps, in 2008. Another controversial example was the purchase of the British software company, Autonomy Corporation, by Hewlett Packard in 2011. Also Google purchased the mobile device producer, Motorola Mobility, in 2012. However the deal did not last long as Google sold the firm to the Chinese personal computer and mobile device producer, Lenovo, in 2014. The purchase of Motorola Mobility by Lenovo is another example of a horizontal merger.
- A *conglomerate merger* is where firms in totally unrelated industries merge. Many of the big multinational corporations operate in a number of sectors and regularly buy other firms. For example, in 2004 the US conglomerate group General Electric purchased Vivendi, the conglomerate multimedia firm which owned the US media and entertainment firms NBC and Universal. Google has also acquired a large number of firms in a range of different sectors. For example in 2014 it acquired a company that makes thermostats (Nest) and one that makes high-altitude drones (Titan).

Why merge?

Why do firms want to merge with or take over others? Is it purely that they want to grow: are mergers simply evidence of the hypothesis that firms are growth maximisers? Or are there other motives that influence the predatory drive?

Merger for growth. Mergers provide a much quicker means to growth than does internal expansion. Not only does the firm acquire new capacity, but it also acquires additional consumer demand. Building up this level of consumer demand by internal expansion might have taken a considerable length of time.

The telecommunications, media and technology sector has seen many mergers in recent times where companies in different market segments have come together. The acquisition in 2000 for $162 billion of Time Warner by America Online (AOL), the Internet group, brought together a firm strong in media distribution with a media content provider. The two businesses were clearly complementary and allowed AOL to grow and expand its range of media-based interests. Google has also used mergers as a key part of its growth strategy. Up until April 2015, it had purchased over 180 companies as part of its expansion plans. Some of the bigger deals included the acquisitions of YouTube, DoubleClick and Motorola.

Definitions

Merger The outcome of a mutual agreement made by two firms to combine their business activities.

Takeover Where one business acquires another. A takeover may not necessarily involve mutual agreement between the two parties. In such cases, the takeover might be viewed as 'hostile'.

Horizontal merger Where two firms in the same industry at the same stage of the production process merge.

Vertical merger Where two firms in the same industry at different stages of the production process merge.

Conglomerate merger Where two firms in different industries merge.

Merger for economies of scale. Once the merger has taken place, the constituent parts can be reorganised through a process of 'rationalisation'. The result can be a reduction in costs. For example, only one head office will now be needed. On the marketing side, the two parts of the newly merged company may now share distribution and retail channels, benefiting from each other's knowledge and operation in distinct market segments or geographical locations.

The merger of SBC Communications Inc. and AT&T Corp. in 2005 has made the new company, AT&T Inc., the largest telecommunications company in the USA and one of the largest in the world. According to the *Financial Times* in February 2006, the merger was expected ultimately to result in total cost savings of $18 billion, largely as a result of rationalisation in the combined business. It also resulted in dramatic growth in parts of the business as customers saw the benefits of being on a larger telecommunications network.

Pause for thought

Which of the three types of merger (horizontal, vertical and conglomerate) are most likely to lead to (a) reductions in average costs; (b) increased market power?

Merger for monopoly power. Here the motive is to reduce competition and thereby gain greater market power and larger profits. With less competition, the firm will face a less elastic demand and be able to charge a higher percentage above marginal cost. What is more, the new more powerful company will be in a stronger position to regulate entry into the market by erecting effective entry barriers, thereby enhancing its monopoly position yet further.

Merger for increased market valuation. A merger can benefit shareholders of *both* firms if it leads to an increase in the stock market valuation of the merged firm. If both sets of shareholders believe that they will make a capital gain on their shares, then they are more likely to give the go-ahead for the merger.

Merger to reduce uncertainty. Firms face uncertainty at two levels. The first is in their own markets. The behaviour of rivals may be highly unpredictable. Mergers, by reducing the number of rivals, can correspondingly reduce uncertainty. At the same time, they can reduce the *costs* of competition (e.g. reducing the need to advertise).

The second source of uncertainty is the economic environment. In a period of rapid change, such as often accompanies a boom, firms may seek to protect themselves by merging with others.

BOX 15.1   GLOBAL MERGER ACTIVITY

An international perspective

What have been the trends, patterns and driving factors in mergers and acquisitions (M&A) around the world in recent years? An overview of cross-border M&A is given in diagram (a).

The 1990s saw a rapid growth in M&As as the world economy boomed. Then with a slowing down in economic growth after 2000, M&A activity declined, both in value and in the number of deals. But from 2004 to 2007 they rose back dramatically with the rapid growth in the world economy.

Then in 2008, there was a global banking crisis followed by the credit crunch and recession, leading to a substantial decline in M&A activity. From 2009 to 2011 the number of M&As started to rise again as firms restructured following the crisis (see diagram (a)). Many large firms attempted to acquire weakened competitors or purchase undervalued complementary businesses. However, activity slowed down again from 2011 to 2013 before increasing once more in 2014.

The 1990s

The early years of the 1990s saw relatively low M&A activity as the world was in recession, but as world economic growth picked up, so worldwide M&A activity increased. Economic growth was particularly rapid in the USA, which became the major target for acquisitions.

There was also an acceleration in the process of 'globalisation'. With the dismantling of trade barriers around the world and increasing financial deregulation, so international competition increased. Companies felt the need to become bigger in order to compete more effectively.

In Europe, M&A activity was boosted by the development of the single European market, which came into being in January 1993. Companies took advantage of the abolition of trade barriers in the EU, which made it easier for them to operate on an EU-wide basis. As 1999 approached, and with it the arrival of the euro, so European merger activity reached fever pitch, stimulated also by the strong economic growth experienced throughout the EU.

By 2000, the number of annual worldwide M&As was some three times the level of 1990. Around this time there were some very large mergers indeed. These included a $67 billion marriage of pharmaceutical companies Zeneca of the UK and Astra of Sweden in 1998, a $183 billion takeover of telecoms giant Mannesmann of Germany by Vodafone of the UK in 1999 and a $40.3 billion takeover of Orange of the UK by France Telecom in 2000.

Other sectors in which merger activity was rife included financial services and the privatised utilities sector. In the UK, in particular, most of the privatised water and electricity companies were taken over, with buyers attracted by the sector's monopoly profits. French and US buyers were prominent.

The 2000s

The number of cross-border deals peaked at 10 576 in 2000 and had a combined total value of over $950 billion. However, a worldwide economic slowdown after 2000 led to a fall in both the number and value of mergers throughout most of the

Merger due to opportunity. A widely held theory concerning merger activity is that it occurs simply as a consequence of opportunities that may arise: opportunities that are often unforeseen. Therefore business mergers are largely unplanned and, as such, virtually impossible to predict. Dynamic business organisations will be constantly on the lookout for new business opportunities as they arise.

Other motives. Other motives for mergers include:

- Getting bigger so as to become less likely to be taken over oneself.
- Merging with another firm so as to defend it from an unwanted predator (the 'White Knight' strategy).
- Asset stripping. This is where a firm takes over another and then breaks it up, selling off the profitable bits and probably closing down the remainder.
- Empire building. This is where owners or managers favour takeovers because of the power or prestige of owning or controlling several (preferably well-known) companies.
- Geographical expansion. The motive here is to broaden the geographical base of the company by merging with a firm in a different part of the country or the world.
- Reducing levels of taxation. It has been argued that a number of takeovers in the pharmaceutical industry have

been motivated by the desire to reduce the company's tax bill. Under certain conditions if an American firm purchases a business outside of the USA, it can switch its residence for tax purposes to the country of the firm it has acquired. This was one reason why the American pharmaceutical company Pfizer made a $100 billion bid to purchase the UK company AstraZeneca in April 2014. The move could have cut its rate of corporation tax from 27 per cent to 20 per cent. The bid was rejected.

Mergers will generally have the effect of increasing the market power of those firms involved. This could lead to less choice and higher prices for the consumer. For this reason, mergers have become the target for government competition policy. (Such policy is the subject of Chapter 21.)

Do mergers result in the anticipated gains?

The record of many mergers and acquisitions appears to be rather disappointing. A recent example that appears to have gone badly wrong was the $11.1 billion takeover of Autonomy by Hewlett Packard (HP) in October 2011. HP had purchased Autonomy in order to help it move into the software market. In November 2012 HP shocked the business world by announcing that the company it had purchased just a year earlier had fallen in value by $8.8 billion. HP accused

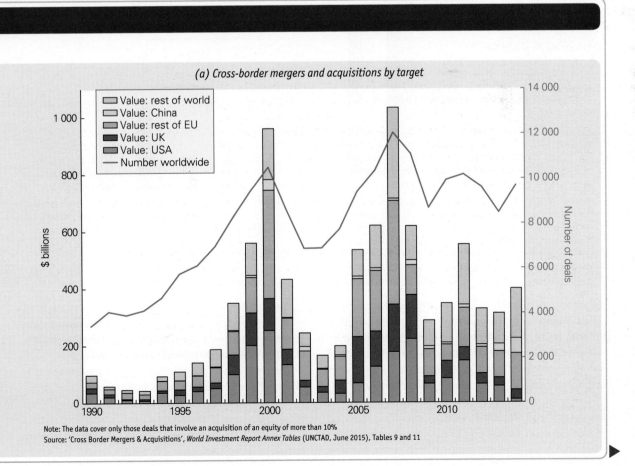

(a) Cross-border mergers and acquisitions by target

Note: The data cover only those deals that involve an acquisition of an equity of more than 10%
Source: 'Cross Border Mergers & Acquisitions', *World Investment Report Annex Tables* (UNCTAD, June 2015), Tables 9 and 11

world. The value of cross-border M&As in 2003 was just under $167 billion – a fall of 82.5 per cent from the peak of three years earlier. Activity began to increase again after 2003 as economic growth in the world economy began to accelerate.

In 2007 the number of cross-border mergers reached a new peak of 12 044 and had a combined total value of over $1000 billion. However, in 2008 and 2009, as recession took hold, both the number and value of cross-border M&As fell quite dramatically. Recession is a difficult time for deal making and the number of withdrawn mergers – that is, where two firms agree in principle to merge but later pull out of a deal – increased. As diagram (a) shows, the value of cross-border M&As in 2009 was just $288 billion– a fall of 72 per cent from the record high in 2007.

With the faltering recovery of 2010 there was a small increase in global M&A. However, the eurozone crisis and fears about the state of the public finances of the USA had a negative impact on M&A activity in 2012 and 2013.

Furthermore, the worldwide pattern of cross-border M&A activity had changed between the mid-1990s and the post-financial crisis period of 2008–14. Diagram (b) illustrates three interesting trends.

■ First, North America saw a fall in its global share of cross-border M&As from 24.6 per cent in the mid-1990s to 20.1 per cent between 2009 and 2014; and its share measured by value fell from 32.2 per cent to 25.6 per cent.

■ Second, Asian countries (excluding Japan) saw a dramatic growth in their share of the number of cross-border M&As from 7.7 per cent in the mid-1990s to 16.4 per cent for the period 2009–14. The growth in their share of the value increased from 5.2 per cent to 13.2 per cent. Two nations in the region, China and India, have been particularly attractive because their economies are growing rapidly; they have low costs, notably cheap skilled labour and low tax rates; and they are becoming more receptive to all forms of foreign direct investment, including M&As.

■ Third, EU countries saw a reduction in their share of the number of cross-border M&As from 49.4 per cent to 37.7 per cent; and a fall in their share of the value, from 42.1 per cent to 36.7 per cent. In 2007, the biggest completed cross-border M&A was the €70 billion ($98.3 billion) purchase of the Dutch Bank ABN-AMRO by RFS Holdings, a consortium of the Royal Bank of Scotland, Santander and Fortis. This occurred just before the banking crisis, which put a huge strain on the finances of the acquiring companies and was a major contributing factor to RBS having to be bailed out by the UK government in October 2008.

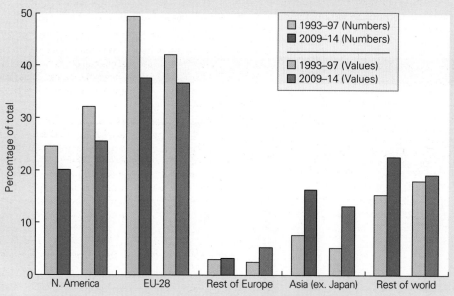

(b) Cross-border mergers and acquisitions by target region (% of total number and value)

Legend:
- 1993–97 (Numbers)
- 2009–14 (Numbers)
- 1993–97 (Values)
- 2009–14 (Values)

Source: 'Cross Border Mergers & Acquisitions', *World Investment Report Annex Tables* (UNCTAD, June 2015), Tables 9 and 11

the management at Autonomy of using illegal accounting activities before the takeover in order deliberately to inflate the true value of the business. Executives at Autonomy accused HP of completely mismanaging the integration of Autonomy into its business after the merger. At the time of writing both parties were involved in a bitter legal case.

The previous example is an extreme case, so how can you judge if most M&As have been successful?

One common method is to look at what happens to the share price of the acquiring company both before and after the takeover. If the merged company manages to attain all of the perceived benefits from the deal (economies of scale, greater revenue, etc.) then it should become more profitable and this should be reflected in the share price.

However, other factors will affect share prices and this needs to be controlled for. Most studies use the share price of other firms in the same sector as a control group. Thus if the share price of the merged firm outperforms that of other firms in the same sector then it can be argued that the merger has been a success.

There were also some high-value cross-border M&As in the EU nations during this latter period, and some of these deals were between firms within the EU. In 2011, for example, the biggest completed cross-border M&A was the $25.1 billion purchase of International Power PLC, an electricity generation company, by GDF Suez Energy.

Other big cross-border purchases in 2011 involving firms based in EU countries included a $21.2 billion deal for the French pharmaceutical company Sanofi-Aventis to purchase the US biotech company Genzyme Corp and a $10.8 billion deal for the UK-based firm SABMiller to purchase Foster's Group in Australia. In 2013 AB-InBev completed an $18 billion acquisition of Grupo Modelo, a Mexican owned brewer.[1]

Some consequences of cross-border M&A activity

When viewed in terms of long-run trends, cross-border M&As are becoming more common as globalisation gathers pace. In the mid-1990s they accounted for about 16 per cent of all deals, whereas now they account for over 40 per cent.

In the UK, cross-border deals are more frequent than internal deals. The Office for National Statistics reported that in 2014 there were 203 acquisitions by UK companies abroad or by foreign companies into the UK. By contrast, there were 173 acquisitions of UK companies by other UK companies.[2]

M&As are a rapid entry strategy for firms that want to gain an immediate entry hold on an overseas market. However, they can raise concerns about national sovereignty, i.e. the extent to which governments have control over their industrial base when foreign firms are present in the domestic economy. For example, the takeover of the nuclear electricity generator, British Energy, by the French firm EDF in 2008 raises issues about the direction of long-term nuclear energy strategy in the UK.

Horizontal cross-border mergers. A horizontal merger or acquisition of a domestic firm by an overseas firm may not alter the number of firms competing in the sector if the foreign firm is new to the market and merely replaces an existing firm. However, its presence may generate greater competition and innovation in the industry if the new owners bring with them fresh techniques and ways of doing business.

On the other hand, if the foreign firm is already present in the domestic economy and it then takes over a rival, the number of firms in the industry is reduced. Again, this may be beneficial for consumers if the costs of the merged firms fall and they subsequently compete vigorously with other firms in the domestic market on price and product range. However, as Chapters 11 and 12 show, it is also possible that fewer firms in the industry means less competition and higher prices.

Vertical cross-border mergers. Vertical and conglomerate cross-border M&As are less common than their horizontal counterparts but they too come with potential costs as well as benefits. For example, a backward vertical M&A can help a firm compete globally by reducing its supply costs, but it can impose harsh terms on suppliers in the domestic economy where it operates in order to achieve this. Forward vertical M&A into, say, the retail sector can help a foreign firm secure a domestic market and offer customers a better service, but they may now move away from supplying rival retailers on comparable terms so that customer choice is reduced.

Conglomerate cross-border mergers. Conglomerate M&As can have the same positive and detrimental impacts as those associated with horizontal and vertical M&A. However, the large size and diverse product range of the conglomerate bring with it additional costs and benefits.

For example, acquired subsidiaries of conglomerates can gain access to considerable managerial expertise and other resources, including technology and cheaper finance. This can mean greater benefits for customers if competition prevails. But if acquired subsidiaries can access cheaper finance than domestic firms, this may deter new investment by home-based firms, thereby reducing competition.

In addition, access to cheaper finance may allow conglomerate subsidiaries the opportunity to engage in predatory pricing behaviour, i.e. offering prices below cost in order to drive rival businesses out of the market. Once rivals have left the sector, the predator firm can raise prices once again (see pages 287 and 373).

Most cross-border M&As are good for society. That they exist is a sign of healthy global capital markets, where funds can be borrowed or shares purchased in order that new firms can replace older, possibly under-performing firms. Whilst there are often job losses through M&As, new owners often provide stability and generate new employment growth. That said, to maximise the benefits of cross-border M&As, governments have to be wary of the potential downsides.

1. *Are the motives for merger likely to be different in a recession from in a period of rapid economic growth?*

2. *Use newspaper and other resources to identify the costs and benefits of a recent cross-border merger or acquisition.*

[1] *World Investment Report*, Annex Tables (UNCTAD, September 2014).
[2] *Mergers and Acquisitions involving UK Companies, Q4 2014* (ONS, March 2015).

Recent studies that have adopted this approach have found that about a third of deals increase shareholder value; about a third perform no better than other firms in the same sector; and about a third actually perform worse. This implies that approximately two-thirds of deals fail to achieve the anticipated gains.

A survey of over 350 executives carried out by the Economics Intelligence Unit in 2012 identified the five most important factors that resulted in disappointing M&As.

These are illustrated below with the percentage of respondents who considered it a major or very major factor:

- Due diligence failed to highlight critical issues (59 per cent).
- Overestimated synergies: i.e. cost reductions, growth in revenue (55 per cent).
- Failed to recognise insufficient strategic fit (49 per cent).
- Failed to assess cultural fit during (46 per cent).
- Problems integrating management teams and retaining staff (46 per cent).

15.6 EXTERNAL GROWTH THROUGH STRATEGIC ALLIANCE

We noted (section 15.3) that a major form of growth for firms was that of strategic alliances – a broad term that covers a number of collaborative arrangements across one or more sectors. These alliances may involve some joint ownership and sharing of resources; they may be contractual arrangements or agreements based on trust between parties to supply and distribute goods. Strategic alliances may be horizontal or vertical, or involve networks of firms across industries (see Figure 15.1 on page 246).

Types of strategic alliance

Horizontal strategic alliances

Horizontal strategic alliances are formal or informal arrangements between firms to co-operate on a particular activity at the same stage of production. This may involve the establishment of a **joint venture**. Examples of this include the decision in 2012 by Kellogg Company and Wilmar International to enter into a joint venture for the manufacture, sale and distribution of cereal and snacks in China. Jaguar Land Rover also entered into a deal with Chery Automobile in 2012 to manufacture and sell cars in the Chinese market.

Figure 15.2 shows the current status of the major strategic alliances in the airline industry. In addition to the global alliances illustrated in Figure 15.2, there are many bilateral arrangements between the airlines on specific routes. Indeed, many airlines see these as more significant than belonging to one of the three global airline alliances. For example, Emirates, whilst refusing to join one of the three global alliances, formed a 10-year strategic alliance with Qantas in September 2012 to align ticket prices and flight schedules between Europe and Australia. This agreement led to Qantas switching its stopover destination for many of its European flights from Singapore to Dubai. It previously had been in a similar arrangement with BA. This agreement

Definitions

Horizontal strategic alliances A formal or informal arrangement between firms jointly to provide a particular activity at a similar stage of the same technical process.

Joint venture Where two or more firms set up and jointly own a new independent firm.

Figure 15.2 Airline strategic alliances

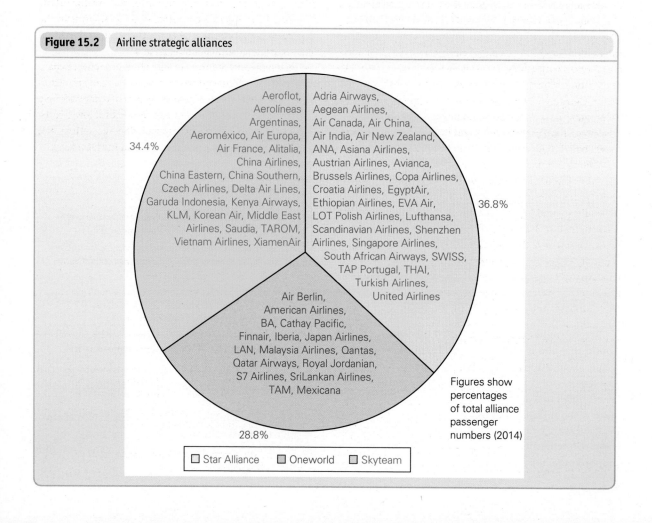

34.4%

Aeroflot, Aerolíneas Argentinas, Aeroméxico, Air Europa, Air France, Alitalia, China Airlines, China Eastern, China Southern, Czech Airlines, Delta Air Lines, Garuda Indonesia, Kenya Airways, KLM, Korean Air, Middle East Airlines, Saudia, TAROM, Vietnam Airlines, XiamenAir

Adria Airways, Aegean Airlines, Air Canada, Air China, Air India, Air New Zealand, ANA, Asiana Airlines, Austrian Airlines, Avianca, Brussels Airlines, Copa Airlines, Croatia Airlines, EgyptAir, Ethiopian Airlines, EVA Air, LOT Polish Airlines, Lufthansa, Scandinavian Airlines, Shenzhen Airlines, Singapore Airlines, South African Airways, SWISS, TAP Portugal, THAI, Turkish Airlines, United Airlines

36.8%

Air Berlin, American Airlines, BA, Cathay Pacific, Finnair, Iberia, Japan Airlines, LAN, Malaysia Airlines, Qantas, Qatar Airways, Royal Jordanian, S7 Airlines, SriLankan Airlines, TAM, Mexicana

28.8%

Figures show percentages of total alliance passenger numbers (2014)

☐ Star Alliance   ☐ Oneworld   ☐ Skyteam

had lasted for 17 years. Qantas also remains in the One World Alliance and continues to cross-sell seats with BA.

Contractual agreements between firms at the same stage of production include the establishment of a *franchise* (though there are also vertical franchise agreements). A franchise usually involves another party agreeing to take on the product format of the franchisor in return for a fee. Two of the most famous examples of companies that have grown by using franchise arrangements are Subway and McDonalds.

Another form of contractual agreement is that of *licensing*. Some lagers, beers and soft drinks are sold in the UK under licence. For example Britvic has had licensing agreements with PepsiCo for the bottling of a number of products including Pepsi, Gatorade and Lipton Ice Tea.

Some informal horizontal agreements might focus upon very specific stages in the supply chain. An example here is the decision by three of the world's largest steel manufacturers, NKK, Kawasaki and ThyssenKrupp, to share information on the technology for producing car panels.

Vertical strategic alliances

Vertical strategic alliances are formal or informal arrangements between firms operating at different stages of an activity to provide jointly a particular product or service. Examples of vertical joint ventures include the company FilmFlex, a video-on-demand service, provided for customers in the UK. This service was provided jointly by Walt Disney Television International and Sony Pictures Television. In the UK it operates services with Film4, TalkTalk and mobile operator EE. The venture brings film and TV makers into a specialist retail sector. Customers can order and watch a particular film or TV programme from their own home or mobile device when it is convenient for them. Sony and Disney sold FilmFlex to the US-based company Vubiquity in May 2014.

Where a number of companies join together to provide a good or service, the term *consortium* is used. In recent years, many consortia have been created. A consortium is usually created for very specific projects, such as a large civil engineering work. As such they have a very focused objective and once the project is completed the consortium is usually dissolved. TransManche Link, the Anglo-French company that built the Channel Tunnel, is an example of a defunct consortium. Camelot, the company that runs the UK National Lottery, was previously owned in equal shares by Cadbury Schweppes, De La Rue, Fujitsu Services, Royal Mail Enterprises and Thales Electronics, each of which had particular expertise to bring to the consortium.

It is also possible for firms at different stages of production to form contractual agreements. For example, there are licensing deals between suppliers of mobile phones and software companies such as Adobe. Similarly, Edios and Square Enix create and manufacture games for the PlayStation 3, having been given licences by Sony. Square Enix purchased Eidos for just over £85 million in April 2009 and now produces games for the PlayStation 4. There are also licensing agreements between manufacturers of cosmetics and retailers as well as car manufacturers and car dealers. These are sometimes known in competition policy language as *vertical restraints* because the dealer is restrained by the manufacturer as to how and where it can sell the product.

One of the best-known forms of vertical contractual alliance is that of *outsourcing* or *subcontracting*. When a business outsources, it employs an independent business to manufacture or supply some service rather than conduct the activity itself. Car manufacturers are major subcontractors. Given the multitude and complexity of components that are required to manufacture a car, the use of subcontractors to supply specialist items, such as brakes and lights, seems a logical way to organise the business. Nissan in the UK, for example, has set up a supplier business park so that it can get its inputs at the right price and quality and available 'just-in-time', thereby keeping inventory costs to a minimum. Box 15.2 explores some of the issues associated with outsourcing the Apple iPhone.

Networks

Networks consist of multi-firm alliances across sectors between organisations, some of which may be formal and others informal. Sony is a good example of a company that has expanded abroad over the years through the formation of joint ventures, licensing and informal arrangements with other firms across a number of sectors. Firms in the motor vehicle, electronics, pharmaceutical and other high-tech sectors have similar arrangements.

Some networks of firms are very large and reflect expansion through internal growth as well as via mergers, acquisitions and strategic alliances. Being part of a network may give firms access to technology and resources at lower costs. It may also give greater access to global markets. However, network development is also important at the local level.

Definitions

Franchise A formal agreement whereby a company uses another company to produce or sell some or all of its product.

Licensing Where the owner of a patented product allows another firm to produce it for a fee.

Vertical strategic alliance A formal or informal arrangement between firms operating at different stages of an activity jointly to provide a product or service.

Consortium Where two or more firms work together on a specific project and create a separate company to run the project.

Vertical restraints Where a dealer is restrained by a manufacturer as to how and where it can sell a product.

Outsourcing or subcontracting Where a firm employs another firm to produce part of its output or some of its input(s).

Network The establishment of formal and informal multi-firm alliances across sectors.

Many firms have developed supply-chain clusters to support their operations and they rely increasingly on other organisations from outside the sector, such as banks, insurance companies and government. Thus, the establishment of networks allows firms to develop competitive advantage through their core business activities and other less formal means, including conversations with influential individuals and groups.

Why form strategic alliances?

There are many reasons why firms may decide to set up a strategic alliance. Often these reasons are specific to a particular time or set of circumstances.

New markets. As a business expands, possibly internationally, it may well be advantageous to join with an existing player in the market. Such a business would have local knowledge and an established network of suppliers and distributors. Similar arguments apply if a business is seeking to diversify. Rather than developing the skills, knowledge and networks necessary to succeed, the process might be curtailed by establishing an alliance with a firm already operating in the market.

Risk sharing. Many business ventures might just be too risky for a solitary firm. Creating some form of strategic alliance spreads risk and creates opportunity. The Channel Tunnel and the consortium of firms that built it is one such example. The construction of the Channel Tunnel was a massive undertaking and far too risky for any single firm to embark upon. With the creation of a consortium, risk was spread, and the various consortium members were able to specialise in their areas of expertise.

Capital pooling. Projects that might have prohibitively high start-up costs, or running costs, may become feasible if firms co-operate and pool their capital. In addition, an alliance of firms, with their combined assets and credibility, may find it easier to generate finance, whether from investors in the stock market or from the banking sector.

The past 20 years have seen a flourishing of strategic alliances. They have become a key growth strategy for business both domestically and internationally. They are seen as a way of expanding business operations quickly without the difficulties associated with the more aggressive approach of acquisition or the more lengthy process of merger.

> ### PAUSE FOR THOUGHT
>
> *What are the difficulties associated with acquisitions and mergers?*

BOX 15.2   HOW MANY FIRMS DOES IT TAKE TO MAKE AN IPHONE?

Quite a lot actually

Outsourcing is a growing and strategically important activity for modern businesses. Making decisions about what products to make in-house and what to outsource has important implications for a firm's profitability and growth.

Take the case of the iPhone. The original iPhone was introduced in 2007, and the iPhone 6 and 6Plus were launched in September 2014. Apple does not manufacture this product but instead outsources the production and assembly of the numerous different parts to various companies spread across countries in three continents. For example in 2015 it had 349 suppliers based in China, 139 based in Japan, 60 based in the USA and 42 based in Taiwan. A key issue for Apple is how best to manage this very complex production process.

Apple's main contribution is the design of the device. A specialist team designs the look and feel of the phone and its various features. Apple's engineers design the internal workings of the phone – the hardware and the necessary software – to meet the specifications of the design team. Not surprisingly, there is a lot of negotiation between these two groups before an initial specification is agreed.

At this point the supply chain team comes into operation. The engineering team will itemise the range of components and other materials that are needed and the assembly requirements. The supply chain team will then have to estimate the costs of sourcing the components and their assembly from a range of potential suppliers.

'Apple's consistently reliable and profitable operations have made their supply chain team . . . one of the most envied in the industry – they develop and source from hundreds of suppliers from around the world; manage assembly contractors; set challenging production schedules and deliver better than most in their industry.'[3]

Companies within the supply chain do not stay constant between models. The suppliers chosen by Apple are those that offer the best deal, where 'best' includes not just cost, but also quality, reliability and capacity.

Take the iPhone 6:[4] LG Display (South Korea) is the largest display panel supplier; Sony (Japan) supplies both front and rear cameras; Corning (USA) supplies the Gorilla Glass; TDK (Japan) is the major supplier of inductor coils; Taiwan Semiconductor Manufacturing Company (TSMC) is the leading supplier of the A8 processor; Jabil (USA) and Foxconn (Taiwan) supply the metal phone cases; Toshiba (Japan) and SK Hynix (South Korea) supply storage at 16GB, 64GB and 128GB; TSMC (Taiwan) supply ID sensor and fingerprint technology. Several other manufacturers supply the other parts. It is assembled in China and Brazil by two Taiwanese companies, Foxconn (a subsidiary of Hon Hai Precision Industry) and Pegatron.

---

[3] Ram Ganeshan, 'The iPhone 4 Supply Chain', *Operations Buzz*, 28 November 2010.
[4] Justin Wong, 'iPhone 6: Apple Supply Chain Revisited', OPS rules, 15 December 2014.

15.7 EXPLAINING EXTERNAL FIRM GROWTH: A TRANSACTION COSTS APPROACH

By way of concluding this chapter it is worth considering a theoretical approach to understanding how external growth may occur. We examined the transaction cost approach (see Chapter 3) when explaining why firms exist. This approach, developed by the economist Oliver Williamson, can also be useful in illustrating the growth of firms, particularly by strategic alliance or vertical integration.

Consider two firms, one a motor vehicle manufacturer, the other a supplier of car exhausts. These two parties will have invested heavily in a highly specific set of assets which have little or no alternative use outside of making cars or exhausts, respectively. In other words, they both have sunk costs. Both the car and the exhaust manufacturer will also be involved in frequent transactions with each other. The car manufacturer sells a lot of cars and so will need a lot of exhausts on a regular basis. In addition, if the economic environment is uncertain and there is information asymmetry in the exchange then the potential for moral hazard exists (see pages 98–104).

Consider the following. The car manufacturer is looking for a supplier of exhausts. It puts out an invitation to tender for the contract. A number of potential suppliers put in bids and one supplier is chosen because it offers the best price and can deliver the best quality, and does so 'just-in-time' to keep inventory costs low. Once the contract has been signed, the two parties to the exchange become 'locked in' to the contract. It is at this stage that one or both of the parties could act opportunistically and exploit the situation because they have different sets of information about the markets in which they operate.

For example, the motor vehicle manufacturer could say to the supplier of exhausts that car sales are poorer than expected because of a fall in demand. As a result it might ask the exhaust manufacturer to lower the price at which it sells exhausts. Alternatively, the exhaust manufacturer may claim that it needs a higher price for its exhausts because the cost of steel has risen. The possibility of this renegotiation of the contract arises because each party to the exchange has a different set of information. But what should either party do if they were faced with this problem?

Both firms have invested in highly specific equipment that may have been specially tailored to meet this contract.

With the launch of the iPhone 6, although many of the suppliers remained the same, some had bigger roles to play than previously, while some had smaller ones. For example, for the first time Samsung was not the leading supplier of the A series processors. However, it has been reported that it may replace TSMC as the lead supplier of both A8 chips and A9 chips for future iPhones.

Power and value added

With such a large share of the market, Apple has considerable market power when negotiating with suppliers. It has been estimated that it costs Apple just over $200 in parts and labour to build a 16GB iPhone 6. The biggest expense is the 4.7-inch touchscreen that cost $45. The camera also costs $11.

When these and other costs are subtracted from the price of around $650, this leaves Apple with around $450 of value added to cover R&D, administration, marketing, distribution and pre-tax profit. This gross profit margin of around 69 per cent is very similar to that for the iPhone 5. The gross profit margin on the first iPhone released in 2007 was somewhat lower at 55 per cent. This product has proved to be one of the most profitable in the world. In January 2015 Apple reported record quarterly profits of $18 billion (£11.9 billion) – the largest ever in corporate history. A key factor in explaining these profits was the iPhone. 74.5 million handsets were sold in the final quarter of 2014 and Apple reported revenues of $74.6 billion for the same period.

Apple's market power works in two ways.

First, with suppliers eager to supply parts to such a large purchaser, Apple can use this competition to drive down component and assembly prices. Most of the parts are fairly generic and Apple thus has a choice of suppliers. However, it did experience sourcing problems before the launch of the iPhone 6. Apple supported GTAT as a new supplier of sapphire screens. The company went bankrupt and Apple quickly had to switch designs back to using Gorilla Glass.

Second, with a buoyant demand for iPhones (and other Apple products), Apple can charge a premium price. It has a monopoly on its specific designs and thus demand for the finished product is relatively inelastic.

The story of iPhones applies also to iPods, iPads and Macs. Each uses parts sourced from around the world and each features unique design properties that give the product a loyal following.

1. *What factors determine the size of the value-added for iPhones? Why do you think the figure is larger for later versions of the iPhone?*
2. *Is value-added the same as normal or supernormal profit?*

BOX 15.3   THE DAY THE WORLD STOPPED

Northern Rock: a cautionary tale of business growth

In 1997 Northern Rock converted from a building society – a residential mortgage lender owned by its savers and borrowers – into a bank quoted on the stock market. During the next 10 years it reduced the number of branches from 128 to 76 but expanded its online banking capabilities and mortgage business dramatically.

In January 2007 the bank announced pre-tax profits of £627 million for 2006, 27 per cent above 2005 levels. Its share of the UK mortgage market had grown from 11 per cent in 2006 to 13.4 per cent in December 2006 and to 18.9 per cent in June 2007. Northern Rock had grown from being a small local lender in the north-east of England to being the fifth largest supplier of mortgages in the UK.

However, all was not well. On 13 September 2007 Northern Rock was granted emergency financial support from the Bank of England in its role as lender of the last resort. The share price plummeted (see diagram).

The following day saw the beginning of a 'run on the bank', something that had not occurred since Overend, Gurney & Co. collapsed in 1866. Not only were there queues outside the branch offices of Northern Rock, but the online banking website crashed as depositors withdrew their savings.

Over the next few months the government issued some £25 billion in loans so that the bank could continue operating. In spite of several attempts to find a private-sector 'white knight' to take it over, the government decided to take it into full public ownership on 22 February 2008 and shares were finally suspended.

What went wrong?

Commercial retail banks have two major objectives. They should make profit for their shareholders by engaging in activities that include lending but have sufficient liquidity (e.g. cash) in order to meet the requirements of their customers (see Chapter 28).

Northern Rock relied largely on making profit through mortgage lending, which was in marked contrast to the strategy of other commercial banks which had a more diversified range of services. Northern Rock had an exceptional IT system that not only lowered the costs of mortgage services but also showed mortgage brokers and independent financial advisers, the principal source of its mortgage business, that the company had cheap mortgages for sale.

While house prices were rising (see Box 4.1) the demand for mortgages kept rising, but this also meant that individuals needed bigger mortgages. If an individual wanted a 100 per cent (or even 125 per cent) mortgage at competitive rates, Northern Rock would provide it if they were viewed as being able to pay it back.

A bank makes profit on the interest that it earns from mortgage customers. However, in providing high-value mortgages, banks have to find money from deposits to pay house sellers or borrow from elsewhere. Northern Rock largely adopted the latter strategy, because attracting new deposits is a more costly exercise. The bank bundled its mortgages together and packaged them as financial instruments (bonds), which it then sold to investors on money markets around the world at a favourable interest rate, at least initially. These loans were largely accepted as secure investments in money markets because investors believed that Northern Rock customers were unlikely to default on their mortgages.

This practice of 'securitisation' is legitimate and allowed under international banking regulations, but Northern Rock engaged in extremely high levels of money market lending. According to the BBC, 61 per cent of its lending was from the money market. This was far in excess of its rivals such as HBOS (33 per cent), RBS (23 per cent), Barclays (20 per cent) and Lloyds (16 per cent).[5] In using the money markets to borrow money at low interest rates, it gained a competitive edge over its rivals. The more money it borrowed, the more mortgages it could afford to provide and the more profit it would make.

Mortgage lending backed by securitised assets was the 'goose that laid the golden egg', and so Northern Rock continued to focus its business efforts in this direction. Even though there had been some disquiet among financial commentators about this strategy, the risks were viewed at the time as acceptable by the UK financial regulators – the Financial Services Authority (FSA) and the Bank of England.

In 2007, as monetary policy in the UK tightened faster than expected, Northern Rock issued a tranche of mortgages at interest rates that were lower than those it had to pay in the market to finance them. The bank issued a profits warning in June and its share price fell.

Then the market for obtaining finance from securitised assets crumbled as it became clear that similar mortgage-backed assets in the USA had high levels of repayment arrears and property prices were falling rapidly. Anyone who now held a mortgage-backed asset (bond) would be highly unsure whether they could recoup its value in the presence of mortgage defaults. Thus, credit, once freely available, dried up and the term 'credit crunch' has become part of the lexicon of everyday life. Northern Rock now had mortgages that were not covered by money market loans. The goose had been mortally wounded.

The chief executive of Northern Rock had a vivid recollection of the day in 2007 when he realised the business strategy had failed.

> The world stopped on August 9. It's been astonishing, gobsmacking. Look across the full range of financial products, across the full geography of the world, the entire system has frozen.[6]

[5] See 'The downturn in facts and figures', *BBC News*, 18 February 2008, http://news.bbc.co.uk/1/hi/business/7250498.stm

---

The value of this equipment would be much lower in a transaction with a different business partner. It would therefore cost both firms money if they were to exit the deal and try to find an alternative supplier or purchaser. Williamson suggested that one party might take over or merge with the other – a vertically integrated merger would occur.

However, it is also possible that the parties engage in some other action short of a merger, largely because they

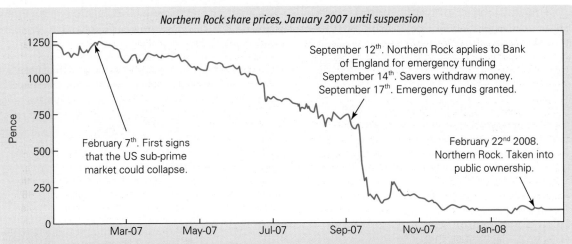

Northern Rock share prices, January 2007 until suspension

September 12th. Northern Rock applies to Bank of England for emergency funding
September 14th. Savers withdraw money.
September 17th. Emergency funds granted.

February 7th. First signs that the US sub-prime market could collapse.

February 22nd 2008. Northern Rock. Taken into public ownership.

Source: Based on data available from http://timesonline.hemscott.com/timesonline/timesonline.jsp?page=company-chart&companyId=3497&from=1/1/2007&to=22/2/2008&returnPeriod=2

The world is different now

The world of Northern Rock is very different seven and a half years after nationalisation. Questions were asked in the press and parliament about the risks involved in the Northern Rock business strategy and about the role of the FSA, the Bank of England and the Treasury as regulators. Questions were also raised about the Basel II arrangements which provide guidance, rules and standards in respect of risk management and supervision at an international level (see Chapter 28, pages 525–9).

In 2010 the bank was split into two parts. The first, Northern Rock Asset Management, now called NRAM, holds the bank's historic mortgage portfolio and toxic loans. The second, Northern Rock PLC, holds the retail and wholesale deposit business. These two banks are informally referred to by staff as the 'bad bank' and the 'good bank'. The 'good bank' with its 75 High Street branches was sold to Virgin Money in November 2011, for just under £1 billion. This was substantially below the amount pumped into the bank by the government to secure its solvency. In January 2012 Virgin Money began the process of fully integrating Northern Rock into its business and, in the process, ended the Northern Rock name. By October 2012 all the previous Northern Rock branches had been rebranded as Virgin Money Stores and the two websites were combined into Virginmoney.com.

As of April 2015 the 'bad bank', NRAM, remains under government ownership. This business has no customer branches and is closed to new business. It only services what remains of the residential mortgage book. The remaining assets of NRAM were combined with those of Bradford and Bingley into a single holding company called UK Asset Resolution (UKAR). This is a state-owned limited company which has the objective

of managing the remaining mortgages and repaying the government loans that were made as part of the bailout. In July 2012 it sold £465 million of high-quality NRAM mortgages to Virgin Money. In October 2014, UKAR announced that it had sold £1.7 billion of mortgages formerly owned by NRAM (and a further £1 billion formerly owned by Bradford and Bingley) to a consortium led by JP Morgan. In November 2015, the Chancellor of the Exchequer announced that a further £13 billion of mortgages originally owned by Northern Rock had been sold to the US business, Cerberus.[7] Some observers have commented that perhaps the assets of the so-called 'bad bank' have not proved to be as bad as people first thought.

In an attempt to reduce the risk of a similar situation in the future, the government passed the Financial Services Act in 2012. The FSA was abolished and a new regulatory framework for the financial system was established. This created two new regulatory bodies that both became operational on 1 April 2013. These were the Prudential Regulation Authority (PRA) which is a subsidiary of the Bank of England and the Financial Conduct Authority (FCA). Both of these new regulators are under the supervision of the Financial Policy Committee of the Bank of England. It is hoped that this regulatory framework will prevent a 'Northern Rock' from happening again.

1. *What are the strengths and weaknesses of diversification as a business growth strategy?*
2. *Follow the story of the successors to Northern Rock using materials from the media and consider how they have developed since Northern Rock was split.*

---

[6] 'Why Northern Rock was doomed to fail', *Daily Telegraph*, 17 September 2007.
[7] GOV.UK News Story, (November 2015).

want to carry out business transactions in a more civilised manner. Contracts can be useful devices for managing the exchange process but they can also be very difficult instruments to apply because they do not allow flexibility.

Williamson suggested, therefore, that many firms would form some intermediate arrangement – a strategic alliance – that might rely partly on contract and also on trust. Parties will have to signal to the other that they want a long-term business relationship as a means of building that trust.

A number of companies, particularly Japanese firms, have these sorts of arrangements. For example, there may be an opportunity for senior executives from each firm to sit on the boards of the other, or there may be meetings between business partners to discuss key issues. Indeed, in our example above, buyers from the car manufacturer might go out on visits with their exhaust manufacturer counterparts so that they can explain to raw materials suppliers the consequences of higher prices further up the supply chain.

Further, firms which signal that they are trustworthy business partners and that they have successfully developed resources over the long term are also more likely to engage in joint ventures.

Thus, where there are large and uncertain costs associated with market transactions, it can be beneficial to have some form of merger or an alliance. The conditions in which these might occur are often specific to the parties involved and depend on the nature of the industry as well as the prevailing and anticipated economic conditions.

In this chapter we have considered the growth of firms and the forms it may take. Although we identified various constraints on growth (section 15.2), a word of caution is still required. There can be real dangers associated with a strategy of rapid external business growth in turbulent or largely unknown environments, as the case of Northern Rock in Box 15.3 demonstrates.

SUMMARY

1a Business growth and business profitability are likely to be inversely related in the short run. A growing firm will bear certain additional costs, such as higher advertising and marketing bills.

1b In the long run, the relationship could be positive. A growing firm may take advantage of new market opportunities and may achieve greater economies of scale and increased market power. On the other hand, a rapidly growing firm may embark on various risky projects or projects with a low rate of return.

2a Constraints on business growth include: (i) financial conditions, (ii) shareholder confidence, (iii) the level and growth of market demand and (iv) managerial conditions.

2b (i) Financial conditions determine the business's ability to raise finance. (ii) Shareholder confidence is likely to be jeopardised if a firm ploughs back too much profit into investment and distributes too little to shareholders. (iii) A firm is unlikely to be able to grow unless it faces a growing demand: either in its existing market, or by diversifying into new markets. (iv) The knowledge, skills and dynamism of the management team will be an important determinant of the firm's growth.

3a A business can expand either internally or externally.

3b Internal expansion involves one or more of the following: expanding the market through product promotion and differentiation; vertical integration; diversification.

3c External expansion entails the firm expanding by merger/acquisition or by strategic alliance.

4a Vertical integration can reduce a firm's costs through various economies of scale. It can also help to reduce uncertainty, as the vertically integrated business can hopefully secure supply routes and/or retail outlets. This strategy can also enhance the business's market power by enabling it to erect various barriers to entry.

4b A vertically integrated business will trade off the security of such a strategy with the reduced ability to respond to change and to exploit the advantages that the market might present.

4c Through a process of tapered vertical integration, many firms make part of a given input themselves and subcontract the production of the remainder to one or more other firms. By making a certain amount of an input itself, the firm is less reliant on suppliers, but does not require as much capital equipment as if it produced all the input itself.

4d The nature and direction of diversification depend upon the skills and abilities of managers, and the type of technology employed.

4e Diversification offers the business a growth strategy that not only frees it from the limitations of a particular market, but also enables it to spread its risks, and seek profit in potentially fast-growing markets.

5a There are three types of merger: horizontal, vertical and conglomerate. The type of merger adopted will be determined by the aims of business: that is, whether to increase market power, improve business security or spread risks.

5b There is a wide range of motives for merger. Some have more statistical backing than others.

6a One means of achieving growth is through the formation of strategic alliances with other firms. They are a means whereby business operations can be expanded relatively quickly and at relatively low cost.

6b Types of strategic alliance include: horizontal and vertical strategic alliances and networks. They may take a number of forms: joint ventures, consortia, franchising, licensing, subcontracting and informal agreements based on trust between the parties.

6c Advantages of strategic alliances include easier access to new markets, risk sharing and capital pooling.

7 An important explanation of business growth relates to the transaction costs in markets where there are large sunk costs, frequent transactions and information differences on both sides of the exchange. This is particularly relevant in explaining the development of strategic alliances and vertical integration.

MyEconLab

This book can be supported by MyEconLab, which contains a range of additional resources, including an online homework and tutorial system designed to test and build your understanding.

You need both an access card and a course ID to access MyEconLab:

1. Is your lecturer using MyEconLab? Ask your lecturer for your course ID.

2. Has an access card been included with the book at a reduced cost? Check the inside back cover of the book.

3. If you have a course ID but no access card, go to: http://www.myeconlab.com/ to buy access to this interactive study programme.

REVIEW QUESTIONS

1 Explain the relationship between a business's rate of growth and its profitability.

2 'Business managers must constantly tread a fine line between investing in business growth and paying shareholders an "adequate" dividend on their holdings.' Explain why this is such a crucial consideration.

3 Distinguish between internal and external growth strategy. Identify a range of factors which might determine whether an internal or external strategy is pursued.

4 What is meant by the term 'vertical integration'? Why might a business wish to pursue such a growth strategy?

5 A firm can grow by merging with or taking over another firm. Such mergers or takeovers can be of three types: horizontal, vertical or conglomerate. Which of the following is an example of which type of merger (takeover)?

a) A soft drinks manufacturer merges with a pharmaceutical company.

b) A car manufacturer merges with a car distribution company.

c) A large supermarket chain takes over a number of independent grocers.

6 To what extent will consumers gain or lose from the three different types of merger identified above?

7 Assume that an independent film company, which has up to now specialised in producing documentaries for a particular television broadcasting company, wishes to expand. Identify some possible horizontal, vertical and other closely related fields. What types of strategic alliance might it seek to form and with what types of company? What possible drawbacks might there be for it in such alliances?

The small-firm sector

Business issues covered in this chapter

- How are small and medium-sized businesses defined?
- How large is the small-firm sector in the UK?
- What competitive advantages do small businesses have?
- What problems are they likely to face?
- What determines how rapidly small businesses are likely to grow?
- What policies towards small businesses do governments pursue?

KI 6
p 37

How often do you hear of small businesses making it big? Not very often, and yet many of the world's major corporations began life as small businesses. From acorns have grown oak trees! But small and large businesses are usually organised and run quite differently and face very different problems.

In this chapter we consider the place of small firms in the economy: their strengths and weaknesses, their ability to grow and the factors that limit expansion. We also consider the small-business policies of governments, both in the UK and in the European Union.

16.1 DEFINING THE SMALL-FIRM SECTOR

Unfortunately, there is no single agreed definition of a 'small' firm. In fact, a firm considered to be small in one sector of business, such as manufacturing, may be considerably different in size from one in, say, the road haulage business. Nevertheless, the most widely used definition is that adopted by the EU for its statistical data. Three categories of SME (small and medium enterprise) are distinguished. These are shown in Table 16.1.

This subdivision of small firms into three categories allows us to distinguish features of enterprises that vary

with the degree of smallness (e.g. practices of hiring and firing, pricing and investment strategies, competition and collusion, innovation). It also enables us to show changes over time in the size and composition of the small-firm sector. However, we might still question the adequacy of such a definition, given the diversity that can be found in business activity, organisational structure and patterns of ownership within the small-firm sector.

Table 16.1	EU SME definitions		
Criterion	**Micro**	**Small**	**Medium**
Maximum number of employees	9	49	249
Maximum annual turnover	€2 million	€10 million	€50 million
Maximum annual balance sheet total	€2 million	€10 million	€43 million
Maximum % owned by one, or jointly by several, enterprise(s) not satisfying the same criteria	25%	25%	25%

Note: To qualify as an SME, both the employee and the independence criteria must be satisfied and either the turnover or the balance sheet total criteria

The small-firm sector in the UK

In the UK, firms are divided into four categories by number of employees: micro (0–9 employees), small (0–49 employees) (includes micro), medium (50–249 employees), large (250 or more employees). The Department for Business, Innovation and Skills publishes annual business population estimates, which are available from its website (www.bis.gov.uk). Table 16.2 is taken from the 2011 dataset.

The most significant feature of the data is that micro businesses (between 0 and 9 employees) accounted for 95.2 per cent of all businesses and provided 26.2 per cent of all employment. The table also shows that there were 5 286 565 micro and small businesses out of a total of 5 332 875 businesses: i.e. 99.1 per cent. Micro and small businesses also accounted for 39 per cent of employment and 31.7 per cent of turnover. From such information we can see that the small-firm sector clearly represents a very important part of the UK's industrial structure.

There are significant variations between sectors in the percentage of SMEs, whether by number of firms, employment or turnover. This is illustrated in Table 16.3.

Service providers (categories G to S in Table 16.3) contribute the overwhelming number of micro and small firms

within the economy, accounting for 3 817 945 businesses, or 72.8 per cent of all small firms.

Changes over time

How has the small-firm sector changed over time? The problems associated with definition and data collection make time-series analysis of the small-firm sector very difficult and prone to various inconsistencies. However, it is possible to identify certain trends.

The Bolton Report on small firms in 1971 estimated that there were approximately 820 000 businesses employing fewer than 200 people. This figure had declined fairly consistently throughout the first part of the twentieth century, before beginning to rise again in the mid-1960s. By the turn of the century it was estimated that there were about 3.5 million small firms (i.e. employing fewer than 250 people). This figure had increased to 5.2 million by 2014. The period between 2010 and 2014 was one of particularly rapid growth, with the number of SMEs increasing by 760 000.

Pause for thought

What inconsistencies might there be in time-series data on the small-firm sector?

What is the explanation for this rise in small businesses in recent years? A wide range of factors have been advanced to explain this phenomenon, and include the following:

- *The growth in the service sector of the economy.* Many services are, by their nature, small in scale and/or specialist. For example, many small businesses have developed in the area of computer support and back-up.
- *The growth in niche markets.* Rising consumer affluence creates a growing demand for specialist products and services. Key examples might be in textiles and in other fashion/craft-based markets. Such goods and services are likely to be supplied by small firms, in which economies of scale and hence price considerations are of less relevance.

Table 16.2	Number of UK businesses, employment and turnover for the whole economy by number of employees (2014)					
Size (number of employees)	**Businesses (number)**	**Employment (000s)**	**Turnover[a] (£m ex VAT)**	**Businesses (%)**	**Employment (%)**	**Turnover (%)**
0–9 (micro)	5 076 540	8 457	666 854	95.2	26.2	17.7
10–49 (small)	210 025	4 116	529 125	3.9	12.8	14.0
50–249 (medium)	37 255	3 731	501 858	0.7	11.6	13.3
250 + (large)	9 055	15 933	2 073 631	0.2	49.4	55.0
All	5 332 875	32 237	3 771 468	100.0	100.0	100.0

[a] Excluding finance sector (Sector K) as data are not available on a comparable basis
Source: *Business Population Estimates for the UK and Regions* (BIS, 2014). Contains public-sector information licensed under the Open Government Licence (OGL) v1.0, www.nationalarchives.gov.uk/doc/open-government-licence

BOX 16.1 CAPTURING GLOBAL ENTREPRENEURIAL SPIRIT

Stimulating the growth of SMEs

There has been considerable interest in the notion of entrepreneurship in recent times and governments around the
world have increasingly made it a focus of their economic
strategy. For example, in 2015, the UK government passed
the Small Business, Enterprise and Employment Act. This
Bill aims to reduce the barriers that can sometimes limit the
ability of small businesses to innovate, grow and compete. It
includes measures to improve SMEs' access to finance, reduce
unnecessary regulation and make it easier for SMEs to bid for
government contracts. When the Act was passed the government stated that it was 'committed to fostering and encouraging the entrepreneurial spirit'.

But what exactly is an entrepreneur? Entrepreneurs are
sources of new ideas and new ways of doing things. That is,
they are at the forefront of invention and innovation, providing new products and developing markets.

The GEM

The Global Entrepreneurship Monitor (GEM) provides a
framework for analysing entrepreneurship. It suggests that
entrepreneurship is a complex phenomenon that can exist at
various stages of the development of a business. So, someone who is just starting a venture and trying to make it in a
highly competitive environment is entrepreneurial. And so
too, but in a different way, are established business owners if
they are innovative, competitive and growth-minded. Focusing on different stages of the 'entrepreneurial cycle' allows
many of the dynamic elements of SMEs to be identified and
analysed.

GEM measures the stage of the life cycle of entrepreneurship
by dividing entrepreneurs into nascent, new and established
business owners. Nascent owners are those who have established a business within the last three months. New owners
are those who have been in business between 3 and 42
months. Together, nascent and new business owners make
up 'early stage entrepreneurs', while 'established owners' –
those in business for more than 42 months – will have come
through the traumas of the initial birth and the early development stages of the firm.

GEM's Global Report[1] measures entrepreneurial activity in
a country by the percentage of those aged 18 to 64 who are
business owners, whether early stage or established. The 2014
report was based on a survey of 206 000 individuals across
73 different countries. The prevalence of all entrepreneurial
activity was highest in Uganda, where 71.4 per cent of those
surveyed indicated that they had entrepreneurial tendencies
(see diagram (a)). Thailand also had a very high incidence
of 57.4 per cent. This can be contrasted with Russia, which
had one of the lowest occurrences, with only 7.5 per cent of
those surveyed indicating an enterprising disposition. The
unweighted average for all the countries surveyed was 25.1
per cent.

Among the 23 European Union countries cited in the GEM
survey of 2014, the UK appears just above midway, with 17.3
per cent noted as early stage or established entrepreneurs. Of
the EU countries, 13 had a lower incidence than the UK, while
nine had a higher incidence. The countries with a lower incidence included France (8.3 per cent), Germany (10.6 per cent)

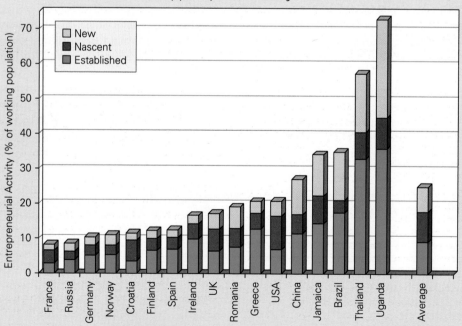

(a) Entrepreneurial activity

Note: Unweighted average is of 73 countries

Source: Based on data in *Global Entrepreneurship Monitor 2014, Executive Report* (Global Enterprise Research Association, 2015)

[1]S. Singer, J. E. Amorós and D. M. Arreola, *Global Entrepreneurship Monitor*, 2014 Global Report (GERA, 2014).

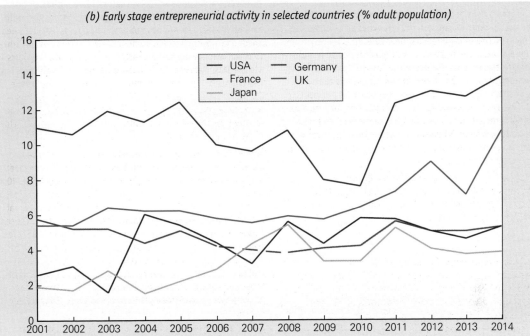

(b) Early stage entrepreneurial activity in selected countries (% adult population)

Note: Survey data was not available for Germany in 2007

Source: After data accessed 2014 from *Key Indicators* database, *Global Entrepreneurship Monitor* (Global Entrepreneurship Research Association)

and Spain (12.5 per cent), while those with higher incidence included Austria (18.8 per cent), The Netherlands (19.3 per cent) and Greece (20.8 per cent). The UK was also behind the USA (20.9 per cent) and China (27.2 per cent) in all measures of entrepreneurship.

Unfortunately, consistent time-series data are not available. Not all countries report every year and the concept of 'established entrepreneurs' was only introduced in 2005. However, there is data relevant for comparison purposes on nascent and new business owners (early stage entrepreneurial activity) for industrialised countries over the period 2001 to 2014. Diagram (b) illustrates that the UK is above France, Germany and Japan but below the USA in being involved in new venture creation, although the UK figure increased more rapidly than in the USA in the two years up to 2014.

The GEM report also includes data on the motivation for starting a business. A necessity-driven entrepreneur is someone who reports that they started a business because there were no better options available to obtain work. An opportunity-driven entrepreneur is someone who reports that they started a business because of a recognised opportunity in the market rather than having no other options for work.

Information from the 2014 GEM report indicates that the proportion of early stage entrepreneurs in the UK who established a business because of necessity-driven motives was 12.9 per cent. This compares favourably with a figure of 23.2 per cent in Germany, 34.8 per cent in Greece and 46.6 per cent in Croatia. Also 83.6 per cent of early stage entrepreneurs in the UK reported an opportunity-driven motive for starting their business compared with 75.8 per cent in

Germany, 61.5 per cent in Greece and 51.3 per cent in Croatia. The figures for the UK were very similar to the USA, which had 13.5 per cent and 81.5 per cent respectively.[2]

Challenges for UK entrepreneurs

Thus, the UK seems to be performing fairly well compared to similar nations. However, challenges remain.

Survival rates. First, longer-term survival has to be improved. The Office for National Statistics reported in November 2014 that the three-year survival rate of UK VAT-registered businesses that were established in 2008 (i.e. which were still active in 2010) was 58 per cent.[3] This figure was 7 per cent lower than the three-year survival rate for those firms that started in 2004.

The five-year survival rate was also low, with only 41.3 per cent of businesses established in 2008 still active in 2012. The five-year survival rate varied substantially by sector, ranging from a high of 53.4 per cent for businesses related to health to a low of 31.4 per cent for businesses in the finance and insurance industry. It also varied by region, with the South West having the highest survival rate of 45.5 per cent, while London had the lowest of 37.1 per cent.

Improving survival rates is important because fear of failure is commonly cited as part of the explanation for differences in enterprise and business formation rates between the UK and

---

[2]Singer et al., *Global Entrepreneurship Monitor*.
[3]'Business demography, 2013' (Office for National Statistics, 27 November 2014).

USA: 36.8 per cent of people seeking entrepreneurial opportunities in the UK, compared with 29.7 per cent in the USA, said that fear of failure would prevent them from starting a business.

Female entrepreneurs. Second, the UK needs to address the issue of low rates of female entrepreneurship. Figures from the GEM report for 2014 show that the incidence of female early stage entrepreneurial activity in the UK was 7.5 per cent whereas the figure for the USA was 11.2 per cent. The Small Business Survey for 2014[4] reports that 18 per cent of SMEs were women-led – either controlled by a woman or with a management team that is over 50 per cent female. Although low, this figure has increased from 3.2 per cent in 2001.

High-growth firms. The OECD defines high-growth firms as those with annual growth rates of at least 20 per cent (of either turnover or employment) over a three-year period, and having more than 10 employees at the beginning of the observation period. Approximately 7 per cent of SMEs in the UK meet this definition. A subset of these high-growth firms – those which were less than five years old – are referred to as 'gazelles'.

High-growth SMEs contribute dramatically to an economy's employment, innovation and growth and their presence in large numbers demonstrates a higher order of entrepreneurial dynamism within an economy. They create around a quarter of all new jobs among existing businesses. A 2014 survey of 100 fast-growing firms in the UK revealed that 70 had 150 or fewer employees and 67 had sales of £50 million or less. Almost half (44) were in the broad services sector. Examples ranged from a gym operator to a pet insurance provider. The second largest group was companies in the retail sector (36), many of whom were selling a large portion of their output via the Internet. Examples included a number of online wine merchants.[5]

However, it seems very difficult to turn fast-growing small firms in the UK from 'gazelles' into 'gorillas' – firms less than 10 (perhaps 15) years old with a presence in at least three countries and employing over 500 people. In the USA, companies such as Google, Facebook, eBay and Amazon stand out as recent examples of firms that have developed from gazelles into gorillas. In the UK, however, these beasts are much more elusive.

1. *Under what economic conditions is 'necessity' entrepreneurship likely to increase?*

2. *Is business failure necessarily a 'bad thing' for a country?*

[4] 'Small Business Survey, 2014: SME employers' (Department for Business Innovation & Skills, March 2015).
[5] 'Sunday Times Virgin Fast Track 100 Research Report 2014' (Fast Track, December 2014).

■ *New working practices which require greater labour force flexibility.* Forms of employment such as ***subcontracting*** have become more pronounced, as businesses attempt to achieve certain cost and flexibility advantages over their rivals. This often forces individuals either to set up their own companies to provide such services, or to become self-employed.

■ *Rises in the level of unemployment.* The higher the level of unemployment, the more people turn to self-employment as an alternative to trying to find work with an employer. The rise in unemployment in the 1980s, early 1990s and from 2008 to 2011 were all associated with increases in self-employment. According to the Office for National Statistics, 4.6 million people were self-employed in their main job in the UK in 2014. This represents 15 per cent of the total number of people in work and is the highest figure since the data were first collected over 40 years ago. It compares to a figure of 13 per cent in 2008 and just 8.7 per cent in 1975.

Total employment in the second quarter of 2014 was 1.1 million higher than it had been in the first quarter of 2008, just before the economic downturn began. The majority of this increase – 732 000 or 67 per cent – was due to a rise in self-employment. Surprisingly, this recent large increase was not caused by a greater percentage of people entering self-employment; over the five-year period 2009–14, this inflow rate had remained fairly constant at around 37 per cent. The big change was a fall in the percentage of people *leaving* self-employment; this outflow figure had been around 35 per cent in previous five-year periods, but fell to 23 per cent in the 2009–14 period. One reason for this fall may have been the negative impact of the recession on the number of opportunities for people to move from self-employment back into employment.

■ *The role of government.* Government attitudes and policy initiatives shifted in favour of small-business creation during the 1980s. The development of an ***enterprise culture***, in which individuals were to be given the opportunity, and various financial incentives, to start their own businesses, has been one of the principal aims of all governments in recent times. (In section 16.3 we shall consider government policy initiatives in more detail.)

Definitions

Subcontracting The business practice where various forms of labour (frequently specialist) are hired for a given period of time. Such workers are not directly employed by the hiring business, but either employed by a third party or self-employed.

Enterprise culture One in which individuals are encouraged to become wealth creators through their own initiative and effort.

Table 16.3 SME share of UK private-sector businesses, employment and turnover by industrial sector (2015)

Industrial sector SIC 2007	Businesses		Employment		Turnover	
	Total number	SME (% share)	Total employment (000s)	SME (% share)	Total turnover (£m)	SME (% share)
All industries	5 389 450	99.9	25 871	60.3	3 710 278	47.3
A Agriculture, forestry and fishing	153 360	99.9	46	94.8	41 710	91.8
B, D, E Mining, electricity, gas, water	29 390	99.7	365	n.a.	204 014	18.2
C Manufacturing	275 565	99.6	2 640	57.5	601 966	30.2
F Construction	956 105	100.0	2 042	85.5	245 291	74.9
G Wholesale, retail and repairs	522 690	99.8	4 970	46.0	1 359 547	45.5
H Transportation and storage	274 840	99.8	1 364	47.1	172 244	42.0
I Hotels and restaurants	183 180	99.6	2 163	60.5	86 631	56.5
J Information and communication	338 905	99.9	1 301	61.5	213 914	44.4
K Financial and insurance activities	84 140	99.6	1 063	27.6	n.a.	n.a.
L Real estate activities	105 045	99.9	471	75.3	51 332	75.1
M Professional, scientific and technical activities	792 885	99.9	2 455	76.5	266 398	66.3
N Administrative and support service activities	443 400	99.7	2 820	47.4	218 703	61.8
P Education	267 550	100.0	552	84.1	22 173	78.1
Q Health and social work	371 375	99.8	1 785	71.8	74 515	76.8
R Arts, entertainment and recreation	268 365	100.0	711	69.3	119 421	21.1
S Other service activities	322 655	100.0	707	n.a.	32 419	n.a.

Note: n.a. = not available
Source: *Business Population Estimates for the UK and Regions* (BIS, 2015). Contains public-sector information licensed under the Open Government Licence (OGL) v1.0, http://www.nationalarchives.gov.uk/doc/open-government-licence

The growth in small businesses in the UK has been pronounced since the early 1970s. But has a similar trend been apparent in other developed economies?

International comparisons

Poor-quality data made international comparisons on small-firm activity and entrepreneurship very difficult in the past. However, this challenge is starting to be met because of their importance in job creation (look at Tables 16.2 and 16.3 again), in productivity, in innovation and, ultimately, economic growth. For example, a consortium of academics in universities across the world has compiled a Global Entrepreneurial Monitor (GEM). This is reported on in Box 16.1.

16.2 THE SURVIVAL, GROWTH AND FAILURE OF SMALL BUSINESSES

Evidence suggests that a small business stands a significantly higher chance of failure than a large business, and yet many small businesses survive and some grow. What characteristics distinguish a successful small business from one that is likely to fail? The following section looks at this issue.

Competitive advantage and the small-firm sector

The following have been found to be the key competitive advantages that small firms might hold.

> **Pause for thought**
>
> *Before you read on, try to identify what competitive advantages a small business might have over larger rivals.*

- *Flexibility.* Small firms are better able to respond to changes in market conditions and to meet customer requirements effectively. For example, they may be able to develop or adapt products for specific needs. Small firms may also be able to make decisions quickly, avoiding the bureaucratic and formal decision-making processes that typify many larger companies.
- *Quality of service.* Small firms are better able to deal with customers in a personal manner and offer a more effective after-sales service.
- *Production efficiency and low overhead costs.* Small firms can avoid some of the diseconomies of scale that beset large companies. A small firm can benefit from: management that avoids waste; good labour relations; the employment of a skilled and motivated workforce; lower premises costs. In a survey of SME managers,[6] 78 per cent ranked themselves as having strong people management skills.
- *Product development.* As we have seen, many small businesses operate in niche markets, offering specialist goods or services. The distinctiveness of such products gives the small firm a crucial advantage over its larger rivals. A successful small business strategy, therefore, would be to produce products that are clearly differentiated from those of large firms in the market, thereby avoiding head-on competition – competition which the small firm would probably not be able to survive.
- *Innovation.* Small businesses, especially those located in high-technology markets, are frequently product or process innovators. Such businesses, usually through entrepreneurial vision, manage successfully to match such innovations to changing market needs. Many small businesses are, in this respect, path breakers or market leaders.

Small businesses do, however, suffer from a number of significant limitations.

Problems facing small businesses

The following points have been found to hinder the success of small firms. They are often collectively referred to as the 'liabilities of smallness'.

- *Selling and marketing.* Small firms face many problems in selling and marketing their products, especially overseas. Small firms are perceived by their customers to be less stable and reliable than their larger rivals. This lack of

credibility is likely to hinder their ability to trade. This is a particular problem for 'new' small firms which have not had long enough to establish a sound reputation. Only 28 per cent of SME managers ranked themselves as 'strong' at the task of entering new markets.[7]
- *Funding R&D.* Given the specialist nature of many small firms, their long-run survival may depend upon developing new products and processes in order to keep pace with changing market needs. Such developments may require significant R&D investment. However, the ability of small firms to attract finance is limited, as many of them have virtually no collateral and they are frequently perceived by banks as a highly risky investment. Only 27 per cent of SME managers ranked themselves as 'strong' at accessing external finance.[8]
- *Management skills.* A crucial element in ensuring that small businesses not only survive but also grow is the quality of management. If key management skills, such as being able to market a product effectively, are limited, then this will limit the success of the business.
- *Economies of scale.* Small firms will have fewer opportunities and scope to gain economies of scale, and hence their costs are likely to be somewhat higher than those of their larger rivals. This will obviously limit their ability to compete on price.

The question often arises whether it is possible to distinguish between those small businesses which are likely to grow and prosper and those that are likely to fail. In the section below we will consider not only how businesses grow, but also whether there is a key to success.

How do small businesses grow?

It is commonly assumed that all businesses wish to grow. But is it true? Do small businesses want to become big businesses? It may well be that the owners of a small firm have no aspirations to expand the operations of their enterprise. They might earn sufficient profits and experience a level of job satisfaction that would in no way be enhanced with a bigger business operation. In fact the negative aspects of big business – formalised management structure, less customer contact and a fear of failure – might reduce the owner's level of satisfaction.

If growth is a small business objective, what are the chances of success? Evidence from the UK and the USA suggests that for every 100 firms established, after a five-year period only 41 and 51, respectively, will survive; but they are more likely to survive if they have grown.

The process of growth
Small businesses are frequently perceived to grow in five stages. These are shown in Table 16.4.

[6]Steve Lomax, June Wiseman and Emma Parry, 'Small Business Survey 2014: SME Employers', *BIS Research Paper Number 214* (Department for Business, Innovation and Skills, March 2015), p. 4.

[7]Ibid.
[8]Ibid.

Table 16.4	Management role and style in the five stages of small business growth		
Stage	**Top management role**	**Management style**	**Organisation structure**
1 Inception	Direct supervision	Entrepreneurial, individualistic	Unstructured
2 Survival	Supervised supervision	Entrepreneurial, administrative	Simple
3 Growth	Delegation/co-ordination	Entrepreneurial, co-ordinate	Functional, centralised
4 Expansion	Decentralisation	Professional, administrative	Functional, decentralised
5 Maturity	Decentralisation	Watchdog	Decentralised, functional/product

Source: D. J. Storey, *Understanding the Small-Business Sector* (Routledge, 1994). Reproduced with permission of Cengage Learning (EMEA) Ltd.

In the initial stage, *inception*, the entrepreneur plays the key role in managing the enterprise with little, if any, formalised management structure. In the next two stages we see the firm establish itself (the *survival* stage) and then *begin to grow*. The entrepreneur devolves management responsibility to non-owner managers. Such non-owner managers are able to add certain skills to the business which might enhance its chances of growth and success. The fourth and fifth phases, *expansion* and *maturity*, see the firm become more bureaucratic and rationalised; power within the organisation becomes more dispersed.

This picture of the growth of small businesses is *descriptive* rather than explanatory. To *explain* why a small firm grows we need to examine a number of factors. It is useful to group them under three headings – the entrepreneur, the firm and strategy.

The entrepreneur

Factors in this section relate predominantly to the attributes and experience of the individual entrepreneur. They include the following.

- *Entrepreneurial motivation and a desire to succeed.* Motivation, drive and determination are clearly important attributes for a successful entrepreneur. On their own, however, they are unlikely to be sufficient. If motivation is not complemented with things such as good business knowledge and decision making, then a business is likely to fail irrespective of its owner's motives.
- *Educational attainment.* Although educational attainment does not necessarily generate business success (indeed, it is often claimed that running a business is not an 'intellectual' activity), the level of education of an entrepreneur is positively related to the rate of growth of the firm.
- *Prior management experience and business knowledge.* Previous experience by the owner in the same or a related industry is likely to offer a small firm a far greater chance of survival and growth. 'Learning by doing' will enable the new business owner to avoid past mistakes or to take advantage of missed previous opportunities.

The firm

The following are the key characteristics of a small business that determine its rate of growth.

- *The age of the business.* New businesses grow faster than mature businesses.
- *The sector of the economy in which the business is operating.* A firm is more likely to experience growth if it is operating in a growing market. Examples include the financial services sector during the 1980s, and specialist high-technology sectors today.
- *Legal forms.* Limited companies have been found to grow faster than sole proprietorships or partnerships. Evidence suggests that limited companies tend to have greater market credibility with both banks and customers.
- *Location.* Small firms tend to be highly dependent for their performance on a localised market. Being in the right place is thus a key determinant of a small business's growth.

Strategy

Various strategies adopted by the small firm will affect its rate of growth. Strategies that are likely to lead to fast growth include the following:

- *Workforce and management training.* Training is a form of investment. It adds to the firm's stock of human capital, and thereby increases the quantity, and possibly also the quality, of output per head. This, in turn, is likely to increase the long-term growth of the firm.
- *The use of external finance.* Taking on additional partners, or, more significantly, taking on shareholders, will increase the finance available to firms and therefore allow a more rapid expansion.
- *Product innovation.* Firms that introduce new products have been found on the whole to grow faster than those that do not.
- *Export markets.* Even though small firms tend to export relatively little, export markets can frequently offer additional opportunities for growth. This is especially important when the firm faces stiff competition in the domestic market.

BOX 16.2 | HOTEL CHOCOLAT

A small, fast-growing, ethical business

Hotel Chocolat is a UK-based luxury chocolate manufacturer founded in 1993 by Angus Thirwell and Peter Harris. They had previous experience of the confectionery sector, having established the Mint Marketing Company in 1988 which sold packaged mints to the corporate market. A number of their customers asked them if they sold confectionary other than mints, which led them to move into the chocolate business with the creation of Choc Express in 2003.

Their initial sales were primarily from mail-order catalogue-based customers. They then developed an online store to complement their catalogue sales.

In 2003, Choc Express was rebranded as Hotel Chocolat, and the owners embraced a new means of selling when their first retail store was launched. By October 2014 it had grown into a multi-million pound business with 81 shops, 8 cafés, 2 restaurants and a hotel, including outlets in Denmark and Australia.

Initially most of the stores were located in the south of England, but Hotel Chocolat now has 10 outlets in the north of England, 12 in the Midlands and 4 in Scotland. A limited selection of their range of chocolates can also be purchased in John Lewis stores.

A tasting club was created, where, for a fee, customers receive a monthly box of new chocolates, which they have to rate on a 'taste scorecard'. This tasting club has over 100 000 members and provides valuable market research data on the public's tastes.

The rapid growth in the business has been helped by its use of 'chocolate bonds'. These pay investors' interest in chocolate and have helped to raise over £5 million. However, the firm's attempts to expand into the American market have been less successful. Both of its stores in Boston and Long Island have recently been closed.

The company's growth has been based on premium chocolates with authentic, wholesome ingredients, i.e. without artificial flavourings or hydrogenated fats. The product range covers chocolate slabs, boxed chocolates, gift boxes and chocolate fancies, such as chocolate-covered 'Amaretto and Almond Sultanas' and 'Dark with Chilli and Cocoa Nibs'. They also offer products for the corporate sector, vegetarians, vegans and diabetics. A range of beauty products was launched in November 2012.

The company has also engaged in forward vertical integration. It originally outsourced the production of its chocolates, but they are all now produced at its own factory in Cambridgeshire.

Fair trading

In 2004 the Hotel Chocolat engaged in backward vertical integration and purchased a 140-acre cocoa plantation on the Caribbean island of St Lucia. As part of the first phase of developing the St Lucia plantation, the company refurbished the estate, began to plant new seedlings and worked towards gaining full organic accreditation. It also started phase 2 of the project, the establishment of a chocolate factory in St Lucia, and it developed a hotel on the plantation.

The company realised early on in St Lucia that developing a sustainable industry for the long term, offering a high-quality and consistent supply of cocoa, required that it support local cocoa growers. For over 20 years prior to the purchase of the plantation, cocoa in St Lucia had been in decline. Local growers had no guarantee that harvested crops would be bought and, when crops were sold, payment could take up to six months to arrive. Under these circumstances cocoa production was loss making.

The company has developed a programme of 'engaged ethics' to develop sustainable production and fair standards. Hotel Chocolat now guarantees that farmers who embrace the programme will be able to sell all the cocoa they produce at 30 to 40 per cent above the market price and will be paid within one week. The company buys all of the cocoa 'wet' (unfermented), to ensure consistent quality, allowing farmers to concentrate on growing and replanting. All of this is supported by advice and technical expertise. By early 2009, 42 farmers had benefited from the programme.

As it develops the chocolate factory, Hotel Chocolat plans to bring other St Lucians into the supply chain, including chocolate workers, drivers, tour guides, engineers and support staff, all of whom will be trained and developed.

In October 2010 a hurricane passed through the estate. Co-founder Angus Thirlwell takes up the story:

> There were two main things I saw which gave me real confidence about the strength of our Engaged Ethics culture in Saint Lucia: Firstly, the day after the devastating hurricane, we opened our fermentation station as usual. It was essential that farmers who were not badly hit and who could make it with wet cocoa deliveries, could keep on doing business with us and earning much needed funds to help with rebuilding and replanting. It would have been all too easy to have kept it closed, but our team made exceptional efforts to keep the promises we made – we will buy all your cocoa, you can rely on us – fantastic to see! Secondly, the day after the hurricane we despatched our carpenters and stone-masons into the community to help put new roofs on, clear roads and distribute food. We had our own building programme to finish off but more important to help people in desperate straits first.[9]

This programme of engaged ethics has also been a mainstay of the company's approach in Ghana, the world's second largest cocoa producer. In 2002 the company began sourcing cocoa in the Osuben Basin Region. Here it provided direct funding and management skills to help launch and sustain projects that would help cocoa growers: for example, by subsidising health insurance, supporting local schools and sinking boreholes for clean drinking water.

Tapping into a growing market

The chocolate market in the UK has seen modest volume growth from 2008 to 2013 of 5.3 per cent, but strong sales revenue growth over the same period of 25.7 per cent. According to Mintel, in 2013 this market was worth £4063 million and is forecast to grow to £4793 million by 2018.[10]

---

[9] *Our Unique Cocoa Plantation – The Rabot Estate, St Lucia* (www.hotelchocolat.co.uk, September 2012).
[10] *Chocolate Confectionery – UK* (Mintel, April 2014).

Hotel Chocolat's approach to excellence in chocolate products and its strong sense of corporate and social responsibility have clearly helped it to tap into this growing market and appeal to the ethical consumer. In the six months to 28 December 2014, its profits increased by 144 per cent to £8.3 million. This was the first time it had made greater profits than its main high street rival, Thorntons.

Its success has been acknowledged by various awards. *Retail Week* awarded it 'Emerging Retailer of the Year' in 2007. It

also won Speciality Retailer of the year for 2013 and a Cosmopolitan Beauty Product Award in 2013 for its Cocoa Juvenate Body Butter.

1. *What conditions existed to enable Hotel Chocolat's small business to do so well in such a short period of time?*

2. *What dangers do you see in the growth strategy adopted by Hotel Chocolat?*

■ *The use of professional managers.* The devolving of power to non-owning managers is identified as a major characteristic of fast-growth small firms. Such managers, as previously mentioned, widen the skills and knowledge base of the organisation, and shift the reliance of the business away from the entrepreneur, whose skills might be limited to specific areas.

What the above factors suggest is that, if a small business is to be successful and subsequently grow, it must consider its business strategy – the organisation of the business, and the utilisation of individuals' abilities and experience. It is a

combination of these factors which is likely to generate success, and only those businesses that co-ordinate such characteristics are likely to grow. Conversely, those businesses that fail to embrace these key characteristics are likely to fall by the wayside.

A potentially crucial factor in aiding success is the contribution and role of public policy. In the next section we shall consider the attitude of the UK government to small business and the policy initiatives it has introduced. We will also assess how such initiatives differ from, complement or duplicate those provided by the EU.

16.3 GOVERNMENT ASSISTANCE AND THE SMALL FIRM

When the UK Conservative–Liberal coalition government was elected in 2010, it stated that its principal economic objective was to develop a strategy that would enable the country to achieve its full economic potential. A key element of the strategy was the encouragement and promotion of entrepreneurial talent; and one way of achieving this was by supporting small and medium-sized enterprises.

SME policy in the UK

UK governments in recent years have recognised the strategic importance of small firms to the economy and have introduced various forms of advisory services and tax concessions. In particular, they have tried to encourage the establishment of new small firms. In the UK, the level of small business start-ups is about three businesses per 100 adults. In the USA, it is over seven businesses per 100 adults.

A new Department for Business, Innovation and Skills (BIS) was created in June 2009. This became the lead authority for small business policy. The Treasury, however, provides the financial opportunities and establishes the macro-economic policy framework for industry, including small firms. The government and the EU also offer grants and other forms of assistance through regional, urban, social and industrial policy that small firms may be able to tap into (see sections 21.2, 21.3, 31.3 and 31.4). In this section we concentrate on the strategic framework and specific policies aimed at SMEs.

Strategic framework

In October 2010 the UK government launched a new vision for growth and enterprise, entitled 'Local growth: realising every place's potential'. This set out how it intended to support enterprise, innovation, global trade and inward investment. It developed a framework centred around the idea of 'Local Enterprise Partnerships'. These are joint bodies bringing together the private and public sector to promote the economic interests of each part of the country.

In October 2011, Lord Young was appointed as an advisor to the Prime Minister on Enterprise. He undertook a three-part review on enterprise and small firms.

Pause for thought

Why might the government wish to distinguish SME start-up policies from SME growth and performance policies?

- The first review, Make Business Your Business, was published in May 2012. This report stressed the record number of new start-up businesses and the growing culture of entrepreneurship.
- The second review, Growing Your Business, was published in 2013 and focused on ways of helping small firms to grow.
- The final review, Enterprise For All, was published in June 2014 and focused on the best ways of developing enterprise in the education system.

Forms of government support to small business in the UK

Raising finance The government created the British Business Bank on 1 November 2014. This is a state-owned bank, and one of its key aims is to increase the supply of lending to SMEs. It manages all government schemes that try to help smaller firms obtain access to finance. The current schemes operated by the British Business Bank include:

- *Enterprise Finance Guarantee.* The aim of this scheme is to facilitate lending to small businesses that have had a loan application declined because they lack either adequate security or a proven track record. The Enterprise Finance Guarantee (EFG) provides the lender with a government-backed guarantee that covers 75 per cent of the value of an individual loan.

  The decision of whether or not to lend the money is still left entirely at the discretion of the private provider. However, given the extra protection afforded by the scheme, loan applications by SMEs have a much greater chance of being successful.

  To be eligible for a loan with the EFG, a firm must have a turnover no greater than £41 million and be seeking finance of between £1000 and £1.2 million. It must also agree to a repayment period of between 3 months and 10 years. In the 4th quarter of 2014, 575 EFG loans had been made with a total value of £65.5 million. This was a big reduction on the 4th quarter of 2013 when 900 EFG loans were made with a total value of £99.9 million.

- *The Angel CoFund.* Rather than seeking finance from a traditional lender, SMEs may seek investment from groups or individuals and offer a share of their business in return. Individuals who invest their own money into a new business in return for a share of that business (i.e. ownership equity) are referred to as 'angel investors' (or as 'Dragons' in the popular TV programme, *Dragons' Den*). As well as providing finance, these angel investors may also offer managerial guidance and enable the firm to make use of their business contacts.

  'Venture capitalists' invest other people's money that has been pooled into a managed fund. Once again, venture capitalists expect a share of the business in return for the investment.

Some people have argued that SMEs face an equity gap. They may have viable investment opportunities, but the level of finance required is greater than the amount angel investors would invest and less than venture capitalists would normally invest. The Angel CoFund aims to promote and develop the angel investment market. It offers support for angel investors who have organised themselves into groups or syndicates and are looking to make an equity investment of between £100 000 and £1 million in an eligible SME. The scheme provides government money for up to a maximum of 49 per cent of the investment.

Since its launch in November 2011 the fund has invested over £24 million in 54 SMEs, with supporting investments of £95 million from business angel syndicates.

- *Enterprise Capital Funds.* The aim of this scheme is to encourage venture capital funds to invest in fast growing SMEs. The scheme combines both private and public money in Enterprise Capital Funds (ECFs) that are available to SMEs.

  Each ECF is run by managers in the private sector and they are often organised on a matched-fund basis – the government invests £1 in a fund for every £1 raised by the fund manager from the private sector. The maximum amount the government will invest in any individual ECF is capped at £50 million or two-thirds of the total fund size. As of 2014, 16 ECF funds had been created which had raised £543.5 million in total with £321.2 million coming from the government.

Grants Governments from all political parties have introduced a large range of different grants to support SMEs. For example, the 2010–15 Coalition government invested £50 million through the 'Smart' scheme to help small firms meet the costs of running R&D projects to develop new products, processes or services. Firms can apply for grants of between £25 000 and £250 000 to fund up to 60 per cent of their project costs.

Another example is the broadband connection voucher scheme introduced in December 2013. SMEs employing fewer than 250 people can apply for a grant of up to £3000 to help cover the cost of installing faster broadband. The initial take-up of the scheme was disappointing, with only 3000 SMEs taking up the vouchers.

How effective have the various grants been? Have they really helped small firms or have they simply been a waste of taxpayers' money used to finance small business activities that would have still taken place without any government support?

The government tried to address this issue with the way a new 'Growth Vouchers programme' was implemented. This £30 million, 15-month programme was launched in January 2014 with the aim of helping SMEs find innovative ways of overcoming any barriers that were preventing them from growing. Companies that have been running for at least a year, employ fewer than 50 employees and have not paid for strategic external advice in the previous three years could apply for a £2000 grant. The grant could be used to pay 50 per cent of the cost of receiving expert advice from private providers in areas such as recruiting staff, raising finance and marketing.

Firms which receive the grant were chosen at random from those that successfully completed the application process. The firms that received the funding would be monitored for the following two to three years and compared with those which were successful with the application process but did not receive the grant. This randomised trial, it was hoped, would allow the effectiveness of government-funded business advice to be properly assessed.

Tax concessions. Every year the Chancellor of the Exchequer sets out the tax rates and exemptions for the economy. In most instances there are some tax concessions to encourage enterprise and SME development. For example, a new lower rate of corporation tax of 20 per cent was introduced in April 2012 for small firms with a turnover of up to £300 000. Larger firms paid a rate of 24 per cent. However, from April 2015 all firms will pay the lower 20 per cent rate.

The government also introduced Employment Allowance in April 2014. All firms are able to claim up to £2000 per year through this scheme towards the cost of their employer National Insurance Contributions (NICs). It has been estimated that 90 per cent of the benefit from this tax cut will go to small firms and it will lead to 450 000 SMEs being completely exempt from having to pay any NICs.

Small businesses can also get extra reductions off their business rates if they only use one property that has a rateable value of less than £12 000.

Regulations. The coalition government introduced the 'red tape challenge' in 2011. Businesses were invited to identify regulations which they believed could be simplified or removed. In January 2014, the government announced that more than 3000 regulations had been discovered that could be either scrapped or amended. It was estimated that these changes could result in cost savings for firms of over £800 million a year once the challenge was fully implemented.

Mentoring. Survival rates of small businesses that receive mentoring are significantly higher than those which do not. For this reason the government has been willing to fund various mentoring schemes to help SMEs. Perhaps the most important in recent years was the 'Get Mentoring' project, which ran from September 2011 until December 2012. It was a private/public-sector partnership delivered by the Small Firms Enterprise Development Initiative that received £1.9 million of government funding to pay for the recruitment and training of volunteer mentors from the small business community. In excess of 1500 people successfully completed the training over the 16-month period.

SMEs looking for mentoring services can contact the trained mentors via the Mentorsme website that is owned and operated by the British Bankers' Association.

In November 2014 the government announced that it was spending a further £150 000 to fund 'Meet a Mentor' events designed to get female owners of SMEs into contact with each other.

The Business Growth Service that now incorporates the 'Growth Accelerator' provides mentoring and consultancy services to assist SMEs in developing and acting upon growth plans.

Small-firm policy in the EU

The need for an EU policy for SMEs was first recognised in the Colonna report on industrial policy back in 1970. However, it was not until 1985 that the European Council gave top priority to SME policy and launched the SME Action Programme in 1986.

A more significant move towards a fully integrated SME policy occurred in 1993 when, as part of the EU's enterprise policy, SME initiatives were given an independent budget of ECU112.2 billion (where 1 ECU = €1) for the period 1993 to 1996. In conjunction with this, it was stated that the impact of community policies on SMEs was to be more tightly monitored, co-ordinated and scrutinised.

By June 2008 the EU had reached the point of adopting the Small Business Act, its first comprehensive SME policy framework aiming to level the playing field for SMEs. This act focuses upon issues such as access to finance, the time taken to set up a company and how the public sector interacts with SMEs.

In 2011 the original act was revisited, and new actions were implemented. These new actions included strengthening loan guarantee schemes, improving access to venture capital markets and streamlining legislation. In September 2014 the European Commission carried out a public consultation exercise to gather feedback on how the Small Business Act could be improved.

One of the more recent and important schemes run by the EU to support SMEs was the Competition and Innovation Framework Programme (CIP) which had a budget of €3.62 billion and operated from 2007 to 2013. It had a number of objectives that were focused on SMEs, including: providing better access to finance, supporting their innovation activities and delivering business support services.

COSME and the Horizon 2020 programme

CIP was replaced by the programme for the Competitiveness of Enterprises and Small and Medium-sized Enterprises (COSME) which has a planned budget of €2.3 billion and runs from 2014–20. A new Executive Agency for Small and Medium-sized Enterprises (EASME) was created in January 2014 to manage most parts of COSME on behalf of the EU. The programme has four key objectives:

- To improve access to finance for SMEs.
- To improve access to markets inside the EU and globally.
- To promote entrepreneurship.
- To improve conditions for the competitiveness and sustainability of EU businesses.

The objectives of COSME are very similar to those of the CIP. However, all the innovation actions and policies that were previously carried out under CIP have now been transferred to the Horizon 2020 (H2020) programme. H2020 will also run from 2014 to 2020 and has a budget of €80 billion to help implement the Innovation Union Initiative.

Some of the policies that have been implemented under the COSME programme include:

- *The Loan Guarantee Facility (LGF).* This is similar to the EFG scheme in the UK. It provides guarantees for loans to SMEs of up to €150 000 which might otherwise have not taken place because of the lack of collateral. It is estimated that the LGF will enable 330 000 SMEs to obtain loans with a total value of €21 billion. It is also expected that 90 per cent of the firms that benefit from the scheme will have 10 or fewer employees.

- *Equity Facility for Growth (EFG).* This is similar to Enterprise Capital Funds in the UK and provides financial support for venture capital funds that invest in SMEs. The EU predicts that the scheme will help over 500 firms obtain equity financing.

- *Enterprise Europe Network (EEN).* The aim of this scheme is to help SMEs get access to different markets. Staff from the SME can get into contact with a local partner from the EEN, who can provide support on issues such as how to obtain market information and overcome any legal obstacles. They can also identify potential business partners across Europe.

An important part of the H2020 programme is the *SME Instrument*. This scheme has a €2.8 billion budget and aims to support the growth of SMEs which have innovative ideas and EU or global potential. Applicants can receive up to €2.5 million of funding.

The EU's commitment to SMEs has clearly grown in recent years and it has recognised the valuable role that they play within the economy, not only as employers and contributors to output, but in respect of their ability to innovate and initiate technological change – vital components in a successful and thriving regional economy. However, it also recognises that there is more to be done.

SUMMARY

1a The small-firm sector is difficult to define. Different criteria might be used. However, the level of employment tends to be the most widely used.

1b The difficulties in defining what a small firm is mean that measuring the size of the small-firm sector is also difficult and subject to a degree of error. However, it appears that in the UK the small-firm sector has been growing since the mid-1960s. This is the result of a variety of influences including: industrial structure, working practices, the level of unemployment, the role of government and consumer affluence.

1c The growth in the small-firm sector in the UK is not mirrored elsewhere in the major European nations other than in Italy.

2a Small firms survive because they provide or hold distinct advantages over their larger rivals. Such advantages include: greater flexibility, greater quality of service, production efficiency, low overhead costs and product innovation.

2b Small businesses are prone to high rates of failure, however. This is due to problems of credibility, finance and limited management skills.

2c Of those small businesses that manage to survive, a small fraction will grow. The growth of business tends to proceed through a series of stages, in which the organisation and management of the firm evolve, becoming less and less dependent upon the owner-manager.

2d Those small businesses that do grow are likely to have distinct characteristics relating to individual abilities, business organisation and business strategy. Combinations of variables from these three categories will tend to favour growth of the SME.

3a Government policy aimed at the small firm within the UK is particularly concerned with business start-ups, although we can also identify initiatives that look to stimulate growth and improve performance.

3b Small business policy within the EU seeks to complement national programmes. It provides a wide range of grants, projects and information for SMEs. A large emphasis is placed upon the development and transmission of technological innovations within the SME sector.

MyEconLab

This book can be supported by MyEconLab, which contains a range of additional resources, including an online homework and tutorial system designed to test and build your understanding.

You need both an access card and a course ID to access MyEconLab:

1. Is your lecturer using MyEconLab? Ask your lecturer for your course ID.

2. Has an access card been included with the book at a reduced cost? Check the inside back cover of the book.

3. If you have a course ID but no access card, go to: http://www.myeconlab.com/ to buy access to this interactive study programme.

REVIEW QUESTIONS

1 Why is it so difficult to define the small-firm sector? What problems does this create?

2 'Small businesses are crucial to the vitality of the economy.' Explain.

3 Compare and contrast the competitive advantages held by both small and big business.

4 It is often argued that the success of a small business depends upon a number of conditions. Such conditions can be placed under the general headings of: the entrepreneur, the firm and the strategy. How are conditions under each of these headings likely to contribute to small business success?

5 Compare and contrast UK and EU approaches to SME policy.

on longer lasting

Pricing strategy

Business issues covered in this chapter

■ How are prices determined in practice?
■ What determines the power that a firm has to determine its prices?
■ Why do some firms base prices on average costs of production?
■ Why do firms sometimes charge different prices to different customers for the same product (e.g. seats on a plane)?
    What forms can such 'price discrimination' take?
■ What types of pricing strategy is a firm likely to pursue if it is producing multiple products?
■ How does pricing vary with the stage in the life of a product? Will newly launched products be priced differently from
    products that have been on the market a long time?

How are prices determined in practice? Is there such a thing as an 'equilibrium price' for a product, which will be charged to all customers and by all firms in the industry? In most cases the answer is no.

Take the case of the price of a rail ticket. On asking, 'What's the train fare to London?', you are likely to receive any of the following replies: 'Do you want an "Advance" ticket?' 'Do you want a single or return?' 'How old are you?' 'Do you have a railcard (family & friends, young person's, student, senior)?' 'Do you want an off-peak or Anytime return?' 'Will you be travelling out before 10 a.m.?' 'Will you be leaving London between 4 p.m. and 6 p.m.?' 'Do you want to reserve a seat?' 'Do you want to take advantage of our special low-priced winter Saturday fare?'

How you respond to the above questions will determine the price you pay, a price that can vary several hundred per cent from the lowest to the highest. And it is not just train fares that vary in this way: air fares and holidays are other examples. In some situations, selling the same product to different groups of consumers at different prices is an example of **price discrimination**. The key question is whether the different prices can be explained by any differences in the costs of supplying the good. (We shall examine price discrimination in detail later in this chapter.) But prices for a product do not just vary according to the customer. They vary according to a number of other factors as well.

Definition

Price discrimination Where a firm sells the same or similar product at different prices and the difference in price cannot be fully accounted for by any differences in the costs of supply.

- *The competition that the firm faces.* Firms operating under monopoly or collusive oligopoly are likely to charge very different prices from firms operating in highly competitive markets
- *Information on costs and demand.* Firms in the real world may have very scant information about the elasticity of demand for their product and for the products of their competitors, and how demand is likely to change. It is the same with information on costs: firms may have only a rough idea of how costs are likely to change over time and over different levels of output. The picture of a firm choosing its price by a careful calculation of marginal cost and marginal revenue may be far from reality.
- *The aims of the firm.* Is the firm aiming to maximise profits, or is it seeking to maximise sales or growth, or does it have a series of aims? Which aim or aims that it pursues will determine the price it charges?
- *The life cycle of the product.* When a firm launches a product, it may charge a very different price from when the product has become established in the market, or, later, when it is beginning to be replaced by more up-to-date products.

In this chapter we will explore the pricing strategies of business. We will identify different pricing models, show how a firm's pricing policy is likely to change over a product's life cycle, and how and under what circumstances businesses might practise price discrimination. We will also consider a number of other pricing issues, such as those linked to a multi-product business and the use of a practice known as 'transfer pricing'.

17.1 PRICING AND MARKET STRUCTURE

The firm's power over prices

In a free and competitive market we know that the quantity bought and sold, and the actual price of the product, are determined by the forces of supply and demand. If the quantity demanded is in excess of the quantity supplied, the consequent market shortage will cause the price level to rise. Equally, if the quantity supplied is in excess of the quantity demanded, the resulting market surplus will cause the market price to fall. At some point we have an equilibrium or market-clearing price, to which the market will naturally move. In such an environment, the firm cannot have a 'pricing strategy': the price is set for it by the market. It is a price taker and has no influence over the setting of prices.

But even if a firm were able to identify the market demand and supply schedules, which is not at all certain given the problem of acquiring accurate market information, the market equilibrium price is likely to be short lived as market conditions change and demand and supply shift. This would be particularly the case for those goods or services that are fashionable and subject to changing consumer preferences, or where production technology is undergoing a period of innovation, influencing both the cost structure of the product and the potential output decisions open to the business. The best business could hope for, given the uncertainty of demand and supply, is to be flexible enough to continue making a profit when market conditions shift.

When a firm has a degree of market power, however, it will have some discretion over the price it can charge for its product. The smaller the number of competitors, and the more distinct its product is from those of its rivals, the more

inelastic the firm's demand will become at any given price. This will provide it with greater control over price.

We saw (Chapter 12) that, in oligopolistic markets, firms are dependent on each other: what one firm does, in terms of pricing, product design, product promotion, etc., will affect its rivals. The degree of interdependence, and the extent to which firms acknowledge it, will affect the degree to which they either compete or collude. This, in turn, will affect their pricing strategy. The result is that prices may be very difficult to predict in advance and bear little resemblance to those that would have been determined through the operation of free-market forces.

At one time there may be an all-out price war, with firms desperately trying to undercut each other in order to grab market share, or even drive their rivals out of business. At other times, prices may be very high, with the oligopolists colluding with each other to achieve maximum industry profits. In such cases the price may be even higher than if the industry were an unregulated monopoly because there might still be considerable *non*-price competition, which would add to costs and hence to the profit-maximising price.

Pause for thought

Would prices generally be lower or higher if a business was aiming to maximise long-run growth rather than short-run profits?

It is clear from this that, under oligopoly, pricing is likely to be highly strategic. One of the key strategic issues is the effect of prices on potential new entrants, and here it is not only the oligopolist, but also the monopolist that must think strategically. If the firm sets its prices at a level that maximises its short-run profits, will this encourage new firms to take the risk of entering the market? If so, should the firm keep its price down and thereby deliberately limit the size of its profits so as not to attract new entrants?

Limit pricing

This policy of *limit pricing* is illustrated in Figure 17.1. To simplify the explanation it is assumed that both the existing firm and potential new entrant have constant marginal costs. It is also assumed that neither firm has any fixed costs so that $AC = MC$.

Two AC curves are drawn: one for the existing firm and one for a new entrant. The existing firm, being experienced and with a capital base and established supply channels, is shown having a lower AC curve. Any potential new entrant, if it is to compete successfully with the existing firm, must charge the same price or a lower one: i.e. we are assuming there is no product differentiation.

The short-run profit maximising position for the existing firm is to produce where $MC = MR$. This is illustrated at point *a* in Figure 17.1. The firm will produce an output of Q_1 and charge a price of P_1. However, given that the potential new entrant's average costs are below this price, it could enter the industry and earn supernormal profits.

If, instead, the existing firm produced an output of Q_2 at a price of P_L, then it would be more difficult for the potential

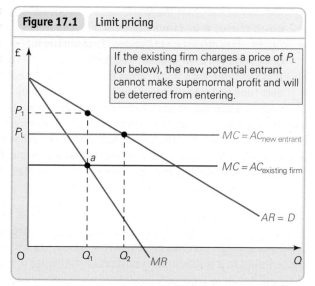

Figure 17.1 Limit pricing

If the existing firm charges a price of P_L (or below), the new potential entrant cannot make supernormal profit and will be deterred from entering.

new entrant to enter the market. If it did enter and the existing firm continued to produce Q_2, then the market price would fall below P_L and the new entrant would make a loss. Thus, provided the existing firm does not raise price above P_L, the other firm, unable to make supernormal profit, will not be attracted into the industry.

P_L may well be below the existing firm's short-run profit-maximising price, but it may prefer to limit its price to P_L to protect its long-run profits from damage by competition.

17.2 ALTERNATIVE PRICING STRATEGIES

What is the typical procedure by which firms set prices? Do they construct marginal cost and marginal revenue curves (or equations) and find the output where they are equal? Do they then use an average revenue curve (or equation) to work out the price at that output?

To do this requires a detailed knowledge of costs and revenues that few firms possess. To work out *marginal* cost, the firm must know how costs will *change* as output changes. In reality this is highly unlikely. The business environment is in a constant state of change and uncertainty. The costs of production and the potential revenues from sales will be difficult to predict, shaped as they are by many complex and interrelated variables (changes in tastes, advertising, technological innovation, etc.).

Similarly, to work out *marginal* revenue, the firm requires information not just on current price and sales. It must know what will happen to demand if price *changes*. In other words, it must know the price elasticity of demand for its product. Under oligopoly in particular, it is virtually impossible to identify a demand curve for the firm's product. Demand for one firm's product will depend on what its rivals do: and that can never be predicted with any certainty. As a consequence, managers' 'knowledge' of future demand and costs will take the form of estimates (or even 'guesstimates').

Trying to equate marginal costs and marginal revenue, therefore, is likely to be a highly unreliable means of achieving maximum profits (if, indeed, that were the aim).

If, then, the marginalist principle of traditional theory is not followed by most businesses, what alternative pricing strategy can be adopted? In practice, firms look for rules of pricing that are relatively simple to apply.

Cost-based pricing

One alternative to marginalist pricing is average-cost or *mark-up pricing*. In this case, producers derive a price by simply adding a certain percentage (mark-up) for profit on top of average costs (average fixed costs plus average variable costs).

> ### Definitions
>
> **Limit pricing** Where a business strategically sets its price below the level that would maximise its profits in the short run in an attempt to deter new rivals entering the market. This enables the firm to make greater profits in the long run.
>
> **Mark-up pricing** A pricing strategy adopted by business in which a profit mark-up is added to average costs.

$$P = AFC + AVC + \text{profit mark-up}$$

The size of the profit mark-up will depend on the firm's aims: whether it is aiming for high or even maximum profits, or merely a target based on previous profit.

Choosing the level of output

Although calculating price in this manner does away with the firm's need to know its marginal cost and revenue curves, it still requires the firm to estimate how much output it intends to produce. The reason is that average cost varies with output. If the firm estimates that it will be working to full capacity, its average cost is likely to be quite different from that if it only works at 80 or 60 per cent of capacity.

Businesses tend to base their mark-up on *short-run* average costs. This is because estimates of short-run costs are more reliable than those of long-run costs. Long-run costs are based on *all* factors being variable, including capital. But by the time new capital investment has taken place, factors such as technological change and changes in factor prices will have shifted the long-run average cost curve, thereby making initial estimations inaccurate.

Figure 17.2 shows a firm's typical short-run average cost curves. The AVC curve is assumed to be saucer shaped. It falls at first as a result of increasing marginal returns; then is probably flat, or virtually so, over a range of output; then rises as a result of diminishing marginal returns and possibly the need to pay overtime. The flat range of the average variable cost curve reflects the *reserve capacity* held by the business. This is spare capacity that the business can draw upon, if needed, to respond to changes in the market. For example, demand for the product may be subject to seasonal variation. The point is that many businesses can accommodate such changes with very little change in their average variable costs.

Most firms that use average-cost pricing will base their price on this horizontal section of the AVC curve (between points a and b in Figure 17.2). This section represents the firm's *normal* range of output. This normal range of output

is that within which the plant has been designed to operate, and the business expects to be producing.

Average fixed costs will carry on falling as more is produced: overheads are spread over a greater output. This is illustrated in Figure 17.2. The result is that average (total) cost (AC) will continue falling over the range of output where AVC is constant, with minimum AC being reached at point c – beyond the flat section of the AVC curve. In practice, many firms do not regard average fixed costs in this way. Instead, they focus on average variable costs and then just add an element for overheads (AFC).

Choosing the mark-up

The level of profit mark-up on top of average cost will be influenced by a range of possible considerations, such as fairness and the response of rivals. However, the most significant consideration is likely to be the implications of price for the level of market demand.

If a firm could estimate its demand curve, it could then set its output and profit mark-up at levels to avoid a shortage or surplus. Thus in Figure 17.3 it could choose a lower output (Q_1) with a higher mark-up (fg), or a higher output (Q_2) with a lower mark-up (hj). If a firm could not estimate its demand curve, then it could adjust its mark-up and output over time by a process of trial and error, according to its success in meeting profit and sales aims.

One problem here is that prices have to be set in advance of the firm knowing just how much it will sell and therefore how much it will need to produce. In practice, firms will usually base their assumptions about next year's sales on this year's figures, add a certain percentage to allow for growth in demand and then finally adjust this up or down if they decide to change the mark-up.

Definition

Reserve capacity A range of output over which business costs will tend to remain relatively constant.

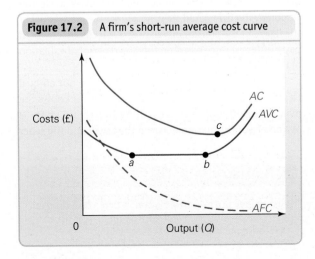

Figure 17.2 A firm's short-run average cost curve

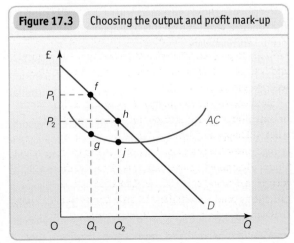

Figure 17.3 Choosing the output and profit mark-up

Variations in the mark-up

In most firms, the mark-up is not rigid. In expanding markets, or markets where firms have monopoly/oligopoly power, the size of the mark-up is likely to be greater. In contracting markets, or under conditions of rising costs and constant demand, a firm may well be forced to accept lower profits and thus reduce the mark-up.

Multi-product firms often have different mark-ups for their different products depending on their various market conditions. Such firms will often distribute their overhead costs unequally among their products. The potentially most profitable products, often those with the least elastic demands, will probably be required to make the greatest contribution to overheads.

The firm is likely to take account of the actions and possible reactions of its competitors. It may well be unwilling to change prices when costs or demand change, for fear of the reactions of competitors (see the kinked demand curve theory on pages 201–4). If prices are kept constant and yet costs change, either due to a movement along the *AC* curve in response to a change in demand, or due to a shift in the *AC* curve, the firm must necessarily change the size of the mark-up.

Pause for thought

If the firm adjusts the size of its mark-up according to changes in demand and the actions of competitors, could its actions approximate to setting price and output where MC = MR?

17.3 PRICE DISCRIMINATION

Up until this point in the chapter it has been assumed that a firm sells each unit of its output for the same price. This is sometimes referred to as *uniform pricing*. However, if a firm implements a uniform pricing policy then it is missing out on potential profit. Given that some customers gain a higher utility from the product and thus have a greater willingness to pay, they would still have purchased the good if the price was higher.

The firm might be tempted to increase prices to try to capture some of this consumer surplus and convert it into profit. However it faces a trade-off. A higher price will increase the profit *per transaction*, but it will also cause some of its customers to stop buying the product. These would be the people gaining a lower utility and hence putting a lower valuation on the product. Indeed, if it is already producing where $MC = MR$, it would lose more from people stopping buying the product than it would gain from charging remaining customers the higher price.

This trade-off could be avoided, however, if the firm could charge a higher price to those customers with a high valuation for the product (i.e. gaining a high utility) and a lower price to those consumers with a lower valuation for the product. Firms can do this by implementing a strategy of *price discrimination*.

If the cost to a firm of supplying different customers does not vary then price discrimination can be defined in the following way: it is the practice of selling the same or similar products to different customers for different prices.

If the costs of supplying the good to different customers *do* vary, then the previous definition is incomplete. For example, if differences in the cost of supplying each customer could *fully* explain the variation in prices. Price discrimination is where the mark-up of price over the marginal cost of supplying the product varies between different sales.

Price discrimination is often split into three broad categories: first, second and third degree. However, there is

some debate about whether to classify some specific examples as either second or third degree.

First-degree price discrimination

First-degree price discrimination is also sometimes referred to as 'perfect price discrimination' or 'personalised pricing'. It is a pricing strategy where the seller of the product is able to charge each consumer the maximum price he or she is prepared to pay for each unit of the product.

The following simple scenario will help to illustrate the concept. Assume a firm has developed a tablet computer that is unique and different from all the others on the market. In other words, the firm has some market power. It has a website which has photos and details of the tablet's specifications. However, the website contains no information about the price. When each customer contacts the website and enquires about the product, they receive an automated email response. The wording of the email is as follows: 'What is the maximum amount you are willing to pay for this tablet?' If consumers had to provide a truthful response, the firm could then simply set the price equal to the figure in the consumer's answer. Each customer would pay a different price based on their own personal valuation of the product.

Unfortunately for the firm, consumers are not obliged to provide an honest response. Only the buyer knows the maximum amount they are willing to pay: i.e. there is asymmetric information between the buyer and the seller

Definition

First-degree price discrimination Where a firm charges each consumer for each unit the maximum price which that consumer is willing to pay for that unit.

BOX 17.1	EASY PRICING

Getting the most revenue from the demand curve

Low-cost airlines such as easyJet and Ryanair adopted an approach to pricing in the late 1990s that was novel at the time, but is now being increasingly used by other airlines and in other industries. The approach is a form of price discrimination.

The principle is simple: with a fixed number of seats per flight, as the seats are sold, so the prices go up. Thus the first few seats are sold at really low prices. Indeed, when particular flights first come on sale, many people go online very quickly to try to get the lowest priced seats. This rush to purchase seats at reasonable prices helps to drive sales and gets people to commit to a purchase when otherwise they may have waited and perhaps changed their minds.

The idea is also to take advantage of the different prices people are willing to pay. Business passengers, for example, may be willing to pay very high prices (or at least their employers may) but might want to book a flight at the last minute. The pricing model means that with a plane that is nearly fully booked at that stage, the price will be high and the airline will be able to charge a price closer to the business passenger's willingness to pay.

In fact, in the perfect case of such a pricing model, each passenger is paying the maximum they would be willing to pay – a case of first-degree price discrimination. This means that all the consumer surplus (see pages 91–2) that would have gone to the consumer instead goes as revenue to the airline.

This is illustrated in the diagram. Assume that the plane has 156 seats (the typical easyJet Airbus A319-100 configuration) and that the demand for seats is given by the demand curve (*D*).

If each passenger pays what he or she would be willing to pay, the total revenue from a full plane is given by the total grey and pink shaded areas. If, by contrast, a single price were charged to fill the plane, this would have to be P_1, giving total revenue of just the pink area, with passengers gaining consumer surplus of the grey area.

The easyGroup

Stelios Haji-Ioannou, the original owner of easyJet, founded the easyGroup holding company of 'easy' subsidiaries in 1998. In addition to easyJet, these include or have included easyCinema, easyMobile and easyCruise, amongst others. In several of these easyGroup companies prices rise as sales increase, just as with easyJet. Take the case of easy-Cinema. Prices started very low and then rose as the cinema filled up for any given screening. EasyCinema customers had no tickets: they booked online and printed out a bar-coded entry pass.

Unfortunately, for Mr Haji-Ioannou, the easyCinema venture failed. Faced with an effective cartel of film distributors, which chose not to sell to the cut-price easyCinema, it could only show old or less popular films. It was forced to close in 2006.

Other similar ventures, such as easyCruise and easyMobile, have also closed or been sold. Nevertheless, the number of ventures in easyGroup now number over 20, including easyCar, easyVan, easyOffice (serviced office rental), easyJobs (employment agency), easyGym and easyBus (airport transfers).

But the most successful of the easyGroup businesses remains easyJet, the UK's largest airline by number of passengers carried. It has seen turnover grow in every year since 2000. Its load factor has steadily increased, with an average seat occupancy in 2014 of over 90 per cent.

Unlike Ryanair, it has targeted the business market and flies to main airports rather than small ones in remote locations. The pricing model particularly suits easyJet's market, with holidaymakers being able to take advantage of low-priced seats booked a long time in advance and business travellers having the flexibility of buying tickets at the last minute, but at much higher prices.

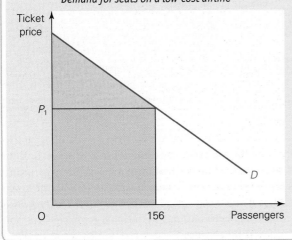

Demand for seats on a low-cost airline

1. *Distinguish between first-, second- and third-degree price discrimination.*
2. *Is easyJet's pricing model one of pure first-degree price discrimination? Explain whether or not the total revenue for a full plane will be the full amount shown by the grey and pink areas in the diagram.*
3. *What other policies of easyJet have made it so successful?*

(see page 38). Buyers also have an incentive to withhold this information if they believe it will have an influence on the price they are charged.

In reality first-degree price discrimination is more of a theoretical benchmark than a viable business strategy. However, there may be some real-world cases where sellers have a pricing strategy that approaches one of perfect price discrimination. It is more likely in any sector where there is scope for bargaining over price. Through observation and

negotiation a seller may be able to 'size up' a customer and obtain some information about their willingness to pay.

Take the example of stall-holders in a bazaar or a new car dealer. In both of these cases the same product is often sold to different consumers for different prices. As they haggle, the stall-holders may try to find out the nationality of a customer, because it may indicate something about their willingness to pay. The car dealers may try to find out a customer's address for similar reasons. Accountants, lawyers, architects and other firms offering professional services often bargain over price and, in the process, charge different prices to different customers.

Although the seller may try, it is highly unlikely that they will ever succeed in obtaining enough information to charge every customer a price equal to the maximum amount they are willing to pay. Possibilities for sellers engaging in first-degree price discrimination, therefore, are very rare. Also, bargaining is a time-consuming activity. A supplier will have to judge whether the extra revenue it generates outweighs the extra costs.

Pause for thought

Is the pricing system adopted by the 'easy' group of companies a form of first-degree price discrimination (see Box 17.1)?

Figure 17.4 demonstrates the impact of first-degree price discrimination if it could be implemented. To simplify the explanation, we assume that marginal cost (*MC*) is constant and that there are no fixed costs, so that average cost $AC = MC$.

If the profit-maximising firm charged the same price to all of its customers, it would be P_1 and output would correspondingly be Q_1 (i.e. where $MC = MR$). Area 1 would represent the supernormal profit made by the firm. However, if the firm knew the demand curve for its product, and could sell every unit at the maximum price that each consumer was prepared to pay, it could make additional gains.

First, it could make more profit from the same number of sales, Q_1. All of the consumer surplus that existed when it charged one price (area 2) would be converted by a policy of first-degree price discrimination into profits.

Second, its profit-maximising level of output would be greater than Q_1. If the firm could charge each customer a separate price then the *MR* changes – it is no longer below the *AR* curve. Instead $MR = AR$, as the firm no longer has to pass any price reductions on to other customers. This

means that the new profit-maximising level of output is Q_2. This further increases its total profit by area 3.

The impact on consumers is mixed. Those who previously purchased the product under a single pricing strategy are now paying higher prices than they were before. However, new customers are able to purchase the product under first-degree price discrimination who would not have purchased it if a single price had been charged.

Although it is unlikely to occur in the real world, perfect price discrimination still provides a useful benchmark against which to judge the impact of other pricing strategies.

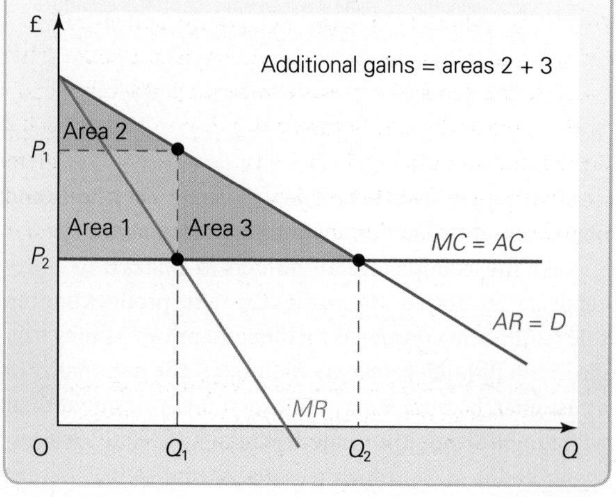

Third-degree price discrimination

Third-degree price discrimination is where the firm charges a different price to different groups of consumers. There is no bargaining, haggling or discussion between buyers and sellers. Instead, the firm needs to find some consumer characteristic, trait or attribute that could be used as a basis to split them into different groups.

To be successful the characteristic must have four important properties:

- It must be relatively easy for the firm to observe;
- It must provide some indication of the consumer's willingness to pay: i.e. consumers allocated to one group should generally be less price sensitive at any given price than those allocated to another group – in other words, price elasticity of demand must differ between the groups;
- It must be impossible or very costly for a consumer to change characteristics so that they switch from being a member of a high-price group to a member of low-price group, i.e. a customer is unable to reclassify themselves as a child or a pensioner in order to qualify for the lower price.
- It must be legal to charge different prices based on the characteristic. Using either ethnicity or gender is often judged to be unlawful. For example 'Ladies nights' have been prohibited in the USA in California, New Jersey, Maryland and Pennsylvania

Having allocated its customers into these groups, the seller then sets a different price for each group according to its price elasticity of demand: the group with the lowest price elasticity of demand will be charged the highest price. However, each consumer in the same group pays the same price for the product.

Figure 17.4   First-degree price discrimination

Definition

Third-degree price discrimination Where a firm divides consumers into different groups based on some characteristic that is relatively easy to observe and acceptable to the consumer. The firm then charges a different price to consumers in different groups, but the same price to all the consumers within a group.

Figure 17.5 Third-degree price discrimination

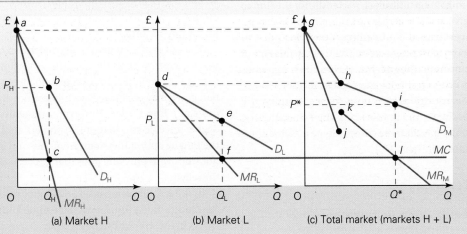

(a) Market H   (b) Market L   (c) Total market (markets H + L)

Third-degree price discrimination is more viable than first-degree price discrimination as the informational demands it places on the firm are much lower: i.e. it only needs to have information about how the willingness to pay varies between different groups of customers rather than between each individual consumer. However, the firm still needs to be able to find an informative, acceptable and easily observable characteristic.

One possibility would be to split consumers into different groups based on their incomes. In many instances it is highly probable that most consumers with higher incomes would be willing to pay more for a given product than those on lower incomes. They would tend to be less price sensitive at any given price. Therefore the firm could set a relatively higher price for those consumers on higher incomes and a relatively low price for those on lower incomes. For example, supermarkets could charge higher prices in stores located in wealthy areas than in those located in poorer areas. Figure 17.5 illustrates a simple example.

Assume a firm decides to split its customers into two different groups – those earning at or above £40 000 per year and those earning less than £40 000. Panel (a) in Figure 17.5 illustrates the demand curve for the firm's product of those earning at or above £40 000, while panel (b) illustrates the demand curve for those earning less than £40 000.

Equilibrium for a single-price firm. If the firm were unable to split its customers into these two different groups, then a market demand curve could be derived. This is illustrated in panel (c) and is obtained by horizontally aggregating the demand curves in panel (a) and (b). The market demand curve is the same as the demand curve in market H from point *g* to *h*. This is because no consumers in market L are willing to pay a price above *d*. As the price falls below *d* consumers in both markets, H and L, are willing to buy the good, so horizontal aggregation of both demand curves must take place from this point onwards. This creates a kink in the market demand curve at point *h*. This kink also creates a discon-

tinuity in the *MR* curve between points *j* and *k*. To simplify the explanation, it is also assumed that the firm's marginal cost is constant and that it has no fixed costs. Thus $AC = MC$.

To understand how a firm would behave if it could only set one price for all of its customers we need to focus on the market demand curve in panel (c). If it was a profit-maximising firm then it would produce where the market MR: i.e. $MR_M = MC$. This occurs at point *l* in panel (c) of Figure 17.5. It would therefore produce an output of Q^* and sell all of this output at the same price of P^*.

Equilibrium under third-degree price discrimination. What happens if the firm could now charge a different price to the customers in market H from those in market L? At the single price of P^* the price elasticity of demand in market H is lower than it is in market L. (Note that demand is nevertheless elastic in both markets at this price as MR is positive.) Therefore the firm could increase its profits by charging a price above P^* in market H and below P^* in market L. Once again this can be illustrated in Figure 17.5.

In market H the profit-maximising firm should produce where $MR_H = MC$. Therefore it should sell an output of Q_H for a price of P_H.

In market L it should produce where $MR_L = MC$ at point *f*. Therefore it should sell an output of Q_L for a price of P_L.

Note that P_L is below P^*, while P_H is above P^*. Also, because the demand curves are linear the total output sold is the same under third-degree price discrimination as it is under uniform pricing: i.e. $Q^* = Q_H + Q_L$. We will see later in the chapter that this is a key point when considering whether or not price discrimination is in the public interest.

Pause for thought

Can you think of any real-world examples of strategies used by firms to prevent the re-sale of a product between customers who are paying different prices for the same or similar product?

Splitting customers into different groups based on their incomes might be informative about their willingness to pay. However, it might be a difficult characteristic for the firm to directly observe. It might perhaps ask to see a copy of the customer's salary slip in order to qualify for the lower price. In reality, however, most people are unlikely to keep this type of proof on their person. They might also object on the grounds that it was an unacceptable invasion of their privacy.

To implement this pricing strategy successfully, the seller might have to find another consumer characteristic that successfully met all three criteria. Some possible alternatives are shown in Table 17.1.

> ### Pause for thought
>
> *To what extent does each of the characteristics in Table 17.1 indicate to the firm differences in consumers' incomes?*

Third-degree price discrimination by the non-profit-maximising firm

If a firm does not set a profit-maximising price, either because it has some alternative aim, or because it uses cost-based methods of pricing, which, owing to a lack of information, do not lead to the profit-maximising price, then we cannot predict precisely what the discriminatory prices will be. All we can say is that price discrimination will allow the firm to achieve higher profits, which most firms will prefer to lower profits.

Table 17.1	Examples of third-degree price discrimination
Characteristic	**Example**
Age	16–25 or senior railcard; half-price children's tickets in the cinema.
Gender	'Ladies' night' in a bar or club where men pay the full price for drinks while women can get the same drinks at a discounted price.
Ethnicity	A study by Levitt and Venkatech found that prostitutes charged black customers less than either white or Hispanic customers.
Location	Pharmaceutical companies often charge different prices for the same medicine/drug in different countries. Consumers in the USA are often charged more than those from other countries.
Occupation	Apple, Microsoft and Orange provide price discounts to employees of educational institutions.
Business or individual	Publishers of academic journals charge much lower subscription rates to individuals than university libraries.
Past buying behaviour	Firms often charge new customers a lower price than existing customers for the same product or service as an 'introductory offer'.

Second-degree price discrimination

Second-degree price discrimination is where customers are offered a range of different prices for the same or similar product by the firm.

The prices offered may be dependent on one of a number of factors, such as the quantity or version of the product that is purchased. For example, the first so many units purchased may be charged at a higher price and subsequent units at a lower price. However, unlike first- and third-degree price discrimination, customers are free to choose the pricing option they want from those on offer. They are not stuck with only one price that has been determined by the seller.

In order to implement second-degree price discrimination successfully, firms must have some knowledge about their customers' willingness to pay. They may be aware that some of their customers are more price sensitive, while others are less so. The problem for firms is that they cannot tell which consumers belong to which group. There may not be any easy-to-observe consumer characteristics that would suggest individuals' price elasticity of demand at any given price. For the strategy to work, therefore, a firm would need to find a way to offer a range of prices in such a way that a relatively price insensitive customer would pay the higher price and the more price sensitive consumer the lower price(s). Here are some examples of second-degree price discrimination where price differences purely reflect differences in price elasticity of demand.

Discounts for greater purchases. This is where price is dependent on the amount purchased. Many suppliers of inputs to other firms offer lower prices to large customers. Another example is the use by supermarkets of promotions such as 'buy two, get an additional one free' or 'buy six bottles of wine and get a 5 per cent discount'.

Similarly, electricity companies in some countries charge a high price for the first so many kilowatts. This is the amount of electricity that would typically be used for lighting and running appliances: in other words, the uses for which there is no substitute fuel. Additional kilowatts are charged at a much lower rate. This is electricity that is typically used for heating and cooking, where there are alternative fuels.

Figure 17.6 illustrates how second-degree price discrimination can increase revenue. Assume that the firm is currently charging a price of P_1 and hence selling an

> ### Definition
>
> **Second-degree price discrimination** Where a firm offers consumers a range of different pricing options for the same or similar product. Consumers are then free to choose whichever option they wish, but the price is often dependent on either the quantity or the exact version of the product purchased.

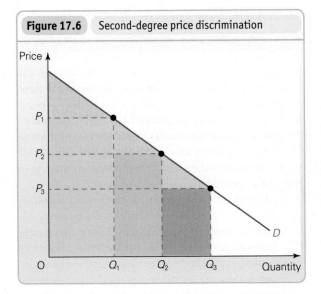

Figure 17.6 Second-degree price discrimination

output of Q_1. Its revenue is shown by the blue area. If it now reduces the price to P_2 for *additional* sales above Q_1, its sales will increase to Q_2. Its revenue will now increase by the pink area. If it reduces the price further, to P_3, for sales above Q_2, sales will rise to Q_3 and revenue will increase further, by the green area. Thus a large amount of consumer surplus has been captured by the firm. But this is not as much as under first-degree price discrimination (see Figure 17.4). Consumer surplus of the grey areas still remains.

Coupons/vouchers. A firm can use coupons or vouchers that enable a consumer to purchase the product for a lower price. For this pricing strategy to work, consumers must have to exert some time and effort in order to obtain and use the coupons or vouchers. The firm must not make it too easy to find and use them as it does not want customers who would have bought the product anyway to use them!

For example, the vouchers may be on a flyer inside a local newspaper or included in junk mail. The customer will then have to search through the flyers or junk mail to see if there are any coupons or vouchers for products they are interested in buying. Only those consumers who are relatively more price sensitive at the non-discounted price of the product will take the time and effort involved in order to get the voucher. Those who are relatively less price sensitive will not find the search costs involved worthwhile and will end up paying the full price.

Inter-temporal pricing. This pricing strategy can be used where different customers have a different willingness to pay at different points in time. When a product is launched, some consumers are desperate to get hold of it. For example, some consumers want to have the most up-to-date technology and are willing to pay more for a new mobile phone that is released with innovative features. Similarly, when computers or tablets are first available with a new, faster processing chip, the price tends to be higher. Over time the price of such products is reduced, which enables firms to sell to people less anxious to switch to the latest version.

Another example is the pricing of seats on certain airlines. As the plane fills up, so the price of the seat rises. If you book a seat on a budget airline a long time in advance, for example, you may be able to get it at a very low price. If, on the other hand, you want a seat at the last minute, you may well have to pay a very high price. Although this is the other way around from the case of high-tech products, it again reflects price elasticity of demand. The business traveller who needs to travel the next day for a meeting will have a very low price sensitivity and may well be prepared to pay a very high price indeed.

In both the above cases, customers are not being assigned to a time period by the firm, so it is not classed as an example of third-degree price discrimination. Instead, it is up to customer preferences. In the high-tech case, the least price-sensitive customers reveal themselves by paying the higher price when the good is first launched, whereas customers who are more price sensitive simply wait for the price to come down. In the case of airlines, the more price sensitive consumers reveal themselves early on, while the less price sensitive ones reveal themselves later.

A mixture of second-degree price discrimination and product differentiation

Unlike the above cases, most examples of second-degree price discrimination are a mixture of price discrimination and product differentiation. Although this is not 'pure' price discrimination, as the more expensive product will normally be a higher quality product, there is an *element* of price discrimination if the price difference partly reflects the price elasticity of demand and not just differences in costs of production. Here are some examples:

Product size. It is common for small-sized packets or containers of everyday items, such as breakfast cereal or milk, to be sold at a higher unit price (i.e. per weight or volume) than large packets. It may be that the small sized packets cost more per unit of product to produce and distribute, but it is unlikely that this accounts for the entire difference in price.

Versioning. This is where a firm produces different versions of the same core product. The different versions of the product should be perceived as having different levels of quality by the customer. Examples include first class versus economy seats on aeroplanes or trains; 'value' versus 'finest' ranges of a product sold in supermarkets; different specifications of computers or software packages.

The less price sensitive consumers will voluntarily choose to purchase the more expensive version of the good with the perceived higher quality. The more price sensitive customers, by contrast, will buy the cheaper version of the good with the perceived lower quality.

For the strategy to work, the consumer surplus for the relatively less price sensitive customers from purchasing the more expensive version of the product must be greater than the consumer surplus they would receive if they purchased the cheaper version of the product.

Versioning is not *pure* price discrimination for two reasons. First, by definition, the products are not the same: they differ in quality and/or specification. Second, the costs of producing the different versions of the good are likely to vary. Generally, the higher quality product will have a higher marginal cost. For there to be an element of price discrimination, therefore, the difference in the price between the different versions of the good must be *greater* than the difference in the marginal cost of producing them. More specifically the mark-up of price over marginal cost must be greater for the version of the product purchased by the relatively less price sensitive consumers than for that purchased by the relatively more price sensitive consumers.

Combinations of versioning and inter-temporal pricing. Some new products are released in a higher quality, more expensive version first. For example, a book written by a celebrity author is often released in the higher-priced hardback form to capture the desire of more avid fans before being released in the lower-priced paperback version sometime later. Again, the hardback version costs a little bit more to produce than the paperback one (but only a little), but the price difference can be huge.

> ### Pause for thought
>
> *How would profit-maximising output and price be determined under third-degree price discrimination if there were three separate markets? Draw a diagram to illustrate your answer.*

Conditions necessary for price discrimination to operate

Given that firms can generate greater revenue and profits by implementing a strategy of price discrimination, why don't all firms implement the policy? Unfortunately for some firms it might not be possible for a number of reasons. The following are the conditions necessary for price discrimination to operate:

Conditions necessary for all types of price discrimination

- The firm must have some market power: in other words, it must face a downward-sloping demand curve and hence can set its price. Thus price discrimination would be impossible under perfect competition, where firms are price takers. **KI 21 p175**

- Re-sale of the product must not be possible between consumers. A potentially profitable strategy of price discrimination may fail if consumers in the low-price market are able to re-sell the good to those consumers who are in the high-price market.

  For example with second-degree price discrimination, can the customer who obtains the quantity discount sell some of the units they have purchased to another customer who does not purchase enough to receive the discount? Can consumers allocated to one group under a pricing strategy of third-degree price discrimination re-sell the product to a customer allocated to another group? If re-sale *is* possible, then entrepreneurial consumers who can obtain the product in the low-price market may purchase large amounts of the good and make a profit selling it to customers in the high-price market. With the advent of online retailing, such as eBay, this might be easy for consumers to do. If this happens the firm may quickly discover that it does not make any sales at the higher price.

  In some cases the nature of the product means that re-sale is impossible: e.g. you can't re-sell a haircut! It is similar with many services or with goods that are consumed at the time of purchase, such as a restaurant meal. In other circumstances, even though re-sale may be possible, the transactions costs might outweigh the benefits: for example, the good might be relatively inexpensive so the potential gains from re-sale are small, or it may be difficult to transport and distribute the goods to the customers in the high-price market. **KI 5 p36**

  In other cases it might be both possible and potentially profitable to re-sell the good. This is most likely when the good is non-perishable, relatively expensive and easy to transport to consumers in the high-price market: i.e. the transaction costs are low. In these situations the firm may have to intervene more directly to prevent re-sale between its customers.

- Demand elasticity must vary between consumers at any given price. The firm will charge the higher price in the market where demand is less elastic, and thus less sensitive to a price rise. **KI 12 p 68**

Price discrimination and the public interest

The word 'discrimination' carries with it negative connotations, so people often assume that this pricing strategy must not be in the public interest. It is also tempting to think that anything that increases a firm's profits must be at the expense of consumers' welfare. It is true that some consumers will benefit from price discrimination while others will be worse off. However, in certain circumstances economists may judge that it is in the public interest. The following factors need to be taken into account when assessing the impact of price discrimination on a market.

Distribution effects on those customers who previously purchased the good at a uniform price

KI 32
p343

Those paying the higher price will probably feel that price discrimination is unfair to them. Price has risen for them and their consumer surplus is lower. On the other hand, those who previously purchased the good but are now paying a lower price will feel better off. Their consumer surplus will be higher. Judgements could be made about whether the gains were more socially desirable than the losses.

The impact of any extra sales

In Figure 17.5 the quantity of sales under price discrimination remained the same as under uniform pricing. However, in some circumstances the quantity of sales may increase. There may be some consumers, such as old-age pensioners, who previously could not afford to buy the good when the firm used uniform pricing. The lower price, which has been made possible by a policy of price discrimination, enables them to purchase the good. These extra sales will have a positive impact on the welfare of society. They will increase both consumer and producer surplus.

Misallocation effects

Price discrimination may cause a negative allocation effect. Under uniform pricing the product is allocated through the pricing mechanism to those consumers who value it the most, given their incomes. The implementation of third-degree price discrimination could result in some units of the product being re-allocated away from those consumers with a higher willingness to pay to those with a lower willingness to pay.

Without any restrictions, mutually beneficial trade could take place between the buyers. Those consumers with a higher valuation of the good could purchase it from those with a lower valuation at a price that would improve the welfare of both parties. However, the seller blocks this re-sale from taking place and, in the process, reduces society's welfare.

If the number of sales does not increase, then price discrimination is usually judged to be against the public interest because of the misallocation effect. If the pricing strategy does have a positive impact on the number of sales, then economists judge that it might be in the public interest. It all depends on the relative sizes of the positive impact of the extra sales and the negative impact of the misallocation effect.

Anti-competitive effects

The analysis of the impact of price discrimination often focuses on a pure monopoly. However, price discrimination could take place in an oligopolistic market. In this case it is possible that a firm may use price discrimination to drive competitors out of business. This is known as *predatory pricing*. Under this practice, a company charges a price below average cost in one market by cross-subsidising that part of the business with profits from another part of the business. It does this until its rival stops competing in that market.

Predatory pricing, however, is illegal under UK and European competition law. Even though consumers gain from lower prices in the short run, the long-run strategy of predatory firms is to raise their prices once their competitor has been driven from the market.

On the other hand, a firm that engages in price discrimination might use its profits from its high-priced market to break into another market and withstand a possible price war. This would increase competition and hence consumer welfare. Alternatively, it might use the higher profits to invest in new and improved products that enhance consumer choice.

Other examples of price discrimination

There are various other pricing strategies used by firms that involve an element of price discrimination. They include the following:

Peak-load pricing. This is where people are charged more at times of peak demand and less at off-peak times (see Case study F.6 in MyEconLab). For example, bus and train fares are often highest during the 'rush hours' when consumers want to get to work. Similarly, the price of land-line telephone calls is highest during the working day. During 'off-peak' times, prices are lower.

Part of the reason for this practice is the lower price elasticity of demand at peak times. For example, many commuters have little option but to pay higher rail fares at peak times. This is genuine price discrimination. But part of the reason has to do with higher marginal costs incurred at peak times, as capacity limits are reached.

Two-part tariff. This is a pricing system that requires customers to pay an access and a usage price for a product. This practice is used in a variety of settings but particularly in the telecommunications and energy sectors. For example, most customers who use gas have to pay a fixed standing

---

Definitions

Predatory pricing Where a firm sets its average price below average cost in order to drive competitors out of business.

Peak-load pricing The practice of charging higher prices at times when demand is highest because the constraints on capacity lead to higher marginal cost.

Two-part tariff A pricing system that requires customers to pay both an access and a usage price for a product.

BOX 17.2 A QUANTITY DISCOUNT PRICING STRATEGY

A strategy to get consumers to identify themselves!

Assume that a firm knows that it has two types of customers for its product. Type 'I' customers have a lower price elasticity of demand than type 'E' customers at any given price for the product. Unfortunately for the firm, it has no way of knowing into which category any individual customer falls. There are no easy-to-observe consumer characteristics that would provide some indication of their willingness to pay.

Ideally, the firm would like the customers to sort themselves voluntarily into the two different groups. It could then charge type I consumers a higher price than type E consumers and transfer some consumer surplus into profit. However, if it simply offered the good for sale at two different prices all the consumers, whether they were type I or type E, would simply choose the lower price.

In order to try to get the consumers to self-select voluntarily into the two different groups, the firm could introduce a *quantity discount*. This pricing strategy is illustrated in

the figure. To simplify the example, it is assumed that the firm's marginal cost is constant and it has no fixed costs of production, so that $AC = MC$. Consumers can obtain the product for the lower discounted price of P_L if they purchase a minimum quantity of the product (Q^*). The new lower price applies to all the units of the good they purchase and not just those in excess of Q^*. (This is different from a block declining tariff where the lower price would only apply to the incremental units purchased in excess of Q^*.) If the consumers purchase less than Q^*, then they have to pay the higher price of P_H.

Which pricing option will a type I consumer choose?

All consumers, if they are rational, will choose the pricing option that provides them with the most satisfaction: i.e. the option that gives them the greatest level of consumer surplus.

A quantity discount

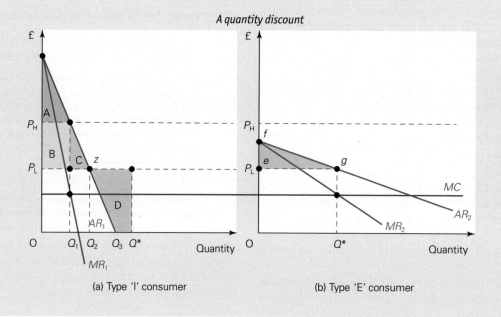

(a) Type 'I' consumer

(b) Type 'E' consumer

charge per period of time and then pay so much per therm of gas used.

The aim of these schemes is to increase the firm's revenue, by giving it a lump-sum payment per customer (particularly relevant where the firm has high fixed costs) on top of the price per unit. The problem is setting the appropriate two-part tariff. This is particularly difficult

when there is a lot of competition between firms and when customers are quite prepared to switch supplier. It is for this reason that there are a number of mobile phone two-part tariff plans for customers with an average to high usage, as well as a 'Pay-As-You-Go' option aimed at lighter users.

If type I consumers pay the higher price for the product, P_H, then they will buy Q_1 units of the good – see diagram (a) in the figure. Their consumer surplus would be area A (the green area). If, instead, consumers purchased the quantity required (Q^*) to get the discounted price (P_L) then there are potentially three effects on their welfare. Two are positive and one is negative.

- The first positive effect on consumers' welfare comes from the quantity of the product that they would still have purchased at a price of P_H: i.e. Q_1. The consumer is now able to purchase Q_1 for the lower price of P_L. The extra consumer surplus obtained from buying Q_1 at the lower price is shown by area B (the blue area).
- The second positive effect comes from some of the additional units of the product that the consumer purchases at the discounted price of P_L. From diagram (a) it can be seen that at a price of P_L a type I consumer would purchase Q_2 units of the product: i.e. the quantity where P_L meets the consumer's demand curve. This will generate an increase in consumer surplus as the maximum willingness to pay for these additional units from Q_1 to Q_2 is greater than the price. This gain in consumer surplus is represented in by area C (the orange area).
- The negative effect on consumer welfare comes from the extra units of the product from Q_2 to Q^* that the consumer has to buy to obtain the lower price of P_L. Type I consumers would maximise their consumer surplus by purchasing Q_2 at a price of P_L. However, this lower price is not available to them if they only purchase Q_2. They have to buy Q^* in order to obtain the quantity discount. This means that between Q_2 and Q^* the consumers' maximum willingness to pay for the product is less than the price they have to pay: i.e. the section of the demand curve from point z to Q_3 is below the price of P_L. The quantity from Q_3 to Q^* does not provide the consumer with any utility at all. Their maximum willingness to pay for these additional units is zero. This negative impact on consumer surplus can be represented by area D (the lilac area).

The net gain for a type I customer of purchasing the product at the lower price is area B + area C – area D. Therefore, if area D is greater than areas B + C, this consumer would be worse off from buying the good at the lower price. Such consumers would voluntarily pay the higher price for the product where the total consumer surplus they receive is at its greatest.

Which pricing option will a type E consumer choose?

Type E consumers, with the relatively more price sensitive demand at any given price, as shown in diagram (b) in the figure, would choose to purchase the product at the lower price. They would not buy any of the product at a price of P_H as it is above the maximum amount they are willing to pay for the first unit: i.e. the intercept of the demand curve (AR_2) on the price axis at point f is below P_H. By purchasing Q^* at a price of P_L they can obtain consumer surplus equal to the pink area in diagram (b).

The discount quantity pricing strategy has managed to get the type I customers to identify themselves and self-select to pay a higher price for the same product than a type E customer. In this case, the firm has not had to use an easily identifiable consumer characteristic in order to separate its consumers into different groups.

1. The quantity discount is an example of what type of price discrimination?
2. Explain any conditions that must be met for this type of price discrimination to be a viable strategy for the firm.
3. Both type I and type E consumers are still able to obtain some consumer surplus. Under what type of price discrimination is the firm able to extract all the consumers' surplus and convert it into profit?
4. Re-draw the diagram to illustrate a situation where both types of consumer would purchase the product for a lower price.
5. It is assumed in this example that MC is constant. If MC and AC fell as the firm produced more would a quantity discount still be an example of price discrimination? Explain your answer.

17.4 MULTIPLE PRODUCT PRICING

Thus far in our analysis of pricing strategy, we have been concerned only with a single product produced by a single firm. However, many businesses produce a range of products. Such products might be totally distinct and sold in different markets, or the firm might offer a range of models in the same market that differ in design and performance. For example, a vacuum cleaner manufacturer might also produce other household appliances such as irons, as well as offering a range of vacuums with different suction abilities and design features.

Each of these products and product ranges will require its own distinct price, and probably a longer-term pricing strategy. However, multi-product pricing raises a wider set of issues owing to the interrelated nature of demand and production.

Interrelated demand

Many of the large supermarkets or DIY stores are in fierce competition for business. It is quite normal to see them offering 'bargain buys', whose prices are cut dramatically in order to attract customers to the store. Often their price is even below average cost. Such cases are known as *loss leaders*. The hope is that customers will purchase not just the loss leader, but additional amounts of other products with full profit mark-ups, thereby bringing a net gain in profits.

This strategy is known as *full-range pricing* and involves the business assessing the prices of all its products together, and deciding from this how it might improve its profit performance. One of the most important considerations is the price elasticity of demand for the loss leader. The more elastic it is, the more customers will tend to be attracted into the store by the bargain. The business will also consider additional factors such as advertising the loss leaders and their positioning in the store, so as to attract customers to see other items at full price that they had not intended to buy.

Other demand interrelations that might influence the pricing policy of a business are where a business produces either complementary or substitute products.

If a business produces complementary products, then increased sales of one product, such as Apple's iPod, will raise the revenue gained from the other, such as the use of the iTunes store.

Alternatively, if the products produced by a business are substitutes, such as those of a breakfast cereal manufacturer like Kellogg's, then the increased sales of one product within its range may well detract from the revenue gained from the others.

Businesses like Apple and Kellogg's should therefore determine the prices of all their substitute and complementary products jointly so as to assess the total revenue implications. Here it is vital for the firm to have estimates of the cross-price elasticities of demand for their products (see section 5.3).

Interrelated production

The production of **by-products** is the most common form of interrelated production. A by-product is a good or service that is produced as a consequence of producing another good or service. For example, whey is a by-product of cheese. By-products have their own distinct market demand. However, the by-product is only produced following demand for the main production good: it may well not be profitable to produce as a separate product.

To consider whether the by-product is profitable to sell, it is important to allocate the correct costs to its production. The raw materials and much of the other inputs to produce it can be considered to have a zero cost, since they have already been paid in producing the main product. But packaging, marketing and distributing the by-product clearly involve costs that have to be allocated directly to it, and the price it sells for must more than cover these costs.

It is not as simple as this, however, since the pricing of the by-product, and the subsequent revenue gained from its sale, might significantly influence the pricing of the main production good. Given that the two products share joint costs, a business must carefully consider how to allocate costs between them and what pricing policy it is going to pursue.

If it is aiming to maximise profits, it should add the marginal costs from both products to get an *MC* curve for the 'combined' product. Similarly, it should add the marginal revenues from both products at each output to get an *MR* curve for the combined product. It should then choose the combined output where the combined *MC* equals the combined *MR*. It should read off the price at this output for each of the two products from their separate demand curves.

In practice, many firms simply decide on the viability of selling by-products *after* a decision has been made on producing the main product. If the specific costs associated with the by-product can be more than covered, then the firm will go ahead and sell it.

17.5 TRANSFER PRICING

The growth of modern business, both national and international, has meant that its organisation has become ever more complex. In an attempt to reduce the diseconomies that stem from coordinating such large business enterprises, the setting of price and output levels is frequently decentralised to individual divisions or profit centres. Such divisions or profit centres are assumed to operate in a semi-independent way, aiming to maximise their individual performance and, in so doing, benefit the business as a whole.

However, the decentralisation of pricing and output decision making can become problematic. This is particularly the case when the various divisions within the firm represent distinct stages in the production process. In these instances, certain divisions may well produce intermediate products that they will sell to other divisions within the business. There then

Definitions

Loss leader A product whose price is cut by the business in order to attract custom.

Full-range pricing A pricing strategy in which a business, seeking to improve its profit performance, assesses the pricing of its goods as a whole rather than individually.

By-product A good or service that is produced as a consequence of producing another good or service.

arises the difficulty of how such intermediate products should be priced. This is known as the problem of *transfer pricing*.

One implication of this is that a division which is seeking to maximise its own profits when selling to another division will attempt to exploit its 'monopoly' position and increase the transfer price. As it does so, the purchasing division, unless it, in turn, can pass on the higher cost, will see its profits fall. Indeed, if it could, the purchasing division would seek to drive down the purchase price as low as possible.

This conflict between divisions may not necessarily be in the interests of the business as a whole. The solution to this problem is for divisions to base their pricing of intermediate products on marginal costs. The marginal cost of the final product produced by the business will then be a 'true' marginal cost. If the business is seeking to maximise overall profits, it can then compare this final marginal cost with marginal revenue in order to decide on the level of total output. The lesson is that, for maximum company profits, individual divisions should seek to be efficient and produce with the lowest possible marginal costs, but not seek to maximise their own division's profits.

Transfer pricing and tax liability

Transfer pricing within multinational companies is an area of concern for tax authorities. The price used to transfer goods or services between plants and divisions located in different countries is not determined by a market. Instead, the price is often set to avoid tax, ensuring that profits appear in countries where taxes on profits are lowest.

In recent years there have been many high-profile cases of companies setting transfer prices so as to avoid tax. Companies such as Starbucks, Apple, Amazon and Coca-Cola have charged themselves high prices for the use of things such as logos, brands or business services owned or 'provided by' a subsidiary located in a low-tax country or region, such as Luxembourg, Jersey or the Cayman Islands and have thereby diverted a large proportion of their profits to these 'tax havens'. Often the 'subsidiary' is little more than a small office with one employee, a telephone and a bank account.

OECD countries have agreed that tax liabilities on profits should be calculated using prices that would have arisen if the transfers had taken place between independent firms, rather than within one firm. In practice this is difficult to achieve and extremely hard to police. We examine this issue further in section 23.6 (see pages 433–4).

KI 22
p181

> **Definition**
>
> **Transfer pricing** The pricing system used within a business organisation to transfer intermediate products between the business's various divisions.

17.6 PRICING AND THE PRODUCT LIFE CYCLE

New products are launched and then become established. Later they may be replaced by more up-to-date products. Many products go through such a 'life cycle'. Four stages can be identified in a typical life cycle (see Figure 17.7):

1. Being launched.
2. A rapid growth in sales.
3. Maturity: a levelling off in sales.
4. Decline: sales begin to fall as the market becomes saturated, or as the product becomes out of date.

Analogue televisions, audio cassettes and traditional mobile phones have all reached stage 4. Writable DVDs, DIY products and automatic washing machines have

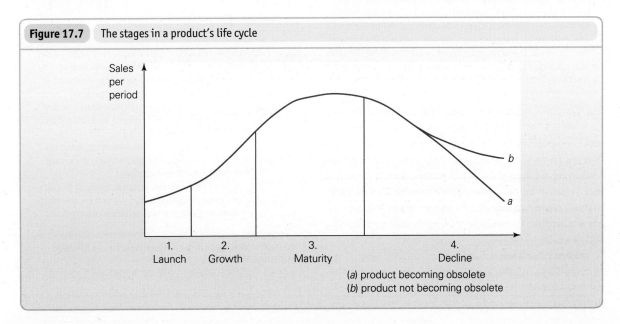

Figure 17.7 The stages in a product's life cycle

(a) product becoming obsolete
(b) product not becoming obsolete

BOX 17.3 HOW DO EUROPEAN COMPANIES SET PRICES?

In 2005 the European Central Bank published a summary of surveys of the pricing behaviour of 11 000 firms by the national central banks of nine countries in the eurozone (Austria, Belgium, France, Germany, Italy, Luxembourg, the Netherlands, Portugal and Spain).[1] This work mirrored much of the work carried out in other countries, including a study of pricing by UK firms in the mid-1990s.[2]

A number of questions were asked. Among these were: how do firms set prices? The findings, illustrated in table (a), show that firms engage largely in imperfect competition. For the eurozone as a whole, over half of firms engage in mark-up

pricing, and for German firms this proportion is as high as 73 per cent. Where the country surveys asked firms to distinguish between constant and variable mark-up, the latter type dominates. Moreover, the survey revealed that the lower the level of competition, the more frequently mark-up pricing is used.

More recently published evidence for the UK economy supports the finding that firms operate under conditions of imperfect competition.[3] Sixty-eight per cent of UK firms said that competitor price levels were important when determining their own prices. Fifty-eight per cent of firms said variable mark-ups, and 44 per cent said fixed mark-ups, were important considerations when setting prices.

(a) How do firms set prices? (%)

	Belgium	Germany	Spain	France	Italy	Netherlands	Portugal	Eurozone
Mark-up	46	73	52	40	42	56	65	54
Competitors' price	36	17	27	38	32	22	13	27
Other (mainly customer and regulator set)	18	10	21	22	26	21	23	18

Note: Figures do not necessarily add up to 100 per cent because of rounding.

Another question asked in the European surveys was whether firms charged a uniform price to each customer, or based their pricing on the quantity that each firm bought, or whether they priced on a case-by-case basis. The survey found that, on average, 80 per cent of eurozone firms use price discrimination tactics, setting prices on case-by-case or quantity sold basis. Figures range from 92 per cent of German firms to 65 per cent of Spanish firms.

There seems to be no clear relationship between the size of firm and price discrimination, though Luxembourg reported a positive relationship. If anything, smaller firms seem to differentiate their prices in France, Italy and Portugal. There was also no overall pattern as to the relationship between the frequency of price discrimination and the degree of competition in the domestic market. However, firms in the retail and wholesale trade were more likely to use uniform pricing.

Surveys conducted in Belgium, Spain and Luxembourg included questions directed at firms operating in foreign as well as domestic markets. Table (b) reveals the pricing behaviour of these firms. The survey suggests that some of the differences in pricing between markets seem to be accounted for by exchange rate movements, transport costs, market rules and the tax system. However, two of the most important determinants of overseas pricing by these firms are the prices charged by competitors and the cyclical nature of demand in these locations. In other words, pricing in foreign markets is determined more by the market power of the firms than by costs of transacting abroad.

The survey also sought to establish those factors which could cause prices to change – either up or down. The summary

results are presented in table (c). Changes in costs are the main factor underlying price increases, whereas changes in market conditions, such as competitors' prices and demand, are more important explanations of price reductions. Furthermore, prices seem to be more flexible downwards in response to demand shocks, while the opposite holds true in the case of cost shocks. Generally, prices did not seem to be sensitive to the economic outlook prevailing at the time the surveys were conducted.

(c) Factors leading to a rise or fall in price in the eurozone (mean scores: 4 = very important; 1 = completely unimportant)

	Rise	Fall
Labour costs	3.0	2.1
Costs of raw materials	3.1	2.6
Financial costs, including interest rates	2.2	1.9
Demand	2.2	2.6
Competitors' price	2.4	2.8

1. Which of the following is more likely to be consistent with the aim of maximising profits: pricing on the basis of
   (a) cost per unit plus a variable percentage mark-up;
   (b) cost per unit plus a fixed percentage mark-up?
2. Explain the differences between the importance attached to the different factors leading to price increases and those leading to price reductions.
3. What type of price discrimination is occurring, according to table (b), where firms have the possibility of charging different prices in different locations?
4. Why might we require a more detailed analysis of firm size and the different industrial sectors within the survey in order to evaluate the price-setting data presented above?

(b) Pricing behaviour in foreign markets (%)

	Belgium	Spain	Luxembourg
Price in euros is same for all countries	33	47	56
Price in euros is same for eurozone countries	9	6	5
Price in euros is different for all countries	58	47	39

[1] The Pricing Behaviour of Firms in the Euro Area: New Survey Evidence (Eurosystem Inflation Persistence Network, Working Paper series, no. 535, European Central Bank, October 2005).
[2] S. Hall, M. Walsh and T. Yates, 'How do UK companies set prices?', Bank of England Quarterly Bulletin, May 1996.
[3] J. Greenslade and M. Parker, 'New insights into price-setting behaviour in the UK: introduction and survey results', The Economic Journal, February 2012.

reached stage 3. Large LED TVs, speed-dating events, fair-trade herbal teas, induction hobs, music downloads and smartphones are probably still in stage 2. Electric cars, HD multimedia entertainment devices and biodiesel are probably still in stage 1 (at least they were when we wrote this – but things move quickly!).

At each stage, the firm is likely to be faced with quite different market conditions: not only in terms of consumer demand, but also in terms of competition from rivals. What does this mean for pricing strategy?

The launch stage

In this stage the firm will probably have a monopoly (unless there is a simultaneous launch by rivals).

Given the lack of substitutes, the firm may be able to charge very high prices and make large profits. This will be especially true if it is a radically new product – like the ball-point pen, the home computer and the mobile phone were. Such products are likely to have a rapidly expanding and price-inelastic demand.

> **Pause for thought**
>
> *If entry barriers are high, should a firm always charge a high price during this phase?*

The danger of a high-price policy is that the resulting high profits may tempt competitors to break into the industry, even if barriers are quite high. As an alternative, then, the firm may go for maximum 'market penetration': keeping the price low to get as many sales and as much brand loyalty as possible, before rivals can become established.

Which policy the firm adopts will depend on its assessment of its current price elasticity of demand and the likelihood of an early entry by rivals.

The growth stage

Unless entry barriers are very high, the rapid growth in sales will attract new firms. The industry becomes oligopolistic.

Despite the growth in the number of firms, sales are expanding so rapidly that all firms can increase their sales. Some price competition may emerge, but it is unlikely to be intense at this stage. New entrants may choose to compete in terms of minor product differences, while following the price lead set by the original firm.

The maturity stage

Now that the market has grown large, there are many firms competing. New firms – or, more likely, firms diversifying into this market – will be entering to get 'a piece of the action'. At the same time, the growth in sales is slowing down.

Competition is now likely to be more intense and collusion may well begin to break down. Pricing policy may become more aggressive as businesses attempt to hold on to their market share. Price wars may break out, only to be followed later by a 'truce' and a degree of price collusion.

It is in this stage particularly that firms may invest considerably in product innovation in order to 'breathe new life' into old products, especially if there is competition from new types of product. Thus the upgrading of hi-fi cassette recorders, with additional features such as Dolby S, was one way in which it was hoped to beat off competition from digital cassette recorders.

> **Pause for thought**
>
> *Why have audio cassettes and cassette recorders virtually disappeared while vinyl records and turntables have seen a resurgence in sales?*

The decline stage

Eventually, as the market becomes saturated, or as new superior alternative products are launched, sales will start to fall. For example, once most households had a fridge, the demand for fridges fell back as people simply bought them to replace worn-out ones, or to obtain a more up-to-date one. Initially in this stage, competition is likely to be intense. All sorts of price offers, extended guarantees, better after-sales service, added features, etc., will be introduced as firms seek to maintain their sales. Some firms may be driven out of the market, unable to survive the competition.

After a time, however, the level of sales may stop falling. Provided the product has not become obsolete, people still need replacements. This is illustrated in Figure 17.7 by line *b*. The market may thus return to a stable oligopoly with a high degree of tacit price collusion.

Alternatively, the product becomes obsolete (line *a*) and sales dry up. Firms will leave the market. It is pointless trying to compete.

SUMMARY

1a Prices are determined by a wide range of factors, principal among which are demand and supply, market structure and the aims of managers.

1b Firms with market power will not always attempt to maximise short-run profits, even if maximum profit is the aim. They may well limit prices so as to forestall the entry of new firms.

2a Traditional economic theory assumes that businesses will set prices corresponding to the output where the marginal costs of production are equal to marginal revenue. They will do so in pursuit of maximum profits.

2b The difficulties that a business faces in deriving its marginal cost and revenue curves suggest that this is unlikely to be a widely practised pricing strategy.

2c Cost-based pricing involves the business adding a profit mark-up to its average costs of production. The profit mark-up set by the business is likely to alter depending upon market conditions, such as the level of consumer demand and the degree of market competition.

3a Many businesses practise price discrimination in an attempt to maximise profits from the sale of a product. There are different types of price discrimination that a business might practise.

3b First-degree price discrimination is where is consumer is charged the maximum he or she is prepared to pay. Second-degree price discrimination is where the same consumer is charged different prices according to the amount, timing or other features of the purchase. Third-degree price discrimination is where consumers are divided into groups and the groups with the lower price elasticity of demand are charged the higher prices.

3c For a business to practise price discrimination it must be able to set prices and separate markets so as to prevent re-sale from the cheap to the expensive market. Also, consumers must have different price elasticities of demand that the firm can exploit in its pricing.

3d Whether price discrimination is in the consumer's interest or not is uncertain. Some individuals will gain and some will lose.

4 Businesses that produce many products need to consider the demand and production interrelations between them when setting prices.

5a The organisation of a business as a series of divisions, each pursuing an independent strategy, has implications for pricing policy, especially when products are sold within a business enterprise.

5b The optimum transfer price between divisions from the point of view of the whole organisation is likely to be equal to marginal cost.

6a Products will be priced differently depending upon where they are in the product's life cycle.

6b New products can be priced cheaply so as to gain market share, or priced expensively to recoup cost. Later on in the product's life cycle, prices will have to reflect the degree of competition, which may become intense as the market stabilises or even declines.

MyEconLab

This book can be supported by MyEconLab, which contains a range of additional resources, including an online homework and tutorial system designed to test and build your understanding.

You need both an access card and a course ID to access MyEconLab:

1. Is your lecturer using MyEconLab? Ask your lecturer for your course ID.

2. Has an access card been included with the book at a reduced cost? Check the inside back cover of the book.

3. If you have a course ID but no access card, go to: http://www.myeconlab.com/ to buy access to this interactive study programme.

REVIEW QUESTIONS

1 Explain why a business will find it difficult to set prices following the $MC = MR$ rule of traditional economic theory.

2 Could an existing firm implement a policy of limit pricing if it had the same cost schedule as potential new entrants? (In the example used in the text it is assumed that the existing firm has lower costs than the potential new entrant.)

3 'Basing prices on average cost is no less problematical than using marginal cost and marginal revenue.' Assess this statement.

4 Outline the main factors that might influence the size of the profit mark-up set by a business.

5 If customers were all charged the same price for a product could this ever be classed as an example of price discrimination? Explain your answer.

6 In Figure 17.4 on page 282 it is assumed that the costs to the firm are the same whether they have a policy of uniform pricing or implement a strategy of price discrimination. In reality explain why the costs may vary. What impact would this have on Figure 17.4?

7 A salesperson often asks a customer the following question 'how much are you thinking of spending?' Why might the salesperson ask this question? Is it in the interests of the customer to tell him/her the truth?

8 There are websites that collect together information on the various discounts that are available at any given point in time. Some of them make statements like 'Our staff spend several hours every day scouring the internet for great deals so that you don't have to.' Discuss the implications of these websites for retailers who want to use coupons as a means of implementing a policy of second-degree price discrimination.

9 If a cinema could sell all its seats to adults in the evenings at the end of the week, but only a few on Mondays and Tuesdays, what price discrimination policy would you recommend to the cinema in order for it to maximise its weekly revenue?

10 What is the role of a loss leader and what lessons might a business learn when pricing a range of products? Are there any supermarket products that would *not* be suitable to sell as loss leaders?

11 How will a business's pricing strategy differ at each stage of its product's life cycle? First assume that the business has a monopoly position at the launch stage; then assume that it faces a high degree of competition right from the outset.

ADDITIONAL PART F CASE STUDIES IN THE *ECONOMICS FOR BUSINESS* MyEconLab (www.pearsoned.co.uk/sloman)

F.1 What do you maximise? An examination of 'rational' behaviour from an individual's point of view – including individual managers.

F.2 When is a theory not a theory? A light-hearted examination of the difficulties of formulating theories from evidence.

F.3 Business divorce. A case study of the demergers of ICI and Hanson.

F.4 Enron. A cautionary tale of business growth.

F.5 Hypergrowth companies. Why do some companies grow quickly and are they likely to be a long-term success?

F.6 Peak-load pricing. An example of price discrimination: charging more when it costs more to produce.

F.7 Price discrimination in the cinema. An illustration of why it might be in a cinema's interests to offer concessionary prices at off-peak times, but not at peak times.

F.8 How do UK companies set prices? The findings of a Bank of England survey.

WEBSITES RELEVANT TO PART F

Numbers and sections refer to websites listed in the Web appendix and hotlinked from this text's website at **www.pearsoned.co.uk/sloman**

■ For news articles relevant to Part F, see the *Economics News Articles* link from MyEconLab or go directly to the Sloman Economics News site.

■ For general news relevant to alternative strategies, see websites in section A, and particularly A2, 3, 8, 9, 23, 24, 25, 26, 35, 36. See also A38–44 for links to newspapers worldwide.

■ For student resources relevant to Part F, see sites C1–7, 9, 10, 19.

■ For models and simulations on business strategy see sites C3, 5, 7, 8, 10, 13, 14, 17–20.

■ For information on mergers, see sites E4, 10, 18, 20; G7, 8.

■ For data on SME, see the SME database in B3. Also see sites E10 and G7.

■ For information on pricing, see site E10 and the sites of the regulators of the privatised industries: E15, 16, 19, 22.

■ For sites that look at companies, their scale of operation and market share, see B32; D2; E4, 10; G7, 8.

The firm in the factor market

The FT Reports . . .

The Financial Times, 11 October 2015

FT

US women fall behind in jobs market

By Sam Fleming

Last year the labour force participation rate of prime-age American women fell behind that of Japan — a country traditionally viewed as being a global laggard — leaving it languishing below the majority of OECD nations including Sweden, France, and even Greece.

The experience of women like Charlotte Brock . . . After finding she was pregnant, Ms Brock did what many working women are forced do in the US when confronted with a system that offers no guaranteed right to paid parental leave and hugely costly childcare: she quit her job to look after her baby. . .

. . . The reasons for declines in US labour force participation, which measures people in work or looking for a post, are complex and heavily contested. However, experts believe one driver is threadbare support for working parents. "We don't have the same incentives other countries have for women to stay in the labour force after they have kids," said Elise Gould of the Economic Policy Institute in Washington DC.

The share of US women either in work or looking for a post soared from just 33 per cent of 25-54-year-olds in the 1940s to 77 per cent at the start of the 2000s. Yet since then it has trended to around 73 per cent — even as other countries' participation rates improved. . .

. . . The issue shows signs of featuring in the presidential election, said Michael Strain, a resident scholar at the American Enterprise Institute, amid concerns that US economic prospects are being impaired by the large share of the population that has become detached from the jobs market. . . .

But political attention on female participation touches only one aspect of a broader, worrying trend. While unemployment has dropped since the recession and the US still benefits from a flexible labour market, the overall workforce participation rate including men has slid to its lowest level since 1977.

The ageing population explains a chunk of the departures from the labour force, but dismal numbers among individuals aged 25–54 point to other forces at work. Among prime-age men, only Italy and Israel have lower participation rates among 34 countries tracked by the OECD.

Gary Burtless at the Brookings Institution think-tank said lower levels of participation are apparent among the least-skilled men, which could reflect changes in the nature of the jobs on offer, as well as the recent downturn, when there was heavy attrition in sectors such as construction. Women have also suffered, in part because of public sector job cuts, he added.

So far we have considered the role of the firm as a supplier of goods and services. In other words, we have looked at the operation of firms in the goods market. But to produce goods and services involves using factors of production: labour, capital and raw materials. In Part G, therefore, we turn to examine the behaviour of firms in factor markets and, in particular, the market for labour and the market for capital.

In factor markets, the supply and demand roles are reversed. The firm is *demanding* factors of production in order to *produce* goods and services. This demand for factors is thus a *derived* demand: one that is derived from consumers' demand for the firm's products. Households, on the other hand, in order to earn the money to buy goods and services, are *supplying* labour. Chapter 18 focuses upon labour and the determination of wage rates. It also shows how the existence of power, whether of employers or trade unions, affects the wage rate and the level of employment in a given labour market. In addition to the issue of wage determination, we will consider the problem of low pay and discrimination, and the implications for the labour market of growing levels of flexibility in employment practices (see the quote above). We also look at the effects of the minimum wage and at gender and the labour market (see the *Financial Times* article).

In Chapter 19 we will consider the employment of capital by firms and look at the relationship between the business and investment. We will consider how businesses appraise the profitability of investment. We will also examine the various sources of finance for investment. The chapter finishes by examining the stock market. We ask whether it is an efficient means of allocating capital.

Key terms

Derived demand
Wage taker
Wage setter
Marginal revenue product
Monopsony
Bilateral monopoly
Trade union
Collective bargaining
Efficiency wages
Minimum wage rates
Discrimination
The flexible firm
Core and peripheral
    workers
Insiders and outsiders
Capital
Capital services
Investment
Discounting
Net present value
Financial intermediaries
Maturity transformation
Risk transformation
Retail and wholesale
    banking
Efficient capital markets
Weak, semi-strong and
    strong efficiency
Random walk

18

Labour markets, wages and industrial relations

<table>
<tr><td>

Business issues covered in this chapter

</td></tr>
<tr><td>

■ How has the UK labour market changed over the years?

■ How are wage rates determined in a perfect labour market?

■ What are the determinants of the demand and supply of labour and their respective elasticities?

■ What forms of market power exist in the labour market and what determines the power of employers and labour?

■ What effects do powerful employers and trade unions have on wages and employment?

■ What are the causes of low pay?

■ How has the minimum wage affected business and employment?

■ What is meant by a 'flexible' labour market and how has increased flexibility affected working practices, employment and wages?

</td></tr>
</table>

In this chapter we will consider how labour markets operate. In particular, we will focus on the determination of wage rates in different types of market: ones where employers are wage takers, ones where they can choose the wage rate, and ones where wage rates are determined by a process of collective bargaining.

We start by examining some of the key trends in the structure of the labour market.

18.1 MARKET-DETERMINED WAGE RATES AND EMPLOYMENT

The labour market has undergone great changes in recent years. Advances in technology, changes in the pattern of output, a need to be competitive in international markets and various social changes have all contributed to changes in work practices and in the structure and composition of the workforce. Major changes in the UK are discussed in Case study G.1 in MyEconLab.

In this chapter we shall be focusing on wage rates. An obvious question is why do some people earn very high

wages, whereas others, who perhaps work just as hard, if not harder, earn much less.

Why, for example, do top sportsmen and sportswomen get paid so much, but, perhaps more interestingly, why do only *some* of them get paid so much? Frank Lampard, Michael Ballack and Emmanuel Adebayo are great footballers and earn very high wages. But have you ever wondered why they earn so much more than Lin Dan and Domagoj Duvnjak? Probably not. They are Chinese and Croatian

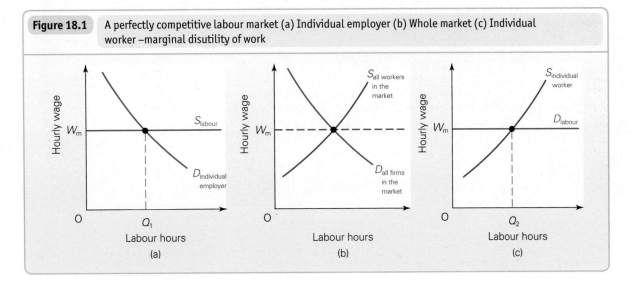

Figure 18.1 A perfectly competitive labour market (a) Individual employer (b) Whole market (c) Individual worker –marginal disutility of work

and are seen as world greats in badminton and handball, respectively.

Economics allows us to develop a theory that explains why the greatest ever sportsman in one discipline can be paid so little relative to merely great sportsmen in other disciplines. You can read about the salaries of footballers and the revenues and costs of their clubs on the Sloman Economics News site in the blog, *Why is it so difficult to make a profit? The problem of players' pay in the English Premier League.*

Perfect labour markets

Before we can answer such questions, we first need to consider how wages are determined, and to do this we must make a similar distinction to that made in the theory of the firm: the distinction between perfect and imperfect markets. Although in practice few labour markets are totally perfect, many do at least approximate to it.

The key assumption of a perfect labour market is that everyone is a *wage taker*. In other words, neither employers nor employees have any economic power to affect wage rates. This situation is not uncommon. Small employers are likely to have to pay the 'going wage rate' to their employees, especially where the employee is of a clear category, such as an electrician, a bar worker, a secretary or a porter. As far as employees are concerned, being a wage taker means not being a member of a union and therefore not being able to use collective bargaining to push up the wage rate.

The other assumptions of a perfect labour market are as follows:

■ *Freedom of entry.* There are no restrictions on the movement of labour. For example, workers are free to move to alternative jobs or to areas of the country where wage rates are higher. There are no barriers erected by, say, unions, professional associations or the government. Of course, it takes time for workers to change jobs and maybe to retrain. This assumption therefore applies only in the long run.

■ *Perfect knowledge.* Workers are fully aware of what jobs are available at what wage rates and with what conditions of employment. Likewise employers know what labour is available and how productive that labour is.

■ *Homogeneous labour.* It is usually assumed that, in perfect markets, workers of a given category are identical in terms of productivity. For example, it would be assumed that all bricklayers are equally skilled and motivated.

Pause for thought

Which of these assumptions do you think would be correct in each of the following cases? (a) Supermarket checkout operators. (b) Agricultural workers. (c) Crane operators. (d) Business studies teachers. (e) Call centre workers.

Wage rates and employment under perfect competition are determined by the interaction of the market demand and supply of labour. This is illustrated in Figure 18.1(b).

Generally it would be expected that the supply and demand curves slope the same way as in goods markets. The higher the wage paid for a certain type of job, the more workers will want to do that job. This gives an upward-sloping supply curve of labour. On the other hand, the higher the wage that employers have to pay, the less labour they will want to employ. Either they will simply produce less output, or they will substitute other factors of production, like machinery, for labour. Thus the demand curve for labour slopes downwards.

Figure 18.1(a) shows how an individual employer has to accept this wage. The supply of labour to that employer is infinitely elastic. In other words, at the market wage W_m, there is no limit to the number of workers available to that

Definition

Wage taker The wage rate is determined by market forces.

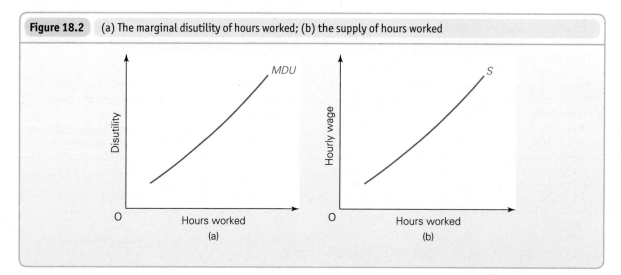

Figure 18.2 (a) The marginal disutility of hours worked; (b) the supply of hours worked

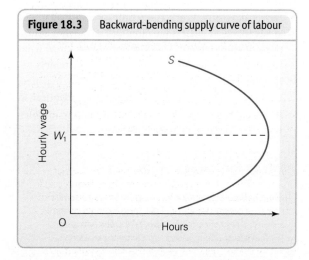

Figure 18.3 Backward-bending supply curve of labour

employer (but no workers at all will be available below it: they will all be working elsewhere). At the market wage W_m, the employer will employ Q_1 hours of labour.

Figure 18.1(c) shows how an individual worker also has to accept this wage. In this case it is the demand curve for that worker that is infinitely elastic. In other words, there is as much work as the worker cares to do at this wage (but none at all above it).

We now turn to look at the supply and demand for labour in more detail.

The supply of labour

We can look at the supply of labour at three levels: the supply of hours by an individual worker (Figure 18.1(c)), the supply of workers to an individual employer (Figure 18.1(a)) and the total market supply of a given category of labour (Figure 18.1(b)). Let us examine each in turn.

The supply of hours by an individual worker

Work involves two major costs (or 'disutilities') to the worker:

KI 9
p 51

■ When people work they sacrifice leisure.
■ The work itself may be unpleasant.

Each extra hour worked will involve additional disutility. This **marginal disutility of work** (*MDU*) will tend to *increase* as people work more hours. There are two reasons for this. First, the less the leisure they have left, the greater the disutility they experience in sacrificing a further hour of leisure. Second, the unpleasantness they experience in doing the job will tend to increase due to boredom or tiredness.

This increasing marginal disutility (see Figure 18.2(a)) will tend to give an upward-sloping supply curve of hours by an individual worker (see Figure 18.2(b)). The reason is that, in order to persuade people to work more hours, a higher hourly wage must be paid to compensate for the higher marginal disutility incurred. This helps explain why overtime rates are higher than standard rates.

Under certain circumstances, however, the supply of hours curve might bend backwards (see Figure 18.3). The reason is that, when wage rates go up, there will be two opposing forces operating on the individual's labour supply.

On the one hand, with higher wage rates people will tend to work more hours, since leisure would now involve a greater sacrifice of income and hence consumption. They substitute income for leisure. This is called the **substitution effect** of the increase in wage rates.

On the other hand, people may feel that with higher wage rates they can afford to work less and have more leisure. This is called the **income effect**.

Definitions

Marginal disutility of work The extra sacrifice/hardship to a worker of working an extra unit of time in any given time period (e.g. an extra hour per day).

Substitution effect of a rise in wages Workers will tend to substitute income for leisure as leisure now has a higher opportunity cost. This effect leads to *more* hours being worked as wages rise.

Income effect of a rise in wages Workers get a higher income for a given number of hours worked and may thus feel they need to work fewer hours as wages rise.

BOX 18.1	'TELECOMMUTERS'

The electronic cottage

The increasing sophistication of information technology, with direct computer linking, broadband access to the Internet, fax machines, mobile phones and Skype, has meant increased flexibility in the labour market. Many people can work from home – either all the time or for part of the week.

The number of these home workers or 'telecommuters' has grown steadily since the information technology revolution of the early 1980s. The *Monthly Labour Review* indicates that some 24 per cent of US workers telecommute all or part of the time.[1] According to the ONS, in the UK in 2014 there were 4.2 million home workers or 13.9 per cent of the 30.2 million people in work, up from 11.1 per cent in 1998.

> Of these home workers, around 1.5 million (or 5 per cent of those in work) worked within their home or its grounds, while the remaining 2.7 million people (8.9 per cent of those in work) used their home as a base but worked in different places.[2]

It has been found that where 'telecommuting networks' have been established, gains in productivity levels have been significant, when compared with comparable office workers. Most studies indicate rises in productivity of over 35 per cent and at the same time a reduction in staff absenteeism. With fewer interruptions and less chatting with fellow workers, less working time is lost. Add to this the stress-free environment, free from the strain of commuting, and the individual worker's performance is enhanced and workers are found to be more attentive.

Some of the most recent evidence from China reinforces the above.[3] The study looked at over 12 000 workers at a Chinese travel agency and experimented by having 200 of these employees telecommute. The findings found that those telecommuting took more calls, worked longer hours and had fewer sick days. By the end of the experiment, it was estimated that $2000 per employee would be saved every year by employees working at home and thus the option was offered to all workers across the firm.

In another study by O2, the company's entire UK head office workforce (2500 people) was asked to work from home on 8 February 2012: 36 per cent of them reported that they were more productive from home, with 52 per cent of time saved commuting being spent working.[4]

With further savings in time, in the renting and maintenance of offices (often in high-cost inner-city locations) and in heating and lighting costs, the economic arguments in favour of telecommuting seem very persuasive.

What is more, concerns that managers lose control over their employees, and that the quality of work falls, appear unfounded. In fact the reverse seems to have occurred: the quality of work in many cases has improved.

The technological developments that have permitted this rise in home working have been the equivalent of an increase in labour mobility. Work can be taken to the workers rather than the workers coming to the work. The effect is to reduce the premium that needs to be paid to workers in commercial centres, such as the City of London.

Then there are the broader gains to society. Telecommuting opens up the labour market to a wider group of workers who might find it relatively difficult to leave the home – groups such as single parents and the disabled. This not only improves efficiency, as a better use is made of the full labour force, but enhances equity as well. Also there are environmental gains, as fewer journeys to work mean less traffic congestion and less pollution.

But do people working from home feel isolated? For many people, work is an important part of their social environment, providing them with an opportunity to meet others and to work as a team. Interestingly, in the Chinese travel agency study above, only 50 per cent of those telecommuting said they would like to continue to do it, as they missed the social interactions of the office. The existence of video call software, such as Skype, has reduced some of these problems. However, for many, this technology is a poor substitute for being in the same room.

There is the question of whether employers sometimes exploit telecommuters. The Low Pay Commission has found that many homeworkers are paid well below the minimum wage because employers pay by the amount of work done and underestimate the amount of time it takes to complete work.

International telecommuting

There is no reason, of course, why telecommuters cannot work in different countries. With the creation of transoceanic fibre optical cable networks, international data transmission has become both faster and cheaper. Increasingly companies in developed countries have employed relatively low-wage workers in the developing world to do data processing, telesales and various types of 'back-office' work – work that is often highly skilled. More than 500 multinational companies employ IT workers in Bangalore alone.

Some of the international teleworkers work in call centres; others work from their own homes. Increasingly telecommuters in India are being provided with computers and broadband connections to enable them to do so.

> Call-centres of tomorrow will not be the ones operating from under a single roof. Instead, it will be a network of customer service agents (CSAs) working from their own home miles away from each other . . . With all the push that the [Indian] government is giving to increase broadband penetration, this concept will trigger a revolution in the way call-centres of today operate.[5]

International telecommuting can be closer to home. Growing numbers of UK workers have moved to France or Spain, where property is much cheaper and, thanks to broadband, they can carry on their UK jobs from there. When they do have to come into the office, cheap travel by budget airlines makes that possible.

1. What effect is telecommuting likely to have on (a) trade union membership; (b) trade union power?
2. How are the developments referred to in this box likely to affect relative house prices between capital cities and the regions?

[1] Mary C. Noonan. and Jennifer L. Glass, 'The hard truth about telecommuting', *Monthly Labour Review* (June 2012).
[2] 'Record proportion of people in employment are home workers', *Characteristics of Home Workers* (ONS, 4 June 2014).
[3] N. Bloom, J. Liang and Z. J. Ying, 'Does working from home work? Evidence from a Chinese Experiment', *CEP Discussion Paper No. 1194* (March 2013).
[4] 'O2 releases the results of the UK's biggest ever flexible working pilot', *The Blue*, 3 April 2012.
[5] 'Telecommuting: the work-from-home option', DQ Channels of India, www.dqchannels.com/content/mirror/105021801.asp.

The relative magnitude of these two effects determines the slope of the individual's supply curve. It is normally assumed that the substitution effect outweighs the income effect, especially at lower wage rates. A rise in wage rates acts as an incentive: it encourages a person to work more hours. It is possible, however, that the income effect will outweigh the substitution effect. Particularly at very high wage rates people say: 'There's not so much point now in doing overtime. I can afford to spend more time at home.'

If the wage rate becomes high enough for the income effect to dominate, the supply curve will begin to slope backward. This occurs above a wage rate of W_1 in Figure 18.3.

These considerations are particularly important for a government considering tax cuts. Cuts in income tax rates are like giving people a pay rise, and thus provide an incentive for people to work harder. This analysis is only correct, however, if the substitution effect dominates. If the income effect dominates, people will work less after the tax cut.

The supply of labour to an individual employer

Under perfect competition, the supply of labour to a particular firm will be perfectly elastic, as in Figure 18.1(a). The firm is a 'wage taker' and thus has no power to influence wages.

The market supply of a given type of labour

This will typically be upward sloping. The higher the wage rate offered in a particular type of job, the more people will want to do that job.

The *position* of the market supply curve of labour will depend on the number of people willing and able to do the job at each given wage rate. This depends on three things:

- the number of qualified people;
- the non-wage benefits or costs of the job, such as the pleasantness or otherwise of the working environment, job satisfaction or dissatisfaction, status, power, the degree of job security, holidays, perks and other fringe benefits;
- the wages and non-wage benefits in alternative jobs.

> ### Pause for thought
>
> *Which way will the supply curve shift if the wage rates in alternative jobs rise?*

A change in the wage rate will cause a movement along the supply curve. A change in any of these other three determinants will shift the whole curve.

The elasticity of the market supply of labour

How *responsive* will the supply of labour be to a change in the wage rate? If the market wage rate goes up, will a lot more labour become available or only a little? This responsiveness (elasticity) depends on (a) the difficulties and costs of changing jobs and (b) the time period.

Another way of looking at the elasticity of supply of labour is in terms of the **mobility of labour**: the willingness and ability of labour to move to another job, whether in a different location (geographical mobility) or in a different industry (occupational mobility). The mobility of labour (and hence the elasticity of supply of labour) will be higher when there are alternative jobs in the same location, when alternative jobs require similar skills and when people have good information about these jobs.

It is also much higher in the long run, when people have the time to acquire new skills and when the education system has had time to adapt to the changing demands of industry.

> ### Pause for thought
>
> *What effect has the expansion of the EU, in particular the accession of the central and eastern European countries (CEECs), had on the position and elasticity of the supply curve of various types of labour?*

The demand for labour: the marginal productivity theory

The traditional 'neoclassical' theory of the firm assumes that firms aim to maximise profits. The same assumption is made in the neoclassical theory of labour demand. This theory is generally known as the **marginal productivity theory**.

The profit-maximising approach

How many workers will a profit-maximising firm want to employ? The firm will answer this question by weighing up the costs of employing extra labour against the benefits. It will use exactly the same principles as in deciding how much output to produce.

In the goods market, the firm will maximise profits where the marginal cost of an extra unit of *goods* produced equals the marginal revenue from selling it: $MC = MR$.

In the labour market, the firm will maximise profits where the marginal cost of employing an extra *worker* equals the marginal revenue that the worker's output earns for the firm: MC of labour = MR of labour. The reasoning is simple. If an extra worker adds more to a firm's revenue than to its costs, the firm's profits will increase. It will be worth employing that worker. But as more

> ### Definitions
>
> **Mobility of labour** The ease with which labour can either shift between jobs (occupational mobility) or move to other parts of the country in search of work (geographical mobility).
>
> **Marginal productivity theory** The theory that the demand for a factor depends on its marginal revenue product.

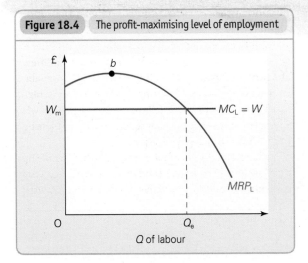

Figure 18.4 The profit-maximising level of employment

workers are employed, diminishing returns to labour will set in (see page 142). Each extra worker will produce less than the previous one, and thus earn less revenue for the firm. Eventually the marginal revenue from extra workers will fall to the level of their marginal cost. At that point the firm will stop employing extra workers. There are no additional profits to be gained. Profits are at a maximum.

Measuring the marginal cost and revenue of labour

Marginal cost of labour (MCL). This is the extra cost of employing one more worker. Under perfect competition the firm is too small to affect the market wage. It faces a horizontal supply curve (see Figure 18.1(a) on page 299). In other words, it can employ as many workers as it chooses at the market wage rate. Thus the additional cost of employing one more person will simply be the wage rate: $MC_L = W$.

Marginal revenue of labour (MRP_L). The marginal revenue that the firm gains from employing one more worker is called the **marginal revenue product of labour** (MRP_L). The MRP_L is found by multiplying two elements – the marginal physical product of labour (MPP_L) and the marginal revenue gained by selling one more unit of output (MR).

$$MRP_L = MPP_L \times MR$$

The MPP_L is the extra output produced by the last worker. Thus if the last worker produces 100 tonnes of output per week (MPP_L), and if the firm earns an extra £2 for each additional tonne sold (MR), then the worker's MRP is £200. This extra worker is adding £200 to the firm's revenue.

The profit-maximising level of employment for a firm

KI 20
p 142

The MRP_L curve is illustrated in Figure 18.4. As more workers are employed, there will come a point when diminishing returns set in (point *b*). Thereafter the MRP_L curve slopes downwards. The figure also shows the MC_L 'curve' at the current market wage W_m.

KI 4
p 25

Pause for thought

Why is the MC_L curve horizontal?

Profits are maximised at an employment level of Q_e, where MC_L (i.e. W) = MRP_L. Why? At levels of employment below Q_e, MRP_L exceeds MC_L. The firm will increase profits by employing more labour. At levels of employment above Q_e, MC_L exceeds MRP_L. In this case the firm will increase profits by reducing employment.

Derivation of the firm's demand curve for labour

No matter what the wage rate, the quantity of labour demanded will be found from the intersection of W and MRP_L (see Figure 18.5). At a wage rate of W_1, Q_1 labour is demanded (point *a*); at W_2, Q_2 is demanded (point *b*); at W_3, Q_3 is demanded (point *c*).

The MRP_L curve therefore shows the quantity of labour employed at each wage rate. But this is just what the demand curve for labour shows. Thus the MRP_L curve is the demand curve for labour.

There are three determinants of the demand for labour:

- *The wage rate.* This determines the position *on* the demand curve. (Strictly speaking, we would refer here to the wage determining the 'quantity demanded' rather than the 'demand'.)
- *The productivity of labour (MPP_L).* This determines the position *of* the demand curve.
- *The demand for the good.* The higher the market demand for the good, the higher will be its market price, and hence the higher will be the MR, and thus the MRP_L. This too determines the position of the demand curve. It shows how the demand for labour (and other factors) is a ***derived demand***: i.e. one derived from the demand for the good. For example, the higher the demand for houses, and hence the higher their price, the higher will be the demand for bricklayers.

Pause for thought

If the productivity of a group of workers rises by 10 per cent, will the wage rate they are paid also rise by 10 per cent? Explain why or why not.

Definitions

Marginal revenue product of labour The extra revenue a firm earns from employing one more unit of labour.

Derived demand The demand for a factor of production depends on the demand for the good which uses it.

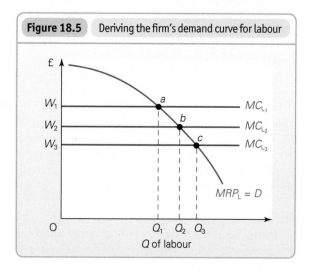

Figure 18.5 Deriving the firm's demand curve for labour

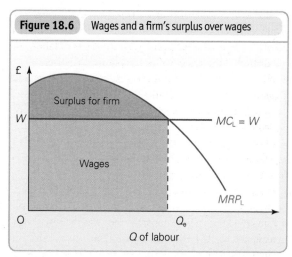

Figure 18.6 Wages and a firm's surplus over wages

A change in the wage rate is represented by a movement *along* the demand curve for labour. A change in the productivity of labour or in the demand for the good *shifts* the curve.

The elasticity of demand for labour

The elasticity of demand for labour (with respect to changes in the wage rate) will be greater:

The greater the price elasticity of demand for the good. A rise in the wage rate, being a cost of production, will drive up the price of the good. If the market demand for the good is elastic, this rise in price will lead to a significant fall in sales and hence a bigger drop in the number of people employed.

The easier it is to substitute labour for other factors and vice versa. If labour can be readily replaced by other inputs (e.g. machinery), then a rise in the wage rate will lead to a large reduction in labour as workers are replaced by these other inputs.

The greater the wage cost as a proportion of total costs. If wages are a large proportion of total costs and the wage rate rises, total costs will rise significantly; therefore production will fall significantly, and so too will the demand for labour.

The longer the time period. Given sufficient time, firms can respond to a rise in wage rates by reorganising their production processes. For example, they could introduce robotic production lines.

Wages and profits under perfect competition

The wage rate (W) is determined by the interaction of demand and supply in the labour market. This will be equal to the value of the output that the last person produces (MRP_L).

Profits to the individual firm will arise from the fact that the MRP_L curve slopes downward (diminishing returns). Thus the last worker adds less to the revenue of firms than previous workers already employed.

If *all* workers in the firm receive a wage equal to the *MRP* of the *last* worker, everyone but the last worker will receive a wage less than their *MRP*. This excess of MRP_L over W of previous workers provides a surplus to the firm over its wages bill (see Figure 18.6). Part of this will be required for paying non-wage costs; part will be the profits for the firm.

Perfect competition between firms will ensure that profits are kept down to *normal* profits. If the surplus over wages is such that *supernormal* profits are made, new firms will enter the industry. The price of the good (and hence MRP_L) will fall, and the wage and hence costs will be bid up, until only normal profits remain.

18.2 POWER IN THE LABOUR MARKET

Power may exist on either side of the labour market. Firms may have market power as employers; workers may have market power is they are members of powerful trade unions. In this section, we consider both types of labour market 'imperfection'.

Firms with market power

In the real world, many firms have the power to influence wage rates – they are not wage takers. When a firm is the only employer of a particular type of labour, this situation is called a ***monopsony***. Royal Mail used to be a monopsony employer of postal workers.[6] Another example is when a factory is the only employer of certain types of labour in that district. It therefore has local monopsony power.

When there are just a few employers, this is called ***oligopsony***. The big supermarkets are often considered to be oligopsonists, not because they are the only employers of a particular type of labour, but because they are the main buyers of certain products. Thus, they have significant power over farmers and other suppliers and can use that power to force down the prices they pay, thus cutting their costs.

Monopsonists (and oligopsonists) in the labour market are 'wage setters', not 'wage takers'. Thus a large employer in a small town may have considerable power to resist wage increases or even to force wage rates down.

Such firms face an upward-sloping supply curve of labour. This is illustrated in Figure 18.7. If the firm wants to take on more labour, it will have to pay a higher wage rate to attract workers away from other industries. But conversely, by employing less labour it can get away with paying a lower wage rate.

The supply curve shows the wage that must be paid to attract a given quantity of labour. The wage it pays is the *average cost* to the firm of employing labour (AC_L): i.e. the cost per worker. The supply curve is also therefore the AC_L curve.

The *marginal* cost of employing one more worker (MC_L) will be above the wage (AC_L): see Figure 18.7. The reason is that the wage rate has to be raised to attract extra workers. The MC_L will thus be the new higher wage paid to the new employee *plus* the small rise in the total wages bill for existing employees: after all, they will be paid the higher wage too.

The profit-maximising employment of labour would be at Q_1, where $MC_L = MRP_L$. The wage (found from the AC_L curve) would thus be W_1.

If this had been a perfectly competitive labour market, employment would have been at the higher level Q_2, with the wage rate at the higher level W_2, where $W = MRP_L$. What in effect the monopsonist is doing, therefore, is forcing the wage rate down by restricting the number of workers employed.

Workers with market power: the role of trade unions

How can unions influence the determination of wages, and what might be the consequences of their actions?

The extent to which unions will succeed in pushing up wage rates depends on their power and militancy. It also depends on the power of firms to resist and on their ability to pay higher wages. In particular, the scope for unions to gain a better deal for their members depends on the sort of market in which the employers are producing.

---

[6]Until 2005, Royal Mail had a statutory monopoly in the delivery of letters.

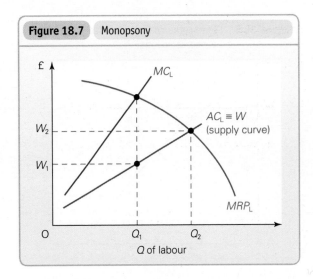

Figure 18.7　Monopsony

Unions facing competitive employers

If the employers are producing under perfect or monopolistic competition, unions can raise wages only at the expense of employment. Firms are only earning normal profit. Thus if unions force up wages, the marginal firms will go bankrupt and leave the industry. Fewer workers will be employed. The fall in output will lead to higher prices. This will enable the remaining firms to pay a higher wage rate.

> ### Pause for thought
>
> *Which of the following unions find themselves in a weak bargaining position for the reasons given?*
> a) *The maritime workers union (Nautilus).*
> b) *The shopworkers' union (USDAW).*
> c) *The National Union of Mineworkers (NUM).*
> d) *The farmworkers' union (part of the Unite Union).*

Figure 18.8 illustrates these effects. If unions force the wage rate up from W_1 to W_2, employment will fall from Q_1 to Q_2. There will be a surplus of people ($Q_3 - Q_2$) wishing to work in this industry, for whom no jobs are available.

The union is in a doubly weak position. Not only will jobs be lost as a result of forcing up the wage rate, but also there is a danger that these unemployed people could undercut the union wage, unless the union can prevent firms employing non-unionised labour.

> ### Definitions
>
> **Monopsony** A market with a single buyer or employer.
> **Oligopsony** A market with just a few buyers or employers.

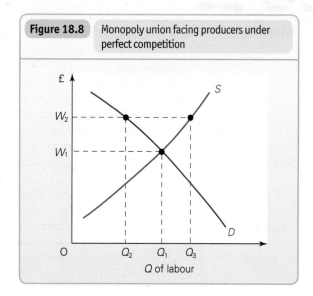

Figure 18.8 Monopoly union facing producers under perfect competition

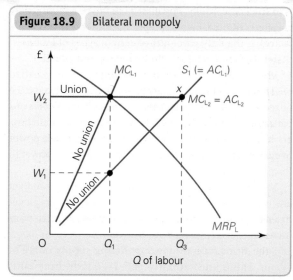

Figure 18.9 Bilateral monopoly

In a competitive market, then, the union is faced with the choice between wages and jobs. Its actions will depend on its objectives.

Wages can be increased without a reduction in the level of employment only if, as part of the bargain, the productivity of labour is increased. This is called a ***productivity deal***. The *MRP* curve, and hence the demand curve in Figure 18.8, shifts to the right.

Power on both sides of the labour market: bilateral monopoly

One interesting observation is that the largest and most powerful trade unions are often in industries where there are monopsonist or oligopsonist employers. In such cases, trade unions act as a countervailing power to the large employer.

So, what happens when a union monopoly faces a monopsony employer? What will the wage rate and level of employment be? Unfortunately, economic theory cannot give a precise answer to this question. There is no 'equilibrium' level as such. Ultimately, the wage rate and level of employment will depend on the relative bargaining strengths and skills of unions and management.

Strange as it may seem, unions may be in a better position to make substantial gains for their members when they are facing a powerful employer. There is often considerable scope for them to increase wage rates *without* this leading to a reduction in employment, or even for them to increase both the wage rate *and* employment. Figure 18.9 shows how this can be so.

Assume first that there is no union. The monopsonist will maximise profits by employing Q_1 workers at a wage rate of W_1 (Q_1 is where $MRP_L = MC_L$).

What happens when a union is introduced into this situation? Wages will now be set by negotiation between unions and management. Once the wage rate has been agreed, the employer can no longer drive the wage rate

down by employing fewer workers. If it tried to pay less than the agreed wage, it could well be faced by a strike, and thus have a zero supply of labour!

Similarly, if the employer decided to take on *more* workers, it would not have to *increase* the wage rate as long as the negotiated wage was above the free-market wage: as long as the wage rate was above that given by the supply curve S_1.

The effect of this is to give a new supply curve that is horizontal up to the point where it meets the original supply curve. For example, let us assume that the union succeeds in negotiating a wage rate of W_2 in Figure 18.9. The supply curve will be horizontal at this level to the left of point x. To the right of this point it will follow the original supply curve S_1, since to acquire more than Q_3 workers the employer would have to raise the wage rate above W_2.

If the supply curve is horizontal to the left of point x at a level of W_2, so too will be the MC_L curve. The reason is simply that the extra cost to the employer of taking on an extra worker (up to Q_3) is merely the negotiated wage rate: no rise has to be given to existing employees. If MC_L is equal to the wage, the profit-maximising employment ($MC_L = MRP_L$) will now be where $W = MRP_L$. At a negotiated wage rate of W_2, the firm will therefore choose to employ Q_1 workers.

What this means is that the union can push the wage right up from W_1 to W_2 and the firm will still *want* to employ Q_1. In other words, a wage rise can be obtained *without* a reduction in employment.

The union could go further still. By threatening industrial action, it may be able to push the wage rate above W_2

Definition

Productivity deal Where, in return for a wage increase, a union agrees to changes in working practices that will increase output per worker.

and still insist that Q_1 workers are employed (i.e. no redundancies). The firm may be prepared to see profits drop right down to a normal level rather than face a strike and risk losses. The absolute upper limit to the wage rate will be that at which the firm is forced to close down.

The actual wage rate under bilateral monopoly is usually determined through a process of negotiation or 'collective bargaining'. The outcome of this bargaining will depend on a wide range of factors, which vary substantially from one industry or firm to another.

Collective bargaining

Sometimes when unions and management negotiate, *both* sides can gain from the resulting agreement. For example, the introduction of new technology may allow higher wages, improved working conditions and higher profits. Usually, however, one side's gain is the other's loss. Higher wages mean lower profits. Either way, both sides will want to gain the maximum for themselves.

The outcome of the negotiations will depend on the relative bargaining strengths of both sides. In bargaining there are various threats or promises that either side can make. For these to be effective, of course, the other side must believe that they will be carried out.

Union threats might include strike action, *picketing, working to rule* or refusing to co-operate with management, for example in the introduction of new technology. Alternatively, in return for higher wages or better working conditions, unions might offer no-strike agreements (or an informal promise not to take industrial action), increased productivity, reductions in the workforce or long-term deals over pay.

In turn, employers might *threaten* employees with plant closure, *lock-outs*, redundancies or the employment of non-union labour. Or they might offer, in return for lower wage increases, various 'perks' such as productivity bonuses, profit-sharing schemes, better working conditions, more overtime, longer holidays or security of employment.

Industrial action imposes costs on both unions and firms. Unions lose pay; firms lose revenue. It is usually in both sides' interests, therefore, to settle by negotiation. Nevertheless, to gain the maximum advantage, each side must persuade the other that it will carry out its threats if pushed. In 1978/79, the UK experienced a period known as the Winter of Discontent, where strikes took place at the same time across a huge number of sectors. A blog on the Sloman News Site, *The Winter of Discontent: the sequel?*, considers a similar period of industrial unrest that could have occurred in 2009. This is also discussed in Box 18.2.

The approach described so far has essentially been one of confrontation. The alternative is for both sides to concentrate on increasing the total net income of the firm by co-operating on ways to increase efficiency or the quality of the product. This approach is more likely when unions and management have built up an atmosphere of trust over time.

Union membership. Trade union membership in the UK stands at about 6.5 million (25.6 per cent of employees) in the mid-2010s. This number is around half of that seen in the late 1970s. The fall in membership can be explained by a number of factors: the shift to a service-based economy; continued privatisation and the introduction of private-sector management practices, such as local pay bargaining; and contracted-out services into many of the remaining parts of the public sector. More women working and more part-time and casual work, with many people having no guaranteed hours, so-called 'zero-hour contracts' (see Box 6.1), are also contributory factors, as are the attitudes of many firms to union recognition.

Union membership remains highest in areas of the public sector with high levels of monopsony power, such as education, but there is no doubt that, even here, their power has declined. Case G.4 in MyEconLab charts the rise and decline of the labour movement in the UK.

The role of government

The government can influence the outcome of collective bargaining in a number of ways. One is to try to set an example. It may take a tough line in resisting wage demands by public-sector workers, hoping thereby to persuade employers in the private sector to do likewise.

Alternatively, it could set up arbitration or conciliation machinery. For example, in the UK, the Advisory Conciliation and Arbitration Service (ACAS) conciliates in around 1000 disputes each year, roughly half of these involving pay-related issues. It also provides, on request by both sides, an arbitration service, where its findings will be binding.

Another approach is to use legislation. The government could pass laws that restrict the behaviour of employers or unions. It could pass laws that set a minimum wage rate (see pages 312–14), or prevent discrimination against workers on various grounds. Similarly, it could pass laws that curtail the power of unions.

The Conservative governments between 1979 and 1997 put considerable emphasis on reducing the power of trade unions and making labour markets more 'flexible'. Several Acts of Parliament were passed during these years, which significantly reduced the power of trade unions in the UK. However, in recent years, we have seen many incidents of trade union action in the UK and in many other countries (see Box 18.2).

Definitions

Picketing Where people on strike gather at the entrance to the firm and attempt to dissuade workers or delivery vehicles from entering.

Working to rule Workers do no more than they are supposed to, as set out in their job descriptions.

Lock-outs Union members are temporarily laid off until they are prepared to agree to the firm's conditions.

BOX 18.2　WINTERS OF DISCONTENT

The sequel?

In the winter of 1978/79 (dubbed the 'Winter of Discontent'), the UK economy almost ground to a halt when workers across the country went on strike. Miners, postal workers, bin-men, grave diggers, healthcare ancillaries, train and bus drivers, gas and electricity workers, lorry drivers for companies such as BP and Esso and workers at Ford all went on strike; there were even unofficial strikes by ambulance drivers. The strike was partly the cause of the Labour government losing the 1979 election.

Industrial action continued into 1980 and 1981 as the UK economy plunged into recession and unemployment rose to 3 million. Then again, in 1984–85, there was large-scale disruption as the National Union of Miners struck over pit closures. The chart illustrates the huge loss of working hours during these periods.

It looked as though history was about to repeat itself just a few years ago in 2009 as the world economy plunged into a deep recession in the aftermath of the credit crunch.

There were fears that Britain was entering months of industrial unrest, as bus drivers, bin-men, airline and underground staff and firefighters followed the postal workers' lead and protested at changes to their pay, shift patterns and working conditions.

In the latter half of 2009 and early 2010, industrial action spread rapidly in the UK (and in other countries across the world). From bins to buses, and trains to planes, there was massive disruption, affecting everyone and reducing output at a time when it was the last thing the country needed. The effects were serious for many parts of the economy, although, as the chart shows, there were far fewer days lost this time.

Postal services

Throughout 2009, members of the Communication Workers Union (CWU) held intermittent one-day strikes, and in October 2009 a national strike went ahead. The confrontation was concerned with pay, working conditions, a pension deficit and the introduction of modern, efficient technology, which the CWU expected to lead to job losses and office closures.

So, what were the effects?

- Post was obviously delayed (over 150 million undelivered letters and packets).
- Greetings cards companies were concerned that people would not send cards, affecting profitability at their busiest time of year.
- Households faced delays in paying bills and receiving payments.
- Businesses experienced delays in supplies, orders and customer service was restricted.
- eBay traders had to delay sending packages.
- Businesses had to employ other delivery services, raising costs, cutting profits and causing lost customers.

Research by the London Chamber of Commerce suggested that it cost London more than £500 million in lost business. The Chief Executive of the organisation said:

Not being able to rely on a normal postal service forces companies to pay extra for couriers, delays consumer spending, damages client relationships and plays havoc with a firm's cash flow.[7]

But the news was not all bad, at least not for the Royal Mail's competitors, such as TNT, Fedex and DHL, with TNT handling an extra 16 000 items in the first 24 hours!

Airlines

While post failed to get from A to B, so did passengers, as talks with BA cabin crew over pay freezes, working practices and redundancies broke down. Strikes occurred over Christmas and then again in 2010, with those in March 2010 estimated to have cost BA between £40 and £45 million.[8]

The Spanish airline, Iberia, experienced strikes over the renewal of contracts in 2009, which led to 400 flights cancelled in two days, pushing up costs to stranded passengers, as they tried to get home on more expensive airlines. Pilots from India's Jet Airways held a five-day strike during September 2009, and Germany's Lufthansa had to cancel thousands of flights in early 2010, when 4000 pilots went on strike, with fears of foreign pilots being used to maintain the airline's profitability. Estimates suggest this cost the company some £21.9 million per day.

Airlines were severely hit by the recession, as holidays abroad became an unaffordable luxury for many cash-strapped consumers. While many airlines had other problems as well, lower revenues and profits meant that cost savings were needed, and so staff had to be cut. BA lost over £400 million in 2008, due to lower passenger numbers, and the resulting strike action imposed further costs.

The financial impact of these strikes included not only lost revenue but also the cost of hiring in planes and crew, as well as buying seats on rival carriers.

Other problems

Over 800 drivers in Bolton, Bury and Wigan held numerous 24-hour strikes during 2009, because of disputes with First Bus over pay. At the same time, 1.5 million customers were affected when thousands of Underground workers went on strike and this occurred again in February 2015. These strikes cost businesses, as staff struggled to get to work, meaning lost hours, and as shoppers had problems getting to London, meaning lost sales.

Members of the National Union of Teachers and the National Association of Headteachers boycotted Sats tests in 2010, in part to 'protect their terms and conditions of employment'[9] and in Leeds, 92 per cent of refuse workers went on strike for several weeks after refusing the Council's offer relating to their working

---

[7] Tom Sands, 'Postal strike costs London £500m', Parcl2Go.com News, 26 October 2009.
[8] 'BA strike: talks between airline and union resume', BBC News, 7 April 2010.
[9] 'Headteachers vote to boycott Sats tests', The Guardian, 16 April 2010.

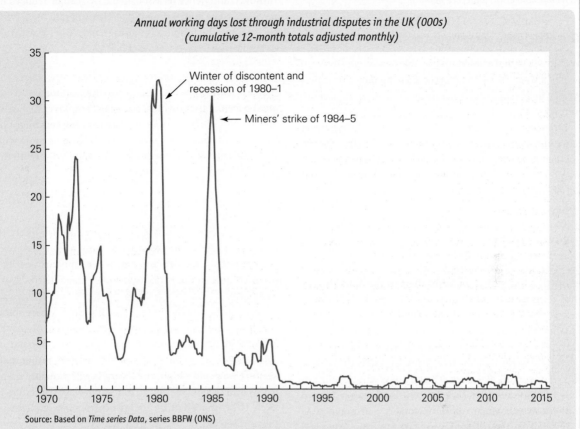

Annual working days lost through industrial disputes in the UK (000s)
(cumulative 12-month totals adjusted monthly)

Winter of discontent and recession of 1980–1

Miners' strike of 1984–5

Source: Based on *Time series Data*, series BBFW (ONS)

week and pay. Piles of rubbish built up, which although not imposing direct costs on business, did adversely affect them. It was an 'external cost' imposed on consumers as it reduced the incentive to shop. We consider external costs in Chapter 20.

A trilogy or quadrilogy or . . .?

The 2009 strikes did not compare with the Winter of Discontent of 1978/79, but did still disrupt the lives of millions and cost the economy at a very bad time. Then, with the election of the Coalition government and the start of its 'austerity policies', many trade unions quickly began to mobilise.

Public-sector unions were particularly vocal in response to curbs on their pay and pensions and further industrial action ensued. In mid-2010, the Public and Commercial Services Union threatened to re-launch strikes which had begun in March involving 200 000 civil servants, but which had been suspended for the election. In March 2013, the Public and Commercial Services Union (PCS) voted to strike in response to job losses, changes in pensions and public-sector pay being frozen for two years for those earning above £21 000.

Further postal strikes took place over the 2013 Easter weekend and again in the run-up to Christmas in 2014. Baggage handlers at Stansted airport threatened to walk out following shift changes which could adversely affect their pay. This followed a four-day strike over the Jubilee weekend in June 2012.

Civil servants were called in to cover UK border control posts, which was the first time that the government recruited other members of the civil service to break a strike by immigration officials. Further strikes by a variety of airlines and air traffic controllers have also occurred, with the latest (writing in April 2015) by French air traffic controllers in April 2015.[10]

Despite the volume of industrial action we have observed over the past six to seven years, there has been growing recognition that employers and employees can learn from each other and with co-operation everyone can be made better off. However, negotiations across the UK have failed to resolve many issues, and estimates across all affected industries now paint a stark picture of the economic costs incurred by recent industrial action and possible action to come.

1. Are strikes the best course of action for workers? In the cases outlined above, would you have advised any other responses by either side?
2. Which strike do you think was the most costly to (a) consumers, (b) businesses and (c) the economy? Explain.
3. Why did strains on public finances lead to industrial unrest?

---

[10]'French air-traffic strike: a formidable power to disrupt', *The Independent*, 5 May 2015.

On the Sloman News Site, you will find blogs written about strikes and industrial action in posts entitled *The Royal Mail, Quiet Underground: Busy Overground, PCS vote to strike, A News blackout* and *Turbulence in the air*.

The efficiency wage hypothesis

We have seen that a union may be able to force an employer to pay a wage above the market-clearing rate. But it may well be in an employer's interests to do so, even in non-unionised sectors.

One explanation for this phenomenon is the *efficiency wage hypothesis*. This states that the productivity of workers rises as the wage rate rises. As a result, employers are frequently prepared to offer wage rates above the market-clearing level, attempting to balance increased wage costs against gains in productivity. But why may higher wage rates lead to higher productivity? There are three main explanations.

Less 'shirking'. In many jobs it is difficult to monitor the effort that individuals put into their work. Workers may thus get away with shirking or careless behaviour. The business could attempt to reduce shirking by imposing a series of sanctions, the most serious of which would be dismissal. The greater the wage rate currently received, the greater will be the cost to the individual of dismissal, and the less likely it is that workers will shirk. The business will benefit not only from the additional output, but also from a reduction in the costs of having to monitor workers' performance. As a consequence the *efficiency wage rate* for the business will lie above the market-determined wage rate.

Reduced labour turnover. If workers receive on-the-job training or retraining, then losing a worker once the training has been completed is a significant cost to the business. Labour turnover, and hence its associated costs, can be reduced by paying a wage above the market-clearing rate. By paying such a wage, the business is seeking a degree of loyalty from its employees.

Morale. A simple reason for offering wage rates above the market-clearing level is to motivate the workforce – to create the feeling that the firm is a 'good' employer that cares about its employees. As a consequence, workers might be more industrious, show more initiative and be more willing to accept the introduction of new technology (with the reorganisation that it involves).

The paying of efficiency wages above the market-clearing wage will depend upon the type of work involved.

Workers who occupy skilled positions are likely to receive efficiency wages considerably above the market wage. This is especially true where the business has invested time in their training, which makes them costly to replace.

By contrast, workers in unskilled positions, where shirking can be easily monitored, little training takes place and workers can be easily replaced, are unlikely to command an 'efficiency wage premium'. In such situations, rather than keeping wage rates high, the business will probably try to pay as little as possible and so minimum wage legislation is likely to be important for such workers, as we shall see in the next section.

18.3 LOW PAY AND DISCRIMINATION

Low pay

Identifying workers as being low paid clearly involves making certain value judgements about what constitutes 'low'.

One way is to consider pay relative to living standards. The problem here, though, is that pay is only one of the determinants of living standards. Pay of a certain level may give a reasonable living standard for a single person, especially if he or she has property, such as a house and furniture. The same pay may result in dire poverty for a large household with several dependants living on that one income, and considerable outgoings.

It is more usual, therefore, to define low pay relative to average rates of pay. Low pay will be anything below a certain percentage of the average wage rate. The larger the percentage selected, the bigger the low-paid sector will become.

A decency threshold. The Council of Europe defines low pay as anything below 60 per cent of a country's mean net (i.e. post-tax) earnings. It refers to this as the 'decency threshold'. Previously the decency threshold was defined as anything below 68 per cent of a country's mean gross wage rate, which gave a higher figure. If a minimum hourly wage were to be based on even the new lower decency threshold, then

Definitions

Efficiency wage hypothesis A hypothesis that states that a worker's productivity is linked to the wage he or she receives.

Efficiency wage rate The profit-maximising wage rate for the firm after taking into account the effects of wage rates on worker motivation, turnover and recruitment.

in the UK it would be set at around £8.60 and would raise wages for about 35 per cent of workers. Other studies have identified the low-pay threshold at two-thirds of *median* hourly earnings of *male* workers.[11] A minimum hourly wage set at this level would also be around £8.60 for full-time workers.

A minimum wage. Another way of defining low pay is anything below an agreed minimum wage. As of January 2015, 22 of the 28 EU member countries had a national minimum wage. These rates varied considerably. But, three broad groupings can be identified: one where minimum wages were lower than €500 a month (Bulgaria, Romania, Lithuania, the Czech Republic, Hungary, Latvia, Slovakia, Estonia, Croatia and Poland), an intermediate set where minimum wages range from €500 to less than €1000 a month (Portugal, Greece, Malta, Spain and Slovenia) and a final set where the national minimum wage was €1000 or above per month (United Kingdom, France, Ireland, Germany, the Netherlands, Belgium and Luxembourg).

The UK minimum in October 2015 was £6.70 per hour for those aged 21 and over, £5.30 per hour for those aged 18–20 and £3.87 for 16- and 17-year-olds. In 2014, the minimum wage was 56.0 per cent of the median hourly wage for all workers and 49.4 per cent of that for full-time workers. In 1999, the year that the minimum wage was introduced, it was 45.6 per cent of the median for all workers, but when evidence suggested that the minimum wage seemed to be having little effect on unemployment, it was raised faster than wages, to reach over 52 per cent of the median wage by 2008. Since then the minimum wage has fallen in real terms (i.e. after adjusting for inflation).

You can read about the impact of the minimum wage in two articles on the Sloman News Site: 'An above-inflation rise in the NMW' and 'Effects of raising the minimum wage'.

A living wage. Although the minimum wage has increased since its introduction in 1999, many critics still argue that it is insufficient and is not a 'living wage'. In particular, due to variations in the cost of living in different parts of the UK, there are suggestions that minimum wages should vary depending on where you live. In recent years there has been a campaign in the UK for a 'living wage' – one which would lift those working full-time out of poverty. The Living Wage Foundation has estimated that for 2015 the UK average hourly wage would need to have been £7.85, while in London, where the cost of living is highest, this would have required an hourly rate of £9.15.

Changes in relative wages over time. Another approach to the analysis of low pay is to see how the wage rates of the

lowest-paid workers have changed over time compared to the average worker. Evidence from various editions of the Annual Survey of Hours and Earnings (National Statistics) indicates that inequality in pay in the UK has widened. In 1979, the lowest 10 per cent of wage earners received a wage that was 70 per cent of the median wage. Provisional data for 2014 calculates the median weekly wage for full-time workers at £518. However, the lowest 10 per cent of workers earn less than £287.90 or approximately 55 per cent of the median wage. On the other hand, the top 10 per cent of earners received a weekly wage of more than £1024.40, which is 198 per cent of the median weekly wage.

Low pay in particular sectors/industries. Low pay tends to be concentrated in certain sectors and occupations. Sales, customer service workers, accommodation and food service workers are classic examples. Weekly wages of workers in the latter two occupations are only 61.8 per cent of the UK average. Low pay also occurs disproportionately between women and men. In 2014, the median hourly wage for women was £10.37, while the figure for men was 24.6 per cent higher at £12.92. When only considering full-time workers, the differential falls to 11.45 per cent, reflecting the lower pay for part-time workers and the higher proportion of women working part time.

The growth in low pay

A number of factors have contributed to the progressive rise in the size of the low-paid sector and the widening disparity between high- and low-income earners over the past 30 years.

With technological development, it is the demand for skilled labour that has increased, thus pushing up their wages, while demand for unskilled labour has fallen, pushing down wages. Developing nations, such as China, Brazil and India, have also contributed to the growth in low pay by exporting goods that compete with domestic products. Over time this has led to the decline of those industries struggling to compete with cheap imports from these countries. The impact of the decline in such industries is that skilled workers in countries like the UK have lost their jobs, becoming unskilled workers in different sectors. This increase in supply of unskilled labour pushed wages down.

There has also been a general shift in power from workers to employers, which really began with the high unemployment that existed in the early 1980s and 1990s. With such a high jobless rates, wages of unskilled and semi-skilled workers in particular were forced downwards and have never fully recovered, despite falling unemployment in the late 1990s and early 2000s.

A rise in part-time employment, from 20.5 per cent of employees in 1984 to 29.2 per cent in 2014, has been a key change in the UK. In recent years growing numbers of workers are on 'zero-hour' contracts, where there is no guaranteed work in any week. At the end of 2014 it was estimated that 697 000 employees were employed on such contracts

---

[11] The mean hourly wage is the arithmetical average: i.e. the total level of gross wage payments divided by the total number of hours worked by the population (over a specified time period). The median hourly wage is found by ranking the working population from lowest to highest paid, and then finding the hourly pay of the middle person in the ranking.

Figure 18.10 Minimum hourly wage rates (2014)

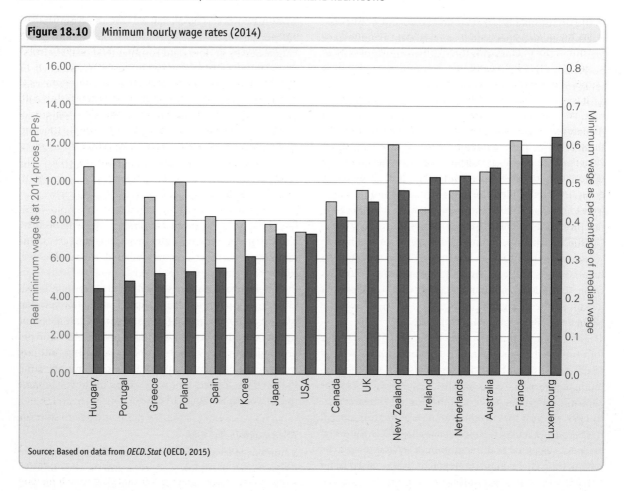

Source: Based on data from *OECD.Stat* (OECD, 2015)

(2.3 per cent of all employees: up from 0.6 per cent in 2011). As part-time workers do not receive the same rights, privileges and hourly pay as their full-time equivalents, this has contributed towards the growth in the low-pay sector.

The introduction of the UK national minimum wage in 1999 has gone some way to arresting the growth in low pay, but is it enough and is it an effective method of protecting the low paid?

Minimum wages

Minimum wages are used widely in developed countries. Figure 18.10 shows the minimum wage rates in a number of countries in 2013. The red bars show real minimum hourly wage rates. They are adjusted for inflation and given in 2013 prices and converted to US dollars at 'purchasing-power parity (PPP)' exchange rates, which adjust the market exchange rate to reflect purchasing power: i.e. the exchange rates at which one dollar would be worth the same in purchasing power in each country. This allows more meaningful comparisons between countries. The blue bars show minimum hourly wage rates as a percentage of each country's median hourly wage rate.

Critics of a national minimum wage argue that it can cause unemployment and with it a *rise* in poverty. Support-

ers argue that it not only helps to reduce poverty among the low paid, but also has little or no adverse effects on employment and may even *increase* employment.

In order to assess the background to this debate, we need to revisit our earlier analysis of the demand and supply of labour.

Minimum wages in a competitive labour market

In a competitive labour market, workers will be hired up to the point where the marginal revenue product of labour (MRP_L), i.e. the demand for labour, is equal to the marginal cost of labour (MC_L), which gives the supply curve. Referring back to Figure 18.8 (on page 306), the free-market equilibrium wage is W_1 and the level of employment is Q_1. A national minimum wage, set at W_2, will reduce the level of employment to Q_2 and increase the supply of labour to Q_3, thereby creating unemployment of the amount $Q_3 - Q_2$.

The level of unemployment created as a result of the national minimum wage will be determined not only by the level of the minimum wage, but also by the elasticity of labour demand and supply. The more elastic the demand and supply of labour, the bigger the unemployment effect will be. Evidence suggests that the demand for low-skilled workers is likely to be relatively wage sensitive. The most likely reason for this is that many of the goods or services

KI 12
p 68

produced by low-paid workers are very price sensitive, the firms frequently operating in very competitive markets. It would seem at first sight, therefore, that any increase in wage rates is likely to force up prices and thereby reduce output and employment.

It is important to be careful in using this argument, however. What is relevant is not so much the price elasticity of demand for *individual* firms' products, but rather for the products of the low-paid sector as a whole. If one firm alone raised its prices, it might well lose a considerable number of sales. But with minimum wage legislation applying to *all* firms, if all the firms in an industry or sector put up their prices, demand for any one firm would fall much less. Here the problem of consumers switching away from a firm's products, and hence of that firm being forced to reduce its workforce, would mainly occur (a) if there were cheaper competitor products from abroad, where the new minimum wage legislation would not apply, or (b) if other firms produced the products with more capital-intensive techniques, involving fewer workers to whom the minimum wage legislation applied.

Minimum wages and monopsony employers

In an imperfect labour market where the employer has some influence over rates of pay, the impact of the national minimum wage on levels of employment is even less clear-cut.

The situation is illustrated in Figure 18.11 (which is similar to Figure 18.9 on page 306). A monopsonistic employer will employ Q_1 workers: where MC_{L2} is equal to MRP_L. At this point the firm is maximising its return from the labour it employs. Remember that the MC_L curve lies above the supply of labour curve (AC_L), since the additional cost of employing one more unit of labour involves paying all existing employees the new wage. The wage rate paid by the monopsonist will be W_1.

If the minimum wage is set above W_1 (but below W_2), the level of employment within the firm is likely to grow! Why should this be so? The reason is that the minimum wage cannot be bid down by the monopsonist cutting back on its workforce. Assume, for example, that the minimum wage was set at a rate of W_3. The minimum wage rate is thus both the new AC_{L2} and also the new MC_{L2}: the additional cost of employing one more worker (up to Q_2) is simply the minimum wage rate. The $MC_{L2} = AC_{L2}$ line is thus a horizontal straight line up to the original supply curve ($S_1 = AC_1$). The level of employment that maximises the monopsonist's profits will be found from the intersection of this new $MC_L = AC_L$ line with the MRP_L curve: namely, an employment level of Q_2. In fact, with a wage rate anywhere between W_1 and W_2 this intersection will be to the right of Q_1: i.e. the imposition of a minimum wage rate will *increase* the level of employment.

Clearly, if the minimum wage rate were very high, then, other things being equal, the level of employment would fall. This would occur in Figure 18.11 if the minimum wage rate were above W_3. But even this argument is not clear-cut, given that (a) a higher wage rate may increase labour productivity by improving worker motivation and (b) other firms, with which the firm might compete in the product market, will also be faced with paying the higher minimum wage rate. The resulting rise in prices is likely to shift the MRP_L curve to the right.

On the other hand, to the extent that the imposition of a minimum wage rate reduces a firm's profits, this may lead it to cut down on investment, which may threaten long-term employment prospects.

> ### Pause for thought
>
> 1. If an increase in wage rates for the low paid led to their being more motivated, how would this affect the marginal revenue product and the demand for such workers? What implications does your answer have for the effect on employment in such cases?
> 2. If minimum wages encourage employers to substitute machines for workers, will this necessarily lead to higher long-term unemployment in (a) that industry and (b) the economy in general?

Evidence on the effect of minimum wages

Which of the views concerning the effects of a national minimum wage are we to believe? Evidence from various countries suggests that modest increases in the minimum wage have had a neutral effect upon employment. It has been found that there exists a 'range of indeterminacy' over which wage rates can fluctuate with little impact upon levels of employment. Even above this 'range', research findings have suggested that, whereas some employers might reduce the quantity of labour they employ, others might respond to their higher wage bill, and hence higher costs, by improving productive efficiency.

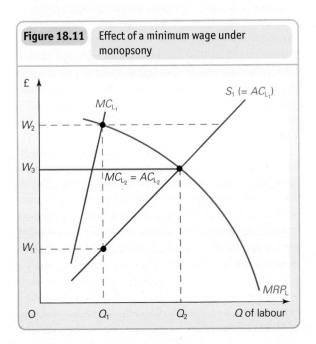

Figure 18.11 Effect of a minimum wage under monopsony

| **Figure 18.12** | Mean gross hourly earnings of full-time employees |

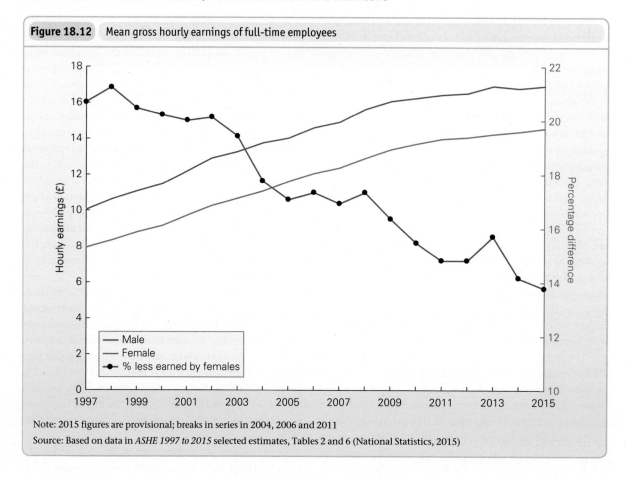

Note: 2015 figures are provisional; breaks in series in 2004, 2006 and 2011

Source: Based on data in *ASHE 1997 to 2015* selected estimates, Tables 2 and 6 (National Statistics, 2015)

Since the introduction of the minimum wage in the UK in 1999, there is little evidence to suggest that employers have responded by employing fewer workers. In fact, until 2008 unemployment rates fell, despite the minimum wage rising relative to both median and medial hourly wage rate. This, however, can be explained by a buoyant economy and increasing labour market flexibility (see section 18.4).

With the recession of 2009/10, however, many employers were claiming that it would be difficult to pay the minimum wage without reducing their workforce, given falling demand for their products and, in some cases, falling prices. Also, firms may make significant cuts in employment if the minimum wage were to rise substantially. Indeed, the minimum wage fell as a percentage of both median and mean hourly wage rates from 2008. The issue here is how *high* can the minimum wage be set before unemployment begins to rise?

Gender and the labour market

Women earn less than men. How much less depends on how earnings are measured, but on the most widely used definition, mean gross earnings per hour, women in the UK earned some 14 per cent less per hour than men in 2014 (see Figure 18.12). This is based on figures in the *Annual Survey of Hours and Earnings (ASHE)*. As the chart shows, the gender wage gap has narrowed in recent years. And this trend has been continuing for much longer. Women typically earned 37 per cent less in 1970, 26 per cent less by 1980, 23 per cent less by 1990 and 20 per cent less by 2000.

A similar picture of gender inequality in pay can be seen throughout the EU. In 2013, women's gross average hourly pay was 16.4 per cent less than men's. The figure varies from one country to another. For example, in Germany women earned 21.6 per cent less, in France 15.2 per cent less and in Italy 7.3 less. This gender pay gap exists, despite females doing better at school and university than their male counterparts. You can read more about the gender pay gap in a 2014 report, produced by the European Commission.[12]

The inequality between male and female earnings can in part be explained by the fact that men and women are occupationally segregated. Seeing that women predominate in poorly paid occupations, the difference in earnings is somewhat to be expected. But if you consider Table 18.1, you can see that quite substantial earning differentials persist *within* particular occupations, partly because a smaller proportion of women are in senior positions.

---

[12]*Tackling the Gender Pay Gap in the European Union* (Publications Office of the European Union, 2014).

Table 18.1	Average gross hourly pay, excluding overtime, for selected occupations, full-time UK employees on adult rates, 2014		
	Men	**Women**	
Occupation	**£ per hour**		**Women's pay as % of men's**
Chief executives and senior officials	51.27	36.88	71.9
Medical practitioners	36.50	28.91	79.2
Solicitors	41.27	33.74	81.8
Laboratory technicians	13.14	10.96	83.4
Senior police officers	29.83	25.12	84.2
Librarians	17.13	14.44	84.3
Accountants	22.57	19.16	84.9
Communication operators	15.11	13.95	92.3
Management consultants and business analysts	23.69	21.96	92.7
Sales and retail assistants	8.74	8.12	92.9
Secondary school teachers	22.83	21.24	93.0
Assemblers and routine operatives	8.86	8.34	94.1
Hairdressers, barbers	7.91	7.55	95.4
Nurses	17.36	16.62	95.7
Bar staff	7.04	6.75	95.9
Social workers	17.45	16.76	96.0
Chefs	8.79	8.63	98.2
All occupations	**16.77**	**14.39**	**85.8**
Average gross weekly pay (incl. overtime)	673.00	539.20	80.1
Average weekly hours worked (incl. overtime)	40.20	37.50	
Average weekly overtime	1.40	0.60	

Source: *Annual Survey of Hours and Earnings* (National Statistics, 2015)

So why has this inequality persisted? There are a number of possible reasons:

■ The marginal productivity of labour in typically female occupations may be lower than in typically male occupations. This may in small part be due to simple questions of physical strength. More often, however, it is due to the fact that women tend to work in more labour-intensive occupations. If there is less capital equipment per female worker than there is per male worker, then the marginal product of a woman is likely to be less than that of a man. Evidence from the EU as a whole suggests that occupational segregation is a significant factor in explaining pay differences.

■ Many women take career breaks to have children. For this reason, employers are sometimes more willing to invest money in training men (thereby increasing their marginal productivity), and more willing to promote men.

■ Women tend to be less geographically mobile than men. If social norms are such that the man's job is seen as somehow more 'important' than the woman's, then a couple will often move if that is necessary for the man to get promotion. The woman, however, will have to settle for whatever job she can get in the same locality as her partner. Additionally this may reduce a woman's bargaining power when negotiating for wage increases in her current job, if her employer knows that her outside options are more limited than a man's would be.

■ A smaller proportion of women workers are members of unions than men. Even when they are members of unions, they are often in jobs where unions are weak (e.g. clothing industry workers, shop assistants and secretaries).

■ Part-time workers (mainly women) have less bargaining power, less influence and less chance of obtaining promotion.

■ Custom and practice. Despite equal pay legislation, many jobs done wholly or mainly by women continue to be low paid, irrespective of questions of productivity.

■ Prejudice. In many jobs women are discriminated against when it comes to promotion, especially to senior positions. A report published in 2015 for the UK government[13] confirmed that women remain seriously under-represented in boardrooms. Of the FTSE 100 companies, only 23.5 per cent of board members were women (but nearly double the figure of 12.5 per cent in 2011). This phenomenon is known as the 'glass ceiling' and it is very difficult to legislate against. Businesses can simply claim that the 'better' person was promoted or that women do not put themselves forward. The report suggests various measures to increase the number of female board members, including discussions with chairmen on the issue, Women on Boards conferences, pressure from investors and requiring companies to report on their diversity policies.

Which of the above reasons could be counted as economically 'irrational' (i.e. paying different wage rates to women and men for other than purely economic reasons)? Certainly the last two would qualify. Paying different wage rates on these grounds would *not* be in the profit interests of the employer.

Some of the others, however, are more difficult to classify. The causes of inequality in wage rates may be traced back beyond the workplace: perhaps to the educational system, or to a culture which discourages women from being so aggressive in seeking promotion or to more generous maternity than paternity leave. Even if it is a manifestation of profit-maximising behaviour by employers that women in some circumstances are paid less than their male counterparts, the reason why it is more profitable for employers to pay men more than women may indeed reflect discrimination elsewhere or at some other point in time.

> ### Pause for thought
>
> *If we were to look at weekly rather than hourly pay and included the effects of overtime, what do you think would happen to the pay differentials in Table 18.1?*

> ### Pause for thought
>
> *If employers were forced to give genuinely equal pay for equal work, how would this affect the employment of women and men? What would determine the magnitude of these effects?*

18.4 THE FLEXIBLE FIRM AND THE MARKET FOR LABOUR

The past 30 years have seen sweeping changes in the ways that firms organise their workforce. Three world recessions combined with rapid changes in technology have led many firms to question the wisdom of appointing workers on a permanent basis to specific jobs. Instead, they want to have the greatest flexibility possible to respond to new situations. If demand falls, they want to be able to 'shed' labour without facing large redundancy costs. If demand rises, they want rapid access to additional labour supplies. If technology changes, say with the introduction of new computerised processes, they want to have the flexibility to move workers around, or to take on new workers in some areas and lose workers in others.

What many firms seek, therefore, is flexibility in employing and allocating labour. What countries are experiencing is an increasingly flexible labour market, as workers and employment agencies respond to the new 'flexible firm'.

There are three main types of flexibility in the use of labour:

■ *Functional flexibility*. This is where an employer is able to transfer labour between different tasks within the production process. It contrasts with traditional forms of organisation where people were employed to do a specific job, and then stuck to it. A functionally flexible labour force will tend to be multi-skilled and relatively highly trained.

■ *Numerical flexibility*. This is where the firm is able to adjust the size and composition of its workforce according to changing market conditions. To achieve this, the firm is likely to employ a large proportion of its labour on a part-time or casual basis, or even subcontract out specialist requirements, rather than employing such labour skills itself.

■ *Financial flexibility*. This is where the firm has flexibility in its wage costs. In large part it is a result of functional and numerical flexibility. Financial flexibility can be achieved by rewarding individual effort and productivity rather than paying a given rate for a particular job. Such rates of pay are increasingly negotiated at the local level rather than being nationally set. The result is not only a widening of pay differentials between skilled and unskilled workers, but also growing differentials in pay between workers within the same industry but in different parts of the country.

> ### Definitions
>
> **Functional flexibility** Where employers can switch workers from job to job as requirements change.
>
> **Numerical flexibility** Where employers can change the size of their workforce as their labour requirements change.
>
> **Financial flexibility** Where employers can vary their wage costs by changing the composition of their workforce or the terms on which workers are employed.

KI 6
p 37

---

[13] 'Women on Boards', Davies Review Annual Report 2015 (GOV.UK. March 2015).

Figure 18.13 The flexible firm

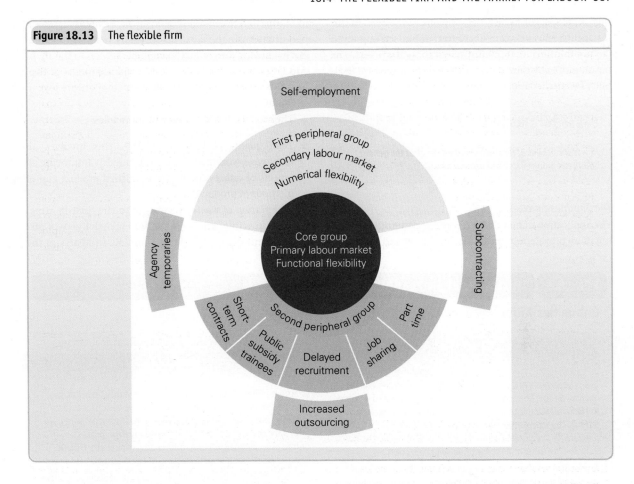

Figure 18.13 shows how these three forms of flexibility are reflected in the organisation of a *flexible firm*, an organisation quite different from that of the traditional firm.

 KEY IDEA 26 | *Flexible firm.* A firm that has the flexibility to respond to changing market conditions by changing the composition of its workforce and its working practices.

The most significant difference is that the labour force is segmented. The core group, drawn from the *primary labour market*, will be composed of *functionally* flexible workers, who have relatively secure employment and are generally on full-time permanent contracts. Such workers will be relatively well paid and receive wages reflecting their scarce skills.

The periphery, drawn from the *secondary labour market*, is more fragmented than the core, and can be subdivided into a first and a second peripheral group. The first peripheral group is composed of workers with a lower level of skill than those in the core, skills that tend to be general rather than firm-specific. Thus workers in the first peripheral group can usually be drawn from the external labour market. Such workers may be employed on full-time contracts, but they will generally face less secure employment than those workers in the core. An example is workers in the hotel industry, many of whom have little job security and who are on short-term or zero-hour contracts.[14]

The business gains a greater level of numerical flexibility by drawing labour from the second peripheral group. Here workers are employed on a variety of short-term, part-time contracts, often through a recruitment agency. Some of these workers may be working from home, or online from another country, such as India, where wage rates are much lower. Workers in the second peripheral group have little job security.

As well as supplementing the level of labour in the first peripheral group, the second periphery can also provide

Definitions

Flexible firm A firm that has the flexibility to respond to changing market conditions.

Primary labour market The market for permanent full-time core workers.

Secondary labour market The market for peripheral workers, usually employed on a temporary or part-time basis, or a less secure 'permanent' basis.

---

[14] Margaret Deery and Leo K. Jago, *The Core and the Periphery: An Examination of the Flexible Workforce Model in the Hotel Industry* (Centre for Hospitality and Tourism Research, Victoria University, Melbourne, 2002).

high-level specialist skills that supplement the core. In this instance the business can subcontract or hire self-employed labour, minimising its commitment to such workers. The business thereby gains both functional and numerical flexibility simultaneously.

Pause for thought

How is the advent of flexible firms likely to alter the gender balance of employment and unemployment?

The Japanese model

The application of new flexible working patterns is becoming more prevalent in businesses in the UK and elsewhere in Europe and North America. In Japan, flexibility has been part of the business way of life for many years and was crucial in shaping the country's economic success in the 1970s and 1980s. In fact we now talk of a Japanese model of business organisation, which many of its competitors seek to emulate.

The model is based around four principles:

■ *Total quality management (TQM).* This involves all employees working towards continuously improving all aspects of quality, both of the finished product and of methods of production.

■ *Elimination of waste.* According to the 'just-in-time' (JIT) principle, businesses should take delivery of just sufficient quantities of raw materials and parts, at the

---

| BOX 18.3 | THE INTERNET AND LABOUR MOBILITY |

Online flexibility

A firm may wish to be flexible, but is the labour market sufficiently flexible to meet the firm's needs?

It is all well and good a firm looking to expand employment in a prosperous period, but how will it find the individuals it needs, whether they be self-employed, subcontracted or added to the core labour group? This question becomes far more critical, the more highly skilled (and hence scarce) the workers that the firm requires. Generally, it is the core/skilled workers that flexible firms find most difficulty in recruiting.

A solution to enhancing labour market flexibility, it seems, may lie in the development of online recruitment technologies and there are many firms emerging in this area.

Keynote, a market research company, reported that in 2012, 44 per cent of survey respondents had used the Internet for job search.[15] Firms not only have their own online vacancy boards but are also using social networking sites to target different audiences. Four per cent of respondents had used social media sites to search for jobs. This figure is expected to increase in coming years. Many candidates use online sites such as Monster.co.uk and Fish4jobs.com to register for job alerts by e-mail or mobile phone and to register their CV. On the downside, Keynote reports that use of e-recruitment is leading to increased numbers of unsuitable candidates applying for vacancies. Filtering out these candidates wastes time and money.

The Internet improves the efficiency with which information is relayed to the employers and suppliers of labour and increases their search horizons. As well as reaching a wider and more targeted audience, recruitment costs are lowered and the recruitment cycle is shortened and made more efficient by the use of Internet technologies. According to the Chartered Institute of Personnel and Development:

> Technology plays an increasingly important role in recruitment, ranging from attracting candidates through to the selection process. Electronic techniques are also being used to slim down the number of potential candidates. In particular, using online recruitment can

mean employers receive large numbers of applications from unsuitable candidates, so it can be helpful also to use technology to help manage the application forms.[16]

A large number of companies have been established which provide software that can manage e-recruitment processes: e.g. jobtrain.co.uk and recruitactive.com. These companies offer services such as managing the application process, online psychometric testing, online advertising etc. Helene Cavalli, Vice President of Marketing at Lee Hecht Harrison said:

> I was really excited to see how many job seekers are active on social media . . . As strong advocates, we spend a lot of time coaching job seekers on how to develop a sold social media strategy. While it isn't the only strategy for finding a job, it's becoming increasingly important.[17]

There are big benefits for job seekers too. It may lead to increased spatial search for employment. For example, workers based in London no longer have to travel to Manchester and scout around; they can peruse jobs online.

It can also widen the range of industries that firms and individuals might target. So, shipyard workers might look to use their welding skills in the offshore industry. It can also enhance the likelihood of matching the skills of the unemployed with job vacancies and so lower the average length of time it takes to fill a vacancy.

The days of pounding the streets, looking in employment agency windows, or circling a vacancy in the newspaper with a pen are not over, but the opportunity afforded by online recruitment is dramatically enhancing labour market flexibility.

1. *Explain how a flexible firm's flexibility would be enhanced by online recruitment.*
2. *If a firm is trying to achieve flexibility in its use of labour, do you think this would be harder or easier in a period of recession? Explain why.*

---

[15]'E-Recruitment market assessment 2012' (Keynote, 2012), www.keynote.co.uk/market-intelligence/view/product/ 10553/e-recruitment

[16]'Selection methods', *CIPD Factsheet* (CIPD, 2013).

[17]Jacquelyn Smith, 'How social media can help (or hurt) you in your job search', *Forbes*, 16 April 2013.

right time and place. Stocks are kept to a minimum and hence the whole system of production runs with little, if any, slack. For example, supermarkets today have smaller storerooms relative to the total shopping area than they did in the past, and take more frequent deliveries.

■ *A belief in the superiority of team work in the core group.* Collective effort is a vital element in Japanese working practices. Team work is seen not only to enhance individual performance, but also to involve the individual in the running of the business, and thus to create a sense of commitment.

■ *Functional and numerical flexibility.* Both are seen as vital components in maintaining high levels of productivity.

The principles of this model are now widely accepted as being important in creating and maintaining a competitive business in a competitive marketplace.

Within the EU, the UK has been one of the most successful in cutting unemployment and creating jobs. Much of this has been attributed to increased labour market flexibility. As a result, other EU countries, such as Italy and Germany, continue to seek to emulate many of the measures the UK has adopted.

SUMMARY

1a The UK labour market has undergone many changes with the growth of technology, changes in the social structure and the movement towards service-sector employment. Other changes include the rise in part-time working; the growth in female employment levels; a rise in the proportion of temporary, short-term contracts and casual employment.

1b Wages in a competitive labour market are determined by the interaction of demand and supply. The individual's supply of labour will be determined by the substitution and income effects from a given increase in the wage rate. At low wage levels, it is likely that individuals will substitute work for leisure. At high wage levels, it is possible that individuals will work less and consume more leisure time, giving a backward-bending supply curve of labour by the individual.

1c The elasticity of labour supply will largely depend upon the geographical and occupational mobility of labour. The more readily labour can transfer between jobs and regions, the more elastic the supply.

1d The demand for labour is traditionally assumed to be based upon labour's productivity. Marginal productivity theory assumes that the employer will demand labour up to the point where the cost of employing one additional worker (MC_L) is equal to the revenue earned from the output of that worker (MRP_L). The firm's demand curve for labour is its MRP_L curve.

1e The elasticity of demand for labour is determined by: the price elasticity of demand for the good that labour produces; the substitutability of labour for other factors; the proportion of wages to total costs; and time.

2a In an imperfect labour market, where a business has monopoly power in employing labour, it is known as a monopsonist. Such a firm will employ workers to the point where the $MRP_L = MC_L$. Since the wage is below the MC_L, the monopsonist, other things being equal, will employ fewer workers at a lower wage than would be employed in a perfectly competitive labour market.

2b If a union has monopoly power, its power to raise wages will be limited if the employer operates under perfect or monopolistic competition in the goods market. A rise in wage rates will force the employer to cut back on employment, unless there is a corresponding rise in productivity.

2c In a situation of bilateral monopoly (where a monopoly union faces a monopsony employer), the union may have considerable scope to raise wages above the monopsony level, without the employer wishing to reduce the level of employment. There is no unique equilibrium wage. The wage will depend on the outcome of a process of collective bargaining between union and management.

2d The efficiency wage hypothesis states that business might hold wages above the market-clearing wage rate so as to: reduce shirking; reduce labour turnover; improve the quality of labour recruited; and stimulate worker morale. The level of efficiency wage will be determined largely by the type of job the worker does, and the level and scarcity of skill they possess.

3a Low pay is difficult to define. There is no accepted definition. The widening disparity in wages between high- and low-income earners is due to: unemployment resulting from recession; unemployment resulting from a shift in technology; the growth in part-time employment; and changes in labour market legislation.

3b A statutory minimum wage is one way of tackling the problem of low pay. It is argued, however, that in a perfect labour market, where employers are forced to accept the wage as determined by the marketplace, any attempt to impose a minimum wage above this level will create unemployment. In an imperfect labour market, where an employer has some monopsonistic power, the impact of a minimum wage is uncertain. The impact will depend largely upon how much workers are currently paid below their MRP and whether a higher wage encourages them to work more productively.

3c Differences between male and female earnings between occupations can in part be explained by differences in the types of work that men and women do; they are occupationally segregated. Differences within occupations are less easily accounted for. It would seem that some measure of discrimination is being practised.

4a Changes in technology have had a massive impact upon the process of production and the experience of work. Labour markets and business organisations have become more flexible: functionally, numerically and financially. The flexible firm will incorporate these different forms of flexibility into its business operations, with a core workforce, supplemented by workers and skills drawn from a periphery, who are likely to be on part-time and temporary contracts.

4b The application of the flexible firm model is closely mirrored in the practices of Japanese business. Commitments to improve quality, reduce waste, build teamwork and introduce flexible labour markets are seen as key components in the success of Japanese business organisation.

MyEconLab

This book can be supported by MyEconLab, which contains a range of additional resources, including an online homework and tutorial system designed to test and build your understanding.

You need both an access card and a course ID to access MyEconLab:

1. Is your lecturer using MyEconLab? Ask your lecturer for your course ID.

2. Has an access card been included with the book at a reduced cost? Check the inside back cover of the book.

3. If you have a course ID but no access card, go to: http://www.myeconlab.com/ to buy access to this interactive study programme.

REVIEW QUESTIONS

1 If a firm faces a shortage of workers with very specific skills, it may decide to undertake the necessary training itself. If, on the other hand, it faces a shortage of unskilled workers, it may well offer a small wage increase in order to obtain the extra labour. In the first case it is responding to an increase in demand for labour by attempting to shift the supply curve. In the second case it is merely allowing a movement along the supply curve. Use a demand and supply diagram to illustrate each case. Given that elasticity of supply is different in each case, do you think that these are the best policies for the firm to follow?

2 The wage rate a firm has to pay and the output it can produce varies with the number of workers as follows (all figures are hourly):

Number of workers	1	2	3	4	5	6	7	8
Wage rate (AC_L) (£)	3	4	5	6	7	8	9	10
Total output (TPP_L)	10	22	32	40	46	50	52	52

Assume that output sells at £2 per unit.

a) Copy the table and add additional rows for TC_L, MC_L, TRP_L and MRP_L. Put the figures for MC_L and MRP_L in the spaces between the columns.

b) How many workers will the firm employ in order to maximise profits?

c) What will be its hourly wage bill at this level of employment?

d) How much hourly revenue will it earn at this level of employment?

e) Assuming that the firm faces other (fixed) costs of £30 per hour, how much hourly profit will it make?

f) Assume that the workers now form a union and that the firm agrees to pay the negotiated wage rate to all employees. What is the maximum to which the hourly wage rate could rise without causing the firm to try to reduce employment below that in (b) above? (See Figure 18.9.)

g) What would be the firm's hourly profit now?

3 If, unlike a perfectly competitive employer, a monopsonist has to pay a higher wage to attract more workers, why, other things being equal, will a monopsonist pay a lower wage than a perfectly competitive employer?

4 The following are figures for a monopsonist employer:

Number of workers (1)	Wage rate (£) (2)	Total cost of labour (£) (3)	Marginal cost of labour (£) (4)	Marginal revenue product (£) (5)
1	100	100		
			110	230
2	105	210		
			120	240
3	110	230		
				240
4	115			
				230
5	120			
				210
6	125			
				190
7	130			
				170
8	135			
				150
9	140			
				130
10	145			

Fill in the missing figures for columns (3) and (4). How many workers should the firm employ if it wishes to maximise profits?

5 To what extent could a trade union succeed in gaining a pay increase from an employer with no loss in employment?

6 Do any of the following contradict marginal productivity theory: wage scales related to length of service (incremental scales), nationally negotiated wage rates, discrimination, firms taking the lead from other firms in determining this year's pay increase?

7 Using the analysis of sections 18.1 and 18.2, explain why a Premier League footballer will be paid such a high wage.

8 Apply the same analysis to top handball, lacrosse or badminton players. Why are they paid a relatively low wage compared to Premier League footballers, despite their exceptional talent and skill?

9 What is the efficiency wage hypothesis? Explain what employers might gain from paying wages above the market-clearing level.

10 'Minimum wages will cause unemployment.' Is this so?

11 How might we explain why men earn more than women?

12 Identify the potential costs and benefits of the flexible firm to (a) employers and (b) employees.

Investment and the employment of capital

Business issues covered in this chapter

- What determines the amount of capital a firm will employ?
- How can a firm judge whether a proposed investment should go ahead? What techniques are there for investment appraisal?
- How can investment be financed? What types of financial institution are involved in financing investment?
- What are the relative merits of alternative sources of finance?
- What are the functions of the stock market?
- Is the stock market efficient as a means of allocating capital?

19.1 THE PRICING OF CAPITAL AND CAPITAL SERVICES

Capital includes all manufactured products that are used to produce goods and services. Thus capital includes such diverse items as a blast furnace, a bus, a cinema projector, a computer, a factory building and a screwdriver.

The capital goods described above are physical assets and are known as *physical* capital. The word 'capital' is also used to refer to various *paper* assets, such as shares and bonds. These are the means by which firms raise finance to purchase physical capital, and are known as *financial* capital. Being merely paper assets, however, they do not count as factors of production. Nevertheless, financial markets have an important role in determining the level of investment in physical capital, and we shall be examining these markets in the final two sections of this chapter.

The price of capital versus the price of capital services

A feature of most manufactured factors of production is that they last a period of time. A machine may last 10 years; a factory may last 20 years or more. This leads to an important distinction: the income for the owner from *selling* capital and the income from *using* it or *hiring* it out.

- Income can be earned from selling capital and this is known as its *price*. It is a once-and-for-all payment. Thus a factory might sell for £1 million, a machine for £20 000 or a screwdriver for £1.
- Income can be gained from using capital, for example as part of the production process and this is known as its *return*. Alternatively, income can be gained from hiring out capital and this is known as its *rental*. This income therefore represents the value or price of the *services* of capital, expressed per period of time. Thus a firm might have to pay a rental of £1000 per year for a photocopier.

Obviously the price of capital will be linked to the value of its services: to its return. A highly productive machine will sell for a higher price than one producing a lower output and hence yielding a lower return.

Figure 19.1 (a) Perfectly competitive factor market; (b) firm with monopsony power in factor market

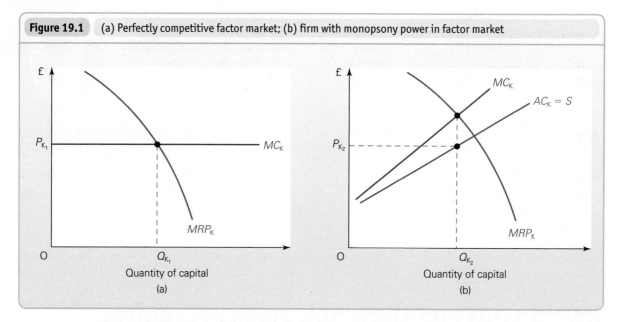

Quantity of capital
(a)

Quantity of capital
(b)

The discussion of the rewards to capital leads to a very important distinction: that between stocks and flows.

A *stock* is a quantity of something held. You may have £1000 in a savings account. A factory may contain 100 machines. These are both stocks: they are quantities held at a given point in time. A *flow* is an increase or decrease in quantity over a specified time period. You may save £10 per month. The factory may invest in another 20 machines next year.

> **KEY IDEA 27**
>
> **Stocks and flows.** A stock is a quantity of something at a given point in time. A flow is an increase or decrease in something over a specified period of time. This is an important distinction and a common cause of confusion.

Wages, rental and interest are all rewards to *flows*. Wages are the amount paid not to purchase a person (as a slave!), but for the services of that person's labour for a period of time. Rental is the amount paid per period of time to use the services of machinery or equipment, not to buy it outright. Likewise interest is the reward paid to people per year for the use of their money.

Pause for thought

Which of the following are stocks and which are flows?
a. *Unemployment.*
b. *Redundancies.*
c. *Profits.*
d. *A firm's stock market valuation.*
e. *The value of property after a period of inflation.*

An important example of stocks and flows arises with capital and investment. If a firm has 100 machines, that is a stock of capital. It may choose to build up its stock by investing. Investment is a flow concept. The firm may choose to invest in 10 new machines each year. This may not add 10 to the stock of machines, however, as some may be wearing out (a negative flow).

The profit-maximising employment of capital

On the demand side, the same rules apply for capital as for labour, if a firm wishes to maximise profits. Namely, it should demand additional capital (K) up to the point where the **marginal cost of capital** equals its **marginal revenue product**: $MC_K = MRP_K$. This same rule applies whether the firm is buying the capital outright, or merely hiring it.

Figure 19.1 illustrates the two cases of perfect competition and monopsony. In both diagrams the MRP curve slopes downwards. This is just another illustration of the law of diminishing returns, but this time applied to capital. If a firm increases the amount of capital while *holding other factors constant*, diminishing returns to capital will occur. Diminishing returns will equally apply whether the firm is buying the extra capital or hiring it.

In diagram (a) the firm is a price taker. The capital price is given at P_{K_1} Profits are maximised at Q_{K_1} where $MRP_K = P_K$ (since $P_K = MC_K$).

In diagram (b) the firm has monopsony power. The price it pays for capital will vary, therefore, with the amount it uses. The firm will again buy or hire capital to the point where $MRP_K = MC_K$. In this case, it will mean using Q_{K_1} at a price of P_{K_1}

What is the difference when applying these principles between buying capital and hiring it? Although the

Definitions

Stock The quantity of something held.

Flow An increase or decrease in quantity over a specified period.

Marginal cost of capital The cost of one additional unit of capital.

Marginal revenue product The additional revenue earned from employing one additional unit of capital.

$MRP_K = MC_K$ rule remains the same, there are differences. As far as buying capital is concerned, MC_K is the extra outlay for the firm in *purchasing* one more unit of capital – say, a machine – and MRP_K is all the revenue produced by that machine over its *whole life* (but measured in terms of what this is worth when purchased: see section 19.3). In the case of hiring the machine, MC_K is the extra outlay for the firm in rental *per period of time*, while MRP_K is the extra revenue earned from it *per period of time*.

19.2 THE DEMAND FOR AND SUPPLY OF CAPITAL SERVICES

In this section we will consider the *hiring* of capital equipment for a given period of time.

Demand for capital services

The analysis is virtually identical to that of the demand for labour. As with labour we can distinguish between an individual firm's demand for capital services (K) and the whole-market demand for capital services.

Individual firm's demand
Take the case of a small painting and decorating firm that requires some scaffolding in order to complete a job. It could use ladders, but the job would take longer to complete. It goes along to a company that hires out scaffolding and is quoted a daily rate.

If it hires the scaffolding for one day, it can perhaps shorten the job by two or three days. If it hires it for a second day, it can perhaps save another one or two days. Hiring it for additional days may save extra still. But diminishing returns are occurring: the longer the scaffolding is up, the less intensively it will be used, and the less additional time it will save. Perhaps for some of the time it will be used when ladders could have been used equally easily.

The time saved allows the firm to take on extra work. Thus each extra day the scaffolding is hired gives the firm extra revenue. This is the scaffolding's marginal revenue product of capital (MRP_K). Diminishing returns to the scaffolding mean that the MRP_K curve has the normal downward-sloping shape (see Figure 19.1).

Market demand
The market demand for capital services depends on the demand by individual firms (determined by the productivity of the capital and the price of the product it produces). The higher the MRP_K for individual firms, the greater will be the market demand.

Supply of capital services

It is necessary to distinguish (a) the supply *to* a single firm, (b) the supply *by* a single firm and (c) the market supply.

Supply to a single firm
This is illustrated in Figure 19.2(a). The small firm renting capital equipment is probably a price taker. If so, it faces a horizontal supply curve at the going rental rate (R_e). This is the firm's AC_K and MC_K curve. If, however, it has monopsony power, it will face an upward-sloping supply curve as in Figure 19.1(b).

Supply by a single firm
This is illustrated in Figure 19.2(c). Here the firm supplying the capital equipment is likely to be a price taker, facing a

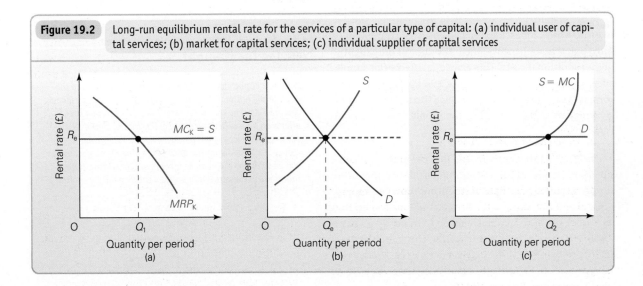

Figure 19.2 Long-run equilibrium rental rate for the services of a particular type of capital: (a) individual user of capital services; (b) market for capital services; (c) individual supplier of capital services

horizontal demand curve. It has to accept the going rental rate (R_e) established in the market. If it tries to charge more, then customers are likely to turn to rival suppliers.

It will maximise profit by supplying an amount Q_2, where the market rental rate is equal to the marginal cost of supplying the equipment. This is the profit-maximising rule for perfect competition that we established on page 179.

There is a problem, however, in working out the marginal cost of renting out capital equipment: the piece of equipment probably cost a lot to buy in the first place, but lasts a long time. How are these large costs to be apportioned to each new rental? The answer is that it depends on the time period under consideration.

The short run. In the short run the hire company is not buying any new equipment: it is simply hiring out its existing equipment. In the case of our scaffolding firm, the marginal costs of doing this will include the following:

■ *Depreciation.* Scaffolding has second-hand value. Each time the scaffolding is hired out it deteriorates, and thus its second-hand value falls. This loss in value is called 'depreciation'.

■ *Maintenance and handling.* When equipment is hired out, it can get damaged and thus incur repair costs. The equipment might need servicing. Also, hiring out equipment involves labour time (e.g. in the office) and possibly transport costs.

> ## Pause for thought
>
> *Assume now that the firm has monopoly power in hiring out equipment, and thus faces a downward-sloping demand curve. Draw in two such demand curves on a diagram like Figure 19.2(c), one crossing the MC curve in the horizontal section, and one in the vertical section. How much will the firm supply in each case and at what price? (You will need to draw in MR curves too.) Is the MC curve still the supply curve?*

These marginal costs are likely to rise relatively slowly. In other words, for each extra day a piece of equipment is hired out, the company will incur the same or only slightly higher additional costs. This gives a relatively flat supply curve of capital services in Figure 19.2(c) up to the hire company's maximum capacity. Once the scaffolding firm is hiring out all its scaffolding, the supply curve becomes vertical.

The long run. In the long run, the hire company will consider purchasing additional equipment. It can therefore supply as much as it likes in the long run. The supply

curve will be relatively elastic, or if it is a price taker itself (i.e. if the scaffolding firm simply buys scaffolding at the market price), the supply curve will be horizontal (i.e. perfectly elastic). This long-run supply curve will be vertically higher than the short-run curve, since the long-run *MC* includes the cost of purchasing each additional piece of equipment.

Market supply

This is illustrated in Figure 19.2(b). The market supply curve of capital services is the sum of the quantities supplied by all the individual firms.

In the short run, the market supply will be relatively inelastic, given that it takes time to manufacture new equipment and that stocks of equipment currently held by manufacturers are likely to be relatively small. Moreover, hire companies may be unwilling to purchase (expensive) new equipment immediately there is a rise in demand: after all, the upsurge in demand may turn out to be short lived.

In the long run, the supply curve will be more elastic because extra capital equipment can be produced.

Determination of the price of capital services

As Figure 19.2(b) shows, in a perfect market the market rental rate for capital services will be determined by the interaction of market demand and supply.

If there is monopsony power on the part of the users of hired capital, this will have the effect of depressing the rental rate below the MRP_K (see Figure 19.1(b)), as we saw in the case of a monopsony buyer of labour. If, on the other hand, there is monopoly power on the part of hire companies, the analysis is similar to that of monopoly in the goods market (see Figure 11.5 on page 185). The firm, by reducing the supply of capital for hire, can drive up the rental rate. It will maximise profit where the marginal revenue from hiring out the equipment is equal to the marginal cost of so doing: at a rental rate (price) *above* the marginal cost.

> ## Pause for thought
>
> *What will happen to the demand for capital services and the equilibrium rental if the price of some other factor, say labour, changes? Assume that wage rates fall. Trace through the effects on a three-section diagram like that of Figure 19.2. (Clue: a fall in wages will have two significant effects: it will reduce costs and hence the price of the product, so that more will be sold; and it will make labour cheaper relative to capital. How will these two things affect the demand for capital?)*

19.3 INVESTMENT APPRAISAL

The alternative to hiring capital is to buy it outright. This section examines the demand and supply of capital for purchase.

The demand for capital: investment

How many computers will an engineering firm want to buy? Should a steelworks install another blast furnace? Should a removal firm buy another furniture lorry? Should it buy another warehouse? These are all ***investment*** decisions. Investment is the purchasing of additional capital.

The demand for capital, or 'investment demand', by a profit-maximising firm is based on exactly the same principles as the demand for labour or the demand for capital services. The firm must weigh up the marginal revenue product of that investment (i.e. the money it will earn for the firm) against its marginal cost.

However, capital is durable. It goes on producing goods, and hence yielding revenue for the firm, for a considerable period of time. Calculating these benefits, therefore, involves taking account of their *timing*.

There are two ways of approaching this question of timing: the ***present value approach*** and the ***rate of return approach***. In both cases the firm is comparing the marginal benefits with the marginal costs of the investment.

Present value approach

To work out the benefit of an investment (its *MRP*), the firm must estimate all the future earnings it will bring and then convert them to a *present value*. Let us take a simple example.

Assume that a firm is considering buying a machine. It will produce profits of £1000 per year for four years and then wear out and sell for £1000 as scrap. What is the benefit of this machine to the firm? At first sight the answer would seem to be £5000. This, after all, is the total income earned from the machine. Unfortunately, it is not as simple as this. The reason is that money earned in the future is less beneficial to the firm than having the same amount of money today: after all, if the firm has the money today, it can earn interest on it by putting it in the bank or reinvesting it in some other project. (Note that this has nothing to do with inflation. In the case we are considering, we are assuming constant prices.)

To illustrate this, assume that you have £100 today and can earn 10 per cent interest by putting it in a bank. In one year's time that £100 will have grown to £110, in two years' time to £121, in three years' time to £133.10, and so on. This process is known as ***compounding***.

It follows that, if someone offered to give you £121 in two years' time, it would be no better than giving you £100 today, since, with interest, £100 would grow to £121 in two years. What we say, then, is that with a 10 per cent interest rate, £121 in two years' time has a *present value* of £100.

The procedure of reducing future values back to a present value is known as ***discounting***.

The principle of discounting. People generally prefer to have benefits today than in the future. Thus future benefits have to be reduced (discounted) to give them a present value.

When we do discounting, the rate which we use is called the ***rate of discount***: in this case 10 per cent. The formula for discounting is given by:

$$PV = \sum \frac{X_t}{(1 + r)^t}$$

Where PV is the present value

X_t is the earnings from the investment in year t

r is the rate of discount (expressed as a decimal: i.e. 10 per cent = 0.1)

$\sum$ is the sum of each of the years' discounted earnings.

So what is the present value of the investment in the machine that produced £1000 for four years and then is sold as scrap for £1000 at the end of the four years? According to the formula it is:

$$\frac{£1000}{1.1} + \frac{£1000}{(1.1)^2} + \frac{£1000}{(1.1)^3} + \frac{£2000}{(1.1)^4}$$
$$= £909 + £826 + £751 + £1366$$
$$= £3852$$

Thus the present value of the investment (i.e. its *MRP*) is £3852, *not* £5000 as it might seem at first sight. In other words, if the firm had £3852 today and deposited it in a bank at a 10 per cent interest rate, the firm would earn exactly the same as it would by investing in the machine.

So is the investment worthwhile? It is now simply a question of comparing the £3852 benefit with the cost of buying the machine. If the machine costs less than £3852, it will be worth buying. If it costs more, the firm would be

Definitions

Investment The purchase by the firm of equipment or materials that will add to its stock of capital.

Present value approach to appraising investment This involves estimating the value now of a flow of future benefits (or costs).

Rate of return approach The benefits from investment are calculated as a percentage of the costs of investment. This rate is then compared to the rate at which money has to be borrowed in order to see whether the investment should be undertaken.

Compounding The process of adding interest each year to an initial capital sum.

Discounting The process of reducing the value of future flows to give them a present valuation.

Rate of discount The rate that is used to reduce future values to present values.

BOX 19.1   INVESTING IN ROADS

The assessment of costs and benefits

In the UK, the Department of Transport uses the following procedure to evaluate new road schemes, a procedure very similar to that used in many countries.

Estimating demand

The first thing to be done is to estimate likely future traffic flows. These are based on the government's National Road Traffic Forecast. This makes two predictions: a 'low-growth case', based on the assumption of low economic growth and high fuel prices, and a 'high-growth case', based on the assumption of high economic growth and low fuel prices. The actual growth in traffic, therefore, is likely to lie between the two.

Identifying possible schemes

Various road construction and improvement schemes are constantly under examination by the government, especially in parts of the network where traffic growth is predicted to be high and where congestion is likely to occur. In each case forecasts are then made of the likely use of the new roads and the diversion of traffic away from existing parts of the network. Again, two forecasts are made in each case: a 'low-growth' and a 'high-growth' one.

The use of cost–benefit analysis

The costs and benefits of each scheme are assigned monetary values and are compared with those of merely maintaining the existing network. The government uses a computer program known as COBA to assist it in the calculations.

Estimating the benefits of a scheme (relative to the existing network)

Three types of benefit are included in the analysis:

■ *Time saved*. This is broken down into two categories: working time and non-working time (including travelling to and from work). The evaluation of working time is based on average national wage rates, while that of non-working time is based on surveys and the examination of traveller behaviour (the aim being to assess the value placed by the traveller on time saved). This results in non-working time per minute being given a value of approximately a quarter of that given to working time.
■ *Reductions in vehicle operating costs*. These include: fuel, oil, tyres, maintenance and depreciation from usage. There will be savings if the scheme reduces the distance of journeys or allows a more economical speed to be maintained.
■ *Reductions in accidents*. There are two types of benefit here: (a) the reduction in the human costs of casualties (divided into three categories – fatal, serious non-fatal and slight); and (b) the reduction in monetary costs, such as lost output, vehicle repair or replacement, medical costs and police, fire service and ambulance costs.

The reductions in monetary costs are relatively easy to estimate. The human benefits from the reduction in casualties

are more difficult. The current method of evaluating them is based on the amount people are prepared to pay to reduce the risks of accidents. This clearly has the drawback that people are often unaware of the risks of accidents or of the extent of the resulting pain and suffering.

The following figures are used to value each casualty prevented (in 2013 prices, up-rated each year for inflation, changes in fuel costs, etc.):

■ fatal: £1 742 988
■ serious non-fatal: £195 863
■ slight: £15 099.

The human cost element for each type of accident in 2013 prices is valued at £1 152 221, £158 611 and £11 621 respectively.[1] Other costs include lost output and medical and ambulance costs.

Estimating the costs of the scheme (relative to the existing network)

There are two main categories of cost: construction costs and additional road maintenance costs. If the new scheme results in a saving in road maintenance compared with merely retaining the existing network, then the maintenance costs will be negative.

The analysis

The costs and benefits of the scheme are assessed for the period of construction and for a standard life (in the UK this is 30 years). The costs and benefits are discounted back to a present value. The rate of discount recommended by the UK Treasury is 3.5 per cent. If the discounted benefits exceed the discounted costs, there is a positive net present value, and the scheme is regarded as justified on economic grounds. If there is more than one scheme, then their net present values will be compared so as to identify the preferable scheme.

It is only at this final stage that environmental considerations are taken into account. In other words, they are not included in the calculation of costs and benefits, but may have some influence in determining the choice between schemes. Clearly, if a socially efficient allocation of road space is to be determined, such externalities need to be included in the cost and benefit calculations.

If you are interested in finding out more about the approach used to assess new road investment, then you may want to visit the Department for Transport's website and in particular read through the economic analysis of the Road Investment Strategy.

 Are there any other drawbacks of using a willingness to pay principle to evaluate human costs?

---

[1] *Reported Road Casualties Great Britain: 2013* (Department for Transport, September 2014), pp. 250 and 252.

KI 28
p 325

better off keeping its money in the bank and earning the 10 per cent rate of interest.

The difference between the present value of the benefits (PV_b) of the investment and its cost (C) is known as the **net present value (NPV)**.

$$NPV = PV_b - C$$

If the *NPV* is positive, the investment is worthwhile.

> ## Pause for thought
>
> *What is the present value of a machine that lasts three years, earns £100 in year 1, £200 in year 2, and £200 in year 3, and then has a scrap value of £100? Assume that the rate of discount is 5 per cent. If the machine costs £500, is the investment worthwhile? Would it be worthwhile if the rate of discount were 10 per cent?*

Rate of return approach

The alternative approach when estimating whether an investment is worthwhile is to calculate the investment's *rate of return*. This rate of return is known as the firm's **marginal efficiency of capital (MEC)** or **internal rate of return (IRR)**.

We use the same formula as for calculating present value:

$$PV = \sum \frac{X_t}{(1 + r)^t}$$

and then calculate what value of *r* would make the *PV* equal to the cost of investment: in other words, the rate of discount that would make the investment just break even. Say this worked out at 5 per cent. What we would be saying is that the investment will just cover its costs if the current rate of interest (rate of discount) is 5 per cent. In other words, this investment is equivalent to receiving 20 per cent interest: it has a 5 per cent rate of return (*IRR*).

 So should the investment go ahead? Yes, if the actual rate of interest (*i*) is less than 5 per cent. In such a case the firm is better off investing its money in this project than keeping its money in the bank: i.e. if *IRR* > *i*, the investment should go ahead.

This is just one more application of the general rule that if $MRP_K > MC_K$ then more capital should be used: only in this case MRP_K is expressed as a rate of return (*IRR*), and the MC_K is expressed as a rate of interest (*i*).

The risks of investment

One of the problems with investment is that the future is uncertain. The return on an investment will depend on the value of the goods it produces, which will depend on the goods market. For example, the return on investment in the car industry will depend on the demand and price of cars. But future markets cannot be predicted with accuracy: they depend on consumer tastes, the actions of rivals and the whole state of the economy. Investment is thus risky.

Risk may also be incurred in terms of the output from an investment. Take the case of prospecting for oil. An oil

company may be lucky and have a major strike, but it may simply drill dry well after dry well. If it does get a major strike and hence earn a large return on its investment, these profits will not be competed away by competitors prospecting in other fields, because they too still run the risk of drilling dry holes.

How is this risk accounted for when calculating the benefits of an investment? The answer is to use a higher rate of discount. The higher the risk, the bigger the premium that must be added to the rate.

The supply of capital

It is important to distinguish between the supply of *physical* capital and the supply of *finance* to be used by firms for the purchase of capital.

Supply of physical capital. The principles here are just the same as those in the goods market. It does not matter whether a firm is supplying lorries (capital) or cars (a consumer good): it will still produce up to the point where $MC = MR$ if it wishes to maximise profits.

Supply of finance. When firms borrow to invest, this creates a demand for finance (or 'loanable funds'). The supply of loanable funds comes from the deposits that individuals and firms make in financial institutions. These deposits are savings, the level of which depends on the rate of interest that depositors receive. The higher the rate of interest, the more people will be encouraged to save. This is illustrated by an upward-sloping supply curve of loanable funds, as shown in Figure 19.3.

Saving also depends on the level of people's incomes, their expectations of future price changes, and their general level of 'thriftiness' (their willingness to forgo present consumption in order to be able to have more in the future). A change in any of these other determinants will shift the supply curve.

Determination of the rate of interest

The rate of interest is determined by the interaction of supply and demand in the market for loanable funds. This is illustrated in Figure 19.3.

As we have seen, supply represents accumulated savings. The demand curve includes the demand by households for credit and the demand by firms for funds to finance their investment. This demand curve slopes downward for two

> ## Definitions
>
> **Net present value of an investment (*NPV*)** The discounted benefits of an investment minus the cost of the investment.
>
> **Marginal efficiency of capital (*MEC*) or internal rate of return (*IRR*)** The rate of return of an investment: the discount rate that makes the net present value of an investment equal to zero.

BOX 19.2 THE RATIOS TO MEASURE SUCCESS

Using numbers to decide

Whenever a firm makes a decision, numerous factors will be considered. Market opportunities will be analysed, the actions of competitors predicted and the economic environment studied. However, crucial to any decision will be the health of the business itself. Owners and managers will need to look at all the firm's numbers before taking any action and there are some ratios that will give a business some key information.

We typically classify ratios into groups based on the information that they show. In this box, we split the ratios into three categories and outline the main ratios within each.

Profitability ratios

These ratios do exactly what they suggest: they provide information about a business's profitability. By measuring a firm's ability to generate earnings and profits, they indicate the success of a firm over time and provide a means of comparison with its competitors. The three main ratios are:

- *Gross Profit Margin*: this measures the ratio of gross profit to sales revenue. Gross profit is calculated by subtracting the variable costs of goods sold from gross revenue and so measures the profitability of a company before fixed costs (overheads) have been taken into account. It is expressed as a percentage and is calculated as:

$$\text{Gross Profit Margin} = \frac{\text{Gross profit}}{\text{Sales turnover}} \times 100$$

- *Net Profit Margin*: this measures the ratio of net profit to sales revenue. Net profit is revenue minus all costs: that is, not only the variable costs of production, but also fixed costs, such as rent, insurance, heating and lighting, salaries (unrelated to output) and also taxes. It gives us information about how effective a firm is in turning sales into profits and thus whether or not a business adds value during the production process. Given its close relationship to gross profit margin, it is important that these first two profitability ratios are compared, as they provide key information about a firm's financial performance. Net profit margin is calculated as:

$$\text{Net Profit Margin} = \frac{\text{Net profit}}{\text{Sales turnover}} \times 100$$

- *Return on Capital Employed (ROCE)*: this measures the efficiency with which a business uses its funds to generate returns. Capital employed refers to the company's total assets minus its current liabilities and the ROCE is calculated as:

$$\text{ROCE} = \frac{\text{Earnings (before interest and taxes)}}{\text{Capital employed}} \times 100$$

High gross and net profit margins are good indicators that a firm is performing effectively, but looking at these two ratios separately can often be misleading. For example, if a firm's gross profit margin is rising, but its net profit margin is falling, then it means that the firm is generating more profit from its sales, but that its costs are increasing at an even faster rate. That is, the company is becoming inefficient.

Just as it is important to examine the trends in profit margins, analysing a firm's ROCE over time is also essential and an upward trend suggests that the firm is earning more in revenue for every £1 of capital employed in the business. Profit margins and ROCE should always be compared between firms within an industry and it is always worth remembering that what is seen as a high profit margin or ROCE in one industry may be a low one in another industry.

 1. *What steps might a firm take to improve (a) gross profit margin, (b) net profit margin and (c) ROCE?*

Financial efficiency ratios

These are ratios that analyse the efficiency with which a business manages its resources and assets. Once again, there are three key ratios:

- *Asset Turnover*: this ratio looks at the assets (or resources) that a firm has and analyses the amount of sales that are generated from this asset base. Consider a pizza kitchen that has a given level of assets (e.g. work-space, ovens). This ratio will measure the level of sales generated relative to this asset base. The higher the sales, the more efficiently is this firm using its assets; so a higher asset turnover figure is a good indicator of financial efficiency. It is calculated as:

$$\text{Asset Turnover} = \frac{\text{Sales}}{\text{Net assets}} \times 100$$

- *Stock Turnover*: this measures the frequency with which a firm orders in new stock. Holding stock can be extremely costly, as it means that money has already been spent on purchasing or producing the items, but no income has been received from their sale. Thus, a higher figure for stock turnover implies that less money is tied up in stock. This particular ratio will vary significantly from one industry to another and you would expect some industries to have a very high level of stock turnover, due to the nature of the products they are selling. For example, firms whose sales are subject to fluctuation (due, say, to the weather) may need to hold higher stocks. Therefore, although it is suggested that a higher figure for stock turnover is better, it is not always the case. Stock turnover is calculated as:

$$\text{Stock Turnover} = \frac{\text{Cost of sales}}{\text{Average stock held}}$$

■ *Debtor and Creditor Days*: these two ratios measure the effectiveness of a firm in collecting payments from and making payments to other traders. Many businesses offer trade credit, where you can buy something today, but pay for it later. Such incentives can be crucial, but it can cause problems when you are the firm offering the trade credit. Debtor days show how long a firm's customers on average take to pay their bill and creditor days show how long a firm takes to pay the bills that it owes. As you will probably realise, comparing these two figures is essential. Ideally, debtor days should be lower than creditor days, as this implies that firm A receives the money it is owed before it has to make payments to those to whom it owes money. They are calculated as follows:

$$\text{Debtor Days} = \frac{\text{Trade debtors}}{\text{Revenue}} \times 365$$

and

$$\text{Creditor Days} = \frac{\text{Trade payables}}{\text{Cost of sales}} \times 365$$

With the business environment under continuing financial pressure, using resources efficiently is vitally important for most firms. Businesses in all sectors will want to analyse trends in these financial efficiency ratios, as a means of identifying areas where improvements can be made.

 2. *What type of figure would you expect a greengrocer to have for its stock turnover? How might this compare with a furniture store?*

3. *What are the advantages and disadvantages of offering trade credit?*

Liquidity ratios

Many businesses have debts, but the key question is whether they have the ability to repay these debts. We have already considered two key ratios; gearing and the debt/equity ratio. Two additional liquidity ratios provide further information:

■ *Current Ratio*: this ratio is a basic measure of how a firm's current assets compare with its current liabilities. If a firm's assets are higher than its liabilities, this suggests that the firm has sufficient funds for the day-to-day running of the business. It is calculated as:

$$\text{Current Ratio} = \frac{\text{Current assests}}{\text{Current liabilities}}$$

■ *Acid Test Ratio* (or *Quick Ratio*): this is a very similar to the current ratio. However, instead of comparing all current assets with liabilities, the acid test ratio excludes stocks, sometimes called 'inventories' (e.g. raw materials), as these cannot readily be turned into cash and hence are termed 'illiquid'. They would first have to be made into the finished product before any cash could be earned. The calculation is therefore very similar to the one above:

$$\text{Acid Test Ratio} = \frac{\text{Current assests} - \text{Stock}}{\text{Current liabilities}}$$

Some businesses will need to carry much higher levels of stocks (or 'inventories') than others and will therefore have a low acid test ratio relative to their current ratio. Thus most manufacturers will need to have a much higher proportion of stocks than most service-sector firms, such as solicitors or accountants. This does not make their businesses necessarily more risky. Ratios need to be judged, therefore, according to what would be expected in a particular industry.

With weak trading conditions across the economy following the banking crisis of 2007/8, liquidity is a word that has been used many times in recent years, as all firms need cash to survive. A current ratio of between 1.5 and 2 suggests that a firm has sufficient cash, without having excessive working capital. Again, comparing this ratio over time and with other firms in the same sector is important to give an indication of relative performance.

 4. *Would you expect the Current Ratio or the Acid Test to have a higher figure for any given firm?*

While the ratios discussed should never be analysed independently and can give misleading results if they are not interpreted correctly, they remain a good numerical measure of business performance. Before undertaking any changes relating to market penetration, scale of operation, diversification, etc., a firm will consider the above ratios (and many more) to ensure that it is making the best use of its existing resources and that it has sufficient funds to carry out its plans.

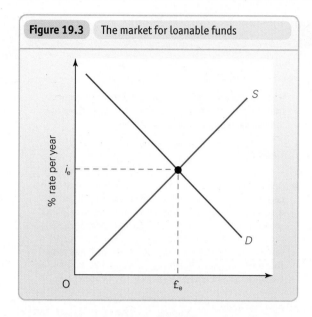

Figure 19.3 The market for loanable funds

reasons. First, households will borrow more at lower rates of interest. It effectively makes goods cheaper for them to buy. Second, it reflects the falling rate of return on investment as investment increases. This is simply due to diminishing returns to investment. As rates of interest fall, it will now become profitable for firms to invest in projects that have a lower rate of return: the quantity of loanable funds demanded thus rises.

Equilibrium will be achieved where demand equals supply at an interest rate of i_e and a quantity of loanable funds $£_e$.

How will this market adjust to a change in demand or supply? Assume that there is a rise in demand for capital equipment, due, say, to an improvement in technology which increases the productivity of capital. There is thus an increase in demand for loanable funds. The demand curve shifts to the right in Figure 19.3. The equilibrium rate of interest will rise and this will encourage more savings. The end result is that more money will be spent on capital equipment.

Calculating the costs of capital

When calculating the net present value or internal rate of return of an investment, it is clearly important for the firm to estimate the cost of the investment. The cost includes both the cost of the equipment that the firm buys and the costs of raising the finance to pay for the investment.

A firm can finance investment from three major sources:

■ retaining profits;
■ borrowing from the banking sector – either domestic or overseas;
■ issuing new shares (equities) or debentures (fixed-interest loan stock).

It is quite common for a firm to raise finance for a particular project from a mixture of all three sources. The problem is that each source of finance will have a different cost. What is needed, then, for each project is a weighted average

of the interest rate (or equivalent) charged or implied by each component of finance.

For investment financed by retained profits, the opportunity cost depends on what would have been done with the profits as the next best alternative. It might be the interest forgone by not putting the money into a bank or other financial institution, or by not purchasing assets. If the next best alternative was to distribute the profits to shareholders, then the opportunity cost would be the cost associated with the increased risks of the firm's share price falling, and the consequent risks of a takeover by another company. (Share prices would fall if shareholders, disillusioned with the reduced dividends, sold their shares.) For a bank loan, or for debentures, the cost is simply the rate of interest paid on the loan. The only estimation problem here is that of forecasting future rates of interest on loans where the rate of interest is variable.

For equity finance, the cost is the rate of return that must be paid to shareholders to persuade them not to sell their shares. This will depend on the rate of return on shares elsewhere. The greater the return on shares generally, the higher must be the dividends paid by any given firm in order to persuade its shareholders not to switch into other companies' shares.

Leverage and the cost of capital

The cost of capital will increase as the risks for those supplying finance to the company increase: they will need a higher rate of return to warrant incurring the higher risks. One of the most important determinants of the risk to suppliers of finance is the company's leverage. *Leverage* is a measure of the extent to which the company relies on debt finance (i.e. loans) as opposed to equity finance.

There are two common measures of leverage. The first is the *gearing ratio*. This is the ratio of debt finance (debentures and borrowing from banks) to total finance. The other is the *debt/equity ratio*. This is the ratio of debt finance to equity finance.

The greater the company's leverage, the higher will be the risks to creditors and hence the higher will be the interest charged (see Figure 19.4). But why should this be so? The reason is that interest on loans (bank loans and debentures) has to be paid, irrespective of the company's profits. If there is a downturn in the company's profits then, if it has 'low gearing' (i.e. a low debt/equity ratio), it can simply cut its dividends and as a result will find it relatively easy to make

> ### Definitions
>
> **Leverage** The extent to which a company relies upon debt finance as opposed to equity finance.
>
> **Gearing ratio** The ratio of debt finance to total finance.
>
> **Debt/equity ratio** The ratio of debt finance to equity finance.
>
> **Risk premium** As a business's gearing rises, investors require a higher average dividend from their investment.

Figure 19.4   The debt/equity ratio

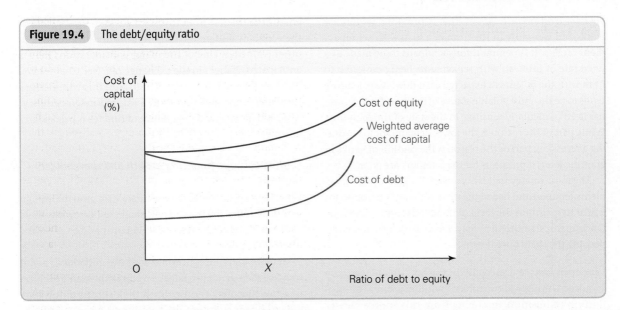

its interest payments. If, however, it is 'highly geared', it may find it impossible to pay all the interest due, even by cutting dividends, in which case it will be forced into receivership.

Given that a highly geared company poses greater risks to creditors, they will demand a higher interest rate to compensate. Similarly with shareholders: given that dividends are likely to fluctuate more with a highly geared company, shareholders will require a higher average dividend over the years. In other words, investors in a highly geared company – whether banks, debenture holders or shareholders – will demand a higher **risk premium**. As gearing increases, so the risk premium, and hence the average cost of capital, will rise at an accelerating rate (see Figure 19.4).

19.4   FINANCING INVESTMENT

It is often claimed that the UK has 'fair weather' bankers: that is, bankers who are prepared to lend when things are going well, but less inclined to lend when times are hard. This criticism has intensified in recent years, with banks accused of holding back recovery in the economy by being reluctant to lend to many businesses, especially SMEs. They are also accused of taking a short-term perspective in their lending practices and of being over-eager to charge high rates of interest on loans, thereby discouraging investment.

But the problem for business does not end there. Dealers on the stock market are also accused of focusing their speculative behaviour on short-run returns (see Boxes 4.2 and 5.4), thereby generating volatility in share prices and creating business caution, as firms seek ways of maintaining shareholder confidence in their stock (usually through paying high dividends).

In this section we will consider the sources from which business might draw finance, and the roles played by the various UK financial institutions. We will assess the extent to which 'short-termism' is an endemic problem in the capital market.

Sources of business finance

The firm can finance growth by borrowing, by retaining profits or by a new issue of shares (see section 19.3).

Internal funds

As we noted (see Chapter 15), the largest source of finance for investment in the UK is firms' own internal funds (i.e. retained profits). Given that business profitability depends in large part on the general state of the economy, internal funds as a source of business finance are likely to show considerable cyclical variation. When profits are squeezed in a recession, this source of investment will decline – but so also will the *demand* for investment: after all, what is the point in investing if your market is declining?

Furthermore, if retained profits are used, the firm will have less profit available to pay out in dividends. This could cause shareholders to consider selling their shares, which could cause a fall in share prices.

External funds

Other sources of finance, which include borrowing and the issue of shares and debentures, are known as 'external funds'. These are then categorised as short-term, medium-term or long-term sources of finance.

Short-term finance. This is usually in the form of a short-term bank loan or overdraft facility, and is used by firms as a form of working capital to aid them in their day-to-day business operations. Another way of borrowing for a short period of time is for a firm to issue *commercial bills of exchange* (see page 522).

KI 14
p 82

Medium-term finance. Again, this is provided largely by banks and is usually in the form of a loan with set repayment targets. It is common for such loans to be made at a fixed rate of interest, with repayments being designed to fit in with the business's expected cash flow. Bank lending tends to be the most volatile source of business finance, and has been particularly sensitive to the state of the economy. While part of the reason is the lower demand for loans during a recession, part of the reason is the caution of banks in granting loans if prospects for the economy are poor.

The more money that is borrowed, the greater the repayments required and hence the more difficult it becomes for a firm to maintain the level of dividends to shareholders. Once again, shareholders may decide to sell their shares, pushing the share price down.

Long-term finance. Especially in the UK, this tends to be acquired through the stock and bond markets. The proportion of business financing from this source clearly depends on the state of the stock market. In the late 1990s, with a buoyant stock market, the proportion of funds obtained through share issue increased. Then with a decline in stock market prices from 2000 to 2003, this proportion fell, only to rise again as the stock market surged ahead after 2004. From late 2007 through to early 2009, however, with growing worries about difficulties of raising finance following the 'credit crunch' (see Chapter 28) and fears of an impending recession, the stock market plummeted once more. The stock market did recover, though it took quite a few years to return to the pre-crisis level, as we saw in Box 4.3.

Despite the traditional reliance on the stock market for external long-term sources of finance in the UK, there has been a growing involvement of banks in recent years, though criticisms of their caution and short-termism still remain. This change does provide a more similar approach to other European countries, notably Germany and France. In these countries, banks provide a significant amount of *long-term*, fixed interest rate finance. While this tends to increase companies' gearing ratios and thus increases the risk of bankruptcy, it does provide a much more stable source of finance and creates an environment where banks are much more committed to the long-run health of companies. For this reason the net effect may be to *reduce* the risks associated with financing investment.

Other sources of long-term finance include various forms of grants from government, local authorities and the EU, often for specific purposes, such as R&D or training, or just for SMEs. Another source is 'venture capital', where an established business or a 'business angel' invests in a new or small business seeking to expand in exchange for a share of the business.

Another source of finance is that from outside the country. This might be direct investment by externally based companies in the domestic economy or from foreign financial institutions. In either case, a major determinant of the amount of finance from this source is the current state of the economy and predictions of its future state relative to other countries. One of the major considerations here is anticipated changes in the exchange rate (see Chapter 27). If the exchange rate is expected to rise, this will increase the value of any given profit in terms of foreign currency. As would be expected, this source of finance is particularly volatile.

Conflict between financing growth and shareholders' interests

Whether a firm chooses to raise finance for growth through retained profits, the issue of new shares or borrowing, there could be an adverse effect on dividends and thus on the firm's share price.

Shareholders are concerned with their dividends and if they see their dividends fall as a result of the firm's decision to grow, they may choose to sell their shares, unless they are confident that *long-run* profits and hence dividends will rise again. If shareholders do sell their shares, the supply curve of shares will shift to the right, pushing the share price down.

Firms must therefore weigh up the benefits of growth with the potential costs of a falling share price. The problem is that if share prices fall too far, firms may become susceptible to being taken over and of certain managers losing their jobs. This is known as the ***takeover constraint*** (section 15.2, page 244), and to avoid it, growth-maximising firms need to ensure that they have sufficient profits to distribute in the short run. This is the idea of profit 'satisficing': making sufficient profits to keep shareholders happy, as we discussed in Chapter 14.

The role of the financial sector

Before we look at the financial institutions operating within the UK, and assess their differing financial roles, it should be noted that they all have the common function of providing a link between those who wish to lend and those who wish to borrow. In other words, they act as the mechanism whereby the supply of funds is matched to the demand for funds.

As ***financial intermediaries***, these institutions provide four important services.

Definitions

Takeover constraint The effect that the fear of being taken over has on a firm's willingness to undertake projects that reduce distributed profits

Financial intermediaries The general name for financial institutions (banks, building societies, etc.) which act as a means of channelling funds from depositors to borrowers.

BOX 19.3   FINANCING INNOVATION

A flourishing domestic economy is, in no small part, the result of firms successfully innovating and responding to the changing conditions and technologies within the marketplace. Through such adaptation and innovation the economy prospers, stimulating growth, income and employment. Conversely, an economy that fails to innovate and respond to change is likely to be set upon the rocky road to stagnation and decline.

Given the stark contrast in these alternative realities, not only is the development of new ideas and their diffusion throughout the economy crucial to its vitality, but also it is essential that the financial system supports such innovation, and does so in the most efficient way. It must ensure not only that finance is available, but also that it goes to those projects with the greatest potential.

Unfortunately, the projects with the greatest potential may involve considerable risk and uncertainty. Because of this, the private sector may be unwilling to fund their development. It may also be unwilling to finance various forms of research, where the outcomes are uncertain: something that is inevitable in much basic research.

As a result of this reluctance by the private sector, innovation funding has traditionally operated at three levels:

- Level one: government financing of 'upstream' or basic research, where outcomes are likely to yield few if any financial returns.
- Level two: self-financed business R&D (i.e. financed out of ploughed-back profit), where the profitability of such R&D activity is difficult to assess, especially by those outside of the business, and thus where banks and other financial institutions would be reluctant to provide finance.
- Level three: external financing using accepted financial assessment criteria for risk and uncertainty.

In this traditional model, the state's role in financing innovation and investment does not end at the level of basic research. It will also compensate for market failures at later stages of the innovation-financing process. For example, it may adopt measures to improve the self-financing capacity of firms (e.g. tax relief), or measures to facilitate easier access to external finance (e.g. interest rate subsidies), or measures to extend and protect the ownership of intellectual property rights (e.g. tightening up and/or extending patent or copyright legislation).

The offshore wind generation sector

The offshore wind generation sector is an excellent example of a sector that has been moving through the levels. When compared to onshore facilities, offshore wind farms offer considerable potential. There is more energy to capture and planning regulations are less restrictive. However, this potential needs to be offset against the high costs of offshore production. At present these costs remain prohibitively high. However, the technology is improving rapidly and costs are expected to decline substantially.

Seen as 'the most scalable of the UK's bulk renewable technologies', offshore wind has huge potential to help meet the UK's 2020 green energy targets. The UK's existing capacity has increased significantly, but further investment of between £16 and £21 billion is needed by 2020 to deliver 10GW of capacity.

The private sector has been unwilling to invest in this sector, due to the high degree of risk and uncertainty, given the emerging nature of this technology. As such, public subsidy has been essential to meet the required degree of investment and this has occurred over the past 15 years. This public investment has led to the UK becoming the world leader in offshore wind in terms of its capacity and the UK is now consistently ranked as the best place in the world to invest in this new means of generating energy.

While this success does not mean the removal of public subsidy and investment, a growing number of international equity investors have already invested in UK operational or construction projects in the sector. As the technology continues to develop and becomes more commercially viable, the sector will move into level three and the government subsidy may well be fully removed. Further details of the UK' investment in offshore wind can be found in a UK Trade and Investment report.[2]

Effects of financial liberalisation

The traditional model of financing innovation appears to be changing and, along with it, the role of governments in the process is diminishing.

The most significant of these changes can be found in the liberalisation of global finance. Three of the major effects of this on innovation financing are as follows:

- Channels of finance have diversified, widening the range of potential investment sources.
- Financial innovations have increased the ability of potential innovators to locate and negotiate favourable financial deals.
- Government regulations over capital market activities have diminished.

The implications of these changes have been to increase the efficiency and flexibility of the financial system. This has resulted in a reduction in international differences in the costs of capital for any businesses having access to global financing. Projects with high earning potential, but high risk, have been able to raise finance from a wider range of sources, national and international.

Although such financial globalisation has not removed the need for state support, it appears that financial changes are certainly diminishing its significance as a supporter of innovation finance.

1. *What market failures could account for a less than optimal amount of innovation in the absence of government support?*
2. *If financial markets were perfectly competitive and could price risk accurately, would there be any case at all for government support of innovation?*

---

[2]*UK Offshore Wind: Opportunities for Trade and Investment* (UK Trade and Investment, 2014).

Expert advice

Financial intermediaries can advise their customers on financial matters: on the best way of investing their funds and on alternative ways of obtaining finance. This should help to encourage the flow of savings and the efficient use of them. As far as businesses are concerned, banks often play a central role in advising on investment and on possible mergers and acquisitions. They also support small firms, for example in assisting with the development of business plans. There is considerable competition between banks in terms of the advisory services that they offer to businesses.

Expertise in channelling funds

Financial intermediaries have the specialist knowledge to be able to channel funds to those areas that yield the highest return. This too encourages the flow of saving as it gives savers the confidence that their savings will earn a good rate of interest. Financial intermediaries help to ensure that projects that are potentially profitable, at least in the short run, are able to obtain finance. They thereby help to increase allocative efficiency.

Maturity transformation

Many people and firms want to borrow money for long periods of time, and yet many depositors want to be able to withdraw their deposits on demand or at short notice. If people had to rely on borrowing directly from other people, there would be a problem: the lenders would not be prepared to lend for a long enough period. If you had £100 000 of savings, would you be prepared to lend it to a friend to buy a house if the friend was going to take 25 years to pay it back? Even if there was no risk whatsoever of your friend defaulting, most people would be totally unwilling to tie up their savings for so long.

This is where a bank or building society comes in. It borrows money from a vast number of small savers, who are able to withdraw their money on demand or at short notice. It then lends the money to house purchasers for a long period of time by granting mortgages (typically these are paid back over 20 to 30 years).

This process whereby financial intermediaries lend for longer periods of time than they borrow is known as *maturity transformation*. They are able to do this because with a large number of depositors it is highly unlikely that they would all want to withdraw their deposits at the same time. On any one day, although some people will be withdrawing money, others will be making new deposits.

There is still the problem, however, that long-term loans by banks, especially to industry, often carry greater risks. With banking tradition, especially in the UK, being to err on the side of caution, this can limit the extent to which maturity transformation takes place, and can result in a less than optimum amount of investment finance, when viewed from a long-term perspective.

Pause for thought

What dangers are there in maturity transformation for (a) financial institutions; (b) society generally?

Risk transformation

You may be unwilling to lend money directly to another person in case they do not pay up. You are unwilling to take the risk. Financial intermediaries, however, by lending to large numbers of people, are willing to risk the odd case of default. They can absorb the loss because of the interest they earn on all the other loans. This spreading of risk is known as *risk transformation*. What is more, financial intermediaries may have the expertise to be able to assess just how risky a loan is.

Pause for thought

Which of the above are examples of economies of scale?

In addition to channelling funds from depositors to borrowers, certain financial institutions have another important function. This is to provide a means of transmitting payments. Thus, by the use of debit cards, credit cards, cheques, standing orders, etc., money can be transferred from one person or institution to another without having to rely on cash.

The banking system

Banking can be divided into two main types: *retail banking* and *wholesale banking*. Most banks today conduct both types of business and are thus known as 'universal banks'.

Retail banking. This is the business conducted by the familiar high street banks, such as Barclays, Lloyds, HSBC, Royal Bank of Scotland, NatWest (part of the RBS group), Santander and

Definitions

Maturity transformation The transformation of deposits into loans of a longer maturity.

Risk transformation The process whereby banks can spread the risks of lending by having a large number of borrowers.

Retail banking Branch, telephone, postal and Internet banking for individuals and businesses at published rates of interest and charges. Retail banking involves the operation of extensive branch networks.

Wholesale banking Where banks deal in large-scale deposits and loans, mainly with companies and other banks and financial institutions. Interest rates and charges may be negotiable.

TSB. They operate bank accounts for individuals and businesses, attracting deposits and granting loans at published rates of interest. Some of these accounts are accessed through the banks' branches and some via telephone or Internet banking.

Wholesale banking. This involves receiving large deposits from and making large loans to companies or other banks and financial institutions; these are known as **wholesale deposits and loans**.

As far as companies are concerned, these may be for short periods of time to account for the non-matching of a firm's payments and receipts from its business. They may be for longer periods of time, for various investment purposes. As wholesale deposits and loans involve very large sums of money, banks compete against each other for them and negotiate individual terms with the firm to suit the firm's particular requirements.

In the past, there were many independent wholesale banks, known as *investment banks*. These included famous names such as Morgan Stanley, Rothschild, S. G. Hambros and Goldman Sachs. Since the deregulation of the mid-1980s, banks have diversified their business, now providing a range of financial services, such as insurance, share dealing, pensions, mortgages and estate agency. We have also seen many of the independent investment banks merging with universal banks, so that they now conduct both retail and wholesale activities.

Concerns about universal banks. One of the major causes of the banking crisis of 2008 was the growth in dealing in highly complex financial products by the investment arms of these universal banks. Many of these products bundled up sound assets with highly risky ones, such as mortgage loans to borrowers in the USA who had little chance of repaying, especially with the fall in US house prices. These 'toxic' assets caused serious problems for many banks and forced governments around the world to intervene to rescue ailing banks (we look at this in more detail in Chapter 28).

The UK's Coalition government set up the Independent Commission on Banking (ICB) in 2010. It was charged with investigating the structure of the banking system and proposed *functional separation*, whereby retail banking was ring-fenced from wholesale banking. It was argued that, for the stability of the financial system, it was necessary to isolate the core activities of retail banks from the potential contagion from risky wholesale banking activities.

The principal recommendations of the ICB were accepted and the Financial Services (Banking Reform) Act became law in December 2013. The Act defines core activities as facilities for accepting deposits, facilities for withdrawing money or making payments from deposit accounts and the provision of overdraft facilities. It gives regulators the power to exercise ring-fencing rules to ensure the effective provision of core activities. These include restricting the power of a ring-fenced body to enter into contracts and payments with other members of the banking group. The Act also gives the regulator restructuring powers so as to split banks up to safeguard their future.

Inter-bank lending. Banks also lend and borrow wholesale funds to and from each other. Banks that are short of funds borrow large sums from others with surplus funds, thus ensuring that the banking sector as a whole does not have funds surplus to its requirements. The rate at which they lend to each other is known as the IBOR (inter-bank offer rate). The IBOR has a major influence on the other rates that banks charge. In the eurozone, the IBOR is known as Euribor. In the UK, it is known as LIBOR (where 'L' stands for 'London'). As inter-bank loans can be anything from overnight to 12 months, the IBOR will vary from one length of loan to another. You can read about the revelations regarding the fixing of LIBOR on the Sloman News Site, in the blog post *Liability for LIBOR*.

19.5 THE STOCK MARKET

In this section, we will look at the role of the stock market and consider the advantages and limitations of raising finance through it. We will also consider whether the stock market is efficient.

The role of the Stock Exchange

The London Stock Exchange operates as both a primary and secondary market in capital.

The primary market. As a **primary market** the Stock Exchange provides a means for public limited companies (see page 40) to raise finance by issuing new shares, whether to new shareholders or to existing ones. To raise finance on the Stock Exchange a business must be 'listed'. The Listing Agreement involves directors agreeing to abide by a strict set of rules governing

Definitions

Wholesale deposits and loans Large-scale deposits and loans made by and to firms at negotiated interest rates.

Primary market in capital Where shares are sold by the issuer of the shares (i.e. the firm) and where, therefore, finance is channelled directly from the purchasers (i.e. the shareholders) to the firm.

behaviour and levels of reporting to shareholders. Companies must have at least three years' trading experience and make at least 25 per cent of their shares available to the public.

At the end of March 2015, there were 982 UK and 298 international companies on the Main Market List, with a market value of £4.3 trillion. During 2014, companies on this list raised £26.2 billion of equity capital on the London Stock Exchange, £3.6 billion of which was raised by international companies.

As well as those on the Main Market List, there are some 1008 companies on what is known as the Alternative Investment Market (AIM). Companies listed here tend to be young but with growth potential, and do not have to meet the strict criteria or pay such high costs as companies on the Main Market List.

In 2014, companies on the AIM list raised £5.9 billion of new capital, which is higher than in 2013 when £3.9 billion was raised and despite year on year growth, it is still considerably down on 2007 when £16.2 billion was raised. The reason for this fall had been the persistence of economic uncertainty created by the recession that began in 2008.

The secondary market. As a *secondary market*, the Stock Exchange operates as a market where investors can sell existing shares to one another. In 2014, on an average day's trading, around £4.6 billion worth of trades in listed equities took place.

The advantages and disadvantages of using the stock market to raise capital

As a market for raising capital the stock market has a number of advantages:

- It brings together those who wish to invest and those who seek investment. It thus represents a way that savings can be mobilised to create output, and does so in a relatively low-cost way.
- Firms that are listed on the stock exchange are subject to strict regulations. This is likely to stimulate investor confidence, making it easier for business to raise finance.
- The process of merger and acquisition is facilitated by having a share system. It enables business more effectively to pursue this as a growth strategy.

The main weaknesses of the stock market for raising capital are:

- The cost to a business of getting listed can be immense, not only in a financial sense, but also in being open to public scrutiny. Directors' and senior managers' decisions will often be driven by how the market is likely to react, rather than by what they perceive to be in the business's best interests. They always have to think

about the reactions of those large shareholders in the City that control a large proportion of their shares.
- It is often claimed that the stock market suffers from *short-termism*. Investors on the Stock Exchange are more concerned with a company's short-term performance and its share value. In responding to this, the business might neglect its long-term performance and potential.

Is the stock market efficient?

One of the arguments made in favour of the stock market is that it acts as an arena within which share values can be accurately or efficiently priced. If new information comes on to the market concerning a business and its performance, this will be quickly and rationally transferred into the business's share value. This is known as the *efficient market hypothesis*. So, for example, if an investment analyst found that, in terms of its actual and expected dividends, a particular share was under-priced and thus represented a 'bargain', the analyst would advise investors to buy. As people then bought the shares, their price would rise, pushing their value up to their full worth. So by attempting to gain from inefficiently priced securities, investors will encourage the market to become more efficient.

> **KEY IDEA 29**
>
> *Efficient capital markets.* Capital markets are efficient when the prices of shares accurately reflect information about companies' current and expected future performance.

So how efficient is the stock market in pricing securities? Is information rationally and quickly conveyed into the share's price? Or are investors able to prosper from the stock market's inefficiencies?

We can identify three levels of efficiency.

Weak form of efficiency. Share prices often move in cycles which do not reflect the underlying performance of the firm. If information is imperfect, those with a better understanding of such cycles gain from buying shares at the

> ### Definitions
>
> **Secondary market in capital** Where shareholders sell shares to others. This is thus a market in 'second-hand' shares.
>
> **Short-termism** Where firms and investors take decisions based on the likely short-term performance of a company, rather than on its long-term prospects. Firms may thus sacrifice long-term profits and growth for the sake of quick return.
>
> **Efficient (capital) market hypothesis** The hypothesis that new information about a company's current or future performance will be quickly and accurately reflected in its share price.

trough and selling them at the peak of the cycles. They are taking advantage of the market's inefficiency.

The technical analysis used by investment analysts to track share cycles is a complex science, but more and more analysts are using the techniques. As they do so and knowledge becomes more perfect, so the market will become more efficient and the cycles will tend to disappear. But why?

As more people buy a company's shares as the price falls towards its trough, so this extra demand will prevent the price falling so far. Similarly, as people sell as the price rises towards its peak, so this extra supply will prevent the price rising so far. This is an example of stabilising speculation (see pages 77–9). As more and more people react in this way, so the cycle all but disappears. When this happens, *weak efficiency* has been achieved.

The semi-strong form of efficiency. **Semi-strong efficiency** is when share prices adjust fully to publicly available information. In practice, not all investors will interpret such information correctly: their knowledge is imperfect. But as investors become more and more sophisticated, and as more and more advice is available to shareholders (through stockbrokers, newspapers, published accounts, etc.), and as many shares are purchased by professional fund managers, so the interpretation of public information becomes more and more perfect and the market becomes more and more efficient in the semi-strong sense.

If the market were efficient in the semi-strong sense, then no gain could be made from studying a company's performance and prospects, as any such information would *already* be included in the current share price. In selecting shares, you would do just as well by pinning the financial pages of a newspaper on the wall, throwing darts at them, and buying the shares the darts hit!

The strong form of efficiency. If the stock market showed the **strong form of efficiency**, then share prices would fully reflect *all* available information – whether public or not. For this to be so, all 'inside' information would have to be reflected in the share price the moment the information is available.

If the market is *not* efficient at this level, then people who have access to privileged information will be able to make large returns from their investments by acting on such information. For example, directors of a company would know if the company was soon to announce better than expected profits. In the meantime, they could gain by buying shares in the company, knowing that the share price would rise when the information about the profits became public. Gains made from such 'insider dealing' are illegal, but proving whether individuals are engaging in it

is very difficult. Nevertheless, there are people in prison for insider dealing: so it does happen!

Given the penalties for insider dealing and the amount of private information that firms possess, it is unlikely that all such information will be reflected in share prices. Thus the strong form of stock market efficiency is unlikely to hold.

If stock markets were fully efficient, the expected returns from every share would be the same. The return is referred to as the *yield*: this is measured as the dividends paid on the share as a percentage of the share's market price. For example, if you hold shares whose market price is £1 per share and you receive an annual dividend of 3p per share, then the yield on the shares is 3 per cent. But why should the expected returns on shares be the same? If any share was expected to yield a higher-than-average return, people would buy it; its price would rise and its yield would correspondingly fall.

It is only unanticipated information, therefore, that would cause share prices to deviate from that which reflected expected average yields. Such information must, by its nature, be random, and as such would cause share prices to deviate randomly from their expected price, or follow what we call a *random walk*. Evidence suggests that share prices do tend to follow random patterns.

> ### Pause for thought
>
> *Would the stock market be more efficient if insider dealing were made legal?*

> ### Definitions
>
> **Weak efficiency (of share markets)** Where share dealing prevents cyclical movements in shares.
>
> **Semi-strong efficiency (of share markets)** Where share prices adjust quickly, fully and accurately to publicly available information.
>
> **Strong efficiency (of share markets)** Where share prices adjust quickly, fully and accurately to all available information, both public and that available only to insiders.
>
> **Yield on a share** The dividend received per share expressed as a percentage of the current market price of the share.
>
> **Random walk** Where fluctuations in the value of a share away from its 'correct' value are random: i.e. have no systematic pattern. When charted over time, these share price movements would appear like a 'random walk': like the path of someone staggering along drunk!

SUMMARY

1a We need to distinguish between factor prices and factor services. A factor's price is income from its sale, whereas a factor's service is the income from its use.

1b The profit-maximising employment of capital will be at the point where the marginal cost of capital equals the marginal revenue product.

2a The demand for capital services will be equal to MRP_K. As a result of diminishing returns, this will decline as more capital is used.

2b The supply of capital services to a firm will be horizontal or upward sloping, depending on whether the firm is perfectly competitive or has monopsony power.

2c The supply curve of capital services by a firm in the short run will be relatively elastic up to capacity supply. In the long run, the supply curve will be very elastic, but at a higher rental rate than in the short run, given that the cost of purchasing the equipment must be taken into account in the rental rate.

2d The market supply of capital services is likely to be highly inelastic in the short run, given that capital equipment tends to have very specific uses and cannot normally be transferred from one use to another. In the long run it will be more elastic.

2e The price of capital services is determined by the interaction of demand and supply.

3a The demand for capital for purchase will depend on the return it earns for the firm. To calculate the return, all future earnings from the investment have to be reduced to present value by discounting at a market rate of interest. If the present value exceeds the cost of the investment, the investment is worthwhile. Alternatively, a rate of return from the investment (IRR) can be calculated and then this can be compared with the return that the firm could have earned by investing elsewhere.

3b The supply of finance for investment depends on the supply of loanable funds, which in turn depends, in large part, on the rate of interest.

3c The rate of interest is determined by the demand and supply of loanable funds.

3d The costs of capital supplied to the firm will rise the more it is in debt, and hence the more risky the investment becomes.

4a Business finance can come from internal and external sources. Sources external to the firm include borrowing, the issue of shares, venture capital and government grants.

4b The role of the financial sector is to act as a financial intermediary between those who wish to borrow and those who wish to lend.

4c UK financial institutions specialise in different types of deposit taking and lending. It is useful to distinguish between retail and wholesale banking.

5a The stock market operates as both a primary and secondary market in capital. As a primary market it channels finance to companies as people purchase new shares. It is also a market for existing shares.

5b It helps to stimulate growth and investment by bringing together companies and people who want to invest in them. By regulating firms and by keeping transaction costs of investment low, it helps to ensure that investment is efficient.

5c It does impose costs on firms, as it is expensive for firms to be listed and the public exposure may make them too keen to 'please' the market. It can also foster short-termism.

5d The stock market is relatively efficient. It achieves weak efficiency by reducing cyclical movements in share prices. It achieves semi-strong efficiency by allowing share prices to respond quickly and fully to publicly available information. Whether it achieves strong efficiency by adjusting quickly and fully to *all* information (both public and insider), however, is more doubtful.

MyEconLab

This book can be supported by MyEconLab, which contains a range of additional resources, including an online homework and tutorial system designed to test and build your understanding.

You need both an access card and a course ID to access MyEconLab:

1. Is your lecturer using MyEconLab? Ask your lecturer for your course ID.

2. Has an access card been included with the book at a reduced cost? Check the inside back cover of the book.

3. If you have a course ID but no access card, go to: http://www.myeconlab.com/ to buy access to this interactive study programme.

REVIEW QUESTIONS

1 Draw the MRP_K, AC_K and MC_K curves for a firm which has monopsony power when hiring capital equipment. Mark the amount of capital equipment it will choose to hire and show what hire charge it will pay.

2 Using a diagram like Figure 19.2, demonstrate what will happen under perfect competition (in the short run) when there is an increase in the productivity of a particular type of capital. Consider the effects on the

demand, price (rental rate) and quantity supplied of the services of this type of capital. In what way will the long-run effect differ from the short-run one that you have illustrated?

3 If capital supply is totally inelastic, what determines the rental value of capital equipment in the short run?

4 Suppose an investment costs £12 000 and yields £5000 per year for three years. At the end of the three years, the equipment has no value. Work out whether the investment will be profitable if the rate of discount is: (a) 5% (b) 10% (c) 20%.

5 If a project's costs occur throughout the life of the project, how will this affect the appraisal of whether the project is profitable?

6 What factors would cause a rise in the market rate of interest?

7 What is meant by the two terms 'gearing ratio' and 'debt/equity ratio'? What is their significance?

8 Explain the various roles that financial intermediaries play within the finance sector.

9 In what circumstances is the stock market likely to be 'efficient' in the various senses of the term?

ADDITIONAL PART G CASE STUDIES IN THE ECONOMICS FOR BUSINESS MyEconLab (www.pearsoned.co.uk/sloman)

G.1 Labour market trends. This case study describes the changing patterns of employment in the UK, from the rise in service-sector employment and fall in manufacturing employment, to the rise in part-time working and a rise in female participation rates.

G.2 Stocks and flows. This examines one of the most important distinctions in economics and one which we shall come across on several occasions.

G.3 Poverty in the past. Extreme poverty in Victorian England.

G.4 The rise and decline of the labour movement. A brief history of trade unions in the UK.

G.5 How useful is marginal productivity theory? How accurately does the theory describe employment decisions by firms?

G.6 Profit sharing. An examination of the case for and against profit sharing as a means of rewarding workers.

G.7 How can we define poverty? This examines different definitions of poverty and, in particular, distinguishes between absolute and relative measures of poverty.

G.8 How to reverse the UK's increased inequality. Recommendations of the Rowntree Foundation.

G.9 Net present value in cost–benefit analysis. A numerical example using discounting techniques to show how net present value is calculated.

G.10 Catastrophic risk. This examines the difficulties in assigning a monetary value to the remote chance of a catastrophe happening (such as an explosion at a nuclear power station).

WEBSITES RELEVANT TO PART G

Numbers and sections refer to websites listed in the Web appendix and hotlinked from this text's website at **www.pearsoned.co.uk/sloman**

■ For news articles relevant to Part G, see the *Economics News Articles* link from the text's website.

■ For general news on labour and capital markets, see websites in section A, and particularly A1–5, 7, 8, 21–26, 35, 36. See also A38–44 for links to economics news articles from newspapers worldwide.

■ For data on labour markets, see links in B1 or 3, especially to *Labour Market Trends* on the National Statistics site. Also see B9 and links in B19. Also see the labour topic in B33 and the resources > statistics links in H3.

■ For information on international labour standards and employment rights, see site H3.

■ Site I11 contains links to *Labour Economics*. You can search for data on *Labour Economics* in site J5.

■ Links to the TUC and Confederation of British Industry sites can be found at E32 and 33.

■ For information on poverty and inequality, see sites B18; E9, 13, 31, 40; G5.

■ For information on taxes, benefits and the redistribution of income, see E9, 30, 36; G5, 13. See also *The Virtual Chancellor* at D1.

■ For information on stock markets, see sites F18 and A3, 31, 40; G5.

■ Sites I8, 11, 14, 18 contain links to *Financial Economics and Markets*.

■ For student resources relevant to Part G, see sites C1–7, 9, 10, 19; D3, 7, 8, 12–14, 16–18, 20.

The relationship between government and business

The FT Reports . . .

The Financial Times, 6 January 2015

FT

Global fines for price-fixing hit $5.3bn record high

By Caroline Binham, Legal Correspondent

Fines meted out to companies for price-fixing reached a record high in 2014, as antitrust authorities cracked down on cartels that rigged the markets for products ranging from auto parts to sausages.

Competition agencies across the world levied fines totalling $5.3bn last year, a 31 per cent increase on 2013's own record-breaking total. Several authorities in emerging markets and Europe took their most rigorous action to date against individual and corporate cartel members, according to data compiled by Allen & Overy, the law firm.

France and Germany both imposed their highest fines, with French authorities levying a $1.2bn penalty on a single cartel, and Germany fining three cartels nearly $1bn in total.

Hotels and bistros were revealed as the preferred venue for price-fixing deals. Investigators found that the price of wurst was being rigged by a cartel that included leading makers Herta, Böklunder, and Wiesenhof, which met at the Atlantic hotel in Hamburg. Similarly, French authorities raided a Parisian restaurant as part of a probe into the price fixing of household and personal-care products, involving such companies as L'Oréal and Unilever.

Brazil emerged as one of the toughest enforcers of competition law, imposing fines of $1.6bn over the year, including its highest ever single fine of $1.4bn, levied on a cement cartel. A Brazilian court also imposed the longest jail sentence for price-fixing last year, ordering a Brazilian executive found guilty of bid rigging between two airlines to spend more than 10 years in prison and pay a $156m fine.

'Individual accountability is slowly becoming a mantra of more and more authorities globally, with antitrust offenders now facing prison time on multiple continents,' said John Terzaken, an antitrust partner at A&O. 'This is a particularly sobering reality for senior executives responsible for global business lines, who risk severe sanctions for their own conduct as well as for wilfully ignoring violations of their subordinates.'...

Auto-parts makers across the globe have also come under scrutiny from competition authorities, in what Mr Terzaken called 'unquestionably the broadest and deepest international cartel case on record.' Agencies from the EU, South Korea, China and Canada fined companies ranging from SKF of Sweden to Hitachi and Mitsubishi of Japan, as part of parallel probes into the industry in 2014.

While I have been a lifelong capitalist, I could never accept that laissez faire is a good solution for a society. It was John Ralston Saul who said that 'unregulated competition is just a naïve metaphor for anarchy' – we don't need that. What we need are regulated markets. And the challenge is to maximise our prosperity by finding the most efficient ways to regulate them.

Neelie Kroes, European Commission Competition Commissioner, 'Competition, the crisis and the road to recovery', Address at the Economic Club of Toronto, 30 March 2009

Despite the fact that most countries today can be classified as 'market economies', governments nevertheless intervene substantially in the activities of business in order to protect the interests of consumers, workers or the environment.

Firms might collude to fix prices, use misleading advertising, create pollution, produce unsafe products, or use unacceptable employment practices. In such cases, government is expected to intervene to correct for the failings of the market system: for example, by outlawing collusion, by establishing advertising standards, by taxing or otherwise penalising polluting firms, by imposing safety standards on firms' behaviour and products, or by protecting employment rights.

In Part H, we explore the relationship between business and government. In Chapter 20 we will consider how markets might fail to achieve ideal outcomes, and what government can do to correct such problems. We will also consider how far firms should go in adopting a more socially responsible position.

In Chapter 21 we will focus upon the relationship between the government and the individual firm, and consider three policy areas: monopolies and oligopolies, research and technology, and training. In their attempt to control price fixing by monopolies and oligopolies, competition authorities in many countries may impose fines on firms, as the *Financial Times* article shows.

In Chapter 22, we will broaden our analysis and look at government policy aimed at the level of the market, and its impact upon all firms. Here we will consider environmental policy, transport policy and the issue of privatisation and regulation.

Perhaps, like Neelie Kroes (see the quote above), you believe that markets need government intervention in order to make them more efficient. There is, however, a problem. Unless government intervention is carefully designed, it can have unintended consequences. The 'cure' might even be worse than the 'disease'.

Key terms

Social efficiency
Equity
Market failure
Externalities
Private and social costs and benefits
Deadweight welfare loss
Public goods
Free-rider problem
Merit goods
Government intervention
Coase theorem
Laissez-faire
Social responsibility
Competition policy
Restrictive practices
Technology policy
Training policy
Environmental policy
Green taxes
Tradable permits
Cost–benefit analysis
Road pricing
Transport policy
Privatisation
Regulation
Price-cap regulation
Deregulation
Franchising

20 Chapter

Reasons for government intervention in the market

Business issues covered in this chapter

- To what extent does business meet the interests of consumers and society in general?
- In what sense are perfect markets 'socially efficient' and why do most markets fail to achieve social efficiency?
- In what ways do governments intervene in markets and attempt to influence business behaviour?
- Can taxation be used to correct the shortcomings of markets, or is it better to use the law?
- What are the drawbacks of government intervention?
- What is meant by 'corporate social responsibility' and what determines firms' attitudes towards society and the environment?
- What is the relationship between business ethics and business performance?

20.1 MARKETS AND THE ROLE OF GOVERNMENT

Government intervention and social objectives

In order to decide the optimum amount of government intervention, it is first necessary to identify the various social goals that intervention is designed to meet. Two of the major objectives of government intervention identified by economists are *social efficiency* and *equity*.

Social efficiency. If the marginal benefits to society – or 'marginal social benefits' (*MSB*) – of producing any given good or service exceed the marginal costs to society or 'marginal

> **Definitions**
>
> **Social efficiency** Production and consumption at the point where $MSB = MSC$.
>
> **Equity** The fair distribution of a society's resources.

social costs' (*MSC*), it is said to be socially efficient to produce more. For example, if people's gains from having additional motorways exceed *all* the additional costs to society (both financial and non-financial) then it is socially efficient to construct more motorways.

If, however, the marginal social costs of producing any good or service exceed the marginal social benefits, then it is socially efficient to produce less.

It follows that if the marginal social benefits of any activity are equal to the marginal social costs, then the current level is the optimum. To summarise: for social efficiency in the production of any good or service:

$MSB > MSC \rightarrow$ produce more
$MSC > MSB \rightarrow$ produce less
$MSB = MSC \rightarrow$ keep production at its current level

Similar rules apply to consumption. For example, if the marginal social benefits of consuming more of any good or service exceed the marginal social costs, then society would benefit from more of the good being consumed.

Social efficiency is an example of 'allocative efficiency': in other words, the best allocation of resources between alternative uses.

> **KEY IDEA 30**
>
> *Allocative efficiency in any activity is achieved where any reallocation would lead to a decline in net benefit.* It is achieved where marginal benefit equals marginal cost. Private efficiency is achieved where marginal private benefit equals marginal private cost (*MB = MC*). Social efficiency is achieved where marginal social benefit equals marginal social cost (*MSB = MSC*).

In the real world, the market rarely leads to social efficiency: the marginal social benefits of most goods and services do not equal the marginal social costs. In this chapter we examine why the free market fails to lead to social efficiency and what the government can do to rectify the situation. We also examine why the government itself may fail to achieve social efficiency.

> **KEY IDEA 31**
>
> *Markets generally fail to achieve social efficiency.* There are various types of market failure. Market failures provide one of the major justifications for government intervention in the economy.

Equity. Most people would argue that the free market fails to lead to a *fair* distribution of resources, if it results in some people living in great affluence while others live in dire poverty. Clearly what constitutes 'fairness' is a highly contentious issue: those on the political right generally have a quite different view from those on the political left. Nevertheless, most people would argue that the government does have some duty to redistribute incomes from the rich to the poor through the tax and benefit system, and perhaps to provide various forms of legal protection for the poor (such as a minimum wage rate).

> **KEY IDEA 32**
>
> *Equity is where income is distributed in a way that is considered to be fair or just.* Note that an equitable distribution is not the same as a totally equal distribution and that different people have different views on what is equitable.

Although our prime concern in this chapter is the question of social efficiency, we will be touching on questions of distribution too.

20.2 TYPES OF MARKET FAILURE

Market power

Whenever markets are imperfect, whether as pure monopoly or monopsony or whether as some form of imperfect competition, the market will fail to equate *MSB* and *MSC*.

Let us assume that all the costs and benefits to society accrue solely to the firm and its customers (we drop this assumption in the section on externalities below). This means that the firm's marginal cost is the marginal social cost (*MC = MSC*) and the price (*AR*), i.e. what consumers are willing to pay for one more unit, is the marginal social benefit (*AR = MSB*).

Take the case of monopoly. A monopoly will produce less than the socially efficient output. This is illustrated in Figure 20.1. A monopoly faces a downward-sloping demand curve, and therefore marginal revenue (*MR*) is below average revenue (= *MSB*).

Profits are maximised at an output of Q_1, where marginal revenue equals marginal cost (see Figure 11.6 on page 185). If there are no other sources of market failure, the socially efficient output will be at the higher level of Q_2, where *MSB = MSC*.

Deadweight loss under monopoly

One way of analysing the welfare loss that occurs in any market is to use the concepts of *consumer* and *producer surplus*. The two concepts are illustrated in Figure 20.2. The diagram shows an industry which is initially under perfect

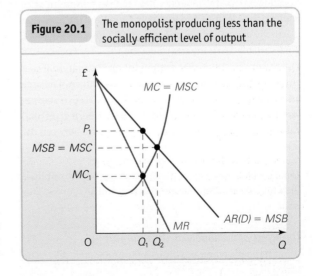

> **Figure 20.1** The monopolist producing less than the socially efficient level of output

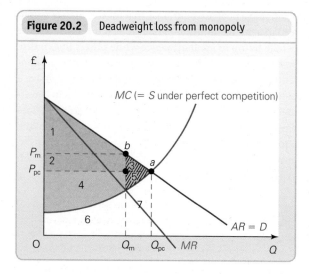

Figure 20.2 Deadweight loss from monopoly

is $P_m \times Q_m$ (areas $2 + 4 + 6$). Total cost is the area under the *MC* curve (area 6). Thus the producer surplus is areas $2 + 4$. This is clearly a *larger* surplus than under perfect competition (since area 2 is larger than area 5): monopoly profits are larger than profits under perfect competition.

Consumer surplus, however, will be much smaller. With consumption at Q_m, total utility is given by areas $1 + 2 + 4 + 6$, whereas consumer expenditure is given by areas $2 + 4 + 6$. Consumer surplus, then, is simply area 1. (Note that area 2 has been transformed from consumer surplus to producer surplus.)

Total surplus under monopoly is therefore areas $1 + 2 + 4$: a smaller surplus than under perfect competition. 'Monopolisation' of the industry has resulted in a loss of total surplus of areas $3 + 5$. The producer's gain has been more than offset by the consumers' loss. This loss of surplus is known as ***deadweight welfare loss*** of monopoly.

Externalities

Markets tend to work more effectively when the benefits and costs to the consumers and producers directly involved in the transaction are the same as the benefits and costs to society. But this may not always be the case. There may be benefits or costs to people *other* than the consumer or producer. We call these benefits and costs ***external benefits*** and ***external costs***. Together, we refer to them as ***externalities***.

So far in this text it has been assumed that there are no externalities. As far as consumption is concerned, we have assumed that the only people who benefit are the customers

competition and then becomes a monopoly (but faces the same revenue and cost curves).

Consumer surplus. **Consumer surplus** from a good is the difference between the total utility (satisfaction) received by consumers and their total expenditure on the good (see pages 91–2). It can be thought of as the difference between the maximum amount people are willing to pay for a good and the price they actually do pay. Under *perfect competition* the industry will produce an output of Q_{pc} at a price of P_{pc}, where $MC(= S) = P(= AR)$: i.e. at point *a*. Consumers' total utility is given by the area under the demand (*MU*) curve (the sum of all the areas 1–7). Consumers' total expenditure is $P_{pc} \times Q_{pc}$ (areas $4 + 5 + 6 + 7$). Consumers' surplus is thus the area between the price and the demand curve (areas $1 + 2 + 3$).

Producer surplus. **Producer surplus** is similar to profit. It is the difference between total revenue and total variable cost. (It will be more than profit if there are any fixed costs.) It can be thought of as the difference between the minimum price required in order for a firm to supply a good and the price that is actually paid. Total revenue is $P_{pc} \times Q_{pc}$ (areas $4 + 5 + 6 + 7$). Total variable cost is the area under the *MC* curve (areas $6 + 7$). The reason for this is that each point on the marginal cost curve shows what the last unit costs to produce. The area under the *MC* curve thus gives all the marginal costs starting from an output of zero to the current output: i.e. it gives total variable costs. Producer surplus is thus the area between the price and the *MC* curve (areas $4 + 5$).

Total (private) surplus. Total consumer plus producer surplus is therefore the area between the demand and *MC* curves. This is shown by the total shaded area (areas $1 + 2 + 3 + 4 + 5$).

The effect of monopoly on total surplus

What happens when the industry is under *monopoly*? The firm will produce where $MC = MR$, at an output of Q_m and a price of P_m (at point *b* on the demand curve). Total revenue

KI 31
p 343

Definitions

Consumer surplus The difference between the maximum a person would have been prepared to pay for a good (i.e. the utility measured in money terms) over what that person actually pays. Total consumer surplus equals total utility minus total expenditure.

Producer surplus The difference between the minimum price required for a firm to supply a good and the price that is actually paid. Total producer surplus is the excess of firms' total revenue over total (variable) costs.

Deadweight welfare loss The reduction in total surplus (consumer plus producer surplus) below the maximum amount that is possible.

External benefits Benefits from production (or consumption) experienced by people *other* than the producer (or consumer) directly involved in the transaction.

External costs Costs of production (or consumption) borne by people *other* than the producer (or consumer) directly involved in the transaction.

Externalities Costs or benefits of production or consumption experienced by people *other* than the producers and consumers directly involved in the transaction. They are sometimes referred to as 'spillover' or 'third-party' costs or benefits.

who purchase the good and derive pleasure from it. We used consumer surplus as a way of measuring consumers' satisfaction or benefit from consuming the product.

Likewise we have assumed that all the opportunity costs to society in the production of a good are incurred by the firm producing it. These include the payments for the time/effort of the workers in the form of wages, the cost of raw materials and the opportunity cost of using capital goods. Society misses out on the best alternative things that these factor inputs could have produced. We used producer surplus as a way of measuring the benefit to firms from production.

External effects of consumption and production. But sometimes consumption and production *do* affect other people. In this case the marginal social benefit (*MSB*) will be different from the marginal private benefit (*MPB*) and/or the marginal social cost (*MSC*) will be different from the marginal private cost (*MPC*).

Take the case of consumption. Imagine a situation where your consumption of a good has either a positive or negative impact on people around you (other than the firm that sold you the good). This could be on other consumers or other firms. In other words there are either *external* benefits or costs of your actions. In this situation the full benefit to society from your consumption of the good are different from the private benefits that you receive. These external or 'third-party' effects are called **consumption externalities**. When we add consumption externalities to private benefits we get **social benefits**.

Now imagine a situation where you are the owner of a firm. Each unit you produce generates costs or benefits that are experienced by your firm. However, production may also generate benefits or costs for other people. These could be the general public, other than your direct consumers, or other firms that are not your suppliers or customers. Once again, there are external benefits or costs, but this time from the firm's actions. The full costs or benefits to society from the production of the good in this case are different from the private costs borne by the firm. These external effects are called **production externalities**. When we add production externalities to private costs we get **social costs**.

In a market environment, where everyone is acting purely in their own interests, these externalities will not be taken into account; neither consumers nor firms make any payments or receive any compensation from other people not directly involved in the market transaction.

In the following section we will consider four different types of externality. Each one will be considered in isolation, although it would be possible to have more than one in any particular market. It will be assumed in each case that, apart from the existence of an externality, the market is otherwise perfect.

KEY IDEA 33 *Externalities are costs or benefits* experienced by people not directly involved in the market transaction that created them. Where these exist, even an otherwise perfect market will fail to achieve social efficiency.

Figure 20.3 Negative externalities in production

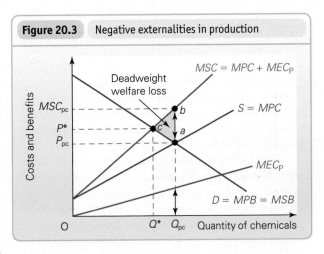

External costs of production (*MSC* > *MPC*) with no external costs/benefits of consumption (*MSB* = *MPB*)

When firms in the chemical industry dump waste into a river or pollute the air, the community bears additional costs to those borne by the firms. There are marginal external costs (MEC_p) of chemical production. This is illustrated in Figure 20.3. In this example we assume that they begin with the first unit of production and increase at a constant rate.

The marginal *social* costs (*MSC*) of chemical production will equal the marginal private costs (*MPC*) plus the MEC_p. This means that the *MSC* curve is above the *MPC* curve. The vertical distance between them is equal to the MEC_p. It is also assumed that there are no externalities in consumption, which means that the marginal social benefit (*MSB*) curve is the same as the marginal private benefit (*MPB*) curve.

Firms will maximise profit where *M(P)C* = *MR*. But under perfect competition, firms are price takers and thus can sell as much as they choose at the market price. Thus, for them, *P* = *AR* = *MR* (see section 11.2 on pages 178–9). This makes the *industry MPC* curve also the market supply curve, since at any price, firms will choose to supply the output where price equals marginal cost. Thus in Figure 20.3, *S* = *MPC*.

The market demand curve will be the sum of individuals' demand curves, which are equal to their marginal utility curves (see Figure 6.3 on page 93). In the context of consumption, marginal utility is the same thing as marginal private benefit. As we are assuming there are no externalities on the consumption side, *D* = *MPB* = *MSB*.

Definitions

Consumption externalities Spillover effects on other people of consumers' consumption.

Social benefits Private benefits plus consumption externalities.

Production externalities Spillover effects on other people of firms' production.

Social costs Private costs plus production externalities.

Competitive market forces, with producers and consumers only responding to private costs and benefits, will result in a market equilibrium at point *a* in Figure 20.3: i.e. where demand equals supply. The market equilibrium price is P_{pc}, while the market equilibrium quantity is Q_{pc}.

At P_{pc}, MPB is equal to MSB. The market price reflects both the private and social benefits from the last unit consumed. However, the presence of external costs in production means that $MSC > MPC$.

The socially optimal output would be Q^*, where $P = MSB = MSC$. This is illustrated at point *c* and clearly shows how external costs of production in a perfectly competitive market result in overproduction: i.e. $Q_{pc} > Q^*$. From society's point of view, too much waste is being dumped in rivers.

The deadweight welfare loss caused by this overproduction is illustrated by the area *abc*. This is where the MSC of the units produced and consumed between Q_{pc} and Q^* are greater than the MSB they provide.

One of the reasons why external costs cause problems in a free-market economy is because no one has legal ownership of factors such as the air or rivers. Therefore, nobody has the ability either to prevent or to charge for their use as a dumping ground for waste. Such a 'market' is *missing*. Control must, therefore, be left to the government, local authorities or regulators.

Other examples of external costs of production include extensive farming that destroys hedgerows and wildlife, and global warming caused by CO_2 emissions from power stations.

External benefits of production (MSC < MPC) with no external costs/benefits of consumption (MSB = MPB)

If companies in the forestry industry plant new woodlands, there is a benefit not only to the companies themselves, but also to the world through a reduction of CO_2 in the atmosphere (forests are a carbon sink). In this case there are marginal external benefits (MEB_p) of production. These are shown in Figure 20.4. We assume that they begin with the first tree planted but that the marginal benefit declines with each additional tree. In other words, the MEB_p is a downward-sloping line.

Pause for thought

Why are marginal external benefits typically likely to decline as output increases? Why in some cases might marginal external benefits be constant at all levels of output or even increase as more is produced?

Given these positive externalities, the marginal *social* cost (MSC) of providing timber is less than the marginal private cost: $MSC = MPC - MEB_p$. This means that the MSC curve is *below* the MPC curve. The vertical distance between the curves is equal to the MEB_p. Once again, it is assumed that there are no externalities in consumption so that $MSB = MPB$.

Competitive market forces will result in an equilibrium output of Q_{pc}, where market demand ($= MPB$) equals market supply ($= MPC$) (point *a*). The socially efficient level of output, however, is Q^*: i.e. where $MSB = MSC$ (point *c*). The external benefits of production thus result in a level of output *below* the socially efficient level. From society's point of view not enough trees are being planted. The deadweight welfare loss caused by this underproduction is illustrated by the area *abc*. Output is not being produced between Q_{pc} and Q^* even though $MSB > MSC$.

Another example of external benefits in production is that of research and development. An interesting recent example has been the development of touch-screen technology for tablets and mobile phones. If other firms have access to the results of the research, then clearly the benefits extend beyond the firm which finances it. Since the firm only receives the private benefits, it may conduct a less than optimal amount of research. In turn, this may reduce the pace of innovation and so negatively affect economic growth over the longer term.

Figure 20.4   Positive externalities in production

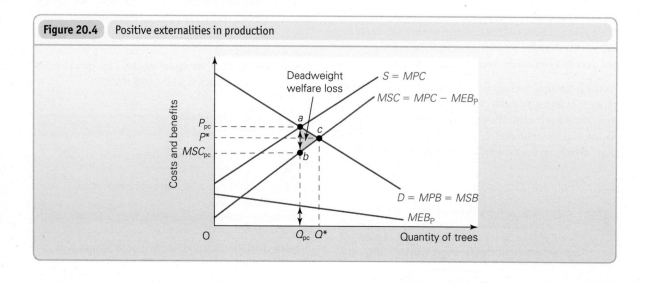

External costs of consumption (MSB < MB) with no external costs/benefits of production (MSC = MPC)

Drinking alcohol can sometimes lead to marginal external costs of consumption. For example, there are the extra nightly policing costs to deal with the increased chance of social disorder. Public health costs may also be greater as a direct consequence of people's drinking behaviour: e.g. through an increase in hospitalisations. It may also lead to a number of alcohol-related road accidents. These marginal external costs of consumption (MEC_c) result in the marginal social benefit of alcohol consumption being lower than the marginal private benefit: i.e. $MSB = MPB - MEC_c$.

This is illustrated in Figure 20.5, where the MSB curve is below the MPB curve. In this example it is assumed that there are no externalities in production so that $MSC = MPC$.

Competitive market forces will result in an equilibrium output of Q_{pc} (point a) whereas the socially efficient level of output is Q^*: i.e. where $MSB = MSC$ (point c). The external costs of consumption result in level of output *above* the socially efficient level: i.e. $Q_{pc} > Q^*$. From society's point of view, too much alcohol is being produced and consumed.

The deadweight welfare loss caused by this overconsumption is illustrated by the area *abc*.

Other possible examples of negative externalities of consumption include taking a journey by car, noisy radios in public places, the smoke from cigarettes and litter.

External benefits of consumption (MSB > MPB) with no external costs/benefits of production (MSC = MPC)

How do people travel to a city centre to go shopping on a Saturday? How do people travel to a football match? If they use the train, then other people benefit, as there is less congestion and exhaust fumes and fewer accidents on the roads. These marginal external benefits of consumption (MEB_c) result in the marginal social benefit of rail travel being *greater* than the marginal private benefit (i.e. $MSB = MPB + MEB_c$).

This is illustrated in Figure 20.6, where the MSB curve is above the MPB curve. The vertical distance between the curves is equal to the MEB_c. Once again it is assumed that there are no externalities in production so that $MSC = MPC$.

Figure 20.5   Negative externalities in consumption

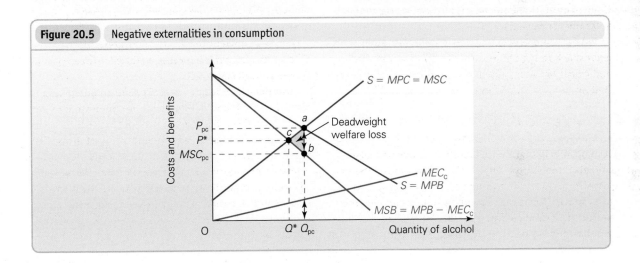

Figure 20.6   Positive externalities in consumption

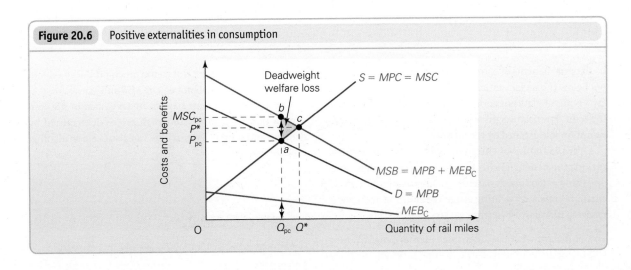

BOX 20.1   CAN THE MARKET PROVIDE ADEQUATE PROTECTION FOR THE ENVIRONMENT?

In recent years people have become acutely aware of the damage being done to the environment by pollution. But if the tipping of chemicals and sewage into the rivers and seas and the spewing of toxic gases into the atmosphere cause so much damage, why does it continue? If we all suffer from these activities, both consumers and producers alike, then why will a pure market system not deal with the problem? After all, a market should respond to people's interests.

The reason is that the costs of pollution are largely *external* costs. They are borne by society at large and only very slightly (if at all) by the polluter. If, for example, 10 000 people suffer from the smoke from a factory (including the factory owner), then that owner will bear only approximately 1/10 000 of the suffering. That personal cost may be quite insignificant when the owner is deciding whether the factory is profitable. And if the owner lives far away, the personal cost of the pollution will be zero.

Thus the *social* costs of polluting activities exceed the *private* costs. If people behave selfishly and only take into account the effect their actions have on themselves, there will be an *overproduction* of polluting activities.

Thus it is argued that governments must intervene to prevent or regulate pollution, or alternatively to tax the polluting activities or subsidise measures to reduce the pollution (see section 22.1).

But if people are purely selfish, why do they buy 'green' products? Why do they buy, for example, 'ozone-friendly' aerosols? After all, the amount of damage done to the ozone layer from their own personal use of 'non-friendly' aerosols would be absolutely minute. The answer is that many people have a social conscience. They *do* sometimes take into account the effect their actions have on other people. They are not totally selfish. They like to do their own little bit, however small, towards protecting the environment.

Nevertheless, to rely on people's consciences may be a very unsatisfactory method of controlling pollution. In a market environment where people are all the time being encouraged to consume more and more goods and where materialism is the religion of the age, there would have to be a massive shift towards 'green thinking' if the market were to be a sufficient answer to the problem of pollution.

Certain types of environmental problem may get high priority in the media, such as global warming or toxic waste. However, the sheer range of polluting activities makes reliance on people's awareness of the problems and their social consciences far too arbitrary.

 The table gives the costs and benefits for a perfectly competitive industry where the activities of the firms create a certain amount of pollution. (It is assumed that the costs of this pollution to society can be accurately measured.)

a. What is the perfectly competitive market price and output?

b. What is the socially efficient level of output?

c. Why might the marginal pollution costs increase in the way illustrated in this example?

Output (000s units)	Price per unit (MSB) (£)	Marginal (private) costs to the firm (MC) (£)	Marginal external (pollution) costs (MEC) (£)	Marginal social costs (MSC = MC + MEC) (£)
1	180	30	20	50
2	160	30	22	52
3	140	35	25	60
4	120	45	30	75
5	100	60	40	100
6	80	80	55	135
7	60	105	77	182
8	40	135	110	245

External benefits of consumption result in a level of output below the socially efficient level i.e. $Q_{pc} < Q'$. From society's point of view not enough journeys are being made on the train. The deadweight welfare caused by this underconsumption is illustrated by the area *abc*.

Other examples of external benefits of consumption include the beneficial effects for other people from someone using a deodorant, parents getting their children vaccinated, somebody wearing attractive clothing and people planting flowers in their front garden.

To summarise: whenever there are external benefits, there will be too little produced or consumed. Whenever there

are external costs, there will be too much produced or consumed. The market will not equate *MSB* and *MSC*.

The above arguments have been developed in the context of perfect competition with prices determined by demand and supply. Externalities can also occur in all other types of market.

Pause for thought

Give other examples of each of the four types of externality.

Public goods

There is a category of goods where the positive externalities are so great that the free market, whether perfect or imperfect, may not produce at all. They are called *public goods*. In order to understand exactly what a public good is it is important to discuss two of their key characteristics – *non-rivalry* and *non-excludability*. Before looking specifically at public goods, let us explore the concepts of rivalry and excludability.

The degree of rivalry

Rivalry occurs when one person's consumption of a good reduces the amount of it available for other consumers. Goods vary in their degree of rivalry.

Perfectly rivalrous goods. At one extreme are goods that are perfectly rivalrous. A good has this characteristic if as one or more people increase their consumption of the product, it prevents all other or 'rival' consumers from enjoying it. This is typical with non-durable goods such as food, alcohol and fuel. For example, imagine that you have purchased a bar of chocolate for your own consumption. Each chunk of the chocolate bar that you eat means that there is less available for other or 'rival' consumers to enjoy. They cannot eat the same piece that you have eaten! The good gets 'used up' when it is consumed.

Many durable goods such as mobile phones also have the property of being rivalrous. For example if you use your mobile phone it usually prevents other people from using it. Although the mobile phone does not get 'used up', only one person can usually consume the benefits it provides at a time: i.e. sending a text or calling someone.

Perfectly non-rivalrous goods. At the other extreme are goods that are perfectly non-rivalrous. A good has this characteristic if as one or more people increase their consumption of the product it has no impact on the ability of other or 'rival' consumers to enjoy the good. For example, imagine that you turn on either your tablet or television to watch a live football match or an episode of your favourite TV programme. Your decision to watch the programme has no impact on the ability of other people to enjoy watching the same programme on a different device. The television set may be rivalrous but the broadcast is not.

Goods with a degree of rivalry and non-rivalry. In reality, many goods and services will be neither perfectly rival nor non-rival. For example, it may be possible for more than one person to enjoy watching a video clip on a mobile phone. However a 'crowding effect' will soon occur. As additional people try watching the video it will prevent others from seeing it on the same phone.

There are a number of goods and services that may have the characteristic of being relatively non-rival with low numbers of consumers before becoming more rivalrous at high levels of consumption. For example, some goods cover a relatively small geographic range. Here overcrowding, and hence rivalry, will set in with relatively few consumers. Viewing a carnival procession, for example, may be non-rivalrous with just a few people watching, but quickly any given location along the route will become crowded and getting a good view becomes rivalrous. In other cases, such as access to the Internet, rivalry might only set in beyond very high levels of usage, when global demand is exceptionally high.

Rather than trying to categorise many goods as either rival or non-rival it makes more sense to think of them as having different *degrees* of rivalry. They could be placed on a scale of rivalry as illustrated along the horizontal axis in Figure 20.7.

The ease of excludability

Excludability occurs when the supplier of a good can restrict who consumes it. This is the case for goods sold in the market. Suppliers only allow those consumers who are prepared to pay for the good to have it. For those goods already in the hands of consumers, excludability occurs when they can prevent other people benefiting too. Just as with rivalry, goods vary in their ease of excludability.

Easily excludable goods. At one extreme some goods have the property of being very easily excludable. In this case a relatively low-cost and effective system can be implemented which guarantees that only those people who have paid for the good are able to enjoy the benefits it provides. The system must also prevent anyone who does not pay from obtaining any of the benefits that consuming the good provides. For example, although television broadcasts have a high degree of non-rivalry, a relatively straightforward and reasonably effective system of encryption could

---

> **Pause for thought**
>
> *How rivalrous in consumption are each of the following: (a) a can of drink; (b) public transport; (c) a commercial radio broadcast; (d) the sight of flowers in a public park?*

> **Definitions**
>
> **Public good** A good or service that has the features of non-rivalry and non-excludability.
>
> **Non-rivalry** Where the consumption of a good or service by one person will not prevent others from enjoying it.
>
> **Non-excludability** Where it is too costly to implement a system that would effectively prevent people who have not paid from enjoying the benefits from consuming a good.

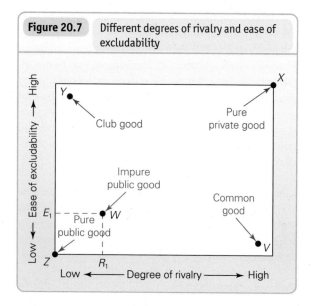

Figure 20.7   Different degrees of rivalry and ease of excludability

---

Pure public goods

Good Z in Figure 20.7 has the characteristics of being perfectly non-rival and completely non-excludable. This is a known as a *pure public good*. Once a given quantity of a pure public good is produced, everyone can obtain the same level of benefits it provides. Therefore the marginal cost of supplying another customer with a given quantity of a public good is zero. However, this should not be confused with the marginal cost of producing another unit of the good. This would involve using additional resources; so the marginal cost of producing another unit would be positive.

Another way to think about the characteristics of pure public goods is that they cannot be sold in separate units to different customers. For example, it is impossible for you to consume 5 units of a pure public good while somebody else consumes an additional 2 units of the good. Once 5 units are produced for one person's consumption, those same 5 units are freely available for everyone else to consume.

There is some debate whether pure public goods actually exist or whether they are purely a theoretical idea. Perhaps one of the closest real-world examples is that of national defence. Once a given investment in national defence has been made, additional people can often benefit from the protection it provides at no additional cost. It would also be very difficult to exclude anyone within a country from obtaining the benefits from the increase in security.

---

be implemented to exclude non-payers from watching the programmes. If this was not possible then pay television channels and pay per view broadcasting could not exist. YouTube has also introduced a number of subscription channels.

Advances in technology may also change the ease of excludability for any given good or service over time.

Perfectly non-excludable goods. At the other extreme there may be some goods for which excludability is impossible: i.e. they have the property of being non-excludable. A good has this characteristic if it is too costly or simply not feasible to implement a system that would effectively prevent those people who have not paid from enjoying the benefits it provides.

In some circumstances it may be theoretically possible to exclude non-payers but in reality the transaction costs involved are too great. For example, it may be very difficult to prevent anyone from fishing in the open ocean or enjoying the benefits of walking in a country park.

Once again, many goods will be neither perfectly excludable nor non-excludable. In these cases it makes more sense to think about the differing levels of ease with which non-payers can be excluded from consuming the good. This is also illustrated in Figure 20.7, this time along the vertical axis.

Pure private goods

Good X in Figure 20.7 is a pure private good. It is very easy to exclude any non-payers from consuming the product, while it is also perfectly rivalrous. A pure private good is one where the benefits can be enjoyed only by the consumer who owns (or rents) them.

In reality many goods will be close to point X and have significant degrees of rivalry and ease of excludability. Products that fall into this category can normally be provided by the market mechanism.

Pause for thought

To what extent is national defence a pure public good? Can it ever be rivalrous or excludable in consumption?

Impure public goods

Good W in Figure 20.7 is an example of an *impure public good*. It has a low level of rivalry, without being perfectly rivalrous, and it is difficult, but not impossible, to exclude non-payers. In reality, many public goods will fall into this category, with some being more impure than others. We will see later that as the degree of rivalry and ease of excludability fall it becomes increasingly difficult for the good to be provided by the market mechanism.

Good Y has a low degree of rivalry but exclusion is relatively easy. This is called a *club good*. Wireless Internet

---

Definitions

Pure public good A good or service which has the features of being perfectly non-rivalrous and completely non-excludable and as a result would not be provided by the free market.

Impure public good A good that is partially non-rivalrous and non-excludable.

Club good A good which has a low degree of rivalry but is easily excludable.

Figure 20.8 Socially efficient output level of a pure public good

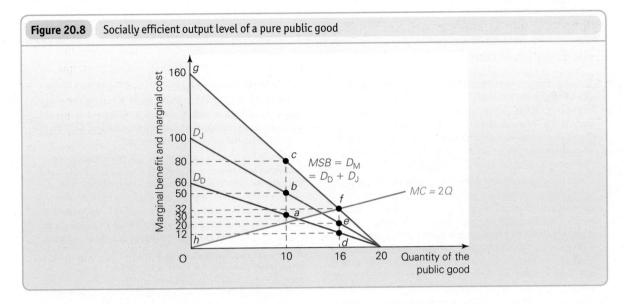

connection in a café could be an example of a club good if a password is required.

Good V has a high degree of rivalry but the exclusion of non-payers is very difficult. This is called a **common good or resource**. Examples include cutting down trees in the rainforests and fishing in the open ocean.

> ### Pause for thought
>
> *Where would you place each of the following in Figure 20.7: (a) an inner city road at 3.00am (b) an inner city road at 8.00 am (c) a toll motorway at 3.00am (d) a toll motorway at 8.00 am?*

The efficient level of output for a pure public good

The socially efficient level of output is the quantity at which the marginal social benefit is equal to the marginal social cost. In a competitive market without externalities the marginal social benefit curve is the same as the market demand curve.

The market demand curve for a private good illustrates the sum of all the quantities demanded by all consumers at each possible price. Different consumers will each want to purchase varying amounts at each price. These different individual demands at each price are simply added together in order to derive the market demand curve for a private good. This is known as horizontal aggregation or summation of individual demand curves.

The market demand curve for a pure public good cannot be derived in the same way, because consumers are unable to purchase and consume different quantities of the good. Once a given amount of a pure public good is produced for one customer, every other customer can consume that same amount at no additional cost.

Therefore, instead of thinking about how much people are willing to buy at each different price, we have to work out how much people are willing to pay *in total* for each possible level of output. In other words, we have to add together the maximum amount each consumer is willing to pay for each possible level of output. This is illustrated in Figure 20.8.

To keep the example simple, it is assumed that there are just two consumers of the public good – Dean and Jon. In most real-world examples there would be many more. The maximum amount Dean would be willing to pay to consume the tenth unit of the good is illustrated at point *a* on his demand curve (D_D) and is £30. The maximum amount Jon would be willing to pay for the tenth unit of the good is illustrated at point *b* on his demand curve (D_J) and is £50.

Therefore if we simply add these willingness-to-pay figures together we obtain the marginal benefit to society from producing the tenth unit of the public good. This is illustrated at point *c* and is £80. This provides us with one point on the marginal social benefit curve. If we continue this exercise for each different level of output, the marginal social benefit (*MSB*) can be derived as illustrated in Figure 20.8. The curve has been derived in this example by vertically aggregating Dean and Jon's individual demand curves: $MSB = D_D + D_J$.

Producing a public good would normally have the same characteristics as producing a private good. Costs would vary with output in a very similar manner. Therefore the marginal cost (*MC*) for the market as a whole would be derived in the same way as it would be for a private good: i.e. by adding together the quantities that each firm would want to supply at each price – the horizontal summation of all the individual firms' marginal cost curves. Hence it is drawn as an upward-sloping line.

> ### Definition
>
> **Common good or resource** A good or resource that has a high degree of rivalry but the exclusion of non-payers is difficult.

BOX 20.2 THE TRAGEDY OF THE COMMONS

The depletion of common resources

Common resources are not owned but are available free of charge to anyone. Examples include the air we breathe and the oceans for fishing. Like public goods, they are non-excludable. For example, in the absence of intervention, fishing boats can take as many fish as they are able from the open seas. There is no 'owner' of the fish to stop them. As long as there are plentiful stocks of fish, there is no problem.

But as more people fish the seas, so fish stocks are likely to run down. This is where common resources differ from public goods. There *is* rivalry. One person's use of a common resource diminishes the amount available for others. This result is an overuse of common resources. This is why many fish stocks are severely depleted, why rainforests are disappearing (cut down for timber or firewood), why many roads are congested and why the atmosphere is so polluted (being used as a common 'dump' for emissions). In each case, a resource that is freely available is overused. This has become known as the **tragedy of the commons**.

How can we analyse the overuse of common resources? The simplest way is in terms of externalities. When I use a common resource, I am reducing the amount available for others. I am imposing a cost on other people: an external cost. If I am motivated by self-interest, I will not take these external costs into account. Overuse of the resource thus occurs.

Another way of analysing it is to examine the effect of one person's use of a resource on other people's output. Take the case of fishing grounds. In the diagram the horizontal axis measures

the use of this common resource, say, in terms of the number of fishing boats per day. The average cost of operating a boat (e.g. the wages of the crew and the fuel) is taken to be constant and is thus equal to the marginal cost. For the sake of simplicity, the price of fish is also assumed to be constant.

As the number of boats increases and fish stocks decline, so each extra boat entering will add less and less to the total catch. The revenue added by each extra boat – the marginal revenue product (MRP) – thus declines. Eventually, at point B_2, no more fish can be caught: $MRP = 0$. The catch is at the maximum. The average revenue product (ARP) is the revenue earned per boat: i.e. the total value of the catch divided by the number of boats.

The average and marginal revenue product curves have to be interpreted with care. Say one additional boat enters the fishing ground. The MRP curve shows the extra revenue accruing to the boat operators collectively. It does *not* show the revenue actually earned by the additional boat. The extra boat gets an average catch (which has been reduced somewhat because of the additional boat) and hence gains the average revenue product of all the boats.

What will be the equilibrium? Note first that the optimal number of boats for the boat operators collectively is B_1, where the marginal cost of an extra boat equals its marginal revenue product. In other words, this maximises the collective profit. At point B_1, however, there will be an incentive for extra boats to enter the fishery because the average revenue product (that is, the return that an additional boat gets) is greater than the cost of operating the boat.

More boats will enter as long as the value earned by each boat (ARP) is greater than the cost of operating it: as long as the ARP curve is above the $AC = MC$ line. Equilibrium is reached with B_3 boats: considerably above the collective profit-maximising number. Note also that the way the diagram is drawn, marginal revenue product is negative. The last boat has *decreased* the total value of the catch.

In many parts of the world, fish stocks have become so severely depleted that governments, individually or collectively, have had to act. Measures have included quotas on catches or the number of boats, minimum net mesh sizes (to allow young fish to escape), or banning fishing altogether in certain areas or for certain species.

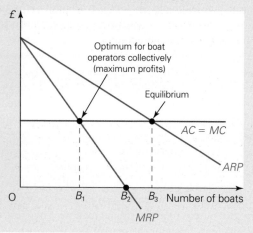

Fishing in open-access fishing grounds

£

Optimum for boat operators collectively (maximum profits)

Equilibrium

$AC = MC$

ARP

O B_1 B_2 B_3 Number of boats

MRP

To what extent can the following be regarded as common resources: (a) rainforests; (b) children's playgrounds in public parks; (c) silence in a library; (d) the Internet?

Assuming there are no externalities in production, the private marginal cost curve is the same as the social marginal cost curve ($MC = MSC$). The socially efficient quantity can be found where $MC = MSB$ which is at point f at an output of 16.

Provision of pure public goods and the free-rider problem

Assume a private firm produced 16 units of the good and charged Jon a price of £20 per unit (point e) and Dean £12 per unit (point d). These prices would equal their

maximum willingness to pay for 16 units. If Jon acts in a perfectly rational and selfish manner we can predict that he will not pay for the good. Why? Because once the

Definition

Tragedy of the commons When resources are commonly available at no charge, people are likely to overexploit them.

16 units are produced he can consume them whether he has paid for them or not. He can act as a *free-rider* by enjoying the benefits of a good which have been paid for by Dean.

Unfortunately for Jon, if Dean thinks the same way, then he will not pay for the good either. If neither of them pays for the good, then the firm will not generate any revenue and quickly go out of business. As a result, both Dean and Jon will be worse off. Because of the free-riding problem, firms cannot produce the good and make a profit in a private market; so the output will be zero. The social inefficiency this creates can be illustrated by the area of deadweight welfare loss in Figure 20.8 – i.e. the shaded area *fgh*.

 The free-rider problem. This occurs when people are able to enjoy the benefits from consuming a good that someone else has bought without having to pay anything towards the cost of providing it themselves. This problem can lead to a situation where a good or service is not produced even though the benefits to society outweigh the costs of producing it.

With just two people it may be possible for the consumers to agree on contribution levels. However, as the number of people who benefit from the public good gets larger, free-riding becomes more likely. This will make it increasingly difficult for private firms to produce public goods in an unregulated market without any government support. If they charge a price they are in effect asking for a voluntary contribution from each customer who can consume the good whether they have paid or not. If no voluntary contributions are forthcoming, then the good will not be provided.

The more closely an impure public good resembles a pure public good, the more likely the free-riding problem becomes. It is then increasingly unlikely that the market mechanism will produce the socially efficient level of the good. In these circumstances the good may have to be provided by the government or by the government subsidising private firms. (Note that not all goods and services produced by the public sector come into the category of public goods and services: thus education and health are publicly provided, but they *can* be, and indeed are, privately provided as well.)

Pause for thought

When studying at school, college or university students are often asked to produce assessed group work. To what extent is group work an example of an impure public good? How could any potential free-riding problems be overcome?

Ignorance and uncertainty

Perfect competition assumes that consumers, firms and factor suppliers have perfect knowledge of costs and benefits.

In the real world there is often a great deal of ignorance and uncertainty. Thus people are unable to equate marginal benefit with marginal cost.

Consumers purchase many goods only once or a few times in a lifetime. Cars, washing machines, televisions and other consumer durables fall into this category. Consumers may not be aware of the quality of such goods until they have purchased them, by which time it is too late. Advertising may contribute to people's ignorance by misleading them as to the benefits of a good.

Firms are often ignorant of market opportunities, prices, costs, the productivity of workers (especially white-collar workers), the activity of rivals, etc. Many economic decisions are based on expected future conditions. Since the future can never be known for certain, many decisions may turn out to be wrong.

Asymmetric information

 One form of imperfect information is when the different sides in an economic relationship have different amounts of information. This is known as 'asymmetric information' (see pages 37–8) and is at the heart of the principal–agent problem.

Take the case of a firm (the principal) using the services of a bank (the agent) to finance its investments. The bank is likely to have a much better knowledge of its range of products and of the current state of financial markets and may mis-sell products to the firm in order to earn a larger profit for the bank. For example, it could provide loans at fixed rates of interest, knowing that rates were likely to fall. The firm would end up being locked into paying a higher rate of interest than if it had taken out a variable rate loan and the bank would consequently make more profit. This practice came to light in 2012, with banks accused of mis-selling such products to some 28 000 SMEs.

Immobility of factors and time lags in response

Even under conditions of perfect competition, factors may be very slow to respond to changes in demand or supply. Labour, for example, may be highly immobile both occupationally and geographically. This can lead to large price changes and hence to large supernormal profits and high wages for those in the sectors of rising demand or falling costs. The long run may be a very long time coming!

In the meantime, there will be further changes in the conditions of demand and supply. Thus the economy is in a constant state of disequilibrium and the long run never comes. As firms and consumers respond to market signals

Definition

Free-rider problem When people enjoy the benefits from consuming a good without paying anything towards the cost of providing it.

and move towards equilibrium, so the equilibrium position moves and the social optimum is never achieved.

KEY IDEA 35

The problem of time lags. Many economic actions can take a long time to take effect. This can cause problems of instability and an inability of the economy to achieve social efficiency.

Whenever monopoly/monopsony power exists, the problem is made worse as firms or unions put up barriers to the entry of new firms or factors of production.

Protecting people's interests

The government may feel that people need protecting from poor economic decisions that they make on their *own* behalf. It may feel that in a free market people will consume too many harmful things. This may be a particular problem when the benefit from consuming a good is immediate while the costs happen at some point in the future. People may put too much weight on the immediate benefits and too little on the long-run costs of their decisions. Products where this might be an issue include tobacco, alcohol and fast/unhealthy food.

If the government wants to discourage consumption of these goods, it can put taxes on them. In more extreme cases it could make various activities illegal: activities such as prostitution, certain types of gambling, and the sale and consumption of drugs.

On the other hand, the government may feel that people consume too little of things that are good for them: things such as education, health care and sports facilities. Such goods are known as *merit goods*. The government could either provide them free or subsidise their production.

Definition

Merit goods Goods which the government feels that people will under-consume and which therefore ought to be subsidised or provided free.

20.3 GOVERNMENT INTERVENTION IN THE MARKET

Faced with all the problems of the free market, what is a government to do?

There are several policy instruments that the government can use. At one extreme, it can totally replace the market by providing goods and services itself. At the other extreme, it can merely seek to persuade producers, consumers or workers to act differently. Between the two extremes the government has a number of instruments it can use to change the way markets operate. These include taxes, subsidies, laws and regulatory bodies. In this section we examine these different forms of government intervention.

KEY IDEA 36

Government intervention may be able to rectify various failings of the market. Government intervention in the market can be used to achieve various economic objectives which may not be best achieved by the market. Governments, however, are not perfect, and their actions may bring adverse as well as beneficial consequences.

Taxes and subsidies

When there are imperfections in the market, social efficiency will not be achieved. Marginal social benefit (*MSB*) will not equal marginal social cost (*MSC*). A different level of output would be more desirable.

Taxes and subsidies can be used to correct these imperfections. Essentially the approach is to tax those goods or activities where the market produces too much, and subsidise those where the market produces too little.

Taxes and subsidies to correct for monopoly. If the problem of monopoly that the government wishes to tackle is that of *excessive profits*, it can impose a lump-sum tax on the monopolist: that is, a tax of a fixed absolute amount irrespective of how much the monopolist produces, or the price it charges. Since a lump-sum tax is an additional *fixed* cost to the firm, and hence will not affect the firm's marginal cost, it will not reduce the amount that the monopolist produces (which *would* be the case with a per-unit tax). An example of such a tax was the 'windfall tax' imposed by the UK Labour government in 1997. This was on the profits of various privatised utilities. Then, in 2005, there was another tax on the 'excess' profits of oil companies operating in the North Sea. These had been the result of large increases in world oil prices.

If the government is concerned that the monopolist produces *less* than the socially efficient output, it could give the monopolist a per-unit *subsidy* (which would encourage the monopolist to produce more). But would this not *increase* the monopolist's profit? The answer to this is to impose a harsh lump-sum tax in addition to the subsidy. The tax would not undo the subsidy's benefit of encouraging the monopolist to produce more, but it could be used to reduce the monopolist's profits below the original (i.e. pre-subsidy) level.

Taxes and subsidies to correct externalities. The rule here is simple: the government should impose a tax equal to the marginal external cost (or grant a subsidy equal to the marginal external benefit). This is known as a Pigouvian tax (or Pigouvian subsidy) named after the economist Arthur Pigou.

Previously we examined the impact of external costs of pollution created by the chemical industry as a whole. We will now focus on one firm in that industry, which otherwise

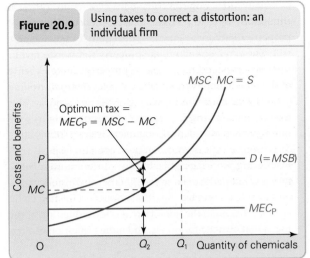

Figure 20.9 Using taxes to correct a distortion: an individual firm

is perfectly competitive. Our firm is thus a price taker. Assume that this particular chemical company emits smoke from a chimney and thus pollutes the atmosphere. This creates external costs for the people who breathe in the smoke. The marginal social cost of producing the chemicals thus exceeds the marginal private cost to the firm: $MSC > MC$.

This is illustrated in Figure 20.9. In this example it is assumed the marginal external pollution cost begins with the first unit of production but remains constant. Hence the MEC_P is drawn as a horizontal line. The vertical distance between the MC and MSC curves is equal to the MEC_P. The firm produces Q_1 where $P = MC$ (its profit-maximising output), but in doing so takes no account of the external pollution costs it imposes on society.

If the government now imposes a tax on production equal to the marginal pollution cost, it will effectively 'internalise' the externality. The firm will have to pay an amount equal to the external cost it creates. It will therefore now maximise profits at Q_2, which is the socially optimum output where $MSB = MSC$.

Advantages of taxes and subsidies

Many economists favour the tax/subsidy solution to market imperfections (especially the problem of externalities) because it still allows the market to operate. It forces firms to take on board the full social costs and benefits of their actions. It is also adjustable according to the magnitude of the problem.

KI 9
p 51

What is more, by taxing firms for polluting, say, they are encouraged to find cleaner ways of producing. The tax thus acts as an incentive over the longer run to reduce pollution: the more a firm can reduce its pollution, the more taxes it can save.

Likewise, when *good* practices are subsidised, firms are given the incentive to adopt more good practices.

Disadvantages of taxes and subsidies

Infeasible to use different tax and subsidy rates. Each firm produces different levels and types of externality and operates

under different degrees of imperfect competition. It would be expensive and administratively very difficult, if not impossible, to charge every offending firm its own particular tax rate (or grant every relevant firm its own particular rate of subsidy).

> **Pause for thought**
>
> *Why is it easier to use taxes and subsidies to tackle the problem of car exhaust pollution than to tackle the problem of peak-time traffic congestion in cities?*

Lack of knowledge. Even if a government did decide to charge a tax equal to each offending firm's marginal external costs, it would still have the problem of measuring that cost and apportioning blame. The damage to lakes and forests from acid rain has been a major concern since the beginning of the 1980s. But just how serious is that damage? What is its current monetary cost? How long lasting is the damage?

Just what and who are to blame? These are questions that cannot be answered precisely. It is thus impossible to fix the 'correct' pollution tax on, say, a particular coal-fired power station.

Despite these problems, it is nevertheless possible to charge firms by the amount of a particular emission. For example, firms could be charged for chimney smoke by so many parts per million of a given pollutant. Although it is difficult to 'fine-tune' such a system so that the charge reflects the precise number of people affected by the pollutant and by how much, it does go some way to internalising the externality.

Changes in property rights

One cause of market failure is the limited nature of property rights. If someone dumps a load of rubble in your garden, you can insist that it is removed and claim compensation for the disutility it has caused you. If, however, someone dumps a load of rubble in his or her *own* garden, which is next door to yours, what can you do? You can still see it from your window. It is still an eyesore. But you have no property rights over the next-door garden.

Property rights define who owns property, to what uses it can be put, the rights other people have over it and how it may be transferred. By *extending* these rights, individuals may be able to prevent other people imposing costs on them, or charge them for doing so.

> **Pause for thought**
>
> *If the sufferers had no property rights, show how it would still be in their interests to 'bribe' the firm to produce the socially efficient level of output.*

The socially efficient compensation rate would be one that was equal to the marginal external cost (and would have the same effect as the government charging a tax on the firm of that amount (see Figure 20.9). The *Coase theorem*[1] states that when there are well-defined property rights and there are no bargaining or negotiation costs, then the socially efficient charge *will* be levied. But why?

Let us take the case of river pollution by a chemical works that imposes a cost on people fishing in the river. If property rights to the river were now given to the fishing community, they could impose a charge on the chemical works per unit of output. If they charged *less* than the marginal external cost, they would suffer more from the last unit (in terms of lost fish) than they were being compensated. If they charged *more*, and thereby caused the firm to cut back its output below the socially efficient level, they would be sacrificing a level of compensation that would be greater than the marginal suffering. It will be in the sufferers' best interests, therefore, to charge an amount *equal* to the marginal externality.

Alternatively the property rights to the river could be awarded to the chemical works. In this situation the fishing community could offer payments to the firm on condition that it did not pollute the river.

One interesting result is that the efficient solution to the problem caused by the externality does not depend on which party is assigned the property rights: i.e. the fishing community or the chemical works. All that matters is that the property rights are fully assigned to either one or the other and that there are no bargaining costs.

In most instances, however, this type of solution is totally impractical. It is impractical when *many* people are *slightly* inconvenienced, especially if there are many culprits imposing the costs. For example, if I were disturbed by noisy lorries outside my home, it would not be practical to negotiate with every haulage company involved. What if I wanted to ban the lorries from the street, but my next-door neighbour wanted to charge them 10p per journey? Who gets their way?

The extension of private property rights becomes a more practical solution where the culprits are few in number, are easily identifiable and impose clearly defined costs. Thus a noise abatement act could be passed which allowed me to prevent my neighbours playing noisy radios, having noisy parties or otherwise disturbing the peace in my home. The onus would be on me to report them. Or I could agree not to report them if they paid me adequate compensation.

But even in cases where only a few people are involved, there may still be the problem of litigation. I may have to incur the time and expense of taking people to court. Justice may not be free, and there is thus a conflict with equity. The rich can afford 'better' justice. They can employ top lawyers. Thus even if I have a right to sue a large company for dumping toxic waste near me, I may not have the legal muscle to win.

Finally, there is the broader question of *equity*. Although the socially efficient outcome does not depend on who the property rights are assigned to, the equity of the outcome will. The extension of private property rights may favour the rich (who tend to have more property) at the expense of the poor. Ramblers may get great pleasure from strolling across a great country estate, along public rights of way. This may annoy the owner. If the owner's property rights were now extended to exclude the ramblers, is this a social gain?

Of course, equity considerations can also be dealt with by altering property rights, but in a different way. *Public* property like parks, open spaces, libraries and historic buildings could be extended. Also the property of the rich could be redistributed to the poor. Here it is less a question of the rights that ownership confers, and more a question of altering the ownership itself.

> **Pause for thought**
>
> *Would it be a good idea to extend countries' territorial waters in order to bring key open seas fishing grounds within countries' territory? Could it help to solve the problem of overfishing?*

Laws prohibiting or regulating undesirable structures or behaviour

Laws are frequently used to correct market imperfections. Laws can be of three main types: those that prohibit or regulate behaviour that imposes external costs; those that prevent firms providing false or misleading information; and those that prevent or regulate monopolies and oligopolies (see Chapter 21).

Advantages of legal restrictions

- They are usually simple and clear to understand and are often relatively easy to administer. For example, various polluting activities could be banned or restricted by placing quotas on the amounts firms can produce.

> **Definition**
>
> **Coase theorem** When there are well-defined property rights and zero bargaining costs, then negotiations between the party creating the externality and the party affected by the externality can bring about the socially efficient market quantity.
>
> **Government surplus (from a tax on a good)** The total tax revenue earned by the government from sales of a good.
>
> **Excess burden (of a tax on a good)** The amount by which the loss in consumer plus producer surplus exceeds the government surplus.

---

[1] Named after Ronald Coase, who developed the theory. See his article, 'The problem of social cost', *Journal of Law and Economics*, vol. 3 (1960), pp. 1–44.

BOX 20.3 DEADWEIGHT LOSS FROM TAXES ON GOODS AND SERVICES

The excess burden of taxes

Subsidies can be used to correct for social inefficiencies caused by positive externalities, monopoly power and public goods. However, the government might have to impose or raise taxes on other goods in order to finance any subsidies. These taxes might have adverse effects themselves. One such effect is the deadweight loss that results when taxes are imposed on goods and services in a perfectly competitive market.

The diagram shows the demand and supply of a particular good. Equilibrium is initially at a price of P_1 and a level of sales of Q_1 (i.e. where $D = S$). Now an excise tax is imposed on this market in order to raise revenue to fund a subsidy in another market. The supply curve shifts upwards by the amount of the tax, to $S + $ tax. Equilibrium price rises to P_2 and equilibrium quantity falls to Q_2. Producers receive an after-tax price of $P_2 - $ tax.

Consumer surplus falls from areas $1 + 2 + 3$, to area 1 (the upper grey area). Producer surplus falls from areas $4 + 5 + 6$

to area 6 (the lower grey area). Does this mean, therefore, that total surplus falls by areas $2 + 3 + 4 + 5$? The answer is no, because there is a gain to the government from the tax revenue (and hence a gain to the population from the resulting government expenditure). The revenue from the tax is known as the **government surplus**. It is given by areas $2 + 4$ (the blue area).

But even after including government surplus there is still a fall in total surplus of areas $3 + 5$ (the pink area). This is the deadweight loss of the tax. It is sometimes known as the **excess burden** of the tax.

Does this loss of total surplus from taxation imply that taxes on goods to fund subsidies are always a 'bad thing'? The answer is no. A comparison would have to be made between the negative impact of the tax in one market with the positive impact of the subsidy it funded in the other market. We have also assumed that there were no market failures in the market where the tax was imposed. This might not be true. For example, if there is a negative externality then the tax could have a positive impact on social efficiency in the market in which it was implemented.

In the real world of imperfect markets and inequality, taxes can do more good than harm. As we have shown in this section, they can help to correct for externalities. They can also be used as a means of redistributing incomes. Nevertheless, the excess burden of taxes is something that ideally ought to be considered when weighing up the desirability of imposing taxes on goods and services, or of increasing their rate.

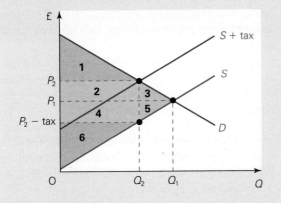

1. *How would the burden of taxation change if (a) demand was more inelastic and (b) supply was more inelastic?*
2. *How far can an economist contribute to this highly political debate over the desirability of an excise tax?*

- When the danger is very great, it might be much safer to ban various practices altogether (e.g. the use of various toxic chemicals) rather than to rely on taxes or on individuals attempting to assert their property rights through the civil courts.
- When a decision needs to be taken quickly, it might be possible to invoke emergency action. For example, in a city like Athens it has been found to be simpler to ban or restrict the use of private cars during a chemical smog emergency than to tax their use.
- Because consumers suffer from imperfect information, consumer protection laws can make it illegal for firms to sell shoddy or unsafe goods, or to make false or misleading claims about their products.

Disadvantages of legal restrictions

The main problem is that legal restrictions tend to be a rather blunt weapon. If, for example, a firm were required to reduce the effluent of a toxic chemical to 20 tonnes per week, there would be no incentive for the firm to reduce it

further. With a tax on the effluent, however, the more the firm reduced the effluent, the less tax it would pay. Thus with a system of taxes there is a *continuing* incentive to cut pollution, to improve safety, or whatever.

Regulatory bodies

Rather than using the blunt weapon of general legislation to ban or restrict various activities, a more 'subtle' approach can be adopted. This involves the use of various regulatory bodies. Having identified possible cases where action might be required (e.g. potential cases of pollution, misleading information or the abuse of monopoly power), the regulatory body would probably conduct an investigation and then prepare a report containing its findings and recommendations. It might also have the power to enforce its decisions or this might be up to some higher authority.

An example of such a body is the Competition and Markets Authority, the work of which will be examined in section 21.1. Other examples are the bodies set up to regulate the privatised utilities: e.g. Ofwat (the Office of Water Services) and Ofgem (the Office of Gas and Electricity Markets). These are examined in section 22.3.

The advantage of this approach is that a case-by-case method can be used and, as a result, the most appropriate solution adopted. However, investigations may be expensive and time-consuming; only a few cases may be examined; and offending firms may make various promises of good behaviour which, if not followed up by the regulatory body, may not in fact be carried out.

> **Pause for thought**
>
> *What other forms of intervention are likely to be necessary to back up the work of regulatory bodies?*

Price controls

Price controls can be used either to raise prices above, or to reduce them below, the free-market level.

The government, or another body, could set prices below the market level to prevent a monopoly or oligopoly from charging prices above the socially efficient level. This is one of the major roles of the regulatory bodies for the privatised utilities. Typically, an industry has not been allowed to raise its prices by more than a certain amount below the rate of inflation (as we shall see in section 22.3). However, above-inflation increases are permitted where it can be argued to be in the wider social interest to do so. For example, in recent years water companies have been permitted to raise some charges by more than inflation to fund investment in infrastructure.

The government could set prices *above* the competitive market equilibrium to reduce the level of social inefficiency caused by a negative externality. An efficient outcome would be reached if a minimum price was set at a level where the marginal social benefit was equal to the marginal social cost. Governments have considered introducing minimum unit prices for alcohol in order to correct for the external costs of consumption.

Price controls could be used with the objective of redistributing incomes. Thus (high) farm prices can be used to protect the incomes of farmers, and minimum wage legislation can help those on low incomes. On the consumption side, low maximum rents might be put in place with the intention of helping those on low incomes afford housing. However, as was argued in Box 4.3, price controls can cause shortages and surpluses.

Provision of information

When ignorance is a reason for market failure, the direct provision of information by the government or one of its

agencies may help to correct that failure. An example is the information on jobs provided by job centres to those looking for work. They thus help the labour market to work better and increase the elasticity of supply of labour. Another example is the provision of consumer information: for example, on the effects of smoking, or of eating certain foodstuffs. Another is the provision of government statistics on prices, costs, employment, sales trends, etc. This enables firms to plan with greater certainty.

The direct provision of goods and services

In the case of public goods and services, such as streets, pavements, seaside illuminations and national defence, the market mechanism may fail to provide the socially efficient amount because of the free-riding problem. Governments may have to finance the optimal provision of the public good by requiring compulsory payments from members of society. One way of obtaining the compulsory payments is through the central/local tax system. Central government, local government or some other public agency could then manage the production of the goods and services directly. Alternatively, they could pay private firms to do so.

The government could also provide goods and services directly which are *not* public goods. Examples include health and education. There are four reasons why such things are provided free or at well below cost.

Social justice. Society may feel that these things should not be provided according to ability to pay. Rather they should be provided as of right: an equal right based on need.

Large positive externalities. People other than the consumer may benefit substantially. If a person decides to get treatment for an infectious disease, other people benefit by not being infected. A free health service thus helps to combat the spread of disease.

Dependants. If education were not free, and if the quality of education depended on the amount spent, and if parents could choose how much or little to buy, then the quality of children's education would depend not just on their parents' income, but also on how much they cared. A government may choose to provide such things free in order to protect children from 'bad' parents. A similar argument is used for providing free prescriptions and dental treatment for all children.

Ignorance. Consumers may not realise how much they will benefit. If they have to pay, they may choose (unwisely) to go without. Providing health care free may persuade people to consult their doctors before a complaint becomes serious.

20.4 THE CASE FOR LESS GOVERNMENT INTERVENTION

Government intervention in the market can itself lead to problems. The case for less government intervention is not that the market is the *perfect* means of achieving given social goals, but rather that the problems created by intervention are greater than the problems overcome by that intervention.

Drawbacks of government intervention

Shortages and surpluses. If the government intervenes by fixing prices at levels other than the equilibrium, this will create either shortages or surpluses.

If the price is fixed *below* the equilibrium, there will be a shortage. For example, if the rent of council houses is fixed below the equilibrium in order to provide cheap housing for poor people, demand will exceed supply. In the case of such shortages the government will have to adopt a system of waiting lists, or rationing, or giving certain people preferential treatment. Alternatively it will have to allow allocation to be on a first-come, first-served basis or allow queues to develop. Underground markets are likely to occur.

If the price is fixed *above* the equilibrium price, there will be a surplus. For example, if the price of food is fixed above the equilibrium in order to support farmers' incomes, supply will exceed demand. Either government will have to purchase such surpluses and then perhaps store them, throw them away or sell them cheaply in another market, or it will have to ration suppliers by allowing them to produce only a certain quota, or allow them to sell to whomever they can.

Poor information. The government may not know the full costs and benefits of its policies. It may genuinely wish to pursue the interests of consumers or any other group and yet may be unaware of people's wishes or misinterpret their behaviour.

Bureaucracy and inefficiency. Government intervention involves administrative costs. The more wide-reaching and detailed the intervention, the greater the number of people and material resources that will be involved. These resources may be used wastefully.

Lack of market incentives. If government intervention removes market forces or cushions their effect (by the use of subsidies, welfare provisions, guaranteed prices or wages, etc.), it may remove certain useful incentives. Subsidies may allow inefficient firms to survive. Welfare payments may discourage effort. The market may be imperfect, but it does tend to encourage efficiency by allowing the efficient to receive greater rewards.

Shifts in government policy. The economic efficiency of industry may suffer if government intervention changes too frequently. It makes it difficult for firms to plan if they cannot predict tax rates, subsidies, price and wage controls, etc.

Lack of freedom for the individual. Government intervention involves a loss of freedom for individuals to make economic choices. The argument is not just that the pursuit of individual gain is seen to lead to the social good, but that it is desirable in itself that individuals should be as free as possible to pursue their own interests with the minimum of government interference: that minimum being largely confined to the maintenance of laws consistent with the protection of life, liberty and property.

Advantages of the free market

Although markets in the real world are not perfect, even imperfect markets can be argued to have positive advantages over government provision or even government regulation. These might include the following.

Automatic adjustments. Government intervention requires administration. A free-market economy, on the other hand, leads to the automatic, albeit imperfect, adjustment to demand and supply changes.

Dynamic advantages of capitalism. The chances of making high monopoly/oligopoly profits will encourage entrepreneurs to invest in new products and new techniques. Prices may be high initially, but consumers will gain from the extra choice of products. Furthermore, if profits are high, new firms will sooner or later break into the market and competition will ensue.

> ### Pause for thought
>
> *Are there any features of the free market that would discourage innovation?*

A high degree of competition even under monopoly/oligopoly. Even though an industry at first sight may seem to be highly monopolistic, competitive forces may still work as a result of the following:

- A fear that excessively high profits might encourage firms to attempt to break into the industry (assuming that the market is contestable).
- Competition from closely related industries (e.g. coach services for rail services, or electricity for gas).
- The threat of foreign competition.
- Countervailing powers (see page 204). Large powerful producers often sell to large powerful buyers. For example, the power of detergent manufacturers to drive up the price of washing powder is countered by the power of supermarket chains to drive down the price at which they purchase it. Thus power is to some extent neutralised.
- The competition for corporate control (see page 188).

KI 8
p42

KI 9
p51

KI 10
p52

KI 9
p51

20.5 FIRMS AND SOCIAL RESPONSIBILITY

It is often assumed that firms are simply concerned to maximise profits: that they are not concerned with broader issues of *corporate social responsibility (CSR)*. What this assumption means is that firms are only concerned with the interests of shareholders (or managers) and are not concerned for the well-being of the community at large.

It is then argued, however, that competitive forces could result in society *benefiting* from the self-interested behaviour of firms: i.e. that profit maximisation will lead to social efficiency under conditions of perfect competition and the absence of externalities.

But, as we have seen, in the real world markets are not perfect and there are often considerable externalities. In such cases, a lack of social responsibility on the part of firms can have profoundly adverse effects on society. Indeed, many forms of market failure can be attributed directly to business practices that could not be classified as 'socially responsible': advertising campaigns that seek to misinform, or in some way deceive the consumer; monopoly producers exploiting their monopoly position through charging excessively high prices; the conscious decision to ignore water and air pollution limits, knowing that the chances of being caught are slim.

So should businesses be concerned only with profit, or should they take broader social issues into account? If they do behave in an anti-social way, is the only answer to rely on government intervention, or are there any social pressures that can be brought to bear to persuade businesses to modify their behaviour?

Two views of corporate social responsibility

The classical view. According to this view, business managers are responsible only to their shareholders, and as such should be concerned solely with profit maximisation. If managers in their business decisions take into account a wider set of social responsibilities, not only will they tend to undermine the market mechanism, but also they will be making social policy decisions in fields where they may have little skill or expertise. If being socially responsible ultimately reduces profits, then the shareholder loses and managers have failed to discharge their duty. By diluting their purpose in pursuit of *social* goals, businesses extend their influence over society as a whole, which cannot be good given the lack of public accountability to which business leaders are subject.

The socioeconomic view. This view argues that the role of modern business has changed, and that society expects business to adhere to certain moral and social responsibilities. Modern businesses are seen as more than economic institutions, as they are actively involved in society's social, political and legal environments. As such, all businesses are responsible not only to their shareholders but also to all *stakeholders*. Stakeholders are all those affected by the business's operations: not only shareholders, but also workers, customers, suppliers, creditors and people living in the neighbourhood. Given the far-reaching environmental effects of many businesses, stakeholding might extend to the whole of society.

In this view of corporate social responsibility, it is not just a moral argument that managers should take into account broader social and environmental issues, but also a financial one. It is argued that a business will maximise profits over the *long term* only if its various social responsibilities are taken into account. If a business is seen as ignoring the interests of the wider community and failing to protect society's welfare, then this will be 'bad for business': the firm's reputation and image will suffer.

In many top corporations, *environmental scanning* is now an integral part of the planning process. This involves the business surveying changing political, economic, social, technological, environmental and legal trends in the external environment in order to remain in tune with consumer concerns (see section 1.1). For example, the general public's growing concern over 'green' issues has significantly influenced many businesses' product development programmes and R&D strategies (see Box 20.4). The more successful a business is in being able to associate the image of 'environmentally friendly' to a particular product or brand, the more likely it is to enhance its sales or establish a measure of brand loyalty, and thereby to strengthen its competitive position.

Several companies in recent years have made great play of their social responsibility. For instance, in 2007, Marks and Spencer launched its 'Plan A'. The original plan centred on meeting 100 social and environmental targets across five areas: climate change, waste, natural resources, ethical trading and health and well-being. In 2010, M&S announced that it was adding a further 80 commitments and extending some of its original commitments.[2]

> ### Definitions
>
> **Corporate social responsibility** Where a firm takes into account the interests and concerns of a community rather than just its shareholders.
>
> **Stakeholder** An individual affected by the operations of a business.
>
> **Environmental scanning** Where a business surveys political, economic, social, technological, environmental and legal trends in the external environment to aid its decision-making process.

---

[2]http://plana.marksandspencer.com/about

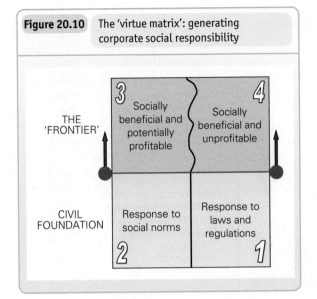

Figure 20.10 The 'virtue matrix': generating corporate social responsibility

small children; manufacturers may landscape the surroundings to their factories or build factories of a pleasant design so as to make them more attractive to local residents and visitors. They are not obliged to take such actions by law, but feel that it is expected of them.

A key point about actions in the civil foundation is that they are likely to be consistent with the aim of profit maximisation or maximising shareholder value. In other words, shareholders' and society's interests are likely to coincide. This is obvious in the case of abiding by the law. Except in cases where breaking the law can go undetected, firms must abide by the law if they are to avoid prosecution with all the risks to profits that this entails. But abiding by social norms (cell 2) is also likely to contribute towards profit. The extra costs associated with such actions will probably be recouped from extra sales associated with achieving a good public image or extra productivity from a contented workforce.

The frontier

The top two cells represent the frontier. These refer to activities that are not directly in the interests of shareholders, but have a moral or social motivation.

Cell 3 represents those actions that are not immediately profitable, but could possibly become so in the future because of positive reactions from consumers, employees, competitors or government. To quote from Martin: 'When Prudential allowed people with AIDS to tap the death benefits in their life assurance policies to pay for medical expenses, the move generated so much goodwill that competing insurers soon offered [such] settlements as well. Very quickly, corporate behavior that had seemed radical became business as usual throughout the insurance industry.'[4] Generally activities in cell 3 are risky and the willingness of firms to engage in them depends on their attitudes towards risk.

Cell 4 represents the most radical departure from shareholders' interests. Here managers take action that benefits society but at the *expense* of profit. Managers are not always ruthless profit maximisers (see Chapter 14). They can be motivated by a range of objectives. One of these is 'to do the right thing' by employees, customers or society generally. For example, improving working conditions for employees is seen not just as a way of improving productivity, but also as a moral duty towards the workforce. Likewise managers may control toxic emissions beyond the legal minimum requirement because of their genuine concern for the environment.

The development of corporate social responsibility over time

Pressures from various stakeholders are likely to increase corporate social responsibility over time. These pressures are

What we increasingly observe today is business feeling that it is not enough to be seen merely *complying* with laws on the environment, product standards or workplace conditions: i.e. just to be doing the legal minimum. Hence, there is a growing philosophy of 'compliance plus' which motivates businesses to compete against each other in terms of their social image.

The virtue matrix: generating corporate social responsibility

In an article in the Harvard Business Review,[3] Roger L. Martin developed a framework for analysing corporate social responsibility and the factors that influence it. The framework is the 'virtue matrix' and an adaptation of it is illustrated in Figure 20.10.

The matrix is divided into four cells, each of which shows types of action taken by a firm that have social effects.

The civil foundation

The bottom two cells are in what is termed *the civil foundation*. They refer to socially responsible actions that society expects firms to take, and firms will normally do so.

Cell 1 refers to actions in response to laws and regulations. For example, firms may control the emissions of toxic waste because they are obliged to do so by law. Similarly, they may provide a clean and safe environment for their workers because of health and safety legislation.

Cell 2 refers to the types of behaviour expected of firms by society and where firms would come in for criticism, or even condemnation, if they did not abide by these social norms. For example, employers may operate flexible working hours or set up nursery facilities to help workers with

[3]Roger L. Martin, 'The virtue matrix: calculating the return on corporate responsibility', *Harvard Business Review* (March 2002).

[4]Ibid., p. 8.

Figure 20.11 Pressures on companies to be more socially responsible

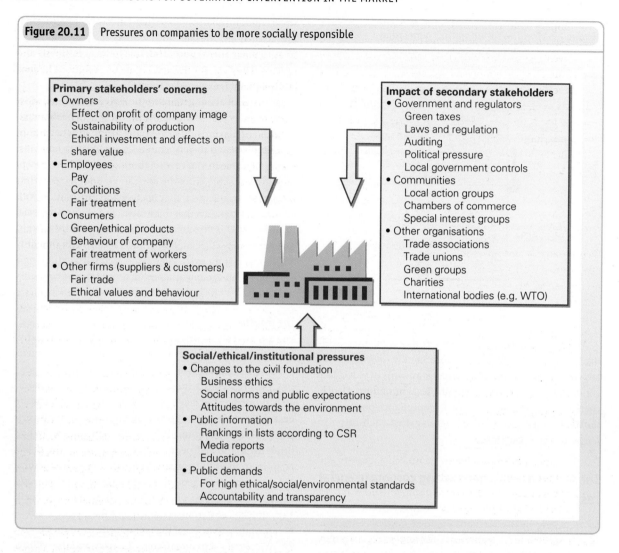

Primary stakeholders' concerns
- Owners
  - Effect on profit of company image
  - Sustainability of production
  - Ethical investment and effects on share value
- Employees
  - Pay
  - Conditions
  - Fair treatment
- Consumers
  - Green/ethical products
  - Behaviour of company
  - Fair treatment of workers
- Other firms (suppliers & customers)
  - Fair trade
  - Ethical values and behaviour

Impact of secondary stakeholders
- Government and regulators
  - Green taxes
  - Laws and regulation
  - Auditing
  - Political pressure
  - Local government controls
- Communities
  - Local action groups
  - Chambers of commerce
  - Special interest groups
- Other organisations
  - Trade associations
  - Trade unions
  - Green groups
  - Charities
  - International bodies (e.g. WTO)

Social/ethical/institutional pressures
- Changes to the civil foundation
  - Business ethics
  - Social norms and public expectations
  - Attitudes towards the environment
- Public information
  - Rankings in lists according to CSR
  - Media reports
  - Education
- Public demands
  - For high ethical/social/environmental standards
  - Accountability and transparency

summarised in Figure 20.11. They come from three sources: from the primary stakeholders, such as shareholders, employees, customers and suppliers; from secondary stakeholders, such as the government and other local, national and international organisations; and from changes to the whole civil foundation, with its norms and values and what is regarded as 'acceptable' corporate behaviour.

These pressures have tended to grow over time. This has resulted in the boundary between the civil foundation and the frontier moving upwards as activities that start in the frontier and then are copied by competitor firms become the norm. The norms of corporate behaviour in Victorian Britain would seem totally unacceptable in Britain today. The long hours, child labour, appalling working conditions, lack of redress for grievances, the filthy conditions of the workplace, the smoke and other pollution pouring from factories are not only illegal nowadays, but totally alien to the norms of society.

Although the boundary tends to move upwards, this is not necessarily the case. Martin gives the example of Russia in the immediate post-communist period, where a collapse of the old order and the development of 'cowboy' capital-

ism led to a decline in standards and the non-enforcement of many regulations governing things such as working conditions and child labour. Many developing countries have a very much lower boundary, which is constantly in danger of being pushed lower by ruthless forces of globalisation and non-representative governments conniving in the process.

Another factor leading to the development of corporate social responsibility is the movement of activities from cell 4 to cell 3. Activities that start as socially desirable but unprofitable tend to become profitable as consumers come to expect firms to behave in socially responsible ways and punish firms that do not by boycotting their products. Thus companies such as Nestlé, McDonald's and Nike have been very concerned to 'clean up' their corporate image because of adverse publicity. Of course, part of the reaction of companies to social pressure may be simply to improve their public relations, but part may be a genuine improvement in their behaviour.

Globalisation and corporate social responsibility
As the world economy becomes ever more intertwined, many companies in rich countries, with a relatively deep civil foundation, are outsourcing much of their production

to developing countries, which have a relatively shallow and less secure civil foundation. This can have the effect of either levelling up or levelling down. Nike and Gap, which produce much of their footwear and clothing in South East Asia, have been accused of operating sweatshops in these countries, with low wages and poor working conditions – a case of levelling down to the civil foundation of these developing countries. Nike and Gap reply that, compared with other factories in these countries, pay and conditions are better – a case of levelling up.

Economic performance and social responsibility

If corporate social responsibility has grown as a business objective, has this in any way impinged upon business performance? Studies, empirical and otherwise, suggest that rather than detracting from business performance and harming shareholder value, in fact the opposite appears to be the case. Corporate social responsibility appears to offer a positive contribution to business performance, especially over the longer term.

The following factors have been identified as some of the positive economic benefits that firms have gained from adopting a more socially responsible position.

Improved economic performance

A large number of studies have attempted to identify and evaluate the economic returns from social responsibility. Factors that have been considered include business growth rates, stock prices and sales and revenue. A survey by van Beurden and Gössling[5] evaluated the findings of 34 studies that considered the link between business ethics and enhanced profits. They concluded that 23 studies showed a positive link, 9 suggested neutral effects or were inconclusive, and the remaining 2 suggested that there was a negative relationship.

Although this evidence would on balance favour an argument that corporate social responsibility is good business practice, the whole area of linking ethics and responsibility to profit is a contentious one. When considering ethics and social responsibility, what are we including within this definition? Is the business merely complying with a business code, developed either within the business or by a third party? Such codes essentially state 'what is not acceptable business behaviour', such as taking bribes or pursuing anti-competitive behaviour. They can be seen as lying in the civil foundation. Or does the understanding of an 'ethical business' go further and entail positive social actions, ranging from giving money to good causes to contributing to particular programmes in which the business has competency? For example, a pharmaceutical company might develop a drug that benefits the populations of the world's poorest countries, with no possibility of profit. Such actions lie in the frontier.

So at what level do we identify an ethical business, and to what degree might this level of responsibility influence profitability?

The concept of profitability is also contentious, most crucially in respect to the time frame over which the assessment takes place. Linking long-run profitability with an ethical or socially responsible programme is fraught with difficulties. How are all the other factors that influence business performance over the longer term accounted for? How do you attribute a given percentage or contribution to profit to the adoption of a more socially responsible business position? Can it ever be this precise, or are we merely left with intimating that a link exists, and is this good enough?

Enhancing the brand

Related to profitability is the issue of how far corporate social responsibility enhances brand image and the firm's reputation. This would not only strengthen consumer loyalty but also aid the firm in raising finance and attracting trading partners.

Surveys have identified that the ethical dimension of the firm is becoming increasingly important in consumer buying decisions. For example, The Co-operative's Ethical Consumer Markets Report shows that the total value of **ethical consumerism**, where consumer decisions, including those concerning financial investments, are motivated by concerns over human rights, social justice, the environment or animal welfare, was some £47.2 billion in 2012. This was 250 per cent higher than in 2000 (in nominal terms), when ethical consumerism was recorded at £13.5 billion.

The survey also shows that the proportion of people who purchased a product at least once a year for ethical reasons rose from 27 per cent in 2000 to 42 per cent in 2012.[6] The report also shows that, in 2012, 50 per cent of people surveyed avoided buying a product or service from a company because of its reputation; the comparable figure in 2000 was 44 per cent. Moreover, 24 per cent of people had actively campaigned on a social or environmental issue in 2012 compared with 15 per cent in 2000.

Thus, environmental responsibility and active participation in the community are the social factors most likely to influence consumers' purchasing behaviour.

> ### Definition
>
> **Ethical consumerism** Where consumers' decisions about what to buy are influenced by ethical concerns such as the producer's human rights record and care for the environment.

---

[5] P. van Beurden and T. Gössling, 'The worth of values – a literature review on the relation between corporate social and financial performance', *Journal of Business Ethics*, vol. 82, no. 2, October 2008, pp. 407–24.

[6] Co-operative Bank, *The Ethical Consumer Markets Report* (2012).

Firms may be further encouraged to develop the social image of their brand with the increasing number of awards given to recognise and promote corporate social responsibility. 'Most admired companies' lists, such as those presented by *Management Today* in the UK and *Fortune* in America, are based on criteria such as reputation for ethics and honesty, use of corporate assets, and community and environmental responsibility. The public relations and marketing potential that can be gained from such awards help firms to strengthen further their socially responsible image.

Attracting and retaining employees

It increasingly appears to be the case that companies with clear ethical and social positions find it easier not only to recruit, but to hold on to their employees. In a number of surveys of graduate employment intentions, students have claimed that they would be prepared to take a lower salary in order to work for a business with high ethical standards and a commitment to socially responsible business practices.

An international survey in 2005 in 15 European, Middle Eastern and African countries[7] showed that 28 per cent of job seekers considered the ethical conduct and values of an employer to be an important factor in deciding whether to apply for work there. Top of the list was security and stability (47 per cent), followed by pay (42 per cent).

Access to capital

Investment in ethically screened investment funds has grown rapidly in recent years. This has been driven not only by the demands of shareholders for ethical funds, but also by a realisation from investors generally that socially responsible business has the potential to be hugely profitable.

The Co-operative's 2012 Ethical Consumer Markets Report shows that the value of funds invested by households in ethical financial products had risen from £6.5 billion in 2000 to £21.1 billion in 2011, an increase of 225 per cent.

The likelihood of returns being lower in ethically screened funds has been questioned by a number of papers.[8]

Indeed, evidence shows that investing in ethical funds in the UK, USA, Germany and Canada does not lead to returns that are significantly different from those obtained from conventional funds.[9] It is difficult to ascertain precisely why this is. However, it could be that environmental performance is a good indicator of general management quality, which is the main determinant of stock price.

Social responsibility appears not only to bring a range of benefits to business and society, but also to be generally profitable. It is likely to enhance business performance, strengthen brand image, reduce employee turnover and increase access to stock market funds. Box 20.4 gives an example of a company that built its reputation on being socially and environmentally responsible – The Body Shop. (See also Box 16.2 on page 270.)

However, perhaps what is even more important is the cost of *not* being socially responsible. In 2010, the massive oil spill from the Deepwater Horizon rig in the Gulf of Mexico, which killed 11 workers, was blamed on poor safety standards and taking excessive risks with the environment. From the blowout on 20 April to the final capping in August, some 4.9 million barrels of oil leaked into the Gulf, causing immense environmental damage and destroying the livelihoods of people in the fishing and tourist industries. It cost the owner, BP, some $3.5 billion in containment and clear-up operations, although the final cost to the company could be many times that amount. Its reputation plummeted in the USA, with motorists boycotting fuel stations. Its share price plummeted from £628 in April 2010 to £296 just three months later.

Despite the concern about cases like this and evidence that firms are increasingly competing with others over their social image, there are still many firms and consumers who care relatively little about the social or natural environment. There is thus a strong case for government intervention to correct market failures.

---

[7] *What Makes a Great Employer?* (MORI survey for Manpower, October 2005).

[8] See, for example, MISTRA, The Foundation for Strategic Environmental Research, *Screening of Screening Companies* (2001) and P. Rivoli, 'Making a difference or making a statement? Finance research and socially responsible investment', *Business Ethics Quarterly* vol. 13, no. 3, 2003, pp. 271–87.

---

[9] See R. Bauer, J. Derwall and R. Otten, 'The ethical mutual fund performance debate: new evidence from Canada', *Journal of Business Ethics*, vol. 70, 2007, pp. 111–124; and R. Bauer, K. Koedijk and R. Otten, 'International evidence on ethical mutual fund performance and investment style', *Journal of Banking and Finance*, vol. 29, 2005, pp. 1751–67.

BOX 20.4	THE BODY SHOP

Is it 'worth it'?

The Body Shop shot to fame in the 1980s. It stood for environmental awareness and an ethical approach to business. But its success had as much to do with what it sold as what it stood for. It sold natural cosmetics, Raspberry Ripple Bathing Bubbles and Camomile Shampoo, products that were immensely popular with consumers.

Its profits increased from a little over €1.7 million in 1985 to nearly €64 million in 2007 and €71.9 million in 2013 and €65.3 million in 2014. Sales, meanwhile, grew even more dramatically, from €8.4 million to €873.4 million in 2014. By the end of 2014, The Body Shop had over 2800 stores in over 60 countries.

What makes this success so remarkable is that The Body Shop did virtually no advertising. Its promotion has largely stemmed from the activities and environmental campaigning of its founder, Anita Roddick, and the company's uncompromising claims that it sold only 'green' products and conducted its business operations with high ethical standards. It actively supported green causes, such as saving whales and protecting rainforests, and it refused to allow its products to be tested on animals. Perhaps most surprising in the world of big business was its high-profile initiative 'trade not aid', whereby it claimed to pay 'fair' prices for its ingredients, especially those supplied from people in developing countries, who were open to exploitation by large companies.

The growth strategy of The Body Shop, since its founding in 1976, has focused upon developing a distinctive and highly innovative product range, and at the same time identifying such products with major social issues of the day such as the environment and animal rights.

Its initial expansion was based on a process of franchising.

> ... franchising. We didn't know what it was, but all these women came to us and said, 'if you can do this and you can't even read a balance sheet, then we can do it'. I had a cabal of female friends all around Brighton, Hove and Chichester, and they started opening little units, all called the Body Shop. I just supplied them with gallons of products – we only had 19 different products, but we made it look like more as we sold them in five different sizes![10]

In 1984 the company went public. In the 1990s, however, sales growth was less rapid and in 1998 Anita Roddick stepped down as chief executive, but for a while she and her husband remained as co-chairmen. In 2003 she was awarded a knighthood and became Dame Anita Roddick. Sales began to grow rapidly from 2004 to 2006 from €553 million to €709 million.

Acquisition of The Body Shop by L'Oréal

A dramatic strategic event occurred in 2006 when The Body Shop was sold to the French cosmetics giant L'Oréal, which was 26 per cent owned by Nestlé. The event resulted in the magazine, *Ethical Consumer*, downgrading The Body Shop's ethical rating from 11 out of 20 to a mere 2.5 and calling for a

boycott of the company. Three weeks after the sale, the daily BrandIndex recorded an 11 point drop in The Body Shop's consumer satisfaction rating from 25 to 14.

There were a number of reasons for this. L'Oréal's animal-testing policies conflict with those of The Body Shop and L'Oréal has been accused of being involved in price fixing with other French perfume houses. L'Oréal's part-owner, Nestlé, has also been subject to various criticisms for ethical misconduct, including promoting formula milk to mothers with babies in poor countries rather than breast milk and using slave labour in cocoa farms in West Africa.

Anita Roddick, however, believed that, by taking over The Body Shop, L'Oréal would develop a more ethical approach to business. L'Oréal publicly recognised that it would have to develop its ethical policies.

Sadly, Anita Roddick died in 2007 and so has not been able to witness changes. L'Oréal though has begun to address its ethical approach. It adopted a new Code of Business Ethics in 2007 and it is gaining some external accreditation for its approach to sustainability and ethics. Notably, L'Oréal was ranked as one of the world's 100 most ethical companies by Ethisphere in 2007. It has also allowed The Body Shop to continue with its ethical policies of no animal testing and 100 per cent vegetarian ingredients.

However, L'Oréal, and with it The Body Shop, continues to attract criticism. Although animal testing for cosmetics is now banned in the EU, L'Oréal still continues to engage in such practices in other countries, including in its own research facility in China. For this reason, animal rights campaigners continue to urge a boycott of all L'Oréal products, including those sold by The Body Shop. Nevertheless, in its 'Sharing beauty with all' sustainability commitment announced in October 2013, L'Oréal announced that 'By 2020, we will innovate so that 100% of products have an environmental or social benefit'.

L'Oréal has injected greater finance into The Body Shop aimed at improving the marketing of products. In autumn 2006 a transactional website was launched and there have been greater press marketing campaigns. And new store designs have helped to boost sales. Although profits fell quite dramatically from €64 million in 2007 to €36 million in 2008 as recession hit the high street, since then profits have risen (as we saw at the beginning of the box).

So, it is probably too early to answer the question of 'Why did L'Oréal acquire the Body Shop?' with the answer from its own advertising slogan, 'Because they're worth it' – but time will tell.

1. *What assumptions has The Body Shop made about the 'rational consumer'?*

2. *How has The Body Shop's economic performance been affected by its attitudes towards ethical issues? (You could do an Internet search to find further evidence about its performance and the effects of its sale to L'Oréal.)*

[10]Anita Roddick interview, Startups.co.uk

SUMMARY

1 Government intervention in the market sets out to attain two goals: social efficiency and equity. Social efficiency is achieved at the point where the marginal benefits to society for either production or consumption are equal to the marginal costs of either production or consumption. Issues of equity are difficult to judge due to the subjective assessment of what is, and what is not, a fair distribution of resources.

2a Monopoly power will (other things being equal) lead to a level of output below the socially efficient level. It will lead to a deadweight welfare loss: a loss of consumer plus producer surplus.

2b Externalities are spillover costs or benefits. Whenever there are external costs, the market will (other things being equal) lead to a level of production and consumption above the socially efficient level. Whenever there are external benefits, the market will (other things being equal) lead to a level of production and consumption below the socially efficient level.

2c Public goods will be underprovided by the market or in the case of pure public goods will not be provided at all. The problem is that they have large external benefits relative to private benefits, and without government intervention it would not be possible to prevent people having a 'free ride' and thereby escaping contributing to their cost of production.

2d Ignorance and uncertainty may prevent people from consuming or producing at the levels they would otherwise choose. Information may sometimes be provided (at a price) by the market, but it may be imperfect; in some cases it may not be available at all.

2e Markets may respond sluggishly to changes in demand and supply. The time lags in adjustment can lead to a permanent state of disequilibrium and to problems of instability.

2f In a free market there may be inadequate provision for dependants and an inadequate output of merit goods.

3a Taxes and subsidies are one means of correcting market distortions. They can be used to affect monopoly price, output and profit. Subsidies can be used to persuade a monopolist to increase output to the competitive level. Lump-sum taxes can be used to reduce monopoly profits without affecting price or output.

3b Externalities can be corrected by imposing tax rates equal to the size of the marginal external cost, and granting rates of subsidy equal to marginal external benefits.

3c Taxes and subsidies have the advantages of 'internalising' externalities and of providing incentives to reduce external costs. On the other hand, they may be impractical to use when different rates are required for each case, or when it is impossible to know the full effects of the activities that the taxes or subsidies are being used to correct.

3d An extension of property rights may allow individuals to prevent others from imposing costs on them. This is not practical, however, when many people are affected to a small degree, or where several people are affected but differ in their attitudes towards what they want doing about the 'problem'.

3e Laws can be used to regulate activities that impose external costs, to regulate monopolies and oligopolies, and to provide consumer protection. Legal controls are often simpler and easier to operate than taxes, and are safer when the danger is potentially great. However, they tend to be rather a blunt weapon.

3f Regulatory bodies can be set up to monitor and control activities that are against the public interest (e.g. anti-competitive behaviour of oligopolists). They can conduct investigations of specific cases, but these may be expensive and time-consuming, and may not be acted on by the authorities.

3g The government may provide information in cases where the private sector fails to provide an adequate level. It may also provide goods and services directly. These could be either public goods or other goods where the government feels that provision by the market is inadequate. The government could also influence production in publicly owned industries.

4a Government intervention in the market may lead to shortages or surpluses; it may be based on poor information; it may be costly in terms of administration; it may stifle incentives; it may be disruptive if government policies change too frequently; it may not represent the majority of voters' interests if the government is elected by a minority, or if voters did not fully understand the issues at election time, or if the policies were not in the government's manifesto; it may remove certain liberties.

4b By contrast, a free market leads to automatic adjustments to changes in economic conditions; the prospect of monopoly/oligopoly profits may stimulate risk taking and hence research and development and innovation, and this advantage may outweigh any problems of resource misallocation; there may still be a high degree of actual or potential competition under monopoly and oligopoly.

5a There are two views of corporate social responsibility (CSR). The first states that it should be of no concern to business, which would do best for society by serving the interests of its shareholders. Social policy should be left to politicians. The alternative view is that business needs to consider the impact of its actions upon society, and to take changing social and political considerations into account when making decisions. This, anyway, is generally good business.

5b The virtue matrix is a means of illustrating the drivers of CSR. Firms will take socially responsible actions if they are required to by law or if social norms dictate. These pressures on firms represent the 'civil foundation'. Some firms will take corporate social responsibility further and thus move into the 'frontier'. Here they may do things that are socially beneficial and may only possibly lead to higher profits, or may even clearly reduce profits. As firms become more socially responsible over time and as social pressures on business increase, so the civil foundation is likely to grow.

5c Evidence suggests that economic performance is likely to be enhanced as the corporate responsibility of firms grows.

MyEconLab

This book can be supported by MyEconLab, which contains a range of additional resources, including an online homework and tutorial system designed to test and build your understanding.

You need both an access card and a course ID to access MyEconLab:

1. Is your lecturer using MyEconLab? Ask your lecturer for your course ID.

2. Has an access card been included with the book at a reduced cost? Check the inside back cover of the book.

3. If you have a course ID but no access card, go to: http://www.myeconlab.com/ to buy access to this interactive study programme.

REVIEW QUESTIONS

1 Assume that a firm discharges waste into a river. As a result, the marginal social costs (*MSC*) are greater than the firm's marginal (private) costs (*MC*). The following table shows how *MC*, *MSC*, *AR* and *MR* vary with output.

Output	1	2	3	4	5	6	7	8
MC(£)	23	21	23	25	27	30	35	42
MSC(£)	35	34	38	42	46	52	60	72
TR(£)	60	102	138	168	195	219	238	252
AR(£)	60	51	46	42	39	36.5	34	31.5
MR(£)	60	42	36	30	27	24	19	14

a) How much will the firm produce if it seeks to maximise profits?

b) What is the socially efficient level of output (assuming no externalities on the demand side)?

c) How much is the marginal external cost at this level of output?

d) What size tax would be necessary for the firm to reduce its output to the socially efficient level?

e) Why is the tax less than the marginal externality?

f) Why might it be equitable to impose a lump-sum tax on this firm?

g) Why will a lump-sum tax not affect the firm's output (assuming that in the long run the firm can still make at least normal profit)?

2 Distinguish between publicly provided goods, public goods and merit goods.

3 Name some goods or services provided by the government or local authorities that are not public goods.

4 Some roads could be regarded as a public good, but some could be provided by the market. Which types of road could be provided by the market? Why? Would it be a good idea?

5 Assume that you wanted the information given in (a)–(h) below. In which cases could you (i) buy perfect information; (ii) buy imperfect information; (iii) be able to obtain information without paying for it; (iv) not be able to obtain information?

a) Which washing machine is the most reliable?

b) Which of two jobs that are vacant is the most satisfying?

c) Which builder will repair my roof most cheaply?

d) Which builder will make the best job of repairing my roof?

e) Which builder is best value for money?

f) How big a mortgage would it be wise for me to take out?

g) What course of higher education should I follow?

h) What brand of washing powder washes whiter?

In which cases are there non-monetary costs to you of finding out the information? How can you know whether the information you acquire is accurate or not?

6 Make a list of pieces of information a firm might want to know and consider whether it could buy the information and how reliable that information might be.

7 Why might it be better to ban certain activities that cause environmental damage rather than to tax them?

8 Consider the advantages and disadvantages of extending property rights so that everyone would have the right to prevent people imposing any costs on them whatsoever (or charging them to do so).

9 How suitable are legal restrictions in the following cases?

a) Ensuring adequate vehicle safety (e.g. that tyres have sufficient tread or that the vehicle is roadworthy).

b) Reducing traffic congestion.

c) Preventing the use of monopoly power.

d) Ensuring that mergers are in the public interest.

e) Ensuring that firms charge a price equal to marginal cost.

10 Evaluate the following statement: 'Despite the weaknesses of a free market, the replacing of the market by the government generally makes the problem worse.'

11 In what ways might business be socially responsible?

12 What economic costs and benefits might a business experience if it decided to adopt a more socially responsible position? How might such costs and benefits change over the longer term?

Government and the firm

Business issues covered in this chapter

- How do governments attempt to prevent both the abuse of monopoly power and collusion by oligopolists through competition policy?
- How effective is competition policy?
- Why does a free market fail to achieve the optimal amount of research and development?
- What can the government do to encourage technological development and innovation?
- Why is training so important for a country's economic performance?
- Why do governments pursue a training policy and not just leave it to employers?
- How do training policies differ between countries?

KI 36
p 354

In this chapter we shall consider the relationship between government and the individual firm. This relationship is not simply one of regulation and control, but can involve the active intervention of government in attempting to improve the economic performance of business. We shall consider government attitudes and policy towards enhancing research and technology development, and training, as well as the more punitive area of business regulation through the use of monopolies and mergers legislation.

21.1 COMPETITION POLICY

Competition, monopoly and the public interest

KI 21
p 175

Most markets in the real world are imperfect, with firms having varying degrees of market power. But will this power be against the public interest? This question has been addressed by successive governments in framing legislation to deal with monopolies and oligopolies.

It might be thought that market power is always 'a bad thing', certainly as far as the consumer is concerned. After all, it enables firms to make supernormal profit, thereby 'exploiting' the consumer. The greater the firm's power, the higher prices will be relative to the costs of production. Also, a lack of competition removes the incentive to become more efficient.

But market power is not necessarily a bad thing. Firms may not fully exploit their position of power – perhaps for fear that very high profits would eventually lead to other firms overcoming entry barriers, or perhaps because they are not aggressive profit maximisers. Even if they do make large supernormal profits, they may still charge a lower price than more competitive sectors of the industry because of their economies of scale. Finally, they may use their profits for research and development and for capital investment. The consumer might then benefit from improved products at lower prices.

Competition policy could seek to ban various structures. For example, it could ban mergers leading to market share of more than a certain amount. Most countries, however, prefer to focus on whether the *practices* of particular monopolists or oligopolists are anti-competitive. Some of these practices may be made illegal, such as price fixing by oligopolists; others may be assessed on a case-by-case approach to determine whether or not they should be permitted. Such an approach does not presume that the mere possession of power is against the public interest, but rather that certain uses of that power may be.

There are three possible targets of competition policy:

- *monopoly policy* – the abuse of the existing power of monopolies and oligopolies;
- *merger policy* – the growth of power through mergers and acquisitions;
- *restrictive practices policy* – oligopolistic collusion.

Competition policy in the European Union

Relevant EU legislation is contained in Articles 101 and 102 of the 2009 Treaty of the Functioning of the European Union. Additional regulations covering mergers came into force in 1990 and were amended in 2004. Further minor amendments have been put in place since then, which have focused on specific market regulation.

Article 101 is concerned with restrictive practices and Article 102 with the abuse of market power. The Articles predominately apply to firms trading between EU members and so do not cover monopolies or oligopolies operating solely within a member country. The policy is implemented by the European Commission. If any firm appears to be breaking the provisions of either of the Articles, the Commission can refer it to the European Court of Justice.

EU restrictive practices policy

Article 101 covers *agreements* between firms, *joint decisions* and concerted *practices* which prevent, restrict or distort competition. In other words it covers all types of oligopolistic collusion that are judged to be against the interests of consumers.

Article 101 is designed to prevent collusive *behaviour rather than* oligopolistic *structures* (i.e. the simple existence of co-operation between firms).

Practices considered anti-competitive include firms colluding to do any of the following:

- fix prices (i.e. above competitive levels);
- limit production, markets, technical development or investment;
- share out markets or sources of supply;

- charge discriminatory prices or operate discriminatory trading conditions, such as to benefit the colluding parties and disadvantage others;
- make other firms who sign contracts with any of the colluding firms accept unfavourable obligations which, by their nature, have no connection with the subject of such contracts.

If companies are found guilty of undertaking any of these anti-competitive practices that are in contravention of Article 101, they are subject to financial penalties. Box 21.1 lists some of the cases that were settled in 2014.

The size of any fine imposed on an organisation depends on a number of factors. Initially the authorities calculate the firm's annual sales of the product or products that were affected by the activities that restricted competition. These are referred to as the 'relevant sales'. For example, in the paper envelope case referred to in Box 21.1 the Commission estimated that the company 'Bong' had made sales worth €140 million from the cartel activities it had undertaken with four other companies.

The initial size of the basic fine is then calculated by taking a percentage of the value of these annual relevant sales. The percentage figure can be up to a maximum of 30 per cent but is usually in the range of 15 to 20 per cent in most cases. The final figure chosen by the authorities depends on how severe they consider the case to be. The level of severity depends on factors such as the market shares of the companies involved and the size of the geographical area affected by the practices.

Once this initial figure has been calculated it is then adjusted to take into account the duration of the activities that have been judged to be in contravention of Article 101. For example, a cartel that existed for five years is judged to be five times more damaging than one that only lasted a year. In this case, the initial figure would be increased by a 'multiplier' of five.

An additional amount is then added to the size of the fine and is known as an 'entry fee'. This is once again calculated as a percentage of the value of the firm's relevant sales. However, this figure is not multiplied by the duration of the cartel agreement.

Once this additional amount has been added, more adjustments can be made for either aggravating or mitigating factors. For example, the fine on a company could be increased if it was a repeat offender or was seen as the ring leader. Alternatively, the fine could be reduced if the firm was judged to have been far less actively involved in the cartel's activities.

The final size of the basic fine imposed on a firm is capped and cannot be greater than 10 per cent of that firm's annual total turnover. If the products/geographical area affected by the restrictive practices are only a small fraction of a firm's total sales, then this limit is unlikely to be reached. It is only in cases where the cartel activities make up a large fraction of the firm's turnover that the cap would have an effect. This was the case in the paper envelope investigation discussed in Box 21.1.

Once a figure has finally been reached for the size of the basic fine, firms can take actions that reduce the amount they have to pay. For example, if members of a cartel come forward with information that helps the Commission with its investigations, then they can receive a percentage reduction. This is referred to as a 'Leniency Notice'.

In order to qualify for a Leniency Notice, firms would have to provide detailed information about cartel meetings and exactly how the anti-competitive practices operated. The first company to supply this type of information can receive a reduction of up to 100 per cent: i.e. they obtain full immunity and do not have to pay anything. The second company to come forward with this type of information can receive a reduction of up to 50 per cent, the third up to 30 per cent and any firm after this can receive reductions of up to 20 per cent.

Another discount is applied if firms accept the Commission's decision and the size of any financial penalties imposed on them. This is referred to as a Settlement. If a firm enters into a 'Settlement Discussion' it can obtain a 10 per cent reduction in the size of the fine. The advantage of a Settlement is that it speeds up the final decision process and hence reduces the administrative costs to the parties involved. It also removes the potential legal costs to both parties if a firm appeals against the decision and takes its case to court.

The aim of all these reductions is to encourage the co-operation of firms. There is a prisoner's dilemma game here. Although the optimum position for firms collectively might be for them all to refuse to co-operate and make it difficult for the Commission to uncover cartel activity, firms have an incentive to be the first to own up and thereby escape or minimise the fines. The Nash equilibrium, therefore, is one where cartel activity is reduced.

EU monopoly policy

Article 102 relates to the abuse of market power and has also been extended to cover mergers. As with Article 101, it is the *behaviour* of firms that is the target of the legislation. The following are cited as examples of abuses of market power. As you can see, they are very similar to those in Article 101.

- Charging unfairly high prices to consumers, or paying unfairly low prices to suppliers.
- Limiting production, markets or technical developments to the detriment of consumers.
- Using price discrimination or other discriminatory practices to the detriment of certain parties.
- Making other firms that sign contracts with it accept unfavourable obligations which, by their nature, have no connection with the subject of such contracts.

Under Article 102, such practices can be banned and firms can be fined where they are found to have abused a dominant position (see Box 11.3 for an example in relation to Microsoft). A firm does not need to have some specified minimum market share before Article 102 can be invoked. Instead, if firms are able to conduct anti-competitive practices, it is simply assumed that they must be in a position of market power. This approach seems sensible, given the difficulties of identifying the boundaries of a market, in terms of either geography or type of product.

EU merger policy

Under current regulations (2004), mergers that would significantly reduce competition in the EU are prohibited. For example, a merger could be blocked if there were concerns that the new firm would have significant market power that might lead to higher prices for consumers.

Therefore the EU investigates 'large' mergers that have an 'EU dimension'. A merger is judged as having an 'EU dimension' when no more than two-thirds of each firm's EU-wide business is conducted in a single member state. If a firm does conduct more than two-thirds of its business in one country then investigation of the merger would be the responsibility of that member state's competition authority.

A merger is deemed as 'large' if it exceeds either one of two turnover thresholds. These thresholds include combinations of both worldwide and EU sales. They also relate to both the sales of individual firms and the combined sales of the firms involved in the merger.

The first threshold is exceeded if (a) the firms involved have combined worldwide sales greater than €5 billion; and (b) at least two of the firms individually have sales of more than €250 million within the EU. The second threshold is exceeded if (a) the firms involved have combined worldwide sales of more than €2.5 billion; (b) in each of at least three member states, combined sales of all firms involved are greater than €100 million; (c) in each of those three member states, at least two of the firms each have domestic sales greater than €25 million; and (d) EU-wide sales of each of at least two firms is greater than €100 million.

If either of these thresholds is exceeded and the merger is judged to have an EU dimension, then formal notification of the merger has to be made by the firms to the European Commission. There were 337 notifications in 2015 and the figure has been around 300 per year since 2000.

Once a notification is made the Commission must carry out a preliminary investigation (Phase 1), which is normally completed within 25 working days. At the end of Phase 1 the majority of cases (over 90 per cent) are usually settled and the merger is either allowed to proceed unconditionally or with some minor stipulations attached.

In a small number of cases, competition concerns are raised at the end of Phase 1 and a decision is made to conduct a formal investigation into the potential impact of the merger (Phase 2). In 2015, eleven of the 337 notifications made to the European Commission were referred to this part of the process. The more in-depth Phase 2 investigations must normally be completed within 90 working days or 110 in more complex cases. The whole process is overseen by a Chief Competition Economist and a panel that scrutinises the investigating team's conclusions.

At the end of Phase 2 there are three possibilities: (a) the merger is allowed to proceed with no conditions attached; (b) the merger is allowed to proceed subject to certain conditions being met; (c) the merger is prohibited.

The process of EU merger control is thus very rapid and administratively inexpensive. The regulations are also potentially quite tough. Mergers are disallowed if they result in 'a concentration which would significantly impede effective competition, in particular by the creation or strengthening of a dominant position'. But the regulations are also flexible, since they recognise that mergers *may* be in the interests of consumers if they result in cost reductions. In such cases, they are permitted.

This flexibility has led to criticism that the Commission has been too easily persuaded by firms, allowing mergers to go ahead with few, if any, restrictions. Indeed, since the current merger control measures were put in place in 1990, over 6063 mergers have been notified, but only around 240 have been referred to Phase 2 of the process and, of these, only 24 had been prohibited (as of December 2015). No mergers were prevented from taking place in either 2014 or 2015, while just two cases were prohibited in 2013. These were Ryanair's proposed takeover of Aer Lingus and UPS's proposed takeover of TNT Express.

This issue highlights a problem for EU policy makers: there is a trade-off between encouraging competition within the EU and supporting European companies to become world leaders. The ability to compete in *world* markets normally requires that companies are large, which may well lead to them having monopoly power within the EU.

> ### Pause for thought
>
> *To what extent is Article 102 consistent with both these points of view?*

UK competition policy

There have been substantial changes to UK competition policy since the first legislation was introduced in 1948. The current approach is based on the 1998 Competition Act and the 2002 Enterprise Act, together with Part 3 of the 2013 Enterprise and Regulatory Reform Act.

The Competition Act brought UK policy in line with EU policy, detailed above. The Act has two key sets (or 'chapters') of prohibitions. Chapter I prohibits various restrictive practices, and mirrors EU Article 101. Chapter II prohibits various abuses of monopoly power, and mirrors EU Article 102.

The Enterprise Act strengthened the Competition Act and introduced new measures for the control of mergers.

Under the 1998 and 2002 Acts, the body charged with ensuring that the prohibitions were carried out was the Office of Fair Trading (OFT). The OFT could investigate any firms suspected of engaging in one or more of the prohibited practices. Its officers had the power to enter and search premises and could require the production and explanation of documents. When the OFT decided that an infringement of one of the prohibitions had occurred, it would be able to direct the offending firms to modify their behaviour or cease their practices altogether.

The Competition Act also set up a Competition Commission (CC) to which the OFT could refer cases for further investigation. The CC was charged with determining whether the structure of an industry or the practices of firms within it were detrimental to competition.

The Enterprise Act made the OFT and CC independent of government. It also set up a Markets and Policy Initiatives Division (MPI) of the OFT. This carried out investigations into particular markets suspected of not working in the best interests of consumers. The MPI's investigations could lead to the OFT enforcing its findings if anti-competitive practices were taking place (see below). Alternatively, the MPI could refer the case to the CC or make proposals to the government for changes in the law.

If a case was referred to the Competition Commission, it would carry out an investigation to establish whether competition had been adversely affected. If it found that it was, it would decide on the appropriate remedies, such as prohibiting various practices.

Firms affected by an OFT or CC ruling had the right of appeal to the Competition Appeal Tribunal (CAT), which could uphold or quash the original decision. The CAT is entirely independent of the CC and OFT.

The Competition and Markets Authority. Following the outcome of a consultation on the links between competition and economic growth, the government introduced the 2013 Enterprise and Regulatory Reform Act. While retaining the principles and broad procedures of the 1998 and 2002 Acts, the 2013 Act resulted in the setting up of a new unified body – the Competition and Markets Authority (CMA). Since April 2014, the CMA has undertaken much of the work that was previously carried out by the OFT and CC. This has involved taking over any investigations that had been instigated by the OFT or were being carried out by the CC.

It is hoped that the new combined organisation will be able to deploy its resources more effectively. In particular, a key rationale for the change is the belief that it will reduce the duplication of processes that occurred when there were two separate competition bodies. Less duplication should lead to lower administration costs.

Another key aim of the change was to reduce the length of time it takes to carry out investigations and reach final decisions. A number of new statutory limits have been placed on the length of time the CMA has to complete its studies.

Some specific amendments have also been made to both restrictive practices and merger policy. These will be discussed in the following sections.

UK restrictive practices policy

The 1998 Competition Act brought UK restrictive practices policy more into line with EU policy. For example, the way fines were calculated and implemented for anti-competitive behaviour was changed so that it was more comparable to the method used by the European Commission: i.e. the penalties imposed could be up to 10 per cent of the firm's annual turnover.

The 2002 Enterprise Act made it a *criminal* offence to engage in cartel agreements (i.e. horizontal, rather than vertical, collusive agreements between firms), irrespective of whether there are appreciable effects on competition. Convicted offenders can receive a prison sentence of up to five years and/or an unlimited fine. Prosecutions can be brought by the Serious Fraud Office or the CMA. The CMA also has substantial powers to enter premises, seize documents and require people to answer questions or provide information.

It was anticipated at the time of the 2002 Act that it would result in between six and ten prosecutions/year. In reality, the authorities found it more difficult to implement and only two cases were prosecuted between 2002 and 2013, and only one of those successfully: three UK executives were jailed in 2008 for their part in operating a cartel in the marine hose industry. In order to address this issue the 2013 Act included a number of legal amendments to try to make it easier for the CMA to bring successful prosecutions against executives involved in cartel behaviour.

The types of practices that constitute 'cartel agreements' were also made more consistent with EU policy: e.g. price fixing, limiting supply, sharing out markets, limiting supply or bid-rigging. Each of these is discussed in more detail below:

- Horizontal price-fixing agreements. These are agreements between competitors to set one or more of the following: fixed prices, minimum prices, the amount or percentage by which prices may be increased, or a range outside which prices may not move. The object is to restrict price competition and thus to keep prices higher than they would otherwise be.
- Agreements to share out markets. These may be by geographical area, type or size of customer, or nature of outlet. By limiting or even eliminating competition within each part of the market, such agreements can be an effective means of keeping prices high (or quality low).
- Agreements to limit production. This may involve output quotas or a looser agreement not to increase output wherever this would drive down prices.
- Agreements to limit or co-ordinate investment. By restraining capacity, this will help firms to keep output down and prices up.
- *Collusive tendering*. This is where two or more firms put in a tender for a contract at secretly agreed (high) prices. A well-known case throughout most of the 1980s and 1990s was that of firms supplying ready-mixed concrete agreeing on prices they would tender to local authorities (see Case study H.5 in MyEconLab).

- Agreements between purchasers. These could be to reduce prices paid to suppliers. For example, large supermarkets could collude to keep prices to farmers low. An alternative form of agreement would be to deal with certain suppliers only.
- Agreements to boycott suppliers or distributors that deal with competitors to the colluding firms.

Pause for thought

Are all such agreements necessarily against the interests of consumers?

In the case of other types of agreement, the CMA has the discretion to decide, on a case-by-case basis, whether or not competition is appreciably restricted, and whether, therefore, they should be terminated or the firms should be exempted. Such cases include the following:

- Vertical price-fixing agreements. These are price agreements between purchasing firms and their suppliers. An example of this is ***resale price maintenance***. This is where a manufacturer or distributor sets the price for retailers to charge. It may well distribute a price list to retailers (e.g. a car manufacturer may distribute a price list to car showrooms). Resale price maintenance is a way of preventing competition between retailers driving down retail prices and ultimately the price they pay to the manufacturer. Both manufacturers and retailers, therefore, are likely to gain from resale price maintenance.
- Agreements to exchange information that could have the effect of reducing competition. For example, if producers exchange information on their price intentions, it is a way of allowing price leadership, a form of tacit collusion, to continue.

UK monopoly policy

Under the Chapter II prohibition of the 1998 Competition Act, it is illegal for a dominant firm to exercise its market power in such a way as to reduce competition. Any suspected case is investigated by the CMA, which uses a two-stage process in deciding whether an abuse has taken place.

The first stage is to establish whether a firm has a position of dominance. The firm does not literally have to be a monopoly. Rather, 'dominance' normally involves the firm

---

Definitions

Collusive tendering Where two or more firms secretly agree on the prices they will tender for a contract. These prices will be above those which would be put in under a genuinely competitive tendering process.

Resale price maintenance Where the manufacturer of a product (legally) insists that the product should be sold at a specified retail price.

having at least a 40 per cent share of the market (national or local, whichever is appropriate), although this figure will vary from industry to industry. Also dominance depends on the barriers to entry to new competitors. The higher the barriers to the entry of new firms, the less contestable will be the market (see section 11.4), and the more dominant a firm is likely to be for any given current market share.

If the firm *is* deemed to be dominant, the second stage involves the CMA having to decide whether the firm's practices constitute an abuse of its position. As with restrictive practices, Chapter II follows EU legislation. It specifies the same four types of market abuse as does Article 102 (see above). Within these four categories, the CMA identifies the following practices as being overtly anti-competitive:

- *Charging excessively high prices*. These are prices above those the firm would charge if it faced effective competition. One sign of excessively high prices is abnormally high rates of profit.

- *Price discrimination*. This is regarded as an abuse only to the extent that the higher prices are excessive or the lower prices are used to exclude competitors.

- *Predatory pricing*. This is where prices are set at loss-making levels, so as to drive competitors out of business (see page 287). The test is to look at the dominant firm's price in relation to its average costs. If its price is below average variable cost, predation would be assumed. If its price is above average variable cost, but below average total cost, then the Director General would need to establish whether the reason was to eliminate a competitor.

  In November 2008 the OFT decided that Cardiff Bus engaged in predatory conduct intended to eliminate a competitor, 2 Travel, during the period April 2004 to February 2005. Before 2 Travel's entry into the market, Cardiff Bus had a substantial market share, carrying 80 000 passengers per day. However, 'Cardiff Bus responded to the introduction of a new no-frills bus service by another bus company, 2 Travel, by introducing its own no-frills bus services which ran on the same routes, at similar times as 2 Travel's services and made a loss for Cardiff Bus. Shortly after 2 Travel's exit from the market Cardiff Bus withdrew its own no-frills services'.[1]

- ***Vertical restraints***. This is where a supplying firm imposes conditions on a purchasing firm (or vice versa). For example, a manufacturer may impose rules on retailers about displaying the product or the provision of after-sales service, or it may refuse to supply certain outlets (e.g. perfume manufacturers refusing to supply discount chains, such as Superdrug). Another example is *tie-in sales*. This is where a firm controlling the supply of a first product insists that its customers buy a second product from it rather than from its rivals.

The simple *existence* of any of these practices may not constitute an abuse. The CMA has to decide whether their *effect* is to restrict competition. This may require a detailed investigation to establish whether competition is restricted or distorted. If this is found to be the case, the CMA decides what actions must be taken to remedy the situation.

UK merger policy

The framework for merger policy is set out in the 2002 Enterprise Act. This Act made two significant changes.

First, much of the decision-making power was removed from government ministers. Prior to this Act the competition authorities made recommendations but these could be overruled by a minister. The final judgement is now left to the authorities apart from a few exceptional circumstances when a minister can still intervene. These are cases where the proposed merger would have an impact on national security, media plurality or the stability of the financial system. For example, the government intervened in 2008 and allowed the proposed merger between Lloyds TSB and the troubled bank HBOS to go ahead, overruling any objections raised by the competition authorities.

Second, the criterion used to assess mergers was changed. Previously they were judged using a broad public interest test. The authorities had to take into account 'all matters which appear to them in the particular circumstances to be relevant'. This was changed in the 2002 Act so that the assessment was made solely on competition issues. More specifically, a merger could be prevented if it was likely to result in a substantial lessening of competition (SLC).

A merger or takeover is investigated by the CMA if the target company has a UK turnover that exceeds £70 million, or if the merger results in the new company having a market share of 25 per cent or more.

One unusual aspect of UK policy is that there are no obligations on the participating firms to pre-notify the authorities about a merger that meets either of these two conditions. A voluntary notice can be made or the CMA can initiate an investigation following information received from third parties. Between 2010 and 2014 around 30–40 per cent of merger investigations were instigated by the authorities as no notification had been made by the firms involved.

A merger can also be completed before it has been officially cleared by the CMA. If the CMA then decides to prevent the merger, the firms face the costs of having

---

[1] 'Cardiff Bus engaged in predatory conduct against competitor, OFT decides', *OFT press release, 133/08*, 18 November 2008. In this instance, the OFT decided not to fine Cardiff Bus because its turnover did not exceed £50 million at the time of the infringement of Chapter II of the Competition Act 1998.

---

to split the business back into two separate entities. The 2013 Act increased the CMA's power to force companies to reverse integration activities undertaken prior to an investigation.

In other respects UK policy is similar to EU policy. The CMA conducts a preliminary or Phase 1 investigation to see whether competition is likely to be threatened. The 2013 Act introduced a statutory deadline of 40 working days to complete Phase 1 of the process. Prior to this, deadlines had been non-binding and were often not met. The Act also gave the CMA greater information-gathering powers in Phase 1 investigations.

At the end of the 40-day period the CMA has to decide whether there is a significant chance that the merger would result in a substantial lessening of competition (SLC). If the

CMA concludes that this might be the case, it begins Phase 2 of the process – a much more in-depth assessment. If no SLC issues are raised, the merger is allowed to go ahead.

In 2014/15 only six out of the 82 Phase 1 cases were referred for a Phase 2 investigation; 63 cases were cleared unconditionally, while 10 cases were judged not to qualify. One example in February 2015 was the acquisition of 143 stores by Vodafone from Phones4U. This was cleared by the CMA after a Phase 1 investigation.

There is a 24-week statutory time limit for Phase 2 decisions to be made. This can be extended in special circumstances by up to eight weeks. The membership of the team that carries out Phase 2 of the process differs from that which carried out Phase 1 of the investigation. The reasoning behind this is that it is thought to be useful to get a

---

BOX 21.1 FROM PAPER ENVELOPES TO CANNED MUSHROOMS: THE UMPIRE STRIKES BACK

EU procedures for dealing with cartels

EU competition policy applies to companies operating in two or more EU countries. The policy is implemented by the European Commission, which has the power to levy substantial fines on companies found to be in breach of the legislation. In 2008, in order to simplify administrative processes and to reduce the number of cases going to the courts, new settlement procedures were introduced. If, on seeing the evidence against them, firms co-operate, then fines can be reduced by 10 per cent. Meanwhile, firms that have participated in a cartel but that reveal details of its existence can be granted either immunity or further reductions in fines through a Leniency Notice (see pages 369–70).

The following table summarises six cases that were settled in 2014.

Date	Industry/sector	Number of firms involved	Commission fine (€m)
December 2014	Paper envelopes	5	19.485
October 2014	Interest rate derivatives	4	32.355
September 2014	Smart card chips	4	138.048
June 2014	Canned mushrooms	3	32.225
April 2014	Steel abrasives	4	30.707
April 2014	High voltage power cables	11	301.639

Fixing prices at a mini-golf meeting

In September 2010, the European Commission began an investigation into the market for both standardised and customised paper envelopes in the EU. In December 2014, the Commission found Bong (of Sweden), GPV and Hamelin (of France), Mayer-Kuvert (of Germany) and Tompla (of Spain) guilty of participating in activities that restricted competition in this market. The meetings at which the details of the cartel arrangements were discussed were referred to by the participating firms as 'golf' or 'mini-golf' meetings!

The cartel arrangements directly affected the market for envelopes in Denmark, France, Germany, Norway, Sweden and the UK. The firms were judged to have been involved in the following restrictive practices that were in violation of Article 101:

- allocating customers amongst members of the cartel: i.e. agreeing not to target customers that 'belonged' to other firms;
- agreeing on price increases;
- co-ordinating responses to tenders initiated by major European customers;
- exchanging commercially sensitive information on customers and sales volumes.

Public versions of the documents that outline the decisions made by the European Commission often do not disclose information that is considered to be commercially sensitive. This means that in many reports details about the value of sales directly affected by the anti-competitive practices are omitted. However, in the envelope case this information was published and is illustrated in the first row of the next table.

The proportion of the value of sales used to calculate the size of the fine was set at 15 per cent in this case (see table row 2). Four out of the five firms began taking part in the cartel on 8 October 2003 and their involvement in anti-competitive activities lasted until 22 April 2008. Therefore for these firms the duration multiplier (row 3) was set at 4.5. Hamelin was judged to have entered the cartel a month later than the other participants so the multiplier in their case was set at 4.416. A percentage rate of 15 per cent was also used to calculate the entry fee (row 5). The final figures for the basic amounts of the fine are illustrated in the last row of the table, which the Commission rounded down to the nearest €1000.

It was considered to be an exceptional case as the sales of envelopes affected by the cartel activities made up a large fraction of each firm's total turnover. Therefore the basic fines would exceed the 10 per cent cap on turnover set by the authorities. The fines were reduced in a way that took account of (a) the value of affected sales for each firm as a

'fresh pair of eyes' to look at a case. At the end of Phase 2 the CMA has to make one of the following decisions:

Unconditional clearance of the merger. In 2014/15 this happened in 2 out of the 4 cases. For example, in September 2015 the acquisition of 99p Stores Ltd by Poundland plc was cleared after a Phase 2 investigation.

Conditional clearance subject to the firms taking certain actions that are legally binding. These are referred to as 'remedies'. Four out of the 12 cases in 2013/14 involved remedies.

An example of a remedy is a firm having to sell off parts of the company it has acquired to maintain an acceptable level of competition. For example, the acquisition of City Screen by Cineworld raised certain issues for the competition authorities. In particular it was judged that it would cause a substantial lessening of competition in three areas – Aberdeen, Bury St Edmunds and Cambridge. This could lead to limited choice and higher prices for cinema-goers. The acquisition was only allowed to proceed on the condition that Cineworld sold one of the cinemas it owned in each of these three areas to a company approved by the authorities. The acquisition was finally cleared by the CMA in February 2015, when Cineworld sold one of its cinemas in Cambridge to an independent operator. The sale of Cineworld-owned cinemas in Aberdeen and Bury St Edmunds had already been approved in 2014.

Prohibition of the merger. In the 11 years between 2004/05 and 2014/15 only nine mergers were prohibited out of the 114 Phase 2 investigations that took place.

	Bong	GPV group	Hamelin	Mayer-Kuvert	Tompla
1. Value of relevant sales (€)	140 000 000	125 086 629	185 521 000	70 023 181	143 316 000
2. Percentage (15%) of the value of relevant sales (€)	21 000 000	18 762 994	27 828 150	10 503 477	21 497 400
3. Duration multiplier	4.5	4.5	4.416	4.5	4.5
4. Duration multiplier × 15% of sales (€)	94 500 000	84 433 473	122 889 110	47 265 646	96 738 300
5. Entry fee (€)(= row 2))	21 000 000	18 762 994	27 828 150	10 503 477	21 497 400
6. Basic fine (€)(= rows 4 + 5 rounded down to nearest €1000)	115 500 000	103 196 000	150 717 000	57 769 000	118 235 000

proportion of their turnover and (b) the level of involvement in the restrictive practices. Unfortunately the size of each firm's basic fine, after these adjustments, are not published in the non-confidential report.

Under the Commission's 2006 Leniency Notice we do know that Tompla received a 50 per cent reduction in the size of its adjusted basic fine, Hamelin received a reduction of 25 per cent and Mayer-Kuvert received a reduction of 10 per cent. All five firms obtained an additional 10 per cent reduction for agreeing to the Settlements and not taking their cases to court. Two firms also claimed that they were unable to pay the fine without getting into serious final difficulties and were granted a further reduction.

The final sizes of the fines paid by the companies are illustrated in the table below.

Firm	Fine (€)
Bong	3 118 000
GPV	1 651 000
Hamelin	4 996 000
Mayer-Kuvert	4 991 000
Tompla	4 729 000

Commissioner Margrethe Vestager in charge of competition policy said: 'Everybody uses envelopes. When cartelists raise the prices of everyday household objects they do so at the expense of millions of Europeans. The Commission's fight against cartels penalises such behaviour and also acts as a deterrent, protecting consumers from harm. On this case we have closed the envelope, sealed it and returned it to the sender with a clear message: don't cheat your customers, don't cartelise.'[2]

 Why might global cartels be harder to identify and eradicate than cartels solely located within the domestic economy? What problems does this raise for competition policy?

[2]'Antitrust: Commission fines five envelope producers over €19.4 million in cartel settlement', *Press Release*, European Commission (11 December 2014).

Assessment of EU and UK competition policy

With UK competition legislation having been brought in line with EU legislation, it is possible to consider the two together.

It is generally agreed by commentators that the policy is correct to concentrate on anti-competitive *practices* and their *effects* rather than simply on the existence of agreements or on the size of a firm's market share. After all, economic power is only a problem when it is abused. When, by contrast, it enables firms to achieve economies of scale, or more finance for investment, the result can be to the benefit of consumers. In other words, the assumption that structure determines conduct and performance (see pages 14–15 and 176–7) is not necessarily true, and certainly it is not necessarily true that market power is always bad or competitive industries are always good.

Secondly, most commentators favour the system of certain practices being *prohibited*, with fines applicable to the first offence. This acts as an important deterrent to anti-competitive behaviour.

Similar conclusions have been reached in the USA, where the application of competition law has undergone changes in recent years. In the past, the focus was on the structure of an industry. Under the Sherman Act of 1890, oligopolistic collusion in the 'restraint of trade' was made illegal, as was any attempt to establish a monopoly. Although, under the Clayton Act of 1914, various potentially anti-competitive practices (such as price discrimination) were only illegal when they substantially lessened competition, the application of these two 'anti-trust' laws was largely directed to breaking up large firms. Today, the approach is to focus on efficiency, rather than on market share; and on the effects on consumers of any collusion or co-operation between firms, rather than on the simple collusion itself.

A problem with any policy to deal with collusion is the difficulty in rooting it out. When firms do all their deals 'behind closed doors' and are careful not to keep records or give clues, then collusion can be very hard to spot. The cases that have come to light, such as that of collusive tendering between firms supplying ready-mixed concrete, may be just the tip of an iceberg.

Merger policy remains the most controversial part of competition policy, with criticisms that far too many are allowed to go ahead. Specific areas of contention with UK policy are whether: (a) firms should be forced to notify the authorities of proposed mergers and be prevented from undertaking any integration activities until the merger is cleared; (b) there should be a return to a broad public interest test rather than judging mergers purely by their impact on competition.

21.2 POLICIES TOWARDS RESEARCH AND DEVELOPMENT (R&D)

The impact of technology, not only on the practice of business but also on the economy in general, is vividly illustrated by the development and use of the Internet. In 1997, worldwide some 40 million people and 25 000 firms used the Internet. By 2014, there were over 3 billion users (around 40 per cent of the world's population).

The commercial possibilities of the Internet range from the selling of information and services to global forms of catalogue shopping. The Internet is just one example of how technology and technological change are shaping the whole structure and organisation of business (see Chapter 3) on the flat organisation), the experience of work for the worker, and the productivity of business and hence the competitive performance of national economies.

If a business fails to embrace new technology, its productivity and profitability will almost certainly lag behind those businesses that do.

It is the same for countries. Unless they embrace new technology, the productivity gap between them and those that do is likely to widen. Once such a gap has been opened, it will prove very difficult to close. Those countries ahead in the technological race will tend to get further ahead as the dynamic forces of technology enhance their competitiveness, improve their profits and provide yet greater potential for technological advance. In other words, the rate of technological advance can have dramatic effects on a country's living standards. This helps to explain why understanding the nature and drivers of technological advance is an important part of the literature on long-term economic growth. So how can countries compete more effectively in the technological race? *Technology policy* refers to a series of government initiatives to affect the process of technological change and its rate of adoption. The nature of the policy will depend on which stage of the introduction of new technology it is designed to affect. Three stages can be identified:

- *Invention*. In this initial stage, research leads to new ideas and new products. Sometimes the ideas arise from general research; sometimes the research is directed towards a particular goal, such as the development of a new type of car engine or computer chip.
- *Innovation*. In this stage, the new ideas are put into practice. A firm will introduce the new technology, and will hopefully gain a commercial advantage from so doing.

Definition

Technology policy Involves government initiatives to affect the process and rate of technological change.

■ *Diffusion*. In the final stage, the new products and processes are copied, and possibly adapted, by competitor firms. The effects of the new technology thus spread throughout the economy, affecting general productivity levels and competitiveness.

Technology policy can be focused on any or all of these stages of technological change.

Technological change and market failure

Why is a technology policy needed in the first place? The main reason is that the market system might fail to provide those factors vital to initiate technological change, and there are a number of reasons for this, including the following.

R&D free riders. If an individual business can benefit from the results of *other* businesses conducting R&D, with all its associated costs and risks, then it is less likely to conduct R&D itself. It will simply 'free ride' on such activity. R&D spending might be an example of a positive externality in production. As a consequence, it would be in the interest of the firm conducting R&D to keep its findings secret or under some kind of property right, such as a patent, so as to gain as much competitive advantage as possible from its investment.

Although it is desirable to encourage firms to conduct R&D, and for this purpose it may be necessary to have a strict patent system in force, it is also desirable that there is the maximum *social* benefit from such R&D. This would occur only if such findings were widely disseminated. It is thus important that technology policy finds the optimum balance between the two objectives of (a) encouraging individual firms to conduct research and (b) disseminating the results.

Monopolistic and oligopolistic market structures. The more a market is dominated by a few large producers, the less incentive they will have to conduct R&D and innovate as a means of reducing costs or developing innovative new products or experiences for consumers. The problem is most acute under monopoly. Nevertheless, despite a lower incentive to innovate, the higher profits of firms with monopoly power will at least provide a source of finance that might enable them to conduct more research. The problems of having to borrow money to finance R&D are discussed below.

Duplication. Not only is it likely that there is too little R&D being conducted, there is also the danger that resources may be wasted in duplicating research. The more firms there are conducting R&D, the greater the likelihood of some form of duplication. Given the scarcity of R&D resources, any duplication would be a highly inefficient way to organise production.

Risk and uncertainty. Because the payoffs from R&D activity are so uncertain, there will tend to be a natural caution on the part of both the business conducting R&D and (if different) the financier. Only R&D activity which has a clear market potential, or is of low risk, is likely to be considered. It has been found that financial markets in particular will tend to adopt a risk-averting strategy and fail to provide an adequate pool of long-term funds. (This is another manifestation of the 'short-termism' we considered in section 19.4.)

Forms of intervention

Attempts to correct the above market failures and develop a technology policy might include the use of the following.

The patent system. The strengthening of legal rights over the development of new products will encourage businesses to conduct R&D, as they will be able to reap greater rewards from successful R&D investment.

> ### Pause for thought
>
> *Before you read on, can you identify the main forms of intervention the government might use in order to encourage and support R&D?*

Public provision. In an attempt to overcome the free-rider problem and the inefficiency of R&D duplication, government might provide R&D itself, either through its own research institutions or via funding to universities and other research organisations. This is of particular importance in the case of basic research, where the potential outcomes are far less certain than those of applied research.

R&D subsidies. If the government provided subsidies to businesses conducting R&D activity, it would not only reduce the cost and hence the risk for business, but could also ensure that the outcome from the R&D activity is more rapidly diffused throughout the economy than might otherwise be expected. This would help improve general levels of technological innovation.

Co-operative R&D. Given that the benefits of technological developments are of widespread use, the government could encourage co-operative R&D. The government could take various roles here, from being actively involved in the R&D process to acting as a facilitator, bringing private-sector businesses together. The key advantages of this policy are that it will not only reduce the potential for duplication, but also encourage the pooling of scarce R&D resources.

Diffusion policies. Such policies tend to be of two types: the provision of information concerning new technology, and the use of subsidies to encourage businesses to adopt new technology.

Other policies. A wide range of other policies, primarily adopted for other purposes, might also influence R&D. These might include: education and training policy; competition policy; national defence policies and initiatives; and policies on standards and compatibility.

Technology policy in the UK and EU

The UK's poor technological performance since 1945 can be attributed to many factors, from a lack of entrepreneurial vision on the part of business to the excessive short-termism of the UK's financial institutions. There also appears to have been a failure on the part of government to initiate suitable strategies to overcome such problems.

In the UK, the attitude towards technology policy has tended to be market-driven, with the role of government relatively limited. More interventionist strategies have typically been kept to a minimum, focusing largely on military and defence technologies. Recent UK governments have looked to provide financial support for R&D by enabling companies to reduce their profits liable to corporation tax by a proportion of their R&D expenditure (see section 31.2).

Despite a sizeable number of UK-based companies regularly making a list of the world's largest R&D-spending companies, the UK's R&D performance compares less favourably when measured relative to GDP. In part, this reflects the limited R&D expenditure by government. But, it also reflects the low R&D intensity across the private sector. In other words, total R&D expenditure by British firms is low *relative* to the income generated by sales (see Box 21.2). Since 1995, UK gross expenditure on research and

---

BOX 21.2   THE R&D SCOREBOARD

For many years, it has been suggested that the UK's poor international competitive record has been in no small part due to its failure to invest in research and development. The UK's R&D intensity – that is, the ratio of R&D spending to sales – has been considerably lower than that of its main economic rivals.

Each year the European Union publishes the *EU Industrial R&D Investment Scoreboard*. This gives details of the R&D expenditures by the top R&D spending companies both in the EU and worldwide. It also investigates emerging trends and patterns in R&D spending.

The data used in the majority of the report is based on the 2500 largest R&D-spending companies in the world. Of these 2500 firms, 633 were based in the EU, while 1867 were based outside the EU. A separate part of the report focuses on the top 1000 R&D investing companies based in the EU. Out of these 1000 firms, 258 were based in the UK, 221 were based in Germany and 120 were based in France.

Here we look at some of the patterns that emerge from the 2014 Scoreboard, which looks at 2013 data.

Geographical concentration

During 2013, R&D spending by the world's top 2500 companies rose by 4.9 per cent to €538.5 billion. This followed a 6.8 per cent per cent increase in 2012. However, there were significant geographic differences in growth rates. The 804 US companies in the sample reported an increase of 5 per cent, the 387 Japanese companies reported an increase of 5.5 per cent while the 633 EU companies reported a lower increase of 2.5 per cent. The best performing countries in the world were South Korea with a growth rate of 16.6 per cent and China with a growth rate 9.8 per cent.

The three biggest R&D investing countries in the EU are Germany, the UK and France. However, there were big differences in their performance in 2013. The German companies in the sample reported a growth rate of 6 per cent, while the UK companies reported a growth rate of 5.2 per cent. However, the French companies in the sample reported a decrease of R&D spending of 3.4 per cent.

R&D intensity

Across the highest-spending 2500 companies, R&D intensity stood at 3.2 per cent in 2013. In other words, the value of R&D expenditure was equivalent to 3.2 per cent of their sales. The figure for EU companies only was 2.7 per cent, which compares unfavourably to the USA, which had a figure of 5 per cent. The UK had one of the lowest rates in the EU with an intensity figure of approximately 1.5 per cent.

R&D by firm and sector

R&D spending is concentrated amongst a relatively small number of firms. The top 100 companies accounted for 53.1 per cent of the total R&D spending of the 2500 firms in the study.

The table below shows the ranking of the biggest 20 R&D spending companies worldwide. Volkswagen came top of the list spending over €11.7 billion, with Samsung in second place spending over €10 billion. The top ranked UK-based companies were GlaxoSmithKline in 21st place, spending just over €4 billion, and Astrazeneca in 37th place, spending €3.2 billion.

The table also illustrates the intensity of R&D, as measured relative to sales. Based on this measure Intel would be top of the table with Volkswagen in 15th place. Interestingly, a number of companies which were considered the most innovative in the world in 2014 in surveys carried out by organisations such as the Boston Consulting Group are not in the top 20 R&D investors. This includes Apple and Amazon.

R&D investment is also heavily concentrated in three out of the 40 industrial sectors: *Pharmaceuticals and biotechnology* (18 per cent), *Technology hardware and equipment* (16.1 per cent) and *Automobiles and parts* (15.5 per cent). These three sectors alone accounted for nearly 50 per cent of the total R&D investment by the Scoreboard companies.

Out of the top 20 companies listed in the table, eight were in *Automobile and parts*, six were in the *Pharmaceutical*

development as a percentage of GDP has been lower than that of its main economic rivals (see Figure 21.1). For instance, the UK's share of R&D expenditure in GDP has typically been only 72 per cent of that in Germany and only 57 per cent of that in Japan.

As Figure 21.1 shows, the aggregate level of R&D spending across the 27 member states of the EU is relatively low, averaging only 1.75 per cent of GDP since 1995. Member countries, however, have been encouraged to invest 3 per cent of their GDP in R&D (2 per cent private investment, 1 per cent public finding). The principal EU fund for allocating funds for R&D is the *EU Framework for Research and Technological Development*. The budget for the Seventh

Framework Programme from 2007 to 2013 was €50.5 billion, while that for the Eighth Framework Programme from 2014 to 2020 has been raised to €80 billion.

The framework programmes are designed, amongst other things, to foster collaboration in research, including between academia and industry, to fund frontier science, help develop knowledge and science clusters, provide scholarships for young researchers and to fund R&D by small businesses. In doing so, the intention is to improve the EU's competitive stance and to promote new growth and jobs. The hope is that this interventionist approach will raise the productive potential of the wider EU economy not only in the short term, but also in the longer term.

Research and development by firm

Sector	Country	Expenditure (€m)	Intensity (% of net)
Volkswagen	Germany	11 743.0	6.0
Samsung Electronics	S. Korea	10 154.9	6.5
Microsoft	USA	8252.5	13.1
Intel	USA	7694.1	20.1
Novartis	Switzerland	7173.5	17.1
Roche	Switzerland	7076.2	18.6
Toyota Motors	Japan	6269.9	3.5
Johnson & Johnson	USA	5933.6	11.5
Google	USA	5735.6	13.2
Daimler	Germany	5379.0	4.6
General Motors	USA	5220.8	4.6
Merck US	USA	5165.0	16.2
BMW	Germany	4792.0	6.3
Sanofi-Aventis	France	4757.0	14.4
Pfizer	USA	4750.2	12.7
Robert Bosch	Germany	4653.0	10.1
Ford Motor	USA	4640.7	4.4
Cisco Systems	USA	4563.8	13.4
Siemens	Germany	4556.0	6.0
Honda Motor	Japan	4366.7	5.4

Source: Based on data from *2014 EU Industrial R&D Investment Scoreboard* (European Commission)

and *biotechnology* and two were in *Technology hardware and equipment* sectors. Both of the top-ranked UK companies were in the *Pharmaceuticals and biotechnology* sector. The sectors with the fastest growth of R&D investment in 2013 were *Construction and materials* (13.6 per cent) followed by *Software and computer services* (11.4 per cent).

1. What are the economic costs and benefits of R&D spending to the national economy? Distinguish between the short and long run.
2. R&D is only one indicator, albeit an important one, of innovation potential. What other factors are likely to affect innovation?
3. What is the economic case for and against government intervention in the field of R&D?

Figure 21.1   Gross expenditure on R&D as a percentage of GDP

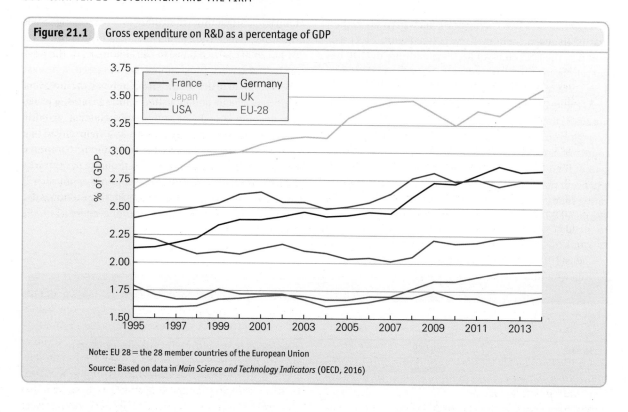

Note: EU 28 = the 28 member countries of the European Union

Source: Based on data in *Main Science and Technology Indicators* (OECD, 2016)

21.3   POLICIES TOWARDS TRAINING

It is generally recognised by economists and politicians alike that improvements in training and education can yield significant supply-side gains. Indeed, the UK's failure to invest as much in training as many of its major competitors is seen as a key explanation for the country's poor economic performance since the early 1970s. OECD figures[3] show that in the UK in 2012 the percentage of the population aged 25 to 64 with at least upper secondary education, such as A-levels or vocational equivalents, was 78 per cent. Although this figure was above the OECD average of 75 per cent, it was below the figures of 86 per cent in Germany and 89 per cent in the USA.

Training and economic performance

Training and economic performance are linked in three main ways.

Labour productivity. In various studies comparing the productivity of UK and German industry, education and training was seen as the principal reason for the productivity gap between the two countries.

Innovation and change. A key factor in shaping a firm's willingness to introduce new products or processes will

be the adaptability and skills of its workforce. If the firm has to spend a lot of money on retraining, or on attracting skilled workers away from other firms, the costs may prove prohibitive.

Costs of production. A shortage of skilled workers will quickly create labour bottlenecks and cause production costs to increase. This will stifle economic growth.

Training policy

If training is financed by the employer, the benefits will become an externality if the employees leave to work elsewhere. Society will have obtained benefits from the training that have not been captured by the firm which financed it. The free market, therefore, will provide less than the optimal amount of training. The more mobile the labour force, and the more 'transferable' the skills acquired from training, the more likely it is that workers will leave, and the less willing will firms be to invest in training.

In the UK, there is a high level of labour turnover. What is more, wage differentials between skilled and unskilled workers are narrower than in many other countries, and so there is less incentive for workers to train.

[3]*Education at a Glance 2014* (OECD, 2015).

How can increased training be achieved? There are several different approaches:

■ Workers could be encouraged to stay with their employer so that employers would be more willing to invest in training. Externalities would be reduced.

■ Firms could pass the costs on to the employee while they were training. They could do this by paying the trainee a wage below the value of their work or their marginal revenue product. Regulation and minimum wage legislation may make this more difficult.

■ The government could provide subsidies for training. Alternatively, the government or some other agency could provide education and training directly.

■ Firms could co-operate to prevent 'poaching' and set up industry-wide training programmes, perhaps in partnership with the government and unions.

Training policy in various countries

As far as the first approach is concerned, most countries have seen a movement towards *greater* labour mobility. The rise in the 'flexible firm' (see page 317) has involved the employment of fewer permanent workers and more part-time and temporary workers.

Some countries, such as Japan and Germany, however, have a generally lower rate of labour turnover than most. In Japan, in particular, it is common for workers to stay with one employer throughout their career. There the relationship between employer and employee extends well beyond a simple short-term economic arrangement. Workers give loyalty and commitment to their employer, which in return virtually guarantees long-term employment and provides various fringe benefits (such as housing, child care, holiday schemes and health care). It is not surprising that Japanese firms invest highly in training.

In the USA, labour turnover is very high and yet there is little in the way of industry-wide training. Instead, by having a high percentage of young people in further and higher education, the US government hopes that sufficient numbers and quality of workers are available for industry. The Organisation for Economic Co-operation and Development (OECD) publishes entry rates to tertiary education on an internationally comparable basis. As of 2012, the data indicated that 71 per cent of young adults in the US population will enter higher education over their lifetime. This was slightly higher than in the UK where the figure was 67 per cent. The percentage of the population taking vocational training courses is very low. Total public-sector expenditure on all types of training programmes averaged just 0.05 per cent of GDP between 2005 and 2010.

In Germany, the 2012 OECD data indicated that 53 per cent of young adults will enter higher education over their lifetime. This figure is considerably lower than in the USA (and the UK). However, public-sector expenditure on training accounts for 0.3 per cent of GDP, six times larger than the share in the USA. Three-quarters of this training is

categorised as institutional training, whereby young people who do not enter higher education embark on some form of apprenticeship, attending college for part of the week and receiving work-based training for the rest.

In the German model, the state, unions and employers' associations work closely in determining training provision, and they have developed a set of vocational qualifications based around the apprenticeship system. Given that virtually all firms are involved in training, the 'free-rider' problem of firms poaching labour without themselves paying for training is virtually eliminated. The result is that the German workforce is highly skilled. Many of the skills, however, are highly specific. This is a problem when the demand for particular skills declines.

The UK approach

There has been considerable concern in the UK about the quantity and appropriateness of training. For instance, in 2004 the then Labour government set up a committee under Lord Leitch to consider the most effective forms of training for increasing economic prosperity and productivity, and improving social justice. The report looked at the UK record on skills training and came to some rather gloomy conclusions. Some of the key observations were that:

■ The UK had a relatively poor productivity performance and lagged behind some of its major rivals. At the time output per worker per hour was over 10 per cent lower than in Germany and the USA.

■ An important factor that helped to explain this relatively poor productivity performance was the UK's low level of skills.

■ The proportion of adults in the UK without a basic school-leaving qualification was double that of Canada and Germany.

■ Over 5 million people of working age in the UK had no qualifications at all.

■ One in six adults did not have the literacy skills expected of an 11-year-old.

The Leitch Committee stated in its interim report that the UK had to 'raise its game'. So to what extent has the UK approach to training evolved?

The institutional arrangements introduced to support the provision of training in the UK have changed frequently over the past 25 years. Some people have argued that they have been changed far too frequently and this has created a very complicated system. The following section will discuss some of the major reforms.

The approach adopted by the Conservative government elected in 1979 was initially influenced by its free-market approach. Training was left largely to employers. However, with growing worries over the UK's *productivity gap* (see Box 31.2 for empirical evidence), the government set up Training and Enterprise Councils (TECs) in 1988. The

TECs identified regional skills needs, organised training and financed work-based training schemes.

Pause for thought

What advantages and drawbacks are there in leaving training provision to employers? Clue: think about how training provision might be influenced by the business cycle (the cycle of booms and recessions in the economy).

In 2001, the then Labour government replaced the TECs with the Learning and Skills Council (LSC). In total the LSC had a budget of over £10 billion and was responsible for planning and funding training in sixth forms and further education colleges, work-based training for young people aged 16 to 24 ('Apprenticeships' and 'Advanced Apprenticeships'), adult and community learning, the provision of information, advice and guidance for adults, and developing links between education and business.

In addition, a support service called 'Connexions' was established and funded by the government. It offered careers, training and employment advice and support for young people between the ages of 13 and 19.

In March 2008 it was announced that the LSC was to be abolished. Its previous responsibilities were split between two new organisations – the Skills Funding Agency (SFA) and the Young Peoples Funding Agency (YPFA). The SFA took over the role of supporting and allocating government money for training, while the YPFA managed the provision of further education for 16–19-year-olds in England. Both the SFA and the YPFA were established in April 2010. The YPFA only lasted two years before being abolished in March 2012.

The Educational Funding Agency. The YPFA was replaced by the Education Funding Agency (EFA). The EFA took over other responsibilities as well as those of the YPFA. As of April 2015 it is responsible for distributing government funding for state education in England for all 3–19-year-olds. It also has responsibility for managing the estates of schools and colleges. It distributes over £50 billion of government spending and funds every state school place in the country.

The Skills Funding Agency. The role of the SFA has also evolved since it was first established. The National Apprenticeship Service that was created in 2009 to manage apprenticeship frameworks is now a division of the SFA.

As of April 2015 the SFA is responsible for distributing over £4 billion of government spending to fund skills training. It allocates money to over 1000 colleges, private training organisations and employers.

The National Careers Service. The 'Connexions' careers service was replaced by the National Careers Service (NCS) in April 2012. The NCS also replaced Next Step, the adult advisory service, and so brought access to careers advice for both young people and adults together into one organisation. Advisers are available both online and by phone. People aged 19 and over can also make face-to-face appointments. The NCS has also become a division of the SFA.

Qualifications

The past 25 years have seen various new vocational qualifications introduced. The National Vocational Qualification (NVQ) was launched in 1991 specifically to support workplace learning for young people. A young person works for an employer and receives on-the-job training. They also attend college on an occasional basis. The NVQ is awarded when they have achieved sufficient competence. In addition, the government launched General National Vocational Qualifications (GNVQs). These further-education qualifications were aimed to bridge the gap between education and work, by ensuring that education was more work relevant.

The GNVQ system was modelled on that in France, where a clear vocational educational route is seen as the key to reducing skills shortages. At the age of 14, French students can choose to pursue academic or vocational education routes. The vocational route provides high-level, broad-based skills (unlike in Germany, where skills tend to be more job specific).

However, GNVQs were competing alongside other well-established vocational qualifications such as City and Guilds and BTEC certificates and diplomas. Such competition led to the withdrawal of the GNVQ by October 2007. The NVQ survives largely because it complements other vocational qualifications, for example on apprenticeship schemes.

In 2008, 14–19 diplomas were launched. By 2011, these were offered in 14 vocational areas or 'lines of learning', such as engineering, IT, hair and beauty studies, retail business, construction and hospitality. They were studied in schools or colleges. All diplomas are available at three levels: Foundation (level 1), Higher (level 2: equivalent to GCSE grades A* to C) and Advanced (level 3: equivalent to $3\frac{1}{2}$ A-levels).

The Wolf Report. In 2010 the government commissioned a review of vocational education led by Professor Alison Wolf.[4] The final report published in 2011 was quite critical of many of the courses that governments had introduced. The study suggested that around 350 000 16–19-year-olds were working towards vocational qualifications that were of little or no value and were not recognised by employers.

The report blamed the incentive structure created by league tables that had caused colleges and schools to enrol people on courses that would boost league table positions but would not help them to get a job. With over 5000 vocational qualifications, it concluded that the whole system had

---

[4]Alison Wolf, *Review of Vocational Education – The Wolf Report* (GOV.UK, March 2011).

Figure 21.2 Total government-funded apprenticeship starts, England

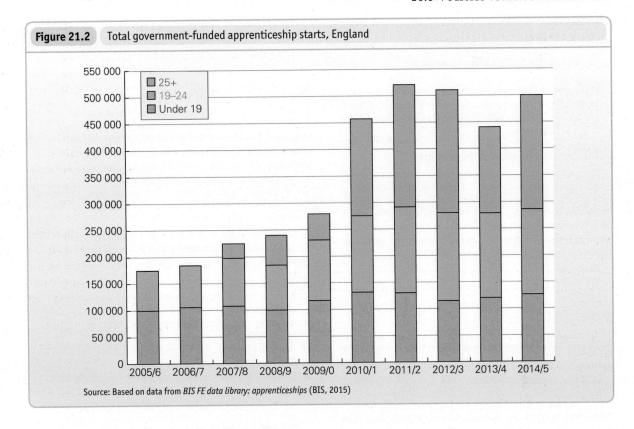

Source: Based on data from *BIS FE data library: apprenticeships* (BIS, 2015)

become far too complex and should be simplified as soon as possible. It also recommended that the government should fund coherent study programmes rather than just qualifications. It also called for greater employer involvement in the design of qualifications and courses.

Following the publication of this review, the Department of Education abolished 14–19 diplomas in August 2013. The SFA also removed the funding from 1800 vocational qualifications in July 2013. It announced that a further 1000 qualifications would have their funding removed in 2014.

The government unveiled 142 new 'Tech level' vocational qualifications in December 2013. These qualifications are supported by leading businesses and trade organisations such as Vauxhall, Procter & Gamble and Kawasaki. Only vocational qualifications that have 'Tech level' status will be counted in school and college league tables. The government also announced new broader based vocational qualifications called Applied General Qualifications, which have the support of some universities.

The report also stressed the importance of young people obtaining English and Maths at grades A* to C in order for them to be successful in the labour market. It noted that only 4 per cent of those students who failed to get grade C or above in Maths and English by the age of 16 achieved this outcome during their 16–18 education. Another recommendation of the report was that everyone who fails to get at least a 'C' in GCSE English or Maths must continue to study those subjects post-16.

It has also been widely accepted across the political spectrum that all young people should continue in learning until they are 18. The age to which all young people must continue in either education or training was increased to 17 in 2013 and 18 in 2015.

Apprenticeships

A second important and influential review commissioned by the government was carried out by Doug Richard.[5] This review focused on the apprenticeship system. An apprenticeship is a paid job where the employee receives both off- and on-the-job training. The government currently subsidises some of the training costs of an apprenticeship if it meets certain quality standards. These are known as 'Apprenticeship Frameworks' and they have become an increasingly important part of government policy on training.

The growth, and more recent decline, in the number of people starting on government-funded apprenticeships in England is illustrated in Figure 21.2. There were 244 900 starts in 2014/15, which was an increase of 23 300 on the number in 2007/8, but a decline from the peak of 515 000 in 2011/12. On average, apprenticeships last longer than a year, so the numbers starting are less than the total number on the scheme. The total number in England in 2013/14 was 852 000. The amount spent by the government on funding the scheme was just under £1.5 billion.

Figure 21.2 also clearly illustrates how apprenticeships have formed an important plank of training not only for

[5]Doug Richard, *The Richard Review of Apprenticeships* (School for Startups, November, 2012).

BOX 21.3 RADICAL CHANGES TO APPRENTICESHIPS

Tackling the UK's skills shortage?

In October 2013 the government announced a number of proposals to change the way apprenticeships are structured and funded. These proposals followed the recommendations of the Richard review.[6]

The existing funding arrangements

The government funds part of the cost of providing apprenticeships as long as they meet certain quality standards. These are called Apprenticeship Frameworks. As of April 2015, the size of the subsidy paid by the government is dependent on a number of factors including the age of the apprentice and the framework being followed. The impact of age on the size of the subsidy is shown in the table below.

Age of apprentice	% of course fee subsidised
16–18	100
19–23	50
24 and over	Up to 50

The size of the course fee being either fully or partly funded by the government depends on which of the 200 available frameworks the apprentice is following. Each framework specifies the qualifications that must be taken in order to successfully complete a particular apprenticeship. The Skills Funding Agency publishes a list of over 3500 of these eligible qualifications with fees ranging from over £10 000 to less than a £100. This results in large variations in the total course fees for each of the different frameworks. The table below illustrates the average level of public funding per Advanced Apprenticeship for some of the different subject groups.

Subject/framework group	Level 3
Retail and Commercial Enterprise	£3 700
Business, Administration and Law	£3 900
Information and Communication Technology	£10 200
Construction, Planning and Built Environment	£14 700
Engineering and Manufacturing Technologies	£20 000

[6]Ibid.

The important role of training providers

In about 10 per cent of apprenticeship frameworks the subsidy is paid directly to the firm. This is usually the case in larger organisations that have their own training staff capable of providing any off-the-job training. However, the majority of firms do not have their own specialist staff and so have to use an external training organisation instead. These external training organisations can be of two different types: independent training providers or colleges of further education.

When they are involved, external training providers carry out the majority of the work in organising and delivering an apprenticeship. This includes:

■ Discussing timetables for the training and developing training plans to fit the needs of both the employer and employee.
■ Managing the recruitment process and shortlisting suitable candidates for interview.
■ Managing the paperwork once potential apprentices has been selected.
■ Providing the training and claiming the subsidy payment from the government.
■ Claiming money from the firm for that part of any course fees not covered by the government subsidy: i.e. for apprentices aged 19 and over.
■ Providing ongoing assessment and advice to both the employer and apprentice.

Criticisms of the system

The Richard review made a number of criticisms of the apprenticeship framework system. Given the significant role played by training providers, he argued that in the majority of apprenticeships firms take a very passive role. Instead of being actively involved in designing the content of the training, the evidence suggested that firms treated the frameworks as state-managed programmes. They saw their role as one of simply offering work placements to people on a government-run training scheme. Evidence to support this argument came from data on apprenticeships for people aged 19 and over. In theory the course fees on these programmes should be co-funded by the government and the employer. However, only 11 per cent of employers paid any training fees, which suggests only limited involvement.

---

young people but also for older age groups too. In 2014/15, 36 per cent of all apprenticeship starts were aged 25 or over.

The skills and training received on an apprenticeship. These can be broken down into a number of different areas. There is a competency element that measures work-based skills. This normally involves the apprentice taking National Vocational Qualifications.

There is also an element that develops and measures the theoretical knowledge that underpins the practical skills. This will involve the apprentice taking a Technical Certificate.

Another area to the training is one that develops and tests transferable skills, such as numeracy and literacy. This may involve the apprentice studying and passing qualifications in Maths and English at GCSE level.

A final element focuses on activities other than those that result in a qualification. This includes the apprentice gaining an understanding of employee rights and responsibilities.

Richard argued that in order for the apprenticeship system to deliver the high-quality training required for a successful economy, it was vital to get employers more actively involved. In particular it was extremely important that employers should take a leading role in managing and designing high-value training programmes that met their skill requirements.

Changes to funding and the trailblazers

Following the recommendations of the Richard review, the government announced a number of radical proposals to change the way apprenticeship frameworks are funded. One of these proposals is that the subsidy for course fees should be paid directly to the firm rather than the training provider. Another suggestion was to change the way the size of course fees were decided. Instead of these being set at a national level by the SFA, it is proposed that they are determined at a local level following negotiations between the firm and the training provider. The key rationale behind these changes is to try and get firms more directly involved in decisions about the relevance, quality and cost of training.

Changes were also proposed to the method used to calculate the size of the subsidy. Firms would now be expected to pay course fees to the relevant training provider. They would then be able to claim back £2 off the government for every £1 spent on fees up to a maximum limit or cap. The government proposed five different levels for this cap. Firms might also be able to claim some additional payments based on the age of the apprentice, the size of the firm and whether the person successfully completes the apprenticeship. These payments are illustrated in the table below.

	Cap 1	Cap 2	Cap 3	Cap 4	Cap 5
Size of the cap	£2000	£3000	£6000	£8 000	£18 000
Employer contribution if money is claimed up to the maximum cap	£1000	£1500	£3000	£4 000	£9 000
Additional payments					
Apprentice aged 16–18	£600	£900	£1800	£2 400	£5 400
Firm employs < 50	£500	£500	£900	£1 200	£2 700
Successful completion	£500	£500	£900	£1 200	£2 700
Maximum size of government subsidy	£3600	£4900	£9600	£12 800	£28 800

The government also launched the 'Trailblazers' initiative in October 2013. Trailblazers are groups of leading employers within a sector, who work together to determine the content of new apprenticeship standards. In March 2014 the government published the first 20 standards developed in phase 1 of the initiative. It hoped that these new employer-designed standard will eventually replace the frameworks.

Business Secretary Vince Cable said: 'Our reforms have empowered businesses large and small to design and deliver world-beating apprenticeships that offer a real route to a successful career.'[7]

However, some people have expressed concerns about the potential impact of these changes. The reforms move much of the administrative burden of the system from training providers back on to firms. Some fear these potential extra costs will deter many employees from becoming involved and result in a significant reduction in the number of apprenticeships. This maybe particularly true for small and medium-sized enterprises. The requirement to fund some of the course fees of 16–18-year-old apprentices might also deter firms from recruiting younger people.

1. What is the economic rationale for governments to finance the training provided to apprentices?
2. The government subsidises course fees for qualifications taken by a trainee as part of an apprenticeship. However, course fees only represent one element of the costs of training a worker. What are the other economic costs?
3. Explain some of the potential impacts of the funding changes on the provision of apprenticeships.

---

[7]'More than 700 employers to design top quality apprenticeships', *Press Release*, Department of Business, Innovation and Skills (23 October 2014).

Apprenticeships can be taken at three different levels.

- Intermediate apprenticeships – level 2 qualifications, equivalent to 5 GCSEs.
- Advanced apprenticeships – level 3 qualifications, equivalent to 2 A levels.
- Higher apprenticeships – level 4 qualifications and above.

Increasing the provision of Higher Apprenticeships has been a policy priority for the government in recent years. A Higher Apprenticeship Fund of £25 million was used to finance the development of 29 Higher Apprenticeship projects and 20 000 new starts. A further £40 million of funding for the scheme was announced in the Autumn Statement of 2013. In 2014/15 only 3 per cent of apprenticeships were at a higher level – see Figure 21.3.

Funding was also made available to encourage smaller firms to hire apprentices. The Apprenticeship Grant for Employers of 16–24-year-olds is a scheme that pays £1500 to firms employing 50 or fewer employees if they take on an apprentice. To be eligible the firm must not have taken on an apprentice in the previous 12 months.

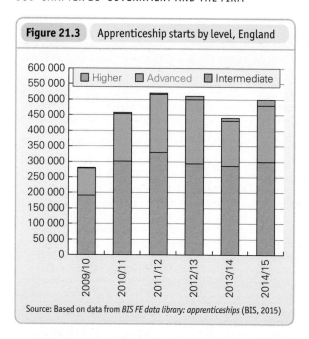

Figure 21.3 Apprenticeship starts by level, England

Source: Based on data from *BIS FE data library: apprenticeships* (BIS, 2015)

The Richard review recommended a move away from Apprenticeship Frameworks based on groups of qualifications towards a more rounded approach. In particular it called for greater involvement and input from employers in the design of the frameworks. More details of changes being made to the system as a result of the Richard review are discussed in Box 21.3.

UK governments have introduced a whole range of initiatives to take on the challenges posed by the Leitch Review. The OECD data suggest that the UK's performance has improved. However, the 2012 data show that, even after all these changes, the UK's skills performance lags behind some of its leading international rivals. For example, in 2012 the proportion of 25–64-year-olds whose highest level of educational attainment is below upper secondary level was 22 per cent in the UK. The corresponding figures for the USA and Germany were 11 per cent and 14 per cent respectively. We await with interest the extent to which the UK performance improves over the next few years.

SUMMARY

1a Competition policy in most countries recognises that monopolies, mergers and restrictive practices can bring both costs and benefits to the consumer. Generally, though, restrictive practices tend to be more damaging to consumers' interests than simple monopoly power or mergers.

1b European Union legislation applies to firms trading between EU countries. Article 101 applies to restrictive practices. Article 102 applies to dominant firms. There are also separate merger control provisions.

1c UK legislation is largely covered by the 1998 Competition Act, the 2002 Enterprise Act and Part 3 of the 2013 Enterprise and Regulatory Reform Act. The Chapter I prohibition of the 1998 Act applies to restrictive practices and is similar to Article 101. The Chapter II prohibition applies to dominant firms and is similar to Article 102. The 2002 Act made certain cartel agreements a criminal offence and required mergers over a certain size to be investigated by the Office of Fair Trading with possible reference to the Competition Commission. Both the OFT and CC were made independent of government. The 2013 Enterprise and Regulatory Reform Act merged the OFT and CC to create the Competition and Markets Authority (CMA).

1d The focus of both EU and UK legislation is on anti-competitive practices rather than on the simple existence of agreements between firms or market dominance. Practices that are found after investigation to be detrimental to competition are prohibited and heavy fines can be imposed, even for a first offence. Since 2008 the EU has operated a streamlined settlement procedure for firms suspected of operating in cartels. Co-operation results in fines being reduced and firms acting as 'whistle-blowers' can receive immunity from fines.

2a The importance of technology in determining national economic success is growing. There is now a need for government to formulate a technology policy to ensure that the national economy has every chance to remain competitive.

2b Technological change, when left to the market, is unlikely to proceed rapidly enough or to a socially desirable level. Reasons for this include R&D free riders, monopolistic market structures, duplication of R&D activities, and risk and uncertainty.

2c Government technology policy might involve intervention at different levels of the technology process (invention, innovation and diffusion). Such intervention might involve extending ownership rights over new products, providing R&D directly or using subsidies to encourage third parties. Government might also act in an advisory/co-ordinating capacity.

2d Technology policy in the UK has tended to emphasise the market as the principal provider of technological change. Where possible, government's role has been kept to a minimum. Within the EU, policy has been more interventionist and a wide range of initiatives have been launched to encourage greater levels of R&D.

3a A well-trained workforce contributes to economic performance by enhancing productivity, encouraging and enabling change and, in respect to supplying scarce skills to the workplace, helps to reduce wage costs.

3b Training policy in the UK has gone through numerous changes in the past 25 years. At times the level of government intervention has increased and at other times training provision has been predominately left to employers. The result of all the changes seems to be a system that delivers less than the optimum amount of training. In other countries, such as Germany, the state plays a far greater role in training provision.

3c The apprenticeship system has become a very important part of the UK government's policy on vocational training. The number of employees doing an apprenticeship has increased rapidly over the past few years.

MyEconLab

This book can be supported by MyEconLab, which contains a range of additional resources, including an online homework and tutorial system designed to test and build your understanding.

You need both an access card and a course ID to access MyEconLab:

1. Is your lecturer using MyEconLab? Ask your lecturer for your course ID.

2. Has an access card been included with the book at a reduced cost? Check the inside back cover of the book.

3. If you have a course ID but no access card, go to: http://www.myeconlab.com/ to buy access to this interactive study programme.

REVIEW QUESTIONS

1 Try to formulate a definition of the public interest.

2 What are the advantages and disadvantages of the current system of controlling restrictive practices?

3 What problems are likely to arise in identifying which firms' practices are anti-competitive? Should regulators take firms' assurances into account when deciding whether to grant an exemption?

4 If anti-monopoly legislation is effective enough, is there ever any need to prevent mergers from going ahead?

5 Discuss some of the problems involved in defining the relevant market for the purposes of competition policy.

6 If two or more firms were charging similar prices, what types of evidence would you look for to prove that this was collusion rather than mere coincidence?

7 Should governments or regulators always attempt to eliminate the supernormal profits of monopolists/oligopolists?

8 We can distinguish three clear stages in the development and application of technology: invention, innovation and diffusion. How might forms of technology policy intervention change at each stage of this process?

9 Governments and educationalists generally regard it as desirable that trainees acquire transferable skills. Why may many employers disagree?

10 There are externalities (benefits) when employers provide training. What externalities are there from the undergoing of training by the individual? Do they imply that individuals will choose to receive more or less than the socially optimal amount of training?

Government and the market

In the previous chapter we considered examples of the relationship between the government and the individual firm. In this chapter we turn to examine government policy at the level of the whole market. Although such policies are generally directed at a whole industry or sector, they nevertheless still affect individual businesses, and indeed the effects may well vary from one firm to another.

22.1 ENVIRONMENTAL POLICY

Scarcely a day goes by without some environmental issue or other featuring in the news: another warning about global warming; a company fined for illegally dumping waste; a drought or flood blamed on pollution/global warming; smog in some major cities. Also attempts by policy makers to improve the environment are often controversial and hit the headlines: for example, the impact of government climate change policies on the size of people's energy bills.

Why does the environment appear to be so misused and policies that attempt to improve the situation so controversial? To answer these questions we have to understand the nature of the economic relationship between humans and the natural world.

The environment as a resource

We all benefit from the environment in three ways:

- as an amenity to be enjoyed;
- as a source of primary products (food, raw materials and other resources);
- as a place where we can dump waste.

Unfortunately these three different uses are often in conflict with each other. For example, we extract and burn fossil fuels such as coal, oil and gas, for power generation and industrial uses. However, the extraction of these fuels may have a negative impact on the amenity value of the environment. One only has to think of some of the concerns raised by people about the impact of drilling for shale gas on their local communities. The burning of fossil fuels also creates greenhouse gases that are emitted into the atmosphere and cause climate change. Some of the CO_2 gets absorbed into the oceans, which increases their level of acidity and kills marine life.

Policies that try to reduce our current use of the environment as a source of primary products and/or reduce the volume of emissions we generate come at cost. These higher costs are often passed on to consumers in the form of higher prices – an outcome they often dislike and complain about.

The subject of environmental degradation lies clearly within the realm of economics, since it is a direct consequence of production and consumption decisions. So how can economic analysis help us to understand the nature of the problem and design effective policies that will result in the optimal use of the environment? What will be the impact of these policies on business?

Market failures

An unregulated market system may fail to provide adequate protection of the environment for a number of reasons.

Externalities. Pollution could be classified as a 'negative externality' of production or consumption, as we saw in section 20.2. In the case of production, there are marginal external costs (*MEC*), which means that the marginal social costs (*MSC*) are greater than the marginal private costs (*MC*) to the polluter. The failure of the market system to equate *MSC* and marginal social benefit (*MSB*) is due to either consumers or firms lacking the appropriate property rights.

The environment as a common resource. The air, the seas and many other parts of the environment are not privately owned. It is argued that they are a global 'commons'. As such, it is extremely difficult to exclude non-payers from consuming the benefits they provide. Because of this property of 'non-excludability' (see page 349), the environment can often be consumed at a zero price. If the price of any good or service to the user is zero, there is no incentive to economise on its use.

Many parts of the environment, however, are *scarce*: there is *rivalry* in their use. As people increase their use of the environment, it may prevent other or rival consumers from enjoying it. Overfishing in the open oceans can lead to the depletion of fish stocks (see Box 20.2 on page 352).

Ignorance. There have been many cases of people causing environmental damage without realising it, especially when the effects build up over a long time. Even when the problems are known to scientists, consumers and producers may not appreciate the full environmental costs of their actions. Firms may want to act in a more 'environmentally friendly' manner but lack the appropriate knowledge to do so.

Intergenerational problems. The environmentally harmful effects of many activities are long term, whereas the benefits are immediate. Thus consumers and firms are frequently prepared to continue with various practices and leave future generations to worry about their environmental consequences. The problem, then, is a reflection of the importance that people attach to the present relative to the future.

In order to ensure that the environment is taken sufficiently into account by both firms and consumers, the government must intervene. It must devise an appropriate *environmental policy*.

Such a policy will involve measures to ensure that at least a specified minimum level of environmental quality is achieved. Ideally, the policy would ensure that all externalities are fully 'internalised'. This means that firms and consumers are forced to pay the *full* costs of production or consumption: i.e. their marginal private costs *plus* any external costs. It also needs to make sure that the effects of actions taken by the current generation on the welfare of future generations are fully taken into account when devising policy. For more detail see Box 22.1.

Problems with policy intervention

Valuing the environment

The principal difficulty facing government in constructing its environmental policy is that of *valuing* the environment and hence of estimating the costs of its pollution. If policy is based upon the principle that the polluter pays, then an accurate assessment of pollution costs is vital if the policy is to establish a socially efficient level of production.

Three common methods used for valuing environmental damage are: the financial costs to *other* users; revealed preferences; and 'contingent valuation' (or stated preference).

The financial costs to other users. In this method, environmental costs are calculated by considering the financial costs imposed on other businesses or individuals by polluting activities. For example, if firm A feeds chemical waste into a local stream, then firm B, which is downstream and requires a clean water supply, may have to introduce a water purification process. The expense of this to firm B can be seen as an external cost of firm A.

The main problem with this method is that not all external costs entail a direct financial cost for the sufferers. Many external costs may therefore be overlooked.

| BOX 22.1 | A STERN REBUKE ABOUT CLIMATE CHANGE INACTION |

Economists can offer solutions, but they can't solve the problem

The analysis of global warming is not just for climate scientists. Economists have a major part to play in examining its causes and consequences and the possible solutions. And these solutions are likely to have a major impact on business.

Perhaps the most influential study of climate change in recent times was the Stern Review. This was an independent review led by Sir Nicholas Stern, the then head of the Government Economic Service and former chief economist of the World Bank. Here was an economist using the methods of economics to analyse perhaps the most serious problem facing the world.

> Climate change presents a unique challenge for economics: it is the greatest and widest-ranging market failure ever seen. The economic analysis must therefore be global, deal with long time horizons, have the economics of risk and uncertainty at centre stage, and examine the possibility of major, non-marginal change.[1]

Dealing with long time horizons presents some interesting problems. The benefits to society from acting on climate change today will occur in the future. The problem is that the cost of these policies will be felt today: e.g. higher prices and less consumption. In order to carry out an assessment of environmental policies the future benefits need to be *discounted* so that they can be compared with the current costs. The problem is in choosing the most appropriate social discount rate. Unfortunately many economists disagree!

What makes matters worse is that the results obtained from any economic assessment that involve costs and benefits over such a long period of time are very sensitive to the discount rate used. Stern used a relatively low social discount rate, which meant that the future benefits and costs were more highly valued. Other economists criticised the report, claiming that a much higher discount rate should have been chosen.

First the bad news

According to the Stern Report, if no action were taken, global temperatures would rise by some 2–3 °C within the next 50 years. As a result the world economy would shrink by an average of up to 20 per cent. The economies of the countries most seriously affected by floods, drought and crop failure could shrink by considerably more. Rising sea levels could displace some 200 million people; droughts could create tens or even hundreds of millions of 'climate refugees'. Because of the low discount rate used, these future costs were weighted heavily.

Then the good

However, Stern concluded that these consequences could be averted – and at relatively low cost – if action were taken early enough. According to the report, a sacrifice of just 1 per cent of global GDP (global income) could be enough to stabilise greenhouse gases to a sustainable level. To achieve this, action would need to be taken to cut emissions from their various sources (see the chart). This would involve a mixture of four things:

- Reducing consumer demand for emissions-intensive goods and services.
- Increased efficiency, which can save both money and emissions.
- Action on non-energy emissions, such as avoiding deforestation.
- Switching to lower-carbon technologies for power, heat and transport.

As one might expect from a report produced by an economist, the policy proposals focused on altering incentives. This could involve taxing polluting activities; subsidising green alternatives, including the development of green technology; establishing a price for carbon through trading carbon (see section on tradable permits on pages 395–6) and regulating its production; and encouraging behavioural change through education, better labelling of products and encouraging public debate.

Heeding the warnings?

So, nearly 10 years after the Stern Report, how much progress has been made? The OECD is very concerned about the environmental impact on growth and is pressing for a global response. So are national governments therefore acting with urgency?

In 2014, the Intergovernmental Panel on Climate Change (IPCC) issued its *Fifth Assessment Report (AR5)*[2] – the first one had been published in 1990. This major document consists of three working group reports and an overarching synthesis. The first working group looked at the physical science; the second considered impacts, adaptation and vulnerability; while the third focused on mitigation of climate change. Economists contributed substantially to both the second and third groups.

---

[1] *Stern Review on the Economics of Climate Change* (TSO, 2006).
[2] *The Fifth Assessment Report (AR5)* (IPCC, 2014).

Revealed preferences. If the direct financial costs of pollution are difficult to identify, let alone calculate, then an alternative approach to valuing the environment might be to consider how individuals or businesses change their behaviour in response to environmental changes. Such changes in behaviour frequently carry a financial cost, which makes calculation easier. For example, the building of a new superstore on a greenfield site overlooked by your house might cause you to move. Moving house entails a financial cost, including the

loss in value of your property resulting from the opening of the store. Clearly, in such a case, by choosing to move you would be regarding the cost of moving to be less than the cost to you of the deterioration in your environment.

Contingency valuation. In this method, people likely to be affected are asked to evaluate the effect on them of any proposed change to their environment. In the case of the superstore, local residents might be asked how much they

KI 28
p 325

Greenhouse gas emissions in 2000, by source

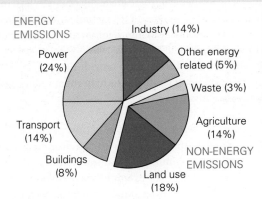

Total emissions in 2000: 42 GtCO₂e.

Energy emissions are mostly CO_2 (some non-CO_2 in industry and other energy related).

Non-energy emissions are CO_2 (land use) and non-CO_2 (agriculture and waste).

Source: *Stern Review on the Economics of Climate Change*. Office of Climate Change (OCC) (Stem Review, 2006), Executive Summary, Figure 1 based on data drawn from World Resources Institute *Climate Analysis Indicators Tool (CAIT)* online database version 3.0

The report on impact[3] confirmed that the effects of climate change are already occurring on all continents and across the oceans. It concluded that the world is ill-prepared for risks from a changing climate.

As with Stern, it stated that that there are currently opportunities to respond to such risks, though this will be difficult to manage with high levels of warming.

The report details the impacts of climate change to date, the future risks from a changing climate, and the opportunities for effective action to reduce risks. It identifies vulnerable people, industries and ecosystems around the world. It finds that risk from a changing climate comes from vulnerability (lack of preparedness) and exposure (people or assets in harm's way) overlapping with hazards (triggering climate events or trends). Each of these three components can be a target for smart actions to decrease risk.

Adaptation to reduce the risks from a changing climate is now starting to occur, but with a stronger focus on reacting to past events than on preparing for a changing future. According to Chris Field, the Co-Chair of Working Group II:

> Climate-change adaptation is not an exotic agenda that has never been tried. Governments, firms, and communities around the world are building experience with adaptation. This experience forms a starting point for bolder, more ambitious adaptations that will be important, as climate and society continue to change.[4]

Less than a month after this report, the working group on mitigation published its own findings.[5] It summarised the diverse options open to policy makers and reaffirmed the conclusion that the worst effects of climate can be prevented, if action is taken.

Part of the Mitigation report takes the form of a summary for policy makers. It acknowledges that substantial reductions in emissions will require major changes in investment patterns. The report finds that some progress in policy development has been achieved, particularly at a national level. These policies are often at sectoral level and involve the regulatory, financial and information measures that economists have recommended for some time.

There is, however, a substantial time lag between the implementation of policies and the impact on the environment. AR5 found that since 2008 emission growth has not yet deviated from the previous trend.

Of course, a major characteristic of climate change is that it is not restricted by national boundaries. This highlights the potential for international cooperation. Attempts to reach international agreement on tackling climate change are examined in Case study H.22 in MyEconLab.

1. *Would it be in the interests of a business to reduce its carbon emissions if this involved it in increased costs?*

2. *How is the concept of 'opportunity cost' relevant in analysing the impact of business decisions on the environment?*

3. *The Stern Report was produced in 2006. Why has progress to date been slow? Does this reflect a lack of political will or scepticism about the extent of climate change?*

---

[3] *Climate Change 2014: Impacts, Adaptation, and Vulnerability, from Working Group II of the IPCC* (IPCC, 2014).
[4] www.unep.org/newscentre/Default.aspx?DocumentID=2764&ArticleID=10773
[5] *Climate Change 2014: Mitigation from Climate Change, from Working Group III of the IPCC* (IPCC, 2014).

---

would be willing to pay in order for the development not to take place, or alternatively, how much they would need to be compensated if it were to take place.

The principal concern with this method is how reliable the answers to the questionnaires would be. There are two major problems:

■ *Ignorance*. People will not know just how much they will suffer *until* the project goes ahead.

■ *Dishonesty*. People will tend to exaggerate the compensation they would need. After all, if compensation is actually going to be paid, people will want to get as much as possible. But even if it is not, the more people exaggerate the costs to them, the more likely it is that they can get the project stopped.

These problems can be lessened if people who have already experienced a similar project elsewhere are questioned. They are more knowledgeable and have less to gain from being dishonest.

Research on contingency valuation has focused heavily on the questioning process and how monetary values of costs and benefits might be accurately established. Of all the methods, contingency valuation has grown most in popularity over recent years, despite its limitations.

Other problems

As well as the problems of value, other aspects of environmental damage make policy making particularly difficult. These include the following:

- *Spatial issues.* The place where pollution is produced and the places where it is deposited may be geographically very far apart. Pollution crosses borders (e.g. acid rain) or can be global (e.g. greenhouse gases). In both cases, national policies might be of little value, especially if you are a receiver of others' pollution! In such circumstances, international agreements would be needed, and these can be very difficult to reach.
- *Temporal issues.* Environmental problems such as acid rain and the depletion of the ozone layer have been occurring over many decades. Thus the full effect of pollution on the environment may be identifiable only in the long term. As a consequence, policy initiatives are required to be forward looking and proactive, if the cumulative effects of pollution are to be avoided. Most policy tends to be reactive, however, dealing only with problems as they arise. In such cases, damage to the environment may have already been done.
- *Irreversibility issues.* Much environmental damage might be irreversible: once a species is extinct, for example, it cannot normally be reintroduced.

Environmental policy options

KI 36
p 354 Environmental policy can take many forms. However, it is useful to put the different types of policy into three broad categories: (a) those that attempt to work through the market by changing property rights or by changing market signals (e.g. through the use of charges, taxes or subsidies); (b) those that involve the use of laws, regulations and controls (e.g. legal limits on the volume of sulphur dioxide emissions); (c) those that attempt to combine the approaches (e.g. 'cap and trade'). The following sections will examine each of these three categories in more detail.

Market-based policies

Extending private property rights

If those suffering from pollution, or causing it, are granted property rights, they can charge the polluters for the right to pollute. According to the Coase theorem (see pages 355-6) this could result in the socially efficient level of output being produced. For example, if the sufferers are awarded the property rights, they can impose a charge

on the polluter that is greater than the sufferers' marginal pollution cost but less than the polluter's marginal profit. Similarly, if the polluting firm is given the right to pollute, victims could offer a payment to persuade it not to pollute.

Extending property rights in this way is normally impractical whenever there are many polluters and many victims. But the principle of the victims paying polluters to reduce pollution is sometimes followed by governments. Thus, under Article 11 of the 1997 Kyoto Protocol, the developed countries agreed to provide financial assistance to the developing countries to help them reduce greenhouse gas emissions.

Introducing charges for the use of the environment

We previously discussed how the environment can be thought of as a common or natural resource where the user pays no price. For example, the emissions created by a coal-burning power station can be spewed into the atmosphere at no cost to the firm even though it imposes costs on society. A firm could also use resources from the environment in its production process at a zero price. For example it could extract water, cut down trees for timber or extract minerals out of the ground (assuming it owned or rented the land). With a zero price these resources will tend to be depleted at rate that is not optimal for society: i.e. too quickly.

To overcome these problems the government could introduce charges for the use of the environment which would otherwise be free to the user.

Environmental ('green') taxes and subsidies

Rather than charging for the use of the environment, a tax could be imposed on the output (or consumption) of a good whenever external environmental costs are generated. Such taxes are known as ***green taxes***. In this case, the good already has a price but it does not fully reflect the full costs to society.

To achieve the socially efficient output level the rate of tax should be equal to the marginal external cost (see Figure 20.9 on page 355). As such, it should fully internalise the costs of the externality.

An alternative is to subsidise activities that reduce pollution (such as the installation of loft insulation). Here the rate of subsidy should be equal to the marginal external benefit.

Taxes and charges have the advantage of relating the size of the penalty to the amount of pollution. This means that there is continuous pressure to cut down on production or consumption of polluting products or activities in order to save tax.

Definition

Green tax A tax on output or consumption to charge for the adverse effect on the environment. The socially efficient level of a green tax is equal to the marginal environmental cost of production.

Table 22.1	Types of environmental taxes and charges

Motor fuels
  Leaded/unleaded
  Diesel (quality differential)
  Carbon/energy taxation
  Sulphur tax
Other energy products
  Carbon/energy tax
  Sulphur tax or charge
  NO_2 charge
  Methane charge
Agricultural inputs
  Fertilisers
  Pesticides
  Manure
Vehicle-related taxation
  Sales tax depends on car size
  Road tax depends on car size

Other goods
  Batteries
  Plastic carrier bags
  Glass containers
  Drink cans
  Tyres
  CFCs/halons
  Disposable razors/cameras
  Lubricant oil charge
  Oil pollutant charge
  Solvents
Waste disposal
  Municipal waste charges
  Waste-disposal charges
  Hazardous waste charges
  Landfill tax or charges
  Duties on waste water

Air transport
  Noise charges
  Aviation fuels
Water
  Water charges
  Sewage charges
  Water effluent charges
  Manure charges
Direct tax provisions
  Tax relief on green investment
  Taxation on free company cars
  Employer-paid commuting expenses taxable
  Employer-paid parking expenses taxable
  Commuter use of public transport tax deductible

One approach is to modify *existing* taxes. In most developed countries there are now higher taxes on high-emission cars.

Increasingly, however, countries are introducing *new* 'green' taxes or charges in order to discourage pollution as goods are produced, consumed or disposed of. Table 22.1 shows the wide range of green taxes and charges used around the world and Figure 22.1 shows green tax revenues as a percentage of GDP in various countries.

As you can see, they are higher than average in the Netherlands and the Scandinavian nations, reflecting the strength of their environmental concerns. They are lowest in the USA. By far the largest green tax revenues come from fuel taxes. Fuel taxes are relatively high in the UK and so, therefore, are green tax revenues.

Problems with taxes and charges

There are various problems with using taxes and charges in the fight against pollution.

Identifying the socially efficient tax rate. It will be difficult to identify the marginal pollution cost of each firm, given that each one is likely to produce different amounts of pollutants for any given level of output. Even if two firms produce identical amounts of pollutants, the environmental damage might be quite different, because the ability of the environment to cope with it will differ between the two locations. Also, the number of people suffering will differ (a factor that is very important when considering the *human* impact of pollution). What is more, the harmful effects are likely to build up over time, and predicting these effects is fraught with difficulty.

Problems of demand inelasticity. The less elastic the demand for the product at its current price, the less effective will a tax be in cutting production and hence in cutting pollution. Thus taxes on petrol would have to be very high indeed to make significant reductions in the consumption of petrol and hence

significant reductions in the exhaust gases that contribute towards global warming and acid rain.

Redistributive effects. The poor spend a higher proportion of their income on domestic fuel than the rich. A 'carbon tax' on such fuel will, therefore, have the effect of redistributing incomes away from the poor. The poor also spend a larger proportion of their income on food than do the rich. Taxes on agriculture, designed to reduce intensive use of fertilisers and pesticides, will again tend to hit the poor proportionately more than the rich.

However, not all green taxes hit the poor more than the rich. The rich spend a higher proportion of their income on motoring than the poor. Thus petrol and other motoring taxes could help to reduce inequality.

Problems with international trade. If a country imposes pollution taxes on its industries, its products will become less competitive in world trade. To compensate for this, the industries may need to be given tax rebates for exports. Also taxes would need to be imposed on imports of competitors' products from countries where there is no equivalent green tax.

Evidence on the adverse effect of environmental taxes on a country's exports is inconclusive, however. Over the long term, in countries with high environmental taxes (or other tough environmental measures), firms will be stimulated to invest in low-pollution processes and products. This will later give such countries a competitive advantage if *other* countries then impose tougher environmental standards.

Effects on employment. Reduced output in the industries affected by green taxes will lead to a reduction in employment. If, however, the effect was to encourage investment in new cleaner technology, employment might not fall. Furthermore, employment opportunities could be generated elsewhere if the extra revenues from the green taxes were spent on alternative products, such as buses and trains rather than cars.

KI 9
p51

KI 32
p343

KI 12
p68

Figure 22.1 Green tax revenues as a percentage of GDP

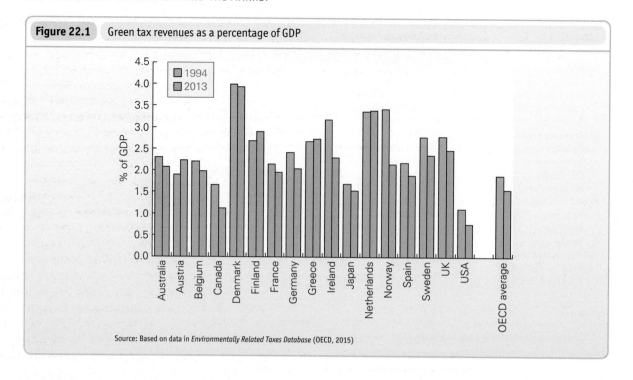

Source: Based on data in *Environmentally Related Taxes Database* (OECD, 2015)

Non-market-based policies

Command-and-control systems (laws and regulations)

The traditional way of tackling pollution has been to set maximum permitted levels of emission or resource use, or minimum acceptable levels of environmental quality, and then to fine firms contravening these limits. Measures of this type are known as ***command-and-control (CAC) systems***. Clearly, there have to be inspectors to monitor the amount of pollution, and the fines have to be large enough to deter firms from exceeding the limit.

Virtually all countries have environmental regulations of one sort or another. For example, the EU has over 200 items of legislation covering areas such as air and water pollution, noise, the marketing and use of dangerous chemicals, waste management, the environmental impacts of new projects (such as power stations, roads and quarries), recycling, depletion of the ozone layer and global warming.

Typically there are three approaches to devising CAC systems.[6]

- ***Technology-based standards.*** The focus could be on the amount of pollution generated, irrespective of its environmental impact. As technology for reducing pollutants improves, so tougher standards could be imposed, based on the 'best available technology' (as long as the cost was not excessive). Thus car manufacturers could be required to ensure that new car engines meet lower CO_2 emission levels as the technology enabled them to do so.

- ***Ambient-based standards.*** Here the focus is on the environmental impact. For example, standards could be set for air or water purity. Depending on the location and the number of polluters in that area, a given standard would be achieved with different levels of discharge. If the object is a cleaner environment, then this approach is more efficient than technology-based standards.

- ***Social-impact standards.*** Here the focus is on the effect on people. Thus tougher standards would be imposed in densely populated areas. Whether this approach is more efficient than that of ambient-based standards depends on the approach to sustainability. If the objective is to achieve social efficiency, then human-impact standards are preferable. If the objective is to protect the environment for its own sake (a 'deeper green' approach), then ambient standards would be preferable.

Definitions

Command-and-control (CAC) systems The use of laws or regulations backed up by inspections and penalties (such as fines) for non-compliance.

Technology-based standards Pollution control that requires firms' emissions to reflect the levels that could be achieved from using the best available pollution control technology.

Ambient-based standards Pollution control that requires firms to meet minimum standards for the environment (e.g. air or water quality).

Social-impact standards Pollution control that focuses on the effects on people (e.g. on health or happiness).

---

[6]See R. K. Turner, D. Pearce and I. Bateman, *Environmental Economics* (Harvester Wheatsheaf, 1994), p. 198.

Assessing CAC systems. Given the uncertainty over the environmental impacts of pollutants, especially over the longer term, it is often better to play safe and set tough emissions or ambient standards. These could always be relaxed at a later stage if the effects turn out not to be so damaging, but it might be too late to reverse damage if the effects turn out to be more serious. Taxes may be a more sophisticated means of reaching a socially efficient output, but CAC methods are usually more straightforward to devise, easier to understand by firms and easier to implement.

Where command-and-control systems are weak is that they fail to offer business any incentive to do better than the legally specified level. By contrast, with a pollution tax, the lower the pollution level, the less tax there will be to pay. There is thus a continuing incentive for businesses progressively to cut pollution levels and introduce cleaner technology.

Voluntary agreements

Rather than imposing laws and regulations, the government can seek to enter into voluntary agreements (VAs) with firms for them to cut pollution. Such agreements may involve a formal contract, and hence be legally binding, or they may be looser commitments by firms. VAs will be helped if (a) companies believe that this will improve their image with customers and hence improve sales; (b) there is an underlying threat by the government of introducing laws and regulations should VAs fail

Firms often prefer VAs to regulations, because they can negotiate such agreements to suit their own particular circumstances and build them into their planning. The result is that the firms may be able to meet environmental objectives at a lower cost. This clearly helps their competitive position.

The effectiveness of VAs depends on how tightly specified the agreements are and how easy they are for government inspectors to monitor. It also depends on there being genuine goodwill from firms. Without it, they may try to draw up agreements in a way that allows them to cut emissions by less than the level originally intended by the government.

Education

People's attitudes are very important in determining the environmental consequences of their actions. Fortunately for the environment, people are not always out to simply maximise their own self-interest. If they were, then why would they buy more expensive 'green' products, such as environmentally friendly detergents? The answer is that many people like to do their bit, however small, towards protecting the environment. There is evidence that attitudes have changed markedly over the past few years.

This is where education can come in. If children, and adults for that matter, were made more aware of environmental issues and the consequences of their actions, then people's consumption habits could change and more pressure would be put on firms to improve their 'green' credentials'.

Tradable permits (a CAC and market based system)

A policy measure that has grown in popularity in recent years is that of **tradable permits**, also known as a 'cap-and-trade' system. This is a combination of command-and-control and market-based systems.

Capping pollution

Initially some criteria have to be set in order to determine which factories, power plants and installations will be covered by the scheme. Policy makers then have to set a limit or 'cap' on the total volume of pollution these organisations will be collectively allowed to produce before any financial penalties are incurred.

The biggest cap-and-trade system in the world is the European Union's Emissions Trading Scheme (EU ETS) – for more details see Box 22.2. It covers energy-intensive installations in four broad sectors that have emissions above certain threshold levels. The four sectors are energy (electricity, oil, coal), ferrous metals (iron, steel), minerals (cement, glass, ceramics) and wood pulp (paper and card). In 2013, the EU set a total cap on the aggregate CO_2 emissions produced by organisations in these sectors of 2 084 301 856 tonnes. The cap decreases by 38,264,246 tonnes (1.74% of the average total quantity of allowances issued annually between 2008 and 2012) per year until 2020.

Once an aggregate cap has been set, pollution permits, sometimes called allowances, are either issued or sold to the firms. Each allowance held by a firm gives it the right to produce a given volume of pollution. The maximum allowance value of all the permits issued by the authorities in a given year should be equal to the size of the aggregate cap set on total pollution.

The number of permits allocated to an individual plant, factory or installation is often based on its current level of pollution. The number of allowances awarded in subsequent years of the scheme is then calculated by requiring all firms to reduce their pollution levels by the same percentage. This approach is known as **grandfathering**. The major criticism of this method is that it seems to be unfair on those firms that have already invested in cleaner technology. Why should they be required to make the same

---

Definitions

Tradable permits Firms are issued or sold permits by the authorities that give them the right to produce a given level of pollution. Firms that do not have permits to match their pollution levels can purchase additional permits to cover the difference, while those that reduce their pollution levels can sell any surplus permits for a profit.

Grandfathering Where the number of emission permits allocated to a firm is based on its *current* levels of emission (e.g. permitted levels for all firms could be 80 per cent of their current emission levels).

reductions in the future as firms currently using older polluting technology?

All firms covered by the scheme must monitor and report the pollution level caused by their production activity. At the end of the year they must then submit enough allowances to the authorities to match the level of pollution they have caused. Each allowance can only be used once. If a firm fails to submit enough allowances then it is subject to heavy fines.

Trading under a cap-and-trade system

So far only the 'cap' part of the 'cap-and-trade' system has been explained. The 'trade' part of the scheme refers to the ability of firms to buy and sell allowances in a secondary market once they have been allocated by the authorities. However, in what circumstances would a firm wish either to buy or to sell an allowance?

Take the example of an organisation that estimates it will not have enough permits at the end of the year to match its forecast level of pollution. It has two options. Firstly, it could invest in new technology that reduces the level of pollution created by its production process. Alternatively it could leave its production process unchanged and purchase extra permits. Obviously its final decision will depend on the relative cost of introducing more energy-efficient technology versus the price of purchasing any additional permits.

In order to buy allowances in the secondary market there must be other firms that have excess permits and hence are willing to sell. These may be firms which have recently made large investments in a more energy-efficient production process. If an organisation forecasts that it will have more permits than the number required, then it can sell the excess allowances in the secondary market.

The price that firms pay either to buy or to sell the allowances in the secondary market will depend on the levels of demand and supply. The levels of demand and supply will be heavily influenced by the initial number of permits allocated by the authorities, the state of the economy and developments in technology.

The principle of tradable permits can be used as the basis of international agreements on pollution reduction. Each country could be required to achieve a certain percentage reduction in a pollutant (e.g. CO_2 or SO_2), but any country exceeding its reduction could sell its right to these emissions to other (presumably richer) countries. A similar principle can be adopted for using natural resources. Thus fish quotas could be assigned to fishing boats or fleets or countries. Any parts of these quotas not used could then be sold.

Assessing the system of tradable permits

It is argued that one major advantage of the cap-and-trade system over most CAC methods is that it can reduce pollution at a much lower cost to society. This can be illustrated by using the following simple example.

Assume there are just two firms which each own one plant that pollutes the environment. Firm A and B's production processes currently result in 2000 tonnes of CO_2 being emitted into the atmosphere each year – 1000 tonnes by each firm. Decreasing emissions of CO_2 would cost firm A £100 per tonne, whereas it would cost firm B £200 per tonne.

Assume that the government wishes to reduce emissions from 2000 to 1600 tonnes. It could set an emissions cap on both firms of 800 tonnes of CO_2. Each would be given permits for that amount. Without the possibility of trading the permits, firm A would have to spend £20 000 to comply with the cap (200 tonnes × £100), while firm B would have to spend £40 000 (200 tonnes × £200). Thus the cost to society of reducing total emissions from 2000 to 1600 tonnes is £60 000.

With trading, however, the cost can be reduced below £60 000. If the two firms traded permits at a price somewhere between £100 and £200 per tonne, say £150, both could gain. Firm A would have an incentive to reduce its emissions to 600 tonnes, costing £40 000 (400 × £100). It could then sell the unused permits (200 tonnes) to firm B for £30 000 (200 × £150), which could then maintain emissions at 1000 tonnes. The net cost to firm A is now only £10 000 (£40 000 – £30 000), rather than the £20 000 from reducing its production to 800 without trade. The cost to Firm B is £30 000, rather than the £40 000 from reducing its production to 800.

Society will have achieved the same total reduction in pollution (i.e. from 2000 tonnes to 1600 tonnes) but at a much lower cost: i.e. £40 000 instead of £60 000. The lower increase in costs means that price increases in the sector for consumers will be lower than they would otherwise have been.

In theory the same outcome could be obtained in a CAC system if the policy makers knew the compliance costs of the different firms. In this case, an emission standard of 600 tonnes could be placed on firm A and a 1000 tonnes on firm B. However, this would require the authorities collecting enormous amounts of detailed information on plant-specific costs in order to calculate the appropriate emissions standard for each business. The cap-and-trade system allows policy makers to achieve the same outcome without the need to collect such large amounts of detailed information.

An interesting comparison can also be made between green taxes/charges and tradable permits. With the cap-and-trade scheme, the authorities determine the quantity of pollution, while the market determines the price. With a green tax, the authorities determine the price of pollution, while the market determines the quantity. In certain circumstances green taxes and tradable permits will produce the same outcome.

Environmental policy in the UK and EU

UK policy

In the UK, current policy is embodied in the 1990 Environmental Protection Act, the 1995 Environment Act (which set up the Environment Agency), the 2003 Waste and Emissions Trading Act and the 2005 Neighbourhoods and Environment Act. The Acts are an attempt to establish an integrated pollution control strategy. This has been the approach in other European countries, notably the Netherlands.

Following a number of energy White Papers and Reviews, the UK government introduced the Climate Change and Sustainable Energy Act and Climate Change Programme in 2006. This obliged government to report to Parliament on greenhouse gas emissions and measures taken to reduce these emissions.

In 2008 the Climate Change Act established legally binding targets on the UK to achieve reductions in greenhouse gases of at least 80 per cent by 2050 on 1990 levels, and a 26 per cent reduction in carbon dioxide emissions by 2020. A key policy to help the UK achieve these reductions is its involvement in the EU ETS. The Climate Change Levy (CCL) was also introduced on 1 April 2001 with the aim of reducing emissions. The CCL is a tax on the use of energy by businesses in the industrial, commercial, agricultural and public services sectors. It is added to the company's fuel bill for electricity, gas, liquefied petroleum and solid fuels. For 2015/16 the rate per kilowatt hour was set at 0.554 pence for electricity and 0.193 pence for gas. The rate per kilogram was set at 1.240 pence for liquefied petroleum and 1.240 pence for any other taxable commodity covered by the scheme. It is estimated that the CCL adds around 3 to 6 per cent to the energy bills of the affected companies.

The CCL has been criticised on a number of grounds. Some people argued that it would have been more effective to introduce an upstream tax on energy production rather than a downstream tax on energy consumption by business. The government in 2001 favoured the downstream approach as it argued that the charges could be targeted on business, leaving households exempt from the tax. However, some of the increase in costs is likely to have been passed on to consumers in the form of higher prices. The policy has also been criticised because the CCL rates do not reflect the carbon content of the fuels.

Reductions in the main rates of the CCL can be obtained by businesses if they enter into a voluntary Climate Change Agreement (CCA) with the Environment Agency. Approximately 9000 sites have entered into these agreements spread across 54 sectors. The agreements set targets for firms to increase energy efficiency and reduce CO_2 emissions. If the targets are achieved, the organisation can claim up to a 90 per cent reduction in the CCL for electricity and 65 per cent for their use of other energy sources.

Another important government policy to reduce emissions is the Renewals Obligation (RO). Introduced in 2002, it places an obligation on UK electricity suppliers to source a certain proportion of the electricity they provide to customers using renewable energy sources. The proportion is set by the government each year and increases annually. The Energy Company Obligation (ECO) was also introduced in January 2013 to reduce domestic energy consumption by placing obligations on large energy suppliers to fund energy improvements in people's homes – e.g. installing insulation. In 2013 it was estimated that the expense to the industry of meeting the RO added around £30 to the average household energy bill while the cost of meeting ECO added a further £47.

In the Autumn Statement of 2011 the government announced its plans to introduce a carbon price floor. This was prompted by concerns about the volatility and relatively low prices for EUAs in the EU ETS. It has been argued that a stable price of £30 per tonne of CO_2 emissions is required for strong enough incentives for investment in low-carbon electricity generation. The aim of the carbon price floor was to ensure that electricity power generators burning fossil fuels paid a minimum price of around £16 per tonne of CO_2 they emitted in 2013/14. The minimum price was set to increase by £2 per year so by 2020 it would be £30 per tonne.

The policy works by charging suppliers of coal and gas to the electricity market a 'top-up' tax if the price of EUAs falls below the carbon price floor. This 'top-up' tax is added to the existing Climate Change Levy (CCL) and is called the carbon price support (CPS) rate of the CCL. The rate is based on the carbon content of primary fuels.

The precise size of the tax is actually set two years in advance. It is calculated by comparing the two-year future traded price of EUAs with the carbon price floor. The tax is set as the difference between these two figures: i.e. the carbon price floor minus the future traded price of EUAs. In 2013 the tax was set at £4.94 per tonne of CO_2.

Given that the CPS rates are set in advance and the EUA price fluctuates it is not a strict price cap. For example, if the EUR price falls in the future then the actual carbon price paid will be below the minimum price set by the government.

Because the carbon price floor was only introduced in the UK there were concerns that it was harming the competitiveness of UK firms. As a result the Chancellor announced in the 2014 Budget that the carbon price floor would remain frozen at £18 for the foreseeable future rather than increasing at the rate of £2 per year.

The challenge for the government continues to be one of finding policies that reduce emissions while being mindful of their impact on energy prices and the competitiveness of UK firms.

EU policy

A major plank of EU environmental policy is its carbon trading scheme. The broader framework for environmental policy has typically been detailed in EU Environment Action

BOX 22.2 TRADING OUR WAY OUT OF CLIMATE CHANGE

The EU carbon trading system

The EU introduced a carbon Emissions Trading Scheme (EU ETS) in January 2005 as its principal policy to meet environmental targets set by the international treaty, the Kyoto Protocol (which entered into force in February 2005). Article 17 of this treaty supported the use of emissions trading and a similar scheme had already reduced emissions of both sulphur dioxide and nitrous oxide in the USA. The EU ETS created a market in carbon permits or allowances. Its ultimate objective is to give companies greater financial incentives to reduce their emissions of CO_2.

Phases I and II

The first phase of the scheme ran from January 2005 until December 2007. Around 12 000 industrial plants across 27 countries were allocated approximately 2.2 billion CO_2 permits, called Emission Unit Allowances (EUAs). Each EUA issued to a firm gives it the right to emit 1 tonne of carbon dioxide into the atmosphere. The factories covered by the scheme were collectively responsible for around 40 per cent of the EU's CO_2 emissions each year.

Companies that do not have enough EUAs to match their annual emissions can purchase additional EUAs to cover the difference, while those that reduce their emissions are able to sell any surplus EUAs for a profit. Companies are able to trade directly with each other or via brokers operating throughout Europe.

At the end of December 2007 all existing allowances became invalid and the second Trading Period began, to last until the end of 2012. Although this was run under the same general principles as Trading Period 1, it also allowed companies to use 'Joint Implementation' and 'Clean Development Mechanism' credits earned under the Kyoto Protocol's project-based mechanisms (see Case study H.22 in MyEconLab). In other words, companies could offset emissions in the EU against emission reductions they achieve in countries outside the EU.

Phase III

Phase III of the EU ETS came into operation on 1 January 2013. It built on the experience gained from operating Phases I and II of the system and included two significant changes.

Move to an EU-wide cap. The cap on total emissions in both Phases I and II of the system were set in a decentralised manner. Each member state had to develop a National Allocation Plan (NAP). The NAP set out the total cap on emissions for that country, the total quantity of EUAs that would be issued and how they would be assigned to each industrial plant or factory. Each NAP had to be approved by the European Commission before it could be implemented. The numerous NAPs have been replaced in Phase III of the EU ETS by a single EU-wide cap on the volume of emissions and on the total number of EUAs to be issued. The size of this EU-wide cap is to be reduced by 38 264 246 tonnes per year so that emissions in 2020 are 21 per cent lower than 2005.

Move to auctioning permits. In Phase I and II of the EU ETS the majority of EUAs were freely allocated to the plants and factories covered by the scheme. The grandfathering method (see page 395) was used to determine the number of EUAs each factory would receive: i.e. it was based on their current emissions. The European Commission allowed member states to auction up to a maximum of 5 per cent of the EUAs in Phase 1 and 10 per cent in Phase II. However this option was seldom chosen.

In Phase III a big increase is planned in the proportion of EUAs that are auctioned. Since 2013 most of the firms in the power sector have already had to purchase all of their allowances by auction. The average in other sectors is planned to increase from 20 per cent in 2013 to 70 per cent by 2020. Only firms in manufacturing and the power industry in certain member states will continue to be allocated the majority of their allowances at no charge.

It has also been recommended by the EU that half of the revenue generated from the auctions should be used to fund measures to reduce greenhouse gas emissions.

In December 2009, the EU also agreed to a '20/20/20' package to tackle climate change. This would involve cutting greenhouse gases by 20 per cent by 2020 compared with 1990 levels, raising the use of renewable energy sources to 20 per cent of total energy usage and cutting energy consumption by 20 per cent.

Much of the emissions reductions would be achieved by tighter caps under the ETS, with binding national targets for non-ETS sectors, such as agriculture, transport, buildings and services. However, over half of the reductions could be achieved by international carbon trading, where permits could be bought from abroad: e.g. under the Clean Development Mechanism.

Assessing the ETS

The introduction of the world's largest market-based policy to address climate change was welcomed by many economists and policy makers. However, others have raised concerns about both the operation of the scheme and its likely impact on overall emissions.

The size of the cap. What matters crucially for the impact of the scheme is the total number of permits issued by the authorities: i.e. the size of the overall cap. If the supply of the permits exceeds demand in the secondary market then the price will be relatively low and firms will lack the necessary incentives to invest in new energy-efficient technology.

Some people have argued that the number of EUAs issued in the past has been far too generous. One reason for this may have been the decentralised manner in which the EUAs were allocated through the NAPs. This gave some countries a strong incentive to game the system by setting an aggregate cap in its NAP that was greater than the volume of emissions actually being produced. By doing this, costs could be kept down for firms operating in that country, which would help to maintain its national economic competitiveness.

Another reason why the number of EUAs may have been too great is because of successful lobbying of governments by firms. In particular, they may have exaggerated claims about the potential negative impact of issuing fewer EUAs on their costs and future competitiveness.

This over-allocation of EUAs clearly seems to have been a problem in Phase I of the scheme. Emission levels across the EU actually rose by 1.9 per cent while the price of EUAs fell from a peak of €30 to just €0.02.

The scrutiny of NAPs by the EU became more rigorous in Phase II of the scheme and the cap on emissions was tightened by 7 per cent. However, there were still big variations between countries, and it appears that the Commission still had limited capacity to check the accuracy of each NAP. Phase III of the system seems to have addressed some of these issues with the removal of the NAPs and the introduction of a single EU-wide cap.

Move from free allocation of permits to auctions. Another major issue with Phases I and II of the scheme was that the majority of EUAs were freely allocated to plants and factories. It was argued by many policy makers that this was important because firms needed time to adjust gradually to a system where they would have to start paying for the pollution they generated. Some people were particularly concerned that selling the permits for a positive price would have large adverse effects on some firms' costs. This might make it increasingly difficult for them to compete with companies outside the EU. However, after the system was introduced, there were accusations that firms in the power sector had simply used the free allocation of permits to make 'windfall profits'.

The increasing use of auctioning in Phase III of the scheme has been adopted to address this issue. It is also assumed that, after eight years of experience with permits, firms will be better able to adapt to having to buy EUAs.

Other concerns included:

- The annual rate of decline in the number of EUAs issued being determined at the beginning of the trading period. Although this provides certainty for firms, it also reduced the ability of the scheme to respond to changing conditions.
- This was clearly illustrated during the global economic downturn. The reduction in industrial output resulted in much lower emissions and this put downward pressure on the price of EUAs. With EUAs trading at such a low price there was very little incentive for firms to reduce their pollution levels. This led to some debate about whether the cap should be tightened within Phase II to take account of this, though this did not in fact happen.
- Some countries appearing to have set tough targets in their NAPs, while others appearing to have 'gamed' the system. This raised issues about the equity of the scheme.
- A perceived lack of willingness to prosecute those infringing the rules.
- Credits earned through Credit Development Mechanisms and Joint Implementation coming from new investments that would have taken place anyway. These 'bogus' credits then enabled companies to maintain their emission levels.

Transport emissions. From 2012 the EU ETS scheme was also extended to aircraft emissions. Originally the scheme was supposed to cover emissions from all flights either arriving or departing from airports in the EU. Following a huge outcry from the aviation industry, the scheme was temporarily amended so that it would only include flights where both arrival and departure were at EU airports. This was known as 'Stop the Clock' and an initial cap was set at 86 million tonnes of CO_2.

Plans to bring shipping emissions within the scheme have been delayed. Shipping is a large and growing source of emissions. As a first step towards cutting these, the European Commission has proposed that owners of large ships using EU ports should report their verified emissions from 2018. Similarly, road transport, responsible for around 20 per cent of all emissions, remains outside the scheme.

Overall, it is still difficult to assess the impact of the ETS, even though we are now well inside Phase 3 of the scheme. Disaggregating the effect of emission allowances from the effects of other economic factors and policy changes is enormously complicated. However, there is general agreement that the systems and processes set in place do have the potential to be effective. The question remains, however, whether there is the political will to tighten the cap in order to reduce emissions further.

 Consider a situation where all firms are of identical size and each is allocated credits that allows it to produce 10 per cent less than its current emissions. How would this compare with a situation where permits are allocated to 90 per cent of firms only? Consider both efficiency and equity in your answer.

Programmes. There have been a series of such programmes since 1973. The Seventh Programme came into force in January 2014 and will run until 2020. The programme identifies three priority areas to which environmental policy should be directed: protect, conserve and enhance the EU's natural capital; boost resource-efficient, low-carbon growth; reduce threats to human health and well-being linked to pollution, chemical substances and the impacts of climate change.

Natural capital refers to the soil, productive land, seas/fresh water, clean air and biodiversity of the EU. In order to transform the EU into a resource-efficient, low-carbon economy, the programme identifies three key requirements: full delivery of the climate and energy package to achieve the 20-20-20 targets; significant improvements to the environmental performance of products; reductions

in the environmental impact of consumption such as cutting food waste. The third priority on human health and well-being is in response to a study by the World Health Organization which estimated that up to 20 per cent of all deaths in Europe could be caused by environmental factors.

The programme also includes four objectives that will help it to deliver on its three key priory areas. These 'enabling' objectives are: better implementation of existing legislation; improving the knowledge base and making it more available for EU citizens and policy makers; better investments for the environment based on market signals that reflect the true costs to the environment; full integration of environmental requirements into other policies. This will involve systematically assessing the environmental impact of any policy initiatives.

22.2 TRANSPORT POLICY

Traffic congestion is a problem faced by many countries, especially in large cities and at certain peak times. This problem has become more acute as our lives have become increasingly dominated by the motor car. Sitting in a traffic jam is both time-wasting and frustrating. It adds considerably to the costs and stress of modern living.

And it is not only the motorist that suffers. Congested streets make life less pleasant for the pedestrian, and increased traffic leads to increased accidents. What is more, the inexorable growth of traffic has led to significant problems of pollution. Traffic is noisy and car fumes are unpleasant and lead to substantial environmental damage.

Between 1960 and 2013 road traffic in Great Britain rose by 338 per cent, whereas the length of public roads rose by only 26 per cent (albeit some roads were widened). Most passenger and freight transport is by road. In 2013, just under 90 per cent of passenger kilometres and 68 per cent of domestic freight tonnage kilometres in Great Britain were by road, whereas rail accounted for a mere 9 per cent of passenger traffic and 9 per cent of freight tonnage. Of

road passenger kilometres, 92 per cent was by car in 2013, and, as Table 22.2 shows, this proportion has grown significantly up to 2010 before showing a slight fall in the last few years. Average weekly household expenditure on transport in 2013 was £70.40, equating to 14 per cent of total expenditure. Out of this total figure on transport, households spent £15.70 (22 per cent) on petrol, £5.70 (8 per cent) on repairs and services, £8.30 (12 per cent) on the purchase of new cars and vans, £12 (17 per cent) on the purchase of old cars and vans and £15.30 (22 per cent) on train/bus fares.

But should the government do anything about the problem? Is traffic congestion a price worth paying for the benefits we gain from using cars? Or are there things that can be done to ease the problem without greatly inconveniencing the traveller?

The existing system of allocating road space

The allocation of road space depends on both demand and supply. Demand is by individuals who base their decisions

Table 22.2	Passenger transport in Great Britain: percentage of passenger kilometres by mode of transport					
Year	Cars, vans and taxis	Motor cycles	Buses and coaches	Bicycles	Rail	Air
1960	49	4	28	4	14	0.3
1970	74	1	15	1	9	0.5
1980	79	2	11	1	7	0.6
1990	85	1	7	1	6	0.8
2000	85	1	6	1	6	1.0
2014	83	1	5	1	10	1.1

Source: *Transport Statistics Great Britain 2015* (Department for Transport, National Statistics 2015). Contains public-sector information licensed under the Open Government Licence (OGL) v1.0. http://www.nationalarchives.gov.uk/doc/open-government-licence

on largely private considerations. Supply, by contrast, is usually by the central government or local authorities. Let us examine each in turn.

Demand for road space (by car users)

The demand for road space can be seen largely as a *derived* demand. What people want is not the car journey for its own sake, but to get to their destination. The greater the benefit they gain at their destination, the greater the benefit they gain from using their car to get there.

The demand for road space, like the demand for other goods and services, has a number of determinants. If congestion is to be reduced, it is important to know how responsive demand is to a change in any of these: it is important to consider the various elasticities of demand.

Price. This is the *marginal cost* to the motorist of a journey. It includes petrol, oil, maintenance, depreciation and any toll charges.

The price elasticity of demand for motoring at current prices seems to be relatively low. There can thus be a substantial rise in the price of petrol and there will be only a modest fall in traffic.

Estimates of the short-run price elasticity of demand for road fuel in industrialised countries typically range from −0.15 to −0.28. Long-run elasticities are somewhat higher, but are still generally inelastic.[7] The low price

elasticity of demand suggests that any schemes to tackle traffic congestion that merely involve raising the costs of motoring will have only limited success.

In addition to the monetary costs, there are also the time costs of travel. Data from the Department for Transport indicated that in 2013 the average time spent travelling to work by car in Great Britain was 26 minutes. However, if the workplace was in central London this figure increased to 55 minutes. The opportunity cost of sitting in a car is the next best alternative activity you could have pursued during this time – relaxing, working, sleeping or even studying economics! Congestion by increasing the duration of the journey increases the opportunity cost.

Income. The demand for road space also depends on people's income. As incomes rise, so car ownership and hence car usage increase substantially. Demand is elastic with respect to income. Figure 22.2 shows the increase in car ownership in various countries.

Price of substitutes. If bus and train fares came down, people might switch from travelling by car. However, the cross-price elasticity of demand is likely to be relatively low. For many journeys people regard bus and trains as a poor substitute for travelling in their own car. Cars are often considered to be more comfortable and convenient.

The price of substitutes also includes the time taken to travel by these alternatives. The quicker a train journey is

---

[7] See *Environmentally Related Taxes in OECD Countries: Issues and Strategies* (OECD, 2001), pp. 99–103.

| Figure 22.2 | Increase in car ownership in various European countries |

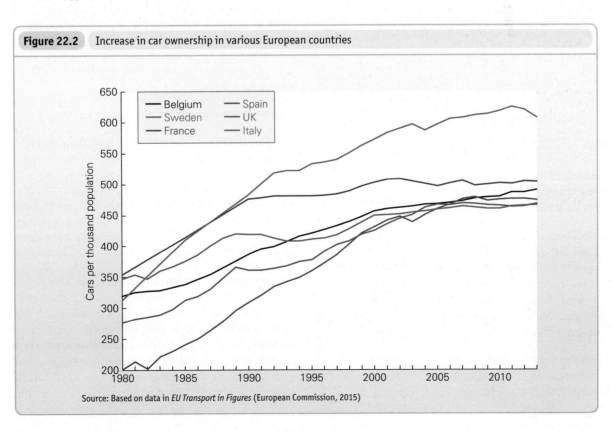

Source: Based on data in *EU Transport in Figures* (European Commission, 2015)

compared with a car journey, the lower will be its time cost to the traveller and thus more people will switch from car to rail. Data from the Department of Transport showed that on average in 2013 69 per cent of people travelled to work by car. However, if the workplace was in central London then this figure fell to 9 per cent. Most journeys instead, 69 per cent, were made by train.

Price of complements. Demand for road space will depend on the price of cars. The higher the price of cars, the fewer people will own cars and so there will not be so many on the road.

> ### Pause for thought
>
> *Go through each of the determinants we have identified so far and show how the respective elasticity of demand makes the problem of traffic congestion difficult to tackle.*

Demand will also depend on the price of complementary services, such as parking. A rise in car parking charges will reduce the demand for car journeys. But here again the cross-elasticity is likely to be relatively low. In most cases, the motorist will either pay the higher charge or park elsewhere, such as in side streets.

Tastes/utility. Another factor explaining the preference of many people for travelling by car is the pleasure they gain from driving compared with alternative modes of transport. Car ownership is regarded by many people as highly desirable, and once accustomed to travelling in their own car, most people are highly reluctant to give it up.

One important feature of the demand for road space is the very large fluctuations. There will be periods of peak demand, such as during the rush hour or at holiday weekends. At such times, roads can get very congested with drivers spending hours at a standstill. At other times, however, the same roads may be virtually empty.

Supply of road space

The supply of road space can be examined in two contexts: the short run and the long run.

The short run. In the short run, the supply of road space is constant. When there is no congestion, supply is more than enough to satisfy demand. There is spare road capacity. At times of congestion, however, there is pressure on this fixed supply. Maximum supply for any given road is reached at the point where there is the maximum flow of vehicles per minute along the road.

The long run. In the long run, the authorities can build new roads or improve existing ones. This will require an assessment of the costs and benefits of such schemes.

Identifying a socially efficient level of road usage (short run)

The existing system of *government* provision of roads and *private* ownership of cars is unlikely to lead to an optimum allocation of road space. So how do we set about identifying just what the social optimum is?

In the short run, the supply of road space is fixed. The question of the short-run optimum allocation of road space, therefore, is one of the optimum usage of existing road space. It is a question of *consumption* rather than supply. For this reason we must focus on the road user, rather than on road provision.

A socially efficient level of consumption occurs where the marginal social benefit of consumption equals its marginal social cost (*MSB = MSC*). So what are the marginal social benefits and costs of using a car?

KI 20
p 142

Marginal social benefit of road usage

Marginal social benefit equals marginal private benefit plus any externalities.

Marginal private benefit is the direct benefit to the car user and is reflected in the demand for car journeys, the determinants of which we examined above. External benefits are few. The one major exception occurs when drivers give lifts to other people.

Marginal social cost of road usage

Marginal social cost equals marginal private cost plus any externalities.

Marginal private costs to the motorist were identified when we looked at demand. They include the costs of petrol, wear and tear, and tolls. They also include the time costs of travel.

There may also be substantial external costs. These include the following.

KI 33
p 345

Congestion costs: time. When a person uses a car on a congested road, it will add to the congestion. This will therefore slow down the traffic even more and increase the journey time of *other* car users.

Congestion costs: monetary. Congestion increases fuel consumption, and the stopping and starting increases the costs of wear and tear. So when a motorist adds to congestion, there will be additional monetary costs imposed on other motorists.

Environmental costs. When motorists use a road, they reduce the quality of the environment for others. Cars emit fumes and create noise. This is bad enough for pedestrians and other car users, but can be particularly distressing for people living along the road. Driving can cause accidents, a problem that increases as drivers become more impatient as a result of delays. Also, as we saw in section 22.1, exhaust emissions contribute to global warming and acid rain. In

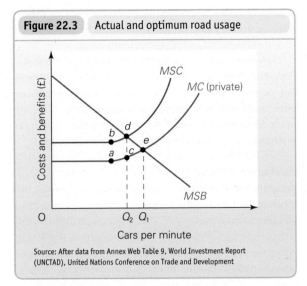

Figure 22.3 Actual and optimum road usage

Source: After data from Annex Web Table 9, World Investment Report (UNCTAD), United Nations Conference on Trade and Development

2012 road transport in the UK generated 108 million tonnes of CO_2 emissions. This was 19 per cent of total domestic emissions of 575 million tonnes.

The socially efficient level of road usage

KI 30 p 343 The optimum level of road use is where the marginal social benefit is equal to the marginal social cost. In Figure 22.3 costs and benefits are shown on the vertical axis and are measured in money terms. Thus any non-monetary costs or benefits (such as time costs) must be given a monetary value. The horizontal axis measures road usage in terms of cars per minute passing a specified point on the road.

For simplicity it is assumed that there are no external benefits from car use and that therefore marginal private and marginal social benefits are the same. The *MSB* curve is shown as downward sloping. The reason for this is that different road users put a different value on this particular journey. If the marginal (private) cost of making the journey were high, only those for whom the journey had a high marginal benefit would travel along the road. If the marginal cost of making the journey fell, more people would make the journey: people would choose to make the journey at the point at which the marginal cost of using their car had fallen to the level of their marginal benefit. Thus the greater the number of cars in a given time period, the lower the marginal benefit.

The marginal (private) cost curve (*MC*) is likely to be constant up to the level of traffic flow at which congestion begins to occur. This is shown as point *a* in Figure 22.3. Beyond this point, marginal cost is likely to rise as time costs increase and as fuel consumption rises.

The marginal *social* cost curve (*MSC*) is drawn above the marginal private cost curve. The vertical difference between the two represents the external costs. Up to point *b*, external costs are simply the environmental costs. It is assumed that these environmental external costs remain constant. Beyond point *b*, there are also external congestion costs,

since additional road users slow down the journey of *other* road users. These external costs get progressively greater as the level of traffic increases.

The actual level of traffic flow will be at Q_1, where marginal private costs and benefits are equal (point *e*). The socially efficient level of traffic flow, however, will be at the lower level of Q_2, where marginal social costs and benefits are equal (point *d*). In other words, the existing system of allocating road space is likely to lead to an excessive level of road usage.

Identifying a socially optimum level of road space (long run)

In the long run, the supply of road space is not fixed. The authorities must therefore assess what new road schemes (if any) to adopt. This will involve the use of some form of *cost–benefit analysis*.

The socially efficient level of construction will be where KI 30 p 343 the marginal social benefit from construction is equal to the marginal social cost. This means that schemes should be adopted as long as their marginal social benefit exceeds their marginal social cost. But how are these costs and benefits assessed in practice? Case study H.15 in MyEconLab examines the procedure used in the UK.

We now turn to look at different solutions to traffic congestion. These can be grouped into three broad types.

Solution 1: direct provision (supply-side solutions)

The road solution

One obvious solution to traffic congestion is to build more roads. At first sight this may seem an optimum strategy, provided the costs and benefits of road-building schemes are carefully assessed and only those schemes where the benefits exceed the costs are adopted.

However, there are serious problems with this approach.

The objective of equity. The first problem concerns that of KI 32 p 343 equity. After all, social efficiency is not the only possible economic objective. For example, when an urban motorway is built, those living beside it will suffer from noise and fumes. Motorway users gain, but the local residents lose. The question is whether this is fair.

The more the government tries to appeal to the car user by building more and better roads, the less will people use public transport, and thus the more will public transport

---

Definition

Cost–benefit analysis The identification, measurement and weighing up of the costs and benefits of a project in order to decide whether or not it should go ahead.

decline. Those without cars lose, and these tend to be from the most vulnerable groups – the poor, the elderly, children and the disabled.

Congestion may not be solved. Increasing the amount of road space may encourage more people to use cars. A good example is the London orbital motorway, the M25. In planning the motorway, not only did the government underestimate the general rate of traffic growth, but it also underestimated the direct effect it would have on encouraging people to use the motorway rather than some alternative route, or some alternative means of transport, or even not making the journey at all. It also underestimated the effect it would have on encouraging people to live further from their place of work and to commute along the motorway. The result is that there is now serious congestion on the motorway and many sections have been widened from the original dual three-lane model to dual four, five and in some parts, six lanes.

Thus new roads may simply generate extra traffic, with little overall effect on congestion.

The environmental impact of new roads. New roads lead to loss of agricultural land, the destruction of many natural habitats, noise, the splitting of communities and disruption to local residents. To the extent that they encourage a growth in traffic, they add to atmospheric pollution and a depletion of oil reserves.

Government or local authority provision of public transport

An alternative supply-side solution is to increase the provision of public transport. If, for example, a local authority ran a local bus service and decided to invest in additional buses, open up new routes, including park-and-ride, and operate a low-fare policy, these services might encourage people to switch from using their cars.

To be effective, this would have to be an attractive alternative. Many people would switch only if the buses were frequent, cheap, comfortable and reliable, and if there were enough routes to take people close to where they wanted to go.

A policy that has proved popular with many local authorities is to adopt park-and-ride schemes. Here the authority provides free out-of-town parking and cheap bus services from the car park to the town centre. These schemes are likely to be more effective when used in combination with charges for private cars entering the inner city.

Solution 2: regulation and legislation

An alternative strategy is to restrict car use by various forms of regulation and legislation.

Restricting car access

One approach involves reducing car access to areas that are subject to high levels of congestion. The following measures are widely used: bus and cycle lanes, no entry to side streets, 'high-occupancy vehicle lanes' (confined to cars with two or more occupants) and pedestrian-only areas.

However, there is a serious problem with these measures. They tend not to solve the problem of congestion, but merely to divert it. Bus lanes tend to make the car lanes more congested; no entry to side streets tends to make the main roads more congested; and pedestrian-only areas often make the roads round these areas more congested.

Parking restrictions

An alternative to restricting road access is to restrict parking. If cars are not allowed to park along congested streets, this will improve the traffic flow. Also, if parking is difficult, this will discourage people from using their cars to travel into city centres. Apart from being unpopular with people who want to park, there are some serious drawbacks with parking restrictions: The problems with this solution include:

- People may well 'park in orbit', driving round and round looking for a parking space, and in the meantime adding to congestion.
- People may park illegally. This may add to rather than reduce congestion, and may create a safety hazard.
- People may feel forced to park down side streets in residential areas, thereby causing a nuisance for local residents.

Solution 3: changing market signals

The solution favoured by many economists is to use the price mechanism. As we have seen, one of the causes of traffic congestion is that road users do not pay the full marginal social costs of using the roads. If they could be forced to do so, a social optimum usage of road space could be achieved.

In Figure 22.3 this would involve imposing a charge on motorists of $d - c$. By 'internalising' the congestion and environmental externalities in this way, traffic flow will be reduced to the social optimum of Q_2.

So how can these external costs be charged to the motorist? There are several possible ways.

Extending existing taxes

Three major types of tax are levied on the motorist: fuel tax, taxes on new cars and car licences. Could increasing these taxes lead to the optimum level of road use being achieved?

Increasing the rates of new car tax and car licences may have some effect on reducing the total level of car ownership, but will probably have little effect on car use. The problem is that these taxes do not increase the marginal cost of car use. They are fixed costs. Once you have paid these taxes, there is no extra to pay for each extra journey you make. They do not discourage you from using your car.

Unlike the other two, fuel taxes are a marginal cost of car use. The more you use your car, the more fuel you consume and therefore the more fuel tax you pay. They are also mildly related to the level of congestion, since fuel consumption tends to increase as congestion increases. Nevertheless, they are not ideal. The problem is that all motorists would pay an increase in fuel tax, even those travelling on uncongested roads. To have a significant effect on congestion, there would have to be a very large increase in fuel taxes and this would be unfair on those who are not causing congestion, especially those who have to travel long distances. There is also a political problem. Most motorists already regard fuel taxes as too high and would resent paying even higher rates.

Pause for thought

Would a tax on car tyres be a good way of restricting car usage?

Road pricing

Charging people for using roads is a direct means of achieving an efficient use of road space. The higher the congestion, the higher should be the charge.

Variable tolls. Tolls are used in many countries, and could be adapted to reflect marginal social costs. One obvious problem, however, is that even with a system of automatic tolls, there could be considerable tailbacks at peak times. Another problem is that it may simply encourage people to use minor roads into cities, thereby causing congestion on these roads. Cities have networks of streets and thus in most cases it is not difficult to avoid the tolls. Finally, if the tolls are charged on people entering a city, they will not affect local commuters. It is often these short-distance commuters within a city who are most likely to be able to find some alternative means of transport and so could make a substantial contribution to reducing congestion.

Area charges. One simple and practical means of charging people to use congested streets is the area charge. People would have to pay (normally by the day) for using their car in a city centre. Earlier versions of this scheme involved people having to purchase and display a ticket on their car, rather like a 'pay-and-display' parking system.

More recently, electronic versions have been developed. The London Congestion Charge is an example. Car drivers must pay £11.50 per day to enter the inner London area (or 'congestion zone') any time between 7.00 and 18.00, Monday to Friday. Payment can be made by various means, including post, Internet telephone, text message, mobile phone SMS and at various shops and petrol stations. Drivers can pay in advance, within 24 hours for an extra £2, or can register for auto-pay. In this case they are billed for all charges and receive a £1 per day discount.

Cars entering the congestion zone have their number plate recorded by camera and a computer check then leads to a fine of £130 being sent to those who have not paid.

The London congestion charging system has reduced traffic in the zone by nearly 20 per cent and has significantly increased the rate of traffic flow. The charge is not a marginal one, however, in the sense that it does not vary with the degree of congestion or the amount of time spent or distance travelled by a motorist within the zone. This is an intrinsic problem of area charges. Nevertheless, their simplicity makes the system easy to understand and relatively cheap to operate.

The London system does not address pollution directly. However, the original scheme did exempt electric (or petrol–electric hybrid) cars, and those fuelled by natural gas or LPG, from paying the charge under an 'alternative fuel discount'. The alternative fuel discount was subsequently replaced by a 'greener vehicle discount' exempting cars that emit 100 g/km of CO_2 or less. This has however led to a big increase in low emission diesel cars in London as they qualified for the discount. This prompted Transport for London to replace the 'greener vehicle discount' in April 2013 with the 'Ultra Low Emission Discount'. Vehicles will now have to either be purely electric or emit 75g/km of CO_2 or less to qualify. Transport for London believed that no diesel cars on the market at that time would meet this new lower emission rate.

There does appear to be a growing commitment to combine both congestion and emission external costs within the charge.

Variable electronic road pricing. The scheme most favoured by many economists and traffic planners is that of variable electronic road pricing. It is the scheme that can most directly relate the price that the motorist is charged to the specific level of marginal social cost. The greater the congestion, the greater the charge imposed on the motorist. Ideally, the charge would be equal to the marginal congestion cost plus any marginal environmental costs additional to those created on non-charged roads.

Various systems have been adopted in various parts of the world, or are under consideration. One involves devices in the road which record the number plates of cars as they pass; alternatively cars must be fitted with sensors. A charge is registered to that car on a central computer. The car owner then receives a bill at periodic intervals, in much the same way as a telephone bill. Several cities around the world are already operating such schemes, including Barcelona, Dallas, Orlando, Lisbon, Oklahoma City and Oslo.

Another system involves having a device installed in the car into which a 'smart card' (like a telephone or photocopying card) is inserted. The cards have to be purchased and contain a certain number of units. Beacons or overhead gantries automatically deduct units from the smart cards at times of congestion. If the card is empty, the number of the car is recorded and the driver fined. Such a system was introduced in 1997 on Stockholm's ring road, and in 1998 in Singapore (see Box 22.3).

BOX 22.3   ROAD PRICING IN SINGAPORE

Part of an integrated transport policy

Singapore has some 280 vehicles per kilometre of road (this compares with 271 in Hong Kong, 222 in Japan, 77 in the UK, 75 in Germany and 37 in the USA). The average car in Singapore is driven some 19 000 kilometres per year, but with low car ownership (see below), this translates into a relatively low figure for kilometres travelled by car per person. Part of the reason is that Singapore has an integrated transport policy. This includes the following

- A 153-kilometre-long mass rail transit (MRT) system with five main lines, 113 stations and subsidised fares. Trains are comfortable, clean and frequent. Stations are air-conditioned.
- A programme of building new estates near MRT stations.
- Cheap, frequent buses, serving all parts of the island.
- A modest expansion of expressways.

But it is in respect to road usage that the Singaporean authorities have been most innovative.

Area licences

The first innovation came in 1975 when the Area Licensing Scheme (ALS) was introduced. The city centre was made a restricted zone. Motorists who wished to enter this zone had to buy a ticket (an 'area licence') at any one of 33 entry points. Police were stationed at these entry points to check that cars had paid and displayed. This scheme was extended to the major expressways in 1995 with the introduction of the Road Pricing Scheme (RPS).

The Vehicle Quota System

In 1990 the government also introduced restrictions on the number of new cars, known as the Vehicle Quota System. In order to register and drive a new vehicle in Singapore, the owner has to purchase a Certificate of Entitlement (COE), which is valid for 10 years. The quantity of COEs issued by the government is limited and the number available each year is announced in April. The COEs are then sold to the public via monthly auctions which are operated in a similar manner to those on the eBay system. Buyers specify a maximum price and bids are automatically revised upwards until that maximum price is reached. The price of COEs increases until the quantity demanded is just equal to the number of certificates on offer.

Partly as a result of the quota system, there are only 114 private cars per 1000 population. As was shown in Figure 22.2, this is only a fraction of the figure for European countries.

A problem with the licences is that they are a once-and-for-all payment, which does not vary with the amount people use their car. In other words, their marginal cost (for additional miles driven) is zero. Many people feel that, having paid such a high price for their licence, they ought to use their car as much as possible in order to get value for money!

Electronic road pricing

With traffic congestion steadily worsening, it was recognised that something more had to be done. In 1998 a new Electronic Road Pricing Scheme (ERP) replaced the Area Licensing Scheme for restricted areas and the Road Pricing Scheme for expressways. This alternative not only saves on police labour costs, but also enables charge rates to be varied according to levels of congestion, times of the day, and locality. How does it work?

All vehicles in Singapore are fitted with an in-vehicle unit (IU). Every journey made requires the driver to insert a smart card into the IU. On specified roads, overhead gantries read the IU and deduct the appropriate charge from the card. If a car does not have sufficient funds on its smart card, the car's details are relayed to a control centre and a fine is imposed. The system has the benefit of operating on three-lane highways and does not require traffic to slow down.

The ERP system operates on roads subject to congestion and charges can vary every 5, 20 or 30 minutes according to predicted traffic flows. Rates are published in advance for a three-month period: e.g. from 2 February 2015 until 3 May 2015. A review of traffic conditions takes place every quarter and the results can lead to rates being adjusted in future periods. The system is thus very flexible to allow traffic to be kept at the desired level.

One potential problem with charging different rates at different times is that some drivers may substantially speed up or slow down as they approach the gantries to avoid paying higher ERP charges. To try and overcome this problem, the ERP rates are adjusted gradually for the first five minutes of a time slot with either new higher or lower charges.

The authorities in Singapore are now testing the use of a Global Navigation Satellite System. This would remove the need for the overhead gantries. It would also make it possible to alter the size of the charge with the length of the congested road the driver has travelled along.

The ERP system was expensive to set up, however. Cheaper schemes have been adopted elsewhere, such as Norway and parts of the USA. These operate by funnelling traffic into a single lane in order to register the car, but they have the disadvantage of slowing the traffic down.

One message is clear from the Singapore solution. Road pricing alone is not enough. Unless there are fast, comfortable and affordable public transport alternatives, the demand for cars will be highly price inelastic. People have to get to work!

 Explain how, by varying the charge debited from the smart card according to the time of day or level of congestion, a socially optimal level of road use can be achieved.

With both these types, the rate can easily be varied electronically according to the level of congestion (and pollution too). The rates could be in bands and the current bands displayed by the roadside and/or broadcast on local radio so that motorists would know what they were being charged.

The most sophisticated scheme, still under development, involves equipping all vehicles with a receiver. Their position is located by satellites, which then send this information to a dashboard unit that deducts charges according to location, distance travelled, time of day and type of vehicle. The charges can operate through either smart cards or central computerised billing. It is likely that such schemes would initially be confined to lorries.

Despite the enthusiasm for such schemes amongst economists, there are nevertheless various problems associated with them:

■ Estimates of the level of external costs are difficult to make.
■ Motorists will have to be informed in advance what the charges will be, so that they can plan the timing of their journeys.
■ There may be political resistance. Politicians may be reluctant to introduce road pricing for fear of losing popular support.
■ If demand is relatively inelastic, the charges might have to be very high to have a significant effect on congestion.
■ The costs of installing road-pricing equipment could be very high.
■ If road pricing was introduced only in certain areas, shoppers and businesses would tend to move to areas without the charge.
■ A new industry in electronic evasion may spring up!

Subsidising alternative means of transport

An alternative to charging for the use of cars is to subsidise the price of alternatives, such as buses and trains. But cheaper fares alone may not be enough. The government may also have to invest directly in or subsidise an *improved* public transport service: more frequent services, more routes, more comfortable buses and trains.

Subsidising public transport need not be seen as an alternative to road pricing: it can be seen as complementary. If road pricing is to persuade people not to travel by car, the alternatives must be attractive. Unless public transport can be made to be seen by the traveller as a close substitute for cars, the elasticity of demand for car use is likely to remain low. This problem is recognised by the UK government, which encourages local authorities to use various forms of road pricing and charges on businesses for employee car parking spaces on condition that the revenues generated are ploughed back into improved public transport. All local authorities have to produce five-year Local Transport Plans covering all forms of transport. These include targets for traffic reduction and increases in public transport.

Subsidising public transport can also be justified on grounds of equity. It benefits poorer members of society who cannot afford to travel by car.

It is unlikely that any one policy can provide the complete solution. Certain policies or combinations of policies are better suited to some situations than others. It is important for governments to learn from experiences both within their own country and in others, in order to find the optimum solution to each specific problem.

22.3 PRIVATISATION AND REGULATION

One solution to market failure, advocated by some on the political left, is nationalisation. If industries are not being run in the public interest by the private sector, then bring them into public ownership. This way, so the argument goes, the market failures can be corrected. Problems of monopoly power, externalities, inequality, etc. can be dealt with directly if these industries are run with the public interest, rather than private gain, at heart.

In the late 1940s and early 1950s the Labour government of the time nationalised many of the key transport, communications and power industries, such as the railways, freight transport, airlines, coal, gas, electricity and steel.

However, by the mid-1970s the performance of the nationalised industries was being increasingly questioned. A change of policy was introduced in the early 1980s, when successive Conservative governments engaged in an extensive programme of 'privatisation', returning virtually all of the *nationalised industries* to the private sector. These included telecommunications, gas, water, steel, electricity and the railways. By 1997, the year the Conservatives left office, with the exception of the rail industry in Northern Ireland and the water industry in Northern Ireland and Scotland, the only nationalised industry remaining in the UK was the Post Office (including post offices and mail). The Post Office and Royal Mail was split in 2012 and Royal Mail was privatised in October 2013. Post Office Ltd remains state owned but, under the 2011 Postal Services Act, there is the option for it to become a mutual organisation in the future.

Definition

Nationalised industries State-owned industries that produce goods or services that are sold in the market.

Other countries have followed similar programmes of privatisation in what has become a worldwide phenomenon. Privatisation has been seen as a means of revitalising ailing industries and as a golden opportunity to raise revenues to ease budgetary problems.

In 2008, however, many governments returned to the use of nationalisation, in order to 'rescue' banks which were at risk of going bankrupt. This was facilitated by the EU giving permission for Member States to support financial institutions, subject to conditions under EU state aid rules.

The arguments for and against privatisation

The following are the major arguments that have been used for and against privatisation.

Arguments for privatisation

Market forces. The first argument is that privatisation will expose these industries to market forces, from which will flow the benefits of greater efficiency, faster growth and greater responsiveness to the wishes of the consumer.

If privatisation involved splitting an industry into competing companies, this greater competition in the goods market may force the companies to drive down costs and reduce prices in order to stay in business.

Privatised companies do not have direct access to government finance. To finance investment they must now go to the market: they must issue shares or borrow from banks or other financial institutions. In doing so, they will be competing for funds with other companies, and thus must be seen as capable of using these funds profitably.

Market discipline will also be enforced by shareholders. Shareholders want a good return on their shares and will thus put pressure on the privatised company to perform well. If the company does not make sufficient profits, shareholders will sell their shares. The share price will fall, and the company will be in danger of being taken over. The market for corporate control (see page 188) thus provides incentives for firms to be efficient. There has been considerable takeover activity in the water and electricity industries with many acquisitions, often by non-UK companies.

Reduced government interference. In nationalised industries, managers may frequently be required to adjust their targets for political reasons. At one time they may have to keep prices low as part of a government drive against inflation. At another they may have to raise their prices substantially in order to raise extra revenue for the government and help finance tax cuts. Privatisation frees the company from these constraints and allows it to make more rational economic decisions and plan future investments with greater certainty.

Financing tax cuts. The privatisation issue of shares directly earns money for the government and thus reduces the amount it needs to borrow. Effectively, then, the government can use the proceeds of privatisation to finance tax cuts. There is a danger here, however, that in order to raise the maximum revenue the government will want to make the industries as potentially profitable as possible. This may involve selling them as monopolies. But this, of course, would probably be against the interests of the consumer.

Arguments against privatisation

Natural monopolies. Some industries have the characteristic of being a natural monopoly. Having just one company leads to much lower average costs in the industry than having a number of firms. In these situations it would not be in the interests of society to introduce competition when privatisation takes place. The market forces argument for privatisation largely breaks down if a public monopoly is simply replaced by a private monopoly, as in the case of the water companies, each of which has a monopoly in its own area. Critics of privatisation argue that at least a public-sector monopoly is not out to maximise profits and thereby exploit the consumer.

The public interest. Will the questions of externalities and social justice not be ignored after privatisation? Critics of privatisation argue that only the most glaring examples of externalities and injustice can be taken into account, given that the whole ethos of a private company is different from that of a nationalised one: private profit rather than public service is the goal. Externalities, they argue, are extremely widespread and need to be taken into account by the industry itself and not just by an occasionally intervening government. A railway or an underground line, for example, may considerably ease congestion on the roads, thus benefiting road as well as rail users. Other industries may cause substantial external costs. Nuclear power stations may produce nuclear waste that is costly to dispose of safely, and/or provides hazards for future generations. Coal-fired power stations may pollute the atmosphere and cause acid rain.

In assessing these arguments, a lot depends on the toughness of government legislation and the attitudes and powers of regulatory agencies after privatisation.

> ### Pause for thought
>
> *To what extent can the problems with privatisation be seen as arguments in favour of nationalisation?*

Regulation

Identifying the short-run optimum price and output

Privatised industries, if left free to operate in the market, may have large degrees of monopoly power; may create externalities; and may be unlikely to take into account questions of fairness. An answer to these problems is for the government or some independent agency to regulate their behaviour so that they produce at the socially optimum price and output. This has been the approach adopted for the major privatisations in the UK.

Regulation in practice

To some extent the behaviour of privatised industries may be governed by general monopoly and restrictive practice legislation. For example in the UK, privatised firms can be investigated by the CMA (Competition and Markets Authority) (see section 21.1). In addition to this, there is a separate regulatory office to oversee the structure and behaviour of each of the privatised utilities. These regulators are as follows: the Office for Gas and Electricity Markets (Ofgem), the Office of Communications (Ofcom), the Office of Rail Regulation (ORR) and the Office of Water Services (Ofwat).

As well as supervising the competitive behaviour of the privatised utility, they set terms under which the industries have to operate. For example, the ORR sets the terms under which rail companies have access to track and stations. The terms set by the regulator can be reviewed by negotiation between the regulator and the industry. If agreement cannot be reached, the CMA as an appeal court and its decision is binding.

The regulator for each industry also sets limits to the prices that certain parts of the industry can charge. These parts are those where there is little or no competition: for example, the charges made to electricity and gas retailers by National Grid, the owner of the electricity grid and major gas pipelines.

The price-setting formulae have largely been of the 'RPI minus X' variety (although other factors, including competition and excessive profits are also taken into account). What this means is that the industries can raise their prices by the rate of increase in the retail price index (i.e. by the rate of inflation) *minus* a certain percentage (X) to take account of expected increases in efficiency. Thus if the rate of inflation were 3 per cent, and if the regulator considered that the industry (or firm) could be expected to reduce its costs by 2 per cent ($X = 2\%$), then price rises would be capped at 1 per cent. The $RPI - X$ system is thus an example of **price-cap regulation**. The idea of this system of regulation is that it forces the industry to pass cost savings on to the consumer.

Pause for thought

If an industry regulator adopts an RPI −X formula for price regulation, is it desirable that the value of X should be adjusted as soon as cost conditions change?

Assessing the system of regulation in the UK

The system that has evolved in the UK has various advantages over that employed in the USA and elsewhere, where regulation often focuses on the level of *profits* (see Web Case H.17).

- It is a discretionary system, with the regulator able to judge individual examples of the behaviour of the industry on their own merits. The regulator has a detailed knowledge of the industry which would not be available to government ministers or other bodies such as the CMA. The regulator could thus be argued to be the best body to decide on whether the industry is acting in the public interest.
- The system is flexible, since it allows for the licence and price formula to be changed as circumstances change.
- The '*RPI* minus X' formula provides an incentive for the privatised firms to be as efficient as possible. If they can lower their costs by more than X, they will, in theory, be able to make larger profits and keep them. If, on the other hand, they do not succeed in reducing costs sufficiently, they will make a loss. There is thus a continuing pressure on them to cut costs. (In the US system, where *profits* rather than *prices* are regulated, there is little incentive to increase efficiency, since any cost reductions must be passed on to the consumer in lower prices, and do not, therefore, result in higher profits.)

There are, however, some inherent problems with the way in which regulation operates in the UK:

- The '*RPI* minus X' formula was designed to provide an incentive for the firms to cut costs. But if X is too low, the firm might make excessive profits. Frequently, regulators have underestimated the scope for cost reductions resulting from new technology and reorganisation, and have thus initially set X too low. As a result, instead of X remaining constant for a number of years, as intended, new higher values for X have been set after only one or two years. Alternatively, one-off price cuts have been ordered, as happened when the water companies were required by Ofwat to cut prices by an average of 10 per cent in 2000. In either case, the incentive for the industry to cut costs is reduced. What is the point of being more efficient if the regulator is merely going to insist on a higher value for X and thus take away the extra profits?
- The '*RPI minus X*' formula might reduce firms' profits and lead to reduced investment and innovation. Given the need for greater investment in power generation, Ofgem introduced a new system for controlling prices in the distribution part of the energy sector in 2013. This is called RIIO (Revenue − Incentives + Innovation + Outputs). This is a new performance-based model which aims to incentivise innovation and a reduction in future costs. It also allows the climate change agenda to be addressed as part of the price control process.
- Regulation is becoming increasingly complex. This makes it difficult for the industries to plan and may

---

Definition

Price-cap regulation Where the regulator puts a ceiling on the amount by which a firm can raise its price.

BOX 22.4 THE RIGHT TRACK TO REFORM?

Reorganising the railways in the UK

Few train routes across Europe are profitable and thus they have to be subsidised by governments. Such has been the strain placed upon public finances that European governments in recent years have been looking for ways of reforming their railways. The most radical approach has been adopted in the UK, which involved dividing up the rail system and privatising its various parts.

Privatisation of the rail system in the UK

The UK Conservative government in 1993 stated that the aim of rail privatisation was to 'improve the quality of rail services for the travelling public and for freight customers'. The 1993 Railways Act detailed the privatisation programme. The management of rail infrastructure, such as track, signalling and stations, was to be separated from the responsibility for running trains. There would be 25 passenger train operating companies (TOCs), each having a franchise lasting between 7–15 years. These companies would have few assets, being forced to rent track and lease stations from the infrastructure owner (Railtrack), and to lease trains and rolling stock from three new rolling-stock companies. There would be three freight companies, which would also pay Railtrack for the use of track and signalling. In practice, the 25 franchises were operated by just 11 companies (with one, National Express, having nine of the franchises).

Railtrack would be responsible for maintaining and improving the rail infrastructure, but rather than providing this itself, it would be required to purchase the necessary services from private contractors.

To oversee the new rail network, two new posts were created. The first was a rail franchising director, who would be responsible for specifying the length and cost of franchises, as well as for outlining passenger service requirements, including minimum train frequency, stations served and weekend provision. The second post created was that of the rail regulator, who would be responsible both for promoting competition and for protecting consumer interests, which might include specifying maximum permitted fares.

Although the individual train operators generally have a monopoly over a given route, many saw themselves directly competing with coaches and private cars. Several began replacing or refurbishing rolling stock and running additional services.

Developments in the UK since privatisation

Problems with the operation of the rail infrastructure. Following the Hatfield rail disaster in October 2000, when lives were lost as a result of a faulty rail, the UK rail network was reduced to a virtual state of crisis. Trains were unreliable; fares were rising by more than the rate of inflation; services were being reduced; and passenger complaints were increasing. There seemed to be few, if any, benefits from privatisation.

In fact, part of the industry was 'semi' renationalised, when Railtrack, the privatised track owner, was placed into receivership in 2002. It was replaced by Network Rail, which is a not-for-profit company, wholly dependent upon the UK Treasury for any shortfall in its funds. The shareholders of Railtrack were replaced by an oversight group of 100 members appointed from the TOCs, engineering firms and members of the public. Any profits are reinvested in the rail infrastructure. Network Rail has increasingly taken over control of infrastructure maintenance following concerns about the quality of the work carried out by private firms awarded contracts by Railtrack. It is now responsible for 20 000 miles of track and 40 000 bridges and tunnels. Its performance has also been subject to criticism. For example, the Office for Rail Regulation launched an investigation in December 2014 into the major disruption caused by the overrunning of engineering work in London.

Problems with the TOCs and the franchise system. Some private-sector TOCs performed so poorly that their franchise contracts had to be temporarily taken over by a state-owned operator. For example, in June 2003 the Strategic Rail Authority (SRA) decided to withdraw the operating licence of the French company Connex South Eastern. Not only were one in every five of its trains running late, its financial performance was also very poor even though it had received £58 million of public money. It had actually requested a further £200 million in state aid when the government terminated its contract. The franchise was temporarily taken over by the publicly owned South Eastern Trains from November 2003 until March 2006 before being returned to a private operator. In another case, National Express was awarded the Intercity East Coast franchise contract which ran from December 2007 until February 2015. However, the company defaulted on its contract in July 2009 and the service had to be taken back into public ownership. It was run by Directly Operated Railways, a subsidiary of the Department for Transport. After a number of delays the

lead to a growth of 'short-termism'. One of the claimed advantages of privatisation was to give greater independence to the industries from short-term government interference, and allow them to plan for the longer term. In practice, one type of interference may have been replaced by another.

- As regulation becomes more detailed and complex and as the regulator becomes more and more involved in the detailed running of the industry, so managers and regulators will become increasingly involved in a game of strategy: each trying to outwit the other. Informa-

tion will become distorted and time and energy will be wasted in playing this game of cat and mouse.

- There may also be the danger of *regulatory capture*. As regulators become more and more involved in their

Definition

Regulatory capture Where the regulator is persuaded to operate in the industry's interests rather than those of the consumer.

government finally announced in November 2014 that it had managed to award the East Coast Franchise back to a company in the private sector. It has been operated from 1 March 2015 by Inter City Railways, a consortium of Stagecoach and Virgin.

There have also been difficulties with the process of awarding franchises. In 2012 the InterCity West Coast franchise, which had been operated by Virgin since 1997, was put out to tender by the government. Four bidders were initially short-listed – Virgin, Abellio, First Group and SNCF/Keolis. The government announced on 15 August 2012 that the franchise contract of 13 years and 4 months had been awarded to First Group. Virgin immediately launched a legal challenge to the decision. However, before the case went to a judicial review the government announced that the award had been cancelled as technical mistakes had been discovered with the way the bids were evaluated by staff at the Department for Transport. These related to the way inflation and passenger numbers were taken into account. A short-term Direct Award was agreed with Virgin to continue running the franchise until April 2017. Three other franchise competitions were paused because of the problems that had been uncovered and the government launched a review into the whole bidding process. Some critics of the system have argued that stricter minimum standards and maximum fares should have been set at the beginning of the contracts.

Turning the railways around? The government took more direct control of the railways by winding up the Strategic Rail Authority in December 2006 and passing most of its functions, including the awarding of franchises, to the Department of Transport. At the same time, government spending in the mid-2000s was also much higher than it had been in the 1980s and 1990s. Total government support peaked at £7.51 billion in real terms in 2006/7 (at 2014/15 prices) before falling back to £4.8 billion in 2014/15. On 31 March 2014 the government announced a new five-year plan to invest £38 billion in the railways.

As new franchises came up for renewal, so some contracts were merged, so that by 2015, the 25 franchises had been reduced to 19. It was recognised that the benefits of economies of scale and co-ordinated services within a region exceeded any reduction in competition from having fewer franchises and fewer operators

The government's aim is to shift the balance of paying for the railway to the customer and the TOCs. Fare increases have reg-ularly been in excess of inflation. In 2013/14, revenue from fares was 61 per cent of rail industry income, up from 55.6 per cent in 2010/11.

At the same time, the government is also looking at ways in which to reduce the costs of running the railways. In May 2011, Sir Roy McNulty, in a report jointly commissioned by the Department for Transport and the Office of the Rail Regulator,[8] argued that the rail industry should be looking to reduce its unit costs, i.e. costs per passenger kilometre, by 30 per cent by 2018/19.

With improvements in the infrastructure, investment by the TOCs in new rolling stock and building more slack into timetables, rail punctuality improved and passenger numbers and freight tonnage increased. In the second quarter of 2015/16, 90.3 per cent of trains were recorded as arriving on time, compared with 79 per cent in 2002/3. Between 1994/95 and 2014/15, passenger kilometres increased from 28.8 billion to 62.9 billion – an increase of 115 per cent. Freight kilometre tonnage increased by some 75 per cent between 1994 and 2014.

Has the model been adopted elsewhere?

Other countries, such as Japan and Germany, have rejected the UK model in favour of maintaining a vertically integrated rail network, where rail infrastructure and train services are managed by the same company. It is suggested that a single management would be far more capable of successfully co-ordinating infrastructure and train service activities than two. Indeed, the 2011 McNulty Report recognises that the fragmentation of the UK rail structure and the lack of an effective supply chain are the principal reasons why there is an 'efficiency gap' in the costs of running the UK rail industry compared with other countries.

Nevertheless, some aspects of the UK model have been adopted under EC Directive 91/440, which allows European train operators access to the rail networks of other companies. This means that several companies (say, from different EU countries) can offer competing services on the same international route.

 Why are subsidies more likely to be needed for commuter and regional services than for medium-to-long-distance passenger services?

[8] *Realising the Potential of GB Rail, Report of the Rail Value for Money Study: Summary Report* (Crown Copyright, 2011).

industry and get to know the senior managers at a personal level, so they are increasingly likely to see the managers' points of view and become less and less tough. Commentators do not believe that this has happened yet: the regulators are generally independently minded. But it remains a potential danger.

■ Alternatively, regulators could be captured by government. Instead of being totally independent, there to serve the interests of the consumer, they might bend to pressures from the government to do things which might help the government win the next election.

One way in which the dangers of ineffective or over-intrusive regulation can be avoided is to replace regulation with competition wherever this is possible. Indeed, one of the major concerns of the regulators has been to do just this. (See Case study H.16 in MyEconLab for ways in which competition has been increased in the electricity industry.)

Increasing competition in the privatised industries

Where natural monopoly exists (see pages 182–3), competition is impossible in a free market. Of course, the industry *could* be broken up by the government, with firms prohibited from owning more than a certain percentage of the industry. But this would lead to higher costs of production. Firms would be operating further back up a downward-sloping long-run average cost curve.

But many parts of the privatised industries are not natural monopolies. Generally it is only the *grid* that is a natural monopoly. In the case of gas and water, it is the pipelines. It would be wasteful to duplicate these. In the case of electricity, it is the power lines: the national grid and the local power lines. In the case of the railways, it is the track.

Other parts of these industries, however, have generally been opened up to competition (with the exception of water). Thus there are now many producers and sellers of electricity and gas. This is possible because they are given access, by law, to the national and local electricity grids and gas pipelines.

To help the opening up of competition, regulators have sometimes restricted the behaviour of the established firms (like BT or British Gas), to prevent them using their dominance in the market as a barrier to entry of new firms. For example, an agreement was reached with British Gas in 1995 to limit its share of the industrial gas market to 40 per cent.

As competition has been introduced into these industries, so price-cap regulation has been progressively abandoned. For example, in 2006 Ofcom abandoned price control of BT and other phone companies over line rentals and phone charges. This was in response to the growth in competition from cable operators, mobile phones and free Internet calls from companies such as Skype via VoIP (voice internet protocol).

Even for the parts of industry where there is a natural monopoly, they could be made contestable monopolies. One way of doing this is by granting operators a licence for a specific period of time. This is known as *franchising*. This has been the approach used for the railways (see Box 22.4). Once a company has been granted a franchise, it has the monopoly of passenger rail services over specific routes. But the awarding of the franchise can be highly competitive, with rival companies putting in competitive bids, in terms of both price (or, in the case of railways, the level of government subsidy required) and the quality of service.

Another approach is to give all companies equal access to the relevant grid. For example, regional electricity companies have to charge the same price for using their local power lines to both rival companies and themselves.

But despite attempts to introduce competition into the privatised industries, they are still dominated by giant companies. Even if they are no longer strictly monopolies, they still have considerable market power and the scope for price leadership or other forms of oligopolistic collusion is great. Thus although regulation through the price formula has been progressively abandoned as elements of competition have been introduced, the regulators have retained an important role in preventing collusion and the abuse of monopoly power. The companies, however, do have the right of appeal.

Definition

Franchising Where a firm is granted the licence to operate a given part of an industry for a specified length of time.

SUMMARY

1a The market fails to achieve a socially efficient use of the environment because large parts of the environment are a common resource, because production or consumption often generates environmental externalities, because of ignorance of the environmental effects of our actions and because of a lack of concern for future generations. Environmental policy attempts to ensure that the full costs of production or consumption are paid for by those who produce and consume.

1b The environment is difficult to value, so it is difficult to estimate the costs of environmental pollution. This is a major problem in being able to devise an efficient environmental policy.

1c Environmental policy can be either market based or non-market based, or a mixture of the two. Market-based solutions include extending property rights and imposing charges for using the environment or taxes/subsidies per unit of output. The use of taxes, subsidies and charges is to correct market signals. Non-market-based solutions involve the use of regulations and controls over polluting activities.

1d The problem with using charges, taxes and subsidies is in identifying the appropriate rates, since these will vary according to the environmental impact.

1e Command-and-control systems, such as making certain practices illegal or putting limits on discharges, are a less sophisticated alternative to taxes or subsidies. However, they may be preferable when the environmental costs of certain actions are unknown and it is wise to play safe.

1f Tradable permits are a mix of command-and-control and market-based systems. Firms are either given or sold permits to emit a certain level of pollution and then these can be traded. A firm that can relatively cheaply reduce its pollution below its permitted level can sell excess permits to another firm which finds it more costly to do so. The system is an efficient and administratively cheap way of limiting pollution to a designated level. It can, however, lead to pollution being concentrated in certain areas and can reduce the pressure on firms to find cleaner methods of production.

2a The allocation of road space depends on demand and supply. Demand depends on the price to motorists of using their cars, incomes, the cost of alternative means of transport, the price of cars and complementary services (such as parking), and the comfort and convenience of car transport. The price and cross-price elasticities of demand for car usage tend to be low: many people are unwilling to switch to alternative modes of transport. The income elasticity, on the other hand, is high. The demand for cars and car usage grows rapidly as incomes grow.

2b With road space fixed (at least in the short term), allocation depends on the private decisions of motorists. The problem is that motorists create two types of external cost: pollution costs and congestion costs. Thus $MSC > MC$. Because of these externalities, the actual use of road space (where $MB = MC$) is likely to be greater than the optimum (where $MSB = MSC$).

2c There are various types of solution to traffic congestion. These include direct provision by the government or local authorities (of additional road space or better public transport); regulation and legislation (such as restricting car access – by the use of bus and cycle lanes, no entry to side streets and pedestrian-only areas – and various forms of parking restrictions); and changing market signals (by the use of taxes, by road pricing, and by subsidising alternative means of transport).

2d Problems associated with building additional roads include the decline of public transport, attracting additional traffic on to the roads and environmental costs.

2e The main problem with restricting car access is that it tends merely to divert congestion elsewhere. The main problem with parking restrictions is that they may actually increase congestion.

2f Increasing taxes is effective in reducing congestion only if it increases the *marginal* cost of motoring. Even when it does, as in the case of additional fuel tax, the additional cost is only indirectly related to congestion costs, since it applies to all motorists and not just those causing congestion.

2g Road pricing is the preferred solution of many economists. By the use of electronic devices, motorists can be charged whenever they add to congestion. This should encourage less essential road users to travel at off-peak times or to use alternative modes of transport, while those who gain a high utility from car transport can still use their cars, but at a price. Variable tolls and area charges are alternative forms of congestion pricing, but are generally less effective than the use of variable electronic road pricing.

2h If road pricing is to be effective, there must be attractive substitutes available. A comprehensive policy, therefore, should include subsidising efficient public transport. The revenues required for this could be obtained from road pricing.

3a From around 1983 the Conservative government in the UK embarked on a large programme of privatisation. Many other countries followed suit.

3b The economic arguments for privatisation include: greater competition, not only in the goods market but in the market for finance and for corporate control; reduced government interference; and raising revenue to finance tax cuts.

3c The economic arguments against privatisation are largely the market failure arguments that were used to justify nationalisation. In reply, the advocates of privatisation argue that these problems can be overcome through appropriate regulation and increasing the amount of competition.

3d Regulation in the UK has involved setting up regulatory offices for the major privatised utilities. These generally operate informally, using negotiation and bargaining to persuade the industries to behave in the public interest. They also set the terms under which the firms can operate (e.g. access rights to the respective grid).

3e As far as prices are concerned, the industries are required to abide by an 'RPI minus X' formula. This forces them to pass potential cost reductions on to the consumer. At the same time they are allowed to retain any additional profits gained from cost reductions greater than X. This provides them with an incentive to achieve even greater increases in efficiency.

3f Many parts of the privatised industries are not natural monopolies. In these parts, competition may be a more effective means of pursuing the public interest. Various attempts have been made to make the privatised industries more competitive, often at the instigation of the regulator. Nevertheless, considerable market power remains in the hands of many privatised firms, and thus the need for regulation will continue.

MyEconLab

This book can be supported by MyEconLab, which contains a range of additional resources, including an online homework and tutorial system designed to test and build your understanding.

You need both an access card and a course ID to access MyEconLab:

1. Is your lecturer using MyEconLab? Ask your lecturer for your course ID.

2. Has an access card been included with the book at a reduced cost? Check the inside back cover of the book.

3. If you have a course ID but no access card, go to: http://www.myeconlab.com/ to buy access to this interactive study programme.

REVIEW QUESTIONS

1 Why is it so difficult to value the environment? What are the implications of this for government policy on the environment?

2 Is it a good idea to use the revenues from green taxes to subsidise green alternatives (e.g. using petrol taxes for subsidising rail transport)?

3 Compare the relative merits of increased road fuel taxes, electronic road pricing and tolls as means of reducing urban traffic congestion. Why is the price inelasticity of demand for private car transport a problem here, whichever of the three policies is adopted? What could be done to increase the price elasticity of demand?

4 How would you set about measuring the external costs of road transport?

5 Consider the argument that whether an industry is in the public sector or private sector has far less bearing on its performance than the degree of competition it faces.

6 To what extent do the various goals of privatisation conflict?

7 Is it desirable after an industry has been privatised for profitable parts of the industry to cross-subsidise unprofitable parts if they are of public benefit (e.g. profitable railway lines cross-subsidising unprofitable ones)?

8 Should regulators of utilities that have been privatised into several separate companies permit (a) horizontal mergers (within the industry); (b) vertical mergers; (c) mergers with firms in other related industries (e.g. gas and electricity suppliers)?

ADDITIONAL PART H CASE STUDIES *IN THE ECONOMICS FOR BUSINESS* MyEconLab (www.pearsoned.co.uk/sloman)

H.1 **The police as a public service.** The extent to which policing can be classified as a public good.

H.2 **Should health care provision be left to the market?** An examination of the market failures that would occur if health care provision were left to the free market.

H.3 **Corporate social responsibility.** An examination of social responsibility as a goal of firms and its effect on business performance.

H.4 **Public choice theory.** This examines how economists have attempted to extend their analysis of markets to the field of political decision making.

H.5 **Cartels set in concrete, steel and cardboard.** This examines some of the best-known Europe-wide cartels of recent years.

H.6 **Taking your vitamins – at a price.** A case study of a global vitamins cartel.

H.7 **Productivity performance and the UK economy.** A detailed examination of how the UK's productivity compares with that in other countries.

H.8 **Technology and economic change.** How to get the benefits from technological advance.

H.9 **The economics of non-renewable resources.** An examination of how the price of non-renewable resources rises as stocks become depleted, and of how the current price reflects this.

H.10 **A deeper shade of green.** This looks at different perspectives on how we should treat the environment.

H.11 **Perverse subsidies.** An examination of the use of subsidies around the world that are harmful to the environment.

H.12 **Can the market provide adequate protection for the environment?** This explains why markets generally fail to take into account environmental externalities.

H.13 **Environmental auditing.** Are businesses becoming greener? A growing number of firms are subjecting themselves to an 'environmental audit' to judge just how 'green' they are.

H.14 **Restricting car access to Athens.** A case study that examines how the Greeks have attempted to reduce local atmospheric pollution from road traffic.

H.15 **Evaluating new road schemes.** The system used in the UK of assessing the costs and benefits of proposed new roads.

H.16 **Selling power to the people.** Attempts to introduce competition into the UK electricity industry.

H.17 **Regulation US-style.** This examines rate-of-return regulation: an alternative to price-cap regulation.

H.18 **Price-cap regulation in the UK.** How *RPI – X* regulation has applied to the various privatised industries.

H.19 **Competition on the buses.** An examination of the impact of the deregulation of UK bus services in the mid-1980s.

H.20 **A lift to profits?** The EC imposes a record fine on four companies operating a lift and escalator cartel.

H.21 **Are we all green now?** Changing attitudes to the environment.

H.22 **Selling the environment.** An examination of the Kyoto Protocol and successive attempts to reach international agreement on tackling climate change.

WEBSITES RELEVANT TO PART H

Numbers and sections refer to websites listed in the Web appendix and hotlinked from this text's website at *www.pearsoned.co. uk/sloman*

- For news articles relevant to Part H, see the *Economics News Articles* link from the text's website.

- For general news on market failures and government intervention, see websites in section A, and particularly A1–5, 18, 19, 24, 31. See also links to newspapers worldwide in A38–44.

- Sites I8, 11, 14, 18 contain links to competition and monopoly policy, regulation, transport, environmental economics and policy, and corporate social responsibility.

- For information on taxes and subsidies, see E18, 25, 30, 36; G13. For use of green taxes, see E2, 14, 30; G11; H5.

- For information on health and the economics of health care (Case study H.2 in MyEconLab: see above), see E8; H8, 9. See also links in I8, 11, 14, 18.

- For sites favouring the free market, see C17; E34. See also C18 for the development of ideas on the market and government intervention.

- For information on training, see E5; G14; H3.

- For the economics of the environment, see links in I8, 11, 14, 18. For policy on the environment and transport, see E2, 7, 11, 14, 29; G10, 11, 19. See also H11.

- UK and EU departments relevant to competition policy can be found at sites E4, 10; G7, 8.

- UK regulatory bodies can be found at sites E4, 11, 15, 16, 18, 19, 21, 22, 25, 29.

- For student resources relevant to Part H see sites C1–7, 9, 10, 19.

Business in the international environment

The FT Reports . . .

The Financial Times, 17 May 2015

Investment from emerging nations surges

By Shawn Donnan

Foreign direct investment by emerging economies surged by almost a third last year as companies in China and elsewhere sought new opportunities offshore as a respite from slowing growth at home, according to new UN figures to be released on Monday.

The data highlight one of the big developing trends in the global economy. Once a target for multinational companies eager to invest and reap the benefits of their rapid growth, emerging economies are becoming rivals to the US and Europe as a source of investment.

The flow of FDI from emerging economies hit a record $484bn in 2014, an increase of 30 per cent on the year before, according to new figures compiled by the Geneva-based UN Conference on Trade and Development, or Unctad.

But that surge was driven almost entirely by Asian investors, with Developing Asia accounting for $440bn in outbound investment last year and overtaking North America and Europe as the world's biggest regional source of foreign direct investment.

Behind that is a big shift in China in particular, said James Zhan, the head of investment for Unctad.

Together, mainland China and Hong Kong accounted for $266bn in outbound investment in 2014, putting China second only to the US in the national league tables for foreign direct investment. That status is a reflection of a remarkable shift in China's place in the world. A decade ago, mainland China saw 18 times more inbound than outbound investment, said Mr Zhan, but last year, for the first time, outbound investment overtook that coming into China.

Mr Zhan said the importance of China as a source of investment was only likely to grow in the years to come.

. . .Investments by multinational companies in developed economies such as the EU, US and Japan were flat last year at $792bn. While there had been 'modest increases' in investment by European and US companies, offshore bets by Japanese companies fell 16 per cent in 2014, according to the UN.

The composition of investments in 2014 was also telling. More than half of the investments made in 2014 by companies from developing economies were in equity and amounted to new projects or acquisitions. However, as much as 80 per cent of the FDI outflows from companies based in developed countries were in the form of reinvested earnings and the result of record cash reserves held by their foreign subsidiaries, according to the UN figures.

Globalization is the target of many critics today. The young see it as a malign force in regard to social agendas. The workers see it as a pernicious force in regard to their economic well-being. But both sets of fears, and resulting opposition to (economic) globalization, especially via trade and multinationals, are mistaken.

Jagdish Bhagwati, 'Why the critics of globalization are mistaken', *Handelsblatt*, August 2008, www.columbia.edu/~jb38/

With falling barriers to international trade, with improved communications and with an increasingly global financial system, so nations have found that their economies have become ever more intimately linked. Economic events in one part of the world, such as changes in interest rates or a downturn in economic growth, will have a myriad of knock-on effects for the international community at large – from the international investor, to the foreign exchange dealer, to the domestic policy maker, to the business which exports or imports, or which has subsidiaries abroad.

In Part I we explore the international environment and its impact on business. Chapter 23 considers the issue of *globalisation* and the rise and spread of multinational enterprises within the world economy. It not only looks at why certain businesses become multinational, but evaluates their impact upon host nations, within both the developed and the developing worlds.

In Chapter 24 we focus on *international trade*. We consider why trading is advantageous and why, nevertheless, certain countries feel the need to restrict trade and protect domestic industries by raising tariffs or dumping goods on foreign markets at prices below marginal cost (see the *Financial Times* article opposite).

Finally, in Chapter 25, we examine one of the most significant trends in international trade over the past 50 years – namely, the rise of the *trade bloc*. We outline the advantages and disadvantages of regional trading. We also look briefly at trading blocs in North America and South East Asia and the Pacific. Then, as an extended case study, we consider the position of the European Union and the effects of the creation of a single European market on both businesses and consumers.

Key terms

Globalisation
Foreign direct investment (FDI)
Multinational corporation
Transnationality index
Comparative advantage
The gains from trade
Terms of trade
Protectionism
Tariffs
Quotas
Infant and senile industries
World Trade Organization (WTO)
Trade bloc
Preferential trading
Free trade areas, customs unions and common markets
Trade creation and diversion
North America Free Trade Association (NAFTA)
Asian-Pacific Economic Cooperation forum (APEC)
European Union (EU)
Single European market

Globalisation and multinational business

Business issues covered in this chapter

- What is meant by globalisation and what is its impact on business?
- What is driving the process of globalisation?
- Does the world benefit from the process of the globalisation of business?
- What forms do multinational corporations take?
- What is the magnitude and pattern of global foreign direct investment?
- For what reasons do companies become multinational ones? Are there any disadvantages for companies of operating internationally?
- How can multinationals use their position to gain the best deal from the host state?
- What is the impact on developing countries of multinational investment?

23.1 GLOBALISATION: SETTING THE SCENE

The nature of global production continually evolves. In the past, many multinational companies (also known as transnational companies) located much of their manufacturing in developing countries. Now they increasingly locate service and 'knowledge-based' jobs there too. Such jobs range from telesales to research and development.

Some of these jobs require high levels of skills and training, once seen as the preserve of the rich economies and the source of their competitive advantage in international trade. However, countries such as India and China, as well as many others, produce a massive number of well-trained and well-educated engineers and IT specialists every year. Such workers are predictably cheap to employ compared to their US, European and Japanese counterparts, many of whom have lost their jobs or find their wages being driven down. But it is not all bad news for the developed economies. By outsourcing to develop-

ing countries, many companies have seen their costs fall and their profits rise. At the same time, consumers benefit from lower prices.

For developing economies, such as India and China, the benefits of this new wave of globalisation are substantial. Foreign companies invest in high-value-added, knowledge-rich production, most of which is subsequently exported. Economic growth is stimulated and wages rise. Increased consumption then spreads the benefits more widely throughout the economy. There are, however, costs. Many are left behind by the growth and inequalities deepen. There are also often significant environmental externalities as rapid growth leads to increased pollution and environmental degradation.

The exodus of jobs from developed to developing countries is a good example of the process of globalisation. In this chapter we are going to explore what *globalisation* is, how it is evolving, the impacts it is likely to have on different groups of people throughout the world and the motivations behind the increasing 'multinationalisation' of business.

Defining globalisation

Economically we are bound through trade, investment, production and finance. Politically we are bound through organisations such as the United Nations, the World Trade Organization (WTO), the International Monetary Fund (IMF) and the G20. Through such organisations we attempt to establish frameworks and rules to govern almost every aspect of our lives. Culturally we are subject to the same advertising and branding; we migrate; we go on holiday; we share ideas, fashions and music; we compete in global sporting events, such as the Olympics; and increasingly we communicate globally through the Internet.

Globalisation is, then, the *process* of developing these links. As Phillipe Legrain suggests, globalisation is 'shorthand for how our lives are becoming increasingly intertwined with those of distant people and places around the world – economically, politically and culturally'.[1]

Supporters and critics of globalisation alike tend to agree that globalisation is nothing new. There has always been a degree of economic, financial, political and cultural interdependence. But what makes globalisation an issue today is the speed at which these interdependences have grown. This has been partly the result of unprecedented technological change, particularly in respect to transport and communication, and partly the result of a political

---

[1]P. Legrain, *Open World: The Truth about Globalisation* (Abacus, 2003).

drive to remove barriers between countries and embrace foreign influences.

Business, caught within this process of globalisation, will invariably seek to take advantage of what it has to offer, which is essentially a borderless world or one that is increasingly so. A global economy enables a business to locate the different dimensions of its value chain wherever it might get the best deal to lower costs or improve quality or both. Globalisation encourages this process of relocation and the framing of business strategy within a global context.

What drives globalisation?

Within any global system, certain industries and markets are likely to be more prone to the forces of globalisation than others. This becomes apparent when you attempt to identify the conditions influencing the globalisation process. These globalisation drivers can be categorised in a number of ways. George Yip suggests that the globalisation potential of an industry – that is, its ability to set global strategy and compete in a global marketplace – can be analysed under four headings:

- market drivers;
- cost drivers;
- government drivers;
- competitive drivers.

These are shown in Table 23.1.

Market drivers. Market drivers focus on the extent to which markets throughout the world are becoming similar. The more similar consumers are in respect to income and taste,

---

Table 23.1	The drivers of globalisation

Market drivers
- Per capita income converging among industrialised nations
- Convergence of lifestyles and tastes
- Organisations beginning to behave as global customers
- Increasing travel creating global consumers
- Growth of global and regional channels
- Establishment of world brands
- Push to develop global advertising

Cost drivers
- Continuing push for economies of scale
- Accelerating technological innovation
- Advances in transportation
- Emergence of newly industrialised countries with productive capability and low labour costs

- Increasing cost of product development relative to market life

Government drivers
- Reduction of tariff barriers
- Reduction of non-tariff barriers
- Creation of blocs
- Decline in role of governments as producers and customers
- Privatisation in previously state-dominated economies
- Shift to open-market economies from closed communist systems in eastern Europe
- Increasing participation of China and India in the global economy

Competitive drivers
- Continuing increases in the level of world trade

- Increased ownership of corporations by foreign acquirers
- Rise of new competitors intent upon becoming global competitors
- Growth of global networks making countries interdependent in particular industries
- More companies becoming globally centred rather than nationally centred
- Increased formation of global strategic alliances

Other drivers
- Revolution in information and communication
- Globalisation of financial markets
- Improvements in business travel

Source: G. Yip, *Total Global Strategy* (Prentice Hall, 1995)

the more significant globalisation market drivers will become.

Cost drivers. Cost drivers present the business with the potential to reorganise its operations globally and reduce costs as a consequence. Global economies of scale, and transport and distribution issues, will be significant.

Government drivers. Governments often play a key role in driving the process of globalisation. The speed of globalisation is likely to be faster when governments openly welcome trade and inward investment.

Global political agreements, such as those made at the WTO covering world trade and related issues (see section 24.4), not only directly affect the operation of markets, but also help establish global rules and protocols.

Competition drivers. As competitiveness builds, whether in the domestic market or overseas, businesses will be forced to consider how to maintain their competitive position. This often involves embracing a global business strategy, which invariably contributes towards globalisation. Global business networks and cross-border strategic alliances are key reflections of this growing competitive global process.

What is clear is that globalisation is both shaped and driven by a wide variety of conditions. These conditions will vary from industry to industry, reflecting why certain industries are more global than others. Furthermore, these conditions will vary over time, so affecting the nature and magnitude of cross-border activities.

Globalisation: the good and the bad

Even though supporters and critics of globalisation are in agreement that globalisation is nothing new, and that it is primarily driven by technological change and shifting political attitudes, they are far from agreeing about the consequences of globalisation and whether these are beneficial or harmful.

The supporters

Supporters of globalisation argue that it has massive potential to benefit the entire global economy. With freer trade and greater competition, countries and businesses within them are encouraged to think, plan and act globally. Technology spreads faster; countries specialise in particular products and processes, and thereby exploit their core competitive advantages.

Both rich and poor, it is argued, benefit from such a process. Politically, globalisation brings us closer together. Political ties help stabilise relationships and offer the opportunity for countries to discuss their differences. However imperfect the current global political system might be, the alternative of independent nations is seen as potentially far worse. The globalisation of

culture is also seen as beneficial, as a world of experience is opened, whether in respect of our holiday destinations, or the food we eat, or the music we listen to or the movies we watch.

Supporters of globalisation recognise that not all countries benefit equally from globalisation: those that have wealth will, as always, possess more opportunity to benefit from the globalisation process, whether from lower prices, global political agreements or cultural experience. However, long term, supporters of globalisation see it as ultimately being for the benefit of all – rich and poor alike.

The critics

Critics of globalisation argue that it contributes to growing inequality and further impoverishes poor nations. As an economic philosophy, globalisation allows multinational corporations (MNCs), based largely in the USA, Europe and Japan, to exploit their dominant position in foreign markets. Without effective competition in these markets, such companies are able to pursue profit with few constraints.

By 'exploiting' low-wage labour, companies are able to compete more effectively on world markets. As competitive pressures intensify and companies seek to cut costs further, this can put downward pressure on such wages.

In political terms, critics of globalisation see the world being dominated by big business. Multinationals put pressure on their home governments to promote their interests in their dealings with other countries, thereby heightening the domination of rich countries over the poor.

Critics are no less damning of the cultural aspects of globalisation. They see the world dominated by multinational brands, Western fashion, music and TV. Rather than globalisation fostering a mix of cultural expression, critics suggest that cultural differences are being replaced by the dominant (Western) culture of the day.

The above views represent the extremes, and to a greater or lesser degree both have elements of truth within them. The impact of globalisation on different groups is not even, and never will be. However, to suggest that big business rules is also an exaggeration. Clearly big business is influential, but it is a question of degree. Influence will invariably fluctuate over time, between events, and between and within countries.

In recent years, at least until the global financial crisis of 2008/9, the momentum has been for barriers to come down. This has had profound effects on both multinational business and the peoples of the world.

In the following sections we consider why it is that businesses decide to go multinational, and evaluate what impact they have on their host countries. Before we do this we shall first offer a definition of multinational business and assess the importance of multinational investment within the global economy.

23.2 WHAT IS A MULTINATIONAL CORPORATION?

Despite their gigantic size and importance within the global economy, *multinational corporations* (MNCs) defy simple definition. At the most basic level, a MNC is a business that owns and controls foreign subsidiaries in more than one country. It is this ownership and control of productive assets in other countries which makes the MNC distinct from an enterprise that does business overseas simply by exporting goods or services.

To achieve control over foreign productive assets, MNCs engage in foreign direct investment (FDI) (rather than merely portfolio investment).[2] This may involve building a new subsidiary overseas or expanding an existing one, or acquiring an existing business operation through either merger or acquisition.

According to the 2015 World Investment Report the 100 largest non-financial MNCs had a combined turnover in 2014 of $9.2 trillion – 3.1 times greater than UK GDP. Table 23.2 shows how some of the largest MNCs have turnovers which exceed the national income of many smaller economies!

Sales by the foreign affiliates of MNCs accounted for $36.4 trillion in 2013 (47 per cent of global GDP), while their value added, a measure of their output, was estimated at $7.9 trillion (47 per cent of global GDP). Foreign affiliates employed 75.1 million people in 2014.

---

[2] Portfolio investment involves purchasing shares and other financial assets in overseas organisations but with little or no strategic and operational control over their investment decisions.

> **Definition**
>
> **Multinational corporations** Businesses that own and control foreign subsidiaries in more than one country.

Table 23.2	Comparison of the 15 largest non-financial MNCs (by turnover) and selected countries (by GDP): 2014			
MNC rank	**Country or company**	**Company headquarters**	**Sector**	**GDP ($bn) or turnover ($bn)**
	China			17 617.3
	USA			17 418.9
	UK			2 548.9
1	Royal Dutch Shell	UK	Oil and gas producers	476.9
2	Wal-Mart Stores	USA	General retailers	476.3
	Switzerland			472.8
3	Sinopec	China	Oil and gas producers	468.0
4	BP	UK	Oil and gas producers	400.7
	Hong Kong			397.5
5	Exxon Mobil	USA	Oil and gas producers	390.2
6	PetroChina	China	Oil and gas producers	373.0
7	Volkswagen	Germany	Automobiles and parts	270.6
	Denmark			249.5
8	Glencore Xstrata	UK	Mining	245.9
9	Total	France	Oil and gas producers	235.9
10	Toyota Motor	Japan	Automobiles and parts	234.1
	Ireland			226.8
11	Samsung Electronics	South Korea	Leisure goods	216.6
12	Chevron	USA	Oil and gas producers	211.8
	Angola			175.6
13	Phillips 66	USA	Oil and gas producers	171.6
14	Apple	USA	Technology hardware and equipment	170.9
15	E.On	Germany	Gas, water and multi-utilities	168.2
	New Zealand			158.9

Sources: Companies: FT Global 500 2014; Countries: *World Economic Outlook* database, IMF

In 2014, the global stock of foreign direct investment (FDI) was around $26 trillion, the equivalent of 34 per cent of global GDP. Of this, 65 per cent was located in developed economies (with 39 per cent in Europe), 32 per cent in developing economies and 3 per cent in transitional economies. The share of the global stock of FDI located in developed economies has declined in recent times. At the end of the 1990s, developed economies hosted 77 per cent of the global stock of FDI compared with just 22 per cent in developing economies and a mere 0.6 per cent in transitional economies.

Diversity among MNCs

There is an immense diversity among MNCs.

Size. Any list of the world's largest firms is dominated by multinationals. As we saw in Table 23.2, their turnovers can be enormous. And yet there are also thousands of very small, often specialist multinationals, which are a mere fraction of the size of the giants.

The nature of business. MNCs cover the entire spectrum of business activity, from manufacturing to extraction, agricultural production, chemicals, processing, service provision and finance. There is no 'typical' line of activity of a multinational.

Overseas business relative to total business. MNCs differ in respect of how extensive their overseas operations are relative to their total business. Nearly 30 per cent of Wal-Mart's sales come from overseas subsidiaries, while 90 per cent of Samsung's sales come from its foreign affiliates. Some smaller MNCs also have a large global presence. The Canadian firm Barrick Gold Corporation, for example, had one of the highest rankings on the United Nation's transnationality index in 2013, but had sales of less than 3 per cent of those achieved by Wal-Mart.

Production locations. Some MNCs are truly 'global', with production located in a wide variety of countries and regions. Other MNCs, by contrast, only locate in one other region, or in a very narrow range of countries.

There are, however, a number of potentially constraining factors on the location of multinational businesses. For example, businesses concerned with the extraction of raw materials will locate as nature dictates. Businesses that provide services will tend to locate in the rich markets of developed regions of the world economy, where the demand for services is high. Others locate according to the factor intensity of the stage of production. Thus, a labour-intensive stage might be located in a developing country where wage rates are relatively low, while another stage which requires a high level of automation might be located in an industrially advanced country.

KI 23
p 197
Ownership patterns. As businesses expand overseas, they are faced with a number of options. They can decide to go it

alone and create wholly owned subsidiaries. Alternatively, they might share ownership, and hence some of the risk, by establishing joint ventures. In such cases the MNC might have a majority or minority stake in the overseas enterprise. Increasingly, though, MNCs are looking at a third option: non-equity modes of operation. In this scenario, the MNC has no ownership stake in the partner firm overseas, but exerts control over operations through contractual arrangements such as franchising or strategic alliances. This non-equity mode of operation by MNCs begins to challenge our understanding and, hence, our definition of MNCs.

In certain countries, where MNC investment is regulated, many governments insist on owning or controlling a share in the enterprise. Whether this is a majority or minority stake varies from country to country. It also depends on the nature of the business and its perceived national importance.

There have been two significant developments in terms of ownership in recent times.

First, there has been a rise in state-owned MNCs. These are MNCs where the government has a significant interest in the parent enterprise and its foreign affiliates. Operationally this means that government has at least 10 per cent of the voting power or is the single largest shareholder. In 2013, it was estimated that there were 550 state-owned MNCs with assets in excess of $2 trillion.

Second, there has been a growth in sovereign wealth funds (SWFs). These are state-owned organisations investing internationally in a range of assets, such as shares, bonds and property. In 2014 there were over 100 SWFs with combined assets valued at $7 trillion (about one-tenth of the world's total assets under management). They have tended to focus their growth in the retail and commercial property sectors.

Organisational structure. We discussed (see Chapter 3) the variety of organisational forms that MNCs might adopt – from the model where the headquarters, or parent company, is dominant and the overseas subsidiary subservient, to that where international subsidiaries operate as self-standing organisations, bound together only in so far as they strive towards a set of global objectives.

KI 6
p 37

The above characteristics of MNCs reveal that they represent a wide and very diverse group of enterprises. Beyond sharing the common link of having production activities in more than one country, MNCs differ widely in the nature and forms of their overseas business, and in the relationship between the parent and its subsidiaries.

> ## Pause For thought
>
> *Given the diverse nature of multinational business, how useful is the definition given on page 421 for describing a multinational corporation?*

23.3 TRENDS IN MULTINATIONAL INVESTMENT

Successful multinational businesses are constantly adapting to the economic environment. In recent times they have been shrinking the size of their headquarters, removing layers of bureaucracy, and reorganising their global operations into smaller autonomous profit centres. Gone is the philosophy that big companies will inevitably do better than small ones. Many modern multinationals are organisations that combine the advantages of size (i.e. economies of scale) with the responsiveness and market knowledge of smaller firms.

The key for the modern multinational is flexibility, and to be at one and the same time both global and local.

The size of multinational investment

We can estimate the size of multinational investment by looking at figures for foreign direct investment (FDI). Figure 23.1 shows FDI inflows in billions of dollars. Global FDI inflows in 2014 were $1.23 trillion, equivalent to 1.6 per cent of global GDP. This was down from $1.56 trillion in 2011 (2.2 per cent of GDP) and the peak of $1.87 trillion in 2007 (3.3 per cent of GDP).

From the chart we also can observe relatively rapid rates of increase in FDI between 1998 and 2000 and again between 2004 and 2007. In 2000 global FDI flows were the equivalent of 4.1 per cent of global GDP and in 2007 they were the equivalent of 3.3 per cent of global GDP. Both periods saw a surge in cross-border merger and acquisition (M&A) activity.

In contrast, when the value of M&A activity contracted sharply following the financial crisis of 2008/9, global FDI inflows fell. Box 23.1 looks in more detail at M&A activity and at greenfield FDI investment, which involves a multinational company setting up a new subsidiary or expanding an existing one.

The significance of inward investment relative to total investment (or 'gross fixed capital formation' – GFCF) is shown in Figure 23.2. Increasing globalisation has meant that the trend in inward investment as a proportion of GFCF has been upwards for both developed and developing nations. However, for the majority of the period since the 1990s the proportion of inward FDI to total investment has been lower in developed than in developing and transition economies.

Historically developed economies have been the main destination for FDI. However, this pattern is changing, especially following the financial crisis of the late 2000s and the subsequent economic downturn. As Table 23.3

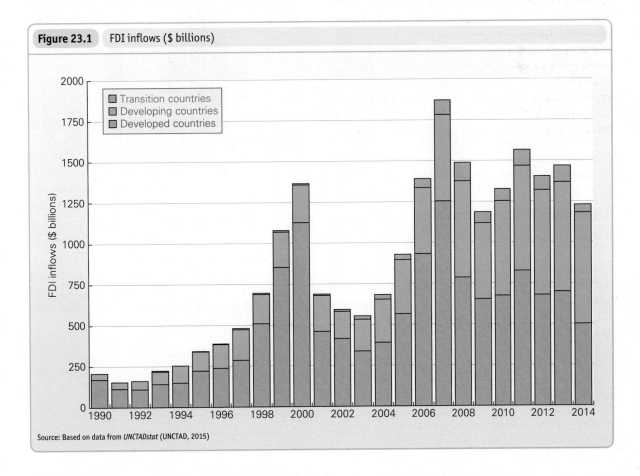

Figure 23.1 FDI inflows ($ billions)

Source: Based on data from *UNCTADstat* (UNCTAD, 2015)

BOX 23.1 M&As AND GREENFIELD FDI

Modes of FDI entry

There are two principal forms of foreign direct investment (FDI), known as 'modes of FDI entry'. The first is *greenfield investment*. This involves multinational companies investing in a new subsidiary overseas or expanding an existing one. The second mode of entry is through *cross-border mergers and acquisitions* (M&As).

Typically, the value of greenfield FDI is higher than investment through M&As. In 2014, for example, greenfield FDI was $695.6 billion, whereas cross-border M&As were worth $398.9 billion

The geography of M&As and greenfield FDI

We now analyse the geography of the two modes of FDI entry.

Cross-border M&As. Consider chart (a) which shows the value of cross-border M&As by the **destination** economy, i.e. the economy of the acquired company.

The host economy for the majority of cross-border M&As is a developed economy. However, the size of this majority has been falling. In the 1990s, developed countries were the destination of 87 per cent of cross-border M&As. In the 2000s this had fallen to 85 per cent and in the first half of the 2010s it had fallen to 76 per cent.

As well as the growing importance of developing and transition economies as a destination for cross-border M&As, especially since the late 2000s, investors from these economies are themselves becoming an important source of global M&A activity. The table shows the recent marked decline in the share of M&A activity originating in developed countries. In the three years 2012–14, around 43 per cent of M&A activity originated in developing and transition countries. This compares with under 20 per cent in the mid-2000s.

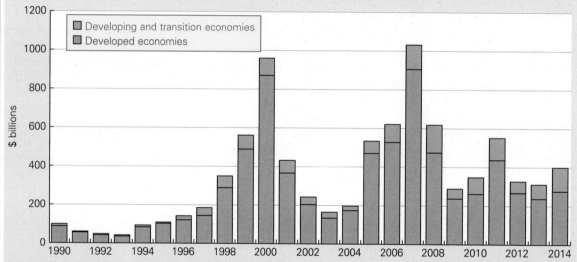

(a) Value of cross-border M&As by destination ($ billions)

Source: Based on data from *World Investment Report 2015*, Annex Web Table 9 (UNCTAD, 2015)

Percentage of FDI originating from developed economies

		2005	2006	2007	2008	2009	2010	2011	2012	2013	2014
M&As	Developed	83.4	80.7	84.0	77.6	66.5	64.8	78.0	56.0	57.2	57.3
	Europe	58.7	49.8	57.5	61.8	46.0	12.8	31.3	12.7	11.0	8.3
	USA	16.9	18.6	17.5	−5.0	8.4	24.5	24.9	22.1	18.8	21.8
Greenfield FDI	Developed	76.9	71.8	71.5	72.5	72.9	72.6	69.4	68.6	67.7	69.2
	Europe	37.4	39.2	46.5	42.2	43.4	44.0	38.2	38.5	37.7	37.3
	USA	22.9	17.9	15.0	18.0	17.0	17.2	17.5	16.8	17.6	18.1

Source: Based on data from *World Investment Report 2015*, Annex Tables 10 and 18 (UNCTAD)

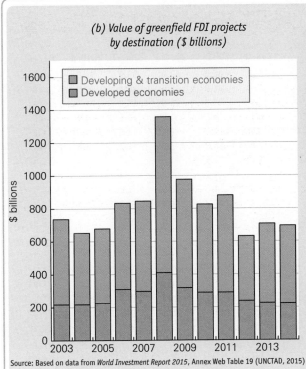

(b) Value of greenfield FDI projects by destination ($ billions)

Source: Based on data from *World Investment Report 2015*, Annex Web Table 19 (UNCTAD, 2015)

Greenfield FDI. Consider now chart (b) which shows the value of greenfield FDI projects by destination. From it, we observe that developing and transition economies have consistently attracted around two-thirds of global greenfield FDI investment since 2003.

Despite the growth of cross-border M&A activity in developing and transition economies, the value of greenfield FDI remains substantially higher in these economies. Over the period 2010–14, the value of greenfield FDI investment in developing and transition economies was 5.6 times greater than that from cross-border M&A activity, whereas in developed countries it was around 16 per cent less.

As the table shows, developing and transition economies during the 2010s have been the source of around 30 per cent of global greenfield FDI. When viewed alongside the growing funds these countries now contribute to global M&A activity, it is clear that developing and transition economies are now important participants in cross-border investment.

 What factors might explain the significance of developing and transition economies not only as a destination for FDI but also increasingly as a source of FDI?

Figure 23.2   FDI inflows (percentage of gross fixed capital formation)

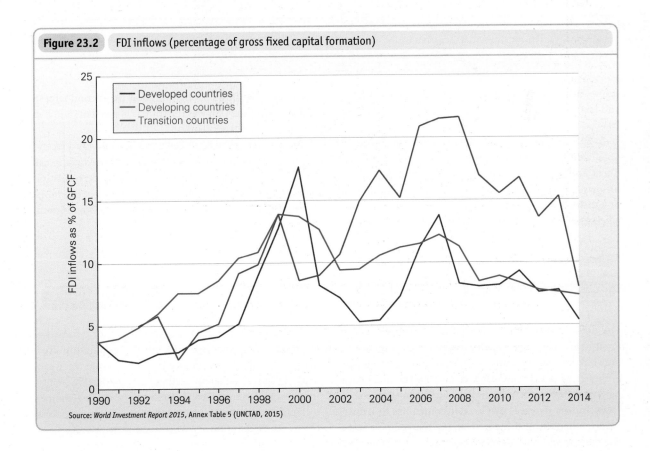

Source: *World Investment Report 2015*, Annex Table 5 (UNCTAD, 2015)

| Table 23.3 | Distribution of world FDI inflows, 1986–2014 (percentage of world FDI inflows) | | | | | | | | | |

Region	1986–7	1988–9	1990–2	1993–7	1998–00	2001–3	2004–7	2008–9	2010–1	2012–4
Developed countries	**82.9**	**82.8**	**74.5**	**61.6**	**78.4**	**66.2**	**63.0**	**53.9**	**51.8**	**45.5**
Europe	29.7	39.7	49.6	35.3	48.1	44.9	41.6	29.6	30.9	24.8
Eurozone	16.4	23.2	32.7	21.8	29.9	33.3	21.5	15.2	21.7	15.9
Australia	5.0	4.6	3.3	2.0	0.7	1.6	1.7	2.9	3.2	4.0
France	3.4	5.5	10.0	6.2	3.6	2.5	2.1	2.6	1.5	1.8
Germany	2.1	2.1	1.1	2.1	7.8	6.3	3.0	1.3	4.6	0.9
Ireland	0.3	0.1	0.7	0.5	1.6	3.5	−1.0	0.5	2.4	2.1
Japan	0.6	−0.4	1.1	0.2	0.8	1.2	0.5	1.3	−0.1	0.2
UK	10.1	13.5	11.3	5.9	9.3	4.0	12.3	7.0	3.6	4.5
USA	42.6	35.3	16.7	20.2	24.9	15.2	14.9	16.3	14.8	11.8
Developing countries	**17.1**	**17.2**	**25.1**	**37.1**	**20.9**	**31.8**	**32.9**	**39.2**	**42.3**	**48.9**
Africa	1.9	2.1	2.0	2.1	1.2	2.9	2.7	4.2	3.2	4.0
Caribbean	0.1	0.1	0.3	0.3	0.2	0.4	0.3	0.4	0.3	0.4
South America	2.1	3.0	4.2	6.7	6.1	4.8	4.3	5.6	7.7	9.6
Brazil	0.6	1.1	0.8	1.9	3.1	2.6	1.9	2.6	4.0	4.7
Asia (exc Japan)	10.5	10.1	15.8	24.8	11.6	19.3	22.7	26.7	28.7	31.9
China	2.1	1.8	3.8	11.4	4.4	8.5	6.6	7.6	8.3	9.2
Hong Kong	3.4	2.0	1.5	2.6	2.8	2.7	3.5	4.3	5.7	6.2
India	0.1	0.1	0.1	0.5	0.3	0.8	1.1	3.1	2.2	2.1
Singapore	2.0	1.8	2.4	3.0	1.3	2.2	2.7	1.4	3.6	4.7
Least developed economies	0.3	0.5	0.7	0.6	0.6	1.4	0.9	1.3	1.6	1.7
Transition economies	**0.0**	**0.0**	**0.4**	**1.3**	**0.7**	**2.0**	**4.2**	**6.9**	**5.9**	**5.6**
Russia				0.6	0.3	0.8	2.4	4.1	3.4	3.3

Note: Shaded areas represent years of declining global FDI
Source: Based on data from *UNCTADstat* (UNCTAD); http://unctadstat.unctad.org/EN/

shows, nearly 55 per cent of FDI flowed into developing and transition economies over the period from 2012 to 2014.

In 2014, the five largest recipients outside of the developed world (China (mainland), Hong Kong, Singapore, Brazil and India) received 32 per cent of all global FDI inflows and 54 per cent of all FDI inflows to developing or transition economies. Mainland China was the world's largest recipient of FDI in 2014, accounting for 10.5 per cent

of global FDI inflows. Hong Kong was the second largest (8.4 per cent); the USA was the third (7.5 per cent) and the UK the fourth (5.9 per cent).

As these figures suggest, FDI remains relatively concentrated, although less so than in the past. This geographical concentration means that Africa as a whole accounts for only around 4 per cent of global FDI and much of this flows to the resource-rich countries of Nigeria, Angola and South Africa.

23.4 WHY DO BUSINESSES GO MULTINATIONAL?

The global marketplace can provide massive opportunities for firms to expand. Once markets within the domestic economy have become saturated, and opportunities for growth diminish, dynamic firms may seek new markets and hence new opportunities by expanding production overseas.

Expansion overseas may enable companies to reduce costs, perhaps by utilising new supply sources, new ideas and skills. A vertically integrated multinational, for example, may be able to locate each part of the production process in the country where the relevant factor prices are lowest.

Businesses can look to expand in one of two ways: through either internal or external expansion (see Chapter 15). MNCs are no exception to this rule. They can expand overseas, either by creating a new production facility from scratch (such as Nissan in the north-east of England), or by merging with, or taking over, existing foreign producers (such as the acquisition of ASDA by Wal-Mart). They can also engage in an international strategic alliance (e.g. the joint venture in 2006 between Finland's Nokia and Japan's Sanyo to produce mobile phones for the North American market).

The decision whether to go multinational will depend on the nature of firms' business and their corporate strategy. MNCs are a diverse group of enterprises and their motives for going overseas will vary. We will examine two theories that have been used to explain the development of the MNC: *the product life cycle* and *the Eclectic Paradigm*.

The product life cycle and the multinational company

The product life cycle hypothesis was discussed at length (Chapter 17). However, it is worth reviewing its elements here in order to identify how an MNC, by altering the geographical production of a good, might extend its profitability.

A product's life cycle can be split into four phases: launch, growth, maturity and decline.

The launch phase. This will tend to see the new product produced in the economy where the product is developed. It will be exported to the rest of the world. At this stage of the product's life cycle, the novelty of the product and the monopoly position of the producer enable the business to charge high prices and make high profits.

The growth phase. As the market begins to grow, other producers will seek to copy or imitate the new product. Prices begin to fall. In order to maintain competitiveness, the business will look to reduce costs, and at this stage might consider shifting production overseas to lower-cost production centres.

Maturity. At the early stage of maturity, the business is still looking to sell its product in the markets of the developed economies. Thus it may still be happy to locate some of its plants in such economies. As the original market becomes increasingly saturated, however, the MNC will seek to expand into markets overseas which are at an earlier stage of development. Part of this expansion will be by the MNC simply exporting to these economies, but increasingly it will involve relocating its production there too.

Maturity and decline. By the time the original markets are fully mature and moving into decline, the only way to extend the product's life is to cut costs and sell the product in the markets of developing countries. The location of production may shift once again, this time to even lower-cost countries. By this stage, the country in which the product was developed will almost certainly be a net importer (if there is a market left for the product), but it may well be importing the product from a subsidiary of the same company that produced it within that country in the first place!

Thus the product life cycle model explains how firms might first export and then engage in FDI. It explains how firms transfer production to different locations to reduce costs and enable profits to be made from a product that could have become unprofitable if its production had continued from its original production base.

The theory was developed in the 1960s when MNC activity was less sophisticated than it is today. It can be useful in explaining horizontally and vertically integrated MNCs, but it cannot explain the more modern forms of MNC growth through strategic alliances. We thus turn to the second theory.

The Eclectic Paradigm

John Dunning[3] developed an organising framework, known as the Eclectic Paradigm. This helps to explain the pattern and growth of international production as well as identifying the gains to firms from being multinational. Dunning identifies three categories of gains:

- MNCs can exploit their core competencies in competing with companies in other countries. These are described by Dunning as 'ownership advantages': in other words, advantages deriving from *ownership-specific assets*.
- They can exploit *locational advantages* in host countries, such as the availability of key raw materials or high demand for the good.
- They may also derive *internalisation advantages*. These occur when the MNC gains from investing overseas rather than exporting to an overseas agent or licensing a foreign firm (i.e. using a market solution). In other words, the MNC gains from keeping control of the product within its organisation.

As firms and nations evolve the distribution of ownership, location and internalisation advantages between firms and nations change so that we observe ever-changing patterns of international production.

Ownership advantages

An MNC may be able to exploit its ownership of assets that reflect its core competencies and which give the business a specific advantage over its foreign rivals in their home markets. Such advantages might include the following:

> ### Definitions
>
> **Ownership-specific assets** Assets owned by the firm – such as technology, product differentiation and managerial skills – which reflect its core competencies.
>
> **Locational advantages** Those features of a host economy that MNCs believe will lower costs, improve quality and/or facilitate greater sales.
>
> **Internalisation advantages** Where the net benefits of extending the organisational structure of the MNC by setting up an overseas subsidiary are greater than those of arranging a contract with an external part.

---

[3] J. H. Dunning, *The Globalisation of Business* (Routledge, 1993).

The ownership of superior technology. Such ownership will not only enhance the productivity levels of the MNC, but probably also contribute to the production of superior-quality products.

Research and development capacity. MNCs are likely to invest heavily in R&D in an attempt to maintain their global competitiveness. The global scale of their operations allows them to spread the costs of this R&D over a large output (i.e. the R&D has a low average fixed cost). MNCs, therefore, are often world leaders in process innovation and product development.

Product differentiation. MNCs often combine innovation with successful product differentiation in international markets. They may invest heavily in advertising and often develop global brand names (e.g. Kellogg's, Ikea, Samsung).

Entrepreneurial and managerial skills. Managers in MNCs are often innovative in the way they do business and organise the value chain. With the arrival of Japanese multinationals in the UK, it became instantly apparent that Japanese managers conducted business in a very different way from their British counterparts. The most fundamental difference concerned working practices. Japanese MNCs quickly established themselves as among the most efficient and productive businesses in the UK (see section 18.7 on the flexible firm).

Pause for thought

Before reading on, can you think of the host country locational advantages that might be attractive to MNCs?

Locational advantages

MNCs will take advantage of the most appropriate locations to make their goods and services. Locational advantages are those features of a host economy that MNCs believe will lower costs, improve quality and/or facilitate greater sales relative to investing in their home country. In addition, by going overseas a firm must be effective at using its ownership-specific advantages over domestic firms, otherwise the locational advantage is muted. MNCs will consider a range of factors when comparing potential locations.

The availability of raw materials. Nations, like individuals, are not equally endowed with factors of production. Some nations are rich in labour, some in capital, some in raw materials. In other words, individual nations might have specific advantages over others. Because such factors of production are largely immobile, especially between nations, businesses respond by becoming multinational: that is, they locate where the necessary factors of production they require can be found. In the case of a business that wishes to extract raw materials, it has little choice but to do this.

The relative cost of inputs. Although it is possible that firms seek out lower-cost land and capital, perhaps because of host government subsidies, one of the main reasons firms want to move overseas is because labour is relatively cheaper. For example, a firm might locate an assembly plant in a developing country (i.e. a country with relatively low labour costs), if that plant uses large amounts of labour relative to the value added to the product at that stage. Thus foreign countries, with different cost conditions, are able to provide business with a more competitive environment within which to produce its products.

As an example, take the case of Nike, the American sportswear manufacturer. It looks to exploit cost differences between countries. Nike has organised itself globally so that it can respond rapidly to changing cost conditions in its international subsidiaries. Its product development operations are carried out in the USA, but all of its production operations are subcontracted out to over 40 overseas locations, mostly in South and South East Asia. If wage rates, and hence costs, rise in one host country, then production can be transferred to a more profitable subsidiary.

So long as Nike headquarters has adequate information regarding the cost conditions of its subsidiaries, management decision-making concerning the location of production simply follows the operation of market forces. In recent times, Nike has begun to consolidate its supply base, while attempting to maintain sufficient flexibility in what is a very dynamic sector. The consolidation is intended to allow Nike to develop more focused relationships with suppliers in what are termed 'focus factories' and so develop a more sustainable and effective sourcing base.

The quality of inputs. The location of multinational operations does not simply depend on factor prices: it also depends on factor quality. For example, a country might have a highly skilled or highly industrious workforce, and it is this, rather than simple wage rates, that attracts multinational investment. The issue here is still largely one of costs. Highly skilled workers might cost more to employ per hour, but if their productivity is higher, they might well cost less to employ per unit of output. It is also the case, however, that highly skilled workers might produce a better-quality product, and thus increase the firm's sales.

If a country has both lower-priced factors and high-quality factors, it will be very attractive to multinational investors. In recent years, the UK government has sought to attract multinational investment through having lower labour costs and more flexible employment conditions than its European rivals, while still having a relatively highly trained labour force compared with those in developing countries. However, as the relocation of many call-centre and IT jobs to developing countries illustrated, such advantages can be transitory.

Avoiding transport and tariff costs. Locating production in a foreign country can also reduce costs in other ways. For example, a business locating production overseas would be

KI 19
p 142

KI 5
p 36

able to reduce transport costs if those overseas plants served local or regional markets, or used local raw materials. One of the biggest cost advantages concerns the avoidance of tariffs (customs duties). If a country imposes tariffs on imports, then by locating *within* that country (i.e. behind the 'tariff wall') the MNC gains a competitive advantage over its rivals which are attempting to import their products from outside the country and are thus having to pay the tariff.

Government policy towards FDI. In order to attract FDI, a government might offer an MNC a whole range of financial and cost-reducing incentives, many of which help reduce the fixed (or 'sunk') costs of the investment, thereby reducing the investment's risk. The granting of favourable tax differentials and depreciation allowances, and the provision of premises, are all widely used government strategies to attract foreign business.

The general economic climate in host nations. FDI is more likely to occur if a nation has buoyant economic growth, large market size, high disposable income, an appropriate demographic mix, low inflation, low taxation, few restrictive regulations on business, a good transport network, an excellent education system, a significant research culture, etc. In highly competitive global markets, such factors may make the difference between success and failure.

The financial crisis of the late 2000s, the subsequent economic downturn and fiscal measures to reduce levels of government borrowing (see Chapter 30) affected developed economies, particularly in Europe, especially hard. This only helped to make developing economies even more attractive to foreign investors (see Table 23.3), including investors based in developing economies.

Internalisation advantages

As well as ownership and locational advantages, FDI can bring internalisation advantages. These are where the benefits of setting up an overseas subsidiary (thereby internalising its production in that country) are greater than the costs of arranging a contract with an external party (e.g. an overseas import agent or a firm in a host country which would make the product under licence).

FDI occurs where (in the language of sections 3.1 and 15.7, see page 36) the *transaction costs* of using the market in an overseas country are too high. Thus, the problems of finding the right partner to contract with, agreeing the terms of the contract, determining the price of the transaction and monitoring the contractual agreement are all compounded in foreign locations where different cultures and legal systems create uncertainties for firms considering expansion overseas. In order to minimise opportunistic behaviour in such situations (i.e. to reduce moral hazard), the firm will engage in FDI rather than exporting via an overseas import agent or licensing a domestic firm in the host nation.

Of course, many firms that start to venture into overseas markets will engage in exporting, rather than FDI, and use an import agent. However, it is also the case that many of the first multinational subsidiaries are sales and distribution outlets. The first plant set up by Hoover in the UK during the 1930s, for example, was a sales establishment through which it distributed its vacuum cleaners. Hoover found it more profitable to control sales than to use a third party.

Many firms go through a sequence from exporting to overseas investment. Toyota, for example, exported its cars to the UK using local motor vehicle retailers to distribute them prior to establishing a greenfield manufacturing site in Burnaston in Derbyshire in the early 1990s. Honda also set up a manufacturing plant in Swindon, Wiltshire, in 1992 after years of exporting cars to the UK.

The usefulness of the Eclectic Paradigm

The Eclectic Paradigm is thus a useful tool for explaining why MNCs arise. It explains how firms use combinations of ownership, locational and internalisation advantages to engage in various forms of FDI and strategic alliance.

Horizontally integrated multinationals. It can explain the development of **horizontally integrated multinationals**. Firms may initially manufacture in their home nation and export to a foreign location but then decide to switch out of exporting and establish a subsidiary producing the same product overseas.

Thus, FDI may be part of a sequence of expansion into new markets. The sequence may begin with exporting and then involve investment in one or more countries. Firms see that by combining their ownership-specific assets (e.g. technology and managerial skills) with locational advantages in the host nation (e.g. market size and government grants) their revenue streams will be greatest from internalising those assets and establishing an overseas subsidiary instead of exporting to it.

Alternatively, firms that engage in a cross-border horizontal merger or acquisition may do so to take advantage of the potential synergies in ownership-specific assets.

Vertically integrated multinationals. Likewise the eclectic paradigm can also explain **vertically integrated multinationals** with various stages of production taking place in different countries. We can follow similar reasoning to that presented in section 15.7. Consider two firms – one a manufacturer and the other a raw material producer – each with its own set of ownership-specific assets, but located in different countries. Further, these two firms are locked into a

---

> ### Definitions
>
> **Horizontally integrated multinational** A multinational that produces the same product in many different countries.
>
> **Vertically integrated multinational** A multinational that undertakes the various stages of production for a given product in different countries.

contract whereby they trade with each other on a frequent basis and have invested heavily in maintaining the relationship. If there is incomplete information or uncertainty about the other's activities and one firm feels that the other is not fulfilling its side of the bargain, then vertical FDI may take place. Here the driving force in the FDI process is the internalisation advantage achieved by vertical integration because the transaction costs of continuing the market relationship are too high.

Oil companies such as Shell and Exxon (Esso) are good examples of vertically integrated multinationals, undertaking in a global operation the extraction of crude oil, controlling its transportation, refining it and producing by-products, and controlling the retail sale of petrol and other oil products.

Conglomerate multinationals. Many of the big MNCs have become **conglomerate multinationals** and the Eclectic Paradigm helps to explain this organisational form. Conglomerates exist because firms have specialised managerial talent (i.e. ownership-specific advantages). Such managers can deal with establishing and running large, complex organisations. Further, there are internalisation advantages from establishing a conglomerate MNC because operating across a number of unrelated sectors and locations using market solutions would be prohibitively costly. Conglomerate expansion overseas allows the firm to spread its risks and gain other economies of scope (see page 184).

Unilever is a good example of a conglomerate multinational. It is a British–Dutch MNC employing over 170 000 people in 190 countries, producing various food, home care and personal care products. It has around 400 brands, including: Walls and Ben & Jerry's ice cream; Knorr soups; Bovril and Marmite; Bertorelli pasta sauces; Hellman's mayonnaise; Lipton and PG Tips tea; Flora, Blue Band and Rama margarines and spreads; Signal toothpaste; Domestos, Cif, Omo, Persil and Comfort; Timotei, TRESemmé and SunSilk shampoos; VO5, Toni and Guy, and Brylcreem hair products; Vaseline, Dove, Simple and Lux soaps; Pond's skin care products; Impulse, Lynx, Sure and Brut fragrances and antiperspirants.

Joint ventures. Finally, the Eclectic Paradigm offers insights into the establishment of joint ventures (see page 255). Evidence shows that new-product joint ventures, where risks and development costs are high, occur among the larger MNCs that have complementary ownership-specific assets.[4] Because the costs and risks are great, these investments are likely to take place in markets with high perceived growth. This would help to explain, for example, the decision by Sony and Panasonic in 2014 to join forces to produce displays for tablet devices.

Joint ventures also occur among new and smaller MNCs that have limited ownership-specific assets. These firms look for suitable partners that can complement their resources in countries with high market potential. In addition, all joint ventures require that there are limited contractual disadvantages in signing an agreement to share resources and develop products, indicating that the joint venture relationship is built on trust as well as sound strategic reasoning.

Problems facing multinationals

Although multinational corporations are successful in developing overseas subsidiaries, they also face a number of problems resulting from their geographical expansion:

■ *Language barriers.* The problem of working in different languages is a necessary barrier for the MNC to overcome. Clearly this problem varies according to the degree to which a common language is spoken. Further, if an MNC tends to employ expatriates, communication will be more difficult and local staff may feel alienated and thus be less productive.

■ *Selling and marketing in foreign markets.* Strategies that work at home might fail overseas, given wide social and cultural differences. Many US multinationals, such as McDonald's and Coca-Cola, are frequently accused of imposing American values in the design and promotion of their products, irrespective of the country and its culture. This can lead to resentment and hostility in the host country, which may ultimately backfire on the MNC.

■ *Attitudes of host governments.* Governments will often try to get the best possible deal for their country from multinationals. This could result in governments insisting on part ownership in the subsidiary (either by themselves or by domestic firms), or tight rules and regulations governing the MNC's behaviour, or harsh tax regimes. In response, the MNC can always threaten to locate elsewhere.

■ *Communication and coordination between subsidiaries.* Diseconomies of scale may result from an expanding global business. Lines of communication become longer and more complex. The greater the attempted level of control exerted by the parent company the greater are these problems likely to be: in other words, the more the parent company attempts to conduct business as though the subsidiaries were regional branches. Multinational organisational structures where international subsidiaries operate largely independently of the parent state will tend to minimise such problems.

[4] See S. Agarwal and S. N. Ramaswami, 'Choice of foreign market entry mode: impact of ownership, location and internalization factors', *Journal of International Business Studies*, vol. 23, no. 1 (1992), pp. 1–28. See also A. Madhok, 'Revisiting multinational firms' tolerance for joint ventures: a trust-based approach', *JIBS*, vol. 26, no. 1 (1995), pp. 117–37.

Definition

Conglomerate multinational A multinational that produces different products in different countries.

23.5 THE ADVANTAGES OF MNC INVESTMENT FOR THE HOST STATE

As mentioned previously, host governments are always on the lookout to attract foreign direct investment, and are prepared to put up considerable finance and make significant concessions to attract overseas business. So what benefits do MNCs bring to the economy? (See Box 23.2 for examples relating to the UK experience.)

Employment

If MNC investment is in new plants (as opposed to merely taking over an existing company), this will generate employment. Most countries attempt to entice MNCs to depressed regions where investment is low and unemployment is high. Often these will be regions where a major industry has closed (e.g. the coal mining regions of South Wales). The employment that MNCs create is both direct, in the form of people employed in the new production facility, and indirect, through the impact that the MNC has on the local economy. This might be the consequence of establishing a new supply network, or simply the result of the increase in local incomes and expenditure, and hence the stimulus to local business.

It is possible, however, that jobs created in one region of a country by a new MNC venture, with its superior technology and working practices, might cause a business to fold elsewhere, thus leading to increased unemployment in that region.

Pause for thought

Why might the size of these regional 'knock-on effects' of inward investment be difficult to estimate?

The balance of payments

A country's balance of payments (see Chapter 27) is likely to improve on a number of counts as a result of inward MNC investment. First, the investment will represent a direct flow of capital into the country. Second, and perhaps more important (especially in the long term), MNC investment is likely to result in both *import substitution* and export promotion. Import substitution will occur as products, previously purchased as imports, are now pro-

duced domestically. Export promotion will be enhanced as many multinationals use their new production facilities as export platforms. For example, many Japanese MNCs invest in the UK in order to gain access to the European Union.

The beneficial effect on the balance of payments, however, will be offset to the extent that profits earned from the investment are repatriated to the parent country, and to the extent that the exports of the MNC displace the exports of domestic producers.

Technology transfer

Technology transfer refers to the benefits gained by domestic producers from the technology imported by the MNC. Such benefits can occur in a number of ways. The most common is where domestic producers implement or replicate the production technology and working practices of the MNC. This is referred to as the 'demonstration effect' and has occurred widely in the UK as British businesses have attempted to emulate many of the practices brought into the country by Japanese multinationals.

In addition to replicating best practice, technology might also be transferred through the training of workers. When workers move jobs from the MNC to other firms in the industry, or to other industrial sectors, they take their newly acquired technical knowledge and skills with them.

Taxation

MNCs, like domestic producers, are required to pay tax and therefore contribute to public finances. Given the highly profitable nature of many MNCs, the level of tax revenue raised from this source could be highly significant (but see section 23.6 on ways in which MNCs can avoid tax).

Definitions

Import substitution The replacement of imports by domestically produced goods or services.

Technology transfer Where a host state benefits from the new technology that an MNC brings with its investment.

BOX 23.2 | LOCATION. LOCATION. LOCATION

The potential benefits and risks of inward FDI to the UK

Countries that have a large foreign multinational sector, such as the UK, are significantly affected by the actions of foreign companies – their product designs, the technologies they use, their management expertise and their decisions about where to locate and invest.

In 2014, global flows of FDI were $1.23 trillion. Inward FDI to the UK was $72.2 billion, equating to 5.9 per cent of global inward FDI. This is a lower share than in the late 2000s but higher than the average for 2010–14 (see chart (a)).

As chart (b) demonstrates, inward investment into the UK is dominated by other EU countries and the USA. At the end of 2014, US companies held £262.5 billion of investment in the UK, roughly 24.5 per cent of the UK's inward FDI stock, while other EU countries held $495.8 billion or 47.9 per cent of the UK's inward FDI stock. The single largest investor-country in the UK from within the EU is the Netherlands, holding £176.0 billion or 17.0 per cent of the UK's stock of foreign investment.

The service sector dominates inward investment. In 2014 it accounted for about 64 per cent of the UK's stock of foreign investment. Financial services alone account for 27 per cent of the stock of inward FDI.

According to an Ernst & Young survey:

> While the UK remains unrivalled in Europe in attracting both North American investments and follow on projects from existing investors worldwide, it lags behind Germany in attracting new projects from first-time investors, and securing projects from some of the world's fastest-growing FDI sources — notably China.

It is also still punching below its weight in attracting manufacturing projects, securing just 12% of manufacturing investments into Europe compared to its 20% share of overall FDI. More worryingly, it won only half as many new manufacturing projects as Germany, which is now beating even the lower-wage destinations of Central and Eastern Europe in the battle for first-time manufacturing investments.

Finally, the sheer pulling power of London for global FDI means it risks overshadowing the rest of the UK, especially the regions.[5]

Effects on productivity and R&D

As well as offering employment, it is argued that foreign firms have higher rates of productivity than domestic firms, which puts competitive pressure on domestic firms to increase their productivity. Some work by Hubert and Pain in 2000 showed that a 1 per cent rise in the output of foreign firms in a particular industry will raise technical progress by 0.53 per cent in domestic firms in that industry.[6]

It is evident that foreign investment, largely through foreign firms operating in the UK, is crucial for research and development expenditure by businesses in the UK. Annual surveys of business research and development conducted

---

[5] '2014 UK attractiveness survey' (Ernst & Young, 2015).

[6] F. Hubert and N. Pain, 'Inward investment and technical progress in the UK manufacturing sector', OECD Economics Department, Working Paper no. 268 (2000).

(a) UK's share of global FDI inflows

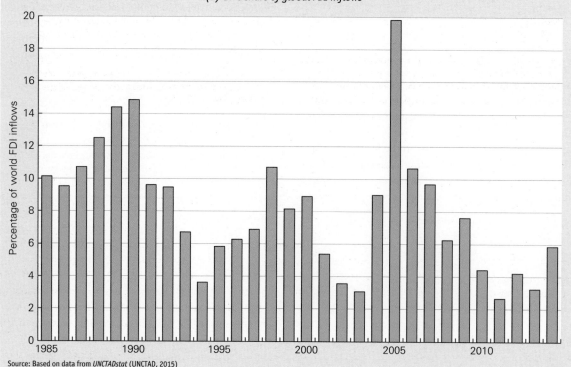

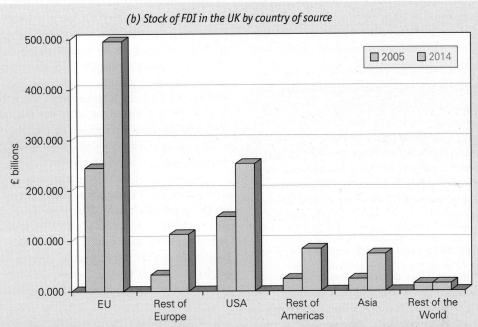

(b) Stock of FDI in the UK by country of source

Legend: 2005, 2014

Source: Based on data in *Foreign Direct Investment (FDI) Involving UK Companies, 2014 (Directional Principle)* (ONS, December 2015)

by the Office for National Statistics typically show around one-quarter of all R&D expenditure in the UK is funded from overseas.

Competition for FDI

Because of the huge potential benefits, the competition between nations to attract new investment, whether from indigenous or foreign firms, is intense. Highly mobile MNCs seek out those locational opportunities that allow them to gain a competitive advantage over other global producers.

As recent figures show, the UK's position in attracting FDI is increasingly under threat. As well as eastern European countries, developing nations such as China and India are increasingly attractive to mobile MNCs and this is only partly due to low relative wage costs. More important in recent times are the additional locational advantages these nations have gained through substantial investments in education and science, thereby raising the quality of their skills base and enhancing their technological capability. As companies become more effective in managing these distant locations

and different cultures, higher value-added activities are increasingly likely to be located there.

Notably the UK continues to struggle to secure manufacturing projects. According to the 2014 Ernst and Young survey, about half of the FDI projects in Europe in 2013 were manufacturing projects, creating an average of around 160 jobs each. The survey points to the potential for such jobs to be located across the UK regions, rather than being focused in London, to where inward FDI is often attracted, and for them to be suitable for younger people.

Attracting a broader range of FDI projects with a wider geographical spread points to the need for supply-side policies (see Chapter 31) which, among other things, can help improve the skills base of the workforce and improve the country-wide infrastructure.

 What do you think the UK government might do either to minimise FDI outflows, or to attract a greater volume of FDI inflow?

23.6 THE DISADVANTAGES OF MNC INVESTMENT FOR THE HOST STATE

Thus far we have focused on the positive effects resulting from multinational investment. However, multinational investment may not always be beneficial in either the short or the long term.

Uncertainty. MNCs are often 'footloose', meaning that they can simply close down their operations in foreign countries and move (see Box 23.2 for an example relating to the closure

of the Peugeot plant in Coventry). This is especially likely with older plants which would need updating if the MNC were to remain, or with plants that can be easily sold without too much loss. The ability to close down its business operations and shift production, while being a distinct economic advantage to the MNC, is a prime concern facing the host nation.

If a country has a large foreign multinational sector within the economy, it will become very vulnerable to such footloose activity, and face great uncertainty in the long term. It may thus be forced to offer the multinational 'perks' (e.g. grants, special tax relief or specific facilities) in order to persuade it to remain. These perks are clearly costly to the taxpayer.

Control. The fact that an MNC can shift production locations not only gives it economic flexibility, but enables it to exert various controls over its host. This is particularly so in many developing countries, where MNCs are not only major employers but in many cases the principal wealth creators. Thus attempts by the host state to improve worker safety or impose pollution controls, for example, may be against what the MNC sees as its own best interests. It might thus oppose such measures or even threaten to withdraw from the country if such measures are not modified or dropped. The host nation is in a very weak position.

Transfer pricing. MNCs, like domestic producers, are always attempting to reduce their tax liabilities. One unique way that an MNC can do this is through a process known as *transfer pricing* (see pages 290–1). The practice of transfer pricing is pervasive and governments are losing vast sums in tax revenue every day because of it. The practice enables the MNC to reduce its profits in countries with high rates of profit tax, and increase them in countries with low rates of profit tax. This can be achieved by simply manipulating its internal pricing structure.

For example, take a vertically integrated MNC where subsidiary A in one country supplies components to subsidiary B in another. The price at which the components are transferred between the two subsidiaries (the 'transfer price') will ultimately determine the costs and hence the levels of profit made in each country. Assume that in the country where subsidiary A is located, the level of corporation tax is half that of the country where subsidiary B is located. If components are transferred from A to B at very high prices, then B's costs will rise and its profitability will fall. Conversely, A's profitability will rise. The MNC clearly benefits as more profit is taxed at the lower rather than the higher rate. Had it been the other way around, with subsidiary B facing the lower rate of tax, then the components would be transferred at a low price. This would increase subsidiary B's profits and reduce A's.

The practice of transfer pricing was mostly starkly revealed in *The Guardian* newspaper in February 2009. Citing a paper that examined the flows of goods priced from US subsidiaries in Africa back to the USA, it stated that 'the public may be horrified to learn that companies have priced flash bulbs at $321.90 each, pillow cases at $909.29 each and a ton of sand at $1993.67, when the average world trade price was 66 cents, 62 cents and $11.20 respectively'.[7]

The environment. Many MNCs are accused of simply investing in countries to gain access to natural resources, which are subsequently extracted or used in a way that is not sensitive to the environment. Host nations, especially developing countries, that are keen for investment are frequently prepared to allow MNCs to do this. They often put more store on the short-run gains from the MNC's presence than on the long-run depletion of precious natural resources or damage to the environment. Governments, like many businesses, often have a very short-term focus: they are concerned more with their political survival (whether through the ballot box or through military force) than with the long-term interests of their people.

23.7 MULTINATIONAL CORPORATIONS AND DEVELOPING ECONOMIES

Many of the benefits and costs of MNC investment that we have considered so far are most acutely felt in developing countries. The poorest countries of the world are most in need of investment and yet are most vulnerable to exploitation by multinationals and have the least power to resist it. There tends, therefore, to be a love–hate relationship between the peoples of the developing world and the giant corporations that are seen to be increasingly dominating their lives: from the spread of agribusiness into the countryside through the ownership and control of plantations, to international mining corporations despoiling vast tracts of land; from industrial giants dominating manufacturing, to international banks controlling the flow of finance; from international tour operators and hotels bringing the socially disruptive effects of affluent tourists from North America, Japan, Europe and Australasia, to the products of the rich industrialised countries fashioning consumer tastes and eroding traditional culture.

Although MNCs employ only a small proportion of the total labour force in most developing countries, they have a powerful effect on these countries' economies, often dominating the import and export sectors. They also often exert considerable power and influence over political leaders and their policies and over civil servants, and are frequently accused of 'meddling' in politics.

It is easy to see the harmful social, environmental and economic effects of multinationals on developing countries, and yet governments in these countries are so eager to attract overseas investment that they are frequently prepared to offer considerable perks to MNCs and to turn a blind eye to many of their excesses.

---

[7]Prem Sikka, 'Shifting profits across borders', *The Guardian*, 12 February 2009 (http://www.theguardian.com/commentisfree/2009/feb/11/taxavoidance-tax)

Does MNC investment aid development?

Whether investment by multinationals in developing countries is seen to be a net benefit or a net cost to these countries depends on what are perceived to be their development goals. If maximising the growth in national income is the goal, then MNC investment has probably made a positive contribution. If, however, the objectives of development are seen as more wide-reaching, and include goals such as greater equality, the relief of poverty, a growth in the provision of basic needs (such as food, health care, housing and sanitation) and a general growth in the freedom and sense of well-being of the mass of the population, then the net effect of multinational investment could be argued to be anti-developmental.

Advantages to the host country

In order for countries to achieve economic growth, there must be *investment*. In general, the higher the rate of investment, the higher will be the rate of economic growth. The need for economic growth tends to be more pressing in developing countries than in advanced countries. One obvious reason is their lower level of income. If they are ever to aspire to the living standards of the rich North, then income per head will have to grow at a considerably faster rate than in rich countries and for many years. Another reason is the higher rates of population growth in developing countries – often some 2 percentage points higher than in the rich countries. This means that for income per head to grow at merely the *same* rate as in rich countries, developing countries will have to achieve growth rates 2 percentage points higher.

Investment requires finance. But developing countries are generally acutely short of funds: FDI can help to make up the shortfall. Specifically, there are key 'gaps' that FDI can help to fill.

The savings gap. A country's rate of economic growth (g) depends crucially on two factors:

- The amount of extra capital that is required to produce an extra unit of output per year: i.e. the marginal capital/output ratio (k). The greater the marginal capital/output ratio, the lower will be the output per year that results from a given amount of investment.
- The proportion of national income that a country saves (s). The higher this proportion, the greater the amount of investment that can be financed.

There is a simple formula that relates the rate of economic growth to these two factors. It is known as the *Harrod–Domar model* (after the two economists Sir Roy Harrod and Evsey Domar, who independently developed the model). The formula is:

$$g = s/k$$

Thus if a developing country saved 10 per cent of its national income ($s = 10\%$), and if £4 of additional capital were required to produce £1 of extra output per annum ($k = 4$), then the rate of economic growth would be 10%/4 = 2.5 per cent.

If that developing country wanted to achieve a rate of economic growth of 5 per cent, then it would require a rate of saving of 20 per cent (5% = 20%/4). There would thus be a shortfall of savings: a *savings gap*. Most, if not all, developing countries perceive themselves as having a savings gap. Not only do they require relatively high rates of economic growth in order to keep ahead of population growth and to break out of poverty, but they also tend to have relatively low rates of saving. Poor people cannot afford to save much out of their income.

This is where FDI comes in. It can help to fill the savings gap by directly financing the investment required to achieve the target rate of growth.

The foreign exchange gap. There are many items, especially various raw materials and machinery, that many developing countries do not produce themselves and yet which are vital if they are to develop. Such items have to be imported. But this requires foreign exchange, and most developing countries suffer from a chronic shortage of foreign exchange. Their demand for imports grows rapidly: they have a high income elasticity of demand for imports – for both capital goods and consumer goods. Yet their exports tend to grow relatively slowly. Reasons include: the development of synthetic substitutes for the raw material exports of developing countries (e.g. plastics for rubber and metal) and the relatively low income elasticity of demand for certain primary products (the demand for things such as tea, coffee, sugar cane and rice tends to grow relatively slowly).

FDI can help to alleviate the shortage of foreign exchange: it can help to close the *foreign exchange gap*. Not only will the MNC bring in capital which might otherwise have had to be purchased with scarce foreign exchange, but also any resulting exports by the MNC will increase the country's future foreign exchange earnings.

Public finance gap. Governments in developing countries find it difficult to raise enough tax revenues to finance all

---

Definitions

Harrod–Domar model A model that relates a country's rate of economic growth to the proportion of national income saved and the ratio of capital to output.

Savings gap The shortfall in savings to achieve a given rate of economic growth.

Foreign exchange gap The shortfall in foreign exchange that a country needs to purchase necessary imports such as raw materials and machinery.

the projects they would like to. MNC profits provide an additional source of tax revenue.

Skills and technology gaps. The capital that flows into the developing countries with MNC investment often embodies the latest technology, access to which the developing country would otherwise be denied. MNCs bring management expertise and often provide training programmes for local labour. Hence, MNCs may not only provide capital but also potentially help to increase the *productivity* of capital and labour, particularly through the spread of knowledge and ideas. These effects may help to foster economic development in developing countries.

Disadvantages to the host country

Whereas there is the potential for MNCs to make a significant contribution to closing the above gaps, in practice they often close them only slightly, or even make them bigger! The following are the main problems:

■ They may use their power in the markets of host countries to drive domestic producers out of business, thereby lowering domestic profits and domestic investment.

■ They may buy few, if any, of their components from domestic firms, but import them instead: perhaps from one of their subsidiaries.

■ The bulk of their profits may simply be repatriated to shareholders in the rich countries, with little, if any, reinvested in the developing country. This, plus the previous point, will tend to make the foreign exchange gap worse.

■ Their practice of transfer pricing may give little scope for the host government to raise tax revenue from them. Governments of developing countries are effectively put in competition with each other, each trying to undercut the others' tax rates in order to persuade the MNC to price its intermediate products in such a way as to make its profits in their country.

■ Similarly, governments of developing countries compete with each other to offer the most favourable terms to MNCs (e.g. government grants, government contracts, tax concessions and rent-free sites). The more favourable the terms, the less the gain for developing countries as a whole.

Pause for thought

What problems is a developing country likely to experience if it adopts a policy of restricting, or even preventing, access to its markets by multinational business?

■ The technology and skills brought in by the multinationals may be fiercely guarded by the MNC. What is more, the dominance of the domestic market by MNCs may lead to the demise of domestic firms and indigenous technology, thereby worsening the skill and technology base of the country.

In addition to these problems, MNCs can alter the whole course of development in ways that many would argue are undesirable. By locating in cities, they tend to attract floods of migrants from the countryside looking for work, but of those only a small fraction will find employment in these industries. The rest swell the ranks of the urban unemployed, often dwelling in squatter settlements on the outskirts of cities and living in appalling conditions.

More fundamentally, they are accused of distorting the whole pattern of development and of worsening the gap between the rich and poor. Their technology is capital intensive (compared with indigenous technology). The result is too few job opportunities. Those who are employed, however, receive relatively high wages, and are able to buy their products. These are the products consumed in affluent countries – from cars, to luxury foodstuffs, to household appliances – products that the MNCs often advertise heavily, and where they have considerable monopoly/oligopoly power. The resulting 'coca-colanisation', as it has been called, creates wants for the mass of people, but wants that they have no means of satisfying.

What can developing countries do?

Can developing countries gain the benefits of FDI while avoiding the effects of growing inequality and inappropriate products and technologies? If a developing country is large and is seen as an important market for the multinational, if it would be costly for the multinational to relocate, and if the government is well informed about the multinational's costs, then the country's bargaining position will be relatively strong. It may be able to get away with relatively high taxes on the MNC's profits and tight regulation of its behaviour (e.g. its employment practices and its care for the environment). If, however, the country is economically weak and the MNC is footloose, then the deal it can negotiate is unlikely to be very favourable.

The bargaining position of developing countries would be enhanced if they could act jointly in imposing conditions on multinational investment and behaviour. Such agreement is unlikely, however, given the diverse nature of developing countries' governments and economies, and the pro-free market, deregulated world of the early twenty-first century.

BOX 23.3 **GROCERS GO GLOBAL**

Carrefour has a fresh snake counter alongside the fish department in its Chinese stores. Wal-Mart boasts that in its Chinese stores you can find local delicacies such as whole roasted pigs and live frogs. Are fresh snakes and live frogs what's needed

to succeed in China? It would seem so. Global companies thinking local, customising themselves to each market, are increasingly seen as the key to success in Asia and elsewhere around the world.

The expansion of European and American grocer retailers into global markets has been under way for a number of years. Driven by stagnant markets at home with limited growth opportunities, the major players in Europe, such as Wal-Mart from the USA, Carrefour and Casino from France, Tesco from the UK, Ahold from Holland and Metro from Germany, have been looking to expand their overseas operations – but with mixed success.

In recent times, Asia has been the market's growth sector, with China a particular attraction. In the five years to 2013, the Chinese supermarket sector grew at an average annual rate of 12.3 per cent, although the rate has slowed slightly since.

But, it has not just been China where foreign retailers have invested. Tesco, for example, entered the Thai market in 1998. Tesco Lotus, the company's regional subsidiary, is now the country's number-one retailer. In 2015 it had over 1700 stores across Thailand, employing over 50 000 full-time staff. Meanwhile, Carrefour and Wal-Mart have also opened hundreds of new outlets within the region in recent times.

The advantages that international retailers have over their domestic competitors are expertise in systems, distribution, the range of products and merchandising. However, given the distinctive nature of markets within Asia, business must learn to adapt to local conditions. Joint ventures and local knowledge are seen as the key ingredients to success

Facing up to the big boys

With the rapid expansion of hypermarkets throughout Asia, the retail landscape has undergone revolutionary change. With a wide range of products all under one roof, from groceries to pharmaceuticals to white goods, and at cut-rate prices, local neighbourhood stores have often stood little chance in the competitive battle. 'Mom and pop operations have no economies of scale.' As well as local retailers, local suppliers are also facing a squeeze on profits, as hypermarkets demand lower prices and use their buying power as leverage.

Such has been the dramatic impact these stores have had upon the retail and grocery sector that a number of Asian economies, such as Malaysia and Thailand, have introduced restrictions on the building of new outlets.

China, one of the toughest markets to enter, restricted foreign companies to joint venture arrangements until 2004. Tesco's answer to these restrictions had been to go into a 50:50 partnership with Taiwanese food supplier Ting Hsing.

Initially, the stores were not the Tesco supermarkets with which customers in the UK are familiar. Instead, they had an orange colour scheme and few brands that the average UK shopper would recognise. In 2006 Tesco increased its stake to 90 per cent and with this came the familiar Tesco branding.

This marked a period of expansion by Tesco and other global retailers in China. By mid-2015, Carrefour, the biggest international retailer in the Chinese market had over 230 hypermarkets, having opened 11 more in 2014 and expected to open a further 15 hypermarkets in 2015.

However, the expansion into China and other Asian markets has not been without difficulties for global retailers. In 2012 Tesco announced that it was to leave Japan after nine years, while in 2014 Carrefour announced that it was leaving India, less than four years after having opened its first store in the country.

Even in markets like China the pace of growth of expansion is tending to slow. In May 2014 Tesco completed the establishment of a joint venture with state-run China Resources Enterprise (CRE). This left Tesco owning 20 per cent of the business and CRE 80 per cent. The venture brought together Tesco's 131 stores in China with CRE's nearly 3000 outlets.

> With relatively slower economic growth in China and complex local market conditions, Tesco, Carrefour and Wal-Mart did begin to pull back on their global expansions and although they are continuing, it is at a slower rate. Philip Clarke, Tesco's CEO said about China:

> 'It's more of a marathon than a sprint. Many retailers putting down more space in the market; few seeing that translate into profitable growth.'[8]

A Bloomberg industry analyst added:

> The rate of same-store sales increases is not what they [chains] were expecting it to be. The rate of addition of capacity has probably exceeded the growth of the market.[9]

 What are the ownership, location and internalisation advantages associated with retail FDI in Asia?

---

[8]Tesco stumbles with Wal-Mart as China shoppers buy local', *Bloomberg*, 19 October 2012.
[9]Ibid.

SUMMARY

1a The process of globalisation can have profound effects on economies. One current feature of globalisation is the relocating of various service and knowledge-based jobs from developed to developing countries.

1b There are various drivers of globalisation, including market, cost, government and competitive drivers.

1c Supporters of globalisation point to its potential to lead to faster growth and greater efficiency through trade, competition and investment. It also has the potential to draw the world closer together politically.

1d Critics of globalisation argue that it contributes to growing inequality and further impoverishes poor nations. It also erodes national cultures and can have adverse environmental consequences.

2 There is great diversity among multinationals in respect of size, nature of business, size of overseas operations, location, ownership and organisational structure.

3a Foreign direct investment (FDI) tends to fluctuate with the ups and downs of the world economy. For example, in 2008/9, with a slowdown in global economic growth, worldwide FDI fell. Over the years, however, FDI has grown substantially, and has accounted for a larger and larger proportion of total investment.

3b Developing countries are both an ever-increasingly important destination for FDI and source of FDI.

4a Why businesses go multinational depends largely upon the nature of their business and their corporate strategy.

4b One theoretical explanation of MNC development is the product life cycle hypothesis. In this theory, a business will shift production around the world seeking to reduce costs and extend a given product's life. The phases of a product's life will be conducted in different countries. As the product nears maturity and competition grows, reducing costs to maintain competitiveness will force businesses to locate production in low-cost markets, such as developing economies.

4c A more modern approach to explaining international production and MNC development is provided by the Eclectic Paradigm. According to this approach, firms have certain ownership-specific advantages (core competencies), such as managerial skills, product differentiation and technological advantages, which they can use in the most appropriate locations. They internalise their ownership-specific advantages and engage in FDI because the costs and risks are lower than licensing an overseas firm or using an import agent (i.e. engaging in an external market transaction).

4d Although becoming an MNC is largely advantageous to the business, it can experience problems with language barriers, selling and marketing in foreign markets, attitudes of the host state and the communication and coordination of global business activities.

5 Host states find multinational investment advantageous in respect to employment creation, contributions to the balance of payments, the transfer of technology and the contribution to taxation.

6 Host states find multinational investment disadvantageous in so far as it creates uncertainty; foreign business can control or manipulate the country or regions within it; tax payments can be avoided by transfer pricing; and MNCs might misuse the environment.

7a The benefits of MNCs to developing countries depend upon the developing countries' development goals.

7b MNCs bring with them investment, which is crucial to economic growth. They also provide the host state with foreign exchange, which might be crucial in helping purchase vital imports.

7c MNCs might prove to be disadvantageous to developing economies if they drive domestic producers out of business, source production completely from other countries, repatriate profits, practise transfer pricing to avoid tax, force host states to offer favourable tax deals or subsidies for further expansion, and guard technology to prevent its transfer to domestic producers.

MyEconLab

This book can be supported by MyEconLab, which contains a range of additional resources, including an online homework and tutorial system designed to test and build your understanding.

You need both an access card and a course ID to access MyEconLab:

1. Is your lecturer using MyEconLab? Ask your lecturer for your course ID.

2. Has an access card been included with the book at a reduced cost? Check the inside back cover of the book.

3. If you have a course ID but no access card, go to: http://www.myeconlab.com/ to buy access to this interactive study programme.

REVIEW QUESTIONS

1 Using the UNCTAD FDI database in the statistics section of the UNCTAD website at (www.unctad.org), find out what has happened to FDI flows over the past five years (a) worldwide; (b) to and from developed countries; (c) to and from developing countries; (d) to and from the UK. Explain any patterns that emerge.

2 What are the advantages and disadvantages to an economy, like that of the UK, of having a large multinational sector?

3 How might the structure of a multinational differ depending upon whether its objective of being multinational is to reduce costs or to grow?

4 If reducing costs is so important for many multinationals, why is it that many locate production not in low-cost developing economies, but in economies within the developed world?

5 'Going global, thinking local.' Explain this phrase, and identify the potential conflicts for a business in behaving in this way.

6 Explain the link between the life cycle of a product and multinational business.

7 Assess the advantages and disadvantages facing a host state when receiving MNC investment.

8 Debate the following: 'Multinational investment can be nothing but good for developing economies seeking to grow and prosper.'

International trade

KI 2 p 18

> **Business issues covered in this chapter**
>
> ■ How has international trade grown over the years? Have countries become more or less interdependent?
> ■ What are the benefits to countries and firms of international trade?
> ■ Which goods should a country export and which should it import?
> ■ Why do countries sometimes try to restrict trade and protect their domestic industries?
> ■ What is the role of the World Trade Organization (WTO) in international trade?

Without international trade we would all be much poorer. There would be some items like pineapples, coffee, cotton clothes, foreign holidays and uranium that we would simply have to go without. Then there would be other items like pineapples and spacecraft that we could produce only very inefficiently.

International trade has the potential to benefit *all* participating countries. This chapter explains why.

Totally free trade, however, may bring problems to countries or to groups of people within those countries. Many people argue strongly for restrictions on trade. Textile workers see their jobs threatened by cheap imported cloth. Car manufacturers worry about falling sales as customers switch to Japanese models or other East Asian ones. This chapter, therefore, also examines the arguments for restricting trade. Are people justified in fearing international competition, or are they merely trying to protect some vested interest at the expense of everyone else?

24.1 TRADING PATTERNS

International trade has been growing as a proportion of countries' national income for many years. This is illustrated in Figure 24.1, which shows the growth in the global volume of exports of goods and in world real GDP. It shows that exports have been growing much more rapidly than GDP.

Over the 60-year period from 1955 to 2014 the average annual growth in world output was 3.6 per cent, whereas the average annual growth in world exports was over 6.3 per cent. The chart also shows the significant negative impact of the global financial crisis at the end of the 2000s on both world output and, in particular, the volume of exports. The fall in total world output in 2009 was the first since the 1930s.

Despite the impact of the global slowdown at the end of the 2000s, it is likely that trade will continue to increase as a percentage of world GDP. This will further increase countries' interdependence and so their vulnerability to world trade fluctuations.

Figure 24.1 Annual growth in global output and exports of goods

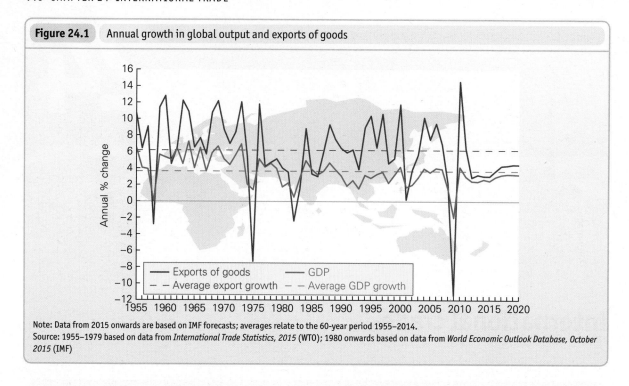

Note: Data from 2015 onwards are based on IMF forecasts; averages relate to the 60-year period 1955–2014.

Source: 1955–1979 based on data from *International Trade Statistics, 2015* (WTO); 1980 onwards based on data from *World Economic Outlook Database, October 2015* (IMF)

Figure 24.2 Share of world merchandise exports, by value (2014)

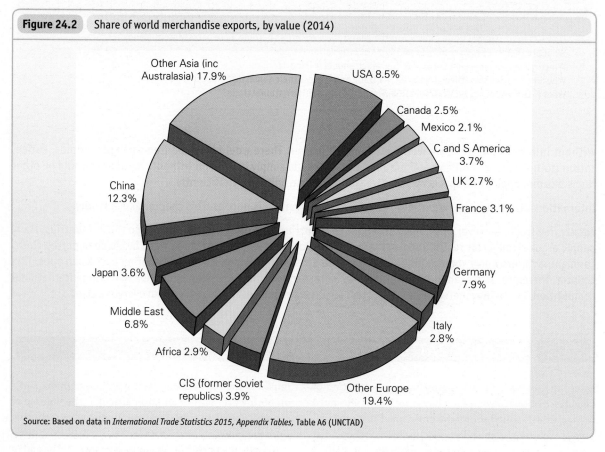

Source: Based on data in *International Trade Statistics 2015, Appendix Tables*, Table A6 (UNCTAD)

The geography of international trade

Developed countries have dominated world trade. But this pattern is changing. In 2014 developing countries accounted for 43 per cent (by value) of all world merchandise trade (see Figure 24.2); in 2000 they accounted for just 23 per cent. Their share of world trade has risen because countries with the fastest *growth* in exports are found in the developing world.

Figure 24.3 Share of world merchandise exports of BRICS, by value (%)

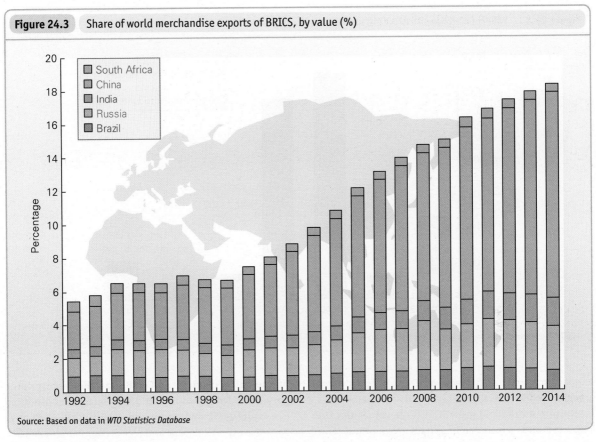

Source: Based on data in *WTO Statistics Database*

Figure 24.4 Average annual rate of growth in value of merchandise trade, 1992–2014

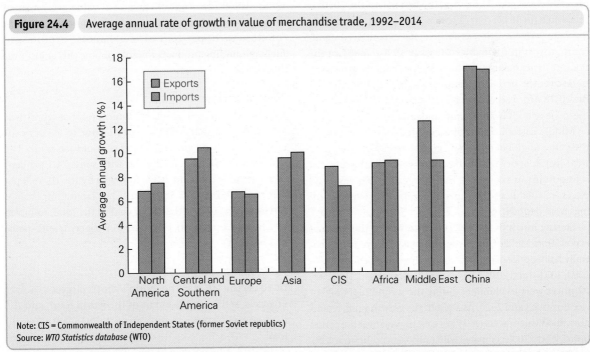

Note: CIS = Commonwealth of Independent States (former Soviet republics)
Source: *WTO Statistics database* (WTO)

The growth in exports from the group of developing nations collectively known as the BRICS[1] (Brazil, Russia, India, China and South Africa) has been especially rapid. Between them they accounted for just 5.4 per cent of world

exports (by value) in 1992; by 2014 this share had more than tripled to 18.3 per cent (see Figure 24.3).

Figure 24.4 shows the *growth* of exports and imports by region. It helps in assessing the openness of economies and provides further evidence that nations are becoming increasingly interdependent. It again illustrates the spectacular growth rate in trade witnessed by China: its

[1]Sometimes the term is used to refer just to the first four countries. When South Africa is excluded, the term is written BRICs rather than BRICS.

Figure 24.5 Value of merchandise exports by region: $ billions, 2014

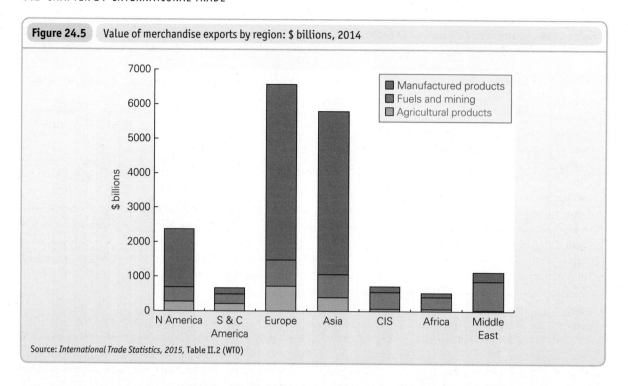

Source: *International Trade Statistics, 2015,* Table II.2 (WTO)

exports increased in value by an average of 17 per cent per year from 1992 to 2014.

Despite more rapid growth in trade values in other regions, Europe remains an important geographical centre for trade (see Figure 24.5). Over the first half of the 2010s it accounted for 36 per cent of both world exports and imports (by value). While Africa, as a whole, has experienced significant growth in trade since the early 1990s, many of the poorest African countries have seen negligible growth in trade over the period. Consequently, over the first half of the 2010s Africa accounted for only around 3.25 per cent of the value of both world exports and imports.

Middle Eastern countries accounted for 6.8 per cent of the value of global exports from 2010 to 2014 compared with just 3.9 per cent of the global value of imports. Oil is important in explaining this differential. However, oil prices are volatile and this affects the growth in export earnings from period to period.

During much of the 1990s, the growth in the value of exports from Middle Eastern countries was weak due to the generally falling price of oil. This changed over the periods 1999–2000, 2003–8 and 2010–11 as world oil prices surged. However, oil prices were to plummet during the second half of 2014 (see Boxes 5.3 and 26.3). As a result, the growth in merchandise export values averaged 19 per cent per year over the period from 1999 to 2008 compared with only 0.6 per cent from 1991 to 1998 and a fall of 6.7 per cent per year across 2013 and 2014.

The composition of international trade

Trade in goods
In 2014 the value of global merchandise exports was $18.9 trillion, which is equivalent to 24.5 per cent of the value of global GDP. By far the largest category of traded goods is that of manufactured products (see Figure 24.5), making up almost two-thirds of all merchandise exports. Europe and Asia account almost equally for around 80 per cent of the global value of exports of manufactures. Meanwhile agricultural products account for close to 10 per cent of merchandise exports and fuels and mining products roughly double this at just over 20 per cent.

Trade in services
In 2014 the global value of commercial services was $4.9 trillion which is equivalent in value to 6.3 per cent of global GDP and about 20.4 per cent of total trade. The USA is by far the largest exporter with some 14.1 per cent of all service exports in 2014, followed by the UK (6.8 per cent) and Germany (5.5 per cent). The largest importer of services is the USA with 9.6 per cent of the total, followed by China (8.1 per cent), Germany (6.9 per cent) and France (5.1 per cent).

Trade and the UK
In 2014, the UK was the world's tenth largest exporter of goods, selling 2.7 per cent of the world total, and the fifth largest importer, consuming 3.6 per cent of world total.

In 2014, 42.9 per cent of the UK's exports of goods went to EU countries, 13.0 per cent went to Switzerland, 11.5 per cent to the USA and 3.3 per cent to China.

UK imports, like UK exports, are strongly tied to Europe. In 2013, 53.1 per cent of the imports of goods came from EU countries, 8.8 per cent from China, 8.3 per cent from the USA and 3.9 per cent from Norway.

24.2 THE ADVANTAGES OF TRADE

Specialisation as the basis for trade

Why do countries trade with each other and what do they gain out of it? The reasons for international trade are really only an extension of the reasons for trade *within* a nation. Rather than people trying to be self-sufficient and do everything for themselves, it makes sense to specialise.

Firms specialise in producing certain types of goods. This allows them to gain economies of scale and to exploit their entrepreneurial and management skills and the skills of their labour force. It also allows them to benefit from their particular location and from the ownership of any particular capital equipment or other assets they might possess. With the revenues that firms earn, they buy in the inputs they need from other firms and the labour they require. Firms thus trade with each other.

Countries also specialise. They produce more than they need of certain goods. What is not consumed domestically is exported. The revenues earned from the exports are used to import goods which are not produced in sufficient amounts at home.

But which goods should a country specialise in? What should it export and what should it import? The answer is that it should specialise in those goods in which it has a *comparative advantage*. Let us examine what this means.

The law of comparative advantage

Countries have different endowments of factors of production. They differ in population density, labour skills, climate, raw materials, capital equipment, etc. These differences tend to persist because factors are relatively immobile between countries. Obviously land and climate are totally immobile, but even with labour and capital there tend to be more restrictions (physical, social, cultural or legal) on their international movement than on their movement within countries. Thus the ability to supply goods differs between countries.

What this means is that the relative costs of producing goods will vary from country to country. For example, one country may be able to produce 1 fridge for the same cost as 6 tonnes of wheat or 3 MP3 players, whereas another country may be able to produce 1 fridge for the same cost as only 3 tonnes of wheat but 4 MP3 players. It is these differences in relative costs that form the basis of trade.

At this stage we need to distinguish between *absolute advantage* and *comparative advantage*.

Absolute advantage

When one country can produce a good with fewer resources than another country, it is said to have an ***absolute advantage*** in that good. If France can produce wine with fewer resources than the UK, and the UK can produce gin

Table 24.1	Production possibilities for two countries				
			Kilos of wheat		Metres of cloth
Less developed country	Either		2	or	1
Developed country	Either		4	or	8

with fewer resources than France, then France has an absolute advantage in wine and the UK an absolute advantage in gin. Production of both wine and gin will be maximised by each country specialising and then trading with the other country. Both will gain.

Comparative advantage

The above seems obvious, but trade between two countries can still be beneficial even if one country could produce *all* goods with fewer resources than the other, providing the *relative* efficiency with which goods can be produced differs between the two countries.

Take the case of a developed country that is absolutely more efficient than a less developed country at producing both wheat and cloth. Assume that with a given amount of resources (labour, land and capital) the alternatives shown in Table 24.1 can be produced in each country.

Despite the developed country having an absolute advantage in both wheat and cloth, the less developed country (LDC) has a ***comparative advantage*** in wheat, and the developed country has a *comparative* advantage in cloth. This is because wheat is relatively cheaper in the LDC: only 1 metre of cloth has to be sacrificed to produce 2 kilos of wheat, whereas 8 metres of cloth would have to be sacrificed in the developed country to produce 4 kilos of wheat. In other words, the opportunity cost of wheat is 4 times higher in the developed country (8/4 compared with 1/2).

On the other hand, cloth is relatively cheaper in the developed country. Here the opportunity cost of producing 8 metres of cloth is only 4 kilos of wheat, whereas in the LDC 1 metre of cloth costs 2 kilos of wheat. Thus the opportunity cost of cloth is 4 times higher in the LDC (2/1 compared with 4/8).

KI 3
p 23

Definitions

Absolute advantage A country has an absolute advantage over another in the production of a good if it can produce it with less resources than the other country.

Comparative advantage A country has a comparative advantage over another in the production of a good if it can produce it at a lower opportunity cost: i.e. if it has to forgo less of other goods in order to produce it.

To summarise: countries have a comparative advantage in those goods that can be produced at a lower opportunity cost than in other countries.

> ## Pause for thought
>
> *Draw up a similar table to Table 24.1, only this time assume that the figures are: LDC 6 wheat or 2 cloth; DC 8 wheat or 20 cloth. What are the opportunity cost ratios now?*

If countries are to gain from trade, they should export those goods in which they have a comparative advantage and import those goods in which they have a comparative disadvantage. Given this, we can state a *law of comparative advantage*.

 The law of comparative advantage. Provided opportunity costs of various goods differ in two countries, both of them can gain from mutual trade if they specialise in producing (and exporting) those goods that have relatively low opportunity costs compared with the other country.

But why do they gain if they specialise according to this law? And just what will that gain be? We will consider these questions next.

The gains from trade based on comparative advantage

Before trade, unless markets are very imperfect, the prices of the two goods are likely to reflect their opportunity costs. For example, in Table 24.1, since the less developed country can produce 2 kilos of wheat for 1 metre of cloth, the *price* of 2 kilos of wheat will roughly equal 1 metre of cloth.

Assume, then, that the pre-trade exchange ratios of wheat for cloth are as follows:

LDC   : 2 wheat for 1 cloth
Developed country : 1 wheat for 2 cloth (i.e. 4 for 8)

Both countries will now gain from trade, provided the exchange ratio is somewhere between 2:1 and 1:2. Assume, for the sake of argument, that it is 1:1. In other words, 1 wheat trades internationally for 1 cloth. How will each country gain?

The LDC gains by exporting wheat and importing cloth. At an exchange ratio of 1:1, it now has to give up only 1 kilo of wheat to obtain a metre of cloth, whereas before trade it had to give up 2 kilos of wheat.

> ## Definition
>
> **The law of comparative advantage** Trade can benefit all countries if they specialise in the goods in which they have a comparative advantage.

The developed country gains by exporting cloth and importing wheat. Again at an exchange ratio of 1:1, it now has to give up only 1 metre of cloth to obtain a kilo of wheat, whereas before it had to give up 2 metres of cloth.

Thus both countries have gained from trade.

The actual exchange ratios will depend on the relative prices of wheat and cloth after trade takes place. These prices will depend on total demand for and supply of the two goods. It may be that the trade exchange ratio is nearer to the pre-trade exchange ratio of one country than the other. Thus the gains to the two countries need not be equal.

> ## Pause for thought
>
> *Show how each country could gain from trade if the LDC could produce (before trade) 3 wheat for 1 cloth and the developed country could produce (before trade) 2 wheat for 5 cloth, and if the exchange ratio (with trade) was 1 wheat for 2 cloth. Would they both still gain if the exchange ratio was (a) 1 wheat for 1 cloth; (b) 1 wheat for 3 cloth?*

The limits to specialisation and trade

Does the law of comparative advantage suggest that countries will completely specialise in just a few products? In practice, countries are likely to experience *increasing* opportunity costs. The reason for this is that, as a country increasingly specialises in one good, it will have to use resources that are less and less suited to its production and which were more suited to other goods. Thus ever-increasing amounts of the other goods will have to be sacrificed. For example, as a country specialises more and more in grain production, it will have to use land that is less and less suited to growing grain.

These increasing costs as a country becomes more and more specialised will lead to the disappearance of its comparative cost advantage. When this happens, there will be no point in further specialisation. Thus, whereas a country like Germany has a comparative advantage in capital-intensive manufactures, it does not produce only manufactures. It would make no sense not to use its fertile lands to produce food or its forests to produce timber. The opportunity costs of diverting all agricultural labour to industry would be very high.

Other reasons for gains from trade

Decreasing costs. Even if there are no initial comparative cost differences between two countries, it will still benefit both to specialise in industries where economies of scale can be gained, and then to trade. Once the economies of scale begin to appear, comparative cost differences will also appear, and thus the countries will have gained a comparative advantage in these industries.

Figure 24.6 Terms of trade for selected countries (2010 = 100)

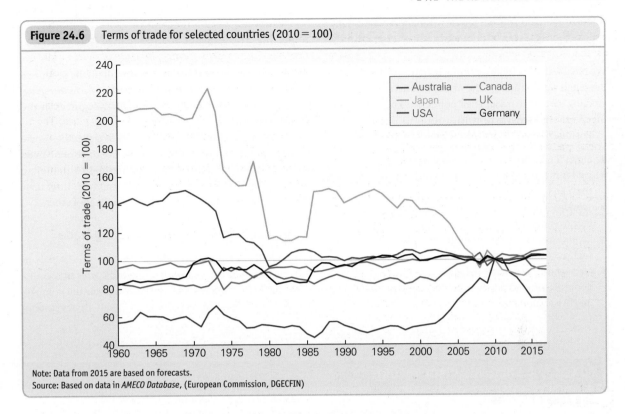

Note: Data from 2015 are based on forecasts.
Source: Based on data in *AMECO Database*, (European Commission, DGECFIN)

This reason for trade is particularly relevant for small countries where the domestic market is not large enough to support large-scale industries. Thus exports form a much higher percentage of GDP in small countries such as Singapore than in large countries such as the USA.

Differences in demand. Even with no comparative cost differences and no potential economies of scale, trade can benefit both countries if demand conditions differ.

If people in country A like beef more than lamb, and people in country B like lamb more than beef, then rather than A using resources better suited for lamb to produce beef, and B using resources better suited for producing beef to produce lamb, it will benefit both to produce beef *and* lamb and to export the one they like less in return for the one they like more.

Increased competition. If a country trades, the competition from imports may stimulate greater efficiency at home. This extra competition may prevent domestic monopolies/oligopolies from charging high prices. It may stimulate greater research and development and the more rapid adoption of new technology. It may lead to a greater variety of products being made available to consumers.

Trade as an 'engine of growth'. In a growing world economy, the demand for a country's exports is likely to grow over time, especially when these exports have a high income elasticity of demand. This will provide a stimulus to growth in the exporting country.

Non-economic advantages. There may be political, social and cultural advantages to be gained by fostering trading links between countries.

The terms of trade

What price will our exports fetch abroad? What will we have to pay for imports? The answer to these questions is given by the terms of trade. The *terms of trade* are defined as:

$$\frac{\text{the average price of exports}}{\text{the average price of imports}}$$

expressed as an index, where prices are measured against a base year in which the terms of trade are assumed to be 100. Thus if the average price of exports relative to the average price of imports has risen by 25 per cent since the base year, the terms of trade will now be 125. The terms of trade for selected countries are shown in Figure 24.6 (with 2010 as the base year).

If the terms of trade rise (export prices rising relative to import prices), they are said to have 'improved', since fewer exports now have to be sold to purchase any given quantity of imports. Changes in the terms of trade are caused by changes in the demand and supply of imports and exports, and by changes in the exchange rate.

Pause for thought

In Figure 24.6, which countries have experienced an improvement in their terms of trade in recent years?

Definition

Terms of trade The price index of exports divided by the price index of imports and then expressed as a percentage. This means that the terms of trade will be 100 in the base year.

24.3 ARGUMENTS FOR RESTRICTING TRADE

We have seen how trade can bring benefits to all countries. But when we look around the world, we often see countries erecting barriers to trade. Their politicians know that trade involves costs as well as benefits.

Possible barriers to imports include the following:

- *tariffs* (i.e. customs duties) on imports;
- *quotas* (i.e. restrictions on the amount of certain goods that can be imported);
- *subsidies on domestic products* to give them a price advantage over imports;
- *administrative regulations* designed to exclude imports, such as customs delays or excessive paperwork;
- *procurement procedures* whereby governments favour domestic producers when purchasing equipment (e.g. defence equipment).

Alternatively, governments may favour domestic producers by subsidising their exports in a process known as *dumping*. The goods are 'dumped' at artificially low prices in the foreign market.

In looking at the costs and benefits of trade, the choice is not the stark one of whether to have free trade or no trade at all. Although countries may sometimes contemplate having completely free trade, typically countries limit their trade. However, they certainly do not ban it altogether.

Arguments in favour of restricting trade

Arguments having some general validity

The infant industry argument. Some industries in a country may be in their infancy but have a potential comparative advantage. This is particularly likely in developing

---

BOX 24.1 STRATEGIC TRADE THEORY

The case of Airbus

Supporters of *strategic trade theory* hold that comparative advantage need not be the result of luck or circumstance, but may in fact be created by government. By diverting resources into selective industries, usually high tech and high skilled, a comparative advantage can be created through intervention.

An example of such intervention was the European aircraft industry, and in particular the creation of the European Airbus Consortium.

The European Airbus Consortium was established in the late 1960s, its four members being Aérospatiale (France), British Aerospace (now BAE Systems) (UK), CASA (Spain) and DASA (Germany). The setting up of this consortium was seen as essential for the future of the European aircraft industry for three reasons:

- to share high R&D costs;
- to generate economies of scale;
- to compete successfully with the market's major players in the USA – Boeing and McDonnell Douglas (which have since merged).

The consortium, although privately owned, was sponsored by government and received state aid, especially in its early years when the company failed to make a profit. Then, in 2000, the French, German and Spanish partners merged to form the European Aeronautic Defence and Space Company (EADS), which had an 80 per cent share of Airbus (BAE Systems having the remaining 20 per cent share). Shortly afterwards, it was announced that enough orders had been secured for the new 550+ seater A380 for production to go ahead. This new jumbo, which had its maiden flight in April 2005, is a serious competitor to the long-established Boeing 747. In 2006, BAE Systems announced that it was planning to sell its 20 per cent stake in Airbus to EADS to concentrate on its core transatlantic defence and aerospace business.

By the early 2000s, Airbus had become very successful and in 2003 for the first time it delivered more passenger aircraft than Boeing (305 compared with 281 for Boeing). This lead continued up to 2012, when Boeing overtook Airbus and delivered 22 more aircraft than its rival (see chart). Boeing continued to deliver more in 2013 and 2014.

In the light of Airbus's growth, it should come as no surprise to find that the Americans, and Boeing in particular, have brought accusations that Airbus is founded upon unfair trading practices and ought not to receive the level of governmental support that it does (see Box 25.1).

Aside from the legal wrangles, other issues were becoming apparent. Considerable delays (up to two years) and cost overruns were being experienced with the new superjumbo, the A380. With falling profitability and falling orders, in February 2007 Airbus announced plans to cut 10 000 jobs from its 57 000 workforce.

The development of the A380 put significant financial strains on Airbus. Its launch was 2½ years late and 50 per cent over budget. Airbus sought to avoid such problems with its new A350, which is seen as competing with Boeing's 787 Dreamliner and 777 series. As of May 2015, it had received 780 orders from 40 customers. But the A350 has also experienced delays and in June 2014, Emirates cancelled an order for 70 of the aircraft, citing frustrations with its development.

So does the experience of Airbus support the arguments of the strategic trade theorists? Essentially three kinds of benefit were expected to flow from Airbus and its presence in the aircraft market: lower prices, economic spillovers and profits.

- Without Airbus the civil aircraft market would have been dominated by two American firms, Boeing and McDonnell Douglas (and possibly one, if the 1997 merger had still gone ahead if Airbus had not existed). The only other

countries. Such industries are too small yet to have gained economies of scale; their workers are inexperienced; there is a lack of back-up facilities – communications networks, specialist research and development, specialist suppliers, etc. – and they may have only limited access to finance for expansion. Without protection, these *infant industries* will not survive competition from abroad.

Protection from foreign competition, however, will allow them to expand and become more efficient. Once they have achieved a comparative advantage, the protection can then be removed to enable them to compete internationally. A risk here, however, is that the protectionist measure is not removed once the industry has become established and thus the incentive for efficiency may disappear.

To reduce reliance on goods with little dynamic potential. Many developing countries have traditionally exported primaries: foodstuffs and raw materials. The world demand for these, however, is fairly income inelastic and has thus tended to grow relatively slowly. For these countries, free

trade is not an engine of growth. Instead, if it encourages their economies to become locked into a pattern of primary production, it may prevent them from expanding in sectors like manufacturing which have a higher income elasticity of demand. There may thus be a valid argument for protecting or promoting manufacturing industry. Note, however, that with the rapid growth of China and the other BRICs, the demand for and prices of various raw materials and foodstuffs in recent years have often increased more rapidly than the demand for and prices of manufactures – at least until 2011 (see figure in Box 26.3 on page 488).

Definitions

Dumping Where exports are sold at prices below marginal cost – often as a result of government subsidy.

Infant industry An industry which has a potential comparative advantage, but which is as yet too underdeveloped to be able to realise this potential.

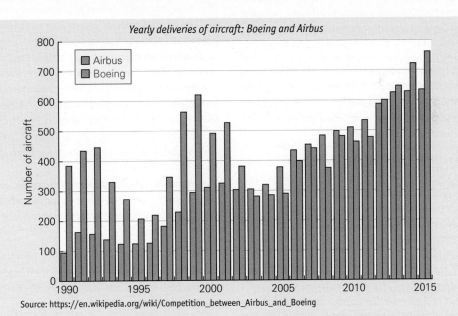

Yearly deliveries of aircraft: Boeing and Airbus

Source: https://en.wikipedia.org/wiki/Competition_between_Airbus_and_Boeing

significant competitors, and only in the small civil aircraft market, are Embraer of Brazil and Bombardier of Canada. Therefore the presence of Airbus would be expected to promote competition and thereby keep prices down. Studies in the 1980s and 1990s tended to support this view, suggesting that consumers have seen significant gains from lower prices. One survey estimated that without Airbus commercial aircraft prices would have been 3.5 per cent higher than they currently are, and without both Airbus and McDonnell Douglas they would have been 15 per cent higher.
■ Economic spillovers from the Airbus Consortium, such as skills and technology developments, might be expected to benefit other industries. Findings are inconclusive on this point.

It is clear, however, that although aggregate R&D in the whole aircraft industry has risen, so has the level of R&D duplication.

On balance it appears that Airbus has had many positive effects and that the strategic trade theory that has underpinned state aid, in this instance, has been largely vindicated. Boeing has a genuine competitor in Airbus and passengers worldwide have benefited from this competition.

1. *In what other industries could the setting up of a consortium, backed by government aid, be justified as a means of exploiting a potential comparative advantage?*
2. *Is it only in industries that could be characterised as world oligopolies that strategic trade theory is relevant?*

To prevent 'dumping' and other unfair trade practices. A country may engage in dumping by subsidising its exports. Alternatively, firms may practise price discrimination by selling at a higher price in home markets and a lower price in foreign markets in order to increase their profits. Either way, prices may no longer reflect comparative costs. Thus the world would benefit from tariffs being imposed by importers to counteract the subsidy.

It can also be argued that there is a case for retaliating against countries which impose restrictions on your exports. In the *short* run, both countries are likely to be made worse off by a contraction in trade. But if the retaliation persuades the other country to remove its restrictions, it may have a longer-term benefit. In some cases, the mere threat of retaliation may be enough to get another country to remove its protection.

KI 21
p 175

To prevent the establishment of a foreign-based monopoly. Competition from abroad could drive domestic producers out of business. The foreign company, now having a monopoly of the market, could charge high prices with a resulting misallocation of resources. The problem could be tackled either by restricting imports or by subsidising the domestic producer(s).

All the above arguments suggest that governments should adopt a 'strategic' approach to trade. **Strategic trade theory** argues that protecting certain industries allows a net gain in the *long* run from increased competition in the market (see Box 24.1).

To spread the risks of fluctuating markets. A highly specialised economy – Zambia with copper, Cuba with sugar – will be highly susceptible to world market fluctuations. Greater diversity and greater self-sufficiency, although maybe leading to less efficiency, can reduce these risks.

To reduce the influence of trade on consumer tastes. The assumption of fixed consumer tastes dictating the pattern of production through trade is false. Multinational companies through their advertising and other forms of sales promotion may influence consumer tastes. Many developing countries object to the insidious influence of Western consumerist values expounded by companies such as Coca-Cola and McDonald's. Thus some restriction on trade may be justified in order to reduce this 'producer sovereignty'.

To prevent the importation of harmful goods. A country may want to ban or severely curtail the importation of things such as drugs, pornographic literature and live animals.

Definition

Strategic trade theory The theory that protecting/supporting certain industries can enable them to compete more effectively with large monopolistic rivals abroad. The effect of the protection is to increase long-run competition and may enable the protected firms to exploit a comparative advantage that they could not have done otherwise.

To take account of externalities. Free trade will tend to reflect private costs. Both imports and exports, however, can involve externalities. The mining of many minerals for export may adversely affect the health of miners; the production of chemicals for export may involve pollution; the importation of juggernaut lorries may lead to structural damage to houses; shipping involves large amounts of CO_2 emissions (estimates typically put this at between 3 to 5 per cent of total world emissions).

KI 33
p 345

Arguments having some validity for specific groups or countries

The arguments considered so far are of general validity: restricting trade for such reasons could be of net benefit to the world. There are two other arguments, however, that are used by individual governments for restricting trade, where their country will gain, but at the *expense* of other countries, such that there will be a net loss to the world.

The first argument concerns taking advantage of market power in world trade. If a country, or a group of countries, has monopsony power in the purchase of imports (i.e. they are individually or collectively a very large economy, such as the USA or the EU), then they could gain by restricting imports so as to drive down their price. Similarly, if countries have monopoly power in the sale of some export (e.g. OPEC countries with oil), then they could gain by restricting exports, thereby forcing up the price.

KI 21
p 175

The second argument concerns giving protection to declining industries. The human costs of sudden industrial closures can be very high. In such circumstances, temporary protection may be justified to allow the industry to decline more slowly, thus avoiding excessive structural unemployment. Such policies will be at the expense of the consumer, who will be denied access to cheaper foreign imports.

'Non-economic' arguments for restricting trade. A country may be prepared to forgo the direct economic advantages of free trade in order to achieve objectives that are often described as 'non-economic':

- It may wish to maintain a degree of self-sufficiency in case trade is cut off or disrupted – for instance, in times of war. This may apply particularly to the production of food and armaments.
- It may decide not to trade with certain countries with which it disagrees politically.
- It may wish to preserve traditional ways of life. Rural communities or communities built around old traditional industries may be destroyed by foreign competition.
- It may prefer to retain as diverse a society as possible, rather than one too narrowly based on certain industries.

Pursuing such objectives, however, will involve costs. Preserving a traditional way of life, for example, may mean that consumers are denied access to cheaper goods from abroad. Society must therefore weigh up the benefits against the costs of such policies.

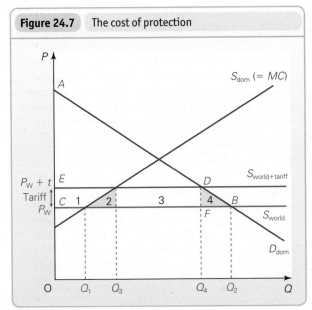

Figure 24.7 The cost of protection

Problems with protection

Tariffs and other forms of protection impose a cost on society. Figure 24.7 illustrates the case of a good that is partly home produced and partly imported. Domestic demand and supply are given by D_{dom} and S_{dom}. It is assumed that firms in the country produce under perfect competition and that therefore the supply curve is the sum of the firms' marginal cost curves.

Let us assume that the country is too small to affect world prices: it is a price taker. The world price is given, at P_w. At P_w, Q_2 is demanded, Q_1 is supplied by domestic suppliers and hence $Q_2 - Q_1$ is imported.

Now a tariff is imposed. This increases the price to consumers by the amount of the tariff. Price rises to $P_w + t$. Domestic production increases to Q_3, consumption falls to Q_4, and hence imports fall to $Q_4 - Q_3$.

What are the costs of this tariff to the country? Consumers are having to pay a higher price, and hence consumer surplus falls from area ABC to ADE (see pages 91–2 and 344 if you are unsure about consumer surplus). The cost to consumers in lost consumer surplus is thus $EDBC$ (i.e. areas $1 + 2 + 3 + 4$). *Part* of this cost, however, is redistributed as a *benefit* to other sections in society. *Firms* get a higher price, and thus gain extra profits (area 1): where profit is given by the area between the price and the MC curve. The *government* receives extra revenue from the tariff payments (area 3): i.e. $Q_4 - Q_3 \times$ tariff. These revenues can be used, for example, to reduce taxes.

But *part* of this cost is not recouped elsewhere. It is a net cost to society (areas 2 and 4).

Area 2 represents the extra costs of producing $Q_3 - Q_1$ at home, rather than importing it. If $Q_3 - Q_1$ were still

imported, the country would only be paying P_w. By producing it at home, however, the costs are given by the domestic supply curve ($= MC$). The difference between MC and P_w (area 2) is thus the efficiency loss on the production side.

Area 4 represents the loss of consumer surplus by the reduction in consumption from Q_2 to Q_4. Consumers have saved area FBQ_2Q_4 of expenditure, but have sacrificed area DBQ_2Q_4 of utility in so doing – a net loss of area 4.

The government should ideally weigh up such costs against any benefits that are gained from protection.

Apart from these direct costs to the consumer, there are several other problems with protection. Some are a direct effect of the protection; others follow from the reactions of other nations.

Protection as 'second-best'. Many of the arguments for protection amount merely to arguments for some type of government intervention in the economy. Protection, however, may not be the best way of dealing with the problem, since protection may have undesirable side effects. There may be a more direct form of intervention that has no side effects. In such a case, protection will be no more than a *second-best* solution.

For example, using tariffs to protect old inefficient industries from foreign competition may help prevent unemployment in those parts of the economy, but the consumer will suffer from higher prices. A better solution would be to subsidise retraining and investment in those areas of the country in *new efficient* industries – industries with a comparative advantage. In this way, unemployment is avoided, but the consumer does not suffer.

> ### Pause for thought
>
> 1. *Protection to allow the exploitation of monopoly/monopsony power can be seen as a 'first-best' policy for the country concerned. Similarly, the use of tariffs to counteract externalities directly involved in the trade process (e.g. the environmental costs of an oil tanker disaster) could be seen to be a first-best policy. Explain why.*
> 2. *Most of the other arguments for tariffs or other forms of protection that we have considered can really be seen as arguments for intervention, with protection being no more than a second-best form of intervention. Go through each of the arguments and consider what would be a 'first-best' form of intervention.*

Retaliation. If the USA imposes restrictions on, say, imports from the EU, then the EU may impose restrictions on imports from the USA. Any gain to US firms competing with EU imports is offset by a loss to US exporters. What is more, US consumers suffer, since the benefits from comparative advantage have been lost.

BOX 24.2 **GIVING TRADE A BAD NAME**

Arguments that don't add up

'Why buy goods from abroad and deny jobs to workers in this country?' This is typical of the concerns that many people have about an open trade policy. However, these concerns are often based on arguments that do not stand up to close inspection. Here are four of them.

'Imports should be reduced since they lower the standard of living. The money goes abroad rather than into the domestic economy.' Imports are consumed and thus add directly to consumer welfare. Also, provided they are matched by exports, there is no net outflow of money. Trade, because of the law of comparative advantage, allows countries to increase their standard of living: to consume beyond their production possibility curve.

'Protection is needed from cheap foreign labour.' Importing cheap goods from, say, China, allows more goods to be consumed. The UK uses less resources by buying these goods through the production and sale of exports than by producing them at home. However, there will be a cost to certain UK workers whose jobs are lost through foreign competition.

'Protection reduces unemployment.' At a microeconomic level, protecting industries from foreign competition may

allow workers in those industries to retain their jobs. But if foreigners sell fewer goods to the UK, they will not be able to buy so many UK exports. Thus unemployment will rise in UK export industries. Overall unemployment, therefore, is little affected, and in the meantime the benefits from trade to consumers are reduced. Temporary protection given to declining industries, however, may help to reduce structural unemployment.

'Dumping is always a bad thing, and thus a country should restrict subsidised imports.' Dumping may well reduce world economic welfare: it goes against the law of comparative advantage. The importing country, however, may well gain from dumping. Provided the dumping is not used to drive domestic producers out of business and establish a foreign monopoly, the consumer gains from lower prices. The losers are the taxpayers in the foreign country and the workers in competing industries in the home country.

 Go through each of these five arguments and provide a reply to the criticisms of them.

The increased use of tariffs and other restrictions can lead to a trade war, with each country cutting back on imports from other countries. In the end, with retaliation, everyone loses.

Protection may allow firms to remain inefficient. By removing or reducing foreign competition, tariffs etc. may reduce firms' incentive to reduce costs. Thus if protection is being given to an infant industry, the government must ensure

that the lack of competition does not prevent it 'growing up'. Protection should not be excessive and should be removed as soon as possible.

Bureaucracy. If a government is to avoid giving excessive protection to firms, it should examine each case carefully. This can lead to large administrative costs. It could also lead to corrupt officials accepting bribes from importers to give them favourable treatment.

24.4 THE WORLD TRADING SYSTEM AND THE WTO

After the Wall Street crash of 1929 (when share prices on the US stock exchange plummeted), the world plunged into the Great Depression. Countries found their exports falling dramatically and many suffered severe balance of payments difficulties. The response of many countries was to restrict imports by the use of tariffs and quotas. Of course, this reduced other countries' exports, which encouraged them to resort to even greater protectionism. The net effect of the Depression and the rise in protectionism was a dramatic fall in world trade. The volume of world trade in manufactures fell by more than a third in the three years following the Wall Street crash. Clearly there was a net economic loss to the world from this decline in trade.

After the Second World War there was a general desire to reduce trade restrictions, so that all countries could gain the maximum benefits from trade. There was no desire to return to the beggar-my-neighbour policies of the 1930s.

In 1947, 23 countries got together and signed the General Agreement on Tariffs and Trade (GATT). By April 2015 there were 161 members of its successor organisation, the World Trade Organization, which was formed in 1995. Between them, the members of the WTO account for around 98 per cent of world trade.

The aims of GATT, and now the WTO, have been to liberalise trade. But whereas GATT focused on the trade in goods, the WTO and its agreements also relate to the trade in services and in inventions and designs, sometimes referred to as intellectual property.

WTO rules

The WTO requires its members to operate according to various rules. These include the following:

- *Non-discrimination.* Under the 'most-favoured-nations clause', any trade concession that a country makes to one member must be granted to *all* signatories. The only exception is with free-trade areas and customs unions (such as the EU). Here countries are permitted to abolish tariffs between themselves while still maintaining them with the rest of the world.
- *Reciprocity.* Any nation benefiting from a tariff reduction made by another country must reciprocate by making similar tariff reductions itself.
- *The general prohibition of quotas.*
- *Fair competition.* If unfair barriers are erected against a particular country, the WTO can sanction retaliatory action by that country. The country is not allowed, however, to take such action without permission.
- *Binding tariffs.* Countries cannot raise existing tariffs without negotiating with their trading partners.

Unlike the GATT, the WTO has the power to impose sanctions on countries breaking trade agreements. If there are disputes between member nations, these will be settled by the WTO, and if an offending country continues to impose trade restrictions, permission will be granted for other countries to retaliate.

For example, in March 2002, the Bush administration imposed tariffs on steel imports into the USA in order to protect the ailing US steel industry (see Case study I.15 in MyEconLab). The EU and other countries referred the case to the WTO, which in December 2003 ruled that they were illegal. This ruling made it legitimate for the EU and other countries to impose retaliatory tariffs on US products. President Bush consequently announced that the steel tariffs would be abolished.

The greater power of the WTO has persuaded many countries to bring their disputes to it. From January 1995 to June 2015 496 disputes had been brought to the WTO (compared with 300 to GATT over the whole of its 48 years).

Pause for thought

Could US action to protect its steel industry from foreign competition be justified in terms of the interests of the USA as a whole (as opposed to the steel industry in particular)?

Trade rounds

Periodically, member countries have met to negotiate reductions in tariffs and other trade restrictions. There have been eight 'rounds' of such negotiations since the signing of GATT in 1947. The last major round to be completed was the Uruguay Round, which began in Uruguay in 1986, continued at meetings around the world and culminated in a deal being signed in April 1994. By that time, the average tariff on manufactured products was 4 per cent and falling. In 1947 the figure was nearly 40 per cent. The Uruguay Round agreement also involved a programme of phasing in substantial reductions in tariffs and other restrictions up to the year 2002 (see Case study I.6 in MyEconLab).

Despite the reduction in tariffs, many countries have still tried to restrict trade by various other means, such as quotas and administrative barriers. Also, barriers have been particularly high on certain non-manufactures. Agricultural protection in particular has come in for sustained criticism by developing countries. High fixed prices and subsidies given to farmers in the EU, the USA and other advanced countries mean that the industrialised world continues to export food to many developing countries which have a comparative advantage in food production! Farmers in developing countries often find it impossible to compete with subsidised food imports from the rich countries.

The most recent round of trade negotiations began in Doha, Qatar, in 2001 (see Box 24.3). The negotiations have focused on both trade liberalisation and measures to encourage development of poorer countries. In particular, the Doha Development Agenda, as it is called, is concerned with measures to make trade fairer so that its benefits are spread more evenly around the world. This would involve improved access for developing countries to markets in the rich world. The Agenda is also concerned with the environmental impacts of trade and development.

The negotiations were originally due to be completed in 2005, but, as Box 24.3 explains, deadlines continued to be missed. December 2013, however, saw a series of agreements at a WTO ministerial conference in Bali. The so-called Bali Package included commitments to streamline trade, boost trade among least developed countries and provide 'food security' for developing countries. The deal was proclaimed as the first substantial agreement since the WTO was formed in 1995. Nonetheless, considerable work remained in meeting the goals set in Doha.

BOX 24.3 THE DOHA DEVELOPMENT AGENDA

A new direction for the WTO?

Globalisation, based on the free play of comparative advantage, economies of scale and innovation, has produced a genuinely radical force, in the true sense of the word. It essentially amplifies and reinforces the strengths, but also the weaknesses, of market capitalism: its efficiency, its instability, and its inequality. If we want globalisation not only to be efficiency-boosting but also fair, we need more international rules and stronger multilateral institutions.[2]

In November 1999, the members of the World Trade Organization met in Seattle in the USA. What ensued became known as the 'battle of Seattle' (see Case study I.3 in MyEconLab). Anti-globalisation protesters fought with police; the world's developing economies fell out with the world's developed economies; and the very future of the WTO was called into question. The WTO was accused of being a free trader's charter, in which the objective of free trade was allowed to ride rough-shod over anything that might stand in its way. Whatever the issue – the environment, the plight of developing countries, the dominance of trade by multinationals – free trade was king.

At Seattle, both the protesters and developing countries argued that things had gone far enough. The WTO must redefine its role, they argued, to respect *all* stakeholders. More radical voices called for the organisation to be scrapped. As Pascal Lamy, then EU Trade Commissioner, made clear in the quote above, rules had to be strengthened, and the WTO had to ensure that the gains from trade were fairer and more sustainable.

The rebuilding process of the WTO began in Doha, Qatar in November 2001. The meeting between the then 142 members of the WTO concluded with the decision to launch a new round of WTO trade talks, to be called the 'Doha Development Agenda'. The talks are designed to increase the liberalisation of trade. However, such a goal is to be tempered by a policy of strengthening assistance to developing economies.

Other areas identified for discussion include: greater liberalisation of agriculture; rules to govern foreign direct investment; the co-ordination of countries' competition policies; the use and abuse of patents on medicines and the needs of developing countries.

The talks were originally scheduled for completion by January 2005, but this deadline was extended several times as new talks were arranged and failed to reach agreement. A particular sticking point was the unwillingness of rich countries, and the USA and the EU in particular, to liberalise trade in agricultural products, given the pressure from their domestic farmers. The USA was unwilling to make substantial cuts in agricultural subsidies and the EU in agricultural tariffs.

There was also an unwillingness by large developing countries, such as India and Brazil, to reduce protection of their industrial and service sectors. What is more, there were large divergences in opinion between developing countries on how much they should reduce their own agricultural protection.

Breakdown of the talks

The talks seemed finally to have broken down at a meeting in Geneva in July 2008. Despite the willingness of developing

countries to reduce industrial tariffs by more than 50 per cent, and by the USA and the EU to make deep cuts in agricultural subsidies and tariffs, the talks foundered over the question of agricultural protection for developing countries. This was item 18 on a 'to-do' list of 20 items; items 1 to 17 had already been agreed. China and India wanted to protect poor farmers by retaining the ability to impose temporary tariffs on food imports in the event of a drop in food prices or a surge in imports. The USA objected. When neither side would budge, the talks collapsed.

But even 'success' would not have addressed some thorny issues, such as achieving equal access to rich countries' markets by all banana-producing countries (see Box 25.1) and protecting cotton producers in developing countries from cheap subsidised cotton grown in the USA. And Africa's interests would not have been properly addressed. In fact, no African country was present in the inner circle of talks at the end.

Many commentators, however, argued that failure was no catastrophe. The gain from total liberalisation of trade would have boosted developing countries' GDP by no more than 1 per cent. And anyway, tariffs were generally falling and were already at an all-time low. But with the global economic downturn of 2008/9, there were worries that protectionism would begin to rise again. This was a classic prisoner's dilemma (see page 206–7). Policies that seemed to be in the interests of countries separately would be to the overall detriment of the world. The Nash equilibrium of such a 'game', therefore, is one where countries are generally worse off. As it turned out, the worries were largely unfounded

The Bali Package and the push to agreement

At the WTO's Bali Ministerial Conference in December 2013, an agreement was reached on a package of issues. The result was a streamlining of trade, allowing developing countries more options for providing food security, boosting least developed countries' trade and, more generally, promoting development. The deal was the first substantial agreement since the WTO was formed in 1995.

At the heart of the agreement is the simplifying of customs procedures, making them more transparent, and ensuring that trade is made 'easier, faster and cheaper'. Meanwhile, the deal also permits developing countries to continue subsidising their agriculture in order to promote food security, provided the practice does not distort international trade.

According to the EU's trade commissioner Karel De Gucht, about one-quarter of the goals set for the Doha Round have been achieved in this agreement. This, of course, still leaves a long way to go if all the Doha objectives are to be met. World trade, although now likely to be somewhat freer, is still not free; developing countries will still find access restricted for their agricultural products, and manufactures too, to many markets in the rich world; rich countries will still find access restricted for their manufactured products and services to many markets in the developing world.

By the time you read this, a final agreement may have been reached – or perhaps not!

[2]'Global policy without democracy' (speech by Pascal Lamy, EU Trade Commissioner, given in 2001).

 Outline the advantages and drawbacks of adopting a free trade strategy for developing economies. How might the Doha Development Agenda go some way to reducing these drawbacks?

SUMMARY

1a World trade has grown, for many years, significantly faster than the growth in world output.

1b The developed nations have tended to dominate world trade. However, the share of world trade accounted for by developing countries has risen rapidly in recent times and is now over 43 per cent. The growth in exports from the BRICS (Brazil, Russia, India, China and South Africa) has been especially rapid.

1c The composition of world trade is largely dominated by manufacturing products, although trade in services has expanded over recent years.

2a Countries can gain from trade if they specialise in producing those goods in which they have a comparative advantage, i.e. those goods that can be produced at relatively low opportunity costs. This is merely an extension of the argument that gains can be made from the specialisation and division of labour.

2b If two countries trade, then, provided that the trade price ratio of exports and imports is between the pre-trade price ratios of these goods in the two countries, both countries can gain.

2c With increasing opportunity costs there will be a limit to specialisation and trade. As a country increasingly specialises, its (marginal) comparative advantage will eventually disappear.

2d Gains from trade also arise from decreasing costs (economies of scale), differences in demand between countries, increased competition from trade and the transmission of growth from one country to another. There may also be non-economic advantages from trade.

2e The terms of trade give the price of exports relative to the price of imports expressed as an index, where the base year is 100.

3a Countries use various methods to restrict trade, including tariffs, quotas, exchange controls, import licensing, export taxes, and legal and administrative barriers. Countries may also promote their own industries by subsidies.

3b Reasons for restricting trade that have some validity in a world context include the infant industry argument, the problems of relying on exporting goods whose market is growing slowly or even declining, dumping and other unfair trade practices, the danger of the establishment of a foreign-based monopoly, the need to spread the risks of fluctuating export prices, and the problems that free trade may adversely affect consumer tastes, may allow the importation of harmful goods and may not take account of externalities.

3c Often, however, the arguments for restricting trade are in the context of one country benefiting even though other countries may lose more. Countries may intervene in trade in order to exploit their monopoly/monopsony power or to protect declining industries.

3d Finally, a country may have other objectives in restricting trade, such as remaining self-sufficient in certain strategic products, not trading with certain countries of which it disapproves, protecting traditional ways of life or simply retaining a non-specialised economy.

3e Arguments for restricting trade, however, are often fallacious. In general, trade brings benefits to countries, and protection to achieve one objective may be at a very high opportunity cost. Even if government intervention to protect certain parts of the economy is desirable, restricting trade is unlikely to be a first-best solution to the problem, since it involves side-effect costs. What is more, restricting trade may encourage retaliation; it may allow inefficient firms to remain inefficient; it may involve considerable bureaucracy.

4 Most countries of the world are members of the WTO and in theory are in favour of moves towards freer trade. The WTO is more powerful than its predecessor, GATT. It has a disputes procedure and can enforce its rulings. In practice, however, countries have been very unwilling to abandon restrictions if they believe that they can gain from them, even though they might be at the expense of other countries.

MyEconLab

This book can be supported by MyEconLab, which contains a range of additional resources, including an online homework and tutorial system designed to test and build your understanding.

You need both an access card and a course ID to access MyEconLab:

1. Is your lecturer using MyEconLab? Ask your lecturer for your course ID.

2. Has an access card been included with the book at a reduced cost? Check the inside back cover of the book.

3. If you have a course ID but no access card, go to: http://www.myeconlab.com/ to buy access to this interactive study programme.

REVIEW QUESTIONS

1 What is likely to be the impact of rising levels of intra-regional trade for the world economy?

2 Imagine that two countries, Richland and Poorland, can produce just two goods, computers and coal. Assume that for a given amount of land and capital, the output of these two products requires the following constant amounts of labour:

	Richland	Poorland
1 computer	2	4
100 tonnes of coal	4	5

Assume that each country has 20 million workers.

a) Draw the production possibility curves for the two countries (on two separate diagrams).

b) If there is no trade, and in each country 12 million workers produce computers and 8 million workers produce coal, how many computers and tonnes of coal will each country produce? What will be the total production of each product?

c) What is the opportunity cost of a computer in (i) Richland; (ii) Poorland?

d) What is the opportunity cost of 100 tonnes of coal in (i) Richland: (ii) Poorland?

e) Which country has a comparative advantage in which product?

f) Assuming that price equals marginal cost, which of the following would represent possible exchange ratios?
   (i)   1 computer for 40 tonnes of coal;
   (ii) 2 computers for 140 tonnes of coal;
   (iii) 1 computer for 100 tonnes of coal;
   (iv) 1 computer for 60 tonnes of coal;
   (v)   4 computers for 360 tonnes of coal.

g) Assume that trade now takes place and that 1 computer exchanges for 65 tonnes of coal. Both countries specialise completely in the product in which they have a comparative advantage. How much does each country produce of its respective product?

h) The country producing computers sells 6 million domestically. How many does it export to the other country?

i) How much coal does the other country consume?

3 Why doesn't the USA specialise as much as General Motors or Texaco? Why doesn't the UK specialise as much as GlaxoSmithKline? Is the answer to these questions similar to the answer to the questions, 'Why doesn't the USA specialise as much as Luxembourg?', and 'Why doesn't ICI or Unilever specialise as much as the local florist?'

4 To what extent are the arguments for countries specialising and then trading with each other the same as those for individuals specialising in doing the jobs to which they are relatively well suited?

5 The following are four items that are traded internationally: wheat; computers; textiles; insurance. In which one of the four is each of the following most likely to have a comparative advantage: India; the UK; Canada; Japan? Give reasons for your answer.

6 Go through each of the arguments for restricting trade (both those of general validity and those having some validity for specific countries) and provide a counterargument for not restricting trade.

7 If countries are so keen to reduce the barriers to trade, why do many countries frequently attempt to erect barriers?

8 Debate the following: 'All arguments for restricting trade boil down to special pleading for particular interest groups. Ultimately there will be a net social cost from any trade restrictions.'

9 If rich countries stand to gain substantially from freer trade, why have they been so reluctant to reduce the levels of protection of agriculture?

10 Make out a case for restricting trade between the UK and Japan. Are there any arguments here that could not equally apply to a case for restricting trade between Scotland and England or between Liverpool or Manchester?

25 Chapter

Trading blocs

Business issues covered in this chapter

■ Why do countries form free trade areas and other types of trading alliance, and what forms can they take?
■ Do they result in a creation of trade or a mere diversion of trade from outside to inside the area?
■ What trading alliances exist around the world and what are their features?
■ How has the EU evolved and to what extent is it a true common market?
■ How has the single market in the EU benefited companies and member states?

The world economy seems to have been increasingly forming into a series of trade blocs, based upon regional groupings of countries: a European region centred on the European Union, an Asian region on Japan, a North American region on the USA and a Latin American region. Such trade blocs are examples of *preferential trading arrangements*. These arrangements involve trade restrictions with the rest of the world, and lower or zero restrictions between the members.

Although trade blocs clearly encourage trade between their members (intra-regional trade has been growing significantly faster than trade between regions), many countries outside these blocs complain that they benefit the members at the expense of the rest of the world. For many developing economies, in need of access to the most prosperous nations in the world, this represents a significant check on their ability to grow and develop.

In this chapter we shall first consider why groups of countries might wish to establish trade blocs, and what they seek to gain beyond the benefits that result from free and open trade. We will then look at the world's trade blocs as they currently stand, paying particular attention to the European Union, which is by far the most advanced in respect to establishing a high level of regional integration.

Definition

Preferential trading arrangement A trading arrangement whereby trade between the signatories is freer than trade with the rest of the world.

25.1 PREFERENTIAL TRADING

Types of preferential trading arrangement

There are three possible forms that such trading arrangements might take.

Free trade areas

A **free trade area** is where member countries remove tariffs and quotas between themselves, but retain whatever restrictions *each member chooses* with non-member countries. Some provision will have to be made to prevent imports from outside coming into the area via the country with the lowest external tariff.

Customs unions

A **customs union** is like a free trade area, but in addition members must adopt *common* external tariffs and quotas with non-member countries.

Common markets

A **common market** is where member countries operate as a *single* market. Like a customs union there are no tariffs and quotas between member countries and there are common external tariffs and quotas. But a common market goes further than this. A full common market includes the following features:

- *A common system of taxation.* In the case of a *perfect* common market, this will involve identical rates of tax in all member countries.
- *A common system of laws and regulations governing production, employment and trade.* For example, in a perfect common market there would be a *single* set of laws governing issues such as product specification (e.g. permissible artificial additives to foods, or levels of exhaust emissions from cars), the employment and dismissal of labour, mergers and takeovers, and monopolies and restrictive practices.
- *Free movement of labour, capital and materials, and of goods and services.* In a perfect common market, this will involve a total absence of border controls between member states, the freedom of workers to work in any member country, and the freedom of firms to expand into any member state.
- *The absence of special treatment by member governments of their own domestic industries.* Governments are large purchasers of goods and services. In a perfect common market, they should buy from whichever companies within the market offer the most competitive deal and not show favouritism towards domestic suppliers: they should operate a *common procurement policy*.

The definition of a common market is sometimes extended to include the following two features of *economic and monetary union*.

- *A fixed exchange rate between the member countries' currencies.* In the extreme case, this would involve a single currency for the whole market.
- *Common macroeconomic policies.* To some extent this must follow from a fixed exchange rate, but in the extreme case it will involve a single macroeconomic management of the whole market, and hence the abolition of separate fiscal or monetary intervention by individual member states. We will examine European economic and monetary union in section 32.3.

The direct effects of a customs union: trade creation and trade diversion

By joining a customs union (or free trade area), a country will find that its trade patterns change. Two such changes can be distinguished: trade creation and trade diversion.

Trade creation

Trade creation is where consumption shifts from a high-cost producer to a low-cost producer. The removal of trade barriers allows greater specialisation according to comparative advantage. Instead of consumers having to pay high prices for domestically produced goods in which the country has a comparative disadvantage, the goods can now be obtained more cheaply from other members of the customs union. In return, the country can export to them goods in which it has a comparative advantage.

KI 37 p 444

Trade diversion

Trade diversion is where consumption shifts from a lower-cost producer outside the customs union to a higher-cost producer within the union.

Definitions

Free trade area A group of countries with no trade barriers between themselves.

Customs union A free trade area with common external tariffs and quotas.

Common market A customs union where the member countries act as a single market with free movement of labour and capital, common taxes and common trade laws.

Trade creation Where a customs union leads to greater specialisation according to comparative advantage and thus a shift in production from higher-cost to lower-cost sources.

Trade diversion Where a customs union diverts consumption from goods produced at a lower cost outside the union to goods produced at a higher cost (but tariff free) within the union.

Assume that the most efficient producer of good y in the world is New Zealand – outside the EU. Assume that before membership of the EU, the UK paid a similar tariff on good y from any country, and thus imported the product from New Zealand rather than from the EU.

After the UK joined the EU, however, the removal of the tariff made the EU product cheaper, since the tariff remained on the New Zealand product. Consumption thus switched to a higher-cost producer. There was thus a net loss in world efficiency. As far as the UK was concerned, consumers still gained, since they were paying a lower price than before. However, there was a loss to domestic producers (from the reduction in protection, and hence reduced prices and profits) and to the government (from reduced tariff revenue). These losses may have been smaller or larger than the gain to consumers: in other words, there may have still been a net gain to the UK, but there could have been a net loss, depending on the circumstances.

Pause for thought

Is joining a customs union more likely to lead to trade creation or trade diversion in each of the following cases? (a) The union has a very high external tariff. (b) Cost differences are very great between the country and members of the union.

Longer-term effects of a customs union

Over the longer term, there may be other gains and losses from being a member of a customs union.

Longer-term advantages

- Increased market size may allow a country's firms to exploit *(internal) economies of scale*. This argument is more important for small countries, which therefore have more to gain from an enlargement of their markets.
- *External economies of scale*. Increased trade may lead to improvements in the infrastructure of the members of the customs union (better roads, railways, financial services, etc.). This, in turn, could then bring greater long-term benefits from trade between members, and from external trade too, by making the transport and handling of imports and exports cheaper.
- The bargaining power of the whole customs union with the rest of the world may allow member countries to gain *better terms of trade*. This, of course, will necessarily involve a degree of political co-operation between the members.
- *Increased competition* between member countries may stimulate efficiency, encourage investment and reduce monopoly power. Of course, a similar advantage could be gained by the simple removal of tariffs with any competing country.
- Integration may encourage a *more rapid spread of technology*.

Longer-term disadvantages

- Resources may flow from the country to more efficient members of the customs union, or to the geographical centre of the union (so as to minimise transport costs). This can be a major problem for a *common market* (where there is free movement of labour and capital). The country could become a depressed 'region' of the community.
- If integration encourages greater co-operation between firms in member countries, it may also encourage *greater oligopolistic collusion*, thus keeping prices higher to the consumer. It may also encourage mergers and takeovers, which would increase monopoly power.
- *Diseconomies of scale*. If the union leads to the development of very large companies, they may become bureaucratic and inefficient.
- *The costs of administering* the customs union may be high. This problem is likely to worsen the more intervention there is in the affairs of individual members.

25.2 PREFERENTIAL TRADING IN PRACTICE

Preferential trading has the greatest potential to benefit countries whose domestic market is too small, taken on its own, to enable them to benefit from economies of scale, and where they face substantial barriers to their exports. Most developing countries fall into this category and as a result many have attempted to form preferential trading arrangements.

Examples in Latin America and the Caribbean include the Latin American Integration Association (LAIA), the Andean Community, the Central American Integration System (SICA) and the Caribbean Community (CARICOM). A Southern Common Market (MerCoSur) was formed in 1991, consisting of Argentina, Brazil, Paraguay and Uruguay. It has a common external tariff and most of its internal trade is free of tariffs.

In 1993, the six original ASEAN nations (Brunei, Indonesia, Malaysia, the Philippines, Singapore and Thailand) agreed to work towards an ASEAN Free Trade Area (AFTA). ASEAN (the Association of South-East Asian Nations) now has ten members (the new ones being Laos, Myanmar, Vietnam and Cambodia) and is dedicated to increased economic co-operation within the region. What progress has been made in achieving AFTA? Virtually all tariffs between the six original members were eliminated by 2010 and there were plans to eliminate them for the remaining countries by 2015. ASEAN hoped to announce the establishment of a common market known as the ASEAN Economic Community (AEC) by the end of 2015.

In Africa, the Economic Community of West African States (ECOWAS) has been attempting to create a common market between its 15 members. The West African franc is used in eight of the countries by a population of over 100 million people. A further six countries plan to introduce a common currency, as part of the West African Monetary Zone (WAMZ). However, the start date for the Eco, as the currency is to be known, has had to be put back several times as countries struggle to meet a series of convergence criteria. The ultimate goal is to combine the two currency areas and adopt a single currency for all member states.

North America Free Trade Agreement (NAFTA)

NAFTA is one of the two most powerful trading blocs in the world (the other being the EU). It came into force in 1994 and consists of the USA, Canada and Mexico. The three countries have agreed to abolish tariffs between themselves in the hope that increased trade and co-operation will follow. Tariffs between the USA and Canada were phased out by 1999 and tariffs between all three countries were eliminated as of 1 January 2008. New non-tariff restrictions will not be permitted either, but many existing ones can remain in force, thus preventing the development of true free trade between the members. Indeed, some industries, such as textiles and agriculture, will continue to have major non-tariff restrictions.

NAFTA members hope that, with a market similar in size to the EU, they will be able to rival the EU's economic power in world trade. Other countries may join in the future, so NAFTA may eventually develop into a Western Hemisphere free trade association.

NAFTA is principally a free trade area and not a common market. Unlike the EU, it does not seek to harmonise laws and regulations, except in very specific areas such as environmental management and labour standards. Member countries are permitted total legal independence, subject to the one proviso that they must treat firms of other member countries equally with their own firms – the principle of 'fair competition'. Nevertheless, NAFTA has encouraged a growth in trade between its members, most of which is trade creation rather than trade diversion.

Case study I.11 in MyEconLab looks at the costs and benefits of NAFTA membership to the three countries involved.

The Asia-Pacific Economic Cooperation forum (APEC)

The most significant move towards establishing a more widespread regional economic organisation in East Asia appeared with the creation of the Asia-Pacific Economic Cooperation forum in 1989 (APEC). APEC links 21 economies of the Pacific Rim, including Asian, Australasian and North and South American countries (19 countries, plus Hong Kong and Taiwan). These countries account for around 57 per cent of the world's total output and 46 per cent of world merchandise trade. At the 1994 meeting of APEC leaders, it was resolved to create a free trade area across the Pacific by 2010 for the developed industrial countries, and by 2020 for the rest.

Unlike the EU and NAFTA, APEC is likely to remain solely a free trade area and not to develop into a customs union, let alone a common market. Within the region there exists a wide disparity in GDP per capita, ranging in 2015 from $56 400 in the USA, $52 400 in Australia and $33 200 in Japan to a mere $2600 in Papua New Guinea and $2200 in Vietnam. Such disparities create a wide range of national interests and goals. Countries are unlikely to share common economic problems or concerns. In addition, political differences and conflicts within the region are widespread, reducing the likelihood that any organisational agreement beyond a simple economic one would succeed. However, the economic benefits from free trade, and the resulting closer regional ties, could be immense.

The longest established and most comprehensive preferential trading arrangement is the EU. In the remainder of this chapter we will consider the development of the EU and its implications for business.

25.3 THE EUROPEAN UNION

The European Economic Community (EEC) was formed by the signing of the Treaty of Rome in 1957 and came into operation on 1 January 1958.

The original six member countries of the EEC (Belgium, France, Italy, Luxembourg, Netherlands and West Germany) had already made a move towards integration with the formation of the European Coal and Steel Community in 1952. This had removed all restrictions on trade in coal, steel and iron ore between the six countries. The aim had been to gain economies of scale and allow more effective competition with the USA and other foreign producers.

The EEC extended this principle and aimed eventually to be a full common market with completely free trade between members in all products, and with completely free movement of labour, enterprise and capital.

All internal tariffs between the six members had been abolished and common external tariffs established by 1968. But this still only made the EEC a *customs union*, since a number of restrictions on internal trade remained (legal, administrative, fiscal, etc.). Nevertheless, the aim was eventually to create a full common market.

In 1973 the UK, Denmark and Ireland became members. Greece joined in 1981, Spain and Portugal in 1986, and Sweden, Austria and Finland in 1995. Then in May 2004 a further 10 countries joined: Cyprus, the Czech Republic, Estonia, Hungary, Latvia, Lithuania, Malta, Poland, Slovakia and Slovenia. Bulgaria and Romania joined in 2007. With the accession of Croatia in July 2013, the European Union now has 28 members.

From customs union to common market

The EU is clearly a customs union. It has common external tariffs and no internal tariffs. But is it also a common market? For years there have been certain common economic policies.

Common Agricultural Policy (CAP). The EU has traditionally set common high prices for farm products. This has involved charging variable import duties to bring foreign food imports up to EU prices and intervention to buy up surpluses of food produced within the EU at these above-equilibrium prices. Although the main method of support has shifted to providing subsidies (or 'income support') unrelated to current output, this still represents a common economic policy of agricultural support.

Regional policy. EU regional policy provides grants to firms and local authorities in relatively deprived regions of the Union.

Competition policy. EU policy here has applied primarily to companies operating in more than one member state (see section 21.1). For example, Article 101 of the Treaty of Lisbon prohibits agreements between firms operating in more than one EU country (e.g. over pricing or sharing out markets) which adversely affect competition in trade between member states.

Harmonisation of taxation. VAT is the standard form of indirect tax throughout the EU. However, there are substantial differences in VAT rates between member states, as there are with other tax rates.

Social policy. In 1989 the European Commission presented a Social Charter to the EU heads of state (see Case study I.12 in MyEconLab). This spelt out a series of worker and social rights that should apply in all member states. These rights were grouped under 12 headings covering areas such as the guarantee of decent levels of income for both the employed and the non-employed, freedom of movement of labour between EU countries, freedom to belong to a trade union and equal treatment of women and men in the labour market. The Social Charter was only a recommendation and each element had to be approved separately by the European Council of Ministers.

The Social Chapter of the Maastricht Treaty (1991) attempted to move the Community forward in implementing the details of the Social Charter in areas such as maximum working hours, minimum working conditions, health and safety protection, the provision of information to and consultation with workers, and equal opportunities.

The UK Conservative government at the time refused to sign this part of the Maastricht Treaty. It maintained that such measures would increase costs of production and would, therefore, make EU goods less competitive in world trade and increase unemployment. Critics of the UK position argued that the refusal to adopt minimum working conditions (and also a minimum wage rate) would make the UK the 'cheap labour sweat-shop' of Europe. One of the first acts of the incoming Labour government in 1997 was to sign up to the Social Chapter.

> ### Pause for thought
>
> *Does the adoption of laws enforcing improved working conditions necessarily lead to higher costs per unit of output?*

Despite these various common policies, in other respects the Community of the 1970s and 1980s was far from a true common market: there were all sorts of non-tariff barriers, such as high taxes on wine by non-wine-producing countries, special regulations designed to favour domestic producers, governments giving contracts to domestic producers (e.g. for defence equipment), and so on.

The Single European Act of 1986, however, sought to remove these barriers and to form a genuine common market by the end of 1992. One of the most crucial aspects of the Act was its acceptance of the principle of **mutual recognition**. This is the principle whereby if a firm or individual is permitted to do something under the rules and regulations of *one* EU country, it must thereby also be permitted to do it in all other EU countries. This means that firms and individuals can choose the country's rules that are least constraining. It also means that individual governments can no longer devise special rules and regulations that keep out competitors from other EU countries.

> ### Definition
>
> **Mutual recognition** The EU principle that one country's rules and regulations must apply throughout the Union. If they conflict with those of another country, individuals and firms should be able to choose which to obey.

The benefits and costs of the single market

It is difficult to quantify the benefits and costs of the single market, given that many occur over a long period. Also it is difficult to know to what extent the changes taking place are the direct result of the single market.

In 2012, the European Commission published *20 Years of the European Single Market*. This stated that: 'EU27 GDP in 2008 was 2.13 per cent or €233 billion higher than it would have been if the Single Market had not been launched in 1992. In 2008 alone, this amounted to an average of €500 extra in income per person in the EU27. The gains come from the Single Market programme, liberalisation in network industries such as energy and telecommunication, and the enlargement of the EU to 27 member countries.'

Even though the precise magnitude of the benefits is difficult to estimate, it is possible to identify the *types* of benefit that have resulted, many of which have been substantial.

Trade creation. Costs and prices have fallen as a result of a greater exploitation of comparative advantage. Member countries can now specialise further in those goods and services that they can produce at a comparatively low opportunity cost.

Reduction in the direct costs of barriers. This category includes administrative costs, border delays and technical regulations. Their abolition or harmonisation has led to substantial cost savings.

Economies of scale. With industries based on a Europe-wide scale, many firms and their plants can be large enough to gain the full potential economies of scale. Yet the whole European market is large enough for there still to be adequate competition. Such gains have varied from industry to industry depending on the minimum efficient scale of a plant or firm (see Box 9.4 on p. 156). Economies of scale have also been gained from mergers and other forms of industrial restructuring.

Greater competition. Increased competition between firms has led to lower costs, lower prices and a wider range of products available to consumers. This has been particularly so in newly liberalised service sectors such as transport, financial services, telecommunications and broadcasting. In the long run, greater competition can stimulate greater innovation, the greater flow of technical information and the rationalisation of production.

Despite these gains, the single market has not received universal welcome within the EU. Its critics argue that, in a Europe of oligopolies, unequal ownership of resources, rapidly changing technologies and industrial practices, and factor immobility, the removal of internal barriers to trade has merely exaggerated the problems of inequality and economic power. More specifically, the following criticisms are made.

Radical economic change is costly. Substantial economic change is necessary to achieve the full economies of scale and efficiency gains from a single European market. These changes necessarily involve redundancies – from bankruptcies, takeovers, rationalisation and the introduction of new technology. The severity of this 'structural' and 'technological' unemployment (see section 26.3) depends on (a) the pace of economic change and (b) the mobility of labour – both occupational and geographical. Clearly, the more integrated markets become across the EU, the less the costs of future economic change.

Adverse regional effects. Firms are likely to locate as near as possible to the 'centre of gravity' of their markets and sources of supply. If, before barriers are removed, a firm's prime market is the UK, it might well locate in the Midlands or the north of England. If, however, with barriers now removed, its market has become Europe as a whole, it may choose to locate in the south of England or in France, Germany or the Benelux countries instead. The creation of a single European market thus tends to attract capital and jobs away from the edges of the Union to its geographical centre.

In an ideal market situation, areas like Cornwall, the south of Italy, Portugal and parts of eastern Europe should attract resources from other parts of the Union. As these are relatively depressed areas, wage rates and land prices are lower. The resulting lower industrial costs should encourage firms to move there. In practice, however, as capital and labour (and especially young and skilled workers) leave the extremities of the Union, so these regions are likely to become more depressed. If, as a result, their infrastructure is neglected, they then become even less attractive to new investment.

The development of monopoly/oligopoly power. The free movement of capital can encourage the development of giant 'Euro-firms' with substantial economic power. Indeed, recent years have seen some very large European mergers (see Box 15.1). This can lead to higher, not lower prices and less choice for the consumer. It all depends on just how effective competition is, and how effective EU competition policy is in preventing monopolistic and collusive practices.

Trade diversion. Just as trade creation has been a potential advantage of completing the internal market, so trade diversion has been a possibility too. This is more likely if *external* barriers remain high (or are even increased) and internal barriers are *completely* abolished.

Pause for thought

Why may the newer members of the EU have the most to gain from the single market, but also the most to lose?

BOX 25.1   BEYOND BANANAS

EU/US trade disputes

Trade relations between the EU and USA have been strained in recent years. The World Trade Organization (WTO), set up to manage trade and prevent such disputes arising, has been slow in resolving the issues and restoring order.

The problems between the EU and USA started over bananas.

Bananas

The EU/US 'banana war' began in 1993 when the EU adopted a tariff and quota system that favoured banana producers in African, Caribbean and Pacific (ACP) countries, mostly ex-European colonies. Predictably, Latin American banana producers, owned by large American multinationals like Chiquita and Dole, took exception to this move. Latin American producers, with huge economies of scale, were able to produce bananas at considerably lower cost than producers in the ACP countries. But, faced with significant tariffs on entry into the EU market, their bananas became more expensive. Championed by the USA, the Latin American producers won the case at the WTO for removing the agreement.

The EU, however, failed to comply, arguing that the preferential access to EU markets for ACP producers was part of a general development strategy, known as the 'Lomé Convention', to support developing economies. Without preferential access, it was argued, ACP banana producers could simply not compete on world markets. As a European Commission document highlighted: 'The destruction of the Caribbean banana industry would provoke severe economic hardship and political instability in a region already struggling against deprivation.'[1]

As the EU refused to comply with the WTO ruling, the USA imposed $191 million worth of tariffs on EU exports in March 1999. After a series of battles over the issue at the WTO, the EU finally agreed in 2009 to reform its banana protocol and to cut tariffs on non-ACP bananas from $234 per tonne to $196 per tonne straight away and to $150 by 2016. In return, it would pay compensation to ACP nations. The deal, however, is dependent on agreement of the Doha round of trade negotiations, which is still on-going, as discussed in Box 24.3.

Hormone-treated beef

Trade disputes between the EU and the USA have not just concerned bananas. A dispute over hormone-treated beef has been going on for a staggering 20 years. In January 1996 the US requested 'consultations' with the EU following an EU directive prohibiting the use in livestock farming of certain substances 'having a hormonal action'. In 1998, the WTO panel ruled against a ban by the EU on imports of hormone-treated beef from the USA and Canada. The ruling permitted the two countries to impose retaliatory sanctions on EU imports. After a process of arbitration, the values were set at $116.8 million for the USA and CDN$11.1 million for Canada.

Despite this, the EU continued to refuse to import any animal products, live or processed, that had received growth hormones. The ban was made on grounds of public health, and this remains the crux of the dispute. The EU argues that it has not been proven that hormone-treated beef is safe. In reply,

the Americans argue that the EU has not provided evidence that it is otherwise.

Following an independent assessment of the risks to consumers of hormone-treated meat, which resulted in the EU banning certain hormones by its farmers, the EU argued that the sanctions should be lifted as it was no longer in breach of the WTO rules. In November 2004, the EU asked the WTO to rule that continued US and Canadian sanctions related to the beef hormone ruling were illegal. In February 2005, a WTO panel was set up to consider the case. The EU, Canada and the USA would all make representations. In addition Australia, Mexico, China and Taiwan were permitted to make 'third-party' representations.

In April 2008, a WTO disputes panel ruled that the EU violated WTO rules in continuing to ban one of the hormones at issue, but also ruled that the USA and Canada were wrong in taking unilateral actions in imposing sanctions against the EU. Both sides appealed but the USA put in place a modified set of duties in January 2009.

However, in April 2009 the USA and EU resolved to work through the dispute: the EU would maintain its ban on hormone-treated beef, but the USA would start to remove its sanctions if the EU's duty-free import quotas of hormone-free beef increased significantly. The volumes of hormone-free beef exempted from taxation would increase to 48 200 tonnes and so, in May 2012, the USA removed its import duties on all targeted European luxury foods.

Genetically modified (GM) foods

A more recent trade dispute, again in the field of public health, concerns the development of GM food. GM strains of maize and soya have been available in the USA for many years, but the export of such products, whether as seed or food, is banned from the EU. The US position is that EU consumers should be free to choose whether they have GM food or not. This, not surprisingly, is rejected by the EU on the basis that GM foods might contaminate the entire food supply once introduced. In July 2000, the EU decided to continue with its GM food ban indefinitely.

In response to a complaint to the WTO by the USA, Canada and Argentina, a panel was set up in March 2004 to consider the case. In 2006 the WTO concluded that the EU's GM ban was illegal because the risks shown by the scientific evidence did not warrant the ban. Accordingly, WTO rules should apply across EU member states. In January 2008, the US and the EU informed the Dispute Settlement Board that they had reached an agreement on 'procedures' for the EU implementing the WTO's ruling.

Signs that the dispute was ending emerged in 2010, with GM crops being permitted to be grown under strict regulations throughout Europe. Barack Obama has called for a free-trade agreement between the EU and USA, but despite the progress, GM crops do continue to be tightly regulated across Europe, including the requirement that products are clearly labelled.

---

[1] 'EC fact sheet on Caribbean bananas and the WTO', *Press Release*, European Commission (18 March 1997).

Airbus

Another recent branch of the current EU/US trade dispute concerns Airbus and EU industrial policy (an area which has been a bone of contention for the USA for many years). The issue concerns the new superjumbo, the A380. The Americans are very unhappy with the loans and subsidies, claimed to be $15 billion, which have been provided by EU members to companies within the Airbus Consortium to develop the aircraft. The American complaint is that such subsidies have broken the WTO subsidy code and, as such, are unfair.

In October 2004, the USA requested the establishment of a WTO panel to consider the case. This provoked a counter-request by Airbus, claiming unfair subsidies of $27.3 billion for Boeing by the US government since 1992. In July 2005, two panels were set up to deal with the two sets of allegations.

In June 2010, the WTO panel found Airbus guilty of using some illegal subsidies to win contracts through predatory pricing, but dismissed several of Boeing's claims because many of the subsidies were reimbursable at commercial rates of interest. However, some of the 'launch aid' for research and development was given at below market rates and so violated WTO rules. The report evoked appeal and counter-appeal from both sides, but the WTO's Appellate Body reported in May 2011 upholding the case that 'certain subsidies' provided by the EU and member states were incompatible with WTO rules. In June 2011, the EU accepted the findings.

In March 2011, the WTO panel found Boeing guilty of three violations of WTO rules on subsidies, including subsidies between 1989 and 2006 worth at least $5.3 billion. These subsidies were adjudged to have resulted in lost sales, especially to third-country markets, and in significantly suppressing the price of Airbus aircraft.

In April 2011, the USA notified the WTO of its intention to appeal the judgment. The WTO's Appellate Body reported back in March 2012. While some of the detailed findings of the initial 2011 panel report were overturned, it nonetheless agreed that in broad terms that there had been breaches of the SCM agreement on subsidies and, as a result, serious prejudice to the interests of the EU. In April 2012, the USA informed the WTO's Dispute Settlement Board that it intended to implement the recommendations and rulings to respect the SCM Agreement.

However, the dispute was to continue. In October 2012, the European Union requested the establishment of a compliance panel, arguing that the USA had failed to comply with the recommendations and rulings of the Dispute Settlement Board. Shortly after, the USA said that it objected to the level of suspension of concessions and other obligations.

Because of the complexities around the dispute, rulings were delayed and, at the time of writing, proceedings continue. Furthermore, with continuous development and investment in both existing and new models of aircraft, the prospect of further wrangles remains.

 Why does the WTO appear to be so ineffective in resolving the disputes between the EU and USA?

Perhaps the biggest objection raised against the single European market is a political one: the loss of national sovereignty. Governments find it much more difficult to intervene at a microeconomic level in their own economies.

Completing the internal market

Despite the reduction in barriers, the internal market is still not 'complete'. In other words, various barriers to trade between member states still remain.

To monitor progress an 'Internal Market Scoreboard' was established in 1997. This is published every six months and shows progress towards the total abandonment of any forms of internal trade restrictions (see Box 25.2). It shows the percentage of EU Internal Market Directives still to be transposed into national law. In addition to giving each country's 'transposition deficit', the Scoreboard identifies the number of infringements of the internal market that have taken place. The hope is that the 'naming and shaming' of countries will encourage them to make more rapid progress towards totally free trade within the EU.

In 1997, the average transposition deficit of member countries was 6.3 per cent. By 1999, this had fallen to 3.5 per cent. An average deficit target of 1 per cent was set in 2007 and this was reached by 2008. Data for 2014 show the average transposition deficit at just 0.7 per cent.

Nevertheless, national governments continued to introduce *new* technical standards, several of which have had the effect of erecting new barriers to trade. Also, infringements of single market rules by governments have not always been dealt with. The net result is that, although trade is much freer today than in the early 1990s, especially given the transparency of pricing with the euro, there still exist various barriers, especially to the free movement of goods.

To counteract new barriers, the EU periodically issues new Directives. If this process is more rapid than that of the transposition of existing Directives into national law, the transposition deficit increases.

The effect of the new member states

Given the very different nature of the economies of many of the new entrants to the EU, and their lower levels of GDP per head, the potential for gain from membership has been substantial. The gains come through trade creation, increased competition, technological transfer and inward investment, both from other EU countries and from outside the EU.

BOX 25.2 | **THE INTERNAL MARKET SCOREBOARD**

Keeping a tally on progress to a true single market

This success or otherwise of implementing EU internal market directives is measured by the Internal Market Scoreboard. The Scoreboard tracks the transposition deficit for each country.

This is the percentage of directives that have failed to be implemented into national law by their agreed deadline.

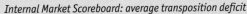

Internal Market Scoreboard: average transposition deficit

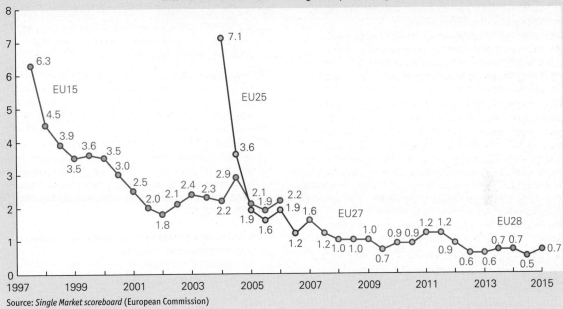

Source: *Single Market scoreboard* (European Commission)

The Scoreboard has been published every six months since 1997 and, in addition to tracking the deficit for each country, also shows the average deficit across all EU countries. The chart shows that the average deficit was falling until May 2002, but then rose somewhat. Part of the problem is that new directives are being issued as existing ones are being implemented.

After 2004, the transposition deficit tended to fall, even with the accession of ten new members in 2004 and two more in 2007. An average deficit target of 1 per cent was set in 2007 and this was reached by 2008. The average deficit fell further in 2009 to 0.7 per cent but then rose to 0.9 per cent in 2010 and to 1.2 in 2011. But then it rose to 0.9 per cent in 2010 and to 1.2 in 2011.

Behind the rise in the average deficit in 2010 and 2011 was a reduction in the speed with which directives were being enacted. To tackle delays, a target of 'zero tolerance' operates for delays of two years or more in transposing directives. Overly long delays are seen as impairing the functioning of Single Market.

In the 2011 Single Market Act the European Commission proposed a target transposition deficit of close to 0.5 per cent.

The transposition deficit began to decline and by November 2014 the EU average had fallen to 0.5 per cent. However, by May 2015 the transposition deficit had again risen above target to stand at 0.7 per cent.

As well as the transposition deficit, the Scoreboard also measures the compliance deficit: the percentage of transposed directives where infringement proceedings for non-conformity have been initiated by the Commission. The proposed target for the compliance deficit is 0.5 per cent. In recent times the compliance deficit has been relatively stable. Through 2014 and into 2015 it stood at between 0.5 and 0.7 per cent.

1. *What value are scoreboards for member states and the European Commission?*
2. *Why do you think that it is so important that legislation, such as that governing the Internal Market, is in place in all member states at the same time?*

Note: Internal Market Scoreboards can be accessed at http://ec.europa.eu/internal_market/score/index_en.htm

A study in 2004[2] concluded that Poland's GDP would rise by 3.4 per cent and Hungary's by almost 7 per cent. Real wages would rise, with those of unskilled workers rising faster than those of skilled workers, in accordance with these countries' comparative advantage. There would also be benefits for the 15 pre-2004 members from increased trade and investment, but these would be relatively minor in comparison to the gains to the new members.

In future years, now that the euro is used by 19 of the 28 member states, with the possibility of others adopting it at some time, trade within the EU is likely to continue to grow as a proportion of GDP. We examine the benefits and costs of the single currency and the whole process of economic and monetary union in the EU in Section 32.3.

[2]M. Maliszewska, *Benefits of the Single Market Expansion for Current and New Members States* (Centrum Analiz Spoleczno-Ekonomicznych, 2004).

SUMMARY

1a Countries may make a partial movement towards free trade by the adoption of a preferential trading system. This involves free trade between the members, but restrictions on trade with the rest of the world. Such a system can be either a simple free trade area, or a customs union (where there are common restrictions with the rest of the world), or a common market (where in addition there is free movement of capital and labour, and common taxes and trade laws).

1b A preferential trading area can lead to trade creation where production shifts to low-cost producers within the area, or to trade diversion where trade shifts away from lower-cost producers outside the area to higher-cost producers within the area.

1c Preferential trading may bring dynamic advantages of increased external economies of scale, improved terms of trade from increased bargaining power with the rest of the world, increased efficiency from greater competition between member countries, and a more rapid spread of technology. On the other hand, it can lead to increased regional problems for members, greater oligopolistic collusion and various diseconomies of scale. There may also be large costs of administering the system.

2 There have been several attempts around the world to form preferential trading systems. The two most powerful are the European Union and the North America Free Trade Association (NAFTA).

3a The European Union is a customs union in that it has common external tariffs and no internal ones. But virtually from the outset it has also had elements of a common market, particularly in the areas of agricultural policy, regional policy and competition policy, and to some extent in the areas of tax harmonisation, transport policy and social policy.

3b The Single European Act of 1986 sought to sweep away any remaining restrictions and to establish a genuine free market within the EU: to establish a full common market. Benefits from completing the internal market have included trade creation, cost savings from no longer having to administer barriers, economies of scale for firms now able to operate on a Europe-wide scale, and greater competition leading to reduced costs and prices, greater flows of technical information and more innovation.

3c The actual costs and benefits of EU membership to the various countries vary with their particular economic circumstances – for example, the extent to which they gain from trade creation, or lose from adverse regional effects – and with their contributions to and receipts from the EU budget.

3d These costs and benefits in the future will depend on just how completely the barriers to trade are abolished, on the extent of monetary union and on the effects of the enlargement of the Union.

MyEconLab

This book can be supported by MyEconLab, which contains a range of additional resources, including an online homework and tutorial system designed to test and build your understanding.

You need both an access card and a course ID to access MyEconLab:

1. Is your lecturer using MyEconLab? Ask your lecturer for your course ID.

2. Has an access card been included with the book at a reduced cost? Check the inside back cover of the book.

3. If you have a course ID but no access card, go to: http://www.myeconlab.com/ to buy access to this interactive study programme.

REVIEW QUESTIONS

1 What factors will determine whether a country's joining a customs union will lead to trade creation or trade diversion?

2 Assume that a group of countries forms a customs union. Is trade diversion in the union more likely or less likely in the following cases?

   a) Producers in the union gain monopoly power in world trade.

   b) Modern developments in technology and communications reduce the differences in production costs associated with different locations.

   c) The development of an internal market within the union produces substantial economies of scale in many industries.

3 Are NAFTA and APEC likely to develop along the same lines as the EU? Explain your answer.

4 Why is it difficult to estimate the magnitude of the benefits of completing the internal market of the EU?

5 Look through the costs and benefits that we identified from the single European market. Do the same costs and benefits arise from a substantially enlarged EU?

6 To what extent do non-EU countries gain or lose from the existence of the EU?

7 If there have been clear benefits from the single market programme, why do individual member governments still try to erect barriers, such as new technical standards?

ADDITIONAL PART I CASE STUDIES IN *THE ECONOMICS FOR BUSINESS* MyEconLab (www.pearsoned.co.uk/sloman)

I.1 **Investing in Wales.** The factors influencing the investment in Wales by the Korean multinational, LG.

I.2 **The Maharaja Mac.** An examination of activities of McDonald's in India.

I.3 **Ethical business.** An examination of the likelihood of success of companies which trade fairly with developing countries.

I.4 **Free trade and the environment.** Do whales, the rainforests and the atmosphere gain from free trade?

I.5 **The Uruguay round.** An examination of the negotiations that led to substantial cuts in trade barriers.

I.6 **The Battle of Seattle.** This looks at the protests against the WTO at Seattle in November 1999 and considers the arguments for and against the free trade policies of the WTO.

I.7 **The World Trade Organization.** This looks at the various opportunities and threats posed by this major international organisation.

I.8 **High oil prices.** What is their effect on the world economy?

I.9 **Crisis in South East Asia.** Causes of the severe recession in many South East Asian countries in 1997/8.

I.10 **A miracle gone wrong.** Lessons from East Asian crisis of the late 1990s.

I.11 **Assessing NAFTA.** Who are the winners and losers from NAFTA?

I.12 **The benefits of the Single Market.** Evidence of achievements and the Single Market Action Plan of 1997.

I.13 **The social dimension of the EU** The principles of the Social Charter.

I.14 **Steel barriers.** Looking after the US steel industry.

I.15 **Banana, banana.** A more detailed examination than that in Box 25.1 of the dispute between the USA and the EU over banana imports.

I.16 **Immigration, the Single European Market and the UK labour market.** This case study looks at efforts to quantify the impact of immigration on the UK labour market following the expansion of the EU in 2004.

WEBSITES RELEVANT TO PART I

Numbers and sections refer to websites listed in the Web appendix and hotlinked from this text's website at **www.pearsoned. co.uk/sloman**

- For news articles relevant to Part I, see the *Economics News Articles* link from the text's website.

- For general news on business in the international environment, see websites in section A, and particularly A1–5, 7–9, 21–25, 31. See also links to newspapers worldwide in A38, 39 and 43, and the news search feature in Google at A41. See also links to economics news in A42.

- For articles on various aspects of trade and developing countries, see A27, 28; I9.

- For international data on imports and exports, see site H16 > *Documents, Data and Resources > Statistics*. See also World Economic Outlook in H4 and trade data in B24. See also the trade topic in I14.

- For UK data, see B1, *1. National Statistics > Publications > Books > Annual Abstract > External trade and investment*. See also B4 and 34. For EU data, see B38, 47.

- For discussion papers on trade, see H4, 7, 12.

- For trade disputes, see H16.

- For various pressure groups critical of the effects of free trade and globalisation, see H13, 14.

- For information on various preferential trading arrangements, see H20–23.

- For EU sites, see G1, 7, 20.

- For information on trade and developing countries, see H4, 7, 9, 10, 16, 17. See also links to development sites in I9.

- Sites I8, 11, 14, 16 contain links to various topics in International Economics.

- For information and data on trade, development, finance and cross-border investment flows see site H2.

- For student resources relevant to this chapter, see sites C1–7, 9, 10, 19.

The macroeconomic environment

The FT Reports...

The Financial Times, 11 March 2015 FT

China data point to sharper downturn

By Jamil Anderlini in Beijing and Gabriel Wildau in Shanghai

China's economy slowed at its sharpest rate in the first two months of the year since the global financial crisis, heightening fears that this deceleration will undermine global growth.

Chinese industrial production, regarded as a good proxy for broader economic growth, expanded 6.8 per cent in January and February from a year earlier. Excluding the financial crisis, it was the slowest reading since records started in 1995, Goldman Sachs said.

Fixed asset investment and retail sales also slowed significantly, data showed on Wednesday.

'Today's disappointing data release highlights just how quickly domestic demand is deteriorating as the ongoing property downturn continues to spread its negative impact through the economy,' said Wang Tao, UBS chief China economist.

Weakening Chinese demand has been one of the main causes of falling global commodity prices and weaker emerging markets. An extended slowdown in the economy could further sharpen the divergence developing between the US, whose prospects have been brightening, and other important global economies.

Expectations that the US Federal Reserve will soon raise rates is sending the dollar rocketing higher, while central banks in the eurozone, China and many emerging markets are all easing to fight falling inflation and shore up growth.

China expanded at the slowest pace since 1990 last year, contrasting with the decades of double-digit growth since the late 1970s. The International Monetary Fund has already cut its gross domestic product estimate to 6.8 per cent this year and 6.5 per cent in 2016, the first time the IMF forecast lower growth in China than in India for decades.

Fixed asset investment, key in an economy where investment contributes more to growth than almost any other in history, expanded 13.9 per cent in the first two months from a year earlier, down from an annual expansion of 15.7 per cent last year.

Retail sales, one measure of how successful China has been at shifting to a more consumption-based growth model, also slowed in the first two months, expanding 10.7 per cent compared with 11.9 per cent growth in December.

The broad slowdown is being led by a serious decline in China's previously overheated real estate sector, where prices and sales have fallen since the start of last year.

In a sign of further pain to come, housing sales in the first two months of the year fell 16.3 per cent in terms of floor space from a year earlier, after falling 7.6 per cent in December.

China's housing market has only existed since the late 1990s when the government privatised and commercialised housing that was previously assigned to people by the government or their 'work unit'.

The latest figures confirm the worst fall in the market since at least the financial crisis, following more than a decade of frantic building that has created massive oversupply and left countless half-built and half-empty apartment complexes across the country.

The full impact of the housing slump is yet to be felt.

Property investment increased more than 10 per cent last year to Rmb9.5tn ($1.5tn) while sales fell roughly 8 per cent in terms of floor area.

This has exacerbated oversupply and thus the prospect of much slower overall economic growth once investment follows sales down.

'Economic momentum appears markedly weaker than suggested by the recent recovery in export growth and Purchasing Managers' index readings,' said Julian Evans-Pritchard, China economist at Capital Economics. 'As such, a further slowdown in GDP growth in this quarter now looks likely.'

The growth in fixed asset investment in the first two months was the weakest in China since December 2000, when the country's banking system was technically bankrupt following a massive build-up of bad loans in the 1990s.

The latest industrial production figures are the worst since December 2008, in the immediate aftermath of Lehman Brothers' bankruptcy and a subsequent collapse in Chinese exports.

China is also struggling with a huge and growing debt load and the threat of deflation.

At 282 per cent of GDP by the middle of last year, according to estimates from McKinsey, China's overall debt load is higher than that of the US or Germany.

The economy expanded 7.4 per cent last year, the slowest pace in almost a quarter of a century and the government has lowered its growth target this year to 'around 7 per cent' from last year's 'around 7.5 per cent'.

Still, many economists believe the slowdown in the property market will make it difficult for Beijing to achieve that lower goal.

'The extremely weak activity data at the beginning of the year suggest that China needs to engage into more aggressive policy easing,' Li-Gang Liu, chief greater China economist at ANZ, wrote in a note, adding that China's first-quarter growth could miss 7 per cent.

Banks are dangerous institutions. They borrow short and lend long. They create liabilities which promise to be liquid and hold few liquid assets themselves. That though is hugely valuable for the rest of the economy. Household savings can be channelled to finance illiquid investment projects while providing access to liquidity for those savers who may need it.

Mervyn King, Former Governor of the Bank of England, 'Finance: a return from risk', speech to the Worshipful Company of International Bankers, at the Mansion House, 17 March 2009 (www.bankofengland.co.uk); see www.bankofengland.co.uk/mfsd/iadb/notesiadb/Revisions.htm for the Revisions Policy.

The success of an individual business depends not only on its own particular market and its own particular decisions. It also depends on the whole macroeconomic environment in which it operates, as can be seen in the Financial Times article opposite.

If the economy is booming, then individual businesses are likely to be more profitable than if the economy is in recession. If the exchange rate rises (or falls), this will have an impact on the competitiveness of businesses trading overseas, and on the costs and profitability of business in general. Similarly, business profitability will be affected by interest rates, the general level of prices and wages and the level of unemployment.

It is thus important for managers to understand the forces that affect the performance of the economy. In the remaining chapters of the text, we will examine these macroeconomic forces and their effects on the business sector.

In Chapter 26 we examine the macroeconomic environment in which businesses operate. We identify the main macroeconomic variables that determine this environment and analyse how they are interrelated. In particular, we look at the objectives of economic growth, low unemployment and low inflation. We also consider the trade-offs facing policy makers in trying to achieve these objectives and how policy impacts on business.

Chapter 27 looks at macroeconomic issues arising from a country's economic relationships with the rest of the world. In particular, it looks at the balance of payments and the role of exchange rates in influencing economic performance.

Chapter 28 looks at the significance of the financial system for both individual businesses and the economy. In particular, it looks at the behaviour of financial institutions and the role of money. You will be able to judge whether 'Banks are dangerous institutions', as Mervyn King states.

Finally, in Chapter 29 we examine various theories about how the economy operates and the implications for business. We look at the relationship between inflation and unemployment and examine the possible causes of the business cycle. We also see the important role played by the expectations of both business and consumers.

Key terms

Actual and potential economic growth
Output gap
Aggregate demand
Aggregate supply
Business cycle
Unemployment
Inflation
Circular flow of income
Injections and withdrawals
The balance of payments
The exchange rate
Fixed and floating exchange rates
Functions of money
Assets and liabilities (of banks)
Central bank
Money market
Money supply
Credit creation
Deposits multiplier
Money multiplier
Demand for money
Keynesian
New classical
Aggregate expenditure
Marginal propensity to consume
The multiplier
The accelerator
The quantity theory of money
Expectations
The Phillips curve
Real business cycles

The macroeconomic environment of business

Business issues covered in this chapter

■ What determines the level of activity in the economy and hence the overall business climate?
■ If a stimulus is given to the economy, what will be the effect on business output?
■ Why do economies experience periods of boom followed by periods of recession? What determines the length and magnitude of these 'phases' of the business cycle?
■ What are the causes of unemployment and how does unemployment relate to the level of business activity?
■ What are the causes of inflation and how does inflation relate to the level of business activity?
■ What is meant by 'GDP' and how is it measured?

We have seen how the success or failure of businesses can be affected by market conditions and by the strategic choices that firms make. Yet the macroeconomic environment is very important too. Recent history shows this very clearly indeed. In 2009 global output fell by 2 per cent in the aftermath of the financial crisis. A greater understanding of the macroeconomic environment and how it is influenced can help firms to plan and make decisions to boost their profitability.

In this chapter we shall identify what the main macroeconomic variables are and how they are related. We shall also have a preliminary look at how policy makers, such as the government and the central bank, can influence these variables in order to create a more favourable environment for business. Macroeconomic policy will be discussed in more detail in Part K.

26.1 INTRODUCTION TO THE MACROECONOMIC ENVIRONMENT

The macroeconomic environment can be described by a series of interrelated macroeconomic variables. We can group them under the following headings: economic growth, unemployment, inflation and the economic relationships with the rest of the world, the financial well-being of individuals, businesses and other organisations, governments and nations and the relationship between the financial system and the economy.

Economic growth. Governments hope to achieve high *rates of economic growth* over the long term: in other words, growth that is sustained over the years and is not just a temporary phenomenon. They also try to achieve *stable* growth, avoiding both recessions and excessive short-term growth that cannot be sustained. In practice, however, this can often prove difficult to achieve, as recent history has shown.

> **KEY IDEA 38**
> *Economies suffer from inherent instability.* As a result, economic growth and other macroeconomic indicators tend to fluctuate.

Unemployment. Reducing unemployment is another major macroeconomic aim of governments not only for the sake of the unemployed themselves, but also because it represents a waste of human resources and because unemployment benefits are a drain on government revenues.

Inflation. By **inflation** we mean a general rise in prices throughout the economy. The annual rate of inflation is the percentage increase in prices over a 12-month period. Government policy here is to keep inflation both low and stable. In fact, this has led many governments to adopt an inflation rate target and to delegate responsibility to its central bank for interventions in money markets to affect interest rates (we consider these interventions in section 30.3). The hope is that by demonstrating a commitment to low inflation and depoliticising the determination of interest rates, peoples' expectations of inflation will be lower than they otherwise would be. In turn, lower expectations of inflation help to keep actual rates of inflation lower.

Low and stable inflation is thought to aid the process of economic decision making. For example, businesses will be able to set prices and wage rates, and make investment decisions, with far more confidence. We have become used to low inflation rates and in some countries, like Japan, periods of deflation, where prices in general fall. Even though inflation rates rose in many countries in 2008 and then again in 2010–11, figures remained much lower than in the past; in 1975, UK inflation reached over 23 per cent.

The balance of payments. Governments aim to provide an environment in which exports can grow without an excessive growth in imports. They also aim to make the economy attractive to inward investment. In other words, they seek to create a climate in which the country's earnings of foreign currency at least match, or preferably exceed, the country's expenditure of foreign currency: they seek to achieve a favourable **balance of payments**.

The achievement of a favourable balance of payments depends, in part, on whether changes in **exchange rates** allow the country's goods and services to remain price competitive on international markets. A lower exchange rate (i.e. fewer dollars, yen, euros, etc. to the pound) will make UK goods cheaper to overseas buyers, and thus help to boost UK exports. On the other hand, it will make imports more expensive and could increase the rate of inflation. The government or central bank may thus seek to manipulate exchange rates to make them 'more favourable', whether lower or higher.

Financial well-being. It is increasingly recognised that the behaviour of individuals, businesses (including financial institutions), governments and nations is affected by their financial well-being. In analysing their well-being we can look at trends in three key accounts which are compiled for the main sectors of the economy: the household, corporate and government sectors and the economy as whole.

First, there is the *income account* which records the various flows of income and receipts alongside the amounts either spent or saved. In the case of the national accounts, economic growth refers to the annual real growth in a country's income flows (i.e. after taking inflation into account).

Second, there is the *financial account*. The financial *balance sheet* gives a complete record of the stocks of financial assets (arising from saving) and financial liabilities (arising from borrowing) of a sector, and includes things such as currency, bank deposits, loans, bonds and shares. *Changes in such balances over time (flows of new saving and bor-*

> ### Definitions
>
> **Balance of payments account** A record of the country's transactions with the rest of the world. It shows the country's payments to or deposits in other countries (debits) and its receipts or deposits from other countries (credits). It also shows the balance between these debits and credits under various headings.
>
> **Exchange rate** The rate at which one national currency exchanges for another. The rate is expressed as the amount of one currency that is necessary to purchase one unit of another currency (e.g. £1 = €1.30).
>
> **Rate of economic growth** The percentage increase in output over a 12-month period.
>
> **Rate of inflation** The percentage increase in prices over a 12-month period.

rowing) were important in explaining the credit crunch and subsequent deep recession of the late 2000s/early 2010s.

Third, there is the *capital account* which records the stock of non-financial (physical) wealth, arising from acquiring or disposing of physical assets, such as property and machinery. *Changes* over time (inflows and outflows) in the capital balance sheets of the different sectors give important insights into relationships between the sectors of the economy and to possible growing tensions.

The *national balance sheet* is a measure of the wealth of a country. It can be presented so as to show the contribution of each sector and/or the composition of wealth. The balance of a sector's or country's stock of both financial and non-financial wealth is referred to as its **net worth**.

 Balance sheets affect people's behaviour. The size and structure of governments', institutions' and individuals' liabilities (and assets too) affect economic well-being and can have significant effects on behaviour and economic activity.

Financial stability. A core aim of the government and the central bank is to ensure the stability of the financial system. After all, financial markets and institutions are an integral part of economies. Their well-being is crucial to the well-being of an economy.

Because of the global interconnectedness of financial institutions and markets, problems can spread globally like a contagion. The financial crisis of the late 2000s showed how financially distressed financial institutions can cause serious economic upheaval on a global scale. A major part of the global response to the financial crisis has been to try to ensure that financial institutions are more financially resilient, as we shall see in Chapter 28. In particular, financial institutions should have more loss-absorbing capacity and therefore be better able to withstand 'shocks' and deteriorating macroeconomic conditions.

From the above issues we can identify a series of macroeconomic policy objectives that policy makers, including governments, might typically pursue:

- High and stable economic growth.
- Low unemployment.
- Low rates of inflation.
- The avoidance of balance of payments deficits and excessive exchange rate fluctuations.
- A stable financial system.
- The avoidance of excessively financially distressed sectors of the economy, including government.

Unfortunately, these policy objectives may conflict. For example, a policy designed to accelerate the rate of economic growth may result in a higher rate of inflation, a balance of payments deficit and excessive borrowing. Governments are thus often faced with awkward policy choices, illustrating how societies face trade-offs between economic objectives.

In understanding these choices and their implications, it is important to analyse the determinants of the key issues that shape the macroeconomic environment. In this chapter we will examine economic growth, unemployment and inflation. In Chapter 27 we will focus on the balance of payments and its relation to the exchange rate before then in Chapter 28 considering the financial system and the financial well-being of economic agents (i.e. households, businesses and governments).

 Societies face trade-offs between economic objectives. For example, the goal of faster growth may conflict with that of greater equality; the goal of lower unemployment may conflict with that of lower inflation (at least in the short run). This is an example of opportunity cost: the cost of achieving more of one objective may be achieving less of another. The existence of trade-offs means that policy makers must make choices.

Definition

Net worth The market value of a sector's stock of financial and non-financial wealth.

26.2 **ECONOMIC GROWTH**

The distinction between actual and potential growth

Before examining the causes of economic growth, it is essential to distinguish between *actual* and *potential* economic growth.

Actual growth is the percentage annual increase in national output or 'GDP' (gross domestic product): in other words, the rate of growth in actual output produced. When statistics on GDP growth rates are published, it is actual growth they are referring to. (We examine the measurement

of GDP in the appendix to this chapter.) Figure 26.1 shows annual growth rates for four economies.

Potential growth is the speed at which the economy *could* grow. It is the percentage annual increase in the economy's *capacity* to produce: the rate of growth in **potential output**.

 Living standards are limited by a country's ability to produce. Potential national output depends on the country's resources, technology and productivity.

| **Figure 26.1** | Growth rates in selected industrialised economies |

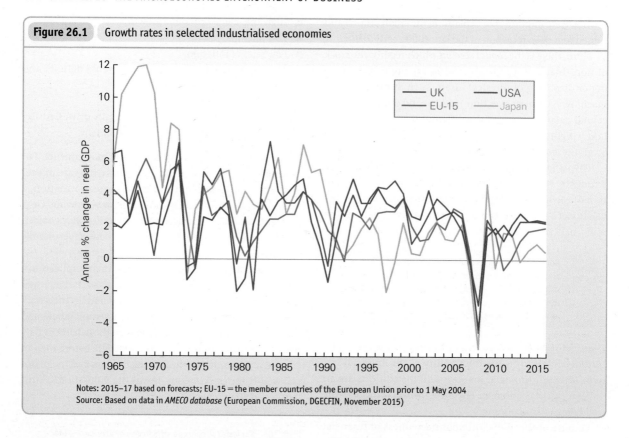

Notes: 2015–17 based on forecasts; EU-15 = the member countries of the European Union prior to 1 May 2004
Source: Based on data in *AMECO database* (European Commission, DGECFIN, November 2015)

Potential output (i.e. potential GDP) is the level of output when the economy is operating at 'normal capacity utilisation'. This allows for firms having a planned degree of spare capacity to meet unexpected demand or for hold-ups in supply. It also allows for some unemployment as people move from job to job. Potential output is thus somewhat below full-capacity output, which is the absolute maximum that could be produced with firms working flat-out.

The difference between actual and potential output is known as the *output gap*. Thus if actual output exceeds potential output, the output gap is positive: the economy is operating above normal capacity utilisation. If actual output is below potential output, the output gap is negative: the economy is operating below normal capacity utilisation. Box 26.1 looks at the output gap for the UK and three other economies since the mid-1980s.

If the actual growth rate is less than the potential growth rate, there will be an increase in spare capacity and an increase in unemployment: the output gap will become more negative (or less positive). To close a negative output gap, the actual growth rate would temporarily have to exceed the potential growth rate. In the long run, however, the actual growth rate will be limited to the potential growth rate.

There are two key issues around economic growth: the rate of growth over the long term and short-term fluctuations. To help illustrate them, consider Figure 26.2, which shows for the UK the level of output (real GDP) alongside the annual rate of growth in output since the 1850s. We can see how short-term economic growth rates vary

considerably. This illustrates the inherent volatility of economies. But we also observe how output levels rise over the longer term.

These two issues pose challenges for policy makers. First, what can be done to ensure that actual output is kept as close as possible to potential output and fluctuations in growth kept to a minimum? Second, what determines the rate of potential economic growth and what can be done to increase it?

Actual economic growth and the business cycle

Although growth in potential output varies to some extent over the years – depending on the rate of advance of technology, the level of investment and the discovery of new

Definitions

Actual growth The percentage annual increase in national output actually produced.

Potential growth The percentage annual increase in the capacity of the economy to produce.

Potential output The output that could be produced in the economy if all firms were operating at their normal level of capacity utilisation.

Output gap Actual output minus potential output.

Business cycle or **trade cycle** The periodic fluctuations of national output around its long-term trend.

Figure 26.2 Output and economic growth in the UK since 1850

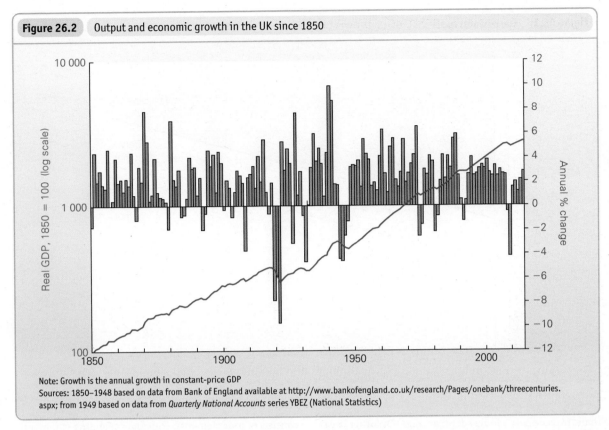

Note: Growth is the annual growth in constant-price GDP
Sources: 1850–1948 based on data from Bank of England available at http://www.bankofengland.co.uk/research/Pages/onebank/threecenturies.
aspx; from 1949 based on data from *Quarterly National Accounts* series YBEZ (National Statistics)

raw materials – it nevertheless tends to be much steadier than the growth in actual output.

As we have seen, actual growth tends to fluctuate. In some years there is a high rate of economic growth: the country experiences a boom. In other years, economic growth is low or even negative: the country experiences a recession.[1] This cycle of booms and recessions is known as the *business cycle* or *trade cycle*.

There are four 'phases' of the business cycle. They are illustrated in Figure 26.3.

1 *The upturn.* In this phase, a stagnant economy begins to recover and growth in actual output resumes.
2 *The rapid expansion.* During this phase, there is rapid economic growth: the economy is booming. A fuller use is made of resources and the gap between actual and full-capacity output narrows.
3 *The peaking out.* During this phase, growth slows down or even ceases.
4 *The slowdown, recession or slump.* During this phase, there is little or no growth or even a decline in output. Increasing slack develops in the economy.

Long-term output trend. A line can be drawn showing the trend of national output over time (i.e. ignoring the cyclical fluctuations around the trend). This is shown as the dashed line in Figure 26.3. If, over time, firms on average operate with a 'normal' degree of capacity utilisation, the trend out-

put line will be the same as the potential output line. If the average level of capacity that is unutilised stays constant from one cycle to another, the trend line will have the same slope as the full-capacity output line. In other words, the trend (or potential) rate of growth will be the same as the rate of growth of capacity.

If, however, the level of unutilised capacity changes from one cycle to another, then the trend line will have a different slope from the full-capacity output line. For example, if unemployment and unused industrial capacity *rise* from one peak to another, or from one trough to another, then the trend line will move further away from the full-capacity output line (i.e. it will be less steep).

Pause for thought

If the average percentage (as opposed to the average level) of full-capacity output that was unutilised remained constant, would the trend line have the same slope as the potential output line?

The business cycle in practice

The business cycle illustrated in Figure 26.3 is a 'stylised' cycle. It is nice and smooth and regular. Drawing it this way allows us to make a clear distinction between each of the four phases. In practice business cycles are highly irregular. They are irregular in two ways.

The magnitude of the phases. Sometimes in phase 2 there is a very high rate of economic growth, considerably higher

[1] In official statistics, a recession is defined as when an economy experiences falling national output (negative growth) for two or more quarters.

| Figure 26.3 | The business cycle |

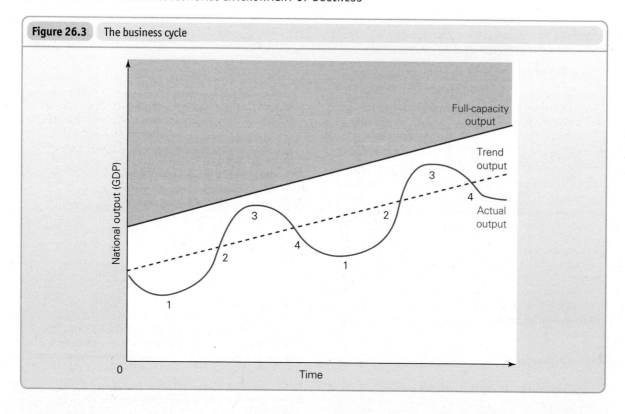

than the economy's longer-term average. On other occasions in phase 2 growth is much gentler. Sometimes in phase 4 there is a recession, with an actual decline in output as occurred in 2008/9. On other occasions, phase 4 is merely a 'pause', with growth simply being low.

The length of the phases. Some booms are short lived, lasting only a few months or so. Others are much longer, lasting perhaps three or four years. Likewise some recessions are short, while others are long. Sometimes a recession can be closely followed by another recession with the economic upturn only short-lived. Economists refer to this as a double-dip recession. Such a situation occurred when the recession of 1973/4 was followed by another recession in 1975.

Nevertheless, despite the irregularity of the fluctuations, cycles are still clearly discernible. These cycles are more readily apparent when we focus on *growth* rather than the *level* of output. We can see this by revisiting Figure 26.2 (on page 473). While the plot of real GDP gives us a sense that growth is irregular, since if growth was constant we would have a straight line (as it is plotted on a log scale), it is by looking at the annual rates of change (growth) that we can see the true extent of this.

Causes of fluctuations in actual growth

Economists typically focus on variations in the growth of 'aggregate demand' in explaining variations in the rate of actual growth in the *short run*.

Aggregate demand (*AD*) is the total spending on goods and services made within the country. This spending consists of four elements: consumer spending (*C*), investment expenditure by firms (*I*), government spending (*G*) and the expenditure by foreign residents on the country's goods and services (i.e. their purchases of its exports) (*X*). From these four must be subtracted any expenditure that goes on imports (*M*), since this is expenditure that 'leaks' abroad and is not spent on domestic goods and services. Thus:

$$AD = C + I + G + X - M$$

A rapid rise in aggregate demand will create shortages. This will tend to stimulate firms to increase output, thereby reducing slack in the economy. Likewise, a reduction in aggregate demand will leave firms with increased stocks of unsold goods. They will therefore tend to reduce output.

Aggregate demand and actual output therefore tend to fluctuate together in the short run. A boom is associated with a rapid rise in aggregate demand: the faster the rise in aggregate demand, the higher the short-run growth rate. A recession, by contrast, is associated with a reduction in aggregate demand.

Definition

Aggregate demand Total spending on goods and services made in the economy. It consists of four elements: consumer spending (*C*), investment (*I*), government spending (*G*) and the expenditure on exports (*X*), less any expenditure on foreign goods and services (*M*): $AD = C + I + G + X - M$

BOX 26.1 OUTPUT GAPS

An alternative measure of excess or deficient demand

If the economy grows, how fast and for how long can it grow before it runs into inflationary problems? On the other hand, what minimum rate must be achieved to avoid rising unemployment?

To answer these questions, economists have developed the concept of 'output gaps'.[2] The output gap is the difference between actual output and potential output.

If actual output is below potential output (the gap is negative), there will be a higher than normal level of unemployment as firms are operating below their normal level of capacity utilisation. There will, however, be a downward pressure on inflation, resulting from a lower than normal level of demand for labour and other resources. If actual output is above potential output (the gap is positive), there will be excess demand and a rise in inflation.

Generally, the gap will be negative in a recession and positive in a boom. In other words, output gaps follow the course of the business cycle.

But how do we measure output gaps? There are two principal statistical techniques.

De-trending techniques. This approach is a purely mechanical exercise which involves smoothing the actual GDP figures. In doing this, it attempts to fit a trend growth path along the lines of the dashed line in Figure 26.3. The main disadvantage of this approach is that it is not grounded in economic theory and therefore does not take into consideration those factors that economists consider to be important in determining output levels over time.

Production function approach. Many forecasting bodies use an approach which borrows ideas from economic theory. Specifically, it uses the idea of a production function which relates output to a set of inputs. Estimates of potential output are generated by using statistics on the size of a country's capital stock, the potential available labour input and, finally, the productivity or effectiveness of these inputs in producing output.

In addition to these statistical approaches, use could be made of business surveys. In other words, we ask businesses directly. However, survey-based evidence can provide only a broad guide to rates of capacity utilisation and whether there is deficient or excess demand.

International evidence

The diagram shows output gaps for six economies from 1970 estimated using a production function approach. What is apparent from the chart is that all the economies have experienced significant output gaps, both positive and negative. This helps to illustrate that economies are inherently volatile. However, while output gaps vary from year to year, over the longer term the average output gap tends towards zero.

The diagram shows how the characteristics of countries' business cycles can differ, particularly in terms of depth and duration. But, we also see evidence of an international business cycle (see page 622), where national cycles appear to share characteristics. This is true of the late 2000s and early 2010s. Increasing global interconnectedness from financial and trading links meant that the financial crisis of the late 2000s spread like a contagion.

 How might the behaviour of firms differ during periods of negative and positive output gaps?

[2] See C. Giorno et al., 'Potential output, output gaps and structural budget balances', *OECD Economic Studies*, no. 24 (1995), p. 1.

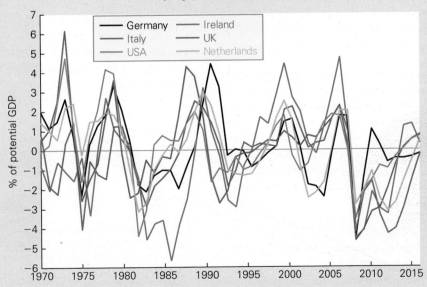

Output gaps, 1970–2017

Note: Figures for Germany based on West Germany only up to 1991; data from 2015 based on forecasts
Source: Based on data from *AMECO database* (European Commission, DGECFIN)

While much of the analysis of business cycles focuses on fluctuations in aggregate demand, shifts in 'aggregate supply' can also lead to fluctuations in the rate of economic growth. *Aggregate supply* (AS) is the total amount of goods and services supplied by firms within the country. Sudden sharp changes to input prices could affect firms' output decisions. For instance, increases in input costs, such as those in employing labour, could result in firms reducing production levels.

When viewing economic growth over the longer term, aggregate supply takes on increasing importance. This is because a rapid rise in aggregate demand is not enough to ensure a continuing high level of growth over a *number* of years. Without an expansion of potential output too, rises in actual output must eventually come to an end as spare capacity is used up.

In the long run, therefore, there are two determinants of actual growth:

■ the growth in aggregate demand, which determines whether potential output will be realised;
■ the growth in potential output.

Potential economic growth

Potential economic growth represents an increase in the capacity of the economy to produce. Here, therefore, we are focusing on aggregate *supply*.

Figure 26.4 shows estimates of potential output from 1970 for five developed economies. We observe varia-tions across countries in the rate at which potential output increases. To understand why this might be the case we need to consider the principal determinants of potential output. These can be grouped in two main categories: (a) the amount of resources available and (b) their productivity.

Increases in the quantity of resources

Capital. The nation's output depends on its stock of capi-tal (*K*). An increase in this stock (through investment) will increase output. If we ignore the problem of machines wearing out or becoming obsolete and needing replacing, then the stock of capital will increase by the amount of investment. The rise in output that results will depend on the productivity of capital.

The rate of growth, as we saw in section 23.7 (page 435), depends on the marginal capital/output ratio (*k*). This is the amount of extra capital (Δ*K*) divided by the amount of extra annual output that it produces (Δ*Y*). The lower the value of *k*, the higher is the productivity of capital (i.e. the less extra capital you need to produce extra out-put). The rate of growth in potential output also depends on the proportion of national income that is invested (*i*), which, assuming that all saving is invested, will equal the

---

Definition

Aggregate supply The total amount of goods and ser-vices produced in the economy.

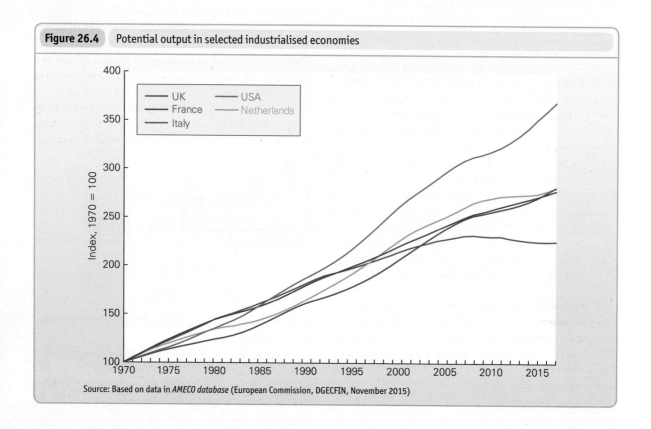

Figure 26.4 Potential output in selected industrialised economies

proportion of national income that is saved (*s*). The formula for growth becomes:

$$g = i/k \text{ (or } g = s/k)$$

Thus if 20 per cent of national income went in new investment (*i* = 20%), and if each £1 of new investment yielded 25p of extra income per year (*k* = 4), then the growth rate would be 5 per cent. A simple example will demonstrate this. If national income is £2 trillion (i.e. £2000 billion), then £400 billion will be invested (*i* = 20%). This will lead to extra annual output of £100 billion (*k* = 4). Thus national income grows to £2.1 trillion (i.e. £2100 billion): a growth of 5 per cent.

But what determines the rate of investment? There are a number of determinants. These include the confidence of businesspeople about the future demand for their products, the ability of firms to finance investment projects, the profitability of business, the tax regime, the rate of growth in the economy and the rate of interest.

Over the long term, if investment is to increase, then *saving* must increase in order to finance that investment. Put another way, people must be prepared to forgo a certain amount of consumption in order to allow resources to be diverted into producing more capital goods: factories, machines, etc.

Note that if investment is to increase, there may also need to be a steady increase in *aggregate demand*. In other words, if firms are to be encouraged to increase their capacity by installing new machines or building new factories, they may need first to see the *demand* for their products growing. Here a growth in *potential* output is the result of a growth in aggregate demand and hence *actual* output.

Labour. If there is an increase in the working population, there will be an increase in potential output. This increase in working population may result from a larger 'participation rate': a larger proportion of the total population in work or seeking work. For example, if a greater proportion of women with children decide to join the labour market, the working population will rise.

Alternatively, a rise in the working population may be the result of an increase in total population. There is a problem here. If a rise in total population does not result in a greater *proportion* of the population working, output *per head of the population* may not rise at all. In practice, many developed countries are faced with a growing proportion of their population above retirement age, and thus a potential *fall* in output per head of the population.

Land and raw materials. The scope for generating growth here is usually very limited. Land is virtually fixed in quantity. Land reclamation schemes and the opening up of marginal land can add only tiny amounts to GDP. Even if new raw materials are discovered (e.g. oil), this will only result in *short-term* growth: i.e. while the rate of extraction is building up. Once the rate of extraction is at a maximum,

economic growth will cease. Output will simply remain at the new higher level, until eventually the raw materials begin to run out. Output will then fall back again.

The problem of diminishing returns. If a single factor of production increases in supply while others remain fixed, diminishing returns will set in. For example, if the quantity of capital increases with no increase in other factors of production, then diminishing returns to capital will set in. The rate of return on capital will fall. Unless *all* factors of production increase, therefore, the rate of growth is likely to slow down.

Then there is the problem of the environment. If a rise in labour and capital leads to a more *intensive* use of land and natural resources, the resulting growth in output may be environmentally unsustainable. The solution to the problem of diminishing returns is for there to be an increase in the *productivity* of resources.

Increases in the productivity of resources

Technological improvements can increase the marginal productivity of capital. Much of the investment in new machines is not just in extra machines, but in superior machines producing a higher rate of return. Consider the microchip revolution of recent years. Modern computers can do the work of many people and have replaced many machines which were cumbersome and expensive to build. Improved methods of transport have reduced the costs of moving goods and materials. Improved communications (such as the Internet) have reduced the costs of transmitting information. The high-tech world of today would seem a wonderland to a person of 100 years ago.

As a result of technical progress, the productivity of capital has tended to increase over time. Similarly, as a result of new skills, improved education and training, and better health, the productivity of labour has also tended to increase over time.

But technical progress on its own is not enough. There must also be the institutions and attitudes that encourage *innovation*. In other words, the inventions must be exploited.

> ### Pause for thought
>
> *Will the rate of actual growth have any effect on the rate of potential growth?*

Policies to achieve growth

How can governments increase a country's growth rate? Policies differ in two ways.

First, they may focus on the demand side or the supply side of the economy. In other words, they may attempt to create sufficient *aggregate demand* to ensure that firms wish to invest and that potential output is realised. Or alternatively, they may seek to increase *aggregate supply* by concentrating on measures to increase potential output: measures to encourage research and development, innovation and training. (Chapter 30 looks at demand-side policies, while Chapter 31 looks at supply-side ones.)

Second, they may be market-orientated or interventionist policies. Many economists and politicians, especially those on the political right, believe that the best environment for encouraging economic growth is one where private enterprise is allowed to flourish: where entrepreneurs are able to reap substantial rewards from investment in new techniques and new products. Such economists therefore advocate policies designed to free up the market. Others, however, argue that a free market will be subject to considerable cyclical fluctuations and market distortions. Such economists, therefore, tend to advocate intervention by the government to reduce these fluctuations and compensate for market failures.

26.3 UNEMPLOYMENT

The meaning of unemployment

Unemployment can be expressed either as a number (e.g. 3 million) or as a percentage (e.g. 10 per cent). But just who should be included in the statistics? Should it be everyone without a job? The answer is clearly no, since we would not want to include children and pensioners. We would probably also want to exclude those who were not looking for work, such as parents choosing to stay at home to look after children.

The most usual definition that economists use for the **number unemployed** is: *those of working age who are without work, but who are available for work at current wage rates.* If the figure is to be expressed as a percentage, then it is a percentage of the total **labour force**. The labour force is defined as: *those in employment plus those unemployed.* Thus if 30 million people were employed and 2 million people were unemployed, the **unemployment rate** would be:

$$\frac{2}{30 + 2} \times 100 = 6.25$$

Official measures of unemployment

Two common measures of unemployment are used in official statistics. The first is **claimant unemployment**. This is simply a measure of all those in receipt of unemployment-related benefits. In the UK, claimants receive the 'job-seeker's allowance'.

The second measure is the **standardised unemployment rate**. Since 1998, this has been the main measure used by the UK government. It is the measure used by the International Labour Organization (ILO) and the Organisation for Economic Co-operation and Development (OECD), two international organisations that publish unemployment statistics for many countries.

In this measure, the unemployed are defined as people of working age who are without work, available to start work within two weeks and *actively seeking employment* or waiting to take up an appointment. The figures are compiled from the results of national labour force surveys. In the UK the labour force survey is conducted quarterly.

But is the standardised unemployment rate likely to be higher or lower than the claimant unemployment rate? The standardised rate is likely to be higher to the extent that it includes people seeking work who are nevertheless not entitled to claim benefits, but lower to the extent that it excludes those who are claiming benefits and yet who are not actively seeking work. Clearly, the tougher the benefit regulations, the lower the claimant rate will be relative to the standardised rate. In the three months to December 2014 standardised unemployment in the UK (for those aged 16 and over) was estimated at 1.86 million (5.7 per cent) while the claimant count in December 2014 was 0.86 million (2.5 per cent).

The costs of unemployment

The most obvious cost of unemployment is to the *unemployed themselves*. There is the direct financial cost of the loss in their earnings, measured as the difference between their previous wage and their unemployment benefit. Then there are the personal costs of being unemployed. The longer people are unemployed, the more dispirited they may become. Their self-esteem is likely to fall, and they are more likely to succumb to stress-related illness.

Then there are the costs to the *family and friends* of the unemployed. Personal relations can become strained, and there may be an increase in domestic violence and the number of families splitting up.

Definitions

Number unemployed (economist's definition) Those of working age who are without work, but who are available for work at current wage rates.

Labour force The number employed plus the number unemployed.

Unemployment rate The number unemployed expressed as a percentage of the labour force.

Claimant unemployment Those in receipt of unemployment-related benefits.

Standardised unemployment rate The measure of the unemployment rate used by the ILO and OECD. The unemployed are defined as people of working age who are without work, available for work and actively seeking employment.

Then there are the *broader costs to the economy*. Unemployment benefits are a cost borne by taxpayers. There may also have to be extra public spending on benefit offices, social services, health care and the police. What is more, unemployment represents a loss of output. Apart from the lack of income to the unemployed themselves, this under-utilisation of resources leads to lower incomes for other people too:

■ Firms lose the profits that could have been made, had there been full employment.
■ The government loses tax revenues, since the unemployed pay no income tax and national insurance, and, given that the unemployed spend less, they pay less VAT and excise duties.
■ Other workers lose any additional wages they could have earned from higher national output.

The costs of unemployment are to some extent offset by benefits. If workers voluntarily quit their job to look for a better one, then they must reckon that the benefits of a better job more than compensate for their temporary loss of income. From the nation's point of view, a workforce that is prepared to quit jobs and spend a short time unemployed will be a more adaptable, more mobile workforce – one that is responsive to changing economic circumstances. Such a workforce will lead to greater allocative efficiency in the short run and more rapid economic growth over the longer run.

Long-term involuntary unemployment is quite another matter. The costs clearly outweigh any benefits, both for the individuals concerned and for the economy as a whole. A demotivated, deskilled pool of long-term unemployed is a serious economic and social problem.

Unemployment and the labour market

We now turn to the causes of unemployment. These causes fall into two broad categories: *equilibrium* unemployment and *disequilibrium* unemployment. To make clear the distinction between the two, it is necessary to look at how the labour market works.

Figure 26.5 shows the aggregate demand for labour and the aggregate supply of labour: that is, the total demand and supply of labour in the whole economy. The *real* average wage rate is plotted on the vertical axis. This is the average wage rate expressed in terms of its purchasing power: in other words, after taking inflation into account.

The *aggregate supply of labour curve* (AS_L) shows the number of workers *willing to accept jobs* at each wage rate. This curve is relatively inelastic, since the size of the workforce at any one time cannot change significantly. Nevertheless, it is not totally inelastic because (a) a higher wage rate will encourage some people to enter the labour market (e.g. parents raising children) and (b) the unemployed will be more willing to accept job offers rather than continuing to search for a better-paid job.

The *aggregate demand for labour curve* (AD_L) slopes downward. The higher the wage rate, the more will firms

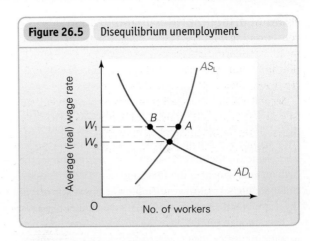

Figure 26.5 Disequilibrium unemployment

attempt to economise on labour and to substitute other factors of production for labour.

The labour market is in equilibrium at a wage of W_e in Figure 26.5, where the demand for labour equals the supply. If the wage were above W_e, the labour market would be in a state of disequilibrium. At a wage rate of W_1, there is an excess supply of labour of $A - B$. This is called *disequilibrium unemployment*.

For disequilibrium unemployment to occur, two conditions must hold:

■ The aggregate supply of labour must exceed the aggregate demand.
■ There must be a 'stickiness' in wages. In other words, the wage rate must not immediately fall to W_e.

Even when the labour market *is* in equilibrium, however, not everyone looking for work will be employed. Some people will hold out, hoping to find a better job. The curve N in Figure 26.6 shows the total number in the labour force. The horizontal difference between it and the aggregate supply of labour curve (AS_L) represents the excess of people looking for work over those actually willing to accept jobs. Q_e represents the equilibrium level of employment and the distance $D - E$ represents the *equilibrium level of unemployment*. This is sometimes known as the *natural level of unemployment*.

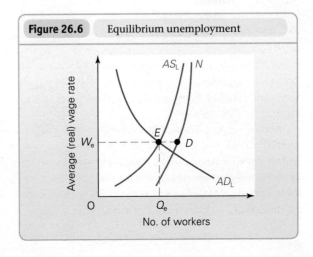

Figure 26.6 Equilibrium unemployment

Types of disequilibrium unemployment

There are three possible causes of disequilibrium unemployment.

Real-wage unemployment

This is where trade unions use their monopoly power to drive wages above the market-clearing level. In Figure 26.5, the wage rate is driven up above W_e. Excessive real wage rates were blamed by the Thatcher and Major governments for the high unemployment of the 1980s and early 1990s. The possibility of higher real-wage unemployment was also one of the reasons for their rejection of a national minimum wage.

Even though unions have the power to drive up wages in some industries, their power to do so has waned in recent years. Labour markets have become more flexible (see section 18.4). What is more, the process of globalisation has meant that many firms face intense competition from rivals in China, India and many other countries. This makes it impossible for them to concede large pay increases. In many cases, they can simply use labour in other countries if domestic labour is too expensive. For example, many firms employ call-centre workers in India, where wages are much lower.

As far as the national minimum wage is concerned, evidence from the UK suggests that the rate has not been high enough to have significant adverse effects on employment (see pages 313–14.

Demand-deficient or cyclical unemployment

KI 38
p470

Demand-deficient or ***cyclical unemployment*** is associated with recessions, such as that of 2008/9. As the economy moves into recession, consumer demand falls. Firms find that they are unable to sell their current level of output. For a time they may be prepared to build up stocks of unsold goods, but sooner or later they will start to cut back on production and cut back on the amount of labour they employ. In Figure 26.5 the AD_L curve shifts to the left. The deeper the recession becomes and the longer it lasts, the higher will demand-deficient unemployment become.

Later, as the economy recovers and begins to grow again, so demand-deficient unemployment will start to fall. Because demand-deficient unemployment fluctuates with the business cycle, it is sometimes referred to as 'cyclical unemployment'. Figure 26.7 shows the fluctuations in

> ## Definitions
>
> **Aggregate supply of labour curve** A curve showing the total number of people willing and able to work at different average real wage rates.
>
> **Aggregate demand for labour curve** A curve showing the total demand for labour in the economy at different average real wage rates.
>
> **Disequilibrium unemployment** Unemployment resulting from real wages in the economy being above the equilibrium level.
>
> **Equilibrium ('natural') unemployment** The difference between those who would like employment at the current wage rate and those willing and able to take a job.
>
> **Demand-deficient** or **cyclical unemployment** Disequilibrium unemployment caused by a fall in aggregate demand with no corresponding fall in the real wage rate.

Figure 26.7   Standardised unemployment rates in selected industrialised economies

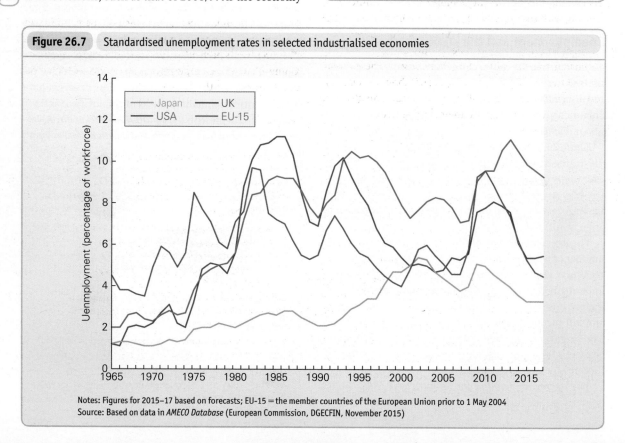

Notes: Figures for 2015–17 based on forecasts; EU-15 = the member countries of the European Union prior to 1 May 2004
Source: Based on data in *AMECO Database* (European Commission, DGECFIN, November 2015)

unemployment in various industrial countries. If you compare this figure with Figure 26.1, you can see how unemployment tends to rise in recessions and fall in booms.

Growth in the labour supply

If labour supply rises with no corresponding increase in the demand for labour, the equilibrium real wage rate will fall. If the real wage rate is 'sticky' downwards, unemployment will occur. This tends not to be such a serious cause of unemployment as demand deficiency, since the supply of labour changes relatively slowly. Nevertheless, there is a problem of providing jobs for school leavers each year with the sudden influx of new workers on to the labour market.

There is also a potential problem over the longer term if social trends lead to more couples with children both seeking employment. In practice, however, with the rapid growth of part-time employment and the high cost of childcare, this has not been a major cause of excess labour supply.

Equilibrium unemployment

If you look at Figure 26.7, you can see how unemployment was higher in the 1980s and 1990s than in the 1970s. Part of the reason for this was the growth in equilibrium unemployment. In the 2000s, unemployment fell in many countries – at least until the financial crisis of 2007/8. Again, part of the reason for this was a change in equilibrium unemployment, but this time a fall.

Although there may be overall *macro*economic equilibrium, with the *aggregate* demand for labour equal to the *aggregate* supply, and thus no disequilibrium unemployment, at a *micro*economic level supply and demand may not match. In other words, there may be vacancies in some parts of the economy, but an excess of labour (unemployment) in others. This is equilibrium unemployment. There are various types of equilibrium unemployment.

Frictional (search) unemployment

Frictional unemployment occurs when people leave their jobs, either voluntarily or because they are sacked or made redundant, and are then unemployed for a period of time while they are looking for a new job. They may not get the first job they apply for, despite a vacancy existing. The employer may continue searching, hoping to find a better-qualified person. Likewise, unemployed people may choose not to take the first job they are offered. Instead they may continue searching, hoping that a better one will turn up.

KI 8
p42
The problem is that information is imperfect. Employers are not fully informed about what labour is available; workers are not fully informed about what jobs are available and what they entail. Both employers and workers, therefore, have to search: employers search for the right labour and workers search for the right jobs.

Structural unemployment

Structural unemployment is where the structure of the economy changes. Employment in some industries may expand while in others it contracts. There are two main reasons for this.

A change in the pattern of demand. Some industries experience declining demand. This may be due to a change in consumer tastes. Certain goods may go out of fashion. Or it may be due to competition from other industries. For example, consumer demand may shift away from coal and to other fuels. This will lead to structural unemployment in mining areas.

A change in the methods of production (technological unemployment). New techniques of production often allow the same level of output to be produced with fewer workers. This is known as 'labour-saving technical progress'. Unless output expands sufficiently to absorb the surplus labour, people will be made redundant. This creates **technological unemployment**. An example is the job losses in the banking industry caused by the increase in the number of cash machines and by the development of telephone and Internet banking.

Structural unemployment often occurs in particular regions of the country. When it does, it is referred to as **regional unemployment**. This is most likely to occur when particular industries are concentrated in particular areas. For example, the decline in the South Wales coal-mining industry led to high unemployment in the Welsh valleys.

Seasonal unemployment

Seasonal unemployment occurs when the demand for certain types of labour fluctuates with the seasons of the year. This problem is particularly severe in holiday areas such as Cornwall, where unemployment can reach very high levels in the winter months.

Definitions

Frictional (search) unemployment Unemployment that occurs as a result of imperfect information in the labour market. It often takes time for workers to find jobs (even though there are vacancies) and in the meantime they are unemployed.

Structural unemployment Unemployment that arises from changes in the pattern of demand or supply in the economy. People made redundant in one part of the economy cannot immediately take up jobs in other parts (even though there are vacancies).

Technological unemployment Structural unemployment that occurs as a result of the introduction of labour-saving technology.

Regional unemployment Structural unemployment occurring in specific regions of the country.

Seasonal unemployment Unemployment associated with industries or regions where the demand for labour is lower at certain times of the year.

BOX 26.2	THE DURATION OF UNEMPLOYMENT

Taking a dip in the unemployment pool

A few of the unemployed may never have had a job and maybe never will. For most, however, unemployment lasts only a certain period. For some it may be just a few days while they are between jobs. For others it may be a few months. For others – the long-term unemployed – it could be several years. Long-term unemployment negatively affects a country's potential output, particularly by reducing a country's stock of human capital. Therefore, the length of time people spend unemployed is an important labour market issue.

Long-term unemployment is normally defined as those who have been unemployed for over 12 months. Chart (a) shows the composition of standardised unemployment in the UK by duration since the early 1990s. It shows how long-term unemployment fell from the mid-1990s until the economic downturn in the late 2000s. As a result, the percentage of unemployed people classified as long-term unemployed, which had hit 45 per cent in 1994, fell to just below 20 per cent by 2005, before rising to 37 per cent during 2014 before then easing again in 2015.

But what determines the average duration of unemployment? There are three important factors here.

The number unemployed (the size of the stock of unemployment)

Unemployment is a 'stock' concept: it measures a quantity of people unemployed at a particular point in time. The higher the stock of unemployment, the longer will tend to be the duration of unemployment. There will be more people competing for vacant jobs.

The rate of inflow and outflow from the stock of unemployment

The people making up the unemployment total are constantly changing. Each week some people are made redundant or quit their jobs. They represent an inflow to the stock of unemployment. Other people find jobs and thus represent an outflow from the stock of unemployment. Unemployment is often referred to as 'the pool of unemployment'.

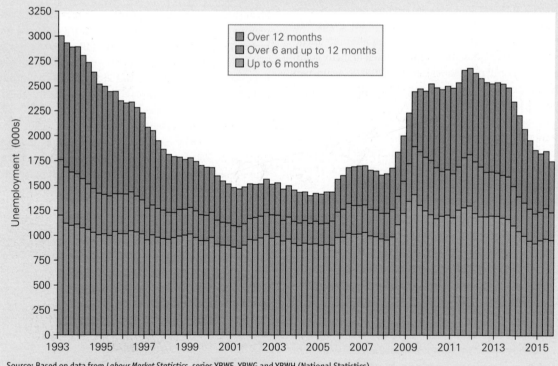

(a) UK unemployment by duration

Source: Based on data from *Labour Market Statistics*, series YBWF, YBWG and YBWH (National Statistics)

26.4	INFLATION

Inflation refers to rising price levels; deflation refers to falling price levels. The annual rate of inflation measures the annual percentage *increase* in prices. If the rate of inflation is negative, then prices are falling and we are measuring the rate of deflation.

Typically inflation relates to *consumer* prices. The government publishes a 'consumer prices index' (CPI) each month, and the rate of inflation is the percentage increase in that index over the previous 12 months.

If the inflow of people into the unemployment pool exceeds the outflow, the pool of unemployed people will rise. The duration of unemployment will depend on the rate of inflow and outflow. The rate is expressed as the number of people per period of time. Chart (b) shows the total inflows and outflows in the UK since 1989.

In each of the years, the outflows (and inflows) exceed the total number unemployed. The bigger the flows are relative to the total number unemployed, the less will be the average duration of unemployment. This is because people move into and out of the unemployment pool more quickly, and hence their average stay will be shorter.

The phase of the business cycle

The duration of unemployment will also depend on the phase of the business cycle. At the onset of a recession,

unemployment will rise, but as yet the average length of unemployment is likely to have been relatively short. Once a recession has lasted for a period of time, however, people will on average have been out of work longer; and this long-term unemployment is likely to persist even when the economy is pulling out of recession.

1. *If the number unemployed exceeded the total annual outflow, what could we conclude about the average duration of unemployment?*
2. *Make a list of the various inflows to and outflows from employment from and to (a) unemployment; (b) outside the workforce?*

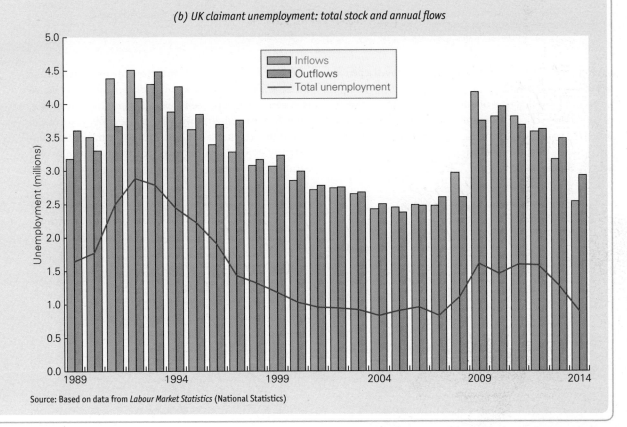

(b) UK claimant unemployment: total stock and annual flows

Source: Based on data from *Labour Market Statistics* (National Statistics)

A broader measure of inflation relates to the rate at which the prices of all domestically produced goods and services are changing. The price index used in this case is known as the *GDP deflator*. Figure 26.8 shows the annual rates of change in the GDP deflator for the USA, Japan, the UK and the EU-15. As you can see, inflation was particularly severe in the mid-1970s, but rates have been relatively low

Definition

GDP deflator The price index of all final domestically produced goods and services: i.e. all items that contribute towards GDP.

Figure 26.8 Inflation rates in selected industrialised economies

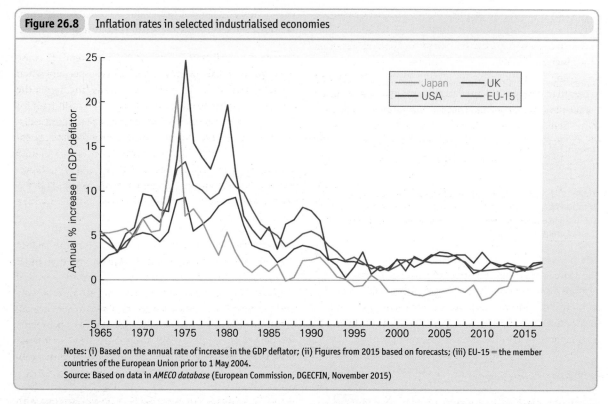

Notes: (i) Based on the annual rate of increase in the GDP deflator; (ii) Figures from 2015 based on forecasts; (iii) EU-15 = the member countries of the European Union prior to 1 May 2004.
Source: Based on data in *AMECO database* (European Commission, DGECFIN, November 2015)

in more recent years and indeed Japan experienced a period of prolonged deflation.

You will also find rates of inflation reported for a variety of goods and services. For example, inflation rates are published for wages (wage inflation), commodity prices, food prices, house prices, import prices, prices after taking taxes into account and so on.

Figure 26.9 shows three inflation rate measures for the UK from 2001. The three annual inflation rates have varied between –3 and 6 per cent over the period. Interestingly, from 2008 to mid-2014 we see that the annual rate of CPI inflation – the Bank of England's target measure – consistently exceeded the annual growth of average weekly earnings. This meant that the purchasing power of aver-

Figure 26.9 Selection of UK inflation rates

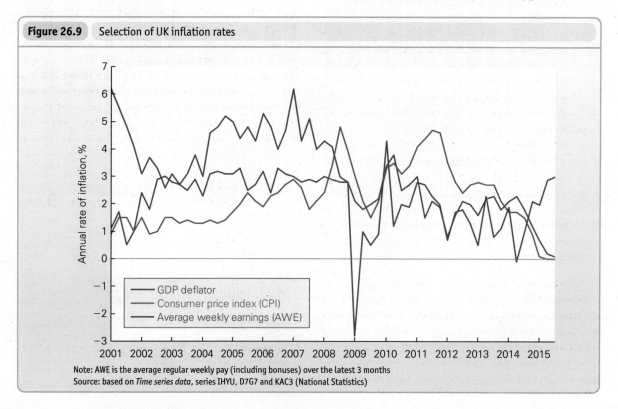

Note: AWE is the average regular weekly pay (including bonuses) over the latest 3 months
Source: based on *Time series data*, series IHYU, D7G7 and KAC3 (National Statistics)

age weekly earnings was being eroded by higher consumer prices.

When there is inflation, we have to be careful in assessing how much national output, consumption, wages, etc. are increasing. Take the case of GDP. GDP in year 2 may seem higher than in year 1, but this may be partly (or even wholly) the result of higher prices. Thus GDP in money terms may have risen by 5 per cent, but if inflation is 3 per cent, *real growth in GDP* will be only 2 per cent. In other words, the volume of output will be only 2 per cent higher.

> **KEY IDEA 42** *The distinction between nominal and real figures.* Nominal figures are those using current prices, interest rates, etc. Real figures are figures corrected for inflation.

Before we proceed, a word of caution: be careful not to confuse a rise or fall in *inflation* with a rise or fall in *prices*. A rise in inflation means a *faster* increase in prices. A fall in inflation means a *slower* increase in prices (but still an increase as long as inflation is positive).

The costs of inflation

A lack of growth is obviously a problem if people want higher living standards. Unemployment is obviously a problem, both for the unemployed themselves and also for society, which suffers a loss in output and has to support the unemployed. But why is inflation a problem? If firms are faced with rising costs, does it really matter if they can simply pass them on in higher prices? Similarly for workers, if their wages keep up with prices, there will not be a cut in their living standards.

If people could correctly anticipate the rate of inflation and fully adjust prices and incomes to take account of it, then the costs of inflation would indeed be relatively small. For us as consumers, they would simply be the relatively minor inconvenience of having to adjust our notions of what a 'fair' price is for each item when we go shopping. For firms, they would again be the relatively minor costs of having to change price labels, or prices in catalogues or on menus, or to adjust slot machines. These are known as *menu costs*.

 In reality, people frequently make mistakes when predicting the rate of inflation and are not able to adapt to it fully. This leads to the following problems, which are likely to be more serious the higher the rate of inflation becomes and the more the rate fluctuates.

 Redistribution. Inflation redistributes income away from those on fixed incomes and those in a weak bargaining position, to those who can use their economic power to gain large pay, rent or profit increases. It redistributes wealth to those with assets (e.g. property) that rise in value particularly rapidly during periods of inflation, and away from those with savings that pay rates of interest below the rate of inflation and hence whose value is eroded by inflation. Pensioners may be particularly badly hit by rapid inflation.

Uncertainty and lack of investment. Inflation tends to cause uncertainty in the business community, especially when the rate of inflation fluctuates. (Generally, the higher the rate of inflation, the more it fluctuates.) If it is difficult for firms to predict their costs and revenues, they may be discouraged from investing. This will reduce the rate of economic growth. On the other hand, as will be explained below, policies to reduce the rate of inflation may themselves reduce the rate of economic growth, especially in the short run. This may then provide the government with a policy dilemma.

Balance of payments. Inflation is likely to worsen the balance of payments. If a country suffers from relatively high inflation rates, its exports will become less competitive in world markets. At the same time, imports will become relatively cheaper than home-produced goods. Thus exports will fall and imports will rise. As a result the balance of payments will deteriorate and/or the exchange rate will fall, or interest rates will have to rise. Each of these effects can cause problems. This is examined in more detail in the next chapter.

Resources. Extra resources are likely to be used to cope with the effects of inflation. Accountants and other financial experts may have to be employed by companies to help them cope with the uncertainties caused by inflation.

The costs of inflation may be relatively mild if the inflation rate is kept to single figures. They can be very serious, however, if inflation gets out of hand. If inflation develops into 'hyperinflation', with prices rising perhaps by several hundred or even thousand per cent per year, the whole basis of the market economy will be undermined. Firms constantly raise prices in an attempt to cover their rocketing costs. Workers demand huge pay increases in an attempt to stay ahead of the rocketing cost of living. Thus prices and wages chase each other in an ever-rising inflationary spiral. People will no longer want to save money. Instead they will spend it as quickly as possible before its value falls any further. People may even resort to barter in an attempt to avoid using money altogether.

Hyperinflation has occurred in various countries. Extreme examples include Germany in the early 1920s,

> **Definitions**
>
> **Real growth values** Values of the rate of growth of GDP or any other variable after taking inflation into account. The real value of the growth in a variable equals its growth in money (or 'nominal') value minus the rate of inflation.
>
> **Menu costs of inflation** The costs associated with having to adjust price lists or labels.

Serbia and Montenegro in 1993–5 and Zimbabwe in 2006–8. In each case, inflation peaked at several million per cent.

> **Pause for thought**
>
> *Do you personally gain or lose from inflation? Why?*

Aggregate demand and supply and the level of prices

The level of prices in the economy is determined by the interaction of aggregate demand and aggregate supply. The analysis is similar to that of demand and supply in individual markets, but there are some crucial differences. Figure 26.10 shows aggregate demand and supply curves. Let us examine each in turn.

Aggregate demand curve

The aggregate demand curve shows how much national output (real GDP) will be demanded at each level of prices (GDP deflator). But why does the *AD* curve slope downwards: why do people demand fewer products as prices rise? There are three main reasons:

- *International substitution effect.* If prices rise, people will be encouraged to buy fewer of the country's products and more imports instead (which are now relatively cheaper); also the country will sell fewer exports. Thus aggregate demand will be lower.
- *Inter-temporal substitution effect.* As prices rise, people will need more money to pay for their purchases. With a given supply of money in the economy, this will have the effect of driving up interest rates (we will explore this in Chapter 28). The effect of higher interest rates will be to discourage borrowing and encourage saving. Both will have the effect of reducing spending and hence reducing aggregate demand.

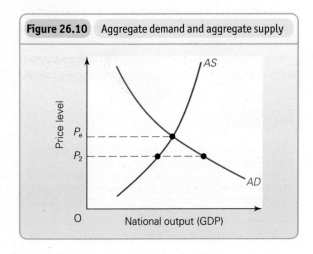

Figure 26.10 Aggregate demand and aggregate supply

- *Real balance effect.* If prices rise, the real value of people's savings will be eroded. They may thus save more (and spend less) to compensate.

The above three effects are *substitution effects* of the rise in prices (see page 53). They involve a switch to *alternatives* – either imports or saving.

There may also be an *income effect*. This will occur provided consumers' incomes do not rise as fast as prices, causing a fall in consumers' *real* incomes. Consumers cut down on consumption as they cannot afford to buy so much. Firms, on the other hand, with falling real wage costs, are likely to find their profit per unit rising. However, they are unlikely to spend much more on investment, if at all, as consumer expenditure is falling. The net effect is a fall in aggregate demand.

Aggregate supply curve

The aggregate supply curve slopes upwards – at least in the short run. In other words, the higher the level of prices, the more will be produced. The reason is simple: provided that factor prices (and, in particular, wage rates) do not rise as rapidly as product prices, firms' profitability at each level of output will be higher than before. This will encourage them to produce more.

Equilibrium

The equilibrium price level will be where aggregate demand equals aggregate supply. To demonstrate this, consider what would happen if aggregate demand exceeded aggregate supply: for example, at P_2 in Figure 26.10. The resulting shortages throughout the economy would drive up prices. This would cause a movement up along both the *AD* and *AS* curves until $AD = AS$ (at P_e).

Shifts in the AD or AS curves

If there is a change in the price level there will be a movement *along* the *AD* and *AS* curves. If any other determinant of *AD* or *AS* changes, the respective curve will shift. The analysis here is very similar to shifts and movements along demand and supply curves in individual markets (see pages 55 and 57–8).

The aggregate demand curve will shift if there is a change in any of its components: consumption, investment, government expenditure or exports minus imports. Thus if the government decides to spend more, or if consumers spend more as a result of lower taxes, or if business confidence increases so that firms decide to invest more, the *AD* curve will shift to the right.

> **Pause for thought**
>
> *Give some examples of events that could shift (a) the AD curve to the left; (b) the AS curve to the left.*

Similarly, the aggregate supply curve will shift to the right if there is a rise in labour productivity or in the stock of capital: in other words, if there is a rise in potential output.

Causes of inflation

Demand-pull inflation

Demand-pull inflation is caused by continuing rises in aggregate demand. In Figure 26.10, the *AD* curve shifts to the right, and continues doing so. Firms will respond to the rise in aggregate demand partly by raising prices and partly by increasing output (there is a move up along the *AS* curve). Just how much they raise prices depends on how much their costs rise as a result of increasing output. This in turn depends upon how close actual output is to potential output. The less slack there is in the economy, the more will firms respond to a rise in demand by raising their prices (the steeper will be the *AS* curve).

Demand-pull inflation is typically associated with a booming economy. Many economists therefore argue that it is the counterpart of demand-deficient unemployment. When the economy is in recession, demand-deficient unemployment will be high, but demand-pull inflation will be low. When, on the other hand, the economy is near the peak of the business cycle, demand-pull inflation will be high, but demand-deficient unemployment will be low.

Cost-push inflation

Cost-push inflation is associated with continuing rises in costs and hence continuing leftward (upward) shifts in the *AS* curve. Such shifts occur when costs of production rise *independently* of aggregate demand. If firms face a rise in costs, they will respond partly by raising prices and passing the costs on to the consumer, and partly by cutting back on production (there is a movement back along the *AD* curve).

Just how much firms raise prices and cut back on production depends on the shape of the aggregate demand curve. The less elastic the *AD* curve, the less sales will fall as a result of any price rise, and hence the more will firms be able to pass on the rise in their costs to consumers as higher prices.

Note that the effect on output and employment is the opposite of demand-pull inflation. With demand-pull inflation, output and hence employment tend to rise. With cost-push inflation, however, output and employment tend to fall.

It is important to distinguish between *single* shifts in the aggregate supply curve (known as 'supply shocks') and *continuing* shifts. If there is a single leftward shift in aggregate supply, there will be a single rise in the price level. For example, if the government raises the excise duty on petrol and diesel, there will be a single rise in road fuel prices and hence in industry's fuel costs. This will cause *temporary* inflation while the price rise is passed on through the economy. Once this has occurred, prices will stabilise at the new level and the rate of inflation will fall back to zero again. If cost-push inflation is to continue over a number of years, therefore, the aggregate supply curve must *continually* shift to the left. If cost-push inflation is to *rise*, these shifts must get more rapid.

Rises in costs may originate from a number of different sources, such as trade unions pushing up wages, firms with monopoly power raising prices in order to increase their profits, or increases in international commodity prices. With the process of globalisation and increased international competition, cost-push pressures have tended to decrease in recent years. The major exception is the price of various commodities and especially oil. For example, the near tripling of oil prices from $51 per barrel in January 2007 to $147 per barrel in July 2008 and again from $41 a barrel in January 2009 to $126 a barrel in April 2011 put upward pressure on costs and prices around the world.

Demand-pull and cost-push inflation can occur together, since wage and price rises can be caused both by increases in aggregate demand and by independent causes pushing up costs. Even when an inflationary process *starts* as either demand-pull or cost-push, it is often difficult to separate the two. An initial cost-push inflation may encourage the government to expand aggregate demand to offset rises in unemployment. Alternatively, an initial demand-pull inflation may strengthen the power of certain groups, which then use this power to drive up costs. Either way, the result is likely to be continuing rightward shifts in the *AD* curve and leftward shifts in the *AS* curve. Prices will carry on rising.

Expectations and inflation

Workers and firms take account of the *expected* rate of inflation when making decisions.

Imagine that a union and an employer are negotiating a wage increase. Let us assume that both sides expect a rate of inflation of 5 per cent. The union will be happy to receive a wage rise somewhat above 5 per cent. That way the members would be getting a *real* rise in incomes. The employers will be happy to pay a wage rise somewhat below 5 per cent.

> ### Definitions
>
> **Demand-pull inflation** Inflation caused by persistent rises in aggregate demand.
>
> **Cost-push inflation** Inflation caused by persistent rises in costs of production (independently of demand).

| BOX 26.3 | INFLATION OR DEFLATION |

Where's the danger?

During the first half of the 2000s it appeared that inflation was no longer a serious worry in many developed economies. Instead, 'deflation' (i.e. falling prices) had become a source of concern. One of the main reasons for this was dubbed the 'China price effect'. The rapid growth in cheap Chinese imports into developed countries was exerting downward pressure on prices.

The Japanese economy has been in deflation for a decade or so and central banks, including the US Federal Reserve and the European Central Bank, were now sounding warnings that deflation was a real and present danger to their economies too.

A return of inflation?

The USA and other OECD economies staged a rapid recovery after 2003. Between 2004 and 2007 global growth averaged 3.9 per cent each year. The UK and USA saw average annual economic growth rates of 2.7 and 2.9 per cent respectively. These rates, however, were dwarfed by China and India, which experienced growth rates of 12.1 per cent and 9.0 per cent respectively over the same period.

The rapid growth in aggregate demand in many OECD countries put upward pressure on prices and wages but, unlike previously, a new China price effect was beginning to reinforce this upward pressure.

By 2007/8, the growth in China, India and other rapidly developing countries was causing significant inflation in commodity prices, i.e. in the prices of raw material and primary agricultural products. This emergence of rapid commodity price inflation can be clearly seen in the chart.

Swinging between inflation and deflation?

However, with the onset of recession in mid-2008, inflation started to fall and the new China price effect seemed to have gone away. Once more there seemed to be a spectre of deflation. By 2009, many people were asking themselves why they should buy now when, by delaying, they might be able to get an item more cheaply later on. The effect of this would be a leftward shift in the AD curve, which forces prices down even further.

But the worry about deflation was short-lived. In 2010, the global economy expanded by 4.1 per cent and by a further 3.0 per cent in 2011. This was mirrored by the likes of China and India which saw their respective economies expand by 10.6 per cent and 10.3 per cent in 2010 and by 9.5 per cent and 6.6 per cent in 2011. In the UK, the annual rate of CPI inflation peaked at 5.2 per cent in the 12 months to September 2011, significantly above the Bank of England's central inflation target of 2 per cent.

The period 2012 to 2014 saw a slight easing of global growth, with the world economy expanding by around 2.5 per cent each year. This was reflected in a cooling of the rate of commodity price inflation. By 2014 commodity prices in general and oil prices in particular were falling. The fall in oil prices from around $100 per barrel to around $60 in the second half of the year reflected both worries for the prospects of economic growth, especially in the eurozone, and increased supply, especially from shale deposits in the USA.

Falling commodity prices helped to moderate consumer price inflation rates. At the start of 2015, the annual rate of CPI inflation in the UK had fallen back significantly to around zero per cent. Meanwhile in the eurozone there was deflation, with the CPI inflation rate as low as −0.6 per cent in January and then around zero for the rest of the year.

1. *What long-term economic benefits might deflation generate for business and the economy in general?*
2. *Would an inflationary China price effect be an example of demand-pull or cost-push inflation?*

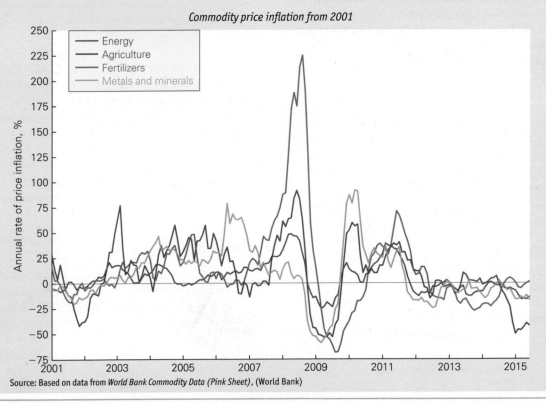

Commodity price inflation from 2001

Source: Based on data from *World Bank Commodity Data (Pink Sheet)*, (World Bank)

After all, they can put their price up by 5 per cent, knowing that their rivals will do approximately the same. The actual wage rise that the two sides agree on will thus be somewhere around 5 per cent.

Now let us assume that the expected rate of inflation is 10 per cent. Both sides will now negotiate around this benchmark, with the outcome being somewhere round about 10 per cent.

Thus the higher the expected rate of inflation, the higher will be the level of pay settlements and price rises, and hence the higher will be the resulting actual rate of inflation.

In recent years the importance of expectations in explaining the actual rate of inflation has been increasingly recognised by economists. (We examine this in Chapter 29.)

26.5 THE BUSINESS CYCLE AND KEY MACROECONOMIC VARIABLES

KI 38
p 470

In the short term (up to about two years), several of our key macroeconomic variables identified in section 26.1 are likely to be related. This happens when they depend on aggregate demand and so vary with the course of the business cycle. This is illustrated in Figure 26.11

In the expansionary phase of the business cycle (phase 2), aggregate demand grows rapidly. There will be relatively rapid growth in output, with a positive output gap emerging, and (demand-deficient) unemployment will fall. However, the growing shortages lead to higher (demand-pull) inflation and a deteriorating balance of payments as the extra demand 'sucks in' more imports and as higher prices make domestic goods less competitive internationally.

At the peak of the cycle (phase 3), unemployment is probably at its lowest and output at its highest (for the time being). But growth has already ceased or at least slowed

down. Inflation and balance of payments problems are probably acute.

As the economy moves into phase 4 (let us assume that this is an actual recession with falling output), the reverse will happen to that of phase 2. Falling aggregate demand will make growth negative and demand-deficient unemployment higher, but inflation is likely to slow down and the balance of payments will improve. These two improvements may take some time to occur, however.

We might also expect the financial well-being of economic agents to change over the course of the business cycle. For example, in phase 2 as aggregate demand increases the increase in national income allows economic agents to accumulate financial and non-financial assets and/or to reduce holdings of financial liabilities. But, exactly how the balance sheets are affected will depend on the actual behaviour of economic agents.

Figure 26.11   The business cycle and macroeconomic objectives

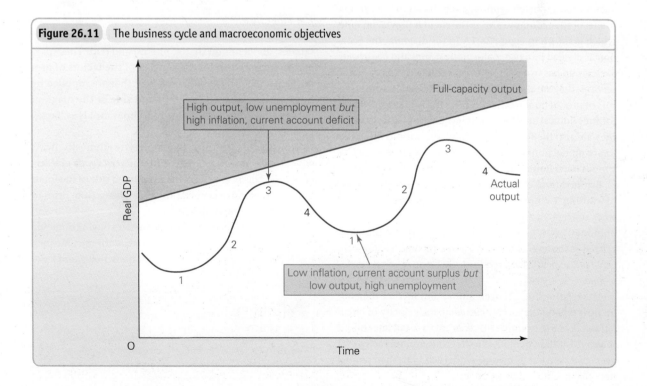

Some economists argue that while the balance sheets of people, businesses, governments and even whole nations are affected by the business cycle, these balance sheets can affect the actual path of the economy. In other words, there is a feedback loop from the health of the balance sheets to the macroeconomy. Financial well-being is affected by the macroeconomic environment, but the macroeconomic environment can be affected by financial well-being.

For example, the slowdown phase of the business cycle (phase 4) could be the result of financially distressed economic agents. A **balance sheet recession** is said to occur when high levels of private-sector indebtedness result in the private sector looking to increase its saving and/or pay down debt. Unfortunately, this only helps to dampen aggregate demand and reduce the rate of economic growth. It is argued that this process contributed to the economic slowdown that took place in the late 2000s following the financial crisis.

As we saw earlier (page 485), policy makers are often faced with a dilemma. If they reflate the economy, this will stimulate economic growth and reduce unemployment, but the rate of inflation will rise and the balance of exports over imports (net exports) will deteriorate. If they deflate the economy, it is the other way round: inflation and net exports will improve, but unemployment will rise and growth, or even output, will fall.

The situation is further complicated by the behaviour of financial institutions and the financial well-being of economic agents. This suggests that policy makers need also to be concerned by the risks to the economy arising from the financial system. This is a theme we return to in Chapter 28.

Definition

Balance sheet recession An economic slowdown or recession caused by the private sector looking to improve their financial well-being by increasing their saving and/or paying down debt.

26.6 THE CIRCULAR FLOW OF INCOME

Another way of understanding the relationship between some of the key macroeconomic variables is to use a simple model of the economy. This is the circular flow of income, which is shown in Figure 26.12. In the diagram, the economy is divided into two major groups: *firms* and *households*. Each group has two roles. Firms are producers of goods and services; they are also the employers of labour and other factors of production. Households (which is the word we use for individuals) are the consumers of goods and services; they are also the suppliers of labour and various other factors of production. In the diagram there is an inner flow and various outer flows of income between these two groups.

Before we look at the various parts of the diagram, a word of warning. Do not confuse *money* and *income*. Money is a stock concept. At any given time, there is a certain quantity of money in the economy (e.g. £1 trillion). But that does not tell us the level of national *income*. Income is a flow concept (as is expenditure). It is measured as so much *per period of time*.

The relationship between money and income depends on how rapidly the money *circulates*: its 'velocity of circulation'. (We will examine this concept in detail later on.) If there is £1 trillion of money in the economy and each £1 on average is paid out as income twice each year, then annual national income will be £2 trillion.

The inner flow, withdrawals and injections

The inner flow

Firms pay money to households in the form of wages and salaries, dividends on shares, interest and rent. These payments are in return for the services of the factors of production – labour, capital and land – that are supplied by households. Thus on the left-hand side of the diagram money flows directly from firms to households as 'factor payments'.

Households, in turn, pay money to domestic firms when they **consume domestically produced goods and services (C_d)**. This is shown on the right-hand side of the inner flow. There is thus a circular flow of payments from firms to households to firms and so on.

If households spend *all* their incomes on buying domestic goods and services, and if firms pay out *all* this income they receive as factor payments to domestic households, and if the

Definition

The consumption of domestically produced goods and services (C_d) The direct flow of money payments from households to firms.

Figure 26.12   The circular flow of income

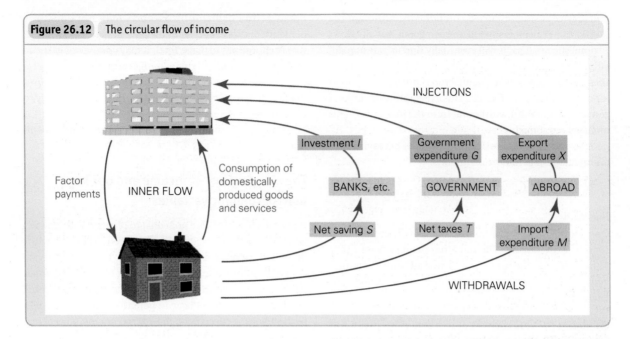

velocity of circulation does not change, the flow will continue at the same level indefinitely. The money just goes round and round at the same speed and incomes remain unchanged.

In the real world, of course, it is not as simple as this. Not all income gets passed on round the inner flow; some is *withdrawn*. At the same time, incomes are injected into the flow from outside. Let us examine these withdrawals and injections.

Withdrawals

Only part of the incomes received by households will be spent on the goods and services of domestic firms. The remainder will be withdrawn from the inner flow. Likewise, only part of the incomes generated by firms will be paid to domestic households. The remainder of this will also be withdrawn. There are three forms of **withdrawals (W)** (or 'leakages' as they are sometimes called).

Net saving (S). Saving is income that households choose not to spend but to put aside for the future. Savings are normally deposited in financial institutions such as banks and building societies. This is shown in the bottom right of the diagram. Money flows from households to 'banks, etc.'. What we are seeking to measure here, however, is the net flow from households to the banking sector. We therefore have to subtract from saving any borrowing or drawing on past savings by households in order to get the *net* saving flow. Of course, if household borrowing exceeded saving, the net flow would be in the other direction: it would be negative.

Net taxes (T). When people pay taxes (to either central or local government), this represents a withdrawal of money from the inner flow in much the same way as saving: only in this case people have no choice. Some taxes, such as income tax and employees' national insurance contributions, are paid out of household incomes. Others, such as VAT and excise duties, are paid out of consumer expenditure. Others, such as corporation tax, are paid out of firms' incomes before being received by households as dividends on shares. (For simplicity, however, we show taxes being withdrawn at just one point. It does not affect the argument.)

When, however, people receive *benefits* from the government, such as working tax credit, child benefit and pensions, the money flows the other way. Benefits are thus equivalent to a 'negative tax'. These benefits are known as **transfer payments**. They transfer money from one group of people (taxpayers) to others (the recipients).

In the model, 'net taxes' (T) represent the *net* flow to the government from households and firms. It consists of total taxes minus benefits.

Import expenditure (M). Not all consumption is of totally home-produced goods. Households spend some of their incomes on imported goods and services, or on goods

Pause for thought

Would this argument still hold if prices rose?

Definitions

Withdrawals (W) (or leakages) Incomes of households or firms that are not passed on round the inner flow. Withdrawals equal net saving (S) plus net taxes (T) plus import expenditure (M): $W = S + T + M$.

Transfer payments Moneys transferred from one person or group to another (e.g. from the government to individuals) without production taking place.

and services using imported components. Although the money that consumers spend on such goods initially flows to domestic retailers, it will eventually find its way abroad, either when the retailers or wholesalers themselves import them, or when domestic manufacturers purchase imported inputs to make their products. This expenditure on imports constitutes the third withdrawal from the inner flow. This money flows abroad.

Total withdrawals are simply the sum of net saving, net taxes and the expenditure on imports:

$$W = S + T + M$$

Injections

Only part of the demand for firms' output arises from consumers' expenditure. The remainder comes from other sources outside the inner flow. These additional components of aggregate demand are known as *injections (J)*. There are three types of injection.

Investment (I). This consists of investment in plant and equipment. It also includes the building up of stocks of inputs, semi-finished or finished goods. When firms invest, they obtain the money from various financial institutions, either from past savings or from loans, or through a new issues of shares.

Government expenditure (G). When the government spends money on goods and services produced by firms, this counts as an injection. Examples of such government expenditure are spending on roads, hospitals and schools. (Note that government expenditure in this model does not include state benefits. These transfer payments, as we saw above, are the equivalent of negative taxes and have the effect of reducing the T component of withdrawals.)

Export expenditure (X). Money flows into the circular flow from abroad when residents abroad buy our exports of goods and services.

Total injections are thus the sum of investment, government expenditure and exports:

$$J = I + G + X$$

Aggregate demand, which is the total spending on output, is thus $C_d + J$.

The relationship between withdrawals and injections

There are indirect links between saving and investment via financial institutions, between taxation and government expenditure via the government (central and local), and between imports and exports via foreign countries. These links, however, do not guarantee that $S = I$ or $G = T$ or $M = X$.

Take investment and saving. The point here is that the decisions to save and invest are made by different people, and thus they plan to save and invest different amounts.

Likewise the demand for imports may not equal the demand for exports. As far as the government is concerned, it may choose not to make $T = G$. It may choose not to spend all its tax revenues: to run a 'budget surplus' ($T > G$); or it may choose to spend more than it receives in taxes: to run a 'budget deficit' ($G > T$), by borrowing or printing money to make up the difference.

Thus planned injections (J) may not equal planned withdrawals (W).

The circular flow of income and our key macroeconomic variables

If planned injections are not equal to planned withdrawals, what will be the consequences? If injections exceed withdrawals, the level of expenditure will rise. The extra aggregate demand will generate extra incomes. In other words, *actual* national income will rise. If this rise in actual income exceeds any rise there may have been in potential income, there will be the following effects upon the macroeconomic objectives:

- There will be economic growth. The greater the initial excess of injections over withdrawals, the bigger will be the rise in national income.
- Unemployment will fall as firms take on more workers in order to meet the extra demand for output.
- The rate of inflation will tend to rise. The more the gap is closed between actual and potential income, the more difficult will firms find it to meet extra demand, and the more likely they will be to raise prices.
- The exports and imports part of the balance of payments will tend to deteriorate. The higher demand sucks more imports into the country, and higher domestic inflation makes exports less competitive and imports relatively cheaper compared with home-produced goods. Thus imports will tend to rise and exports will tend to fall (*net exports fall*).
- An increase in national income allows economic agents to accumulate financial and non-financial assets and/or to reduce holdings of financial liabilities.

Changes in injections and withdrawals thus have a crucial effect on the whole macroeconomic environment in which businesses operate. We will examine some of these effects in more detail in the following chapters.

> ### Pause for thought
>
> *What will be the effect on each of the key macroeconomic variables if planned injections are less than planned withdrawals?*

> ### Definition
>
> **Injections (J)** Expenditure on the production of domestic firms coming from outside the inner flow of the circular flow of income. Injections equal investment (*I*) plus government expenditure (*G*) plus expenditure on exports (*X*).

SUMMARY

1   The macroeconomic environment is characterised by a series of interrelated macroeconomic variables. These include: economic growth, unemployment, inflation, the balance of payments, exchange rates, the financial well-being of economic agents (i.e. households, businesses, governments and nations) and the stability of the financial system (e.g. flows of credit).

2a Actual growth must be distinguished from potential growth. The actual growth rate is the percentage annual increase in the output that is actually produced, whereas potential growth is the percentage annual increase in the capacity of the economy to produce (whether or not it is actually produced).

2b Actual growth will fluctuate with the course of the business cycle. The cycle can be broken down into four phases: the upturn, the rapid expansion, the peaking-out, and the slowdown or recession. In practice the length and magnitude of these phases will vary: the cycle is thus irregular.

2c Actual growth is determined by potential growth and by the level of aggregate demand. If actual output is below potential output, actual growth can temporarily exceed potential growth, if aggregate demand is rising sufficiently. In the long term, however, actual output can only grow as fast as potential output will permit.

2d Potential growth is determined by the rate of increase in the *quantity* of resources: capital, labour, land and raw materials; and by the *productivity* of resources. The productivity of capital can be increased by technological improvements and the more efficient use of the capital stock; the productivity of labour can be increased by better education, training, motivation and organisation.

3a The two most common measures of unemployment are claimant unemployment (those claiming unemployment-related benefits) and ILO/OECD standardised unemployment (those available for work and actively seeking work or waiting to take up an appointment).

3b The costs of unemployment include the financial and other personal costs to the unemployed person, the costs to relatives and friends, and the costs to society at large in terms of lost tax revenues, lost profits and lost wages to other workers, and in terms of social disruption.

3c Unemployment can be divided into disequilibrium and equilibrium unemployment.

3d Disequilibrium unemployment occurs when the average real wage rate is above the level that will equate the aggregate demand and supply of labour. It can be caused by unions or government pushing up wages (real-wage unemployment), by a fall in aggregate demand but a downward 'stickiness' in real wages (demand-deficient unemployment), or by an increase in the supply of labour.

3e Equilibrium unemployment occurs when there are people unable or unwilling to fill job vacancies. This may be due to poor information in the labour market and hence a time lag before people find suitable jobs (frictional unemployment), to a changing pattern of demand or

supply in the economy and hence a mismatching of labour with jobs (structural unemployment – specific types being technological and regional unemployment), or to seasonal fluctuations in the demand for labour.

4a Inflation redistributes incomes from the economically weak to the economically powerful; it causes uncertainty in the business community and as a result reduces investment; it tends to lead to balance of payments problems and/or a fall in the exchange rate; it leads to resources being used to offset its effects. The costs of inflation can be very great indeed in the case of hyperinflation.

4b Equilibrium in the economy occurs when aggregate demand equals aggregate supply. Inflation can occur if there is a rightward shift in the aggregate demand curve or an upward (leftward) shift in the aggregate supply curve.

4c Demand-pull inflation occurs as a result of increases in aggregate demand. This can be due to monetary or non-monetary causes.

4d Cost-push inflation occurs when there are increases in the costs of production independent of rises in aggregate demand. Cost-push inflation can be of a number of different varieties: wage push, profit push or import-price push.

4e Cost-push and demand-pull inflation can interact to form spiralling inflation.

4f Expectations play a crucial role in determining the rate of inflation. The higher people expect inflation to be, the higher it will be.

5   In the short run, several important macroeconomic variables are related to aggregate demand and the business cycle. In the expansion phase, growth is high and unemployment is falling, but inflation is rising and the current account of the balance of payments is moving into deficit. In the recession, the reverse is the case.

6a The circular flow of income model depicts the flows of money around the economy. The inner flow shows the direct flows between firms and households. Money flows from firms to households in the form of factor payments, and back again as consumer expenditure on domestically produced goods and services.

6b Not all income gets passed on directly around the inner flow. Some is withdrawn in the form of saving, some is paid in taxes, and some goes abroad as expenditure on imports.

6c Likewise not all expenditure on domestic firms is by domestic consumers. Some is injected from outside the inner flow in the form of investment expenditure, government expenditure and expenditure on the country's exports.

6d Planned injections and withdrawals are unlikely to be the same. If injections exceed withdrawals, national income will rise, unemployment will tend to fall, inflation will tend to rise and the current account of the balance of payments will tend to deteriorate. The reverse will happen if withdrawals exceed injections.

MyEconLab

This book can be supported by MyEconLab, which contains a range of additional resources, including an online homework and tutorial system designed to test and build your understanding.

You need both an access card and a course ID to access MyEconLab:

1. Is your lecturer using MyEconLab? Ask your lecturer for your course ID.

2. Has an access card been included with the book at a reduced cost? Check the inside back cover of the book.

3. If you have a course ID but no access card, go to: http://www.myeconlab.com/ to buy access to this interactive study programme.

REVIEW QUESTIONS

1 The following table shows index numbers for real GDP (national output) for various countries (2007=100). Using the formula $g = (Y_t - Y_{t-1})/Y_{t-1} \times 100$ (where g is the rate of growth, Y is the index number of output, t is any given years and $t - 1$ is the previous year):

	2007	2008	2009	2010	2011	2012	2013	2014	2015
EU-15	100.0	100.3	95.8	97.8	99.4	98.8	98.7	99.9	101.7
UK	100.0	99.7	95.4	97.2	98.8	99.4	101.1	104.0	106.6
USA	100.0	99.7	96.9	99.4	101.0	103.3	105.6	108.2	111.5
Japan	100.0	99.0	93.5	97.8	97.4	99.1	100.7	100.7	101.8

Source: *AMECO* database (European Commission, DGECFIN)

a) (i) Work out the growth rate (g) for each country for each year from 2008 to 2015.

(ii) Plot the figures on a graph.

(iii) Describe the patterns that emerge.

b) (i) For each country work out the percentage increase in real GDP between 2007 and 2015.

(ii) Prepare a column chart showing the percentage increase in output over this period with the countries ranked from largest to smallest by the size of increase.

(iii) Comment on your findings.

2 In 1974 the UK economy shrank by 2.5 per cent before shrinking by a further 1.5 per cent in 1975. However, the figures for GDP showed a rise of 12 per cent in 1974 and 24 per cent in 1975. What explains these apparently contradictory results?

3 Figure 26.3 shows a decline in actual output in recessions. Redraw the diagram, only this time show a mere slowing down of growth in phase 4.

4 At what point of the business cycle is the country now? What do you predict will happen to growth over the next two years? On what basis do you make your prediction?

5 For what possible reasons may one country experience a persistently faster rate of economic growth than another?

6 Would it be desirable to have zero unemployment?

7 What major structural changes have taken place in the UK economy in the past 10 years that have contributed to structural unemployment?

8 What would be the benefits and costs of increasing the rate of unemployment benefit?

9 Do any groups of people gain from inflation?

10 If everyone's incomes rose in line with inflation, would it matter if inflation were 100 per cent or even 1000 per cent per annum?

11 Imagine that you had to determine whether a particular period of inflation was demand-pull, or cost-push, or a combination of the two. What information would you require in order to conduct your analysis?

12 In terms of the UK circular flow of income, are the following net injections, net withdrawals or neither? If there is uncertainty, explain your assumptions.

a) Firms are forced to take a cut in profits in order to give a pay rise.

b) Firms spend money on research.

c) The government increases personal tax allowances.

d) The general public invests more money in building societies.

e) UK investors earn higher dividends on overseas investments.

f) The government purchases US military aircraft.

g) People draw on their savings to finance holidays abroad.

h) People draw on their savings to finance holidays in the UK.

i) The government runs a budget deficit (spends more than it receives in tax revenues) and finances it by borrowing from the general public.

j) The government runs a budget deficit and finances it by printing more money.

k) As consumer confidence rises, households decrease their precautionary saving.

APPENDIX: MEASURING NATIONAL INCOME AND OUTPUT

Three routes: one destination

KI 27
p 322

To assess how fast the economy has grown, we must have a means of *measuring* the value of the nation's output. The measure we use is called *gross domestic product* (GDP).

GDP can be calculated in three different ways, which should all result in the same figure. These three methods are illustrated in the simplified circular flow of income shown in Figure 26.13.

The product method

This first method of measuring GDP is to add up the value of all the goods and services produced in the country, industry by industry. In other words, we focus on firms and add up all their production. This method is known as the *product method*.

In the national accounts these figures are grouped together into broad categories such as manufacturing, construction and distribution. The figures for the UK economy for 2013 are shown in the top part of Figure 26.14.

When we add up the output of various firms, we must be careful to avoid *double counting*. For example, if a manufacturer sells a television to a retailer for £200 and the retailer sells it to the consumer for £300, how much has this television contributed to GDP? The answer is *not* £500. We do not add the £200 received by the manufacturer to the £300 received by the retailer: that would be double counting. Instead we either just count the final value (£300) or the value added at each stage (£200 by the manufacturer + £100 by the retailer).

The sum of all the values added by all the various industries in the economy is known as *gross value added (GVA) at basic prices*.

How do we get from GVA to GDP? The answer has to do with taxes and subsidies on products and is shown in the bottom part of Figure 26.14. Taxes paid on goods and services (such as VAT and duties on petrol and alcohol) and any subsidies on products are *excluded* from gross value added (GVA), since they are not part of the value added in production. Nevertheless, the way GDP is measured throughout the EU is at *market prices*: i.e. at the prices actually paid at each stage of production. Thus **GDP at market prices** (sometimes referred to simply as GDP) is GVA *plus* taxes on products *minus* subsidies on products.

The income method

The second approach is to focus on the incomes generated from the production of goods and services. A moment's reflection will show that this must be the same as the sum of all values added at each stage of production. Value added is simply the difference between a firm's revenue from sales and the costs of its purchases from other firms. This difference is made up of wages and salaries, rent, interest and profit. In other words, it consists of the incomes earned by those involved in the production process.

Since GVA is the sum of all values added, it must also be the sum of all incomes generated: the sum of all wages and salaries, rent, interest and profit.

The second part of Figure 26.14 shows how these incomes are grouped together in the official statistics. As you can see, the total is the same as that in the top part Figure 26.14, even though the components are quite different.

Note that we do not include *transfer payments* such as social security benefits and pensions. Since these are not payments for the production of goods and services, they are excluded from GVA. Conversely, part of people's gross income is paid in income taxes. Since it is this *gross* (pretax) income that arises from the production of goods and services, we count wages, profits, interest and rent *before* the deduction of income taxes.

As with the product approach, if we are working out GVA, we measure incomes before the payment of taxes on products or the receipt of subsidies on products, since it is

---

Figure 26.13	The circular flow of income and expenditure

(1) Production

(2) Incomes

(3) Expenditure

Definitions

Gross value added (GVA) at basic prices The sum of all the values added by all industries in the economy over a year. The figures exclude taxes on products (such as VAT) and include subsidies on products.

Gross domestic product (GDP) (at market prices) The value of output produced within a country over a 12-month period in terms of the prices actually paid. GDP = GVA + taxes on products − subsidies on products.

Figure 26.14   UK GDP: 2013

UK GVA (product based measure): 2013	£m	% of GVA
Agriculture, forestry and fishing	9 937	0.7
Mining & quarrying; electricity & gas; water supply & sewerage	67 460	4.4
Manufacturing	147 697	9.7
Construction	92 363	6.1
Wholesale & retail trade; repair of motor vehicles	171 940	11.3
Hotels, restaurants & food services	43 044	2.8
Transportation; information & communication	159 424	10.5
Financial and insurance activities	122 587	8.0
Real estate	175 678	11.5
Public administration & defence	79 298	5.2
Education; human health & social work	206 336	13.5
Other services	249 540	16.4
GVA (gross value added at basic prices)	**1 525 304**	**100.0**

UK GVA by category of income: 2013		
Compensation of employees (wages and salaries)	877 883	57.6
Operating surplus (gross profit, rent and interest of firms government and other institutions)	523 351	34.3
Mixed incomes	98 848	6.5
Tax less subsidies on production (other than those on products) plus statistical discrepancy	25 222	1.7
GVA (gross value added at basic prices)	**1 525 304**	**100.0**

UK GDP: 2013		
GVA (gross value added at basic prices)	1 525 304	
plus VAT and other taxes on products	194 735	
less Subsidies on products	–6 737	
GDP (at market prices)	**1 713 302**	

---

these pre-tax-and-subsidy incomes that arise from the value added by production. When working out GDP, however, we add in these taxes and subtract these subsidies to arrive at a *market price* valuation.

Pause for thought

If a retailer buys a product from a wholesaler for £80 and sells it to a consumer for £100, then the £20 of value that has been added will go partly in wages, partly in rent and partly in profits. Thus £20 of income has been generated at the retail stage. But the good actually contributes a total of £100 to GDP. Where, then, is the remaining £80 worth of income recorded?

The expenditure method

The final approach to calculating GDP is to add up all expenditure on final output (which will be at market prices). This will include the following:

■ Consumer expenditure (*C*). This includes all expenditure on goods and services by households and by non-profit institutions serving households (NPISH) (e.g. clubs and societies).

■ Government expenditure (*G*). This includes central and local government expenditure on final goods and services. Note that it includes non-marketed services (such as health and education), but excludes transfer payments, such as pensions and social security payments.

- Investment expenditure (*I*). This includes investment in capital, such as buildings and machinery. It also includes the value of any increase (+) or decrease (–) in inventories, whether of raw materials, semi-finished goods or finished goods.
- Exports of goods and services (*X*).
- Imports of goods and services (*M*). These have to be subtracted from the total in order to leave just the expenditure on domestic product. In other words, we subtract the part of consumer expenditure, government expenditure and investment that goes on imports. We also subtract the imported component (e.g. raw materials) from exports.

GDP (at market prices) = $C + G + I + X - M$

Table 26.1 shows the calculation of UK GDP by the expenditure approach.

From GDP to national income

Gross national income

Some of the incomes earned in the country will go abroad. These include wages, interest, profit and rent earned in this country by foreign residents and remitted abroad, and taxes on production paid to foreign governments and institutions (e.g. the EU). On the other hand, some of the incomes earned by domestic residents will come from abroad. Again, these can be in the form of wages, interest, profit or rent, or in the form of subsidies received from governments or institutions abroad. Gross domestic product, however, is concerned with those incomes generated within the country, irrespective of ownership. If, then, we are to take 'net income from abroad' into account (i.e. these inflows minus outflows), we need a new measure. This is *gross national income (GNY)*.[3] It is defined as follows:

Table 26.1	UK GDP at market prices by category of expenditure, 2013	
	£ million	**% of GDP**
Consumption expenditure of households and NPISH (C)	1 110 807	64.8
Government final consumption (G)	346 774	20.2
Gross capital formation (I)	291 717	17.0
Exports of goods and services (X)	511 275	29.8
less Imports of goods and services (M)	−543 375	−31.7
Statistical discrepancy	−3 896	−0.2
GDP at market prices	**1 713 302**	**100.0**

Source: *United Kingdom National Accounts* (National Statistics)

GNY at market prices = GDP at market prices
+ net income from abroad

Thus GDP focuses on the value of domestic production, whereas GNY focuses on the value of incomes earned by domestic residents.

Net national income

The measures we have used so far ignore the fact that each year some of the country's capital equipment will wear out or become obsolete: in other words, they ignore capital *depreciation*. If we subtract an allowance for depreciation (or 'capital consumption') we get *net national income (NNY)*:

NNY at market prices = GNY at market prices
– depreciation

Table 26.2 shows GDP, GNY and NNY figures for the UK.

Households' disposable income

Finally, we come to a term called *households' disposable income*. It measures the income people have available for spending (or saving): i.e. after any deductions for income tax, national insurance, etc. have been made. It is the best measure to use if want to see how changes in household income affect consumption.

How do we get from GNY at market prices to households' disposable income? We start with the incomes that

Table 26.2	UK GDP, GNY and NNY at market prices: 2013
	£ million
Gross domestic product (GDP)	**1 713 302**
Plus net income from abroad	−13 132
Gross national income (GNY)	**1 700 170**
Less capital consumption (depreciation)	227 981
Net national income (NNY)	**1 472 189**

Source: *United Kingdom National Accounts* (National Statistics).

Definitions

Gross national income (GNY) GDP plus net income from abroad.

Depreciation The decline in value of capital equipment due to age or wear and tear.

Net national income (NNY) GNY minus depreciation.

---

[3] In the official statistics, this is referred to as *GNI*. We use *Y* to stand for income, however, to avoid confusion with investment.

[4] We also include income from any public-sector production of goods or services (e.g. health and education) and production by non-profit institutions serving households.

firms receive [4] from production (plus income from abroad) and then deduct that part of their income that is *not* distributed to households. This means that we must deduct taxes that firms pay – taxes on goods and services (such as VAT), taxes on profits (such as corporation tax) and any other taxes – and add in any subsidies they receive. We must then subtract allowances for depreciation and any undistributed profits. This gives us the gross income that households receive from firms in the form of wages, salaries, rent, interest and distributed profits.

To get from this what is available for households to spend we must subtract the money households pay in income taxes and national insurance contributions, but add all benefits to households such as pensions and child benefit.

Households' = GNY at market prices – taxes paid by
disposable   firms + subsidies received by firms
income   – depreciation – undistributed profits
               – personal taxes + benefits

Definition

Households' disposable income The income available for households to spend: i.e. personal incomes after deducting taxes on incomes and adding benefits.

SUMMARY TO APPENDIX

1 National income is usually expressed in terms of gross domestic product. This is simply the value of domestic production over the course of the year. It can be measured by the product, expenditure or income methods.

2 The product method measures the values added in all parts of the economy.

3 The income method measures all the incomes generated from domestic production: wages and salaries, rent and profit.

4 The expenditure method adds up all the categories of expenditure: consumer expenditure, government expenditure, investment and exports. We then have to deduct the element of each that goes on imports in order to arrive at expenditure on domestic products. Thus GDP $= C + G + I + X - M$.

5 GDP at market prices measures what consumers pay for output (including taxes and subsidies on what they buy). Gross value added (GVA) measures what factors of production actually receive. GVA, therefore, is GDP at market prices minus taxes on products plus subsidies on products.

6 Gross national income (GNY) takes account of incomes earned from abroad (+) and incomes earned by people abroad from this country (–). Thus GNY = GDP plus net income from abroad.

7 Net national income (NNY) takes account of the depreciation of capital. Thus NNY = GNY – depreciation.

8 Households' disposable income is a measure of household income after the deduction of income taxes and the addition of benefits.

REVIEW QUESTIONS TO APPENDIX

1 Should we include the sale of used items in the GDP statistics? For example, if you sell your car to a garage for £2000 and it then sells it to someone else for £2500, has this added £2500 to GDP, or nothing at all, or merely the value that the garage adds to the car, i.e. £500?

2 What items are excluded from national income statistics which would be important to take account of if we were to get a true indication of a country's standard of living?

Today's rates

		We buy	We sell
	EURO	1.2836	1.1604
	USA	1.7730	1.920
	AUSTRALIA	2.0089	1.789
	TURKEY	3.6534	3.1968
	THAILAND	59.5440	47.8915
	HONG KONG	14.2542	11.7390
	DENMARK	9.8041	8.4503
	CANADA	1.9061	1.6867

27 Chapter

The balance of payments and exchange rates

Business issues covered in this chapter

- What is meant by 'the balance of payments' and how do trade and financial movements affect it?
- How are exchange rates determined?
- What are the implications for business of changes in the exchange rate?
- What is the relationship between the balance of payments and exchange rates?
- How do governments and/or central banks seek to influence the exchange rate and what are the implications for other macroeconomic policies and for business?

In Part I we examined the role of international trade for a country and for business, and saw how trade has grown rapidly since 1945. The world economy has become progressively more interlinked, with multinational corporations dominating a large proportion of international business. In this chapter we return to look at international trade and the financial flows associated with it. In particular, we shall examine the relationship between the domestic economy and the international trading environment. This will involve considering both the balance of payments and the exchange rate.

We will first explain what is meant by the balance of payments. In doing so, we will see just how the various monetary transactions between the domestic economy and the rest of the world are recorded.

Then we will examine how rates of exchange are determined, and how they are related to the balance of payments. Then we will see what causes exchange rate fluctuations, and what will happen if the government intervenes in the foreign exchange market to prevent these fluctuations. Finally, we will consider how exchange rates have been managed in practice.

27.1 THE BALANCE OF PAYMENTS ACCOUNT

KI 27
p 322

A country's balance of payments account records all the flows of money between residents of that country and the rest of the world. *Receipts* of money from abroad are regarded as *credits* and are entered in the accounts with a positive sign. *Outflows* of money from the country are regarded as *debits* and are entered with a negative sign.

There are three main parts of the balance of payments account: the *current account*, the *capital account* and the *financial account*. Each part is then subdivided. We shall look at each part in turn, and take the UK as an example. Table 27.1 gives a summary of the UK balance of payments for 2014, while also providing an historical perspective.

KI 27
p 322

Table 27.1	UK balance of payments		
	2014		**Average 1987–2014 as % of GDP**
	£m	% of GDP	
CURRENT ACCOUNT			
Balance on trade in goods	−123 143	−6.8	−4.1
Balance on trade in services	88 741	4.9	2.4
Balance of trade	**−34 402**	**−1.9**	**−1.7**
Income balance	−32 901	−1.8	0.4
Net current transfers	−25 166	−1.4	−0.9
Current account balance	**−92 469**	**−5.1**	**−2.2**
CAPITAL ACCOUNT			
Capital account balance	**−415**	**0.0**	**0.0**
FINANCIAL ACCOUNT			
Net direct investment	81 600	4.5	−1.2
Portfolio investment balance	114 735	6.3	1.8
Other investment balance	−102 982	−5.7	1.5
Balance of financial derivatives	14 741	0.8	−0.1
Reserve assets	−7 113	−0.4	−0.2
Financial account balance	**100 981**	**5.6**	**1.9**
Net errors and omissions	**−8 097**	**−0.4**	**0.4**
Balance	0	0	0

Source: *Balance of Payments, Quarter 3 (July to Sept) 2015* and *Quarterly National Accounts, Quarter 3 (July to Sept) 2015* (Office for National Statistics, 2015)

The current account

The *current account* records payments for imports and exports of goods and services, plus incomes flowing into and out of the country, plus net transfers of money into and out of the country. It is normally divided into four subdivisions.

The trade in goods account. This records imports and exports of physical goods (previously known as 'visibles'). Exports result in an inflow of money and are therefore a credit item. Imports result in an outflow of money and are therefore a debit item. The balance of these is called the *balance on trade in goods* or *balance of visible trade* or *merchan-* *dise balance*. A *surplus* is when exports exceed imports. A *deficit* is when imports exceed exports.

The trade in services account. This records imports and exports of services (such as transport, tourism and insurance). Thus the purchase of a foreign holiday would be a debit since it represents an outflow of money, whereas the purchase by an overseas resident of a UK insurance policy would be a credit to the UK services account. The balance of these is called the *services balance*.

The balance of both the goods and services accounts together is known as the *balance on trade in goods and services* or simply the *balance of trade*.

Definitions

Current account of the balance of payments The record of a country's imports and exports of goods and services, plus incomes and transfers of money to and from abroad.

Balance on trade in goods or **balance of visible trade** or **merchandise balance** Exports of goods minus imports of goods.

Services balance Exports of services minus imports of services.

Balance of trade in goods and services or **balance of trade** Exports of goods and services minus imports of goods and services.

Figure 27.1 Current account balance in selected industrial countries

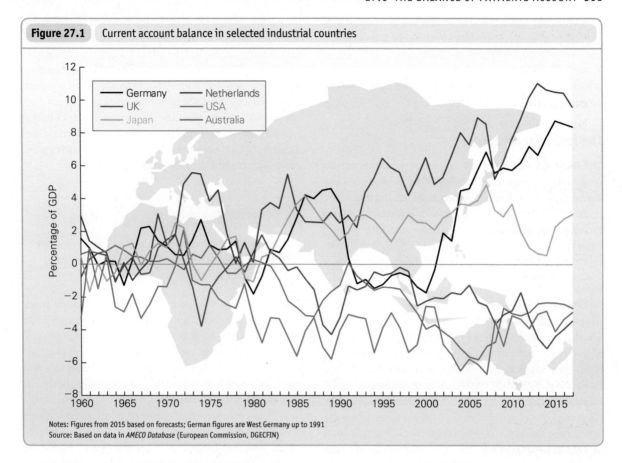

Notes: Figures from 2015 based on forecasts; German figures are West Germany up to 1991
Source: Based on data in *AMECO Database* (European Commission, DGECFIN)

The balance of trade directly affects the level of aggregate demand. To see this we return to the circular flow of income model introduced in Section 26.6. A balance of trade deficit, which as Table 27.1 shows has been the norm in the UK for some time, represents a net leakage from the circular flow. This is because imports (a withdrawal) are greater than exports (an injection). Their effect is to reduce aggregate demand. Conversely, a balance of trade surplus is a net injection for an economy. Trade surpluses act to increase aggregate demand.

In equilibrium, injections must equal withdrawals. Thus a net withdrawal on the balance of trade must be offset by a net injection elsewhere: either investment exceeding saving and/or government expenditure exceeding tax revenue. This is why we often see countries with trade deficits also running government budget deficits. The USA and the UK are two notable examples of countries with 'twin deficits'.

Income flows. These consist of wages, interest and profits flowing into and out of the country. For example, dividends earned by a foreign resident from shares in a UK company would be an outflow of money (a debit item).

Current transfers of money. These include government contributions to and receipts from the EU and international organisations, and international transfers of money by private individuals and firms. Transfers out of the country are debits. Transfers into the country (e.g. money sent from Greece to a Greek student studying in the UK) would be a credit item.

The *current account balance* is the overall balance of all the above four subdivisions. A *current account surplus* is where credits exceed debits. A *current account deficit* is where debits exceed credits.

Figure 27.1 shows the current account balance expressed as a percentage of GDP for a sample of countries. Since 1984, the UK has consistently experienced a current account deficit.

The capital account

The *capital account* relates to the acquisition and disposal of non-financial assets. This comprises two elements.

First, *capital transfers* are the flows of funds, into the country (credits) and out of the country (debits), associated with the transfer of ownership of fixed assets (e.g. land). These transfers include money that migrants bring into the country and official debt forgiveness by governments.

Definitions

Balance of payments on current account The balance on trade in goods and services plus net incomes and current transfers.

Capital account of the balance of payments The record of transfers of capital to and from abroad.

Second, the *acquisition or disposal of non-produced, non-financial assets* covers intangibles such as the sales and purchases of patents, copyrights and trademarks.

As Table 27.1 shows, the balance on the capital account is small in comparison to that on the current and financial accounts.

The financial account[1]

The **financial account** of the balance of payments records cross-border changes in the holding of shares, property, bank deposits and loans, government securities, etc. In other words, unlike the current account which is concerned with money incomes, the financial account is concerned with the purchase and sale of assets. Case Study J.7 in MyEconLab considers some of the statistics behind the UK's financial account.

Direct investment. This involves a significant and lasting interest in a business in another country. If a foreign company invests money from abroad in one of its branches or associated companies in the UK, this represents an inflow of money when the investment is made and is thus a credit item. (Any subsequent profit from this investment that flows abroad will be recorded as an investment income outflow on the current account.) Investment abroad by UK companies represents an outflow of money when the investment is made. It is thus a debit item. Note that what we are talking about here is the acquisition or sale of assets: e.g. a factory or farm, or the takeover of a whole firm, not the imports or exports of equipment.

Portfolio investment. This relates to transactions in debt and equity securities (shares) which do not result in the investor having any significant influence on the operations of a particular business. If a UK resident buys shares in an overseas company, this is an outflow of funds and is hence a debit item.

Other investment and financial flows. While direct and portfolio investments are concerned primarily with long-term investment, these consist primarily of various types of short-term monetary flows between the UK and the rest of the world. Deposits by overseas residents in banks in the UK and loans to the UK from abroad are credit items, since they represent an inflow of money. Deposits by UK residents in overseas banks and loans by UK banks to overseas residents are debit items. They represent an outflow of money.

Short-term monetary flows are common between international financial centres to take advantage of differences in countries' interest rates and changes in exchange rates.

In the financial account, credits and debits are recorded *net*. For example, UK investment abroad consists of the net

acquisition of assets abroad (i.e. the purchase less the sale of assets abroad). Similarly, foreign investment in the UK consists of the purchase less the sale of UK assets by foreign residents. By recording financial account items net, the flows seem misleadingly modest. For example, if UK residents deposited an extra £100 billion in banks abroad but drew out £99 billion, this would be recorded as a mere £1 billion net outflow on the other investment and financial flows account. In fact, *total* financial account flows vastly exceed current plus capital account flows.

> ### Pause for thought
>
> *Where would interest payments on short-term foreign deposits in UK banks be entered on the balance of payments account?*

Flows to and from the reserves. The UK, like all other countries, holds reserves of gold and foreign currencies. From time to time the Bank of England (acting as the government's agent) will sell some of these reserves to purchase sterling on the foreign exchange market. It does this normally as a means of supporting the rate of exchange (as we shall see below). Drawing on reserves represents a *credit* item in the balance of payments accounts: money drawn from the reserves represents an *inflow* to the balance of payments (albeit an outflow from the reserves account). The reserves can thus be used to support a deficit elsewhere in the balance of payments.

Conversely, if there is a surplus elsewhere in the balance of payments, the Bank of England can use it to build up the reserves. Building up the reserves counts as a debit item in the balance of payments, since it represents an outflow from it (to the reserves).

When all the components of the balance of payments account are taken together, the balance of payments should exactly balance: credits should equal debits. As we shall see below, if they were not equal, the rate of exchange would have to adjust until they were, or the government would have to intervene to make them equal.

When the statistics are compiled, however, a number of errors are likely to occur. As a result there will not be a balance. To 'correct' for this, a **net errors and omissions** *item*

> ### Definitions
>
> **Financial account of the balance of payments** The record of the flows of money into and out of the country for the purpose of investment or as deposits in banks and other financial institutions.
>
> **Net errors and omissions** A statistical adjustment to ensure that the two sides of the balance of payments account balance. It is necessary because of errors in compiling the statistics.

---

[1] Prior to October 1998, this account was called the 'capital account'. The account that is *now* called the capital account used to be included in the transfers section of the current account. This potentially confusing change of names was adopted in order to bring the UK accounts in line with the system used by the International Monetary Fund (IMF), the EU and most individual countries.

Figure 27.2 UK balance of payments as a percentage of GDP

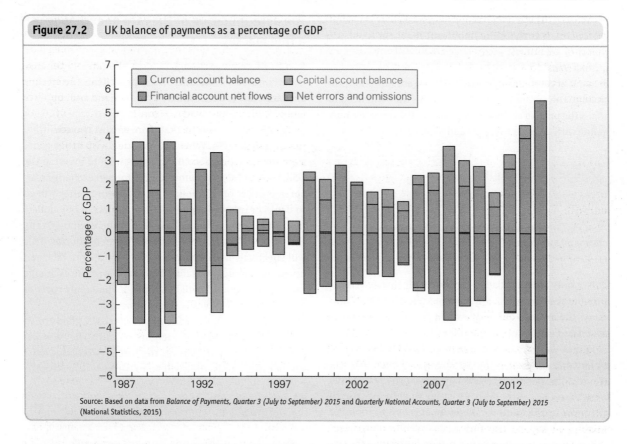

Source: Based on data from *Balance of Payments, Quarter 3 (July to September) 2015* and *Quarterly National Accounts, Quarter 3 (July to September) 2015* (National Statistics, 2015)

is included in the accounts. This ensures that there will be an exact balance. The main reason for the errors is that the statistics are obtained from a number of sources, and there are often delays before items are recorded and sometimes omissions too.

Figure 27.2 graphically summarises the main accounts of the UK's balance of payments: current, capital and financial accounts. It presents each as a percentage of national income (see also right-hand column of Table 27.1). In conjunction with the net errors and omissions item, which averages close to zero over the long run, we can see how the accounts combine to give a zero overall balance. For much of the period since the late 1980s, current account deficits

have been offset by surpluses on the financial account. The persistence of the UK's current account deficit is discussed further in Case Study J.6 in MyEconLab.

> ### Pause for thought
>
> *With reference to Table 27.1 and Figure 27.2, compare the 2014 balance of payments figures (as percentages of GDP) with the averages for the period from 1987. In what senses were the 2014 figures more or less favourable than the averages since 1987?*

27.2 THE EXCHANGE RATE

An exchange rate is the rate at which one currency trades for another on the foreign exchange market.

If you want to go abroad, you will need to exchange your pounds into euros, dollars, Swiss francs or whatever. To do this you may go to a bank. The bank will quote you that day's exchange rates: for example, €1.35 to the pound, or $1.50 to the pound. It is similar for firms. If an importer wants to buy, say, some machinery from Japan, it will require yen to pay the Japanese supplier. It will thus ask the foreign exchange section of a bank to quote it a rate of exchange of the pound into yen. Similarly, if you want to buy some foreign stocks and shares, or if companies based

in the UK want to invest abroad, sterling will have to be exchanged into the appropriate foreign currency.

Likewise, if Americans want to come on holiday to the UK or to buy UK assets, or American firms want to import UK goods or to invest in the UK, they will require sterling. They will be quoted an exchange rate for the pound in the USA: say, £1 = $1.50. This means that they will have to pay $1.50 to obtain £1 worth of UK goods or assets.

Exchange rates are quoted between each of the major currencies of the world. These exchange rates are constantly changing. Minute by minute, dealers in the foreign exchange dealing rooms of the banks are adjusting the rates of exchange. They charge commission when they exchange currencies. It is therefore important for them to ensure that they are not left with a large amount of any currency unsold. What they need to do is to balance the supply and demand of each currency: to balance the amount they purchase to the amount they sell. To do this they will need to adjust the price of each currency, namely the exchange rate, in line with changes in supply and demand.

Pause for thought

How did the pound 'fare' compared with the US dollar, Australian dollar and the yen in the period since 1980? What conclusions can be drawn about the relative movements of these three currencies?

Not only are there day-to-day fluctuations in exchange rates, but also there are long-term changes in them. Figure 27.3 shows the average quarterly exchange rates between the pound and various currencies since 1985.

One of the problems in assessing what is happening to a particular currency is that its rate of exchange may rise against some currencies (weak currencies) and fall against others (strong currencies). In order to gain an overall picture of its fluctuations, therefore, it is best to look at a weighted average exchange rate against all other currencies. This is known as the *exchange rate index* or the *effective exchange rate*. The weight given to each currency in the index depends on the proportion of trade done with that country. Figure 27.3 also shows the sterling exchange rate index based on January 2005 = 100.

The determination of the rate of exchange in a free market

In a free foreign exchange market, the rate of exchange is determined by demand and supply. Thus the sterling exchange rate is determined by the demand and supply of pounds. This is illustrated in Figure 27.4.

For simplicity, assume that there are just two countries: the UK and the USA. When UK importers wish to buy goods from the USA, or when UK residents wish to invest in the USA, they will *supply* pounds on the foreign exchange market in order to obtain dollars. In other words, they will go to banks or other foreign exchange dealers to buy dollars in exchange for pounds. The higher the exchange rate, the more dollars they will obtain for their pounds. This will effectively make American goods cheaper to buy, and investment more profitable. Thus the *higher* the exchange rate, the *more* pounds will be supplied. The supply curve of pounds therefore typically slopes upwards.

When US residents wish to purchase UK goods or to invest in the UK, they will require pounds. They *demand* pounds by selling dollars on the foreign exchange market. In other words, they will go to banks or other foreign

Definition

Exchange rate index or **effective exchange rate**
A weighted average exchange rate expressed as an index, where the value of the index is 100 in a given base year. The weights of the different currencies in the index add up to 1.

Figure 27.3 Sterling exchange rates against selected currencies

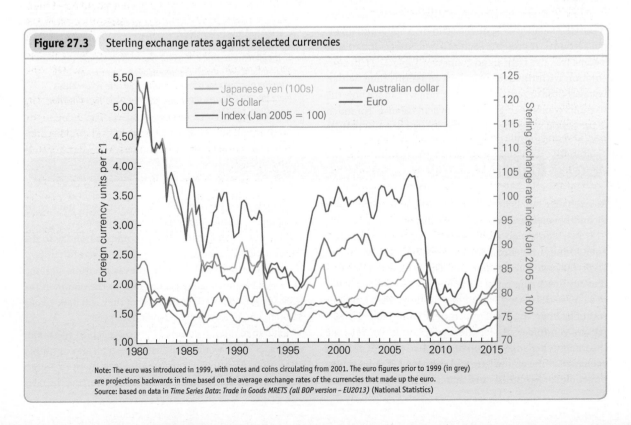

Note: The euro was introduced in 1999, with notes and coins circulating from 2001. The euro figures prior to 1999 (in grey) are projections backwards in time based on the average exchange rates of the currencies that made up the euro.
Source: based on data in *Time Series Data: Trade in Goods MRETS (all BOP version – EU2013)* (National Statistics)

Figure 27.4 Determination of the rate of exchange

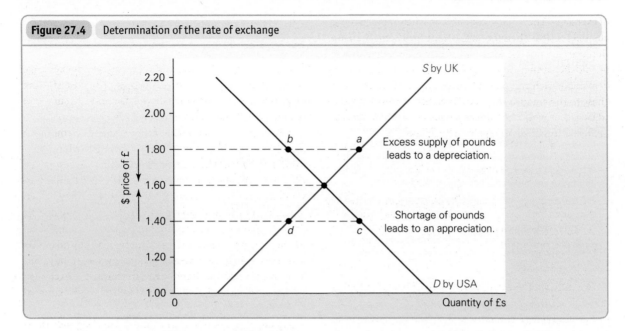

exchange dealers to buy pounds in exchange for dollars. The lower the dollar price of the pound (the exchange rate), the cheaper it will be for them to obtain UK goods and assets, and hence the more pounds they are likely to demand. The demand curve for pounds, therefore, typically slopes downwards.

The equilibrium exchange rate will be where the demand for pounds equals the supply. In Figure 27.4 this will be at an exchange rate of £1 = $1.60. But what is the mechanism that equates demand and supply?

If the current exchange rate were above the equilibrium, the supply of pounds being offered to the banks would exceed the demand. For example, in Figure 27.4 if the exchange rate were $1.80, there would be an excess supply of pounds of $a - b$. Banks would not have enough dollars to exchange for all these pounds. But the banks make money by *exchanging* currency, not by holding on to it. They would thus lower the exchange rate in order to encourage a greater demand for pounds and reduce the excessive supply. They would continue lowering the rate until demand equalled supply.

Similarly, if the rate were below the equilibrium, say at $1.40, there would be a shortage of pounds of $c - d$. The banks would find themselves with too few pounds to meet all the demand. At the same time, they would have an excess supply of dollars. The banks would thus raise the exchange rate until demand equalled supply.

In practice, the process of reaching equilibrium is extremely rapid. The foreign exchange dealers in the banks are continually adjusting the rate as new customers make new demands for currencies. What is more, each bank has to watch closely what the others are doing. They are constantly in competition with each other and thus have to keep their rates in line. The dealers receive minute-by-minute updates on their computer screens of the rates being offered round the world.

Shifts in the currency demand and supply curves

Any shift in the demand or supply curves will cause the exchange rate to change. This is illustrated in Figure 27.5, which this time shows the euro/sterling exchange rate. If the demand and supply curves shift from D_1 and S_1 to D_2 and S_2 respectively, the exchange rate will fall from €1.40 to €1.30. A fall in the exchange rate is called a ***depreciation***. A rise in the exchange rate is called an ***appreciation***.

But why should the demand and supply curves shift? The following are the major possible causes of a depreciation:

■ *A fall in domestic interest rates*. UK rates would now be less competitive for savers and other depositors. More UK residents would be likely to deposit their money abroad (the supply of sterling would rise), and fewer people abroad would deposit their money in the UK (the demand for sterling would fall).

■ *Higher inflation in the domestic economy than abroad*. UK exports will become less competitive. The demand for sterling will fall. At the same time, imports will become relatively cheaper for UK consumers. The supply of sterling will rise.

■ *A rise in domestic incomes relative to incomes abroad*. If UK incomes rise, the demand for imports, and hence the supply of sterling, will rise. If incomes in other countries fall, the demand for UK exports, and hence the demand for sterling will fall.

Definitions

Depreciation A fall in the free-market exchange rate of the domestic currency with foreign currencies.

Appreciation A rise in the free-market exchange rate of the domestic currency with foreign currencies.

BOX 27.1 NOMINAL AND REAL EXCHANGE RATES

Searching for a real advantage

We have seen on several occasions just how important the distinction between nominal and real is. But, what does this distinction mean when applied to exchange rates? A *nominal* bilateral exchange rate is simply the rate at which one currency exchanges for another. All exchange rates that you see quoted in the newspapers, on television or the Internet, or at travel agents, banks or airports, are nominal rates. Up to this point we have solely considered nominal rates.

The *real* exchange rate is the exchange rate index adjusted for changes in the prices of exports (measured in the domestic currency) and imports (measured in foreign currencies): in other words, adjusted for the **terms of trade**, where the terms of trade are defined as the price index of exports divided by the weighted price index of imports (P_X/P_M), expressed as a percentage. Thus if a country has a higher rate of inflation for its exports than the weighted average inflation of the imports it buys from other countries, its terms of trade will improve and its real exchange rate index (RERI) will rise relative to its nominal exchange rate index (NERI).

The **real exchange rate index** can thus be defined as:

$$RERI = NERI \times P_X/P_M$$

Thus if (a) a country's inflation is 5 per cent higher than the trade-weighted average of its trading partners (P_X/P_M rises by 5 per cent per year) and (b) its nominal exchange rate depreciates by 5 per cent per year (NERI falls by 5 per cent per year), its real exchange rate index will stay the same.

Take another example: if a country's export prices rise faster than the foreign currency prices of its imports (P_X/P_M rises),

its real exchange rate will appreciate relative to its nominal exchange rate.

The real exchange rate thus gives us a better idea of the *quantity* of imports a country can obtain from selling a given quantity of exports. If the real exchange rate rises, the country can get more imports for a given volume of exports.

The chart shows the nominal and real exchange rate indices of sterling. As you can see, the real exchange rate has tended to rise over time relative to the nominal exchange rate. This is because the UK has typically had a higher rate of inflation than the weighted average of its trading partners.

The real exchange rate also gives a better idea than the nominal exchange rate of how competitive a country is. The lower the real exchange rate, the more competitive will the country's exports be. From the chart we can see that the UK became less competitive between 1996 and 2001, and remained at similarly uncompetitive levels until 2008, thanks not only to a rise in the nominal exchange rate index, but also to higher inflation than its trading partners. However, as the financial crisis of the late 2000s unfolded, sterling depreciated sharply. Between July 2007 and October 2009 the nominal and real exchange rate indices fell by 26 per cent and 23 per cent respectively.

 If differences in inflation rates were to be reflected in longer-term changes in real exchange rates what pattern should we observe in real exchange rates? Is this supported by the data in the chart?

Definitions

Terms of trade The price index of exports divided by the price index of imports and then expressed as a percentage. This means that the terms of trade will be 100 in the base year.

Real exchange rate index (RERI) The nominal exchange rate index (NERI) adjusted for changes in the relative prices of exports and imports: $RERI = NERI \times P_X/P_M$

Sterling nominal and real exchange rate indices (Jan 1970 = 100)

Note: Exchange rate indices are BIS narrow indices comprising 27 countries, re-based by the authors, Jan 1970 = 100

Source: Based on data from *Bank for International Settlements*

Figure 27.5 Floating exchange rates: movement to a new equilibrium

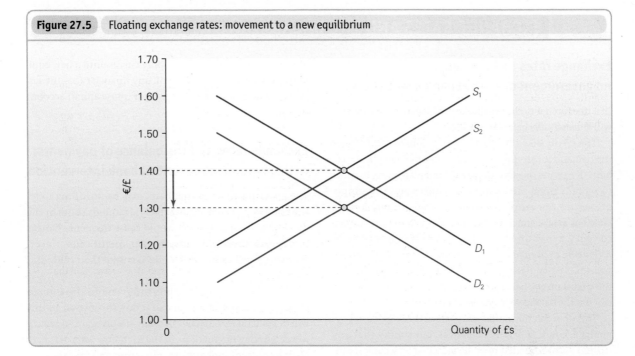

- *Relative investment prospects improving abroad*. If investment prospects become brighter abroad than in the UK, perhaps because of better incentives abroad, or because of worries about an impending recession in the UK, again the demand for sterling will fall and the supply of sterling will rise.

- *Speculation that the exchange rate will fall*. If businesses involved in importing and exporting, and also banks and other foreign exchange dealers, think that the exchange rate is about to fall, they will sell

pounds now before the rate does fall. The supply of sterling will thus rise.

Pause for thought

Go through each of the above reasons for shifts in the demand for and supply of sterling and consider what would cause an appreciation of the pound.

BOX 27.2 DEALING IN FOREIGN EXCHANGE

A daily juggling act

Imagine that a large car importer in the UK wants to import 5000 cars from Japan costing ¥15 billion. What does it do?

It will probably contact a number of banks' foreign exchange dealing rooms in London and ask them for exchange rate quotes. It thus puts all the banks in competition with each other. Each bank will want to get the business and thereby obtain the commission on the deal. To do this it must offer a higher rate than the other banks, since the higher the ¥/£ exchange rate, the more yen the firm will get for its money. (For an importer a rate of, say, ¥180 to £1 is better than a rate of, say, ¥150.)

Now it is highly unlikely that any of the banks will have a spare ¥15 billion. But a bank cannot say to the importer: 'Sorry, you will have to wait before we can agree to sell them to you.' Instead the bank will offer a deal and then, if the firm agrees, the bank will have to set about obtaining the ¥15 billion. To do this it must offer Japanese who are *supplying* yen to obtain pounds at a sufficiently *low* ¥/£ exchange rate.

(The lower the ¥/£ exchange rate, the fewer yen the Japanese will have to pay to obtain pounds.)

The banks' dealers thus find themselves in the delicate position of wanting to offer a *high* enough exchange rate to the car importer in order to gain its business, but a *low* enough exchange rate in order to obtain the required amount of yen. The dealers are thus constantly having to adjust the rates of exchange in order to balance the demand and supply of each currency.

In general, the more of any foreign currency that dealers are asked to supply (by being offered sterling), the lower will be the exchange rate they will offer. In other words, a higher supply of sterling pushes down the foreign currency price of sterling.

 Assume that an American firm wants to import Scotch whisky from the UK. Describe how foreign exchange dealers will respond.

27.3 EXCHANGE RATES AND THE BALANCE OF PAYMENTS

Exchange rates and the balance of payments: no government or central bank intervention

In a free foreign exchange market, the balance of payments will *automatically* balance. But why?

The credit side of the balance of payments constitutes the demand for sterling. For example, when people abroad buy UK exports or assets they will demand sterling in order to pay for them. The debit side constitutes the supply of sterling. For example, when UK residents buy foreign goods or assets, the importers of them will require foreign currency to pay for them. They will thus supply pounds. A *floating exchange rate* will ensure that the demand for pounds is equal to the supply. It will thus also ensure that the credits on the balance of payments are equal to the debits: that the balance of payments balances.

This does not mean that each part of the balance of payments account separately balances, but simply that any current account deficit must be matched by a capital plus financial account surplus and vice versa.

For example, suppose initially that each part of the balance of payments did separately balance. Then let us assume that interest rates rise. This will encourage larger short-term financial inflows as people abroad are attracted to deposit money in the UK: the demand for sterling would shift to the right (e.g. from D_2 to D_1 in Figure 27.5). It will also cause smaller short-term financial outflows as UK residents keep more of their money in the country: the supply of sterling shifts to the left (e.g. from S_2 to S_1 in Figure 27.5). The financial account will go into surplus. The exchange rate will appreciate.

As the exchange rate rises, this will cause imports to be cheaper and exports to be more expensive. The current account will move into deficit. There is a movement up

along the new demand and supply curves until a new equilibrium is reached. At this point, any financial account surplus is matched by an equal current (plus capital) account deficit.

Exchange rates and the balance of payments: with government or central bank intervention

The government or central bank may be unwilling to let the country's currency float freely. Frequent shifts in the demand and supply curves would cause frequent changes in the exchange rate. This, in turn, might cause uncertainty for businesses, which might curtail their trade and investment.

The central bank may thus intervene in the foreign exchange market. But what can it do? The answer to this will depend on its objectives. It may simply want to reduce the day-to-day fluctuations in the exchange rate, or it may want to prevent longer-term, more fundamental shifts in the rate.

Reducing short-term fluctuations

Assume that the UK government believes that an exchange rate of €1.40 to the pound is approximately the long-term equilibrium rate. Short-term leftward shifts in the demand

> **Definition**
>
> **Floating exchange rate** When the government does not intervene in the foreign exchange markets, but simply allows the exchange rate to be freely determined by demand and supply.

BOX 27.3 THE IMPORTANCE OF INTERNATIONAL FINANCIAL MOVEMENTS

How a current account deficit can coincide with an appreciating exchange rate

Since the early 1970s, most of the major economies of the world have operated with floating exchange rates. The opportunities that this gives for speculative gain have led to a huge increase in short-term international financial movements. Vast amounts of money transfer from country to country in search of higher interest rates or a currency that is likely to appreciate. This can have a bizarre effect on exchange rates.

If a country pursues an expansionary fiscal policy (i.e. cutting taxes and/or raising government expenditure), the current account will tend to go into deficit as extra imports are 'sucked in'. What effect will this have on exchange rates? You might think that the answer is obvious: the higher demand for imports will create an extra supply of domestic currency on the foreign exchange market and hence drive down the exchange rate.

In fact the opposite is likely. The higher interest rates resulting from the higher domestic demand can lead to a massive inflow of short-term finance. The financial account can thus move sharply into surplus. This is likely to outweigh the current account deficit and cause an *appreciation* of the exchange rate.

Exchange rate movements, especially in the short term, are largely brought about by changes on the financial rather than the current account.

 Why do high international financial mobility and an absence of exchange controls severely limit a country's ability to choose its interest rate?

for sterling and rightward shifts in the supply, however, are causing the exchange rate to fall below this level (see Figure 27.5). What can the government do to keep the rate at €1.40?

Using reserves. The Bank of England can sell gold and foreign currencies from the reserves to buy pounds. This will shift the demand for sterling back to the right.

Borrowing from abroad. The government can negotiate a foreign currency loan from other countries or from an international agency such as the International Monetary Fund. It can then use these moneys to buy pounds on the foreign exchange market, thus again shifting the demand for sterling back to the right.

Raising interest rates. If the Bank of England raises interest rates, it will encourage people to deposit money in the UK and encourage UK residents to keep their money in the country. The demand for sterling will increase and the supply of sterling will decrease. However, the changes in interest rates necessary to manage the exchange rate may come into conflict with other economic objectives, such as keeping the rate of inflation on target.

Maintaining a fixed rate of exchange over the longer term

Governments may choose to maintain a fixed rate over a number of months or even years. The following are possible methods it can use to achieve this (we are assuming that there are downward pressures on the exchange rate: e.g. as a result of higher aggregate demand and higher inflation).

Contractionary policies. This is where the government deliberately curtails aggregate demand by either *fiscal policy* or *monetary policy* or both.

Contractionary fiscal policy will involve raising taxes and/or reducing government expenditure. Contractionary monetary policy involves raising interest rates. Note that in this case we are not just talking about the tempo-

rary raising of interest rates to prevent a short-term outflow of money from the country, but the use of higher interest rates to reduce borrowing and hence dampen aggregate demand.

A reduction in aggregate demand will work in two ways:

- It reduces the level of consumer spending. This will directly cut imports since there will be reduced spending on Japanese electronics, German cars, Spanish holidays and so on. The supply of sterling coming on to the foreign exchange market thus decreases.
- It reduces the rate of inflation. If inflation falls below that of other countries, this will make UK goods more competitive abroad, thus increasing the demand for sterling. It will also cut back on imports as UK consumers switch to the now more competitive home-produced goods. The supply of sterling falls.

Supply-side policies. This is where the government attempts to increase the long-term competitiveness of UK goods by encouraging reductions in the costs of production and/ or improvements in the quality of UK goods. For example, the government may attempt to improve the quantity and quality of training and research and development.

Controls on imports and or foreign exchange dealing. This is where the government restricts the outflow of money, either by restricting people's access to foreign exchange, or by the use of tariffs (customs duties) and quotas. For instance, the Icelandic government put in place controls on foreign currency exchanges in the aftermath of the collapse of its largest banks in 2008 in order to bolster the krona and to build up foreign reserves.

> ### Pause for thought
>
> *What problems might arise if the government were to adopt this third method of maintaining a fixed exchange rate?*

27.4 FIXED VERSUS FLOATING EXCHANGE RATES

Are exchange rates best left free to fluctuate and be determined purely by market forces, or should the government or central bank intervene to fix exchange rates, either rigidly or within bands?

Advantages of fixed exchange rates

Surveys reveal that most businesspeople prefer relatively rigid exchange rates: if not totally fixed, then pegged for periods of time, or at least where fluctuations are kept to a minimum. The following arguments are used to justify this preference.

Certainty. With fixed exchange rates, international trade and investment become much less risky, since profits are not affected by movements in the exchange rate.

Assume a firm correctly forecasts that its product will sell in the USA for $1.50. It costs 80p to produce. If the rate of exchange is fixed at £1 = $1.50, each unit will earn £1 and hence make a 20p profit. If, however, the rate of exchange were not fixed, exchange rate fluctuations could wipe out this profit. If, say, the rate appreciated to £1 = $2, and if units continued to sell for $1.50, they would now earn only 75p each, and hence make a 5p loss.

Little or no speculation. Provided the rate is *absolutely* fixed – and people believe that it will remain so – there is no point in speculating. For example, between 1999 and 2001, when the old currencies of the eurozone countries were still used, but were totally fixed to the euro, there was no speculation that the German mark, say, would change in value against the French franc or the Dutch guilder.

Prevents governments pursuing 'irresponsible' macroeconomic policies. If a government deliberately and excessively expands aggregate demand – perhaps in an attempt to gain short-term popularity with the electorate – the resulting balance of payments deficit will force it to constrain demand again (unless it resorts to import controls).

Governments cannot allow their economies to have a persistently higher inflation rate than competitor countries without running into balance of payments crises, and hence a depletion of reserves. Fixed rates thus force governments (in the absence of trade restrictions) to keep the rate of inflation roughly to world levels.

Disadvantages of fixed exchange rates

Exchange rate policy may conflict with the interests of domestic business and the economy as a whole. A balance of payments deficit can occur even if there is no excess demand. For example, there can be a fall in the demand for the country's exports as a result of an external shock or because of increased foreign competition. If protectionism is to be avoided, and if supply-side policies work only over the long run, the government (or central bank) will be forced to raise interest rates. This is likely to have two adverse effects on the domestic economy:

- Higher interest rates may discourage business investment. This in turn will lower firms' profits in the long term and reduce the country's long-term rate of economic growth. The country's capacity to produce will be restricted and businesses are likely to fall behind in the competitive race with their international rivals to develop new products and improve existing ones.
- Higher interest rates will have a dampening effect on the economy by making borrowing more expensive and thereby cutting back on both consumer demand and investment. This can result in a recession with rising unemployment.

The problem is that, with fixed exchange rates, domestic policy is entirely constrained by the balance of payments. Any attempt to cure unemployment by cutting interest rates will simply lead to a balance of payments deficit and thus force governments to raise interest rates again.

Competitive contractionary policies leading to world depression. If deficit countries pursued contractionary policies, but surplus countries pursued expansionary policies, there would be no overall world contraction or expansion. Countries may be quite happy, however, to run a balance of payments

surplus and build up reserves. Countries may thus competitively deflate – all trying to achieve a balance of payments surplus. But this is beggar-my-neighbour policy. Not all countries can have a surplus. Overall the world must be in balance. The result of these policies is to lead to general world recession and a restriction in growth.

Problems of international liquidity. If trade is to expand, there must be an expansion in the supply of currencies acceptable for world trade (dollars, euros, pounds, gold, etc.): there must be adequate **international liquidity**. Countries' reserves of these currencies must grow if they are to be sufficient to maintain a fixed rate at times of balance of payments disequilibrium. Conversely, there must not be excessive international liquidity. Otherwise the extra demand that would result would lead to world inflation. It is important under fixed exchange rates, therefore, to avoid too much or too little international liquidity.

The problem is how to maintain adequate control of international liquidity. The supply of dollars, for example, depends largely on US policy, which may be dominated by its internal economic situation rather than by a concern for the well-being of the international community. Similarly, the supply of euros depends on the policy of the European Central Bank, which is governed by the internal situation in the eurozone countries.

Inability to adjust to shocks. With sticky prices and wage rates, there is no swift mechanism for dealing with sudden balance of payments crises – like that caused by a sudden increase in oil prices. In the short run, countries will need huge reserves or loan facilities to support their currencies. There may be insufficient international liquidity to permit this. In the longer run, countries may be forced into a depression, by having to deflate. The alternative may be to resort to protectionism, or to abandon the fixed rate and **devalue.**

Speculation. If speculators believe that a fixed rate simply cannot be maintained, speculation is likely to be massive. If, for example, there is a large balance of payments deficit, speculative selling will worsen the deficit, and may itself force a devaluation. For example, speculation of this sort had disastrous effects on the Argentinean peso in 2002 (see Case Study J.11) and on the Mexican peso in 1995 and the Thai baht in 1997 (see Case Study J.12).

Definitions

International liquidity The supply of currencies in the world acceptable for financing international trade and investment.

Devaluation Where the government refixes the exchange rate at a lower level.

Advantages of a free-floating exchange rate

The advantages and disadvantages of free-floating rates are to a large extent the opposite of fixed rates.

 Automatic correction. The government simply lets the exchange rate move freely to the equilibrium. In this way, balance of payments disequilibria are automatically and instantaneously corrected without the need for specific government policies.

No problem of international liquidity and reserves. Since there is no central bank intervention in the foreign exchange market, there is no need to hold reserves. A currency is automatically convertible at the current market exchange rate.

Insulation from external economic events. A country is not tied to a possibly unacceptably high world inflation rate, as it could be under a fixed exchange rate. It is also to some extent protected against world economic fluctuations and shocks.

Governments are free to choose their domestic policy. Under a floating rate the government can choose whatever level of domestic demand it considers appropriate, and simply leave exchange rate movements to take care of any balance of payments effect. Similarly, the central bank can choose whatever rate of interest is necessary to meet domestic objectives, such as achieving a target rate of inflation. The exchange rate will simply adjust to the new rate of interest – a rise in interest rates causing an appreciation, a fall causing a depreciation. This freedom for the government and central bank is a major advantage, especially when the effectiveness of contractionary policies under fixed exchange rates is reduced by downward wage and price rigidity, and when competitive contractionary policies between countries may end up causing a world recession.

Disadvantages of a free-floating exchange rate

Despite these advantages there are still some potentially serious problems with free-floating exchange rates.

 Unstable exchange rates. The less elastic are the demand and supply curves for the currency in Figure 27.4, the greater the change in exchange rate that will be necessary to restore equilibrium following a shift in either demand or supply. In the long run, in a competitive world with domestic substitutes for imports and foreign substitutes for exports, demand and supply curves are relatively elastic. Nevertheless, in the short run, given that many firms have contracts with specific overseas suppliers or distributors, the demands for imports and exports are less elastic.

 Speculation. In an uncertain world, where there are few restrictions on currency speculation, where the fortunes and policies of governments can change rapidly, and where large amounts of short-term deposits are internationally 'foot-loose', speculation can be highly destabilising in the short run. At times of international currency turmoil such speculation can be enormous. In 2014 over $5.3 trillion dollars on average passed daily across the foreign exchanges: greatly in excess of countries' foreign exchange reserves! If people think that the exchange rate will fall, then they will sell the currency, and this will cause the exchange rate to fall even further, perhaps overshooting the eventual equilibrium.

An example of such overshooting occurred between July 2008 and March 2009 when the pound depreciated 14 per cent against the euro, 29 per cent against the US dollar, 35 per cent against the yen and the exchange rate index fell 17 per cent (see Figure 27.6). Speculators were predicting that interest rates in the UK would fall further than in other countries and stay lower for longer. This was because recession was likely to be deeper in the UK, with inflation undershooting the Bank of England's 2 per cent target and perhaps even becoming negative. But the fall in the exchange rate represented considerable overshooting and the exchange rate index rose 9 per cent between March and June 2009.

This is just one example of the violent swings in exchange rates that have occurred in recent years.

> ### Pause for thought
>
> *If speculators on average gain from their speculation, who loses?*

Uncertainty for traders and investors. The uncertainty caused by currency fluctuations can discourage international trade and investment. To some extent this problem can be overcome by using the **forward exchange market**. Here traders agree with a bank *today* the rate of exchange for some point in the future (say, six months' time). This allows traders to plan future purchases of imports or sales of exports at a known rate of exchange. Of course, banks charge for this service, since they are taking on the risks themselves of adverse exchange rate fluctuations.

But dealing in the futures market only takes care of short-run uncertainty. Banks will not be prepared to take on the risks of offering forward contracts for several years hence. Thus firms simply have to live with the uncertainty over exchange rates in future years. This may discourage long-term investment. For example, the possibility of exchange rate appreciation may well discourage firms from investing abroad, since a higher exchange rate will mean that foreign exchange earnings will be worth less in the domestic currency.

> ### Definition
>
> **Forward exchange market** Where contracts are made today for the price at which a currency will be exchanged at some specified future date.

| **Figure 27.6** | Depreciating and then appreciating sterling from 2008 |

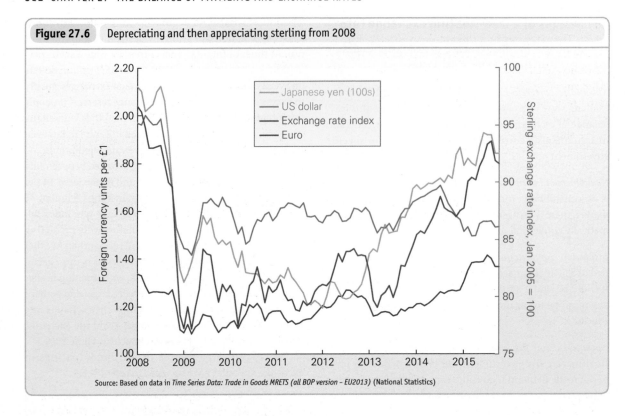

Source: Based on data in *Time Series Data: Trade in Goods MRETS (all BOP version – EU2013)* (National Statistics)

As Figure 27.3 showed (see page 504), there have been large changes in exchange rates. Such changes not only make it difficult for exporters. Importers too will be hesitant about making long-term deals. For example, a UK manufacturing firm signing a contract to buy US components in March 2008, when $2.00 worth of components could be purchased for £1, would find it a struggle to make a profit some four years later when less than $1.60 worth of US components could be purchased for £1!

Lack of discipline on the domestic economy. Governments may pursue irresponsibly inflationary policies (e.g. for short-term political gain). This will have adverse effects over the longer term as the government will at some point have to deflate the economy again, with a resulting fall in output and rise in unemployment.

Exchange rates in practice

Most countries today have a relatively free exchange rate. Nevertheless, the problems of instability that this can bring are well recognised, and thus many countries seek to regulate or manage their exchange rate.

There have been many attempts to regulate exchange rates since 1945. By far the most successful was the Bretton Woods system, which was adopted worldwide from the end of the Second World War until 1971. This was a form of *adjustable peg* exchange rate, where countries pegged (i.e. fixed) their exchange rate to the US dollar, but could

repeg it at a lower or higher level ('devalue' or 'revalue' their exchange rate) if there was a persistent and substantial balance of payments deficit or surplus.

With growing world inflation and instability from the mid-1960s, it became more and more difficult to maintain fixed exchange rates, and the growing likelihood of devaluations and revaluations fuelled speculation. The system was abandoned in the early 1970s. What followed was a period of exchange rate management known as *managed flexibility*. Under this system, exchange rates were not pegged but allowed to float. However, central banks intervened from time to time to prevent excessive exchange rate fluctuations. This system largely continues to this day.

However, on a regional basis, especially within Europe, there were attempts to create greater exchange rate stability. The European system, which began in 1979, involved establishing exchange rate bands: upper and lower limits within which exchange rates were allowed to fluctuate. The name

Definitions

Adjustable peg A system whereby exchange rates are fixed for a period of time, but may be devalued (or revalued) if a deficit (or surplus) becomes substantial.

Managed flexibility (dirty floating) A system of flexible exchange rates, but where the government intervenes to prevent excessive fluctuations or even to achieve an unofficial target exchange rate.

given to the EU system was the ***exchange rate mechanism (ERM)***. The hope was that this would eventually lead to a single European currency. With a single currency there can be no exchange rate fluctuations between the member states, any more than there can be fluctuations between the Californian and New York dollar, or between the English, Scottish and Welsh pound.

The single currency, the euro, finally came into being in January 1999 (although notes and coins were not introduced until January 2002). (We examine the euro and its

effects on the economies of the member states, and those outside too, in section 32.3.)

Definition

ERM (exchange rate mechanism) A semi-fixed system whereby participating EU countries allowed fluctuations against each other's currencies only within agreed bands. Collectively they floated freely against all other currencies.

BOX 27.4 | THE EURO/DOLLAR SEESAW

Ups and downs in the currency market

For periods of time, world currency markets can be quite peaceful, with only modest changes in exchange rates. But with the ability to move vast sums of money very rapidly from one part of the world to another and from one currency to another, speculators can suddenly turn this relatively peaceful world into one of extreme turmoil.

In this box we examine the huge swings of the euro against the dollar since the euro's launch in 1999. In Case Study J.12 in MyEconLab we examine other examples of currency turmoil.

First the down . . .

On 1 January 1999, the euro was launched and exchanged for $1.16. By October 2000 the euro had fallen to $0.85. What was the cause of this 27 per cent depreciation? The main cause was the growing fear that inflationary pressures were increasing in the USA and that, therefore, the Federal Reserve Bank would have to raise interest rates. At the same time, the

eurozone economy was growing only slowly and inflation was well below the 2 per cent ceiling set by the ECB. There was thus pressure on the ECB to cut interest rates.

The speculators were not wrong. As the diagram shows, US interest rates rose, and ECB interest rates initially fell, and when eventually they did rise (in October 1999), the gap between US and ECB interest rates soon widened again.

In addition to the differences in interest rates, a lack of confidence in the recovery of the eurozone economy and a continuing confidence in the US economy encouraged investment to flow to the USA. This inflow of finance (and lack of inflow to the eurozone) further pushed up the dollar relative to the euro.

The low value of the euro against the dollar meant a high value of the other currencies, including the pound, relative to the euro. This made it very difficult for companies outside the eurozone to export to eurozone countries and also for those

Fluctuations between the euro and the dollar

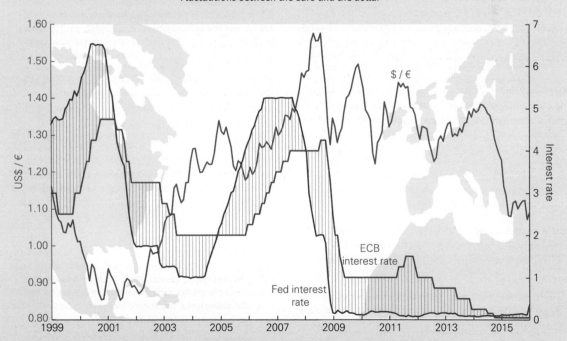

Notes: Federal reserve rate is the federal funds *effective* rate; ECB interest rate is the main refinancing operations rate
Source: *Federal Reserve Bank, European Central Bank, Bank of England;* Exchange rate based on data from *Statistical Interactive Database* (Bank of England)

competing with imports from the eurozone (which had been made cheaper by the fall in the euro).

In October 2000, with the euro trading at around 85¢, the ECB plus the US Federal Reserve Bank, the Bank of England and the Japanese central bank all intervened on the foreign exchange market to buy euros. This arrested the fall, and helped to restore confidence in the currency. People were more willing to hold euros, knowing that central banks would support it.

. . . then the up

The position changed completely in 2001. With the US economy slowing rapidly and fears of an impending recession, the Federal Reserve Bank reduced interest rates 11 times during the year: from 6.5 per cent at the beginning of the year to 1.75 per cent at the end (see the chart). Although the ECB also cut interest rates, the cuts were relatively modest: from 4.75 at the beginning of the year to 3.25 at the end. With eurozone interest rates now considerably above US rates, the euro began to rise.

In addition, a massive deficit on the US current account, and a budget deficit nearing 4 per cent of GDP, made foreign investors reluctant to invest in the US economy. In fact, investors were pulling out of the USA. One estimate suggests that European investors alone sold $70 billion of US assets during 2002. The result of all this was a massive depreciation of the dollar and appreciation of the euro, so that by December 2004 the euro had risen to $1.36: a 60 per cent appreciation since July 2001!

In 2004–5, the US economy began to experience strong economic growth once more (an annual average of 3.4 per cent) and consequently the Fed raised interest rates several times, from 1 per cent in early 2004 to 5.25 per cent by June 2006. With growth in the eurozone averaging just 1.8 per cent in 2004–5, the ECB kept interest rates constant at 2 per cent until early 2006. The result was that the euro depreciated against the dollar in 2005. But then the rise of the euro began again as the US growth slowed and eurozone growth rose and people anticipated a narrowing of the gap between US and eurozone interest rates.

In 2007 and 2008, worries about the credit crunch in the USA led the Fed to make substantial cuts in interest rates to stave off recession. In August 2007 the US federal funds rate was 5.25 per cent. It was then reduced on several occasions to stand at between 0 and 0.25 per cent per cent by December 2008. The ECB, in contrast, kept the eurozone rate constant at 4 per cent for the first part of this period and even raised it to 4.25 temporarily in the face of rapidly rising commodity prices (see Box 26.3). As a result, short-term finance flooded into the eurozone and the euro appreciated again, from $1.37 in mid-2007 to $1.58 in mid-2008.

Eventually, in September 2008, with the eurozone on the edge of recession and predictions that eurozone rates would drop, the euro at last began to fall. It continued to do so as the ECB cut rates. However, with monetary policy in the eurozone remaining tighter than in the USA, the euro began to rise again, only falling once more at the end of 2009 and into 2010 as US growth accelerated and speculators anticipated a tightening of US monetary policy.

. . . then seesawing on the back of economic and fiscal fragility

The first half of the 2010s was characterised by concerns over the weakness of the eurozone economy and the public

finances of several eurozone economies. Growth in the eurozone was often elusive, averaging just 0.8 per cent per year from 2010 to 2015. Meanwhile gross public-sector debt across the eurozone countries rose from 66 per cent in 2007 to 96 per cent of GDP by 2015. These concerns contributed to the volatility of the euro.

In particular, the euro would tend to weaken at times when there were growing fears of debt default as investors became increasingly reluctant to hold the currency. For instance, in early 2010 fear of a Greek default and growing worries about contagion to other highly indebted eurozone countries, such as Portugal, Ireland, Italy and Spain, led to speculation against the euro. In January 2010, the euro stood at $1.44; by early June, it had fallen to $1.19. This represented a 17 per cent depreciation. But by the end of October 2010 the euro was trading at $1.39 as efforts were made to strengthen the funding mechanisms for eurozone countries in financial distress.

In January 2015 on the back of continuing economic fragility, the ECB finally announced what many had being expected: full-scale quantitative easing (see Box 30.4). This marked a crucial stage in monetary easing within the eurozone. Monetary easing creates an increased money supply which, in turn, leads to an increased demand for foreign currencies and drives down the exchange rate. With the ECB reducing interest rates and people increasingly predicting QE, the euro depreciated during 2014. Between March and December 2014 the euro depreciated by 11 per cent against the dollar, while the euro exchange rate index depreciated by 4 per cent. With the announced programme of QE being somewhat larger than markets expected, in the week following the announcement the euro fell a further 2.3 per cent against the dollar, and the euro exchange rate index also fell by 2.3 per cent. The result was the euro was trading at its lowest level against the US dollar since April 2003.

From mid 2015, with the US economy recovering relatively strongly, and with relatively optimistic statements about future prospects for growth and employment from Janet Yellen, the Fed's chair, people began anticipating a rise in US interest rates. The dollar began appreciating again (the euro depreciating). Eventually, in December 2015, the Fed raised interest rates by 0.25 percentage points. Many exporters in the USA were worried that this would lead to a further appreciation and make their products less competitive.

The path of the euro shows that interest-rate volatility and the relative level of interest rates in the USA and the eurozone have been a major contributory factor to exchange-rate volatility between the euro and the dollar. However, more recently, concerns over the eurozone economy and the financial well-being of national eurozone governments have played a particularly important role in explaining fluctuations in the euro.

Find out what has happened to the euro/dollar exchange rate over the past 12 months. (You can find the data from the Bank of England's Statistical Interactive Database at www. bankofengland.co.uk/statistics/index.htm). Explain why the exchange rate has moved the way it has.

SUMMARY

1a The balance of payments account records all payments to and receipts from foreign countries. The current account records payments for imports and exports, plus incomes and transfers of money to and from abroad. The capital account records all transfers of capital to and from abroad. The financial account records inflows and outflows of money for investment and as deposits in banks and other financial institutions. It also includes dealings in the country's foreign exchange reserves.

1b The whole account must balance, but surpluses or deficits can be recorded on any specific part of the account. Thus the current account could be in deficit but it would have to be matched by an equal and opposite capital plus financial account surplus.

2a The rate of exchange is the rate at which one currency exchanges for another. Rates of exchange are determined by demand and supply in the foreign exchange market. Demand for the domestic currency consists of all the credit items in the balance of payments account. Supply consists of all the debit items.

2b The exchange rate will depreciate (fall) if the demand for the domestic currency falls or the supply increases. These shifts can be caused by a fall in domestic interest rates, higher inflation in the domestic economy than abroad, a rise in domestic incomes relative to incomes abroad, relative investment prospects improving abroad, or the belief among speculators that the exchange rate will fall. The opposite in each case would cause an appreciation (rise).

3a The government can attempt to prevent the rate of exchange from falling by central bank purchases of the domestic currency in the foreign exchange market, either by selling foreign currency reserves or by using foreign loans. Alternatively, the central bank can raise interest rates. The reverse actions can be taken if the government wants to prevent the rate from rising.

3b In the longer term it can prevent the rate from falling by pursuing contractionary policies, protectionist policies, or supply-side policies to increase the competitiveness of the country's exports.

4a Fixed exchange rates bring the advantage of certainty for the business community, which encourages trade and foreign investment. They also help to prevent governments from pursuing irresponsible macroeconomic policies.

4b Fixed exchange rates bring the disadvantages of conflicting policy goals, the tendency to lead to competitive contractionary policies, the problems of ensuring adequate international liquidity to enable intervention, and the restrictions that fixed rates place upon countries when attempting to respond to system shocks.

4c The advantages of free-floating exchange rates are that they automatically correct balance of payments disequilibria; they eliminate the need for reserves; and they give governments a greater independence to pursue their chosen domestic policy.

4d On the other hand, a completely free exchange rate can be highly unstable, especially when the elasticities of demand for imports and exports are low; also speculation may be destabilising. This may discourage firms from trading and investing abroad. What is more, a flexible exchange rate, by removing the balance of payments constraint on domestic policy, may encourage governments to pursue irresponsible domestic policies for short-term political gain.

4e There have been various attempts to manage exchange rates, without them being totally fixed. One example was the Bretton Woods system: a system of pegged exchange rates, but where devaluations or revaluations were allowed from time to time. Another was the ERM, which was the forerunner to the euro. Member countries' currencies were allowed to fluctuate against each other within a band.

MyEconLab

This book can be supported by MyEconLab, which contains a range of additional resources, including an online homework and tutorial system designed to test and build your understanding.

You need both an access card and a course ID to access MyEconLab:

1. Is your lecturer using MyEconLab? Ask your lecturer for your course ID.

2. Has an access card been included with the book at a reduced cost? Check the inside back cover of the book.

3. If you have a course ID but no access card, go to: http://www.myeconlab.com/ to buy access to this interactive study programme.

REVIEW QUESTIONS

1 The table below shows the items in the UK's 2007 balance of payments.

a) Fill in the missing totals for (i) the balance of trade, (ii) the current account balance, (iii) the portfolio investment balance; and (iv) for net errors and omissions.

b) UK's GDP in 2007 was estimated at £1 518 675 million. Calculate each item on the balance of payments as a percentage of GDP.

c) Compare the value of each item in £ millions and as percentages of GDP with those for 2014 in Table 27.1.

	£ millions
Current account:	
Balance on trade in goods	−93 926
Balance on trade in services	52 602
Balance of trade	
Income balance	14 065
Net current transfers	−13 996
Current account balance	
Capital account:	
Capital account balance	310
Financial account:	
Net direct investment	−8 722
Portfolio investment balance	
Other investment balance	−24 411
Balance of financial derivatives	−26 989
Reserve assets	−1 191
Financial account net flows	35 592
Net errors and omissions	

2 Assume that there is a free-floating exchange rate. Will the following cause the exchange rate to appreciate or depreciate? In each case you should consider whether there is a shift in the demand or supply curves of sterling (or both) and which way the curve(s) shift(s).

a) More Blu-ray players are imported from Japan.
  Demand curve *shifts left/shifts right/does not shift*
  Supply curve *shifts left/shifts right/does not shift*
  Exchange rate *appreciates/depreciates*

b) Non-UK residents increase their purchases of UK government securities.
  Demand curve *shifts left/shifts right/does not shift*
  Supply curve *shifts left/shifts right/does not shift*
  Exchange rate *appreciates/depreciates*

c) UK interest rates fall relative to those abroad.
  Demand curve *shifts left/shifts right/does not shift*
  Supply curve *shifts left/shifts right/does not shift*
  Exchange rate *appreciates/depreciates*

d) The UK experiences a higher rate of inflation than other countries.
  Demand curve *shifts left/shifts right/does not shift*
  Supply curve *shifts left/shifts right/does not shift*
  Exchange rate *appreciates/depreciates*

e) The result of a further enlargement of the EU is for investment in the UK by the rest of the EU to increase by a greater amount than UK investment in other EU countries.
  Demand curve *shifts left/shifts right/does not shift*
  Supply curve *shifts left/shifts right/does not shift*
  Exchange rate *appreciates/depreciates*

f) Speculators believe that the rate of exchange will fall.
  Demand curve *shifts left/shifts right/does not shift*
  Supply curve *shifts left/shifts right/does not shift*
  Exchange rate *appreciates/depreciates*

3 Explain how the current account of the balance of payments is likely to vary with the course of the business cycle.

4 Is it a 'bad thing' to have a deficit on the direct investment part of the financial account?

5 Why may credits on a country's short-term financial account create problems for its economy in the future?

6 What is the relationship between the balance of payments and the rate of exchange?

7 Consider the argument that in the modern world of large-scale short-term international financial movements, the ability of individual countries to affect their exchange rate is very limited.

8 To what extent can dealing in forward exchange markets remove the problems of a free-floating exchange rate?

9 What adverse effects on the domestic economy may follow from (a) a depreciation of the exchange rate and (b) an appreciation of the exchange rate?

10 What will be the effects on the domestic economy under free-floating exchange rates if there is a rapid expansion in world economic activity? What will determine the size of these effects?

Banking, money and interest rates

Business issues covered in this chapter

- What are the functions of money?
- Why do banks play such a crucial role in the functioning of economies?
- What determines the amount of money in the economy? What causes it to grow and what is the role of banks in this process?
- What is the relationship between money and interest rates?
- How will a change in the money supply and/or interest rates affect the level of business activity?

In this chapter we are going to look at the important role that the banking system plays in the economy. Changes in the behaviour of financial institutions and in the amount of money can have a powerful effect on all the major macroeconomic indicators, such as inflation, unemployment, economic growth, exchange rates, the balance of payments and the financial well-being of different sectors of the economy. Furthermore, the financial crisis of the late 2000s has helped to demonstrate the systemic importance of financial institutions to the economy.

The chapter begins by defining what is meant by money and examining its functions. Then we look at the operation of the financial sector and its role in determining the supply of money.

We then turn to look at the demand for money. Here we are not asking how much money people would like. What we are asking is: how much of people's assets do they want to hold in the form of money?

Next, we put supply and demand together to show how interest rates are determined, or how money supply must be manipulated to achieve a chosen rate of interest. Finally, we see how changes in money supply and/or interest rates affect aggregate demand and the level of business activity.

28.1 THE MEANING AND FUNCTIONS OF MONEY

Before going any further we must define precisely what we mean by 'money' – not as easy a task as it sounds. Money is more than just notes and coins. In fact the main component of a country's money supply is not cash, but deposits in banks and other financial institutions. The bulk of the deposits appear merely as bookkeeping entries in the banks' accounts.

People can access and use this money in their accounts through debit cards, cheques, standing orders, direct debits, etc. without the need for cash. Only a very small proportion of these deposits, therefore, need to be kept by the banks in their safes or tills in the form of cash.

What items should be included in the definition of money? To answer this we need to identify the *functions* of money.

The functions of money

The main purpose of money is for buying and selling goods, services and assets: i.e. as a ***medium of exchange***. It also has two other important functions. Let us examine each in turn.

A medium of exchange

In a subsistence economy where individuals make their own clothes, grow their own food, provide their own entertainments, etc., people do not need money. If people want to exchange any goods, they will do so by barter. In other words, they will do swaps with other people.

The complexities of a modern developed economy, however, make barter totally impractical for most purposes. What is necessary is a medium of exchange which is generally acceptable as a means of payment for goods and services, and as a means of payment for labour and other factor services. 'Money' is any such medium.

To be a suitable physical means of exchange, money must be light enough to carry around, come in a number of denominations, large and small, and not be easy to forge. Alternatively, money must be in a form that enables it to be transferred *indirectly* through some acceptable mechanism. For example, money in the form of bookkeeping entries in bank accounts can be transferred from one account to another by the use of such mechanisms as debit cards, cheques, standing orders and direct debits.

A means of evaluation

Money allows the value of goods, services and assets to be compared. The value of goods is expressed in terms of prices, and prices are expressed in money terms. Money also allows dissimilar things, such as a person's wealth or a company's assets, to be added up. Similarly, a country's GDP is expressed in money terms. Money thus serves as a 'unit of account'.

A means of storing wealth

Individuals and businesses need a means whereby the fruits of today's labour can be used to purchase goods and services in the future. People need to be able to store their wealth: they want a means of saving. Money is one such medium in which to hold wealth. It can be saved.

What should count as money?

What items, then, should be included in the definition of money? Unfortunately, there is no sharp borderline between money and non-money.

Cash (notes and coin) obviously counts as money. It readily meets all the functions of money. Goods (fridges, cars and cabbages) do not count as money. But what about various financial assets such as savings accounts, bonds and shares? Do they count as money? The answer is: it depends on how narrowly money is defined.

> **Pause for thought**
>
> *Why are debit and credit cards not counted as money?*

Countries thus use several different measures of money supply. All include cash, but they vary according to what additional items are included. To understand their significance and the ways in which money supply can be controlled, it is first necessary to look at the various types of account in which money can be held and at the various financial institutions involved.

> **Definition**
>
> **Medium of exchange** Something that is acceptable in exchange for goods and services.

28.2 THE FINANCIAL SYSTEM

In order to understand the role of the financial sector in determining the supply of money, it is important to distinguish different types of financial institution. Each type has a distinct part to play in determining the size of the money supply.

The key role of banks in the monetary system

By far the largest element of money supply is bank deposits. It is not surprising then that banks play an absolutely crucial role in the monetary system. Banking can be divided into two main types: *retail banking* and *wholesale banking* (see Chapter 19). Most banks today conduct both types of business and are thus known as 'universal banks'.

Retail banking is the business conducted by the familiar high street banks, such as Barclays, Lloyds TSB, HSBC, Santander, Royal Bank of Scotland and NatWest (part of the RBS group). They operate bank accounts for individuals and businesses, attracting deposits and granting loans at published rates of interest.

The other major type of banking is **wholesale banking**. This involves receiving large deposits from and making large loans to companies or other banks and financial institutions; these are known as *wholesale deposits and loans*. (See section 19.4 for a more detailed account of their activities.)

In the past, there were many independent wholesale banks, known as *investment banks*. These included famous names such as Morgan Stanley, Rothschild, SG Hambros and Goldman Sachs. With the worldwide financial crisis of 2008, however, most of the independent investment banks merged with universal banks, which conduct both retail and wholesale activities.

The rise of large universal banks has caused concern, however. In the UK in 2010, the Coalition government set up the Independent Commission on Banking (ICB). It was charged with investigating the structure of the banking system. The ICB proposed *functional separation*: the ring-fencing of retail from wholesale banking. It argued that the supply of vital retail banking activities needed isolating from the potential contagion from risky wholesale banking activities.

The principal recommendations of the ICB were accepted and the Financial Services (Banking Reform) Act became law in December 2013. The Act defines *core activities* as facilities for accepting deposits, facilities for withdrawing money or making payments from deposit accounts and the provision of overdraft facilities. It gives regulators the power to exercise ring-fencing rules to ensure the effective provision of core activities. These include restricting the power of a ring-fenced body to enter into contracts and payments with other members of the banking group. The Act also gives the regulator restructuring powers so as to split banks up to safeguard their future.

Building societies are UK institutions that historically have specialised in granting loans (mortgages) for house purchase. But, like banks, they too are deposit-taking financial institutions and so compete for the deposits of the general public. In recent years, many building societies have converted to banks.

Banks and building societies are both examples of what are called *monetary financial institutions (MFIs)*. This term is used to describe all deposit-taking institutions, which also includes central banks (e.g. the Bank of England).

Balance sheets

Banks and building societies provide a range of *financial instruments*. These are financial claims, either by customers

on the bank (e.g. deposits) or by the bank on its customers (e.g. loans). They are best understood by analysing the balance sheets of financial institutions, which itemise their liabilities and assets.

A financial institution's **liabilities** are those financial instruments involving a financial claim on the financial institution itself. As we shall see, these are largely *deposits* by customers, such as current and savings accounts. Its **assets** are financial instruments involving a financial claim on a third party: these are *loans*, such as personal and business loans and mortgages.

The total liabilities and assets for UK banks and building societies are set out in the balance sheet in Table 28.1. The aggregate size of the balance sheet at the start of 2015 was equivalent to around four times the UK's annual GDP. This is perhaps the simplest indicator of the significance of banks in modern economies, like the UK.

Both the *size* and *composition* of banks' balance sheets have become the focus of the international community's effort to ensure the stability of countries' financial systems. The growth of the aggregate balance sheet in the UK is considered in Box 28.2. But, it is to the composition of the balance sheet that we now turn.

Liabilities

Customers' deposits in banks (and other MFIs) are liabilities to these institutions. This means simply that the customers have the claim on these deposits and thus the institutions are legally liable to meet the claims.

There are four major types of deposit: sight deposits, time deposits, certificates of deposit and 'repos'.

Sight deposits. **Sight deposits** are any deposits that can be withdrawn on demand by the depositor without penalty. In the past, sight accounts did not pay interest. Today, however, there are some sight accounts that do.

Definitions

Retail banking Branch, telephone, postal and Internet banking for individuals and businesses at published rates of interest and charges. Retail banking involves the operation of extensive branch networks.

Wholesale banking Where banks deal in large-scale deposits and loans, mainly with companies and other banks and financial institutions. Interest rates and charges may be negotiable.

Monetary financial institutions (MFIs) Deposit-taking financial institutions including banks, building societies and central banks.

Financial instruments Financial products resulting in a financial claim by one party over another.

Liabilities All legal claims for payment that outsiders have on an institution.

Assets Possessions, or claims held on others.

Sight deposits Deposits that can be withdrawn on demand without penalty.

BOX 28.1 **FINANCIAL INTERMEDIATION**

What is it that banks do?

Banks and other financial institutions are known as financial intermediaries. They all have the common function of providing a link between those who wish to lend and those who wish to borrow. In other words, they act as the mechanism whereby the supply of funds is matched to the demand for funds. In this process, they provide four important services.

Expert advice

Financial intermediaries can advise their customers on financial matters: on the best way of investing their funds and on alternative ways of obtaining finance. This should help to encourage the flow of savings and the efficient use of them.

Expertise in channelling funds

Financial intermediaries have the specialist knowledge to be able to channel funds to those areas that yield the highest return. This too encourages the flow of savings as it gives savers the confidence that their savings will earn a good rate of interest. Financial intermediaries also help to ensure that projects that are potentially profitable will be able to obtain finance. They help to increase allocative efficiency.

Maturity transformation

Many people and firms want to borrow money for long periods of time, and yet many depositors want to be able to withdraw their deposits on demand or at short notice. If people had to rely on borrowing directly from other people, there would be a problem here: the lenders would not be prepared to lend for a long enough period. If you had £100 000 of savings, would you be prepared to lend it to a friend to buy a house if the friend was going to take 25 years to pay it back? Even if there was no risk whatsoever of your friend defaulting, most people would be totally unwilling to tie up their savings for so long. This is where a bank or building society comes in. It borrows

money from a vast number of small savers, who are able to withdraw their money on demand or at short notice. It then lends the money to house purchasers for a long period of time by granting mortgages (typically these are paid back over 20 to 30 years). This process whereby financial intermediaries lend for longer periods of time than they borrow is known as maturity transformation. They are able to do this because with a large number of depositors it is highly unlikely that they would all want to withdraw their deposits at the same time. On any one day, although some people will be withdrawing money, others will be making new deposits.

Risk transformation

You may be unwilling to lend money directly to another person in case they do not pay up. You are unwilling to take the risk. Financial intermediaries, however, by lending to large numbers of people, are willing to risk the odd case of default. They can absorb the loss because of the interest they earn on all the other loans. This spreading of risks is known as risk transformation. What is more, financial intermediaries may have the expertise to be able to assess just how risky a loan is.

Transmitting payments

In addition to channelling funds from depositors to borrowers, certain financial institutions have another important function. This is to provide a means of transmitting payments. Thus by the use of debit cards, credit cards, standing orders, cheques, etc., money can be transferred from one person or institution to another without having to rely on cash.

 Which of the above are examples of economies of scale?

The most familiar form of sight deposits are current accounts at banks. Depositors are normally issued with cheque books and/or debit cards (e.g. Visa debit or Mastercard's Maestro) which enable them to spend the money directly without first having to go to the bank and draw the money out in cash. In the case of debit cards, the person's account is electronically debited when the purchase is made and the card is 'swiped' across the machine. This process is known as EFTPOS (electronic funds transfer at point of sale).

An important feature of current accounts is that banks often allow customers to be overdrawn. That is, they can draw on their account and make payments to other people in excess of the amount of money they have deposited.

Time deposits. **Time deposits** require notice of withdrawal. However, they normally pay a higher rate of interest than

sight accounts. With some types of account, a depositor can withdraw a certain amount of money on demand, but will have to pay a penalty of so many days' interest. They are not cheque-book or debit-card accounts. The most familiar forms of time deposits are the deposit and savings accounts in banks and the various savings accounts in building societies. No overdraft facilities exist with time deposits.

Definition

Time deposits Deposits that require notice of withdrawal or where a penalty is charged for withdrawals on demand.

Table 28.1 Balance sheet of UK banks (end of November 2015)

Sterling liabilities	£bn	%	Sterling assets	£bn	%
Sight deposits		44.5	Notes and coin	9.4	0.3
UK banks, etc.	122.5		Balances with Bank of England		9.1
UK public sector	15.3		Reserve balances	304.6	
UK private sector	1215.0		Cash ratio deposits	4.1	
Non-residents	150.5		Market loans		11.2
Time deposits		30.9	UK banks, etc.	264.6	
UK banks, etc.	143.7		UK banks' CDs, etc.	4.0	
UK public sector	19.4		Non-residents	110.0	
UK private sector	681.6		Bills of exchange	10.1	0.3
Non-residents	199.1		Reverse repos	216.7	6.4
Certificates of deposit (CDs)	154.1	4.6	Investments	444.1	13.1
Repos	202.8	6.0	Advances	1943.2	57.3
Sterling capital and other funds	446.7	13.2	Other assets	82.6	2.4
Other liabilities	27.0	0.8			
Total sterling liabilities	3377.8	100.0	**Total sterling assets**	3393.4	100.0
Liabilities in other currencies	3585.8		Assets in other currencies	3570.3	
Total liabilities	6963.6		**Total assets**	6963.6	

Note: Data are not seasonally adjusted
Source: Based on data in *Bankstats (Monetary and Financial Statistics)* (Bank of England), January 2016

A substantial proportion of time deposits are from the *banking sector*: i.e. other banks and other financial institutions. Interbank lending, including that involving foreign banks, had grown over the years with the deregulation of financial markets. But, inter-bank lending virtually dried up in 2008/9. Banks became increasingly fearful that if they lent money to other banks, the other banks might default on payment. The reason was that many banks held assets based on mortgages granted to people unable to pay. As these assets fell in value, so banks became less and less able to raise enough money to pay back interbank loans.

Sale and repurchase agreements ('repos'). If banks have a temporary shortage of funds, they can sell some of their financial assets to other banks or to the central bank – the Bank of England in the UK and the European Central Bank in the eurozone (see below), and later repurchase them on some agreed date, typically a fortnight later. These *sale and repurchase agreements (repos)* are in effect a form of loan, the bank borrowing for a period of time using some of its financial assets as the security for the loan. One of the major assets to use in this way are government bonds, normally called 'gilt-edged securities' or simply 'gilts' (see below). Sale and repurchase agreements involving gilts are known as *gilt repos*. Gilt repos play a vital role in the operation of monetary policy (see section 30.1).

Certificates of deposit. **Certificates of deposit** (CDs) are certificates issued by banks to customers (usually firms) for large deposits of a fixed term (e.g. £100 000 for 18 months). They can be sold by one customer to another, and thus provide a means whereby the holders can get money quickly if they need it without the *banks* that have issued the CD having to supply the money. (This makes them relatively 'liquid' to the depositor but 'illiquid' to the bank: we examine this below.) The use of CDs has grown rapidly in recent years. Their use by firms has meant that, at a wholesale level, sight accounts have become *less* popular.

Capital and other funds. This consists largely of the share capital in banks. Since shareholders cannot take their money out of banks, it provides a source of funding to meet

Definitions

Sale and repurchase agreements (repos) An agreement between two financial institutions whereby one in effect borrows from another by selling it assets, agreeing to buy them back (repurchase them) at a fixed price and on a fixed date.

Certificates of deposit Certificates issued by banks for fixed-term interest-bearing deposits. They can be resold by the owner to another party.

sudden increases in withdrawals from depositors and to cover bad debts. It is vital that banks have sufficient capital. As we shall see, an important part of the response to the financial crisis has been to require banks to hold relatively larger amounts of capital. At the end of 2008, the aggregate amount of sterling capital held by banks based in the UK was equivalent to 9.7 per cent of their sterling liabilities. By the start of 2015 this had risen to over 13 per cent.

Assets

Banks' financial assets are its claims on others. There are three main categories of assets.

Cash and reserve balances in the central bank (Bank of England in the UK, ECB in the eurozone). Banks need to hold a certain amount of their assets as cash. This is largely used to meet the day-to-day demands of customers. This, however, is typically less than 1 per cent of their total sterling assets as the demand for cash at any one time represents only a tiny fraction of total deposits in banks.

They also keep 'reserve balances' in the central bank. In the UK these earn interest at the Bank of England's repo rate (or 'Bank Rate' as it is called), if kept within an agreed target range. These are like the banks' own current accounts and are used for clearing purposes (i.e. for settling the day-to-day payments between banks). They can be withdrawn in cash on demand. With inter-bank lending being seen as too risky during the crisis of 2008, many banks resorted to depositing surplus cash in the Bank of England, even though the Bank Rate was lower than the inter-bank rate (known as 'LIBOR', which stands for the London Inter-Bank Offered Rate).

In the UK, banks and building societies are also required to deposit a small fraction of their assets as 'cash ratio deposits' with the Bank of England. These cannot be drawn on demand and earn no interest. The Bank then invests these funds and the interest it earns helps to finance its operations to implement monetary policy and to ensure financial stability. The financial crisis resulted in the Bank of England increasing the scale of its activities to ensure the stability of the financial system, including taking a greater supervisory role, as detailed in this chapter and Chapter 30. Consequently, the size of CRDs was increased in 2013.

The increase in CRDs alongside an increase in reserve balances led to an increase in banks' cash and balances in the Bank of England. In 2015, they accounted for around 9 per cent of banks' sterling assets compared with just 4 per cent in 2010. Nonetheless, the vast majority of banks' assets remain in the form of various types of loan – to individuals and firms, to other financial institutions and to the government. These are 'assets' because they represent claims that the banks have on other people. Loans can be grouped into two types: short and long term.

Short-term loans. These are in the form of market loans, bills of exchange or reverse repos. The market for these various types of loan is known as the **money market**.

■ *Market loans* are made primarily to other banks or financial institutions. They consist of (a) money lent 'at call' (i.e. reclaimable on demand or at 24 hours' notice), (b) money lent 'at short notice' (i.e. money lent for a few days) and (c) CDs (i.e. certificates of deposit made in other banks or building societies).

■ *Bills of exchange* are loans either to companies (commercial bills) or to the government (Treasury bills). These are, as explained in section 19.4, in effect, an IOU, with the company issuing them (in the case of commercial bills) or the Bank of England (in the case of Treasury bills) promising to pay the holder a specified sum on a particular date (typically three months later). Since bills do not pay interest, they are sold below their face value (at a 'discount') but redeemed on maturity at face value. This enables the purchaser, in this case the bank, to earn a return. The market for new or existing bills is therefore known as the **discount market**.

■ *Reverse repos*. When a sale and repurchase agreement is made, the financial institution *purchasing* the assets (e.g. gilts) is, in effect, giving a short-term loan. The other party agrees to buy back the assets (i.e. pay back the loan) on a set date. The assets temporarily held by the bank making the loan are known as 'reverse repos'.

Longer-term loans. These consist primarily of loans to customers, both personal customers and businesses. These loans, also known as *advances*, are of four main types: fixed-term (repayable in instalments over a set number of years, typically six months to five years), overdrafts (often for an unspecified term), outstanding balances on credit-card accounts and mortgages (typically for 25 years).

Banks also make *investments*. These are partly in government bonds ('gilts'), which are effectively loans to the government. The government sells bonds, which then pay a fixed sum each year in interest. Once issued, bonds can then be bought and sold on the Stock Exchange. Banks are normally only prepared to buy bonds that have

---

Definitions

Money market The market for short-term loans and deposits.

Market loans Loans made to other financial institutions.

Bill of exchange A certificate promising to repay a stated amount on a certain date, typically three months from the issue of the bill. Bills pay no interest as such, but are sold at a discount and redeemed at face value, thereby earning a rate of discount for the purchaser.

Discount market An example of a money market in which new or existing bills are bought and sold.

Reverse repos When gilts or other assets are purchased under a sale and repurchase agreement. They become an asset of the purchaser.

less than five years to maturity. Banks also invest in other financial institutions, including subsidiary financial institutions.

Taxing the balance sheets

In January 2011, the UK Coalition government introduced the bank levy: a tax on the liabilities of banks and building societies operating in the UK. The design of the levy built on proposals presented by the International Monetary Fund in June 2010. There were two key principles. First, the revenues raised should be able to meet the full fiscal costs of any future support for financial institutions. Second, it should provide banks with incentives to reduce risk-taking behaviour and so reduce the likelihood of future financial crises.

The UK bank levy has two rates: a full rate on taxable liabilities with a maturity of less than 1 year and a half rate on taxable liabilities with a maturity of more than 1 year. The intention is to discourage excessive short-term borrowing by the banks in their use of wholesale funding. The tax levy rates were intended to raise at least £2.5 billion each year. When introduced from January 2011 the full rate was set at 0.05 and the half rate at 0.025. However, rates were subsequently raised several times. One reason behind this was that the shrinking balance sheets of MFIs (see Box 28.2) meant that revenues over the period 2011/12 to 2013/14 averaged only £2 billion each year. By April 2015 the full rate had risen to 0.21 per cent and the half rate to 0.105 per cent.

Not all liabilities are subject to the levy. First, it is not imposed on the first £20 billion of liabilities. This is to encourage small banks (note that the largest UK banks, such as HSBC, Barclays and RBS, each have liabilities of over £2 trillion). Second, various liabilities are excluded. These are: (a) gilt repos; (b) retail deposits insured by public schemes such as the UK's Financial Services Compensation Scheme, which guarantees customers' deposits of up to £85,000; (c) a large part of a bank's capital known as Tier 1 capital (see below) – the argument here is that it is important for banks to maintain sufficient funds to meet the demands of its depositors.

Banks are also able to offset against their taxable liabilities holdings of highly liquid assets, such as Treasury bills and cash reserves at the Bank of England. It is hoped that these exclusions and deductions will encourage banks to engage in less risky lending.

Liquidity, profitability and capital adequacy

As we have seen, banks keep a range of liabilities and assets. The balance of items in this range is influenced by three important considerations: profitability, liquidity and capital adequacy.

Profitability

Profits are made by lending money out at a higher rate of interest than that paid to depositors. The average interest rate received by banks on their assets is greater than that paid by them on their liabilities.

Liquidity

The **liquidity** of an asset is the ease with which it can be converted into cash without loss. Cash itself, by definition, is perfectly liquid.

Some assets, such as money lent at call to other financial institutions, are highly liquid. Although not actually cash, these assets can be converted into cash on demand with no financial penalty. Other short-term inter-bank lending is also very liquid. The only issue here is one of confidence that the money will actually be repaid. This was a worry in the financial crisis of 2008/9, when many banks stopped lending to each other on the inter-bank market for fear that the borrowing bank might become insolvent.

Other assets, however, are much less liquid. Personal loans to the general public or mortgages for house purchase can only be redeemed by the bank as each instalment is paid. Other advances for fixed periods are only repaid at the end of that period. This was why securitisation of mortgages became popular with banks as it effectively made their mortgage assets tradable and hence more liquid (see Boxes 28.2 and 28.3).

Banks must always be able to meet the demands of their customers for withdrawals of money. To do this, they must hold sufficient cash or other assets that can be readily turned into cash. In other words, banks must maintain sufficient liquidity.

The balance between profitability and liquidity

Profitability is the major aim of banks and most other financial institutions. However, the aims of profitability and liquidity tend to conflict. In general, the more liquid an asset, the less profitable it is, and vice versa. Personal and business loans to customers are profitable to banks, but highly illiquid. Cash is totally liquid, but earns no profit. Thus financial institutions like to hold a range of assets with varying degrees of liquidity and profitability.

For reasons of *profitability*, banks will want to 'borrow short' (at low rates of interest, such as people's deposits in current accounts) and 'lend long' (at higher rates of interest, such as on personal loans or mortgages). The difference in the average maturity of loans and deposits is known as the **maturity gap**. In general terms, the larger the maturity gap between loans and deposits, the greater the profitability. For reasons of *liquidity*, however, banks

---

Definitions

Liquidity The ease with which an asset can be converted into cash without loss.

Maturity gap The difference in the average maturity of loans and deposits.

will want a relatively small gap: if there is a sudden withdrawal of deposits, banks will need to be able to call in enough loans.

The ratio of an institution's liquid assets to total assets (or liabilities) is known as its *liquidity ratio*. For example, if a bank had £100 million of assets, of which £10 million were liquid and £90 million were illiquid, the bank would have a 10 per cent liquidity ratio. If a financial institution's liquidity ratio is too high, it will make too little profit. If the ratio is too low, there is a risk that customers' demands may not be able to be met: this would cause a crisis of confidence and possible closure. Institutions thus have to make a judgement as to what liquidity ratio is best – one that is neither too high nor too low.

Balances in the central bank, short-term loans (i.e. those listed above) and government bonds with less than 12 months to maturity (and hence tradable now at near their face value) would normally be regarded as liquid assets.

As Box 28.2 explains, over the years, banks had reduced their liquidity ratios (i.e. the ratio of liquid assets to total assets). This was not a problem as long as banks could always finance lending to customers by borrowing on the inter-bank market. In 2008, however, banks became increasingly worried about bad debt. They thus felt the need to increase their liquidity ratios and hence cut back on lending and chose to keep a higher proportion of deposits in liquid form. In the UK, for example, banks

---

BOX 28.2 GROWTH OF BANKS' BALANCE SHEETS

The rise of wholesale funding

Banks' traditional funding model relied heavily on deposits as the source of funds for loans. However, new ways for financial institutions to access funds to generate new loans evolved, especially in the years preceding the financial crisis of 2008. These reflected the deregulation of financial markets and the rapid pace of financial innovation.

Seeds of the crisis

Increasingly financial institutions made greater use of wholesale funds. These are funds obtained mainly from other financial institutions. This coincided too with the emergence of a process known as securitisation. This involves the conversion of non-marketable banks' assets, such as residential mortgages, which have regular income streams (e.g. from payments of interest and capital), into assets that could be traded, known as 'tradable financial instruments'. These asset-backed securities provide lenders who originate the loans with a source of funds for further loans. Therefore, securitisation became another means by which lenders could raise capital. Securitisation is discussed further in Box 28.3.

With an increasing use of money markets by financial institutions, vast sums of funds became available for lending. One consequence of this is illustrated in the chart: the expansion of the aggregate balance sheet. The balance sheet grew from £2.5 trillion (3 times GDP) in 1998 to over £8.5 trillion (5.6 times GDP) in 2010.

The growth in banks' balance sheets was accompanied by a change in their composition.

First, the profile of banks' assets became less liquid as they extended more long-term credit to households and firms. Assets generally became more risky too, as banks increasingly granted mortgages of 100 per cent or more of the value of houses – a problem for banks if house prices fell and they were forced to repossess.

Second, there was a general increase in the use of fixed-interest bonds as opposed to ordinary shares (equities) for raising capital. The ratio of bonds to equity capital is known as *gearing (or leverage) ratio*. The increase in leverage meant that banks were operating with lower and lower levels of loss-absorbing capital, such as ordinary shares. If banks

run at a loss, dividends on shares can be suspended; the payment of interest on fixed interest bonds cannot. This meant that as the crisis unfolded, policy makers were facing a liquidity problem, not among one or two financial institutions, but across the financial system.

The market failure we are describing is a form of *co-ordination failure*. When one bank pursues increased earnings by borrowing from and lending to other financial institutions, this is not necessarily a problem. But if many institutions build their balance sheets by borrowing from and lending to each other, then it becomes a problem for the whole financial system. The apparent increase in liquidity for individual banks, on which they base credit, is not an overall increase in liquidity for the financial system as a whole. The effect is to create a credit bubble.

The dangers of the bubble for the financial system and beyond were magnified by the increasingly tangled web of interdependencies between financial institutions, both nationally and globally. There was a danger that this complexity was masking fundamental weaknesses of many financial institutions and too little overall liquidity.

The financial crisis

Things came to a head in 2007 and 2008. Once one or two financial institutions failed, such as Northern Rock in the UK in September 2007 and Lehman Brothers in the USA in September 2008, the worry was that failures would spread like a contagion. Banks could no longer rely on each other as their main source of liquidity.

The problems arising from the balance sheet expansion, increased leverage and a heightened level of maturity mismatch meant that central banks around the world, including the Bank of England, were faced with addressing a liquidity problem of huge proportions. They had to step in to supply central bank money to prevent a collapse of the banking system.

Subsequently, the international Basel Committee on Banking Supervision (see pages 527–9) agreed a set of measures, to be applied globally, designed to ensure the greater financial resilience of banks and banking systems. It is notable from

substantially increased their level of reserves in the Bank of England.

Capital adequacy

In addition to sufficient liquidity, banks must have sufficient capital (i.e. funds) to allow them to meet all demands from depositors and to cover losses if borrowers default on payment. Capital adequacy is a measure of a bank's capital relative to its assets, where the assets are weighted according to the degree of risk. The more risky the assets, the greater the amount of capital that will be required.

A measure of capital adequacy is given by the *capital adequacy ratio (CAR)*. This is given by the following formula:

$$CAR = \frac{\text{Common Equity Tier 1 capital} + \text{Additional Tier 1 capital} + \text{Tier 2 capital}}{\text{Risk-weighted assets}}$$

Common Equity Tier 1 (CET1) capital includes bank reserves (from retained profits) and ordinary share capital ('equities'), where dividends to shareholders vary with the

> **Definitions**
>
> **Liquidity ratio** The proportion of a bank's total assets held in liquid form.
>
> **Capital adequacy ratio** The ratio of a bank's capital (reserves and shares) to its risk-weighted assets.

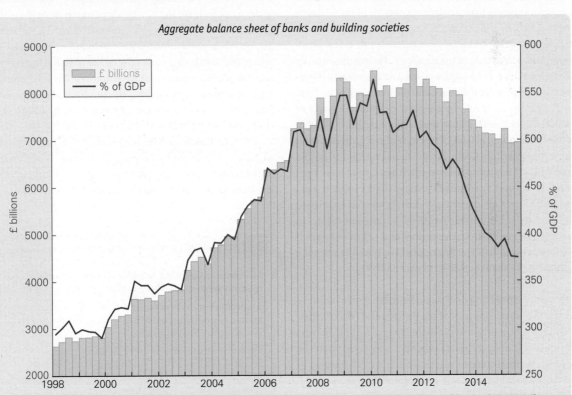

Aggregate balance sheet of banks and building societies

Source: (i) Data showing liabilities of banks and building societies based on series LPMALOA and RPMTBJF (up to the end of 2009) and RPMB3UQ (from 2010) from *Statistical Interactive Database*, Bank of England (data published 4 January 2016, not seasonally adjusted). (ii) GDP data from series YBHA, Office for National Statistics (GDP figures are the sum of the latest four quarters).

the chart how the early 2010s saw a consolidation of the aggregate balance sheet of banks resident in the UK. At the end of 2015 the aggregate balance sheet stood at close to £7 trillion. This was equivalent to 3.75 times GDP, its lowest level since 2003.

Why do you think banks became reluctant to deposit moneys with other banks during the financial crisis of the late 2000s?

> **Definitions**
>
> **Gearing** or **leverage** (US term) The ratio of debt capital to equity capital: in other words, the ratio of borrowed capital (e.g. bonds) to shares.
>
> **Co-ordination failure** When a group of firms (e.g. banks) acting independently could have achieved a more desirable outcome if they had co-ordinated their decision making.

amount of profit the bank makes. Such capital thus places no burden on banks in times of losses as no dividend need be paid. What is more, unlike depositors, shareholders cannot ask for their money back.

Additional Tier 1 (AT1) capital consists largely of preference shares. These pay a fixed dividend (like company bonds), but although preference shareholders have a prior claim over ordinary shareholders on company profits, dividends need not be paid in times of loss.

Tier 2 capital is subordinated debt with a maturity greater than five years. Subordinated debt holders only have a claim on a company after the claims of all other bondholders have been met.

Risk-weighted assets are the total value of assets, where each type of asset is multiplied by a risk factor. Under the internationally agreed Basel II accord, cash and government bonds have a risk factor of zero and are thus not included. Inter-bank lending between the major banks has a risk factor of 0.2 and is thus included at only 20 per cent of its value; residential mortgages have a risk factor of 0.35; personal loans, credit-card debt and overdrafts have a risk factor of 1; loans to companies carry a risk factor of 0.2, 0.5, 1 or 1.5, depending on the credit rating of the company. Thus the greater the average risk factor of a bank's assets, the greater will be the value of its risk-weighted assets, and the lower will be its CAR.

The greater the CAR, the greater the capital adequacy of a bank. Under Basel II, banks were required to have a CAR of at least 8 per cent (i.e. 0.08). They were also required to meet two supplementary CARs. Firstly, banks needed to hold a ratio of Tier 1 capital to risk-weighted assets of at least 4 per cent and, secondly, a ratio of ordinary share capital to risk-weighted assets of at least 2 per cent. It was felt that these three ratios would provide banks with sufficient capital to meet the demands from depositors and to cover losses if borrowers defaulted. The financial crisis, however, meant a rethink (as we shall see below on pages 527-9).

Secondary marketing and securitisation

As we have seen, one way of reconciling the two conflicting aims of liquidity and profitability is to hold a mixture of liquid and illiquid assets. Another way is through the *secondary marketing* of assets. This is where holders of assets sell them to someone else before the maturity date. This allows banks to close the maturity gap for *liquidity* purposes, but maintain the gap for *profitability* purposes.

Certificates of deposit (CDs) are a good example of secondary marketing. CDs are issued for fixed-period deposits in a bank (e.g. one year) at an agreed interest rate. The bank does not have to repay the deposit until the year is up. CDs are thus illiquid liabilities for the bank, and they allow it to increase the proportion of illiquid assets without having a dangerously high maturity gap. But the holder of the CD in the meantime can sell it to someone else (through a broker). It is thus liquid to the holder. Because CDs are liquid to the holder, they can be issued at a relatively *low* rate of interest and thus allow the bank to increase its profitability.

Another example of secondary marketing is when a financial institution sells some of its assets to another financial institution. The advantage to the first institution is that it gains liquidity. The advantage to the second one is that it gains profitable assets. The most common method for the sale of assets has been through a process known as *securitisation*.

Securitisation occurs when a financial institution pools some of its assets, such as residential mortgages, and sells them to an intermediary known as a *special purpose vehicle (SPV)*. SPVs are legal entities created by the financial institution. In turn, the SPV funds its purchase of the assets by issuing bonds to investors (noteholders). These bonds are known as *collateralised debt obligations (CDOs)*. The sellers (e.g. banks) get cash now rather than having to wait and can use it to fund loans to customers. The buyers make a profit if the income yielded by the CDOs is as expected. Such bonds can be very risky, however, as the future cash flows may be *less* than anticipated.

The securitisation chain is illustrated in Figure 28.1. The financial institution looking to sell its assets is referred to as the 'originator' or the 'originator-lender'. Working from left to right, we see the originator-lender sells its assets to

---

Definitions

Secondary marketing Where assets are sold before maturity to another institution or individual.

Securitisation Where future cash flows (e.g. from interest rate or mortgage payments) are turned into marketable securities, such as bonds.

Special purpose vehicle (SPV) Legal entities created by financial institutions for conducting specific financial functions, such as bundling assets together into fixed-interest bonds and selling them.

Collateralised debt obligations (CDOs) These are a type of security consisting of a bundle of fixed-income assets, such as corporate bonds, mortgage debt and credit-card debt.

Figure 28.1 Securitisation chain

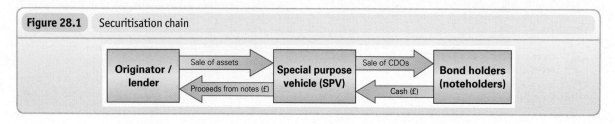

another financial institution, the SPV, which then bundles assets together into CDOs and sells them to investors (e.g. banks or pension funds) as bonds. Now working from right to left, we see that by purchasing the bonds issued by the SPV, the investors provide the funds for the SPV's purchase of the lender's assets. The SPV is then able to use the proceeds from the bond sales (CDO proceeds) to provide the originator-lender with liquidity.

The effect of secondary marketing is to reduce the liquidity ratio that banks feel they need to keep. It has the effect of increasing their maturity gap.

Dangers of secondary marketing. There are dangers to the banking system, however, from secondary marketing. To the extent that banks individually feel that they can operate with a lower liquidity ratio, so this will lead to a lower national liquidity ratio. This may lead to an excessive expansion of credit (illiquid assets) in times of economic boom.

Also, there is an increased danger of banking collapse. If one bank fails, this will have a knock-on effect on those banks which have purchased its assets. In the specific case of securitisation, the strength of the chain is potentially weakened if individual financial institutions move into riskier market segments, such as **sub-prime** residential mortgage markets. Should the income streams of the originator's assets dry up – for instance, if individuals default on their loans – then the impact is felt by the whole of the chain. In other words, institutions and investors are exposed to the risks of the originator's lending strategy.

The issue of securitisation and its impact on the liquidity of the financial system during the 2000s is considered in Box 28.3.

Strengthening international regulation of capital adequacy and liquidity

Capital adequacy

In light of the financial crisis of 2008–9, international capital adequacy requirements were strengthened by the *Basel Committee on Banking Supervision* in 2010/11. The new 'Basel III' capital requirements, as they are called, will be phased in by 2019. They are summarised in Figure 28.2.

From 2013, banks will continue to need a CAR of at least 8 per cent (i.e. 0.08). But, by 2015 they will also be required to operate with a ratio of CET1 to risk-weighted assets of at least 4.5 per cent. The phased introduction of a *capital conservation buffer* from 2016 will raise the CET1 ratio to no less than 7 per cent by 2019. This will take the overall CAR to at least 10.5 per cent.

> ### Definition
>
> **Sub-prime debt** Debt where there is a high risk of default by the borrower (e.g. mortgage holders who are on low incomes facing higher interest rates and falling house prices).

Figure 28.2   Basel III minimum capital requirements, by 1/1/2019

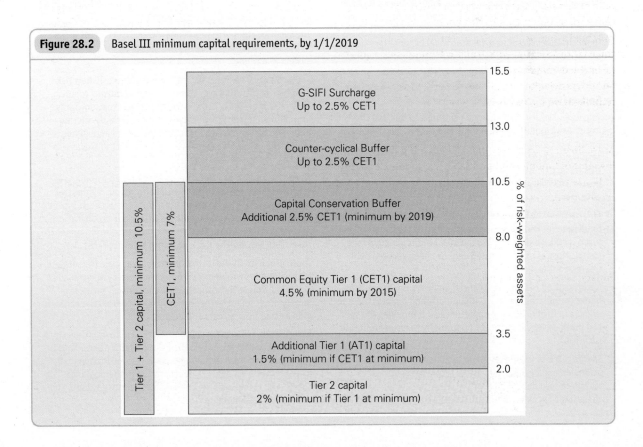

On top of this, national regulators will be required to assess the financial resilience across all financial institutions under its jurisdiction, particularly in light of economic conditions. This is **macro-prudential regulation**. If necessary, it will then apply a *counter-cyclical buffer* to all banks so increasing the CET1 ratio by up to a further 2.5 per cent. The idea is to build up a capital buffer in boom times to allow it to be drawn on in times of recession or financial difficulty.

Large global financial institutions, known as **global systemically important banks (G-SIBs)**, will be required to operate with a CET1 ratio of up to 2.5 per cent higher than other banks. The reason for this extra capital requirement is that the failure of such an institution could trigger a global financial crisis. This would potentially take the overall CAR for very large financial institutions in 2019 to 15.5 per cent (see Figure 28.2).

Net stable funding ratio

As part of Basel III, it is intended to introduce a minimum *net stable funding ratio* (NSFR) by 2018. The NSFR is the ratio of stable liabilities to assets likely to require funding (i.e. assets where there is a likelihood of default or which could not be 'monetised' and thereby converted into money through their sale). The aim of having a minimum NSFR is to limit excessive risk from maturity transformation by taking a longer-term view of the funding profile of banks relative to their assets.

On the liabilities side, these will be weighted by their expected reliability – in other words, by the stability of these funds. This weighting will reflect the maturity of the liabilities and the likelihood of lenders withdrawing their funds. For example, Tier 1 and 2 capital will have a weighting of 100 per cent; term deposits with less than one year to maturity will have a weighting of 50 per cent; and unsecured wholesale funding will have a weighting of 0 per cent. The result of these weightings is a measure of stable funding.

On the assets side, these will be weighted by the likelihood that they will have to be funded over the course of one year. This means that they will be weighted by their

---

KI 14
p 82

BOX 28.3	RESIDENTIAL MORTGAGES AND SECURITISATION

Was this the cause of the credit crunch?

The conflict between profitability and liquidity may have sown the seeds for the credit crunch that affected economies across the globe in the second half of the 2000s.

To understand this, consider the size of the 'advances' item in the banking sector's balance sheet – some 56 per cent of the value of sterling (see Table 28.1). The vast majority of these are to households. Advances secured against property have, in recent times, accounted for around 80 per cent by value of all household advances. Residential mortgages involve institutions lending long.

Securitisation of debt

One way in which individual institutions can achieve the necessary liquidity to expand the size of their mortgage lending (illiquid assets) is through securitisation. Securitisation grew especially rapidly in the UK and USA. In the UK this was particularly true amongst banks; building societies have historically made greater use of retail deposits to fund advances.

Figures from the Bank of England show that the value of lending to individuals which was securitised increased from just over £0.8 billion in 1998 to £103.7 billion in 2008 (see chart). Most of this securitised debt has been secured debt, i.e. residential mortgages.

Securitisation is a form of financial engineering. It provides banks (originator-lenders) with liquidity and enables them to engage in further lending opportunities. It provides the special purpose vehicles with the opportunity to issue profitable securities.

The increase in securitisation up to 2008 highlights the strong demand amongst investors for these securities or 'collateralised debt obligations' (CDOs). The attraction of these fixed-income products for the noteholders was the potential for higher returns than on (what were) similarly rated products. However, investors have no recourse should people with mortgages fall into arrears or, worse still, default on their mortgages.

Risks and the sub-prime market

The securitisation of assets is not without risks for all those in the securitisation chain and consequently for the financial system as a whole.

The pooling of advances in itself reduces the cash-flow risk facing investors. However, there is a **moral hazard** problem here (see page 100). The pooling of the risks may encourage originator-lenders to lower their credit criteria by offering higher income multiples (advances relative to annual household incomes) or higher loan-to-value ratios (advances relative to the price of housing).

Towards the end of 2006 the USA witnessed an increase in the number of defaults by households on residential mortgages. This was a particular problem in the *sub-prime market* – higher-risk households with poor credit ratings. Similarly, the number falling behind with their payments rose. This was on the back of rising interest rates.

These problems in the US sub-prime market were the catalyst for the liquidity problem that beset financial systems in 2007 and 2008. Where these assets were securitised, investors, largely other financial institutions, suffered from the contagion arising from arrears and defaults.

Securitisation also internationalised the contagion. Investors are global so that advances, such as a US family's residential mortgage, can cross national borders. This resulted in institutions writing off debts, a deterioration of their balance sheets, the collapse in the demand for securitised assets and the drying up of liquidity.

KI 17
p 100

KI 7
p 38

liquidity, with more liquid assets requiring less funding. Thus cash will have a zero weighting, while more risky assets will have weightings up to 100 per cent. The result is a measure of required funding.

Banks will need to hold a minimum stable-liabilities-to-required-funding ratio (NSFR) of 100 per cent.

> ### Pause for thought
>
> *Why are government bonds that still have 11 months to run regarded as liquid, whereas overdrafts granted for a few weeks are not?*

The central bank

The Bank of England is the UK's central bank. The European Central Bank (ECB) is the central bank for the countries using the euro. The Federal Reserve Bank of America (the Fed) is the USA's central bank. All countries have a central bank and they fulfil two vital roles in the economy.

The first is to oversee the whole monetary system and ensure that banks and other financial institutions operate as stably and as efficiently as possible.

> ### Definitions
>
> **Macro-prudential regulation** Regulation which focuses on the financial system as a whole and which monitors its impact on the wider economy.
>
> **Global systemically important banks (G-SIBs)** Banks identified by a series of indicators as being significant players in the global financial system.

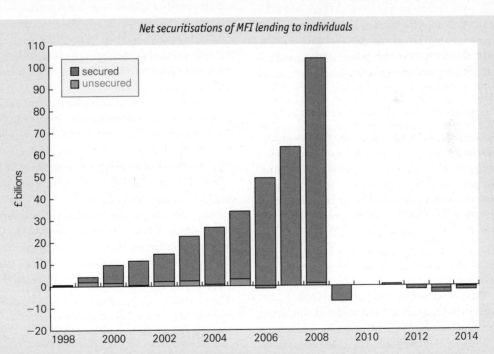

Net securitisations of MFI lending to individuals

Note: Negative totals indicate acquisition of secured and unsecured debt portfolios
Source: Based on data from *Statistical Interactive Database*, Bank of England, series LPQB3XE and LPQB3HK (data published 2/3/15).

The chart shows the collapse of the market for securitised assets. The period from 2009 to 2014 was characterised by banks buying back CDOs from SPVs, including unsold ones.

 Does securitisation necessarily involve a moral hazard problem?

> ### Definition
>
> **Moral hazard** The temptation to take more risks when you know that someone else will cover the risks if you get into difficulties. In the case of banks taking risks, the 'someone else' may be another bank, the central bank or the government.

The second is to act as the government's agent, both as its banker and in carrying out monetary policy. The Bank of England traditionally worked in very close liaison with the Treasury, and there used to be regular meetings between the Governor of the Bank of England and the Chancellor of the Exchequer. Although the Bank may have disagreed with Treasury policy, it always carried it out. With the election of the Labour government in 1997, however, the Bank of England was given independence to decide the course of monetary policy. In particular, this meant that the Bank of England and not the government would now decide interest rates.

Another example of an independent central bank is the European Central Bank (ECB). The ECB operates monetary policy for the countries using the euro and it alone, not the member governments, determines common interest rates for these countries. Similarly, the Fed is independent of both President and Congress, and its chairman is generally regarded as having great power in determining the country's economic policy. Although the degree of independence of central banks from government varies considerably around the world, there has nevertheless been a general trend to make central banks more independent.

If the UK were ever to adopt the euro, there would be a much reduced role for the Bank of England. At present, however, within its two broad roles, it has a number of different functions. Although we shall consider the case of the Bank of England, the same principles apply to other central banks.

It issues notes

The Bank of England is the sole issuer of banknotes in England and Wales (in Scotland and Northern Ireland retail banks issue banknotes). The amount of banknotes issued by the Bank of England depends largely on the demand for notes from the general public. If people draw more cash from their bank accounts, the banks will have to draw more cash from their balances in the Bank of England.

It acts as a bank

To the government. It keeps the two major government accounts: 'The Exchequer' and the 'National Loans Fund'. Taxation and government spending pass through the Exchequer. Government borrowing and lending pass through the National Loans Fund. The government tends to keep its deposits in the Bank of England to a minimum. If the deposits begin to build up (from taxation), the government will probably spend them on paying back government debt. If, on the other hand, the government runs short of money, it will simply borrow more.

To the banks. Banks' deposits in the Bank of England consist of reserve balances and cash ratio deposits (see Table 28.1). The reserve balances are used largely for clearing purposes

between the banks, but are also a means by which banks can manage their liquidity risk. Therefore, the reserve balances provide banks with an important buffer stock of liquid assets.

To overseas central banks. The Bank of England holds deposits of sterling (and similarly the European Central Bank holds deposits of euros) made by overseas authorities as part of their official reserves and/or for purposes of intervening in the foreign exchange market in order to influence the exchange rate of their currency (see page 531).

It operates the country's monetary policy

The Bank of England's Monetary Policy Committee (MPC) sets interest rates (the rate on gilt repos) at its regular meetings. This nine-member committee consists of four experts appointed by the Chancellor of the Exchequer and four senior members of the Bank of England, plus the Governor in the chair.

The Bank of England conducts **open-market operations** to keep interest rates in line with the level decided by the MPC. By purchasing securities (gilts and/or Treasury bills), for example through reverse repos (repos to the banks), the Bank of England provides liquidity, thereby putting downward pressure on interest rates. If it is looking to raise interest rates, the Bank of England will sell securities to banks, so reducing banks' reserves in the Bank. In the process of influencing interest rates through open-market operations the Bank of England affects the size of the money supply. (This is explained in Chapter 30.)

As the financial crisis unfolded it became increasingly difficult for the Bank to meet its monetary policy objectives while maintaining financial stability. New policies were thus adopted. October 2008 also saw the Bank of England stop short-term open-market operations. The key priority was now ensuring sufficient liquidity and so the focus switched to longer-term OMOs.

March 2009 saw the Bank begin a programme of **quantitative easing (QE)** (see Box 30.4). The aim was to increase the amount of money in the financial system and thereby stimulate bank lending and hence aggregate demand. QE involved the Bank creating electronic money and using it to

---

> **Definitions**
>
> **Open-market operations** The sale (or purchase) of government securities in the open market which aim to reduce (or increase) the money supply and thereby affect interest rates.
>
> **Quantitative easing** When the central bank increases the monetary base through an open market purchase of government bonds or other securities. It uses electronic money (reserve liabilities) created specifically for this purpose.

KI 39 p471

purchase assets, mainly government bonds, predominantly from non-deposit-taking financial institutions, such as unit trusts, insurance companies and pension funds. These institutions would then deposit the money in banks, which could lend it to businesses and consumers for purposes of spending.

It provides liquidity, as necessary, to banks

Financial institutions engage in maturity transformation (see Box 28.1), which means that they are typically borrowing funds for a shorter time period than that for which they are loaning funds. While most customer deposits can be withdrawn instantly, financial institutions will have a variety of lending commitments, some of which span many years. Hence, the Bank of England acts as a 'liquidity backstop' for the banking system. It attempts to ensure that there is always an adequate supply of liquidity to meet the legitimate demands of depositors in banks.

Banks' reserve balances provide them with some liquidity insurance. However, the Bank of England needs other means by which to provide both individual banks and the banking system with sufficient liquidity. The financial crisis, for instance, saw incredible pressure on the aggregate liquidity of financial system. The result is that the UK has three principal insurance facilities:

Index long-term repos (ILTRs). Each month the Bank of England provides MFIs with reserves for a six-month period secured against collateral and indexed against the Bank Rate. Financial institutions can borrow reserves against different levels of collateral. These levels reflect the quality and liquidity of the collateral. The reserves are distributed through an auction where financial institutions indicate, for their particular level of collateral, the number of basis points over the Bank Rate (the 'spread') they are prepared to pay. The resulting equilibrium interest rate, paid by all those borrowing, is that which balances the demand from MFIs with the supply of reserves made available. The Bank of England may subsequently provide a greater quantity of reserves if, from the bids, it observes a greater demand for it to provide liquidity insurance.

Discount window facility (DWF). This on-demand facility allows financial institutions to borrow government bonds (gilts) for 30 days against different classes of (less liquid) collateral. They pay a fee to do so. The size of the fee is determined by both the type and quantity of collateral being traded. The gilts can then be used in repo operations as a means of securing liquidity. Financial institutions can look to roll over the gilts obtained from the DWF beyond the normal 30 days if they are still short of liquidity.

Contingent term repo facility (CTRP). This is a facility which the Bank of England can activate in exceptional circumstances. As with the ILTRs, financial institutions can obtain liquidity secured against different levels of collateral through an auction. However, the terms, including the maturity of the funds, are intended to be more flexible.

It oversees the activities of banks and other financial institutions

The Bank of England requires all recognised banks to maintain adequate liquidity: this is called **prudential control**.

In May 1997, the Bank of England ceased to be responsible for the detailed supervision of banks' activities. This responsibility passed to the Financial Services Authority (FSA). But the financial crisis of the late 2000s raised concerns about whether the FSA, the Bank of England and HM Treasury were sufficiently watchful of banks' liquidity and the risks of liquidity shortage. Some commentators argued that a much tighter form of prudential control should have been imposed.

The early 2010s saw the implementation of a new regulatory framework with an enhanced role for the Bank of England.

First, the Bank's *Financial Policy Committee (FPC)* was made responsible for **macro-prudential regulation**: i.e. regulation which takes a broader view of the financial system. It considers, for instance, the resilience of the financial system to possible shocks and its capacity to create macroeconomic instability through excessive credit creation.

Second, the prudential regulation of individual firms was transferred from the FSA to the *Prudential Regulation Authority (PRA)*, a subsidiary of the Bank of England. Third, the *Financial Conduct Authority (FCA)* took responsibility for consumer protection and the regulation of markets for financial services. The FCA is an independent body accountable to HM Treasury. The FSA was wound up.

It operates the government's exchange rate policy

The Bank of England manages the country's gold and foreign currency reserves. This is done through the **exchange equalisation account**. By buying and selling foreign currencies on the foreign exchange market, the Bank of England can affect the exchange rate (see Chapter 27).

> ### Definitions
>
> **Prudential control** The insistence by the Bank of England that banks maintain adequate liquidity.
>
> **Macro-prudential regulation** Regulation of the financial system as a whole to ensure that it is resilient to shocks.
>
> **Exchange equalisation account** The gold and foreign exchange reserves account in the Bank of England.

The role of the money markets

Money markets enable participants, such as banks, to lend to and borrow from each other. The financial instruments traded are short-term ones. As we have seen, central banks use money markets to exercise control over interest rates. But they are very important too in widening the lending and borrowing opportunities for financial institutions.

We take the case of the London money market, which is normally divided into the 'discount and repo' markets and the 'parallel' or 'complementary' markets.

The discount and repo markets

The discount market. The discount market is the market for commercial or government bills. The discount market is also known as the traditional market because it was the market in which many central banks traditionally used to supply central bank money to financial institutions. For instance, if the Bank of England wanted to increase liquidity in the banking system it could purchase from the banks Treasury bills which had yet to reach maturity. This process is known as *rediscounting*. The Bank of England would pay a price below the face value, thus effectively charging interest to the banks. The price could be set so that the 'rediscount rate' reflected the interest rate set by the MPC (see section 30.2).

The repo market. The emergence of the repo market is a more recent development dating in the UK back to the 1990s. As we have just noted, repos have become an important potential source of wholesale funding for financial institutions. They are an important means by which central banks can affect the liquidity of the financial system both to implement monetary policy and to ensure financial stability.

By entering into a repo agreement the Bank of England buys gilts from the banks (thereby supplying them with money) on the condition that the banks buy the gilts back at a fixed price and on a fixed date. The repurchase price will be above the sale price. The difference is the equivalent of the interest that the banks are being charged for having what amounts to a loan from the Bank of England. The repurchase price (and hence the 'repo rate') is set by the Bank of England to reflect the rate chosen by the MPC.

The financial crisis caused the Bank to modify its repo operations to manage liquidity for both purposes of monetary policy and increasingly to ensure financial stability. These changes included a widening of the securities eligible as collateral for loans, a suspension of short-term repo operations and an increased focus on longer-term repo operations.

So central banks, like the Bank of England, are prepared to provide central bank money through the creation of reserves. The central bank is thus the ultimate guarantor of sufficient liquidity in the monetary system and is known as **lender of last resort**.

As a means of supplying liquidity to troubled banks in various eurozone countries, the ECB in late 2011 and into 2012 issued a large amount of three-year repo loans (just over €1 trillion). These long-term repo operations, or LTROs, were seen as vital for staving off a liquidity crisis and potential collapse of certain banks struggling with bad debts.

The parallel money markets

Like repo markets, complementary or parallel money markets have grown rapidly in recent years. In part, this reflects the opening up of markets to international dealing, the deregulation of banking and money market dealing, and the desire of banks to keep funds in a form that can be readily switched from one form of deposit to another, or from one currency to another.

Examples of parallel markets include the markets for certificates of deposit (CDs), foreign currencies markets (dealings in foreign currencies deposited short term in the country) and the inter-bank market. Of these, the *inter-bank market* is particularly important. It has traditionally been a major source of liquidity.

The inter-bank market involves wholesale loans from one bank to another from one day to up to several months. Inter-bank lending has traditionally been a major source of liquidity. Bank with surplus liquidity lend to other banks, which then use this as the basis for loans to individuals and companies. Inter-bank interest rates (known as LIBOR) tend to be higher than those in the discount and repo markets and sensitive to the aggregate level of liquidity in the financial system.

As Figure 28.3 shows, during the financial crisis of 2008 inter-bank lending rates rose significantly above the Bank Rate. At the same time lending virtually ceased as banks became worried that the bank they were lending to might default.

Definitions

Rediscounting bills of exchange Buying bills before they reach maturity.

Lender of last resort The role of the Bank of England as the guarantor of sufficient liquidity in the monetary system.

Figure 28.3 One-month LIBOR and Bank Rate

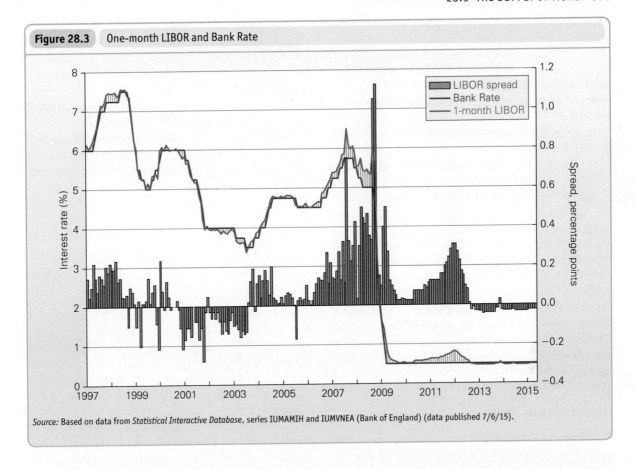

Source: Based on data from *Statistical Interactive Database*, series IUMAMIH and IUMVNEA (Bank of England) (data published 7/6/15).

28.3 THE SUPPLY OF MONEY

If money supply is to be monitored and possibly controlled, it is obviously necessary to measure it. But what should be included in the measure? Here we need to distinguish between the *monetary base* and *broad money*.

The ***monetary base*** (or 'high-powered money' or 'narrow money') consists of cash (notes and coin) in circulation outside the central bank.[1] In 1970, the stock of notes and coins in circulation in the UK was around £4 billion, equivalent to 7 per cent of annual GDP. By 2015 this had grown to over £70 billion, but equivalent to only about 4 per cent of annual GDP.

The monetary base gives us a very poor indication of the effective money supply, however, since it excludes the most important source of liquidity for spending: namely, bank

deposits. The problem is which deposits to include. We need to answer three questions:

- Should we include just sight deposits, or time deposits as well?
- Should we include just retail deposits, or wholesale deposits as well?
- Should we include just bank deposits, or building society (savings institution) deposits as well?

In the past there has been a whole range of measures, each including different combinations of these accounts. However, financial deregulation, the abolition of foreign exchange controls and the development of computer technology have led to huge changes in the financial sector throughout the world. This has led to a blurring of the

---

[1] Before 2006, there used to be a measure of narrow money called M0. This included cash in circulation outside the Bank of England and banks' non-interest-bearing 'operational balances' in the Bank of England, with these balances accounting for a tiny proportion of the whole. Since 2006, the Bank of England has allowed banks to hold interest-bearing reserve accounts, which are much larger than the former operational balances. The Bank of England thus decided to discontinue M0 as a measure and focus on cash in circulation as its measure of the monetary base.

> **Definition**
>
> **Monetary base** Notes and coin outside the central bank.

distinctions between different types of account. It has also made it very easy to switch deposits from one type of account to another. For these reasons, the most usual measure that countries use for money supply is **broad money**, which in most cases includes both time and sight deposits, retail and wholesale deposits, and bank and building society deposits.

In the UK this measure of broad money is known as M4. In most other European countries and the USA it is known as M3. There are, however, minor differences between countries in what is included.

In 1970, the stock of M4 in the UK was around £26 billion, equivalent to 50 per cent of annual GDP. By 2015 this had grown to £2.1 trillion, equivalent to about 120 per cent of annual GDP.

As we have seen, bank deposits of one form or another constitute by far the largest component of (broad) money supply. To understand how money supply expands and contracts, and how it can be controlled, it is thus necessary to understand what determines the size of bank deposits. Banks can themselves expand the amount of bank deposits, and hence the money supply, by a process known as 'credit creation'.

The creation of credit

To illustrate this process in its simplest form, assume that banks have just one type of liability – deposits – and two types of asset – balances with the central bank (to achieve liquidity) and advances to customers (to earn profit).

Banks want to achieve profitability while maintaining sufficient liquidity. Assume that they believe that sufficient liquidity will be achieved if 10 per cent of their assets are held as balances with the central bank. The remaining 90 per cent will then be in advances to customers. In other words, the banks operate a 10 per cent liquidity ratio.

Assume initially that the combined balance sheet of the banks is as shown in Table 28.2. Total deposits are £100 billion, of which £10 billion (10 per cent) are kept in balances with the central bank. The remaining £90 billion (90 per cent) are lent to customers.

 Now assume that the government spends more money – £10 billion, say, on roads or education. It pays for this with cheques drawn on its account with the central bank. The people receiving the cheques deposit them in their

Table 28.2	Banks' original balance sheet		
Liabilities	**£bn**	**Assets**	**£bn**
Deposits	100	Balances with the central bank	10
		Advances	90
Total	100	Total	100

banks. Banks return these cheques to the central bank and their balances correspondingly increase by £10 billion. The combined banks' balance sheet now is shown in Table 28.3.

But this is not the end of the story. Banks now have surplus liquidity. With their balances in the central bank having increased to £20 billion, they now have a liquidity ratio of 20/110, or 18.2 per cent. If they are to return to a 10 per cent liquidity ratio, they need only retain £11 billion as balances at the central bank (£11 billion/£110 billion = 10 per cent). The remaining £9 billion they can lend to customers.

Assume now that customers spend this £9 billion in shops and the shopkeepers deposit the cheques in their bank accounts. When the cheques are cleared, the balances in the central bank of the customers' banks will duly be debited by £9 billion, but the balances in the central bank of the shopkeepers' banks will be credited by £9 billion: leaving *overall balances in the central bank unaltered*. There is still a surplus of £9 billion over what is required to maintain the 10 per cent liquidity ratio. The new deposits of £9 billion in the shopkeepers' banks, backed by balances in the central bank, can thus be used as the basis for *further* loans. Ten per cent (i.e. £0.9 billion) must be kept back in the central bank, but the remaining 90 per cent (i.e. £8.1 billion) can be lent out again.

When the money is spent and the cheques are cleared, this £8.1 billion will still remain as surplus balances in the central bank and can therefore be used as the basis for yet more loans. Again, 10 per cent must be retained and the remaining 90 per cent can be lent out. This process goes on and on until eventually the position is as shown in Table 28.4.

The initial increase in balances with the central bank of £10 billion has allowed banks to create new advances (and hence deposits) of £90 billion, making a total increase in money supply of £100 billion.

Table 28.3	The initial effect of an additional deposit of £10 billion		
Liabilities	**£bn**	**Assets**	**£bn**
Deposits (old)	100	Balances with the central bank (old)	10
Deposits (new)	10	Balances with the central bank (new)	10
		Advances	90
Total	110	Total	110

Definitions

Broad money Cash in circulation plus retail and wholesale bank and building society deposits.

Table 28.4	The full effect of an additional deposit of £10 billion			
Liabilities		**£bn**	**Assets**	**£bn**
Deposits (old)		100	Balances with the central bank (old)	10
Deposits (new: initial)		10	Balances with the central bank (new)	10
(new: subsequent)		90	Advances (old)	90
			Advances (new)	90
Total		200	Total	200

This effect is known as the **bank (or bank deposits) multiplier**. In this simple example with a liquidity ratio of $1/_{10}$ (i.e. 10 per cent), the bank deposits multiplier is 10. An initial increase in deposits of £10 billion allowed total deposits to rise by £100 billion. In this simple world, therefore, the deposits multiplier is the inverse of the liquidity ratio (L).

bank deposits multiplier $= 1/L$

Pause for thought

If banks choose to operate with a 5 per cent liquidity ratio and receive an extra £100 million of cash deposits: (a) What is the size of the deposits multiplier? (b) How much will total deposits have expanded after the multiplier has worked through? (c) How much will total credit have expanded?

The creation of credit: the real world

In practice, the creation of credit is not as simple as this. There are three major complications.

Banks' liquidity ratio may vary

Banks may choose a different liquidity ratio. At certain times, banks may decide that it is prudent to hold a bigger proportion of liquid assets. For example, if banks are worried about increased risks of default on loans, they may choose to hold a higher liquidity ratio to ensure that they have enough to meet customers' needs. This was the case in the late 2000s when many banks became less willing to lend to other banks for fear of the other banks' assets containing subprime debt. Banks, as a result, hoarded cash and became more cautious about granting loans.

On the other hand, there may be an upsurge in consumer demand for credit. Banks may be very keen to grant additional loans and thus make more profits, even though they have acquired no additional assets. They may simply go ahead and expand credit, and accept a lower liquidity ratio.

Customers may not want to take up the credit on offer. Banks may wish to make additional loans, but customers may not

want to borrow. There may be insufficient demand. But will the banks not then lower their interest rates, thus encouraging people to borrow? Possibly, but if they lower the rate they charge to borrowers, they must also lower the rate they pay to depositors. But then depositors may switch to other institutions such as building societies.

Banks may not operate a simple liquidity ratio

The fact that banks hold a number of fairly liquid assets, such as money at call, bills of exchange and certificates of deposit, makes it difficult to identify a simple liquidity ratio. If the banks use extra cash to buy such liquid assets, can they then use these assets as the basis for creating credit? It is largely up to banks' judgements on their overall liquidity position. In practice, therefore, the size of the bank deposits multiplier will vary and is thus difficult to predict in advance.

Some of the extra cash may be withdrawn by the public

If extra cash comes into the banking system, and as a result extra deposits are created, part of them may be held by households and non-bank firms (known in this context as the **non-bank private sector**) as cash *outside* the banks. In other words, some of the extra cash leaks out of the banking system. This will result in an overall multiplier effect that is smaller than the full bank deposits multiplier. The overall multiplier is known as the **money multiplier**. It is defined as the change in total money supply expressed as a proportion of the change in the monetary base that caused it: $\Delta M_s/\Delta M_b$ (where M_s is total broad money supply and M_b is the monetary base).

The broad money multiplier in the UK

In the UK, the principal money multiplier measure is the broad money multiplier. This is given by $\Delta M4/\Delta M_b$, where M_b in this case is defined as cash in circulation with the public and in banks' interest-bearing deposits (reserve accounts) at the Bank of England.

Another indicator of the broad money multiplier is simply the ratio of the *level of* (as opposed to the *change in*) M4 relative to the cash in circulation with the public and banks' reserve accounts at the central bank. This 'levels'

Definitions

Bank (or bank deposits) multiplier The number of times greater the expansion of bank deposits is than the additional liquidity in banks that caused it: $1/L$ (the inverse of the liquidity ratio).

Non-bank private sector Household and non-bank firms. The category thus excludes the government and banks.

Money multiplier The number of times greater the expansion of money supply (M_s) is than the expansion of the monetary base (M_b) that caused it: $\Delta M_s/\Delta M_b$.

Figure 28.4 UK broad money multiplier

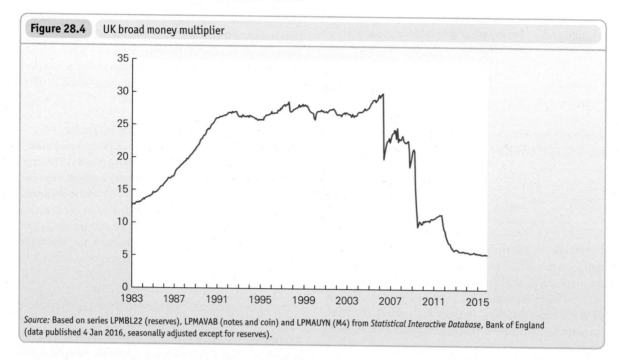

Source: Based on series LPMBL22 (reserves), LPMAVAB (notes and coin) and LPMAUYN (M4) from *Statistical Interactive Database*, Bank of England (data published 4 Jan 2016, seasonally adjusted except for reserves).

relationship is shown in Figure 28.4 and helps us to analyse the longer-term relationship between the stocks of broad money and the monetary base. From it, we can see how the broad money multiplier grew rapidly during the 1980s and into the beginning of the 1990s. From the early 1990s to the mid-2000s, the level of M4 relative to the monetary base fluctuated in a narrow range.

From May 2006 the Bank of England began remunerating banks' reserve accounts at the official Bank Rate. This encouraged banks to increase their reserve accounts at the Bank of England and led to a sharp fall in the broad money multiplier. It then declined further from 2009. The significant decline in 2009 and again in 2011/12 coincided with the Bank of England's programme of asset purchases (quantitative easing) which led to a large increase in banks' reserves at the Bank of England. The point is that the increase in the monetary base did not lead to the same percentage increase in broad money, as banks were more cautious about lending and chose to keep higher reserves. The policy of quantitative easing is discussed more in Chapter 30.

In the next section we look at factors which help explain movements in the money multiplier and changes in the money supply.

What causes money supply to rise?

Money supply can rise for a number of reasons. We examine each below.

Central bank action

The central bank may decide that the stock of money is too low and that this is keeping up interest rates and holding back spending in the economy. In such circumstances, it may choose to create additional money.

As we saw above (page 530), this was the case following the 2007/8 financial crisis when the Bank of England and the US Federal Reserve Bank embarked on programmes of *quantitative easing*. This involved the central bank creating electronic (narrow) money and using it to purchase assets, mainly government bonds. When the recipients of the money (mainly non-bank financial institutions) deposited it in banks, the banks could lend it to businesses and consumers for purposes of spending and, through the bank deposits multiplier, broad money supply would increase.

As we can see from Figure 28.5, however, this was not enough to prevent UK broad money supply falling for much of the period from 2010 to 2014.

Banks choose to hold a lower liquidity ratio

If banks collectively choose to hold a lower liquidity ratio, they will have surplus liquidity. The banks have tended to choose a lower liquidity ratio over time because of the increasing use of direct debits and debit-card and credit-card transactions.

Surplus liquidity can be used to expand advances, which will lead to a multiplied rise in broad money supply (e.g. M4).

An important trend in recent years has been the growth in *inter-bank lending*. Table 28.1 (see page 521) showed that short-term loans to other banks (including overseas banks) is the largest element in banks' liquid assets. These assets may be used by a bank as the basis for expanding loans and thereby starting a chain of credit creation. But although these assets are liquid to an *individual bank*, they do not add to the liquidity of the banking system *as a whole*. By using

Figure 28.5 Annual rate of growth of M4

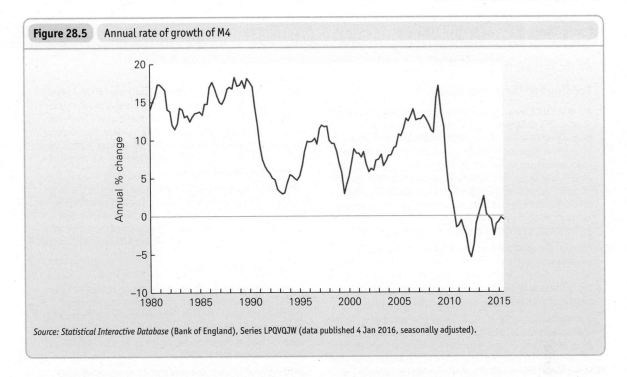

Source: Statistical Interactive Database (Bank of England), Series LPQVQJW (data published 4 Jan 2016, seasonally adjusted).

them for credit creation, the banking system is operating with a lower *overall* liquidity ratio.

This was a major element in the banking crisis of 2008. By operating with a collectively low liquidity ratio, banks were vulnerable to people defaulting on debt, such as mortgages. The problem was compounded by the holding of sub-prime debt in the form of securitised assets. Realising the vulnerability of other banks, banks became increasingly unwilling to lend to each other. The resulting decline in interbank lending reduced the amount of credit created and so depressed the money supply (see Figure 28.5). In Box 28.4 we discuss in more detail the effect of credit cycles on the UK money supply.

Pause for thought

What effects do debit cards and cash machines (ATMs) have on (a) banks' prudent liquidity ratios; (b) the size of the bank deposits multiplier?

The non-bank private sector chooses to hold less cash

Households and non-bank firms may choose to hold less cash. Again, the reason may be a greater use of cards, direct debits, etc. This means that a greater proportion of the cash base will be held as deposits in banks rather than in people's wallets, purses or safes outside banks. The extra cash deposits allow banks to create more credit.

The above two reasons for an expansion of broad money supply (M4) are because more credit is being created for a given monetary base. As Figure 28.4 showed, the money

multiplier rose substantially in the late 1980s and early 1990s and then gradually up to 2006. The other two reasons for an expansion of money supply are reasons why the monetary base itself might expand.

An inflow of funds from abroad

When sterling is used to pay for UK exports and is deposited in UK banks by the exporters, credit can be created on the basis of it. This leads to a *multiplied* increase in money supply.

The money supply will also expand if depositors of sterling in banks overseas then switch these deposits to banks in the UK. This is a direct increase in the money supply. In an open economy like the UK, movements of sterling and other currencies into and out of the country can be very large. This can lead to large fluctuations in the money supply.

A public-sector deficit

A public-sector deficit is the difference between public-sector expenditure and public-sector receipts. To meet this deficit, the government has to borrow money by selling interest-bearing securities (Treasury bills and gilts). In general, the bigger the public sector's deficit, the greater will be the growth in the money supply. Just how the money supply will be affected, however, depends on who buys the securities.

Consider first the case where government securities are purchased by the non-bank private sector (i.e. to the general public and non-bank firms). The money supply will remain unchanged. When people or firms buy the bonds or bills, they will draw money from their banks. When the government spends the money, it will be redeposited in

BOX 28.4 CREDIT, MONEY AND MINSKY'S FINANCIAL INSTABILITY HYPOTHESIS

Are credit cycles inevitable?

Lending and the money supply

M4 is the UK's main broad aggregate measure of the money supply. It is defined as the UK non-bank private sector's holdings of notes and coins, sterling deposits and other short-term financial instruments issued by banks and building societies (up to five years). Its growth is highly variable (see Figure 28.5). This mirrors the variability in the growth in credit. As we saw (on pages 534–6), when banks grant credit, further deposits are created when the non-bank private sector looks to spend this credit. This can result in more credit being extended and more deposits being created.

Chart (a) shows annual flows of net lending to the non-bank private sector: the household sector, non-financial corporations and other financial corporations (OFCs). Net lending is additional credit and is calculated by subtracting repayments from the total amount of gross lending by banks and building societies.

The chart captures the marked growth in credit during the late 1980s, particularly to households, which contributed to the stock of M4 (broad money) increasing at an average rate of 16 per cent year over the second half of the decade. A marked slowdown in the growth of credit followed the recession of the early 1990s. Private non-financial corporations reduced their holdings of bank debt during this period. Unsurprisingly M4 growth slowed too, with the annual growth rate falling to only a little over 2 per cent during 1993.

From the mid-1990s up to the late 2000s we observe a period of prolonged and robust credit growth. Over the period 2006 to 2008 yearly net lending to the non-bank private sector averaged £292 billion. Again this helped to fuel the growth in M4. The average annual rate of growth in M4 over 2006 and 2007 was 13 per cent.

But the story was to change dramatically from 2008 onwards as the 'credit crunch' began to bite. We began to see extraordinarily low levels of net lending to households – levels not seen since the late 1970s. Meanwhile non-financial corporations and OFCs began reducing their existing bank debts by more than they were acquiring new debts: i.e. net lending to these two sectors was negative.

While the repayment of debt by OFCs was aided by the Bank of England's programme of asset purchases (quantitative easing), the late 2000s marked a new phase in the credit cycle. But how inevitable was this slump and the exuberance in lending that preceded it? How inevitable are credit cycles?

Minsky's credit cycles

Hyman Minsky (1919–96) was an American economist known for his work on understanding the relationship between the financial system and the macroeconomy. His *financial instability hypothesis* proposes that financial cycles are an inherent part of the economic cycle and so are a key cause of the fluctuations in real GDP.

Psychological influences are important in explaining the financial instability hypothesis. The extension of credit by MFIs can be seen to go through different phases. During these phases credit criteria and the ability of borrowers to afford their debts vary. Credit flows are dependent on the state of the economy, with the accumulation of debt by the non-bank private sector being pro-cyclical. Consequently, credit flows help to amplify the magnitude of the cycle.

Minsky argued that credit flows will tend to increase in a period of sustained growth. This causes banks and investors to develop a heightened euphoria and confidence in the

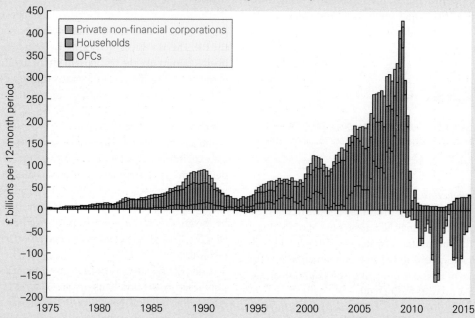

(a) Annual flows of net lending to non-bank private sector

Note: Based on sum of latest four quarters

Source: *Statistical Interactive Database* (Bank of England), Series LPQVWNL, LPQVWNQ and LPQVWNV (data published 4 Jan 2016, seasonally adjusted).

economy and in the returns of assets. As a result, economic agents begin to take on bigger debts to acquire assets. These debts increasingly stretch their financial well-being. A point is reached, perhaps triggered by an economic shock or a tightening of economic policy, when the euphoria stops and confidence is replaced with pessimism. This is sometimes referred to as a 'Minsky moment'.

Some argue that a Minsky moment may have taken place in 2008/9. If we look at chart (b) we can see that the private non-bank sector had become incredibly indebted to MFIs by this point. By the end of March 2009 its stock of MFI debt had peaked at £2.81 trillion, the equivalent to almost 290 per cent of annual GDP.

The consequence of a Minsky moment is that lenders reduce their lending while, more generally, economic agents look to increase their net worth (i.e. reduce debts or increase savings) to ensure their financial well-being. The data in the two charts appear consistent with this behaviour. These individual actions cause a decline in aggregate spending and in national income. In other words, we observe a balance-sheet economic slowdown or, as in the late 2000s, a balance-sheet recession (see section 26.5). Furthermore, the large-scale selling of assets to improve financial well-being causes the value of assets to fall. This paradoxical reduction of net worth is known as the 'paradox of debt'.

Minsky believed that credit cycles are an inherent feature of a free-market economy. Hence, the authorities will need to take action to moderate or thwart credit cycles so as to reduce economic instability. The significance given to macro-prudential regulation by policy makers in the response to the financial crisis can be seen as an example of a 'thwarting mechanism'

to help mitigate the dangers posed to the economy by credit cycles.

While Minsky argued that the ingredients for economic volatility arising from financial instability are ever-present, some argue that other factors are needed for this instability to develop into a financial crisis. These factors may be part of a longer cycle of events. We could view the processes of financial deregulation and innovation that have characterised the past two to three decades as part of this longer cycle.

One interpretation of the financial crisis of the late 2000s is that it was the result of the interaction of the normal Minsky cycle, i.e. short-run variations in the accumulation of credit, with a longer cycle of events or a 'Minsky super-cycle'.

 What demand-side and supply-side factors influence the flows of net lending by financial institutions to the non-bank private sector?

Definition

Financial instability hypothesis During periods of economic growth, economic agents (firms and individuals) tend to borrow more and MFIs are more willing to lend. This fuels the boom. In a period of recession, economic agents tend to cut spending in order to reduce debts and MFIs are less willing to lend. This deepens the recession. Behaviour in financial markets thus tends to amplify the business cycle.

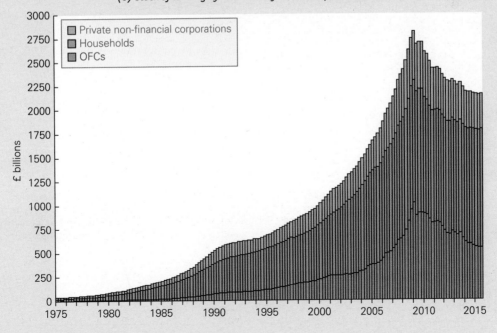

(b) Stock of lending by MFIs held by non-bank private sector

Note: Based on sum of latest four quarters
Source: *Statistical Interactive Database* (Bank of England), Series LPQBC44, LPQBC56 and LPQBC57 (data published 4 Jan 2016, seasonally adjusted).

banks. There is no increase in money supply. It is just a case of existing money changing hands.

This is not the case, however, when the securities are purchased by the banking sector, including the central bank. Consider the purchase of Treasury bills by commercial banks: there will be a multiplied expansion of the money supply. The reason is that, although banks' balances at the central bank will go down when the banks purchase the bills, they will go up again when the government spends the money. In addition, the banks will now have additional liquid assets (bills), which can be used as the basis for credit creation.

The government could attempt to minimise the boost to money supply by financing the deficit through the sale of gilts, since, even if these were partly purchased by the banks, they could not be used as the basis for credit creation.

> ### Pause for thought
>
> *Identify the various factors that could cause a fall in the money supply.*

The relationship between money supply and the rate of interest

Simple monetary theory often assumes that the supply of money is totally independent of interest rates: that money supply is *exogenous*. This is illustrated in Figure 28.6(a). The supply of money is assumed to be determined by the government or central bank ('the authorities'): what the authorities choose it to be, or what they allow it to be by their choice of the level and method of financing public-sector borrowing.

In practice, money supply is *endogenous*, with higher interest rates leading to increases in the supply of money. This is illustrated in Figure 28.6(b). The argument is that the supply of money is responding to the demand for money. If people start borrowing more money, the resulting shortage of money in the banks will drive up interest rates. But if banks have surplus liquidity or are prepared to operate with a lower liquidity ratio, they will create extra credit in response to the increased demand and higher interest rates: money supply has expanded. If banks find themselves short of liquidity, they can always borrow from the central bank through repos.

Some economists go further still. They argue that money supply is not only endogenous, but also the 'curve' is effectively horizontal; money supply expands passively to match the demand for money. It is likely, however, that the shape will vary with the confidence of banks. In periods of optimism banks may be willing to expand credit to meet the demand from customers. In periods of pessimism, such as that following the financial crisis, banks may be unwilling to grant credit when customers seek it.

> ### Definitions
>
> **Exogenous money supply** Money supply that does not depend on the demand for money but is set by the authorities (i.e. the central bank or the government).
>
> **Endogenous money supply** Money supply that is determined (at least in part) by the demand for money.

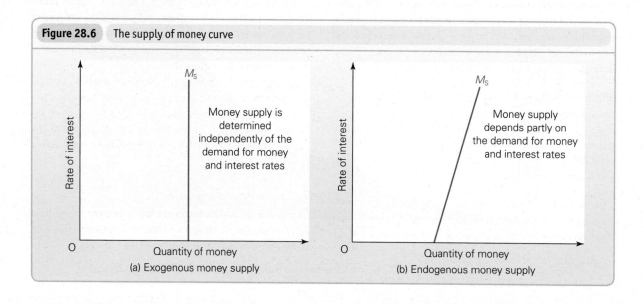

Figure 28.6 The supply of money curve

(a) Exogenous money supply — Money supply is determined independently of the demand for money and interest rates

(b) Endogenous money supply — Money supply depends partly on the demand for money and interest rates

28.4 THE DEMAND FOR MONEY

The demand for money refers to the desire to *hold* money: to keep your wealth in the form of money, rather than spending it on goods and services or using it to purchase financial assets such as bonds or shares. It is usual to distinguish three reasons why people want to hold their assets in the form of money.

The transactions motive. Since money is a medium of exchange, it is required for conducting transactions. But since people only receive money at intervals (e.g. weekly or monthly) and not continuously, they require to hold balances of money in cash or in current accounts.

The precautionary motive. Unforeseen circumstances can arise, such as a car breakdown. Thus individuals often hold some additional money as a precaution. Firms too keep precautionary balances. This may be because of uncertainties about the timing of their receipts and payments. If a large customer is late in making a payment, a firm may be unable to pay its suppliers unless it has spare liquidity. But firms may also hold precautionary balances because of uncertainty surrounding the economic environment in which they operate.

The assets or speculative motive. Money is not just a medium of exchange, it is also a means of storing wealth (see page 518). Keeping some or all of your wealth as money in a bank account has the advantage of carrying no risk. It earns a relatively small, but safe rate of return. Some assets, such as company shares or bonds, may earn you more on average, but there is a chance that their price will fall. In other words, they are risky.

What determines the size of the demand for money?

What would cause the demand for money to rise? We now turn to examine the various determinants of the size of the demand for money (M_D). In particular we will look at the role of the rate of interest. First, however, let us identify the other determinants of the demand for money.

Money national income. The more money people earn, the greater will be their expenditure and hence the greater the transactions demand for money. A rise in money ('nominal') incomes in a country can be caused either by a rise in real GDP (i.e. real output) or by a rise in prices, or by some combination of the two.

The frequency with which people are paid. The less frequently people are paid, the greater the level of money balances that will be required to tide them over until the next payment.

Financial innovations. The increased use of credit cards, debit cards and cash machines, plus the advent of interest-paying current accounts, have resulted in changes in the demand for money. The use of credit cards reduces both the transactions and precautionary demands. Paying once a month for goods requires less money on average than paying separately for each item purchased. Moreover, the possession of a credit card reduces or even eliminates the need to hold precautionary balances for many people. On the other hand, the increased availability of cash machines, the convenience of debit cards and the ability to earn interest on current accounts have all encouraged people to hold more money in bank accounts. The net effect has been an increase in the demand for money.

Speculation about future returns on assets. The assets motive for holding money depends on people's expectations. If they believe that share prices are about to fall on the stock market, they will sell shares and hold larger balances of money in the meantime. The assets demand, therefore, can be quite high when the price of securities is considered certain to fall. Some clever (or lucky) individuals anticipated the 2007–8 stock market decline. They sold shares and 'went liquid'.

Generally, the more risky such alternatives to money become, the more will people want to hold their assets as money balances in a bank or building society.

People also speculate about changes in the exchange rate. If businesses believe that the exchange rate is about to appreciate (rise), they will hold greater balances of domestic currency in the meantime, hoping to buy foreign currencies with them when the rate has risen (since they will then get more foreign currency for their money).

The rate of interest. In terms of the operation of money markets, this is the most important determinant. It is related to the opportunity cost of holding money. The opportunity cost is the interest forgone by not holding higher interest-bearing assets, such as shares, bills or bonds. With most bank accounts today paying interest, this opportunity cost is less than in the past and thus the demand for money for assets purposes has increased.

But what is the relationship between money demand and the rate of interest? Generally, if rates of interest rise, they will rise more on shares, bills and bonds than on bank accounts. The demand for money will thus fall. The demand for money is thus *inversely* related to the rate of interest.

The demand-for-money curve

The demand-for-money curve with respect to interest rates is shown in Figure 28.7. It is downward sloping, showing that lower interest rates will encourage people to hold additional money balances (mainly for speculative purposes).

Pause for thought

Which way is the demand-for-money curve likely to shift in each of the following cases? (a) Prices rise, but real incomes stay the same. (b) Interest rates abroad rise relative to domestic interest rates. (c) People anticipate that share prices are likely to fall in the near future.

A change in interest rates is shown by a movement along the demand-for-money curve. A change in any other determinant of the demand for money (such as national income or expectations about exchange rate movements) will cause the whole curve to shift: a rightward shift represents an increase in demand; a leftward shift represents a decrease.

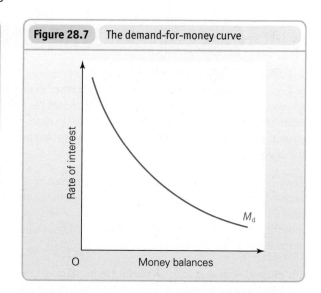

Figure 28.7 The demand-for-money curve

28.5 EQUILIBRIUM

Equilibrium in the money market

Equilibrium in the money market occurs when the demand for money (M_d) is equal to the supply of money (M_s). This equilibrium is achieved through changes in the rate of interest.

In Figure 28.8, assume that the demand for and supply of money are given by M_s and M_d. The equilibrium rate of interest is r_e and the equilibrium quantity of money is M_e. But why?

If the rate of interest were above r_e, people would have money balances surplus to their needs. They would use these to buy shares, bonds and other assets. This would drive up the price of these assets. But the price of assets is inversely related to interest rates. The higher the price of an asset (such as a government bond), the less will any given interest payment be as a percentage of its price (e.g. £10 as a percentage of £100 is 10 per cent, but as a percentage of £200 is only 5 per cent). Thus a higher price of assets will correspond to lower interest rates.

As the rate of interest fell, so there would be a contraction of the money supply (a movement down along the

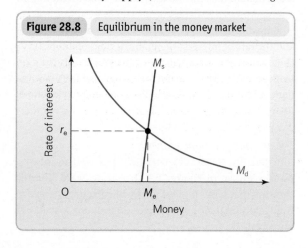

Figure 28.8 Equilibrium in the money market

M_s curve) and an increase in the demand for money balances, especially speculative balances (a movement down along the M_d curve). The interest rate would go on falling until it reached r_e. Equilibrium would then be achieved.

Similarly, if the rate of interest were below r_e, people would have insufficient money balances. They would sell securities, thus lowering their prices and raising the rate of interest until it reached r_e.

A shift in either the M_s or the M_d curve will lead to a new equilibrium quantity of money and rate of interest at the new intersection of the curves. For example, a rise in the supply of money will cause the rate of interest to fall, whereas a rise in the demand for money will cause the rate of interest to rise.

In practice, there is no one single interest rate. Rather, equilibrium in the money markets will be where demand and supply of the various financial instruments separately balance. Generally, however, different interest rates tend to move roughly together as the overall demand for money and other liquid assets (or their supply) changes. Table 28.5 gives some examples of interest rates on various financial instruments. It shows how the various rates of interest move together.

In many countries today interest rates have become a key tool of monetary policy. The Bank of England conducts open-market operations to affect the general structure of interest rates, as we saw in section 28.2. By doing so, it supplies an aggregate level of reserves such that, given the demand for money, it is able to keep inter-bank rates close to its chosen policy rate ('Bank Rate'). This then affects the general structure of the economy's interest rates. We can see how the significant reductions to the policy rate from late 2008 were typically mirrored by falls in other interest rates.

Equilibrium in the foreign exchange market

Changes in the money supply will not only affect interest rates, they will also have an effect on exchange rates.

Table 28.5	Selected rates of interest: January 1997 to November 2015 (monthly averages)						
Financial instrument	**Period of loan**	**Rate of interest, % per annum**					
		Average Jan 1997–Sept 2008	Average Oct 2008–Nov 2015	Jan 1997	Sept 2008	Jan 2009	Nov 2015
Call money	Overnight	5.15	0.56	5.90	4.89	1.34	0.46
Gilt repos	1 week	5.09	0.59	5.91	4.92	1.43	0.51
Inter-bank loans	1 month	5.25	0.77	6.11	5.35	2.52	0.51
Treasury bills	3 months	5.04	0.49	6.01	4.74	0.89	0.48
British government securities[1]	20 years	4.81	3.66	7.74	4.64	4.48	2.69
Bank and building society mortgages[2]	Variable (25 years typical)	6.87	4.30	7.18	6.95	4.73	4.49
Credit card	–	17.72	17.08	22.14	16.12	16.09	17.94
Official Bank Rate (policy rate)	–	5.19	0.67	5.94	5.00	2.00	0.50

Source: *Statistical Interactive Database* (Bank of England), 4 March 2016

[1] Zero coupon, nominal yields (series IUMALNZC)
[2] Standard variable rate for UK MFIs (series IUMTLMV)

Assume, for example, that the money supply increases. This has three direct effects:

- *Part* of the excess balances will be used to purchase foreign assets. This will therefore lead to an increase in the supply of domestic currency coming on to the foreign exchange markets.
- The excess supply of money in the domestic money market will push down the rate of interest. This will reduce the return on domestic assets below that on foreign assets. This, like the first effect, will lead to an increased demand for foreign assets and thus an increased supply of domestic currency on the foreign exchange market.

 KI 13 p78

- Speculators will anticipate that the higher supply of domestic currency will cause the exchange rate to depreciate. They will therefore sell domestic currency and buy foreign currencies.

The effect of all three is to cause the exchange rate to depreciate.

The full effect of changes in the money supply

KI 10 p52

The effect of changes in the money supply on interest rates and exchange rates will in turn affect the level of activity in the economy. Assume that there is a rise in UK money supply. The sequence of events is as follows and is illustrated in Figure 28.9:

- A rise in money supply will lead to a fall in the rate of interest: this is necessary to restore equilibrium in the money market.
- The fall in the rate of interest will make borrowing cheaper. This will lead to a rise in investment and other

forms of borrowing. There may also be a fall in saving as saving now gives a poorer return. (See the top part of Figure 28.9.)

- The fall in the domestic rate of interest and the resulting outflow of money from the country, plus the increased demand for foreign assets resulting from the increased money supply, will cause the exchange rate to depreciate. The fall in the exchange rate will make UK exports cheaper and hence more will be sold. People in the UK will get less foreign currency for a pound. This will make imports more expensive and hence less will be purchased. (See the bottom part of Figure 28.9.)
- The rise in investment and exports will mean increased injections into the circular flow of income (see section 26.6), and the fall in imports will mean reduced withdrawals from it. The effect will be a rise in aggregate demand and a resulting rise in national income and output, and possibly a rise in prices too.

Just how much will aggregate demand, national income and prices change as a result of changes in the money supply? We will examine this in the next chapter. Then in Chapter 30 we will examine how the government can attempt to *control* the level of aggregate demand: both by changing interest rates and the money supply ('monetary policy') and by changing taxation and/or government expenditure ('fiscal policy').

Pause for thought

What determines the amount that real output rises as a result of a rise in the money supply?

Figure 28.9 Monetary transmission mechanisms

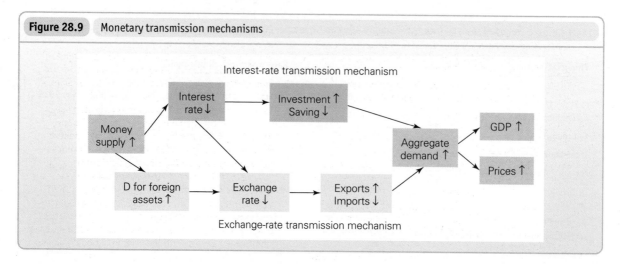

SUMMARY

1 Money's main function is as a medium of exchange. In addition it is a means of storing wealth, a means of evaluation and a means of establishing the value of future claims and payments.

2a Central to the financial system are the retail and wholesale arms of banks. Between them they provide the following important functions: giving expert advice, channelling capital to areas of highest return, maturity transformation, risk transformation and the transmission of payments. Some of these banks had to be rescued by the government in 2008 – they were too important to the health of the economy to allow them to fail.

2b Banks' liabilities include both sight and time deposits. They also include certificates of deposit and repos. Their assets include: notes and coin, balances with the central bank, market loans, bills of exchange (Treasury bills and commercial bills), reverse repos, advances to customers (the biggest item – including overdrafts, personal loans, credit card debt and mortgages) and investments (government bonds and inter-bank investments). In the years up to 2008 they had increasingly included securitised assets.

2c Banks aim to make profits, but they must also have a sufficient capital base and maintain sufficient liquidity. Liquid assets, however, tend to be relatively unprofitable and profitable assets tend to be relatively illiquid. Banks therefore need to keep a balance of profitability and liquidity in their range of assets.

2d The Bank of England is the UK's central bank. It issues notes; it acts as banker to the government, to banks and to various overseas central banks; it ensures sufficient liquidity for the financial sector; it operates the country's monetary and exchange rate policy.

2e The money market is the market in short-term deposits and loans. It consists of the discount and repo markets and the parallel money markets.

2f Through repos the Bank of England provides liquidity to the banks at the rate of interest chosen by the Monetary Policy Committee (Bank Rate). It is always prepared to lend in this way in order to ensure adequate liquidity in the economy. The financial crisis saw the Bank of England supply adapt its operations in the money market

and introduce new ways of providing liquidity insurance, including the Discount Window Facility (DWF) and longer-term repos.

2g The parallel money markets consist of various markets in short-term finance between various financial institutions.

3a Money supply can be defined in a number of different ways, depending on what items are included. A useful distinction is between narrow money and broad money. Narrow money includes just cash, and possibly banks' balances at the central bank. Broad money also includes deposits in banks and possibly various other short-term deposits in the money market. In the UK, M4 is the preferred measure of broad money. In the eurozone it is M3.

3b Bank deposits are a major proportion of broad money supply. The expansion of bank deposits is the major element in the expansion of the money supply.

3c Bank deposits expand through a process of credit creation. If banks' liquid assets increase, they can be used as a base for increasing loans. When the loans are redeposited in banks, they form the base for yet more loans, and thus a process of multiple credit expansion takes place. The ratio of the increase of deposits to an expansion of banks' liquidity base is called the 'bank multiplier'. It is the inverse of the liquidity ratio.

3d In practice it is difficult to predict the precise amount by which money supply will expand if there is an increase in cash. The reasons are that banks may choose to hold a different liquidity ratio; customers may not take up all the credit on offer; there may be no simple liquidity ratio given the range of near-money assets; and some of the extra cash may leak away into extra cash holdings by the public.

3e (Broad) money supply will rise if (a) banks choose to hold a lower liquidity ratio and thus create more credit for an existing amount of liquidity; (b) the non-bank private sector chooses to hold less cash; (c) the government runs a deficit and some of it is financed by borrowing from the banking sector; (d) there is an inflow of funds from abroad.

3f Simple monetary theory assumes that the supply of money is independent of interest rates. In practice, a rise

►

in interest rates will often lead to an increase in money supply. But conversely, if the government raises interest rates, the supply of money may fall in response to a lower demand for money.

4a The three motives for holding money are the transactions, precautionary and assets (or speculative) motives.

4b The demand for money will be higher, (a) the higher the level of money national income (i.e. the higher the level of real national income and the higher the price level), (b) the less frequently people are paid, (c) the greater the advantages of holding money in bank accounts, such as access to cash machines and the use of debit cards, (d) the more risky alternative assets become and the more likely they are to fall in value, and the more likely the exchange rate is to rise, and (e) the lower the opportunity cost of holding money in terms of interest forgone on alternative assets.

4c The demand for money curve with respect to interest rates is downward sloping.

5a Equilibrium in the money market is where the supply of money is equal to the demand. Equilibrium is achieved through changes in the interest rate and the exchange rate.

5b The interest rate mechanism works as follows: a rise in money supply causes money supply to exceed money demand; interest rates fall; this causes investment to rise; this causes a multiplied rise in national income.

5c The exchange rate mechanism works as follows: a rise in money supply causes interest rates to fall; the rise in money supply, plus the fall in interest rates, causes an increased supply of domestic currency to come on to the foreign exchange market; this causes the exchange rate to depreciate; this causes increased exports and reduced imports and hence a multiplied rise in national income.

MyEconLab

This book can be supported by MyEconLab, which contains a range of additional resources, including an online homework and tutorial system designed to test and build your understanding.

You need both an access card and a course ID to access MyEconLab:

1. Is your lecturer using MyEconLab? Ask your lecturer for your course ID.

2. Has an access card been included with the book at a reduced cost? Check the inside back cover of the book.

3. If you have a course ID but no access card, go to: http://www.myeconlab.com/ to buy access to this interactive study programme.

REVIEW QUESTIONS

1 Imagine that the banking system receives additional deposits of £100 million and that all the individual banks wish to retain their current liquidity ratio of 20 per cent.

 a) How much will banks choose to lend out initially?

 b) What will happen to banks' liabilities when the money that is lent out is spent and the recipients of it deposit it in their bank accounts?

 c) How much of these latest deposits will be lent out by the banks?

 d) By how much will total deposits (liabilities) eventually have risen, assuming that none of the additional liquidity is held outside the banking sector?

 e) How much of these are matched by (i) liquid assets; (ii) illiquid assets?

 f) What is the size of the bank multiplier?

 g) If one half of any additional liquidity is held outside the banking sector, by how much less will deposits have risen compared with (d) above?

2 What is meant by the terms *narrow money* and *broad money*? Does broad money fulfil all the functions of money?

3 Why do banks hold a range of assets of varying degrees of liquidity and profitability?

4 What is meant by the securitisation of assets? How might this be (a) beneficial and (b) harmful to banks and the economy?

5 What were the causes of the credit crunch and the banking crisis of the late 2000s?

6 Define the term 'liquidity ratio'. How will changes in the liquidity ratio affect the process of credit creation? Why might a bank's liquidity ratio vary over time?

7 What is measured by the CET1 ratio? What measures would a bank need to take in order to increase its CET1 ratio?

8 Analyse the possible effects on banks' balance sheets of the following:

 a) the Basel III regulatory requirements;

 b) the UK bank levy.

9 Why might the relationship between the demand for money and the rate of interest be an unstable one?

10 What effects will the following have on the equilibrium rate of interest? (You should consider which way the demand and/or supply curves of money shift.)

 a) Banks find that they have a higher liquidity ratio than they need.

 b) A rise in incomes.

 c) A growing belief that interest rates will rise from their current level.

Business activity, employment and inflation

Business issues covered in this chapter

- If there is an increase in investment, how will this affect the economy?
- Why does an increase in aggregate demand of £x lead to a rise in GDP of more than £x?
- To what extent does a rise in the money supply lead to a rise in the economy's output (real GDP) rather than merely a rise in prices?
- What is the relationship between unemployment and inflation? Is the relationship a stable one?
- How do business and consumer expectations affect the relationship between inflation and unemployment? How are such expectations formed?
- How does a policy of targeting the rate of inflation affect the relationship between inflation and unemployment?
- What determines the course of a business cycle and its turning points? Is the business cycle caused by changes in aggregate demand, changes in aggregate supply or both?

In this chapter we examine what determines the level of business activity and why it fluctuates. We also look at the effects of business activity on employment and inflation.

We start, in section 29.1, by looking at the determinants of GDP and, in particular, the role of aggregate demand. We do this by introducing the simple 'Keynesian' model (named after the great economist, John Maynard Keynes (1883–1946). (see Case study J.17 in MyEconLab). We consider how business activity might respond to changes in the level of aggregate demand.

Section 29.2 builds on the analysis of section 29.1 by looking at alternative perspectives on the effect of changes in aggregate demand on the macroeconomy. Some economists argue that changes in aggregate demand may have little or no effect on output and employment, even in the short run, but may have a significant effect on prices. In contrast, some economists argue that there could be quite significant effects on economic activity and that these effects could persist.

In section 29.3, we consider how changes in money and interest rates can have important, but possibly uncertain, effects on aggregate demand and business activity. These debates are particularly significant given that many central banks aggressively used monetary policy in an attempt to stimulate economic activity following the financial crisis of the late 2000s and the subsequent economic downturn.

In sections 29.4 and 29.5, we turn to the problems of unemployment and inflation and the relationship between the two. An important influence on both of them is what people *expect* to happen. Generally, if people are optimistic and believe that the economy will grow and unemployment will fall, this will happen. Similarly, if people expect inflation to stay low, it will do. In other words, people's expectations tend to be self-fulfilling. Getting people to expect low rates of inflation is something that can lead central banks to adopt inflation rate targets (the subject of section 29.4).

Finally, in section 29.6, we examine why real GDP (national output) and business activity fluctuate. In other words, we examine possible causes of the business cycle.

29.1 THE SIMPLE KEYNESIAN MODEL OF BUSINESS ACTIVITY

One of our key macroeconomic variables is the economy's output. This can be measured by real GDP (Y), also known as constant-price GDP. We know that real GDP tends to fluctuate and the patterns that arise result in the *business cycle*. Macroeconomics is characterised by lively debates as to the causes of the business cycle and the role that policy makers can play in alleviating or exacerbating these cycles.

The circular flow of income model (introduced in Chapter 26) allows us to see the flows of income between the various sectors of the economy and how they affect aggregate demand. Understanding the determinants of aggregate demand is important because many economists believe that it is fluctuations in aggregate demand which lie behind the business cycle.

In this section, after briefly revisiting the circular flow model, we develop the simple Keynesian model of the determination of GDP (national income). We can then analyse more closely the impact of changes of aggregate demand on output and hence income. We assume throughout that prices are constant and so there is no inflation. In section 29.2 we relax this assumption and see how a change in aggregate demand could affect prices as well as output.

Revisiting the circular flow of income model

Figure 29.1 shows a simplified version of the circular flow, with injections entering at just one point, and likewise withdrawals leaving at just one point (this simplification does not affect the argument).

If injections (J) do not equal withdrawals (W), a state of disequilibrium exists. What will bring them back into equilibrium is a change in national income (GDP) and employment.

Start with a state of equilibrium, where injections equal withdrawals. If there is now a rise in injections – say, firms decide to invest more – aggregate demand (i.e. the consumption of domestic products (C_d) plus injections (J)) will be higher. Firms will respond to this increased demand by using more labour and other resources and thus paying out more incomes (Y) to households. Household consumption will rise and so firms will sell more.

Firms will respond by producing more, and thus using more labour and other resources. Household incomes will rise again. Consumption and hence production will rise again, and so on. There will thus be a multiplied rise in incomes and employment. This is known as the *multiplier effect*.

> **KEY IDEA 43**
>
> *The principle of cumulative causation.* An initial event can cause an ultimate effect which is much larger.

The process, however, does not go on for ever. Each time household incomes rise, households save more, pay more taxes and buy more imports. In other words, withdrawals rise. When withdrawals have risen to match the increase in injections, equilibrium will be restored and national income (GDP) and employment will stop rising. The process can be summarised as follows:

$$J > W \rightarrow Y\uparrow \rightarrow W\uparrow \text{ until } J = W$$

Similarly, an initial fall in injections (or rise in withdrawals) will lead to a multiplied fall in GDP and employment:

$$J < W \rightarrow Y\downarrow \rightarrow W\downarrow \text{ until } J = W$$

Thus equilibrium in the circular flow of income can be at *any* level of GDP and employment.

Figure 29.1 The circular flow of income

$$J = I + G + X$$

$$C_d$$

$$W = S + T + M$$

Definition

Multiplier effect An initial increase in aggregate demand of £*x*m leads to an eventual rise in national income that is greater than £*x*m.

The simple Keynesian model

The circular flow model is a demand-drive model of the economy. Changes in aggregate demand drive changes in national income (i.e. the value of national output). But to analyse the determination of national income we need to model the income flows that affect aggregate demand. Then we can identify the equilibrium level of national income.

Equilibrium can be shown on a 'Keynesian 45° line diagram' also known as the 'Keynesian Cross'. Keynes argued that equilibrium national income is determined by aggregate demand. Equilibrium can be at any level of capacity. If aggregate demand is buoyant, equilibrium can be where businesses are operating at full capacity with full employment. If aggregate demand is low, however, equilibrium can be at well below full capacity with high unemployment (i.e. a recession). Keynes argued that it is important, therefore, for governments to manage the level of aggregate demand to avoid recessions.

The Keynesian Cross diagram plots various elements of the circular flow of income, such as consumption, withdrawals, injections and aggregate demand, against real GDP (real national income).

In Figure 29.2 two continuous lines are shown. The 45° line out from the origin plots $C_d + W$ against real GDP (Y). It is a 45° line because, by definition, $Y = C_d + W$. To understand this, consider what can happen to the income earned from GDP (national income): either it must be spent on domestically produced goods (C_d) or it must be withdrawn from the circular flow – there is nothing else that can happen to it. Thus if national income (Y) were £100 billion, then $C_d + W$ must also be £100 billion. If you draw a line such that whatever value is plotted on the horizontal axis (Y) is also plotted on the vertical axis ($C_d + W$), the line will be at 45° (assuming that the axes are drawn to the same scale).

The other continuous line plots aggregate demand. In this diagram it is known as the *aggregate expenditure line* (E). It consists of $C_d + J$: in other words, the total spending on domestic firms.

To show how this line is constructed, consider the dashed line. This shows C_d. It is flatter than the 45° line. The reason is that for any given rise in GDP and hence people's incomes, only *part* will be spent on domestic products, while the remainder will be withdrawn: i.e. C_d rises less quickly than GDP (Y). The E line consists of $C_d + J$. But we have assumed that J is constant with respect to changes in national income. Thus the E line is simply the C_d line shifted upward by the amount of J.

If aggregate expenditure exceeded GDP, at say Y_1, there would be excess demand in the economy (of $a – b$). In other words, people would be buying more than was currently being produced. Firms would thus find their stocks dwindling and would therefore increase their level of production. In doing so, they would employ more factors of production. GDP would thus rise. As it did so, C_d and hence E would rise. There would be a movement up along the E line. But because not all the extra incomes earned from the rise in GDP would be consumed (i.e. some would be withdrawn), expenditure would rise less quickly than income: the E line is flatter than the Y line. As income rises towards Y_e, the gap between the Y and E lines gets smaller. Once point e is reached, $Y = E$. There is then no further tendency for GDP to rise.

If GDP exceeded aggregate expenditure, at say Y_2, there would be insufficient demand for the goods and services currently being produced ($c – d$). Firms would find their

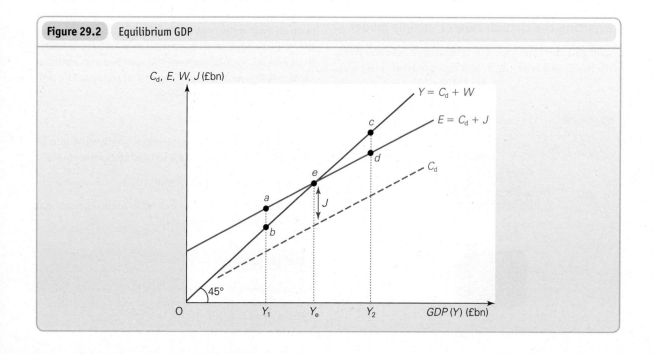

Figure 29.2 Equilibrium GDP

stocks of unsold goods building up. They would thus respond by producing less and employing less factors of production. GDP would thus fall and go on falling until Y_e was reached.

The multiplier

When aggregate expenditure rises, this will cause GDP to rise. But by how much? The answer is that there will be a *multiplied* rise in GDP: i.e. it will rise by more than the rise in aggregate expenditure. The size of the *multiplier* is given by the letter k, where:

$$k = \Delta Y / \Delta E$$

Thus, if aggregate expenditure rose by £10 million (ΔE) and as a result GDP rose by £30 million (ΔY), the multiplier would be 3. Figure 29.3 is drawn on the assumption that the multiplier is 3.

Assume in Figure 29.3 that aggregate expenditure rises by £20 billion, from E_1 to E_2. This could be caused by a rise in injections, or by a fall in withdrawals (and hence a rise in consumption of domestically produced goods) or by some combination of the two. Equilibrium GDP rises by £60 billion, from £100 billion to £160 billion (where the E_2 line crosses the *GDP* line).

What determines the size of the multiplier? The answer is that it depends on the '*marginal propensity to consume domestically produced goods and services*' (mpc_d). The mpc_d is the proportion of any rise in GDP that gets spent on domestically produced goods (in other words the proportion that is not withdrawn as saving, taxes or spending on imports).

$$mpc_d = \Delta C_d / \Delta Y$$

In Figure 29.3, $mpc_d = \Delta C_d / \Delta Y = £49bn/£60bn = {}^2/_3$ (i.e. the slope of the C_d line). The higher the mpc_d the greater the proportion of income generated from GDP that recirculates around the circular flow of income and thus generates extra output.

The *multiplier formula* is given by:

$$k = \frac{1}{1 - mpc_d}$$

In our example, with $mpc_d = {}^2/_3$

$$k = \frac{1}{1 - {}^2/_3} = \frac{1}{{}^1/_3} = 3$$

If the mpc_d were ${}^3/_4$, the multiplier would be 4. Thus the higher the mpc_d, the higher the multiplier.

> ## Pause for thought
>
> *Think of two reasons why a country might have a steep E line, and hence a high value for the multiplier.*

> ## Definitions
>
> **The multiplier** The number of times a rise in GDP (ΔY) is bigger than the initial rise in aggregate expenditure (ΔE) that caused it. Using the letter k to stand for the multiplier, the multiplier is defined as $k = \Delta Y / \Delta E$
>
> **Marginal propensity to consume domestically produced goods and services** The fraction of a rise in national income (Y) that is spent by consumers on domestic product (C_d) and hence is not withdrawn from the circular flow of income: $mpc_d = \Delta C_d / \Delta Y$.
>
> **Multiplier formula** The formula for the multiplier is $k = 1/(1 - mpc_d)$.

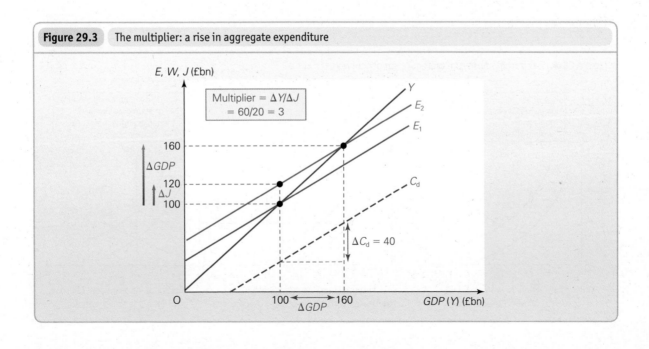

Figure 29.3 The multiplier: a rise in aggregate expenditure

29.2 AGGREGATE DEMAND, OUTPUT AND INFLATION

In the previous section we saw how changes in aggregate demand could lead to a multiplied change in national income. In practice, a rise in aggregate demand is likely to lead to a rise not only in real GDP, but also in prices throughout the economy.

The problem with both the circular flow model and the simple Keynesian multiplier model is that they take no account of just how firms make supply decisions: they assume that firms simply respond to demand. But supply decisions, as well as being influenced by current levels of demand, are also influenced by prices and costs.

To be able to analyse the impact of changes in aggregate demand on national income *and* prices we need to make use of the aggregate demand–aggregate supply (*AD/AS*) model. The debate concerning the impact of changes in aggregate demand on prices and output can best be understood in terms of the nature of the aggregate supply (*AS*) curve. We will start with the short-run *AS* (*SRAS*) curve and then look at the long-run curve.

Assume that there is a rise in aggregate demand. The short-run effect on real GDP (output) and prices will depend on the shape of the *SRAS* curve. The new classical and monetarist position (at least in the long run) is that the result of the rise in demand will simply be a rise in prices. In contrast, the Keynesian position is that there will also (or even solely) be a rise in national output. Let us examine the different analyses of the *SRAS* curve.

The short-run aggregate supply curve

Various approaches to analysing aggregate supply are illustrated in Figure 29.4.

The moderate position

The moderate or mainstream view is that the *SRAS* curve is upward sloping. This is because wages and many other input prices exhibit *some* 'stickiness' in the short term, as we saw in section 26.4. A rise in demand will not simply be absorbed in higher input prices: in other words, output will rise too.

Nevertheless, as more variable factors are used, firms will experience diminishing returns. Marginal costs will rise. The less the spare capacity in firms, the more rapidly marginal costs will rise for any given increase in output and hence the steeper will be the *SRAS* curve.

KI 20
p 142

Therefore, the moderate view is that an increase in *AD* will have some effect on prices and some effect on output and employment (see Figure 29.4(a) and 26.10). The extent of these effects will depend on the economy's current level of output relative to its potential level. The higher actual output is relative to potential output, the less slack in the economy and the steeper the *SRAS* becomes.

KI 12
p 68

The extreme Keynesian position

The extreme Keynesian position mirrors the simple Keynesian model in section 29.1. As shown in Figure 29.4(b), the *SRAS* curve is *horizontal* up to the level of real national income that will generate full employment (Y_F) (similar to the concept of *potential national income*). This level of national income is referred to as the **full-employment level of GDP**. (In practice, there would still be some unemployment at this level because of the existence of equilibrium unemployment – structural, frictional and seasonal.) A rise in aggregate demand from AD_1 to AD_2 will raise output from Y_1 to Y_2, but there will be *no effect on prices* until full employment is reached.

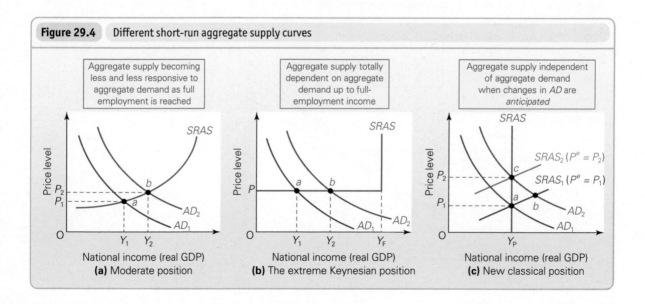

Figure 29.4 Different short-run aggregate supply curves

(a) Moderate position — National income (real GDP)

(b) The extreme Keynesian position — National income (real GDP)

(c) New classical position — National income (real GDP)

In this extreme Keynesian model, aggregate supply up to the full-employment level is determined entirely by the level of aggregate demand. But there is no guarantee that aggregate demand will intersect aggregate supply at full employment. Therefore governments should manage aggregate demand by appropriate fiscal and monetary policies to ensure production at Y_F.

A recessionary gap. If the equilibrium level of GDP (Y_e) is below the full-employment level (Y_F), there will be excess capacity in the economy and hence demand-deficient unemployment. This situation is illustrated in Figure 29.5(a) using the Keynesian cross diagram. If national income is to be raised from Y_e to Y_F, aggregate expenditure (E) will have to be raised, either by increasing injections or by reducing withdrawals, so as to close the gap a–b. This gap is known as the ***recessionary or deflationary gap***.

Note that the size of the recessionary gap is *less* than the amount by which Y_e falls short of Y_F. This is another illustration of the multiplier. If aggregate expenditure is raised by $a - b$, output will rise by $Y_F - Y_e$. The multiplier is thus given by:

$$\frac{Y_F - Y_e}{a - b}$$

An inflationary gap. If, at the full-employment level of output, aggregate expenditure *exceeds* GDP, there will be a problem of excess demand. Y_e will be above Y_F. The problem is that Y_F represents an effective limit to output, other than in the very short term. GDP can only expand beyond this point by firms operating at above normal capacity levels – by employing people overtime or taking other temporary measures to boost output. The result will be demand-pull inflation.

This situation involves an ***inflationary gap***. This is the amount by which aggregate expenditure exceeds national income at the full-employment level of national income. It

is illustrated by the gap e–f in Figure 29.5(b). To eliminate this inflation, the inflationary gap must be closed, either by raising withdrawals or by lowering injections.

KI 43
p 547

> ### Pause for thought
>
> *Assume that full-employment GDP is £500 billion and that current GDP is £450 billion. Assume also that the mpcd is $^4/_5$. (a) Is there an inflationary or deflationary gap? (b) What is the size of this gap?*

The new classical position

In contrast, new classicists argue that the *SRAS* curve may be *vertical* at potential output (Y_p), as in Figure 29.4(c). This rests on two important assumptions. First is the assumption of ***continuous market clearing***. This means that all markets continuously adjust to their equilibrium. Second, is the assumption of ***rational expectations***. This means that people use all available information and predict inflation, or any other macroeconomic variable, as well as they can. The important point here is that forecasting errors are random so that, on average, people's expectations of inflation are correct.

KI 13
p 78

The implication of continuous market clearing and rational expectations is that *anticipated* changes in aggregate demand will simply cause a change in prices, not a

> ### Definitions
>
> **Full-employment level of GDP** The level of GDP at which there is no deficiency of demand.
>
> **Recessionary or deflationary gap** The shortfall of aggregate expenditure below GDP at the full-employment level of GDP.
>
> **Inflationary gap** The excess of aggregate expenditure over GDP at the full-employment level of GDP.

Figure 29.5 (a) Recessionary gap; (b) inflationary gap

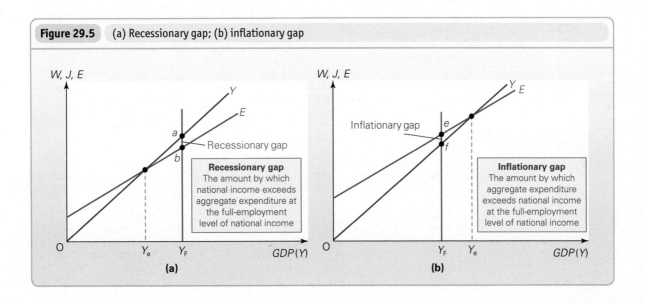

change in output and employment, even in the short run. Hence, an anticipated rise in aggregate demand will quickly work through both goods and factor markets into higher prices. There has been no increase in *real* aggregate demand. Output remains at its potential (normal capacity) level Y_p. Thus it is essential to keep (nominal) demand under control if *prices* are to be kept under control.

Unanticipated change in aggregate demand. An upward-sloping *SRAS* curve would be observable only if changes in aggregate demand were *unanticipated* and even then deviations in output from its potential level would be transitory. If, in Figure 29.4(c), aggregate demand were to rise unexpectedly, say from AD_1 to AD_2, people would not foresee the upward effect on general prices. Hence, workers and firms would have negotiated specific input prices, including wages, on the expectation that the general price level would be P_1. Therefore, the expected price level P^e is P_1 ($P^e = P_1$). As the general price level rises it is profitable for businesses to expand output levels. This is equivalent to the move from *a* to *b* in Figure 29.4(c).

Once people recognise these errors, however, output adjusts back to its potential level Y_p. The economy moves from point *b* to *c*. In the presence of rational expectations and continuous market clearing this adjustment is likely to happen relatively quickly. Hence to raise output and employment *supply-side* policies will be required. If successful, these will shift the vertical *AS* curve to the right.

KI 13
p 78

Pause for thought

If there was an unexpected decrease in aggregate demand would new classicists expect output to fall below its potential level?

The long-run aggregate supply curve

A vertical long-run AS curve

While new classical economists argue that the short-run *AS* curve is typically vertical, most economists argue that it is only the *long-run AS* curve that is vertical at the potential level of output (Y_p): see Figure 29.6(b). Any rise in nominal aggregate demand would lead simply to a rise in prices and no long-term increase in output at all.

The mainstream view is that long-term increases in output could occur only through rightward shifts in this vertical long-run *AS* curve, in other words through increases in potential output. To achieve this, governments should largely focus on supply-side policy, such as policies which help foster technological progress (see Chapter 31).

But why do these economists argue that the long-run *AS* curve is vertical? They justify this by focusing on the *interdependence of markets*. Assume initially that the economy is operating at the potential level of output (Y_p). Now assume that there is an increase in demand, such as from an increase in government expenditure. The increase in aggregate demand will initially lead firms to raise both prices and output, for the reasons we gave above. In other words, the short-run aggregate

Definitions

Continuous market clearing The assumption that all markets in the economy continuously clear so that the economy is permanently in equilibrium.

Rational expectations Expectations based on the current situation. These expectations are based on the information people have to hand. While this information may be imperfect and therefore people will make errors, these errors will be random.

Figure 29.6   Short-run and long-run aggregate supply curves

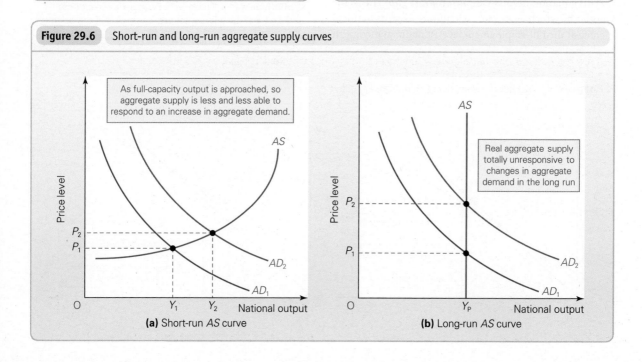

(a) Short-run *AS* curve   (b) Long-run *AS* curve

supply curve is upward sloping. There is a movement from point *a* to point *b* in Figure 29.7. Output rises to Y_2.

However, as raw material and intermediate goods producers raise their prices, so this will raise the costs of production of firms using these inputs. A rise in the price of steel will raise the costs of producing cars and washing machines. At the same time, workers, seeing the prices of goods rising, will demand higher wages. Firms will be relatively willing to grant these wage demands, given that they are experiencing a buoyant demand from their customers. The effect of all this is to raise firms' *costs*, and hence their prices. As prices rise for any given level of output, so the short-run *AS* curve will shift upward. This is shown by a move to $SRAS_2$ in Figure 29.7. The economy moves from point *b* to point *c*. Thus output can only temporarily rise above the potential level (Y_p).

The long-run effect, therefore, of a rise in aggregate demand from AD_1 to AD_2 is a movement from point *a* to point *c*. The long-run aggregate supply curve passes through these two points. It is vertical at the potential level of output. A rise in aggregate demand will therefore have no long-run effect on output. The entire effect will be felt in terms of higher prices.

As we saw above, new classical economists go one step further. Because markets are very flexible, they argue, higher costs will be passed through into higher prices virtually instantly. What is more, people will typically anticipate this and hence take it into account *now*. These assumptions mean that the *short*-run aggregate supply curve will be vertical also (as in Figure 29.4(c)). Even if the change in aggregate demand and/or the impact on prices were a 'surprise', markets would still clear relatively quickly so that any impact on the economy's output would be transitory.

An upward-sloping long-run AS curve

Some Keynesian economists, however, argue that the long-run *AS* curve is upward sloping, not vertical. Indeed, it may be even shallower than the short-run curve. For them, potential output is affected by changes in aggregate demand.

The key here is investment. If the increase in aggregate demand includes an increase in investment (*I*) this can positively affect the economy's *capacity* to produce. More generally, in observing an increase in demand, firms may be encouraged to invest in new plant and machinery. Therefore, an increase in aggregate demand can increase potential output. The result is that firms may well be able to increase output significantly in the long run with little or no increase in their prices. Their long-run *MC* curves are much flatter than their short-run *MC* curves.

Again assume initially that output is at the potential level. In Figure 29.8 this is shown as Y_{P1}. Aggregate demand then increases to AD_2. Equilibrium moves to point *b* with GDP at Y_2. The resulting increased investment shifts the short-run *AS* curve to the right. Equilibrium moves from point *b* to *d*. Point *d* is now at the new potential level of output, Y_{P2}. The long-run *AS* curve thus joins points *a* and *d*.

The way the diagram is drawn, the long-run *AS* curve is more elastic than the short-run curve. There is a relatively large increase in output and a relatively small increase in price. If the rise in costs had been more substantial, curve $SRAS_2$ could be above curve $SRAS_1$. In this case, although the long-run *AS* curve would still be upward sloping, it would be steeper than the short-run curves: point *d* would be above point *b*.

KI 40
p 471

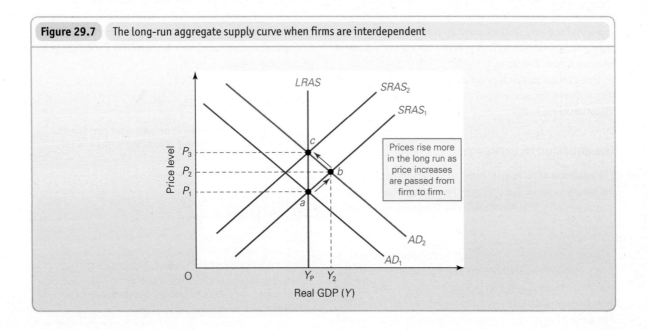

Figure 29.7   The long-run aggregate supply curve when firms are interdependent

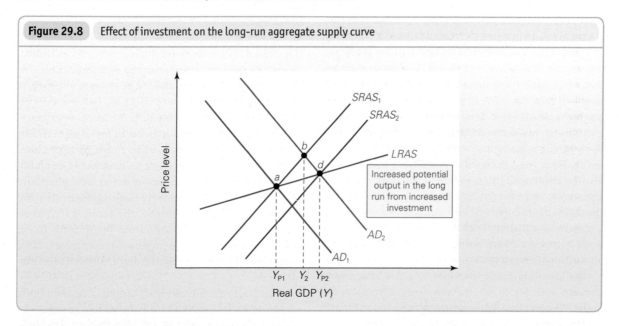

Figure 29.8 Effect of investment on the long-run aggregate supply curve

---

The long-run *AS* curve will be steeper if the extra investment causes significant shortages of materials, machinery or labour. This is more likely when the economy is already operating near its full-capacity output. It will be flatter, and possibly even downward sloping, if the investment involves the introduction of new cost-reducing technology.

29.3 MONEY, AGGREGATE DEMAND AND INFLATION

There has long been particular interest amongst economists about the impact of changes in the money supply on output and prices. In recent times this analysis has been especially pertinent since, following the financial crisis of the late 2000s and the ensuing economic downturn, many central banks aggressively increased the monetary base (narrow money). By doing so they were attempting to stimulate aggregate demand as well as prevent the rate of inflation from undershooting its target level.

One of the simplest ways of understanding the relationship between money, output and prices is in terms of the 'equation of exchange'.

The equation of exchange

The *equation of exchange* shows the relationship between the money value of spending and the money value of output (nominal GDP). This identity may be expressed as follows:

$$MV = PY$$

M is the supply of money in the economy (e.g. M4). *V* is its *velocity of circulation*. This is the number of times per year that money is spent on buying goods and services that have been produced in the economy that year (real GDP). *P* is the level of prices of domestically produced goods and

services, expressed as an index, where the index is 1 in a chosen base year (e.g. 2010). Thus if prices today are 10 per cent higher than those in the base year, *P* is 1.1. *Y* is *real* national income (real GDP): in other words, the quantity of national output produced in that year measured in base-year prices.

PY is thus *nominal* GDP: i.e. GDP measured at current prices. For example, if GDP at base-year prices (*Y*) is £2 trillion and the price index is 1.1, then GDP at current prices (*PY*) is £2.2 trillion.

Definitions

Equation of exchange *MV = PY*. The total level of spending on GDP (*MV*) equals the total value of goods and services produced (*PY*) that go to make up GDP.

Velocity of circulation The number of times annually that money on average is spent on goods and services that made up GDP.

MV is the total spending on the goods and services that make up GDP – in other words, (nominal) aggregate demand. For example, if money supply is £500 billion, and money, as it passes from one person to another, is spent on average four times a year on national output, then total spending (*MV*) is £2 trillion a year. But this too *must* equal GDP at current prices. The reason is that what is spent on output (by consumers, by firms on investment, by the government or by people abroad on exports) must equal the value of goods produced (*PY*).

The equation of exchange (or 'quantity equation') is true by definition. *MV* is *necessarily* equal to *PY* because of the way the terms are defined. Thus a rise in *MV must* be accompanied by a rise in *PY*. What a change in *M* does to *P*, however, is a matter of debate. The controversy centres on the impact of changes in the money supply on aggregate demand and then on the impact of changes in aggregate demand on output. We have seen that the latter depends crucially on the nature of *aggregate supply*. We now focus on the relationship between money supply and aggregate demand, beginning with the short-run relationship.

Money supply and aggregate demand

The short run

Chapter 28 identified two ways in which changes in the money supply could affect aggregate demand: the interest-rate and exchange-rate transmission mechanisms. Taken together, the impact of an increase in the money supply can be summarised as follows:

1 A rise in money supply will lead to a fall in the rate of interest.
2 The fall in the rate of interest will lead to a rise in investment and other forms of borrowing. It will also lead to a fall in the exchange rate and hence a rise in exports and a fall in imports.
3 The rise in investment, and the rise in exports and fall in imports, will mean a rise in aggregate demand.

However, there is considerable debate over how these transmission mechanisms function.

How interest-rate sensitive is money demand? The demand for money as a means of storing wealth (the assets motive) can be large and highly responsive to changes in interest rates on alternative assets. Indeed, large sums of money move around the money market as firms and financial institutions respond to and anticipate changes in interest rates. Thus, with an increase in money supply, only a relatively small fall in interest rates on bonds and other assets may be necessary to persuade people to hold all the extra money in bank accounts, thereby greatly slowing down the average speed at which money circulates. The fall in *V* may virtually offset the rise in *M*.

In other words, the more sensitive is the demand for money to changes in the rate of interest, the less impact changes in money supply have on aggregate demand.

How stable is the money demand function? Another criticism is that the demand for money is unstable and so the demand-for-money curve in Figure 28.8 is frequently shifting. People hold speculative balances of money when they anticipate that the prices of other assets, such as shares, bonds and bills, will fall (and hence the rate of return or interest on these assets will rise).

There are many factors that could affect such expectations, such as changes in foreign interest rates, changes in exchange rates, statements of government intentions on economic policy, good or bad industrial news, or newly published figures on inflation or money supply. With an unstable demand for money, it is difficult to predict the effect of a change in money supply on interest rates and so aggregate demand.

It is largely for this reason that most central banks usually prefer to control interest rates directly, rather than indirectly by controlling the money supply – although increasing the money supply through 'quantitative easing' was a major additional measure used to stimulate aggregate demand in the wake of the world recession. (We examine the conduct of monetary policy in section 30.2.)

How interest-rate sensitive is spending? The problem here is that investment may be insensitive to changes in interest rates. Businesses are more likely to be influenced in their decision to invest by predictions of the future buoyancy of markets. Interest rates do have *some* effect on businesses' investment decisions, but the effect is unpredictable, depending on the confidence of investors.

The impact on household sector spending is likely to be strongest for homeowners with mortgages. If interest rates go down, and mortgage rates follow suit, people will suddenly experience lower monthly repayments (debt servicing costs) and will therefore have more residual income to spend on goods and services.

The impact of interest rate changes also needs to be set in the context of the financial well-being of economic agents. If, as in the early 2010s, people and businesses are looking to reduce their debts, then cuts to interest rates are likely to encourage paying off debts rather than increased spending.

How interest-rate sensitive is the exchange rate? Also the amount that the exchange rate will depreciate is uncertain, since exchange rate movements (as we saw in Chapter 27) depend crucially on expectations about trade prospects and about future world interest rate movements. Thus the effects on imports and exports are also uncertain.

To summarise: the effects on total spending of a change in the money supply *might* be quite strong, but they could be weak. In other words, the effects are highly unpredictable. Therefore, the control of the money supply can be an unreliable means of controlling aggregate demand – at least in the short run.

So what does this imply for effectiveness of quantitative easing in boosting spending? Its impact was to depend crucially on the behaviour of the private sector, since many governments were simultaneously seeking to *reduce* expenditure in order to reduce often very large public-sector deficits. The private-sector response was to depend, in part, on the willingness of banks to provide additional credit and the willingness of households and businesses to accept this credit and to increase their spending.

The long run

In the long run, there is a stronger link between money supply and aggregate demand. In fact, 'monetarists' claim that in the long run V is determined *totally independently* of the money supply (M). Thus an increase in M will leave V unaffected and hence will directly increase expenditure (MV). But why do they claim this?

If money supply increases over the longer term, people will have more money than they require to hold. They will spend this surplus. Much of this spending will go on goods and services, thereby directly increasing aggregate demand.

The theoretical underpinning for this is given by the *theory of portfolio balance*. People have a number of ways of holding their wealth. They can hold it as money, or as financial assets such as bills, bonds and shares, or as physical assets such as houses, cars and televisions. In other words, people hold a whole portfolio of assets of varying degrees of liquidity – from cash to central heating.

If money supply expands, people will find themselves holding more money than they require: their portfolios are 'unnecessarily liquid'. Some of this money will be used to purchase financial assets and some, possibly after a period of time, to purchase *goods and services*. As more assets are purchased, this will drive up their price. This will effectively reduce their 'yield'. For bonds and other *financial* assets, this means a reduction in their rate of interest. For goods

and services, it means an increase in their price relative to their usefulness.

The process will stop when a balance has been restored in people's portfolios. In the meantime, there will have been extra consumption and hence an increase in aggregate demand.

How will a change in money affect output and prices?

Our discussion has shown that the effect of changes in the money supply on aggregate demand is open to considerable debate and difficult to predict, especially in the short run. Even if we assume that changes in the money supply do affect aggregate demand, there is still the question of how much this will lead to a rise in output (i.e. real GDP) and how much it will simply result in a rise in prices.

To consider this, we can return to the analysis of section 29.2. Here we applied the *AD/AS* framework to consider the impact of changes in aggregate demand both on levels of business activity and on prices. The debate centred on the aggregate supply curve. The moderate position is that aggregate supply (output) is relatively responsive in the short run to increases in aggregate demand, provided there is slack in the economy. Similarly, reductions in aggregate demand are likely to lead to reductions in output. Many also argue, however, that aggregate supply is inelastic in the *long run*; that potential output is determined largely or wholly independently of aggregate demand. In the long run, therefore, any rise in MV will be mainly or totally reflected in a rise in prices (P).

In the long run, according to this view, the stock of money therefore determines the price level, and the rate of increase in money supply determines the rate of inflation. It is thus important to ensure that money supply is kept under control if inflation is to be avoided. (We examine monetary policy in section 30.2.)

29.4 THE RELATIONSHIP BETWEEN INFLATION AND UNEMPLOYMENT: THE SHORT RUN

Unemployment and inflation at the same time

We saw in section 29.2 how the extreme Keynesian short-run aggregate supply (*AS*) curve is horizontal up to the full-employment output level, Y_F. The curve is shown again in Figure 29.9 and is labelled AS_1. Up to Y_F, output and employment can rise with no rise in prices at all. The deflationary gap is being closed. At Y_F no further rises in output are possible. Any further rise in aggregate demand is entirely reflected in higher prices. An inflationary gap opens. In other words, this implies that either inflation *or* unemployment can occur, but not both simultaneously.

Two important qualifications need to be made to this analysis to explain the occurrence of both unemployment *and* inflation at the same time.

First, there are *other* types of inflation and unemployment not caused by an excess or deficiency of aggregate demand: for example, cost-push and expectations-generated inflation; frictional and structural unemployment. Box 29.1 looks at the actual relationship between the rate of inflation and the amount of excess or deficient demand, as measured by output gaps, in the UK since the mid-1960s.

Thus, even if a government could manipulate national income so as to get Y_e and Y_F to coincide, this would not

BOX 29.1 MIND THE GAP

Do output gaps explain inflation?

Chapter 26 introduced the concept of output gaps. An output gap measures the difference between an economy's actual level of output and its potential output (the output level when the economy is operating at 'normal capacity utilisation'). A positive output gap shows that the level of actual output is greater than the potential level, while a negative output gap shows that the level of output is below the potential level.

The magnitude of the output gap, which is usually expressed as a percentage of potential output, enables us to assess the extent of any demand deficiency (negative output gap) or the extent of excess demand (positive output gap).

The 'moderate view' of the slope of the short-run aggregate supply (see Figure 29.4(a)) is that it is determined by the amount of slack in the economy. As the economy approaches or exceeds its potential output, the aggregate supply curve becomes steeper as firms' marginal costs rise faster. Consequently, increases in demand at output levels close to or in excess of an economy's potential output will exert more upward pressure on prices than if the economy has a more significant amount of slack. This suggests that the rate of price inflation is positively related to the size of the output gap.

The chart plots the output gap (as a percentage of potential output) and the annual rate of economy-wide inflation (rate of increase of the GDP deflator) for the UK since 1965.

It would appear that for the period from 1965 to the end of the 1980s there was a positive correlation between output gaps and inflation rates, albeit that turning points in the rates of inflation lag those in the size of output gaps – in

other words, it took time for price pressure to fully work through the economy. This reflects, in part, the fact that some prices, such as wage rates, are adjusted relatively infrequently.

Since the 1990s, however, the relationship between output gaps and inflation rates is less clear. Indeed, for much of the rest of the period, there is a general reduction in inflation rates regardless of the size of output gaps. This demonstrates that there are several potential influences on rates of inflation.

One explanation is a reduction in cost-push pressures – at least until the mid- to late 2000s (see Box 26.3). First, labour markets became more competitive and flexible. Second, firms faced greater competition from the EU, China and many other countries in an increasingly globalised market. Third, except for the periods from 2007–8 and late 2009–10 (see the chart in Box 26.3), commodity price inflation has been subdued.

Another explanation is inflation rate expectations. The adoption of clear and credible inflation targets by central banks, such as the Bank of England, has influenced both firms when setting prices and both firms and unions when negotiating wage rates. It has helped to anchor such price and wage setting to the inflation rate target, irrespective of the state of the economy.

1. *What factors may have resulted in the lower inflation rates experienced by the UK from the 1990s?*
2. *Do credible inflation rate targets guarantee low inflation?*

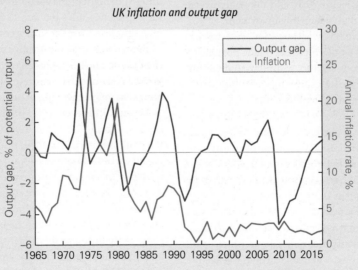

UK inflation and output gap

Notes: (i) Inflation rate is the annual rate of increase in the GDP deflator; (ii) Data from 2015 based on forecasts
Source: Based on data in *AMECO database* (European Commission, DGECFIN)

eliminate all inflation and unemployment – only demand-pull inflation and demand-deficient unemployment. For this reason governments may choose to use a whole package of policies, each tailored to the specific type of problem.

Second, not all firms operate with the same degree of slack. A rise in aggregate demand can lead to *both* a reduction

in unemployment *and* a rise in prices: some firms responding to the rise in demand by taking up slack and hence increasing output; other firms, having little or no slack, responding by raising prices; others doing both. Similarly, labour markets have different degrees of slack and therefore the rise in demand will lead to various mixes of higher wages and lower unemployment.

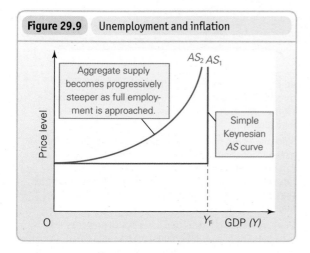

Figure 29.9   Unemployment and inflation

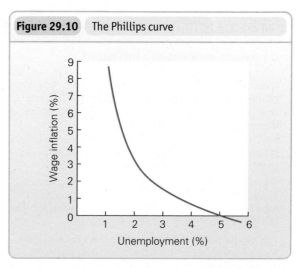

Figure 29.10   The Phillips curve

Thus the moderate view of the short-run *AS* curve is that it will look like AS_2 in Figure 29.9 (see also Figure 29.4(a)).

The Phillips curve

The relationship between inflation and unemployment was examined by A. W. Phillips in 1958. He showed the statistical relationship between wage inflation and unemployment in the UK from 1861 to 1957. With wage inflation on the vertical axis and the unemployment rate on the horizontal axis, a scatter of points was obtained. Each point represented the observation for a particular year. The curve that best fitted the scatter has become known as the ***Phillips curve***. It is illustrated in Figure 29.10 and shows an inverse relationship between inflation and unemployment.

Given that wage increases over the period were approximately 2 per cent above price increases (made possible by increases in labour productivity), a similar-shaped, but lower curve could be plotted showing the relationship between *price* inflation and unemployment.

The curve has often used to illustrate the short-run effects of changes in (real) aggregate demand. When aggregate demand rose (relative to potential output), inflation rose and unemployment fell: there was an upward movement along the curve. When aggregate demand fell, there was a downward movement along the curve.

The Phillips curve was bowed in to the origin. The usual explanation for this is that as aggregate demand expanded, at first there would be plenty of surplus labour, which could be employed to meet the extra demand without the need to raise wage rates very much. But as labour became increasingly scarce, firms would find that they had to offer increas-

ingly higher wage rates to obtain the labour they required, and the position of trade unions would be increasingly strengthened.

The *position* of the Phillips curve depended on *non-demand factors* causing inflation and unemployment: frictional and structural unemployment; and cost-push and expectations-generated inflation. If any of these non-demand factors changed so as to raise inflation or unemployment, the curve would shift outward to the right.

The Phillips curve seemed to present governments with a simple policy choice. They could trade off inflation against unemployment. Lower unemployment could be bought at the cost of higher inflation, and vice versa. Unfortunately, the experience since the late 1960s has suggested that no such simple relationship exists beyond the short run.

From about 1967 the Phillips curve relationship seemed to break down. The UK, along with many other countries in the Western world, began to experience growing unemployment *and* higher rates of inflation as well.

Figure 29.11 shows price inflation and unemployment in the UK from 1960. From 1960 to 1967 a curve similar to the Phillips curve can be fitted through the data. From 1968 to the early 1990s, however, no simple picture emerges. Certainly the original Phillips curve could no longer fit the data; but whether the curve shifted to the right and then back again somewhat (the broken lines), or whether the relationship broke down completely, or whether there was some quite different relationship between inflation and unemployment, is not clear by simply looking at the data.

Since 1997 the Bank of England has been targeting consumer price inflation (see section 29.5). For much of this period, the 'curve' would seem to have become a virtually horizontal straight line at the targeted rate!

However, from the late 2000s, against a backdrop of marked economic volatility, the range of inflation rates increased despite inflation rate targeting. Then in the period from late 2013, inflation fell below the target, reflecting lower commodity prices and sluggish demand in the eurozone and elsewhere.

KI 40
p471

Definition

Phillips curve A curve showing the relationship between (price) inflation and unemployment. The original Phillips curve plotted wage inflation against unemployment for the years 1861–1957.

Figure 29.11 The breakdown of the Phillips curve

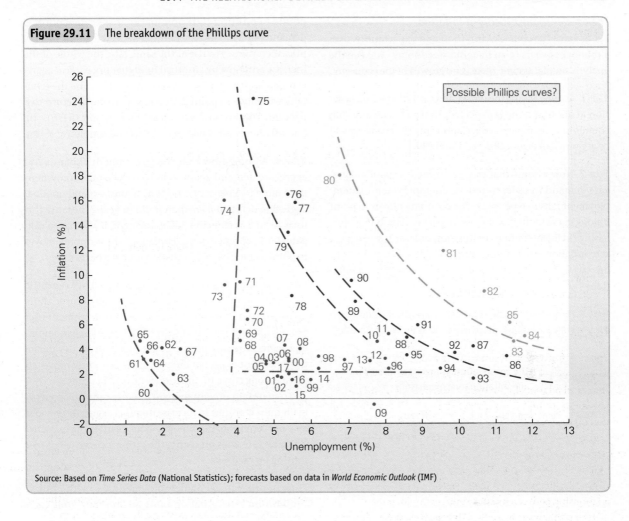

Source: Based on *Time Series Data* (National Statistics); forecasts based on data in *World Economic Outlook* (IMF)

Nonetheless, despite difficulties in keeping inflation to target, many economists continue to argue that expectations concerning future inflation rates are an important influence on the inflation–unemployment relationship and that inflation has become much less volatile since inflation targeting was introduced.

Expectations and the Phillips curve

A major contribution to the theory of unemployment and inflation was made by Milton Friedman and others in the late 1960s. They incorporated people's expectations about the future level of prices into the Phillips curve. In its simplest form, the *expectations-augmented Phillips curve* is given by the following:

$$\pi = f(1/U) + \pi^e$$

What this states is that inflation (π) depends on two things:

■ The inverse of unemployment (1/U). This is simply the normal Phillips curve relationship. The higher the rate of (demand-deficient) unemployment, the lower the rate of inflation.

■ The expected rate of inflation (π^e). The higher the rate of inflation that people expect, the higher will be the level of wage demands and the more willing will firms be to raise prices. Thus the higher will be the actual rate of inflation and thus the vertically higher will be the whole Phillips curve.

Let us assume for simplicity that the rate of inflation people expect this year (π^e_t) (where t represents the current time period: i.e. this year) is the same rate that inflation actually was last year (π_{t-1})

$$\pi^e_t = \pi_{t-1}$$

Thus if unemployment is such as to push up prices by 4 per cent ($f(1/U) = 4\%$) and if last year's inflation was 6 per cent, then inflation this year will be 4 per cent + 6 per cent = 10 per cent.

KI 13
p 78

Definition

Expectations-augmented Phillips curve A (short-run) Phillips curve whose position depends on the expected rate of inflation.

The accelerationist theory of inflation

Let us trace the course of inflation and expectations over a number of years in an imaginary economy. To keep the analysis simple, assume there is no growth in the economy.

Year 1. Assume that at the outset, in year 1, there is no inflation at all; that none is expected; that $AD = AS$; and that equilibrium unemployment is 8 per cent. The economy will be at point *a* in Figure 29.12 and Table 29.1.

Year 2. Now assume that the government expands aggregate demand in order to reduce unemployment. Unemployment falls to 6 per cent. The economy moves to point *b* along curve I. Inflation has risen to 4 per cent, but people, basing their expectations of inflation on year 1, still expect zero inflation. There is therefore no shift as yet in the Phillips curve. Curve I corresponds to an expected rate of inflation of zero.

Year 3. People now revise their expectations of inflation to the level of year 2. The Phillips curve shifts up by 4 percentage

points to position II. If nominal aggregate demand (i.e. demand purely in money terms, irrespective of the level of prices) continues to rise at the same rate, the whole of the increase will now be absorbed in higher prices. *Real* aggregate demand will fall back to its previous level and the economy will move to point *c*. Unemployment will return to 8 per cent. There is no *demand-pull* inflation now ($f(1/U) = 0$), but inflation is still 4 per cent due to expectations ($\pi^e = 4\%$).

Year 4. Assume now that the government expands *real* aggregate demand again so as to reduce unemployment once more to 6 per cent. This time it must expand nominal aggregate demand *more* than it did in year 2, because this time, as well as reducing unemployment, it also has to validate the 4 per cent expected inflation. The economy moves to point *d* along curve II. Inflation is now 8 per cent.

Year 5 onwards. Expected inflation is now 8 per cent (the rate of actual inflation in year 4). The Phillips curve shifts up to position III. If at the same time the government tries to keep unemployment at 6 per cent, it must expand nominal aggregate demand 4 per cent faster in order to validate the 8 per cent expected inflation. The economy moves to point *e* along curve III. Inflation is now 12 per cent.

To maintain unemployment at 6 per cent, the government must continue to increase nominal aggregate demand by 4 per cent more than the previous year. As the expected inflation rate goes on rising, the Phillips curve will go on shifting up each year.

Thus in order to keep unemployment below the initial equilibrium rate, inflation must go on *accelerating* each

Table 29.1	The accelerationist theory of inflation and inflationary expectations						
Year	Point on graph	π	=	$f(1/U)$	+	π^e	
1	*a*	0	=	0	+	0	
2	*b*	4	=	4	+	0	
3	*c*	4	=	0	+	4	
4	*d*	8	=	4	+	4	
5	*e*	12	=	4	+	8	

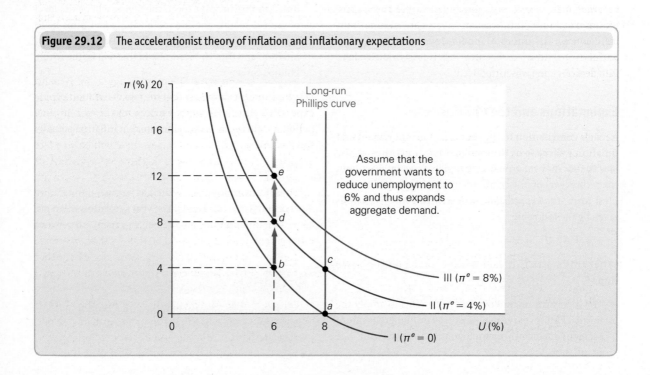

Figure 29.12 The accelerationist theory of inflation and inflationary expectations

year. For this reason, this theory of the Phillips curve is sometimes known as the *accelerationist theory*.

The more the government reduces unemployment, the greater the rise in inflation that year, and the more the rise in expectations the following year and each subsequent year; and hence the more rapidly will price rises accelerate. Thus the true longer-term trade-off is between unemployment and the rate of increase in inflation.

Pause for thought

What determines how rapidly the short-run Phillips curves in Figure 29.12 shift upwards?

The long-run Phillips curve and the natural rate of unemployment

As long as there are demand-pull pressures ($f(1/U) > 0$), inflation will accelerate as the expected rate of inflation (π^e) rises. In the long run, therefore, the Phillips curve will be vertical at the rate of unemployment where *real* aggregate demand equals *real* aggregate supply. This is the *equilibrium* rate of unemployment. It is also known as the *natural rate* or the *non-accelerating-inflation rate of unemployment (NAIRU)*. In Figure 29.12 the equilibrium rate of unemployment is 8 per cent.

The implication for government policy is that expanding aggregate demand can reduce unemployment below the equilibrium rate only in the *short* run. In the long run, the effect will be purely inflationary. On the other hand, a policy of restraining aggregate demand, for example by restraining the growth in the money supply, will *not* in the long run lead to higher unemployment: it will simply lead to lower inflation at the equilibrium rate of unemployment. The implication is that governments should make it a priority to control money supply, perhaps through targeting the size of the public-sector deficit, and thereby nominal aggregate demand and inflation.

Rational expectations

New classical economists go further than the monetarist theory described above. They argue that even the short-run Phillips curve is vertical: that there is *no* trade-off between

unemployment and inflation, even in the short run. They base their arguments on two key assumptions (see section 29.2, page 551) – continuous market clearing and rational expectations.

Because prices and wage rates are flexible, markets clear very rapidly. This means that there will be no disequilibrium unemployment, even in the short run. All unemployment will be equilibrium unemployment, or 'voluntary unemployment' as new classical economists prefer to call it.

In the accelerationist theory, expectations are based on *past* information and thus take time to catch up with changes in aggregate demand. Such expectations are known as *adaptive expectations*. Thus for a short time a rise in nominal aggregate demand will raise output and reduce unemployment below the equilibrium rate, while prices and wages are still relatively low.

The new classical analysis, by contrast, is based on *rational expectations*. Rational expectations are not based on past rates of inflation. Instead they are based on the current state of the economy and the current policies being pursued by the government. Workers and firms look at the information available to them – at the various forecasts that are published, at various economic indicators and the assessments of them by various commentators, at government pronouncements, and so on. From this information they predict the rate of inflation as well as they can. It is in this sense that the expectations are 'rational': people use their reason to assess the future on the basis of current information.

But forecasters frequently get it wrong, and so do economic commentators! And the government does not always do what it says it will. Thus workers and firms will be basing expectations on *imperfect information*. As we saw earlier, the crucial point about the rational expectations theory, however, is that these errors in prediction are *random*. People's predictions of inflation are just as likely to be too high as too low.

Assume that the government raises aggregate demand and that the increase is expected. People will anticipate that this will lead to higher prices and wages. If both goods and labour markets clear continuously because of the flexibility of prices and wages, there will be *no* effect on output and employment. If their expectations of higher inflation are correct, this will thus *fully* absorb the increase in nominal aggregate demand such that there will have been no increase in *real* aggregate demand at all. Firms will not produce any more output or employ any more people: after all, why should they? If they anticipate that people will spend 10 per cent more money but that prices will rise by 10 per cent, their *volume* of sales will remain the same.

Output and employment will only rise, therefore, if people make an error in their predictions (i.e. if they underpredict the rate of inflation and interpret an increase in money spent as an increase in *real* demand). But they are

---

Definitions

Accelerationist theory The theory that unemployment can only be reduced below the natural rate at the cost of accelerating inflation.

Natural rate of unemployment or **non-accelerating-inflation rate of unemployment (NAIRU)** The rate of unemployment consistent with a constant rate of inflation: the rate of unemployment at which the vertical long-run Phillips curve cuts the horizontal axis.

as likely to *over* predict the rate of inflation, in which case output and employment will fall! Thus there is no systematic trade-off between inflation and unemployment, even in the short run.

The vertical short-run Phillips curve is therefore comparable to the vertical short-run aggregate supply curve we saw in section 29.2 (see page 550). As we saw, this shows aggregate supply (output) being determined independently of aggregate demand.

Both the vertical short-run Phillips curve and the vertical *SRAS* curve can be used to illustrate how anticipated changes in economic policy, such as changes in government spending, have no effect on output and employment. Instead they remain at their equilibrium levels. This controversial conclusion is known as the **policy ineffectiveness proposition**.

> ### Pause for thought
>
> *For what reasons would a new classical economist support the policy of the Bank of England publishing its inflation forecasts and the minutes of the deliberations of the Monetary Policy Committee?*

Expectations of output and employment

Many economists, especially those who would describe themselves as 'Keynesian', criticise the approach of focusing exclusively on price expectations. Expectations, they argue, influence *output* and *employment* decisions, not just pricing decisions.

If there is a gradual but sustained expansion of aggregate demand, firms, seeing the economy expanding and seeing their orders growing, will start to invest more and make longer-term plans for expanding their labour force. Business and consumers will generally *expect* a higher level of output, and this optimism will cause businesses to produce more. In other words, expectations will affect output and employment as well as prices. Similarly, if businesses anticipate a recession, they are likely to cut back on production and investment.

Graphically, the increased output and employment from the recovery in investment will shift the Phillips curve to the left, offsetting (partially, wholly or more than wholly) the upward shift from higher inflationary expectations.

The lesson here for governments is that a sustained, but moderate, increase in aggregate demand can lead to a sustained growth in aggregate supply. What should be avoided is an excessive and unsustainable expansion of aggregate demand. In turn, this raises questions about the role that governments should play in managing aggregate demand in order to affect levels of business activity.

Such debates were heightened by the financial crisis of the late 2000s, the subsequent global economic downturn and the fragility of the macroeconomic environment that then characterised the first half of the 2010s. Did the austerity policies pursued in the UK, the eurozone and many other countries affect aggregate supply as well as aggregate demand? Did they reduce *potential* GDP and hence shift the *AS* curve to the left? Chapter 30 looks at government policy in more detail.

29.5 INFLATION RATE TARGETING AND UNEMPLOYMENT

The Phillips curve appeared to have shifted to the right in the 1970s and 1980s and then back to the left in the 1990s. It also seems to have changed its shape. Far from being vertical in the long run, it appears in more recent times to have resembled more of a horizontal line. While inflation rates did vary more than they had for some time in the late 2000s and early 2010s, unemployment rates were to fluctuate markedly as aggregate demand collapsed following

> ### Definition
>
> **Policy ineffectiveness proposition** The conclusion drawn from new classical models that, when economic agents anticipate changes in economic policy, output and employment remain at their equilibrium (or natural) levels.

the financial crisis, followed by a gradual recovery in private-sector expenditure. Figure 29.13 traces out the path of inflation and unemployment since 1967.

What explains the shape of this path? Part of the explanation lies in long-term changes in unemployment. Part lies in the policy of inflation targeting, pursued in the UK since 1992.

Changes in equilibrium unemployment

Why was there a substantial rise in unemployment from the early 1970s to the mid-1980s? Why, as a result, was there an apparent rightward shift in the Phillips curve? Why was there then a substantial fall in unemployment from the mid-1990s? To answer this, we need to look at the labour market and the determinants of the equilibrium level of unemployment (i.e. the natural rate of unemployment or NAIRU).

Figure 29.13 Phillips loops in the UK

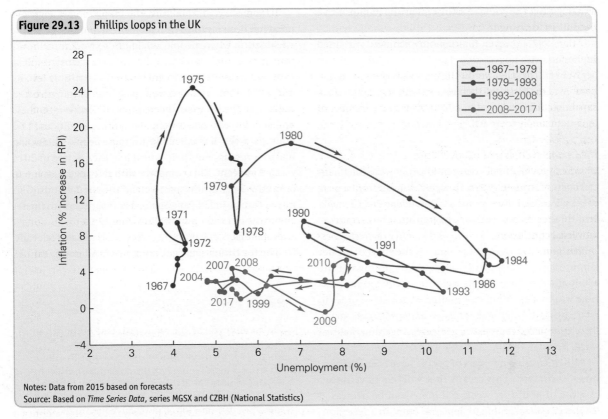

Notes: Data from 2015 based on forecasts
Source: Based on *Time Series Data*, series MGSX and CZBH (National Statistics)

Structural unemployment. The 1970s and 1980s were a period of rapid industrial change. The changes included the following:

■ Dramatic changes in technology. The microchip revolution, for example, has led to many traditional jobs becoming obsolete.

■ Competition from abroad. The introduction of new products from abroad, often of superior quality to domestic goods, or produced at lower costs, has led to the decline of many older industries: e.g. the textile industry.

■ Shifts in demand away from the products of older labour-intensive industries to new capital-intensive products.

The free market seemed unable to cope with these changes without a large rise in structural/technological unemployment. Labour was not sufficiently mobile – either geographically or occupationally – to move to industries where there were labour shortages or into jobs where there were skill shortages. A particular problem here was the lack of investment in education and training, with the result that the labour force was not sufficiently flexible to respond to changes in demand for labour.

From the mid-1980s, however, there were increasing signs that the labour market was becoming more flexible (see section 18.7). People seemed more willing to accept that they would have to move from job to job throughout their career. At the same time, policies were introduced to improve training (see section 31.3).

Another explanation for first the rise of equilibrium unemployment and later the fall is the phenomenon of 'hysteresis'.

Hysteresis If a recession causes a rise in unemployment which is not then fully reversed when the economy recovers, then there is a problem of **hysteresis**. This term, used in physics, refers to the lagging or persistence of an effect, even when the initial cause has been removed. In our context it refers to the persistence of unemployment even when the initial demand deficiency no longer exists.

The recessions of the early 1980s and early 1990s created a growing number of long-term unemployed who were both deskilled and demotivated. What is more, many firms, in an attempt to cut costs, cut down on training programmes. In these circumstances, a rise in aggregate demand would not simply enable the long-term unemployed to be employed again.

The recessions also caused a lack of investment and a reduction in firms' capacity. When demand recovered, many firms were unable to increase output and instead raised prices. Unemployment thus fell only modestly and

KI 35
p354

Definition

Hysteresis The persistence of an effect even when the initial cause has ceased to operate. In economics it refers to the persistence of unemployment even when the demand deficiency that caused it no longer exists.

inflation rose. The NAIRU had increased: the Phillips curve had shifted to the right.

After 1992, however, the economy achieved sustained expansion, with no recession. Equilibrium unemployment began to fall. In other words, the hysteresis was not permanent. As firms increased their investment, the capital stock expanded; firms engaged in more training; the number of long-term unemployed fell.

The financial crisis and its aftermath

UK unemployment rates rose sharply following the financial crisis of the late 2000s. However, the fall from a peak of 8.5 per cent in three months to November 2011 to 6 per cent three years later led some to argue that hysteresis was now less of a problem.

The principal reason, they argue, is the effect of greater labour market flexibility. Consequently, following the economic downturn, firms were able to introduce part-time working or negotiate nominal wage cuts in order to retain workers. Even where there were no wage cuts, many firms introduced nominal wage freezes, meaning that real wages fell.

Also, increasing numbers of people have been on 'zero-hours contracts'. This means that workers have no set number of hours per week and hours can be decreased (or increased) according to demand. Thus, in a recession, employers can simply cut the number of hours offered to workers on such contracts.

To some extent, therefore, the problem of unemployment has been replaced by a problem of **underemployment** – a situation where people would like to work more hours than they are able to obtain, either in their current job or in an alternative job or in an additional part-time job. By mid-2014, some 10 per cent of people in employment (3 million) in the UK were underemployed. On average, these underemployed workers wanted to work an additional 11.3 hours per week. If you include just those people who would like to work more in their *current* job, the UK rate in 2014 was 5.9 per cent. This compares with rates of 2.1, 4.1, 6.0, 6.9 and 9.5 per cent respectively in the Netherlands, Germany, France, Ireland and Spain. A comparison with figures before the recession is shown in Figure 29.14.

Nonetheless, the problem of hysteresis remains relevant. Despite the falling aggregate unemployment rate in the UK,

---

Definition

Underemployment International Labour Organisation (ILO) definition: a situation where people currently working less than 'full time' (40 hours in the UK) would like to work more hours (at current wage rates), either by working more hours in their current job, or by switching to an alternative job with more hours or by taking on an additional part-time job or any combination of the three. Eurostat definition: where people working less than 40 hours per week would like to work more hours in their current job at current wage rates.

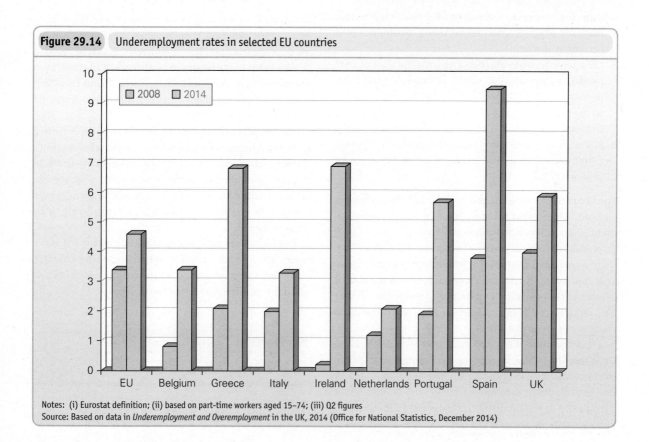

| **Figure 29.14** | Underemployment rates in selected EU countries |

Notes: (i) Eurostat definition; (ii) based on part-time workers aged 15–74; (iii) Q2 figures
Source: Based on data in *Underemployment and Overemployment* in the UK, 2014 (Office for National Statistics, December 2014)

35 per cent of those recorded as unemployed on the claim-ant count measure at the end of 2014 had been so for a year or more (see Box 26.2). Furthermore, youth unemployment rates remain more than double the aggregate level. These factors act as a brake on reductions in unemployment and adversely affect potential output.

Meanwhile, unemployment rates in the first half of the 2010s remained significantly above pre-financial crisis lev-els in many countries in the eurozone, such as Greece, Por-tugal and Spain, which have had to seek bailouts because of their high levels of debt. A condition of being granted bailouts has been to reduce public-sector debt. This has ruled out Keynesian expansionary fiscal policy. The very high levels of unemployment in these countries, especially amongst the young (rates of over 50 per cent in Greece and Spain in the 15–24 age group), has resulted in a problem of entrenchment and hysteresis that will make reductions in unemployment slow and difficult to achieve.

Inflation targeting

As we have seen, a major determinant of the actual rate of inflation is the rate of inflation that people expect. Since 1992, a policy of inflation targeting has been adopted, and in 1997 the Bank of England was given independence in setting interest rates to achieve the target rate of inflation.

The target was initially set in October 1992 as a range from 1 to 4 per cent for RPIX inflation.[1] With the election of the Labour government in 1997, a single point target of 2.5 per cent was adopted. This was changed to a 2 per cent tar-get for CPI inflation in December 2003. CPI inflation is typi-cally about 0.5 to 0.8 percentage points below RPI inflation.

The public's inflation rate expectations appear to have been affected by inflation rate targeting. Figure 29.15 shows forecast and actual RPI inflation since 1998. The forecasts are the average of at least 20 independent forecasts and thus can be taken as an indicator of expectations. As you can see, until the credit crunch of 2008, inflation forecasts were pretty accurate and reflected belief that the Bank of England would be successful in meeting its inflation target.

The credit crunch and the onset of recession began to affect the accuracy of 24-month forecasts. Subsequently, the 12-month forecasts became less accurate too as infla-tion rose as a result of rapid rises in food, oil and other com-modity prices (see Box 26.3).

Implications for the Phillips curve

So, does this mean that the Phillips curve has now become horizontal? The answer is that it depends on policy and, hence, on the central bank's remit. If inflation remains central to this remit, is successfully kept on target and peo-ple believe that it will remain so, the path of inflation and unemployment will be a horizontal straight line.

Even if the central bank does succeed in achieving the target rate of inflation, in the short term unemployment will fluctuate with the business cycle. Thus there may be

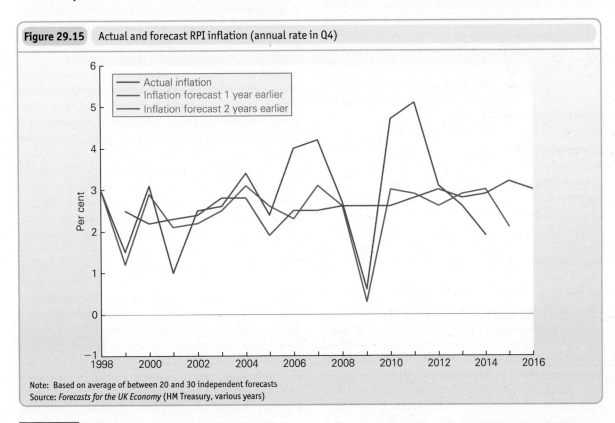

Figure 29.15   Actual and forecast RPI inflation (annual rate in Q4)

Note: Based on average of between 20 and 30 independent forecasts
Source: *Forecasts for the UK Economy* (HM Treasury, various years)

---

[1] RPIX is the retail prices index, excluding mortgage interest payments. CPI is the consumer prices index. Differences in how CPI is compiled means that CPI inflation is typically about 0.5 percentage points below RPIX inflation. Thus the current target of 2 per cent CPI inflation is approximately equivalent to 2.5 per cent RPIX inflation – the target that was used prior to December 2003.

movements left or right along this horizontal line from one year to the next depending on the level of economic activity. Such fluctuations in unemployment are consistent with stable inflation, provided that the fluctuations are mild and are not enough to alter people's expectations of inflation.

Over the medium term (3–6 years), there may be a leftward movement if the economy starts in recession and then the output gap is gradually closed through a process of steady economic growth (growth that avoids 'boom and bust'). Demand-deficient unemployment will be gradually eliminated. Thus between 1992 (the trough of the recession) and 1996, the output gap was closed from –2.6 to +0.1 (see the chart in Box 29.1). Provided the process is gradual, inflation can stay on target.

Over the longer term, movements left (or right) will depend on what happens to equilibrium unemployment. A reduction in equilibrium unemployment will result in a leftward movement. Evidence suggests that between the mid-1980s and the financial crisis of the late 2000s, the

equilibrium unemployment halved from around 10 per cent to 5 per cent. The precise amount, however, is not certain as it is subject to measurement errors.

What if the central bank's remit changed?

If inflation rate targeting were relaxed, perhaps as a shift to a broader remit, or even abandoned, and if aggregate demand expanded rapidly, the traditionally shaped short-run Phillips curve could re-emerge. A rapid expansion of aggregate demand would both reduce unemployment below the equilibrium rate and raise inflation. There would be a positive output gap.

This position could not be sustained, however, as inflationary expectations would rise and the short-run Phillips curve would begin shifting upwards (as in Figure 29.12 on page 560). A long-run vertical Phillips curve would once more become apparent at the natural (equilibrium) rate of unemployment.

29.6 BUSINESS CYCLES

Business cycles and aggregate demand

KI 38
p470
Many economists, particularly Keynesians, blame fluctuations in output and employment largely on fluctuations in aggregate demand. Theirs is therefore a 'demand-side' explanation of the business cycle. In the upturn (phase 1), aggregate demand starts to rise (see Figure 26.3 on page 474). It rises rapidly in the expansionary phase (phase 2). It then slows down and may start to fall in the peaking-out phase (phase 3). It then falls or remains relatively stagnant in the recession (phase 4).

Consumption cycles

Spending by the household sector is the largest component by value of aggregate demand. In the UK, household spending has averaged around 60 per cent of GDP over the past 50 years. Consequently, even relatively small changes in consumer behaviour can have a significant impact on the overall demand for firms' goods and services and so on the level of business activity. Figure 29.16 shows the similarity in annual rates of economic growth and in household spending for the UK. Therefore, in analysing the business cycle it is important to have an understanding of the consumption cycle.

An important influence on consumption is people's incomes. You might think that this implies a relatively straightforward relationship between *disposable income* and consumption. Disposable income is the income people have available for spending or saving after deductions, such as income tax and payments to social insurance schemes (national insurance in the UK), and any additions, such as social benefits.

Consumption smoothing. However, evidence shows that short-run changes in consumption, such as those from one quarter of a year to the next, are typically *less* variable than those in disposable income. The evidence, therefore, points to the short-run *marginal propensity to consume from disposable income* being smaller than it is over the longer term. One explanation is that households do not like their spending to vary too drastically in the short term. For example, many people's income varies with the time of year. Examples include those working in the holiday industry or painting and decorating. However, such people are likely to spread their spending relatively evenly over the year.

The key point here is that because households dislike large changes in their consumption they will tend to engage in *consumption smoothing*. This helps to explain why consumption is less volatile than other components of aggregate demand, especially, as we shall see shortly, investment spending. The act, therefore, of consumption smoothing helps to dampen the business cycle.

The financial system (such as banks and building societies) plays an important part in consumption smoothing. It allows, for instance, households to borrow against *expected future incomes*. Households can borrow when their current income is low and pay back the loans later when income is hopefully higher. Similarly, when income levels are high households may increase their saving to boost their future consumption levels. Therefore, the financial system provides households with greater flexibility over when to spend not just their current income, but their expected future incomes too.

Figure 29.16 Annual rates of growth in UK household-sector consumption, investment and output

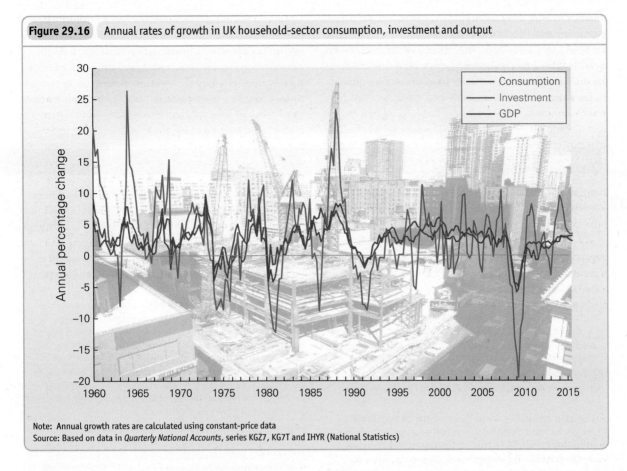

Note: Annual growth rates are calculated using constant-price data
Source: Based on data in *Quarterly National Accounts*, series KGZ7, KG7T and IHYR (National Statistics)

Whilst the financial system typically tends to reduce volatility in consumption, there are times when the opposite is true. We consider two reasons for this.

Availability and price of credit. The ability and willingness of financial institutions to lend may be affected by the phase of the business cycle. In a boom, with bank deposits increasing and banks relatively confident about the future, banks may be willing to lend more or reduce the interest rate charged on credit relative to that paid on saving, thereby further stimulating consumer spending. In a recession, however, banks may fear people's ability to repay loans and may thus cut back on lending or raise the interest rate charged on credit relative to that paid on saving, thereby further dampening consumer demand.

In other words, banks may take the path of output as a signal of the riskiness of lending; they perceive lending to be riskier in a recession than in a boom. This is significant because it can result in the overall flow of credit being dependent on the phase of the business cycle. If true, it

creates an inherently destabilising mechanism *within* the economy.

The idea that the financial sector may amplify shocks to the macroeconomy when conditions in financial markets are affected by the state of the macroeconomy is known as the *financial accelerator*.

Household wealth and the household sector's balance sheets. By borrowing and saving, households accumulate a stock of financial liabilities (debts), financial assets (savings) and physical assets (mainly property). The household sector's

Pause for thought

Other than looking at the current growth of economic output, how else can financial institutions assess the riskiness of their lending?

Definitions

Disposable income Income available for spending or saving after the deduction of direct taxes and the addition of benefits.

Marginal propensity to consume from disposable income The proportion of a rise in disposable income that is spent.

Consumption smoothing The act by households of smoothing their levels of consumption over time despite facing volatile incomes.

Financial accelerator When a change in national income is amplified by changes in the financial sector, such as changes in interest rate differentials or the willingness of banks to lend.

financial balance sheet details the sector's holding of financial assets and liabilities, while its *capital balance* sheet details its physical assets. The balance of financial assets over liabilities is the household sector's *net financial wealth*. The household sector's *net worth* is the sum of its net financial wealth and its *physical wealth*.

Changes to household balance sheets will affect the people's financial health. Such changes can have a significant impact on household spending. For instance, a declining net worth to income ratio, perhaps as the result of falling house prices or falling share prices, may encourage people to save more in an attempt to build up a buffer stock of

---

| **BOX 29.2** | **HOUSEHOLD SECTOR BALANCE SHEETS** |

A country's national balance sheet details its net worth (i.e. wealth). This aggregates the net worth of the household sector, the corporate sector and the public sector. We consider here the net worth of the household sector and the extent to which this may influence consumption (C).[2] The sector's net worth is the sum of its net financial wealth and non-financial assets.

The household sector's net financial wealth is the balance of financial assets over financial liabilities. Financial assets include moneys in savings accounts, shares and pension funds. Financial liabilities include debts secured against property, largely residential mortgages, and unsecured debts, such as overdrafts and unpaid balances on credit cards.

Physical wealth is predominantly the sector's residential housing wealth and is, therefore, affected by changes in house prices.

The table summarises the net worth of the UK household sector. By the end of 2014 the sector had a stock of net worth estimated at over £9.44 trillion compared with £3.55 trillion at the end of 1997 – an increase of 166 per cent. This, of course, is a nominal increase, not a real increase, as part of it merely reflects the rise in asset prices.

Over the period, net worth as a percentage of GDP grew every year with the exceptions of 2001, 2008 and 2013. The most rapid increase in the net worth to GDP ratio was observed in 2009 when it rose by 36 percentage points (partly as a result of a fall in GDP).

Financial balance sheet

The household sector has experienced significant growth in the size of its financial balance sheet. This is captured by the chart, which shows the components of net financial wealth:

financial assets and liabilities. The ratio of financial liabilities to disposable income rose from 105 per cent in 1997 to 168 per cent in 2007; people were taking on more and more debt relative to their incomes, fuelled by the ease of accessing credit – both consumer credit (loans and credit-card debt) and mortgages. Then, in the aftermath of the credit crunch, the ratio began to fall. By 2013, it had fallen to 142 per cent and stood at 143 per cent in 2014.

The longer-term increase in the sector's debt-to-income ratio up to 2007 meant that interest payments involved increasingly significant demands on household budgets and hence on the discretionary income households had for spending. This made the sector's spending more sensitive to changes in interest rates. This became a worry as recovery gathered pace from 2014. A rise in interest rates could place a substantial burden on households, thereby curbing consumer expenditure and causing the recovery to stall.

Higher debt-to-income levels can fuel people's concerns about the potential risks arising from debt. If the prospects for income growth are revised down or become more uncertain, people may decide to cut their spending in order to pay off some of their debts.

Non-financial assets

The accumulation of household debt has gone hand-in-hand with the growth of non-financial assets, mainly housing. This is not a coincidence, since an important reason for the growth in household debt has been the sector's acquisition of property. Secured debt is debt where property acts as collateral. It accounts for nearly 90 per cent of household debt. Between 1998 and 2014 it grew on average by around 7 per cent per year. Over the same period, the stock of dwellings increased in value by around 8 per cent per year.

House prices display two characteristics: they are notoriously volatile in the short term but rise relative to general prices over the long term. House price volatility makes the net worth

---

[2] The household sector in the official statistics also includes 'non-profit institutions serving households (NPISH)' such as charities, clubs and societies, trade unions, political parties and universities.

Household sector summary balance sheet

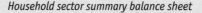

	1997			2014		
	£ billions	**% of disposable income**	**% of GDP**	**£ billions**	**% of disposable income**	**% of GDP**
Financial assets	2658.2	451.4	300.9	5883.1	501.9	323.7
Financial liabilities	617.6	104.9	69.9	1681.2	143.4	92.5
Net financial wealth	**2040.6**	**346.5**	**231.0**	**4201.9**	**358.5**	**231.2**
Non-financial assets	1511.8	256.7	171.1	5241.4	447.2	288.4
Net worth	**3552.3**	**603.2**	**402.1**	**9443.3**	**805.7**	**519.7**

Source: Based on data from *National Balance Sheet, 2015 Estimates and Quarterly National Accounts* (National Statistics)

wealth. This buffer stock acts as a form of security blanket. Alternatively, households may look to repay some of their outstanding debt.

If, in attempting to improve the position of their balance sheets, households were to reduce their spending substantially, the effect could lead to a balance sheet recession (see Chapter 26, page 490). In contrast, improvements to household balance sheets may strengthen the growth of consumption. The household sector's balance sheets are discussed in Box 29.2.

The *financial instability hypothesis* (see Box 28.4 on pages 538–9) argues that a deterioration of the balance sheets of

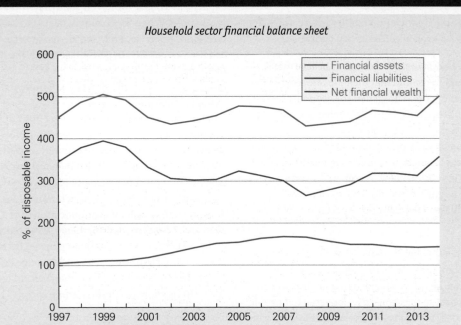

Household sector financial balance sheet

Source: Based on data from *National Balance Sheet, 2015 Estimates* and *Quarterly National Accounts* (National Statistics)

of the household sector volatile too. This impact of house price volatility on net worth had grown over the years as house prices had risen and hence the stocks of both housing assets and secured debt had risen. In 2014, 51 per cent of the household sector's net worth came from the value of dwellings. It had been as high as 57 per cent in 2007.

The precautionary effect. The volatility in net worth from volatile house prices (and potentially the prices of other assets, such as shares) can induce volatility in consumption. If asset prices are falling, households may respond by cutting their spending and increasing saving. This is a precautionary effect. Conversely, higher asset prices enable households to reduce saving and spend more.

The collateral effect. The trend for house prices to rise introduces another means by which the balance sheets affect spending: a collateral effect. As house prices rise, people's housing equity will tend to rise too. Housing equity is the difference between the value of the property and the value of any outstanding loan secured against it. House price movements affect the collateral that households have to secure additional lending.

When house prices are rising, households may look to borrowing additional sums from mortgage lenders for purposes other than transactions involving property or spending on major home improvements. This is known as housing equity withdrawal (HEW). These funds can then be used to fund consumption, purchasing other assets (e.g. shares) or repaying other debts.

When house prices fall, households have less collateral to secure additional lending to fund spending. In these circumstances people may wish to restore, at least partially, their housing equity by increasing mortgage repayments (negative HEW), thereby further reducing consumption.

The period from 2002 to 2007 was one of high levels of HEW, averaging over £7.0 billion per quarter or 3.1 per cent of disposable income. From 2008 to 2015, however, HEW averaged minus £11.25 billion per quarter. This meant that households were increasing housing equity by the equivalent of 3.9 per cent of income per quarter – money that could have been spent on consumption. Case study J.20 in MyEconLab details the patterns in HEW and consumer spending.

Draw up a list of the various factors that could affect the household balance sheet and then consider how these could impact on consumer spending.

economic agents followed by efforts then to rebuild them is an inherent feature of economies. This pattern in the balance sheets reflects a financial cycle primarily driven by psychological influences. A period of growth tends to breed an overconfidence and exuberance across all economic agents, including financial institutions. The result is that, as people borrow more and more, balance sheets become increasingly fragile until a point is reached – a Minsky moment – when a balance sheet consolidation commences: people seek to reduce their debts by cutting back on spending.

In addition to this financial instability, there are other factors that help to explain consumption cycles.

TC 13
p 78 *Expectations of future incomes.* If consumers believe that their incomes are likely to rise and that their jobs are secure, they are likely to spend more. Thus when the economy booms, consumer confidence is likely to rise, thereby further stimulating the economy. If, however, the economy is in recession and consumers are worried about their future income or that they may lose their jobs, they will probably cut back on spending. This is then likely to deepen the recession. In simple terms, the current spending plans of forward-looking households are dependent on expectations of future incomes.

Expectations of future prices. If people expect prices to rise, as is likely in a boom, they tend to buy durable goods such as furniture and cars before this happens. Again, this will give an additional boost to the economy. Conversely, if people expect prices to fall, as is likely in a recession, they may wait, thereby deepening the recession. This has been a problem in Japan for many years, where periods of falling prices (deflation) led many consumers to hold back on spending, thereby weakening aggregate demand and hence economic growth.

The age of durables. If people's car, carpets, clothes, etc. are getting old, they will tend to have a high level of 'replacement' consumption, particularly after a recession when they had cut back on their consumption of durables. This can help to stimulate a recovery from recession. Conversely, as the economy reaches the peak of the boom, people are likely to spend less on durables as they have probably already bought the items they want. This can then contribute to the ending of the boom. Thus spending on durable can help to explain the turning points: the upturn from recession and the downturn from a boom.

Instability of investment

One of the factors contributing to the ups and downs of the business cycle is the instability of investment. Figure 29.16 (page 567) shows that real investment spending (gross capital formation) is markedly more volatile than output (real GDP).

As with household spending, we would expect investment, and in particular private-sector investment, to be affected by expectations and financial market conditions. Therefore, changes in national income can lead to amplified changes in investment expenditure because of their impact on the financial sector.

The investment accelerator. But the extent of the volatility in investment points to another type of accelerator effect. To understand this effect, remember that investment (except for replacement investment) provides businesses with *additional* capacity. This helps to explain why, in a recession, investment in new plant and equipment can all but disappear. After all, what is the point in investing in additional capacity if you cannot even sell what you are currently producing? When an economy begins to recover from a recession, however, and confidence returns, investment can rise very rapidly. In percentage terms, the rise in investment may be *several times that of the rise in income*. When the growth of the economy slows down, however, investment can fall dramatically.

The point is that investment depends not so much on the *level* of GDP and consumer demand, as on their *rate of change*. The reason is that investment (except for replacement investment) is to provide *additional* capacity, and thus depends on how much demand has risen, not on its level. But growth rates change by much more than the level of output. For example, if economic growth is 1 per cent in 2015 and 2 per cent in 2016, then in 2016 output has gone up by 2 per cent, but growth has gone up by 100 per cent! (i.e. it has doubled). Thus percentage changes in investment tend to be much more dramatic than percentage changes in GDP. This is known as the *accelerator theory*. KI 43
p 547

Pause for thought

Under what circumstances would you expect a rise in GDP to cause a large accelerator effect?

These fluctuations in investment, being injections into the circular flow of income, then have a multiplied effect on GDP, thereby magnifying the upswings and downswings of the business cycle.

Fluctuations in stocks

Firms hold stocks of finished goods. These stocks tend to fluctuate with the course of the business cycle, and these fluctuations in stocks themselves contribute to fluctuations in output.

Imagine an economy that is recovering from a recession. KI 13
p 78 At first, firms may be cautious about increasing production. Doing so may involve taking on more labour or making additional investment. Firms may not want to make these commitments if the recovery could soon peter out. They may

---

Definition

Accelerator theory The level of investment depends on the rate of change of national income, and the result tends to be subject to substantial fluctuations.

therefore run down their stocks rather than increase output. Initially, the recovery from recession will be slow.

If the recovery continues, however, firms will start to gain more confidence and will increase their production. Also they will find that their stocks have got rather low and will need building up. This gives a further boost to production, and for a time the growth in output will exceed the growth in demand. This extra growth in output will then, via the multiplier, lead to a further increase in demand.

Once stocks have been built up again, the growth in output will slow down to match the growth in demand. This slowing down in output will, via the accelerator and multiplier, contribute to the ending of the expansionary phase of the business cycle.

As the economy slows down, firms may for a time be prepared to carry on producing and build up stocks. The increase in stocks thus cushions the effect of falling demand on output and employment.

If the recession continues, firms will be unwilling to go on building up stocks. But as firms attempt to reduce their stocks back to the desired level, production will fall *below* the level of sales, despite the fact that sales themselves are lower. This could therefore lead to a dramatic fall in output and, via the multiplier, to an even bigger fall in sales.

Eventually, once stocks have been run down to the minimum, production will have to rise again to match the level of sales. This will contribute to a recovery and the whole cycle will start again.

Aggregate demand and the course of the business cycle

Why do booms and recessions last for several months or even years, and why do they eventually come to an end? Let us examine each in turn.

Why do booms and recessions persist for a period of time?

Time lags. It takes time for changes in injections and withdrawals to be fully reflected in changes in GDP, output and employment. The multiplier process takes time. Moreover, consumers, firms and government may not all respond immediately to new situations. Their responses are spread out over a period of time.

'Bandwagon' effects. Once the economy starts expanding, expectations become buoyant. People think ahead and adjust their expenditure behaviour: they consume and invest more *now*. Likewise in a recession, a mood of pessimism may set in. The effect is cumulative.

The multiplier and accelerator interact: they feed on each other. A rise in GDP causes a rise in investment (the investment accelerator). This, being an injection into the circular flow, causes a multiplied rise in income. This then causes a further accelerator effect, a further multiplier effect, and so on. The increase in investment may be greater

still if credit conditions ease as national income rises. If so, the *financial* accelerator further amplifies the increase in national income.

Group behaviour. Individual consumers and businesses may take their lead from others and so mimic their behaviour. This helps to reinforce bandwagon effects.

For example, during the 2000s many financial institutions loosened their lending criteria. This helped to fuel unsustainable property booms in several countries, including the UK, Ireland and the USA. They engaged in a competitive race, offering ever more favourable terms for borrowers. Often the borrowers could only repay if their assets (e.g. property) appreciated in value, as they tend to do in a boom – but not in a recession. This mirrors the predictions of the financial instability hypothesis.

This rush to lend meant that many banks over-extended themselves and operated with too little capital. This made them much more vulnerable to financial crises and much more likely to cut back lending dramatically in a downturn – as indeed they did from 2008.

Group behaviour can therefore help to amplify economic upturns and downturns. This illustrates how the *interaction* between economic agents affects macroeconomic aggregates, such as national income.

Why do booms and recessions come to an end? What determines the turning points?

Ceilings and floors. Actual output can go on growing more rapidly than potential output only as long as there is slack in the economy. As full employment is approached and as more and more firms reach full capacity, so a ceiling to output is reached.

At the other extreme, there is a basic minimum level of consumption that people tend to maintain. During a recession, people may not buy much in the way of luxury and durable goods, but they will continue to buy food and other basic goods. There is thus a floor to consumption.

The industries supplying these basic goods will need to maintain their level of replacement investment. Also there will always be some minimum investment demand as firms, in order to survive competition, need to install the latest equipment. There is thus a floor to investment too.

Echo effects. Durable consumer goods and capital equipment may last several years, but eventually they will need replacing. The replacement of goods and capital purchased in a previous boom may help to bring a recession to an end.

The investment accelerator. For investment to continue rising, consumer demand must rise at a *faster and faster* rate. If this does not happen, investment will fall back and the boom will break. This can then be amplified by the financial accelerator.

Sentiment and expectations. A change of sentiment and a sense that current rates of growth will not be sustained can lead people to adjust their spending behaviour, so contributing to the very slowdown that was expected. The impact of this will be amplified by bandwagon effects and group behaviour.

Random shocks. National or international political, social or natural events can affect the mood and attitudes of firms, governments and consumers, and thus affect aggregate demand.

Changes in government policy. In a boom, a government may become most worried by inflation and balance of trade deficits and thus pursue contractionary policies. In a recession, it may become most worried by unemployment and lack of growth and thus pursue expansionary policies. These government policies, if successful, will bring about a turning point in the cycle.

> ### Pause for thought
>
> *Why is it difficult to predict precisely when a recession will come to an end and the economy will start growing rapidly?*

KI 36
p 354
Some economists argue that governments should attempt to reduce cyclical fluctuations by the use of active demand-management policies. These could be either fiscal or monetary policies, or both (see Chapter 30). A more stable economy will provide a better climate for long-term investment, which will lead to faster growth in both potential and actual output.

Fluctuations in aggregate supply

While the mainstream view of business cycles stresses the importance of fluctuations in aggregate demand, it recognises that shifts in the aggregate supply curve in Figure 29.6 (see page 552) can also cause fluctuations in output. Sudden sharp changes to input prices, such as in the price of oil, could be one such cause.

Real business cycle theory

But some economists, such as 'new classical economists', go further and argue that shifts in aggregate supply are the *primary* source of economic volatility. One particular theory is known as **real business cycle theory**. In a recession, according to the theory, aggregate supply curves will shift to the left (output falls), while in a boom aggregate supply curves shift to the right (output rises).

But what causes aggregate supply to change in the first place, and why, once there has been an initial change, will the aggregate supply curve *go on* changing, causing a recession or boom to continue?

The initial shifts in aggregate supply are caused by *impulses*. An impulse could come from a structural change, such as a shift in demand from older manufacturing industries to new service industries. Because of the immobility of labour, not all those laid off in the older industries will find work in the new industries. Structural unemployment (part of equilibrium unemployment) rises and output falls. *Aggregate* demand may be the same, but because of a change in its pattern, aggregate supply falls and the Phillips curve shifts to the right.

Alternatively, the impulse could be a change in technology. For example, a technological breakthrough in telecommunications could increase aggregate supply. Or it could come from an oil price increase, shifting aggregate supply to the left.

The persistence of supply-side effects

Real business cycle theory stresses that the effects of impulses persist – aggregate supply *goes on* shifting. There are two main reasons. The first is that several changes may take months to complete. For example, a technological breakthrough does not affect all industries simultaneously.

KI 35
p 354

The second reason is that these changes will affect the profitability of investment. A positive shock (impulse) will raise investment levels, which will increase firms' capacity; hence the aggregate supply curve will shift to the right. Conversely, a negative shock (impulse) will reduce investment, causing the aggregate supply curve to shift to the left. Therefore, changes in the profitability of investment are said to amplify or 'propagate' the impact of the impulses through their effect on aggregate *supply*. This is in contrast to the multiplier effect, where changes in investment affect output through their effect on aggregate demand (see page 549).

By focusing on impulses which have enduring effects on aggregate supply, real business cycle theory offers a rather different perspective on the business cycle. The conventional view of the business cycle is one of fluctuations in actual output (real GDP) around the economy's potential output (see Figure 26.11 on page 489). By contrast, real business cycle theory portrays the business cycle as upward and downward movements in the economy's potential output which then affect the economy's actual output.

Turning points

So far we have seen how the theory of real business cycles explains persistent rises or falls in aggregate supply. But

> ### Definition
>
> **Real business cycle theory** The new classical theory which explains cyclical fluctuations in terms of shifts in aggregate supply, rather than aggregate demand.

how does it explain *turning points*? Why do recessions and booms come to an end? The most likely explanation is that, once a shock has worked its way through, aggregate supply will stop shifting. If there is then any shock in the other direction, aggregate supply will start moving back again. For example, after a period of recession, gluts in various commodities could lead to falls in commodity prices, thereby reducing industries' costs. Since these 'reverse shocks' are likely to occur at irregular intervals, they can help to explain why real-world business cycles are themselves irregular.

SUMMARY

1a In the simple circular flow of income model, equilibrium national income (GDP) is where withdrawals equal injections: where $W = J$.

1b The simple Keynesian model can be illustrated through the Keynesian cross diagram. Prices are assumed constant. Equilibrium is where national income (Y) (i.e. GDP), shown by the 45° line, is equal to aggregate expenditure (E).

1c If there is an initial increase in aggregate expenditure (ΔE), which could result from an increase in injections or a reduction in withdrawals, there will be a multiplied rise in national income (Y). The multiplier is defined as $\Delta Y/\Delta E$.

1d The size of the multiplier depends on the marginal propensity to consume domestically produced goods (mpc_d). The larger the mpc_d, the more will be spent each time incomes are generated around the circular flow, and thus the more will go round again as *additional* demand for domestic product. The multiplier formula is $1/1 - mpc_d$.

2a The impact of changes in aggregate demand on prices (and output) is affected by the nature of aggregate supply (AS) curve.

2b If nominal aggregate demand changes, then in the short run it is likely to affect real GDP according to the degree of slack in the economy. The short-run aggregate supply curve tends to be relatively elastic (except when the economy is operating close to or above potential output). This is because both wage rates and prices tend to be relatively sticky in the short run.

2c In the long run, according to many economists, the aggregate supply curve is vertical because price increases from any rise in aggregate demand tend to be passed on from one firm to another and feed into wage increases.

2d New classicists argue that that the *short-run* aggregate supply curve may be vertical too. This is because of the flexibility of markets and the ability of rational people to forecast the effect of expected changes in aggregate demand on prices.

2e Some argue, however, that even the long-run aggregate supply curve may be upward sloping. If a sustained increase in demand leads to increased investment, this can have the effect of shifting the short-run aggregate supply curve to the right and making the long-run curve upward sloping, not vertical.

3a The quantity equation $MV = PY$ can be used to analyse the possible relationship between money and prices.

3b In the short run, V tends to vary inversely, but unpredictably, with M. Thus the effect of a change in money supply on nominal GDP (PY) is uncertain.

3c The reason is that the interest-rate transmission mechanism between changes in money and changes in GDP is unreliable and possibly weak. The reasons are (a) an unstable and possibly elastic demand for money and (b) an unstable and possibly inelastic investment demand.

3d The exchange-rate transmission mechanism is stronger but still very unpredictable.

3e In the long run, the transmission mechanisms are stronger and relatively stable. If people have an increase in money in their portfolios, they will attempt to restore portfolio balance by purchasing assets, including goods. Thus an increase in money supply is transmitted directly into an increase in aggregate demand. The interest rate and exchange rate mechanisms are also argued to be strong. The demand for money is seen to be more stable in the long run. This leads to a long-run stability in V (unless it changes as a result of other factors, such as institutional arrangements for the handling of money).

3f The short-run effect of a change in money supply on *real* GDP (Y) depends on the degree of slack in the economy. In the long run, Y is determined largely independently of the money supply. A faster growth in the money supply over a long period is likely to result merely in higher inflation.

4a To explain how inflation and unemployment can occur simultaneously we need to allow for other types of inflation and unemployment. Consequently, the AS curve will be upward sloping but getting steeper as full employment is approached and as bottlenecks increasingly occur.

4b The Phillips curve showed the apparent trade-off between inflation and unemployment for more than 100 years prior to 1958. However, after the mid-1960s, the relationship appeared to break down as both inflation and unemployment rose.

4c An explanation for this is given by the adaptive expectations hypothesis. In its simplest form the hypothesis states that the expected rate of inflation this year is what it actually was last year: $\pi_t^e = \pi_{t-1}$

4d If there is excess demand in the economy, producing upward pressure on wages and prices, initially unemployment will fall. The reason is that workers and firms will believe that wage and price increases represent *real* wage and price increases. Thus workers are prepared to take jobs more readily and firms choose to produce more. But as people's expectations adapt upwards to these higher wages and prices, so ever-increasing rises in nominal aggregate demand will be necessary to maintain unemployment below the equilibrium rate. Price and wage rises will accelerate: i.e. inflation will rise.

4e According to this analysis, the Phillips curve is thus vertical at the natural rate of unemployment.

4f The new classical theory assumes flexible prices and wages in the short run as well as in the long run. It also assumes that people base their expectations of inflation

▶

on a rational assessment of the *current* situation. People may predict wrongly, but they are equally likely to under-predict or to overpredict. On average over the years they will predict correctly.

4g The implication of rational expectations and continuous market clearing is that not only the long-run but also the short-run Phillips curve will be vertical. If people correctly predict the rate of inflation, they will correctly predict that any increase in *nominal* aggregate demand will simply be reflected in higher prices. Total output and employment will remain the same: at the equilibrium level.

4h Expectations can also impact upon output and employ-ment. If business is confident that demand will expand and that order books will be healthy, then firms are likely to gear up production and take on extra labour.

5a Data for the UK show its Phillips curve shifting to the right in the 1970s and 1980s. Reasons include a growth in equilibrium unemployment caused by rapid technolog-ical changes and a persistence of unemployment beyond the recessions of the early 1980s and early 1990s (hysteresis).

5b In the late 1990s and early 2000s, equilibrium unem-ployment fell as labour markets became more flexible and as the lagged effects of the recessions of the early 1980s and early 1990s faded.

5c Some argue that the pace with which unemployment fell in the UK in the early 2010s demonstrates that hysteresis is now less of a problem. However, there was a substan-tial rise in underemployment, which reflected a higher degree of slack in the labour market than that implied by the unemployment statistics. Also rates of youth and long-term unemployment remained high and these would be expected to impact on future unemployment rates.

5d Inflation targeting in the UK has seen the rate of inflation typically very close to the target level. Inflation targeting helps to anchor inflationary expectations around the target rate. This has tended to make the time-path of the Phillips curve horizontal at the target rate of inflation.

5e In response to the economic downturn following the financial crisis, the Bank of England introduced a strategy of forward guidance to provide an indication

of the likely medium-term path of interest rates. Some economists argue that this could undermine the credibil-ity of inflation rate policy and raise the public's inflation-ary expectations.

6a Keynesians explain cyclical fluctuations in the economy by examining the causes of fluctuations in the level of aggregate *demand*.

6b Financial institutions may use economic growth as an indicator of the riskiness of lending. This will affect the availability of credit or the price of credit. Weaker growth is likely to result in reduced flows of credit and a higher rate of interest on borrowing relative to that on saving. This creates a financial accelerator effect which amplifies the business cycle. The financial instability hypothesis argues that the financial system swings between fragility and robustness with changes in the confidence of banks and investors. Again, the result is credit cycles which generate macroeconomic instability.

6c A major part of the Keynesian explanation of the business cycle is the instability of investment. The investment accelerator theory helps to explain this instability. It relates the level of investment to *changes* in national income and consumer demand. An initial increase in consumer demand can result in a very large percentage increase in investment; but as soon as the rise in consumer demand begins to level off, investment will fall; and even a slight fall in consumer demand can reduce investment to virtually zero. Investment in stocks is also unstable and tends to amplify the busi-ness cycle.

6d Booms and recessions can persist because of time lags, 'bandwagon' and 'group' effects and the *interaction* of the multiplier, accelerator and credit cycles.

6e Turning points are explained by ceilings and floors to output, echo effects, the investment accelerator, expec-tations and sentiment, random shocks and swings in government policy.

6f Real business cycle theory focuses on aggregate supply shocks (impulses), which then persist for a period of time. Eventually their effect will peter out, and supply shocks in the other direction can lead to turning points in the cycle.

MyEconLab

This book can be supported by MyEconLab, which contains a range of additional resources, including an online homework and tutorial system designed to test and build your understanding.

You need both an access card and a course ID to access MyEconLab:

1. Is your lecturer using MyEconLab? Ask your lecturer for your course ID.

2. Has an access card been included with the book at a reduced cost? Check the inside back cover of the book.

3. If you have a course ID but no access card, go to: http://www.myeconlab.com/ to buy access to this interactive study programme.

REVIEW QUESTIONS

1 Assume that the multiplier has a value of 3. Now assume that the government decides to increase aggregate demand in an attempt to reduce unemployment. It raises government expenditure by £100 million with no increase in taxes. Firms, anticipating a rise in their sales, increase investment by £200 million, of which £50 million consists of purchases of foreign machinery. How much will GDP rise? (Assume *ceteris paribus*.)

2 What factors could explain why some countries have a higher multiplier than others?

3 In what way will the nature of aggregate supply influence the effect of a change in aggregate demand on prices and real national income?

4 What shape do you think the aggregate supply curve would be at the current output if the economy was in a deep recession?

5 What shape of aggregate supply curve is assumed by the simple Keynesian demand-driven model of the economy? Under what circumstances is this shape likely to be a true reflection of the aggregate supply curve?

6 What are the implications of the relationship between the money supply (M) and the V and Y terms in the quantity equation $MV = PY$ for the effectiveness of controlling the amount of money in the economy as a means of controlling inflation?

7 In the adaptive expectations model of the Phillips curve, if the government tries to maintain unemployment below the equilibrium rate, what will determine the speed at which inflation accelerates?

8 For what reasons might the equilibrium rate of unemployment increase?

9 How can adaptive expectations of inflation result in clockwise Phillips loops? Why would these loops not be completely regular?

10 What implications would a vertical short-run aggregate supply curve have for the effectiveness of demand management policy?

11 Explain the persistence of high levels of unemployment after the 1980s recession. What policies would you advocate to reduce unemployment?

12 How can the interaction of the multiplier and accelerator explain cyclical fluctuations in GDP?

13 What is meant by 'real business cycle' theory? How can such theory account for (a) the persistence of periods of rapid or slow growth; (b) turning points in the cycle?

14 What do the financial accelerator and the financial instability hypothesis imply about the determinants of longer-term rates of economic growth?

ADDITIONAL PART J CASE STUDIES IN THE *ECONOMICS FOR BUSINESS* MyEconLab (www.pearsoned.co.uk/sloman)

J.1 **Theories of economic growth.** An overview of classical and more modern theories of growth.

J.2 **The costs of economic growth.** Why economic growth may not be an unmixed blessing.

J.3 **Technology and unemployment.** Does technological progress destroy jobs?

J.4 **The GDP deflator.** An examination of how GDP figures are corrected to take inflation into account.

J.5 **Comparing national income statistics.** The importance of taking the purchasing power of local currencies into account.

J.6 **The UK's balance of payments deficit.** An examination of the UK's persistent trade and current account deficits.

J.7 **Making sense of the financial balances on the balance of payments.** An examination of the three main components of the financial account.

J.8 **A high exchange rate.** This case looks at whether a high exchange rate is necessarily bad news for exporters.

J.9 **The Gold Standard.** A historical example of fixed exchange rates.

J.10 **The importance of international financial movements.** How a current account deficit can coincide with an appreciating exchange rate.

J.11 **Argentina in crisis.** An examination of the collapse of the Argentine economy in 2001/2.

J.12 **Currency turmoil in the 1990s.** Two examples of speculative attacks on currencies: first on the Mexican peso in 1995; then on the Thai baht in 1997.

J.13 **The attributes of money.** What makes something, such as metal, paper or electronic records, suitable as money?

J.14 **Secondary marketing.** This looks at one of the ways of increasing liquidity without sacrificing profitability. It involves selling an asset to someone else before the asset matures.

J.15 **Consolidated MFI balance sheet.** A look at the consolidated balance sheet of UK monetary financial institutions (banks, building societies and the Bank of England).

J.16 **Bailing out the banks.** An overview of the concerted efforts made to rescue the banking system in the crisis of 2007-9.

J.17 **John Maynard Keynes (1883–1946).** Profile of the great economist.

J.18 **The rational expectations revolution.** A profile of two of the most famous economists of the new classical rational expectations school.

J.19 **The phases of the business cycle.** A demand-side analysis of the factors contributing to each of the four phases.

J.20 **How does consumption behave?** The case looks at evidence on the relationship between consumption and disposable income.

▶

J.21 **Trends in housing equity withdrawal (HEW).** An analysis of the patterns in HEW and consumer spending.

J.22 **UK monetary aggregates.** This case shows how UK money supply is measured using both UK measures and eurozone measures.

J.23 **Credit and the business cycle.** This case traces cycles in the growth of credit and relates them to the business cycle. It also looks at some of the implications of the growth in credit.

J.24 **Has there been an accelerator effect over the past 50 years?** This case examines GDP and investment data to see whether the evidence points to an accelerator effect.

J.25 **Modelling the financial accelerator.** This case looks at how we can incorporate the accelerator effect into the simple Keynesian model of the economy.

WEBSITES RELEVANT TO PART J

Numbers and sections refer to websites listed in the Web appendix and hotlinked from this text's website at **www.pearsoned.co.uk/sloman**

■ For news articles relevant to Part J, see the *Economics News Articles* link from the text's website.

■ For general news on macroeconomic issues, both national and international, see websites in section A, and particularly A1–5, 7–9. For general news on money, banking and interest rates, see again A1–5, 7–9 and also 20–22, 25, 31, 35, 36. For all of Part J, see links to newspapers worldwide in A38, 39, 43, 44, and the news search feature in Google at A41.

■ For macroeconomic data, see links in B1, 2 and 3; also see B4 and 35. For UK data, see B2, 3, 5 and 34. For EU data, see B38 and 47. For US data, see Current economic indicators in B6 and the Data section of B17. For international data, see B15, 21, 24, 31, 33. For links to data sets, see B1, 4, 28, 35, 46; I14.

■ For national income statistics for the UK (Appendix to Chapter 26), see B1, *1. National Statistics* > *Publications* > Search "Blue Book" (filter search by Books).

■ For data on UK unemployment, see B1, *1. National Statistics* > *Publications* > Search "UK Labour Market". For International data on unemployment, see B1, 21, 24, 31, 38, 47; H3.

■ For international data on balance of payments and exchange rates, see B1 > sites B.7 (*Statistical Annex of the European Economy*), B.8 (*OECD Economic Outlook: Statistical Annex Tables*), B.10 (*World Economic Outlook*). See also the trade topic in I14.

■ For details of individual countries' balance of payments, see B31.

■ For UK data on balance of payments, see B1, *1. National Statistics* > *Publications* > Search "Pink Book". See also B34. For EU data, see B38.

■ For exchange rates, see A1, 3; B34; F2, 4, 5, 6, 8.

■ For discussion papers on balance of payments and exchange rates, see H4 and 7.

■ For monetary and financial data (including data for money supply and interest rates), see section F and particularly F2. Note that you can link to central banks worldwide from site F17. See also the links in B1.

■ For links to sites on money and monetary policy, see the Financial Economics sections in I4, 7, 11, 17.

■ For information on the development of ideas, see C12, 18; also see links under *Methodology* and *History of Economic Thought* in C14.

■ For student resources relevant to this chapter, see sites C1–7, 9, 10, 12, 19.

Macroeconomic policy

The FT Reports ...

The Financial Times, 5 March 2015

ECB set to fire starting gun on QE programme

By Claire Jones

The European Central Bank will launch its landmark quantitative easing programme on Monday with the first purchases of sovereign bonds to support an accelerating recovery in the eurozone.

An upbeat Mario Draghi said on Thursday that the controversial €1.1tn programme, announced in January, would help support an economy that after years of crisis and stagnation was likely to see a recovery that would 'broaden and strengthen gradually'.

The ECB is expected to buy up to €850bn in government bonds between next week and September 2016. Together with purchases of private sector debt and paper from eurozone institutions such as the European Investment Bank, the eurozone's central bankers will buy €60bn of debt a month. The central bank has promised to extend QE should price pressures remain weak.

'The latest inflation projections suggest that the hurdle to extend the programme beyond September next year is set pretty high,' said Ken Wattret, an economist at BNP Paribas.

Mr Draghi said in Nicosia, the Cypriot capital where Thursday's governing council vote took place, that the ECB would not buy assets trading at negative yields below minus 0.2 per cent, in effect imposing a ceiling on the price it was prepared to pay for government debt. German two-year bonds were trading below this level at the time of the announcement.

Negative yields, which are present in several eurozone bond markets, occur when bondholders pay more to buy a bond than they would receive should they hold the paper until it matures.

The euro rose to $1.1101 during Mr Draghi's statement, but later fell back to $1.1063. Eurozone bond yields fell while share prices rose.

The ECB president made an emphatic appeal to eurozone governments to step up the pace of economic reform, saying the signs of an accelerating economy and the launch of QE were 'no grounds for complacency'.

Swift and credible economic reforms would not only raise longer-term potential growth but lift expectations of higher incomes and encourage companies to bring forward investments, he said.

The governing council kept the central bank's benchmark interest rate at 0.05 per cent while the rate charged on a portion of eurozone banks' deposits parked at the ECB stayed at 0.2 per cent.

When the world economy was plunged into deep crisis in the 1930s, the response, both nationally and internationally, was too little and too late. This failure to act turned a serious downturn into a prolonged depression. We will not repeat those mistakes again.

Alistair Darling. Chancellor of the Exchequer, *Budget speech*, 21 April 2009

The role of government and of central bankers in managing macroeconomic affairs has always been a contentious one. Economists keenly debate the extent to which policy makers should intervene in economies. Such debates concern not only regional and national economies, but also groups of economies such as the 28 member states of the European Union (as the *Financial Times* article points out). Economists keenly debate the role that policy makers can play in reducing the inherent volatility of economies and in fostering more rapid long-term economic growth.

In this final part of the text, we consider the alternative policies open to policy makers in their attempts to manage or influence the macroeconomy. Chapter 30 focuses on fiscal and monetary policy in the context of affecting *aggregate demand*. We consider how such policies are supposed to work and how effective they are in practice.

Up to the financial crisis of the late 2000s, policy makers had taken a more passive approach towards policy, often advocating policy rules. The financial crisis saw fiscal rules relaxed, suspended or even abandoned. Many central banks continue to rely on policy rules: for example, the Bank of England sets interest rates so as to achieve a target rate of inflation of 2 per cent. Nonetheless, even here there is renewed interest in the merit of such rules.

Chapter 31, by contrast, focuses on *aggregate supply* and considers the role of government in attempting to improve economic performance by supply-side reforms: i.e. reforms designed to increase productivity and efficiency and achieve a growth in potential output. Both free-market and interventionist supply-side strategies will be considered.

Finally Chapter 32 takes an international perspective. We shall see how, in a world of interdependent economies, national governments try to harmonise their policies so as to achieve international growth and stability. Unfortunately, there is frequently a conflict between the broader interests of the international community and the narrow interests of individual countries, and in these circumstances, national interests normally dictate policy.

Key terms

Fiscal policy
Fiscal stance
Fine-tuning
Automatic fiscal stabilisers and discretionary fiscal policy
Pure fiscal policy
Crowding out
Monetary policy
Open-market operations
Demand management
Inflation targeting
Market-orientated and interventionist supply-side policies
Regional and urban policy
Industrial policy
International business cycle
Policy co-ordination
International convergence
Economic and monetary union in Europe (EMU)
Single European currency
Currency union

30

Demand-side policy

Business issues covered in this chapter

- What types of macroeconomic policy are there and in what ways might they affect business?
- What will be the impact on the economy and business of various fiscal policy measures?
- What determines the effectiveness of fiscal policy in smoothing out fluctuations in the economy?
- What fiscal rules or frameworks are adopted by governments and what are the economic arguments for such constraints on government policy?
- How does monetary policy work in the UK and the eurozone, and what are the roles of the Bank of England and the European Central Bank?
- How does targeting inflation influence interest rates and hence business activity?
- Are there better rules for determining interest rates than sticking to a simple inflation target?

There are two major types of demand-side policy: fiscal and monetary. In each case, we shall first describe how the policy operates and then examine its effectiveness. We shall also consider the more general question of whether the government and central bank ought to intervene actively to manage the level of aggregate demand, or whether they ought merely to set targets or rules for various indicators – such as money supply, inflation or government budget deficits – and then stick to them.

30.1 FISCAL POLICY

KI 43
p 547

Fiscal policy involves the government manipulating the level of government expenditure and/or rates of tax in order to affect the level of aggregate demand. An *expansionary* fiscal policy will involve raising government expenditure (an injection into the circular flow of income) or reducing taxes (a withdrawal from the circular flow). A *deflationary* (i.e. a

Definition

Fiscal policy Policy to affect aggregate demand by altering government expenditure and/or taxation.

contractionary) fiscal policy will involve cutting government expenditure and/or raising taxes.

But why might a government use fiscal policy?

First, it can try to remove any severe deflationary or inflationary gaps. For instance, an expansionary fiscal policy could be used to try to prevent an economy experiencing a severe or prolonged recession. This was the approach taken around the world from 2008 when substantial tax cuts and increases in government expenditure were undertaken. Likewise, deflationary fiscal policy could be used to prevent rampant inflation, such as that experienced in the 1970s.

Table 30.1 General government deficits/surpluses and debt as percentage of GDP

	General government deficits (−) or surpluses (+)		General government debt	
	Average 1995–2007	Average 2008–16	Average 1995–2007	Average 2008–16
Belgium	−1.3	−3.3	108.3	102.3
France	−2.9	−4.7	61.6	87.1
Germany	−2.9	−0.7	61.0	74.1
Greece	−6.4	−8.4	96.8	157.3
Ireland	+1.2	−10.0	41.7	96.5
Italy	−3.5	−3.2	106.4	121.6
Japan	−5.7	−7.4	148.5	230.8
Netherlands	−2.7	−2.6	55.2	63.8
Portugal	−4.3	−5.9	58.6	110.6
Spain	−1.4	−7.2	52.9	77.5
Sweden	0.0	−0.6	55.0	39.7
UK	−2.2	−6.7	42.0	79.8
USA	−2.8	−7.8	61.7	97.2
EU-15	−1.1	−3.9	64.0	84.0

Note: Data from 2015 based on forecasts

Source: Based on data from *AMECO* database, Tables 16.3 and 18.1 (European Commission, DG ECFIN)

Second, it can try to smooth out the fluctuations in the economy associated with the business cycle by *fine-tuning*. Stabilisation policies involve the government adjusting the level of aggregate demand so as to prevent the economy's actual output level deviating too far from its potential output level – to keep output gaps to a minimum.

Fiscal policy is also likely to affect aggregate supply, and the government will take this into account when designing its tax and spending policies. For example, it could give tax incentives to encourage businesses to invest or to engage in research and development, or it could increase its expenditure on infrastructure, such as roads and telecommunications. The aim would be to increase the economy's *potential* output. We look at supply-side policies in Chapter 31.

Deficits and surpluses

Central government deficits and surpluses

Since an expansionary fiscal policy involves raising government expenditure and/or lowering taxes, this has the effect of either increasing the **budget deficit** or reducing the **budget surplus.** A budget deficit in any one year is where central government's expenditure exceeds its revenue from taxation. A budget surplus is where tax revenues exceed central government expenditure.

For most of the past 50 years, governments around the world have run budget deficits. A deficit in any year adds to the total debt that a government has accumulated over the

years. From the mid-1990s, however, many countries, the UK included, made substantial efforts to reduce their budget deficits, and some achieved budget surpluses for periods of time. The position changed dramatically in 2008–9, however, as governments around the world increased their expenditure and cut taxes in an attempt to stave off recession. Government deficits, and hence stocks of debt, in many countries soared. Since then, governments have once more made efforts to reduce or even eliminate deficits.

General government

'General government' includes central and local government. Table 30.1 shows general government deficits/surpluses and debt for selected countries. They are expressed as a proportion of GDP. Deficits refer to the debt that a government incurs in one year when its spending exceeds its receipts. If the government runs persistent deficits over many years, these debts will accumulate.

As you can see, in the period from 1995 to 2007, all countries, with the exception of Ireland and Sweden, averaged a deficit. Nevertheless, for most countries, these deficits and debts were smaller than in the early 1990s. However, in the period from 2008 to 2016, the average deficit increased for most countries. And the bigger the deficit, the faster debt increased.

The whole public sector

To get a more complete view of public finances, we would need to look at the spending and receipts of the entire public sector: namely, central government, local government and public corporations.

Total public expenditure. First, we need to distinguish between **current** and **capital expenditures**. Current expenditures include items such as wages and salaries of public-sector staff, administration and the payments of welfare benefits. Capital expenditure (gross capital formation) gives rise to a stream of benefits *over time*. Examples include expenditure on roads, hospitals and schools.

Second, we must distinguish between **final expenditure** on goods and services, and **transfers**. This distinction recognises that the public sector directly adds to the economy's aggregate demand through its spending on goods and services, including the wages of public-sector workers, but also that it redistributes incomes between individuals and firms. Transfers include subsidies and benefit payments, such as payments to the unemployed.

Since 1990 the UK's public expenditure has typically split 93 to 7 per cent between current and capital expenditure, and 62 to 38 per cent between final expenditure and transfers.

Public-sector deficits. If the public sector spends more than it earns, it will have to finance the deficit through borrowing: known as **public-sector net borrowing (PSNB)**. Since the 1960s, the UK's public-sector net borrowing has averaged nearly 3 per cent of GDP.

The precise amount of money the public sector requires to borrow in any one year is known as the **public-sector net cash requirement (PSNCR)**. It differs slightly from the PSNB because of time lags in the flows of public-sector incomes and expenditure.

If the public sector runs a surplus (a negative PSNB), it will be able to repay some of the public-sector debts that have accumulated from previous years. If it runs a deficit, the public-sector debt will increase by the size of that deficit.

Cyclically adjusted balances

The size of the deficit or surplus is not entirely due to deliberate government policy. It is influenced by the state of the economy.

If the economy is booming with people earning high incomes, the amount paid in taxes will be high. Also, in a booming economy the level of unemployment will be low. Thus the amount paid out in unemployment benefits will be low. The combined effect of increased tax revenues and reduced benefits is to reduce the public-sector deficit (or increase the surplus).

By contrast, if the economy is depressed, tax revenues will be low and the amount paid in benefits will be high. This will increase the public-sector deficit (or reduce the surplus).

By 'cyclically adjusting' measures of public-sector deficits or surpluses we remove their cyclical component. In other words, we show just the direct effects of government policy, not the effects of the level of economic activity. Figure 30.1 shows both actual and cyclically adjusted public-sector net borrowing as a percentage of GDP since the mid-1970s. Over the long run the economy's output gap is zero (see Box 26.1). Hence, over the period shown, both net borrowing measures average the same (around 3 per cent of GDP).

The deficit or surplus that would arise if the economy were producing at the potential level of national income (see Box 26.1 on page 475) is termed the **structural deficit or surplus**. Remember that the potential level of national income is where there is no excess or deficiency of aggregate demand: where there is a zero output gap.

The use of fiscal policy

Automatic fiscal stabilisers

To some extent, government expenditure and taxation will have the effect of *automatically* stabilising the economy. For example, as national income rises, the amount of tax people

---

Definitions

Current expenditure Recurrent spending on goods and factor payments.

Capital expenditure Investment expenditure; expenditure on assets.

Final expenditure Expenditure on goods and services. This is included in GDP and is part of aggregate demand.

Transfers Transfers of money from taxpayers to recipients of benefits and subsidies. They are not an injection into the circular flow but are the equivalent of a negative tax (i.e. a negative withdrawal).

Public-sector net borrowing (PSNB) The difference between the expenditures of the public sector and its receipts from taxation, the surpluses of public corporations and the sale of assets.

Public-sector net cash requirement (PSNCR) The (annual) deficit of the public sector, and thus the amount that the public sector must borrow.

Structural deficit (or surplus) The public-sector deficit (or surplus) that would occur if the economy were operating at the potential level of national income: i.e. one where there is a zero output gap.

Figure 30.1 UK public-sector net borrowing (% of GDP)

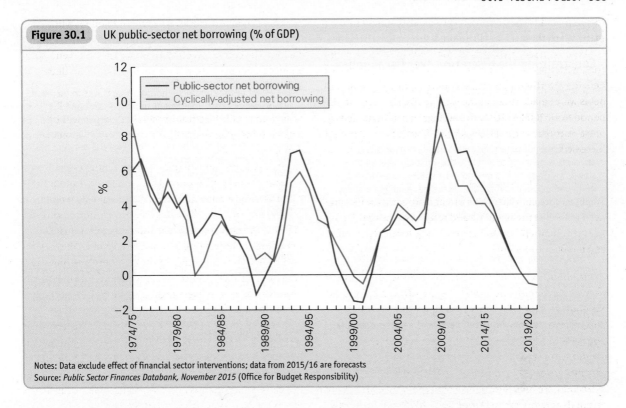

Notes: Data exclude effect of financial sector interventions; data from 2015/16 are forecasts
Source: *Public Sector Finances Databank, November 2015* (Office for Budget Responsibility)

pay automatically rises. This rise in withdrawals from the circular flow of income will help to damp down the rise in national income. This effect will be bigger if taxes are *progressive* (i.e. rise by a bigger percentage than national income). Some government transfers will have a similar effect. For example, the total paid in unemployment benefits will fall, if rises in national income cause a fall in unemployment. This again will have the effect of dampening the rise in national income.

Discretionary fiscal policy

Automatic stabilisers cannot *prevent* fluctuations; they merely reduce their magnitude. If there is a fundamental disequilibrium in the economy or substantial fluctuations in national income, these automatic stabilisers will not be enough. The government may thus choose to *alter* the level of government expenditure or the rates of taxation. This is known as **discretionary fiscal policy**. Box 30.1 looks at discretionary fiscal policy in the UK since the financial crisis of the late 2000s.

If government expenditure on goods and services (roads, health care, education, etc.) is raised, this will create a full multiplied rise in national income. The reason is that all the money gets spent and thus all of it goes to boosting aggregate demand.

Cutting taxes (or increasing benefits), however, will have a smaller effect on national income than raising government expenditure on goods and services by the same amount. The reason is that cutting taxes increases people's *disposable* incomes, of which only part will be spent. Part will be withdrawn into extra saving, imports and other taxes. In other words, not all the tax cuts will be passed on round the circular flow of income as extra expenditure. Thus if one-fifth of a cut in taxes is withdrawn and only

four-fifths is spent, the tax multiplier will be only four-fifths as big as the government expenditure multiplier.

Pause for thought

Why will the multiplier effect of government transfer payments, such as child benefit, pensions and social security benefits, be less than the full multiplier effect from government expenditure on goods and services?

The effectiveness of fiscal policy

How successful will fiscal policy be? Will it be able to 'fine-tune' demand? Will it be able to achieve the level of GDP that the government would like it to achieve?

There are various problems with using fiscal policy to manage the economy. These can be grouped under two broad headings: problems of magnitude and problems of timing.

Problems of magnitude

Before changing government expenditure or taxation, the government will need to calculate the effect of any such change on national income, employment and inflation. Predicting these effects, however, is often very unreliable for a number of reasons.

Definition

Discretionary fiscal policy Deliberate changes in tax rates or the level of government expenditure in order to influence the level of aggregate demand.

BOX 30.1 THE FINANCIAL CRISIS AND THE UK FISCAL POLICY YO-YO

Constraining the discretion over fiscal policy

The impact of the financial crisis on economic growth in the UK was stark. The UK economy had expanded by 3.0 per cent in 2006 and by a further 2.6 in 2007. But in 2008 it contracted by 0.3 per cent and then by 4.3 per cent in 2009.

The UK fiscal policy response was initially expansionary as attempts were made to mitigate the worst of the economic slowdown. Then, with a new government in place and with a burgeoning budget deficit, the UK turned rapidly to a policy of fiscal consolidation. Within a short space of time the stance of fiscal policy changed markedly: a fiscal policy yo-yo.

Expansion

The UK economy entered recession in the second quarter of 2008. In the Pre-Budget Report of November 2008, amongst other measures, the Labour government introduced a 13-month cut in VAT from 17.5 per cent to 15 per cent. It also brought forward from 2010/11 £3 billion of capital spending on projects such as motorways, new social housing, schools and energy efficiency.

The effect of the capital spending projects was to increase public-sector gross investment to 5.2 per cent and 5.3 per cent of GDP in 2008/9 and 2009/10 respectively. In the previous 15 years the typical amount of public-sector gross investment spending had been just 3.3 per cent of GDP. Meanwhile, as chart (a) shows, total government spending (excluding financial interventions) began to rise rapidly, fuelled by rising transfer payments on the back of the faltering economy, peaking at just over 45 per cent in 2009/10.

The UK came out of recession in the third quarter of 2009 after five consecutive quarters of declining output which saw the economy shrink by 6 per cent. Meanwhile, the rate of unemployment, which had stood at 5.2 per cent at the start of 2008, peaked at 8 per cent in early 2010 and stood at 7.8 per cent in May when 13 years of Labour government came to an end. Not only did this mark a change of government as a Conservative–Liberal coalition took charge, but it also a marked a change in the direction of fiscal policy.

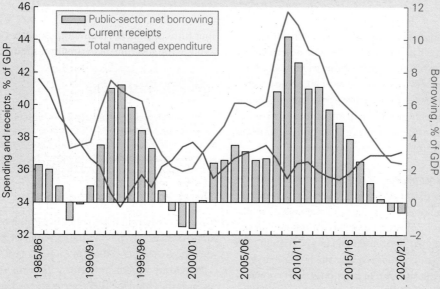

(a) UK public-sector spending and receipts (% of GDP)

Note: Data from 2015/16 based on forecasts
Source: *Public Sector Finances Databank, November 2015* (Office for Budget Responsibility)

Predicting the effect of changes in government expenditure

A rise in government expenditure of £x may lead to a rise in total injections (relative to withdrawals) that is smaller than £x. This will occur if the rise in government expenditure *replaces* a certain amount of private expenditure. For example, a rise in expenditure on state education may dissuade some parents from sending their children to private schools. Similarly, an improvement in the National Health Service may lead to fewer people paying for private treatment.

Crowding out. Another reason for the total rise in injections being smaller than the rise in government expenditure is a phenomenon known as *crowding out*. If the government relies on *pure fiscal policy* – that is, if it does not finance an

Definitions

Crowding out Where increased public expenditure diverts money or resources away from the private sector.

Pure fiscal policy Fiscal policy which does not involve any change in money supply.

Consolidation

In 2009/10, public-sector net borrowing hit 10.2 per cent of GDP, up from 2.7 per cent in 2007/8 (see chart (a)). Consequently, public-sector net debt grew rapidly (see chart (b)). From £561.5 billion (37 per cent of GDP) in 2007/8 it rose to £959.8 billion (62 per cent of GDP) by 2009/10.

The response of the new government was to begin a policy of consolidation. The framework for this was to be known as the 'fiscal mandate'. The initial mandate was for a balanced current budget (after adjusting for the position in the economic cycle) five years ahead. Therefore, at the end of a rolling five-year forecast period public-sector receipts should at least equal public-sector current expenditures, after adjusting for the economy's output gap. This mandate was supplemented by a target for public-sector net debt as a percentage of GDP to be falling by 2015/16.

To achieve this, the government embarked on a series of spending cuts and tax rises. This started with a 'discretionary consolidation' of £8.9 billion in 2010/11 comprising spending cuts of £5.3 billion and tax increases worth £3.6 billion. It

was announced that the consolidation would continue up to 2015/16. By the end of 2015/16 the government planned to have delivered a discretionary consolidation of £122 billion, with £99 billion coming from discretionary reductions in spending and £23 billion from tax increases. As it turned out, however, in real terms total public-sector spending fell by just 0.7 per cent between 2010/11 and 2014/15.

The principal fiscal objectives were thus not met during the 2010–15 parliamentary period, although the government claimed that 'significant progress' had been made on its fiscal consolidation. As the parliament drew to a close an updated fiscal framework was proposed. The fiscal mandate would now aim to return the cyclically adjusted current budget to balance over a three-year rolling horizon, starting with balance in 2017/18. The new supplementary target for debt was that net debt should be falling as a percentage of GDP by 2016/17.

 Which is likely to give a bigger boost to aggregate demand: tax cuts of a given amount targeted to (a) the rich, or (b) the poor?

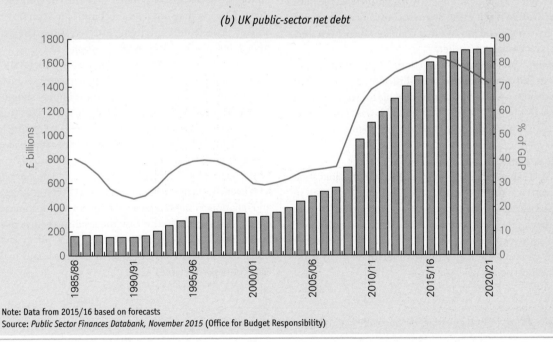

(b) UK public-sector net debt

Note: Data from 2015/16 based on forecasts
Source: *Public Sector Finances Databank, November 2015* (Office for Budget Responsibility)

increase in the budget deficit by increasing the money supply – it will have to borrow the money from the non-bank private sector. It will thus be competing with the private sector for finance and will have to offer higher interest rates. This will force the private sector also to offer higher interest rates, which may discourage firms from investing and individuals from buying on credit. Thus government borrowing *crowds out* private borrowing. In the extreme case, the fall in consumption and investment may completely offset the rise in government expenditure, with the result that aggregate demand does not rise at all.

Predicting the effect of changes in taxes

A cut in taxes, by increasing people's real disposable income, increases not only the amount they spend, but also the amount they save. The problem is that it is not easy to predict the relative size of these two increases. In part it will depend on whether people feel that the cut in tax is only temporary, in which case they may simply save the extra disposable income, or permanent, in which case they may adjust their consumption upwards. More generally, it may depend on a broader set of variables, including confidence and financial well-being.

Predicting the resulting multiplied effect on national income

Even if the government *could* predict the net initial effect on injections and withdrawals, the extent to which national income will change is still hard to predict for the following reasons:

- The size of the *multiplier* may be difficult to predict, since it is difficult to predict how much of any rise in income will be withdrawn. For example, the amount of a rise in income that households save or consume will depend on their expectations about future price and income changes.
- Induced investment through the *accelerator* (see page 570) is also extremely difficult to predict. It may be that a relatively small fiscal stimulus will be all that is necessary to restore business confidence, and that induced investment will rise substantially. Similarly, rising confidence amongst financial institutions could see credit conditions relaxed with the *financial accelerator* (see page 567) resulting in rising levels of investment. In such situations, fiscal policy can be seen as a 'pump primer'. It is used to *start* the process of recovery, and then the *continuation* of the recovery is left to the market. But for pump priming to work, businesspeople must *believe* that it will work. Business confidence can change very rapidly and in ways that could not have been foreseen a few months earlier.
- Multiplier/accelerator interactions. If the initial multiplier and accelerator effects are difficult to estimate, their interaction will be virtually impossible to estimate. Small divergences in investment from what was initially predicted will become magnified as time progresses.

Random shocks

Forecasts cannot take into account the unpredictable, such as the attack on the World Trade Center in New York in September 2001. Even events that, with hindsight, should have been predicted, such as the banking crisis of 2007–9, often are not. Unfortunately, unpredictable or unpredicted events do occur and may seriously undermine the government's fiscal policy.

> ### Pause for thought
>
> *Give some other examples of 'random shocks' that could undermine the government's fiscal policy.*

Problems of timing

Fiscal policy can involve considerable time lags. It may take time to recognise the nature of the problem before the government is willing to take action; tax or government expenditure changes take time to plan and implement – changes will have to wait until the next Budget to be announced and may come into effect some time later; the effects of such changes take time to work their way through the economy via the multiplier and accelerator.

If these time lags are long enough, fiscal policy could even be *de*stabilising. Expansionary policies taken to cure a recession may not come into effect until the economy has *already* recovered and is experiencing a boom. Under these circumstances, expansionary policies are quite inappropriate: they simply worsen the problems of overheating. Similarly, deflationary policies taken to prevent excessive expansion may not take effect until the economy has already peaked and is plunging into recession. The deflationary policies only deepen the recession.

This problem is illustrated in Figure 30.2. Path (a) shows the course of the business cycle without government intervention. Ideally, with no time lags, the economy should be dampened in stage 2 and stimulated in stage 4. This would make the resulting course of the business cycle more like path (b), or even, if the policy were perfectly stabilising, a line that purely reflected the growth in potential output. With the presence of time lags, however, deflationary policies taken in stage 2 may not come into effect until stage 4, and reflationary policies taken in stage 4 may not come into effect until stage 2. In this case the resulting course of the business cycle will be more like path (c). Quite obviously, in these circumstances 'stabilising' fiscal policy actually makes the economy *less* stable.

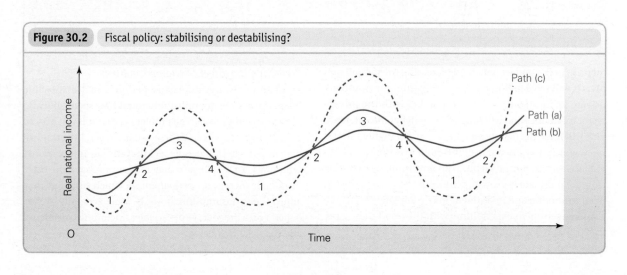

Figure 30.2 Fiscal policy: stabilising or destabilising?

If the fluctuations in aggregate demand can be forecast, and if the lengths of the time lags are known, then all is not lost. At least the fiscal measures can be taken early and their delayed effects can be taken into account.

Fiscal rules

Given the problems of pursuing active fiscal policy, many governments today take a much more passive approach. Instead of changing the policy as the economy changes, countries apply a set of fiscal rules. These rules typically relate to measures of government deficits and to the stock of accumulated debt. Taxes and government expenditure can then be planned to meet these rules.

However, rules cannot cope with severe disruption to the global economy, such as occurred in the credit crunch of 2008. Countries around the world resorted to discretionary fiscal policy to boost aggregate demand. They abandoned fiscal rules – at least temporarily. Rules were generally reinstated around the world, however, as the global economy pulled out of recession. In Box 30.2 we detail how the fiscal rules in the eurozone and the UK evolved following the events of the late 2000s.

In Section 30.3 we review the debate concerning constraints on a government's discretion over both its fiscal and monetary policies.

BOX 30.2	THE EVOLVING FISCAL FRAMEWORKS IN THE UK AND EUROZONE

Constraining the discretion over fiscal policy

If governments persistently run budget deficits, the national debt will rise. If it rises faster than GDP, it will account for a growing proportion of GDP. Governments could find themselves having to borrow more and more to meet the interest payments, and so the national debt could rise faster still. Consequently, a principal aim of fiscal rules or frameworks, which constrain government discretion over fiscal policy, has been to ensure sustainable government finances.

European Union

Stability and Growth Pact (SGP)

In June 1997, at the European Council meeting in Amsterdam, the EU countries agreed a Stability and Growth Pact (SGP). This stated that member states should seek to balance their budgets (or even aim for a surplus) averaged over the course

of the business cycle, and that deficits should not exceed 3 per cent of GDP in any one year. A country's deficit was permitted to exceed 3 per cent only if its GDP had declined by at least 2 per cent (or 0.75 per cent with special permission from the Council of Ministers). Otherwise, countries with deficits exceeding 3 per cent were required to make deposits of money with the European Central Bank. Under the Pact's Excessive Deficit Procedure, these would then become fines if the excessive budget deficit were not eliminated within two years. The UK, however, was not legally bound by this procedure.

There were two main aims of targeting a zero budget deficit over the business cycle. The first was to allow automatic stabilisers to work without 'bumping into' the 3 per cent deficit ceiling in years when economies were slowing. The second was to allow a reduction in government debts as a proportion of GDP (assuming that GDP grew on average at around 2–3 per cent per year).

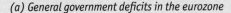

(a) General government deficits in the eurozone

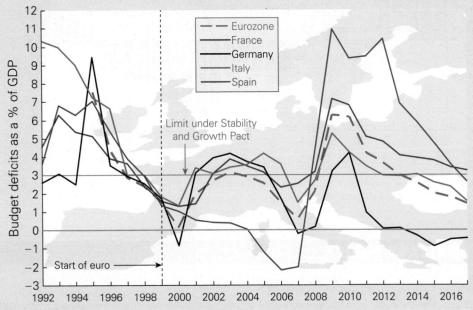

Note: Data from 2015 are based on forecasts

Source: Based on data in *Statistical Annex to the European Economy* (European Commission).

From 2002, with slowing growth, Germany, France and Italy breached the 3 per cent ceiling. By 2007, however, after two years of relatively strong growth, deficits had been reduced well below the ceiling (see chart (a)).

But then the credit crunch hit. As the EU economies slowed, so deficits rose. To combat the recession, in November 2008 the European Commission announced a €200 billion fiscal stimulus plan, mainly in the form of increased public expenditure. €170 billion of the money would come from member governments and €30 billion from the EU, amounting to a total of 1.2 per cent of EU GDP. The money would be for a range of projects, such as job training, help to small businesses, developing green energy technologies and energy efficiency. Most member governments quickly followed by announcing how their specific plans would accord with the overall plan.

The combination of the recession and the fiscal measures pushed most eurozone countries' budget deficits well above the 3 per cent ceiling (see chart (a)). The recession in EU countries deepened markedly in 2009, with GDP declining by 4.5 per cent in the eurozone and by 5.4 per cent in Italy, 5.1 per cent in Germany, 3.8 per cent in Spain and 2.9 per cent in France. Consequently, the deficits were not seen to breach SGP rules.

The Fiscal Compact

As the European economy began to recover in 2010, there was tremendous pressure on member countries to begin reining in their deficits. The average eurozone deficit had risen to 6.2 per cent of GDP, and some countries' deficits were much higher. Indeed, with the Spanish, Greek and Irish deficits being 9.6, 11.0 and 29.3 per cent respectively, reining in the deficits would prove to be especially painful for these and several other eurozone countries.

The SGP was now seen as needing reform. The result was an intense period of negotiation that culminated in early 2012 with a new intergovernmental treaty to limit spending and borrowing. The entire treaty, known as the Fiscal Compact, applies to all eurozone countries. However, non-eurozone member states can choose to be bound by the fiscal rules outlined in the Treaty.

The Fiscal Compact requires that from January 2013 national governments not only abide by the excessive deficit procedure of the SGP but also keep structural deficits no higher than 0.5 per cent of GDP. Structural deficits are that part of a deficit not directly related to the economic cycle and so would exist even if the economy were operating at its potential output. In the cases of countries with a debt-to-GDP ratio significantly below 60 per cent, the structural deficit is permitted to reach 1 per cent of GDP. Finally, where the debt-to-GDP ratio exceeds 60 per cent, countries should, on average, reduce it by one-twentieth per year.

Where a national government is found by the European Court of Justice not to comply with the Fiscal Compact, it has the power to fine that country up to 0.1 per cent of GDP payable to the European Stability Mechanism (ESM). The ESM is a fund from which loans are provided to support a eurozone government in severe financing difficulty or alternatively is used to purchase that country's bonds in the primary market.

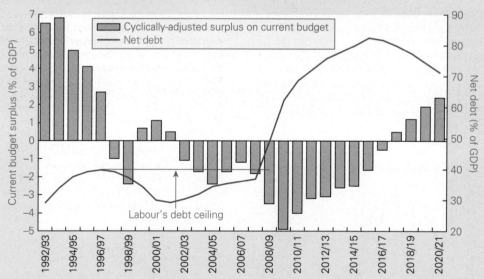

(b) Public-sector net debt and cyclically-adjusted current budget surplus (per cent of GDP)

Notes: Data exclude effect of financial sector interventions; data from 2015/16 are forecasts
Source: *Public Finances Databank* (Office for Budget Responsibility)

30.2 MONETARY POLICY

The Bank of England's Monetary Policy Committee regularly meets to set Bank Rate. The event gets considerable media coverage. Pundits, for two or three days before the meeting, try to predict what the MPC will do and economists give their 'considered' opinions about what the MPC *ought* to do.

The fact is that changes in interest rates have gained a central significance in macroeconomic policy. And it is not just in the UK. Whether it is the European Central Bank setting interest rates for the eurozone countries, or the Federal Reserve Bank setting US interest rates, or any other central

UK policy

Golden and sustainable rules

On being elected in 1997, the Labour government in the UK adopted a similar approach to that of the SGP. It introduced two fiscal rules.

The golden rule. First, under its 'golden rule', the government pledged that over the economic cycle it would borrow only to invest (e.g. in roads, hospitals and schools) and not to fund current spending (e.g. on wages, administration and benefits). In other words, it would seek, over the cycle, to achieve a ***current budget balance***, where total receipts equal total current expenditures (i.e. excluding capital expenditures). Investment was exempted from the zero borrowing rule because it contributes towards the growth of GDP.

Chart (b) shows how the cyclically adjusted current budget balanced across the economic cycle from 1997/8 to 2006/7. By cyclically adjusting, we remove the estimated effects of the economic cycle, such as increased welfare payments and lower tax receipts when output is below its potential.

The sustainable investment rule. Secondly, under its 'sustainable investment rule', the government also set itself the target of maintaining public-sector net debt at no more than 40 per cent of GDP averaged over the economic cycle.

As with the SGP, the argument for the golden rule was that by using an averaging rule over the cycle, automatic stabilisers would be allowed to work. Deficits of receipts over current spending could occur when the economy is in recession or when growth is sluggish (as in 2001–3), helping to stimulate the economy.

The global financial crisis of 2008, however, saw the UK fiscal framework suspended. In the Pre-Budget Report of November 2008, the government argued that its 'immediate priority' was to support the economy by using discretionary fiscal policy. As we saw in Box 30.1, these measures included a 13-month cut in VAT from 17.5 per cent to 15 per cent and bringing forward from 2010/11 £3 billion of capital spending.

However, the deteriorating state of the public finances led the Labour government in late 2009 to introduce through Parliament a Fiscal Responsibility Bill. It required governments to present to Parliament their fiscal plans to deliver sound public finances. The plan of Chancellor Alistair Darling was to halve the size of the deficit over the next parliament.

Fiscal mandate

The fiscal priority of the Conservative–Liberal Democrat coalition government (2010–15) was to get public-sector borrowing down. By 2010 public-sector borrowing had reached 10.4 per cent of GDP, one of the highest percentages in the developed world. The government set itself a 'fiscal mandate': to achieve a cyclically adjusted current balance by 2015/16. This was, therefore, very similar to the golden rule. The fiscal mandate was supplemented by a target for the ratio of public-sector debt to GDP to be falling by 2015/16.

The government embarked on a discretionary consolidation that would see reductions in spending of £99 billion by 2015/16 and increases in tax of £23 billion (Box 30.1). This meant that expenditure cuts would make up 81 per cent of the total fiscal consolidation.

On its own, the much tighter fiscal policy would substantially dampen aggregate demand. The question was whether the recovery in exports, investment and consumer demand would be sufficient to offset this, which, in turn, would be heavily dependent on the confidence of people. Despite growing by 2.9 per cent in 2014, the UK economy grew by an average rate of just 1.7 per cent per year from 2010 to 2014 – almost 0.75 percentage points below its longer-term average.

As it turned out, the government failed to meet both its fiscal mandate and the supplementary debt target. In the Autumn Statement of 2014 – the last before the election in May 2015 – the government presented its new fiscal mandate and supplementary debt rule. These were contained within an updated Charter for Budget Responsibility which, since 2011, sets out before Parliament the government's objectives for fiscal policy and for managing the public debt. The fiscal mandate was now to target returning the cyclically adjusted current budget to balance by 2017/18. Meanwhile the revised supplementary target for debt was for the net debt-to-GDP to begin falling by 2016/17.

The updated Charter for Budget Responsibility signalled the prospect of further significant fiscal consolidation. The government estimated that a further discretionary consolidation of £30 billion was needed over the following two years (2016/17 to 2017/18).

What effects will an increase in government investment expenditure have on public-sector debt (a) in the short run; (b) in the long run?

Definition

Current budget balance The difference between public-sector receipts and those expenditures classified as current rather than capital expenditures.

---

bank around the world choosing what the level of interest rates should be, monetary policy is seen as having a major influence on a whole range of macroeconomic indicators.

But is monetary policy simply the setting of interest rates? In reality, it involves the central bank intervening in the money market to ensure that the interest rate that has been announced is also the *equilibrium* interest rate.

The policy setting

In framing its monetary policy, the government must decide on what the goals of the policy are. Is the aim simply to control inflation, or does the government wish also to affect output and employment, or does it want to control the exchange rate?

KI 36
p 354

The government must also decide where monetary policy fits into the total package of macroeconomic policies. Is it seen as the major or even sole macroeconomic policy instrument, or is it merely one of several?

A decision also has to be made about who is to carry out the policy. There are three possible approaches here.

In the first, the government both sets the policy and decides the measures necessary to achieve it. Here the government would set the interest rate, with the central bank simply influencing money markets to achieve this rate. This first approach was used in the UK before 1997.

The second approach is for the government to set the policy *targets*, but for the central bank to be given independence in deciding interest rates. This is the approach adopted in the UK today. The government has set a target rate of inflation of 2 per cent, but then the MPC is free to choose the rate of interest.

The third approach is for the central bank to be given independence not only in carrying out policy, but also in setting the policy targets itself. The ECB, within the statutory objective of maintaining price stability over the medium term, has decided on the target of keeping inflation below, but close to, 2 per cent over the medium term.

Finally, there is the question of whether the government or central bank should take a long-term or short-term perspective. Should it adopt a target for inflation or money supply growth and stick to it come what may? Or should it adjust its policy as circumstances change and attempt to 'fine-tune' the economy?

We will be looking primarily at *short-term* monetary policy: that is, policy used to keep to a set target for inflation or money supply growth, or policy used to smooth out fluctuations in the business cycle.

It is important first, however, to take a longer-term perspective. Governments generally want to prevent an excessive growth in the money supply over the longer term. If money supply does grow rapidly, then inflation is likely to be high. Likewise they want to ensure that money supply grows enough and that there is not a shortage of credit, such as that during the credit crunch. If money supply grows too rapidly, then inflation is likely to be high; if money supply grows too slowly, or even falls, then recession is likely to result.

Control of the money supply over the medium and long term

In section 28.3 we identified two major sources of monetary growth: (a) banks choosing to hold a lower liquidity ratio; (b) public-sector borrowing financed by borrowing from the banking sector. If the government wishes to restrict monetary growth over the longer term, it could attempt to control either or both of these.

Liquidity of banks

The central bank could impose a statutory **minimum reserve ratio** on the banks, *above* the level that banks would otherwise choose to hold. Such ratios come in various forms. The simplest is where the banks are required to hold a given minimum percentage of deposits in the form of cash or deposits with the central bank.

The effect of a minimum reserve ratio is to prevent banks choosing to reduce their cash or liquidity ratio and creating more credit. This was a popular approach of governments in many countries in the past. Some countries imposed very high ratios indeed in their attempt to slow down the growth in the money supply.

A major problem with imposing restrictions of this kind is that banks may find ways of getting round them. After all, banks would like to lend and customers would like to borrow. It is very difficult to regulate and police every single part of countries' complex financial systems.

Nevertheless, attitudes changed substantially after the excessive lending of the mid-2000s. The expansion of credit had been based on 'liquidity' achieved through secondary marketing between financial institutions and the growth of securitised assets containing sub-prime debt (see Box 28.3). After the credit crunch and the need for central banks or governments to rescue ailing banks, such as Northern Rock and later the Royal Bank of Scotland in the UK and many other banks around the world, there were calls for greater regulation of banks to ensure that they had sufficient capital and operated with sufficient liquidity, and that they were not exposed to excessive risk of default.

KI 14
p 82

Public-sector deficits

Section 28.3 showed how government borrowing tends to lead to an increase in money supply. To prevent this, public-sector deficits must be financed by selling *bonds* (as opposed to bills, which could well be taken up by the banking sector, thereby increasing money supply). However, to sell extra bonds the government will have to offer higher interest rates. This will have a knock-on effect on private-sector interest rates. The government borrowing will thus crowd out private-sector borrowing and investment. This is known as **financial crowding out**.

If governments wish to reduce monetary growth and yet avoid financial crowding out, they must therefore reduce the size of public-sector deficits.

It is partly for this reason that many governments have constrained fiscal policy choices by applying fiscal rules or agreements, such as the Fiscal Compact in the eurozone or the 'fiscal mandate' in the UK (see Box 30.2).

Definitions

Minimum reserve ratio A minimum ratio of cash (or other specified liquid assets) to deposits (either total or selected) that the central bank requires banks to hold.

Financial crowding out Where an increase in government borrowing diverts money away from the private sector.

Short-term monetary measures

KI 36
p354

Inflation may be off target. Alternatively, the government (or central bank) may wish to alter its monetary policy. What can it do? There are various techniques that could be used. These can be grouped into three categories: (a) altering the money supply; (b) altering interest rates; (c) rationing credit. These are illustrated in Figure 30.3, which shows the demand for and supply of money. The equilibrium quantity of money is initially Q_1 and the equilibrium interest rate is r_1.

KI 10
p52

Assume that the central bank wants to tighten monetary policy in order to reduce inflation. It could (a) seek to shift the supply of money curve to the left: e.g. from M_s to M'_s (resulting in the equilibrium rate of interest rising from r_1 to r_2), (b) raise the interest rate directly from r_1 to r_2, and then manipulate the money supply to reduce it to Q_2, or (c) keep interest rates at r_1, but reduce money supply to Q_2 by rationing the amount of credit granted by banks and other institutions.

Credit rationing was widely used in the past, especially during the 1960s. The aim was to keep interest rates low, so as not to discourage investment, but to restrict credit to more risky business customers and/or to consumers. In the UK, the Bank of England could order banks to abide by such a policy, although in practice it always relied on persuasion. The government also, from time to time, imposed restrictions on hire-purchase credit, by specifying minimum deposits or maximum repayment periods.

Such policies were progressively abandoned around the world from the early 1980s. They were seen as stifling competition and preventing efficient banks from expanding. Hire-purchase controls may badly hit certain industries (e.g. cars and other consumer durables), whose products are bought largely on hire-purchase credit. What is more, with the deregulation and globalisation of financial markets up to 2007, it had become very difficult to ration credit. If one financial institution was controlled, borrowers could simply go elsewhere.

With the excessive lending in sub-prime markets that had triggered the credit crunch of 2007–9, there were calls around the world for tighter controls over bank lending. But this was different from credit rationing as we have defined it. In other words, tighter controls, such as applying counter-cyclical buffers of capital to all banks, would be used to prevent reckless behaviour by banks, rather than to achieve a particular level of money at a lower rate of interest.

KI 6
p37

We thus focus on techniques to alter the money supply and to change interest rates.

Techniques to control the money supply

There are four possible techniques that a central bank could use to alter money supply. They have one major feature in common: they involve manipulating the liquid assets of the banking system. The aim is to influence the total money supply by affecting the amount of credit that banks can create.

Open-market operations. **Open-market operations** are the most widely used of the four techniques around the world. They alter the monetary base. This then affects the amount of credit banks can create and hence the level of broad money (M4 in the UK; M3 in the eurozone).

Open-market operations involve the sale or purchase by the central bank of government securities (bonds or bills) in the open market. These sales (or purchases) are *not* in response to changes in the public-sector deficit and are thus best understood in the context of an unchanged deficit.

If the central bank wishes to *reduce* the money supply, it takes money from the banking system in return for securities. It can do this by borrowing from financial institutions against government securities (reverse repos on banks' balance sheets) or by selling securities outright. The borrowing or sale of these securities reduces banks' balances with the central bank. If this brings bank reserves below their prudent ratio, banks will reduce advances. There will be a multiple contraction of credit and hence of (broad) money supply. (Details of how open-market operations work in the UK are given in Box 30.3.)

KI 10
p52

KI 43
p547

Figure 30.3 The demand for and supply of money

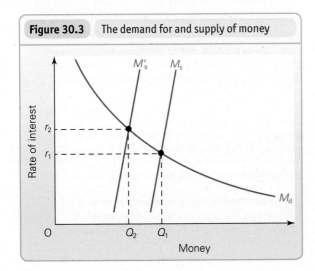

Pause for thought

Explain how open-market operations could be used to increase the money supply.

Definition

Open-market operations The sale (or purchase) by the authorities of government securities in the open market in order to reduce (or increase) money supply.

BOX 30.3   THE DAILY OPERATION OF MONETARY POLICY

What goes on at Threadneedle Street?

The Bank of England (the 'Bank') does not normally attempt to control money supply directly. Instead it seeks to control interest rates by conducting open-market operations (OMOs) through short-term and longer-term repos and through the outright purchase of high-quality bonds. These operations, as we shall see, determine short-term interest rates, which then have a knock-on effect on longer-term rates, as returns on different forms of assets must remain competitive with each other.

Let us assume that the Monetary Policy Committee (MPC) of the Bank of England forecasts that, as a result of a low level of aggregate demand, inflation will fall below target. It thus decides to reduce interest rates. But how is this achieved?

The first thing is that the MPC will announce a cut in Bank Rate. The Bank of England then has to back up the announcement by using OMOs to ensure that the announced interest rate is the equilibrium rate.

Normal operation of the monetary framework

The MPC meets regularly to decide on Bank Rate. From its inception in 1997, it met monthly. However, following an independent report published in December 2014, it announced plans to move to eight meetings a year from 2016.

Changes in the Bank Rate are intended to affect the whole structure of interest rates in the economy, from inter-bank rates to bank deposit rates and rates on mortgages and business loans. The monetary framework works to affect the general structure of interest rates, principally by affecting short-term inter-bank rates.

Central to the process are the reserve accounts of financial institutions at the Bank of England (see section 28.2, page 531). From the inception of the current system in May 2006, commercial banks have agreed with the Bank of England the average amount of reserve balances they would hold between MPC meetings. So long as the actual average over the period is kept within a small range of the agreed target, the reserves are remunerated at Bank Rate.

In order for individual banks to meet their reserve targets, the Bank of England needs to provide sufficient reserves. To do so, it uses OMOs. In normal circumstances, the Bank of England conducts short-term OMOs every week (on a Thursday) at Bank Rate. The size of the weekly OMO is adjusted to help banks maintain reserves at the target level and to reflect variations in the amount of cash withdrawn or deposited in banks.

To supply reserves the Bank of England will either enter into short-term repo operations, lending against collateral ('high-quality' government securities), or buy securities outright. Although there is usually a shortage of liquidity in the banking system, in some weeks there may be a surplus. This would ordinarily drive market interest rates down. In such circumstances the Bank may look to reduce banks' reserves. To do this it can sell government securities on a repo basis, invite bids for Bank of England one-week sterling bills or sell outright some of its portfolio of securities.

At the end of the period between MPC interest rate decisions, the Bank of England conducts a 'fine-tuning' OMO. This is conducted on a Wednesday – the day before the MPC decision on interest rates. The idea is to ensure that banks meet their reserve targets as closely as possible. This OMO could expand or contract liquidity as appropriate.

Longer-term OMOs. Longer-term finance is available through longer-term open-market operations. Prior to the financial crisis of the late 2000s, longer-term OMOs would normally be conducted once per month. As well as the outright purchase of gilts, the Bank would conduct repo lending with 3-, 6-, 9- or 12-month maturities.

The rate of interest on the repos is market determined. Banks bid for the money and the funds are offered to the successful bidders. The bigger the demand for these funds by banks and the lower the supply by the Bank of England, the higher will be the interest rate that banks must pay. By adjusting the supply, therefore, the Bank of England can look to influence longer-term interest rates too.

With the aggregate amount of banks' reserves determined by the Bank of England's OMOs, the task now is for individual banks to meet their agreed reserve targets. This requires that they manage their balance sheets and, in particular, their level of liquidity. In doing so, commercial banks can make use of either the inter-bank market or the 'standing facilities' at the Bank of England. These standing facilities allow individual banks to borrow overnight (secured against high-quality collateral) at a rate above Bank Rate if they are short of liquidity; or to deposit reserves with the Bank at a rate below Bank Rate if they have surplus liquidity. Consequently, banks will trade reserves with each other if inter-bank rates fall within the 'corridor' created by the interest rates of the standing facilities.

The financial crisis and open-market operations

The financial crisis meant that normal OMOs were no longer sufficient to maintain liquidity for purposes of monetary policy. There was a severe liquidity crisis – one which posed grave risks for financial stability.

In response, from January 2009 the Bank of England deliberately injected narrow money in a process known as 'quantitative easing' (see Box 30.4). This involved the Bank of England purchasing assets, largely gilts, from banks. Between January 2009 and July 2012 the Bank of England injected £375 billion by such means. Quantitative easing thus massively extended the scope of OMOs.

As a result of this significant increase in aggregate reserves, banks were no longer required to set reserve targets. The supply of reserves was now being determined by MPC policy decisions. All reserves were to be remunerated at the Bank Rate.

Furthermore, short-term OMOs were temporarily suspended. Long-term repo operations continued but these were modified to allow financial institutions to sell a wider range of securities.

The Bank also adapted its means of providing liquidity insurance (see section 28.2, page 531). This included the introduction of the Discount Window Facility (DWF), which enables banks to borrow government bonds (gilts) against a wide range of collateral. Banks can then sell these bonds through repo operations and thereby secure liquidity.

 Assume that the Bank of England wants to raise interest rates. Trace through the process by which it achieves this.

Central bank lending to the banks. The central bank in most countries is prepared to provide extra money to banks (through gilt repos, rediscounting bills or straight loans). In some countries, it is the policy of the central bank to keep its interest rate to banks *below* market rates, thereby encouraging banks to borrow (or sell back securities) whenever such facilities are available. By cutting back the amount it is willing to provide, the central bank can reduce banks' liquid assets and hence the amount of credit they can create.

In other countries, such as the UK and the eurozone countries, it is not so much the amount of money made available that is controlled, but rather the rate of interest (or discount). The higher this rate is relative to other market rates, the less willing to borrow will banks be, and the lower, therefore, will be the monetary base. Raising this rate, therefore, has the effect of reducing the money supply.

In response to the credit crunch of the late 2000s, central banks in several countries extended their willingness to lend to banks. The pressure on central banks to act as the 'liquidity backstop' grew as the inter-bank market ceased to function effectively in distributing reserves and, hence, liquidity between financial institutions. As a result, inter-bank rates rose sharply relative to the policy rate (see Figure 28.3 on page 533). Increasingly, the focus of central banks was on providing the necessary liquidity to ensure the stability of the financial system. Yet, at the same time, by providing more liquidity, central banks were ensuring monetary policy was not being compromised. The additional liquidity was needed to alleviate the upward pressure on market interest rates.

Funding. Rather than focusing on controlling the monetary base (as in the case of the above two techniques), an alternative is for the authorities (the Debt Management Office in the UK) to alter the overall liquidity position of the banks. An example of this approach is a change in the balance of *funding* government debt. To reduce money supply the authorities issue more bonds and fewer bills. Banks' balances with the central bank will be little affected, but to the extent that banks hold fewer bills, there will be a reduction in their liquidity and hence a reduction in the amount of credit created. Funding is thus the conversion of one type of government debt (liquid) into another (illiquid).

Variable minimum reserve ratios. In some countries (such as the USA), banks are required to hold a certain proportion of their assets in liquid form. The assets which count as liquid are known as 'reserve assets'. These include assets such as balances in the central bank, bills of exchange, certificates of deposit and money market loans. The ratio of such assets to total liabilities is known as the *minimum reserve ratio*. If the central bank raises this ratio (in other words, requires the banks to hold a higher proportion of liquid assets), then banks will have to reduce the amount of credit they grant. The money supply will fall.

Difficulties in controlling money supply

Targets for the growth in broad money were an important part of UK monetary policy from 1976 to 1985. Money targets were then abandoned and have not been used since. The European Central Bank targets the growth of M3 (see Box 30.5), but this is a subsidiary policy to that of setting interest rates in order to keep inflation under control. If, however, a central bank did choose to target money supply as its main monetary policy, how would the policy work?

Assume that money supply is above target and that the central bank wishes to reduce it. It would probably use open-market operations: i.e. it would sell more bonds or bills. The purchasers of the bonds or bills would draw liquidity from the banks. Banks would then supposedly be forced to cut down on the credit they create. But is it as simple as this?

The problem is that banks will normally be unwilling to cut down on loans if people want to borrow – after all, borrowing by customers earns profits for the banks. Banks can always 'top up' their liquidity by borrowing from the central bank and then carry on lending. True, they will have to pay the interest rate charged by the central bank, but they can pass on any rise in the rate to their customers.

The point is that as long as people *want* to borrow, banks and other financial institutions will normally try to find ways of meeting the demand. In other words, in the short run at least, the supply of money is to a large extent demand determined. It is for this reason that central banks prefer to control the *demand* for money by controlling interest rates.

As we shall see in Box 30.4, there are similar difficulties in *expanding* broad money supply by a desired amount. Following the credit crunch, various central banks around the world engaged in a process of quantitative easing. The process results in an increase in the monetary base (narrow money); banks' liquidity increases. But just how much this results in an increase in broad money depends on the willingness of banks to lend and customers to borrow. In the recessionary climate after 2008, confidence was low. Much of the extra liquidity remained in banks and the money multiplier fell (see Figure 28.4 on page 536). The growth of M4 in the UK fell sharply during 2009, despite quantitative easing, and remained weak throughout the first half of the 2010s (see Figure 28.5 on page 537).

Techniques to control interest rates

The approach to monetary control today in most countries is to focus directly on interest rates. Normally an interest rate change will be announced, and then open-market

---

Definitions

Funding Where the authorities alter the balance of bills and bonds for any given level of government borrowing.

Minimum reserve ratio A minimum ratio of cash (or other specified liquid assets) to deposits (either total or selected) that the central bank requires banks to hold.

operations will be conducted by the central bank to ensure that the money supply is adjusted so as to make the announced interest rate the *equilibrium* one. Thus, in Figure 30.3 (on page 591), the central bank might announce a rise in interest rates from r_1 to r_2 and then conduct open-market operations to ensure that the money supply is reduced from Q_1 to Q_2.

Let us assume that the central bank decides to raise interest rates. What does it do? In general, it will seek to keep banks short of liquidity. This will happen automatically on any day when tax payments by banks' customers exceed the money they receive from government expenditure. This excess is effectively withdrawn from banks and ends up in the government's account at the central bank. Even when this does not occur, the issuing of government debt will effectively keep the banking system short of liquidity, at least in the short term.

This 'shortage' can then be used as a way of forcing through interest rate changes. Banks will obtain the necessary liquidity from the central bank through repos (see page 521) or by selling it back bills. The central bank can *choose the rate of interest to charge*: i.e. the repo rate or the bill price. This will then have a knock-on effect on other interest rates throughout the banking system (see Table 28.5 in page 543). Box 30.3 gives more details on just how the Bank of England manipulates interest rates on a day-to-day basis.

The effectiveness of changes in interest rates

Even though central bank adjustment of the repo rate is the current preferred method of monetary control in most countries, it is not without its difficulties. The problems centre on the nature of the demand for loans. If this demand is (a) unresponsive to interest rate changes or (b) unstable because it is significantly affected by other determinants (such as anticipated income or foreign interest rates), then it will be very difficult to control by controlling the rate of interest.

KI 12
p 68
Problem of an inelastic demand for loans. If the demand for loans is inelastic (i.e. a relatively steep M_d curve in Figure 30.3 on page 591), any attempt to reduce demand will involve large rises in interest rates. The problem will be compounded if the demand curve shifts to the right, due, say, to a consumer spending boom. High interest rates lead to the following problems:

KI 41
p 471
- They may discourage business investment and thereby reduce long-term growth.
- They add to the costs of production, to the costs of house purchase and generally to the cost of living. They are thus cost inflationary.
- They are politically unpopular, since the general public do not like paying higher interest rates on overdrafts, credit cards and mortgages.
- The necessary bond issue to restrain liquidity will commit the government to paying high rates on these bonds for the next 20 years or so.

- High interest rates encourage inflows of money from abroad. This drives up the exchange rate. A higher exchange rate makes domestically produced goods expensive relative to goods made abroad. This can be very damaging for export industries and industries competing with imports. Many firms in the UK suffered badly between 1997 and 2007 from a high exchange rate, caused partly by higher interest rates in the UK than in the eurozone and the USA.

Evidence suggests that the demand for loans may indeed be quite inelastic. Especially in the short run, many firms and individuals simply cannot reduce their borrowing commitments. What is more, although high interest rates may discourage many firms from taking out long-term fixed-interest loans, some firms may merely switch to shorter-term variable-interest loans.

Problem of an unstable demand. Accurate monetary control requires the central bank to be able to predict the demand curve for money (in Figure 30.3). Only then can they set the appropriate level of interest rates. Unfortunately, the demand curve may shift unpredictably, making control very difficult. The major reason is *speculation*. For example, if people think interest rates will rise and bond prices fall, in the meantime they will demand to hold their assets in liquid form. The demand for money will rise. Alternatively, if people think exchange rates will rise, they will demand the domestic currency while it is still relatively cheap. The demand for money will rise.

KI 38
p 470

KI 13
p 78

It is very difficult for the central bank to predict what people's expectations will be. Speculation depends so much on world political events, rumour and 'random shocks'.

If the demand curve shifts very much, and if it is inelastic, then monetary control will be very difficult. Furthermore, the central bank will have to make frequent and sizeable adjustments to interest rates. These fluctuations can be very damaging to business confidence and may discourage long-term investment.

> ### Pause for thought
>
> *Assume that the central bank announces a rise in interest rates and backs this up with open-market operations. What determines the size of the resulting fall in aggregate demand?*

The net result of an inelastic and unstable demand for money is that substantial interest rate changes may be necessary to bring about the required change in aggregate demand. For example, central banks had to cut interest rates to virtually zero in their attempt to tackle the global recession of the late 2000s. Indeed, as we see in Box 30.4, central banks took to other methods as the room for further interest rate cuts simply disappeared.

BOX 30.4 QUANTITATIVE EASING

Rethinking monetary policy in hard times

As the economies of the world slid into recession in 2008, central banks became more and more worried that the traditional instrument of monetary policy – controlling interest rates – was insufficient to ward off a slump in demand.

Running out of options?

Interest rates had been cut at an unprecedented rate and central banks were reaching the end of the road for cuts. The Fed was the first to be in this position. By December 2008 the target federal funds rate (the overnight rate at which the Fed lends to banks) had been cut to a range between 0 and 0.25 per cent in December. But you cannot cut nominal rates below zero – otherwise you would be paying people to borrow money, which would be like giving people free money.

The problem was that there was an acute lack of willingness of banks to lend, and firms and consumers to borrow, as people saw the oncoming recession.

Increasing the money supply

So what were central banks to do? The answer was to increase money supply directly, in a process known as **quantitative easing**. This involves an aggressive version of open-market operations, where the central bank buys up a range of assets, such as securitised mortgage debt and long-term government bonds. The effect is to pump large amounts of additional cash into the economy in the hope of stimulating demand and, through the process of credit creation, to boost broad money too.

In the USA, in December 2008, at the same time as the federal funds rate was cut to a range of 0 to 0.25 per cent, the Fed embarked on large-scale quantitative easing. It began buying hundreds of billions of dollars' worth of mortgage-backed securities on the open market and planned also to buy large quantities of long-term government debt. The Federal Open Market Committee (the body setting interest rates in the USA) said that, 'The focus of the committee's policy going forward will be to support the functioning of financial markets and stimulate the economy through open-market operations and other measures that sustain the size of the Federal Reserve's balance sheet at a high level.'[1]

The result was that considerable quantities of new money were injected into the system.

A similar approach was adopted in the UK. In January 2009, the Bank of England was given powers by the Treasury to buy up to £50 billion of high-quality private-sector assets, such as corporate bonds and commercial paper. In March 2009, this was extended to government bonds (or 'gilts') and quantitative easing started.

Between March and November 2009, the MPC decided to purchase £200 billion of financial assets, mostly 'gilts'. The purchases, largely from private investors, such as insurance companies and pension funds, were with newly created electronic money. When the money found its way back into the banking system, it resulted in an increase in banks' reserve balances in the Bank of England.

With recovery still weak, the MPC sanctioned further asset purchases in October 2011 (£75 billion), February 2012 (£50 billion) and July 2012 (£50 billion), bringing the total to £375 billion, virtually all of which were government bonds.

The transmission mechanism of asset purchases

Quantitative easing involves directly increasing the amount of narrow money. It can also, indirectly, increase broad money. There are two main ways this can happen.

The first is through the effects on asset prices and yields. When non-bank financial companies, including insurance companies and pension funds, sell assets to the central bank, they can use the money to purchase other assets. In doing so this will drive up their prices. This, in turn, reduces the yields on these assets (at a higher price there is less dividend or interest per pound spent on them), which should help to reduce interest rates generally and make the cost of borrowing cheaper for households and firms, thereby boosting aggregate demand.

Also, for those holding these now more expensive assets there is a positive wealth effect. For instance, households with longer-term saving plans involving securities will now have greater financial wealth. Again, this will boost spending.

The second mechanism is through bank lending. Commercial banks will find their reserve balances increase at the central bank as the sellers of assets to the central bank deposit the money in their bank accounts. This will increase the liquidity ratio of banks, which, other things being equal, should encourage them to grant more credit.

However, it is all very well increasing the monetary base, but a central bank cannot force banks to lend or people to borrow. That requires confidence. We observed in Box 28.4 the continued weakness of bank lending to the non-bank private sector through the late 2000s and into the early 2010s. This is not to say that quantitative easing failed in the UK and elsewhere: the growth in broad money could have been weaker still. However, it does illustrate the potential danger of this approach if, in the short run, little credit creation takes place. In the equation $MV = PY$, the rise in (narrow) money supply (M) may be largely, or more than, offset by a fall in the velocity of circulation (V) (see page 554).

On the other hand, there is also the danger that if this policy is conducted for too long, the growth in broad money supply could ultimately prove to be excessive, resulting in inflation rising above the target level. It is therefore important for central banks to foresee this and turn the monetary 'tap' off in time. This would involve 'quantitative tightening' – selling assets that the central bank had purchased, thereby driving down asset prices and driving up interest rates.

 Would it be appropriate to define the policy of quantitative easing as 'monetarist'?

Definition

Quantitative easing A deliberate attempt by the central bank to increase the money supply by buying large quantities of securities through open-market operations.

These securities could be securitised mortgage and other private-sector debt or government bonds.

[1] Press release, Board of Governors of the Federal Reserve System (16 December 2008).

BOX 30.5 MONETARY POLICY IN THE EUROZONE

The role of the ECB

The European Central Bank (ECB) is based in Frankfurt and is charged with operating the monetary policy of those EU countries that have adopted the euro. Although the ECB has the overall responsibility for the eurozone's monetary policy, the central banks of the individual countries, such as the Bank of France and Germany's Bundesbank, were not abolished. They are responsible for distributing euros and for carrying out the ECB's policy with respect to institutions in their own countries. The whole system of the ECB and the national central banks is known as the European System of Central Banks (ESCB).

In operating the monetary policy of a 'euro economy' roughly the size of the USA, and in being independent from national governments, the ECB's power is enormous and is equivalent to that of the Fed. So what is the structure of this giant on the European stage, and how does it operate?

The structure of the ECB

The ECB has two major decision-making bodies: the Governing Council and the Executive Board.[2]

The Governing Council consists of the members of the Executive Board and the governors of the central banks of each of the eurozone countries. The Council's role is to set the main targets of monetary policy and to take an oversight of the success (or otherwise) of that policy.

The Executive Board consists of a president, a vice-president and four other members. Each serves for an eight-year, non-renewable term. The Executive Board is responsible for implementing the decisions of the Governing Council and for preparing policies for the Council's consideration. Each member of the Executive Board has a responsibility for some particular aspect of monetary policy.

The targets of monetary policy

The overall responsibility of the ECB is to achieve price stability in the eurozone. The target is a rate of inflation below, but close to, 2 per cent over the medium term. It is a weighted average rate for all the members of the eurozone, not a rate that has to be met by every member individually.

Alongside its definition of price stability, the ECB's monetary policy strategy comprises what it calls 'a two-pillar approach to the analysis of the risks to price stability'. These two pillars are an analysis of (a) monetary developments and (b) economic developments. The former includes an analysis of monetary aggregates, including M3. The latter includes an analysis of economic activity, the labour market, cost indicators, fiscal policy and the balance of payments.

The ECB then attempts to 'steer' short-term interest rates to influence economic activity to maintain price stability in the euro area in the medium term. In May 2015, the rates were as follows: 0.05 per cent for the main 'refinancing operations' of the ESCB (i.e. the minimum rate of interest at which liquidity

is offered once per week to 'monetary financial institutions' (MFIs) by the ESCB); a 'marginal lending' rate of 0.30 per cent (for providing overnight support to the MFIs); and a 'deposit rate' of −0.20 per cent (the rate paid to MFIs for depositing overnight surplus liquidity with the ESCB). The negative deposit rate meant that banks were being charged for 'parking' money with the ECB rather than lending it. The hope was that this would encourage banks to lend to each other or to households and businesses and, consequently, stimulate the economy.

Interest rates are set by the Governing Council by simple majority. In the event of a tie, the president has the casting vote.

The operation of monetary policy

The ECB sets a minimum reserve ratio for eurozone banks. The ratio is designed primarily to prevent excessive lending and hence the need for excessive borrowing from the central bank or from other financial institutions. This, in turn, should help to reduce the volatility in interest rates.

The minimum reserve ratio was not designed, however, to be used to make changes in monetary policy. In other words, it was not used as a variable minimum reserves ratio, and for this reason it was set at a low level. From 1 January 1999 to 17 January 2012 the ratio (also known as the reserve coefficient) was 2 per cent of key liquid and relatively liquid liabilities. However, as of 18 January 2012 the ratio was reduced to 1 per cent in an attempt to help stimulate bank lending. In other words, it was now being used for the first time as part of an active monetary policy.

The main instrument for keeping the ECB's desired interest rate as the equilibrium rate is open-market operations in government bonds and other recognised assets, mainly in the form of repos. These repo operations are conducted by the national central banks, which must ensure that the repo rate does not rise above the marginal overnight lending rate or fall below the deposit rate.

The ECB uses four types of open-market operations:

Main refinancing operations. These are short-term repos with a maturity of one week. They take place weekly and are used to maintain liquidity consistent with the chosen ECB interest rate.

Longer-term refinancing operations (LTROs). These take place monthly and normally have a maturity of three months but, as we shall see below, three-year LTROs were introduced in 2011. They are to provide additional longer-term liquidity to banks as required at rates determined by the market, not the ECB.

Fine-tuning operations. These can be short-term sales or purchases of short-term assets. They are designed to combat

[2] See www.ecb.int/ecb/orga/decisions/govc/html/index.en.html

unexpected changes in liquidity and hence to keep money-market rates at the ECB's chosen rate.

Structural operations. These are used as necessary to adjust the amount of liquidity in the eurozone. They can involve either the purchase or sale of various assets.

ECB independence

The ECB is one of the most independent central banks in the world. It has very little formal accountability to elected politicians. Although its president can be called before the European Parliament, the Parliament has virtually no powers to influence the ECB's actions.

Until its January 2015 meeting, its deliberations were secret and no minutes of Council meetings were published. Subsequently, an account of meetings is published (usually with a lag of around two weeks) with an explanation of the policy stance. However, the minutes do not include details of how Council members voted or of future policy intentions, unlike the minutes published by the Bank of England which, from 2015, are available at the time of the policy announcement.

Response to the financial crisis

The financial crisis for 2007–8 put incredible strains on commercial banks in the eurozone and, hence, on the ECB's monetary framework. Consequently, monetary operations were gradually modified.

A Securities Market Programme (SMP) began in May 2010 designed to supply liquidity to the ailing banking system. It allowed for ECB purchases of central government debt in the secondary market (i.e. not directly from governments) as well as purchases in both primary and secondary markets of private-sector debt instruments. By June 2012, €214 billion of purchases had been made, largely of government bonds issued by countries experiencing financing difficulties, including Portugal, Ireland, Greece and Spain. This led some to question whether the programme was being implemented to meet fiscal rather than monetary policy objectives.

As we noted earlier, the reserve ratio was reduced in January 2012 from 2 per cent to 1 per cent, so helping to alleviate some of the constraints on the volume of bank lending by banks. This move was preceded in December 2011 by three-year refinancing operations (LTROs) worth €529.5 billion and involving some 800 banks. By the end of February 2012, a further €489.2 billion of three-year loans to 523 banks took place, taking the ECB's repo operations to over €1 trillion. The hope was that the funds would help financially distressed banks pay off maturing debt and again increase their lending.

Then in September 2012, with worries about the continuing difficulties of some eurozone countries, such as Greece, Spain and Italy, to borrow at affordable interest rates and whether this would lead to their being driven from the euro, the ECB announced a replacement for the SMP programme.

This would involve a more extensive programme of purchasing existing government bonds of countries in difficulty. The ECB would purchase bonds with up to three years to maturity in the secondary market. The aim would be to drive down these countries' interest rates and thereby make it cheaper to issue new bonds when old ones matured. These Outright Monetary Transactions (OMTs) were in principle unlimited, with the ECB President, Mario Draghi, saying that the ECB would do 'whatever it takes' to hold the single currency together.

Critics argued that this would still not be enough to stimulate the eurozone economy and help bring countries out of recession. They gave two reasons.

The first is that OMTs differ from the quantitative easing programmes used in the UK and USA. ECB purchases of these bonds would not increase the eurozone money supply as the ECB would sell other assets to compensate. This process is known as *sterilisation*.

The second reason is that OMTs would be conducted only if countries stuck to previously agreed strong austerity measures. Despite the eurozone economy contracting by 0.7 per cent in 2012 and by a further 0.4 per cent in 2013, OMTs had still not been used.

Subsequent measures followed. In June 2014, the ECB announced that it was adopting a negative deposit rate (see above), that it was embarking on a further series of targeted long-term refinancing operations so as to provide long-term loans to commercial banks at cheap rates until September 2018, and that it would stop sterilising its SMP programme.

Then in September 2014, it announced that it would be commencing the purchase of asset-backed private-sector securities, such as securitised mortgages and commercial loans (see section 28.2). Nonetheless, concerns remained that the announcements did not go far enough given the problems facing the eurozone economy.

Finally, in January 2015 the ECB launched a large-scale quantitative easing programme. It announced that it would create new money to buy €60 billion of assets every month in the secondary market. Around €10 billion would be private-sector securities that were currently being purchased under September 2014 measures. The remaining €50 billion would be public-sector assets, mainly bonds of governments in the eurozone. This extended programme of asset purchases began in March 2015 and was set to continue until at least September 2016, bringing the total of asset purchased by that time to over €1.1 trillion.

 What are the arguments for and against publishing the minutes of the meetings of the ECB's Governing Council and Executive Board?

Definition

Sterilisation Actions taken by a central bank to offset the effects of foreign exchange flows or its own bond transactions so as to leave money supply unchanged.

Using monetary policy

KI 35
p 354
It is impossible to use monetary policy as a precise means of controlling aggregate demand. It is especially weak when it is pulling against the expectations of firms and consumers and when it is implemented too late. However, if the authorities operate a tight monetary policy firmly enough and long enough, they should eventually be able to reduce lending and aggregate demand. But there will inevitably be time lags and imprecision in the process.

KI 13
p 78
An expansionary monetary policy is even less reliable. If the economy is in recession, no matter how low interest rates are driven, or however much the monetary base is expanded, people cannot be forced to borrow if they do not wish to. Firms will not borrow to invest if they predict a continuing recession.

A particular difficulty in using interest rate reductions to expand the economy arises if the repo rate is nearly zero but this is still not enough to stimulate the economy. The problem is that (nominal) interest rates cannot be negative, for clearly nobody would be willing to lend in these circumstances. Japan was in such a situation in the early 2000s. It was caught in what is known as the *liquidity trap*. The UK and many eurozone countries were in this position in the early 2010s. Despite record low interest rates and high levels of liquidity, borrowing and lending remained low given worries about fiscal austerity and its dampening effects on economic growth.

Forward guidance. One way in which central banks, like the Federal Reserve, the Bank of England and the ECB, attempted to encourage spending following the financial crisis of the late 2000s was by publicly indicating the expected path of future interest rates. By stating that interest rates were likely to remain low for some time, central banks hoped that this *forward guidance* would give economic agents confidence to bring forward their spending.

Despite these problems, changing interest rates can often be quite effective in the medium term. After all, they can be changed very rapidly. There are not the time lags of implementation that there are with fiscal policy. Indeed, since the early 1990s, most governments or central banks in OECD countries have used interest rate changes as the major means of keeping aggregate demand and inflation under control.

In the UK, the eurozone and many other countries, a target is set for the rate of inflation. As we have seen, in the UK and the eurozone the target is 2 per cent. If forecasts suggest that inflation is going to be above the target rate, the government or central bank raises interest rates. The advantage of this is that it sends a very clear message to people that inflation *will* be kept under control. People will therefore be more likely to adjust their expectations accordingly and keep their borrowing in check.

30.3 ATTITUDES TOWARDS DEMAND MANAGEMENT

Debates over the control of demand have shifted ground somewhat in recent years. There is now less debate over the relative effectiveness of fiscal and monetary policy in influencing aggregate demand. There is general agreement that a *combination* of fiscal and monetary policies will have a more powerful effect than either used separately.

Economists have become increasingly interested in the environment within which policy is made. Indeed, many countries have, in recent times, been operating economic policy within a framework of rules. This is known as *constrained discretion*. Most commonly we observe this with monetary policy. Many central banks today have prescribed macroeconomic objectives, such as inflation rate targets, which help to determine the monetary policy decisions they make. Similarly, fiscal frameworks, such as the EU's Fiscal Compact and the UK's fiscal mandate (see Box 30.2), impact on governments' fiscal policy choices.

In this section we analyse debates around the extent to which governments ought to pursue active demand management policies or adhere to a set of policy rules. The financial crisis of the late 2000s, the subsequent global economic downturn and deteriorating public finances have helped to reignite the debate about the merits of constraining the discretion of policy-makers over fiscal and monetary policy.

The case for rules and policy frameworks

Why should governments commit to rules or design policy frameworks which may involve their giving up control of economic instruments? Well, there are two important arguments against discretionary policy.

Definitions

Liquidity trap When interest rates are at their floor and thus any further increases in money supply will not be spent but merely be held in idle balances as people wait for the economy to recover and/or interest rates to rise.

Constrained discretion A set of principles or rules within which economic policy operates. These can be informal or enshrined in law.

Political behaviour. The first concerns the motivation of government. Politicians may attempt to manipulate the economy for their own political purposes – such as the desire to be re-elected. The government, if not constrained by rules, may overstimulate the economy some time before an election so that growth is strong at election time. After the election, the government strongly dampens the economy to deal with the higher inflation and rising public-sector debt, and to create enough slack for another boost in time for the next election.

 When politicians behave in this way, they may lose *credibility* for sound economic management. This can lead to higher inflationary expectations, uncertainty and lower long-term investment.

 Time lags with discretionary policy. Both fiscal and monetary policies can involve long and variable time lags, which can make the policy at best ineffective and at worst destabilising. Taking the measures before the problem arises, and thus lessening the problem of lags, is no answer since forecasting tends to be unreliable.

In contrast, by setting and sticking to rules, and then not interfering further, the government can provide a sound monetary framework in which there is maximum freedom for individual initiative and enterprise, and in which firms are not cushioned from market forces and are therefore encouraged to be efficient. By the government setting a target for a steady reduction in the growth of money supply, or a target for the rate of inflation, and then resolutely sticking to it, people's expectations of inflation will be reduced, thereby making the target easier to achieve.

This sound and stable monetary environment, with no likelihood of sudden contractionary or expansionary fiscal or monetary policy, will encourage firms to take a longer-term perspective and to plan ahead. This could then lead to increased capital investment and raise long-term growth rates.

The optimum situation is for all the major countries to adhere to mutually consistent rules, so that their economies do not get out of line. This will create more stable exchange rates and provide the climate for world growth.

Advocates of this point of view in the 1970s and 1980s were the monetarists and new classical macroeconomists, but in recent years support for the setting of targets has become widespread. As we have seen, in both the UK and the eurozone countries, targets are set for both inflation and public-sector deficits.

The case for discretion

Many economists, especially those in the Keynesian tradition, reject the argument that rules provide the environment for high and stable growth. Demand, they argue, is subject to many and sometimes violent shocks: e.g. changes in expectations, domestic political events (such as an impending election), world economic factors (such

as the world economic recession of 2008–9) or world political events (such as a war). The resulting shifts in injections or withdrawals cause the economy to deviate from a stable full-employment growth path.

 Any change in injections or withdrawals will lead to a cumulative effect on national income via the multiplier and accelerator and via changing expectations. These effects take time and interact with each other, and so a process of expansion or contraction can last many months before a turning point is eventually reached.

Since shocks to demand occur at irregular intervals and are of different magnitudes, the economy is likely to experience cycles of irregular duration and of varying intensity.

 Given that the economy is inherently unstable and is buffeted around by various shocks, Keynesians argue that the government needs actively to intervene to stabilise the economy. Otherwise, the uncertainty caused by unpredictable fluctuations will be very damaging to investment and hence to long-term economic growth (quite apart from the short-term effects of recessions on output and employment).

Difficulties with choice of target

Assume that the government or central bank sets an inflation target. Should it then stick to that rate, come what may? Might not an extended period of relatively low inflation warrant a lower inflation target? The government must at least have the discretion to *change* the rules, even if only occasionally.

Then there is the question of whether success in achieving the target will bring success in achieving other macroeconomic objectives, such as low unemployment and stable economic growth. The problem is that something called *Goodhart's Law* is likely to apply. The law, named after Charles Goodhart, formerly of the Bank of England, states that attempts to control an *indicator* of a problem may, as a result, make it cease to be a good indicator of the problem.

Targeting inflation may make it become a poor indicator of the state of the economy. If people believe that the central bank will be successful in achieving its inflation target, then those expectations will feed into their inflationary expectations, and not surprisingly the target will be met. But that target rate of inflation may now be consistent with

> **KEY IDEA 44**
>
> **Goodhart's law.** Controlling a symptom (i.e. an indicator) of a problem will not cure the problem. Instead, the indicator will merely cease to be a good indicator of the problem.

> ### Definition
>
> **Goodhart's Law** Controlling a symptom of a problem, or only part of the problem, will not cure the problem: it will simply mean that the part that is being controlled now becomes a poor indicator of the problem.

both a buoyant and a depressed economy. It is possible that the Phillips curve may become *horizontal*, as we saw for the UK in Figure 29.13. Thus achieving the inflation target may not tackle the much more serious problem of creating stable economic growth and an environment which will therefore encourage long-term investment.

In extreme cases, as occurred in 2008, the economy may slow down rapidly and yet cost-push factors cause inflation to rise. Targeting inflation in these circumstances will demand *higher* interest rates, which will help to deepen the recession.

Use of a Taylor rule. For this reason, many economists have advocated the use of a **Taylor rule**,[3] rather than a simple inflation target. A Taylor rule takes *two* objectives into account – (1) inflation and (2) either real national income or unemployment – and seeks to get the optimum degree of stability of the two. The degree of importance attached to each of the two objectives can be decided by the government or central bank. The central bank adjusts interest rates when either the rate of inflation diverges from its target or the rate of economic growth (or unemployment) diverges from its sustainable (or equilibrium) level.

Take the case where inflation is above its target level. The central bank following a Taylor rule will raise the rate of interest. It knows, however, that this will reduce real national income below the level at which it would otherwise have been. This, therefore, limits the amount that the central bank is prepared to raise the rate of interest. The more weight it attaches to stabilising inflation, the more it will raise the rate of interest. The more weight it attaches to achieving stable growth in real national income, the less it will raise the rate of interest.

Thus the central bank has to trade off inflation stability against stability in economic growth.

KI 40 p471

Difficulties with the target level

KI 3 p23

When a monetary or an inflation target is first set, the short-term costs of achieving it may be too high. If expectations are slow to adjust downward and inflation remains high, then adherence to a tight monetary or inflation rule may lead to a very deep and unacceptable recession. This was a criticism made by many economists of monetarist policies between 1979 and 1982.

Definition

Taylor rule A rule adopted by a central bank for setting the rate of interest. It will raise the interest rate if (a) inflation is above target or (b) economic growth is above the sustainable level (or unemployment is below the equilibrium rate). The rule states how much interest rates will be changed in each case.

---

[3]Named after John Taylor, from Stanford University, who proposed that for every 1 per cent that GDP rises above sustainable GDP, real interest rates should be raised by 0.5 percentage points, and that for every 1 per cent that inflation rises above its target level, real interest rates should be raised by 0.5 percentage points (i.e. nominal rates should be raised by 1.5 percentage points).

PAUSE FOR THOUGHT

If people believe that the central bank will be successful in keeping inflation on target, does it matter whether a simple inflation rule or a Taylor rule is used? Explain.

When a target has been in force for some time, it may cease to be the appropriate one. Economic circumstances might change. For example, a faster growth in productivity or a large increase in oil revenues may increase potential growth and thus warrant a faster growth in money supply. Or an extended period of relatively low inflation may warrant a lower inflation target. The government must at least have the discretion to *change* the rules, even if only occasionally.

But if rules should not be stuck to religiously, does this mean that the government can engage in fine-tuning? Keynesians today recognise that fine-tuning may not be possible; nevertheless, significant and persistent excess or deficient demand *can* be corrected by demand management policy. For example, the actions taken by central banks in 2007/8 to cut interest rates substantially, and by governments to increase its expenditure and to cut taxes, helped to stave off even deeper recessions in 2008/9.

Improvements in forecasting, a willingness of governments to act quickly and the use of quick-acting policies can all help to increase the effectiveness of discretionary demand management.

Conclusions

The resolution of this debate will depend on the following factors:

- The confidence of people in the effectiveness of either discretionary policies or rules: the greater the confidence, the more successful is either policy likely to be.
- The degree of self-stabilisation of the economy (in the case of rules), or conversely the degree of inherent instability of the economy (in the case of discretion).
- The size and frequency of exogenous shocks to demand: the greater they are, the greater the case for discretionary policy.
- In the case of rules, the ability and determination of governments to stick to the rules and the belief by the public that they will be effective.
- In the case of discretionary policy, the ability of governments to adopt and execute policies of the correct magnitude, the speed with which such policies can be effected and the accuracy of forecasting.

Case study K.12 in MyEconLab looks at the history of fiscal and monetary policies in the UK from the 1950s to the current day. It illustrates the use of both rules and discretion and how the debates about policy shifted with historical events.

SUMMARY

1a Fiscal policy affects the size of government budget deficits or surpluses. They also vary with the business cycle. The structural deficit or surplus measures the deficit or surplus that would occur if the economy were operating at the *potential* level of national income.

1b Automatic fiscal stabilisers are tax revenues that rise and benefits that fall as national income rises. They have the effect of reducing the size of the multiplier and thus reducing cyclical upswings and downswings.

1c Discretionary fiscal policy is where the government deliberately changes taxes or government expenditure in order to alter the level of aggregate demand. Changes in government expenditure on goods and services will have a full multiplier effect. Changes in taxes and benefits will have a smaller multiplier effect as some of the tax/benefit changes will merely affect other withdrawals and thus have a smaller net effect on consumption of domestic product.

1d There are problems in predicting the magnitude of the effects of discretionary fiscal policy. Expansionary fiscal policy can act as a pump primer and stimulate increased private expenditure, or it can crowd out private expenditure. The extent to which it acts as a pump primer depends crucially on business confidence – something that is very difficult to predict beyond a few weeks or months. The extent of crowding out depends on monetary conditions and monetary policy.

1e There are various time lags involved with fiscal policy, which make it difficult to use fiscal policy to 'fine-tune' the economy.

1f In recent years, many governments around the world preferred a more passive approach towards fiscal policy. Targets were set for one or more measures of the public-sector finances, and then taxes and government expenditure were adjusted so as to keep to the target.

1g Nevertheless, in extreme circumstances, as occurred in 2008/9, governments were prepared to abandon rules and give a fiscal stimulus to their economies.

2a Control of the growth of the money supply over the longer term will normally involve governments attempting to restrict the size of the budget deficit. This will be difficult to do, however, in a period of recession.

2b In the short term, the authorities can use monetary policy to restrict/increase the growth in aggregate demand in one of two major ways: (a) reducing/increasing money supply directly, (b) reducing/increasing the demand for money by raising/reducing interest rates.

2c The money supply can be reduced/increased directly by using open-market operations. This involves the central bank selling/buying more government securities and thereby reducing/increasing banks' reserves. Alternatively, the central bank can reduce/increase the amount

it is prepared to lend to banks (other than as a last-resort measure).

2d The money supply is difficult to control precisely, however, and even if it is successfully controlled, there then arises the problem of severe fluctuations in interest rates if the demand for money fluctuates and is relatively inelastic.

2e The current method of control in the UK and other countries involves the central bank influencing interest rates by its operations in the gilt repo and discount markets. The central bank keeps banks short of liquidity and then supplies them with liquidity, largely through gilt repos, at its chosen interest rate (gilt repo rate). This then has a knock-on effect on interest rates throughout the economy.

2f With an inelastic demand for loans, there may have to be substantial changes in interest rates in order to bring the required change in aggregate demand. What is more, controlling aggregate demand through interest rates is made even more difficult by fluctuations in the demand for money. These fluctuations are made more severe by speculation against changes in interest rates, exchange rates, the rate of inflation, etc.

2g Nevertheless, controlling interest rates is a way of responding rapidly to changing forecasts, and can be an important signal to markets that inflation will be kept under control, especially when, as in the UK and the eurozone, there is a firm target for the rate of inflation.

2h Faced with a deepening recession after the financial crisis of 2007–8, central banks embarked on programmes of quantitative easing, which involved their creating large amounts of new narrow money. This was used to purchase bonds and other assets from financial institutions, thereby increasing banks' reserves and allowing them to increase lending and hence increase broad money through the process of credit creation.

3a The case against discretionary policy is that it involves unpredictable time lags that can make the policy destabilising. Also, the government may *ignore* the long-run adverse consequences of policies designed for short-run political gain.

3b The case in favour of rules is that they help to reduce inflationary expectations and thus create a stable environment for investment and growth.

3c The case against sticking to money supply or inflation rules is that they may cause severe fluctuations in interest rates and thus create a less stable economic environment for business planning.

3d Although perfect fine-tuning may not be possible, Keynesians argue that the government must have the discretion to change its policy as circumstances demand.

MyEconLab

This book can be supported by MyEconLab, which contains a range of additional resources, including an online homework and tutorial system designed to test and build your understanding.

You need both an access card and a course ID to access MyEconLab:

1. Is your lecturer using MyEconLab? Ask your lecturer for your course ID.

2. Has an access card been included with the book at a reduced cost? Check the inside back cover of the book.

3. If you have a course ID but no access card, go to: http://www.myeconlab.com/ to buy access to this interactive study programme.

REVIEW QUESTIONS

1 'The existence of a budget deficit or a budget surplus tells us very little about the stance of fiscal policy.' Explain and discuss.

2 Adam Smith remarked in *The Wealth of Nations* concerning the balancing of budgets, 'What is prudence in the conduct of every private family can scarce be folly in that of a great kingdom.' What problems might there be if the government decided to follow a balanced budget approach to its spending?

3 What factors determine the effectiveness of discretionary fiscal policy?

4 Why is it difficult to use fiscal policy to 'fine-tune' the economy?

5 When the Bank of England announces that it is putting up interest rates, how will it achieve this, given that interest rates are determined by demand and supply?

6 How does the Bank of England attempt to achieve the target rate of inflation of 2 per cent? What determines its likelihood of success in meeting the target?

7 Imagine you were called in by the government to advise on whether it should adopt a policy of targeting the money supply. What advice would you give and how would you justify the advice?

8 Imagine you were called in by the government to advise on whether it should attempt to prevent cyclical fluctuations by the use of fiscal policy. What advice would you give and how would you justify the advice?

9 What do you understand by the term 'constrained discretion'? Illustrate your answer with reference to the UK and the eurozone.

10 Is there a compromise between purely discretionary policy and adhering to strict targets?

11 Under what circumstances would adherence to an inflation target lead to (a) more stable interest rates, (b) less stable interest rates than pursuing discretionary demand management policy?

Supply-side policy

Business issues covered in this chapter

- How can supply-side policy influence business and the economy?
- What types of supply-side policy can be pursued and what is their effectiveness?
- What will be the impact on business of a policy of tax cuts?
- How can the government encourage increased competition?
- What is the best way of tackling regional problems and encouraging business investment in relatively deprived areas?
- What is meant by 'industrial policy' and what forms can it take?

31.1 SUPPLY-SIDE PROBLEMS

In considering economic policy up to this point we have focused our attention on the demand side of the economy, where unemployment and slow growth are the result of a lack of aggregate demand, and where inflation and a balance of trade deficit are the result of excessive aggregate demand. Many of the causes of these problems, however, lie on the *supply side* and, as such, require an alternative policy approach.

If successful, **supply-side policies** will shift the aggregate supply curve to the right, thus increasing output for any given level of prices (or reducing the price level for any given level of output). In doing so, they increase an economy's level of *potential output*: the economy's output when firms are operating at normal levels of capacity utilisation.

Effective supply-side initiatives will raise the rate at which the level of potential output grows over time and so the rate at which the aggregate supply curve shifts rightwards. Therefore, supply-side policies can be evaluated on their ability to affect an economy's long-run economic *growth*.

The quantity and productivity of factors of production

The growth of potential output is crucially dependent on an economy's factors of production (i.e. its resources, such as labour and capital). Supply-side policies are designed to influence both the *quantities* of factors employed and their *productivity*.

Physical capital

The rate at which economies accumulate capital, such as machinery and office space, is an important determinant of their long-term economic growth (see section 26.2 and

Definition

Supply-side policies Government policies that attempt to influence aggregate supply directly, rather than through aggregate demand.

Box 31.1). The rate at which the stock of capital grows depends on the size of investment flows. Therefore, supply-side policies need to facilitate investment.

Of course, it is not just the *quantity* of investment that affects economic growth but how *productive* that investment is. The greater the productivity of additional capital, the faster will national income and business profits rise, and the greater the amount of additional investment that can be financed.

The productivity of capital depends crucially on technological progress and innovation. Therefore, effective supply-side policies are those that help to foster new inventions, their incorporation in new capital equipment and their adoption by businesses. These might be policies that encourage investment in 'cutting-edge' technologies or that raise the shares of national income devoted to education, training, and research and development. A key question is what policies can encourage the effective propagation of innovation and technological progress.

The UK's record of low investment. Unfortunately for the UK, it has for several decades experienced lower levels of investment relative to national income than other industrialised countries. This is illustrated in Table 31.1. In particular, investment by the private sector has been weak by international standards: a trend that seems to have persisted over four decades.

Pause for thought

How can the UK's low level of investment relative to national income be explained?

To some extent the UK's poor investment performance has been offset by the fact that wage rates have been lower than in competing countries. This has at least made the UK relatively attractive to inward investment, especially by US, Japanese, Korean and more recently Chinese and Indian companies seeking to set up production plants within the EU.

The poor performance of UK manufacturing firms has resulted in a growing import penetration of the UK market. Imports of manufactured products have grown more rapidly than UK manufactured exports, and since the early 1980s the UK has been a net importer of manufactured products.

Some economists believe that the UK's low-investment economy highlights the need for more government intervention, especially in the fields of education and training, research and development, and the provision of infrastructure. This has been the approach in many countries, including France, Germany and Japan.

Labour

The economy's potential output is also affected by both the quantity and quality of the labour input. In section 26.3 we introduced the concept of equilibrium unemployment: the difference between those who would like to work at the current wage rate and those willing and able to take a job. There can be a mismatch between the aggregate supply of labour and the aggregate demand for labour, which means that vacancies are not filled despite the existence of unemployment. Perhaps workers have the wrong qualifications, or are poorly motivated, or are living a long way away from the job, or are simply unaware of the jobs that are vacant.

Generally, the problem is that labour is not sufficiently mobile, either occupationally or geographically, to respond to changes in the job market. Labour supply for particular jobs is too inelastic. Supply-side policies might look to increase labour market flexibility, to provide better job information, to support retraining and to enhance the skills of the workforce.

KI 12
p 68

| Table 31.1 | Gross fixed capital formation as a percentage of GDP: 1971–2016 |

	1971–93		1994–2016		1971–2016	
	General government	**Private**	**General government**	**Private**	**General government**	**Private**
UK	3.9	18.7	2.4	15.7	3.2	17.2
Denmark	3.4	18.2	3.1	17.2	3.2	17.7
Germany	3.2	18.3	2.3	18.6	2.7	18.4
USA	4.5	17.8	3.7	17.1	4.1	17.5
Italy	3.8	19.9	2.8	16.8	3.3	18.3
Ireland	4.0	18.9	3.1	18.0	3.5	18.5
Netherlands	4.5	18.7	3.8	17.2	4.2	17.9
France	4.4	19.2	4.0	17.4	4.2	18.3
Belgium	4.0	18.9	2.2	20.1	3.1	19.5
Spain	3.6	20.2	3.8	20.5	3.7	20.3
Japan	5.2	25.8	4.4	19.4	4.8	22.6

Source: *AMECO* database, European Commission, DGECFIN, Tables 3.2 and 6.1

BOX 31.1 GETTING INTENSIVE WITH PHYSICAL CAPITAL

Economic growth and capital accumulation

In this box we look at the growth of the physical capital stock in a sample of countries and then compare this with their growth in GDP per worker.

Capital as recorded in a country's national accounts consists of *non-financial fixed assets*. It does not include stocks of goods and services transformed or used up in the course of production, known as *intermediate goods and services*. Furthermore, it does not relate directly to the stock of human capital: the skills and attributes embodied in individuals that affect production (see Box 31.2).

A country's stock of capital can be valued at its replacement cost, regardless of its age: this is its *gross* value. It can also be valued at its written-down value, known as its *net* value. The net value takes into account the *consumption of capital* which occurs through wear and tear (depreciation) or when capital becomes naturally obsolescent. The value of the UK's net capital stock was estimated at £4.27 trillion in 2014, or 2.35 times the value of that year's GDP.

In models of economic growth an important measure of capital is the stock of capital per person employed (per worker). This is also known as *capital intensity*. In the chart we plot the ratio of capital per worker in 2016 to that in 1960 (y-axis) against the ratio of output per worker (x-axis) in 2016 to that in 1960 for a sample of developed countries.

For each country we observe an increase in capital intensity, although the rates of capital accumulation differ quite sig-

nificantly. The data show that the UK ranks relatively lowly in terms of capital accumulation. In the UK the capital stock per worker is 2.3 times higher in 2016, compared with, for example, Japan where it is 5.8 times higher or France where it is 3.7 times higher.

We would expect that the higher the level of capital per worker, the greater will be the level of output (real GDP) per worker. This is largely borne out in the chart. However, while there is a statistical association between capital accumulation and economic growth, economic theory plays an important role in our understanding of this apparent relationship.

There is considerable debate about the determinants of capital accumulation and its significance for growth, especially when analysed alongside technological progress. Although data on increases in capital do to some extent capture advances in technology, the significance of technological change is likely to be underestimated. Furthermore, advances in technology are thought to be crucially important in stimulating capital accumulation.

 Does the type of capital being accumulated impact affect the rate of long-run economic growth?

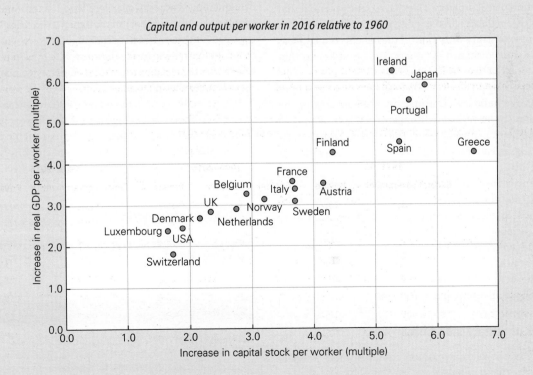

Capital and output per worker in 2016 relative to 1960

Note: 2016 figures are forecasts
Source: Based on data from *AMECO database* (European Commission)

As well as making workers more responsive to job opportunities, supply-side policies may aim to make employers more adaptable and more effective in operating within existing labour constraints.

Pause for thought

How can increasing the effectiveness of labour improve both the productivity of labour and the productivity of capital?

Successful supply-side policies that reduce equilibrium unemployment and increase employment also increase the economy's potential output. The benefits for potential output can be enduring too. A more flexible and skilful workforce increases the economy's stock of **human capital**. The concept of human capital captures the knowledge, skills and attributes that are embodied within the workforce and which affect production activities.

Human and physical capital

An increase in an economy's stock of human capital increases the effectiveness with which the economy's existing stock of physical capital can be employed. This therefore contributes to further accumulation of physical capital.

Greater levels of human capital also contribute to the development of new products, processes and techniques and, hence, in the development of higher quality capital. As we have seen, this can be important in increasing the rate of technological progress. There is also the potential that **knowledge spillovers** hasten progress. These spillovers are a form of externality with some of the benefits of new ideas captured or consumed by others. The point here is that these ideas can then be developed by others.

Supply-side policies can aim to foster the benefits from knowledge spillovers. This may involve encouraging the clustering of businesses within particular sectors so as to enable the exchange of ideas. The development of business parks or enterprise zones (see page 617) are a means of doing this.

Some economists argue that it is competition which helps foster the development of ideas and technological progress. By seeking a competitive advantage over their rivals, firms may look to deliver products and services that provide consumers with greater satisfaction or develop processes which allow them to produce more cost-effectively. Whichever strategy businesses choose, it is argued, the benefits help to drive technological progress.

Types of supply-side policy

Supply-side policies are commonly grouped under two general types: *market-orientated* and *interventionist*.

Market-orientated policies focus on ways of 'freeing up' the market, such as encouraging private enterprise, risk-taking and competition: policies that provide incentives for innovation, hard work and productivity. These are considered in Section 31.2.

Interventionist policies focus on means of counteracting the deficiencies of the free market and typically involve government expenditure on infrastructure and training, and financial support for investment. These are considered in Section 31.3.

However, some policies may draw on elements of both types: for instance, by providing financial support (interventionist) through the use of tax reliefs (market-orientated).

Regional imbalances. Supply-side policies and initiatives should not be seen solely in terms of delivering *national* objectives. There are often marked differences in incomes, unemployment rates and other measures of economic and social well-being *within* a country. Therefore, both national governments and international bodies, such as the EU, may adopt supply-side projects and initiatives that help to tackle regional inequalities. We look at regional policy in the final section of this chapter.

Links between demand-side and supply-side policy

Policies can have both demand-side and supply-side effects. For example, many supply-side policies involve increased government expenditure, whether on retraining schemes, on research and development projects, or on industrial relocation. They will therefore cause a rise in aggregate demand (unless accompanied by a rise in taxes). Similarly, supply-side policies of tax cuts designed to increase incentives will increase aggregate demand (unless accompanied by a cut in government expenditure). It is thus important to consider the consequences for demand when planning various supply-side policies.

Likewise, demand management policies often have supply-side effects. If a cut in interest rates boosts investment, there will be a multiplied rise in national income: a demand-side effect. But that rise in investment will also create increased productive capacity: a supply-side effect.

Pause for thought

Why might it take time for the benefits of supply-side policies to become evident?

Definitions

Human capital The knowledge, skills, competencies and other attributes embodied in individuals or groups of individuals that are used to produce goods and services.

Knowledge spillovers The capture by third parties of benefits from the development by others of new ideas, for example, new products, processes and technologies.

31.2 MARKET-ORIENTATED SUPPLY-SIDE POLICIES

Radical market-orientated supply-side policies were first adopted in the early 1980s by the Thatcher government in the UK and the Reagan administration in the USA, but were subsequently copied by other right and centre-right governments around the world. The essence of these supply-side policies is to encourage and reward individual enterprise and initiative, and to reduce the role of government; to put more reliance on market forces and competition, and less on government intervention and regulation.

Reducing government expenditure

The desire of many governments to cut government expenditure is not just to reduce the size of the public-sector deficit and hence reduce the growth of money supply; it is also an essential ingredient of their supply-side strategy.

The public sector is portrayed by some as more bureaucratic and less efficient than the private sector. What is more, it is claimed that a growing proportion of public money has been spent on administration and other 'non-productive' activities, rather than on the direct provision of goods and services.

Two things are needed, it is argued: (a) a more efficient use of resources within the public sector and (b) a reduction in the size of the public sector. This would allow private investment to increase with no overall rise in aggregate demand. Thus the supply-side benefits of higher investment could be achieved without the demand-side costs of higher inflation.

In practice, governments have found it very difficult to cut their expenditure relative to GDP. However, many countries were faced with trying to do this after the financial crisis and global economic slowdown of the late 2000s (see Figure 31.1). Governments found that this means making difficult choices, particularly concerning the levels of services and the provision of infrastructure.

Pause for thought

Why might a recovering economy (and hence a fall in government expenditure on social security benefits) make the government feel even more concerned to make discretionary cuts in government expenditure?

Tax cuts

The imposition of taxation can distort a variety of choices that individuals make. Changes to the rates of taxation can lead individuals to substitute one activity for another. Three examples which are commonly referred to in the context of aggregate supply are:

- taxation of labour income and its impact on labour supply (including hours worked and choice of occupation);
- taxation of interest income earned on financial products (savings) and its impact on the funds available for investment;

KI 9
p51

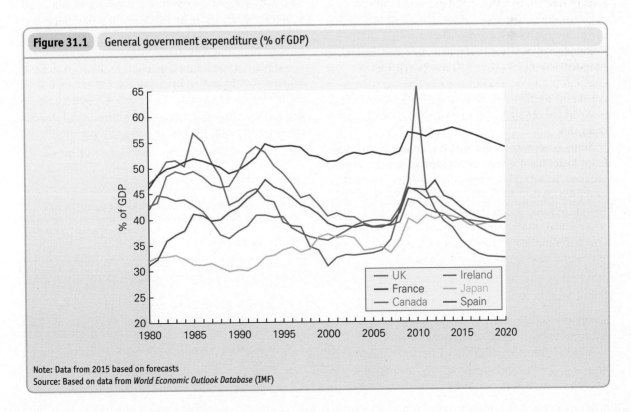

Figure 31.1 General government expenditure (% of GDP)

Note: Data from 2015 based on forecasts
Source: Based on data from *World Economic Outlook Database* (IMF)

BOX 31.2   UK HUMAN CAPITAL

Estimating the capabilities of the workforce

The OECD defines human capital as the knowledge, skills, competencies and other attributes embodied in individuals or groups of individuals acquired during their life and used to produce goods, services or ideas in market circumstances.

In other words, human capital captures the capabilities embodied in people in the workforce that can affect both the nature and extent of production. While trends in human capital have implications for economic growth, there can be microeconomic effects too. For example, individuals with a lower stock of human capital may face a greater probability of unemployment or lower lifetime earnings. This has implications for inequality and social cohesiveness. But how we do we go about measuring human capital?

Measuring human capital

In estimating an individual's human capital, a common approach is to estimate the present value of an individual's *remaining lifetime labour income*. This can be done for representative individuals in categories defined by gender, age and educational attainment. An assumption is then made about the working life of individuals. In compiling the UK estimates it is assumed that the remaining lifetime labour income of individuals aged 65 and over is zero. Then an approach known as *backwards recursion* is applied.

Backwards recursion involves first estimating the remaining lifetime labour income of someone aged 64 with a particular gender, age and educational level. The remaining lifetime income in this case is simply their current annual labour income for the year from their 64th birthday. For someone aged 63 it is their current annual labour income for the year from their 63rd birthday plus the present value[1] of the remaining lifetime income of someone aged 64 with the same gender, age and educational level. This continues back to someone aged 16. In calculating the remaining lifetime labour income of representative individuals, account is also taken of the probability that their level of educational attainment may rise and, with it, their expected future earnings.

Further working assumptions are necessary to complete the calculations. Two of the most important are that: the rate of labour productivity growth is 2 per cent per annum and the discount rate is 3.5 per cent per annum, as recommended by HM Treasury's Green Book (2003) when undertaking appraisal and evaluation studies in central government.

Two measures of the stock of human capital are estimated. The first is for *employed* human capital. It is based on estimating the lifetime labour income of those in employment. The second is *full* human capital. It includes the human capital of the unemployed. This assumes that the human capital of those currently unemployed should be valued at the remaining lifetime labour income of employed individuals with the same characteristics (gender, age and educational attainment). It ignores any so-called scarring effects from being unemployed, such as the depreciation of job-specific or transferable skills. Such effects are likely to increase the longer the duration of unemployment.

Estimates of human capital

The chart shows estimates of employed and full human capital in the UK since 2004. Both follow broadly similar patterns. Between 2004 and 2007, prior to the financial crisis, the stock of human capital increased steadily by a little over 3 per cent per annum. Both employed and full human capital fell in each year from 2009 to 2013. The fall in full human capital was less pronounced because of the impact of rising unemployment on the employed human capital estimates.

In 2014, the UK's full human capital was £18.95 trillion while that for employed human capital was £18.22 trillion. This means that stock of human capital was between 10 and 10.4 times larger than annual GDP, depending on which measure of human capital is used. In Box 31.1 we saw that the net value of the UK's physical capital was £4.27 trillion. Therefore, in 2014, the value of the stock of human capital was estimated to be up to 4.4 times higher than the stock of physical capital.

We can also analyse the *distribution* of human capital by a particular characteristic, such as educational attainment. In 2014 it is estimated that 36.1 per cent of UK employed human capital was embodied in the 27.0 per cent of the population who have a degree (or equivalent). In contrast, only 5.1 per cent of employed human capital was embodied in the 9.0 per cent of the working-age population with no formal qualifications.

Inequality and human capital

Research by the OECD and IMF[2] suggests that there is a correlation between inequality and human capital development

---

[1] 'Present value' in this case is the value in today's terms of income earned in the future. These incomes have to be reduced by the rate of interest that could have been earned if the income had been earned today instead of in the future. This process of reducing future incomes to present values is known as 'discounting' (see page 325).

[2] See: *FOCUS on Inequality and Growth* (Directorate for Employment, Labour and Social Affairs, *OECD*, December 2014); and Jonathan D. Ostry, Andrew Berg and Charalambos G. Tsangarides, 'Redistribution, inequality, and growth', *IMF Staff Discussion Note* (IMF, February 2014).

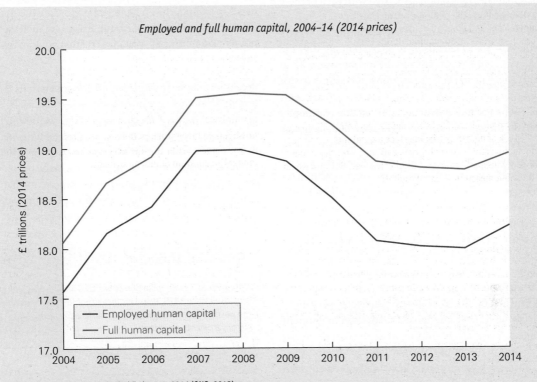

Employed and full human capital, 2004–14 (2014 prices)

Source: Based on data in *Human Capital Estimates, 2014* (ONS, 2015)

and that this impacts on economic growth. Higher inequality reduces economic growth.

Traditionally it has been argued that there is a trade-off between inequality and economic growth: that higher inequality encourages economic growth. Increasing the rewards to those who are more productive or who invest, it is claimed, encourages a growth in productivity and capital investment, which, in turn, leads to faster economic growth. Redistribution from the rich to the poor, by contrast, is argued to reduce incentives by reducing the rewards from harder work, education, training and investment. Risk taking, it is claimed, is discouraged.

However, the OECD and IMF research suggests that when income inequality rises, economic growth falls. Inequality has grown massively in many countries, with average incomes at the top of the distribution seeing particular gains, while many at the bottom have experienced actual declines in real incomes or, at best, little or no growth. This growth in inequality, claims the OECD, has led to a loss in economic growth of around 0.35 percentage points per year over the past 25 years.

According to the OECD and IMF, inequality reduces the development of skills of the lower income groups and reduces social mobility. The lower educational attainment applies to both the length and quality of education: people from poorer backgrounds tend to leave school or college earlier and with fewer qualifications.

But if greater inequality generally results in lower economic growth, will a redistribution from rich to poor necessarily result in faster economic growth? Redistribution policies need to be well designed and implemented and focus on raising incomes of the poor through increased opportunities to increase their productivity. There needs to be increasing access to public services, such as high-quality education, training and health care. Simple transfers from rich to poor via the tax and benefits system may, in fact, undermine economic growth.

1. In what ways might human capital and physical capital be complementary?
2. In what other ways could we consider the distribution of human capital?

- taxation of firms' profits and its impact on capital expenditure by firms.

Over time, many countries have witnessed a decline in the marginal rates of taxation associated with each of these cases. Here we consider the case of the UK.

In 1979, the basic rate of income tax in the UK was 33 per cent, with higher rates rising to 83 per cent. By 1997 the basic rate was only 23 per cent and the top rate was only 40 per cent. The Blair and Brown governments continued with this policy, so that by 2008 the basic rate was 20 per cent. From 2010, an additional 50 per cent tax rate was implemented for those earning in excess of £150 000, largely as a means of plugging the deficit in the public finances. This was subsequently reduced to 45 per cent from 2013.

Similar reductions in rates of tax on business profits have been designed to encourage investment. Reductions in corporation tax (the tax on business profits) have increased after-tax profits, leaving more funds for ploughing back into investment, as well as increasing the after-tax return on investment. In 1983 the main rate of corporation tax in the UK stood at 52 per cent. A series of reductions have taken place since then. By 2011 the main rate had been halved to 26 per cent and by 2015 the rate had fallen to 20 per cent

Governments have also looked to increase investment allowances. These allow firms to offset the cost of investment against pre-tax profit, thereby reducing their tax liability. Successive governments have used a range of such allowances. For example, in the UK companies can offset a multiple of research and development costs against corporation tax. Since April 2012, the rate of relief for small and medium-sized enterprises (SMEs) has been 225 per cent: i.e. taxable profits are reduced by £225 for every £100 of R&D expenditure. For larger companies the rate of relief is 130 per cent.

Since April 2013, firms have been subject to a lower rate of corporation tax on profits earned from inventions they have patented and certain other innovations. The idea is that firms will be provided with financial support to innovate where this results in their acquiring patents. Patents provide protection for intellectual property rights. From April 2013, firms are liable to corporation tax on the profits attributable to qualifying patents at a reduced rate of 10 per cent. The relief is being phased in, so that by 2017 all profits related to the patent will be subject to the reduced rate.

KI 9
p51 *Substitution effects of tax cuts.* The argument for reducing tax rates on incomes and profits is that it contributes to higher levels of economic output. Specifically, it encourages an increased supply of labour hours, more moneys invested with financial institutions and more capital expenditure by firms than would otherwise be the case. The reason is that tax cuts increase the return on such activities. In other words, there is a *substitution effect* inducing more of these beneficial activities. In the case of labour, people are encouraged to substitute work for leisure as their after-tax wage rate is now higher.

Income effects of tax cuts. However, in each case there is a counteracting incentive. This is the *income effect*. Tax cuts increase the returns to working, saving and undertaking capital expenditure. This means that less of each activity needs to be undertaken to generate the same income flow as before. Take the case of labour: if a tax cut increases your hourly take-home pay, you may feel that you can afford to work fewer hours.

Because economic theory offers no firm conclusions as to the benefit of tax cuts, economists and policy makers often look to empirical evidence for guidance. In the case of whether or not tax cuts encourage people to work longer hours, the evidence suggests that the substitution and income effects just about cancel each other out. Anyway, for many people there is no such choice in the short run. There is no chance of doing overtime or working a shorter week. In the long run, there may be some flexibility in that people can change jobs.

> ### Pause for thought
>
> *If tax receipts as a proportion of national income have generally risen since 1979, does this mean that there can have been no positive incentive effects of the various tax measures taken by governments since then?*

Reducing the power of labour

The argument here is that if labour costs to employers are reduced, their profits will probably rise. This could encourage and enable more investment and hence economic growth. If the monopoly power of labour is reduced, then cost-push inflation will also be reduced.

The Thatcher government in the 1980s took a number of measures to curtail the power of unions. These included introducing the right of employees not to join unions, preventing workers taking action other than against their direct employers, and enforcing secret ballots on strike proposals (see page 627). It set a lead in resisting strikes in the public sector.

As labour markets have become more flexible, with increased part-time working and short-term and zero-hour contracts, and as the process of globalisation has exposed more companies to international competition, so this has further eroded the power of labour in many sectors of the economy (see section 18.7).

Reducing welfare

New classical economists claim that a major cause of unemployment is the small difference between the welfare benefits of the unemployed and the take-home pay of the employed. This causes voluntary unemployment (i.e. frictional unemployment). People are caught in a 'poverty trap': if they take a job, they lose their benefits.

A dramatic solution to this problem would be to cut unemployment benefits. A major problem with this approach, however, is that, with changing requirements for labour skills, many of the redundant workers from the older industries are simply not qualified for new jobs that are created. What is more, the longer people are unemployed, the more demoralised they become. Employers would probably be prepared to pay only very low wages to such workers. To persuade these unemployed people to take low-paid jobs, the welfare benefits would have to be slashed. A 'market' solution to the problem, therefore, may be a very cruel solu-tion. A fairer solution would be an interventionist policy: a policy of retraining labour.

Another alternative is to make the payment of unem-ployment benefits conditional on the recipient making a concerted effort to find a job. In the Jobseeker's Allowance introduced in the UK in 1996, claimants must be availa-ble for and actively seeking work and must complete a Claimant Commitment, which sets out the types of work the person is willing to do and the plan to find work. Pay-ment can be refused if the claimant refuses to accept jobs offered.

| BOX 31.3 | LABOUR PRODUCTIVITY |

How effective is UK labour?

A country's potential output depends on the productivity of its factors of production, including labour. There are two common ways of measuring labour productivity. The first is *output per worker*. This is the most straightforward measure to calculate. All that is required is a measure of total output and employment.

A second measure is *output per hour worked*. This has the advantage that it is not influenced by the *number* of hours worked. So for an economy like the UK, with a very high per-centage of part-time workers on the one hand, and long aver-age hours worked by full-time employees on the other, such a measure would be more accurate in gauging worker efficiency.

Both measures focus solely on the productivity of labour. If we want to account directly for the productivity of capital we need to consider the growth in *total* factor productivity (*TFP*). This measure analyses output relative to the amount of all factors used. Changes in total factor productivity over time provide a good indicator of technical progress.

Charts (a) and (b) show comparative productivity levels of various countries and the G7 using GDP per hour worked. Chart (a) shows countries' productivity relative to the UK. As you can see, GDP per hour worked is lower in the UK than the other countries with the exception of Japan. For example, in 2014, compared with the UK, output per hour was 33 per cent higher in Germany and 32 per cent higher in both France and the USA.

Compared with the rest of the G7 countries, UK output per hour was 20 per cent lower – the highest productivity gap since the series began in 1991. A major explanation of lower productivity in the UK is the fact that for decades it has invested a smaller proportion of its national income than most other industrialised nations. Nevertheless, until 2006 the gap had been narrowing with the rest of the G7. This was because UK productivity, although lower than in many other countries, was growing faster. This can be seen in chart (b). Part of the reason for this was the inflow of investment from abroad.

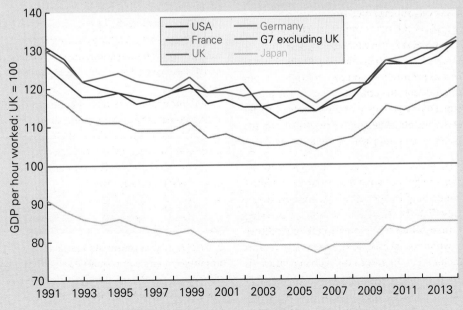

(a) Productivity in selected economies relative to the UK (GDP per hour worked)

Source: Based on data in *International Comparisons of Productivity* (National Statistics, 2015)

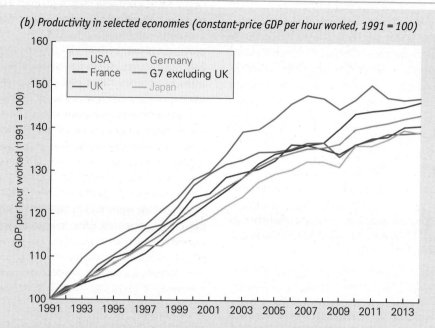

(b) Productivity in selected economies (constant-price GDP per hour worked, 1991 = 100)

Source: Based on data in *International Comparisons of Productivity* (National Statistics, 2015), rebased by authors

Chart (c) compares labour productivity across both measures. Workers in the USA and the UK work longer hours than those in France and Germany. Thus whereas output per hour worked in the USA is on a par with that in France and Germany, output per person employed in the USA is about 25 per cent higher than in France and 32 per cent higher than in Germany.

The evidence points to UK labour productivity being lower than that in the USA, France and Germany on both measures but higher than that in Japan. In understanding the growth in labour productivity it is generally agreed that we need to focus on three factors: physical capital (see Box 31.1), human capital (see Box 31.2), and innovation and technological progress. See also the posts – *UK productivity: a constraint on long-term growth* and *The UK's poor productivity record* – on the Sloman News site.

What could explain the differences in labour productivity between the five countries in chart (c), and why do the differences vary according to which of the two measures is used?

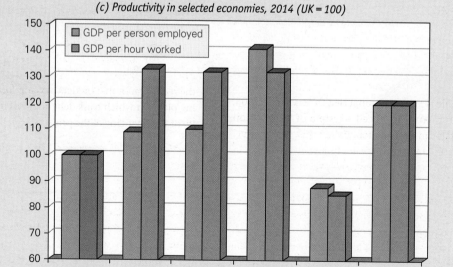

(c) Productivity in selected economies, 2014 (UK = 100)

Note: Current-price GDP per worker

Source: Based on data in *International Comparisons of Productivity* (National Statistics, 2015)

Policies to encourage competition

If the government can encourage more competition, this should have the effect of increasing national output and reducing inflation. Five major types of policy were pursued under this heading.

Privatisation. If privatisation simply involves the transfer of a natural monopoly to private hands (e.g. the water companies), the scope for increased competition is limited. However, where there is genuine scope for increased competition (e.g. in the supply of gas and electricity), privatisation can lead to increased efficiency, more consumer choice and lower prices. There may still be a problem of oligopolistic collusion, however, and thus privatised industries are monitored and regulated with the aim of making them genuinely competitive.

Alternatively, privatisation can involve the introduction of private services into the public sector (e.g. private contractors providing cleaning services in hospitals, or refuse collection for local authorities). Private contractors may compete against each other for the franchise. This may well lower the cost of provision of these services, but the quality of provision may suffer unless closely monitored. The effects on unemployment are uncertain. Private contractors may offer lower wages and thus may use more labour. But if they are trying to supply the service at minimum cost, they are likely to employ less labour.

Deregulation. This involves the removal of monopoly rights: again, largely in the public sector. The deregulation of the bus industry, opening it up to private operators, is a good example of this initiative.

KI 5
p 36
Introducing market relationships into the public sector. This is where the government tries to get different departments or elements within a particular part of the public sector to 'trade' with each other, so as to encourage competition and efficiency. The best-known examples are within health and education.

One example is in the National Health Service. In 2003, the UK government introduced a system of 'foundation trusts'. Hospitals can apply for foundation trust status. If successful, they are given much greater financial autonomy in terms of purchasing, employment and investment decisions. By May 2015, there were 152 NHS foundation trusts. Critics argue that funds were being diverted to foundation hospitals away from the less well-performing hospitals where greater funding could help that performance. In the 2012 Health and Social Care Act the government proposed that in due course all NHS hospitals become foundation trusts.

Primary Care Trusts (PCTs) were abolished in England in April 2013. In their place were Clinical Commissioning Groups (CCGs). These are formed of groups of GP practices. Clinical commissioning groups are responsible for arranging most of the NHS services within their boundaries. They oversee how NHS funds are spent. Therefore, as with GP fundholding, a key principle is to give GPs a choice of 'providers' with the hope of reducing costs and driving up standards.

The Private Finance Initiative (PFI). This is where a private company, after a competitive tender, is contracted by a government department or local authority to finance and build a project, such as a new road or a prison. The government then pays the company to maintain and/or run it, or simply rents the assets from the company. The public sector thus becomes a purchaser of services rather than a direct provider itself.

The aim of these 'public–private partnerships' (PPPs) is to introduce competition (through the tendering process) and private-sector expertise into the provision of public services (see Case study K.15 in MyEconLab). By doing so, the objective is to achieve gains in efficiency which outweigh any extra burden to the taxpayer from private-sector profits.

KI 2
p 18
Critics, however, claim that PPPs result in a poorer quality of provision with weak cost control too, resulting in a higher burden for the taxpayer in the long term. Given mounting criticisms of PPPs and general concerns over levels of government borrowing, the Coalition government in November 2011 set up a review of the PFI. The intention was to develop a new model for delivering public investment and services that takes advantage of private-sector expertise, but at a lower cost to the taxpayer. This review coincided with the introduction in 2010 of a National Investment Plan (NIP): a strategic plan to *target* public investment.

In December 2012 the Treasury published its New Approach to Public Private Partnerships. The publication set out the Government's new approach: PF2. Changes included the following:

- the public sector taking stakes of up to 49 per cent in individual private finance projects;
- publication of an annual report detailing project and financial information on all projects where the government holds a public-sector equity stake;
- removal of 'soft services', such as cleaning and catering, from PF2 projects;
- the requirement that bidders develop long-term financing plans, in which bank debt does not form the majority of the financing of the project.

Free trade and capital movements. The opening up of international trade and investment is central to a market-orientated supply-side policy. One of the first measures of the Thatcher government (in October 1979) was to remove all controls on the purchase and sale of foreign currencies, thereby permitting the free inflow and outflow of capital, both long term and short term. Most other industrialised countries also removed or relaxed exchange controls during the 1980s and early 1990s.

The Single European Act of 1987, which came into force in 1993, was another example of international liberalisation. It created a 'single market' in the EU: a market without barriers to the movement of goods, services, capital and labour (see section 25.3).

31.3 INTERVENTIONIST SUPPLY-SIDE POLICIES

The basis of the case for government intervention is market failure. In particular, in the context of growth of potential output, the free market is likely to provide too little research and development, training and investment.

There are potentially large external benefits from research and development. Firms investing in developing and improving products, and especially firms engaged in more general scientific research, may produce results that provide benefits to many other firms. Thus the *social* rate of return on investment may be much higher than the *private* rate of return. Investment that is privately unprofitable for a firm may therefore still be economically desirable for the nation.

Similarly, investment in training may continue yielding benefits to society that are lost to the firms providing the training when the workers leave.

Investment often involves risks. Firms may be unwilling to take those risks, since the costs of possible failure may be too high. When looked at nationally, however, the benefits of investment might well have substantially outweighed the costs, and thus it would have been socially desirable for firms to have taken the risk. Successes would have outweighed failures.

Even when firms do wish to make such investments, they may find difficulties in raising finance. Banks may be unwilling to lend – a problem that increased after the credit crunch. Alternatively, if firms rely on raising finance by the issue of new shares, this makes them very dependent on the stock market performance of their shares. This depends largely on current profitability and expected profitability in the near future, not on *long-term* profitability. Similarly, the fear of takeovers may make managers over-concerned to keep shareholders happy, further encouraging 'short-termism'.

Types of interventionist supply-side policy

Nationalisation. This is the most extreme form of intervention, and one that most countries had tended to reject, given a worldwide trend for privatisation. Nevertheless, many countries had always stopped short of privatising certain key transport and power industries, such as the railways and electricity generation.

Nationalisation may also be a suitable solution for rescuing vital industries suffering extreme market turbulence. This was the case with the banks in the late 2000s (and beyond) as the financial crisis unfolded. With the credit crunch and the over-exposure to risky investments in securitised sub-prime debt, inadequate levels of capital, declining confidence and plummeting share prices, several banks were taken into full or partial public ownership. In the UK, Northern Rock and Bradford & Bingley were fully nationalised, while the government took a majority shareholding

in the Royal Bank of Scotland and Lloyds Banking Group, although later the government began selling its share of these banks.

Direct provision. Improvements in infrastructure, such as a better motorway system, can be of direct benefit to industry. Alternatively, the government could provide factories or equipment to specific firms.

Funding research and development. Around about one-third of UK research and development (R&D) is financed by the government, but around half of this has been concentrated in the fields of defence, aerospace and the nuclear power industry. As a result, there has been little government sponsorship of research in the majority of industry. Since the mid-1970s, however, there have been several government initiatives in the field of information technology. Even so, the amount of government support in this field has been very small compared with Japan, France and the USA. What is more, the amount of support declined between the mid-1980s and the late 1990s.

As we saw above, the UK uses the tax system to encourage R&D. Despite this, as Figure 31.2 demonstrates, UK gross expenditure on research and development as a percentage of GDP has been lower than that of its main economic rivals.

Lower R&D has contributed to a productivity gap between the UK and other G7 countries, although it was gradually narrowing until 2006, but since then has widened (see chart (a) in Box 31.3). The UK's poor R&D record has occurred even though a sizeable number of UK-based companies regularly make a list of the world's largest R&D spending companies. In part, this reflects the limited R&D expenditure by government. But, it also reflects the low R&D intensity across the private sector. In other words, total R&D expenditure by British firms has often been low *relative* to the income generated by sales.

Training and education. The government may set up training schemes, or encourage educational institutions to make their courses more vocationally relevant, or introduce new vocational qualifications (such as GNVQs, NVQs and foundation degrees in the UK). Alternatively, the government can provide grants or tax relief to firms which themselves provide training schemes. Alternative approaches to training in the UK, Germany, France and the USA are examined in Case study K.16 in MyEconLab.

Assistance to small firms. UK governments in recent years have recognised the importance of small firms to the economy and have introduced various forms of advisory services, grants and tax concessions. For example, they receive financial support for R&D expenditure through corporation tax relief. This means they can reduce the profits liable for tax by engaging

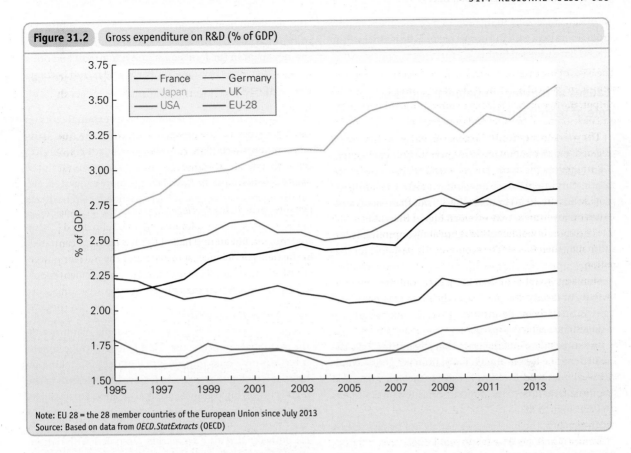

Figure 31.2 Gross expenditure on R&D (% of GDP)

Note: EU 28 = the 28 member countries of the European Union since July 2013
Source: Based on data from *OECD.StatExtracts* (OECD)

in R&D. As we saw above (page 610), the rate of relief for small and medium-sized enterprises (SMEs) is 225 per cent, compared with 130 per cent for larger companies. In addition, small firms are subject to fewer planning and other bureaucratic controls than large companies. Support to small firms in the UK is examined in Case study K.17 in MyEconLab.

Advice and persuasion. The government may engage in discussions with private firms in order to find ways to improve efficiency and innovation. It may bring firms together to exchange information, so as to co-ordinate their decisions and create a climate of greater certainty. It may bring firms and unions together to try to create greater industrial harmony.

Information. The government may provide various information services to firms: technical assistance, the results of public research, information on markets, etc.

In addition to adopting supply-side measures that focus on the economy as a whole, governments might decide to target specific regions of the economy, or specific industries for policy initiatives. Such initiatives are often more interventionist in nature, as the next section shows.

31.4 REGIONAL POLICY

Within most countries, unemployment is not evenly distributed. Take the case of the UK. Northern Ireland and parts of the north and west of England, parts of Wales and parts of Scotland have unemployment rates substantially higher than in the south-east of England.

Similarly, countries experience regional disparities in average incomes, rates of growth and levels of prices, as well as in health, crime, housing, etc. In the UK, these disparities grew wider in the mid-1980s as the recession hit the north, with its traditional heavy industries, much harder than the south. In the recession of the early 1990s, however, it was the service sector that was hardest hit, a sector more concentrated in the south. Regional disparities therefore

narrowed somewhat. Disparities are not only experienced at regional level. They are often more acutely felt in specific *areas*, especially inner cities and urban localities subject to industrial decline.

Within the European Union differences exist not only within individual countries, but also between them. For example, in the EU some countries are much less prosperous than others. Thus, especially with the opening up of the EU in 1993 to the free movement of factors of production, capital and labour may flow to the more prosperous regions of the Union, such as Germany, France and the Benelux countries, and away from the less prosperous regions, such as Portugal, Greece and southern Italy. With the enlargement of the EU since 2004 to include 13 new members, mainly from central and eastern Europe, regional disparities within the EU have widened further.

Causes of regional imbalance and the role of regional policy

KI 10
p52
If the market functioned perfectly, there would be no regional problem. If wages were lower and unemployment were higher in the north, people would simply move to the south. This would reduce unemployment in the north and help to fill vacancies in the south. It would drive up wage rates in the north and reduce wage rates in the south.

The process would continue until regional disparities were eliminated.

KI 29
p336
The capital market would function similarly. New investment would be located in the areas offering the highest rate of return. If land and labour were cheaper in the north, capital would be attracted there. This too would help to eliminate regional disparities.

A similar argument applies between countries. Take the case of the EU. Labour should move from the poorer countries, such as those of eastern Europe, to the richer ones and capital should flow in the opposite direction until disparities are eliminated.

In practice, the market does not always behave as just described. There are three major problems.

KI 12
p68
Labour and capital immobility. Labour may be geographically immobile. The regional pattern of industrial location may change more rapidly than the labour market can adjust to it. Thus jobs may be lost in the depressed areas more rapidly than people can migrate.

Similarly, the existing capital stock is highly immobile. Buildings and most machinery cannot be moved to where the unemployed are! *New* capital is much more mobile. But there may be insufficient new investment, especially during a recession, to halt regional decline, even if some investors are attracted into the depressed areas by low wages and cheap land.

KI 43
p547
Regional multiplier effects. The continuing shift in demand may in part be due to **regional multiplier effects**. In the prosperous regions, the new industries and the new workers attracted there create additional demand. This creates additional output and jobs and hence more migration. There is a multiplied rise in income. In the depressed regions,

the decline in demand and loss of jobs causes a multiplied downward effect. Loss of jobs in manufacturing leads to less money spent in the local community; transport and other service industries lose custom. The whole region becomes more depressed.

Externalities. Labour migration imposes external costs on non-migrants. In the prosperous regions, the new arrivals compete for services with those already there. Services become overstretched; house prices rise; council house waiting lists lengthen; roads become more congested, etc. In the depressed regions, services decline, or alternatively local taxes must rise for those who remain if local services are to be protected. Dereliction, depression and unemployment cause emotional stress for those who remain.

Approaches to regional policy

Market-orientated solutions

Supporters of market-based solutions argue that firms are the best judges of where they should locate. Government intervention would impede efficient decision taking by firms. It is better, they argue, to remove impediments to the market achieving regional and local balance. For example, they favour either or both of the following.

Locally negotiated wage agreements. A problem with nationally negotiated wage rates is that that wages are not driven down in the less prosperous areas and up in the more prosperous ones. This discourages firms from locating in the less prosperous areas. At the same time, firms find it difficult to recruit labour in the more prosperous ones, where wages are not high enough to compensate for the higher cost of living there.

Reducing unemployment benefits. A general reduction in unemployment benefits and other welfare payments would encourage the unemployed in the areas of high unemployment to migrate to the more prosperous areas, or enable firms to offer lower wages in the areas of high unemployment.

The problem with these policies is that they attempt initially to widen the economic divide between workers in the different areas in order to encourage capital and labour to move. Such policies would hardly be welcomed by workers in the poorer areas!

Definition

Regional multiplier effects When a change in injections into or withdrawals from a particular region causes a multiplied change in income in that region. The regional multiplier is given by $1/(1 - mpc_r)$, where mpc_r is the marginal propensity to consume products from the region.

Pause for thought

1. *Think of some other 'pro-market' solutions to the regional problem.*
2. *Do people in the more prosperous areas benefit from pro-market solutions?*

Interventionist solutions

 Interventionist policies involve encouraging firms to move. Such policies include the following.

 Subsidies and tax concessions in the depressed regions. Businesses could be given general subsidies, such as grants to move, or reduced rates of corporation tax. Alternatively, grants or subsidies could be specifically targeted at increasing employment (e.g. reduced employer's national insurance contributions) or at encouraging investment (e.g. investment grants or other measures to reduce the costs of capital).

The provision of facilities in depressed regions. The government or local authorities could provide facilities such as land and buildings at concessionary, or even zero, rents to incoming firms; or spend money on improving the infrastructure of the area (roads and communications, technical colleges, etc.).

The siting of government offices in the depressed regions. The government could move some of its own departments out of the capital and locate them in areas of high unemployment. The siting of the vehicle licensing centre in Swansea is an example.

 It is important to distinguish policies that merely seek to *modify* the market by altering market signals from policies that *replace* the market. *Regulation* replaces the market, and unless very carefully devised and monitored may lead to ill-thought-out decisions being made. *Subsidies* and *taxes* merely modify the market, leaving it to individual firms to make their final location decisions.

Regional policy in England

The focus of the recent approach in England to regional policy has been the development of 'Enterprise Zones'. The approach may be thought of as encompassing both market-based and interventionist ideas. The Coalition government established 21 Enterprise Zones across England in 2012. This number had grown to 24 by 2015. These zones are specific geographic locations where firms can benefit from reduced planning restrictions, tax breaks and improved infrastructure, including access to superfast broadband. Many of the Enterprise Zones encourage clustering: businesses in the same sector grouping together. The hope is that they can mutually benefit from external economies of scale (see page 634) such as co-operation and/or the sorts of technological spillovers that we came across in section 31.1 (see page 606).

To benefit from clustering effects, the zones typically focus on specific sectors, such as automotive and transport (e.g. the MIRA technology park near Hinckley, Leicestershire) or renewable energy (e.g. the Humber Enterprise Zone). The danger of such policies, particularly given the often small geographic area in question, is that they may merely divert investment away from other areas rather than resulting in *additional* investment.

Pause for thought

If you were the government, how would you set about deciding the rate of subsidy to pay a firm thinking of moving to a less prosperous area?

BOX 31.4 EU REGIONAL POLICY

The 2014–20 spending programme

An interesting case study of the use of regional policy is the European Union. The EU has allocated around one-third of its total budget to regional policy for the period 2014–20. This equates to spending of close to €352 billion.

The EU's regional policy should be seen in the context of economic and social disparities and 'Europe 2020' – the EU's growth strategy. The EU estimated prior to the 2007–13 programme that about one-third of EU citizens had a GDP per head below the 'convergence level' of 75 per cent of the EU average. These disparities have grown with the accession of 13 new members since 2004. Meanwhile, the EU's growth strategy emphasises the need to deliver high levels of employment, productivity and social cohesion.

As with the 2007–13 programme, the 2014–20 programme continues to focus primarily on the poorest member states and regions of the EU: i.e. those below the convergence level of GDP per head. The amount available for the less developed regions is €182 billion (52 per cent the €352 billion budget).

In order to allocate its resources and meet its objectives, the EU operates a series of interrelated funds, collectively known as the Structural and Cohesion Funds.

Cohesion Fund (CF). This is aimed at member states whose national income per head is less than 90 per cent of the EU average. Its aim is to support the development of infrastructure projects, particularly trans-European transport networks, and enhance measures that help protect and improve the quality of the environment. For the 2014–20 period, a total of €63.4 billion has been allocated to CF spending.

The European Regional Development Fund (ERDF). This fund allocates grants for projects designed to aid development in poorer regions of the EU and thereby correct for 'imbalances' and enhance economic, social and territorial cohesion. It

▶

focuses investment under the themes of innovation and research, the digital agenda, support for small and medium-sized enterprises (SMEs) and the low-carbon economy.

The European Social Fund (ESF). The fund is designed to improve education and employment opportunities and to help those people most at risk of poverty. Spending is focused on the themes of promoting employment and supporting labour mobility, promoting social inclusion and combating poverty, investing in education, skills and lifelong

learning and enhancing institutional capacity and efficient public administration. Over €80 billion has been allocated for the 2014–20 period to improve human capital across the EU (see Box 31.2 for more on human capital).

 To what extent is the EU's regional policy consistent with those theories of long-term growth theory stressing the importance of innovation and technological progress?

SUMMARY

1a Supply-side policies, if successful, will shift the aggregate supply curve to the right. Supply-side policies look to influence the quantity and productivity of factors of production.

1b The UK has had a lower rate of investment than most other industrialised countries. This has contributed to a historically low rate of economic growth and a growing trade deficit in manufactures.

1c Supply-side policies often have demand-side effects, and demand-side policies often have supply-side effects. It is important for governments to take these secondary effects into account when working out their economic strategy.

2a Market-orientated supply-side policies aim to increase the rate of growth of aggregate supply and reduce the rate of unemployment by encouraging private enterprise and the freer play of market forces.

2b Reducing government expenditure as a proportion of GDP is a major element of such policies.

2c Tax cuts can be used to encourage people to work more and more efficiently, and to encourage investment. The effects of tax cuts will depend on how people respond to incentives. The substitution effect will result in greater output; the income effect in lower output.

2d Reducing the power of trade unions and a reduction in welfare benefits, especially those related to unemploy-

ment, may force workers to accept jobs at lower wages, thereby decreasing equilibrium unemployment.

2e Various policies can be introduced to increase competition. These include privatisation, deregulation, introducing market relationships into the public sector, the Private Finance Initiative, and freer international trade and capital movements.

3 Interventionist supply-side policy can take the form of grants for investment and research and development, advice and persuasion, the direct provision of infrastructure and the provision, funding or encouragement of various training schemes.

4a Regional and local disparities arise from a changing pattern of industrial production. With many of the older industries concentrated in certain parts of the country and especially in the inner cities, and with an acceleration in the rate of industrial change, so the gap between rich and poor areas has widened.

4b Regional disparities can in theory be corrected by the market, with capital being attracted to areas of low wages and workers being attracted to areas of high wages. In practice, regional disparities persist because of capital and labour immobility and regional multiplier effects.

MyEconLab

This book can be supported by MyEconLab, which contains a range of additional resources, including an online homework and tutorial system designed to test and build your understanding.

You need both an access card and a course ID to access MyEconLab:

1. Is your lecturer using MyEconLab? Ask your lecturer for your course ID.

2. Has an access card been included with the book at a reduced cost? Check the inside back cover of the book.

3. If you have a course ID but no access card, go to: http://www.myeconlab.com/ to buy access to this interactive study programme.

REVIEW QUESTIONS

1 Define demand-side and supply-side policies. Are there any ways in which such policies are incompatible?

2 Outline the main supply-side policies that have been introduced in the UK since 1979. Does the evidence suggest that they have achieved what they set out to do?

3 What types of tax cuts are likely to create the greatest (a) incentives, (b) disincentives to effort?

4 Compare the relative merits of pro-market and interventionist solutions to regional imbalances.

5 Is the decline of older industries necessarily undesirable?

6 In what ways can interventionist supply-side policy work with the market, rather than against it? What are the arguments for and against such policy?

International economic policy

Business issues covered in this chapter

- How does the level of business activity in one country impact on that in other countries?
- How do the major economies of the world seek to co-ordinate their policies and what difficulties arise in the process?
- How did the euro evolve and how effective was the system of exchange rates in Europe that preceded the birth of the euro?
- What are the advantages and disadvantages of the euro for members of the eurozone and for businesses both inside and outside the eurozone?
- How can greater currency stability be achieved, thereby creating a more certain global environment for business?

32.1 GLOBAL INTERDEPENDENCE

We live in an interdependent world. Countries are affected by the economic health of other countries and by their governments' policies. Problems in one part of the world can spread like a contagion to other parts, with perhaps no country immune. This was clearly illustrated by the credit crunch of 2007–8. A crisis that started in the sub-prime market in the USA soon snowballed into a worldwide recession.

There are two major ways in which this process of 'globalisation' affects individual economies. The first is through trade. The second is through financial markets.

Interdependence through trade

So long as nations trade with one another, the domestic economic actions of one nation will have implications for those that trade with it. For example, if the US administration feels that the US economy is growing too fast, it might adopt various contractionary fiscal and monetary measures, such as higher tax rates or interest rates.

US consumers will not only consume fewer domestically produced goods, but also reduce their consumption of imported products. But US imports are other countries' exports. A fall in these other countries' exports will lead to a multiplier effect in these countries. Output and employment will fall.

Changes in aggregate demand in one country thus send ripples throughout the global economy. The process whereby changes in imports into (or exports from) one country affect national income in other countries is known as the *international trade multiplier*.

The more open an economy, the more vulnerable it will be to changes in the level of economic activity in the rest

KI 43
p 547

> **Definition**
>
> **International trade multiplier** The effect on national income in country B of a change in exports (or imports) of country A.

of the world. This problem will be particularly acute if a nation is heavily dependent on trade with one other nation (e.g. Canada on the USA) or one other region (e.g. Switzerland on the EU).

In Chapter 24, we saw how international trade has been growing as a proportion of countries' national income for many years. Over the period from 1950 to 2015, while world output grew by close to 3.5 per cent

---

per annum, the volume of exports grew by nearly 6 per cent. With most nations committed to freer trade, and with the World Trade Organization (see section 24.4) overseeing the dismantling of trade barriers, so international trade is likely to continue growing as a proportion of world GDP.

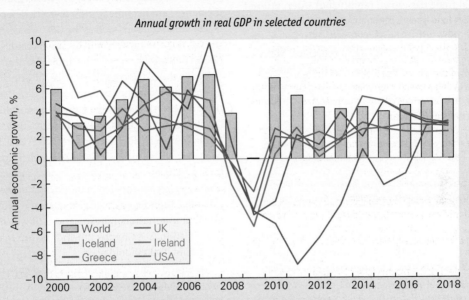

Annual growth in real GDP in selected countries

Note: (i) Figures from 2014 are based on forecasts; (ii) World growth rate based on market exchange rates.
Source: Based on data in *World Economic Outlook, October 2015* (International Monetary Fund)

It also works with developing nations to alleviate poverty and to achieve economic stability. To do this it provides countries with loans.

The IMF has not been without controversy, however. Conditions attached to loans have often been very harsh, especially for some of the most indebted developing countries.

The global economic and financial crisis provided the IMF with a challenge: which countries to support with a limited budget. Between 2007 and spring 2012, the IMF provided some $300 billion of loans to member countries. During this period an increasing amount of assistance was being given to developed economies, especially within the EU.

Following crisis talks with finance ministers in Europe in May 2010, the IMF agreed to set aside €250 billion to support eurozone countries in financial difficulty. This would be in addition to €440 billion supplied by eurozone countries under the 'European Financial Stability Facility' and €60 billion from EU funds under the 'European Financial Stabilisation Mechanism'.

In October 2010 the EU agreed to establish a more permanent funding mechanism for eurozone countries in financial difficulties, known as the European Stability Mechanism (see Box 30.2). The Mechanism became operational in 2013. The IMF is a crucial stakeholder in the funding mechanism, both in committing funds but also in assessing, alongside the European Commission and the European Central Banks, the financial position of any country requesting help. This assessment includes possible 'macroeconomic adjustment programmes' for countries in receipt of funds.

Strengthening the IMF

World leaders meeting as part of the G20 in London in April 2009 announced the need to strengthen global financial institutions. They agreed that the resources available to the IMF should be trebled to US$750 billion. They also agreed that the IMF would work with a new Financial Stability Board (FSB), made up, amongst others, of the G20 countries and the European Commission, so as to help in identifying potential economic and financial risks. Essentially, the G20 countries were looking for a better 'early warning system' to meet some of the challenges of an increasingly interdependent world.

However, the ongoing financial problems facing governments, particularly in the eurozone, led the international community in April 2012 to pledge a further increase of $430 billion in resources for the IMF. Further changes in members' subscriptions were due to be agreed at the end of 2015 as part of the IMF's fifteenth periodic review of the 'quota system'. This is the system which helps determine members' subscriptions, their voting power and their access to financing. The intention was to create a credible 'firewall' to contain future financial crisis.

 Do you see any problems arising from a strengthening of global economic and financial institutions?

The growth in the relative importance of trade increases countries' interdependence and their vulnerability to world trade fluctuations, such as the global recession of the late 2000s. World output fell by 2 per cent in 2009 (at market exchange rates), while worldwide exports fell by 12 per cent. This was the biggest contraction in global trade since the Second World War.

Financial interdependence

International trade has grown rapidly, but international financial flows have grown much more rapidly. It was estimated that during 2013 around $5.3 trillion of assets were being traded daily across the foreign exchanges. Many of the transactions are short-term financial flows, moving to where interest rates are most favourable or to currencies where the exchange rate is likely to appreciate. This again makes countries interdependent.

> ### Pause for thought
>
> *Are exports likely to continue growing faster than GDP indefinitely? What will determine the outcome?*

Financial interdependency impacts not only on financial institutions around the world, but also on national economies. It also illustrates how global responses can be needed. As a result of the credit crunch, world leaders were seriously worried that the whole world would plunge into deep recession. A co-ordinated policy response from governments and central banks began in earnest in October 2008 when governments in Britain, Europe, North America and other parts of the world injected some $2 trillion of extra capital into banks.

Global policy response

As a consequence of both trade and financial interdependence, the world economy, like the economy of any individual country, tends to experience periodic fluctuations in economic activity – an *international* business cycle. The implication of this is that countries will tend to share common problems and concerns at the same time.

This can aid the process of international co-operation between countries.

Countries frequently meet in various groupings – from the narrow group of the world's seven richest countries (the G7) to broader groups such as the G20, which, in addition to the G7 and other rich countries, also includes larger developing countries, such as China, India, Brazil and Indonesia.

Today the G20 is considered to be the principal economic forum. This recognises two important developments. First, there has been a remarkable growth in emerging economies like Brazil, India, China and South Africa which, along with Russia, are often collectively referred to as BRICS (see section 24.1). Second, the increasing scale of interdependency through trade and finance typically requires a co-ordinated response from a larger representation of the international community.

Global interdependence also raises questions about the role that international organisations like the World Trade Organization (see Chapter 24) and the International Monetary Fund (IMF) should play.

The IMF's remit is to promote global growth and stability, to help countries through economic difficulty and to help developing economies achieve macroeconomic stability and reduce poverty. In response to the global economic and financial crisis of the late 2000s, the IMF's budget was substantially increased and it became more actively involved with what were previously defined as 'strong performing economies' (see Box 32.1).

32.2 INTERNATIONAL HARMONISATION OF ECONOMIC POLICIES

What is of crucial importance is to avoid major exchange rate movements between currencies. The five main underlying causes of exchange rate movements are divergences in *interest rates*, *growth rates*, *inflation rates*, *current account balance of payments* and *government deficits*. Such movements, which are often amplified by speculation, can play havoc with the profits of importers and exporters.

Table 32.1 shows the variation in the levels of these indicators across a sample of eight countries. These divergences still remain considerable.

In trying to generate world economic growth without major currency fluctuations it is important that there is a *har-*

> ### Pause for thought
>
> *Referring to Table 32.1, in what respects was there greater convergence between the countries in the period 1995–99 than in the period 2010–14?*

monisation of economic policies between nations. In other words, it is important that all the major countries are pursuing consistent policies aiming at common international goals.

But how can policy harmonisation be achieved? As long as there are significant domestic differences between the major economies, there is likely to be conflict, not harmony. For example, if one country, say the USA, is worried about the size of its budget deficit, it may be unwilling to respond to world demands for a stimulus to aggregate demand to pull the world economy out of recession. What is more, speculators, seeing differences between countries, are likely to exaggerate them by their actions, causing large changes in exchange rates. The G7 countries have therefore sought to achieve greater *convergence* of their economies. But whilst convergence may be a goal of policy, in practice it has proved elusive.

Because of a lack of convergence, there are serious difficulties in achieving international policy harmonisation:

Table 32.1 International macroeconomic indicators

		Australia	Canada	China	France	Germany	Japan	UK	USA
Nominal exchange rate index (annual % change)	1995–9	0.4	−0.1	4.7	1.1	1.7	2.0	4.9	5.4
	2000–4	2.1	2.7	−0.6	1.3	1.7	0.9	1.0	−0.2
	2005–9	0.4	2.5	3.2	0.6	0.6	2.0	−4.6	−1.3
	2010–4	2.7	0.7	2.5	−0.5	−0.5	−2.7	1.6	−0.1
Short–term (3–month) nominal interest rate (%)	1995–9	6.1	5.0	7.7	4.1	3.5	0.6	6.5	5.5
	2000–4	5.2	3.5	2.5	3.3	3.3	0.1	4.7	2.9
	2005–9	5.7	3.1	2.7	3.1	3.1	0.5	4.4	3.5
	2010–4	3.7	1.1	4.4	0.6	0.6	0.3	0.7	0.2
Economic growth (% change in real GDP)	1995–9	4.1	3.6	9.1	2.6	1.6	0.8	2.9	4.0
	2000–4	3.3	2.9	9.2	2.1	1.0	1.4	3.1	2.7
	2005–9	2.9	1.3	11.4	0.7	0.7	−0.3	0.8	0.9
	2010–4	2.7	2.6	8.5	1.0	2.0	1.5	1.7	2.2
Consumer price inflation (% change in CPI)	1995–9	2.0	1.6	5.2	1.3	1.1	0.4	2.0	2.4
	2000–4	3.4	2.4	1.1	2.0	1.5	−0.5	1.2	2.5
	2005–9	2.9	1.8	2.7	1.7	1.8	0.0	2.5	2.6
	2010–4	2.6	1.8	3.2	1.6	1.6	0.4	2.9	2.0
Current account balance (% of GDP)	1995–9	−4.2	−0.6	3.0	2.0	−0.9	2.3	−0.9	−2.0
	2000–4	−4.3	1.9	2.3	1.1	1.1	2.9	−2.0	−4.3
	2005–9	−5.6	0.2	7.6	−0.8	5.8	3.7	−2.6	−4.8
	2010–4	−3.4	−2.9	2.5	−1.2	6.6	1.7	−3.6	−2.7
Unemployment rate (% of labour force)	1995–9	8.0	8.8	3.0	10.3	8.9	3.7	7.2	4.9
	2000–4	6.1	7.3	3.8	8.4	8.9	5.0	5.1	5.2
	2005–9	4.8	6.7	4.2	8.5	8.9	4.3	5.8	5.9
	2010–4	5.5	7.4	4.1	9.8	5.7	4.3	7.6	8.0
General government surplus (% of GDP)	1995–9	−0.2	−1.1	−1.1	−3.3	−3.8	−5.1	−2.2	−1.9
	2000–4	0.8	1.0	−2.5	−2.6	−2.6	−7.1	−1.5	−3.3
	2005–9	−0.1	0.0	−0.9	−3.7	−1.5	−5.0	−5.1	−5.9
	2010–4	−3.9	−3.3	−0.6	−5.0	−0.8	−8.8	−7.3	−8.2

Note: Chinese short-term interest rate 1995–1999 is the central bank discount rate

Sources: *OECD.Stat* (OECD), *Principal Economic Indicators* (IMF) and *AMECO* database (European Commission)

■ Countries' budget deficits and national debt differ substantially as a proportion of their national income. This puts very different pressures on the interest rates necessary to service these debts. In 2015, the ratio of the total stock of general government debt to annual GDP stood at 91 per cent in the UK, compared with 38 per cent for Australia, 69 per cent for Germany 87 per cent for Canada, 97 per cent for France and 246 per cent for Japan.

■ Harmonising rates of monetary growth or inflation targets would involve letting interest rates fluctuate with the demand for money. Without convergence in the demand for money, interest rate fluctuations could be severe.

■ Harmonising interest rates would involve abandoning money, inflation and exchange rate targets (unless interest rate 'harmonisation' meant adjusting interest rates so as to maintain money or inflation targets or a fixed exchange rate).

Definitions

International harmonisation of economic policies
Where countries attempt to co-ordinate their macroeconomic policies so as to achieve common goals.

Convergence of economies When countries achieve similar levels of growth, inflation, budget deficits as a percentage of GDP, balance of payments, etc.

■ Countries have different internal structural relationships. A lack of convergence here means that countries with higher endemic *cost* inflation would require higher interest rates and higher unemployment if international inflation rates were to be harmonised, or higher inflation if interest rates were to be harmonised.

■ Countries have different rates of productivity increase (see Box 31.3), product development, investment and market penetration. A lack of convergence here means that the growth in exports (relative to imports) will differ for any given level of inflation or growth.

■ Countries may be very unwilling to change their domestic policies to fall into line with other countries. They may prefer the other countries to fall into line with them!

If any one of the five – interest rates, growth rates, inflation rates, current account balance of payments or government deficits – could be harmonised across countries, it is likely that the other four would then not be harmonised.

Total convergence and thus total harmonisation may not be possible. Nevertheless, most governments favour some movement in that direction; some is better than none. To achieve this, co-operation is necessary.

Although co-operation is the ideal, in practice discord often tends to dominate international economic relations. The reason is that governments are normally concerned with the economic interests of other countries only if they coincide with those of their own country. This, however, can create a prisoners' dilemma problem (see section 12.3). With each country looking solely after its own interests, the world economy suffers and everyone is worse off.

32.3 EUROPEAN ECONOMIC AND MONETARY UNION

European economic and monetary union (EMU) involves the complete economic and financial integration of the EU countries. It is not just a common market, but a market with a single currency, a single central bank and a single monetary policy.

The ERM

The forerunner to EMU was the exchange rate mechanism (ERM). This came into existence in March 1979 and the majority of the EU countries were members. The UK, however, chose not to join. Spain joined in 1989, the UK joined in 1990 and Portugal in April 1992. Then in September 1992, the UK and Italy indefinitely suspended their membership of the ERM, but Italy rejoined in November 1996 as part of its bid to join the single European currency. Austria joined in 1995, Finland in 1996 and Greece in 1998. By the time the ERM was replaced by the single currency in 1999, only Sweden and the UK were outside the ERM.

Features of the ERM

Under the system, each currency was given a central exchange rate with each of the other ERM currencies in a grid. However, fluctuations were allowed from the central rate within specified bands. For most countries these bands were set at ±2.25 per cent. The central rates could be adjusted from time to time by agreement, thus making the ERM an *adjustable peg* system. All the currencies floated jointly with currencies outside the ERM.

> ### Definition
>
> **Adjustable peg** A system whereby exchange rates are fixed for a period of time, but may be devalued (or revalued) if a deficit (or surplus) becomes substantial.

If a currency approached the upper or lower limit against *any* other ERM currency, intervention would take place to maintain the currencies within the band. This would take the form of central banks in the ERM selling the strong currency and buying the weak one. It could also involve the weak currency countries raising interest rates and the strong currency countries lowering them.

The ERM in practice

In a system of pegged exchange rates, countries should harmonise their policies to avoid excessive currency misalignments and hence the need for large devaluations or revaluations. There should be a convergence of their economies: they should be at a similar point on the business cycle and have similar inflation rates and interest rates.

The ERM in the 1980s. In the early 1980s, however, French and Italian inflation rates were persistently higher than German rates. This meant that there had to be several realignments (devaluations and revaluations). After 1983 realignments became less frequent, and then from 1987 to 1992 they ceased altogether. This was due to a growing convergence of members' internal policies.

By the time the UK joined the ERM in 1990, it was generally seen by its existing members as being a great success. It had created a zone of currency stability in a world of highly unstable exchange rates, and had provided the necessary environment for the establishment of a truly common market by the end of 1992.

Crisis in the ERM. Shortly after the UK joined the ERM, strains began to show. The reunification of Germany involved considerable reconstruction in the eastern part of the country. Financing this reconstruction was causing a growing budget deficit. The Bundesbank (the German central bank) thus felt obliged to maintain high interest rates in order to keep inflation in check. At the same time, the UK was experiencing a massive current account deficit (partly the result of entering the ERM at what many commentators argued was too high an exchange rate). It was thus obliged to raise interest rates in order to protect the pound, despite the fact that the economy was sliding rapidly into recession. The French franc and Italian lira were also perceived to be overvalued, and there were the first signs of worries as to whether their exchange rates within the ERM could be retained.

At the same time, the US economy was moving into recession and, as a result, US interest rates were cut. This led to a large outflow of capital from the USA. With high German interest rates, much of this capital flowed to Germany. This pushed up the value of the German mark and with it the other ERM currencies.

In September 1992, things reached crisis point. First the lira was devalued. Then two days later, on 'Black Wednesday' (16 September), the UK and Italy were forced to suspend their membership of the ERM: the pound and the lira were floated. At the same time, the Spanish peseta was devalued by 5 per cent.

Turmoil returned in the summer of 1993. The French economy was moving into recession and there were calls for cuts in French interest rates. But this was only possible if Germany was prepared to cut its rates too, and it was not. Speculators began to sell francs and it became obvious that the existing franc/mark parity could not be maintained. In an attempt to rescue the ERM, the EU finance ministers agreed to adopt very wide ±15 per cent bands. The result was that the franc and the Danish krone depreciated against the mark.

> ### Pause for thought
>
> *Under what circumstances may a currency bloc like the ERM (a) help to prevent speculation; (b) aggravate the problem of speculation?*

A return of calm. The old ERM appeared to be at an end. The new ±15 per cent bands hardly seemed like a 'pegged' system at all. However, the ERM did not die. Within months, the members were again managing to keep fluctuations within a very narrow range (for most of the time, within ±2.25 per cent!). The scene was being set for the abandonment of separate currencies and the adoption of a single currency: the euro.

The Maastricht Treaty and the road to the single currency

Details of the path towards EMU were finalised in the Maastricht Treaty, which was signed in February 1992. The timetable for EMU involved adoption of a single currency by 1999 at the latest.

One of the first moves was to establish a European Monetary Institute (EMI) as a forerunner of the European Central Bank. Its role was to co-ordinate monetary policy and encourage greater co-operation between EU central banks. It also monitored the operation of the ERM and prepared the ground for the establishment of a European central bank in time for the launch of the single currency.

Before they could join the single currency, member states were obliged to achieve convergence of their economies. Each country had to meet five convergence criteria:

- Inflation: should be no more than 1.5 per cent above the average inflation rate of the three countries in the EU with the lowest inflation rates.
- Interest rates: the rate on long-term government bonds should be no more than 2 per cent above the average of the three countries with the lowest inflation rates.
- Budget deficit: should be no more than 3 per cent of GDP.
- General government debt: should be no more than 60 per cent of GDP.
- Exchange rates: the currency should have been within the normal ERM bands for at least two years with no realignments or excessive intervention.

Before the launch of the single currency, the Council of Ministers had to decide which countries had met the convergence criteria and would thus be eligible to form a *currency union* by fixing their currencies permanently to the euro. Their national currencies would effectively disappear.

At the same time, a European System of Central Banks (ESCB) would be created, consisting of a European Central Bank (ECB) and the central banks of the member states. The ECB would be independent, both from governments and from EU political institutions. It would operate the monetary policy on behalf of the countries which had adopted the single currency.

Birth of the euro

In March 1998, the European Commission ruled that 11 of the 15 member states were eligible to proceed to EMU in January 1999. The UK and Denmark were to exercise their opt-out, negotiated at Maastricht, and Sweden and Greece failed to meet one or more of the convergence criteria. (Greece joined the euro in 2001.)

All 11 countries unambiguously met the interest rate and inflation criteria, but doubts were expressed by many 'Eurosceptics' as to whether they all genuinely met the other three criteria.

The euro came into being on 1 January 1999, but euro banknotes and coins were not introduced until 1 January

> ### Definition
>
> **Currency union** A group of countries (or regions) using a common currency.

2002. In the meantime, national currencies continued to exist alongside the euro, but at irrevocably fixed rates. The old notes and coins were withdrawn a few weeks after the introduction of euro notes and coins.

In May 2004 ten new members joined the EU, in January 2007 another two and in July 2013 another one. Under the Maastricht Treaty, they should all make preparations for joining the euro by meeting the convergence criteria and being in a new version of the exchange rate mechanism with a wide exchange rate band.

Under ERM II, euro candidate countries must keep their exchange rates within ±15 per cent of a central rate against the euro. Estonia, Lithuania and Slovenia were the first to join ERM II in June 2004 with Latvia, Cyprus, Malta and Slovakia following in 2005. Slovenia adopted the euro in 2007, Malta and Cyprus in 2008, Slovakia in 2009, Estonia in 2011, Latvia in 2014 and Lithuania in 2015, making a total of 19 countries using the euro.

How desirable is EMU?

Advantages of the single currency

Elimination of the costs of converting currencies. With separate currencies in each of the EU countries, costs were incurred each time one currency was exchanged into another. The elimination of these costs, however, was probably the least important benefit from the single currency. The European Commission estimated that the effect was to increase the GDP of the countries concerned by an average of only 0.4 per cent. The gains to countries like the UK, which have well-developed financial markets, would be even smaller.

Increased competition and efficiency. Despite the advent of the single market, large price differences remained between member states. Not only has the single currency eliminated the need to convert one currency into another (a barrier to competition), but also it has brought more transparency in pricing, and has put greater downward pressure on prices in high-cost firms and countries.

KI 1
p 10

Elimination of exchange rate uncertainty (between the members). Removal of exchange rate uncertainty has helped to encourage trade between the eurozone countries. Perhaps more importantly, it has encouraged investment by firms that trade between these countries, given the greater certainty in calculating costs and revenues from such trade.

KI 8
p 42

In times of economic uncertainty, exchange rate volatility between currencies can be high, as the experience of sterling showed during the credit crunch of 2008. The associated uncertainty for the UK in its trade with eurozone countries would have been eliminated had it adopted the euro. Without the euro, countries throughout Europe could have suffered considerably during the banking turmoil from wildly diverging exchange rates and interest rates.

Increased inward investment. Investment from the rest of the world is attracted to a eurozone of over 300 million inhabitants, where there is no fear of internal currency movements. By contrast, the UK, by not joining, has found that inward investment has been diverted away to countries within the eurozone.

From 1990 to 1998, the UK's share of inward investment to EU countries (including from other EU countries) was 20.3 per cent (see Figure 32.1). From 1999 to 2003, it

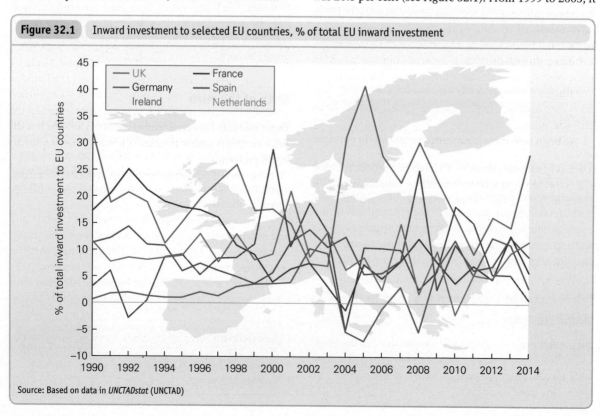

Figure 32.1 Inward investment to selected EU countries, % of total EU inward investment

Source: Based on data in *UNCTADstat* (UNCTAD)

was 13.2 per cent. From 2003 to 2005, as the UK economy grew more strongly than other major economies in the EU, its share increased to 35.3 per cent. This proved to be relatively short-lived, with the volatility of sterling acting as a deterrent to investment. By 2011, the UK's share of inward investment to EU countries had fallen to 10.4 per cent. The share then averaged 18.1 per cent across 2012 and 2013, boosted once more by stronger growth in the UK than in the eurozone.

With the new Conservative government in 2015 committed to a referendum on continuing UK membership of the EU, there were fears that the uncertainty this would cause would lead to a decline in inward investment. A vote to leave the EU, it is argued, would then lead to a further fall in inward investment. In other words, it is not just membership of the eurozone that is seen to be important in attracting inward investment, but also membership of the EU.

Lower inflation and interest rates. A single monetary policy forces convergence in inflation rates (just as inflation rates are very similar between the different regions within a country). With the ECB being independent from short-term political manipulation, this has resulted in a lower average inflation rate in the eurozone countries. This, in turn, has helped to convince markets that the euro will be strong relative to other currencies. The result is lower long-term rates of interest. This, in turn, further encourages investment in the eurozone countries, both by member states and by the rest of the world.

Opposition to EMU

European monetary union has, however, attracted considerable criticism. 'Eurosceptics' see within it a surrender of national political and economic sovereignty. Others, including those more sympathetic to monetary union in principle, raise concerns about the design of the monetary and financial systems within which monetary union operates – a design that, in principle, can be amended (see Boxes 30.2 and 30.5).

We begin with those arguments against EMU in principle.

The lack of national currencies. This can be a serious problem if an economy is at all out of harmony with the rest of the eurozone. For example, if countries such as Greece and Spain have lower productivity growth or higher endemic rates of inflation (due, say, to greater cost-push pressures), then how are they to make their goods competitive with the rest of the eurozone? With separate currencies these countries could allow their currencies to depreciate. With a single currency,

however, they could become depressed 'regions' of Europe, with rising unemployment and all the other regional problems of depressed regions *within* a country.

Proponents of EMU argue that it is better to tackle the problem of high inflation or low productivity in such countries by the discipline of competition from other eurozone countries, than merely to feed that inflation by keeping separate currencies and allowing periodic depreciations, with all the uncertainty that they bring.

What is more, the high-inflation countries tend to be the poorer ones with lower wage levels (albeit faster wage *increases*). With higher mobility of labour and capital as the single market develops, resources are likely to be attracted to such countries. This could help to narrow the gap between the richer and poorer member states.

The critics of EMU argue that labour is relatively immobile, given cultural and language barriers. Thus an unemployed worker in Cork or Kalamata could not easily move to a job in Turin or Helsinki. What the critics are arguing here is that the EU is not an ***optimal currency area*** (see Box 32.2).

Loss of separate monetary policies. The second problem identified is that the same central bank rate of interest must apply to all eurozone countries: the 'one size fits all' criticism. The trouble is that while some countries might require a lower rate of interest in order to ward off recession (such as Portugal, Ireland and Greece in 2010–11), others might require a higher one to prevent inflation. The greater the divergence between economies within the eurozone, the greater this problem becomes. It was hoped, however, that, with common fiscal rules and free trade, these divergences would diminish over time.

Asymmetric shocks. A third and related problem for members of a single currency occurs in adjusting to a shock when that shock affects members to different degrees. These are known as ***asymmetric shocks***. For example, the banking crisis affected the UK more severely than other countries, given that London is a global financial centre. The less the factor mobility between member countries and the less the price flexibility within member countries the more serious is this problem.

Even when shocks are uniformly felt in the member states, however, there is still the problem that policies adopted

---

Pause for thought

Is greater factor mobility likely to increase or decrease the problem of cumulative causation associated with regional multipliers? (See page 616)

Definitions

Optimal currency area The optimal size of a currency area is one that maximises the benefits from having a single currency relative to the costs. If the area were to be increased or decreased in size, the costs would rise relative to the benefits.

Asymmetric shocks Shocks (such as an oil price increase or a recession in another part of the world) that have different-sized effects on different industries, regions or countries.

BOX 32.2   OPTIMAL CURRENCY AREAS

When it pays to pay in the same currency

Imagine that each town and village used a different currency. Think how inconvenient it would be having to keep exchanging one currency into another, and how difficult it would be working out the relative value of items in different parts of the country.

Clearly there are benefits of using a common currency, not only within a country but also across different countries. The benefits include greater transparency in pricing, more open competition, greater certainty for investors and the avoidance of having to pay commission when you change one currency into another. There are also the benefits from having a single monetary policy if that is delivered in a more consistent and effective way than by individual countries.

So why not have a single currency for the whole world? The problem is that the bigger a single currency area gets, the more likely the conditions are to diverge in the different parts of the area. Some parts may have high unemployment and require expansionary policies. Others may have low unemployment and suffer from inflationary pressures. They may require contractionary policies.

What is more, different members of the currency area may experience quite different shocks to their economies, whether from outside the union (e.g. a fall in the price of one of their major exports) or from inside (e.g. a prolonged strike). These 'asymmetric shocks' would imply that different parts of the currency area should adopt different policies. But with a common monetary policy and hence common interest rates, and with no possibility of devaluation/revaluation of the currency of individual members, the scope for separate economic policies is reduced.

The costs of asymmetric shocks (and hence the costs of a single currency area) will be greater, the less the mobility of labour and capital, the less the flexibility of prices and wage rates, and the fewer the alternative policies there are that can be turned to (such as fiscal and regional policies).

So is the eurozone an optimal currency area? Certainly strong doubts have been raised by many economists.

- Labour is relatively immobile.
- There are structural differences between the member states.
- The transmission effects of interest rate changes are different between the member countries, given that countries have different proportions of consumer debt relative to GDP and different proportions of debt at variable interest rates.
- Exports to countries outside the eurozone account for different proportions of the members' GDP and thus their economies are affected differently by a change in the rate of exchange of the euro against other currencies.
- Wage rates are relatively inflexible.
- Under the Stability and Growth Pact and the Fiscal Compact (see Box 30.2), the scope for using discretionary fiscal policy is curtailed, except in times of severe economic difficulty (as in 2009).

This does not necessarily mean, however, that the costs of having a single European currency outweigh the benefits. Also, the problems outlined above should decline over time as the single market develops. Finally, the problem of asymmetric shocks can be exaggerated. European economies are highly diversified; there are often more differences within economies than between them. Thus shocks are more likely to affect different industries or localities, rather than whole countries. Changing the exchange rate, if that were still possible, would hardly be an appropriate policy in these circumstances.

The blog post on the Sloman Economics News site, *Are Scotland and the rest of the UK an optimal currency area?*, considers the issue of optimal currency areas in the context of whether an independent Scotland should continue using the pound.

 Why is a single currency area likely to move towards becoming an optimal currency area over time?

---

centrally will have different impacts on each country. This is because the transmission mechanisms of economic policy (i.e. the way in which policy changes impact of economic variables like growth and inflation) vary across countries.

There are others who are critical of the design of EMU, but who argue that with appropriate changes the problems could be significantly reduced.

Monetary policy. In the case of monetary policy, it is argued that the ECB was not as proactive in tackling the recession that followed the aftermath of the financial crisis. Large-scale programmes of quantitative easing were adopted by the US Federal Reserve and the Bank of England (see Box 30.4).

The ECB, by contrast, was seen as more cautious. Between December 2011 and March 2012 the ECB provided liquidity to the banking system by undertaking large-scale,

long-term repo operations. As a result, over €1 trillion of long-term (three-year) repo loans were provided. Meanwhile, between May 2010 and June 2012 it purchased €214 billion of assets, largely government bonds, under the Securities Market Programme (see Box 30.5). However, the effects on the money supply were sterilised by ECB sales of other assets. In other words, monetary operations were undertaken to offset the injected liquidity.

With the eurozone economy remaining weak, with low growth and increasing fears of a deflationary spiral, it was becoming clear that a more aggressive monetary policy was needed. Gradually, announcements of further monetary easing were made, which saw reductions to the ECB's main interest rates and even the adoption of a negative deposit rate for overnight deposits by financial institutions. Yet by the start of 2015 the annual rate of consumer price inflation had fallen to –0.6 per cent.

Then in late January a large-scale programme of quantitative easing was announced, to begin in March 2015, which would see asset purchases of €60 billion per month until at least September 2016, by which time the total would be €1.1 trillion (see the blog post on the Sloman Economics News site, The ECB takes the plunge – at last). The assets were to be mainly government bonds issued by countries not currently in bail-out programmes.

Critics point to the underlying weakness of a single currency operating alongside separate *national* government debt issues. The greater the divergence of the eurozone countries, in terms of growth, inflation, deficits, debt and the proportions of debt securities maturing in the short term, the greater this problem becomes.

Fiscal policy. Under the Stability and Growth Pact (SGP), countries were supposed to keep public-sector deficits below 3 per cent of GDP and their stocks of debt below 60 per cent of GDP (see Box 30.2). However, the Pact was not rigidly enforced. Furthermore, because the rules allowed for discretion in times of recession, deficits and debt rose sharply in the late 2000s (see Table 30.1 on page 581).

Subsequently, efforts have been made to change the framework within which national governments make their fiscal choices. The result is the Fiscal Compact, signed in March 2012 (see Box 30.2). This reaffirmed the SGP's excessive deficit rules, but added other requirements. For example, eurozone countries would now be required to ensure that their *structural deficits* (i.e. budget deficits that would exist even if economies were operating at their potential output level) did not exceed 0.5 per cent of GDP. Furthermore, tougher penalties would be imposed on countries breaking the rules.

There are those who argue that for eurozone members to benefit fully from monetary union tighter fiscal rules alone are insufficient. Instead, they advocate greater fiscal harmonisation. In other words, the problem, they say, is one of incomplete integration. This would probably require greater fiscal transfers to weaker eurozone countries, such as Greece and Portugal – something that stronger countries, such as Germany and The Netherlands have resisted.

Future of the euro

When Lithuania adopted the euro on 1 January 2015 it became the nineteenth country to do so. Yet debates around the future of the euro intensified during 2015 as the Greek debt crisis raised the prospect of Greece's exit from the euro (Grexit).

The Greek crisis
The perilous state of Greece's public finances had already seen two international bailouts agreed. These involved the IMF, the European Commission and the ECB – the so-called 'Troika' – and were worth €240 billion. However, these loans were contingent on the Greek government undertaking a series of economic measures, including significant fiscal tightening. However, the fiscal austerity measures contributed to a deterioration of the macroeconomic environment (see Box 13.1). Matters came to a head at the end of 2014 when the final tranches of the Greek bailout programme were suspended by the Troika. This followed the formation in December 2014 of a Syriza-led Greek government who had fought the election on an anti-austerity platform.

What followed was a drawn-out set of negotiations between Greece and its international creditors. With no agreement on further aid to Greece yet reached, Greece was unable to meet a €1.55 billion repayment to the IMF on 30 June 2015. This made Greece the first developed country to have defaulted on a loan from the IMF.

Meanwhile conditions for Greek citizens continued to deteriorate. In July the ECB announced that it would maintain its emergency liquidity assurance for the Greek financial system at levels agreed at the end of June. Without further credit for an already financially-distressed banking system, capital controls were imposed with strict limits on withdrawals from bank accounts.

In August 2015 the Greek government and its international creditors reached an agreement on the terms of a third bailout worth €85 billion over three years. Despite winning a referendum to resist the austerity measures demanded by the Troika, the Syriza government felt forced to adopt a large proportion of such measures in order to secure the bailout. For the time being at least, Grexit had been avoided. Nonetheless, fundamental questions remained about the future of the euro and the conditions under which it would be beneficial for other EU member states to join or for existing members to exit.

The single currency and gains from trade
The benefits from a country being a member of a single currency are greater the more it leads to trade creation with other members of the single currency. Table 32.2 shows for a sample of member states of the European Union the proportion of their exports and imports to and from other member states. From the table we can see that about two-thirds of trade in the European Union is between member states. However, there are considerable differences in the importance of intra-EU trade for member states.

On the basis of intra-industry trade, it might be argued that countries like Greece and Malta (and the UK should it have chosen to join) have least to gain from being part of a single currency with other EU nations. But, we need to consider other factors too. The theory of optimal currency areas (see Box 14.5) suggests, for example, that the degree of convergence between economies and the flexibility of labour markets are important considerations for countries considering the costs of relinquishing their national currency.

Table 32.2	Intra-European Union exports and imports, % of total exports or imports			
	Exports		**Imports**	
	2002–8	2009–15	2002–8	2009–15
Belgium	76.6	71.8	71.9	67.4
France	65.3	60.5	69.0	67.9
Germany	64.4	58.9	64.9	64.4
Greece	64.9	50.3	59.8	50.3
Ireland	63.6	58.5	67.3	68.9
Italy	61.8	55.8	60.1	56.0
Lithuania	64.9	59.2	60.7	60.0
Malta	47.8	43.2	72.4	70.2
Portugal	79.0	72.6	77.5	74.4
Spain	72.7	65.7	65.0	57.4
UK	58.9	49.6	55.3	50.2
Eurozone (19 countries)	68.8	64.2	65.3	62.4
EU-28	68.4	64.0	64.9	62.2

Source: *AMECO database* (European Commission, DGECFIN).

Convergence or divergence?

The more similar economies are, the more likely it is that they will face similar or symmetric shocks which can be accommodated by a common monetary policy. Furthermore, greater wage flexibility and mobility of labour provide mechanisms for countries within a single currency to remain internationally competitive.

Table 32.3 shows a series of macroeconomic indicators for a sample of countries within the eurozone. From it we can see that there remain considerable differences in the macroeconomic performance of these countries. These were exacerbated by the financial crisis of the late 2000s and the subsequent deterioration of the macroeconomic environment.

Among the differences captured by Table 32.3 are the contrasting trade positions of eurozone economies. In the period 2002–8 Greece and Spain ran large current account deficits averaging 12 and 7 per cent of GDP respectively. In contrast, Germany ran a current account surplus of around 4.5 per cent of its GDP.

In the absence of nominal exchange rate adjustments, countries like Greece and Spain looking to a fall in the *real* exchange rate to boost competitiveness need to have relatively lower rates of price inflation (see Box 14.1). Therefore, in a single currency productivity growth and wage inflation take on even greater importance in determining a country's competitiveness.

In Table 32.3 labour productivity is captured by the growth in output per hour worked. Again significant variations exist. Where labour productivity growth is lower, it needs lower nominal wage growth to help prevent countries losing their competitiveness. Even in countries where labour productivity is higher, as is often observed in countries with lower levels of income, their competitive position will deteriorate if wage growth exceeds productivity growth. In this scenario unit labour costs (labour costs per unit of output) will increase. In the period from 2002 to 2008, Table 32.3 shows unit labour costs increasing at between 3 and 4 per cent per annum in Greece, Spain and Italy compared with close to zero in Germany. This, other things being equal, puts these countries at a growing competitive disadvantage.

The fiscal framework

The discussion so far highlights the importance of economic convergence in affecting the benefits and costs of being a member of the euro. Fiscal policy can provide some

Table 32.3	Macroeconomic indicators for eurozone, 2002–15											
	2002–8						**2009–15**					
	Euro area	France	Germany	Greece	Italy	Spain	Euro area	France	Germany	Greece	Italy	Spain
Economic growth, % p.a.	1.8	1.6	1.3	3.5	0.8	3.1	0.0	0.5	0.9	−4.0	−1.1	−0.5
Output gap, % of potential output	0.9	1.9	−0.3	1.5	1.0	2.5	−2.4	−1.6	−1.1	−7.6	−3.3	−5.6
Unemployment rate, %	8.5	8.4	9.4	9.4	7.5	10.2	10.9	9.8	5.8	20.6	10.3	22.4
Current account, % of GDP	0.3	−0.1	4.5	−12.0	−1.2	−7.0	1.7	−1.8	6.8	−6.5	−0.5	−1.2
Growth in output per hour worked, % p.a.	0.9	1.2	1.2	1.8	−0.1	0.5	0.8	0.6	0.5	−0.7	0.0	1.9
Growth in unit labour costs, % p.a.	2.0	2.0	0.1	4.0	3.1	3.8	1.3	1.3	2.2	−0.6	1.5	−0.7
Economy-wide inflation rate, %	2.1	2.1	1.0	3.3	2.5	3.6	1.0	0.9	1.5	−0.3	1.1	0.2

Notes: 1) Unit labour costs are the ratio of compensation per employee to real GDP per person employed; 2) The economy-wide inflation rate is the annual rate of change of the GDP deflator; 3) Output per hour worked – data up to 2014 and euro area average excludes Lithuania.
Sources: Output per hour worked based on data from *OECD.Stat* (OECD); other figures based on data from *AMECO database*, (European Commission, DGECFIN)

| Table 32.4 | Public-sector debt relative to GDP and some of its determinants in selected eurozone economies |

	Public sector debt-to-GDP, %		2010–14 averages		
	2010	2014	Primary surplus-to-GDP, %	Real short-term interest rates, %	Economic growth, % p.a.
Eurozone	83.9	94.2	−1.0	−0.4	0.8
Belgium	99.5	106.5	−0.4	−1.1	1.1
France	81.7	95.0	−2.5	−0.4	1.0
Germany	80.5	74.7	1.4	−0.8	1.9
Greece	146.0	177.1	−4.0	1.3	−3.9
Ireland	87.4	109.7	−8.9	0.1	1.8
Italy	115.3	132.1	1.4	−0.4	−0.3
Lithuania	36.2	40.9	−2.7	−1.4	3.4
Malta	67.6	68.0	0.2	−1.7	3.0
Portugal	96.2	130.2	−2.3	0.0	−0.5
Spain	60.1	97.7	−5.6	0.5	0.0

Source: *AMECO database* (European Commission, DGECFIN).

buffer against asymmetric shocks by enabling transfers of income to those areas experiencing lower rates of economic growth. Therefore, the fiscal framework within which the euro operates is important when considering the future of the euro.

To date, the eurozone has resisted a centralisation of national budgets. In a more centralised (or federal) system we would see automatic income transfers between different regions and countries. A country, say Greece, affected by a negative economic shock would pay less tax revenues and receive more expenditures from a central eurozone budget, while in a country, say Germany, experiencing a positive shock the opposite would be the case.

Since national budgets in the eurozone remain largely decentralised, fiscal transfers are principally determined by national fiscal frameworks. But the ability of these to offset the effects of negative economic shocks is constrained by the sustainability of national budgets. This is important because it places limits on the ability of national governments to use fiscal policy to negate the effects of negative economic shocks.

When analysing the sustainability of national budgets economists look at the balance needed between spending and revenues necessary to prevent the ratio of the stock of public-sector debt to annual GDP from rising. The key here is the flow of receipts compared to those expenditures other than the interest payments on servicing the existing public-sector debt. If receipts are greater than expenditures excluding interest payments then a ***primary surplus*** occurs. A primary surplus is needed to maintain the debt-to-GDP ratio if the effective real rate of interest payable on public-sector debt (the nominal interest rate *less* the inflation rate) is greater than the economy's economic growth

rate. Furthermore, the required size of the primary surplus-to-GDP ratio rises the lower the rate of economic growth relative to the real interest rate and the larger the existing debt-to-GDP ratio.[1]

Table 32.4 shows the public-sector debt-to-GDP ratios in a sample of eurozone economies in 2010 and 2014 alongside the factors that affect the path of the ratio. The table illustrates considerable differences between countries in the state of their public finances. Therefore, in a decentralised fiscal environment, countries with an already high debt-to-GDP ratio, such as Greece, Italy and Portugal, will find it considerably more difficult to use fiscal policy to mitigate the impact of future adverse economic shocks. Consequently, the sustainability of the current decentralised approach to fiscal policy in the eurozone is likely to be crucial in determining the future for the euro and those countries using the euro.

Definition

Primary surplus The situation when the sum of public-sector expenditures excluding interest payments on public-sector debt is less than public-sector receipts.

---

[1] As a rule-of-thumb, the primary surplus-to-GDP ratio required to maintain a given public-sector debt to GDP ratio can be calculated by multiplying the existing debt-to-GDP ratio by the sum of the real rate of interest minus the rate of economic growth.

32.4 ALTERNATIVE POLICIES FOR ACHIEVING CURRENCY STABILITY

One important lesson of recent years is that concerted speculation has become virtually unstoppable. This was made clear by the expulsion of the UK and Italy from the ERM in 1992, the dramatic fall of the Mexican peso and rise of the yen in 1995, the collapse of various south-east Asian currencies and the Russian rouble in 1997–98, the collapse of the Argentine peso in 2002, the fall in the pound in 2008 and the fall in the euro in 2010 and 2014–15. In comparison with the vast amounts of short-term finance flowing across the foreign exchanges each day, the reserves of central banks seem trivial.

If there is a consensus in the markets that a currency will depreciate, there is little that central banks can do. For example, if there were a 50 per cent chance of a 10 per cent depreciation in the next week, then selling that currency now would yield an 'expected' return of just over 5 per cent for the week (i.e. 50 per cent of 10 per cent): equivalent to 1200 per cent at an annual rate!

For this reason, many commentators have argued that there are only two types of exchange rate system that can work over the long term. The first is a completely free-floating exchange rate, with no attempt by the central bank to support the exchange rate. With no intervention, there is no problem of a shortage of reserves!

The second is to share a common currency with other countries: to join a common currency area, such as the eurozone, and let the common currency float freely. The country would give up independence in its monetary policy, but at least there would be no problem of exchange rate instability within the currency area. A similar alternative is to adopt a major currency of another country, such as the US dollar or the euro. Many smaller states have done this. For example, Kosovo and Montenegro have adopted the euro and Ecuador has adopted the US dollar.

An attempt by a country to peg its exchange rate is likely to have one of two unfortunate consequences. Either it will end in failure as the country succumbs to a speculative attack, or the country's monetary policy will have to be totally dedicated to maintaining the exchange rate.

So is there any way of 'beating the speculators' and pursuing a policy of greater exchange rate rigidity without establishing a single currency? Or must countries be forced to accept freely floating exchange rates, with all the uncertainty for traders that such a regime brings?

We shall examine two possible solutions. The first is to reduce international financial mobility, by putting various types of restriction on foreign exchange transactions. The second is to move to a new type of exchange rate regime which offers the benefits of a degree of rigidity without being susceptible to massive speculative attacks.

Controlling exchange transactions

Until the early 1990s, many countries retained restrictions of various kinds on financial flows. Such restrictions made it more expensive for speculators to gamble on possible exchange rate movements. It is not the case, as some commentators argue, that it is impossible to reimpose controls. Indeed Malaysia did just that in 1998 when the ringgit was under speculative attack. Many countries in the developing world still retain controls, and the last ERM countries to give them up only did so in 1991. It is true that the complexity of modern financial markets provides the speculator with more opportunity to evade controls, but they will still have the effect of dampening speculation.

In September 1998, the IMF said that controls on inward movements of capital could be a useful tool, especially for countries which were more vulnerable to speculative attack. In its 1998 annual report it argued that the Asian crisis of 1997–98 was the result not only of a weak banking system, but also of open capital accounts, allowing massive withdrawals of funds.

> ### Pause for thought
>
> *Before you read on, see if you can identify (a) the ways exchange transactions might be controlled; (b) the difficulties in using such policy.*

The aim of capital controls is not to prevent capital flows. After all, capital flows are an important source of financing investment. Also, if capital moves from countries with a lower marginal productivity of capital to countries where it is higher, this will lead to an efficient allocation of world savings. The aim of capital controls must therefore be to prevent speculative flows which are based on rumour or herd instinct rather than on economic fundamentals.

Types of control

In what ways can movements of short-term capital be controlled? There are various alternatives, each one with strengths and drawbacks.

Quantitative controls. Here the authorities would restrict the amount of foreign exchange dealing that could take place. Perhaps financial institutions would be allowed to exchange only a certain percentage of their assets. Developed countries and most developing countries have rejected this approach, however, since it is seen to be far too anti-market.

For example, the general principle of the free movement of capital is central to the Single Market of the European Union. The principle of the free movement of capital is defined in Article 63 of the Treaty on the Functioning of the European Union (TFEU). However, Article 66 allows 'safeguard measures' to be taken if 'in exceptional circumstances, movements of capital to or from third countries cause, or threaten to cause, serious difficulties for the operation of economic and monetary union'. Such measures could extend 'for a period not exceeding six months if such measures are strictly necessary'.

KI 9
p51

A Tobin tax. This is named after James Tobin, who in 1972 advocated the imposition of a small tax of 0.1 to 0.5 per cent on all foreign exchange transactions, or on just capital account transactions.[1] This would discourage destabilising speculation (by making it more expensive) and would thus impose some 'friction' in foreign exchange markets, making them less volatile. Such taxes (dubbed 'Robin Hood' taxes) have been advocated by a number of prominent people, such as Bill Gates and the Archbishop of Canterbury.

In November 2001 the French National Assembly became the first national legislature to incorporate into law a Tobin tax of up to 0.1 per cent. Belgium followed in 2002. The EU finance ministers ordered the European Commission to undertake a feasibility study of such a tax. In late 2001, the charity War on Want declared that 13 March 2002 would be international 'Tobin tax day'. Ironically, Tobin died on 11 March 2002. Then in October 2012, 11 of the 17 eurozone countries agreed to adopt a Tobin tax, or 'financial transactions tax' (FTT) of 0.1 per cent on trading in bonds and shares and 0.01 per cent on trading in derivatives. However, subsequent delays concerning details of the tax and legal issues meant that it was unlikely that such a tax would be introduced before 2016 at the earliest.

The UK government, however, has been implacably opposed to such a tax, arguing that the resulting decline in trades would reduce profits for financial institutions, which are a major part of the UK economy. What is more, not all of such trades, it argues, are speculative. The tax could also reduce trades that were for normal trading or investment purposes. However, advocates of the tax argue that, by setting it at a very low rate, such as 0.1 per cent, it should only be speculative trades that are curbed. What is more, a tax is a far less distortionary means of reducing speculation than quantitative controls.

Box 32.3 considers the arguments in more detail for and against Tobin taxes and the European financial transactions tax in particular.

Non-interest-bearing deposits. Here a certain percentage of inflows of finance would have to be deposited with the central bank in a non-interest-bearing account for a set period of time. Chile in the late 1990s used such a system.

It required that 30 per cent of all inflows be deposited with Chile's central bank for a year. This clearly amounted to a considerable tax (i.e. in terms of interest sacrificed) and had the effect of discouraging short-term speculative flows. The problem was that it meant that interest rates in Chile had to be higher in order to attract finance.

One objection to all these measures is that they are likely only to dampen speculation, not eliminate it. If speculators believe that currencies are badly out of equilibrium and will be forced to realign, then no taxes on capital movements or artificial controls will be sufficient to stem the flood.

There are two replies to this objection. The first is that if currencies are badly out of line then exchange rates *should* be adjusted. The second is that *dampening* speculation is probably the ideal. Speculation *can* play the valuable role of bringing exchange rates to their long-term equilibrium more quickly. Controls are unlikely to prevent this aspect of speculation: adjustments to economic fundamentals. If they help to lessen the wilder forms of destabilising speculation, so much the better.

Exchange rate target zones

One type of exchange rate regime that has been much discussed in recent years is that proposed by John Williamson, of Washington's Peterson Institute for International Economics.[2] Williamson advocates a form of 'crawling peg' within broad bands. This system would involve a pegged central rate, where fluctuations around that rate would be allowed within bands (i.e. like the ERM). Unlike the ERM, however, the central value could be adjusted frequently, but only by small amounts: hence the term 'crawling'.

The system would have four major features:

■ Wide bands. For example, currencies could be allowed to fluctuate by 10 per cent of their central parity.

■ Central parity set in *real* terms, at the 'fundamental equilibrium exchange rate' (FEER): i.e. a rate that is consistent with long-run balance of payments equilibrium.

■ Frequent realignments. In order to stay at the FEER, the central parity would be adjusted frequently (e.g. monthly) to take account of the country's rate of inflation. If its rate of inflation were 2 per cent per annum above the trade-weighted average of other countries, then the central parity would be devalued by 2 per cent per annum. Realignments would also reflect other changes in fundamentals, such as changes in the levels of protection, or major political events, such as German reunification.

---

[1]J. Tobin, 'A proposal for international monetary reform', *Eastern Economic Journal*, vol. 4, no. 3–4, 1978, pp. 153–9.

[2]See, for example, J. Williamson and M. Miller, 'Targets and indicators: a blueprint for the co-ordination of economic policy', *Policy Analyses in International Economics*, no. 22 (IIE, 1987).

BOX 32.3   THE TOBIN TAX

Adding a bit of friction

In the mid-1980s, the daily turnover in the world's foreign exchange markets was approximately $150 billion. By 2013 it had risen to a truly massive $5.3 trillion. But only some 5 per cent of this is used for trade in goods and services.

With the massive growth in speculative flows, it is hardly surprising that this can cause great currency instability and financial crises at times of economic uncertainty. Global financial markets have often been decisive in both triggering and intensifying economic crises. The ERM crisis in 1992, the Mexican peso crisis in 1994, the South East Asian crisis in 1997, the Russian rouble meltdown in 1998, the crisis in Argentina in 2001–2 and the currency instability of 2008–9 in the wake of the credit crunch are the most significant in a long list.

The main issue is one of volatility of exchange rates. If currency markets responded to shifts in economic fundamentals, then currency volatility would not be so bad. However, it is increasingly the case that vast quantities of money flow around the global economy purely speculatively, with the herd instinct often driving speculative waves. Invariably, given the volume of speculative flows, exchange rates overshoot their natural equilibrium, intensifying the distortions created. Such currency movements are a huge destabilising force, not just for individual economies but for the global economy as a whole.

So is there anything countries can do to reduce destabilising speculation? One suggestion is the introduction of a Tobin tax.

The Tobin tax

Writing in 1972, James Tobin proposed a system for reducing exchange rate volatility without fundamentally impeding the operation of the market. This involved the imposition of an international tax of some 0.1 to 0.5 per cent payable on all spot or cash exchange rate transactions. He argued that this would make currency trading more costly and would therefore reduce the volume of destabilising short-term financial flows, which would invariably lead to greater exchange rate stability.

Tobin's original proposal suggested that the tax rate would need to be very low so as not to affect 'normal business'. Even if it was very low, speculators working on small margins would be dissuaded from regular movements of money, given that the tax would need to be paid per transaction. If a tax rate of 0.2 per cent was set, speculators who moved a sum of money once a day would face a yearly tax bill of approximately 50 per cent. An investor working on a weekly movement of money would pay tax of 10 per cent per annum, and a monthly movement of currency would represent a tax of 2.4 per cent for the year. Given that 40 per cent of currency transactions have only a two-day time horizon, and 80 per cent a time horizon of fewer than seven days, such a tax would clearly operate to dampen speculative currency movements.

In addition to moderating volatility and speculation, the Tobin tax might yield other benefits. It would, in the face of globalisation, restore to the nation state an element of control over monetary policy. In the face of declining governance over international forces, this might be seen as a positive advantage of the Tobin proposals.

The tax could also generate significant revenue. Estimates range from $150 to $300 billion annually. Many of the world's

leading pressure groups, such as War on Want and Stamp out Poverty, have argued that the revenue from such an international tax could be used to tackle international problems, such as world poverty and environmental degradation. The World Bank estimates that some $225 billion is needed to eliminate the world's worst forms of poverty. The revenue from a Tobin tax would, in a relatively short period of time, easily exceed this amount. Even with a worldwide rate as low as 0.005 per cent (the rate recommended by Stamp out Poverty), the tax could still raise some $50 billion per year.

Problems with the Tobin tax

How far would a tax on currency transactions restrict speculative movements of money? The issue here concerns the rate of return investors might get from moving their money. If a currency was to devalue by as little as 3 to 4 per cent, a Tobin tax of 0.2 per cent would do little to deter a speculative transaction based upon such a potential return. Given devaluations of 50 per cent in Thailand and Indonesia following the 1997 crash and an 82 per cent appreciation of the euro against the dollar from 2002 to 2008, along with severe short-term fluctuations, a 3 to 4 per cent movement in the currency appears rather modest. Raising the rate of the Tobin tax would be no solution, as it would begin to impinge upon 'normal business'.

One response to such a situation has been proposed by a German economist, Paul Bernd Spahn. He suggests that a two-tier system is used. On a day-to-day basis, a minimal tax rate, as originally envisaged by Tobin, is charged against each transaction conducted. However, during periods when exchange rates are highly unstable, a tax surcharge is levied. This would be at a far higher rate, and would only be triggered once a currency moved beyond some predetermined band of exchange rate variation.

A further problem identified with the Tobin tax concerns the costs of its administration. However, given interlinked computer systems and the progressive centralisation of foreign exchange markets, in terms of marketplaces, traders and currencies, effective administration is becoming easier. Most foreign exchange markets are well monitored already and extending such monitoring to include overseeing tax collection would not be overly problematic.

Another problem is tax avoidance. For example, the Tobin tax is a tax payable on spot exchange rate transactions. This could encourage people to deal more in futures. Foreign exchange futures are a type of 'derivative' that allows people to trade currencies in the future at a price agreed today. These would be far more difficult to monitor, since no currency is exchanged today, and hence more difficult to tax. One solution would be to apply a tax on a notional value of a derivative contract. However, derivatives are an important way through which businesses hedge against future risk. Taxing them might seriously erode their use to a business and damage the derivatives market as a whole, making business more risky.

Even with avoidance, however, supporters of the Tobin tax argue that it is still likely to be successful. The main problem is one of political will.

Although some countries, such as France, Canada, Belgium, Brazil and Venezuela, have supported the introduction of a

►

Tobin tax, most of the major economies are opposed to it. With reservations being expressed by the IMF, any concerted international action to control global financial movements will be difficult to put on the agenda, let alone put in place and administer.

Financial transactions tax (FTT)

In 2009, Adair Turner, chairman of the Financial Services Authority, the UK's financial sector regulator at the time, proposed the possible use of Tobin taxes to curb destabilising financial transactions. This was met with criticism from many bankers that the tax would be unworkable at a global level and if applied solely to the UK would divert financial business away from London.

Despite international opinion on the imposition of a financial transactions tax remaining divided, the European Commission favours an FTT. In February 2013, the European Commission tabled a proposal for a Directive which, once passed, will allow participating countries to transpose the directive into national law. The proposals were broadly supported by 11 countries – France, Germany, Austria, Belgium, Estonia, Greece, Italy, Portugal, Slovakia, Slovenia and Spain.

The FTT is to apply whenever at least one of the parties to a trade is based in one of the participating countries. With a rate of 0.1 per cent on trading in bonds and shares and 0.01 per cent on trading in derivatives, the tax is designed to be too small to affect trading in shares or other financial products for purposes of long-term investment. It would, however, dampen speculative trades that take advantage of tiny potential gains from very short-term price movements.

Such trades account for huge financial flows between financial institutions around the world and tend to make markets more volatile. The short-term dealers are known as high-frequency traders (HFTs) and their activities now account for the majority of trading on exchanges. Most of these trades are by computers programmed to seek out minute gains and respond in milliseconds. And whilst they add to short-term liquidity for much of the time, this liquidity can suddenly dry up if HFTs become pessimistic.

Supporters of the tax claim that it will make a major contribution to tackling the deficit problems of many eurozone countries. The Commission estimates that revenues will be around €30 billion to €35 billion, or 0.4 to 0.5 per cent of the GDP of the participating member states.

The UK government remains opposed to such a tax, unless globally adopted, fearing that the UK's large financial services sector would suffer. Critics claim that it will dampen investment and growth and divert financial business away from the participating countries.

The implementation of the FTT was subsequently delayed, partly over concerns about the legality of the central plank of the tax: that it must be paid if one of the counterparties to the trade is based in one of the participating counties. Delays arose too as discussions continued among the 11 participating member states over the details of the tax, including its scope and the distribution of revenues. These discussions led, in December 2015, to Estonia declaring it would no longer be one of the countries introducing the tax. Nonetheless, the remaining participants voiced their hope that a final decision on the implementation of the FTT could be made during 2016.

 George Soros, multi-millionaire currency speculator, has referred to global capital markets as being like a wrecking ball rather than a pendulum, suggesting that such markets are becoming so volatile that they are damaging to all concerned, including speculators. What might lead Soros to such an observation?

- 'Soft buffers'. Governments would not be forced to intervene at the 10 per cent mark or at some specified fraction of it. In fact, from time to time the rate might be allowed to move outside the bands. The point is that the closer the rate approached the band limits, the greater would be the scale of intervention.

This system has two main advantages. First, the exchange rate would stay at roughly the equilibrium level, and therefore the likelihood of large-scale devaluation or revaluation, and with it the opportunities for large-scale speculative gains, would be small. The reason why the narrow-banded ERM broke down in 1992 and 1993 was that the central parities were *not* equilibrium rates.

Second, the wider bands would leave countries freer to follow an independent monetary policy: one that could therefore respond to domestic needs.

The main problem with the system is that it may not allow an independent monetary policy. If the rate of exchange has to be maintained within the zone, then monetary policy may sometimes have to be used for that purpose rather than controlling inflation.

Nevertheless, crawling bands have been used relatively successfully by various countries, such as Chile and Israel over quite long periods of time. What is more, in 1999, Germany's finance minister at the time, Oskar Lafontaine, argued that they might be appropriate for the euro relative to the dollar and yen. A world with three major currencies, each changing gently against the other two in an orderly way, has a lot to commend it.

Pause for thought

Would the Williamson system allow countries to follow a totally independent monetary policy?

SUMMARY

1a The more open the world economy, the more effect changes in economic conditions in one part of the world economy will have on world economic performance.

1b Changes in aggregate demand in one country will affect the amount of imports purchased and thus the amount of exports sold by other countries and hence their GDP. There is thus an international trade multiplier effect.

1c Changes in interest rates in one country will affect financial flows to and from other countries, and hence their exchange rates, interest rates and GDP.

2a Currency fluctuations can be lessened if countries harmonise their economic policies. Ideally this will involve achieving common growth rates, inflation rates, balance of payments and government deficits (as a percentage of GDP) and interest rates. The attempt to harmonise one of these goals, however, may bring conflicts with one of the other goals.

2b Leaders of the G7 and G20 countries meet regularly to discuss ways of harmonising their policies. Usually, however, domestic issues are more important to the leaders than international ones, and frequently they pursue policies that are not in the interests of the other countries.

3a One means of achieving greater currency stability is for a group of countries to peg their internal exchange rates and yet float jointly with the rest of the world. The exchange rate mechanism of the EU (ERM) was an example. Members' currencies were allowed to fluctuate against other member currencies within a band. The band was ±2.25 per cent for the majority of the ERM countries until 1993.

3b The need for realignments seemed to have diminished in the late 1980s as greater convergence was achieved between the members' economies. Growing strains in the system, however, in the early 1990s, led to a crisis in September 1992. The UK and Italy left the ERM. There was a further crisis in July 1993 and the bands were widened to ±15 per cent.

3c Thereafter, as convergence of the economies of ERM members increased, fluctuations decreased and remained largely within ±2.25 per cent.

3d The ERM was seen as an important first stage on the road to complete economic and monetary union (EMU) in the EU.

3e The Maastricht Treaty set out a timetable for achieving EMU. This would culminate with the creation of a currency union: a single European currency with a common monetary policy operated by an independent European Central Bank.

3f The euro was born on 1 January 1999. Twelve countries adopted it, having at least nominally met the Maastricht convergence criteria. Euro notes and coins were introduced on 1 January 2002, with the notes and coins of the old currencies withdrawn a few weeks later.

3g The advantages claimed for EMU are that it eliminates the costs of converting currencies and the uncertainties associated with possible changes in former inter-EU exchange rates. This encourages more investment, both inward and by domestic firms. What is more, a common central bank, independent from domestic governments, will provide the stable monetary environment necessary for a convergence of the EU economies and the encouragement of investment and inter-Union trade.

3h Critics claim, however, that it might make adjustment to domestic economic problems more difficult. The loss of independence in policy making is seen by such people to be a major issue, not only because of the loss of political sovereignty, but also because domestic economic concerns may be at variance with those of the Union as a whole. A single monetary policy is claimed to be inappropriate for dealing with asymmetric shocks. What is more, countries and regions at the periphery of the Union may become depressed unless there is an effective regional policy.

4a Many economists argue that, with the huge flows of short-term finance across the foreign exchanges, governments are forced to adopt one of two extreme forms of exchange rate regime: free floating or being a member of a currency union.

4b If financial flows could be constrained, however, exchange rates could be stabilised somewhat.

4c Forms of control include: quantitative controls, a tax on exchange transactions (a Tobin tax) and non-interest-bearing deposits of a certain percentage of capital inflows with the central bank. Such controls can dampen speculation, but may discourage capital flowing to where it has a higher marginal productivity.

4d An alternative means of stabilising exchange rates is to have exchange rate target zones. Here exchange rates are allowed to fluctuate within broad bands around a central parity which is adjusted to the fundamental equilibrium rate in a gradual fashion.

4e The advantage of this system is that, by keeping the exchange rate at roughly its equilibrium level, destabilising speculation is avoided, and yet there is some freedom for governments to pursue an independent monetary policy. Monetary policy, however, may still from time to time have to be used to keep the exchange rate within the bands.

MyEconLab

This book can be supported by MyEconLab, which contains a range of additional resources, including an online homework and tutorial system designed to test and build your understanding.

You need both an access card and a course ID to access MyEconLab:

1. Is your lecturer using MyEconLab? Ask your lecturer for your course ID.

2. Has an access card been included with the book at a reduced cost? Check the inside back cover of the book.

3. If you have a course ID but no access card, go to: http://www.myeconlab.com/ to buy access to this interactive study programme.

REVIEW QUESTIONS

1   What are the implications for a country attempting to manage its domestic economy if it is subject to an international business cycle? How might it attempt to overcome such problems?

2   What are the economic (as opposed to political) difficulties in achieving an international harmonisation of economic policies so as to avoid damaging currency fluctuations?

3   To what extent can international negotiations over economic policy be seen as a game of strategy? Are there any parallels between the behaviour of countries and the behaviour of oligopolies?

4   What are the causes of exchange rate volatility? Have these problems become greater or lesser in the last ten years? Explain why.

5   Why did the ERM with narrow bands collapse in 1993? Could this have been avoided?

6   Did the exchange rate difficulties experienced by countries under the ERM strengthen or weaken the arguments for progressing to a single European currency?

7   By what means would a depressed country in an economic union with a single currency be able to recover? Would the market provide a satisfactory solution or would (union) government intervention be necessary? If so, what form would the intervention take?

8   Is the eurozone likely to be an optimal currency area now? Is it more or less likely to be so over time? Explain your answer.

9   Assume that just some of the members of a common market like the EU adopt full economic and monetary union, including a common currency. What are the advantages and disadvantages to those members joining the full EMU and to those not joining?

10 Assess the difficulties in attempting to control exchange transactions. Might such a policy restrict the level of trade?

11 Would the Williamson system allow countries to follow a totally independent monetary policy?

12 If the euro were in a crawling peg system against the dollar, what implications would this have for the ECB in sticking to its inflation target of no more than 2 per cent?

ADDITIONAL PART K CASE STUDIES IN THE *ECONOMICS FOR BUSINESS* MyEconLab (www.pearsoned.co.uk/sloman)

K.1   **The national debt.** This explores the question of whether it matters if a country has a high national debt.

K.2   **Trends in public expenditure.** This case examines attempts to control public expenditure in the UK and relates them to the crowding-out debate.

K.3   **The crowding-out effect.** The circumstances in which an increase in public expenditure can replace private expenditure.

K.4   **Any more G and T?** Did the Code for Fiscal Stability mean that the UK government balanced its books? An examination of the evidence.

K.5   **Discretionary fiscal policy in Japan.** How the Japanese government used fiscal policy on various occasions throughout the 1990s and early 2000s in an attempt to bring the economy out of recession.

K.6   **Central banking and monetary policy in the USA.** This case examines how the Fed conducts monetary policy.

K.7   **Goodhart's Law.** An examination of Key Idea 44.

K.8   **Should central banks be independent of government?** An examination of the arguments for and against independent central banks.

K.9   **Monetary targeting: its use around the world.** An expanded version of Box 30.4.

K.10 **Interest rate responses and the financial crisis of 2007/8.** A comparison of the policy responses of the Fed, the ECB and the Bank of England to the credit crunch.

K.11 **Using interest rates to control both aggregate demand and the exchange rate.** A problem of one instrument and two targets.

K.12 **Fiscal and monetary policy in the UK.** An historical overview of UK fiscal and monetary policy.

K.13 **The USA: is it a 'new economy'?** An examination of whether US productivity increases are likely to be sustained.

K.14 **Welfare to work.** An examination of the policy of the UK Labour government whereby welfare payments are designed to encourage people into employment.

K.15 **Assessing PFI.** Has this been the perfect solution to funding investment for the public sector without raising taxes?

K.16 **Alternative approaches to training and education.** This compares the approaches to training and education – a crucial element in supply-side policy – in the UK, France, Germany and the USA.

K.17 **Assistance to small firms in the UK.** An examination of current government measures to assist small firms.

K.18 **The modern approach to industrial policy.** An analysis of the changing role of government in industrial policy.

K.19 **Attempts at harmonisation.** A look at the meetings of the G7 economies where they attempt to come to agreement on means of achieving stable and sustained worldwide economic growth.

K.20 **The UK Labour government's convergence criteria for euro membership.** An examination of the five tests identified as needing to be passed before the question of euro membership would have been put to the electorate in a referendum.

K.21 **Balance of trade and the public finances.** An examination of countries' budget and balance of trade balances.

WEBSITES RELEVANT TO PART K

Numbers and sections refer to websites listed in the Web appendix and hotlinked from this book's website at
www.pearsoned.co.uk/sloman

■ For news articles relevant to Part K, see the *Economics News Articles* link from the book's website.

■ For general news on macroeconomic policy, see websites in section A, and particularly A1–5, 7–9. See also links to newspapers worldwide in A38, 39 and 43, and the news search feature in Google at A41.

■ For information on UK fiscal policy and government borrowing, see sites E18, 30, 36; F2. See also sites A1–8 at Budget time. For fiscal policy in the eurozone, see sites G1 and 13.

■ For a model of the economy (based on the Treasury model), see *The Virtual Chancellor* (site D1).

■ For monetary policy in the UK, see F1 and E30. For monetary policy in the eurozone, see F6 and 5. For monetary policy in the USA, see F8. For monetary policy in other countries, see the respective central bank site in section F.

■ For links to sites on money and monetary policy, see the *Financial Economics* sections in I8, 11, 14, 16.

■ For demand-side policy in the UK, see the latest Budget Report (e.g. section on maintaining macroeconomic stability) at site E30. See also site E18.

■ For inflation targeting in the UK and eurozone, see sites F1 and 6.

■ For the current approach to UK supply-side policy, see the latest Budget Report (e.g. sections on productivity and training) at site E30. See also sites E5 and 9. For EU supply-side policy, see sites G5, 7, 9, 12, 14, 19.

■ For information on training in the UK and Europe, see sites E5, 10; G5, 14.

■ For support for a market-orientated approach to supply-side policy, see C17 and E34.

■ For European Union policies, see sites G1, 3, 6, 16, 17, 18.

■ For information on international harmonisation, see sites H4 and 5.

■ For student resources relevant to Part K, see sites C1–7, 9, 10, 12, 13, 19.

Web appendix

All the following websites can be accessed from the home page of this book's own website (www.pearsoned.co.uk/ sloman). When you enter the site, click on **Hotlinks** button. You will find all the following sites listed. Click on the one you want and the 'hotlink' will take you straight to it.

The sections and numbers below refer to the ones used in the web references at the end of each Part of the text. Thus if the reference were to A21, this would refer to the Moneyextra site.

A General news sources

As the title of this section implies, websites here can be used for finding material on current news issues or tapping into news archives. Most archives are offered free of charge. However, some do require you to register. As well as key UK and American sources, you will also notice some slightly different places from where you can get your news, such as the *Moscow Times* and *Kyodo News* (from Japan). Check out site numbers 38. *Refdesk,* 43. *Guardian World News Guide* and 44. *Online Newspapers* for links to newspapers across the world. Try searching for an article on a particular topic by using site number 41. *Google News Search.*

1. BBC news
2. The Economist
3. The Financial Times
4. The Guardian
5. The Independent
6. ITN
7. The Observer
8. The Telegraph
9. Aljazeera
10. The New York Times
11. Fortune
12. Time Magazine
13. The Washington Post
14. Moscow Times (English)
15. Pravda (English)
16. Straits Times (Singapore)
17. New Straits Times (Malaysia)
18. The Scotsman
19. The Herald
20. Euromoney
21. Moneyextra
22. Market News International
23. Bloomberg Businessweek
24. International Business Times
25. CNN Money
26. Vox (economic analysis and commentary)
27. Asia News Network
28. allAfrica.com
29. Greek News Sources (English)
30. Kyodo News: Japan (English)
31. Euronews
32. Australian Financial Review
33. Sydney Morning Herald
34. Japan Times
35. Reuters
36. Bloomberg
37. David Smith's Economics UK.com
38. Refdesk (links to a whole range of news sources)
39. Newspapers and Magazines on the World Wide Web
40. Yahoo News Search
41. Google News Search
42. ABYZ News Links
43. Guardian World News Guide
44. Onlinenewspapers

B Sources of economic and business data

Using websites to find up-to-date data is of immense value to the economist. The data sources below offer you a range of specialist and non-specialist data information. Universities have free access to the *UK Data Service* site (site 35 in this set), which is a huge database of statistics. Site 34 in this set, the *Treasury Pocket Data Bank*, is a very useful source of key UK and world statistics, and is updated monthly. It downloads as an Excel file. The Economics Network's *Economic data freely available online* (site 1) gives links to various sections in over 40 UK and international sites.

1. Economics Network gateway to economic data
2. UK Office for Budget Responsibility
3. National Statistics
4. Data Archive (Essex)
5. Bank of England Statistical Database
6. Economic Resources (About)
7. Nationwide House Prices Site
8. House Web (data on housing market)
9. Economist global house price data
10. Halifax House Price Index

11. House price indices from ONS
12. Penn World Table
13. Economist economic and financial indicators
14. FT market data
15. Economagic
16. Groningen Growth and Development Centre
17. AEAweb: Resources for economists on the Internet (RFE): data
18. Joseph Rowntree Foundation
19. Intute: Economics resources (archive site)
20. Energy Information Administration
21. OECD Statistics (OECD.Stat)
22. CIA world statistics site (World Factbook)
23. Millennium Development Goals Indicators database (UN)
24. World Bank statistics
25. Federal Reserve Bank of St Louis, US Economic Datasets (FRED)
26. Ministry of Economy Trade and Industry (Japan)
27. Financial data from Yahoo
28. DataMarket
29. Index Mundi
30. Oanda Currency Converter
31. World Economic Outlook Database (IMF)
32. Telegraph shares and markets
33. OFFSTATS links to data sets
34. Treasury Pocket Data Bank (source of UK and world economic data)
35. UK Data Service (incorporating ESDS)
36. BBC News, market data
37. NationMaster
38. Statistical Annex of the European Economy
39. Business and Consumer Surveys (all EU countries)
40. Gapminder
41. WebEc Economics Data
42. WTO International Trade Statistics database
43. UNCTAD trade, investment and development statistics (UNCTADstat)
44. London Metal Exchange
45. Bank for International Settlements, global nominal and real effective exchange rate indices
46. EconStats from EconomyWatch
47. AMECO database

C Sites for students and teachers of economics

The following websites offer useful ideas and resources to those who are studying or teaching economics. It is worth browsing through some just to see what is on offer. Try out the first four sites, for starters. The *Internet for Economists* (site 8) is a very helpful tutorial for economics students on making best use of the Internet for studying the subject.

1. The Economics Network
2. Reaching Resources for Undergraduate Economics (TRUE)
3. Ecedweb
4. Studying Economics
5. Economics and Business Education Association
6. Tutor2U
7. Council for Economic Education
8. Internet for Economics (tutorial on using the Web)
9. Econoclass: Resources for economics teachers
10. Teaching resources for economists (RFE)
11. METAL – Mathematics for Economics: enhancing Teaching And Learning
12. Federal Reserve Bank of San Francisco: Economics Education
13. Excel in Economics Teaching
14. WebEc resources
15. Dr. T's EconLinks: Teaching Resources
16. Online Opinion (Economics)
17. The Idea Channel
18. History of Economic Thought
19. Resources For Economists on the Internet (RFE)
20. Classroom Expernomics
21. Bank of England education resources
22. Why Study Economics?
23. Economic Classroom Experiments
24. Veconlab: Charles Holt's classroom experiments
25. Embedding Threshold Concepts
26. MIT Open Courseware in Economics
27. EconPort

D Economic models and simulations

Economic modelling is an important aspect of economic analysis. There are several sites that offer access to a model for you to use, e.g. Virtual Chancellor (where you can play being Chancellor of the Exchequer). Using such models can be a useful way of finding out how economic theory works within a specific environment. Other sites link to games and experiments, where you can play a particular role, perhaps competing with other students.

1. Virtual Chancellor
2. Virtual factory
3. Interactive simulation models (Economics Web Institute)
4. About.com Economics
5. Classic Economic Models
6. Economics Network Handbook, chapter on simulations, games and role-play
7. Classroom Experiments, Internet Experiments, and Internet Simulations
8. Simulations
9. Experimental economics: Wikipedia
10. Software available on the Economics Network site
11. RFE Software
12. Virtual Worlds
13. Veconlab: Charles Holt's classroom experiments
14. EconPort Experiments

15. Denise Hazlett's Classroom Experiments in Macro-economics
16. Games Economists Play
17. Finance and Economics Experimental Laboratory at Exeter (FEELE)
18. Classroom Expernomics
19. The Economics Network's Guide to Classroom Experiments and Games
20. Economic Classroom Experiments (Wikiversity)

E UK Government and UK Organisations' sites

If you want to see what a government department is up to, then look no further than the list below. Government departments' websites are an excellent source of information and data. They are particularly good at offering information on current legislation and policy initiatives.

1. Gateway site (GOV.UK)
2. Department for Communities and Local Government
3. Prime Minister's Office
4. Competition and Markets Authority (CMA)
5. Department for Education
6. Department for International Development
7. Department for Transport
8. Department of Health
9. Department for Work and Pensions
10. Department for Business, Innovation and Skills
11. Environment Agency
12. Department of Energy and Climate Change
13. Low Pay Commission
14. Department for Environment, Food and Rural Affairs (DEFRA)
15. Office of Communications (Ofcom)
16. Office of Gas and Electricity Markets (Ofgem)
17. Official Documents OnLine
18. Office for Budget Responsibility
19. Office of Rail and Road (ORR)
20. The Takeover Panel
21. Sustainable Development Commission
22. OFWAT
23. Office for National Statistics (ONS)
24. List of ONS releases from UK Data Explorer
25. HM Revenue and Customs
26. UK Intellectual Property Office
27. Parliament website
28. Scottish Government
29. Scottish Environment Protection Agency
30. HM Treasury
31. Equality and Human Rights Commission
32. Trades Union Congress (TUC)
33. Confederation of British Industry
34. Adam Smith Institute
35. Chatham House
36. Institute for Fiscal Studies
37. Advertising Standards Authority
38. Businesses and Self-employed
39. Campaign for Better Transport
40. New Economics Foundation
41. Financial Conduct Authority
42. Prudential Regulation Authority

F Sources of monetary and financial data

As the title suggests, here is a list of useful websites for finding information on financial matters. You will see that the list comprises mainly central banks, both within Europe and further afield.

1. Rank of England
2. Bank of England Monetary and Financial Statistics
3. Banque de France (in English)
4. Bundesbank (German central bank) (in English)
5. Central Bank of Ireland
6. European Central Bank
7. Eurostat
8. US Federal Reserve Bank
9. Netherlands Central Bank (in English)
10. Bank of Japan (in English)
11. Reserve Bank of Australia
12. Bank Negara Malaysia (in English)
13. Monetary Authority of Singapore
14. Bank of Canada
15. National Bank of Denmark (in English)
16. Reserve Bank of India
17. Links to central banks from the Bank for International Settlements
18. The London Stock Exchange

G European Union and related sources

For information on European issues, the following is a wide range of useful sites. The sites maintained by the European Union are an excellent source of information and are provided free of charge.

1. Economic and Financial Affairs (EC DG)
2. European Central Bank
3. EU official Website
4. Eurostat
5. Employment, Social Affairs and Inclusion (EC DG)
6. Booklets on the EU
7. Internal Market, Industry, Entrepreneurship and SMEs (EC DG)
8. Competition (EC DG)
9. Agriculture and Rural Development (EC DC)
10. Energy (EC DG)
11. Environment (EC DG)
12. Regional Policy (EC DG)
13. Taxation and Customs Union (EC DG)
14. Education and Culture (EC DG)

15. European Patent Office
16. European Commission
17. European Parliament
18. European Council
19. Mobility and Transport (EC DG)
20. Trade (EC DG)
21. Internal Market and Services (EC DG)
22. International Cooperation and Development (EC DG)
23. Banking and Finance (EC DG)

H International organisations

This section casts its net beyond Europe and lists the Web addresses of the main international organisations in the global economy. You will notice that some sites are run by charities, such as Oxfam, while others represent organisations set up to manage international affairs, such as the International Monetary Fund and the United Nations.

1. Food and Agriculture Organization
2. United National Conference on Trade and Development (UNCTAD)
3. International Labour Organization (ILO)
4. International Monetary Fund (IMF)
5. Organisation for Economic Co-operation and Development (OECD)
6. OPEC
7. World Bank
8. World Health Organization
9. United Nations
10. United Nations Industrial Development Organisation
11. Friends of the Earth
12. Institute of International Finance
13. Oxfam
14. Christian Aid (reports on development issues)
15. European Bank for Reconstruction and Development (EBRD)
16. World Trade Organization (WTO)
17. United Nations Development Programme
18. UNICEF
19. EURODAD – European Network on Debt and Development
20. NAFTA
21. South American free trade areas
22. ASEAN
23. APEC

I Economics search and link sites

If you are having difficulty finding what you want from the list of sites above, the following sites offer links to other sites and are a very useful resource when you are looking for something a little bit more specialist. Once again, it is worth having a look at what these sites have to offer in order to judge their usefulness.

1. Gateway for UK official sites
2. Alta Plana
3. Data Archive Search
4. Inomics (search engine for economics information)
5. RePEc bibliographic database
6. Estima: Links to economics resources sites
7. Portal sites with links to other sites (Economics Network)
8. WebEc
9. One World (link to economic development sites)
10. Economic development sites (list) from OneWorld.net
11. DMOZ Open Directory: Economics
12. Web links for economists from the Economics Network
13. EconData.net
14. OFFSTATS links to data sets
15. Excite Economics links
16. Internet Resources for Economists
17. National Association of Business Economics links
18. Resources for Economists on the Internet
19. UK university economics departments
20. Economics education links
21. Development Gateway Foundation
22. Find the Data

J Internet search engines

The following search engines have been found to be useful.

1. Google
2. Bing
3. Whoosh UK
4. Excite
5. Zanran (search engine for data and statistics)
6. Search.com
7. MSN
8. Economics Search Engine from RFE
9. Yahoo
10. Ask
11. Kartoo
12. Blinkx (for videos and audio podcasts)

Key ideas

1. **The behaviour and performance of firms is affected by the business environment.** The business environment includes economic, political/legal, social/cultural and technological factors (page 10).

2. **Scarcity** is the excess of human wants over what can actually be produced. Because of scarcity, various choices have to be made between alternatives (page 18).

3. **The opportunity cost** of something is what you give up to get it/do it. In other words, it is cost measured in terms of the best alternative forgone (page 23).

4. **Rational decision making** involves weighing up the marginal benefit and marginal cost of any activity. If the marginal benefit exceeds the marginal cost, it is rational to do the activity (or to do more of it). If the marginal cost exceeds the marginal benefit, it is rational not to do it (or to do less of it) (page 25).

5. **Transactions costs.** The costs incurred when firms buy inputs or services from other firms as opposed to producing them themselves. They include the costs of searching for the best firm to do business with, the costs of drawing up, monitoring and enforcing contracts and the costs of transporting and handling products between the firms. These costs should be weighed against the benefits of outsourcing through the market (page 36).

6. **The nature of institutions and organisations is likely to influence behaviour.** There are various forces influencing people's decisions in complex organisations. Assumptions that an organisation will follow one simple objective (e.g. short-run profit maximisation) is thus too simplistic in many cases (page 37).

7. **The principal-agent problem.** Where people (principals), as a result of a lack of knowledge, cannot ensure that their best interests are served by their agents. Agents may take advantage of this situation to the disadvantage of the principals (page 38).

8. **Good decision making requires good information.** Where information is poor, or poorly used, decisions and their outcomes may be poor. This may be the result of bounded rationality (page 42).

9. **People respond to incentives.** It is important, therefore, that incentives are appropriate and have the desired effect (page 51).

10. **Changes in demand or supply cause markets to adjust.** Whenever such changes occur, the resulting 'disequilibrium' will bring an automatic change in prices, thereby restoring equilibrium (i.e. a balance of demand and supply) (page 52).

11. **Equilibrium** is the point where conflicting interests are balanced. Only at this point is the amount that demanders are willing to purchase the same as the amount that suppliers are willing to supply. It is a point which will be automatically reached in a free market through the operation of the price mechanism (page 59).

12. **Elasticity.** The responsiveness of one variable (e.g. demand) to a change in another (e.g. price). This concept is fundamental to understanding how markets work. The more elastic variables are, the more responsive is the market to changing circumstances (page 68).

13. **People's actions are influenced by their expectations.** People respond not just to what is happening now (such as a change in price), but to what they anticipate will happen in the future (page 78).

14. **People's actions are influenced by their attitudes towards risk.** Many decisions are taken under conditions of risk or uncertainty. Generally, the lower the probability of (or the more uncertain) the desired outcome of an action, the less likely will people be to undertake the action (page 82).

15. **The principle of diminishing marginal utility.** The more of a product a person consumes over a given period of time, the less will be the additional utility gained from one more unit (page 91).

16. **Adverse selection.** Where information is imperfect, high-risk groups will be attracted to profitable market opportunities to the disadvantage of the average buyer (or seller). In the context of insurance, it refers to those who are most likely to take out insurance posing the greatest risks to the insurer (page 99).

17. **Moral hazard.** Following a deal, there is an increased likelihood that one party will engage in problematic (immoral and hazardous) behaviour to the detriment of another. In the context of insurance, it refers to people taking more risks when they have insurance (page 100).

18. **The 'bygones' principle** states that sunk (fixed) costs should be ignored when deciding whether to produce

or sell more or less of a product. Only variable costs should be taken into account (page 141).

19. **Output depends on the amount of resources and how they are used.** Different amounts and combinations of inputs will lead to different amounts of output. If output is to be produced efficiently, then inputs should be combined in the optimum proportions (page 142).

20. **The law of diminishing marginal returns.** When increasing amounts of a variable factor are used with a given amount of a fixed factor, there will come a point when each extra unit of the variable factor will produce less extra output than the previous unit (page 142).

21. **Market power benefits the powerful at the expense of others.** When firms have market power over prices, they can use this to raise prices and profits above the perfectly competitive level. Other things being equal, the firm will gain at the expense of the consumer. Similarly, if consumers or workers have market power, they can use this to their own benefit (page 175).

22. **Economic efficiency** is achieved when each good is produced at the minimum cost and where consumers get maximum benefit from their income (page 181).

23. **People often think and behave strategically.** How you think others will respond to your actions is likely to influence your own behaviour. Firms, for example, when considering a price or product change will often take into account the likely reactions of their rivals (page 197).

24. **Nash equilibrium.** The position resulting from everyone making their optimal decision based on their assumptions about their rivals' decisions. Without collusion, there is no incentive for any firm to move from this position (page 206).

25. **Core competencies.** The key skills of a business that underpin its competitive advantage. A core competence is valuable, rare, costly to imitate and nonsubstitutable. Firms will normally gain from exploiting their core competencies (page 226).

26. **Flexible firm.** A firm that has the flexibility to respond to changing market conditions by changing the composition of its workforce and its working practices (page 317).

27. **Stocks and flows.** A stock is a quantity of something at a given point in time. A flow is an increase or decrease in something over a specified period of time. This is an important distinction and a common cause of confusion (page 322).

28. **The principle of discounting.** People generally prefer to have benefits today than in the future. Thus future benefits have to be reduced (discounted) to give them a present value (page 325).

29. **Efficient capital markets.** Capital markets are efficient when the prices of shares accurately reflect information about companies' current and expected future performance (page 336).

30. **Allocative efficiency** in any activity is achieved where any reallocation would lead to a decline in net benefit. It is achieved where marginal benefit equals marginal cost. Private efficiency is achieved where marginal private benefit equals marginal private cost $(MB = MC)$. Social efficiency is achieved where marginal social benefit equals marginal social cost $(MSB = MSC)$ (page 343).

31. **Markets generally fail to achieve social efficiency.** There are various types of market failure. Market failures provide one of the major justifications for government intervention in the economy (page 343).

32. **Equity** is where income is distributed in a way that is considered to be fair or just. Note that an equitable distribution is not the same as a totally equal distribution and that different people have different views on what is equitable (page 343).

33. **Externalities** are spillover costs or benefits. Where these exist, even an otherwise perfect market will fail to achieve social efficiency (page 345).

34. **The free-rider problem.** People are often unwilling to pay for things if they can make use of things other people have bought. This problem can lead to people not purchasing things which would be to the benefit of them and other members of society to have (page 353).

35. **The problem of time lags.** Many economic actions can take a long time to take effect. This can cause problems of instability and an inability of the economy to achieve social efficiency (page 354).

36. **Government intervention may be able to rectify various failings of the market.** Government intervention in the market can be used to achieve various economic objectives which may not be best achieved by the market. Governments, however, are not perfect, and their actions may bring adverse as well as beneficial consequences (page 354).

37. **The law of comparative advantage.** Provided opportunity costs of various goods differ in two countries, both of them can gain from mutual trade if they specialise in producing (and exporting) those goods that have relatively low opportunity costs compared with the other country (page 444).

38. **Economies suffer from inherent instability.** As a result, economic growth and other macroeconomic indicators tend to fluctuate (page 470).

39. **Balance sheets affect peoples' behaviour.** The size and structure of governments', institutions' and individuals' liabilities (and assets too) affect economic wellbeing and can have significant effects on behaviour and economic activity.

40. **Societies face trade-offs between economic objectives.** For example, the goal of faster growth may conflict with that of greater equality; the goal of lower unemployment may conflict with that of lower inflation (at least in the short run). This is an example of opportunity

cost: the cost of achieving more of one objective may be achieving less of another. The existence of trade-offs means that policy-makers must make choices (page 471).

41. **Living standards are limited by a country's ability to produce.** Potential national output depends on the country's resources, technology and productivity (page 471).

42. **The distinction between nominal and real figures.** Nominal figures are those using current prices, interest rates, etc. Real figures are figures corrected for inflation (page 485).

43. **The principle of cumulative causation.** An initial event can cause an ultimate effect which is much larger (page 547).

44. **Goodhart's Law.** Controlling a symptom (i.e. an indicator) of a problem will not cure the problem. Instead, the indicator will merely cease to be a good indicator of the problem (page 599).

Glossary

Absolute advantage   A country has an absolute advantage over another in the production of a good if it can produce it with less resources than the other country.

Accelerationist theory   The theory that unemployment can only be reduced below the natural rate at the cost of accelerating inflation.

Accelerator theory   The *level* of investment depends on the *rate of change* of national income, and the result tends to be subject to substantial fluctuations.

Actual growth   The percentage annual increase in national output actually produced.

Ad valorem **tariffs**   Tariffs levied as a percentage of the price of the import.

Adjustable peg   A system whereby exchange rates are fixed for a period of time, but may be devalued (or revalued) if a deficit (or surplus) becomes substantial.

Adverse selection   Where information is imperfect, high risk groups will be attracted to profitable market opportunities to the disadvantage of the average buyer (or seller).

Advertising/sales ratio   A ratio that reflects the intensity of advertising within a market.

Aggregate demand (*AD*)   Total spending on goods and services made in the economy. It consists of four elements, consumer spending (*C*), investment (*I*), government spending (*G*) and the expenditure on exports (*X*), less any expenditure on foreign goods and services (*M*): $AD = C + I + G + X - M$.

Aggregate demand for labour curve   A curve showing the total demand for labour in the economy at different average real wage rates.

Aggregate supply   The total amount of output in the economy.

Aggregate supply of labour curve   A curve showing the total number of people willing and able to work at different average real wage rates.

Allocative efficiency   A situation where the current combination of goods produced and sold gives the maximum satisfaction for each consumer at their current levels of income.

Ambient-based standards   Pollution control that requires firms to meet minimum standards for the environment (e.g. air or water quality).

Appreciation   A rise in the free-market exchange rate of the domestic currency with foreign currencies.

Assets   Possessions, or claims held on others.

Assisted areas   Areas of high unemployment qualifying for government regional selective assistance (RSA and SFI) and grants from the European Regional Development Fund (ERDF).

Asymmetric information   A situation in which one party in an economic relationship knows more than another.

Asymmetric shocks   Shocks (such as an oil price increase or a recession in another part of the world) that have different-sized effects on different industries, regions or countries.

Average (total) cost (*AC*)   Total cost (fixed plus variable) per unit of output: $AC = TC/Q = AFC + AVC$.

Average cost pricing   Where a firm sets its price by adding a certain percentage for (average) profit on top of average cost.

Average fixed cost (*AFC*)   Total fixed cost per unit of output: $AFC = TFC/Q$.

Average physical product (*APP*)   Total output (*TPP*) per unit of the variable factor in question: $APP = TPP/Qv$.

Average revenue   Total revenue per unit of output. When all output is sold at the same price, average revenue will be the same as price: $AR = TR/Q = P$.

Average variable cost (*AVC*)   Total variable cost per unit of output: $AVC = TVC/Q$.

Balance of payments account   A record of the country's transactions with the rest of the world. It shows the country's payments to or deposits in other countries (debits) and its receipts or deposits from other countries (credits). It also shows the balance between these debits and credits under various headings.

Balance of payments on current account   The balance on trade in goods and services plus net incomes and current transfers.

Balance of trade   Exports of goods and services minus imports of goods and services. If exports exceed imports, there is a 'balance of trade surplus' (a positive figure). If imports exceed exports, there is a 'balance of trade deficit' (a negative figure).

Balance on trade in goods and services or balance of trade   Exports of goods and services minus imports of goods and services.

Balance on trade in goods or balance of visible trade or merchandise balance   Exports of goods minus imports of goods.

Balance sheet recession An economic slowdown or recession caused by private-sector individuals and firms looking to improve their financial well-being by increasing their saving and/or paying down debt.

Bank (or bank deposits) multiplier The number of times greater the expansion of bank deposits is than the additional liquidity in banks that caused it $1/L$ (the inverse of the liquidity ratio).

Barometric firm price leadership Where the price leader is the one whose prices are believed to reflect market conditions in the most satisfactory way.

Barometric forecasting A technique used to predict future economic trends based upon analysing patterns of time-series data.

Barter economy An economy where people exchange goods and services directly with one another without any payment of money. Workers would be paid with bundles of goods.

Base year (for index numbers) The year whose index number is set at 100.

Behavioural theories of the firm Theories that attempt to predict the actions of firms by studying the behaviour of various groups of people within the firm and their interactions under conditions of potentially conflicting interests.

Bill of exchange A certificate promising to repay a stated amount on a certain date, typically three months from the issue of the bill. Bills pay no interest as such, but are sold at a discount and redeemed at face value, thereby earning a rate of discount for the purchaser.

Bounded rationality Individuals are limited in their ability to absorb and process information. People think in ways conditioned by their experiences (family, education, peer groups, etc.).

Broad money Cash in circulation plus retail and wholesale bank and building society deposits.

Budget deficit The excess of central government's spending over its tax receipts.

Budget surplus The excess of central government's tax receipts over its spending.

Business cycle or trade cycle The periodic fluctuations of national output round its long-term trend.

By-product A good or service that is produced as a consequence of producing another good or service.

Capital All inputs into production that have themselves been produced (e.g. factories, machines and tools).

Capital account of the balance of payments The record of transfers of capital to and from abroad.

Capital adequacy ratio The ratio of a bank's capital (reserves and shares) to its risk-weighted assets.

Cartel A formal collusive agreement.

CDOs See collateralised debt obligations.

Certificates of deposit Certificates issued by banks for fixed-term interest-bearing deposits. They can be resold by the owner to another party.

Change in demand The term used for a shift in the demand curve. It occurs when a determinant of demand *other* than price changes.

Change in supply The term used for a shift in the supply curve. It occurs when a determinant other than price changes.

Change in the quantity demanded The term used for a movement along the demand curve to a new point. It occurs when there is a change in price.

Change in the quantity supplied The term used for a movement along the supply curve to a new point. It occurs when there is a change in price.

Characteristics (or attributes) theory The theory that demonstrates how consumer choice between different varieties of a product depends on the characteristics of these varieties, along with prices of the different varieties, the consumer's budget and the consumer's tastes.

Claimant unemployment Those in receipt of unemployment-related benefits.

Closed shop Where a firm agrees to employ only members of a recognised union.

Collateralised debt obligations (CDOs) These are a type of security consisting of a bundle of fixed-income assets, such as corporate bonds, mortgage debt and credit-card debt.

Collusive oligopoly When oligopolists agree (formally or informally) to limit competition between themselves. They may set output quotas, fix prices, limit product promotion or development, or agree not to 'poach' each other's markets.

Collusive tendering Where two or more firms secretly agree on the prices they will tender for a contract. These prices will be above those which would be put in under a genuinely competitive tendering process.

Command-and-control (CAC) systems The use of laws or regulations backed up by inspections and penalties (such as fines) for non-compliance.

Command or planned economy An economy where all economic decisions are taken by the central (or local) authorities.

Commercial bill A certificate issued by a firm promising to repay a stated amount on a certain date, typically three months from the issue of the bill. Bills pay no interest as such, but are sold at a discount and redeemed at their face value, thereby earning a rate of discount for the purchaser.

Common market A customs union where the member countries act as a single market with free movement of labour and capital, common taxes and common trade laws.

Comparative advantage A country has a comparative advantage over another in the production of a good if it can produce it at a lower opportunity cost, i.e. if it has to forgo less of other goods in order to produce it.

Competition for corporate control The competition for the control of companies through takeovers.

Complementary goods A pair of goods consumed together. As the price of one goes up, the demand for both goods will fall.

Compounding The process of adding interest each year to an initial capital sum.

Conglomerate merger Where two firms in different industries merge.

Conglomerate multinational A multinational that produces different products in different countries.

Consortium Where two or more firms work together on a specific project and create a separate company to run the project.

Consumer durable A consumer good that lasts a period of time, during which the consumer can continue gaining utility from it.

Consumer prices index (CPI) An index of the prices of goods bought by a typical household.

Consumer surplus The excess of what a person would have been prepared to pay for a good (i.e. the utility measured in money terms) over what that person actually pays. Total consumer surplus equals total utility minus total expenditure.

Consumption The act of using goods and services to satisfy wants. This will normally involve purchasing the goods and services.

Consumption externalities Spillover effects on other people of consumers' consumption.

Consumption of domestically produced goods and services (Cd) The direct flow of money payments from households to firms.

Consumption smoothing The act by households of smoothing their levels of consumption over time despite facing volatile incomes.

Continuous market clearing The assumption that all markets in the economy continuously clear so that the economy is permanently in equilibrium.

Convergence of economies When countries achieve similar levels of growth, inflation, budget deficits as a percentage of GDP, balance of payments, etc.

Co-ordination failure When a group of firms (e.g. banks) acting independently could have achieved a more desirable outcome if they had co-ordinated their decision making.

Core competence The key skills of a business that underpin its competitive advantage.

Corporate social responsibility Where a firm takes into account the interests and concerns of a community rather than just its shareholders.

Cost–benefit analysis The identification, measurement and weighing-up of the costs and benefits of a project in order to decide whether or not it should go ahead.

Cost-push inflation Inflation caused by persistent rises in costs of production (independently of demand).

Countervailing power When the power of a monopolistic/oligopolistic seller is offset by powerful buyers who can prevent the price from being pushed up.

Cournot model A model of duopoly where each firm makes its price and output decisions on the assumption that its rival will produce a particular quantity.

Credible threat (or promise) One that is believable to rivals because it is in the threatener's interests to carry it out.

Cross-price elasticity of demand The responsiveness of demand for one good to a change in the price of another; the proportionate change in demand for one good divided by the proportionate change in price of the other.

Cross-section data Information showing how a variable (e.g. the consumption of eggs) differs between different groups or different individuals at a given time.

Crowding out Where increased public expenditure diverts money or resources away from the private sector.

Currency union A group of countries (or regions) using a common currency.

Current account of the balance of payments The record of a country's imports and exports of goods and services, plus incomes and transfers of money to and from abroad.

Customs union A free trade area with common external tariffs and quotas.

Deadweight welfare loss The loss of consumer plus producer surplus in imperfect markets (when compared with perfect competition).

Debt/equity ratio The ratio of debt finance to equity finance.

Decision tree (or game tree) A diagram showing the sequence of possible decisions by competitor firms and the outcome of each combination of decisions.

Deflation (definition 1) A period of falling prices: negative inflation.

Deflation (definition 2) A period of falling real aggregate demand. Note that 'deflation' is more commonly used nowadays to mean negative inflation.

Deflationary or recessionary gap The shortfall of aggregate expenditure below GDP at the full-employment level of GDP.

Deindustrialisation The decline in the contribution to production of the manufacturing sector of the economy.

Demand curve A graph showing the relationship between the price of a good and the quantity of the good demanded over a given time period. Price is measured on the vertical axis; quantity demanded is measured on the horizontal axis. A demand curve can be for an individual consumer or a group of consumers, or more usually for the whole market.

Demand function An equation showing the relationship between the demand for a product and its principal determinants.

Demand schedule for an individual A table showing the different quantities of a good that a person is willing and able to buy at various prices over a given period of time.

Demand: change in demand The term used for a shift in the demand curve. It occurs when a determinant of demand *other* than price changes.

Demand: change in the quantity demanded The term used for a movement along the demand curve to a new point. It occurs when there is a change in price.

Demand-deficient or cyclical unemployment Disequilibrium unemployment caused by a fall in aggregate demand with no corresponding fall in the real wage rate.

Demand-pull inflation Inflation caused by persistent rises in aggregate demand.

Demand-side policy Government policy designed to alter the level of aggregate demand, and thereby the level of output, employment and prices.

Dependent variable That variable whose outcome is determined by other variables within an equation.

Depreciation (capital) The decline in value of capital equipment due to age or to wear and tear.

Depreciation (currency) A fall in the free-market exchange rate of the domestic currency with foreign currencies.

Derived demand The demand for a factor of production depends on the demand for the good which uses it.

Destabilising speculation This is where the actions of speculators tend to make price movements larger.

Devaluation Where the government refixes the exchange rate at a lower level.

Diminishing marginal rate of substitution of characteristics The more a consumer gets of characteristic A and the less of characteristic B, the less and less of B the consumer will be willing to give up to get an extra unit of A.

Diminishing marginal utility of income Where each additional pound earned yields less additional utility.

Discount market An example of a money market in which new or existing bills are bought and sold.

Discounting The process of reducing the value of future flows to give them a present valuation.

Discretionary fiscal policy Deliberate changes in tax rates or the level of government expenditure in order to influence the level of aggregate demand.

Diseconomies of scale Where costs per unit of output increase as the scale of production increases.

Disequilibrium unemployment Unemployment resulting from real wages in the economy being above the equilibrium level.

Disposable income Income available for spending or saving after the deduction of direct taxes and the addition of benefits.

Diversification A business growth strategy in which a business expands into new markets outside of its current interests.

Dominant firm price leadership When firms (the followers) choose the same price as that set by a dominant firm in the industry (the leader).

Dominant strategy game Where the *same* policy is suggested by different strategies.

Downsizing Where a business reorganises and reduces its size, especially in respect to levels of employment, in order to cut costs.

Dumping Where exports are sold at prices below marginal cost – often as a result of government subsidy.

Duopoly An oligopoly where there are just two firms in the market.

Econometrics The branch of economics which applies statistical techniques to economic data.

Economies of scale When increasing the scale of production leads to a lower cost per unit of output.

Economies of scope When increasing the range of products produced by a firm reduces the cost of producing each one.

Efficiency frontier A line showing the maximum attainable combinations of two characteristics for a given budget. These characteristics can be obtained by consuming one or a mixture of two brands or varieties of a product.

Efficiency wage hypothesis A hypothesis that states that a worker's productivity is linked to the wage he or she receives.

Efficiency wage rate The profit-maximising wage rate for the firm after taking into account the effects of wage rates on worker motivation, turnover and recruitment.

Efficient (capital) market hypothesis The hypothesis that new information about a company's current or future performance will be quickly and accurately reflected in its share price.

Elastic If demand is (price) elastic, then any change in price will cause the quantity demanded to change proportionately more. Ignoring the negative sign, it will have a value greater than 1.

Endogenous money supply Money supply that is determined (at least in part) by the demand for money.

Enterprise culture One in which individuals are encouraged to become wealth creators through their own initiative and effort.

Envelope curve A long-run average cost curve drawn as the tangency points of a series of short-run average cost curves.

Environmental policy Initiatives by government to ensure a specified minimum level of environmental quality.

Environmental scanning Where a business surveys social and political trends in order to take account of changes in its decision-making process.

Equation of exchange $MV = PQ$. The total level of spending on GDP (MV) equals the total value of goods and services produced (PQ) that go to make up GDP.

Equilibrium A position of balance. A position from which there is no inherent tendency to move away.

Equilibrium ('natural') unemployment The difference between those who would like employment at the current wage rate and those willing and able to take a job.

Equilibrium price The price where the quantity demanded equals the quantity supplied; the price where there is no shortage or surplus.

Equity The fair distribution of a society's resources.

ERM (the exchange rate mechanism) A semi-fixed system whereby participating EU countries allowed fluctuations against each other's currencies only within agreed bands. Collectively they floated freely against all other currencies.

Ethical consumerism Where consumers' decisions about what to buy are influenced by ethical concerns such as the producer's human rights record and care for the environment.

Excess burden (of a tax on a good) The amount by which the loss in consumer plus producer surplus exceeds the government surplus.

Excess capacity (under monopolistic competition) In the long run, firms under monopolistic competition will produce at an output below that which minimises average cost per unit.

Exchange equalisation account The gold and foreign exchange reserves account in the Bank of England.

Exchange rate The rate at which one national currency exchanges for another. The rate is expressed as the amount of one currency that is necessary to purchase one unit of another currency (e.g. £1 = €1.40).

Exchange rate index A weighted average exchange rate expressed as an index, where the value of the index is 100 in a given base year. The weights of the different currencies in the index add up to 1.

Exogenous money supply Money supply that does not depend on the demand for money but is set by the authorities (i.e. the central bank or the government).

Expectations-augmented Phillips curve A (short-run) Phillips curve whose position depends on the expected rate of inflation.

Explicit costs The payments to outside suppliers of inputs.

External benefits Benefits from production (or consumption) experienced by people *other* than the producer (or consumer).

External costs Costs of production (or consumption) borne by people *other* than the producer (or consumer).

External diseconomies of scale Where a firm's costs per unit of output increase as the size of the whole industry increases.

External economies of scale Where a firm's costs per unit of output decrease as the size of the whole *industry* grows.

External expansion Where business growth is achieved by merger, takeover, joint venture or an agreement.

Externalities Costs or benefits of production or consumption experienced by people other than the producers and consumers directly involved in the transaction. They are sometimes referred to as 'spillover' or 'third-party' costs or benefits.

Factors of production (or resources) The inputs into the production of goods and services labour, land and raw materials, and capital.

Financial accelerator When a change in national income is amplified by changes in the financial sector, such as changes in interest rate differentials or the willingness of banks to lend.

Financial account of the balance of payments The record of the flows of money into and out of the country for the purpose of investment or as deposits in banks and other financial institutions.

Financial crowding out Where an increase in government borrowing diverts money away from the private sector.

Financial flexibility Where employers can vary their wage costs by changing the composition of their workforce or the terms on which workers are employed.

Financial instability hypothesis During periods of economic growth, economic agents (firms and individuals) tend to borrow more and MFIs are more willing to lend. This fuels the boom. In a period of recession, economic agents tend to cut spending in order to reduce debts and MFIs are less willing to lend. This deepens the recession. Behaviour in financial markets thus tends to amplify the business cycle.

Financial instruments Financial products resulting in a financial claim by one party over another.

Financial intermediaries The general name for financial institutions (banks, building societies, etc.) which act as a means of channelling funds from depositors to borrowers.

Fine tuning The use of demand management policy (fiscal or monetary) to smooth out cyclical fluctuations in the economy.

Firm An economic organisation that co-ordinates the process of production and distribution.

First-degree price discrimination Where a firm charges each consumer for each unit the maximum price which that consumer is willing to pay for that unit.

First-mover advantage When a firm gains from being the first one to take action.

Fiscal policy Policy to affect aggregate demand by altering government expenditure and/or taxation.

Fiscal stance How deflationary or reflationary the Budget is.

Fixed costs Total costs that do not vary with the amount of output produced.

Fixed factor An input that cannot be increased in supply within a given time period.

Flat organisation One in which technology enables senior managers to communicate directly with those lower in the organisational structure. Middle managers are bypassed.

Flexible firm A firm that has the flexibility to respond to changing market conditions by changing the composition of its workforce.

Floating exchange rate When the government does not intervene in the foreign exchange markets, but simply allows the exchange rate to be freely determined by demand and supply.

Flow An increase or decrease in quantity over a specified period.

Foreign exchange gap The shortfall in foreign exchange that a country needs to purchase necessary imports such as raw materials and machinery.

Forward exchange market Where contracts are made today for the price at which a currency will be exchanged at some specified future date.

Franchise A formal contractual agreement whereby a company uses another company to produce or sell some or all of its product.

Franchising Where a firm is granted the licence to operate a given part of an industry for a specified length of time.

Free market One in which there is an absence of government intervention. Individual producers and consumers are free to make their own economic decisions.

Free trade area A group of countries with no trade barriers between themselves.

Free-rider problem When it is not possible to exclude other people from consuming a good that someone has bought.

Frictional (search) unemployment Unemployment that occurs as a result of imperfect information in the labour market. It often takes time for workers to find jobs (even though there are vacancies) and in the meantime they are unemployed.

Full-employment level of GDP The level of GDP at which there is no deficiency of demand.

Full-range pricing A pricing strategy in which a business, seeking to improve its profit performance, assesses the pricing of its goods as a whole rather than individually.

Functional flexibility Where employers can switch workers from job to job as requirements change.

Functional relationships The mathematical relationships showing how one variable is affected by one or more others.

Funding Where the authorities alter the balance of bills and bonds for any given level of government borrowing.

Future price A price agreed today at which an item (e.g. commodities) will be exchanged at some set date in the future.

Futures or forward market A market in which contracts are made to buy or sell at some future date at a price agreed today.

Game theory (or the theory of games) The study of alternative strategies that oligopolists may choose to adopt, depending on their assumptions about their rivals' behaviour.

GDP deflator The price index of all final domestically produced goods and services: i.e. all items that contribute towards GDP.

Gearing or leverage (US term) The ratio of debt capital to equity capital: in other words, the ratio of borrowed capital (e.g. bonds) to shares.

General government debt The accumulated central and local government deficits (less surpluses) over the years, i.e. the total amount owed by central and local government, both to domestic and overseas creditors.

Global sourcing Where a company uses production sites in different parts of the world to provide particular components for a final product.

Global systemically important banks (G-SIBs) Banks identified by a series of indicators as being significant players in the global financial system.

Goodhart's Law Controlling a symptom of a problem, or only part of the problem, will not cure the problem; it will simply mean that the part that is being controlled now becomes a poor indicator of the problem.

Goods in joint supply These are two goods where the production of more of one leads to the production of more of the other.

Government surplus (from a tax on a good) The total tax revenue earned by the government from sales of a good.

Grandfathering Where the number of emission permits allocated to a firm is based on its current levels of emission (e.g. permitted levels for all firms could be 80 per cent of their current emission levels).

Gross domestic product (GDP) The value of output produced within the country over a 12-month period.

Gross domestic product (GDP) (at market prices) The value of output produced within a country over a 12-month period in terms of the prices actually paid. GDP = GVA + taxes on products – subsidies on products.

Gross national income (GNY) GDP plus net income from abroad.

Gross value added (GVA) at basic prices The sum of all the values added by all industries in the economy over a year. The figures exclude taxes on products (such as VAT) and include subsidies on products.

Growth maximisation An alternative theory which assumes that managers seek to maximise the growth in sales revenue (or the capital value of the firm) over time.

Growth vector matrix A means by which a business might assess its product/market strategy.

Harrod–Domar model A model that relates a country's rate of economic growth to the proportion of national income saved and the ratio of capital to output.

Historic costs The original amount the firm paid for factors it now owns.

Holding company A business organisation in which the present company holds interests in a number of other companies or subsidiaries.

Horizontal merger Where two firms in the same industry at the same stage of the production process merge.

Horizontal product differentiation Where a firm's product differs from its rivals' products, although the products are seen to be of a similar quality.

Horizontal strategic alliances A formal or informal arrangement between firms to jointly provide a particular activity at a similar stage of the same technical process.

Horizontally integrated multinational A multinational that produces the same product in many different countries.

Households' disposable income The income available for households to spend, i.e. personal incomes after deducting taxes on incomes and adding benefits.

Human capital The knowledge, skills, competencies and other attributes embodied in individuals or groups of individuals that are used to produce goods and services.

Hysteresis The persistence of an effect even when the initial cause has ceased to operate. In economics it refers to the persistence of unemployment even when the demand deficiency that caused it no longer exists.

Imperfect competition The collective name for monopolistic competition and oligopoly.

Implicit costs Costs which do not involve a direct payment of money to a third party, but which nevertheless involve a sacrifice of some alternative.

Import substitution The replacement of imports by domestically produced goods or services.

Income effect The effect of a change in price on quantity demanded arising from the consumer becoming better or worse off as a result of the price change.

Income effect of a rise in wages Workers get a higher income for a given number of hours worked and may thus feel they need to work fewer hours as wages rise.

Income elasticity of demand The responsiveness of demand to a change in consumer incomes; the proportionate change in demand divided by the proportionate change in income.

Independence (of firms in a market) When the decisions of one firm in a market will not have any significant effect on the demand curves of its rivals.

Independent risks Where two risky events are unconnected. The occurrence of one will not affect the likelihood of the occurrence of the other.

Independent variables Those variables that determine the dependent variable, but are themselves determined independently of the equation they are in.

Index number The value of a variable expressed as 100 plus or minus its percentage deviation from a base year.

Indifference curve A line showing all those combinations of two characteristics of a good between which a consumer is indifferent, i.e. those combinations that give a particular level of utility.

Indifference map A diagram showing a whole set of indifference curves. The further away a particular curve is from the origin, the higher the level of utility it represents.

Indivisibilities The impossibility of dividing a factor of production into smaller units.

Industrial concentration The degree to which an industry is dominated by large business enterprises.

Industrial policies Policies to encourage industrial investment and greater industrial efficiency.

Industrial sector A grouping of industries producing similar products or services.

Industry A group of firms producing a particular product or service.

Industry's infrastructure The network of supply agents, communications, skills, training facilities, distribution channels, specialised financial services, etc. that support a particular industry.

Inelastic If demand is (price) inelastic, then any change will cause the quantity demanded to change by a proportionately smaller amount. Ignoring the negative sign, it will have a value less than 1.

Infant industry An industry which has a potential comparative advantage, but which is as yet too underdeveloped to be able to realise this potential.

Inferior goods Goods whose demand falls as people's incomes rise.

Inflationary gap The excess of aggregate expenditure over GDP at the full-employment level of GDP.

Injections (J) Expenditure on the production of domestic firms coming from outside the inner flow of the circular flow of income. Injections equal investment (I) plus government expenditure (G) plus expenditure on exports (X).

Integrated international enterprise One in which an international company pursues a single business strategy. It co-ordinates the business activities of its subsidiaries across different countries.

Interdependence (under oligopoly) This is one of the two key features of oligopoly. Each firm is affected by its rivals' decisions and its decisions will affect its rivals. Firms recognise this interdependence and take it into account when making decisions.

Internal expansion Where a business adds to its productive capacity by adding to existing or by building new plant.

Internal funds Funds used for business expansion that come from ploughed-back profit.

Internal rate of return (IRR) The rate of return of an investment: the discount rate that makes the net present value of an investment equal to zero.

Internalisation advantages Where the benefits of extending the organisational structure of the MNC by setting up an overseas subsidiary are greater than the costs of arranging a contract with an external party.

International harmonisation of economic policies Where countries attempt to coordinate their macroeconomic policies so as to achieve common goals.

International liquidity The supply of currencies in the world acceptable for financing international trade and investment.

International trade multiplier The impact of changing levels of international demand on levels of production and output.

Inter-temporal pricing This occurs where different groups have different price elasticities of demand for a product at different points in time.

Investment The purchase by the firm of equipment or materials that will add to its stock of capital.

Joint-stock company A company where ownership is distributed between a large number of shareholders.

Just-in-time methods Where a firm purchases supplies and produces both components and finished products as they are required. This minimises stock holding and its associated costs.

Kinked demand theory The theory that oligopolists face a demand curve that is kinked at the current price demand being significantly more elastic above the current price than below. The effect of this is to create a situation of price stability.

Knowledge spillover The capture by third parties of benefits from the development by others of new ideas, for example, new products, processes and technologies.

Labour All forms of human input, both physical and mental, into current production.

Labour force The number employed plus the number unemployed.

Land (and raw materials) Inputs into production that are provided by nature (e.g. unimproved land and mineral deposits in the ground).

Law of comparative advantage Trade can benefit all countries if they specialise in the goods in which they have a comparative advantage.

Law of demand The quantity of a good demanded per period of time will fall as the price rises and rise as the price falls, other things being equal (*ceteris paribus*).

Law of diminishing (marginal) returns When one or more factors are held fixed, there will come a point beyond which the extra output from additional units of the variable factor will diminish.

Law of large numbers The larger the number of events of a particular type, the more predictable will be their average outcome.

Leading indicators Indicators that help predict future trends in the economy.

Lender of last resort The role of the Bank of England as the guarantor of sufficient liquidity in the monetary system.

Leverage The extent to which a company relies upon debt finance as opposed to equity finance.

Liabilities All legal claims for payment that outsiders have on an institution.

Licensing Where the owner of a patented product allows another firm to produce it for a fee.

Limit pricing Where a business keeps prices low, restricting its profits, so as to deter new rivals entering the market.

Liquidity The ease with which an asset can be converted into cash without loss.

Liquidity ratio The proportion of a bank's total assets held in liquid form.

Liquidity trap When interest rates are at their floor and thus any further increases in money supply will not be spent but merely be held in idle balances as people wait for the economy to recover and/or interest rates to rise.

Locational advantages Those features of a host economy that MNCs believe will lower costs, improve quality and/or facilitate greater sales.

Lock-outs Union members are temporarily laid off until they are prepared to agree to the firm's conditions.

Logistics The process of managing the supply of inputs to a firm and the outputs from a firm to its customers.

Long run The period of time long enough for *all* factors to be varied.

Long run under perfect competition The period of time which is long enough for new firms to enter the industry.

Long-run average cost (*LRAC*) curve A curve that shows how average cost varies with output on the assumption that *all* factors are variable. (It is assumed that the least-cost method of production will be chosen for each output.)

Long-run profit maximisation An alternative theory which assumes that managers aim to shift cost and revenue curves so as to maximise profits over some longer time period.

Long-run shut-down point This is where the *AR* curve is tangential to the *LRAC* curve. The firm can just make normal profits. Any fall in revenue below this level will cause a profit-maximising firm to shut down once all costs have become variable.

Loss leader A product whose price is cut by the business in order to attract custom.

Macro-prudential regulation Regulation which focuses on the financial system as a whole and which monitors its impact on the wider economy and ensures that it is resilient to shocks.

Macroeconomics The branch of economics that studies economic aggregates (grand totals), for example the overall level of prices, output and employment in the economy.

Managed flexibility (dirty floating) A system of flexible exchange rates, but where the government intervenes to prevent excessive fluctuations or even to achieve an unofficial target exchange rate.

Managerial utility maximisation An alternative theory which assumes that managers are motivated by self-interest. They will adopt whatever policies are perceived to maximise their own utility.

Marginal benefits The additional benefits of doing a little bit more (or *1 unit* more if a unit can be measured) of an activity.

Marginal consumer surplus The excess of utility from the consumption of one more unit of a good (*MU*) over the price paid: $MCS = MU - P$.

Marginal cost (*MC*) The cost of producing one more unit of output: $MC = \Delta TC/\Delta Q$.

Marginal cost of capital The cost of one additional unit of capital.

Marginal costs The additional cost of doing a little bit more (or *1 unit* more if a unit can be measured) of an activity.

Marginal disutility of work The extra sacrifice/hardship to a worker of working an extra unit of time in any given time period (e.g. an extra hour per day).

Marginal efficiency of capital (*MEC*) or internal rate of return (*IRR*) The rate of return of an investment the discount rate that makes the net present value of an investment equal to zero.

Marginal physical product (*MPP*) The extra output gained by the employment of one more unit of the variable factor: $MPP = \Delta TPP/\Delta Qv$.

Marginal productivity theory The theory that the demand for a factor depends on its marginal revenue product.

Marginal propensity to consume The proportion of a rise in national income (Y) that is spent on goods and services by households and non-profit institutions serving households.

Marginal propensity to consume from disposable income The proportion of a rise in disposable income that is spent on goods and services by households and non-profit institutions serving households.

Marginal propensity to consume domestically produced goods and services The fraction of a rise in national income (Y) that is spent on domestic product (Cd) and hence is not withdrawn from the circular flow of income: $mpc_d = \Delta Cd/\Delta Y$.

Marginal revenue The extra revenue gained by selling one or more unit per time period: $MR = \Delta TR/\Delta Q$.

Marginal revenue product of capital The additional revenue earned from employing one additional unit of capital.

Marginal revenue product of labour The extra revenue a firm earns from employing one more unit of labour.

Marginal utility The extra satisfaction gained from consuming one extra unit of a good within a given time period.

Market The interaction between buyers and sellers.

Market clearing A market clears when supply matches demand, leaving no shortage or surplus.

Market demand schedule A table showing the different total quantities of a good that consumers are willing and able to buy at various prices over a given period of time.

Market experiments Information gathered about consumers under artificial or simulated conditions. A method used widely in assessing the effects of advertising on consumers.

Market loans Loans made to other financial institutions.

Market niche A part of a market (or new market) that has not been filled by an existing brand or business.

Market segment A part of a market for a product where the demand is for a particular variety of that product.

Market surveys Information gathered about consumers, usually via a questionnaire, that attempts to enhance the business's understanding of consumer behaviour.

Marketing mix The mix of product, price, place (distribution) and promotion that will determine a business's marketing strategy.

Mark-up pricing A pricing strategy adopted by business in which a profit mark-up is added to average costs.

Maturity gap The difference in the average maturity of loans and deposits.

Maturity transformation The transformation of deposits into loans of a longer maturity.

Maximum price A price ceiling set by the government or some other agency. The price is not allowed to rise above this level (although it is allowed to fall below it).

Medium of exchange Something that is acceptable in exchange for goods and services.

Menu costs of inflation The costs associated with having to adjust price lists or labels.

Merger The outcome of a mutual agreement made by two firms to combine their business activities.

Merit goods Goods which the government feels that people will underconsume and which therefore ought to be subsidised or provided free.

M-form business organisation One in which the business is organised into separate departments, such that responsibility for the day-to-day management enterprise is separated from the formulation of the business's strategic plan.

Microeconomics The branch of economics that studies individual units (e.g. households, firms and industries). It studies the interrelationships between these units in determining the pattern of production and distribution of goods and services.

Minimum efficient scale (MES) The size of the individual factory or of the whole firm, beyond which no significant additional economies of scale can be gained. For an individual factory the MES is known as the *minimum efficient plant size* (MEPS).

Minimum price A price floor set by the government or some other agency. The price is not allowed to fall below this level (although it is allowed to rise above it).

Minimum reserve ratio A minimum ratio of cash (or other specified liquid assets) to deposits (either total or selected) that the central bank requires banks to hold.

Mixed economy An economy where economic decisions are made partly through the market and partly by the government.

Mobility of labour The ease with which labour can either shift between jobs (occupational mobility) or move to other parts of the country in search of work (geographical mobility).

Monetary base Notes and coin in circulation (i.e. outside the central bank).

Monetary financial institutions (MFIs) Deposit-taking financial institutions including banks, building societies and central banks.

Money market The market for short-term loans and deposits.

Money multiplier The number of times greater the expansion of money supply (M_s) is than the expansion of the monetary base (M_b) that caused it: $\Delta M_s/\Delta M_b$

Monopolistic competition A market structure where, like perfect competition, there are many firms and freedom of entry into the industry, but where each firm produces a differentiated product and thus has some control over its price.

Monopoly A market structure where there is only one firm in the industry.

Monopsony A market with a single buyer or employer.

Moral hazard Following a deal, there is an increased likelihood that one party will engage in problematic (immoral and hazardous) behaviour to the detriment of another.

The temptation to take more risks when you know that someone else will cover the risks if you get into difficulties. In the case of banks taking risks, the 'someone else' may be another bank, the central bank or the government.

Multinational corporations Businesses that either own or control foreign subsidiaries in more than one country.

Multiplier The number of times a rise in GDP (ΔGDP) is bigger than the initial rise in aggregate expenditure (ΔE) that caused it. Using the letter k to stand for the multiplier, the multiplier is defined as: $k = \Delta GDP/\Delta E$.

Multiplier effect An initial increase in aggregate demand of £xm leads to an eventual rise in national income that is greater than £xm.

Multiplier formula The formula for the multiplier is: $k = 1/(1 - mpc_d)$.

Mutual recognition The EU principle that one country's rules and regulations must apply throughout the Union. If they conflict with those of another country, individuals and firms should be able to choose which to obey.

Nash equilibrium The position resulting from everyone making their optimal decision based on their assumptions about their rivals' decisions. Without collusion, there is no incentive for any firm to move from this position.

Nationalised industries State-owned industries that produce goods or services that are sold in the market.

Natural monopoly A situation where long-run average costs would be lower if an industry were under monopoly than if it were shared between two or more competitors.

Natural rate of unemployment or non-accelerating-inflation rate of unemployment (NAIRU) The rate of unemployment consistent with a constant rate of inflation; the rate of unemployment at which the vertical long-run Phillips curve cuts the horizontal axis.

Net errors and omissions A statistical adjustment to ensure that the two sides of the balance of payments account balance. It is necessary because of errors in compiling the statistics.

Net national income (NNY) GNY minus depreciation.

Net present value (NPV) of an investment The discounted benefits of an investment minus the cost of the investment.

Network The establishment of formal and informal multi-firm alliances across sectors.

Network economies The benefits to consumers of having a network of other people using the same product or service.

Net worth The market value of a sector's stock of financial and non-financial wealth.

Non-bank private sector Household and non-bank firms. The category thus excludes the government and banks.

Non-collusive oligopoly When oligopolists have no agreement between themselves – formal, informal or tacit.

Non-excludability Where it is not possible to provide a good or service to one person without it thereby being available for others to enjoy.

Non-price competition Competition in terms of product promotion (advertising, packaging, etc.) or product development.

Non-rivalry Where the consumption of a good or service by one person will not prevent others from enjoying it.

Normal goods Goods whose demand rises as people's incomes rise.

Normal profit The opportunity cost of being in business. It consists of the interest that could be earned on a riskless asset, plus a return for risk taking in this particular industry. It is counted as a cost of production.

Numerical flexibility Where employers can change the size of their workforce as their labour requirements change.

Observations of market behaviour Information gathered about consumers from the day-to-day activities of the business within the market.

Oligopoly A market structure where there are few enough firms to enable barriers to be erected against the entry of new firms.

Oligopsony A market with just a few buyers or employers.

Open-market operations The sale (or purchase) by the authorities of government securities in the open market in order to reduce (or increase) money supply and thereby affect interest rates.

Opportunity cost The cost of any activity measured in terms of the best alternative forgone.

Optimal currency area The optimal size of a currency area is one that maximises the benefits from having a single currency relative to the costs. If the area were to be increased or decreased in size, the costs would rise relative to the benefits.

Organisational slack When managers allow spare capacity to exist, thereby enabling them to respond more easily to changed circumstances.

Output gap Actual output minus potential output.

Outsourcing or subcontracting Where a firm employs another firm to produce part of its output or some of its input(s).

Overheads Costs arising from the general running of an organisation, and only indirectly related to the level of output.

Ownership-specific assets Assets owned by the firm, such as technology, product differentiation and managerial skills, which reflect its core competencies.

Peak-load pricing The practice of charging higher prices at times when demand is highest because the constraints on capacity lead to higher marginal cost.

Perfect competition A market structure in which there are many firms; where there is freedom of entry to the industry; where all firms produce an identical product; and where all firms are price takers.

Perfectly contestable market A market where there is free and costless entry and exit.

PEST analysis Where the political, economic, social and technological factors shaping a business environment are assessed by a business so as to devise future business strategy.

Phillips curve A curve showing the relationship between (price) inflation and unemployment. The original Phillips curve plotted *wage* inflation against unemployment for the years 1861–1957.

Picketing Where people on strike gather at the entrance to the firm and attempt to dissuade workers or delivery vehicles from entering.

Planned or **command economy** An economy where all economic decisions are taken by the central (or local) authorities.

Plant economies of scale Economies of scale that arise because of the large size of the factory.

Policy ineffectiveness proposition The conclusion drawn from new classical models that, when economic agents anticipate changes in economic policy, output and employment remain at their equilibrium (or natural) levels.

Potential growth The percentage annual increase in the output that would be produced if all firms were operating at their normal level of capacity utilisation.

Potential output The output that could be produced in the economy if all firms were operating at their normal level of capacity utilisation.

Predatory pricing Where a firm sets its average price below average cost in order to drive competitors out of business.

Preferential trading arrangement A trading arrangement whereby trade between the signatories is freer than trade with the rest of the world.

Present value approach to appraising investment This involves estimating the value *now* of a flow of future benefits (or costs).

Price benchmark This is a price which is typically used. Firms, when raising prices, will usually raise them from one benchmark to another.

Price discrimination Where a firm sells the same product at different prices.

Price elasticity of demand The responsiveness of quantity demanded to a change in price: the proportionate change in quantity demanded divided by the proportionate change in price.

Price elasticity of supply The responsiveness of quantity supplied to a change in price: the proportionate change in quantity supplied divided by the proportionate change in price.

Price maker (Price chooser) A firm that has the ability to influence the price charged for its good or service.

Price mechanism The system in a market economy whereby changes in price in response to changes in demand and supply have the effect of making demand equal to supply.

Price taker A firm that is too small to be able to influence the market price.

Price to book ratio or **Valuation ratio** The ratio of stock market value to book value. The stock market value is an assessment of the firm's past and anticipated future performance. The book value is a calculation of the current value of the firm's assets.

Price-cap regulation Where the regulator puts a ceiling on the amount by which a firm can raise its price.

Primary labour market The market for permanent full-time core workers.

Primary market in capital Where shares are sold by the issuer of the shares (i.e. the firm) and where, therefore, finance is channelled directly from the purchasers (i.e. the shareholders) to the firm.

Primary production The production and extraction of natural resources, plus agriculture.

Principal–agent problem One where people (principals), as a result of lack of knowledge, cannot ensure that their best interests are served by their agents.

Principle of diminishing marginal utility As more units of a good are consumed, additional units will provide less additional satisfaction than previous units.

Prisoners' dilemma Where two or more firms (or people), by attempting independently to choose the best strategy, based upon what other(s) are likely to do, end up in a worse position than if they had cooperated from the start.

Producer surplus The excess of a firm's total revenue over its total (variable) cost.

Product differentiation Where a firm's product is in some way distinct from its rivals' products.

Production The transformation of inputs into outputs by firms in order to earn profit (or meet some other objective).

Production externalities Spillover effects on other people of firms' production.

Production function The mathematical relationship between the output of a good and the inputs used to produce it. It shows how output will be affected by changes in the quantity of one or more of the inputs.

Productive efficiency A situation where firms are producing the maximum output for a given amount of inputs, or producing a given output at the least cost.

Productivity deal Where, in return for a wage increase, a union agrees to changes in working practices that will increase output per worker.

Profit satisficing Where decision makers in a firm aim for a target level of profit rather than the absolute maximum level. By not aiming for the maximum profit, this allows managers to pursue other objectives, such as sales maximisation or their own salary or prestige.

Profit-maximising rule Profit is maximised where marginal revenue equals marginal cost.

Prudential control The insistence by the monetary authorities (e.g. the Bank of England) that banks maintain adequate liquidity.

Public good A good or service which has the features of non-rivalry and non-excludability and as a result would not be provided by the free market.

Public-sector net borrowing (PSNB) The difference between the expenditures of the public sector and its receipts from taxation, the revenues of public corporations and the sale of assets. If expenditures exceed receipts (a deficit), then the government has to borrow to make up the difference.

Public-sector net cash requirement (PSNCR) The (annual) deficit of the public sector (central government, local government and public corporations), and thus the amount that the public sector must borrow.

Pure fiscal policy Fiscal policy which does not involve any change in money supply.

Quantitative easing When the central bank increases the monetary base through an open market purchase of government bonds or other securities. It uses electronic money (reserve liabilities) created specifically for this purpose.

Quantity demanded The amount of a good that a consumer is willing and able to buy at a given price over a given period of time.

Quantity supplied The amount of a good that a firm is willing and able to sell at a given price over a given period of time.

Quantity theory of money The price level (P) is directly related to the quantity of money in the economy (M).

Quota (set by a cartel) The output that a given member of a cartel is allowed to produce (production quota) or sell (sales quota).

Random walk Where fluctuations in the value of a share away from its 'correct' value are random, i.e. have no systematic pattern. When charted over time, these share price movements would appear like a 'random walk' – like the path of someone staggering along drunk!

Rate of discount The rate that is used to reduce future values to present values.

Rate of economic growth The percentage increase in output over a 12-month period.

Rate of inflation The percentage increase in the level of prices over a 12-month period.

Rate of return approach The benefits from investment are calculated as a percentage of the costs of investment. This rate is then compared to the rate at which money has to be borrowed in order to see whether the investment should be undertaken.

Rational choices Choices that involve weighing up the benefit of any activity against its opportunity cost.

Rational consumer behaviour The attempt to maximise total consumer surplus.

Rational expectations Expectations based on the *current* situation. These expectations are based on the information people have to hand. While this information may be imperfect and therefore people will make errors, these errors will be random.

Rationalisation The reorganising of production (often after a merger) so as to cut out waste and duplication and generally to reduce costs.

Real business cycle theory The new classical theory which explains cyclical fluctuations in terms of shifts in aggregate supply, rather than aggregate demand.

Real exchange rate index (RERI) The nominal exchange rate index (NERI) adjusted for changes in the relative prices of exports and imports: $RERI = NERI \times P_X/P_M$.

Real growth values Values of the rate of growth of GDP or any other variable after taking inflation into account. The real value of the growth in a variable equals its growth in money (or 'nominal') value minus the rate of inflation.

Recession A period where national output falls for a few months or more. The official definition is where real GDP declines for two or more consecutive quarters.

Recessionary or deflationary gap The shortfall of aggregate expenditure below GDP at the full-employment level of GDP.

Rediscounting bills of exchange Buying bills before they reach maturity.

Regional Development Agencies (RDAs) Nine agencies, based in English regions, which initiate and administer regional policy within their area.

Regional multiplier effects When a change in injections into or withdrawals from a particular region causes a multiplied change in income in that region. The regional multiplier is given by $1/(1 - mpc_r)$, where mpc_r is the marginal propensity to consume products from the region.

Regional unemployment Structural unemployment occurring in specific regions of the country.

Regression analysis A statistical technique which shows how one variable is related to one or more other variables.

Regulatory capture Where the regulator is persuaded to operate in the industry's interests rather than those of the consumer.

Replacement costs What the firm would have to pay to replace factors it currently owns.

Repo Short for 'sale and repurchase agreement'. An agreement between two financial institutions whereby one in effect borrows from another by selling it assets, agreeing to buy them back (repurchase them) at a fixed price and on a fixed date.

Resale price maintenance Where the manufacturer of a product (legally) insists that the product should be sold at a specified retail price.

Reserve capacity A range of output over which business costs will tend to remain relatively constant.

Reverse repos When gilts or other assets are *purchased* under a sale and repurchase agreement. They become an asset of the purchaser.

Risk This is when an outcome may or may not occur, but where its probability of occurring is known.

Risk premium As a business's gearing rises, investors require a higher average dividend from their investment.

Risk transformation The process whereby banks can spread the risks of lending by having a large number of borrowers.

Sale and repurchase agreements (repos) An agreement between two financial institutions whereby one in effect borrows from another by selling it assets, agreeing to buy them back (repurchase them) at a fixed price and on a fixed date.

Sales revenue maximisation An alternative theory of the firm which assumes that managers aim to maximise the firm's short-run total revenue.

Saving gap The shortfall in savings to achieve a given rate of economic growth.

Scarcity The excess of human wants over what can actually be produced to fulfil these wants.

Seasonal unemployment Unemployment associated with industries or regions where the demand for labour is lower at certain times of the year.

Secondary action Industrial action taken against a firm not directly involved in the dispute.

Secondary labour market The market for peripheral workers, usually employed on a temporary or part-time basis, or a less secure 'permanent' basis.

Secondary market in capital Where shareholders sell shares to others. This is thus a market in 'second-hand' shares.

Secondary marketing Where assets are sold before maturity to another institution or individual.

Secondary production The production from manufacturing and construction sectors of the economy.

Second-degree price discrimination Where a firm charges a consumer so much for the first so many units purchased, a different price for the next so many units purchased, and so on.

Securitisation Where future cash flows (e.g. from interest rate or mortgage payments) are turned into marketable securities, such as bonds.

Self-fulfilling speculation The actions of speculators tend to cause the very effect that they had anticipated.

Semi-strong efficiency (of share markets) Where share prices adjust quickly, fully and accurately to publicly available information.

Sensitivity analysis Assesses how sensitive an outcome is to different variables within an equation.

Services balance Exports of services minus imports of services.

Short run The period of time over which at least one factor is fixed.

Short run under perfect competition The period during which there is too little time for new firms to enter the industry.

Short-run shut-down point This is where the *AR* curve is tangential to the *AVC* curve. The firm can only just cover its variable costs. Any fall in revenue below this level will cause a profit-maximising firm to shut down immediately.

Short-termism Where firms and investors take decisions based on the likely short-term performance of a company, rather than on its long-term prospects. Firms may thus sacrifice long-term profits and growth for the sake of quick return.

Sight deposits Deposits that can be withdrawn on demand without penalty.

Social benefit Private benefit plus externalities in consumption.

Social cost Private cost plus externalities in production.

Social efficiency Production and consumption at the point where *MSB = MSC*.

Social responsibility Where a firm takes into account the interests and concerns of a community rather than just its shareholders.

Social-impact standards Pollution control that focuses on the effects on people (e.g. on health or happiness).

Special purpose vehicle (SPV) Legal entities created by financial institutions for conducting specific financial functions, such as bundling assets together into fixed-interest bonds and selling them.

Specialisation and division of labour Where production is broken down into a number of simpler, more specialised tasks, thus allowing workers to acquire a high degree of efficiency.

Speculation This is where people make buying or selling decisions based on their anticipations of future prices.

Spot price The current market price.

Spreading risks (for an insurance company) The more policies an insurance company issues and the more independent the risks of claims from these policies are, the more predictable will be the number of claims.

Stabilising speculation This is where the actions of speculators tend to reduce price fluctuations.

Stakeholders (in a company) People who are affected by a company's activities and/or performance (customers, employees, owners, creditors, people living in the neighbourhood, etc.). They may or may not be in a position to make decisions, or influence decision making, in the firm.

Standard Industrial Classification (SIC) The name given to the formal classification of firms into industries used by the government in order to collect data on business and industry trends.

Standardised unemployment rate The measure of the unemployment rate used by the ILO and OECD. The unemployed are defined as people of working age who are without work, available for work and actively seeking employment.

STEEPLE analysis Where the social, technological economic, environmental, political, legal and ethical factors shaping a business environment are assessed by a business so as to devise future business strategy.

Sterilisation Actions taken by a central bank to offset the effects of foreign exchange flows or its own bond transactions so as to leave money supply unchanged.

Stock The quantity of something held.

Strategic alliance Where two or more firms work together, formally or informally, to achieve a mutually desirable goal.

Strategic management The management of the strategic long-term activities of the business, which includes strategic analysis, strategic choice and strategic implementation.

Strategic trade theory The theory that protecting/supporting certain industries can enable them to compete more effectively with large monopolistic rivals abroad. The effect of the protection is to increase long-run competition and may enable the protected firms to exploit a comparative advantage that they could not have done otherwise.

Strong efficiency (of share markets) Where share prices adjust quickly, fully and accurately to all available information, both public and that available only to insiders.

Structural deficit (or surplus) The public-sector deficit (or surplus) that would occur if the economy were operating at the potential level of national income: i.e. one where there is a zero output gap.

Structural unemployment Unemployment that arises from changes in the pattern of demand or supply in the economy. People made redundant in one part of the economy cannot immediately take up jobs in other parts (even though there are vacancies).

Subcontracting The business practice where various forms of labour (frequently specialist) are hired for a given period of time. Such workers are not directly employed by the hiring business, but either employed by a third party or self-employed.

Sub-prime debt Debt where there is a high risk of default by the borrower (e.g. mortgage holders who are on low incomes facing higher interest rates and falling house prices).

Substitute goods A pair of goods which are considered by consumers to be alternatives to each other. As the price of one goes up, the demand for the other rises.

Substitutes in supply These are two goods where an increased production of one means diverting resources.

Substitution effect The effect of a change in price on quantity demanded arising from the consumer switching to or from alternative (substitute) products.

Substitution effect of a rise in wages Workers will tend to substitute income for leisure as leisure now has a higher opportunity cost. This effect leads to *more* hours being worked as wages rise.

Sunk costs Costs that cannot be recouped (e.g. by transferring assets to other uses).

Supernormal profit (also known as pure profit, economic profit, abnormal profit or simply profit) The excess of total profit above normal profit.

Supply curve A graph showing the relationship between the price of a good and the quantity of the good supplied over a given period of time.

Supply schedule A table showing the different quantities of a good that producers are willing and able to supply at various prices over a given time period. A supply schedule can be for an individual producer or group of producers, or for all producers (the market supply schedule).

Supply: change in supply The term used for a shift in the supply curve. It occurs when a determinant other than price changes.

Supply: change in the quantity supplied The term used for a movement along the supply curve to a new point. It occurs when there is a change in price.

Supply-side policy Government policy that attempts to alter the level of aggregate supply directly.

Tacit collusion A situation where firms have an unspoken agreement to engage in a joint strategy. For example, oligopolists take care not to engage in price cutting, excessive advertising or other forms of competition. There may be unwritten 'rules' of collusive behaviour such as price leadership.

Takeover Where one business acquires another. A takeover may not necessarily involve mutual agreement between the two parties. In such cases, the takeover might be viewed as 'hostile'.

Takeover bid Where one firm attempts to purchase another by offering to buy the shares of that company from its shareholders.

Takeover constraint The effect that the fear of being taken over has on a firm's willingness to undertake projects that reduce distributed profits.

Tapered vertical integration Where a firm is partially integrated with an earlier stage of production; where it produces *some* of an input itself and buys some from another firm.

Taylor rule A rule adopted by a central bank for setting the rate of interest. It will raise the interest rate if (a) inflation is above target or (b) economic growth is above the sustainable level (or unemployment is below the equilibrium rate). The rule states how much interest rates will be changed in each case.

Technical or productive efficiency The least-cost combination of factors for a given output.

Technological unemployment Structural unemployment that occurs as a result of the introduction of labour-saving technology.

Technology policy Involves government initiatives to affect the process and rate of technological change.

Technology transfer Where a host state benefits from the new technology that an MNC brings with its investment.

Technology-based standards Pollution control that requires firms' emissions to reflect the levels that could be achieved from using the best available pollution control technology.

Terms of trade The price index of exports divided by the price index of imports and then expressed as a percentage. This means that the terms of trade will be 100 in the base year.

Tertiary production The production from the service sector of the economy.

Third-degree price discrimination Where a firm divides consumers into different groups and charges a different price to consumers in different groups, but the same price to all the consumers within a group.

Tie-in-sales Where a firm is only prepared to sell a first product on the condition that its customers buy a second product from it.

Time deposits Deposits that require notice of withdrawal or where a penalty is charged for withdrawals on demand.

Time-series data Information depicting how a variable (e.g. the price of eggs) changes over time.

Tit-for-tat Where a firm will cut prices, or make some other aggressive move, *only* if the rival does so first. If the rival knows this, it will be less likely to make an initial aggressive move.

Total (sales) revenue (*TR*) The amount a firm earns from its sales of a product at a particular price: $TR = P \times Q$. Note that we are referring to *gross* revenue; that is, revenue before the deduction of taxes or any other costs.

Total consumer surplus The excess of a person's total utility from the consumption of a good (*TU*) over the amount that person spends on it (*TE*): $TCS = TU - TE$.

Total cost (*TC*) The sum of total fixed costs (*TFC*) and total variable costs (*TVC*): $TC = TFC + TVC$.

Total physical product The total output of a product per period of time that is obtained from a given amount of inputs.

Total revenue A firm's total earnings from a specified level of sales within a specified period: $TR = P \times Q$.

Total utility The total satisfaction a consumer gets from the consumption of all the units of a good consumed within a given time period.

Tradable permits Firms are issued or sold permits by the authorities that give them the right to produce a given level of pollution. Firms that do not have permits to match their pollution levels can purchase additional permits to cover the difference from firms that have spare permits, while those that reduce their pollution levels can sell any surplus permits for a profit.

Trade creation Where a customs union leads to greater specialisation according to comparative advantage and thus a shift in production from higher-cost to lower-cost sources.

Trade diversion Where a customs union diverts consumption from goods produced at a lower cost outside the union to goods produced at a higher cost (but tariff free) within the union.

Tragedy of the commons When resources are commonly available at no charge, people are likely to overexploit them.

Transactions costs The costs incurred when firms buy inputs or services from other firms as opposed to producing them themselves. They include the costs of searching for the best firm to do business with, the costs of drawing up, monitoring and enforcing contracts and the costs of transporting and handling products between the firms.

Transfer payments Moneys transferred from one person or group to another (e.g. from the government to individuals) without production taking place.

Transfer pricing The pricing system used within a business organisation to transfer intermediate products between the business's various divisions.

Transnational association A form of business organisation in which the subsidiaries of a company in different countries are contractually bound to the parent company to provide output to or receive inputs from other subsidiaries.

Two-part tariff A pricing system that requires customers to pay an access and a usage price for a product.

U-form business organisation One in which the central organisation of the firm (the chief executive or a managerial team) is responsible both for the firm's day-to-day administration and for formulating its business strategy.

Uncertainty This is when an outcome may or may not occur and where its probability of occurring is not known.

Underemployment *International Labour Organisation (ILO) definition*: a situation where people currently working less than 'full time' (40 hours in the UK) would like to work more hours (at current wage rates), either by working more hours in their current job, or by switching to an alternative job with more hours or by taking on an additional part-time job or any combination of the three. *Eurostat definition*: where people working less than 40 hours per week would like to work more hours in their current job at current wage rates.

Unemployment The number of people who are actively looking for work but are currently without a job. (Note that there is much debate as to who should officially be counted as unemployed.)

Unemployment rate The number unemployed expressed as a percentage of the labour force.

Unit elasticity When the price elasticity of demand is unity, this is where quantity demanded changes by the same proportion as the price. Price elasticity is equal to −1.

Valuation ratio or Price to book ratio The ratio of stock market value to book value. The stock market value is an assessment of the firm's past and anticipated future performance. The book value is a calculation of the current value of the firm's assets.

Value chain The stages or activities that help to create product value.

Variable costs Total costs that do vary with the amount of output produced.

Variable factor An input that *can* be increased in supply within a given time period.

Velocity of circulation The number of times annually that money on average is spent on goods and services that make up GDP.

Vertical integration A business growth strategy that involves expanding within an existing market, but at a different stage of production. Vertical integration can be 'forward', such as moving into distribution or retail, or 'backward', such as expanding into extracting raw materials or producing components.

Vertical merger Where two firms in the same industry at different stages in the production process merge.

Vertical product differentiation Where a firm's product differs from its rivals' products in respect to quality.

Vertical restraints Conditions imposed by one firm on another which is either its supplier or its customer.

Vertical strategic alliance A formal or informal arrangement between firms operating at different stages of an activity to jointly provide a product or service.

Vertically integrated multinational A multinational that undertakes the various stages of production for a given product in different countries.

Wage taker The wage rate is determined by market forces.

Weak efficiency (of share markets) Where share dealing prevents cyclical movements in shares.

Weighted average The average of several items where each item is ascribed a weight according to its importance. The weights must add up to 1.

Wholesale deposits and loans Large-scale deposits and loans made by and to firms at negotiated interest rates.

Withdrawals (*W*) (or leakages) Incomes of households or firms that are not passed on round the inner flow. Withdrawals equal net saving (*S*) plus net taxes (*T*) plus import expenditure (*M*): $W = S + T + M$.

Working to rule Workers do no more than they are supposed to, as set out in their job descriptions.

Yield on a share The dividend received per share expressed as a percentage of the current market price of the share.

Index